SOURCEBOOK OF
COMPANY LAW

SOURCEBOOK OF COMPANY LAW

Second Edition

Harry Rajak BA, LLM
of the Inner Temple, Barrister
Professor of Law and Director of the Insolvency
Research Unit
University of Sussex

JORDANS
1995

Published by
Jordan Publishing Limited
21 St Thomas Street
Bristol BS1 6JS

British Library Cataloguing-in-Publication Data
A catalogue record for this book is available from the British Library.

ISBN 0 85308 266 9

Typeset by Interactive Sciences, Gloucester
Printed in Great Britain by Hobbs the Printers of Southampton

PREFACE TO THE SECOND EDITION

Six years is both a long and a short time in the study of contemporary company law. When this book was first published in 1989, the Companies Bill of that year had just appeared; ultra vires (well and truly abolished in company law in February 1991) was still a theoretical hazard for third parties. The mass of cases reported in the last 5 years on issues inspired by insolvency and bad management practices leading to insolvency (eg disqualification of directors, ever inventive forms of instruments seeking status as fixed rather than floating charges and, in part, minority shareholder protection under s 459 of the Companies Act 1985) make 1989 seem a long time ago. On the other hand, we were then waiting eagerly for a new regime for the registration of company charges and another for public issues for which no Stock Exchange listing was desired. We are still waiting for the former and the anticipated demise of the principles enshrined in *Re Mechanisations (Eaglescliffe) Ltd*,[1] as discussed in the first edition, turns out to have been somewhat premature. We have, however, just got the latter, something which was anticipated in the text of this second edition (see p 174) but which was too late to be included in the first edition.

On 19 June 1995, the Public Offers of Securities Regulations 1995 (SI 1995/1537) were enacted under the provisions of s 2(2) of the European Communities Act 1972. These regulations apply '[w]hen securities are offered to the public in the United Kingdom for the first time' (reg 4) subject to a number of exceptions (eg placings and Eurobonds). The regime established by Part IV of the Financial Services Act 1986 (FSA) continues to apply to securities where a listing is sought.

The new regulations effect the repeal of Part III of the Companies Act 1985, left extant to cater for non-listed public offers which had been expected to graduate to the regime set out in Part V of the FSA after a suitable replacement for Sch 3 to the Companies Act 1985 (which specified the Form and Content of prospectuses) had been agreed. In the event, the new regulations themselves include a comprehensive 'Form and Contents' for prospectuses and also repeal the now redundant Part V of the FSA. The statutory liability and compensation provisions for defective prospectuses, which previously were s 56 of and Sch 3 to the CA 1985 (for omissions) and s 67 of the CA 1985 (for misstatements) are now provided by the new regulations (regs 9, 13–15) and are a virtual repeat of the corresponding provisions (ss 163, 167–168) of the now repealed Part V of the FSA.

The fact that these regulations were enacted under the provisions of the European Communities Act 1972 reflects the fact that this area has been the

---

1 [1966] Ch 20; [1964] 3 All ER 840

subject of increasing harmonisation. In particular, these regulations provide for the mutual recognition, with other EC countries, of prospectuses by giving The Stock Exchange the power to pre-vet prospectuses (as it does in the case of Listing Regulations) so as to enable issuing companies to make public offers in other EC countries on the strength of the pre-vetted prospectus. This extension in The Stock Exchange's powers is effected in these regulations by an amendment to Part IV of the FSA. It remains to be seen in practice whether the hopes for co-ordination of regimes in all EC countries as expressed by this harmonisation measure are realised. There is always the possibility that local customs are sufficiently strong to ensure that 'foreign intruders' conform despite permission in the harmonisation measure to do otherwise. To insist on such conformity would, naturally, be a breach of EC law, but such conformity to local custom may often be as much dictated by local market forces as by local regulation.

European Union law continues its onward march into UK company law. This is reflected at various points in this edition, in the functioning of The Stock Exchange,[2] and the relationship of the seat of the company's incorporation and the EU's professed freedom of movement of persons.[3]

The problems of pre-incorporation contracts gave us some while ago our first taste of the application of EC Company Law Harmonisation Directives,[4] therefore it is something of a surprise to see a flurry of recent cases in this formerly sleepy area of company law.[5] Is it too much to hope that soon we shall have legislation enacting the small but welcome reform enabling companies to adopt pre-incorporation contracts?

The public face of company law has been dominated by the recent reports of non-governmental committees looking into the politically exciting questions of corporate governance and director's remuneration.[6] The comparative potential in company law, for so long restricted to the developments of the well-established Commonwealth courts, has been extended into Europe.[7] The last 5 years has also seen detailed judicial studies of the perennial problems of company law. Pride of place must go to *Adams v Cape Industries plc*[8] investigating the question of the separateness of different companies within the same group, and *Guinness plc v Saunders*[9] for a re-working of the director's fiduciary duties in dealing with companies' tangible and intangible assets.

My preparation of this edition has been greatly assisted by my colleague, John Lowry. Our many discussions were of considerable benefit to me and, in particular, I was able to rely on his preparation of the sections dealing with statutory regimes for minority shareholder protection.

---

2 *R v Stock Exchange, ex parte Else* [1993] BCLC 834 (see p 194)
3 *Regina v Her Majesty's Treasury, ex parte Daily Mail and General Trust plc* [1989] BCLC 206 (ECJ, p 54)
4 *Phonogram v Lane* [1982] QB 938; [1981] 3 All ER 182 (see p 219)
5 See p 218
6 An extract of the 'Cadbury Report' on Corporate Governance appears at pp 372ff
7 Hoffmann LJ in *El Ajou v Dollar Land Holdings plc* [1994] 1 BCLC 464, 483 (see pp 289–90)
8 [1990] BCLC 479 (see p 118)
9 [1990] BCLC 402 (see p 487)

My publishers have been the essence of helpfulness at every turn. Martin West and Mollie Dickenson have looked after me well beyond the call of duty, as indeed have others in Jordans whose names I do not know.

My debt to my family and my students is huge and I hope that they may see some meagre return in this volume for their vast investment.

Harry Rajak
University of Sussex
September 1995

"All in favor of a cap on our liability?"

Drawing by Stevenson; Copyright 1986. *THE NEW YORKER, MAGAZINE INC.*

(See p 506)

"I realize, gentlemen, that $30 million is a lot of money to spend. However, it's not real money and it's not our money either."

ABA SECTION OF BUSINESS LAW

(See p 477)

ACKNOWLEDGEMENTS

Law Reports

Extracts from the *Law Reports* and *Weekly Law Reports* are reproduced with the kind permission of the Incorporated Council of Law Reporting for England and Wales, WC2A 3XN.

Extracts from the *All England Law Reports, New Zealand Law Reports* and *Butterworths Company Law Cases* (BCLC) are reproduced with the kind permission of Butterworth & Co (Publishers) Ltd, London WC2B 6AB and Butterworths of New Zealand, Wellington, New Zealand.

Extracts from *British Company Law Cases* (BCC) are reproduced with the kind permission of CCH Editions Limited, Bicester, Oxfordshire OX6 0XD.

Extracts from material from the *Dominion Law Reports* are reproduced with the kind permission of Canada Law Books Inc, 240 Edward Street, Aurora, Ontario L4G 3S9, Canada.

Extracts from the judgments of *Woolfson v Strathclyde Regional Council* and *Cumming v Quartzag Ltd* were taken from the *Scots Law Times* and are reproduced with the kind permission of W. Green & Son Limited, Edinburgh EH1 1PU.

Extracts from *Dadoo Ltd v Krugersdorp Municipality* and *Morrison v Standard Building Society* are reproduced with the kind permission of Juta and Company Limited, PO Box 14373, Kenwyn 7790, South Africa.

Extracts from *Peter's American Delicacy Company Limited v Heath* and *Black v Smallwood* are reproduced with the kind permission of the Law Book Company Limited, 44–50 Waterloo Road, North Ryde, New South Wales 2113, Australia.

Extracts from *R v Her Majesty's Treasury ex parte Daily Mail and General Trust* are reproduced with the kind permission of the European Law Centre, London E14 9FS and the editor of the *Common Market Law Reports*, Dr Neville March Hunnings.

Other Material

The author is grateful for the permission given by the people and organisations in the second column to reproduce extracts from the material described in the first column.

Translation of *Justinian's Digest*, D.47.22.1,4 and D.3.4.1	The University of Pennsylvania Press and Professor Alan Watson
Laski, 'The Early History of the Corporation' and 'The Personality of Associations	The 'Harvard Law Review'
Dubois, Armand, *The English Business Company After the Bubble Act* New York: The Commonwealth Fund, 1938	The Commonwealth Fund, New York
Formoy, *The Historical Foundations of Company Law*	Sweet & Maxwell Ltd
Carr, *Select Charters of Trading Companies*	The Selden Society and its Secretary, Mr Victor Tunkel
Review of Investor Protection 1984; Companies Bill 1973; Report of the Company Law Committee 1962; Report of the Company Law Amendment Committee 1945; Reform of the Ultra Vires Rule; Report of the Committee of Inquiry on Industrial Democracy 1977; Rules of the Supreme Court; Report of the Committee on Insolvency Law and Practice 1982; Report of the Company Law Amendment Committee 1926; A Revised Framework for Insolvency Law 1984; Company Voluntary Arrangements and Administration Orders, A Consultative Document (October 1993)	The Controller of Her Majesty's Stationery Office and the Department of Trade and Industry
Article in the *Modern Law Review*	The Modern Law Review Limited and Lady Kahn Freund

TABLE OF STATUTES

TABLE OF STATUTORY INSTRUMENTS

TABLE OF EC LEGISLATION

TABLE OF SOURCES

INTRODUCTION

Company law is, academically speaking, a comparatively young subject. The weighty volumes by Lindley (originally *Lindley on Partnership* was *Lindley on Company Law and Partnership*), Palmer, Buckley, and Stiebel served the needs of an increasingly active practitioner market, but company law in higher education is distinctly a post-Second World War phenomenon. Much of the credit for this is due to Professor Gower, whose *Modern Company Law* first appeared in 1954. This achieved the rare feat of appealing to practitioners despite its distinctly intellectual, even conceptual, approach. And, not only was there a need for professional lawyers to be trained in the principles of company law, there was firm evidence that this could be done by higher educational institutions. This process was, of course, to be repeated with labour law, revenue law and many others, where a contextual, historical, philosophical or other intellectual approach could engender interest and provoke argument rather than leave the subject condemned to the dull recitation of 'facts' and principles.

Another significant development in rescuing company law from the exclusive control of professional schools was the study of primary materials. Initially, this consisted of judgments in leading cases and statutes. Casebooks or books of primary materials had been a significant part of American legal education even before the Second World War. There, the much admired (by some) and much reviled (by others) Socratic (some would say Spanish inquisitorial) method of law teaching was pioneered by the Harvard Law School and spread widely. In Britain, the earliest of the casebooks dates back to the 1950s, but for company law in the Commonwealth world the pioneer was *Company Law Through the Cases*, first compiled in 1958 by Professor Hahlo, then of the University of Witwatersrand, South Africa.

Now, in this *Sourcebook*, an attempt has been made to complement judgments with other primary material through which to study company law. Judgments are, of course, an essential part of this study, but unless harnessed to the needs of education, they can exercise the same deadening influence as the recitation of 'facts'. If, instead of learning 'the principle', we learn the name of the leading case in which it emerged as the *ratio* and the choice judicial phrases in which it was couched, have we really made much progress? The educational process needs argument and discussion and this can, in company law, be stimulated by a number of sources.

Company law is rich in comment and criticism. There are articles by law teachers, discussions by journalists and reports by official, semi-official and unofficial bodies. Increasingly, comment is contextual and interdisciplinary. All of this helps us to see the issues behind the legal principles. Then there is the debate within the company law cases themselves. Sometimes, our appreciation of company law can be broadened or sharpened by a dissenting judgment,[1]

---

1 See, eg, the dissenting speech of Lord Morris in *Bushell v Faith* [1970] AC 1099; [1970] 1 All ER 53
(Source 118)

even an affirmed judgment[1] and, of course, a judgment overruled; compare
the treatment of *Salomon's* case, between the dull deadening statement that 'it
is authority for the proposition that a company is distinct from its members'
and the intensity of the debate between the Court of Appeal and the House
of Lords.[2] The powerful unanimity of the House of Lords loses something of
its invincibility when confronted by the equally unanimous and confident
judgments which were overruled. Deep issues lie beneath the legal principles
of *Salomon's* case; it is hardly surprising that we still have so much trouble with
the 'corporate veil'.[3]

Another source of inspiration is the context of the problem which gives rise
to litigation. It is somewhat sobering to consider the debt we owe to
insolvency. If there is enough money to go round, there is no need to sort out
who gets paid first, whether a charge is fixed or floating, whether a retention
of title clause is effective and so on. Secondly, many leading cases in company
law reflect the dynamic political and economic times in which they arise, for
example the fight against nationalisation[4] or the resistance to take-overs.[5]

Company law also has its 'characters'. Who cannot spare a thought, for
example, for Greenhalgh? On seven separate occasions, he was involved in
litigation against his business partners, five times going to the Court of
Appeal.[6] On two of those occasions, the decisions made major contributions
to our appreciation of company law.[7] He lost on almost every occasion, yet his
story is not simply colourful; it shows how difficult it is to reconcile majority
rule with protection for the minority.

It is often difficult to follow the facts in many of the cases we read, but this
is essential if we are to understand the applicable legal principles. Here, the
law teacher can play an important role in his or her students' appreciation of
company law. Sorting out the facts, what actually happened – sometimes even
distinguishing the plaintiff from the defendant can be difficult! – is rewarding
and interesting and, ironically, so much closer to what students will face as
practitioners. It is also essential to a proper intellectual examination of how
the legal principles have developed.

Much of company law is, clearly, still based in the common law. The debt to
principles of partnership remains, winding up on the just and equitable
grounds as a remedy against oppression being the most obvious example. Yet
the modern context of company law, the enormous explosion of commercial
and financial activity and the influence of the European Community, has
substantially increased the statutory regulation of companies. This has been
much lamented by some as over-regulation, but no one expects this pattern to
be reversed. Statute now bites deep into the substance of company law and
students are increasingly being allowed to follow the enlightened course of

---

1 See, eg, the different grounds below and in the Court of Appeal in *Hely-Hutchinson v Brayhead Ltd*
  [1968] 1 QB 549; [1967] 3 All ER 98 (Source 98)
2 *Broderip v Salomon* [1895] 2 Ch 323, overruled as *Salomon v Salomon & Co Ltd* [1897] AC 22 (Source 28)
3 See Ottolenghi, 'From Peeping Behind the Corporate Veil to its Total Extinction' (1990) 53 MLR 338;
  Gower's *Principles of Modern Company Law* (4th edn, 1979) at p 138
4 *Ex Parte Westburn Sugar Refineries Ltd* [1951] AC 625; [1951] 1 All ER 881 (Source 281)
5 *Lyle & Scott v Scott's Trustees* [1959] AC 763; [1959] 2 All ER 661 (Source 214)
6 See the engaging biography in Gower's *Principles of Modern Company Law* (4th edn, 1979) at p 624
7 *Greenhalgh v Arderne Cinemas Ltd* [1951] Ch 286; [1950] 2 All ER 1120 (Source 126)

taking copies of these statutes into their examinations. Indeed, the whole nature of the examination process is under review, with some institutions requiring undergraduate and postgraduate students to write dissertations of anything between 5,000 and 20,000 words. If this welcome development is to be sustained and extended, a grasp of the subject's primary materials will be essential.

Chapter 1

HISTORY AND SOURCES OF COMPANY LAW

PART I: THE ORIGINS AND DEVELOPMENT OF CORPORATE STATUS

Corporate status may be defined as the recognition by the state of the legal existence of an association of people. The association itself enters into legal relationships and, itself, benefits or suffers from those relationships. The development of the concept of corporate status seems to have been a gradual process, emerging informally through action and custom eventually culminating in the laying down by a sufficiently strong central authority of the conditions to be satisfied for achieving such status. As a phenomenon in society, it would seem to go back at least to the time of Solon (6th century BC) and is thought to have begun to evolve in English society during the reign of Edward I (1272–1307) (see Sources 1 and 2).

SOURCE 1
The Digest of Justinian

Justinian's Digest was compiled in the 6th century AD from the writings of the greatest of Roman jurists. The extract below is from the writings of Marcian (3rd century AD) and Gaius (2nd century AD). [D. 47.22.1,4.]

22 *Collegia* and Associations
Marcia, *Institutes, book 3:* Provincial governors are directed by imperial instructions not to tolerate secret social *collegia* and that soldiers are not to form *collegia* in camp. But the lower orders are allowed to pay a small monthly fee, provided that they meet only once a month, lest an unlawful association be created under this guise. And the deified Severus stated in a rescript that this applies not only at Rome but also in Italy and the provinces. 1. There is, however, no ban on assembly for religious purposes, so long as there is no contravention of the *senatus consultum* which prohibits unlawful *collegia*. 2. It is not permitted to belong to more than one *collegium*, as was laid down by the deified brothers; and if someone belongs to more than one, it is provided by rescript that he must choose the one to which he wishes to adhere and receive from the association which he leaves the share of the common fund which is due to him.

Gaius, *XII Tables, book 4:* Co-members are those who belong to the same association, what the Greeks call an ἑταιρεία. A statute gives them the power to enter into any agreement they like, so long as they do not contravene the public statute. This statute appears to have been adopted from the law of Solon which says: 'If the inhabitants of a city district or precinct be in association for the purpose of holding religious feasts or of dining together or to provide for their burial or if they be members of the same club or they combine to engage in some enterprise or for profit, anything that they agree between themselves will be valid unless forbidden by public statutes.'

SOURCE 2
Laski, The Early History of the Corporation
[1916–17] 30 HLR 561, pp 578–582

That Bracton could call the town an *universitas* is perhaps accident rather than design. Yet it is the borough which compels our lawyers to recognize the significance of theory. At what day the *liber burgus* becomes in a full sense corporate we may not with any precision speculate; but, of a certainty, the older authorities were wrong who ascribed that change to the middle fifteenth century. The *communitas* of the borough is gaining abstractness as the years of the first Edward draw near their end. In the reign of his successor the courts are talking freely of the bodiliness of towns. The good citizens of Great Yarmouth betray a healthy anger when the townsmen of their smaller brother 'who are not of any community and have no common seal' pretend to burghal rights. The *Liber Assisarum* has not a little to say of the physical substantiality of a city which is not its citizens. Richard II takes compassion upon the good men of Basingstoke who have suffered the scourge of fire, and incorporation is the form his pity takes — with a common seal thereto annexed. Nor, assuredly, may we belittle in this context the meaning of his extension to cities and to boroughs of the provisions of Mortmain. It is made thereby very clear that the nature of corporateness is becoming known to men. The citizens of Plymouth were not less clear about its nature when they petitioned Parliament that for the purchase of free tenements for life they might become *un corps corporat*. The union of the two Droghedas into a single county — a corporate county the record will make it — suggests that we have passed to the language of a new jurisprudence. We have synthesized men into the abstraction of a new being. What has happened is less the acquisition of new rights than the formulation of a means whereby collective action may be taken by that which is not the body of citizens even while it is still the citizen body. The later use of the corporate term to mean that oligarchic body which will with such difficulty be reformed in the nineteenth century, is evidence of how easily the towns absorbed the possibilities laid open by representative action.

. . .

A new commerce, moreover, is beginning, and it casts its shadows across the pathway of our history. The Black Death and the Hundred Years' War brought with them distress in their trail. The social movements which are their consequence are too vast for a local authority to control, and from separatism we pass to the national consolidation which reached its zenith under the Tudors. What is perhaps above all important is its resultant emphasis on the class structure of industrial society. The emergence of the capitalist seems to synchronize with the emergence of new forms of business organization. As early as 1391 Richard II, whose reign seems generally to have marked the onset of a new time, was granting a charter to what is at least the *communitas* of the English merchants in Prussia; and Henry IV was not slow to emulate the novelties of his predecessor. The organization of foreign merchants in England will be encouraged, since a unit permits with satisfactory ease of the assessment the kings hold dear. The very phrases which suggest the corporate idea begin everywhere to make their appearance. Henry VII made the Englishmen of Pisa a corporation in 1490. The great trading companies which are in some sort the parents of empire begin to buy their charters. Henry VII provided the Merchant Adventurers with what protection the written privilege of an English king might afford; and it has been significantly pointed out by Dr Cunningham that the object of the grant was rather the encouragement of commercial speculation than the governmental regulation of commerce. These companies seem to arise with all the spontaneity that marks the communalism of our earliest history. Their appearance is very striking, since the simpler forms of such business organization as the partnership were already well known. But the partnership seems too narrow in its scope for the larger ideas of fellowship these fifteenth-century Englishmen have inherited from their ancestors. Why they should have chosen the corporate form of life is perhaps not wholly clear. But the step is taken, and from the time of Elizabeth it is in them rather than in the municipal corporation that the historian of corporate theory must be interested. Moreover, after 1515 they could not escape from the king's hands even if they remained a voluntary society; the ministers of Henry VIII recked but little of formal matters. The companies, for the most part, deal with a foreign trade in their earlier history. They want privileges because they are journeying into far, strange lands; and it is surely one of the happiest thoughts of Philip and Mary (whose grandparents had tasted the rich fruits of maritime adventure) which led them to incorporate a company of which the great Sebastian Cabot was the governor.

We may not surely deny that this corporateness is inherited from burghal organization. These merchants have learned the value of their fellowships from the gilds of the town; and not seldom they strive, in all the bitterness of a novel rivalry, with the older crafts and mysteries of the towns. It is perhaps from the analogy of the medieval staple towns that we shall find the connection. Its whole point lies in the organization of a group of men into something like an unity; and once the charters are forthcoming, the incidents of corporateness are not wanting. The sense of exclusiveness must have been fostered by the stress of the keen foreign competition they had from the outset to face. Englishmen have had pride in their isolation, and they did not find it difficult to combine against alien rivals. We can imagine that a medieval government which understood the difficulties of evolving a foreign policy would welcome the spontaneous development of groups of men who for the royal protection we term incorporation would call a new world into being.

PART II: GROUPS IN SOCIETY AND THEORIES OF CORPORATE STATUS

A group of people empowered to function as a legal unit may present a greater challenge to the state than does an individual person. This political dimension of corporate status is evident in Source 1. Many political philosophers have considered the wider question of the role of groups in society.

SOURCE 3
Hobbes, Leviathan
(Pelican, 1968 (first published 1651) ed C B Macpherson) pp 374–5

Excessive greatnesse of a town, multitude of corporations. Another infirmity of a Common-wealth, is the immoderate greatnesse of a Town, when it is able to furnish out of its own Circuit, the number, and expence of a great Army: As also the great number of Corporations; which are as it were many lesser Common-wealths in the bowels of a greater, like wormes in the entrayles of a naturall man.

Hobbes, of course, was not speaking of incorporated associations as opposed to unincorporated associations, but of all groups within society. Nevertheless, there is surely a connection between this philosophy and the assertion that incorporated status can be conferred only by the power of the state (ie incorporation is a privilege conceded by the state, hence the concession theory of corporate personality).

Consider the following source as an expression of a different theory (the realist or organic theory) that groups are real by their very existence and should not depend on the state for legal existence.

SOURCE 4
Laski, The Personality of Associations
[1915–16] 29 HLR, pp 404–8, 423–4

The state knows certain persons who are not men. What is the nature of their personality? Are they merely fictitious abstractions, collective names that hide from us the mass of individuals beneath? Is the name that gives them unity no more than a convenience, a means of substituting one action in the courts where, otherwise, there might be actions innumerable? Or is that personality real? Is Professor Dicey right when he urges that 'whenever men act in concert for a common purpose, they tend to create a body which, from no fiction of law but from the very nature of things, differs from the individuals of whom it is constituted'? Does our symbolism, in fact, point to some reality at the bottom of appearance? If we assume that reality, what consequences will flow therefrom?

Certainly no lawyer dare neglect the phenomena of group life, even if on occasion he denies a little angrily the need for him to theorize about them. For man is so essentially an associative animal that his nature is largely determined by the relationships thus formed. The churches express his feeling that he has need of religion. His desire for conversation and the newspapers results in the establishment of clubs. The necessity of social organization gave birth to the state. As his commercial enterprise began to annihilate distance, the trading company came into being. It would not, one urges, be over-emphasis to assert that in every sphere of human activity associations of some kind are to be found. They are the very life-breath of the community.

And, somehow, we are compelled to personalise these associations. They demand their possessive pronouns; the church has 'its' bishops. They govern a singular verb, the railway company 'employs' servants. The United States of America is greater than all Americans; it becomes a single individual, and fraternises, Jonathan-wise, with a John Bull in whom all Englishmen have their being. The Bank of England is — the phrase, surely, is remarkable — the 'little old lady of Threadneedle Street'; but no one would speak of seven distinguished merchants as a little old lady. The House of Commons is distinct from 'its' members, and no less clearly, it is not the chamber in which they meet. We talk of 'its' 'spirit' and 'complexion'; a general election, so we say, changes 'its' 'character.' Eton, we know well enough, is not six hundred boys, nor a collection of ancient buildings. Clearly, there is compulsion in our personalising. We do it because we must. We do it because we feel in these things the red blood of a living personality. Here are no mere abstractions of an over-exuberant imagination. The need is so apparent as to make plain the reality beneath.

II

Now lawyers are practical men dealing with the very practical affairs of everyday life, and they do not like, in Lord Lindley's phrase, 'to introduce metaphysical subtleties which are needless and fallacious.' The law, so they will say, knows persons; by Act of Parliament 'persons' may include bodies corporate. Persons are the subjects of rights and duties which the courts will, at need, enforce. If a body corporate is a person, it will also be the subject of rights and duties. If it is a person, it is so because the state has conferred upon it the gift of personality; for only the state can exercise that power. And the terms of such conference are strictly defined. The corporation is given personality for certain purposes to be found in its history, in its charter, its constituting act, its articles of association. The courts will say whether certain acts come within those purposes; whether, to use technical terms, they are *intra* or *ultra vires*. This limitation is in the public interest. 'The public,' so the courts have held, 'is entitled to hold a registered company to its registered business.' The company has a personality; but it has a personality capable only of very definitised development.

Why is it so limited? English lawyers, at any rate, have no doubt upon this question. The corporation is the creature of the state. Its will is a delegated will; its purpose exists only because it has secured recognition. And, so the lawyers will tend to imply, it is in truth a fictitious thing. Persons, they know well enough, are human beings; the corporation is invisible and *in abstracto*. It has no human wants. 'It cannot,' so an American judge has said, 'eat or drink, or wear clothing, or live in houses'; though hereto a sceptic might retort that a theory of domicile has given some trouble, and ask if there is not a solid reality about the dinners of the Corporation of London. 'It is,' said Marshall CJ, 'an artificial being, invisible, intangible, and existing only in contemplation of law' . . . 'it is precisely,' he says again, 'what the act of incorporation makes it.' 'Persons,' said Best CJ in 1828, 'who, without the sanction of the legislature, presume to act as a corporation, are guilty of a contempt of the King, by usurping on his prerogative.'

Nor are the textbook writers less definite. 'They are legal persons,' says Austin, 'by a figment, and for the sake of brevity in discourse.' 'To the existence of all corporations,' wrote Kyd in 1793, 'it has long been an established maxim that the King's consent is absolutely necessary.' 'Ten men,' notes Professor Salmond satirically, 'do not become in fact one person because they associate themselves together for one end any more than two horses become one animal when they draw the same cart.' 'The most marked distinction,' Mr Holland has written in a famous textbook, 'between abnormal persons is that some are natural . . . while others are artificial . . . which are treated by law for certain purposes as if they were individual human beings.'

Here is clear doctrine enough — a vivid picture of an all-absorptive state. But when this supposed limitation has once been admitted, it is evident that the state is compelled to do remarkable things with the bodies it has called into being. It fails to regulate them with the ease that might be desired. The definition of *ultra vires*, for example, has become a formidable problem; there seems not a little of accident in the formulation of its principles. Corporations will have a curious habit of attempting perpetually to escape from the rigid bonds in which they have been encased. May we not say that, like some Frankenstein, they show ingratitude to their creators? Or, as artificial things, must we deem them incapable of such thought? A corporation will possess itself of an empire, and resent interference with its domain. An American colony will incorporate itself; and when its creator shows signs of wanton interference, will take the lead in rebellion against the state which, in legal theory, at any rate, gave it birth. Truly the supposed sovereignty of the state is not apparent in the relations thus discovered. The orthodox doctrine needs somewhat closer examination before we accept its truth.

III

But even when we have so examined, there are associations which technically at least are not corporations. That trust which Maitland taught us to understand as so typically English will embrace many of them under its all-protecting fold. Contract, as in the club, will account for much, and with the aid of a little fiction we need have no fear of theory. A mighty church will in Scotland be a trust and not a corporation. In America the operations of certain trusts which are not corporations will necessitate a famous Act of Congress. For otherwise they can hardly come into the courts. They have no name by which to be sued. To the law, they are not persons, have no personality; they are bodies unincorporate, bodies — the thought is charmingly English — which are bodiless. Yet, curiously, the technical formulae do not by their absence reveal any essential lack of corporate character. The Stock Exchange has, in any real meaning of the term, a personality as assuredly effective as that of Lloyds. If, to the law, they are essentially distinct, to practical men and women it seems useless to insist on the distinction as other than an empty formalism. The Stock Exchange is simply a property vested in trustees for the benefit of a few proprietors. Is it? Dare those trustees use it as property in that unpublic sense? Dare they so claim it and retain the respect of men with eyes to see? The technical distinction only made Archbishop Laud impatient when a Puritan trust had ruffled his temper. Sour Bishop Montague who avowed that he had 'spent some time in reading bookes of the Lawe,' was beside himself at the unincorporate character of Lincoln's Inn. Certain words of condemnation died out on Lord Eldon's lips when he thought of the silver cup the Middle Temple treasured. Here, as it seemed, was virtual corporateness, without the state's blessing of incorporation. Wrong, may be, it was thus to presume on kingly right; yet, of a truth, it was also significant.

Significant in what sense? In the sense, we argue, that legal practice has improved on legal theory. The judges builded better than they knew; or, mayhap, they have added yet another to the pile of fictions so characteristic of English law. If corporations can alone come up the front stairs, then they will admit the unincorporate association at the back. For, they know well enough, the life of the state would be intolerable did we recognise only the association which has chosen to accept the forms of law.

Clearly there is much behind this fiction-making. A sovereignty that is but doubtfully sovereign, an unincorporate body of which the bodiliness may yet equitably be recognised — certainly our fictions have served to conceal much. What, as a fact, is their justification? Why do they still invite, as they receive, a lip-given, if a heart-denied, profession of faith? ...

We have travelled far, but at least there has been direction in our travelling. We have asked a question: is corporate personality a real thing? Is the collective will that is the inevitable accompaniment of that personality but a figment of the imagination? The thesis that has been here maintained is a simple one. It is that when the man in the street calls (let us say) Lloyds and the Stock Exchange corporations he is profoundly right in his perception. He has brushed aside the technicalities of form and penetrated to the reality, which is but a cloud serving not to reveal but to obscure. This, it may be pointed out, Erle J perceived nearly sixty years ago. 'According to the plaintiff,' he said, 'it is supposed to be a corporation created for the purpose of the navigation, and having the legal incidents of its existence limited for that purpose. But it appears to me that, by common law, the creation of a corporation conferred on it all the rights and liabilities in respect of property, contracts and litigation which existence confers upon a natural subject, modified only by the formalities required for expressing the will of a numerous body.' Here, at any rate, is the basis of much needed innovation. A corporation is simply an organised body of men acting as a unit, and with a will that has become unified through the singleness of their purpose. We assume its reality. We act upon that assumption. Are we not justified in the event?

After all, our legal theories will and must be judged by their applicability to the facts they endeavour to resume. It is clear enough that unless we treat the personality of our group persons as real and apply the fact of that reality throughout the whole realm of law, what we call justice will, in truth, be no more than a chaotic and illogical muddle.

English lawyers, it is said, have a dislike of abstractions. Such excursions as this into the world of legal metaphysics have for them the suspect air of dangerous adventure. But life, after all, is a series of precipices, and we have to act upon the assumptions we make. Here we urge a radical thesis; we say that the distinction between incorporate and voluntary association must be abolished. We say that the trust must be made to reveal the life that glows beneath, that we must have the means of penetrating beyond its fictitious protectiveness. No one doubts that the change will be vast. No one doubts that the application will need courage and high resolve. But it is in its very difficulty that we shall find its supreme worth.

SOURCE 5
Conservative and Unionist Central Office *v* Burrell
(1982, Court of Appeal, affirming the decision of Vinelott J) [1982] 1 WLR 522; [1982] 2 All ER 1

LAWTON LJ: This is an appeal by the Crown from an order of Vinelott J made on 2 April 1980, whereby he adjudged on the hearing of an appeal by way of case stated from a decision of the Commissioners for the Special Purposes of the Income Tax Acts that such decision was erroneous and that assessments to corporation tax on the Conservative and Unionist Central Office for each of the five years ending on 31 March 1972 to 1976, be discharged. The special commissioners had decided that the Central Office was an unincorporated association and as such was chargeable to corporation tax on its profits under the provisions of sections 238(1) and 526(5) of the Income and Corporation Taxes Act 1970.[1] Vinelott J adjudged that it was not such an association so that corporation tax was not chargeable. It was agreed before us that the Central Office was nothing more than an administrative unit of the Conservative and Unionist Party (to which I shall refer hereafter as 'the party'). No point has ever been taken by either side as to the name used for the purpose of the assessments. Both parties to this appeal asked the court to consider the legal nature of the party. If it is an unincorporated association, corporation tax has to be paid on the income identified in the Conservative and Unionist Party income and expenditure accounts for the relevant years as 'investment income and interest.' If it is not such an association, income tax will have to be paid on this income. We have not been concerned to decide who will have to pay income tax but we were told by Mr Park on behalf of the party that whatever income tax is payable will be paid out of the party's central funds. The reason why the party is contesting the assessments to corporation tax which have been made upon it is that for the relevant years the rates at which corporation tax was charged were much higher than the rates for income tax.

---

1 Now ss 6(1), 832 of the Income and Corporation Taxes Act 1988

The charging section of the Income and Corporation Taxes Act 1970 (section 238(1))[1] starts with these words: 'Corporation tax shall be charged on profits of companies . . . ' Section 526[2] is an interpretation section. Subsection (5) defines 'company' as follows:

> '"company" means, subject to subsection (6) below' — which has no relevance in this case — 'any body corporate or unincorporated association, but does not include a partnership, a local authority or a local authority association . . . '

It is against this statutory background that a meaning has to be given to the words 'unincorporated association.' It is sufficiently like a 'company' for it to be put in the charging section within the ambit of that word. The interpretation section makes it clear that the word 'company' has a meaning extending beyond a body corporate but not as far as a partnership or a local authority. I infer that by 'unincorporated association' in this context Parliament meant two or more persons bound together for one or more common purposes, not being business purposes, by mutual undertakings, each having mutual duties and obligations, in an organisation which has rules which identify in whom control of it and its funds rests and upon what terms and which can be joined or left at will. The bond of union between the members of an unincorporated association has to be contractual. This was accepted by the special commissioners and was the basis of their conclusion. The point of law which arises is whether on the facts they found they could properly have come to the conclusion which they did. The facts are set out fully in the case. For the purposes of this judgment I need do no more than refer to those which I consider to be relevant to the point of law.

Since membership of an unincorporated association is based on agreement between the members, a starting point for examining the legal nature of the party is to consider how anyone can join it. To this there is a short answer: no one can join the party directly. Membership can be obtained either through a local constituency association or through the parliamentary party. Members of local constituency associations, and such associations themselves, have no constitutional links with the parliamentary party although there are many political links. These local associations choose their own parliamentary candidates from a list of candidates approved by the party's Standing Advisory Committee. If a candidate of their choice is elected a member of the House of Commons he becomes a member of the parliamentary party when he accepts the Conservative Whip, which he will do on election but which he may refuse later, in which event he will no longer be a member of the parliamentary party. Once elected members of the House of Commons they become representatives of the constituency for which they have been elected, not delegates of the local constituency associations which may have put them up as candidates. On the facts as found I can find nothing which links contractually and directly members of local constituency associations to Conservative members of the House of Commons representing their constituencies. The lack of a contractual link is even more clear in the case of peers who are members of the parliamentary party as long as they accept the Conservative Whip in the House of Lords.

Contrast the approach of the House of Lords in *Clarke v Dunraven*,[3] where the court found that contestants independently entering into a yacht

---

1 Now s 6(1) of the Income and Corporation Taxes Act 1988
2 Now s 832 of the Income and Corporation Taxes Act 1988
3 [1897] AC 59

race were contractually bound with each other on the terms of the rules governing the race.

The connection between theories of corporate personality and company law in operation can be seen when considering the application of the doctrine of ultra vires to companies. The application of this doctrine has undergone much change (see Chapter 4), but in practice it is still important and it also reveals how different assumptions as to the nature of a corporation (corresponding to different theories of corporate personality) influence decisions. Compare Sources 6 and 7.

SOURCE 6
Riche *v* Ashbury Railway Carriage Company
(Blackburn J, Court of Exchequer Chamber) (1874) LR9 Ex 224

Facts: The Ashbury Railway Carriage and Iron Company Limited agreed to advance £26,000 towards the construction of a railway line in Belgium. One instalment of £13,000 was paid, but the company refused to pay the second on the ground that the agreement was ultra vires the company's objects clause. All twelve judges before whom the case was heard (three in the Court of Exchequer, four in the Court of Exchequer Chamber and five in the House of Lords) agreed that as a matter of construction, the company's objects clause did not expressly allow the company to enter into this agreement; on the other hand, it did not forbid it. The case was argued on the basis that all shareholders approved the agreement.

> I do not entertain any doubt that if, on the true construction of a statute creating a corporation, it appears to be the intention of the legislature, expressed or implied, that the corporation shall not enter into a particular contract, every Court, whether of law or equity, is bound to treat a contract entered into contrary to the enactment as illegal, and therefore wholly void; and to hold that a contract wholly void cannot be ratified.
>
> But it is of great importance, when we come to construe a statute creating a corporation, to consider what would be the incidents at common law conferred on a corporation created by charter.
>
> The leading authority on this subject is the case of *Sutton's Hospital*.[1] There were many points raised in that case. Those which I think material to the present point arose on a part of the charter set out in the special verdict, by which the King incorporated the first governors of the Charterhouse.
>
> . . .
>
> The King, . . . by this charter not only did not in express terms give a power of alienation, but by express negative words forbad any alienation except by lease. But the resolution of the Court, as reported by Coke (at p 30b), was that 'when a corporation is duly created all other incidents are tacite annexed; . . . and, therefore, divers clauses subsequent in the charter are not of necessity, but only declaratory, and might well have been left out. As, 1. by the same to have authority, ability, and capacity to purchase; but no clause is added that they may alien, etc, and it need not, for it is incident. 2. To sue and be sued, implead and be impleaded. 3. To have a seal, etc; that is also declaratory, for when they are incorporated they may make or use what seal they will. 4. To restrain them from

---

1 10 Co Rep 1, 77 ER 937

aliening or demising, but in a certain form; that is an ordinance testifying the King's desire, but it is but a precept and doth not bind in law.'

This seems to me an express authority that at common law it is an incident to a corporation to use its common seal for the purpose of binding itself to anything to which a natural person could bind himself, and to deal with its property as a natural person might deal with his own. And further, than an attempt to forbid this on the part of the King, even by express negative words, does not bind at law. Nor am I aware of any authority in conflict with this case.

. . .

I take it that the true rule of law is, that a corporation at common law has, as an incident given by law, the same power to contract, and subject to the same restrictions, that a natural person has. And this is important when we come to construe the statutes creating a corporation. For if it were true that a corporation at common law has a capacity to contract to the extent given it by the instrument creating it, and no further, the question would be, Does the statute creating the corporation by express provision, or by necessary implication, shew an intention in the legislature to confer upon this corporation capacity to make the contract? But if a body corporate has, as incident to it, a general capacity to contract, the question is, Does the statute creating the corporation by express provision, or necessary implication, shew an intention in the legislature to prohibit, and so avoid the making of, a contract of this particular kind?

. . .

And when we are construing a statute creating and regulating a corporation, it is right to bear in mind that, as Lord Coke says, 'It is a maxim in the common law that a statute made in the affirmative, without any negative expressed or implied, doth not take away the common law:' 2 Inst.200. Affirmative words may no doubt be used so as to imply a negative, see Plowden, Com. 113, but I take it the general principle is that thus laid down by Cresswell J in the *Eastern Archipelago Company v R*[1] 'that to make the words giving an express liberty or right have the effect of controlling or limiting that which would otherwise exist, they must be very plain.'

I now come to consider the construction of the Act of 1862, under which the present company is formed. The sections of the Act of 1862 bearing on the present case seem to me to be only sections 6, 8, 9, 10, and 12.

By section 6 of the Act of 1862, any seven persons may, by subscribing their names to a memorandum of association, and otherwise complying with the requisitions of this Act in respect of registration, form an incorporated company with or without limited liability.

Sections 8, 9 and 10 provide that the memorandum of association shall contain the objects for which the proposed company is to be established.

Section 12 provides that the company may make certain specified alterations in the memorandum of association, not including a change in the objects for which the company is to be established, and then, in express negative words, provides that, 'save as aforesaid, no alteration shall be made in the conditions contained in the memorandum of association.'

The objects of the proposed company must, therefore, always remain the same; and that has, I think, two important effects. First. I think that if the company, as a body, propose to do anything beyond these objects, any one dissentient shareholder (who has not precluded himself from doing so) may prevent it from doing so.

---

1 (1853) 2 EB 856; 118 ER 988

Secondly. No person can be entitled to fix the company with a contract made by the board for any purpose beyond those objects, on the ground that the board had an ostensible or apparent authority to make contracts of that kind, but must, in order to fix the company, at least prove an actual authority given to the board to make the particular contract he seeks to enforce.

Now, if I thought that it was at common law an incident to a corporation that its capacity should be limited to the extent conferred on it by the instrument creating it, I should agree that the capacity of a company incorporated under the Act of 1862 was limited to the objects in the memorandum of association. But if I am right in the opinion which I have already expressed, that the general power of contracting is an incident to a corporation which it requires an indication of intention in the legislature to take away, I see no such indication here. There are not even affirmative words, those used in section 25 of 7 & 8 Vict. c. 110, to which I shall now refer, having been (I presume advisedly) not repeated.

Section 25 of 7 & 8 Vict. c. 110 enacts that from the date of the certificate the shareholders shall be incorporated 'by the name of the company as set forth in the deed of settlement, and for the purpose of carrying on the trade or business for which the company was formed, but only according to the provisions of this Act and of such deed as aforesaid.' And then express powers are given to the company to enter into contracts for any 'necessary purpose of the company.'

I think if the question was whether the legislature had conferred on a corporation created under this Act capacity to enter into contracts beyond the provisions of the deed, there could be only one answer. The legislature did not confer such capacity.

But if the question be, as I apprehend it is, whether the legislature have indicated an intention to take away the power of contracting which at common law would be incident to a body corporate and not merely to limit the authority of the managing body and the majority of the shareholders to bind the minority, but also to prohibit and make illegal contracts made by the body corporate in such a manner that they would be binding on the body if incorporated at common law, I think the answer should be the other way. There certainly is ground for suspecting that the person who framed the Act 7 & 8 Vict. c. 110, thought that the corporation would have no other powers than those thus expressly given to it, and perhaps meant to restrict its powers accordingly, but when we remember the canon of construction that affirmative words do not take away the common law right I think he has not used words sufficient to effect such a purpose. It would be different if negative words had been used, and it had been said that the company should not do any other acts than those necessary for the purpose for which it is formed.

SOURCE 7
Ashbury Railway Carriage and Iron Company (Ltd) *v* Riche
(Lord Cairns LC, House of Lords) (1875) LR 7 HL 653; 44 LJ Exch 185

Those being the results of the documents to which I have referred, I will ask your Lordships now to consider the effect of the Act of Parliament — the Joint Stock Companies Act 1862 — on this state of things. And here, my Lords, I cannot but regret that by the two Judges in the Court of Exchequer the accurate and precise bearing of that Act of Parliament upon the present case appears to me to have been entirely overlooked or misapprehended; and that in the Court of Exchequer Chamber, speaking of the opinion of those learned Judges who thought that the decision of the Court of Exchequer should be maintained, the weight which was given to the provisions of this Act of Parliament appears to me to have entirely fallen short of that which ought to have been given to it. Your Lordships are well aware that this is the Act which put upon its present permanent footing the regulation of joint stock companies, and more especially of those joint stock companies which were to be authorized to trade with a limit to their liability.

The provisions under which that system of limiting liability was inaugurated, were provisions not merely, perhaps I might say not mainly, for the benefit of the shareholders for the time being in the company, but were enactments intended also to provide for the interests of two other very important bodies; in the first place, those who might become shareholders in succession to the persons who were shareholders for the time being; and secondly, the outside public, and more particularly those who might be creditors of companies of this kind. And I will ask your Lordships to observe, as I refer to some of the clauses, the marked and entire difference there is between the two documents which form the title deeds of companies of this description — I mean the Memorandum of Association on the one hand, and the Articles of Association on the other hand. With regard to the memorandum of association, your Lordships will find, as has often already been pointed out, although it appears somewhat to have been overlooked in the present case, that that is, as it were, the charter, and defines the limitation of the powers of a company to be established under the Act. With regard to the articles of association, those articles play a part subsidiary to the memorandum of association. They accept the memorandum of association as the charter of incorporation of the company, and so accepting it, the articles proceed to define the duties, the rights and the powers of the governing body as between themselves and the company at large, and the mode and form in which the business of the company is to be carried on, and the mode and form in which changes in the internal regulations of the company may from time to time be made. With regard, therefore, to the memorandum of association, if you find anything which goes beyond that memorandum, or is not warranted by it, the question will arise whether that which is so done is *ultra vires*, not only of the directors of the company, but of the company itself. With regard to the articles of association, if you find anything which, still keeping within the memorandum of association, is a violation of the articles of association, or in excess of them, the question will arise whether that is anything more than an act *extra vires* the directors, but *intra vires* the company.

The clauses of the statute to which it is necessary to refer are four: in the first place, the sixth clause. That provides that 'Any seven or more persons associated for any lawful purpose may, by subscribing their names to a memorandum of association, and otherwise complying with the requisitions of this Act in respect of registration, form an incorporated company, with or without limited liability.' My Lords, this is the first section which speaks of the incorporation of the company; but your Lordships will observe that it does not speak of that incorporation as the creation of a corporation with inherent common law rights, such rights as are by common law possessed by every corporation, and without any other limit than would by common law be assigned to them, but it speaks of the company being incorporated with reference to a memorandum of association; and you are referred thereby to the provisions which subsequently are to be found upon the subject of that memorandum of association.

The next clause which is material is the eighth: 'Where a company is formed on the principle of having the liability of its members limited to the amount unpaid on their shares, hereinafter referred to as a company limited by shares, the Memorandum of Association shall contain the following things' (I pass over the first and second, and I come to the third item which is to be specified): 'The objects for which the proposed company is to be established.' That is, therefore, the memorandum which the persons are to sign as a preliminary to the incorporation of the company. They are to state 'the objects for which the proposed company is to be established;' and the existence, the coming into existence, of the company is to be an existence and to be a coming into existence for those objects and for those objects alone.

Then, my Lords, section 11 provides: 'The memorandum of association shall bear the same stamp as if it were a deed, and shall be signed by each subscriber in the presence of, and be attested by, one witness at the least, and that attestation shall be a sufficient attestation in Scotland, as well as in England and Ireland. It shall, when registered, bind the company and the members thereof to the same extent as if each member had subscribed his name and affixed his seal thereto, and there were in the memorandum contained, on the part of himself, his heirs, executors, and administrators, a covenant to observe all the conditions of such memorandum, subject to the provisions of this Act.' Your Lordships will observe, therefore, that it is to be a covenant in which every member of the company is to covenant that he will observe the conditions of the memorandum, one of which is that the objects for which the company is established are the objects mentioned in the memorandum, and that he not only will observe that, but will observe it subject to the provisions of this Act. Well, but the very next provision of the Act contained in section 12 is this: 'Any company limited by shares may so far modify the conditions contained in its memorandum of association, if authorized to do so by its regulations as originally framed, or as altered by special resolution in manner hereinafter mentioned, as to increase its capital by the issue of new shares of such amount as it thinks expedient, or to consolidate and divide its capital into shares of larger amount than its existing shares, or to convert its paid-up shares into stock, but, save as aforesaid, and save as is hereinafter provided in the case of a change of name, no alteration shall be made by any company in the conditions contained in its memorandum of association.' The covenant, therefore, is not merely that every member will observe the conditions upon which the company is established, but that no change shall be made in those conditions; and if there is a covenant that no change shall be made in the objects for which the company is established, I apprehend that that includes within it the engagement that no object shall be pursued by the company, or attempted to be attained by the company in practice, except an object which is mentioned in the memorandum of association.

Now, my Lords, if that is so — if that is the condition upon which the corporation is established — if that is the purpose for which the corporation is established — it is a mode of incorporation which contains in it both that which is affirmative and that which is negative. It states affirmatively the ambit and extent of vitality and power which by law are given to the corporation and it states, if it is necessary so to state, negatively, that nothing shall be done beyond that ambit, and that no attempt shall be made to use the corporate life for any other purpose than that which is so specified.

PART III: THE GRANT OF CORPORATE STATUS

Is Intervention by the State Necessary?
In the United Kingdom today, incorporated status can be achieved only through the exercise of central power or the act of officials authorised by central power. Thus companies may be chartered (by the exercise of the royal

prerogative power), statutory (effected by individual statute) or registered (under the provisions of an enabling statute, eg Companies Act 1985, Industrial and Provident Societies Act 1965). The requirement for state intervention for the grant of corporate status has been accepted at least from the time of Blackstone.

SOURCE 8
Blackstone, Commentaries on the Laws of England
(First published 1765–69) volume 1, pp 455–61

Of Corporations
We have hitherto considered persons in their natural capacities, and have treated of their rights and duties. But, as all personal rights die with the person; and, as the necessary forms of investing a series of individuals, one after another, with the same identical rights, would be very inconvenient, if not impracticable; it has been found necessary, when it is for the advantage of the public to have any particular rights kept on foot and continued, to constitute artificial persons, who may maintain a perpetual succession, and enjoy a kind of legal immortality.

These artificial persons are called bodies politic, bodies corporate (*corpora corporata*) or corporations: of which there is a great variety subsisting, for the advancement of religion, of learning, and of commerce; in order to preserve entire and for ever those rights and immunities, which, if they were granted only to those individuals of which the body corporate is composed, would upon their death be utterly lost and extinct. To shew the advantages of these incorporations, let us consider the case of a college in either of our universities, founded *ad studendum et orandum*, for the encouragement and support of religion and learning. If this was a mere voluntary assembly, the individuals which compose it might indeed read, pray, study, and perform scholastic exercises together, so long as they could agree to do so: but they could neither frame, nor receive any laws or rules of their conduct; none at least, which would have any binding force, for want of a coercive power to create a sufficient obligation. Neither could they be capable of retaining any privileges or immunities: for, if such privileges be attacked, which of all this unconnected assembly has the right, or ability, to defend them? And, when they are dispersed by death or otherwise, how shall they transfer these advantages to another set of students, equally unconnected as themselves? So also, with regard to holding estates or other property, if land be granted for the purposes of religion or learning to twenty individuals not incorporated, there is no legal way of continuing the property to any other persons for the same purposes, but by endless conveyances from one to the other, as often as the hands are changed. But when they are consolidated and united into a corporation, they and their successors are then considered as one person in law: as one person, they have one will, which is collected from the sense of the majority of the individuals: this one will may establish rules and orders for the regulation of the whole, which are a sort of municipal laws of this little republic; or rules and statutes may be prescribed to it at it's [*sic*] creation, which are then in the place of natural laws: the privileges and immunities, the estates and possessions, of the corporation, when once vested in them, will be for ever vested, without any new conveyance to new successions; for all the individual members that have existed from the foundation to the present time, or that shall ever hereafter exist, are but one person in law, a person that never dies: in like manner as the river Thames is still the same river, though the parts which compose it are changing every instant.

The honour of originally inventing these political constitutions entirely belongs to the Romans. They were introduced, as Plutarch says, by Numa; who finding, upon his accession, the city torn to pieces by the two rival factions of Sabines and Romans, thought it a prudent and politic measure to subdivide these two into many smaller ones, by instituting separate societies of every manual trade and profession. They were afterwards much considered by the civil law, in which they were called *universitates*, as forming one whole out of many individuals; or *collegia*, from being gathered together: they were adopted also by the canon law, for the maintenance of ecclesiastical discipline; and from them our spiritual corporations are derived. But our laws have considerably refined and improved upon the invention, according to the usual genius of the English nation:

. . .

Corporations, by the civil law, seem to have been created by the mere act, and voluntary association of their member; provided such convention was not contrary to law, for then it was *illicitum collegium*. It does not appear that the prince's consent was necessary to be actually given to the foundation of them; but merely that the original founders of these voluntary and friendly societies (for they were little more than such) should not establish any meetings in opposition to the laws of the state.

But, with us in England, the king's consent is absolutely necessary to the erection of any corporation, either impliedly or expressly given. The king's implied consent is to be found in corporations which exist by force of the *common law*, to which our former kings are supposed to have given their concurrence; common law being nothing else but custom, arising from the universal agreement of the whole community. Of this sort are the king himself, all bishops, parsons, vicars, churchwardens, and some others; who by common law have ever been held (as far as our books can shew us) to have been corporations, *virtute officii*: and this incorporation is so inseparably annexed to their offices, that we cannot frame a complete legal idea of any of these persons, but we must also have an idea of a corporation, capable to transmit his rights to his successors, at the same time. Another method of implication, whereby the king's consent is presumed, is as to all corporations by *prescription*, such as the city of London, and many others, which have existed as corporations, time whereof the memory of man runneth not to the contrary; and therefore are looked upon in law to be well created. For though the members thereof can shew no legal charter of incorporation, yet in cases of such high antiquity the law presumes there once was one; and that by the variety of accidents, which a length of time may produce, the charter is lost or destroyed. The methods, by which the king's consent is expressly given, are either by act of parliament or charter. By act of parliament, of which the royal assent is a necessary ingredient, corporations may undoubtedly be created: but it is observable, that most of those statutes, which are usually cited as having created corporations, do either confirm such as have been before created by the king; as in the case of the college of physicians, erected by charter 10 Hen. VIII, which charter was afterwards confirmed in parliament; or, they permit the king to erect a corporation *in futuro* with such and such powers; as is the case of the bank of England, and the society of the British fishery. So that the immediate creative act is usually performed by the king alone, in virtue of his royal prerogative.

All the other methods therefore whereby corporations exist, by common law, by prescription, and by act of parliament, are for the most part reducible to this of the king's letters patent, or charter of incorporation.

Blackstone may have been wrong in describing Roman Law as different from the English Common Law in this regard (see Source 1 and Source 9). Differing attitudes to the possibility of incorporation by prescription can be seen by comparing Sources 10 and 11.

SOURCE 9
The Digest of Justinian

The extract below is from the writings of Gaius and Ulpian, two of the greatest of the Roman jurists who lived in the second and third centuries AD respectively. (D. 3.4.1.)

> Gaius, *Provincial Edict, book 3:* Partnerships, *collegia,* and bodies of this sort may not be formed by everybody at will; for this right is restricted by statutes, *senatus consulta,* and imperial *constitutiones.* In a few cases only are bodies of this sort permitted. For example, partners in tax farming, gold mines, silver mines, and saltworks are allowed to form corporations. Likewise, there are certain *collegia* at Rome whose corporate status has been established by *senatus consulta* and imperial *constitutiones,* for example, those of the bakers and certain others and of the shipowners, who are found in the provinces too. 1. Those permitted to form a corporate body consisting of a *collegium* or partnership or specifically one or the other of these have the right on the pattern of the state to have common property, a common treasury, and an attorney or syndic through whom, as in a state, what should be transacted and done in common is transacted and done. 2. For if no one defends them, the proconsul says that he will order what they have in common to be seized and, if after warning they are not roused to defend their property, to be sold. Furthermore, we consider that there is no attorney or syndic on occasions also when he is away or prevented by ill-health or not qualified to act. 3. And if an outsider wants to defend the corporation, the proconsul allows it, as is the practice in the defense of individuals, because this improves the position of a corporation.
>
> Ulpian, *Edict, book 8:* If members of a municipality or any corporate body appoint an attorney for legal business, it should not be said that he is in the position of a man appointed by several people; for he comes in on behalf of a public authority or corporate body, not on behalf of individuals.

SOURCE 10
Re The Company or Fraternity of Free Fishermen of Faversham
(Court of Appeal 1887) (1887) 36 Ch D 329; 57 LJ Ch 187

This was a petition to wind up a company or association known by the name of The Company or Fraternity of Free Fishermen and Dredgermen of the Manor and Hundred of Faversham, in the County of Kent.

The association had existed from time immemorial, and its early history was very obscure.

. . .

No record had been found of any charter or grant of the fishery to the tenants of the manor or any association of fishermen, but the fishermen of Faversham appear from time immemorial to have paid a yearly rent of £1 3s 4d. to the lords of the manor for the right of fishing.

. . .

By an Act passed in the year 1840, the 3 Vict. c. lix., intituled 'An Act for granting certain powers to the Faversham Oyster Fishery Company,' it was recited that 'there is and from time out of mind hath been a certain company in the nature of a prescriptive corporation called or known by the name of The Company or Fraternity of Free Fishermen and Dredgermen of the Manor and Hundred of Faversham in the County of Kent, and the freemen and members of the said company had bred, laid, dredged for, caught, had and taken oysters and oyster-brood in the waters and creeks within the said fishery exclusive[1] of all other persons, the said company paying in consideration thereof a yearly sum of 23 shillings and 4 pence to the lord of the said manor and hundred and Faversham for the time being;' and further, that 'the said fishery is maintained and preserved at a very considerable yearly sum of money by the said company, and the said fishery is of great benefit to the public as well as to the said company; . . .'

COTTON LJ: . . . In my opinion, although I regret that creditors who have advanced their money should not be paid, yet the result of the argument and evidence which we have had brought before us is this, that no good whatever would result from making a winding-up order; for this reason, that the corporation, assuming it to be a corporation, has no property which could be sold effectually.

The evidence here is not very plain, but we must try and make out, if we can, what is the true position of affairs. The matters go back to very great antiquity, and the evidence has not, as a rule, been brought before us in such a way as to enable us to decide absolutely on that evidence what the facts are. I think one thing is clearly proved, that the only property which the Free Fishermen have is the right to fish or dredge for oysters in the sea. Then the question is, can that be sold so as to produce any benefit for the creditors?

. . .

In my opinion it is a corporation, and I say so for a reason which may be shortly expressed. There is an Act to regulate and give powers to this Fraternity or Company of Free Fishermen (3 Vict. c. lix.) and that recognises that there is in this body of persons property consisting of this free fishery, this right to fish for oysters. It could not be in them unless in fact they were incorporated, either for the purposes of the grant or by virtue of the grant to them from the Crown; and although a grant from anybody but the Crown would not have incorporated this company of Free Fishermen, yet if there was a grant from the Crown to certain persons as the Free Fishermen of Faversham that would incorporate them for the purpose of their being enabled to take the grant which was made to them by the Crown. In my opinion therefore this was a corporation. But that does not settle the matter at all. If this grant was to a corporation, which I think was formed for the purposes of the grant, then undoubtedly subject to the objections which have been taken to winding up a company which has such a grant made to it and selling the franchise so granted, it would be a case for selling and realizing the property of the corporation. But it may be that the corporation as such never had any beneficial interest in this franchise which was granted to it, and in my opinion that is the proper result of the evidence.

SOURCE 11
Morrison v Standard Building Society
(South African Appellate Division 1932) 1932 AD 229

WESSELS JA: The plaintiff in the court below [the Building Society] (respondent in this Court) claimed . . . an order for the ejectment of the appellant from certain premises . . . and for damages. The appellant set up the following defences:

---

1 The privilege of monopoly, see pp 20–22

1. That the Society has no *locus standi in judicio* because it is an unincorporated Society and cannot sue in its own name.

. . .

The first question to decide is whether the Society was entitled to sue in its own name. Mr Hope, on behalf of the appellant, contended that by the Roman law an association of persons for gain, which has not obtained the permission of the State to act as a corporate body, has no *locus standi in judicio*. Such an association is not a *universitas* or corporation and therefore cannot sue in its own name. There are certain exceptions, but Mr Hope contends that a building society does not fall within one of these. He argues that this is also the Roman-Dutch law because that law is based upon the Roman law and there existed no special legislation in Holland dealing with this matter. In order to ascertain the Roman law as to whether an association of persons such as a building society can have a corporate existence without the special sanction of the State, we have been referred to three passages in the Digest — D. 3.4.1, D. 47.22.3.1 and D. 34.5.20. These passages are very brief, and merely state that an association of persons cannot be regarded as a *corpus* because there are statutes, *senatusconsulta* and imperial decrees which prevent it. In a few cases, however, such associations are permitted, as in the case of tax-gatherers, and where people combine to mine for gold, silver, or salt. Now how much of this legislation formed part of the public law of Rome, and how much part of the private law and how much were mere police regulations, we do not know, for we are ignorant of the provisions of the laws mentioned in *lex* D. 3.4.1. The older commentators have endeavoured by piecing together texts from the *Corpus Juris* to arrive at some general idea of the scope of the legislation. Faber in his *Rationalia ad Pandectas*, in commenting on D. 3.4.1, says that the provision in the *lex* was based on the principle *salus populi suprema lex* and that the Legislature thought it dangerous to allow *hujusmodi societates sodalitates et collegia* to exist lest men coming together under some pretext might conspire against the head of the State. Where however such fear did not exist, persons were entitled to combine as in the case of religious bodies or where persons obtained concessions out of which they could make a profit, or where they combined to mine for gold, silver or salt. In the same way workmen could combine . . . Similar associations for a useful purpose were not only permitted but were even privileged . . . The commentators also point out that some associations for public benefit were specially created corporations, others were allowed to act as corporations, whilst yet others were not interfered with . . .

There is little or no doubt that the older commentators thought that according to the Roman law an association or combination of individuals could not form a *corpus* or *universitas* unless it had the sanction of the State. Amongst the more modern jurists skilled in Roman law a controversy exists whether in fact all corporations required the sanction of the State. Owing to the sparsity of authority in the texts it is a very difficult matter to determine exactly what associations required the sanction of the State and what did not need a special sanction in order to give them the character of a corporation. Some jurists are of opinion that we must consider the objects and constitution of the association and judge from these whether it possesses the character of a corporation or not. If it has the characteristics of a corporation, and if such a combination is not specially forbidden, then it did not require special permission of the State in order to function as a corporation . . . Others again hold that the sanction of the State is essential except in the case of religious bodies, institutions *ad pias causas* and combinations for public purposes . . .

It has been urged that an association formed for gain was in a worse position than other associations. There is nothing in the texts to justify this view. If the *ratio legis* was to prevent seditious associations, then this cannot apply to associations for gain. These would be more of the nature of mining associations and could not possibly harm the State or lead to plots against the *princeps*.

I shall now pass on to the Roman-Dutch law. If it is difficult to ascertain the Roman law upon this subject with any degree of accuracy, it is equally difficult to say what the Roman-Dutch law was in the 18th century. It is true that the Roman-Dutch law was built up on a foundation of Roman law, but it never adopted the Roman law *en bloc*. It certainly never took over any part of the Roman public law or police regulations as part of the common law of Holland. As it is difficult to say how much of the legislation in Rome with regard to *universitates* was public and how much was private law, and how much was founded on police regulations, there must be considerable doubt whether the provisions of the Roman law as to the establishment of *universitates* was ever regarded as part of the law of Holland. Voet (3.4.1) deals with the matter and states that unless a corporation has State sanction it has no *locus standi in judicio* nor has it a *patrimonium*, and therefore the Jews and Anabaptists cannot take legacies, but the writer of the Aanhangsel to Kersteman's Woordenboek shows that Voet is in error. Most of the other celebrated Roman-Dutch lawyers are silent on this point. Seeing that we are not at all certain what the Roman law was with regard to the creation of a *universitas*, and seeing that the Roman-Dutch lawyers of the 17th and 18th centuries do not specially refer to this matter and adopt the Roman law as laid down in the Digest, it is impossible for us to say that State sanction was in Holland an essential for the creation of a *universitas*, and that without such sanction it cannot sue in its own name. But even if in this respect the Roman-Dutch law had adopted the law as laid down in the Digest, it would be difficult to say that a building society was not such a society as the Roman law would have recognised. If the object of the Roman law was to prevent associations from holding property which might become seditious, then this *ratio legis* does not apply to such an institution as a building society which is so favoured by our legislation that it is excluded from the Companies Act and is exempted from paying income tax.

. . .

The Society has brought many actions in its own name in the law courts. Even therefore if it has not obtained State sanction, it certainly has been allowed to carry on business in its corporate name, to hold property and to sue. It therefore falls under the category of associations which have been permitted or suffered to act as corporate bodies without let or hindrance. This review of our law upon the subject has led me to the conclusion that Gregorowoski J was right when he held in the case of *Committee of the Johannesburg Public Library v Spence*[1] that an association of individuals does not always require the special sanction of the State in order to enable it to hold property and to sue in its corporate name in our Courts. In order to determine whether an association of individuals is a corporate body which can sue in its own name, the Court has to consider the nature and objects of the association as well as its constitution, and if these show that it possesses the characteristics of a corporation or *universitas* then it can sue in its own name. Nor can I see any valid objection to such a society suing in its own name. It is true that a partnership cannot sue or be sued in its own name, with certain exceptions, but this is because one partner is the agent of the others and the property of its individual members can be executed upon. A building society is not a partnership in any shape or form. One member of a building society is not the agent of the others and his acts cannot bind his fellow members. Nor can

---

[1] 5 Off Rep 54

a member of such a society be held liable for the debts of the society.[1] The society exists as such quite apart from the individuals who compose it, for these may change from day to day. It has perpetual succession and it is capable of owning property apart from its members (*Webb v Northern Rifles*[2]) . . .

It has therefore all the characteristics of a *universitas* and can sue in its own name. No doubt the Companies Acts do create a difficulty, for if an association can be regarded as a corporate body capable of suing in its own name it may be possible, as pointed out by the learned Judge in the court below, for corporations to be formed which could own property in their corporate names and incur debts for which the individual members would not be responsible beyond the moneys they have paid into the coffers of the corporations. . . . Associations, however, which were formed before these Acts are not affected by this provision (*Shaw v Simmons*[3]). I have, however, no intention of deciding that every association formed before the Companies Acts came into force can sue in its corporate name. Whether it can or cannot depends entirely upon the nature of the association, its constitution, its objects and its activities. In this particular case we are dealing with a building society formed in 1891 . . . whose activities have not been interfered with at any time: an association of a peculiar nature favoured in two Acts of Parliament. But for the fact that it has not obtained the special sanction of the State it possesses all the characteristics of a *universitas* or corporate body, and therefore in my opinion it can sue in its own name.

Chartered and Statutory Companies

Chartered companies and the statutory companies of the late eighteenth and the nineteenth centuries were privately financed but enjoyed their privileges because they carried out undertakings of public importance. In many instances, these privileges consisted of *de iure* or *de facto* monopolies as well as corporate status. There is some doubt as to whether limited liability was extended to the investors of charter companies (see Carr, *Select Charters of Trading Companies*, Selden Society, vol 28, 1913 Introduction, xviii; Jenkins, 'Skinning the Pantomime Horse' [1975] CLJ 308) but there is no doubt that statutes incorporating *statutory* companies did extend limited liability to those who invested in such companies.

SOURCE 12

The Charter of the Newfoundland Company
(taken from Carr, *Select Charters of Trading Companies*, Selden Society, volume 28, 1913, pp 51–62)

James by the Grace of God of Great Britain France and Ireland King, Defender of the Faith etc, To all people to whom these presents shall come, Greeting:

Know ye whereas divers our loving and well-disposed subjects are desirous to make plantation to inhabit and establish a colony or colonies in the southern and eastern parts of the country and isle or islands commonly called Newfound Land, unto the coast and harbours whereof the subjects of this our Realm of England have for the space of fifty years and upwards yearly used to resort in no small numbers to fish, intending by such plantation and inhabiting both to secure and

---

1 For an example of the conferment of limited liability on the members of an unincorporated association, according to principles of the Common Law, see *Wise v Perpetual Trustee* [1903] AC 139, PC
2 1908 TS 462
3 12 QBD 117

make safe the said trade of fishing to our subjects for ever, and also to make some commendable benefit for the use of mankind by the lands and profits thereof which hitherto from the beginning (as it seemeth manifest) hath remained unprofitable, and for better performance of such their purpose and intentions have humbly besought our regal authority and assistance,

We being well assured that the same land or country adjoining to the foresaid coasts where our subjects use to fish remaineth so destitute and so desolate of inhabitants that scarce any one savage person hath in many years been seen in the most part thereof, And well knowing that the same lying and being so vacant is as well for the reasons aforesaid as for many other reasons very commodious for Us and our Dominions, And that by the law of nature and nations We may of our royal authority possess our selves and make grant thereof without doing wrong to any other prince or state, considering they cannot justly pretend any sovereignty or right thereunto in respect that the same remaineth so vacant and not actually possessed and inhabited by any Christian or any other whomsoever,

And therefore thinking it a matter and action well beseeming a Christian King to make true use of that which God from the beginning created for mankind, and thereby intending not only to work and procure the benefit and good of many of our subjects but principally to increase the knowledge of the Omnipotent God and the propagation of our Christian faith.

Have graciously accepted of the said intention and suit, And therefore do *of our special grace certain knowledge and mere motion* for Us our heirs and successors give grant and confirm by these presents unto our right dear and right wellbeloved Cousin and Counsellor *Henrie Earle of Northampton,* Keeper of our Privy Seal, and to our trusty and right wellbeloved *Sir Lawrence Tanfield* Knt, Chief Baron of our Exchequer, *Sir John Doddridge* Knt, one of our Sergeants at law, *Sir Frauncis Bacon* Knt, our Solicitor General, . . . [the names of some 40 knights and gentlemen] their heirs and assigns, and to such and so many as they do or shall hereafter admit to be joined with them in form hereafter in these presents expressed, whether they go in their persons to be planted in the said plantation or whether they go not but do adventure their monies goods and chattels, That they shall be one body or communalty perpetual, and shall have perpetual succession, and one common seal to serve for the said body or communalty and they and their successors shall be known called and incorporated by the name of **The Treasurer and the Company of Adventurers and Planters of the City of London and Bristol for the Colony of Plantation in Newfound Land:**

And that they and their successors shall be likewise enabled by the name aforesaid to plead and be impleaded before any our Judges or Justices in any of our Courts and in any actions or suits whatsoever:

And We do also *of our said special grace certain knowledge and mere motion* for Us our heirs and successors give grant and confirm unto the said Treasurer and Company and their successors under the reservations limitations and declarations hereafter expressed, All that part and portion of the said country commonly called Newfound Land

. . .

And also all the lands soil grounds havens ports rivers mines, as well royal mines of gold and silver as other mines, minerals pearls and precious stones woods quarries marshes waters fishings huntings hawkings fowlings commodities and hereditaments whatsoever, together with all prerogatives jurisdictions royalties privileges franchises and preeminences within any the said territories and the precincts thereof whatsoever and thereto or thereabouts both by sea and land being or in any sort belonging or appertaining and which We by our Letters Patents may or can grant, and in as ample manner and sort as We or any of our noble Progenitors have heretofore granted to any company body politic or corporate or to any adventurer or adventurers undertaker or undertakers of any discovery plantation or traffic of in or unto any foreign parts whatsoever, and in as large and ample manner as if the same were herein particularly mentioned and expressed:

Nevertheless our will and pleasure is and We do by these presents express and declare that there will be saved and reserved unto all manner of persons of what nation soever and also to all and every our loving subjects which do at this present or hereafter shall trade or voyage to the parts aforesaid for fishing, all and singular liberties powers easements and all other benefits whatsoever as well concerning their said fishing as all circumstances and incidents thereunto in as large and ample manner as they have heretofore used and enjoyed the same, without any impeachment disturbance or execution, anything in these presents to the contrary notwithstanding:

To have hold possess and enjoy all and singular the said lands countries and territories with all and singular other the premises heretofore by these presents granted or mentioned to be granted to them the said Treasurer and Company their successors or assigns for ever, to the sole and proper use of them the said Treasurer [etc] to be holden of Us our heirs and successors as of our manor of East Greenwich in the County of Kent in free and common socage and not *in capite*, Yielding and paying unto Us our heirs and successors the fifth part of all the ore of gold and silver that from time to time and at all times hereafter shall be there gotten had and obtained for all services duties and demands:

And forasmuch as the good and prosperous success of the said plantation cannot but chiefly depend, next under the Blessing of God and the support of our royal authority, upon the provident and good direction of the whole enterprise by a careful and understanding Council, And that it is not convenient that all the Adventurers shall be so often drawn to meet and assemble as shall be requisite for them to have meetings and conferences about their affairs,

Therefore We do ordain establish and confirm that there shall be perpetually one Council consisting of twelve persons here resident in London which shall govern and order all matters and causes which shall arise grow or happen by reason of the said plantation or which shall or may concern the government of any colony or colonies to be established in any the said territories or countries of Newfound Land before limited or any the precincts thereof, Which Council shall have a seal for the better government and administration of the said plantation besides the legal seal of the Company or Corporation, Each of which seals shall have our arms engraven on the side thereof and our portraiture on the other side, And that the legal seal of the said Treasurer and Company shall have engraven round about on both sides thereof these words, *Sigillum Thesaurarii et Communitatis Terre Noue*, and that the seal of the Council shall have engraven round about on the one side these words, *Sigillum Regis Magne Britannie Franc., et Hibernie*, and on the other side this inscription round about, *Pro Consilio Terre Noue*:

. . .

And lastly because the principal effect which We can desire or expect of this action is the conversion and reduction of the people in those parts (if any be there inhabiting) unto the true worship of God and Christian religion, in which respect We would be loth that any person should be permitted to pass that We suspected to affect the superstitions of the Church of Rome, We do hereby declare that it is our will and pleasure that none be permitted to pass in any voyage from time to time to be made into the said country but such as first shall have taken the Oath of Supremacy, for which purpose We do by these presents give full power and authority to the Treasurer for the time being and any three of the Council and to every three such person or persons as shall be by the said Treasurer and any three of the said Council thereunto authorised (whereof the Treasurer for the time being to be one), and to any our Mayors Bailiffs or any other our chief officer or officers in any our ports havens or towns where any such person or persons shall take shipping to tender and exhibit the said oath to all such persons as shall at any time be sent and employed in the said voyage to remain or plant there:

. . .

SOURCE 13
Act of Parliament 1836, 6 & 7 William 4, c. cvi (local and personal)

This Act incorporated the Eastern Counties Railway Company, which eventually became part of the Great Eastern Railway. The decision in *Colman v Eastern Counties Railway Company*[1] is regarded as the first application to a statutory company of the doctrine of *ultra vires* (Brice, *The Doctrine of Ultra Vires* (3rd edn 1895), Preface)

An Act for making a Railway from London to Norwich and Yarmouth, by Romford, Chelmsford, Colchester, and Ipswich, to be called 'The Eastern Counties Railway.' [4 July 1836]
Whereas the making a railway from London to Norwich and Yarmouth, passing by Romford, Chelmsford, Colchester, and Ipswich, would be of great public advantage by opening an additional, certain, and expeditious communication between those cities and towns and the intermediate and adjacent towns and districts, and also by facilitating the means of intercourse between the Metropolis and the Eastern Districts of England: and whereas the King's most Excellent Majesty, in right of His Crown, is interested in certain property on the line of the said proposed railway: And whereas the several persons herein-after named are willing at their own costs and charges to carry the said undertaking into execution, but the same cannot be effected without the authority of Parliament: may it therefore please Your Majesty that it may be enacted; and be it enacted by the King's most Excellent Majesty, by and with the advice and consent of the Lords Spiritual and Temporal, and Commons, in this present Parliament assembled, and by the authority of the same, that [21 named men] and all other persons and corporations who have subscribed or shall hereafter subscribe towards the said undertaking, and their several and respective successors, executors, administrators, and assigns, shall be and they are hereby united into a company for making and maintaining the said railway and other works by this Act authorized, and for other the purposes herein declared, according to the provisions and restrictions herein-after mentioned, and for that purpose shall be one body corporate by the name and style of 'The Eastern Counties Railway Company,' and by that name shall have perpetual succession and a common seal, and shall and may sue and be sued, and also shall have power and authority to purchase, hold, and sell lands for the use and benefit of the said undertaking without incurring any penalties or forfeitures, and shall also have and exercise all other powers and authorities which are herein-after given or mentioned.

. . .

III. Proprietors to raise Money amongst themselves for the Undertaking, not exceeding £1,600,000, to be divided into Shares of £25 each. And be it further

---

1 (1846) 10 Beaven 1; 50 ER 481

enacted, that it shall be lawful for the said company to raise amongst themselves any sum of money for making and maintaining the said railway and other works by this Act authorized, not exceeding in the whole one million six hundred thousand pounds, the whole to be divided into shares of twenty-five pounds each; and such shares shall be numbered, beginning with number one, in arithmetical progression, and every share shall be distinguished by the number to be applied to the same; and the said shares shall be and are hereby vested in the several parties taking the same, and their several and respective successors, executors, administrators, and assigns, to their proper use and benefit, proportionably to the sum they shall severally contribute; and all corporations and persons, and their several and respective successors, executors, administrators, and assigns, who have subscribed or shall severally subscribe for one or more share or shares, or such sum or sums as shall be demanded in lieu thereof towards the said undertaking and other the purposes of the said subscription, shall be entitled to and shall receive in proportionable parts, according to the respective sums so by them respectively paid, the net profits and advantages which shall arise or accrue from or by the rates, tolls, and other sums of money to be received by the said company as and when the same shall be divided by the authority of this act.

IV. To compel Payment of Subscriptions. And be it further enacted, that the several persons who have subscribed or who shall hereafter subscribe or agree to advance or pay any money for or towards the said undertaking, shall and they are hereby required to pay the sums of money by them respectively subscribed or agreed to be paid, or such parts thereof as shall from time to time be called for by the directors of the said company under the powers of this Act, at such times and places and to such persons as shall be directed by the said directors; and in case any person shall refuse or neglect to pay as aforesaid the money by him so subscribed for, or the part thereof so called for, it shall be lawful for the said company to sue for and recover the same, with full costs of suit, in any court of law or equity, together with interest on every such unpaid sum of money at the rate of five pounds per cent per annum, from the time when the same was directed to be paid as aforesaid up to the day of the actual payment thereof.

V. Application of Money to be raised. And be it further enacted, that the money to be raised by the said company by virtue of this act shall be laid out and applied, in the first place, in paying and discharging all costs and expences incurred in applying for, obtaining, and passing this Act, and all other expences preparatory or relating thereto, and afterwards the remainder of such money shall be applied in, for, and towards purchasing lands, and making and maintaining the said railway and other works, and in otherwise carrying this Act into execution.

VI. Company empowered to make the Railway. And be further enacted, that it shall be lawful for the said company and they are hereby empowered to make and maintain the railway herein-after mentioned, with all proper works and conveniences connected therewith, in the line or course, and upon, across, under, or over the lands delineated upon the amended plan, and described in the amended Book of Reference to be deposited with the respective Clerks of the Peace for the counties of Middlesex, Essex, Suffolk, and Norfolk, and the town and county of the city of Norwich;

. . .

IX. Power to take lands, etc. And be it further enacted, that for the purposes and subject to the provisions and restrictions of this Act it shall be lawful for the said company, their agents and workmen, and all other persons by them authorized, and they are hereby empowered, to enter into and upon the lands of any person or corporation whatsoever, and to survey and take levels of the same or of any part thereof, and to set out and appropriate for the purposes of this Act such parts thereof as they are by this Act empowered to take or use, and in or upon such lands, or any lands adjoining thereto, to bore, dig, cut, embank, and sough, and to remove or lay, and also to use, work, and manufacture, any earth, stone, trees, gravel, or sand, or any other materials or things which may be dug or obtained therein, or otherwise, in the execution of any of the powers of this Act, and which may be proper or necessary for making, maintaining, altering, repairing, or using the said railway and other works by this Act authorized, or which may obstruct the making, maintaining, altering, repairing, or using the same respectively, according to the full and true intent and meaning of this Act;

. . .

CLIX. Power of Directors to make Calls. And be it further enacted, that the directors of the said company shall have power from time to time to make such calls of money from the proprietors of shares in the capital stock of the said company who shall not have already paid the full amount due or payable in respect of their respective shares, to defray the expense of the said railway and carry on the same, as they from time to time shall find necessary, so that no such call shall at any one time exceed the sum of three pounds upon each share which any person or corporation shall be possessed of or entitled unto in the said undertaking, and that there shall be an interval of three calendar months at the least between every two calls, and twenty-one days notice at the least shall be given of every such call by advertisement in one or more newspaper or newspapers published or circulated in each of the counties of Middlesex, Essex, Suffolk and Norfolk; and the several proprietors of shares in the capital stock of the company shall and they are hereby required to pay the sum or sums of money subscribed for or payable in respect or on account of their several and respective shares, or so much thereof as shall not have been previously paid up by such calls or instalments, to such person or persons, at such time or times, at such place or places, and in such manner as the directors of the company shall from time to time direct or appoint, for the use of the said undertaking; and if any proprietor of any such share shall not from time to time pay the rateable proportion or call or instalment due in respect of each such share to the person, at the time and place, and in the manner to be appointed for payment thereof as hereinbefore mentioned, then and in such case and as often as the same shall happen such proprietor shall pay interest for the amount which shall be so unpaid after the rate of five pounds per centum per annum from the day appointed for the payment thereof up to the time when the same shall be actually paid; provided that no proprietor of any share in the capital stock of the said company shall, under the authority of this Act, be called upon or be liable to pay any greater sum of money than, with the principal money already paid on account of the subscription for such shares, will amount to the sum of twenty-five pounds in respect of each such share, over and besides any interest paid or payable by reason of default in payment of calls as aforesaid.

CLX. In default of Payment of Call for Two Months, Directors empowered to recover the same, or to declare Shares to be forfeited, and sell them. Provided always, and be it further enacted, that in case any proprietor of a share or shares in the capital stock of the company shall neglect or refuse to pay the rateable

proportion or call or instalment due in respect of each share taken or held by
him to the person, at the time and place, and in the manner to be appointed for
payment thereof as aforesaid, together with interest (if any) which shall accrue
for the same, for the space of two calendar months after the day appointed for
the payment thereof, then it shall be lawful for the said company to sue for and
recover the same, together with interest at the rate aforesaid up to the time of
actual payment thereof, in any of His Majesty's Courts of Record, by action of
debt or on the case, or by Bill, suit, or information, or the said directors may and
they are hereby authorized to declare the shares belonging to any person or
corporation so refusing or neglecting to pay in manner last aforesaid to be
forfeited, and to be sold, subject to the provisions of this Act: provided
nevertheless, that no advantage shall be taken of any forfeiture of any share in the
said undertaking until notice in writing under the hands of two directors, or
under the hand of the clerk or secretary of the said company, of such share
having been declared by the directors forfeited, shall have been given or sent by
the post unto or delivered to some inmate of the last known usual place of abode
of the owner of such share, nor until the declaration of forfeiture of the said
directors shall have been confirmed either at a general or special general
meeting of the said company, such general or special general meeting being held
after the expiration of three calendar months at the least from the day on which
such notice of forfeiture shall have been given as aforesaid; and after such
declaration of forfeiture shall have been confirmed by such general or special
general meeting, the said company, by an order to be made at the same or at any
subsequent general or special general meeting, shall have power to direct the said
directors to dispose of the shares so forfeited or any of them in manner by this
Act directed, and the said directors may and they are hereby authorized and
empowered to sell and dispose of such forfeited share or shares either by public
auction or by private contract, and together or in lots, or in such other manner
and for such price as they may think fit . . .

PART IV: THE PROBLEMS OF THE UNINCORPORATED ASSOCIATION

Private commercial activity which was neither large enough nor of sufficient
public importance could not take advantage of the machinery offered by
charter or statutory incorporation. This had therefore to be carried on
through bodies lacking corporate status. Two of these, the deed of settlement
company and the partnership derived from the application of the common
law principles of contract, trusts and agency. The skilful manipulation of these
principles resulted in some of the disadvantages of unincorporated status
being overcome (eg transferable shares could be provided for), but many
remained (including unlimited liability, which although theoretically distinct
from incorporation was, at least in the case of the statutory companies,
increasingly integrated with it, see Shannon, 'The Coming of General Limited
Liability', *Economic History II* (1931), reprinted, Carus-Wilson (ed) *Essays in
Economic History* (London, 1954).

SOURCE 14
Dubois, The English Business Company after the Bubble Act
(New York, 1938) pp 217–27

Instead of a charter or act of incorporation, the basis of the unincorporated organization has to be found in the articles of association which were, as a rule, in the form of a deed of settlement signed by those participating in the society. This instrument would make provision for the management of the business through a committee of management and an assembly of the subscribers. The articles of association stand as the constitution of the unincorporated society, and it was clearly understood in the eighteenth century that protests from members would be in order if committeemen sought to depart from its provisions.

The fact that the unincorporated association in this period was a step-child of the law meant that there were serious difficulties to surmount. If the rules of law that had evolved in connection with the partnership of a small number of participants were to be applied without modification to the larger organization, it would mean that each and every member must join in the conveyance of the society's property, and in the bringing and defending of actions, and that the death of a member would necessitate a reorganization of the enterprise.

The trustee device was the means most frequently used to circumvent these difficulties. The organization's real and personal property would be placed in the names of trustees, and trustees selected by the subscribers to the organization would be authorized in certain instances to act on the society's behalf.

The predominance of the trustee in the unincorporated organization varied from plan to plan. An example of a society in which the trustees held the dominating legal position was the scheme devised in 1749 for the Cornfactors of London. The property on which the Corn Exchange was built was conveyed to three trustees by lease for five hundred years in trust for the proprietors. It was recited in the heads of the deed of trust that the purpose of the transaction was 'that the said Premises may be managed to the best advantage . . . and that no inconvenience may arise by the deaths of any of the parties or any other accident. . . .' The trustees, selected by a general assembly of proprietors, were to receive the rents and disburse the surplus under the direction of the general meetings of the proprietors. The proprietors agreed with the trustees to contribute £25 for each of the eighty shares of the organization with the understanding that the trustees 'were not to be answerable for more than they shall respectively receive.' The investment of surplus funds in Bank annuities necessitated a separate deed in 1794 by which the annuities were placed in the names of the trustees. No mention was made, however, of any power of the trustees to bring or defend actions on behalf of the organization.

. . .

Although the trustee device was as a rule an effective method of dealing with the problem of holding the property of an unincorporated association, more difficulty was experienced in regard to the bringing and defending of actions and suits. The secretary or other officer of an unincorporated society might be designated to defend and bring actions, or the trustees who were holding the company's property might be selected. The privilege of so bringing an action, however, was subject to attack in the courts of law. In Chancery, during this period, representative suits by directors or officers were as a rule permitted, although permission was subject to restriction in the Chancellor's discretion.

. . .

The trustee device thus served effectively to give to the unincorporated association at least some of the ease and effectiveness in dealing with property and court procedure that were the characteristics of the corporation. Indeed, extremely rare was the eighteenth century unincorporated organization that did not make at least some use of trustees. Still, the forms involved were complicated, the responsibilities of trustees great, their rewards small, and the question of the succession of trustees bothersome. In most cases, it would have been a relief to turn to the simplicity of the corporation.

It has been indicated that as a result of the Bubble Act, one of the principal problems of the lawyer planning an unincorporated organization in this period was that of making the shares freely transferable. The method and the extent of the freedom of transfer varied greatly from organization to organization. At times articles of association would provide that a transfer could be made only with the consent of the committee of management, or that transfers must be made to a proprietor of the company. In the Joseph Percival and Copper Company of Bristol, a proprietor who wished to dispose of his shares was required to tender them to the committee of management of the company, who, as a rule, purchased them and later resold them to an approved buyer. The Phoenix Fire Office, established in 1781, exercised a supervision of the transfer of its shares through the device of requiring a surrender to the trustees. Since this company existed primarily for the insurance of sugar refineries, sugar refiners were to be preferred in the allotment of shares.

The Bubble Act to the contrary notwithstanding, the articles of association of other unincorporated organizations made provision for the unrestricted transfer of shares. Examples included the Banking Company of Aberdeen, Scotland, in 1767, the Cornish Metal Company in 1785, and the Norwich General Assurance Office of 1792, The proprietors of the Fulham Bridge who had organized as an unincorporated association in 1728 were soon freely transferring their shares by deeds of assignment.

Attempts of an unincorporated society to obtain the privileges of a limited liability of its members were relatively rare in this period. This stands in striking contrast to the situation in the early nineteenth century when the unincorporated groups operating with a joint stock were extremely bold in asserting that there was a limitation of liability. The grounds on which such a limitation could be based varied with the type of enterprise. Thus, in the case of mining, there is some evidence of the existence in the eighteenth century of a customary restricted liability in the organizations that were formed in accordance with mining custom in Cornwall, Derby, and Wales for the purpose of enabling a large number of individuals in association to develop the mines of those regions.

. . .

Not all the cards were stacked in favour of the corporation. There were certain benefits that the unincorporated form of organization would confer. Moreover, some of the apparent disadvantages might well turn out to be playing tricks. Thus while the difficulties of suing might cause inconvenience to the unincorporated society, the corresponding disability to be sued except in the names of all the members might be a welcome boon. Furthermore, the absence of a limitation of liability might loosen the purse strings of money lenders suspicious of a company's prospects.

Another advantage the unincorporated organization had over the corporation was the matter of relative ease in the changing of the basis of association. The tiresome and endless routine of application to the Crown or to Parliament did not have to be gone through. The proprietors might at a general meeting decide to amend the articles of association, for the deed of settlement would generally make provision that the deed might be amended by a stated majority at a general meeting. This very flexibility might give rise to a feeling of impermanence in the minds of creditors and others dealing with the society. The danger of this attitude is seen in the stress on the existence of an adequate fund in various notices and advertisements that the unincorporated insurance offices published to attract insurers.

When difficulties of internal operation arose in the case of the unincorporated association, the only possible forum where adequate relief could be obtained was the Chancellor's court. Since the unincorporated company was definitely not 'the creature of the state,' the state in its turn was less accessible to such a unit. The courts of law, partly because of procedural difficulties, the governmental boards and commissions, and even Parliament did not see fit to occupy themselves with the problems of the unincorporated company, which was more tolerated than encouraged. Nevertheless, for a century in which the business man was at great pains to shun the courts, the unincorporated association did make a fairly frequent use of the aid of the Court of Chancery, which by closing its eyes to the legal irregularity of the unincorporated group with a joint stock, adhered to its well-established practice of welcoming new litigants. The use of the master in Chancery for the consideration of complicated fact situations was found to be convenient.

SOURCE 15
Formoy, The Historical Foundations of Company Law
(London, 1923) pp 32–6

The fact that these large [unincorporated] trading associations were regarded as partnerships led to many legal difficulties. The essential elements of a partnership which gave rise to these difficulties were (1) the interest of the partners in their stock and effects was a modified joint tenancy, that is, modified in the respect that there was no right of accrual to the survivors. (2) The partners had no action against each other in respect of partnership property, not even the common law action of account. (3) Each partner had power singly to dispose of the whole partnership effects, to receive or release debts, and, except in contracting by deed, to bind his co-partners by contract. (4) Each partner was liable for the partnership debts; and (5) where no provision was made for the continuance of the partnership, death of one partner dissolved the partnership. There was, however, some relief to be obtained in the Court of Chancery, for Equity gave one partner a right of account against his co-partner, and gave him relief against fraud and embezzlement, and in such cases entitled him to have the partnership dissolved, but to get these remedies the unfortunate partner was 'driven to the necessity of having recourse to the *dernier resort* of proceedings in Chancery'.

Nor were these all the difficulties; there was the still greater difficulty that if the partnership wished to sue, all the partners had to be joined as plaintiffs, and if the partnership was sued all the partners must be made defendants. The foundation of this rule was the quite reasonable proposition that all persons interested in the subject-matter of the suit ought to be made parties, but the difficulty of bringing a suit with, say, 2,000 plaintiffs is not hard to imagine.

The following illustration taken from a contemporary law book will show the difficulties to be encountered by a company who wished to sue. 'Suppose then that the body consists of 2,000 partners (no very extraordinary number, if we may trust to the "prospectuses" of the day), and that Stiles has bought goods of them at twenty-five different times, the credit for all of which goods is now expired. Suppose, that during this period of time, there have been 300 changes in the members of the firm, by the sale or supposed sale of the interests of that number of members. Suppose, during the same time there have been six deaths, and that in consequence of these deaths ten new individuals as personal representatives of the deceased members have been admitted as partners to hold the interests of the deceased. . . . Now let the exact times of the several sales or transfers, which have led to the supposed 300 changes in the members of the partnership, to be all of them ascertained. Let the times of the deaths of the deceased partners be also supposed to be accurately known, and also whether any and which of those members who have parted with their interests in the "concern" have also died, and when they died. In the next place, let the exact days of the sale of the several parcels of goods to John Stiles be likewise clearly ascertained, and let all these points be clearly capable of proof . . . He (the legal adviser of the company) will then have to consider, first, how many actions must be brought. And here, inasmuch as during the time of the sales to Stiles, of which there are twenty-five, there have been three hundred changes in the members of the firm, exclusive of the changes by death and the admission of the personal representatives of deceased partners, he (the legal adviser of the company) will in all probability soon discover that there must be twenty-five actions. And this must depend upon there having been a change of one or more members of the partnership between each sale of goods, a point to be ascertained by comparing the exact times of the changes of partners with the exact times of the sales of the goods. It has already been stated, in whose names the first action must be brought. . . . The plaintiffs in the second action . . . will embrace all those who have continued partners from the time of the first sale of goods and all those who became partners after the first sale of goods and continued partners at the time of the second sale, which will include all those, who being partners at any time, have since sold their interest in the partnership; but those, if any, who legally ceased to be partners after the first and before the second sale of goods, will not be comprised among the plaintiffs; so neither will the executors of any deceased partner merely as executors, nor any who have become partners since the second sale. The like course will have to be pursued with the supposed remaining three-and-twenty actions'. Similarly in bringing an action founded on contract against a company, all persons who contracted with the plaintiffs (that is, all the members of the company) must be made defendants, otherwise the defendants could plead in abatement, that is, disclose by the plea such facts as would inform him how to 'purchase a better writ'. But the disclosure need not necessarily give the plaintiff all the facts he needs to make his writ regular, and the process of pleading in abatement might be continued indefinitely until the plaintiff had got all the facts he wanted, or had abandoned his action in despair.

Suppose in spite of all this that the action had been brought successfully against a company, and judgment obtained, the execution of the judgment was no easy matter. Execution would be levied against the goods and chattels and a moiety of the lands of the defendants. If judgment cannot be satisfied by this means, the plaintiff could take the bodies of the defendants, and was obliged to keep them all in prison until his judgment was fully satisfied, because the discharge of one defendant upon payment of his aliquot share would be a discharge of them all.

Moreover, if it was desired to levy execution for a separate debt against an individual who was a member of a company, according to the legal position 'the Sheriff must seize all, because the moieties are undivided; for if he seize but a moiety and sell that, the other will have a right to a moiety of that moiety; therefore, he must seize the whole and sell a moiety thereof undivided, and the vendee will be a tenant in common with the other partner', a position easily comprehensible to a lawyer, but scarcely acceptable to a board of directors who found themselves tenants in common with the bailiff! Again, if the partnership sold goods to any of themselves there was no right of action by the partnership against any of their members, because the same persons (or some of them) would have to be both plaintiffs and defendants. All this was avoided in later law when the doctrine of the difference between the company and the individuals composing it had developed.

It is obvious from the foregoing that in its unadapted state it was practically impossible under the law of partnership for an unincorporated company to sue or be sued. One way out of the difficulty was to obtain an Act of Parliament authorising the company to sue or be sued in the name of one of its officers.

SOURCE 16
Re Agriculturist Cattle Insurance Company (Baird's Case)
(Court of Appeal 1870) (1870) 5 Ch App 725; 23 LT 424

SIR W. M. JAMES LJ: In this case the Master of the Rolls, in placing the executrix of a deceased shareholder on the list of contributories, has placed her with a qualification limiting her liability to the death of her testator, and giving consequential directions for ascertaining such liability.

. . .

The conclusion to which the Master of the Rolls has come, and the argument addressed to me in support of that conclusion, are mainly based on the general law of partnership, that a man ceases to be a partner by his death, and that he is therefore a stranger to all subsequent proceedings, dealings, and transactions of the surviving partners after his death, and cannot therefore be under any liability in respect of them; that therefore, in construing the deed of partnership, this, the ordinary law, the natural and ordinary incident and consequence which flows out of the contract of partnership, must always be kept in mind; that the burden of proof is thrown on those who content that such ordinary law is superseded by the express contract of the parties, and that such burden can only be discharged by shewing in the contract express words or plain implication.

. . .

Ordinary partnerships are by the law assumed and presumed to be based on the mutual trust and confidence of each partner in the skill, knowledge, and integrity of every other partner. As between the partners and the outside world (whatever may be their private arrangements between themselves), each partner is the unlimited agent of every other in every matter connected with the partnership business, or which he represents as partnership business, and not being in its nature beyond the scope of the partnership. A partner who may not have a farthing of capital left may take moneys or assets of this partnership to the value of millions, may bind the partnership by contracts to any amount, may give the partnership acceptances for any amount, and may even — as has been shewn in many painful instances in this Court — involve his innocent partners in unlimited amounts for frauds which he has craftily concealed from them.

That being the relation between partners, of course, when the Court had to consider whether a partner could substitute or let in some other person for or with him, or whether a partner's executor could claim to succeed to him, there could be no difficulty in saying that this could not be done without the consent of all the partners. The death of a partner, therefore, necessarily put an end to the partnership, so far as he was concerned; and as, in the absence of express stipulation, the right of the representative was to have all the assets realized and divided, it necessarily put an end to the whole subject matter of the partnership; as indeed, independently of that right, a contract between A., B., and C. to be partners, is essentially a different thing from a contract that they, or the survivors of them, should be partners.

Therefore, when the simple case was presented to the Court of an agreement between A., B., and C. to be partners for a long term of years, and nothing more, it was of course held that, in the absence of express stipulation, the mere length of the term afforded no sufficient presumption to prevent the application of the ordinary law, and therefore it was held that the death of one was the dissolution of the society as to all. But it was because these were the ordinary law and consequences of an ordinary partnership — it was to escape from these, that joint stock companies were invented. That was the very cause and reason of their existence.

At first they existed under the favour of the Crown, which gave them charters of incorporation, and nobody ever supposed that the holders of stock in the Bank of England or the East India Company had anything to do with the law of partnership, or were partners.

But there were large societies on which the sun of royal or legislative favour did not shine, and as to whom the whole desire of the associates, and the whole aim of the ablest legal assistants they could obtain, was to make them as nearly a corporation as possible, with continuous existence, with transmissible and transferable stock, but without any individual right in any associate to bind the other associates, or to deal with the assets of the association.

A joint stock company is not an agreement between a great many persons that they will be co-partners, but is an agreement between the owners of shares, or the owners of stock, that they or their duly recognized assigns, the owners of the shares for the time being, whoever they may be, shall be and continue an association together, sharing profits and bearing losses. No shareholder in a joint stock company is, in the legal sense of the word, any more a partner than the owner of bank stock is; he may not have the same limit of liability, but in every other respect he is the same; he has the same right to take part in public meetings of the body, he has the same right to elect or remove directors, he has the same right to vote for or against the resolutions of the body, he has the same right to such dividends as may be declared, and he has the same right to dispose of his share as a separate and distinct piece of property, and no other rights in or over the association, its assets, or its transactions; and if he is liable under any contracts or obligation, or in respect of any act of the body, it is not because they are the contracts, obligations, or acts of his partners or partner, but because they are the contracts, obligations, and acts of the quasi body corporate (under present legislation the actual body corporate), by its properly constituted agents. It may be, and generally is, no doubt, that the agents, the directors, are shareholders, and in that sense partners, but it is certain that there may be a board of directors perfectly competent to bind the whole body, although every one of them may have disqualified himself by parting with every share.

Starting then, with this view of the relation which exists between the associates in a joint stock adventure, the presumption is that the death of a shareholder makes not the slightest difference, either in right or liability; that the executor of a deceased shareholder, who succeeds in point of property to the share, takes it (of course in his executorial character) on exactly the same terms and conditions as every other owner of a share — equal benefit, equal liability; and the deed has therefore to be scrutinized, not to see whether it gives or creates such equal benefit and liability, but whether it takes away the one or releases the other.

Now when we come to examine the deed, which is substantially like all other joint stock deeds, it seems to me clear that, so far from excluding, it does in every clause, from beginning to the end, attach the same liability to executors as to others.

SOURCE 17
Re Witney Town Football Club
[1994] 2 BCLC 487 (Chancery Division)

MORRITT J. This is an appeal by the petitioner, Western Counties Construction Ltd, supported by four creditors with debts totalling approximately £30,000 from the judgment dated 11 August 1993 of his Honour Judge Harris QC, sitting in the Oxford County Court, whereby he dismissed a petition for the compulsory winding up of Witney Town Football and Social Club.

. . .

The club was founded in 1885 and is now constituted and regulated by rules passed at a special general meeting held on 14 August 1969 as amended at subsequent general meetings. It has 500 members and owns property of considerable value. It is a member of the Football Association and the Southern Football League, known as the Beazer Homes League, and is affiliated to the Oxfordshire Football Association. It employs professional footballers.

The rules, as amended, provide for the club to have officers, trustees, a management committee, a membership paying subscriptions in exchange for which they may enjoy the facilities of the club subject to a power of the management committee to exclude a member for discreditable conduct, audited accounts and a power to amend the rules. The club, as constituted by the rules, is similar to many other social and sporting clubs, but there are three rules which are not usually found in the constitution of such clubs. They are rr 2, 13 and 17, which are in the following terms:

'2. The club shall exist solely as a body for the purpose of professional Association Football. The club will also provide various social amenities for its members . . .

13. The management committee shall have the power to elect honorary day members. Honorary day membership shall be open to officials, members and supporters of visiting clubs for the days of the visit only . . .

17. The club shall only be wound up by a resolution passed at a special general meeting called for that purpose and the assets of the club shall be disposed of after repayment of all outstanding loans and dues in accordance with the resolutions passed at such meeting. Upon dissolution of the club, all net assets of the club shall be devoted to Association Football and not distributed between the members.'

In his judgment the county court judge considered the terms of s 220 of the 1986 Act,

. . .

After quoting from the judgment of the Lord Chancellor in *Re St James's Club*, he concluded:

'I hold that a club like this is not an association within the meaning of s 220. I am confirmed in that view by an extract from *6 Halsbury's Laws* (4th edn reissue) on the subject of clubs under the heading of "Dissolution" at p 88 to which I have been referred.'

The passage in *6 Halsbury's Laws* to which the judge referred deals with the dissolution under the inherent jurisdiction of the court of unincorporated members' clubs and includes the following sentence:

'The court has jurisdiction under the Companies Act 1985 to wind up compulsorily as an "unregistered company", a working men's club which is not registered as a friendly society, but it has no such jurisdiction in the case of an unincorporated members' club.'

In *Re St James's Club* (1852) 2 De GM & G 383 at 387, 42 ER 920 at 922 the Lord Chancellor started his judgment by considering the nature and constitution of such clubs, namely 'clubs in the ordinary acceptation of the term'. He said:

'... they are, generally speaking (and there is nothing particular in this club) all formed on this principle: the candidate must be elected, he must then pay an entrance fee, and also an annual sum or subscription. In this club there was a rule under which, if the person elected did not pay the entrance fee and annual subscription, he ceased to be a member; there was also an express rule, that if a member's conduct was objectionable out of the house, he might be dismissed from being a member. What, then, were the interests and liabilities of a member? He had an interest in the general assets as long as he remained a member, and if the club was broken up while he was a member, he might file a bill to have its assets administered in this Court, and he would be entitled to share in the furniture and effects of the club; but he had no transmissible interest, he had not an interest, in the ordinary sense of the term capital in partnership transactions; it was a simple right of admission to, and enjoyment of, the club while it continued.'

In relation to the words in the statute 'any association', he concluded ((1852) 2 De GM & G 383 at 389, 42 ER 920 at 923):

'The words are very wide, no doubt; but still, I must give a reasonable construction to the Act, which is *in pari materia*, and incorporated with the Act of the preceding year. I cannot hold it to apply to every association or company. If I were to do so, I might be called upon to carry the application much lower than to such a club as that now in question. A cricket club, an archery society, or a charitable society, would come under the operation of the Act, and indeed every club would be included. Though "associations" are mentioned I cannot think that word is to be treated without regard to the particulars with which it is associated. I shall do as Lord Bacon did in treating of the Statute of Uses, when he said "The nature of the use is best discerned by considering what it is not" . . . so I will not say what associations are within the Act; but bearing in mind that the individuals who form a club do not constitute a partnership, nor incur any liability as such, I think associations of that nature are not within the Winding-up Acts. I find in all these Acts to which I have referred, that every provision is inconsistent with including such an association as this club is. If such had been the intention of the Legislature, why should not the word "club" have been expressly mentioned? If, however, the Legislature has used ambiguous expressions, I will not extend their signification beyond their natural import. At first sight, the word "association" would seem to include the case of clubs, but in looking at the context, I am clearly of opinion that it does not.'

As was submitted for the club, it is plain that the members did not constitute a partnership, nor, under the rules, did they incur any liability as members except for their subscriptions: see *Wise v Perpetual Trustee Co Ltd* [1903] AC 139. Thus they do not come within either of the exceptions which the Lord Chancellor envisaged. Accordingly, the only remaining question is whether the respects in which the club has legal attributes other than those referred to by the Lord Chancellor, renders it not a club within 'the ordinary acceptation' of the term. If that were the case, it would still be necessary to consider whether that attribute was one from which it should be inferred that Parliament must have intended that the court should have jurisdiction to wind up the club.

I do not think that the purposes expressed in r 2 can have either of those results. The judgment of the Lord Chancellor in *Re St James's Club* in terms recognised that clubs of the type he was considering might exist for sporting purposes. He does not consider professional sports or games but I can see no reason why that should give rise to a material distinction. Likewise, I do not see how the provisions of r 13 could take this club out of the category of club with which the Lord Chancellor was dealing. Certainly it provides no reason for thinking that Parliament must have intended a club of this nature to be susceptible of being wound up under the 1986 Act.

Lastly, there is r 17. Counsel did not argue for or against the validity of the final sentence. Both were prepared to proceed on the basis that, whether valid or not, it indicated that the members did not intend that they should share in any surplus assets on the dissolution of the club. But the essential question, it seems to me, is whether the club had the requisite legal attributes whilst it continued as a going concern. In that respect the rights of the members are in all material respects the same as those of the members in the cases predicated by the Lord Chancellor.

In so far as the rights of members on a dissolution are different from those of the members of a conventional members' club, that is assuming the rule to be valid, I do not think that that distinction warrants any implication that Parliament must have intended this type of club to be capable of being wound up under the provisions of the 1986 Act for, in appropriate cases, it could be wound up by the High Court under its inherent jurisdiction without bringing in all the detailed provisions of the 1986 Act and rules: (compare *Re William Denby & Sons Sick and Benevolent Fund* [1972] 2 All ER 1196, [1971] 1 WLR 973).

In my judgment, the judge as right for essentially the reasons he gave. The remedy of the creditors lies against the individuals with whom the contracts were made. In the circumstances, I dismiss the appeal, and the consequential question of substituting another creditor as the petitioner does not arise.

PART V: ESTABLISHING LIMITED LIABILITY

Statutory companies could limit the liability of their investors (p 25), but when incorporation by registration was eventually achieved (in 1844), limited liability was excluded and only achieved after a spirited campaign with the enactment of the Limited Liability Act 1855. One factor in this campaign was the inequality between investors in statutory and registered companies (see Shannon, 'The Coming of General Limited Liability' (1931–32) *Economic History II* 267).

What of investors in the unincorporated deed of settlement companies? In *R v Dodd*[1] (discussed in Source 19), this idea was described as a 'mischievous delusion'. Many such companies purported to restrict the liability of investors by a clause to this effect in the deed of settlement

---

1 9 East 516; 103 ER 670 (see p 41)

(Source 14), but this device was held ineffectual (Source 18). The court did, however, accept that this limitation of liability could be achieved through express provision in the contract between the company and the third party, even where this was by way of reference to a clause in the deed of settlement (Source 19). Recently, the court has had to consider the liability of the members of an international organisation (Source 20).

SOURCE 18
Re Sea Fire and Life Assurance Company (Greenwood's Case)
(Court of Appeal 1854) (1854) 3 DeGM & G 459; 43 ER 180

In the winding up of the company, a call was made on all the shareholders, including the applicant who resisted the call on the ground that he had paid the full stated capital in respect of the shares which he held.

> LORD CRANWORTH LC: . . . As we are of opinion that it was necessary for the purposes of winding up the company that the money should be raised, and as it is obviously incompetent for parties entering into a partnership to stipulate that they will not be liable for the costs of any proceedings that may be instituted against then for winding up the concern — as it is absurd to say that they could thus oust the jurisdiction of the Court, it would be sufficient for us to state, as a reason for not concurring with the Vice-Chancellor, that the order for the call was the only practicable method of raising the funds necessary for proceeding with the winding up of the company, treating it as a partnership for the winding up of the affairs of which there had been a decree in this Court. The grounds, however, on which the Vice-Chancellor proceeded, stated very clearly and fully in his judgment and supported in argument here, involve principles so extensive, so important, and so interesting to a commercial community, that we think it right to say, not merely that we do not concur in the order made by His Honour upon the narrow ground I have already stated, but that, with all deference to His Honour's judgment, we cannot go along with him upon the construction he has put upon the statute,[1] and his view of the rights of parties in joint stock companies arising out of it.
>
> In the first place, the Vice-Chancellor has assumed that it was one of the terms of the deed of this company that the shareholders should not be liable for anything beyond £1 per share; and if our only difference from His Honour had been on the construction of the eighty-ninth clause to which he referred, it might not have been very material to advert to it, as it would have applied to this company only. I am bound, however, to say that I think that, whatever may be the meaning of the clause (and it is not easy to say what its precise meaning is),[2] it could never be intended to nullify the other clauses in the deed conferring upon the directors powers necessary for the proper conduct of business, according to the general scope of dealing and object of the company, yet such would be the effect of the construction put upon it by the Vice-Chancellor.
>
> I will now proceed to state the grounds why, upon the main question of the liability of the shareholders, I cannot agree with the Vice-Chancellor. Supposing that the parties had really stipulated that, in no contingency and under no circumstances whatever, whether the affairs of the company prospered or failed, should any one of the shareholders be liable for more than £1 per share, what

---

1 Joint Stock Companies Registration Act, 7 & 8 Vict. c. 110
2 For the text of this clause, see Clause 89 at p 39

would be the consequence of such a stipulation. His Honour's judgment proceeds upon the ground that no creditor could then come upon a shareholder beyond the £1 per share. That is a very strong assumption, for it militates against the principle of a partnership as hitherto understood in this country. Whether the principle is a right or wrong one is a matter now under investigation before the legislature, but that it is the principle cannot, I think, for one moment be disputed, namely, that every person engaged in a partnership is liable solidarily, as they say upon the Continent, for everything. Thus A., B. and C., carrying on business together, may stipulate among themselves that no one of them shall be liable for more than £1000, yet, if in the conduct of their business they incur a debt to the extent of £10,000, every one of them would be liable for it, notwithstanding any stipulation they might have made with one another. That doctrine does not depend upon the persons dealing with the partners having notice, and any notice would be quite immaterial, for creditors would only know what engagements the partners had made between themselves, whereas the rights of creditors are wholly extrinsic of any such engagements. If the deed of partnership, containing such a provision as I have mentioned, were hung up in the shop, it would make no difference; for how could a person dealing with the firm tell whether each partner would be liable to him or not. They might have already incurred debts with other persons to the extent provided, and thus it would not be possible for him to ascertain the limit of their liability. Whether there ought to be such a limited liability is not now the question; the Court has only to enunciate what is the law, and that is, that such a notice would be of no avail at all.

The law as to common partnerships being such as I have stated, what is the case of a joint stock company? It might be rather a curious and interesting speculation to inquire in what manner exactly, and when, these partnerships became distinguished from ordinary partnerships, and by what steps they advanced to their present position. That long before the Joint Stock Acts they were distinguished, is a proposition that cannot be controverted, although it may be difficult to say precisely in what points they differed. They certainly differed in this, that whereas, according to the ordinary laws of partnership, any one partner acting within the scope of the partnership might bind all the other partners, it was not so with a joint stock company; for, independently of the Joint Stock Companies Act, partnerships consisting of a number of persons too numerous to act in the way that an ordinary partnership does, had been in the habit of exercising many of their functions, accepting bills, giving orders for goods, etc, solely through the means of directors. I have never, however, heard it suggested that, independently of the Act, partners could absolve themselves from the ordinary liabilities of partnership *quoad* third parties because they were very numerous, though Lord Eldon frequently said that it would be extremely difficult to enforce the rights of third parties against bodies so numerous, and he therefore, I believe, doubted whether they were not illegal. But it is idle to speculate upon that point; for these companies, being consonant with the wants of a growing and wealthy community, have forced their way into existence, whether fostered by the law or opposed to it; they have not, however, proceeded to the extent of enabling their members to enter into arrangements absolving themselves from liabilities without the circle of their own deed, that is, from liabilities to third persons.

So stands the matter independently of the Act of Parliament (the Joint Stock Companies Registration Act 1844), and it therefore becomes necessary to see what alteration has been effected by it. The Act has its origin in the numerous schemes, either actually bubble schemes or very similar to them, which were started, and into which the unwary were entrapped; and the legislature, with the view of providing some security against the impositions which were being practised, declared that it should not be lawful for any persons to engage in forming themselves into a company, or to receive subscriptions, without at once registering themselves, so as to give public notice of the object they were engaged in. They might then receive subscriptions, and, after complying with certain requisites, proceed to complete registration, and prosecute their scheme under the sanction of the law. Among the things thus required was, the execution of a deed shewing the terms of partnership, and, this being done, the company became incorporated from the date of the certificate of complete registration by the name of the company for the purpose of carrying on business in that name; and the Act provides (section 25) 'that such company shall continue so incorporated until it shall be dissolved, and all its affairs wound up; but so as not in anywise to restrict the liability of any of the shareholders of the company, under any judgment, decree, or order for the payment of money which shall be obtained against such company, or any of the members thereof, in any action or suit prosecuted by or against such company in any Court of law or Equity.' Thus, while the name of an incorporated company is given to the undertaking, one of the essential incidents of a corporation is taken away, or rather is not conferred, for although the individual members no longer trade separately, yet this section enacts they are to be liable nearly as they were before. Section 66 provides, that every judgment and decree obtained against the company shall take effect and be enforced, not only against the property of the company, but also against the person, property, and effects of any shareholder, until such judgment or decree is fully satisfied, except that, in the case of a former shareholder, no execution shall be issued on such judgment or decree after the expiration of three years next after he shall have ceased to be a shareholder of the company. Thus it is clear that the liability to creditors is not materially affected, and the legislature has not only not exempted the shareholders from their ordinary obligations as partners, but has expressly enacted that they shall remain liable, subject only to the limitation as to three years in a particular case, which is not now in question. . . . Other cases were referred to, *Hallett v Dowdall*[1], and *Lord Talbot's case*[2] but they went upon a totally different principle, depending, not upon any contract which the members of the company had made *inter se*, but upon the terms of the contract entered into between the company and the creditor. That is quite a different question. In the present instance, it may be that creditors would have no claim against the company, if all the policies had been entered into upon the terms that nothing was to be liable to the party claiming upon the policy but the £1 per share which each member was to contribute, nothing but the capital of the company whatever that means: some of the cases have so stated the law. If the terms of the contract between the insuring party or the dealing party and the company are that nothing shall be liable but a particular fund, then no principle arising from the nature of joint stock companies or from the Joint Stock Companies Winding-up Act is wanted to shew that the individual members would not be liable. That is not by reason of any contract that the body of individuals have made with each other, but by reason of the very contract made with the creditor. The cases which were pressed in the argument by the Respondent were of this kind, and they evidently have no bearing upon the present discussion. One of the policies was handed up to us, to shew that the form used was such as I have alluded to. I did not examine it, but if the policy was so worded the individual members of the company may not be personally liable under it; but this will be

1 21 LJ QB 98 (see p 39)
2 5 De G & Sm 386; 64 ER 1165

because by the terms of the contract they have not made themselves personally liable, and that is a principle equally applicable to a joint stock company, or an ordinary partnership, or a single individual. If I say to a man, 'I will insure you against all losses either by fire or sea, provided always that my estate of Blackacre only shall be liable to make good to you the loss,' he would have no right to say that I am bound personally to pay: my answer would be, 'Personal liability is beyond my contract, "non hæc in fædera veni," I agreed with you to such an extent but no further.'

Clause 89 of the Deed of Settlement

89. That, on and after complete registration of the company, there shall be paid by the shareholders, on execution by them of these presents, or any deed of accession thereto, or duplicate thereof, in full of all future calls and instalments, the whole of the sum or sums representing the amount of their subscription towards the capital stock of the company, at and after the rate of 20s. in the £1 on the declared value of each share; and that, on payment thereof within the time hereinafter limited for the same, no further call shall be made on any shareholder in respect of the share or shares subscribed for or held by him under the provisions of these presents; and that every shareholder shall be entitled to receive from the company interest at and after the rate of £5 per cent per annum, payable half-yearly (irrespective of any profits to be declared on the capital of the company in manner hereinbefore directed), in proportion to and *pro ratâ* for the number and amount of shares in the capital stock subscribed for and actually paid up by him.

SOURCE 19
Hallett *v* Dowdall
(Queen's Bench Division (1852)) 21 LJ QB 98

MARTIN B: This is an action on a policy of insurance on the ship *Vindicator*, dated 18 November 1846, and signed by three directors of a maritime insurance company called the General Maritime Assurance Company.

. . .

In the argument of the learned counsel for the plaintiffs in error, it was contended, that the partnership created by the deed of settlement of 23 April 1840 was a lawful partnership that there was nothing illegal in the capital of the partnership being divided into shares, and in the partners or shareholders agreeing that no one should be liable to be called upon to pay more than the amount agreed to be subscribed by him; that the plaintiff below had agreed with the company by an express term contained in the policy that the capital stock and funds of the company should alone be liable to make good all claims under the policy, and that no proprietor should be in anywise subject or liable to a claim made by reason of the policy beyond the amount of his share or shares in the capital stock, it being one of the original and fundamental principles of the company that the responsibility of the individual proprietors should in all cases and under all circumstances be limited to their respective shares in the said capital stock; that, except as against the individuals who signed the policy, the plaintiff below could not, in any event, maintain an action against more than one shareholder without a violation of the express condition that the liability of each shareholder should be restricted to the amount of his own share, and that he should not be responsible for his co-shareholders.

. . .

On the other hand it was contended on behalf of the defendant in error that the General Maritime Assurance Company was a mere trading partnership; that in law there was no distinction as to liability between a joint-stock partnership, as this is called, and an ordinary partnership; that throughout this policy the company were universally described as the contracting party, and that in this action, there having been no plea in abatement, the plaintiff below was entitled by law to consider every shareholder as the company, and as if the company were named as defendants upon the record; that the true rule as to partnership liability was that laid down in *Hawken v Bourne*,[1] namely, that the partner authorized to make a contract was in the nature of a general agent, and had by law authority to bind his co-partners in contracts usually made in the partnership business, although in direct contradiction to the actual authority given by the co-partners; and the case of *Smith v Hull Glass Company*[2] was cited to shew that there was no distinction between joint-stock companies and other partnerships.

The question which arises here is one of great importance. There are very many companies (Life Insurances and others) carrying on business under deeds similar to that in the present instance; and provisions substantially the same as those contained in the present policy are, I believe, universally inserted, with the view of restricting the liability of the shareholders. The circumstance that Gooden was himself a director will make no difference, for assuming that the liability of a director who has not signed the policy is different from that of a mere shareholder, there are, in the present case, other defendants who are mere shareholders, and it is quite clear that in order to fix the defendant Gooden on the plea of non assumpsit evidence must be given of the liability of all the defendants upon the promise alleged in the declaration. The question of the general liability of the shareholders, therefore, directly arises. The first question is, are the stipulations in the deed, as to each subscriber or partner being responsible only to the amount subscribed for by him, lawful and valid as amongst themselves? I entertain no doubt that they are. Such stipulations have been long in general use. Their object is to restrict, as far as possible, the liability of the partners to the same extent as that of shareholders in the various corporations which have for a long period been created by acts of parliament for the purpose of effecting great public works. The partners agree amongst each other that each shall subscribe for, and be responsible for, a certain amount only, and that in the event of one being compelled to pay a demand, the others will indemnify him separately, and in proportion to the extent of their respective interests, and no further; and it seems to me clear that, as amongst themselves, when one has paid up the whole amount subscribed for by him, he is no longer responsible to any further amount to his co-shareholders, their liability to each other being precisely the same as that of shareholders in the ordinary joint-stock corporations created by the acts of parliament, in which the subscribers are liable to the extent of their subscriptions only, and when they have once paid up all their calls, the legal liability to contribute further is at an end. The further question then arises, what is the liability of shareholders and partners in such companies to third parties, on contracts made by the directors in the ordinary course of business? and it seems clearly established by the authorities, that with respect to third persons who have no notice of the terms of the partnership, the shareholders and partners in joint-stock companies are liable to the same extent, and in the same manner as the partners in ordinary partnerships, and that the law pays no regard to the stipulations contained in the partnership deed as to the

---

1 [1841] 8 McW 703; 151 ER 1223
2 11 CB 897; 138 ER 729

restriction of liability, or to any particular provision as to the mode of carrying on the business different from that ordinarily used in such concerns. In the case of *R v Dodd*[1] Lord Ellenborough, in delivering the judgment of the Court, stated that the holding out in the prospectus of two proposed trading companies, one for manufacturing paper and the other for distilling spirits, that no subscriber would be responsible beyond the amount of the shares for which he subscribed, was a mischievous delusion; that as amongst the subscribers themselves, they might stipulate with each other for such restricted liability, but that as to the rest of the world it was clear that each subscriber was liable to the whole amount of the debts contracted by the partnership. So also Lord Eldon, in *Carlen v Drury*[2] stated that he held it to be clear law that each individual in a joint-stock brewery company was answerable for the whole of the debts of the concern. The case of *Hawken v Bourne* before mentioned as relied upon by the defendant in error, was as follows: The defendant was a shareholder in a company that worked a mine in Cornwall. There were directors of the company, of whom the defendant was not one. There was a stipulation among the directors and shareholders that all supplies for the mine were to be paid for in cash, and that no debt was to be incurred; the order for the goods, for the price of which the action was brought, was given by the purser or agent of the directors, which was the customary course in such concerns. The plaintiff knew nothing of the defendant's being a shareholder, but it was not proved that he had any notice of the agreement as to not dealing on credit. It was objected on behalf of the defendant that there was no authority in the purser to bind him on a contract upon credit; that there was no liability by reason of the defendant's appearing to be a partner, as the plaintiff knew nothing of him, and that as making a contract upon his credit was absolutely forbidden by him to the directors, a purser or agent appointed by them could not have any authority to pledge his credit. My Brother Maule, who tried the case, was of opinion that the mine being worked with the knowledge, and for the benefit of the defendant, he was liable in a contract entered into for articles ordered in the usual way of conducting such concerns on behalf of the owners, unless the party ordering them was in fact not authorized by the defendant, and the party supplying them had notice of that fact. This ruling was objected to in the court above, but the Court was of opinion it was right. My Brother Parke delivered the judgment of the Court. He stated that there was evidence that the defendant was a complete partner with the directors in working the mines in the manner in which they were worked, and that one partner, by virtue of that relation, is constituted a general agent for the others as to all matters within the scope of the partnership dealing, and had communicated to him by virtue of that relation all authorities necessary for carrying on the partnership, and all such as are usually exercised by partners in the business in which they are engaged; that any restriction which, by agreement among the partners, is attempted to be imposed upon the authority which one possesses as a general agent for the other, is operative only between the partners themselves, and does not limit the authority as to third persons, who acquire rights by its exercise, unless they know such restriction has been made; and that as it was usual to buy the articles in question on credit, and also to buy them through a purser appointed by the directors, the defendant was liable. The judgment in the case of *Smith v Hull Glass Company* is to the same effect, and lays down also that in this respect there is no distinction between the liability of partners in joint-stock

1 9 East 516; 103 ER 670

2 (1812) 1 V & B 154; 35 ER 61

trading companies and partners in ordinary partnerships. The result of these authorities, therefore, is, that when persons constitute a partnership, whether in the form of a joint-stock company, or otherwise, the individual or individuals who are authorized to make contracts for the partnership have authority to bind all the partners in the manner usual and customary in the same trade or business, and even to delegate to others the authority so to bind them if it be usual so to do, notwithstanding an express agreement not so to deal; and it is, I apprehend, upon this principle that partners in a trading company in a business in which bills of exchange are usually issued can bind their co-partners, notwithstanding the issuing of bills is expressly prohibited by the partnership agreement. In the present case, therefore, if the policy contained no notice of a restricted liability, proprietors, shareholders, or partners by whatever name they may be called, would be liable upon it, for it was a contract made in the way of their business and by partners authorized to make such contracts for the company.

But the plaintiff had express notice on the face of the policy of the restriction, and he agreed that the capital stock and funds should alone be liable to him, and that no proprietor should be in anywise subject to his claim beyond the amount of his shares, which the defendant Gooden would certainly be if the plaintiff was entitled to recover on the promise alleged in this declaration; for to hold that the defendants promised as alleged, would render them all liable to any extent, and each for the other; which is directly contrary to the restrictive clauses. It was argued that this view was repugnant to the contract contained in the policy, and that a contract cannot be at the same time made and a provision inserted that no action shall be maintained in the event of its being broken, and that the case of *Furnivall v Coombes*[1] is an authority to this effect. This may be so, but I think that this principle does not apply to the present case. There are two sets of actions, which, in my opinion, may be maintained upon a policy in the present form. First, I think upon the authority of *Andrews v Ellison*[2] and *Dawson v Wrench*,[3] that the individuals that signed the policy personally contracted that the capital stock or funds of the company should be applied to answer the claim on the policy: and, secondly, that each individual shareholder may be sued and recovered against to the extent of his unpaid subscription. The contract is contained in a policy which I have no doubt was in a great measure copied from the form of the policy used by the two incorporated companies, the Royal Exchange and the London Assurance Companies, who were respectively authorized by act of parliament to insure as companies, or partnerships, on joint capital. The policy expressly declares that the capital stock and funds of the company shall alone be liable to make good all claims under it; and the meaning of this seems to me to be that the plaintiff agreed or consented to look, not to the general property of all the shareholders, but to confine themselves, first, to a fund expected to be accumulated from the payment of the shareholders of a portion of a sum subscribed from time to time, and the premiums received in the course of business and kept by the directors for the purpose of current demands upon the company; and, secondly, as a sort of reserved fund, to the liability of each shareholder to the extent of his shares not paid up. But the policy proceeds further, and expressly declares that no shareholder shall be liable to any claim, nor be in anywise charged, by reason of the policy, beyond the amount of his shares in the capital stock. Now, it seems to me that it is here declared, first, that the shareholder shall be liable to the extent of his unpaid shares; and, secondly,

---

1 (1843) 12 LJ CP 265
2 6 J.B. Moore 199
3 3 Ex 359; 154 ER 883

that he shall not be liable further; and to hold the defendants liable in the present action might render them further liable, and would render them jointly liable, which is equally inconsistent with the above provision, which clearly contemplates a separate liability only. The plaintiff was under no obligation to insure with the company, but as he thought proper to do so, he is in my opinion bound by the express declaration in the policy. I am unable to understand how a shareholder can, upon a contract, or in other words, by his own agreement, be rendered liable to an unlimited extent, when he, and the party with whom he has contracted have, as it appears to me, in the most plain and unambiguous terms, agreed that he shall be liable only to a limited extent. If this agreement be illegal it is of course void and of no effect, but I see nothing illegal in it, and if it be legal the proper duty of the court of law is to carry it out. And even if it were incapable of being carried out, I do not think that such incapacity would empower a court of law to impose upon the shareholders a liability or obligation which they and the parties with whom they contracted expressly agreed they should not bear. In my opinion, however, the contract is capable of being carried out; and although the remedy is an inconvenient one, and may probably lead to a multiplicity of actions, I see no objection in point of law to a separate action being maintained against a shareholder to recover from him upon the policy to the extent of his unpaid shares. Upon a common marine policy each underwriter incurs a separate liability and to a limited amount. Upon the present policy I think also each shareholder incurs a separate liability, and to an amount limited to his unpaid shares. It seems to me that each shareholder authorizes the pledging of his personal liability to this extent. This liability is referred to in the judgment of the Court in *Reid v Allan*[1] and as I have already observed, I see no objection to it in point of law, as it seems to me to be entirely consonant to the interests of the parties expressed in their contract.

SOURCE 20
JH Rayner Mincing Lane Ltd and Others *v* Department of Trade and Industry and Others
[1990] 2 AC 418; [1990] BCLC 102 (House of Lords), affirming; [1989] Ch 253; (1988) 4 BCC 559 (Court of Appeal), affirming; [1987] BCLC 667; [1989] Ch 72 (Staughton J)

The International Tin Council (ITC) was an international organisation established by international treaty with the function of adjusting world production and consumption of tin. Its headquarters were in London and its members were the United Kingdom (represented by the Department of Trade and Industry), 22 sovereign states and the European Economic Community. The ITC was recognised under English Law by the International Tin Council (Immunities and Privileges) Order 1972, SI 1972/120 which conferred on it the status and legal capacities of a corporate body. It dealt on the London Metal Exchange and incurred substantial debts to the plaintiff named above, other tin brokers and various banks on all of which debts it defaulted and in respect of which this action and others were brought to seek payment from the members of the ITC. These were struck out and the consolidated appeal dismissed.

Aside from these several actions, there were other proceedings, namely an application for the appointment of a receiver to the assets of the ITC, a

1 4 Ex 326; 154 ER 1237

petition for the winding up of the ITC and an application for the examination of an officer of the ITC (for details see [1989] Ch 253; (1988) 4 BCC 559). All these failed and the consolidated appeals were dismissed by the Court of Appeal and the House of Lords. The extract below is taken from the judgment of Staughton J at first instance in the action for the recovery of the debt from the members of the ITC.

> STAUGHTON J: .... As I have already said, it is open to question whether in international law legal personality necessarily excludes direct liability of the members of an association to its creditors. I now turn to consider the same topic in English domestic law. But it becomes rather more complicated. There may be two questions: (a) Does having the legal capacities of a body corporate equal legal personality? (b) Does legal personality mean that the members are not directly liable to creditors?
>
> In *Blackstone's Commentaries* (3 Bl Com (15th edn 1809), p 472) it is said that corporations may exist at common law (such as vicars and churchwardens), or by prescription (such as the City of London) or by Act of Parliament or Royal Charter. See also 9 Halsbury's Laws (4th edn) para 1231; and 7 Halsbury's Laws para 1:
>
>> 'The word "company" imports an association of a number of individuals formed for some common purpose. Such an association may be incorporated (that is, a body corporate with perpetual succession and a common seal) or it may be unincorporated. An incorporated company is a legal person separate and distinct from the individual members of the company, whereas an unincorporated company has no such separate existence and it is not in law distinguishable from its members.'
>
> *Lindley on Partnership* (3rd edn 1873), vol 1, p 4 has this passage:
>
>> 'A corporation is a fictitious person, created by special authority (and by the law of England by the Crown or by parliament), and endowed by that authority with a capacity to acquire rights and incur obligations, as a means to the end for the attainment of which the corporation is created. A corporation, it is true, consists of a number of individuals, but the rights and obligations of these individuals are not the rights and obligations of the fictitious person composed of those individuals; nor are the rights and obligations of the body corporate exerciseable by or enforceable against the individual members thereof, either jointly or separately, but only collectively, as one fictitious whole. As the civilians neatly express it' [and then the author cites the passage from Ulpian in the Digest which was quoted in the *Westland Helicopters'* case].[1]
>
> So one has the position that a corporation, created by any of the methods mentioned, is a separate legal person distinct from its members; and its obligations are not enforceable against the members. On the other hand, an unincorporated company has no separate existence; its members, some or all of them, are liable for its obligations.
>
> The law relating to companies did not initially follow that path. The Joint Stock Companies Act 1844 provided by section 25 that a company on registration

---

1 (1984) 23 ILM 1071 (see p 16)

should be incorporated by its name, for the purpose of suing and being sued; but the shareholders continued to be liable for the obligations of the company. Section 66 provided that judgments against the company could be enforced against shareholders, provided that due diligence had been used to recover from the company. However, later Companies Acts took a different view; there was no provision that members should be directly liable for the obligations of a company, once incorporated; there was only the question what contribution they should be liable to make to the company or its liquidator. That was a matter within the province of Millett J in the two applications that came before him. It is no concern of mine.

By the end of the nineteenth century the effect of the separate existence of a corporate body had become clear. In *Re Sheffield and South Yorkshire Permanent Building Society*[1] Cave J said:

'But Mr Grosvenor Woods took a different point, with which it is necessary for us to deal. He argued that persons who unite together for trading or making profits in any way are, at common law, liable for all debts which are incurred during the time they are members of the association, and that, if the association has ultimately to be wound up, past members must pay their shares of the debts. As a general rule — apart from legislation — that is perfectly true with respect to partners, and with respect to associations in the nature of partnership where there is no incorporation, but with respect to corporations the case is entirely different where the legislature has not thought fit to intervene, or where the charter under which the body is incorporated does not provide otherwise. A corporation is a legal *persona* just as much as an individual; and, if a man trusts a corporation, he trusts that legal *persona*, and must look to its assets for payment: he can only call upon individual members to contribute in case the Act or charter has so provided.'

. . .

See also *Salomon v Salomon & Co Ltd*[2] and *Gower's Principles of Modern Company Law* (4th edn 1979), p 100:

'It follows from the fact that a corporation is a separate legal person that its members are not as such liable for its debts.'

Some doubt as to the connection between separate personality and separate liability may be said to have lasted until the judgment of Phillimore LJ in *Von Hellfeld v Rechnitzer and Mayer Frères & Co*;[3] but I do not think that any should persist today.

So I conclude that if by English legislation the I.T.C. had been made a corporation, or body corporate, or a separate legal person in those very words, its members would have had no direct liability for the obligations of the I.T.C. unless the legislature had said so in express terms. Otherwise separate legal personality is, in English law, inconsistent with the members of an association being liable for its debts. But the Order in Council does not make the I.T.C. a corporation, or a body corporate, or in terms grant it legal personality. There may well have been good and valid reasons why it did not do so, for example, it may not have been desired that the English court should have jurisdiction to wind it up. So I shall have to consider the effect of what the Order in Council did say, that the I.T.C.

---

1 (1889) 22 QBD 470
2 [1897] AC 22; 66 LJ Ch 35
3 [1914] 1 Ch 748; 83 LJ Ch 521

should have the legal capacities of a body corporate. On this issue, the judge ruled that the expression in the Order in Council that the I.T.C. had the 'legal capacities of a body corporate', meant that the members of the association should not by virtue of their membership alone be liable for its obligations.

(v) Trade union and other cases

These are said to be important as showing that there can, in English law, be a creature which is not a corporation or body corporate strictly so called, but is a separate legal person with the consequence that its members are not themselves liable for its obligations. The journey through the cases is laborious. What in my judgment they do establish is this: (a) Parliament is sovereign in the United Kingdom, and can create a body with any attributes that it chooses. (b) What sort of body Parliament has created is to be determined by interpretation of the legislation in question. (c) In past cases indications were to be found in the legislation which pointed in one direction or in another. It is also argued that the courts have not found it inherently improbable that Parliament should create such a body.

It scarcely needed authority to establish propositions (a) and (b); and the indications mentioned in proposition (c) are often relevant only to the particular case that was being considered. So it is for the question of inherent probability or improbability that the cases are important.

The heart of the matter is now to be found in the case of *Bonsor v Musicians' Union*.[1] Mr Bonsor played the clarinet, until he was wrongfully expelled from his union. He, and subsequently his widow, sought to claim damages from the union. The House of Lords held unanimously that she was entitled to do so. But there was a difference of view in the reasons given for that conclusion. Lord Morton and Lord Porter considered that the union was 'an entity recognised by the law and distinct from the individual members' and 'a thing created by statute . . . an entity, a body, a near-corporation, which, by statute has in certain respects, an existence apart from its member . . .' On the other hand Lord MacDermott said:

> 'I base this opinion primarily on the statutes. The more closely they are examined the clearer it seems to be that the legislature, though minded to bestow on registered unions some of the gifts and attributes of legal personality, had no intention of doing more and was, indeed, averse to the idea of going the whole length and making those unions new creatures, distinct in law from their membership, and fundamentally different from the "combination" of persons which the definition requires all trade unions to be. I need not go over the various provisions of the Acts again. If they point in more than one direction, on balance they seem to me to lead away from the appellant's contention; and, taken together, it would, I think, be right to say of them that they make of registration and its results something of far less consequence than might fairly be expected had that process meant to bring into being a new juridical person. The comparative ease with which the garb of registration may be donned and doffed hardly accords with the view that each change means the taking up or the laying down of a legal personality; there is, however, nothing so casual or anomalous about the position if all that happens is that the union concerned gains or loses, as the case may be, certain advantages or "privileges" with their attendant responsibilities. But perhaps the most weighty consideration of all lies in the

---

1 [1956] AC 104; [1955] 3 All ER 518

fact that Parliament has made no effort to incorporate the registered trade union. In the latter half of the last century, incorporation was the recognized and usual way of conferring on an association of persons the status of a distinct legal entity, and it is clear that the draftsman of the Act of 1871 had the Companies Act of 1862 before him. Yet there is not a word about the members becoming, on registration, a body corporate, and the only reference to a seal is in relation to the work of the registry. Parliament is not, of course, restricted in its choice of possible methods for producing a given result. But when, as here, it studiously avoids a familiar and appropriate method without purporting to adopt another in its stead, its intention to reach that result may well be open to doubt. For these reasons, I am of opinion that a registered trade union is not a juridical person.'

However he went on to hold that the union could be sued for damages in its own name, and that execution must be confined to the property of the union.

. . .

So it was certainly contemplated that Parliament might create an association with separate legal personality, without making it a corporation or body corporate in the strict sense. The question whether Parliament had done so was a matter of construction of the statute. In *Inland Revenue Comrs v Bew Estates Ltd*[1] Roxburgh J said:

'Parliament has recently shown an increasing fondness for creating quasi-corporations, ie, bodies different from the aggregate of the members, eg, a members' club, and yet not corporations in the language of jurisprudence. In my judgment, the War Damage Commission is such a quasi-corporation, though counsel have argued that it is nothing but the aggregate of its members.'

I think that the judge gave a members' club as an example, not of a quasi-corporation, but of something that *was* the aggregate of the members.

Also helpful is *Chaff and Hay Acquisition Committee v J A Hemphill & Sons Pty Ltd.*[2] That was a decision of the High Court of Australia, a court which has been held in the highest regard in this country, amongst other reasons because it combines the Anglo-Saxon tradition and methods, almost unadulterated, with the special problems of a federal constitution.

The committee was constituted by a statute of South Australia. It sought to sue in New South Wales. The High Court held that, although the South Australian statute formed no part of the law of New South Wales, and although the committee was not a corporation, (i) it was a legal entity, and (ii) as a matter of private international law its existence and capacity would be recognised in New South Wales. It is the first point that is relevant here. I cite only some brief extracts from the judgment of Williams J as illustrating the reasoning of the majority:

'The Act does not expressly incorporate the committee or provide for a common seal. It is not therefore a corporation in the strict sense. But it can contract to buy and sell chaff and hay as a corporate body, and the chaff and hay and other property which it acquires for the purposes of the Act becomes the property of the committee as a corporate body . . . The committee is therefore not only empowered to contract and hold property

---

1 [1956] Ch 407; [1956] 2 All ER 210
2 [1947] 74 CLR 375

as a corporate body, but it is also empowered to sue or be sued as a corporate body with respect to any matters arising out of the Act. And its individual members are protected against liability for all matters and things done or suffered by the committee or any member thereof in the bona fide execution of the Act, or the exercise of discharge of any of its or his powers or duties. Thus the effect of the Act is to create for certain purposes an artificial corporate entity which is separate and distinct from its individual members ... I agree with the opinion of the majority of that Court. The effect of the Act is, in my opinion, to form the committee into a separate corporate body from that of its members for the purposes of the Act. It has the corporate powers already mentioned. Persons who sell chaff or hay to the committee sell their goods to the corporate body. It is to the corporate body that they must look for payment. The members of the committee are not liable as individuals for the chaff or hay purchased by the committee. The vendors of the chaff and hay are liable to the committee and not to the individual members for any breach of contracts on their part ... In my opinion the Chaff and Hay Acquisition Committee is a statutory entity created by the law of South Australia which should be recognised in the courts of New South Wales as a foreign quasi-corporation, having the corporate powers conferred upon it by the Act. It is a quasi-corporation which is an instrumentality, that is to say an agent, of the Crown in right of the State of South Australia.'

So that again is authority that a legislature can create a body which, though not a corporation in the strict sense, can function as a legal person distinct from its members.

PART VI: MODERN COMPANY LAW

Modern company law is the story of the registered company. Since its inception in 1844 (Joint Stock Companies Act, 7 & 8 Vict cc 110, 111) it has replaced the statutory company and all forms of unincorporated association as the chief vehicle for privately financed (and quite a lot of state financed) commercial operations. The deed of settlement company has all but disappeared and partnership is used mainly for associations of practising professionals. A substantial amount of investment and loan business is, on the other hand, conducted through a variety of different organisations including unit trusts, building societies, industrial and provident societies and friendly societies, all of which fall outside company law.

An increasing amount of non-commercial, non-profit-making activity, eg of a cultural or scientific kind or of community organisations such as neighbourhood law centres, is conducted through the means of the company limited by guarantee. This, like the company limited by shares and the unlimited company is incorporated by registration under the provisions of the same enabling general statute (since 1862 called the Companies Act). It is insignificant in any commercial sense, but occasionally makes an important contribution to the development of the principles of company law (see eg

Gaiman v National Association of Mental Health;[1] *Hickman v Kent or Romney Marsh Sheepbreeders' Association*,[2] see p 303).

Company law, today, is an integrated blend of statute and case-law which both interprets and applies the statutory provisions and also maintains the vigorous common law contribution to the content of modern company law principles. A fresh consolidating statute (at intervals of 20 to 40 years) provides the overall structure for the incorporation of companies limited by shares, limited by guarantee and unlimited companies, as well as an increasing number of provisions in response to fast developing commercial institutions and problems (eg floating charges, insider trading, directors' duties and the oppression of minority shareholders, see Chapters 7, 8, 9 and 10).

The case-law shows company law's rich borrowings from contract, agency, trusts and even public law. On the other hand, company law has also been a benefactor in the donation of legal principles (eg legal personality and the doctrine of ultra vires borrowed by the courts for the governance of trade unions, see *Taff Vale Railway Company v Amalgamated Society of Railway Servants*,[3] *Amalgamated Society of Railway Servants v Osborne*,[4] *Bonsor v Musicians' Union*[5] discussed above, see p 46).

But the student of company law must also be familiar with the unending stream of governmental and non-governmental reports, pamphlets, discussion papers, regulations and so on concerning questions of company law and of the operations of the various agencies which govern some aspect of companies (eg the Department of Trade and Industry, The Stock Exchange and, most recently, the Securities and Investment Board which, incidentally, is a company limited by guarantee).

The major common law developments are reflected in the pages of this source collection. But students must obtain and maintain a working familiarity with the governing statutes as well.

Since 1862, at any one time there has been a consolidated Companies Act which has provided the structure for the establishment and operation of companies registered under its provisions. The latest consolidation is that of 1985 which appeared in four separate Acts: the Companies Act 1985, the Business Names Act 1985, the Company Securities (Insider Dealing) Act 1985 and the Companies Consolidation (Consequential Provisions) Act 1985. The Insider Dealing Act and the Business Names Act, together with the enactment the following year of the Insolvency Act, the Company Directors Disqualification Act and the Financial Services Act illustrate the increasingly specialised development of company law.

The Companies Act 1985 is the major consolidating Act providing the jurisdiction and machinery for the registration and operation of companies. Previous Companies Acts also included the machinery for the liquidation and dissolution of companies, but this has now been hived off to the Insolvency Act 1986. Since 1986, apart from dozens, if not hundreds, of amendments to

---

1 [1971] 1 Ch 317; [1970] 2 All ER 362
2 [1915] 1 Ch 881; 84 LJ Ch 688
3 [1901] AC 426
4 [1910] AC 87; 79 LJ Ch 87
5 [1956] AC 104; [1955] 3 All ER 518

most of these Acts, there has been one further major Companies Act (in 1989) — which, like the previous inter-consolidation Companies Acts of 1980 and 1981, includes the implementation of European Community Law Harmonisation Directives (see below) — and the repeal of the Company Securities (Insider Dealing) Act and the enactment of revised provisions to outlaw insider dealing in the Criminal Justice Act 1993 (Part V, ss 52–64, also, in part, implementing a European Community Directive).

In addition to this primary legislation, delegated legislation plays an important part in the administration of companies. The model constitution for a registered company (which prior to the 1985 consolidation was included as a schedule to the Companies Act) is now contained in the Companies (Tables A to F) Regulations 1985. Dozens of other sets of Regulations have a direct and significant bearing on the operation of companies, for example the Insolvency Regulations 1986.

There is, furthermore, an occasional general discussion by an official committee established by the government on the current state of company law, usually preceding the passing of the next consolidation statute (see Gower's *Principles of Modern Company Law* (5th edn 1992), p 49.

Aside from these occasional general reports, many other governmental committees have made important contributions to our understanding of company law. Some have led directly to legislation (eg the Cork Report to the Insolvency Act, Professor Gower's Review of Investor Protection to the Financial Services Act); others have attracted less favour (eg Bullock Report on Industrial Democracy). Often the content of such Reports is deep, reflective and radical (see Source 133 in Chapter 6) as well as detailed.

An increasingly significant source of official analysis and legislation affecting company law, is the European Community (EC). By the force of one of its legislative instruments — the Directive — it has brought substantial changes to United Kingdom company law. These changes are implemented by UK legislation itself.

In addition to the Directive, the European Community legislates by Regulation. This form of legislation is directly effective and requires no domestic implementing legislation. One Regulation touching on company law has been enacted — the European Economic Interest Grouping Regulation[1] — creating a business organisation intended to encourage cross-border co-operation between business organisations in different Member States of the EC. In addition, since at least 1970 there has been a proposal for the establishment of a European Community Company (the so-called Societas Europaea). The most recent draft statute (in the form of a directly applicable Regulation) dates from July 1989.

The role of the European Court of Justice (ECJ) (which, like the Council of Ministers, the Commission and the Parliament, is a major institution of the EC) is increasingly significant. One of its major functions[2] is to answer

---

1 EC Council Regulation No 2137/85 (OJ 1985 L199/1)
2 See art 177, European Community Treaty

questions concerning the treaties and legislation of the EC put to it by the courts of the Member States when the latter are seised of litigation in which the answer to such questions is necessary for a proper decision to be reached by the domestic court. Sources 21 and 22 illustrate this process.

The EC influence can also be seen in the decision of *R v Stock Exchange, ex parte Else*, [1993] BCLC 834, where the Court of Appeal overruled the court below. The latter made a reference of certain questions to the European Court of Justice under Article 177 of the EC treaty, but the Court of Appeal took the view that these questions could be answered properly by an English court. It is interesting to note that, whereas there is generally no obligation on a court of first instance or on the Court of Appeal to make a reference to the ECJ (under Article 177, this only becomes an obligation where the issue is before a court against whose judgment there is no appeal), in the *Else* case the Court of Appeal also refused leave to the plaintiff (which supported the reference to the European Court) appeal to the House of Lords. The *Else* case is extracted in Chapter 3 (Source 63).

SOURCE 21
R v Her Majesty's Treasury *ex parte* Daily Mail and General Trust plc (Queen's Bench Division 1987)
[1987] 1 FTLR 394; [1987] STC 157; [1987] 2 CMLR 1

MACPHERSON J: [1] The applicants in this case, Daily Mail and General Trust plc, seek judicial review of HM Treasury's refusal to acknowledge that consent is not required under section 482(1)(a) of the Income and Corporation Taxes Act 1970 for the applicants to cease to be resident in the United Kingdom for the purpose of establishing their residence in the Netherlands. Alternatively the applicants seek to review the refusal or implied refusal of HM Treasury to grant the applicants' application for such consent.
[2] Three declarations are sought and an order of *mandamus*. And at the heart of the case lies the question whether or not Article 52 of the EEC Treaty protects the applicants and effectively entitles them to transfer their residence to the Netherlands without Treasury consent, or alternatively entitles them to immediate and unconditional consent to that proposed transfer. The question is thus whether or not in the light of the facts of this case section 482 is overcome by Article 52.
[3] Section 482(1)[1] of the 1970 Act provides, so far as is relevant, as follows: Subject to the provisions of this section, all transactions of the following classes shall be unlawful unless carried out with the consent of the Treasury that is to say:

'(a) for a body corporation resident in the United Kingdom to cease to be so resident.'

[4] The test for determining whether or not a body corporate is 'resident' is set out in section 482(7)[1] as follows: 'A body corporate shall be deemed for the purposes of this section to be resident or not to be resident in the United Kingdom according as the central management and control of its trade or business is or is not exercised in the United Kingdom.'
. . .

---

1 See now s 765 of the Income and Corporation Taxes Act 1988

[7] On 1 March 1984 the applicant's solicitors submitted to the Treasury an application to cease to be resident in the United Kingdom. That application put all the applicants' cards on the table. It is purposeless to rehearse them in this judgment. There are subsidiary reasons for the application, but it is obvious that the primary reasons are fiscal.

. . .

[11] On 20 September 1985 the Revenue made it plain that they were minded to recommend rejection of the applicants' application. Counsel advised that the EEC Treaty entitled the applicants to transfer their residence, and these proceedings were eventually launched in the summer of 1986.

[12] The applicants submit that the Treasury's refusal to accept that in this case the force of section 482 is undermined by Article 52 EEC and section 2(1) of the European Communities Act should be declared to be unlawful.

[13] The applicants say that this case raises substantial and important issues in EEC law, and that a decision on these issues is necessary in order to determine this case.

[14] The respondents do not agree. But I have detected both from the correspondence and parts of their argument that they too believe that sooner or later this case will cross the Channel.

[15] I have come firmly to the conclusion that it is right and necessary that I should myself refer the case to the European Court under the provisions of Article 177 of the Treaty, in the exercise of my discretion.

. . .

[18] It seems to me necessary to set out the arguments on each side shortly. They have been succinct.

[19] The applicants say as follows:

1. Article 52 has 'direct effect'.
2. The beneficiaries of the rights under Article 52 are individuals who are nationals of a member-State and (by Article 58) companies formed in accordance with the law of a member-State and having their registered office, central administration or principal place of business within the Community.
3. The applicants must be treated in the same way as individuals with regard to their rights of 'establishment'.
4. The actual operation of an investment company is an economic activity, to be protected and covered by the economic objectives and rights set out in the Treaty.

[20] Mr Vaughan[1] argues that in this case the combined forces of the Treasury and the Inland Revenue are acting contrary to the letter and the spirit of Articles 52 to 58, and that the applicants are wrongly being prevented from establishing themselves in Holland and from setting up their permanent physical presence and their central management and residence in that country.

[21] Mr Vaughan[1] points to Directive 73/148, and says that just as the restrictions on emigration of nationals are to be barred so are restrictions upon establishment, whether such restrictions are discriminatory or not. And he relies upon two cases which involve the establishment of lawyers in other countries than their own (*Reyners*[2] and *Klopp*.[3])

[22] The freedom to leave, both for nationals and for companies or firms, is, says Mr Vaughan,[1] a necessary component or corollary of the right to establish in another State. The right to establish elsewhere does not exist without the right to

---

1 Counsel for the *Daily Mail and General Trust plc*
2 [1974] ECR 631; [1974] 2 CMLR 305
3 [1984] ECR 2971; [1985] 1 CMLR 99

leave one's own member-State. And it is no answer to say that a branch can be set up abroad, since that is simply another way of restricting the full right to establish which is enshrined in Articles 52 to 58.

[23] Mr Vaughan[1] adds that the motives for exercising rights under the Treaty are not relevant and should not be taken into consideration and he says that the European Court has made it clear that (for example) the risk of tax avoidance or evasion cannot justify derogation from a fundamental freedom (see Case 270/83 *France*[2]) so that section 482 cannot be justified in its application to this case.

[24] Mr Buxton[3] stresses the continuing English 'nature' of the applicants. He says that the ambition of the applicants to avoid United Kingdom tax is in this case solely the concern of English domestic law. In the absence of any contention that the United Kingdom tax provisions are contrary to Community law Mr Buxton[3] argues that Community law rightly permits the United Kingdom, without interference, to seek to prevent avoidance of its tax system.

[25] In particular Mr Buxton[3] argues that the fundamental basis of Article 52 is to prohibit discrimination by the authorities of a member-State against the nationals of another member-State who wish to establish themselves in order to perform economic activities in their chosen country.

[26] Section 482[4] does not prevent the applicants from performing economic activities in the Netherlands. Furthermore Article 52 and Directive 73/148 confer general rights of exit which are plainly confined to national human beings. And any right of exit that might apply in the case of corporations does not give a right to establish central management and residence for fiscal purposes, as opposed to other forms of establishment.

[27] Even if his argument is wrong on these fundamental matters Mr Buxton[3] says that an overriding principle of Community law is that freedoms afforded by the Treaty are not to be used to frustrate national measures aimed at tax avoidance.

[28] Mr Buxton[3] points out that the true effect of the case of *Reyners* is to outlaw discrimination against nationals upon grounds of nationality; and he says that such cases as *Fearon*[5] illustrate the implementation of the Community's rule of non-discrimination in this way. And he says that section 482[4] is non-discriminatory and therefore not caught by Article 52 at all.

[29] Section 482[4] does not restrict the applicants' wish to become active participants in economic activity in Holland, since they can do that by establishing an agency, branch or subsidiary. And thus since a change of residence is unnecessary for the applicants to engage in their economic activity in Holland the force of section 482[4] should not be restricted when its aim is the legitimate one of curbing tax avoidance and the upsetting of domestic fiscal and budgetary arrangements.

[30] As to the applicants' argument based upon Directive 73/184 Mr Buxton refers to the case of Royer.[6] And he says that neither the principles nor the detailed rules implementing the Treaty rights which are set out in the directive have any application to corporations. Neither expressly nor by analogy, says Mr Buxton, can it be right to apply to corporations provisions so clearly designed to allow the freedom of movement of individual human beings.

---

1 Counsel for the *Daily Mail and General Trust plc*
2 [1987] 1 CMLR 401
3 Counsel for HM Treasury
4 Now s 765 of the Income and Corporation Taxes Act 1988
5 [1984] ECR 3677; [1985] 2 CMLR 228
6 [1976] ECR 497; [1976] 2 CMLR 619

[31] And Mr Buxton stresses throughout his argument that nothing should be allowed to derogate from the Community's overall interests, which include the outlawing of avoidance of national taxes.

[32] These are of course somewhat abbreviated summaries of the arguments on both sides. Section 482 survives of course from the days in 1950 to 1960 when United Kingdom companies wished to avoid the high taxation in operation in the United Kingdom and so manipulated their shareholdings as to divert dividends beyond the reach of HM Revenue.

[33] My own inclination has been to doubt whether section 482 should be allowed to prevent or to fetter the voluntary movement of residence of a corporation which wishes to take advantage of a better fiscal climate in another member-State within the EEC. The aim being of course not to evade tax altogether but to exchange one fiscal system for another, and not to remove to a foreign tax shelter. And the object of the Treaty being the removal of barriers and the creation of an economic community without protective barriers of any kind either for persons or for corporations or for trade generally. The creation in other words of a true Common Market. But as the argument developed it seemed to me more and more appropriate that the European Court should be asked now to consider the matter. The relevant or possibly relevant directives require consideration. There are no specific instances dealing with the rights of exit or the right to restrict exit by corporations in order to maintain revenue in comparable circumstances.

[34] And I am now sure that the matter should be referred by myself. I bear in mind that this Court should not only look to see whether the matter is so clear that there can be no doubt about the answer, but that it should be wary before saying that the matter is indeed thus clear in any event.

[35] Of course I could reach a conclusion. But as the argument developed I have resisted the temptation to do so; partly because the competing arguments both have considerable force; partly because the matter appears to me instinctively and upon the facts to be eminently one for early reference; and partly because it seems to me that eventual reference is almost certain.

[36] Without more ado, therefore, and in the hope that the Luxembourg Court will agree that no more is necessary to be said in judgment at this stage, I make the necessary reference since I believe that it is necessary so to do to enable this court eventually to give its judgment.

SOURCE 22
Before the European Court of Justice
[1989] BCLC 206
The Judge Rapporteur (O. Due) . . .

By order of 6 February 1987 the national court decided to stay proceedings until the Court of Justice had given a preliminary ruling on the following questions:

'1. Do Articles 52 and 58 of the EEC Treaty preclude a Member State from prohibiting a body corporate with its central management and control in that Member State from transferring without prior consent or approval that central management and control to another Member State in one or both of the following circumstances, namely where: (i) payment of tax upon profits or gains which have already arisen may be avoided; (ii) were the company to transfer its central management and control, tax that might have been chargeable had the company retained its central management and control in that Member State would be avoided?

2. Does Council Directive 73/148/EEC give a right to a corporate body

with its central management and control in a Member State to transfer without prior consent or approval its central management and control to another Member State in the conditions set out in Question 1? If so, are the relevant provisions directly applicable in this case?

3. If such prior consent or approval may be required, is a Member State entitled to refuse consent on the grounds set out in Question 1?

4. What difference does it make, if any, that under the relevant law of the Member State no consent is required in the case of a change of residence to another Member State of an individual or firm?'

Observations of the applicant

The applicant in the main proceedings suggests that the questions asked by the national court should be answered as follows:

'1. Where under the law of a member state unrealised profits or gains have accrued, but no tax liability in respect thereof has arisen, and where the transfer of central management and control of a corporate body from the member state to another member state does not amount to a taxable event, arts 52 and 58 of the EEC Treaty preclude the former member state from prohibiting a body corporate with its central management and control in that state from transferring, without prior consent or approval, its central management and control to another member state, notwithstanding the fact that no tax on unrealised gains will be payable to the first member state as a result of such transfer. Furthermore, where the tax liabilities of bodies corporate accrue from time to time under the law of a member state by virtue of the presence in that state of the central management and control of such bodies corporate, arts 52 to 58 of the EEC Treaty preclude that member state from prohibiting a body corporate from transferring its central management and control to another member state in order to ensure continued tax under the law of the former member state.

2. Article 2(1) and (4) of the EC Council Directive 73/148, in conjunction with arts 52 to 58 of the EEC Treaty, gives a right to a corporate body with its central management and control in a member state to transfer without prior consent or approval its central management and control to another member state in the circumstances referred to in the first question referred by the Divisional Court.

3. Since no consent or approval is required, a member state is not entitled to refuse consent in the circumstances set out in the first question referred by the Divisional Court.

4. Since arts 52 to 58 of the EEC Treaty give expression to the principle that natural and legal persons must be free to choose the appropriate legal form in which to pursue their activities in other member states, it is incompatible with arts 52 to 58 to subject a transfer of corporate residence to another member state to prior consent or approval, where no such prior consent or approval is required in the case of a change of residence to another member state of an individual or a firm.'

Observations of the United Kingdom

...

In its case law the court has recognised a principle preventing individuals from using Community freedoms in order to avoid the application of legitimate national rules. In regard to freedom to provide services, the court decided in *van Binsbergen v Bestuur van de Bedrijfsvereniging voor de Metaalnijverheid* Case 33/74

[1974] ECR 1299 that specific requirements imposed on the person providing a service cannot be considered incompatible with the Treaty where they have as their purpose the general good and are binding on any person established in the member state in question, where the person providing the service would escape from the ambit of those rules by being established in another member state. In regard to freedom of establishment, the court decided in *Knoors v Secretary of State for Economic Affairs* Case 115/78 [1979] ECR 399 that it is not possible to disregard the legitimate interest which a member state may have in preventing certain of its nationals, by means of facilities created under the Treaty, from attempting wrongly to evade the application of their national legislation as regards training for a trade.

...

According to the United Kingdom, the above-mentioned principle justifies a national provision such as that at issue in the main proceedings since it enables the authorities to control a change of company residence in any case where the sole or main objective of that change is the avoidance of liability for United Kingdom taxation.

Finally, the United Kingdom observes that there are sound practical reasons for a difference of treatment between individuals and companies inasmuch as only the latter are subject to the obligation to obtain the approval of the authorities for a transfer of residence. Article 58 treats companies in the same way as individuals for the purposes of the provisions of the Treaty on freedom of establishment but does not require the member states to apply in every case the same rules of domestic law to companies as to individuals.

The United Kingdom therefore submits that the questions posed by the national court should be answered as follows:

'1. Articles 52 to 58 of the EEC Treaty do not preclude the member state from prohibiting the transfer of central management and control in either of the stated circumstances.

2. EC Council Directive 73/148 gives no rights to corporate bodies. The second part of the question accordingly does not arise.

3. The prior consent or approval referred to may be required, and the member state is entitled to refuse consent on either of the grounds set out in question 1.

4. The provisions of the domestic law of the member state referred to make no difference to the above replies.'

Observations of the Commission

...

There is no doubt, as far as individuals are concerned, that Community law recognises a right of exit from the member state of origin. That point has been expressly dealt with by art 2 of the EC Council Directive 73/148 of 21 May 1973 on the abolition of restrictions on movement and residence within the Community for nationals of member states with regard to establishment and the provision of services. The Commission considers that that directive cannot apply to legal persons since the terms in which it is drafted are such as to make it clear that it applies only to natural persons. However, in the view of the Commission, whether one is dealing with natural or legal persons, the rights conferred under art 52ff of the Treaty would be rendered meaningless if the state of nationality could actually prevent emigration. Any legal person may be wound up and reincorporated in another member state, and a legal person has the right to change its residence, where that possibility is provided for under national company law. The Commission therefore considers that where national company law draws a distinction between nationality and residence, and provides for the retention of nationality by companies which decide to establish residence abroad, art 52 of the Treaty confers on a company the right to exercise that choice without being dependent on an authorisation from national fiscal authorities. However, there would appear to be no objection to a requirement that notice be given.

The Commission concludes by proposing that the Court of Justice should give the following answers to the questions submitted by the national court:

'1. Articles 52 and 58 of the EEC Treaty preclude a member state from prohibiting a body corporate with its central management and control in that member state from transferring without prior consent or approval that central management and control to another member state in one or both of the following circumstances, namely where (i) payment of tax on profits or gains which have already arisen may be avoided; (ii) were the company to transfer its central management and control tax that might have become chargeable had the company retained its central management and control in that member state would be avoided.

2. EC Council Directive 73/148 confers no rights on bodies corporate.

3. In the light of the answer given to question 1, this question is not applicable.

4. The answer to question 1 is not affected by the legal situation attaching to an individual or firm.'

The Advocate General's opinion

. . .

8. In order to determine whether the transfer of the central management and control of a company constitutes establishment within the meaning of the Treaty it is therefore necessary to take into consideration a range of factors. The place at which the management of the company meets is undoubtedly one of the foremost of those factors, as is the place, normally the same, at which general policy decisions are made. However, in certain circumstances those factors may be neither exclusive nor even decisive. It might be necessary to take account of the residence of the principal managers, the place at which general meetings are held, the place at which administrative and accounting documents are kept and the place at which the company's principal financial activities are carried on, in particular, the place at which it operates a bank account. That list cannot be regarded as exhaustive. Moreover, those factors may have to be given different weight according to whether, for example, the company is engaged in production or investment. In the latter case, it may be perfectly legitimate to take account of the market on which the company's commercial or stock exchange transactions are mainly carried out and the scale of those transactions.

9. In the light of the judgment in *Association des Centres distributeurs Édouard Leclerc v Sàrl 'Au blé vert'* Case 229/83 [1985] ER 1 it is clear that Community law offers no assistance where 'objective factors' show that a particular activity was carried out 'in order to circumvent' national legislation: see *Leclerc*'s case (at 35 (para 27)). The fact that the essential activities of a company take place on the territory of a member state other than that to which it intends to transfer its central management may not be ignored. Such circumstances may, in certain cases, constitute an indication that what is involved is not genuine establishment, in particular when the effect of the transfer of the central management is to cause the company to cease to be subject to legislation which would otherwise apply to it, I believe that that conclusion can be drawn from the judgments of the court

in *van Binsbergen v Bestuur van de Bedrijfsvereniging voor de Metaalnijverheid* Case 33/74 [1974] ECR 1299 and *Knoors v Secretary of State for Economic Affairs* Case 115/78 [1979] ECR 399. As a general rule it appears that the national court may assess whether, in a specific case and having regard to the circumstances, there is a suggestion of abuse of a right or circumvention of the law and whether it should decide to apply Community law.

10. However, when the proper conclusion to be drawn from the circumstances is that the transfer of the central management genuinely constitutes establishment within the meaning of the Treaty, the question then arises whether the right to make such a transfer may be made subject to the authorisation of the national authorities and whether those authorities may object to the transfer for fiscal reasons.

11. Generally, in most of the member states, the transfer of the central management of a company, in the sense of its real head office, may take place only through the winding up of the company and its reconstruction in the host member state. That solution, the 'legal death' of the company, involves the settlement of its tax position, determined on the day of the winding up, both in regard to the existing debt and in regard to matters in respect of which the event normally giving rise to tax liability has not yet occurred. Capital gains are thus taxed even though no disposition of assets has taken place. In regard to the member states referred to above, the transfer of the central management of a company without loss of legal personality or nationality may take place under agreements between member states of the kind provided for in art 220 of the Treaty.

12. No prior authorisation may be required for the exercise of a fundamental freedom laid down in the Treaty. Similarly, a member state cannot prevent a company from exercising its right of establishment on the ground that such exercise entails a loss of revenue in respect of taxes which would have been due on the basis of the company's future activities if it had remained subject to the tax laws of that state.

13. However, I consider that, as Community law now stands, member states are not prevented from requiring a company to settle its fiscal position on any transfer of its central management, even where winding up is not required. It is generally accepted that the winding up required by national legislation as a condition for the emigration of a company is not contrary to Community law (see *Renauld* p 2.47). It would be paradoxical if a member state not requiring winding up were to find itself placed by Community law in a less favourable fiscal position precisely because its legislation on companies is more consistent with Community objectives in regard to establishment. A company set up under the legislation of a member state in which 'fiscal allegiance' (this expression comes from *Rivier* p 15) is determined in the light of the location of the central administration will maintain its registered office in that country and continue to have that country's nationality even after transferring its residence, or, more precisely, the seat of its management, to another member state. However, for the reasons indicated above, that does not seem to me, in the present state of Community law, to preclude national authorities from attaching to such a transfer fiscal consequences similar to those of winding up.

14. The guidelines which I propose should enable the court to reply to the first and third questions referred to it by the Queen's Bench Division of the High Court. They make a reply to the fourth question unnecessary. The remaining question does not require any long discussion. Although the first paragraph of art 58 provides that companies or firms are, for the purposes of the provisions of the Treaty on freedom of establishment, to be treated in the same way as natural persons who are nationals of member states, they clearly cannot be placed

entirely on the same footing; along with the United Kingdom and the Commission, therefore, I consider that EC Council Directive 72/148 does not apply to legal persons.

15. Consequently, I propose that the court should rule that: (1) the transfer to another member state of the central management of a company may constitute a form of exercise of the right of establishment, subject to the assessment by the national court of any elements of fact showing whether or not such a transfer reflects a genuine integration of the said company into the economic life of the host member state; (2) under Community law a member state may not require a company wishing to establish itself in another member state, by transferring its central management there, to obtain prior authorisation for such transfer; (3) however, Community law does not prohibit a member state from requiring a company established on its territory, on establishing itself in another member state by transferring its central management there, to settle its tax position in regard to the part of its assets affected by the transfer, the value of which is to be determined at the date of transfer; (4) EC Council Directive 73/148 is applicable only to natural persons.

The Judgment of the Court of Justice
First question

11. The first question seeks in essence to determine whether arts 52 and 58 of the Treaty give a company incorporated under the legislation of a member state and having its registered office there the right to transfer its central management and control to another member state. If that is so, the national court goes on to ask whether the member state of origin can make that right subject to the consent of national authorities, the grant of which is linked to the company's tax position.

12. With regard to the first part of the question, the applicant claims essentially that art 58 of the Treaty expressly confers on the companies to which it applies the same right of primary establishment in another member state as is conferred on natural persons by art 52. The transfer of the central management and control of a company to another member state amounts to the establishment of the company in that member state because the company is locating its centre of decision-making there, which constitutes genuine and effective economic activity.

13. The United Kingdom argues essentially that provisions of the Treaty do not give companies a general right to move their central management and control from one member state to another. The fact that the central management and control of a company is located in a member state does not itself necessarily imply any genuine and effective economic activity on the territory of that member state and cannot therefore be regarded as establishment within the meaning of art 52 of the Treaty.

14. The Commission emphasises, first of all, that in the present state of Community law, the conditions under which a company may transfer its central management and control from one member state to another are still governed by the national law in which it is incorporated and of the state to which it wishes to move. In that regard the Commission refers to the differences between the national systems of company law. Some of them permit the transfer of the central management and control of a company and, among those, certain attach no legal consequences to such a transfer, even in regard to taxation. Under other systems the transfer of the management or the centre of decision-making of a company out of the member state in which it is incorporated results in the loss of legal personality However, all the systems permit the winding up of a company in one

member state and its reincorporation in another. The Commission considers that, where the transfer of central management and control is possible under national legislation, the right to transfer it to another member state is a right protected by art 52 of the Treaty.

15. Faced with those diverging opinions, the court must first point out, as it has done on numerous occasions, that freedom of establishment constitutes one of the fundamental principles of the Community and that the provisions of the Treaty guaranteeing that freedom have been directly applicable since the end of the transitional period. Those provisions secure the right of establishment in another member state not merely for Community nationals but also for the companies referred to in art 58.

16. Even though those provisions are directed mainly to ensuring that foreign nationals and companies are treated in the host member state in the same way as nationals of that state, they also prohibit the member state of origin from hindering the establishment in another member state of one of its nationals or of a company incorporated under its legislation which comes within the definition contained in art 58. As the Commission rightly observed, the rights guaranteed by art 52 ff would be rendered meaningless if the member state of origin could prohibit undertakings from leaving in order to establish themselves in another member state. In regard to natural persons, the right to leave their territory for that purpose is expressly provided for EC Council Directive 73/148, which is the subject of the second question to the court.

17. In the case of a company, the right of establishment is generally exercised by the setting up of agencies, branches or subsidiaries, as is expressly provided for in the second sentence of the first paragraph of art 52. Indeed, that is the form of establishment in which the applicant engaged in this case by opening an investment management office in the Netherlands. A company may also exercise its right of establishment by taking part in the incorporation of a company in another member state, and in that regard art 221 of the Treaty ensures that it will receive the same treatment as nationals of that member state as regards participation in the capital of the new company.

18. The provision of United Kingdom law at issue in the main proceedings imposes no restriction on transactions such as those described above. Nor does it stand in the way of a partial or total transfer of the activities of a company incorporated in the United Kingdom to a company newly incorporated in another member state, if necessary after winding up and, consequently, the settlement of the tax position of the United Kingdom company. It requires Treasury consent only where such a company seeks to transfer its central management and control out of the United Kingdom while maintaining its legal personality and its status as a United Kingdom company.

19. In that regard it should be borne in mind that, unlike natural persons, companies are creatures of the law and, in the present state of Community law, creatures of national law. They exist only by virtue of the varying national legislation which determines their incorporation and functioning.

20. As the Commission has emphasised, the legislation of the member states varies widely in regard to both the factor providing a connection to the national territory required for the incorporation of a company and the question whether a company incorporated under the legislation of a member state may subsequently modify that connecting factor. Certain states require that not merely the registered office but also the real head office, that is to say the central administration of the company, should be situated on their territory, and the removal of the central administration from that territory thus presupposes the winding up of the company with all the consequences that winding up entails in

company law and tax law. The legislation of other states permits companies to transfer their central administration to a foreign country but certain of them, such as the United Kingdom, make that right subject to certain restrictions, and the legal consequences of a transfer, particularly in regard to taxation, vary from one member state to another.

21. The Treaty has taken account of that variety in national legislation. In defining, in art 58, the companies which enjoy the right of establishment, the Treaty places on the same footing, as connecting factors, the registered office, central administration and principal place of business of a company. Moreover, art 220 of the Treaty provides for the conclusion, so far as is necessary, of agreements between the member states which a view to securing, inter alia, the retention of legal personality in the event of transfer of the registered office of companies from one country to another. No convention in this area has yet come into force.

22. It should be added that none of the directives on the co-ordination of company law adopted under art 54(3)(g) of the Treaty deal with the differences at issue here.

23. It must therefore be held that the Treaty regards the differences in national legislation concerning the required connecting factor and the question whether, and if so how, the registered office or real head office of a company incorporated under national law may be transferred from one member state to another as problems which are not resolved by the rules concerning the right of establishment but must be dealt with by future legislation or conventions.

24. Under those circumstances, arts 52 and 58 of the Treaty cannot be interpreted as conferring on companies incorporated under the law of a member state a right to transfer their central management and control and their central administration to another member state while retaining their status as companies incorporated under the legislation of the first member state.

25. The answer to the first part of the first question must therefore be that in the present state of Community law arts 52 and 58 of the Treaty, properly construed, confer no right on a company incorporated under the legislation of a member state and having its registered office there to transfer its central management and control to another member state.

26. Having regard to that answer, there is no need to reply to the second part of the first question.

Second question

27. In its second question, the national court asks whether the provisions of EC Council Directive 73/148 of 21 May 1973 on the abolition of restrictions on movement and residence within the Community for nationals of member states with regard to establishment and the provision of services give a company a right to transfer its central management and control to another member state.

28. It need merely be pointed out in that regard that the title and provisions of that directive refer solely to the movement and residence of natural persons and that the provisions of the directive cannot, by their nature, be applied by analogy to legal persons.

29. The answer to the second question must therefore be that EC Council Directive 73/148, properly construed, confers no right on a company to transfer its central management and control to another member state.

PART VII: COMPANIES — PRIVATE LAW INSTITUTIONS IN A PUBLIC LAW FRAMEWORK

It is important to appreciate the different ways in which the words 'public' and 'private' are used. When we talk of public law (as opposed to private law) we are speaking of the set of legal principles which govern the legal relationship between the State (acting through a range of different institutions eg government ministries and statutorily created subordinate executives and legislatures such as local authorities) and persons (individual and corporate). Public law recognises and creates such public bodies, establishes their rights and duties vis à vis persons and constitutes the principles under which disputes between the State and persons are resolved. Private law, on the other hand, is the set of legal principles which governs the legal relationship between two or more legal persons. Private law constitutes the framework and concepts within which legal persons (individual and corporate) establish legal contact voluntarily (trusts, contract, partnership) and involuntarily (torts) and within which disputes between them are resolved.

In Company law, 'private' and 'public' are generally used to signify how a company is financed. A company which draws its finance from the common mix of a bank loan and the private resources of the few people who make up the company's directors and employees, is a private company, whereas a company which is financed in whole or in part from public subscription derived by a general invitation issued by the company is a public company. This distinction is clearly laid down by statute and the technical aspects are considered in Chapter 3. Thus both private companies and public companies are privately financed, as opposed to *public corporations* which are one species of the public bodies referred to above, and which belong to administrative law and are generally financed from public funds.

Companies, as legal persons, are major contributors to the development of the UK's private law principles and institutions. A superficial glance at the names of the litigants of reported and unreported cases in the typical private law fields of contract, torts, commercial law and trusts, or an appreciation of the central role of the company in the management of private wealth, is testimony to this contribution. Yet it would be misleading to view companies as operating exclusively within private law. The public law connections and context for companies can be seen from a cursory glance at the history of company law. The insistent distinction between incorporated and unincorporated associations (see Sources 4 and 5) and, despite the earlier authorities, the now general acceptance in English law of Blackstone's view that 'with us in England, the king's consent is absolutely necessary to the erection of any corporation' (see Source 8, and also Sources 10 and 11) inevitably gives the company a place in public law as well as private law. The fact that the charter and statutory companies from the fifteenth to the nineteenth centuries played such a major public role in the development of Britain and its Empire (see Sources 12 and 13), while being privately financed is another illustration of the public face of the private company.

There is a close and sometimes overlapping relationship between the public and private law principles which govern companies. The birth of a company (see Chapter 3) occurs with its registration by the public official created by the Companies Act (the Registrar of Companies) and the issue by that official of the company's 'birth certificate' (its certificate of incorporation). The name selected for a company is subject to certain restrictions (Chapter 3, section A) and disputes concerned with these aspects of a company's life may be the subject of public law remedies (see Chapter 3, Sources 48 and 49). At the same time, such disputes also have a private law dimension (Chapter 3, Sources 50 and 51). Likewise, the death of a company — the liquidation process — is a mix of public and private processes.

At various points throughout its life, a registered company may find that its operations bring it into a direct relationship with the State, with the latter acting either through the appropriate ministry (usually the Department of Trade and Industry) or through one or other of a large number of bodies specially created to carry out the policy of the government as expressed in the Acts of Parliament.

Thus, every company must comply with regulations under which it discloses certain information about itself and must permit inspection of this information by any member of the public. Failure to do so may result in a criminal penalty or a public law remedy requiring that the company make such disclosure or, in extreme cases, the removal of the company from the register of companies (see Companies Act 1985, ss 10, 12, 228, 230–236, 239, 241(3)(a), 363–364A, 395–409, 652, 709, 713; Insolvency Act 1986, s 21(3), 109). In addition, any company which seeks to raise finance from the public must comply with various sets of regulations (see Chapter 3 Part III). It may be that it is simply seeking finance, but its relationship with the public and the problems of the market in the securities which are issued ensure that the public dimension is never far away.

NOTES AND QUESTIONS

1. *Laski, in Source 4 seems to be arguing that:*
   (i) *all groups should be recognised by the state whether they have undergone the formality of incorporation or not; and*
   (ii) *the courts have, in fact, on many occasions done just that.*
2. *On the second of these points, see* Wedderburn, *'Corporate Personality and Social Policy' [1965] 28 MLR 62 and the judgment of Staughton J in the International Tin Council litigation (Source 20, p 43) as, valuable contributions to this debate illustrating how judicial attitudes to trade unions have effected, in part, the 'informal incorporation', in favour of which Laski was arguing.*
3. *On the first point, that unincorporated groups should be so recognised, consider the practicality of such a policy. Would it be necessary to establish criteria for when an* unincorporated *association came into existence? Consider Source 5, p 7.*
4. *The procedural difficulties for suits by and against partnerships were solved by the introduction, in 1891, of a rule of the Supreme Court allowing such suits by and against partnerships in the* name *of the partnership. The present rule is Order 81:*

> '*Actions by and against firms within jurisdiction (Ord 81, r 1)*
> *1. Subject to the provisions of any enactment, any two or more persons claiming to be entitled, or alleged to be liable, as partners in respect of a cause of action and carrying on business within the jurisdiction may sue or be sued, in the name of the firm (if any) of which they were partners at the time when the cause of action accrued.*'

5. *Sources 16 and 18 emphasise the growing divergence between partnerships and joint stock companies. There is, however, still much in company law which derives from partnership, eg the winding up of small companies on the ground that this is just and equitable (see pp 561ff).*

6. *The development of company law can also be seen in the stirring battles in which companies broke away from the partnership regime, eg in the subjection of companies to the* ultra vires *doctrine (compare the judgments of Blackburn J and Lord Cairns LC in the Court of Exchequer Chamber and the House of Lords respectively in* Ashbury Railway Carriage Company v Riche[1]) *and in the right of the company to issue fresh shares despite the prejudice to the existing shareholders (*Andrews v Gas Meter,[2] *overruling* Hutton v Scarborough Hotels).[3] *Another illustration can be seen in the question of the transferability of shares, see* Re Gresham Life Assurance Society, Ex Parte Penney.[4]

---

1 (1875) LR 7 HL 653; 44 LJ Exch 185 (see pp 9–13)
2 [1897] 1 ChD 361; 66 LJ Ch 246
3 (1865) 2 Dr Sm 521; 13 LT 57
4 (1873) 8 Ch App 446 (see p 599)

Chapter 2

THE COMPANY AS A LEGAL ENTITY

PART I: THE COMPANY — DEPENDENCE AND INDEPENDENCE

When registration is effected under the provisions of the Companies Act, the creature that emerges is an entity recognised by the law. *It* can enter into relationships which the law will recognise and enforce. Thus, it can own property, enter into contracts, contract debts, be liable for the negligence of its employees and so on. It also follows that the company's own property and money can and should be used to meet its liabilities. Other fundamental principles of company law express the company's apparent independence — the directors owe their duties *to the company* (see p 438), any alteration of the articles of association must be bona fide for the benefit of the *company as a whole* (see p 330) and the company is the proper plaintiff in any action against those responsible for damaging the company (see p 530ff).

At the same time, there is a fundamental and apparently contradictory reality — the company is utterly dependent for its every operation on the thoughts and actions of the human beings who are directly connected with it. An apparently powerful and prosperous company may be liquidated on the say so of its shareholders. Consider the facts of the well known *Regal (Hastings) Ltd v Gulliver*[1] (see p 477) where the company vindicated its rights of property and ownership; yet, if Lord Russell is correct, those rights could have been made to evaporate into thin air if the shareholders so chose.

It is, furthermore, axiomatic, first, that a company limited by shares is run for the benefit of its members and, secondly, that its decisions and actions are dictated by the majority vote of the members, either directly or, more commonly, through their elected representatives (see Chapter 6); a decision by the company to buy a factory or close down a plant is a decision by the directors acting within their powers given to them by the company's constitution which, in turn, represents the rules of governance of the company as agreed by the shareholders.

Not surprisingly, this superficial picture with the company as an independent subject of rights and duties sometimes comes under great strain. The benefit of the company as a whole is an inadequate principle where for example the proposed alteration of the articles takes place within the context of an internecine fight between two factions of shareholders (see *Greenhalgh v Arderne Cinemas Ltd*[2] (see p 343). Then again the company may not be able to take the appropriate action to redress wrongs done to itself, as the wrongdoers may, themselves, be in control of the company (see p 529ff). Finally, where there is a contract between the company and, say, a supplier of

---

1 [1967] 2 AC 134n; [1942] 1 All ER 378
2 [1951] Ch 286; [1950] 2 All ER 1120

goods, when (a) the company is unable to pay for the goods, (b) the members of the company have benefited from the delivery of the goods, and (c) the goods were ordered at a time when it was known that the company would probably be unable to pay for them, to insist that the company alone be responsible for payment would amount to a denial of justice. It is then that we may need to supplement the legal structure with the wishes of other legal entities (usually human beings) to produce a satisfactory legal result — one which, in effect, may exclude the company from the picture.

We are required, therefore, to be aware of two worlds. The first consists only of human beings, where some people, the shareholders, have pooled their resources and elected part of their number, the directors, to make decisions and carry out operations in the expectation of making profits for the shareholders in the use of those resources. This will commonly involve entering into transactions with third parties. Here, the world consists of direct relationships between the shareholders and the directors, and through the directors, between the shareholders and the third parties.

The second world, however, in which the company is interposed as a dominant actor makes for different *legal* relationships. There is no contract of agency between shareholders and directors, nor contracts between shareholders and third parties negotiated by the directors. Instead, all three interest groups, shareholders, directors and third parties have separate legal relationships with the company. It is this second world which will constitute the legal framework for the resolution of any dispute unless the result is, for one reason or another, unsatisfactory.

This legal structure may, and often does satisfy the expectations of all these interest groups. The debts of creditors are paid, directors who have powers to govern the company get their salaries and shareholders get their dividends. But if it does not, if someone who is directly connected with the company is dissatisfied by the result which the application of this legal structure dictates, he may urge that the court have regard to the 'reality' which underlies this structure, in order to bring him the satisfaction which the application of the legal structure denies. If a shareholder has benefited from the supply of goods to the company, where the company is insolvent and unable to pay for those goods, insisting that the company alone be responsible for that debt, may not be acceptable.

PART II: WHY HAVE COMPANIES?

Why, then, should we have companies, legal institutions that are independent in law but dependent in fact, which provide for the creation of legal relationships which obscure the true relationships of the human beings who deal with one another and which may need to be denied from time to time in order to produce a just result? The fact is that although the company is utterly dependent on the human beings connected with it, its legal independence is commercially indispensable.

Partnership was hopelessly inadequate as the means for conducting a commercial venture in which a large number of people were engaged (see

Source 15 in Chapter 1). Partners of a partnership retain their *legal* as well as their actual existence and the larger their number (eg where a great deal of money has to be raised) the more unwieldy the management of the partnership.

The genius of the company lies in the suppression of the *legal* existence of the people who create, service and direct the venture. Multiple identities are replaced by one. Contracts and other transactions are effected by that single entity. This facilitates dealings with outsiders and streamlines internal management. Shareholders may have a right to vote, but they do not have a right to manage.

There is no necessary connection between the registration of a company under the provisions of the Companies Act and the limited liability of its shareholders (witness the unlimited company, s 1(2)(c) of the Companies Act 1985). Nevertheless, the demands of commerce forced company personality and limited liability into a tight, fruitful relationship. It is also the limited liability of the shareholders and directors which is probably the single most significant reason why the court may, whether in the interests of justice or under direction of the legislature, ignore the existence of the company, or why, to use the traditional, colourful and perhaps obscuring metaphor, a court may lift (or pierce) the veil of incorporation.

PART III: WHY DENY THE COMPANY'S EXISTENCE?

Where people have elected to run their business through the medium of a company, they must be taken to be aware of the legal structure. Similarly, when a trader agrees to supply goods to a limited liability company, he or she must be taken to know that the company, *alone*, is the other contracting party. Why, then, should this legal structure be ignored in a given instance? This is a legal question and should, therefore, be translatable into: what are the legal principles in accordance with which the court decides that the company's veil is to be lifted or held down?

Commentators are uniformly sceptical as to the chances of discerning clear and coherent *principles*. The closest we might get is some vague, public policy generalisation, that, for example 'justice demands it'[1]. Should we strive for greater certainty? What are the advantages and disadvantages of a lack of principle? ('The results in individual cases may be commendable, but it smacks of palm-tree justice rather than the application of legal rules'[2]).

PART IV: HOW IS THE COMPANY'S EXISTENCE DENIED?

The court must act in accordance with legal norms.

---

1 Gower, *Principles of Modern Company Law* (4th edn, 1979) 138
2 Ibid. Neither of these quotations is repeated in Gower's 5th edn (1992)

Statute

An Act of Parliament might provide that in given circumstances, despite the existence of a company, a benefit might be enjoyed or a detriment suffered by persons who, but for the statute might not suffer the detriment or enjoy the benefit. The circumstances may necessitate a finding by the court of fraud or negligence (eg ss 213 and 214 of the Insolvency Act 1986; Source 23, *Re William C Leitch Brothers Ltd*[1]) or may arise on the happening of a particular contingency (eg ss 24 and 349(4) of the Companies Act 1985).

In addition, where two or more companies are within the same group by reason of one being the parent of the other or others (see s 736, CA), s 227 places an obligation on the directors to prepare group accounts so as to ensure a true and fair view of the group as a whole. As we shall soon see, the question whether each individually incorporated company is to be treated as legally wholly independent, despite being dominated by another company or other companies or whether the law should recognise the group of companies as one entity, is far from resolved by the common law.

The danger of unlimited liability created by s 24 has been much reduced by the Companies (Single Member Private Limited Companies) Regulations 1992, SI 1992/1699 which implements the 12th European Community Company Law Harmonisation Directive. Until the enactment of these Regulations, a person who was the sole member of a private company in the circumstances set out in this section, was jointly and severally liable in respect of debts contracted by the company. This penalty is now suffered only where the company in question is a public limited company.

Section 349(4) is concerned with the description of the company's name. The inaccurate description of the company's name on certain documents (eg a cheque or negotiable instrument) may also result in the personal liability of the company's responsible officer. Sources illustrating this jurisdiction are dealt with in Chapter 3 in the section dealing with the company's name.

Consider what flexibility these powers give to the court. Compare for example the interpretation of 'fraudulent' in 'fraudulent trading' (Source 23) with 'fraudulent' in 'fraudulent preference' (s 615 of the Companies Act 1985, now repealed and replaced by s 239 of the Insolvency Act 1986 where the word 'fraudulent' is omitted, Source 24 and Chapter 11, pp 899ff).

The Principles of the Common Law

A company, as a person in law, enjoys certain relationships. It may be an agent to a principal or a principal to an agent; it may be a beneficiary or a trustee and, therefore entitled or subject to the benefit or liability respectively, of the fiduciary relationship. Any such finding may disturb the conventional legal structure which radiates from a company (see Sources 27, 32, 33, 34, 37, 40).

Certain principles developed by the courts in the resolution of disputes involving companies may be seen as veil-lifting, although not expressed as such. An excellent example is the principle of informality which has been encouraged by the courts to ensure that the wishes of the members prevail

---

1 [1932] 2 Ch 71

despite the failure to abide by the prescribed procedure. The procedural impropriety might be seen as fatally tainting the act in question, but where the court is satisfied that the act accords with the wishes of the individual members, it will apply the informality principle. The court must, therefore, look behind the constitutional or other impropriety in applying this principle. The sources illustrating this principle are to be found in Chapter 5, which deals with the management of the company.

Other illustrations of the court giving effect to the agreement of the shareholders rather than to implementing the provisions of the company's constitution can be seen in the jurisdiction, borrowed from partnership, to wind up the company where this is just and equitable (ie where the majority is attempting, seemingly quite constitutionally, to cause the company to act contrary to the original agreement of the incorporators). The sources covering this jurisdiction are dealt with as part of the protection of minority shareholders in Chapter 8.

PART V: STATUTORY VEIL-LIFTING

SOURCE 23
Re William C Leitch Brothers Ltd
(Chancery Division 1932) [1932] 2 Ch 71

By this summons the liquidator of William C. Leitch Brothers Ltd (hereinafter called 'the company'), asked for declarations that William Cleghorn Leitch, governing director of the company (hereinafter called 'the respondent'), having been knowingly a party to carrying on the business of the company with intent to defraud its creditors, was personally liable for all the company's debts and was liable also to contribute to the company's assets specified sums as compensation for specified acts of misfeasance.

. . .

　　Towards the end of 1929 the company was in financial difficulties which by March 1930, had become so serious that the company was unable to pay its debts as they became due. By 1 March 1930, the company to the knowledge of the respondent owed about £6500 for goods which had been supplied to it and had no means of paying these debts. The respondent ordered goods to an amount of about £6000 after that date, which goods became subject to the charge contained in the debenture held by the respondent. On 20 June 1929, the respondent lent to the company £600, of which £100 was repaid on 6 December 1929, £100 on 2 January 1930, £150 on 10 March 1930 and £150 on 1 April 1930. Between 5 April and 5 May 1930, seven writs were issued by creditors of the company. On 9 May 1930, the respondent, as debenture holder, appointed a receiver on the ground that interest on the debenture had not been paid, and the receiver appointed the respondent manager of the business. The respondent removed from the shops which he managed for the receiver £260 worth of goods to a shop which he had opened in Glasgow in his wife's name and, also as manager for the receiver, collected debts due to the company to the amount of £1300. He kept the sums of money which he so collected on account of interest due to him under the debenture, and later gave receipts for them to the receiver, who dismissed him from the position of manager.

The company had with the Midland Bank Ltd, an account which, on 4 April 1930, was overdrawn to the amount of £800 10s. The amount to which the bank had originally allowed the overdraft, on a guarantee by the respondent, was £600. The overdraft had, however, increased, and was secured by the respondent's guarantee and by his depositing title deeds with the bank. Between 10 April and 5 June 1930, £684 6s. 8d. of the overdraft was paid off. From the beginning of January 1930, to the end of May 1930, the respondent ordered goods greatly in excess of what was required for the company's business and of what had generally been ordered for the company over a like period . . .

MAUGHAM J: . . . That leads me to the question of the true construction of section 275[1] of the Companies Act, 1929, a question of great difficulty. In my opinion I must hold with regard to the meaning of the phrase carrying on business 'with intent to defraud creditors' that, if a company continues to carry on business and to incur debts at a time when there is to the knowledge of the directors no reasonable prospect of the creditors ever receiving payment of those debts, it is, in general, a proper inference that the company is carrying on business with intent to defraud: and, as I have intimated, I am satisfied that the respondent knew what the position was as from 1 March 1930; and I hold further that the respondent deliberately went on trading in the name of the company in order, as he hoped, to safeguard his own position, and without any regard to the interests of the creditors.

SOURCE 24
Re Patrick and Lyon
(Chancery Division 1933) [1933] Ch 786; 102 LJ Ch 300

MAUGHAM J: I will begin by stating that section 275[2] of the Companies Act 1929, under which relief is claimed is a very remarkable section and one which is by no means easy to construe.

. . .

I will express the opinion that the words 'defraud' and 'fraudulent purpose,' where they appear in the section in question, are words which connote actual dishonesty involving, according to current notions of fair trading among commercial men, real moral blame. No judge, I think, has ever been willing to define 'fraud,' and I am attempting no definition. I am merely stating what, in my opinion, must be one of the elements of the word as used in this section. In my opinion it is not used in the same sense as that in which the word 'fraud' is used in section 265[3] of the Act. There, following the example set by section 44 of the Bankruptcy Act 1914, and by section 92 of the Bankruptcy Act 1869, both of which deal with the avoidance of fraudulent preferences, the Legislature has thought fit to state that certain acts are to be deemed a fraudulent preference and to be invalid accordingly. A fraudulent preference within the meaning of the Companies Act 1929, or the Bankruptcy Act 1914, whether in the case of a company or of an individual, possibly may not involve moral blame at all. For example, there may be a discrimination between creditors, irrespective of pressure, on grounds with which most people would sympathize. Again, there is nothing in the language of section 266 of the Companies Act 1929[4] (which enables a floating charge created within six months of a winding up to be

---

1 See now s 213 of the Insolvency Act 1986
2 See now s 213 of the Insolvency Act 1986
3 See now s 239 of the Insolvency Act 1986
4 See now s 245 of the Insolvency Act 1986

attacked in certain circumstances), to indicate that the Legislature took the view that the creation of such a charge when the company is insolvent is fraudulent, however blameworthy it may be. That appears from the fact that the right to attack such a floating charge is limited to cases where the company goes into liquidation within six months of the creation of it. Coming to the present case, I think that in exercising jurisdiction under section 275 the Court, however little it may approve of the conduct of the director who is being attacked, is bound to consider whether he has been guilty of a dishonest fraud, and it is hardly necessary for me to point out that the onus is upon the person who seeks to make good the charge, whether he be the official receiver, or the liquidator, or a creditor, or a contributory.

. . .

The question which I have to determine is whether, within the meaning of section 275 of the Companies Act 1929, and construing the reference therein to fraud as I construe it, the business of the company was carried on for a fraudulent purpose. In my opinion, on the whole, I am not justified in coming to such a conclusion. The business of the company, so far as it was carried on during the latter part of its career, was carried on in order to clear up the position by getting in debts and by effecting sales of stock, and not with a view to securing by purchases on credit assets available as security for debentures. I am not clear in my mind that the first respondent was deliberately intending to carry out any fraudulent purpose or to defraud creditors. That is a matter which cannot be left to conjecture. I must be perfectly satisfied that there is enough evidence to justify the charge. To my mind the case has not been made out and I dismiss the summons.

The insistence by the court on the criminal standard of proof in establishing the business of the company has been carried with intent to defraud the creditors led to the general demise of this jurisdiction. In the 1986 Insolvency Act, there was created — for the first time — a jurisdiction for holding liable any director who caused the company to continue trading after the time when he or she knew or ought to have concluded that there was no reasonable prospect of the company avoiding insolvent liquidation (Insolvency Act 1986, s 214).

This jurisdiction has serious problems. Source 25 — the *Produce Marketing Consortium* case — is the first of only three or four reported instances of the use of s 214 in eight years. It may be that this jurisdiction is successful as a threat, ie former directors are agreeing to make payments and formal proceedings are unnecessary. There is insufficient evidence for any conclusion on this. A further problem is the expense and time involved. *Produce Marketing Consortium* was an eight-day court hearing and few liquidators can contemplate this use of scarce resources (see Hicks, [1993] Insolvency Law & Practice 134, [1993] Company Lawyer 16 at 55). Is there not some tension between inviting people to form limited liability companies and to take risks, on the one hand, and a jurisdiction which punishes risk-taking, on the other?

Following the *Produce Marketing Consortium* source is a further example of the fraudulent trading jurisdiction (*Re A Company*, Source 26). One possible development is that the limited value of s 214 may induce the courts to take a more liberal interpretation of s 213.

SOURCE 25
Re Produce Marketing Consortium (No 2)
[1989] BCLC 520 (Chancery Division)

KNOX J: In this amended originating summons Mr Nigel John Halls, the
liquidator of Produce Marketing Consortium Ltd (PMC), seeks an order that
the respondents Mr Eric Peter David and Mr Ronald William Murphy, and
each of them, contribute £107,946 and such figure for interest and costs or
such other sum as the court may think proper to the assets of PMC. This relief
was originally sought both under s 213 of the Insolvency Act 1986, which
applies to fraudulent trading, and s 214 of that Act, which deals with what the
sidenote calls 'wrongful trading' although those words are not in the body of
the section. The fraudulent trading claim was dropped at the outset of the
hearing and I am therefore only concerned with the claim under s 214.

. . .

The general drift towards insolvency is clearly visible from PMC's audited
accounts. The end of its accounting year was 30 September in each year. The
following table illustrates some of the salient features of the years preceding those
with which this application is primarily concerned:

Year ending 30 September	Turnover	Net profit (Loss)	Net assets (Liabilities)	Bank overdraft
1980	£952,189	(£93)	£14,655	nil
1981	£611,639	(£14,581)	£74	£2,158
1982	not stated	(£25,076)	(£32,652)	£21,105
1983	£662,400	(£21,283)	(£58,635)	£53,551
1984	£899,965	£43	(£58,592)	£91,756

From a relatively healthy position in 1980, when there was no overdraft, assets
exceeded liabilities and trading produced no significant loss, by 1984 a very
different picture emerged of an overdraft of £91,756 and an excess of liabilities
over assets of £58,592 caused by successive years of loss-making operations. Even
the small profit of £43 in the latter year was to prove illusory because the
following year's accounts for the year ending 30 September 1985 contained an
adjustment of an addition of £18,461 loss for the preceding year, turning the
original profit of £43 into a loss of £18,418 and increasing the deficiency of
liabilities over assets from £58,592 to £77,053. The directors' report for the year
ending 30 September 1984 (dated 23 July 1985) contained the following
passage:

> 'At the balance sheet date the company was insolvent, but the directors are
> confident that if the company continues to trade it will be able to meet its
> liabilities.'

The auditor's certificate attached to the accounts of the same date included the
following:

> 'At the balance sheet date the company was insolvent and continuation of its
> activities is dependent upon the continued facilities from its Bankers being
> granted.'

. . .

In addition to the debenture mentioned above the bank took a personal
guarantee from Mr David. The overdraft facility, granted on 22 August 1984 until
the end of that year, was one of £50,000 and it was secured by the debenture and
Mr David's guarantee for £30,000 given on or about 4 May 1984. It was renewed

on 21 January 1985 until the end of March 1985 in the same sum of £50,000 but although the bank requested an increase in Mr David's personal guarantee to £50,000, this was not apparently given at that stage because when the facility was extended until 30 June 1985 it was agreed to be secured on the debenture and Mr David's guarantee for up to £30,000, the pre-existing figure.

. . .

By far the most important shipper for PMC in the last two years of its existence, and by far the largest unsecured creditor with a debt of £175,062.48 in the liquidation of PMC, was a Cypriot company called Ramona Ltd, which exports citrus fruit, lemons, grapefruits and oranges, Valencia lates, from Cyprus principally to the United Kingdom but also elsewhere in Europe and, to a limited extent, the Middle East. In addition to PMC Ramona had two agents in the United Kingdom, EMG (Continental) Ltd (which I will call 'EMG') and Pascual Fruit Importers Ltd (which I will call 'Pascual').

. . .

Ramona did decide to entrust some of their United Kingdom business to PMC, in addition to their other two established agents EMG and Pascual, for the 1985/86 season. That season's trading between Ramona and PMC passed off reasonably successfully, the only fly in the ointment being that PMC was unable to pay Ramona the final payments due to it in proper time. This led to protests by telex from Ramona and excuses from PMC. The underlying reason for PMC's increasingly straightened financial circumstances in the autumn of 1986 was that the year ending 30 September 1985 was a bad one in which, disregarding the prior year's adjustments, a loss of £55,817 was suffered by PMC taking its deficiency of liabilities over assets over £114,000, again writing back the prior year adjustment. The turnover in the year 1984/85 had dropped substantially to £526,457 in contrast to the previous year's turnover of £899,965. These figures for the year 1984/85 are taken from the audited accounts for that year which were only signed on 5 February 1987, over 6 months beyond the time limit for private companies of 10 months by s 242 of the Companies Act 1985 for laying and delivering accounts. Draft accounts containing this material were, I find, provided to the directors in January of 1987. There was a history of PMC's accounts being prepared well out of time as the following table shows:

Year ending 30 September	Date accounts signed
1982	14 December 1982
1983	1 March 1985
1984	23 July 1985
1985	5 February 1987
1986	12 February 1987

. . .

At long last in January 1987 draft accounts for 1984/85 and 1985/86 were submitted by the auditor Mr Tough to the respondents. They showed a grim picture. The former (1984/85 draft) showed turnover down to £526,459. That meant that commission at 3.5% could not exceed £18,500 and a substantial loss was inevitable. The loss for the year was in fact £55,817, and there was also the prior year's adjustment mentioned earlier to the previous year's profit and loss of £18,461. This drove up the excess of liabilities over assets to £132,870. Trade creditors were £85,004, and the bank overdraft was £98,546. The second set of accounts did nothing to alleviate that gloomy picture. Turnover, it is true, picked up to £960,282 which, at 3.5% commission, reflected a gross income of £33,610 but in fact a further loss for the year of £29,937 was the result, coupled with another prior year's adjustment of £12,341 in a downward direction, and that produced an excess of liabilities over assets of £175,148. Trade creditors at 30 September 1986 had risen to £143,454 and the bank overdraft to £118,171.

The 1984/85 and the 1985/86 accounts contained directors' reports which included the same statement as the previous accounts, namely that at the balance sheet date the company was insolvent but the directors were confident that if the company continued to trade it would be able to meet its liabilities. The auditors' certificates were not quite in identical terms. In the 1984/95 accounts it included the following:

> 'At the Balance Sheet date, the Company was insolvent and continuation of its activities is dependent upon the continued facilities from its Bankers being granted. The Financial Statements have been drawn up on a going concern basis which assumes that adequate facilities will be available.'

The 1985/86 accounts included the following:

> 'At the Balance Sheet date, the Company was insolvent and continuation of its activities is dependent upon the continued facilities from its Bankers being granted. The Company is currently negotiating for a renewal of facilities and continuation of the Company's activities is dependent on a successful outcome to these negotiations.'

The two accounts were signed on 5 and 12 February 1987 respectively.

After these two sets of accounts were sent in draft there followed a telephone call between Mr David and Mr Tough when the latter voiced fears that the directors of PMC might be liable for fraudulent trading. This was followed by an important letter written by Mr Tough on 4 February 1987 to Mr David and Mr Murphy. It read:

> 'Dear Peter and Ron,
>   I am enclosing the following: — 1) A copy of the cash flow forecast for the 8 months to the 30.9.1987 which I propose to give to the Bank on Friday. This shows a turnover of £1.6m for the current year and a small reduction in the overdraft from £75,000 down to £68,158 by 30.9.1987, which I would think should please them. If you have any queries, please contact me. 2) A draft letter which I intend to take with me to the meeting and leave with the Bank. 3) Copies of the Accounts for the years ended 30.9.1985 and 30.9.1986. These Accounts show that the Company is insolvent to the extent of some £195,000 at 30.9.1986.'

Pausing there for a moment, that, I think, is a clerical error for '£175,000', which is the correct figure in round terms.

> 'If you do not agree with any of the figures please let me know as soon as possible. In the event that you accept the figures as they appear, I must make the following points: — a) As I have pointed out at previous meetings, there is a possibility that the Directors may be held to be liable for fraudulent trading, on the grounds that the Company has continued to carry on business and to incur debts at a time when there is, to the knowledge of the Directors, no reasonable prospect of the creditors receiving payment of those debts. I refer you to the enclosed pages from our Company Law Text Books for your careful study. b) Even if the Company should attain its targets and make a modest profit for the year ending 30.9.87, it could be many years before the Company's past losses are eliminated and the Company becomes

solvent once again. During that period any pressure from creditors, including the Bank, would probably be catastrophic as it is unlikely the Company could find another Bank to grant the required facilities.'

Mr Tough was not called as a witness by either side, and both Mr David and Mr Murphy denied that there had been warnings given to them at previous meetings of a possibility of a finding of fraudulent trading. There is no direct admissible evidence of such warnings having been given but, given the accounting history of PMC, I find, on a balance of probabilities, that the possibility of insolvent liquidation had been the subject of some discussion between its directors and auditor at intervals during the latter part of 1986.

Both Mr David and Mr Murphy accepted that Mr Tough sent them copies of ss 213 and 214 of the 1986 Act as a result of the telephone call mentioned above.

. . .

There was an interview at the bank on 10 February when Mr Tough accompanied Mr David and Mr Murphy to their meeting with officials at the bank. Mr David in his evidence identified the 'substantial Importer/Broker in the industry' referred to in para 2(d) of Mr Tough's letter of 10 February 1987. In common with large numbers of Mr David's hopes and prognostications not much came of this association.

Initially the bank's response was unfavourable. They wrote on 24 February 1987:

'In reply to your letters of 24th January 1987, 18th February 1987 and the meeting with you and your accountant on the 10th instant, we inform you that the Bank cannot continue granting you overdraft facilities due to the accumulated losses of £186,845 and lack of security but we will be prepared to reconsider this matter if the directors can provide some tangible security of at least for a minimum amount of £25,000.00. Please note that unless you can provide the additional security within the next few days we will have no alternative but to cancel our facility and therefore please note that the overdraft is repayable on demand and we are giving you formal notice to do so by the 5th of March 1987.'

For some reason which remained unexplained in evidence the bank had a change of heart and wrote on 12 March 1987:

'In reply to your letter of 24th January, we are pleased to inform you that we are prepared to renew your overdraft facilities up to a maximum of £70,000 (seventy thousands pounds) only, which must be reduced to £65,000.00 by 15.4.87 and to £60,000.00 by 31.7.87, for normal trading purposes, against the security of a Debenture over all the assets of the Company, a personal guarantee for up to £50,000.00 signed by Mr. Peter David and a charge over a Trade Indemnity Policy.'

It will be noted that this continued support from the bank was at a significantly lower level than that before in that an immediate reduction of £5,000 in the facilities afforded to PMC to £70,000 was called for coupled with two further reductions of £5,000 each in April and at the end of July 1987.

Such reductions were incompatible with the programme contained in the cash flow forecast which did not envisage enough profit being generated during the period covered to allow a reduction of £15,000 on the bank facilities of PMC. In addition the cash flow projection made no provision, other than out of the modest profit of £9,842, for the payment off of existing trade creditors whose debts totalled £143,454 as at 30 September 1986. It was very evident that PMC was going to have to rely on all those creditors and the bank being almost indefinitely willing to allow their indebtedness to remain outstanding if it was to continue trading. Mr Tough was not consulted about the repercussions of the reduced bank facilities.

. . .

A meeting was duly held on 25 August 1987 attended by, *inter alios*, Mr David, Mr Murphy, Mr Tough, Mr Locke of Messrs Richards Butler (Ramona's London solicitors), and Mr Zenon Eliades. There was produced by the Ramona representatives a short report by Messrs Coopers & Lybrands of Nicosia (dated 21 August 1987) assessing the amount due by PMC to Ramona at £168,499.04, made up as to £272,472 in respect of cargoes for which account sales had been rendered by PMC, and an estimate of £45,839.41 as due in respect of cargoes for which account sales had not been rendered, giving a total indebtedness of £318,311.90 from which PMC's remittances of £149,812.86 fell to be deducted leaving £168,499.04 estimated to be owing.

Mr David and Mr Murphy could only say the cupboard was bare and no further payments would be made. There was discussion of a rescue plan involving an association of PMC and Ramona under the title of 'Ramona (UK)' but no details at all were gone into. The two alternatives were liquidation and allowing PMC, in one guise or another, to try to trade out of the difficulties it was in. Mr David and Mr Murphy offered their services as consultants. Mr Zenon Eliades agreed to put the rescue proposal to his board and reply within seven days, but he did not do so because his board had had enough and were not willing to continue allowing PMC to try and trade out. Nothing came out of the proposal and the inevitable occurred in that PMC went into creditors' voluntary liquidation on 2 October 1987.

. . .

The liquidator wrote to Mr David and Mr Murphy after his appointment asking for their explanation of PMC's trading while insolvent. What he wrote was this:

'As you are aware I have been appointed liquidator of the above company. I have recently seen copies of the company's accounts from which it is apparent that the company had been insolvent for some considerable time. The accounts for the year ended 30th September 1986 were available to the directors on 12th February 1987. They showed a deficiency on Profit and Loss Account of £187,748 and the company making losses. Please give details as to what action you took as a director of the company to rectify the situation. Please include details of all board meetings held and provide copies of any documentation you think relevant. Please ensure that your reply is received by myself within the next 7 days or this most serious matter will be passed to my solicitors.'

He wrote similarly to Mr Murphy. He received the following reply from Mr David:

'Thank you for your letter of 25th JAN. 1988. Upon receipt of the accounts on 12th February 1987, it was apparent to the Directors that notwithstanding strenuous efforts to rectify the company's situation, . . . entrance into voluntary liquidation was inevitable. However, a highly inhibiting factor at that time, was that we (PMC LTD) had in cold stores in Hampshire, some 28,000 cartons of lemons and grapefruit. We were most worried that were we to cease trading that our principals (RAMONA LTD, of LIMASSOL CYPRUS) would inevitably suffer extreme damage at the hands of any Receiver taking into account the highly perishable nature of the goods and the complexities of marketing same in the UK. We advised our Accountants that we proposed to market and clear the goods concerned as a matter of duty and in defence of our Principal's interests. At that time a very adverse market situation obtained, which in fact maintained itself on a continuing basis (I refer specifically to Lemons and Grapefruit). After completion of sales and receipt of proceeds thereof, the Company went into voluntary liquidation.'

And from Mr Murphy he received this:

'I refer to your letter dated 25/1/88 and would like to make clear the following. At the time in question, i.e. Feb 87, the company was in the position that with the suggestion of Messrs Ramona Ltd we had placed into the cold stores consignments of Grapefruit and Lemons totalling 28/30,000 cartons, this being carried out because the market was very poor and sales slow. It would have been an easy way out to have closed the company and abandoned the goods in the store to the liquidator. We felt that we had an obligation to try and protect the goods and the exporter in the best possible way, also taking into account that the other two receivers of goods from Ramona Ltd [were] in the same situation with having goods in store and not being able to handle any other quantities. Throughout this period we kept Ramona Ltd advised and asked them on several occasions to control shipments for we could not keep up the schedule of payments to them that they needed. Our bank was kept informed of our situation and continued to keep our overdraft facilities open and it was hoped that we could have realized for Ramona a substantial sum. The market never recovered from the swamping of Grapefruit etc. and immediately at the end of the season (August 1987) Ramona were made aware of the situation and they made several suggestions to keep the company going, but at the beginning of Sept, they ceased all communication with us. We then on the advice of our solicitor and accountant placed PMC Ltd in voluntary liquidation.'

[The judge then referred to section 214 and continued:]

The first question is whether it appears that sub-s (2) applies to Mr David and Mr Murphy. There is no question but that they were directors at all material times and that PMC has gone into insolvent liquidation. The issue is whether at some time after 27 April 1986 and before 2 October 1987, when it went into insolvent liquidation, they knew or ought to have concluded that there was no reasonable prospect that PMC would avoid going into insolvent liquidation. It was inevitably conceded by counsel for the first respondent that this question has to be answered by the standards postulated by sub-s (4), so that the facts which Mr David and Mr Murphy ought to have known or ascertained and the conclusions that they ought to have reached are not limited to those which they themselves showing reasonable diligence and having the general knowledge, skill and experience which they respectively had, would have known, ascertained or reached but also those that a person with the general knowledge, skill and experience of someone carrying out their functions would have known, ascertained or reached.

This was a new provision in the Insolvency Act 1985, s 15. It contrasts with s 213 of the 1986 Act in relation to fraudulent trading, which is derived from s 630 of the Companies Act 1985, itself derived with some amendments from s 332 of the Companies Act 1948, in turn derived from the Companies Act 1929 s 275. Under these latter successive enactments the intent to defraud had to be established in relation to the particular person sought to be charged, and although in *Re William C Leitch Bros Ltd* [1932] 2 Ch 71 at 77, [1932] All ER Rep 892 at 897 Maugham J held that, if a company continued to carry on business and to incur debts at a time when there was to the knowledge of the directors no reasonable prospect of the creditors ever receiving payment of those debts, it was, in general, a proper inference that the company was carrying on business with intent to defraud, there were authorities which exonerated from liability under the fraudulent trading legislation persons who honestly hoped that creditors would be paid off one day albeit that this was not a reasonable expectation by any objective standard. Thus I was referred to a decision of Buckley J in *Re White & Osmond (Parkstone) Ltd* (30 June 1960, unreported) in the course of which he said this:

'In my judgment, there is nothing wrong in the fact that directors incur credit at a time when, to their knowledge, the company is not able to meet all its liabilities as they fall due. What is manifestly wrong is if directors allow a company to incur credit at a time when the business is being carried on in such circumstances that it is clear the company will never be able to satisfy its creditors. However, there is nothing to say that directors who genuinely believe that the clouds will roll away and the sunshine of prosperity will shine on them again and disperse the fog of their depression are not entitled to incur credit to help them to get over the bad time.'

Buckley J also referred to another decision of Maugham J in *Re Patrick & Lyon Ltd* [1933] Ch 786 at 790, [1933] All ER Rep. 590 at 593, where he expressed the opinion regarding s 275 of the Companies Act 1929:

'... that the words "defraud" and "fraudulent purpose", where they appear in the section in question, are words which connote actual dishonesty involving, according to current notions of fair trading among commercial men, real moral blame.'

The 1986 Act now has two separate provisions; s 213 dealing with fraudulent trading, to which the passages which I have quoted from the judgments of Maugham J and Buckley J no doubt are still applicable and s 214 which deals with what the sidenote calls 'wrongful trading'. It is evident that Parliament intended to widen the scope of the legislation under which directors who trade on when the company is insolvent may, in appropriate circumstances, be required to make a contribution to the assets of the company which, in practical terms, means its creditors.

Two steps in particular were taken in the legislative enlargement of the court's jurisdiction. First, the requirement for an intent to defraud and fraudulent purpose was not retained as an essential, and with it goes what Maugham J called 'the need for actual dishonesty involving real moral blame'.

I pause here to observe that at no stage before me has it been suggested that either Mr David or Mr Murphy fell into this category.

The second enlargement is that the test to be applied by the court has become one under which the director in question is to be judged by the standards of what can reasonably be expected of a person fulfilling his functions, and showing reasonable diligence in doing so. I accept the submission of counsel for the first respondent in this connection, that the requirement to have regard to the functions to be carried out by the director in question, in relation to the company in question, involves having regard to the particular company and its business. It follows that the general knowledge, skill and experience postulated will be much less extensive in a small company in a modest way of business, with simple accounting procedures and equipment, than it will be in a large company with sophisticated procedures.

Nevertheless, certain minimum standards are to be assumed to be attained. Notably there is an obligation laid on companies to cause accounting records to be kept which are such as to disclose with reasonable accuracy at any time the financial position of the company at that time: see the Companies Act 1985, s 221(1) and (2)(*a*). In addition directors are required to prepare a profit and loss account for each financial year and a balance sheet as at the end of it: Companies Act 1985, s 227(1) and (3). Directors are also required, in respect of each financial year, to lay before the company in general meeting copies of the accounts of the company for that year and to deliver to the registrar of companies a copy of those accounts, in the case of a private company, within 10 months after the end of the relevant accounting reference period (see the Companies Act 1985, ss 241(1) and (3) and 242(1) and (2)).

As I have already mentioned, the liquidator gave evidence that the accounting records of PMC were adequate for the purposes of its business. The preparation of accounts was woefully late, more especially in relation to those dealing with the year ending 30 September 1985 which should have been laid and delivered by the end of July 1986.

The knowledge to be imputed in testing whether or not directors knew or ought to have concluded that there was no reasonable prospect of the company avoiding insolvent liquidation is not limited to the documentary material actually available at the given time. This appears from s 214(4) which includes a reference to facts which a director of a company ought not only to know but those which he ought to ascertain, a word which does not appear in sub-s (2)(*b*). In my judgment this indicates that there is to be included by way of factual information not only what was actually there but what, given reasonable diligence and an appropriate level of general knowledge, skill and experience, was ascertainable. This leads me to the conclusion in this case that I should assume, for the purposes of applying the test in s 214(2), that the financial results for the year ending 30 September 1985 were known at the end of July 1986 at least to the extent of the size of the deficiency of assets over liabilities.

Mr David and Mr Murphy, although they did not have the accounts in their hands until January 1987, did, I find, know that the previous trading year had been a very bad one. They had a close and intimate knowledge of the business and they had a shrewd idea whether the turnover was up or down. In fact it was badly down in that year to £526,459 and although I have no doubt that they did not know in July 1986 that it was that precise figure, I have no doubt that they had a good rough idea of what it was and in particular that it was well down on the previous year. A major drop in turnover meant almost as night follows day that there was a substantial loss incurred, as indeed there was. That in turn meant again, as surely as night follows day, a substantial increase in the deficit of assets over liabilities.

That deals with their actual knowledge but in addition I have to have regard to what they have to be treated as having known or ascertained and that includes the actual deficit of assets over liabilities of £132,870. This was £80,000 over Mr David's personal guarantee. It was a deficit that, for an indefinite period in the future could not be made good even if the optimistic prognostications of level of turnover entertained by Mr David and Mr Murphy were achieved. They later estimated, when they visited the bank on 16 February 1987, a turnover of £1.6m. If one assumes half as much again, at £2.4m, the gross income of the company would only have risen to £84,000 and the overheads were accepted as being not less than £65,000. That gives a notional profit of £19,000 per annum. If one takes the figure of £1.6m, overheads of £65,000 would not have been covered.

Counsel for the first respondent was not able to advance any particular calculation as constituting a basis for concluding that there was a prospect of insolvent liquidation being avoided. He is not to be criticised for that for in my judgment there was none available. Once the loss in the year ending 30 September 1985 was incurred PMC was in irreversible decline, assuming (as I must) that the respondents had no plans for altering the company's business and proposed to go on drawing the level of reasonable remuneration that they were currently receiving.

It was stated by Mr David that the persons and companies with whom PMC did business were in the main long established trading partners. In fact that could not be said of Ramona which was, by July 1986, a very important creditor. But even if one disregards that aspect, it would not be right to assume that even old established trading partners will wait indefinitely to have their debts paid. Nor, in my judgment, do the facts that the bank was throughout willing to continue its facilities and that Mr Tough, although expressing the grave warnings that he did when the accounts for the years ending 30 September 1985 and 1986 were available to him, was willing to accompany Mr David and Mr Murphy to the bank in February 1987 to see if further facilities would be granted, detract from the conclusion I have reached that Mr David and Mr Murphy ought to have concluded at the end of July 1986 that there was no reasonable prospect that PMC would avoid going into insolvent liquidation. The bank was secured by Mr David's guarantee, if not to any significant extent by the other securities which it took, and Mr Tough's attitude was never more than one of doubt and caution.

The next question which arises is whether there is a case under s 214(3) for saying that after the end of July 1986 the respondents took every step with a view to minimising the potential loss to the creditors of PMC as, assuming them to have known that there was no reasonable prospect of PMC avoiding insolvent liquidation, they ought to have taken. This clearly has to be answered No, since they went on trading for another year.

Counsel for the first respondent gallantly attempted to establish that, assuming that the first time when the respondents ought to have concluded that there was no such reasonable prospect was February 1987 when they actually signed the preceding two years' accounts, their decision to trade on so as to realise the fruit in cold store to the best advantage satisfied the requirement of s 214(3). I would not have accepted that submission in any event because the continued trading was far from limited to the realisation of the fruit in cold store, and Ramona were not told, as they should have been, what the true financial picture was so as to be given the opportunity of deciding for themselves what to do; but this is academic because that submission, even if correct in relation to February 1987, quite plainly was untenable in relation to the end of July 1986.

I am therefore driven to the conclusion that the court's discretion arises under s 214(1). On the nature of that discretion there were conflicting submissions made to me. Counsel for the first respondent submitted that the court's discretion is entirely at large, and he pointed to no less than three sets of words indicating the existence of a wide discretion: the court *may* declare that the person is to be liable to make *such* contribution (*if any*) to the company's assets as the court thinks *proper.* He also submitted that the provision is both compensatory and penal in character. He referred me to *Re William C Leitch Bros Ltd* [1932] 2 Ch 71 at 79, [1932] All ER Rep 892 at 896 where Maugham J said of s 275 of the Companies Act 1929:

'I am inclined to the view that s 275 is in the nature of a punitive provision, and that where the Court makes such a declaration in relation to "all or any of the debts or other liabilities of the company", it is in the discretion of the Court to make an order without limiting the order to the amount of the debts of those creditors proved to have been defrauded by the acts of the director in question, though no doubt the order would in general be so limited.'

However, counsel for the first respondent also submitted that the amount which the court concluded had been lost as a result of the wrongful trading should provide a ceiling for the figure which the court declared should be contributed to the company's assets, which is of course the exact opposite of what Maugham J said in that regard. He also relied on the provisions of s 214(3) which prevent the exercise of the discretion under sub-s (1) in any case where, to put it briefly, the director has done everything possible to minimise loss to creditors, and he suggested that it would be inequitable for a director who has just failed to escape scot-free under the provision because he had only done nearly but not quite everything to that end to be treated on a par with a director who had done nothing to minimise loss to creditors.

Counsel for the liquidator (Miss Arden QC) submitted that s 214 of the 1986 Act gave a purely civil remedy, unlike the predecessors of s 213 of that Act, such as s 275 of the Companies Act 1929 and s 332 of the Companies Act 1948 which combined the civil and criminal. More significantly for my purpose she submitted that s 214 was compensatory rather than penal. What is ordered to be contributed goes to increase the company's assets for the benefit of the general body of creditors. On that basis she submitted that the proper measure was the reduction in the net assets which could be identified as caused by the wrongful activities of the persons ordered to contribute. This jurisdiction, it was submitted, is an enhanced version of the right which any company would have to sue its directors for breach of duty, enhanced in the sense that the standard of knowledge, skill and experience required is made objective.

On this analysis, once the circumstances required for the exercise of discretion under s 214(1) are shown to exist, she submitted that the situation was analogous to that obtaining where a tort such as negligence was shown to have been committed in that quantum was a matter of causation and not culpability. The discretion given to the court was to enable allowance to be made for questions of causation and also to avoid unjust results such as unwarranted windfalls for creditors. Thus in *West Mercia Safetywear Ltd (in liq) v Dodd* [1988] BCLC 250 at 253, Dillon LJ said of s 333 of the Companies Act 1948:

'The section in question, however, s 333 of the Companies Act 1948, provides that the court may order the delinquent director to repay or restore the money, with interest at such rate as the court thinks fit, or to contribute such sum to the assets of the company by way of compensation in respect of the misapplication as the court thinks fit. The court has a discretion over the matter of relief, and it is permissible for the delinquent director to submit that the wind should be tempered because, for instance, full repayment would produce a windfall to third parties, or, alternatively, because it would involve money going round in a circle or passing through the hands of someone else whose position is equally tainted.'

In my judgment the jurisdiction under s 214 is primarily compensatory rather than penal. Prima facie the appropriate amount that a director is declared to be liable to contribute is the amount by which the company's assets can be discerned to have been depleted by the director's conduct which caused the discretion under sub-s (1) to arise. But Parliament has indeed chosen very wide words of discretion and it would be undesirable to seek to spell out limits on that discretion, more especially since this is, so far as counsel were aware, the first case to come to judgment under this section. The fact that there was no fraudulent intent is not of itself a reason for fixing the amount at a nominal or low figure, for that would amount to frustrating what I discern as Parliament's intention in adding s 214 to s 213 in the 1986 Act, but I am not persuaded that it is right to ignore that fact totally.

I take into account the following factors in addition to those set out above, which give rise to the existence of the court's discretion under s 214(1).

This was a case of failure to appreciate what should have been clear rather than a deliberate course of wrongdoing.

There were occasions when positive untruths were stated which cannot just be treated as unwarranted optimism. Mr David in particular is given to a flowing turn of phrase. He referred to PMC's continuing to trade as, 'the ship of state sailing on'. That, in itself, is not to be held against him, although it is doubtless a symptom of his inability to see the realities of the current trading position, but when, as happened more than once, a statement of fact was made which was positively untrue, that is to be held against him.

The most solemn warning given by the auditor in early February 1987 was effectively ignored. I do not regard Mr Tough's attendance at the bank on 10 February as indicating even tacitly that if the bank agreed to extend facilities it would be proper to carry on trading.

Mr David has given a guarantee to the bank with a limit of £50,000. The bank will have a charge over anything which Mr David or Mr Murphy contributes pursuant to my order. Pro tanto that will relieve Mr David from his guarantee liability.

The affairs of PMC were conducted during the last seven months of trading in a way which reduced the indebtedness to the bank, to which Mr David had given a guarantee, at the expense of trade creditors and in particular Ramona. The bank is, if not fully, at least substantially secured. If this jurisdiction is to be exercised, as in my judgment it should be in this case, it needs to be exercised in a way which will benefit unsecured creditors.

The evidence regarding the disappearance of debtors from the statement of affairs is not entirely clear and there remains in my mind an element of speculation on the extent to which it is right to fix on £22,000 as the amount to be treated as having been overstated in September 1986.

Taking all these circumstances into account I propose to declare that Mr David and Mr Murphy are liable to make a contribution to the assets of PMC of £75,000.

As between the two of them it seems to me right that Mr David should indemnify Mr Murphy as to £50,000 and that above that figure they should be jointly liable. As against the liquidator they should be jointly and severally liable for the whole £75,000. I take this view regarding the indemnity to be given by Mr David partly because Mr David was Mr Murphy's senior in every sense, age, standing in the company and personality, but principally because of the existence of Mr David's guarantee to the bank. Naturally counsel for the first respondent was not in a position to make submissions to me how matters should be dealt with as between his two clients, and I should be sorry to see the costs, which must already run the risk of eroding the benefits which the section is intended to confer on creditors, further increased.

SOURCE 26
Re A Company (001418 of 1988)
(Chancery Division) [1991] BCLC 197

JUDGE BROMLEY QC: The application is in respect of alleged fraudulent trading, brought under s 630 of the Companies Act 1985. This is a case where it is quite clear the old law applies. The first defendant at all material times has been the chairman, managing director, secretary and majority shareholder of the company, which went into creditors' voluntary liquidation, as I shall indicate, on 6 June, 1986.

. . .

The principles were established by the Court of Appeal in *R v Grantham* [1984] BCLC 270, [1984] 3 All ER 166, [1984] QB 675, which Mr Hollington cited to me. In that decision the earlier authorities were reviewed. A finding that a person was knowingly party to the business of a company having been carried on with intent to defraud creditors may be made if the following two conditions are satisfied: (1) if that person realised at the time the debts were incurred that there was no reason for thinking that funds would be available to pay the debt in question when it became due or shortly thereafter (see [1984] BCLC 270 at 274, [1984] 3 All ER 166 at 170, [1984] QB 675 at 682) (2) there was actually dishonesty involving, according to current notions of fair trading among commercial men, real moral blame.

The intent to defraud is to be judged by its effect on the person who is the object of the conduct in question.

. . .

As to trade creditors the position is made clear in *R v Grantham* [1984] BCLC 270 at 275–276, [1984] 3 All ER 166 at 170–171, [1984] QB 675 at 683–684. There is intent to defraud within the meaning of the section if the person responsible was intending to deceive or actually deceiving a supplier that he would be paid at the stipulated time or shortly thereafter when the person so intending or deceiving knew perfectly well that there was no hope of that coming about.

As to 'non-choice' creditors, there is no question of deceit. The intent to defraud in my view lies in continuing to incur the liability for tax or national insurance contributions or value added tax when there is no honest belief that those liabilities will be discharged when they become due or shortly thereafter.

. . .

I come to an overview. As I have mentioned, the statement of affairs showed a deficit as to unsecured creditors of £212,681 at the commencement of the liquidation. The debts due to the Inland Revenue for PAYE, on a schedule which the liquidator's firm has prepared, show a deficit for the year ended 5 April 1985 of £15,886, for 1986 of £4,700-odd and for the balance to liquidation on 6 June of £3,035. The liability for national insurance contributions also is shown for the year ended 5 April 1985 and that is of £19,045, the next year of £8,802 and the balancing period of £2,626. I draw attention to the fact that those outstanding liabilities include significant amounts for the year which began on 6 April 1984. The Customs and Excise were also owed value added tax of about £29,000 or £30,000, depending on which figure was taken, and that appears from a schedule the liquidators prepared.

At this stage I refer to a matter which has concerned me, and that is the risk of unfairness by the application of hindsight. For a person to be held knowingly party to carrying on a company's business with intent to defraud creditors requires findings and inferences as to the facts known to that person at the relevant times. At those times the business might either have succeeded or failed.

The certainty that the business failed, which a creditors' liquidation affords, was not a fact known at the time the relevant business decisions were taken. In my judgment accordingly the risk of unfairness through hindsight needs to be borne in mind.

. . .

I come to the directors' remuneration. In my judgment the amounts of remuneration were very high for a company in such a state. For the year ended 31 March 1983 the remuneration was £35,000. That was the year of the substantial profit and I see the case that that might well have been justified. However, for the following year, to 31 March 1984, the remuneration package increased to £37,521. That was the year where there was a sharp swing to loss and a large adverse change in the net assets position. For the year ended 31 March 1985 the directors' remuneration total was £41,726, even higher — and I ask rhetorically: What were the directors doing paying themselves these significant and increasing sums while the debts to the company's creditors mounted?

I also heard evidence about a caravan. The first defendant — not the company — contracted to buy it on hire purchase on 6 August 1983. It was treated as an asset of the company in its books. The company paid the monthly instalments by standing order of £199-odd, and it did that from September 1984 continuously through to May 1986 until just before its liquidation. The Inland Revenue have not accepted those payments as a company trading expense. The position is that while the company's position was deteriorating as it did down to insolvency, the caravan, for which as an asset of the company for its benefit there is no evidence, was continuing to be paid for by the company. In my judgment, in relation to the company's creditors, that was reprehensible.

By the end of July 1984 I find that the first defendant knew (1) that he owed the Customs and Excise for value added tax £10,701, (2) that he owed the Inland Revenue for PAYE and national insurance contributions a sum in excess of £46,000, (3) that there had been a serious deterioration as to the deficiency of net assets, (4) that his bank was continuing to show concern, (5) that he was taking extended credit out of Brewster, (6) that he had no reason to believe that the company was trading profitably, ie that he knew, in my judgment, the position was continuing to deteriorate, nevertheless, (7) large directors' remuneration continued, and (8) the company continued to pay for his caravan.

The first defendant told me that he did not intend to defraud creditors and he did not know about fraudulent trading. I am satisfied that he was in full control of the company and had full knowledge of its affairs. He is an experienced businessman. He told me that his wife's business failed and she was ill, and there appears to be a divorce pending. However, in my judgment, within the principles I have referred to, from the end of July 1984 at least the first defendant had no reason for thinking that the company could pay its debts as they fell due or shortly thereafter. There was in my judgment real moral blame according to current notions of fair trading in his procuring the company to continue to trade, ie within the meaning of the section, dishonestly. I accordingly determine that there was fraudulent trading and, as a convenient date for its start, that it began on 31 July 1984.

. . .

The question now arises as to the form of the relief. Having been helpfully taken through the authorities by Mr Hollington the following principles are in my view relevant on this application by a liquidator.

(1) The declaration should specify responsibility for a definite sum and not be in general terms as, for example, to creditors whose debts were incurred after

commencement of the fraudulent trading (see *Re William C Leitch Bros Ltd* [1932] 2 Ch 71 at 77–79, [1932] All ER Rep 892 at 895–896 per Maugham J).

(2) The provision being applied is in the nature of a punitive provision (see *Re William C Leitch Bros Ltd* [1932] 2 Ch 71 at 80, [1932] All ER Rep 892 at 896). It follows that the declared sum may be or contain a punitive element as well as a compensatory element (see *Re Cyona Distributors Ltd* [1967] 1 All ER 281 at 284, [1967] Ch 889 at 902 per Lord Denning MR).

(3) The usual order on an application by a liquidator is that the sum for which the person concerned is declared to be personally liable ought to be dealt with as part of the general assets in the liquidation (see in *Re William C Leitch Bros Ltd (No 2)* [1933] Ch 261, [1932] All ER Rep 897, per Eve J approved by Lord Denning MR in *Re Cyona Distributors Ltd* [1967] 1 All ER 281 at 284, [1967] Ch 889 at 902).

(4) So far as the sum for which the person in question is declared to be responsible is compensatory, then in my judgment it is more appropriate under this particular statutory provision to adopt the approach of Maugham J in the first *Leitch* case, [1932] 2 Ch 71 at 80, [1932] All ER Rep 892 at 896, ie to limit the sum to the amount of the debts of the creditors proved to have been defrauded by the fraudulent trading. Mr Hollington urged me to adopt the formulation of Knox J in *Re Produce Marketing Consortium Ltd (No 2)* [1989] BCLC 520 at 553 where he said:

> 'Prima facie the appropriate amount that a director is declared to be liable to contribute is the amount by which the company's assets can be discerned to have been depleted by the director's conduct which caused the discretion under [s 214(1)] to arise.'

That is a reference to the Insolvency Act 1986. The preceding section, s 213 of the 1986 Act, is the re-enactment of s 630 of the Companies Act 1985, with which I am concerned. Knox J was however concerned with a different statutory provision and it is, I think, preferable to found myself on a direct nexus with the statutory language before me, particularly in the light of Maugham J's observations to which I have referred. (I add that there may not be a difference of principle and I am in no way dissenting from what Knox J said.) Where the context is fraudulent trading with intent to defraud creditors, there is a clear logic in asking what the creditors have lost as a result of the fraudulent trading. I agree with Mr Hollington that an adequate measure of the maximum compensatory element (I emphasise maximum) is the amount of the trading loss during the period of fraudulent trading.

. . .

I am satisfied that there are elements in this case which point to a need for a considerable punitive element, thus: firstly, the first defendant well knew from the years of the bank's concern expressed to him and the accounts that he was providing that he was trading dangerously. There were large excesses of current liabilities over the current assets which did not come down, and there were serious cash-flow difficulties. Secondly, the fraudulent trading continued for a long period after 31 July 1984 for some 22 months drawing more creditors into the net. Thirdly, the directors' remuneration was high in relation to a company in such a long-continued parlous financial state. Fourthly, the change of name and the reverse at the least must have been appreciated to be confusing to creditors, whether or not it was intended to lead to that confusion. Fifthly, the company continued to pay throughout for the caravan as I have indicated. I consider that a punitive element of £25,000 is appropriate.

PART VI: THE COMMON LAW APPROACH

The sources below are set out in chronological order. In each case, it is possible to deduce who the plaintiff was, who the defendant, what the cause of action was and who won. In a world where principles are vague, such facts are important. When you have read the sources, consider the following questions:

(a) Do you agree that Salomon & Co Ltd was not Aron Salomon's agent (Sources 27, 28)?

(b) Is it a satisfactory answer to the judgments of the Court of Appeal in *Broderip v Salomon*[1] that the company when formed is a person in law separate from its shareholders (Sources 27, 28)?

(c) Should there be a doctrine in the terms of the following dictum?

'To say that a company sustains a separate persona and yet in the same breath to argue that in substance the person holding the shares is the company, is an attempt to have it both ways which cannot be allowed' (de Villiers CJ in *Ochberg v CIR*[2])

or, to put it colloquially, should not those who choose to run their businesses through the medium of a company or companies take the rough with the smooth? (consider, in particular, Sources 31, 33, 36, 40, 41).

(d) If you agree with the House of Lords on Salomon, what would be your view if the facts had been as follows:

'Salomon switched to running his business through a limited liability company because he wanted to avoid personal liability if the business failed. He had no reason to expect that it would fail because it was prosperous when the switch was made; he was just prudent and well advised. He only took 1 £1 share and the company only issued the minimum number of shares; the rest of the 'money' for the purchase of the business was raised by a loan from Salomon to the company secured by a fixed and floating charge. When, say six months or a year or two years later the company fell on hard times, Salomon did not seek the assistance of a moneylender, but effected a voluntary winding up of the company (he considered seeking an administration order, but was advised, almost certainly correctly, that none of the grounds for the court's jurisdiction under s 8(3) of the Insolvency Act 1986 could be satisfied.) In the winding up, the company had just sufficient assets to satisfy Salomon's claim. All other creditors — totalling £250,000 — were left unpaid.'

(e) If you disagree with the House of Lords in Salomon, what is the proper legal principle on which Solomon should have been made to indemnify the company? If it is an essential part of your answer that Salomon owned all or practically all of the shares, will your principle also apply to the case where there are two shareholders each holding 50 per cent of the shares and acting in concert (and to three each owning 33 per cent and so on)?

---

1 [1895] 2 Ch 323
2 1931 AD 215 (South African Sup Ct)

(f) It is said that the Daimler case[1] (Source 29) is not about lifting the veil, but is simply 'looking at the corporators to determine the *character* of the corporation as an enemy alien', just as if one were to 'look at the members to determine whether the company is a subsidiary' (Gower, 4th edn, 1979, p 136).

   Would this also apply to *Gilford Motor Co v Horne*,[2] *Jones v Lipman*[3] and *Re FG Films*[4] (Sources 32, 34, 37)?

(g) In these cases, does it matter whether the shareholders are human beings or other companies? Is there a tendency to treat a group of companies as a single unit in circumstances where the court would not lift the veil if the shareholders were human? If so, is this rational? (see Sources 31, 33, 35, 38, 40 and 42)

(h) Can a single, solid principle be deduced from *Gilford Motor Co v Horne*, *Jones v Lipman*, *Re FG Films and Wallersteiner v Moir*[5] (Sources 32, 34, 37, 39)? If so, how would you formulate it?

(i) What is the relationship between the doctrine of lifting the veil, and the alter ego doctrine (see pp 281ff)? Consider the *Daimler* case (Source 29) and the *Dadoo* case[6] (Source 30) in this regard.

(k) The courts have long wrestled with the problem of associated companies and the extent to which each company within a group should be treated as an independent entity and to what extent the group, as a whole, should be treated as an entity. There are many examples in the succeeding cases, eg Sources 33, 38, 40, 41, 42. Source 42 — *Adams v Cape Industries* — is, unfortunately, long and complicated, but it is an important statement by the Court of Appeal on this issue. Is the distinction drawn between the corporate and commercial activities of the group a convincing one? Is it relevant that the claimants here were involuntary (ie tort) creditors as opposed to people who voluntarily trade with a member of a group?

SOURCE 27

Broderip *v* Salomon

(Chancery Division and Court of Appeal 1895) [1895] 2 Ch 323

Aron Salomon carried on business as a leather merchant and hide factor, wholesale and export boot manufacturer, and Government contractor, in White-chapel, and became desirous of forming a company to take over his business. On 20 July 1892, an agreement was entered into between him and a trustee for a company intended to be formed ...

   The total purchase-money (including the price of book debts, which stood at £6782 19s. 7d.) was £38,782 19s. 7d.

   In framing this agreement and in arriving at the sums to be paid by the company, no one acted on behalf of the proposed company, of which A. Salomon himself was the promoter. His books were made up by an accountant employed

1 [1916] 2 AC 307; 85 LJ KB 1333
2 [1933] Ch 935; 102 LJ Ch 21
3 [1962] 1 WLR 832; [1962] 1 All ER 442
4 [1953] 1 WLR 483; [1953] 1 All ER 615
5 [1974] 1 WLR 991; [1974] 3 All ER 217
6 1920 AD 530 (South African Sup Ct)

by him, no one else had anything to do with the matter, and he in fact settled the figures and dictated the terms to be found in the agreement. The prices which the company was to pay considerably exceeded the amounts appearing in the balance-sheet. At the date of the agreement Salomon owed £7679 12s. 6d., but his business was solvent.

On 28 July 1892, a limited company was registered for the purpose of carrying out the above agreement, which such modifications (if any) as might be agreed to, and of carrying on A. Salomon's business. The nominal capital was £40,000, divided in 40,000 shares of £1 each. The memorandum of association was subscribed by Aron Salomon and his wife and daughter and his four sons, each subscribing for one share. Aron Salomon afterwards had 20,000 shares allotted to him. No one else ever had a share in the company.

. . .

On 5 September 1892, the third meeting of directors was held, at which it was resolved that the seal of the company should be affixed to debentures to be issued to Aron Salomon. It was also resolved that 20,000 shares should be allotted to Aron Salomon, he having applied for them.

At the fourth meeting of directors on 26 January 1893, debentures for £10,000 were sealed and delivered to Aron Salomon.

At the fifth meeting of directors on 5 February 1893, the resolution of 26 January 1893, was rescinded and the debentures cancelled. At the same meeting debentures for £10,000 were, at the request of Aron Salomon, issued to Edmund Broderip, as a security for £5000, lent by him to Aron Salomon, which sum Aron Salomon shortly afterwards lent to the company at £10 per cent interest under an agreement dated 6 February 1893. The company having made default in payment of the interest due on these debentures, Mr Broderip in September 1893, gave notice to call in the principal, and on 11 October 1893, commenced his action on behalf of himself and all the debenture-holders to enforce his security, and on 25 October 1893, the official receiver was appointed receiver and manager. On 26 October an order was made for compulsory winding up of the company. The company put in a defence and counter-claim in the action, making Aron Salomon a party to the counter-claim, and alleging that the arrangements made by Aron Salomon for the formation of the company were a fraud on the creditors of the company, and ought to be set aside; that Aron Salomon was the promoter of, and stood in a fiduciary relation to, the company; and that the company was entitled to have the agreements of 20 July and 2 August 1892, rescinded, to have the £10,000 debentures delivered up to be cancelled, and to have judgment against Aron Salomon for £29,257 18s. 1d. with interest (that being the amount which the company alleged Aron Salomon to have received in cash), and a declaration that the company was entitled to a lien on the business and assets for payment thereof. In the alternative, the company claimed a declaration that the company or its liquidator was entitled to be indemnified by Aron Salomon against £7733 8s. 3d., the amount by which the assets of the company were found in the winding-up to be insufficient for payment of its debts, judgment against him for that sum, a declaration that the company had a lien for that sum on all sums which would not be payable to him out of the assets in respect of the debentures or otherwise, and that he was not entitled to make any claim against the assets of the company until that sum had been satisfied.

The values set by Aron Salomon on his assets had not been examined or checked by any one on behalf of the company after its formation, any more than before. The liquidator contended that the values put upon those assets were excessive.

. . .

VAUGHAN WILLIAMS J: ... Now, in these circumstances the legal position seems to me to be this. I do not think that where you have a private company, and all the shareholders in the company are perfectly cognizant of the conditions under which the company is formed and the conditions of the purchase by the company, you can possibly say that purchasing at an exorbitant price (and I have no doubt whatever that the purchase here was at an exorbitant price) is a fraud upon those shareholders or a fraud upon the company. Of course, purchasing at an exorbitant price may be a fraud, even if all the shareholders know of it, if there is an intention to allot further shares at a later period to future allottees. But that is not, and was not, the case here.

It seems to me, however, that when one considers the fact that these shareholders were mere nominees of Mr Salomon's, that he took the whole of the profits, and that his intention was to take the profits without running the risk of the debts and expenses, one must also consider the position of the unsecured trading creditors, whose debts amount to some £11,000. As I have said, the company was a mere nominee of Mr Salomon's and it does not seem to me that it ought to make the slightest difference whether the nominee is a company or an individual — a person; and therefore I wish, if I can, to deal with this case exactly on the basis that I should do if the nominee, instead of being a company, had been some servant or agent of Mr Salomon to whom he had purported to sell this business.

...

... to allow a man who carries on business under another name to set up a debenture in priority to the claims of the creditors of the company would have the effect of defeating and delaying his creditors. There must be an implied agreement by him to indemnify the company. Under the Companies Act of 1862 a man may become what is called a private company so as to obtain the benefits of limited liability. I have already held, in a case where the founder of such a company had become bankrupt and the company claimed his assets, that the company was a mere fraud, and the Court of Appeal supported that decision. In this case I propose to hold the same thing — that this business was Mr Salomon's business and no one else's; that he chose to employ as agent a limited company; that he is bound to indemnify that agent, the company; and that his agent, the company, has a lien on the assets which overrides his claims. The creditors of the company could, in my opinion, have sued Mr Salomon. Their right to do so would depend on the circumstances of the case, whether the company was a mere alias of the founder or not. In this case it is clear that the relationship of principal and agent existed between Mr Salomon and the company.

...

LINDLEY LJ: This is an appeal by Mr Aron Salomon against an order made by Vaughan Williams J, and which, in effect, directs Mr A. Salomon to indemnify a limited company formed by him against the unsecured debts and liabilities incurred by or in the name of the company whilst it carried on business.

The appeal raises a question of very great importance, not only to the persons immediately affected by the decision, but also to a large number of persons who form what are called 'one-man companies.' Such companies were unheard of until a comparatively recent period, but have become very common of late years.

...

... There can be no doubt that in this case an attempt has been made to use the machinery of the Companies Act 1862, for a purpose for which it never was intended. The legislature contemplated the encouragement of trade by enabling a comparatively small number of persons — namely, not less than seven — to carry on business with a limited joint stock or capital, and without the risk of liability beyond the loss of such joint stock or capital. But the legislature never contemplated an extension of limited liability to sole traders or to a fewer number than seven. In truth, the legislature clearly intended to prevent anything of the kind, for section 48[1] takes away the privileges conferred by the Act from those members of limited companies who allow such companies to carry on business with less than seven members; and by section 79[2] the reduction of the number of members below seven is a ground for winding up the company. Although in the present case there were, and are, seven members, yet it is manifest that six of them are members simply in order to enable the seventh himself to carry on business with limited liability. The object of the whole arrangement is to do the very thing which the legislature intended not to be done; and, ingenious as the scheme is, it cannot have the effect desired so long as the law remains unaltered.

. . . As the company must be recognised as a corporation, I feel a difficulty in saying that the company did not carry on business as a principal, and that the debts and liabilities contracted in its name are not enforceable against it in its corporate capacity. But it does not follow that the order made by Vaughan Williams J is wrong. A person may carry on business as a principal and incur debts and liabilities as such, and yet be entitled to be indemnified against those debts and liabilities by the person for whose benefit he carries on the business. The company in this case has been regarded by Vaughan Williams J as the agent of Aron Salomon. I should rather liken the company to a trustee for him — a trustee improperly brought into existence by him to enable him to do what the statute prohibits. It is manifest that the other members of the company have practically no interest in it, and their names have merely been used by Mr Aron Salomon to enable him to form a company, and to use its name in order to screen himself from liability.

. . .

If the legislature thinks it right to extend the principle of limited liability to sole traders it will no doubt do so, with such safeguards, if any, as it may think necessary. But until the law is changed such attempts as these ought to be defeated whenever they are brought to light. They do infinite mischief; they bring into disrepute one of the most useful statutes of modern times, by perverting its legitimate use, and by making it an instrument for cheating honest creditors.

Mr Aron Salomon's scheme is a device to defraud creditors.

LOPES LJ: . . . The incorporation of the company was perfect — the machinery by which it was formed was in every respect perfect, every detail had been observed; but, notwithstanding, the business was, in truth and in fact, the business of Aron Salomon; he had the beneficial interest in it; the company was a mere *nominis umbra*, under cover of which he carried on his business as before, securing himself against loss by a limited liability of £1 per share, all of which shares he practically possessed, and obtaining a priority over the unsecured creditors of the company by the debentures of which he had constituted himself the holder.

It would be lamentable if a scheme like this could not be defeated. If we were to permit it to succeed, we should be authorizing a perversion of the Joint Stock Companies Acts. We should be giving vitality to that which is a myth and a fiction. The transaction is a device to apply the machinery of the Joint Stock Companies

---

1 Section 24 of the Companies Act 1985
2 Section 122(1)(e) of the Insolvency Act 1986

Act to a state of things never contemplated by that Act — an ingenious device to obtain the protection of that Act in a way and for objects not authorized by that Act, and in my judgment in a way inconsistent with and opposed to its policy and provisions. It never was intended that the company to be constituted should consist of one substantial person and six mere dummies, the nominees of that person, without any real interest in the company. The Act contemplated the incorporation of seven independent bonâ fide members, who had a mind and a will of their own, and were not the mere puppets of an individual who, adopting the machinery of the Act, carried on his old business in the same way as before, when he was a sole trader. To legalize such a transaction would be a scandal.

SOURCE 28
Salomon v Salomon & Co Ltd
(House of Lords 1897) [1897] AC 22; 66 LJ Ch 35

LORD HERSCHELL: ... It is to be observed that both Courts treated the company as a legal entity distinct from Salomon and the then members who composed it, and therefore as a validly constituted corporation. This is, indeed, necessarily involved in the judgment which declared that the company was entitled to certain rights as against Salomon. Under these circumstances, I am at a loss to understand what is meant by saying that A. Salomon & Co, Limited, is but an 'alias' for A. Salomon. It is not another name for the same person; the company is ex hypothesi a distinct legal persona. As little am I able to adopt the view that the company was the agent of Salomon to carry on this business for him. In a popular sense, a company may in every case be said to carry on business for and on behalf of its shareholders; but this certainly does not in point of law constitute the relation of principal and agent between them or render the shareholders liable to indemnify the company against the debts which it incurs. Here, it is true, Salomon owned all the shares except six, so that if the business were profitable he would be entitled, substantially, to the whole of the profits. The other shareholders, too, are said to have been 'dummies,' the nominees of Salomon. But when once it is conceded that they were individual members of the company distinct from Salomon, and sufficiently so to bring into existence in conjunction with him a validly constituted corporation, I am unable to see how the facts to which I have just referred can affect the legal position of the company, or give it rights as against its members which it would not otherwise possess.

The Court of Appeal based their judgment on the proposition that the formation of the company and all that followed on it were a mere scheme to enable the appellant to carry on business in the name of the company, with limited liability, contrary to the true intent and meaning of the Companies Act, 1862. The conclusion which they drew from this premiss was, that the company was a trustee and Salomon their *cestui que trust*. I cannot think that the conclusion follows even if the premiss be sound. It seems to me that the logical result would be that the company had not been validly constituted, and therefore had no legal existence. But, apart from this, it is necessary to examine the proposition on which the Court have rested their judgment, as its effect would be far reaching. Many industrial and banking concerns of the highest standing and credit have, in recent years, been, to use a common expression, converted into joint stock companies, and often into what are called 'private' companies, where the whole of the shares are held by the former partners. It appears to me that all these might be pronounced 'schemes to enable' them 'to carry on business in the name of the company, with limited liability,' in the very sense in which those words are used in the judgment of the Court of Appeal. The profits of the concern carried on by the company will go to the persons whose business it was before the transfer, and in the same proportions as before, the only difference being that the liability of those who take the profits will no longer be unlimited. The very object of the creation of the company and the transfer to it of the business is, that whereas the liability of the partners for debts incurred was without limit, the liability of the members for the debts incurred by the company shall be limited. In no other respect is it intended that there shall be any difference: the conduct of the business and the division of the profits are intended to be the same as before. If the judgment of the Court of Appeal be pushed to its logical conclusion, all these companies must, I think, be held to be trustees for the partners who transferred the business to them, and those partners must be declared liable without limit to discharge the debts of the company. For this is the effect of the judgment as regards the respondent company. The position of the members of a company is just the same whether they are declared liable to pay the debts incurred by the company, or by way of indemnity to furnish the company with the means of paying them. I do not think the learned judges in the Court below have contemplated the application of their judgment to such cases as I have been considering; but I can see no solid distinction between those cases and the present one.

It is said that the respondent company is a 'one man' company, and that in this respect it differs from such companies as those to which I have alluded. But it has often happened that a business transferred to a joint stock company has been the property of three or four persons only, and that the other subscribers of the memorandum have been clerks or other persons who possessed little or no interest in the concern. I am unable to see how it can be lawful for three or four or six persons to form a company for the purpose of employing their capital in trading, with the benefit of limited liability, and not for one person to do so, provided, in each case, the requirements of the statute have been complied with and the company has been validly constituted. How does it concern the creditor where the capital of the company is owned by seven persons in equal shares, with the right to an equal share of the profits, or whether it is almost entirely owned by one person, who practically takes the whole of the profits? The creditor has notice that he is dealing with a company the liability of the members of which is limited, and the register of shareholders informs him how the shares are held, and that they are substantially in the hands of one person, if this be the fact. The creditors in the present case gave credit to and contracted with a limited company; the effect of the decision is to give them the benefit, as regards one of the shareholders, of unlimited liability. I have said that the liability of persons carrying on business can only be limited provided the requirements of the statute be complied with; and this leads naturally to the inquiry, What are those requirements?

The Court of Appeal has declared that the formation of the respondent company and the agreement to take over the business of the appellant where a scheme 'contrary to the true intent and meaning of the Companies Act.' I know of no means of ascertaining what is the intent and meaning of the Companies Act except by examining its provisions and finding what regulations it has imposed as a condition of trading with limited liability. The memorandum must state the amount of the capital of the company and the number of shares into which it is divided, and no subscriber is to take less than one share. The shares may, however, be of as small a nominal value as those who form the company please: the statute prescribes no minimum; and though there must be seven shareholders, it is enough if each of them holds one share, however small its denomination. The legislature, therefore, clearly sanctions a scheme by which all the shares except six are owned by a single individual, and these six are of a value little more than nominal.

It was said that in the present case the six shareholders other than the appellant were mere dummies, his nominees, and held their shares in trust for him. I will assume that this was so. In my opinion, it makes no difference. The statute forbids the entry in the register of any trust; and it certainly contains no enactment that each of the seven persons subscribing the memorandum must be beneficially entitled to the share or shares for which he subscribes. The persons who subscribe the memorandum, or who have agreed to become members of the company and whose names are on the register, are alone regarded as, and in fact are, the shareholders. They are subject to all the liability which attaches to the holding of the share. They can be compelled to make any payment which the ownership of a share involves. Whether they are beneficial owners or bare trustees is a matter with which neither the company nor creditors have anything to do: it concerns only them and their *cestuis que trust* if they have any. If, then, in the present case all the requirements of the statute were complied with, and a company was effectually constituted, and this is the hypothesis of the judgment appealed from, what warrant is there for saying that what was done was contrary to the true intent and meaning of the Companies Act?

It may be that a company constituted like that under consideration was not in the contemplation of the legislature at the time when the Act authorizing limited liability was passed; that if what is possible under the enactments as they stand had been foreseen a minimum sum would have been fixed as the least denomination of share permissible; and that it would have been made a condition that each of the seven persons should have a substantial interest in the company. But we have to interpret the law, not to make it; and it must be remembered that no one need trust a limited liability company unless he so please, and that before he does so he can ascertain, if he so please, what is the capital of the company and how it is held.

LORD MACNAGHTEN: . . . When the memorandum is duly signed and registered, though there be only seven shares taken, the subscribers are a body corporate 'capable forthwith,' to use the words of the enactment, 'of exercising all the functions of an incorporated company.' Those are strong words. The company attains maturity on its birth. There is no period of minority — no interval of incapacity. I cannot understand how a body corporate thus made 'capable' by statute can lose its individuality by issuing the bulk of its capital to one person, whether he be a subscriber to the memorandum or not. The company is at law a different person altogether from the subscribers to the memorandum; and, though it may be that after incorporation the business is precisely the same as it was before, and the same persons are managers, and the same hands receive the profits, the company is not in law the agent of the subscribers or trustee for them. Nor are the subscribers as members liable, in any shape or form, except to the extent and in the manner provided by the Act. That is, I think, the declared intention of the enactment. If the view of the learned judge were sound, it would follow that no common law partnership could register as a company limited by shares without remaining subject to unlimited liability.

Mr Salomon appealed; but his appeal was dismissed with costs, though the Appellate Court did not entirely accept the view of the Court below. The decision of the Court of Appeal proceeds on a declaration of opinion embodied in the order which has been already read.[1]

---

1 Set out in Lord Herschell's opinion, above

I must say that I, too, have great difficulty in understanding this declaration. If it only means that Mr Salomon availed himself to the full of the advantages offered by the Act of 1862, what is there wrong in that. Leave out the words 'contrary to the true intent and meaning of the Companies Act 1862,' and bear in mind that 'the creditors of the company' are not the creditors of Mr Salomon, and the declaration is perfectly innocent: it has no sting in it. . . .

Among the principal reasons which induce persons to form private companies, as is stated very clearly by Mr Palmer in his treatise on the subject, are the desire to avoid the risk of bankruptcy, and the increased facility afforded for borrowing money. By means of a private company, as Mr Palmer observes, a trade can be carried on with limited liability, and without exposing the persons interested in it in the event of failure to the harsh provisions of the bankruptcy law. A company, too, can raise money on debentures, which an ordinary trader cannot do. Any member of a company, acting in good faith, is as much entitled to take and hold the company's debentures as any outside creditor. Every creditor is entitled to get and to hold the best security the law allows him to take.

If, however, the declaration of the Court of Appeal means that Mr Salomon acted fraudulently or dishonestly, I must say I can find nothing in the evidence to support such an imputation. The purpose for which Mr Salomon and the other subscribers to the memorandum were associated was 'lawful.' That fact that Mr Salomon raised £5000 for the company on debentures that belonged to him seems to me strong evidence of his good faith and of his confidence in the company. The unsecured creditors of A. Salomon and Company Limited, may be entitled to sympathy, but they have only themselves to blame for their mis-fortunes. They trusted the company, I suppose, because they had long dealt with Mr Salomon, and he had always paid his way; but they had full notice that they were no longer dealing with an individual, and they must be taken to have been cognisant of the memorandum and of the articles of association. For such a catastrophe as has occurred in this case some would blame the law that allows the creation of a floating charge. But a floating charge is too convenient a form of security to be lightly abolished. I have long thought, and I believe some of your Lordships also think, that the ordinary trade creditors of a trading company ought to have a preferential claim on the assets in liquidation in respect of debts incurred within a certain limited time before the winding-up. But that is not the law at present. Everybody knows that when there is a winding-up debenture-holders generally step in and sweep off everything; and a great scandal it is.

It has become the fashion to call companies of this class 'one man companies.' That is a taking nickname, but it does not help one much in the way of argument. If it is intended to convey the meaning that a company which is under the absolute control of one person is not a company legally incorporated, although the requirements of the Act of 1862 may have been complied with, it is inaccurate and misleading: if it merely means that there is a predominant partner possessing an overwhelming influence and entitled practically to the whole of the profits, there is nothing in that that I can see contrary to the true intention of the Act of 1862, or against public policy, or detrimental to the interests of creditors. If the shares are fully paid up, it cannot matter whether they are in the hands of one or many. If the shares are not fully paid, it is as easy to gauge the solvency of an individual as to estimate the financial ability of a crowd.

. . .

LORD HALSBURY LC: [For the oft quoted dicta of Lord Halsbury's speech, see Source 29.]

[The House of Lords was unanimous in upholding Aron Salomon's appeal.]

SOURCE 29
Daimler Company Limited *v* Continental Tyre and Rubber Company (Great Britain) Limited
(House of Lords 1916) [1916] 2 AC 307; 85 LJ KB 1333

On 23 October 1914, an action was commenced in the name of the respondent company [Continental] by specially indorsed writ for £5605 16s. alleged to be due from the appellants for principal, interest, and notarial charges on three bills of exchange drawn by the respondents and accepted by the appellants in payment for goods supplied to them by the respondents prior to the outbreak of the war with Germany. The writ was issued by the solicitors of the respondent company upon the instructions of the secretary. On 30 October 1914, a summons was taken out on behalf of the respondent company under Order xiv for leave to sign judgment for the amount of the claim with interest and costs. This summons was opposed by the appellants on the grounds that the company and its officers were alien enemies and that consequently the company was incapable of instituting these proceedings or of giving a good and valid discharge for the amount claimed; and, further, that the appellants, in paying that amount, would be acting in contravention of the Trading with the Enemy Act 1914. The appellants therefore contended that the proceedings were wrongly instituted and that unconditional leave to defend should be given to them.

The respondent company was incorporated under the Companies Acts on 29 March 1905, with a capital of £10,000, subsequently increased to £25,000, in fully paid £1 shares, and had its registered office in London. It was formed for the purpose of selling in the United Kingdom motor car tyres made in Germany by a company incorporated in that country under German law. At the date of the writ the German company held 23,398 shares in the respondent company, and the remaining shares, except one, were held by subjects of the German Empire. The one share was registered in the name of Mr Wolter, the secretary of the company, who was born in Germany, but resided in this country and in 1910 became a naturalized subject of the Crown. All the directors were subjects of the German Empire, and three of the four directors were resident in Germany when war was declared; the fourth, who had previously resided in England, left this country for Germany on the outbreak of the war.

30 June. EARL OF HALSBURY. My Lords, I am of opinion that this judgment should be reversed. [The Court of Appeal had affirmed the decision of the Master and the Court of first instance entering judgment in favour of the Respondent.]

In my opinion the whole discussion is solved by a very simple proposition that in our law, when the object to be obtained is unlawful, the indirectness of the means by which it is to be obtained will not get rid of the unlawfulness, and in this cause the object of the means adopted is to enable thousands of pounds to be paid to the King's enemies. Before war existed between us and Germany, an associated body of Germans availed themselves of our English law to carry on a business for manufacturing motor machines in Germany and selling them here in England and elsewhere, as they were entitled to do, but in doing so they were bound to observe the directions which the Act of Parliament under which they were incorporated required.

They were entitled to receive in the shape of dividends the profits of the concern in proportion to their shares in it. They were all Germans originally, though one afterwards became a naturalized Englishman. Now the right and proper course to follow in the matter — and I have no reason to suppose that any other course was followed — was to distribute to them rateably, according to their shares, the profits of their adventure. But this machinery, while perfectly lawful in peace time, becomes absolutely unlawful when the German traders are at war with this country. I confess it seems to me that the question becomes very plain, when one applies the language of the law to the condition of things when war is declared, between the German who is in the character of shareholder and in control of the company. They can neither meet here, nor can they authorize any agent to meet on any company business. They can neither trade with us nor can any British subject trade with them. Nor can they comply with the provisions for the government of the company which they were bound by their incorporated character to observe.

Under these circumstances it becomes material to consider what is this thing which is described as a 'corporation.' It is, in fact, a partnership in all that constitutes a partnership except the names, and in some respects the position of those who I shall call the managing partners. No one can doubt that the names and the incorporation were but the machinery by which the purpose (giving money to the enemy) would be accomplished.

LORD PARKER: . . . The principle upon which the judgment under appeal proceeds is that trading with an incorporated company cannot be trading with an enemy where the company is registered in England under the Companies Acts and carries on its business here. Such a company it calls an 'English company,' and obviously likens to a natural-born Englishman, and accordingly holds that payment to it of a debt which is due to it, and of money which is its own, cannot be trading with the enemy, be its corporators who they may. The view is that an English company's enemy officers vacate their office on becoming enemies and so affect it no longer, and that its enemy shareholders, being neither its agents nor its principals, never in law affect it at all.

My Lords, much of the reasoning by which this principle is supported is quite indisputable. No one can question that a corporation is a legal person distinct from its corporators; that the relation of a shareholder to a company, which is limited by shares, is not in itself the relation of principal and agent or the reverse; that the assets of the company belong to it and the acts of its servants and agents are its acts, while its shareholders, as such, have no property in the assets and no personal responsibility for those acts. The law on the subject is clearly laid down in a passage in Lord Halsbury's judgment in *Salomon v Salomon & Co.*[1] 'I am simply here,' he says, 'dealing with the provisions of the statute, and it seems to me to be essential to the artificial creation that the law should recognise only that artificial existence — quite apart from the motives or conduct of individual corporators. . . . Short of such proof' — ie, proof in appropriate proceedings that the company had no real legal existence — 'it seems to me impossible to dispute that once the company is legally incorporated it must be treated like any other independent person with its rights and liabilities appropriate to itself, and that the motives of those who took part in the formation of the company are absolutely irrelevant in discussing what those rights and liabilities are.' I do not think, however, that it is a necessary corollary of this reasoning to say that the character of its corporators must be irrelevant to the character of the company; and this is crucial, for the rule against trading with the enemy depends upon enemy character.

---

1 [1897] AC 22; 66 LJ Ch 35

A natural person, though an English-born subject of His Majesty, may bear an enemy character and be under liability and disability as such by adhering to His Majesty's enemies. If he gives them active aid, he is a traitor; but he may fall far short of that and still be invested with enemy character. If he has what is known in prize law as a commercial domicil among the King's enemies, his merchandise is good prize at sea, just as if it belonged to a subject of the enemy Power. Not only actively, but passively, he may bring himself under the same disability. Voluntary residence among the enemy, however passive or pacific he may be, identifies an English subject with His Majesty's foes. I do not think it necessary to cite authority for these well-known propositions, nor do I doubt that, if they had seemed material to the Court of Appeal, they would have been accepted.

. . .

In the case of an artificial person what is the analogue to voluntary residence among the King's enemies? Its impersonality can hardly put it in a better position than a natural person and lead to its being unaffected by anything equivalent to residence. It is only by a figure of speech that a company can be said to have a nationality or residence at all. If the place of its incorporation under municipal law fixes its residence, then its residence cannot be changed, which is almost a contradiction in terms, and in the case of a company residence must correspond to the birthplace and country of natural allegiance in the case of a living person, and not to residence or commercial domicil. Nevertheless, enemy character depends on these last. It would seem, therefore, logically to follow that, in transferring the application of the rule against trading with the enemy from natural to artificial persons, something more than the mere place or country of registration or incorporation must be looked at.

My Lords, I think that the analogy is to be found in control, an idea which, if not very familiar in law, is of capital importance and is very well understood in commerce and finance. The acts of a company's organs, its directors, managers, secretary, and so forth, functioning within the scope of their authority, are the company's acts and may invest it definitively with enemy character. It seems to me that similarly the character of those who can make and unmake those officers, dictate their conduct mediately or immediately, prescribe their duties and call them to account, may also be material in a question of the enemy character of the company. If not definite and conclusive, it must at least be prima facie relevant, as raising a presumption that those who are purporting to act in the name of the company are, in fact, under the control of those whom it is their interest to satisfy.

. . . I think the law on the subject may be summarized in the following propositions:–

(1) A company incorporated in the United Kingdom is a legal entity, a creation of law with the status and capacity which the law confers. It is not a natural person with mind or conscience. To use the language of Buckley LJ, 'it can be neither loyal nor disloyal. It can be neither friend nor enemy.'

(2) Such a company can only act through agents properly authorized, and so long as it is carrying on business in this country through agents so authorized and residing in this or a friendly country it is prima facie to be regarded as a friend, and all His Majesty's lieges may deal with it as such.

(3) Such a company may, however, assume an enemy character. This will be the case if its agents or the persons in de facto control of its affairs, whether authorized or not, are resident in an enemy country, or, wherever resident, are adhering to the enemy or taking instructions from or acting under the control of enemies. A person knowingly dealing with the company in such a case is trading with the enemy.

(4) The character of individual shareholders cannot of itself affect the character of the company. This is admittedly so in times of peace, during which every shareholder is at liberty to exercise and enjoy such rights as are by law incident to his status as shareholder. It would be anomalous if it were not so also in a time of war, during which all such rights and privileges are in abeyance. The enemy character of individual shareholders and their conduct may, however, be very material on the question whether the company's agents, or the persons in de facto control of its affairs, are in fact adhering to, taking instructions from, or acting under the control of enemies. This materiality will vary with the number of shareholders who are enemies and the value of their holdings. The fact, if it be the fact, that after eliminating the enemy shareholders the number of shareholders remaining is insufficient for the purpose of holding meetings of the company or appointing directors or other officers may well raise a presumption in this respect. For example, in the present case, even if the secretary had been fully authorized to manage the affairs of the company and to institute legal proceedings on its behalf, the fact that he held one share only out of 25,000 shares, and was the only shareholder who was not an enemy, might well throw on the company the onus of proving that he was not acting under the control of, taking his instructions from, or adhering to the King's enemies in such manner as to impose an enemy character on the company itself. It is an *a fortiori* case when the secretary is without authority and necessarily depends for the validity of all he does on the subsequent ratification of enemy shareholders. The circumstances of the present case were, therefore, such as to require close investigation and preclude the propriety of giving leave to sign judgment under Order xiv, r 1.

(5) In a similar way a company registered in the United Kingdom, but carrying on business in a neutral country through agents properly authorized and resident here or in the neutral country, is prima facie to be regarded as a friend, but may, through its agents or persons in de facto control of its affairs, assume an enemy character.

(6) A company registered in the United Kingdom but carrying on business in an enemy country is to be regarded as an enemy.

SOURCE 30
Dadoo Ltd *v* Krugersdorp Municipal Council
(South African Supreme Court 1920) 1920 AD 530

The company took transfer of property in the township of the Krugersdorp Municipal Council. The shareholders of the company were Asiatics, who by the prevailing legislation were prohibited from owning property in that township. The Municipal Council applied for the transfer to be set aside.

INNES CJ: . . . Taking the intention then to be the prohibition of ownership of fixed property by Asiatics and the prohibition of the acquisition and the occupation of mining rights by coloured people, I come to enquire whether the transaction complained of is a contravention of the statutes. In other words, whether ownership by Dadoo Ltd, is in substance ownership by its Asiatic shareholders. Clearly in law it is not. A registered company is a legal *persona* distinct from the members who compose it. In the words of Lord MacNaghten (*Salomon v Salomon & Co*),[1] 'the company is at law a different person altogether from the subscribers to its memorandum; and though it may be that, after incorporation, the business is precisely the same as it was before, and the same

---
1 [1897] AC 22; 66 LJ Ch 35

persons are managers, and the same hands receive the profits, the company is not in law the agent of the subscribers or a trustee for them.' That result follows from the separate legal existence with which such corporations are by statute endowed, and the principle has been accepted in our practice. Nor is the position affected by the circumstance that a controlling interest in the concern may be held by a single member. This conception of the existence of a company as a separate entity distinct from its shareholders is no merely artificial and technical thing. It is a matter of substance; property vested in the company is not, and cannot be, regarded as vested in all or any of its members. Cases may arise concerning the existence of attributes which in the nature of things cannot be associated with a purely legal *persona*. And then it may be necessary to look behind the company and to pay regard to the personality of the shareholders, who compose it. *The Continental Tyre and Rubber Co v The Daimler Co,*[1] was an instance of such a case. There a joint stock corporation registered in England, whose shares, with a single exception, were held by Germans and whose directors were all Germans resident in Germany, sued upon duly accepted bills of exchange. The question arose whether payment to the plaintiff would be payment to an alien enemy and therefore illegal. The Court of Appeal, with one dissentient (Buckley LJ), answered that question in the negative, substantially on the ground that the British character of the company was established by its registration in England and was not affected by the nationality of its shareholders. The decision was reversed in the House of Lords on another ground; but the main question was also dealt with; and though the remarks thereon were *obiter,* they necessarily carry great weight. The House was divided; three agreed with the Court of Appeal five were of a different opinion, the views of four of the latter being expressed in an exhaustive judgment by Lord Parker of Waddington. It was pointed out that an artificial person could only by a figure of speech be said to have any residence or nationality at all. Yet enemy character depended upon these elements. The analogy of control was adopted, and it was held that the character of those who controlled the company could be properly regarded as affecting the question of its enemy character. Lord Halsbury went further; the corporation, he said, 'was in fact a partnership in all that constitutes a partnership except the name,' and the names and the incorporation were but the machinery by which the purpose of giving money to the enemy could be accomplished. The mere machinery to do an illegal act would not purge its illegality. It is difficult to reconcile that judgment with *Salomon v Salomon & Co,* the principle of which was expressly affirmed by Lord Parker, and Lord Halsbury's reasoning was not adopted by any of his colleagues. The difference between the *Daimler* case and the present one is that, there the enquiry related to attributes which in the nature of things could not attach to a mere legal *persona;* here the question is whether the ownership of the company is in reality the ownership of the shareholders. A company cannot have an enemy character; in the words of Buckley LJ, it has neither body, parts nor passions; it cannot be loyal or disloyal. But it can own land; and its right to do so and the consequences of ownership are not merely matters of form.

. . . had Dadoo and Dindar been partners, they could not legally have become owners of these stands; but as shareholders in a company which owns them, they remain, in my opinion, outside the legal prohibition. In that way no doubt a result is secured almost as convenient to Dadoo as if he were the actual owner. So long as he retains his controlling interest he may indirectly cause the property to be sold or mortgaged or burdened practically to the same extent as if he were

1 [1915] 1 KB 893

dominus. That is only another way of saying that he has managed to avoid the restrictions of the statute. But he has done so, not by taking advantage of a mere technicality, but by doing something different in law and in substance from what the statute prohibited. And he is entitled to the advantage of that position.

SOURCE 31
Macaura *v* Northern Assurance Company
(House of Lords (Ir.) 1925); [1925] AC 619; 94 LJ PC 154

LORD BUCKMASTER: My Lords, the appellant is the owner of the Killymoon estate in the county of Tyrone. The respondents are five insurance companies with whom at various dates in January and February of 1922, the appellant effected insurance against fire on timber and wood goods in the open situate on the Killymoon domain not within a hundred yards of any saw mill or any building in which wood working by power other than wind or water was carried on.

. . .

The history of the matter can be stated in a few sentences. The appellant upon whose estate the timber in question was originally standing on 30 December 1919, assigned the whole of it to a company known as the Irish Canadian Saw Mills Ltd, the amount to be paid for the timber felled and unfelled being £27,000, while a further £15,000 was to be paid for the cost incurred by the appellant in felling the timber that was then down. The total price paid was therefore £42,000, satisfied by the allotment to the appellant or his nominees of £42,000 fully paid £1 shares in the company; no further shares than these were ever issued. The company proceeded with the operations of cutting the timber, and by the end of August 1921, it had all been felled and sawn up in the saw mills. In the course of these operations the appellant had become the creditor of the company for £19,000, and beyond this it is stated that the debts of the company were trifling in amount. The timber when cut remained lying on the appellant's land, and on 22 February 1922, the greater part of it was destroyed by fire. The appellant accordingly claimed against the companies upon the policies and, on 30 May 1922, in an answer sent on behalf of all the companies, it was stated that the companies must decline to accept liability for the loss of any timber within a hundred yards of the saw mill.

. . .

Now, no shareholder has any right to any item of property owned by the company, for he has no legal or equitable interest therein. He is entitled to a share in the profits while the company continues to carry on business and a share in the distribution of the surplus assets when the company is wound up. If he were at liberty to effect an insurance against loss by fire of any item of the company's property, the extent of his insurable interest could only be measured by determining the extent to which his share in the ultimate distribution would be diminished by the loss of the asset — a calculation almost impossible to make. There is no means by which such an interest can be definitely measured and no standard which can be fixed of the loss against which the contract of insurance could be regarded as an indemnity.

SOURCE 32
Gilford Motor Company Limited *v* Horne and Another
(Court of Appeal 1933) [1933] Ch 935; 102 LJ Ch 21

In this action the plaintiffs asked for an injunction to restrain the defendant E. B. Horne, either directly or indirectly by means of the defendant company (called J. M. Horne & Co Ltd) or otherwise, and to restrain the defendant company, from soliciting, interfering with or endeavouring to entice away from the plaintiffs any person, firm or company who at any time during or at the date of the determination of the employment of the defendant as managing director of the plaintiffs were customers of or in the habit of dealing with the plaintiffs, and to restrain the defendant Horne from directing or suggesting such solicitation, interference or endeavouring to entice away by the defendant company or any agent or servant thereof in breach of a covenant on the part of the defendant Horne contained in an agreement dated 30 May 1929, and made between the plaintiffs and Horne.

The plaintiff failed before Farwell J, but its appeal was unanimously upheld by the Court of Appeal. The disagreement was as to the construction of the restrictive covenant, Farwell J holding that the covenant was too widely drafted to be unenforceable. Both courts, however, agreed on the approach to be adopted towards the relationship between Horne and J. M. Horne & Co Ltd.

LORD HANWORTH MR: . . . Farwell J heard the evidence about that company and had these documents before him. He says this: 'The defendant company is a company which, on the evidence before me, is obviously carried on wholly by the defendant Horne. Mrs Horne, one of the directors, is not, so far as any evidence I have had before me, taking any part in the business or the management of the business. The son, whose initials are 'J. M.,' is engaged in a subordinate position in that company, and the other director, Howard, is an employee of the company. As one of the witnesses said in the witness-box, in all dealings which he had had with the defendant company the 'boss' or the 'guvnor,' whichever term is the appropriate one, was the defendant Horne, and I have not any doubt on the evidence I have had before me that the defendant company was the channel through which the defendant Horne was carrying on his business. Of course, in law the defendant company is a separate entity from the defendant Horne, but I cannot help feeling quite convinced that at any rate one of the reasons for the creation of that company was the fear of Mr Horne that he might commit breaches of the covenant in carrying on the business, as, for instance, in sending out circulars as he was doing and that he might possibly avoid that liability if he did it through the defendant company. There is no doubt that the defendant company has sent out circulars to persons who were at the crucial time customers of the plaintiff company.' Now I have recalled that portion of the judgment of Farwell J, and I wish in clear terms to say that I agree with every word of it. I am quite satisfied that this company was formed as a device, a stratagem, in order to mask the effective carrying on of a business of Mr E. B. Horne. The purpose of it was to try to enable him, under what is a cloak or a sham, to engage in business which, on consideration of the agreement which had been sent to him just about seven days before the company was incorporated, was a business in respect of which he had a fear that the plaintiffs might intervene and object.

Now this action is brought by the plaintiffs, the Gilford Motor Company Ltd, to enforce the terms of clause 9 of the agreement of 30 May 1929,[1] on the ground that the defendant Horne, and the company, as his agent and under his direction, have committed breaches of the covenant which I have read. . . . [As a matter of construction and on the evidence] we have to say that the plaintiffs are entitled in this action to have this covenant upheld, and an injunction is the proper mode of enforcing that, as against these defendants. . . .

---

1 The restrictive covenant referred to above

In these circumstances the appeal must be allowed, and for the reasons which I have already stated I think the injunction must go against the company.

I do hold that it was a mere device for enabling Mr E. B. Horne to continue to commit breaches of clause 9, and under those circumstances the injunction must go against both defendants.

SOURCE 33
Smith, Stone & Knight *v* Birmingham Corporation
(King's Bench Division 1939) [1939] 4 All ER 116; 101 LT 371

ATKINSON J: This is a motion by a firm of Smith, Stone & Knight Ltd, whom I shall call the company, to set aside an interim award on somewhat unusual grounds. The company was the owner of a factory and a number of small houses in Moland St, Birmingham. They were paper manufacturers and carried on their business on some premises other than those in Moland St. The corporation of Birmingham desired to purchase under their compulsory powers this factory, land and cottages in Moland St, in order to build a technical college, and on 16 February 1935, they served on the company a notice to treat. On 20 February the company lodged a claim, and described themselves as of '84, Colmore Row, Birmingham, paper makers, waste paper merchants and dealers.' They described the property, and under heading 7, where they had to specify the names of occupiers and various details, they said: Factory and offices let to Birmingham Waste Co Ltd, as yearly tenants at £90 a year.

. . .

On 29 April 1937, an amended claim was put in. Under heading 7, they said:

> 'Factory and offices nominally let to the Birmingham Waste Co Ltd, which said company is a subsidiary company of Smith, Stone & Knight Ltd, carrying on this business for and on behalf of Smith, Stone & Knight Ltd, which said company owns the whole of the capital and takes the whole of the profits of the said subsidiary company. The subsidiary company occupies the said premises and carries on its trade as a separate department of and as agents for Smith, Stone & Knight Ltd. The said rent was and is arranged as an inter-departmental charge and is merely a book-keeping entry.'

They added to that final note, or, at any rate, in its final form it read:

> 'These two items of damage will accrue to Smith, Stone & Knight Ltd who are the principles of the Birmingham Waste Co Ltd. The said loss will fall upon Smith, Stone & Knight Ltd.'

The parties were unable to come to terms and finally the matter was referred to arbitration. A preliminary point was at once raised, which was whether, as a matter of law, the company could claim compensation for disturbance of the business which was carried on on these premises, or whether, in law, that claim must be made by the Waste company itself. In the latter event, the corporation would escape paying compensation altogether, by virtue of Lands Clauses Consolidation Act 1845, section 121. That section enables purchasers to get rid of occupiers with no greater interest than a tenancy not exceeding one year, because they can give them notice and thereby terminate their tenancy, and escape paying anything to them.

. . . On 13 March 1913 the claimants caused this new company, the Birmingham Waste Co Ltd, to be registered. It was a company with a subscribed capital of £502, the claimants holding 497 shares. They found all the money, and they had 497 shares registered in their own name, the other five being registered one in the name of each of the five directors. There were five directors of the Waste company and they were all directors of the claimants, and they all executed a declaration of trust for the share which they held, stating they held them in trust for the claimants. At no time did the board get any remuneration from the Waste company. The new company purported to carry on the Waste business in this sense, that their name was placed upon the premises, and on the note-paper, invoices etc. It was an apparent carrying on by the Waste company. I think that these two facts are of the greatest importance. There was no agreement of any kind made between the two companies, and the business was never assigned to the Waste company. There was no suggestion that anything was done to transfer the beneficial ownership of it to the Waste company. A manager was appointed, doubtless by the company, but there was no staff. The books and accounts were all kept by the claimants; the Waste company had no books at all and the manager, it is found, knew nothing at all about what was in the books, and had no access to them. There is no doubt that the claimants had complete control of the operations of the Waste company. Then other businesses were bought by the claimants, but they were not assigned to the Waste company; the Waste company just carried them on. There was no tenancy agreement of any sort with the company; they were just there in name. No rent was paid. Apart from the name, it was really as if the manager was managing a department of the company.

Those being the facts, the corporation rest their contention on *Salomon's* case[1] and their argument is that the Waste company was a distinct legal entity. It was in occupation of the premises, the business was being carried on in its name and the claimants' only interest in law was that of holders of the shares. It is well settled that the mere fact that a man holds all the shares in a company does not make the business carried on by that company his business, nor does it make the company his agents for the carrying on of the business. That proposition is just as true if the shareholder is itself a limited company. It is also well settled that there may be such an arrangement between the shareholders and a company as will constitute the company the shareholders' agent for the purpose of carrying on the business and make the business the business of the shareholders. In *Gramophone & Typewriter Ltd v Stanley*[2] Cozens-Hardy MR said:

> 'The fact that an individual by himself or his nominees holds practically all the shares in a company may give him the control of the company in the sense that it may enable him by exercising his voting powers to turn out the directors and to enforce his own views as to policy, but it does not in any way diminish the rights or powers of the directors, or make the property or assets of the company his, as distinct from the corporation's. Nor does it make any difference if he acquires not practically the whole, but absolutely the whole, of the shares. The business of the company does not thereby become his business. He is still entitled to receive dividends on his shares, but no more. I do not doubt that a person in that position may cause such an arrangement to be entered into between himself and the company as will suffice to constitute the company his agent for the purpose of carrying on the business, and thereupon the business will become, for all taxing purposes, his business. Whether this consequence follows is in each case a matter of fact. In the present case I am unable to discover anything in addition to the holding of the shares which in any way supports this conclusion.'

---

1 [1897] AC 22; 66 LJ Ch 35
2 [1908] 2 KB 89; 77 LJ KB 834

Then Fletcher Moulton LJ, said the same thing on pp 100 and 101. Then in *Inland Revenue Comrs v Sansom*[1] Lord Sterndale said:

> 'There may, as has been said by Lord Cozens-Hardy MR, be a position such that although there is a legal entity within the principle of *Salomon v Salomon & Co*, that legal entity may be acting as the agent of an individual and may really be doing his business and not its own at all. Apart from the technical question of agency it is difficult to see how that could be, but it is conceivable. Therefore the mere fact that the case is one which falls within *Salomon v Salomon & Co* is not of itself conclusive.'

It seems therefore to be a question of fact in each case, and those cases indicate that the question is whether the subsidiary was carrying on the business as the company's business or as its own. I have looked at a number of cases — they are all revenue cases — . . . and I find six points which were deemed relevant for the determination of the question: Who was really carrying on the business? In all the cases, the question was whether the company, an English company here, could be taxed in respect of all the profits made by some other company, a subsidiary company, being carried on elsewhere. The first point was: Were the profits treated as the profits of the company? — when I say 'the company' I mean the parent company — secondly, were the persons conducting the business appointed by the parent company? Thirdly was the company the head and the brain of the trading venture? Fourthly, did the company govern the adventure, decide what should be done and what capital should be embarked on the venture? Fifthly, did the company make the profits by its skill and direction? Sixthly, was the company in effectual and constant control?

. . .

. . . Indeed, if every one company can be said to be the agent or employee, or tool or simulacrum of another, I think the Waste company was in this case a legal entity, because that is all it was. There was nothing to prevent the claimants at any moment saying: 'We will carry on this business in our own name.' They had but to paint out the Waste company's name on the premises, change their business paper and form, and the thing would have been done. I am satisfied that the business belonged to the claimants; they were, in my view, the real occupiers of the premises. If either physically or technically the Waste company was in occupation, it was for the purposes of the service it was rendering to the claimants, such occupation was necessary for that service, and I think that those facts would make that occupation in law the occupation of the claimants.

SOURCE 34
Re FG Films Ltd
(Chancery Division 1953) [1953] 1 WLR 483; [1953] 1 All ER 615

By this summons the applications sought a declaration (1) that they were the 'maker' of the film 'Monsoon' within the meaning of the Act[2] and of the amending Act of 1948;[3] (2) that throughout the time when the film was being made they were a British company within the meaning of the Act; and (3) that the maker of the film was, throughout the time that it was being made, a British company, namely, the applicants.

. . .

---

1 [1921] 2 KB 492
2 Cinematograph Films Act 1938
3 Cinematograph Films Act 1948

VAISEY J: The applicants have a capital of £100, divided into 100 shares of £1 each, 90 of which are held by the American director and the remaining 10 by a British one. The third director has no shareholding. I now understand that they have no place of business apart from their registered office, and they did not employ any staff. It seems to me to be contrary, not only to all sense and reason, but at the proved and admitted facts of the case, to say or to believe that this insignificant company undertook in any real sense of that word the arrangements for the making of this film. I think that their participation in any such undertaking was so small as to be practically negligible, and that they acted, in so far as they acted at all in the matter, merely as the nominee of and agent for an American company called Film Group Incorporated, which seems (among other things) to have financed the making of the film to the extent of at least £80,000 under the auspices and direction of the said American director who happened to be its president. The suggestion that the American company and that director were merely agents for the applicants is, to my mind, inconsistent with and contradicted by the evidence, and a mere travesty of the facts, as I understand and hold them to be.

The applicants' intervention in the matter was purely colourable. They were brought into existence for the sole purpose of being put forward as having undertaken the very elaborate arrangements necessary for the making of this film and of enabling it thereby to qualify as a British film. The attempt has failed, and the respondent's decision not to register 'Monsoon' as a British film was, in my judgment, plainly right.

In lieu of the declarations for which the applicants ask, I will declare that the applicants were not the makers of the film called 'Monsoon' and that that film is not a British film within the meaning of the Cinematograph Films Acts 1938 and 1948.

SOURCE 35
Lee *v* Lee's Air Farming Ltd
(Judicial Committee, Privy Council 1961) [1961] AC 12; [1960] 3 All ER 420

The company was incorporated in New Zealand. All shares issued, bar one, were allotted to Geofrey Lee, who was appointed the governing director and who also entered into a contract with the company under which he carried out his work as an aerial crop sprayer. He was killed in the course of this work and his widow brought a claim for compensation under the Worker's Compensation Act. To qualify for this payment, it had to be established that the deceased was a 'worker'. The New Zealand Court of Appeal found against Mrs Lee. The appeal to the Privy Council succeeded.

The substantial question which arises is, as their Lordships think, whether the deceased was a 'worker' within the meaning of the Worker's Compensation Act 1922, and its amendments. Was he a person who had entered into or worked under a contract of service with an employer? The Court of Appeal thought that his special position as governing director precluded him from being a servant of the company. On this view it is difficult to know what his status and position was when he was performing the arduous and skilful duties of piloting an aeroplane which belonged to the company and when he was carrying out the operation of top-dressing farm lands from the air. He was paid wages for so doing. The company kept a wages book in which these were recorded. The work that was being done was being done at the request of farmers whose contractual rights and obligations were with the company alone. It cannot be suggested that when engaged in the activities above referred to the deceased was discharging his duties as governing director. Their Lordships find it impossible to resist the conclusion that the active aerial operations were performed because the deceased was in some contractual relationship with the company. That relationship came about because the deceased as one legal person was willing to work for and to make a contract with the company which was another legal entity. A contractual relationship could only exist on the basis that there was consensus between two contracting parties. It was never suggested (nor in their Lordships' view could it reasonably have been suggested) that the company was a sham or a mere simulacrum. It is well established that the mere fact that someone is a director of a company is no impediment to his entering into a contract to serve the company. If, then, it be accepted that the respondent company was a legal entity their Lordships see no reason to challenge the validity of any contractual obligations which were created between the company and the deceased. In this connection reference may be made to a passage in the speech of Lord Halsbury LC in *Salomon v Salomon & Co:*[1] 'My Lords, the learned judges appear to me not to have been absolutely certain in their own minds whether to treat the company as a real thing or not. If it was a real thing; if it had a legal existence, and if consequently the law attributed to it certain rights and liabilities in its constitution as a company, it appears to me to follow as a consequence that it is impossible to deny the validity of the transactions into which it has entered.' A similar approach was evidenced in the speech of Lord MacNaghten.

. . .

In their Lordships' view it is a logical consequence of the decision in *Salomon*'s case that one person may function in dual capacities. There is no reason, therefore, to deny the possibility of a contractual relationship being created as between the deceased and the company. If this stage is reached then their lordships see no reason why the range of possible contractual relationships should not include a contract for services, and if the deceased as agent for the company could negotiate a contract for services as between the company and himself there is no reason why a contract of service could not also be negotiated.

. . .

SOURCE 36
Tunstall *v* Steigmann
(Court of Appeal 1962) [1962] 2 QB 593; [1962] 2 All ER 417

The landlord (Steigmann) opposed the grant of a new tenancy to the tenant (Tunstall) on the grounds that she (Steigmann) intended 'to occupy the-. . . premises for the purpose of a business to be carried on by her thereat'.[2] In fact the business was owned by a company in which the landlord held all but two of the shares (which two were held by nominees for the landlord). This was an appeal against the decision of the county court judge who rejected the tenant's claim for a new tenancy. The Court of Appeal reversed the decision of the county court.

ORMEROD LJ: . . . It becomes necessary to consider section 30(1) of the Landlord and Tenant Act 1954. The subsection in question sets out the grounds

---

1 [1897] AC 22; 66 LJ Ch 35
2 A ground on which a claim for a renewal of the tenancy could be resisted, s 30(1)(g) of the Landlord and Tenant Act 1954

upon which a landlord may oppose an application for a new tenancy, and paragraphs (*f*) and (*g*) of that subsection deal with the grounds which a landlord may put forward as showing his intention with regard to the property. Paragraph (*f*) deals with the landlord's intention at the termination of the current tenancy to demolish or reconstruct the premises comprised in the holding and is not relevant in this appeal. Paragraph (*g*) is the one which was relied upon by the landlord in this case and is as follows: 'Subject as hereinafter provided, that on the termination of the current tenancy the landlord intends to occupy the holding for the purpose, or partly for the purposes, of a business to be carried on by him therein, or as his residence.' There is no question, of course, of the premises being required here as a residence for the landlord, and the only question to be considered is whether it was the intention of the landlord to occupy the holding for the purposes of a business to be carried on by her therein. I have formed the view that in these circumstances it cannot be said that it is the intention of the landlord to carry on the business. It was decided in *Salomon v Salomon & Co Ltd*[1] that a company and the individual or individuals forming a company were separate legal entities, however complete the control might be by one or more of those individuals over the company. That is the whole principle of the formation of limited liability companies and it would be contrary to the scheme of the Companies Act to depart from that principle. It has been contended in this case that a realistic view should be taken of the circumstances. It is submitted that any person in the street would say that the business was the landlord's business, notwithstanding that it was being carried on by a limited company, and that in those circumstances it should be held that the provisions of paragraph (*g*), to which I have referred should be considered to be satisfied. That, I think, is a dangerous doctrine. It may be that in practice the landlord will continue to carry on the business as it has been carried on in the past when she was undoubtedly the proprietor of it. It may be that she will derive a profit or otherwise from the business as she has done in the past. But the fact remains that she has disposed of her business to a limited company. It is the limited company which will carry on the business in the future, and if she acts as the manager of the business, it is for and on behalf of the limited company. In my judgment the fact that she holds virtually the whole of the shares in the limited company and has complete control of its affairs makes no difference to this proposition. The object of a limited liability company, as I understand it, is that the shareholders shall have some protection and some limit to the liability which they may incur in the event of the company being unsuccessful. It is to be assumed that the landlord in this case assigned her business to the limited company for some good reason which she considered to be of an advantage to her. She cannot say that in a case of this kind she is entitled to take the benefit of any advantages that the formation of a company gave to her, without at the same time accepting the liabilities arising therefrom. She cannot say that she is carrying on the business or intends to carry on the business in the sense intended by paragraph (*g*) of the subsection and at the same time say that her liability is limited as provided by the Companies Acts.

It has been argued in the course of this case that there have been a number of departures from the principle of *Salomon v Salomon & Co Ltd* in order that the courts may give effect to what has been described as the reality of the situation, and it is submitted in these circumstances that the court should look at the realities of the situation and that those realities are that the business will in future

1 [1897] AC 22; 66 LJ Ch 35

be carried on by the landlord as it has been carried on in the past. We were referred to *In re Yenidje Tobacco Co Ltd*[1] where the Master of the Rolls dealt with a point in his judgment, the effect of which was that the court would look behind the fact of incorporation if the incorporation was in reality the incorporation of a partnership and would treat the matter for the purposes of winding-up as though it were a partnership. We were also referred to a number of cases arising under the Trading with the Enemy legislation of the 1914–18 war, where unquestionable companies registered in this country were treated as enemy aliens, particularly were we referred to *Daimler Co Ltd v Continental Tyre & Rubber (Great Britain) Ltd.*[2] In addition it was submitted that in allying the Rent Restriction Acts the court has always looked to the reality of the transaction and would not allow the purpose of the Acts to be defeated by the use of the Companies Acts.

. . .

Whilst it may be argued that in the above circumstances the courts have departed from a strict observance of the principle laid down in *Salomon v Salomon & Co Ltd*, it is true to say that any departure, if indeed any of the instances given can be treated as a departure, has been made to deal with special circumstances when a limited company might well be a facade concealing the real facts. Counsel was unable to point to any special circumstances in this case other than that the landlord has complete control of the company. In my judgment that is not enough, I see no reason to depart from well-established principles, and I would allow the appeal.

WILLMER LJ: . . . I have certainly felt the force of the argument on behalf of the landlord; but in the end I am satisfied that it cannot prevail. There is no escape from the fact that a company is a legal entity entirely separate from its corporators — see *Salomon v Salomon & Co.* Here the landlord and her company are entirely separate entities. This is no matter of form; it is a matter of substance and reality. Each can sue and be sued in its own right; indeed, there is nothing to prevent the one from suing the other. Even the holder of 100 per cent of the shares in a company does not by such holding become so identified with the company that he or she can be said to carry on the business of the company. This clearly appears from *Gramophone & Typewriter Co Ltd v Stanley*,[3] a decision of this court which seems to me, on due consideration, to be destructive of the argument for the landlord. As was pointed out by Fletcher Moulton LJ control of a company by a corporator is wholly different in fact and law from carrying on the business himself. 'The individual corporator does not carry on the business of the corporation.' This being so, I do not see how it is possible for the landlord in the present case to assert that she intends to occupy the holding for the purpose of a business to be carried on by her. Her intention, as has been made plain, is that the company which she controls shall carry on its business on the holding. But that, unfortunately for her, is something for which the Act makes no provision.

. . .

For these reasons I feel driven to the conclusion that the judge's decision cannot be supported in law. I do not think that the landlord here brings herself within section 30(1)(g) by proving an intention to occupy through the medium of the company which she controls. She cannot, therefore, successfully oppose the grant of a new tenancy.

---

1 [1916] 2 Ch 426; 86 LJ Ch 1
2 [1916] 2 AC 307; 85 LJ KB 1333
3 [1908] 2 KB 89; 77 LJ KB 834

I have reached this conclusion with some reluctance, for it seems to me that the construction of section 30(1)(g), which I have felt compelled to adopt, may well lead to some very bizarre results. Thus it will be possible for an absentee landlord, living in idleness away from the holding, to resist the grant of a new tenancy upon proof of an intention to occupy, through his agent or manager, for the purposes of carrying on his business through such agent or manager. On the other hand, a hard-working landlord, who has transferred his business to a company of which he retains complete control, and who genuinely needs to obtain possession of the holding so that his company's business may be carried on there with the aid of his own labour, will nevertheless apparently be without any right to oppose an application for a new tenancy by a tenant however undeserving. It seems, however, impossible to escape the conclusion that this is the effect of what Parliament has enacted. If the results are thought undesirable, only Parliament can put that right.[1]

SOURCE 37
Jones *v* Lipman
(Chancery Division 1962) [1962] 1 WLR 832; [1962] 1 All ER 422

The defendant agreed to sell his house to the plaintiff. In breach of that agreement, the defendant transferred the house to a company over which he had complete control. This was an action against the defendant and the company for specific performance of the contract.

RUSSELL J: When the matter came on again in chambers the affidavit evidence by the first defendant made it plain (i) that the defendant company was, and at all material times had been, under the complete control of the first defendant, and (ii) that the acquisition of the defendant company by the first defendant and the transfer to it of the real property comprised in the contract with the plaintiffs (for the chattels remained in the ownership of the first defendant) was carried through solely for the purpose of defeating the plaintiffs' rights to specific performance and in order to leave them to claim such damages, if any, as they might establish. So much was, quite rightly, admitted by counsel for the defendants.

For the plaintiffs the argument was twofold. First, that specific performance would be ordered against a party to a contract who has it in his power to compel another person to convey the property in question; and that admittedly the first defendant had this power over the defendant company. Second, that specific performance would also, in circumstances such as the present, be ordered against the defendant company.

For the second proposition reference was made to *Gilford Motor Co Ltd v Horne*.[2]

[Russell J quoted from the judgments of Lord Hanworth MR and Lawrence and Romer LJJ in that case — see p 100 — and continued:]

Those comments on the relationship between the individual and the company apply even more forcibly to the present case. The defendant company is the creature of the first defendant, a device and a sham, a mask which he holds before his face in an attempt to avoid recognition by the eye of equity. The case

---

1 Which it did; s 6 of the Law of Property Act 1969
2 [1933] Ch 935; 102 LJ Ch 21

cited[1] illustrates that an equitable remedy is rightly to be granted directly against the creature in such circumstances.

SOURCE 38
Littlewoods Mail Order Stores *v* IRC
(Court of Appeal 1969)
[1969] 1 WLR 1241; [1969] 3 All ER 855

LORD DENNING MR: Littlewoods Mail Order Stores Ltd carry on a big business at Jubilee House in Oxford Street. In 1947 the building was bought by Oddfellows Friendly Society for £605,000. The Oddfellows let it to Littlewoods on a 99-year lease at a rent of £23,444 a year. That rent gave the Oddfellows a return of only $3\frac{7}{8}$ per cent on their outlay. During the next 11 years the value of money got much less. In 1958 the building was worth about £2,000,000 if sold with vacant possession. And the rent obtainable on a tenancy from year to year granted in 1958 would be £60,000 a year. Yet Littlewoods had a lease with another 88 years to go at a rent of £23,444.

Such being the position, in 1958 the advisers of Oddfellows and Littlewoods carried through a deal which was designed to confer a considerable advantage on both of them. It came to this: the Oddfellows transferred the freehold in Jubilee House to the Fork Manufacturing Co Ltd, which was a wholly-owned subsidiary of Littlewoods. The Fork Company let Jubilee House to the Oddfellows for 22 years and 10 days at a rent of £6 a year. The Oddfellows granted an underlease to Littlewoods for 22 years at a rent of £42,450 a year. The result was that Littlewoods gave up their lease for 88 years at a rent of £23,444 and took instead a lease from the Oddfellows for 22 years at £42,450: and, in addition, Littlewoods through their wholly-owned subsidiary, the Fork Manufacturing Co Ltd, at the end of the 22 years, would have the entire freehold in hand in possession. In return the Oddfellows received a rent of £42,450 for 22 years and then lost all interest in the premises.

The deal was designed to advantage both in this way: on the one hand Oddfellows would receive a rent of £42,450 a year for 22 years, which would be clear of tax as they were a charity. On the other hand, Littlewoods would claim to deduct the full rent of £42,450 from their profits instead of the smaller sum of £23,444. So they would escape a lot of tax. The deal would be to the advantage of both sides, at the expense of the revenue.

The question was whether the additional 'rent' paid by Littlewoods constituted a payment for the acquisition of a capital asset and, therefore, could not be set off against profits. In *Inland Revenue Commissioners v Land Securities Investments*,[2] the House of Lords decided that rent charges could not be debited against incomings where the rent charges constituted the down-price for the acquisition of a capital asset. Here, however, the acquisition would be by the Fork Manufacturing Co Ltd, a wholly owned subsidiary of Littlewoods, not by Littlewoods itself.

That case[3] would be virtually indistinguishable from the present case but for the interposition in this case of the wholly-owned subsidiary, Fork Manufacturing Co Ltd. If that subsidiary were identified with Littlewoods so as to be one with Littlewoods, the net result of the transaction would be that Littlewoods would give up the 88 years outstanding at £23,444 a year, and would get instead the

---

1 *Gilford Motor Co v Horne*
2 [1969] 1 WLR 604; [1969] 2 All ER 430
3 *Inland Revenue Commissioners v Land Securities Investments*

freehold of Jubilee House, paying therefor a rent of £42,450 a year for 22 years. The case would then be on a par with the *Land Securities* case. Littlewoods would acquire the freehold of Jubilee House (a capital asset) by means of paying an extra £19,006 a year (£42,450 less £23,444) for 22 years, and nothing thereafter. The extra £19,006 would be paid for the capital asset and not be deductible. Mr Heyworth Talbot was inclined to agree that the cases would be indistinguishable; but he said that the interposition of the Fork Manufacturing Co Ltd made all the difference, albeit it was a wholly-owned subsidiary of Littlewoods. He said that the Fork Manufacturing Co Ltd was to be regarded as a separate and independent entity, just as if its shares were owned by someone quite unconnected with Littlewoods. In that case the freehold of Jubilee House would be acquired by the Fork Manufacturing Co Ltd. Littlewoods would have acquired no capital assets at all. They would be able to deduct the whole £42,450 a year.

I cannot accept this argument. I decline to treat the Fork Manufacturing Co Ltd as a separate and independent entity. The doctrine laid down in *Salomon v Salomon & Co*[1] has to be watched very carefully. It has often been supposed to cast a veil over the personality of a limited company through which the courts cannot see. But that is not true. The courts can and often do draw aside the veil. They can, and often do, pull off the mask. They look to see what really lies behind. The legislature has shown the way with group accounts and the rest. And the courts should follow suit. I think that we should look at the Fork Manufacturing Co Ltd and see it as it really is — the wholly owned subsidiary of Littlewoods. It is the creature, the puppet, of Littlewoods, in point of *fact*: and it should be so regarded in point of *law*. The basic fact here is that Littlewoods, through their wholly-owned subsidiary, have acquired a capital asset — the freehold of Jubilee House: and they have acquired it by paying an extra £19,006 a year. So regarded, the case is indistinguishable from the *Land Securities* case. Littlewoods are not entitled to deduct this extra £19,006 in computing their profits.

SOURCE 39
Wallersteiner *v* Moir
(Court of Appeal 1974) [1974] 1 WLR 991; [1974] 3 All ER 217

The plaintiff instituted a libel claim against the defendant. The court below struck out the claim. The defendant presented a counter-claim on behalf of the company for compensation for the losses suffered by the company as a result of the plaintiff's fraudulent activities. The plaintiff sought to have the counter-claim struck out but failed. The Court of Appeal dismissed the appeals against the striking out of the libel proceedings and against the refusal to strike out the counter-claim. In this extract, the Court of Appeal is describing two of the allegedly fraudulent activities.

LORD DENNING . . .

11. *The corporate veil*
It is plain that Dr Wallersteiner used many companies, trusts, or other legal entities as if they belonged to him. He was in control of them as much as any 'one-man company' is under the control of the one man who owns all the shares and is the chairman and managing director. He made contracts of enormous magnitude on their behalf on a sheet of note-paper without reference to anyone else. Such as a contract on behalf of the Rothschild Trust to buy shares for £518,786 15s. or to vary it; or a contract on behalf of Stawa A.G. for a commission

1 [1897] AC 22; 66 LJ Ch 35

of £235,000. He used their moneys as if they were his own. When money was paid to him for shares which he himself owned beneficially, he banked it in the name of I.F.T. of Nassau. Such as the £50,000 for the shares in Watford Chemical Co. When he paid out money on personal loans by himself, he drew the cheques on the account in the name of I.F.T. Such as the £125,000 lent to Camp Bird to pay off the Pearl charge. His concerns always used as their bankers the Anglo-Continental Exchange Ltd, the merchant bank of which he was chairman and which he effectively controlled.

Mr Browne-Wilkinson, as *amicus curiae*, suggested that all these various concerns were used by Dr Wallersteiner as a façade: so that each could be treated as his alter ego. Each was in reality Dr Wallersteiner wearing another hat.

Mr Lincoln, for Dr Wallersteiner, repudiated this suggestion. It was quite wrong, he said, to pierce the corporate veil. The principle enunciated in *Salomon v Salomon & Co Ltd*[1] was sacrosanct. If we were to treat each of these concerns as being Dr Wallersteiner himself under another hat, we should not, he said, be lifting a corner of the corporate veil. We should be sending it up in flames.

I am prepared to accept that the English concerns — those governed by English company law or its counterparts in Nassau or Nigeria — were distinct legal entities. I am not so sure about the Liechtenstein concerns — such as the Rothschild Trust, the Cellpa Trust or Stawa A.G. There was no evidence before us to Liechtenstein law. I will assume, too, that they were distinct legal entities, similar to an English limited company. Even so, I am quite clear that they were just the puppets of Dr Wallersteiner. He controlled their every movement. Each danced to his bidding. He pulled the strings. No one else got within reach of them. Transformed into legal language, they were his agents to do as he commanded. He was the principal behind them. I am of the opinion that the court should pull aside the corporate veil and treat these concerns as being his creatures — for whose doings he should be, and is, responsible. At any rate, it was up to him to show that any one else had a say in their affairs and he never did so: cf. *Gilford Motor Co Ltd v Horne*.[2] [See Source 32 at p 100.]

. . .

13. *Section 190*

Section 190 of the Companies Act 1948 says:

> 'It shall not be lawful for a company to make a loan to any person who is its director or a director of its holding company, or to enter into any guarantee or provide any security in connection with a loan made to such a person as aforesaid by any other person . . . '[3]

This section, be it noted, speaks only of a loan to 'any person who is its director.' Suppose the company makes a loan to another company which is wholly owned by the director. Is that lawful or unlawful? If it were lawful, it would be an easy way of getting round the section. Yet where is the line to be drawn? Suppose the director does not own 100 per cent of the shares, but 90 per cent or 51 per cent. In my opinion if the company is the creature of the director — his puppet — the loan should be treated as a loan to him. Such was certainly the case here with the loans to I.F.T., which was the puppet of Dr Wallersteiner.

There was, therefore a breach of section 190 in that the loans of £284,981 11s 4d and £50,000 to I.F.T. were loans to Dr Wallersteiner as it was his puppet.

The loans would be unlawful under section 190. He would be guilty of a

---

1 [1897] AC 22; 66 LJ Ch 35
2 [1933] Ch 935; 102 LJ Ch 21
3 See now s 330 of the Companies Act 1985

misfeasance and liable to indemnifying the company against any loss arising therefrom.

SOURCE 40
DHN Food Distributors Ltd *v* Tower Hamlets London Borough Council
(Court of Appeal 1976) [1976] 1 WLR 852; [1976] 3 All ER 462

LORD DENNING MR: This case might be called the 'Three in one.' Three companies in one. Alternatively, the 'One in three.' One group of three companies. For the moment I will speak of it as 'the firm.' In 1963 at Bow in the east end of London there was a firm of grocery and provision merchants. It imported groceries and provisions and distributed them to shopkeepers. It had a warehouse in Malmesbury Road. The firm had lorries which collected goods from the docks: and distributed them to shopkeepers. Soon afterwards the firm developed a 'cash and carry' business. Private individuals came by car. They brought substantial quantities wholesale. They paid for them in cash and carried them away.

Six years later in 1969 Tower Hamlets London Borough Council made a compulsory purchase order. They wanted to acquire the property of the firm, to demolish the warehouse, and to build houses on the site. In February 1970 there was a local inquiry. The firm made strong objection. They said that if the property was taken, it would mean the end of their business. The acquiring authority realised that the firm would lose its business, but they said that the housing requirements took priority and that the firm would receive compensation for any loss.

The inspector accepted the view of the acquiring authority. He said in his report:

> 'Whatever the cost may be (of acquisition) it would be seen against the gain in housing accommodation which would result from the residential development of the application site.'

So he recommended the implementation of the compulsory purchase order. It was confirmed by the Minister in his decision letter of 12 October 1970. The acquiring authority acted quickly. On 30 October 1970, they gave a notice to treat and a notice of entry. The firm tried to find other accommodation so as to move their business there, but finding none, the business had to be closed down.

Now comes the point. It is about compensation. Compensation under the statute is to be made for the value of the land and also compensation for disturbance of the business: see section 5(2) and (6) of the Land Compensation Act 1961.

If the firm and its property had all been in one ownership, it would have been entitled to compensation under those two heads: first, the value of the land, which has been assessed in excess of £360,000. Second, compensation for disturbance in having its business closed down. The figure has not yet been assessed. But the firm and its property were not in one ownership. It was owned by three companies. The business was owned by the parent company, D.H.N. Food Distributors Ltd. The land was owned at the time of acquisition by a subsidiary, called Bronze Investments Ltd. The vehicles were owned by another subsidiary, D.H.N. Food Transport Ltd. The parent company D.H.N. held all the shares both in the Bronze company and in the Transport company. The directors were the same in all three companies. As the result of the business having to be closed down, all the three companies are in liquidation.

The question is: what is the effect of the firm being in truth the three companies? The acquiring authority say that the owners of the land were Bronze Investments Ltd, and that company are entitled to the value of the land £360,000. They have actually been paid it. But the acquiring authority say that that company are not entitled to compensation for disturbance because they were not disturbed at all. The authority admit that D.H.N. (who ran the business) and the Transport subsidiary (who owned the vehicles) were greatly disturbed in their business. But the acquiring authority say that those two companies are not entitled to any compensation at all, not even for disturbance, because they had no interest in the land, legal or equitable. They say that in 1970 D.H.N. were only licensees of Bronze, the subsidiary which owned the land: and D.H.N. being licensees only, with no interest in the land, their only claim was under section 20(1) of the Compulsory Purchase Act 1965. That section says that if a person has no greater interest than a tenant from year to year in the land, then he is only entitled to compensation for that lesser interest. Seeing that a licensee can be turned out on short notice, the compensation payable to D.H.N. would be negligible.

The strange thing about the case is this, that the acquiring authority admit that at any time from February 1970, during the local inquiry and afterwards (right up to the time in October 1970 when the council gave notice to treat) the people running these three companies could have put their house in order so as to make the claim impregnable. All they had to do was to take a very simple step. Being in control of all three companies, they could have arranged for Bronze to convey the land to D.H.N.

. . .

Third, lifting the corporate veil. A further very interesting point was raised by Mr Dobry[1] on company law. We all know that in many respects a group of companies are treated together for the purpose of general accounts, balance sheet, and profit and loss account. They are treated as one concern. Professor Gower in *Modern Company Law* (3rd edn 1969), p 216 says:

> 'there is evidence of a general tendency to ignore the separate legal entities of various companies within a group, and to look instead at the economic entity of the whole group.'

. . . This is especially the case when a parent company owns all the shares of the subsidiaries — so much so that it can control every movement of the subsidiaries. These subsidiaries are bound hand and foot to the parent company and must do just what the parent company says. A striking instance is the decision of the House of Lords in *Harold Holdsworth & Co (Wakefield) Ltd v Caddies.*[2] So here. This group is virtually the same as the partnership in which all the three companies are partners. They should not be treated separately so as to be defeated on a technical point. They should not be deprived of the compensation which should justly be payable for disturbance. The three companies should, for present purposes, be treated as one, and the parent company D.H.N. should be treated as that one. So D.H.N. are entitled to claim compensation accordingly. It was not necessary for them to go through a conveyancing device to get it.

GOFF LJ . . . this is a case in which one is entitled to look at the realities of the situation and to pierce the corporate veil. I wish to safeguard myself by saying that so far as this ground is concerned, I am relying on the facts of this particular case. I would not at this juncture accept that in every case where one has a group of

---

1 Counsel for the companies
2 [1955] 1 WLR 352; [1955] 1 All ER 725

companies one is entitled to pierce the veil, but in this case the two subsidiaries were both wholly owned; further, they had no separate business operations whatsoever; thirdly, in my judgment, the nature of the question involved is highly relevant, namely, whether the owners of this business have been disturbed in their possession and enjoyment of it.

I find support for this view in a number of cases from which I would make a few brief citations, first from *Harold Holdsworth & Co (Wakefield) Ltd v Caddies*, where Lord Reid said:

> 'It was argued that the subsidiary companies were separate legal entities each under the control of its own board of directors, that in law the board of the appellant company could not assign any duties to anyone in relation to the management of the subsidiary companies and that therefore the agreement cannot be construed as entitling them to assign any such duties to the respondent.
>
> My Lords, in my judgment this is too technical an argument. This is an agreement in re mercatoria and it must be construed in light of the facts and realities of the situation. The appellant company owned the whole share capital of British Textile Manufacturing Co Ltd and under the agreement of 1947 the directors of this company were to be the nominees of the appellants. So, in fact, the appellants could control the internal management of their subsidiary companies, and, in the unlikely event of there being any difficulty, it was only necessary to go through formal procedure in order to make the decision of the appellants' board fully effective.'

That particular passage is, I think, especially cogent having regard to the fact that Mr Eyre[1] was constrained to admit that in this case, if they had thought of it soon enough, D.H.N. could, as it were, by moving the pieces on their chess board, have put themselves in a position in which the question would have been wholly unarguable.

I also refer to *Scottish Co-operative Wholesale Society Ltd v Meyer.*[2]
That was a case under section 210 of the Companies Act 1948, and Viscount Simonds said:

> 'I do not think that my own views could be stated better than in the late Lord President Cooper's words on the first hearing in this case. "In my view," he said, "the section warrants the court in looking at the business realities of a situation and does not confine them to a narrow legalistic view."'

My third citation is from the judgment of Danckwerts LJ in *Merchandise Transport Ltd v British Transport Commission,*[3] . . . where he said:

> '[the cases] show that where the character of a company, or the nature of the persons who control it, is a relevant feature the court will go behind the mere status of the company as a legal entity, and will consider who are the persons as shareholders or even as agents who direct and control the activities of a company which is incapable of doing anything without human assistance.'

---

1 Counsel for the acquiring Authority
2 [1959] AC 324; [1958] 3 All ER 66
3 [1962] 2 QB 173, 206–207; [1961] 3 All ER 495, 518

SOURCE 41
Woolfson *v* Strathclyde Regional Council
(House of Lords on appeal from the Scottish Court of Session 1978)
(1979) 38 P&CR 521; 1977 SC 84

LORD KEITH OF KINKEL: . . . A compulsory purchase order made in 1966 by
Glasgow Corporation, the respondents' predecessors as highway authority in that
city, provided for the acquisition of certain shop premises in St George's Road,
the date of entry being 29 January 1968. Numbers 57 and 59–61 St George's
Road were owned by the first-named appellant Solomon Woolfson ('Woolfson')
and numbers 53–55 were owned by the second-named appellant Solfred Holdings Ltd ('Solfred'), the shares in which at all material times were held as to two-
thirds by Woolfson and as to the remaining one third by his wife. The whole of
the shop premises was occupied by a company called M. & L. Campbell
(Glasgow) Ltd ('Campbell') and used by it for the purpose of its business as
costumiers specialising in wedding garments. The issued share capital of Campbell was 1000 shares, of which 999 were held by Woolfson and one by his wife.
Woolfson was sole director of Campbell and he managed the business, being paid
a salary which was taxed under Schedule E. His wife also worked for Campbell
and provided valuable expertise. Campbell was throughout shown in the
valuation roll as the occupier of the shop premises, but its occupation was not
regulated by lease or any other kind of formal arrangement. Draft leases were at
one time prepared, but they were never put into operation. From 1952 until
1963, when Schedule A taxation was abolished, payments by way of rent for
numbers 59–61 St George's Road were credited to Woolfson in Campbell's books.
No rent was ever paid or credited in respect of number 57 St George's Road.
From 1962 till 1968 Campbell paid rent to Solfred in respect of numbers 53–55
St George's Road. Various financial arrangements were entered into between
Woolfson and Campbell, but it is unnecessary to go into the details of these.
There can be no doubt, and it is not now disputed by the appellants, that
Campbell was throughout the occupier of the shop premises and that the
business carried on there was that of Campbell.

In these circumstances, the appellants jointly claimed a sum of £80,000 as
compensation for the value of the heritage under section 12(2) of the Land
Compensation (Scotland) Act 1963 and a further sum of £95,469 in respect of
disturbance under section 12(6) of that Act. The lands tribunal held a preliminary proof restricted to the matter of the appellants' right to claim compensation
for disturbance, and on 13 May 1975 issued an order finding that the appellants
had no such right. A special case was at their request stated for the opinion of the
Court of Session, and on 3 December 1976 the Second Division (Lord Justice-
Clerk Wheatley, Lords Johnston and Leechman) affirmed the decision of the
lands tribunal.

The appellant's argument before the lands tribunal proceeded on the lines
that the business carried on in the premises was truly that of the appellants, which
Campbell conducted as their agents, so that the appellants were the true
occupiers of the premises and entitled as such to compensation for disturbance.
Reliance was placed on the decision of Atkinson J in *Smith, Stone & Knight Ltd v
Birmingham Corporation.*[1] Before the Second Division this line of argument was
abandoned, and the appellants instead contended that in the circumstances
Woolfson, Campbell and Solfred should all be treated as a single entity embodied
in Woolfson himself. This followed the refusal by the court to allow Campbell and

---

1 [1939] 4 All ER 116; 101 LT 371 (see p 102)

Mrs Woolfson to be joined as additional claimants in the proceedings. It was argued, with reliance on *D.H.N. Food Distributors Ltd v Tower Hamlets London Borough Council*,[1] that the court should set aside the legalistic view that Woolfson, Solfred and Campbell were each a separate legal persona, and concentrate attention upon the 'realities' of the situation, to the effect of finding that Woolfson was the occupier as well as the owner of the whole premises. This argument was rejected by the court for the reasons given in the opinion of the Lord Justice-Clerk. He approached the matter from the point of view of the principles upon which a court may be entitled to ignore the separate legal status of a limited company and its incorporators, which as held in *Salomon v Salomon & Co Ltd*[2] must normally receive full effect in relations between the company and persons dealing with it. He referred to a passage in the judgment of Ormerod LJ in *Tunstall v Steigmann*[3] . . . to the effect that any departure from a strict observance of the principles laid down in *Salomon* has been made to deal with special circumstances when a limited company might well be a facade concealing the true facts. Having examined the facts of the instant case, the Lord Justice-Clerk reached the conclusion that they did not substantiate but negatived the argument advanced in support of the 'unity' proposition and that the decision in the *D.H.N. Food Distributors* case was distinguishable.

It was maintained before this House that the conclusion of the Lord Justice-Clerk was erroneous. In my opinion the conclusion was correct, and I regard as unimpeachable the process of reasoning by which it was reached. I can see no grounds whatever, upon the facts found in the special case, for treating the company structure as a mere façade, nor do I consider that the *D.H.N. Food Distributors* case is, on a proper analysis, of assistance to the appellants' argument. The position there was that compensation for disturbance was claimed by a group of three limited companies associated in a wholesale grocery business. The parent company, D.H.N., carried on the business in the premises which were the subject of compulsory purchase. These premises were owned by Bronze, which had originally been the wholly-owned subsidiary of a bank which had advanced money for the purchase of the premises, but which had later become the wholly-owned subsidiary of D.H.N. Bronze [had] the same directors as D.H.N. and the premises were its only asset. It carried on no activities whatever. The third company, also a wholly owned subsidiary of D.H.N., owned as its only asset the vehicles used in the grocery business, and it too carried on no operations. The compulsory acquisition resulted in the extinction of the grocery business, since no suitable alternative premises could be found. It was held by the Court of Appeal (Lord Denning MR, Goff and Shaw LJJ) that the group was entitled to compensation for disturbance as owners of the business. The grounds for the decision were (1) that since D.H.N. was in a position to control its subsidiaries in every respect, it was proper to pierce the corporate veil and treat the group as a single economic entity for the purpose of awarding compensation for disturbance; (2) that if the companies were to be treated as separate entities, there was by necessary implication from the circumstances an agreement between D.H.N. and Bronze under which the former had an irrevocable licence to occupy the premises for as long as it wished, and that this gave D.H.N. a sufficient interest in the land to found a claim to compensation for disturbance; and (3) (per Goff and Shaw LJJ) that in the circumstances Bronze held the legal title to the

---

1 [1976] 1 WLR 852; [1976] 3 All ER 462 (see p 113)
2 [1897] AC 22; 66 LJ Ch 35 (see p 91)
3 [1962] 2 QB 593; [1962] 2 All ER 417 (see p 106)

premises in trust for D.H.N., which also sufficed to entitle D.H.N. to compensation for disturbance. It is the first of those grounds which alone is relevant for
present purposes. I have some doubts whether in this respect the Court of Appeal
properly applied the principle that it is appropriate to pierce the corporate veil
only where special circumstances exist indicating that it is a mere façade
concealing the true facts. Further, the decisions of this House in *Caddies v Harold
Holdsworth & Co (Wakefield) Ltd*[1] and *Meyer v Scottish Co-operative Wholesale Society
Ltd*,[2] which were founded on by Goff LJ in support of this ground of judgment
and, as to the first of them, to some extent also by Lord Denning MR, do not, with
respect, appear to me to be concerned with that principle. But however that may
be, I consider the *D.H.N. Food* case to be clearly distinguishable on its facts from
the present case. There the company that owned the land was the wholly-owned
subsidiary of the company that carried on the business. The latter was in
complete control of the situation as respects anything which might affect its
business, and there was no one but itself having any kind of interest or right as
respects the assets of the subsidiary. Here, on the other hand, the company that
carried on the business, Campbell, has no sort of control whatever over the
owners of the land, Solfred and Woolfson. Woolfson holds two-thirds only of the
shares in Solfred, and Solfred has no interest in Campbell. Woolfson cannot be
treated as beneficially entitled to the whole shareholding in Campbell, since it is
not found that the one share in Campbell held by his wife is held as his nominee.
In my opinion there is no basis consonant with principle upon which on the facts
of this case the corporate veil can be pierced to the effect of holding Woolfson to
be the true owner of Campbell's business or of the assets of Solfred.

SOURCE 42
Adams *v* Cape Industries plc
(Court of Appeal) [1990] BCLC 479

In three recent cases, the court has stressed the principle that associated
companies are to be treated as separate legal entities unless, in the words of
Lightman J in *Acatos & Hutcheson v Watson* [1995] 1 BCLC 218, 223:

> 'English law insists on recognition of the distinct legal personality of companies
> unless the relevant contract or legislation requires or permits a broad inter-
> pretation to be given to references to members of a group of companies or the
> legal personality is a mere facade or sham or unlawful device' (see *Adams v Cape
> Industries plc* . . .).

Here the judge approved the purchase by Company A of the entire share
capital of Company B (from members and associates of Company A) where
Company B's sole asset was a 29.4 per cent shareholding in Company A. If
Companies A and B had not been recognised as separate legal entities, the
proposed purchase of shares would have been treated as a purchase by one
company of its own shares, an act prohibited by the common law (*Trevor v
Whitworth*, see p 762) and statute (s 143 of the Companies Act 1985).

Similarly, in *National Dock Labour Board v Pinn & Wheeler Ltd* [1989] BCLC
647, where two separate companies were held by an industrial tribunal to
satisfy the definition of 'waterside' manufacturers by reason of the fact that
one company carried on its (non-manufacturing) business on the waterside

---

1 [1955] 1 WLR 352; [1955] 1 All ER 725
2 [1959] AC 324; [1958] 3 All ER 66

and the other carried on its manufacturing business away from the waterside, but both companies were controlled by a third company. In reversing this decision, Macpherson J said (at 651):

' ... where the companies are kept alive as separate legal entities for good commercial or historical reasons in order to keep the company's name fully alive and in order to maintain the loyalty of employees for example, and also probably to avoid redundancy and other problems, I see no reason why the veil should be pierced.'

But what is a 'good commercial reason'? Does the organisation of the group consisting of a parent and one or more subsidiary companies in such a way as to minimise the exposure to claims from creditors qualify as a 'good commercial reason'? And does it matter whether these claims arise voluntarily (ie by reason of a contract between the creditor and the subsidiary company) or involuntarily (ie where the conduct of the subsidiary constitutes a tort or breach of statutory duty or crime as a result of which the creditor suffers loss)? With that note, we will now consider the case of *Adams v Cape Industries plc.*

The plaintiffs in these proceedings are persons, or the personal representatives of persons, in whose favour awards of damages were made by the judgment, dated 12 September 1983, of the Honourable Judge Steger, a United States Federal District Court judge, in the District Court for the Eastern District of Texas, USA (the Tyler Court). The judgment was a default judgment against Cape Industries plc (Cape) and Capasco Ltd (Capasco), companies registered in England and the sole defendants in all the actions before this court. They had taken no part in the proceedings in which the judgment was made. The judgment was for the specific sums payable to individual plaintiffs set out in an appendix to the judgment: $US37,000 each for 67 plaintiffs; $60,000 each for 31 plaintiffs; $85,000 each for 47 plaintiffs and $120,000 each for 61 plaintiffs. The total of the individual awards was $15.654m and the awards were directed to bear interest at 9% from judgment until payment.

The awards were made in respect of claims for damages for personal injuries and consequential loss allegedly suffered by each plaintiff as a result of exposure to asbestos fibres emitted from the premises of a primary asbestos insulation factory in Owentown, Smith County, Texas, which was operated from 1954 to 1962 by Unarco Industries Inc (Unarco) and from 1962 to 1972 by Pittsburgh Corning Corporation (PCC). The basis of liability of Cape and Capasco was alleged to be negligent acts and omissions and breaches of implied and express warranties.

The relationship of Cape and Capasco to the emission of asbestos fibres from the Owentown factory was, in summary, that Cape owned the shares in subsidiary companies in South Africa which had mined the asbestos and in its subsidiary, Capasco. Capasco was concerned in organising the sale of asbestos, mined in South Africa, throughout the world to those who wished to use it in various industrial processes. Between 1953 and 1978 when it was dissolved, another subsidiary of Cape, North American Asbestos Corp (NAAC) assisted in the marketing of asbestos of the Cape group in the United States. The plaintiffs' contention was that the defendants had been responsible for the supply of asbestos fibres directly or indirectly to Unarco and PCC without giving proper warning of the dangers thereof.

. . .

The motions by Cape, Capasco and Egnep to dismiss the Tyler 1 proceedings as against them on the ground of lack of jurisdiction were dismissed by Judge Steger in August 1977. That dismissal was not final and it was open to the Cape companies to take the jurisdiction point at the trial of the action. They filed answers in which they pleaded to the merits of the claim while maintaining their objection to jurisdiction.

The number of claimants in the Tyler 1 proceedings had by mid 1977 risen to more than 400 and was still increasing. Trial was set for 12 September 1977. The purpose of Judge Steger in fixing that date included that of causing the parties to consider settlement. On 12 September 1977 settlement discussions proceeded in which Judge Steger took part in a manner which would be unusual, if not impossible, in this country but which was effective and normal under the United States system of civil justice. By 28 September 1977 a settlement figure of $20m was agreed for all the claimants who then numbered 462. On agreement of the settlement figure it was ordered that as from 28 September 1977 no further intervention in any of the Tyler 1 actions would be permitted.

. . .

On prohibition by the order of Judge Steger of further interventions in the Tyler 1 proceedings, new actions were commenced by claimants in what have been called the Tyler 2 proceedings. There were eight separate actions. They were assigned to Judge Steger. The first was commenced on 19 April 1978 and the last on 19 November 1979. There followed intervention by a very large number of claimants. Cape, Egnep and NAAC were defendants in all the actions. Capasco was a defendant in three only. PCC, PPG, Corning Glassworks Inc and OCAW, a trade union to which some claimants had belonged, were also defendants in all actions. The United States government was a defendant in some actions and third party defendant in others.

In December 1981 Judge Steger gave directions by which each claimant was required to provide specified information with reference to his claim 'on personal knowledge and attested to under penalty of perjury'. As a result of those directions, and of the response, or lack of response, thereto, a large number of claimants had their claims summarily dismissed 'without prejudice'. The number of plaintiffs left in the Tyler 2 actions was about 206. It is to be assumed that each of those remaining claimants had responded to the order of December 1981 by alleging some physical condition that was capable of having been caused by exposure to asbestos dust and of constituting an injury.

Cape, Capasco and Egnep took the decision to play no part in any of the Tyler 2 actions. They had initially regarded the Tyler 1 actions as having little more than nuisance value. They could not understand how tortious liability to the Owentown workers could be imposed on the Cape companies merely on the ground that Cape subsidiary companies had mined the asbestos and sold it into the United States. They had had expectations of success on their jurisdiction objection. They had, however, succumbed to the pressure for settlement. They were unwilling to be left as the only defendants in a large and expensive jury trial. Having joined in the settlement of the Tyler 1 actions the decided, since they had no assets in the United States, to take no part in the Tyler 2 proceedings; to allow default judgments to be obtained against them; and to defend any actions brought in this country for enforcement of any such judgment on the ground that, under the law of this country, the Tyler Court had no jurisdiction over Cape, Capasco or Egnep with reference to the claims of the claimants.

. . .

On 2 February 1983 Judge Steger approved the settlement of the Tyler 2 proceedings as against the settling defendants, and that approval extended to the fairness and reasonableness of the settlement in the case of any minor claimants. The trial date for the outstanding Tyler 2 claims against the United States was fixed for 22 June 1983. Settlement was discussed. An agreement of compromise dated 15 June 1983 was signed. The United States government contributed nothing directly to the claimants but, in settlement of their claims against the United States, it was agreed that the United States would bear the costs of enforcement of default judgments against Cape, Capasco and Egnep in the United Kingdom or in South Africa. It is in performance of that promise that these proceedings have been pursued in this country.

...

The issues at the trial before Scott J and his decision

The circumstances in which our courts will recognise a foreign court as competent to give a judgment in personam capable of enforcement in this country are stated thus in *Dicey & Morris, The Conflict of Laws* (11th edn, 1987) vol 1, pp 436–437:

> 'First Case — If the judgment debtor was, at the time the proceedings were instituted, resident (or, perhaps, present) in the foreign country.
>
> Second Case — If the judgment debtor was plaintiff in, or counter-claimed, in the proceedings in the foreign court.
>
> Third Case — If the judgment debtor, being a defendant in the foreign court, submitted to the jurisdiction of that court by voluntarily appearing in the proceedings.
>
> Fourth Case — If the judgment debtor, being a defendant in the original court, had before the commencement of the proceedings agreed, in respect of the subject matter of the proceedings, to submit to the jurisdiction of that court or of the courts of that country.'

At the trial the plaintiffs relied on three separate grounds for enforcement of the judgment of the Tyler court in England:

(1) that the defendants had voluntarily appeared in the proceedings in the Tyler court;

(2) that the defendants had, before the proceedings commenced, agreed to submit to the jurisdiction of the Tyler court;

(3) that the defendants were resident in the US at the time of the commencement of the plaintiffs' proceedings in the Tyler court.

(A fourth pleaded ground, referred to as 'comity or reciprocity', was not in the event relied on at the trial.)

Scott J concluded that the Tyler Court had been competent to give a judgment against Cape and Capasco on none of the three grounds relied on (*Dicey and Morris'* first, third and fourth cases). The plaintiffs' claim, therefore, failed for this reason, if no other.

However, the judge proceeded to consider certain additional points raised by the defendants by way of defence. The first point arose in this way. According to the case made for the plaintiffs, the presence (if any) of Cape and Capasco was in the State of Illinois where Cape's subsidiary, NAAC, had its office in Chicago from 1953 to 1978 when it was wound up; and where in the same building from 1978 onwards Continental Products Corp (CPC), also an Illinois corporation but not a subsidiary of Cape, carried out similar marketing functions in the United States for the sale of asbestos produced by Cape's South African subsidiaries. The plaintiffs did not contend that Cape or Capasco had been present in Texas. In these circumstances, the defendants contended that under English law presence in Illinois did not suffice to give the Tyler Court (a federal district court sitting in

Texas) jurisdiction to hear a claim in tort against the defendants governed by the law of Texas. This argument, which we will call '*the country issue*', Scott J rejected. He said that if he had felt able to conclude that Cape and Capasco were present in Illinois when the Tyler 2 actions were commenced, he would have held that to be a sufficient basis in English law for the exercise by the Tyler Court of jurisdiction over them.

. . .

On the basis of the findings of fact made by Scott J and the further facts which they submit he ought to have found, the plaintiffs in their amended notice of appeal submit that he was wrong to conclude that:

'(1) NAAC's business was its own business and not the business of Cape or Capasco (2) CPC . . . was . . . an independently owned company and carried on its own business; (3) As from January 31st 1978 NAAC ceased to act on behalf of any of the Cape companies or to carry on any business on its own account save for the purpose of liquidating its assets;
(4) Mr Morgan was in executive control of NAAC's conduct of its business.'

Two important inferences of fact made by the judge (nos (1) and (2)) and two important findings of primary fact (nos (3) and (4)) are thus challenged on this appeal. We shall consider contention (4) in the section of this judgment dealing with the 'single economic unit' argument and in the appendix. We shall consider the contention that CPC was 'not an independently owned company' in the section dealing with the 'corporate veil argument'. We shall consider contention (3) and the contentions that NAAC's business was not 'its own business' and that CPC's business was not 'its own business' in the section dealing with what we will call the 'agency' argument.

. . .

General principles derived from the authorities relating to the 'presence' issue
In relation to trading corporations, we derive the three following propositions from consideration of the many authorities cited to us relating to the 'presence' of and overseas corporation:

(1) The English court will be likely to treat a trading corporation incorporated under the law of one country ('an overseas corporation') as present within the jurisdiction of the courts of another country only if either (i) it has established and maintained at its own expense (whether as owner or lessee) a fixed place of business of its own in the other country and for more than a minimal period of time has carried on its own business at or from such premises by its servants or agents (a 'branch office' case), (ii) a representative of the overseas corporation has for more than a minimal period of time been carrying on *the overseas corporation's* business in the other country at or from some fixed place of business.

(2) In either of these two cases presence can only be established if it can fairly be said that the *overseas corporation's* business (whether or not together with the representative's own business) has been transacted at or from the fixed place of business. In the first case, this condition is likely to present few problems. In the second, the question whether the representative has been carrying on the overseas corporation's business or has been doing no more than carry on his own business will necessitate an investigation of the functions which he has been performing and all aspects of the relationship between him and the overseas corporation.

(3) In particular, but without prejudice to the generality of the foregoing, the

following questions are likely to be relevant on such investigation: (a) whether or not the fixed place of business from which the representative operates was originally acquired for the purpose of enabling him to act on behalf of the overseas corporation; (b) whether the overseas corporation has directly reimbursed him for (i) the cost of his accommodation at the fixed place of business; (ii) the cost of his staff; (c) what other contributions (if any) the overseas corporation makes to the financing of the business carried on by the representative; (d) whether the representative is remunerated by reference to transactions (eg by commission) or by fixed regular payments or in some other way; (e) what degree of control the overseas corporation exercises over the running of the business conducted by the representative; (f) whether the representative reserves (i) part of his accommodation, (ii) part of his staff for conducting business related to the overseas corporation; (g) whether the representative displays the overseas corporation's name at his premises or on his stationery, and if so, whether he does so in such a way as to indicate that he is a representative of the overseas corporation; (h) what business (if any) the representative transacts as principal exclusively on his own behalf; (i) whether the representative makes contracts with customers or other third parties in the name of the overseas corporation, or otherwise in such manner as to bind it; (j) if so, whether the representative requires specific authority in advance before binding the overseas corporation to contractual obligations.

This list of questions is not exhaustive, and the answer to none of them is necessarily conclusive. If the judge was intending to say that in any case, other than a branch office case, the presence of the overseas company can *never* be established unless the representative has authority to contract on behalf of and bind the principal, we would regard this proposition as too widely stated. We accept the submission of counsel for the plaintiffs to this effect. Every case of this character is likely to involve 'a nice examination of all the facts, and inferences must be drawn from a number of facts adjusted together and contrasted': see *La Bourgogne* [1899] P 1 at 18 per Collins LJ.

Nevertheless, we agree with the general principle stated thus by Pearson J in *F & K Jabbour v Custodian of Absentee's Property of State of Israel* [1954] 1 All ER 145 at 152, [1954] 1 WLR 139 at 146:

> 'A corporation resides in a country if it carries on business there at a fixed place of business, and, in the case of an agency, the principal test to be applied in determining whether the corporation is carrying on business at the agency is to ascertain whether the agent has authority to enter into contracts on behalf of the corporation without submitting them to the corporation for approval . . .'

On the authorities, the presence or absence of such authority is clearly regarded as being of great importance one way or the other. A fortiori the fact that a representative, whether with or without prior approval, never makes contracts in the name of the overseas corporation or otherwise in such manner as to bind it must be a powerful factor pointing against the presence of the overseas corporation.

The plaintiffs' submissions on the 'presence' issue
Ordinarily the three propositions set out above will fall to be applied in the same way whether or not the representative is an individual or itself a corporate body. However, the present case has the peculiar feature that one of the representatives in the United States, whose acts are relied on as the carrying on of business by Cape, was itself a subsidiary of Cape, a feature which has not been present in any

of the directly relevant authorities cited to us. We will make some further observations on the legal relevance (if any) of this feature when we come to consider the second of the main submissions of counsel for the plaintiffs on the presence issue.

These three main submissions were substantially as follows: (1) Cape and Capasco were present and carrying on business in the United States, namely marketing and selling the Cape group's asbestos, through NAAC until May 1978, and through CPC (or Associated Mineral Corporation (AMC), a Liechtenstein corporation) until June 1979 from a place of business in Illinois because NAAC and CPC were the agents of Cape. (We will call this 'the agency argument'). (2) Cape/Capasco and NAAC constituted a single commercial unit and for jurisdictional purposes, NAAC's presence in Illinois therefore sufficed to constitute the presence of Cape/Capasco. Likewise, Cape/Capasco and CPC, which performed the same functions as those previously carried on by NAAC, constituted a single economic unit, and CPC's presence in Illinois sufficed to constitute the presence of Cape/Capasco. (We will call this 'the single economic unit argument'). (3) In relation to CPC/AMC the corporate veil should be lifted so that CPC's and AMC's presence in the United States should be treated as the presence of Cape/Capasco. (We will call this argument, which does not extend to NAAC, 'the corporate veil' argument).

We find it convenient to deal with the second and third of these arguments before coming to the first.

The 'single economic unit' argument

There is no general principle that all companies in a group of companies are to be regarded as one. On the contrary, the fundamental principle is that 'each company in a group of companies (a relatively modern concept) is a separate legal entity possessed of separate legal rights and liabilities': see *The Albazero* [1975] 3 All ER 21 at 28, [1977] AC 774 at 807 per Roskill LJ.

It is thus indisputable that each of Cape, Capasco, NAAC and CPC were in law separate legal entities. Counsel for the plaintiffs did not go so far as to submit that the very fact of the parent-subsidiary relationship existing between Cape and NAAC rendered Cape or Capasco present in Illinois. Nevertheless, he submitted that the court will, in appropriate circumstances, ignore the distinction in law between members of a group of companies treating them as one, and that broadly speaking, it will do so whenever it considers that justice so demands. In support of this submission, he referred us to a number of authorities.

In *The Roberta* (1937) 58 Ll LR 159 agents acting on behalf of the Dordtsche Company, had signed bills of lading. It was conceded at the trial that in so doing the agents had made Walford Lines Ltd, the parent company of Dordtsche Company, responsible for the bills of lading. Langton J, who described the concession as properly made, said (at 169):

> 'The Dordtsche Company are a separate entity from Walford Lines, Ltd, in name alone, and probably for the purposes of taxation. Walford Lines, Ltd, own all the issued shares of the Dordtsche Company, and in fact supply two out of the three directors'.

In *Harold Holdsworth & Co (Wakefield) Ltd v Caddies* [1955] 1 All ER 725, [1955] 1 WLR 352 the question arose whether the respondent company, which had entered into a service agreement with Mr Caddies under which he was appointed managing director of the company, was entitled to require him to devote his whole time to duties in relation to subsidiaries of the company. It was argued that the subsidiary companies were separate legal entities each under the control of its own board of directors, that in law the board of the appellant company could not assign any duties to anyone in relation to the management of the subsidiary companies, and that therefore the agreement could not be construed as entitling them to assign any such duties to Mr Caddies. Lord Reid, in agreement with the majority, rejected this argument, saying ([1955] 1 All ER 725 at 738, [1955] 1 WLR 352 at 367):

> 'My Lords, in my judgment this is too technical an argument. This is an agreement in re mercatoria, and it must be construed in the light of the facts and realities of the situation.'

In *Scottish Co-operative Wholesale Society Ltd v Meyer* [1958] 3 All ER 66, [1959] AC 324 the respondent based his complaint on s 210 of the Companies Act 1948, which provided that:

> 'Any member of a company who complains that the affairs of the company are being conducted in a manner oppressive to some part of the members (including himself) . . . may make an application to the court by petition for an order under this section.'

The appellant society had formed a subsidiary company, of which the respondent was a member. It was submitted on behalf of the society that even if it had acted in an oppressive manner, yet it had not conducted the affairs *of the company* in an oppressive manner within the meaning of the section. The House of Lords unanimously rejected this submission. Viscount Simonds said ([1958] 3 All ER 66 at 71, [1959] AC 324 at 342):

> 'My Lords, it may be that the acts of the society of which complaint is made could not be regarded as conduct of the affairs of the company if the society and the company were bodies wholly independent of each other, competitors in the rayon market, and using against each other such methods of trade warfare as custom permitted. But this is to pursue a false analogy. It is not possible to separate the transactions of the society from those of the company. Every step taken by the latter was determined by the policy of the former.'

A little later Viscount Simonds expressly approved words which had been used by Lord President Cooper on the first hearing of the case ([1958] 3 All ER 66 at 71, [1959] AC 324 at 343):

> 'In my view, the section warrants the courts in looking at the business realities of a situation and does not confine them to a narrow legalistic view.'

[The court then discussed the DHN Food Distributors case and quoted from the judgments of Denning MR and Goff LJ — see Source 40 at p 113 — and continued:]

In *Revlon Inc v Cripps & Lee Ltd* [1980] FSR 85 the question (among many other questions) arose as to whether the goods in question were 'connected in the course of trade with the proprietor . . . of the trade mark' within the meaning of s 4(3) of the Trade Marks Act 1938. The proprietor of the trade mark was Revlon Suisse SA, a subsidiary of Revlon Inc. Buckley LJ, in the course of deciding that the goods were connected in the course of trade with Revlon Suisse SA, said this (at 105):

> 'Since, however, all the relevant companies are wholly owned subsidiaries of Revlon, it is undoubted that the mark is, albeit remotely, an asset of Revlon

and its exploitation is for the ultimate benefit of no one but Revlon. It therefore seems to me to be realistic and wholly justifiable to regard Suisse as holding the mark at the disposal of Revlon and for Revlon's benefit. The mark is an asset of the Revlon Group of companies regarded as a whole, which all belongs to Revlon. This view does not, in my opinion, constitute what is sometimes called "piercing the corporate veil"; it recognises the legal and factual position resulting from the mutual relationship of the various companies.'

Principally, in reliance on those authorities and the case next to be mentioned, counsel for the plaintiffs submitted that in deciding whether a company had rendered itself subject to the jurisdiction of a foreign court it is entirely reasonable to approach the question by reference to 'commercial reality'. The risk of litigation in a foreign court, in his submission, is part of the price which those who conduct extensive business activities within the territorial jurisdiction of that court properly have to pay. He invited us to follow the approach of Advocate-General Warner in *Commercial Solvents Corp v EC Commission* (*Nos 6–7/74*) [1974] ECR 223 when considering whether a parent company and subsidiary were separate 'undertakings' within the meaning of arts 85 and 86 of the Treaty of Rome. He said (at 263):

'One starts to my mind from this, that neither Article 85 nor Article 86 anywhere refers to "persons". In both Articles the relevant prohibitions are directed to "undertakings", a much wider and looser concept. This indeed is what one would expect, because it would be inappropriate to apply rigidly in the sphere of competition law the doctrine referred to by English lawyers as that of *Salomon v Salomon & Co Ltd* [1897] AC 22 — ie the doctrine that every company is a separate legal person that cannot be identified with its members. Basically that doctrine exists in order to preserve the principle of limited liability. It is concerned with the rights of creditors in the context of company law. It has been applied, with more or less happy results, in other spheres, such as those of conveyancing, of contracts and of liability for tort. But to export it blindly into branches of the law where it has little relevance, could, in my opinion, serve only to divorce the law from reality. Suppose, my Lords, that CSC had traded in Italy through a branch office. There could have been no doubt then that it was amenable to the jurisdiction of the Commission and of this Court. Could it have made any difference if CSC has chosen to trade in Italy through a wholly owned subsidiary? The difference would have been one only of legal form, not of reality. Why then should it make any difference that it chose to trade in Italy through a subsidiary that it controlled by a 51% majority rather than by a 100% majority? What matters in this field, in my view, is control.'

Advocate-General Warner said (at 264):

'(1) that there is a presumption that a subsidiary will act in accordance with the wishes of its parent — because according to common experience subsidiaries generally do so act; (2) that, unless that presumption is rebutted, it is proper for the parent and the subsidiary to be treated as a single undertaking for the purposes of Article 85 and 86 of the EEC Treaty.'

We have some sympathy with the submissions of counsel for the plaintiffs in this context. To the layman at least the distinction between the case where a company itself trades in a foreign country and the case where it trades in a foreign country through a subsidiary, whose activities it has full power to control, may seem a slender one. Counsel for the plaintiffs referred us to *Bulova Watch Co Inc v Hattori & Co Ltd* (1981) 508 F Supp 1322, where the United States District Court held that it had jurisdiction over a Japanese corporation which was expanding into a new market by setting up subsidiaries and dealing with competition, both on the theory that the corporation was 'doing business' in New York and under the New York 'long-arm statute'. In the course of his judgment, Chief Justice Weinstein said (at 1342):

' . . . these subsidiaries almost by definition are doing for their parent what their parent would otherwise have to do on its own.'

It is not surprising that in many cases such as *Holdsworth, Scottish Co-operative, Revlon* and *Commercial Solvents* the wording of a particular statute or contract has been held to justify the treatment of parent and subsidiary as one unit, at least for some purposes. The relevant parts of the judgments in *DHN* must, we think, likewise be regarded as decisions on the relevant statutory provisions for compensation, even though these parts were somewhat broadly expressed, and the correctness of the decision was doubted by the House of Lords in *Woolfson v Strathclyde Regional Council* 1978 SLT 159 in a passage which will be quoted below.

Counsel for the plaintiffs (Mr Morison QC) described the theme of all these cases as being that where legal technicalities would produce injustice in cases involving members of a group of companies, such technicalities should not be allowed to prevail. We do not think that the cases relied on go nearly so far as this. As counsel for the defendants (Sir Godfray Le Quesne QC) submitted, save in cases which turn on the wording of particular statutes or contracts, the court is not free to disregard the principle of *Salomon v Salomon* merely because it considers that justice so requires. Our law, for better or worse, recognises the creation of subsidiary companies, which though in one sense the creatures of their parent companies, will nevertheless under the general law fall to be treated as separate legal entities with all the rights and liabilities which would normally attach to separate legal entities.

In deciding whether a company is present in a foreign country by a subsidiary, which is itself present in that country, the court is entitled, indeed bound, to investigate the relationship between the parent and the subsidiary. In particular, that relationship may be relevant in determining whether the subsidiary was acting as the parent's agent and, if so, on what terms. In *Firestone Tyre and Rubber Co Ltd v Lewellin* [1957] 1 All ER 561, [1957] 1 WLR 464 (which was referred to by Scott J) the House of Lords upheld an assessment to tax on the footing that, on the facts, the business both of the parent and subsidiary were carried on by the subsidiary as agent for the parent. However, there is no presumption of any such agency. There is no presumption that the subsidiary is the parent company's alter ego. In the court below the judge refused an invitation to infer that there existed an agency agreement between Cape and NAAC comparable to that which had previously existed between Cape and Capasco and that refusal is not challenged on this appeal. If a company chooses to arrange the affairs of its group in such a way that the business carried on in a particular foreign country is the business of its subsidiary and not its own, it is, in our judgment, entitled to do so. Neither in this class of case nor in any other class of case is it open to this court to disregard the principle of *Salomon v Salomon & Co Ltd* [1897] AC 22 merely because it considers it just so to do.

In support of the single commercial unit argument, counsel for the plaintiffs made a number of factual submissions to the following effect: The purpose of NAAC's creation was that it might act as a medium through which goods of the

Cape group might be sold. The purpose of the liquidation of NAAC was likewise to protect Cape. Any major policy decisions concerning NAAC were taken by Cape. Cape's control over NAAC did not depend on corporate form. It exercised the same degree of control both before and after the removal of the Cape directors from the NAAC board. The functions of NAAC's directors were formal only. Dr Gaze effectively controlled its activities. Cape represented NAAC to its customers as its office in the United States. In broad terms, it was submitted, Cape ran a single integrated mining division with little regard to corporate formalities as between members of the group in the way in which it carried on its business.

The plaintiffs further submitted in their notice of appeal that NAAC 'did not deal, and was not permitted to deal with Egnep or Casap, but had to go through Cape or Capasco.' It seems clear that NAAC, as principal, made direct purchases of raw asbestos from Egnep. On the balance of probabilities, we accept the plaintiffs' submission that it made similar direct purchases from Casap. In referring to the absence of dealing with Egnep or Casap, the plaintiffs were, we understand, intending to submit that as a matter of group policy, which Cape could and did enforce by its power of control over the boards of Egnep, Capasco and NAAC, the transmission of information and orders to or from customers had to be effected and was effected by NAAC through Capasco. We accept that submission. We also accept that the matters referred to in this paragraph lend some broad support to the submission that Cape ran a single integrated mining division with little regard to corporate formalities as between members of the group. However, there has been no challenge to the judge's finding that the corporate forms applicable to NAAC as a separate legal entity were observed.

As to the plaintiffs' other factual submissions in this context we will deal with the purpose of NAAC's creation and existence in considering the 'agency' argument. As to the relationship between Cape and NAAC, it is of the very nature of a parent company-subsidiary relationship that the parent company is in a position, if it wishes, to exercise overall control over the general policy of the subsidiary. The plaintiffs, however, submitted that Cape's control extended to the day-to-day running of NAAC. They challenged the finding of fact made by Scott J that 'Mr Morgan was in executive control of NAAC's conduct of its business'. We explore further the facts relative to this finding and to the extent of Cape's control over NAAC's activities in the appendix to this judgment under items (11), (12) and (13). Our conclusion, shortly stated, is that the finding was justified by the evidence. A degree of overall supervision, and to some extent control, was exercised by Cape over NAAC as is common in the case of any parent-subsidiary relationship, to a large extent through Dr Gaze. In particular, Cape would indicate to NAAC the maximum level of expenditure which it should incur and would supervise the level of expenses incurred by Mr Morgan. Mr Morgan knew that he had to defer in carrying out the business activities of NAAC to the policy requirements of Cape as the controlling shareholders of NAAC. Within these policy limits, such as Cape's requirement that NAAC's orders for asbestos for sale by NAAC in the United States be placed through Capasco on behalf of Egnep and Casap, the day-to-day running of NAAC was left to him. There is no challenge to the judge's findings that (a) the corporate financial control exercised by Cape over NAAC in respect of the level of dividends and the level of permitted borrowing was no more and no less than was to be expected in a group of companies such as the Cape group (b) the annual accounts of NAAC were drawn on the footing that NAAC's business was its own business and there was nothing to suggest that the accounts were drawn on a false footing.

In the light of the set-up and operations of the Cape group and of the relationship between Cape/Capasco and NAAC we see the attraction of the approach adopted by Lord Denning MR in the *DHN* case [1976] 3 All ER 462 at 467, [1976] 1 WLR 852 at 860 which counsel for the plaintiffs urged us to adopt:

'This group is virtually the same as a partnership in which all the three partners are companies.'

In our judgment, however, we have no discretion to reject the distinction between the members of the group as a technical point. We agree with Scott J that the observations of Robert Goff LJ in *Bank of Tokyo Ltd v Karoon* [1986] 3 All ER 468 at 485, [1987] AC 45 at 64 are apposite:

'Counsel suggested beguilingly that it would be technical for us to distinguish between parent and subsidiary company in this context; economically, he said, they were one. But we are concerned not with economics but with law. The distinction between the two is, in law, fundamental and cannot here be bridged.'

As to CPC, in the submission of counsel for the plaintiffs, the replacement of NAAC by CPC was simply a substitute arrangement. The creation of CPC was effected and paid for by Cape so that it could perform the same functions on behalf of Cape as NAAC had previously performed. CPC, on behalf of AMC (and thus Cape) made payment arrangements with third parties and received moneys for AMC (Cape). While Mr Morgan held all the shares in CPC for his own benefit, the rights of pre-emption reserved to AMC by the agency agreement of 5 June 1978 left him with little substantial financial interest in CPC's business, save for the office furniture and a right to an account which would be of little value; effectively, it was submitted, CPC's business was owned by AMC (Cape).

Our reasons for rejecting the 'single economic unit' argument in relation to NAAC apply a fortiori in relation to CPC, because CPC was not Cape's subsidiary and its shares were held by Mr Morgan for his own benefit. We give our reasons in the next section of this judgment for agreeing with the judge that CPC was an independently owned company.

The 'corporate veil' point

Quite apart from cases where statute or contract permits a broad interpretation to be given to references to members of a group of companies, there is one well-recognised exception to the rule prohibiting the piercing of 'the corporate veil'. Lord Keith referred to this principle in *Woolfson v Strathclyde Regional Council* 1978 SLT 159 in the course of a speech with which Lord Wilberforce, Lord Fraser and Lord Russell agreed. With reference to the *DHN* decision, he said (at 161):

'I have some doubts whether in this respect the Court of Appeal properly applied the principle that is it appropriate to pierce the corporate veil only where special circumstances exist indicating that it is a mere façade concealing the true facts.'

The only allegation of a façade in the plaintiffs' pleadings was that the formation and use of CPC and AMC in the 'alternative marketing arrangements of 1978 were a device or sham or cloak for grave impropriety on the part of Cape or Capasco, namely to ostensibly remove their assets from the USA to avoid liability for asbestos claims whilst at the same time continuing to trade in asbestos there'. In their notice of appeal (para 2(b)) the plaintiffs referred to their contention made at the trial that CPC 'was set up to replace NAAC in such a way as to disguise the defendants' continued involvement in the marketing of the group's asbestos in the USA.'

Scott J more or less accepted this contention. He found as a fact that 'the arrangements made regarding NAAC, AMC and CPC were part of one composite arrangement designed to enable Cape asbestos to continue to be sold into the United States while reducing, if not eliminating, the appearance of any involvement therein of Cape or its subsidiaries.'

However, he went on to say:

> 'But the question whether CPC's presence in Illinois can, for jurisdiction purposes, be treated as Cape's presence, must, in my view, be answered by considering the nature of the arrangements that were implemented, not the motive behind them. The documentary evidence I have seen has made clear that the senior management of Cape, including Mr Penna, were very anxious that Cape's connections with CPC and the AMC should not become publicly known. Some of the letters and memoranda have a somewhat conspiratorial flavour to them. But this too, although interesting to notice, is not, in my opinion, relevant to the main question.'

If and so far as the judge intended to say that the motive behind the new arrangements was irrelevant as a matter of law, we would respectfully differ from him. In our judgment, as counsel for the plaintiffs submitted, whenever a device or sham or cloak is alleged in cases such as this, the motive of the alleged perpetrator must be legally relevant, and indeed this no doubt is the reason why the question of motive was examined extensively at the trial. The decision in *Jones v Lipman* [1962] 1 All ER 442, [1962] 1 WLR 832 referred to below was one case where the proven motive of the individual defendant clearly had a significant effect on the decision of Russell J.

The judge's finding of fact quoted above as to the motives of Cape behind the new arrangement is accepted (no doubt welcomed) by the plaintiffs, so far as it goes. They submit, rightly in our judgment, that any such motives are relevant to the 'corporate veil' point. They further submit that the learned judge (a) erred in concluding that CPC was an 'independently owned company'; and (b) failed to make a number of findings of fact which are relevant in the context of the 'corporate veil' point.

Counsel for the plaintiffs has taken us though the arrangements which led to the extinction of NAAC and the emergence of AMC and CPC with care and in considerable detail. The additional facts which the appellants say the judge ought to have found, and which are set out in the appendix to this judgment, all relate to these arrangements. It is true that, as the judge said, some of the letters and memoranda have a 'somewhat conspiratorial flavour to them'. Since, contrary to the judge's view, we think motive is relevant in this context, we have thought it right to investigate these contentions in some detail in the appendix.

On analysis, much of the new material does little more than amply support the judge's finding quoted above as to the purpose of the composite arrangement. In this court counsel for the plaintiffs made it clear that the plaintiffs were not alleging any unlawful purpose or impropriety on the part of Cape in the sense of any intention to deceive or to do any unlawful act, either in Illinois or in this country. It was, however, asserted for the plaintiffs that AMC and CPC together constituted a façade which concealed the real activities of Cape. We understand that to mean that the purpose of Cape was to conceal, so far as it lawfully could having regard to the requirements of the law in Illinois and this country, any connection of Cape with AMC or CPC.

Before expressing our own views as to Cape's purpose, we will state our conclusions as to Mr Morgan's position. It is, in our judgment, right to infer, substantially as submitted by counsel for the plaintiffs, that the assistance derived from the presence of Mr Morgan in Illinois, undertaking the task through CPC of marketing agent for the Cape subsidiaries in the United States, was regarded as being at least of great importance to the general purposes of the Cape group, and possibly essential for those purposes, because, if it was not so regarded, there is no apparent reason why Cape should assume the cost and such risk as might have arisen from setting up CPC. Counsel for the defendants, however, was in our view plainly right in submitting that the agreement of Mr Morgan was required for the creation of the alternative marketing arrangements by means of a new independent Illinois company and that his agreement, when given, was real. Cape had obligations of a moral nature to Mr Morgan and to the long-serving staff of NAAC. Cape also, for its own purposes, wanted Mr Morgan and Mrs Holtze to continue with the work previously done by them for NAAC. If Mr Morgan decided to take on the task of providing services to the subsidiaries of the Cape group through CPC, on the terms available to him as owner of the shares in CPC, Cape would get the benefit of his knowledge and experience as the person in charge of CPC. Nothing in the material to which our attention was drawn under these headings, however, causes us to doubt the correctness of Scott J's conclusion that the shares in CPC belonged both at law and in equity to Mr Morgan. It is clear that Cape intended CPC to be in reality Mr Morgan's company because that was part of their purpose. Such as it was, and dependent for almost all of its business on the Cape subsidiaries, CPC was Mr Morgan's company. We therefore reject the challenge to the judge's finding that CPC was an independently owned company.

As the Cape's purpose in making the arrangements for the liquidation of NAAC and the creation of AMC and CPC, we think that the extracts from the evidence set out in the appendix to this judgment (particularly under item (17)), sufficiently reveal both the substance of what the officers of Cape were doing and what they were trying to achieve. The allegation of impropriety was, in our view, rightly abandoned. The inference which we draw from all the evidence was that Cape's intention was to enable sales of asbestos from the South African subsidiaries to continue to be made in the United States while (a) reducing the appearance of any involvement therein of Cape or its subsidiaries, and (b) reducing by any lawful means available to it the risk of any subsidiary or of Cape as parent company being held liable for United States taxation or subject to the jurisdiction of the United States courts, whether state or federal, and the risk of any default judgment by such a court being held to be enforceable in this country. Inference (a) was also made by the judge. Inference (b) is our own addition.

The question of law which we now have to consider is whether the arrangements regarding NAAC, AMC and CPC made by Cape with the intentions which we have inferred constituted a façade such as to justify the lifting of the corporate veil so as that CPC's and AMC's presence in the United States should be treated as the presence of Cape/Capasco for this reason if no other.

In *Merchandise Transport Ltd v British Transport Commission* [1961] 3 All ER 495 at 518, [1962] 2 QB 173 at 206–207 Danckwerts LJ referred to certain authorities as showing that —

> 'where the character of a company, or the nature of the persons who control it, is a relevant feature the court will go behind the mere status of the company as a legal entity, and will consider who are the persons as shareholders or even as agents who direct and control the activities of a company which is incapable of doing anything without human assistance.'

The correctness of this statement has not been disputed, but it does not assist in determining whether 'the character of a company or the nature of the persons who control it' will be relevant in the present case.

Rather greater assistance on this point is to be found in *Jones v Lipman* [1962] 1 All ER 442, [1962] 1 WLR 832. In that case the first defendant had agreed to sell to the plaintiffs some land. Pending completion the first defendant sold and transferred the land to the defendant company. The evidence showed that this company was at all material times under the complete control of the first defendant. It also showed that the acquisition by him of the company and the transfer of the land to the company had been carried through solely for the purpose of defeating the plaintiff's right to specific performance (see [1962] 1 All ER 442 at 445, [1962] 1 WLR 832 at 836). Russell J made an order for specific performance against both defendants. He held that specific performance cannot be resisted by a vendor who, by his absolute ownership and control of a limited company in which the property is vested, is in a position to cause the contract to be completed. As to the defendant company, he described it as being 'the creature of the first defendant, a device and a sham, a mask which he holds before his face in an attempt to avoid recognition by the eye of equity'. (See [1962] 1 All ER 442 at 445, [1962] 1 WLR 832 at 836.) Following *Jones v Lipman*, we agree with counsel for the plaintiffs that, contrary to the judge's view, where a façade is alleged, the motive of the perpetrator may be highly material.
. . .

We were referred to certain broad dicta of Lord Denning MR in *Wallersteiner v Moir* [1974] 3 All ER 217 at 238, [1974] 1 WLR 991 at 1013, and in *Littlewoods Mail Order Store Ltd v IRC* [1969] 3 All ER 855 at 860, [1969] 1 WLR 1241 at 1254. In both these cases he expressed his willingness to pull aside the corporate veil, saying in the latter:

> 'I decline to treat the [subsidiary] as a separate and independent legal entity. . . The courts can and often do draw aside the veil. They can, and often do, pull off the mask. They look to see what really lies behind. The legislature has shown the way with group accounts and the rest. And the courts should follow suit. I think that we should look at the Fork Company and see it as it really is — the wholly-owned subsidiary of the taxpayers. It is the creature, the puppet, of the taxpayer, in point of *fact*: and it should be so regarded in point of *law*.'

However, in *Wallersteiner v Moir* [1974] 3 All ER 217 at 250, 254, [1974] 1 WLR 991 at 1027, 1032, Buckley and Scarman LJJ expressly declined to tear away the corporate veil. In *Littlewoods* [1969] 3 All ER 855 at 861, [1969] 1 WLR 1241 at 1255, Sachs LJ expressly dissociated himself from the suggestion that the subsidiary was not a separate legal entity and Karminski LJ refrained from associating himself with it. We therefore think that the plaintiffs can derive little support from those dicta of Lord Denning MR.

From the authorities cited to us we are left with rather sparse guidance as to the principles which should guide the court in determining whether or not the arrangements of a corporate group involve a façade within the meaning of that word as used by the House of Lords in *Woolfson*. We will not attempt a comprehensive definition of those principles.

Our conclusions are these. In our judgment, the interposition of AMC between Cape and CPC was clearly a façade in the relevant sense. Scott J said it seemed clear that AMC was 'no more than a corporate name' and that he would expect to find, if all the relevant documents were available, that 'AMC acted through employees or officers of either Casap or Egnep'. He rejected Mr Morgan's evidence that he understood AMC to be an independent South African trading company, and was satisfied that he knew very well that it was a 'creature of Cape'. The seller in CPC's time was, nominally, AMC but, in reality still, I think, Egnep or Casap'. In our judgment, however, the revelation of AMC as the creature of Cape does not suffice to enable the plaintiffs to show the presence of Cape/Capasco in the United States, since on the judge's undisputed findings, AMC was not in reality carrying on any business in the United States.

The relationship between Cape/Capasco and CPC is the crucial factor, since CPC was undoubtedly carrying on business in the United States. We have already indicated our acceptance of the judge's findings that CPC was a company independently owned by Mr Morgan and that the shares therein belonged to him in law and in equity. These findings by themselves make it very difficult to contend that the operation of CPC involved a façade which entitles the court to pierce the corporate veil between CPC and Cape/Capasco and treat them all as one. Is the legal position altered by the facts that Cape's intention, in making the relevant arrangements (as we infer), was to enable sales of asbestos from the South African subsidiaries to be made while (a) reducing if not eliminating the appearance of any involvement therein of Cape or its subsidiaries, and (b) reducing by any lawful means available to it the risk of any subsidiary or of Cape as parent company being held liable for United States taxation or subject to the jurisdiction of the United States courts and the risk of any default judgment by such a court being held to be enforceable in this country?

We think not. Counsel for the plaintiff submitted that the court will lift the corporate veil where a defendant by the device of a corporate structure attempts to evade (i) limitations imposed on his conduct by law; (ii) such rights of relief against him as third parties already possess; and (iii) such rights of relief as third parties may in the future acquire. Assuming that the first and second of these three conditions will suffice in law to justify such a course, neither of them apply in the present case. It is not suggested that the arrangements involved any actual or potential illegality or were intended to deprive anyone of their existing rights. Whether or not such a course deserves moral approval, there was nothing illegal as such in Cape arranging its affairs (whether by the use of subsidiaries or otherwise) so as to attract the minimum publicity to its involvement in the sale of Cape asbestos in the United States. As to condition (iii), we do not accept as a matter of law that the court is entitled to lift the corporate veil as against a defendant company which is the member of a corporate group merely because the corporate structure has been used so as to ensure that the legal liability (if any) in respect of particular future activities of the group (and correspondingly the risk of enforcement of that liability) will fall on another member of the group rather than the defendant company. Whether or not this is desirable, the right to use a corporate structure in this manner is inherent in our corporate law. Counsel for the plaintiffs urged on us that the purpose of the operation was in substance that Cape would have the practical benefit of the group's asbestos trade in the United States, without the risks of tortious liability. This may be so. However, in our judgment, Cape was in law entitled to organise the group's affairs in that manner and (save in the case of AMC to which special considerations apply) to expect that the court would apply the principle of *Salomon v Salomon & Co Ltd* [1897] AC 22 in the ordinary way.

The plaintiffs submitted (para 7 of their notice of appeal) that the motive of the defendants in setting up the arrangements regarding NAAC, AMC and CPC as revealed in the documentary evidence were 'consistent only with an acceptance by Cape that they were present in the United States through NAAC and CPC'. We think there is no substance in this point. These arrangements at most indicated an apprehension on the part of the defendants that they might be held to be so present and a desire that they should not be. They involved no admission or acceptance of such presence.

We reject the 'corporate veil' argument.

The 'agency argument' in relation to NAAC

We now proceed to consider the agency argument in relation to NAAC on the footing, which we consider to be the correct one, that NAAC must for all relevant purposes be regarded as a legal entity separate from Cape/Capasco. In an earlier section of this judgment we summarised three propositions which we derived from the authorities relating to the 'presence' of an overseas corporation. There we stated that, save in a 'branch office' case (which the instant case is not), the English court will be likely to treat an overseas trading corporation as present within the jurisdiction of the courts of another country only if a representative of the overseas corporation has for more than a minimal period of time been carrying on the *overseas corporation's* business in the other country at or from some fixed place of business. In the present case NAAC, as representative of Cape/Capasco, unquestionably carried on business at a fixed place of business in the United States, 150 North Wacker Drive, for a substantial period of time. So no difficulty arises on that score. The crucial question is whether it can fairly be said that *Cape's* business has been transacted by NAAC at or from 150 North Wacker Drive. The judge's answer to it was that 'NAAC's business was its own business, not the business of Cape or of Capasco'. The plaintiffs challenge the correctness of this answer to the question.

This question, as we said earlier, will necessitate an investigation of the functions which NAAC performed and all aspects of the relationship between it and Cape.

The factual materials which we have principally in mind in considering whether Cape's business was being transacted at or from 150 North Wacker Drive is to be found in the section of this judgment headed 'The facts on "presence" as found by Scott J', and in our observations on items (1) to (13) in the appendix to this judgment. We summarise below what we consider the most material facts in context, having regard to the list of potentially relevant factors set out in an earlier section of our judgment.

We accept that the intention of Cape in procuring the incorporation of NAAC in the State of Illinois was that NAAC should assist in the marketing of asbestos in the United States on sales by Egnep or Casap to purchasers in the United States and that it was to be the marketing agent of the Cape Group in the United States. Nevertheless, in our judgment, it is indisputable that at very least a substantial part of the business carried on by NAAC at all material times was in every sense its own business. In these contexts we draw attention in particular to the following facts:

(1) Though we were referred to no evidence relating to the original acquisition by NAAC of its premises at 150 North Wacker Drive, we know that NAAC itself was the lessee of the premises and paid the rent for them. Furthermore, it owned the office furniture and employed there its own staff of four persons for whom it ran its own pension scheme.

(2) From time to time it conducted the following activities as principal on its own account: (a) it bought asbestos from United States government stocks or from Egnep or Casap and sold it to United States customers, such purchases representing about 25% of NAAC's business in terms of tonnage; (b) it imported asbestos goods from Japan and sold them to United States customers. (While we accept that the purchase by NAAC of asbestos goods was subordinate to its

business with or for Cape's subsidiaries, we do not accept the plaintiffs' submission that such sales were trivial, having regard to the turnover of NAAC.)

(3) For storing the asbestos which it had purchased from United States government stocks or Egnep or Casap, NAAC rented in its own name and paid for warehousing facilities.

(4) NAAC earned profits and paid United States taxes thereon.

(5) NAAC's creditors and debtors were its own (not those of Cape).

(6) The return to Cape as NAAC's shareholder took the form of an annual dividend passed by a resolution of NAAC's board of directors.

(7) In other respects also the corporate forms applicable to NAAC as a separate entity were observed.

In the face of these facts, now unchallenged, it is in our judgment clear beyond argument that NAAC was carrying on business of its own. The only question is whether, in performing the functions which it performed on behalf of Cape/Capasco, it was carrying on its own business or their business. What, then, were these functions? As we see the position from the findings of the judge and the evidence put before us, its functions were to assist in the marketing of asbestos in the United States on sales by Egnep or Casap and generally to assist and encourage sales in the United States of asbestos of the Cape group. It acted as the channel of communication between Cape/Capasco and United States customers, such as PCC. It organised and arranged the performance of contracts between United States customers and Egnep. It had a co-ordinating role, particularly in arranging delivery. The United States customer would specify to NAAC from time to time the quantity of asbestos which it wished to purchase and the time when it desired delivery to be made. This information would be conveyed through NAAC to Casap and Egnep. Shipping arrangements and delivery dates would be arranged by Casap or Egnep and communicated to the United States customers via NAAC. NAAC would receive documents and pass them on to the customers. It also received requests and complaints which it would normally pass on to Capasco. Generally it assisted in 'nursing' the group's customers for asbestos and ensuring that they were satisfied. For its services NAAC was remunerated by way of a commission paid to it by Casap on sales effected by Egnep or Casap. There was no evidence that NAAC reserved any part of its office premises or any part of its staff exclusively for performing its agency functions.

Our further findings as to the functions which NAAC performed and as to its relationship between NAAC and Cape are to be found set out in the appendix under items (1) to (3). We bear in mind particularly the submissions contained in item (9) that (i) when corresponding with United States customers, Cape referred to NAAC as 'our Chicago office' and NAAC referred to Cape and Capasco as 'our London office'; (ii) NAAC held itself out to a large United States customer as being part of the Cape selling organisation, and (iii) NAAC was treated by the major customer 'as the channel between them and Cape and Capasco'. However, in the appendix we give our reasons for concluding that the matters shown in the evidence considered under this heading do not by themselves show anything inconsistent with the findings of Scott J as to NAAC's role and functions.

There is no doubt that the services rendered by NAAC in acting as intermediary in respect of contracts between the United States customers and Egnep or Casap were active and important services which were of great assistance to Cape/Capasco in arranging the sales of their group's asbestos in the United States. Nevertheless, for all the closeness of the relationship between Cape/Capasco and NAAC, strictly defined limits were imposed on the functions which NAAC were authorised to carry out or did carry out as their representative. First, NAAC had no general authority to bind Cape/Capasco to any contractual obligation. Second, as counsel for the plaintiffs expressly accepted, there is no evidence that NAAC, whether with or without prior authority from Cape/Capasco, ever effected any transaction in such manner that Cape/Capasco thereby became subject to contractual obligations to any person. This significant factor renders the arguments in favour of 'presence', at least in some respects, even less strong than they were in cases such as *The Lalandia* [1933] P 56 and *The Holstein* [1936] 2 All ER 1660 where the argument failed. Having regard to the legal principles stated earlier in this judgment, and looking at the facts of the case overall, our conclusion is that the judge was right to hold that the business carried on by NAAC was exclusively its own business, not the business of Cape or Capasco, and that Cape and Capasco were not present within the United States through NAAC at any material time. We see no sufficient grounds for disturbing this finding of fact.

Under this section of our judgment we should mention one further point. The plaintiffs challenged the judge's finding that as from 31 January 1978, NAAC ceased to act on behalf of any of the Cape companies or to carry on any business on its own account save for the purpose of liquidating its assets. The object of the challenge was to refute the suggestion that Cape could not be regarded as present in the United States through NAAC during the period between 31 January 1978 and NAAC's formal dissolution on 19 May 1978. (They accepted that after 19 May Cape could not be said to be present in the United States, by or through NAAC). The plaintiffs regard this point as having potential legal relevance, since two of the eight actions which comprise Tyler II were begun before 18 May 1978. In the appendix we give our reasons for rejecting the challenge to the judge's finding of fact.

The agency argument in relation to CPC

We now consider whether Cape/Capasco were present in the United States by or through CPC. In dealing with the 'corporate veil' point we have stated our inferences as to Cape's purpose in making the arrangements for the liquidation of NAAC and the creation of AMC and CPC. Part of the very purpose of these arrangements was to enable sales of asbestos from the Cape group to continue to be made in the United States while creating a greater distance both in appearance and reality between Cape and the company (CPC) which was intended to carry out the functions on its behalf in the United States which had previously been carried out by NAAC. Having dealt with the 'corporate veil' point, we agree with the following passage in Scott J's judgment:

> 'I do not think, on analysis, that the plaintiffs' case is any stronger than their case regarding NAAC. If anything, I think the case is weaker. NAAC was at least a wholly-owned subsidiary. CPC, even if incorporated and launched with Cape money, was, on my reading of the facts, an independently owned company. Like NAAC, CPC acted as agent for the purpose of facilitating the sale in the United States of Cape's asbestos. The seller of the asbestos in NAAC's time was Egnep or Casap. The seller in CPC's time was, nominally, AMC but, in reality, still, I think, Egnep or Casap. CPC, like NAAC, had no authority to bind Egnep, Casap or any other of the Cape subsidiaries to any contract, CPC, like NAAC, carried on its own business from its own offices at 150 North Wacker Drive. The provision by Cape of the $160,000 as a starting-up fund does not make the offices Cape's offices or the business Cape's business.'

The interposition of AMC in the new arrangements made in 1978 cannot one way or the other affect the question whether Cape/Capasco were present in the United States thereafter. For all relevant purposes, as we have already indicated, we are prepared to treat Cape and AMC as one. The functions performed by CPC and its relationship with Cape through AMC are the relevant considerations for present purposes. Since Mr Morgan held all the shares in CPC, beneficially Cape had no control as a shareholder over the activities of CPC similar to the control which it had exercised over NAAC. Counsel for the plaintiffs did not dispute the judge's finding that the terms of the agency agreement of 5 June 1978 were a reliable guide to the nature of the relationship between CPC and AMC and hence between CPC and Cape. Under the terms of this agreement, CPC were left free to sell materials and products other than asbestos fibre and to involve itself in other commercial activities. It is clear that it did so. While there is no evidence that it followed NAAC in buying raw asbestos from Egnep or Casap or the United States government, it undoubtedly bought and sold manufactured textiles on its own behalf as principal.

It is thus quite plain that at least a substantial part of CPC's business was in every sense its own business. As with NAAC, the only question is whether, in performing the functions which it performed on behalf of Cape/Capasco, it was carrying on its own business or their business. As the terms of the agency agreement show, these functions were very similar to those which had been performed by NAAC. The services rendered by CPC to Cape/Capasco were similarly active and important. Again, however, strictly defined limits were imposed on the functions which CPC was authorised to carry out or did carry out as the representative of Cape/Capasco (through AMC). CPC had no authority to bind AMC or Cape or Capasco to any contractual obligation. Again too, there is no evidence that CPC, whether with or without prior authority from any of those three companies, ever carried out any transaction in such manner as to subject any of them to contractual obligations to any person. In the light of the legal principles stated above and of the facts of the case looked at as a whole, we see no sufficient grounds for disturbing the judge's finding that the business carried on by CPC was exclusively its own business and that Cape and Capasco were not present within the United States through CPC (or AMC) at any material time.

. . .

V Conclusion

In the result, while we have some doubts as to whether the judge reached the right conclusion on the country issue, we are satisfied that he reached the right conclusions on the presence issue and the natural justice issue. He was accordingly right, in our judgment, to dismiss the plaintiffs' claims and this appeal likewise must be dismissed.

. . .

Appeal dismissed. Leave to appeal to the House of Lords refused.

24 October. The Appeal Committee of the House of Lords (Lord Keith of Kinkel, Lord Griffiths and Lord Ackner) refused leave to appeal.

SOURCE 43
Creasey *v* Breachwood Motors
(Queen's Bench Division) 1993 [BCLC] 480

MR RICHARD SOUTHWELL QC. The plaintiff Mr Creasey worked for Breachwood Welwyn Ltd (Welwyn) pursuant to a written contract of employment dated 4 February 1987 (the term of the contract being from 1 October 1986 to 30

September 1992) as its general manager. Welwyn carried on the business of a garage trading in cars and other vehicles (including Saab cars as an authorised Saab dealer) at 36 Brownfields, Welwyn Garden City, Herts. The premises at 36 Brownfields were and are owned by Breachwood Motors Ltd (Motors). Mr Ford and Mr Seaman were and are the shareholders and directors of both Welwyn and Motors. Motors carried on similar businesses elsewhere.

On 21 March 1988 Mr Creasey was summarily dismissed by Welwyn. On 9 June 1988 a writ was issued in this action, claiming damages for wrongful dismissal against Welwyn. On 25 July 1988 Welwyn's solicitors served a defence by which Welwyn sought to justify the dismissal. It is clear from the affidavit evidence before me that both the claim and the defence were reasonably arguable. On 27 October 1988 a request for further and better particulars of the defence was made.

On 6 September 1988 Mr Ford signed the report of the directors of Welwyn (Mr Ford and Mr Seaman) in respect of its accounts for the period 1 April 1987 to 31 May 1988. Mr Ford stated that Welwyn began to trade at 36 Brownfields on 1 April 1987 and had made a loss of £35,441. As this was a new venture, it had not been anticipated that a profit would be made in the first year or so. He stated that the directors were encouraged by the way Welwyn's business was developing and were confident that it would soon move into profitability.

On 21 November 1988 Welwyn's solicitors wrote to Mr Creasey's solicitors informing them that accounts being prepared for Welwyn appeared to show that Welwyn was insolvent, and it was likely therefore that Welwyn would cease trading fairly shortly thereafter. They also stated that the moment they knew what was happening they would revert to Mr Creasey's solicitors.

In fact Welwyn ceased trading on 30 November 1988. On 1 December 1988 Motors took over the business of Welwyn at 36 Brownfields and thereafter have carried on that business under the same business name, Welwyn Saab. The evidence of Mr Ford shows that Motors took all the assets of Welwyn which from draft accounts of Welwyn at 30 November 1988 appear to have totalled £79,607. Mr Ford's evidence also shows that Motors paid all the debts of Welwyn to its then creditors, shown in the draft accounts at 30 November 1988 as totalling £154,927. But Mr Ford's evidence also shows that this take-over of Welwyn's assets and liabilities by Motors was entirely informal, and without making any provision for Mr Creasey's claim if that were to succeed.

Welwyn did not go and has not since gone into liquidation. If Welwyn had, its assets would have been available (subject to any costs of liquidation) to pay a dividend to all the creditors of Welwyn, including Mr Creasey.

Mr Ford's evidence is that Motors, having taken over the business of Welwyn, had for commercial reasons to pay the debts of that business since otherwise suppliers would have been reluctant to do business with Motors. But Motors did not pay or make any provision for payment of Mr Creasey's claim.

. . .

I assume that throughout this period Welwyn's solicitors did not provide their services free of charge, and I infer that they were paid by Motors. It can no doubt be assumed that Welwyn's solicitors were fully aware of the separate identities of the two companies, and equally aware that the assets of one company cannot simply be stripped and removed to another company at the whim of common directors and shareholders, with the result that a creditor of the first company is left without recourse to any of the assets of the first company.

The action proceeded in default of steps being taken by Welwyn. On 16 May 1989 Master Trench ordered that particulars be given of the defence within 14 days, and in default the defence be struck out and Mr Creasey be at liberty to enter judgment with damages to be assessed. On 3 August 1989 Master Trench ordered that Mr Creasey be at liberty to enter judgment and gave directions for the assessment of damages. Judgment was not entered until 13 September 1990, over a year later. On 13 March 1991 Master Trench having assessed damages made a [*sic*] order giving judgment for damages of £53,835.03 plus interest of £8,075.24.

Meanwhile on 26 February 1991 the Registrar of Companies had given three months' notice to Welwyn that it would be struck off the register and dissolved. On about 11 June 1991 Welwyn was struck off the register, and accordingly dissolved, pursuant to s 652 of the Companies Act 1985.

On 2 May 1991 Mr Creasey's solicitors sent a copy of the judgment to Welwyn's solicitors who still remained on the record. The response dated 7 May 1991 was that Welwyn ceased to trade in November 1988 and was without assets.

In correspondence from 8 May 1991 Mr Creasey's solicitors put forward the contention that Motors was liable in respect of the judgment by reason of the merger of the business of Welwyn into that of Motors. Motors' solicitors disagreed. The principal questions for the decision of this court are whether that contention is correct, and if so, what the legal consequences are.

. . .

The facts can be summarised shortly: (1) The contract was with Welwyn, and at the date when Welwyn ceased to trade (30 November 1988) Welwyn had a contingent liability to Mr Creasey for damages for breach of contract, contingent on Mr Creasey obtaining judgment establishing such liability. (2) On 1 December 1988 Motors took over all Welwyn's assets and its business carried on at 36 Brownfields, and continued that business under the same trade name with the benefit of Welwyn's goodwill and customers. (3) That take-over of Welwyn's assets was carried out without regard to the separate entity of Welwyn and the interests of its creditors, especially Mr Creasey. (4) As a practical matter Motors had to pay off the liabilities of Welwyn (except the contingent and later actual liability to Mr Creasey) in order to carry on the business at 36 Brownfields, and Motors did so. (5) As a result of the actions of Mr Ford, Mr Seaman and Motors, Mr Creasey finds himself with a judgment against Welwyn, an insolvent company, the assets of which they have removed to Motors, a company which refuses to meet any part of the judgment, and which does not even offer to return the assets or their value to Welwyn.

[The judge after analysing the Scottish authorities rejected, as applicable in England, the submission (made on behalf of the plaintiff) that:]

> 'If a company sells its undertaking as a going concern to another person, there is a presumption that its liabilities including its contingent liabilities are also transferred, with the result that the transferee may be sued by a creditor of the company.'

[and continued:]

I turn to Mr Behar's[1] second main argument, based on English authorities as to the lifting of the veil of incorporation. Mr Behar began naturally with the facts which I have tried to summarise. He submitted that the facts reveal an intention on the part of Mr Ford and Mr Seaman, and Motors as another company controlled by them, to take the benefits of Welwyn's business by means of the informal transfer of the business and all Welwyn's assets, but to leave Mr Creasey

---

1 Counsel for the plaintiff

with Welwyn as an insolvent defendant with no assets whatsoever from which even the smallest dividend could be paid.

As regards the law, Mr Behar referred to s 1.3.1 of *Gore-Browne*. He accepted that, as stated in that section:

'It is not possible to formulate any single principle as the basis for these decisions [in which the veil has been lifted], nor are all the decisions, as to when the separate legal entity of the company must be respected or when it may be disregarded, entirely consistent with one another.'

He relied particularly on the next sentence:

'It is well established that the Courts will not allow the corporate form to be used for the purposes of fraud or as a device to evade a contractual or other legal obligation.'

and referred to the well-known cases of *Gilford Motor Co v Horne* [1933] Ch 935, [1933] All ER Rep 109 and *Jones v Lipman* [1962] 1 All ER 422, [1962] 1 WLR 832 per Russell J as examples of cases in which the veil was lifted on this ground. He cited the passage in the judgment of Lord Hanworth MR in *Gilford* [1933] Ch 935 at 955–956, [1933] All ER Rep 109 at 114 in which Lord Hanworth reached the conclusion that Mr Horne had formed the defendant company 'as a device, a stratagem, in order to mask the effective carrying on of a business of Mr E B Horne', in breach of a valid restrictive covenant. This case is different, in that Motors was already in existence and carrying on its own business, and the 'stratagem', if there was one, involved the transfer of the relevant business to Motors. *Jones v Lipman* is also distinguishable on its facts for similar reasons.

Mr Behar submitted that what is important for the present case is the recognition by the courts that separate legal personality should not be allowed to act as a vehicle for fraud or evasion of a legal obligation.

He cited also *Re a company* [1985] BCLC 333. In that case, as summarised in the headnote:

'The evidence established that the defendant had created a network of English and foreign companies and trusts through which he could dispose of his English assets and, when the insolvency of the plaintiffs was imminent and after the alleged fraud had been committed, he had used this network to dispose of his assets. In these circumstances the court would pierce the corporate veil in order to achieve justice and accordingly the order pertaining to the foreign companies and trusts was proper, subject to the limitation that it was restricted to those companies and trusts over which the defendant exercised substantial or effective control.'

In its judgment delivered by Cumming-Bruce LJ the Court of Appeal said (at 337–338):

'In our view the cases before and after *Wallersteiner v Moir* [1974] 3 All ER 217, [1974] 1 WLR 991 show that the court will use its powers to pierce the corporate veil if it is necessary to achieve justice irrespective of the legal efficacy of the corporate structure under consideration. As Lord Denning MR said ([1974] 3 All ER 217 at 238, [1974] 1 WLR 991 at 1013) the companies there identified were distinct legal entities and the principles of *Salomon v Salomon & Co Ltd* [1897] AC 22, [1885–9] All ER Rep 33 prima facie applied. But only prima facie. On the facts of the *Wallersteiner* case, the companies danced to Dr Wallersteiner's bidding. Buckley LJ disagreed on the facts about the position of IFT, but Scarman LJ held that the evidence disclosed liability in Wallersteiner on the ground that he instigated the loan of £50,000.'

The power of the court to lift the corporate veil exists. The problem for a judge of first instance is to decide whether the particular case before the court is one in which that power should be exercised, recognising that this is a strong power which can be exercised to achieve justice where its exercise is necessary for that purpose, but which, misused, would be likely to cause not inconsiderable injustice. The authorities which are collected in *Gore-Browne* and also in *Gower's Principles of Modern Company Law* (5th edn, 1992) provide only limited guidance as to the circumstances in which this power is to be exercised.

I have also considered two other cases, one in the House of Lords, the other in the Court of Appeal, which were not cited to me.

The first is *Woolfson v Strathclyde Regional Council* 1978 SC (HL) 90. That case concerned a claim for statutory compensation for disturbance in respect of premises occupied by a company C, in which Mr Woolfson owned 999 of the 1000 shares (and was the sole director) and Mrs Woolfson owned one share, the premises being owned as to three of the premises by Mr Woolfson, and as to the other two premises by another company S, in which 20 shares were owned by Mr Woolfson and the remaining 10 shares by his wife. The claim for compensation was made by Mr Woolfson and company S on the footing that the business carried on in the premises was really theirs, being conducted by company C as their agent, so that they were the true occupiers of the premises and were therefore entitled to compensation. The House of Lords refused to pierce the corporate veil so as to treat Mr Woolfson as the true owner of company C's business or company S's assets. In distinguishing another Court of Appeal decision, in *DHN Food Distributors v Tower Hamlets London Borough Council* [1976] 3 All ER 462, [1976] 1 WLR 852, Lord Keith said (1978 SC 90 at 96):

'I have some doubts whether in this respect the Court of Appeal [in *DHN*] properly applied the principle that it is appropriate to pierce the corporate veil only where special circumstances exist indicating that this is a mere façade concealing the true facts.'

The second case is *Adams v Cape Industries plc* [1990] BCLC 479 at 515–520, [1990] Ch 433 at 539–544, in which the Court of Appeal dealt with the 'corporate veil' point raised in that case. The Court of Appeal began by citing the above passage from *Woolfson*, and then considered whether on the facts of *Adams* the existence of the separate corporate entities could be treated as 'a mere façade concealing the true facts'. The Court of Appeal said ([1990] BCLC 479 at 519, [1990] Ch 433 at 543–544):

'From the authorities cited to us we are left with rather sparse guidance as to the principles which should guide the court in determining whether or not the arrangements of a corporate group involve a façade within the meaning of that word as used by the House of Lords in *Woolfson* 1978 SLT 159. We will not attempt a comprehensive definition of those principles.'

The Court of Appeal rejected the submission that the veil could be pierced where a defendant by the device of a corporate structure attempts to evade 'such rights of relief as third parties may in the future require'. They assumed for the purposes of *Adams* that the veil could be pierced where the defendant by the device of a corporate structure attempts to evade: '(i) limitations imposed on his conduct by law; (ii) such rights of relief against him as third parties already possess,' but held that on the facts the attempt to pierce the veil in these two ways failed.

The facts of the present case are very different from those in *Woolfson*, and *Adams*; and I do not read the judgment in *Adams* based on Lord Keith's statement of principle in *Woolfson* as barring the piercing of the corporate veil in this case, in which the transfer of assets from Welwyn to Motors would otherwise enable the Breachwood group owned by Mr Ford and Mr Seaman to evade responsibility for the contingent liabilities to Mr Creasey for breach of his contract of employment.

The most important factor in this case is that Mr Ford and Mr Seaman, and through them Motors, themselves deliberately ignored the separate corporate personalities of Welwyn and Motors, and did so with the benefit of the advice of the solicitors acting for Welwyn and Motors.

Nothing I have seen in the evidence could justify their conduct in deliberately shifting Welwyn's assets and business into Motors in total disregard of their duties as directors and shareholders, not least the duties created by Parliament as a protection to all creditors of a company.

Welwyn was not put into liquidation. As a subsisting company it was entitled to retain its business and assets, so that they be available to pay a dividend however small to such of Welwyn's creditors as Motors decided not to pay.

Mr Ford and Mr Seaman decided instead to remove the business and assets of Welwyn to Motors, and, realising that the business could not be carried on satisfactorily unless Welwyn's trade creditors were paid, paid all their then actual creditors, but left Mr Creasey facing a defendant without assets. They did so in full knowledge of Mr Creasey's claim.

On the state of the evidence before me the inference could readily be drawn that one of the reasons why Mr Ford and Mr Seaman acted in the way they did was in order to ensure that Mr Creasey if he succeeded in his claim would not be able to recover anything. But I consider that it would be wrong to draw so strongly adverse an inference at this stage on only the affidavit evidence.

In all the circumstances, however, this is a case in which the court would be justified in lifting the veil and treating Motors as liable for this remaining liability of Welwyn.

. . .

Mr Lydiard[1] met the 'lifting the veil' submission of Mr Behar in three principal ways.

First, he submitted that Motors could not be described as a 'device' like the companies in *Gilford Motor v Horne* and *Jones v Lipman*. It was and is a solid company with its own business. Welwyn was insolvent. That was why Welwyn had to cease trading. He distinguished *Re a company* [1985] BCLC 333 on the ground, he submitted, that here the assets were not transferred to defeat a contractual liability which Welwyn would otherwise have paid. Welwyn was genuinely insolvent *before* the transfer to Motors took place.

However, in my judgment, the facts remain that Welwyn had assets of over £70,000 and a subsisting business, that Mr Creasey is the only unpaid creditor, and that he is now faced with a dissolved company having no assets at all.

Secondly, he submitted that the realities must be seen clearly if justice is to be done between the parties. If Welwyn had been wound up, Mr Creasey would have had a contested action against a company in liquidation. It would not be equitable in these circumstances, he submitted, to allow Mr Creasey to enforce

---

1 Counsel for the defendant

the entire judgment against a solvent company, Motors, since that would put Mr Creasey in a better position.

This seems to me to be a point of greater relevance if the substitution is allowed to remain, in which case I would have to consider what relief, if any, I should give to Motors in relation to the judgment.

Thirdly, he submitted that this form of remedy (the substitution of Motors as defendant) is both wrong and unjust. Mr Creasey should be left to his ordinary rights so far as concerns restoring Welwyn to the register and winding Welwyn up, and any rights in tort which Mr Creasey may have against Mr Ford, Mr Seaman and Motors. He accepted the consequences I have already set out as regards Mr Creasey and the Legal Aid Board, but submitted that those were not good reasons for taking a procedural step which in his submission is wrong and not calculated to do justice.

It is this factor which has caused me most concern. I am satisfied that the court has power to substitute a defendant, even after judgment, under the court's inherent jurisdiction and under RSC Ord 15, r 7, in an appropriate case: compare in relation to a plaintiff, the decision of the Court of Appeal in *Mercer Alloys Corp v Rolls Royce Ltd* [1972] 1 All ER 211, [1971] 1 WLR 1520. But the question remains whether it is right to use this route so as to achieve justice between the parties.

In my judgment Mr Lydiard's submissions would carry greater force if this case involved parties with substantial funds who were well able to bear the costs involved in the ending of the present action and the start of fresh proceedings involving perhaps both the liquidation of Welwyn and the liquidator starting an action against Mr Ford, Mr Seaman and Motors, and also Mr Creasey starting his own action against these three persons. But here the court is concerned with a plaintiff with legal aid, a potential defendant company with reasonable but not large resources and two other individuals as potential defendants. To require these persons to incur large legal costs in pursuit of other proceedings would in my judgment be unfair to each of them, and particularly to Mr Creasey. Indeed I doubt very much whether in view of the sums in issue justice can be done for Mr Creasey if Motors are not substituted.

The court allowed the substitution, but set aside the judgment on certain terms to give the defendant an opportunity of advancing a defence to the claim.

PART VII: THE PERIODICAL LITERATURE

Still of great value, although now 50 years old, is *Kahn-Freund* 'Some Reflections on Company Law Reform'. The following passage includes the often quoted assessment of *Salomon*[1] as being a 'calamitous' decision.

SOURCE 44
Kahn-Freund, Some Reflections on Company Law Reform
[1944] 7 MLR 54

In this country as elsewhere company law has, to a large extent, changed its economic and social function. The privileges of incorporation and of limited

---

1 [1897] AC 22; 66 LJ Ch 35 (see p 91)

liability were originally granted in order to enable a number of capitalists to embark upon risky adventures without shouldering the burden of personal liability. There was, in the second half of the nineteenth century, a definite commercial need for those measures which the various Companies Acts introduced. However, owing to the ease with which companies can be formed in this country, and owing to the rigidity with which the courts applied the corporate entity concept ever since the calamitous decision in *Salomon v Salomon & Co Ltd*, a single trader or a group of traders are almost tempted by the law to conduct their business in the form of a limited company, even where no particular business risk is involved, and where no outside capital is required. The partnership which — either in its normal form or as a limited partnership — ought to be the usual type of business association, has, in many walks of commercial life, been almost completely displaced by the private company.

This state of affairs would not necessarily call for reform, if it were not for the fact that the courts have failed to give that protection to the business creditors which should be the corollary of the privilege of limited liability. The courts have adapted the law of fiduciary relationships to the liabilities of promoters and directors. They have thus given a measure of protection to the shareholders over and above that provided by Parliament, and they have succeeded in introducing into British company law a body of principles which, elsewhere, had to be formulated by legislation. The flexibility of the law governing this topic contrasts with the complete failure of the courts to mitigate, through the mechanism of the law of agency, the rigidities of the 'folklore' of corporate entity in favour of the legitimate interests of the company's creditors. As it is, the company has often become a means of evading liabilities and of concealing the real interests behind the business.

It is not as if the Courts had been unable to look behind the curtain of 'corporate personality,' when they were minded to do so. In the law of income tax, the paramount needs of the national exchequer have induced Parliament to tear to shreds the veil of corporate entity where it was used as a cloak for tax avoidance or evasion. In other branches of the law the Courts themselves have lifted the veil. Thus, a company was treated as a member of a trade association though, strictly speaking, it was not the company but its nominee who was registered as a member, while a member of a bankrupt's committee of inspection was treated as such, though he appeared in the mask of a representative of a limited company. Closely associated companies were treated as identical for the purposes of the law of negotiable instruments, and in the law of carriage by sea. In *Canada Rice Mills v R*,[1] the Judicial Committee refused to regard a transaction between a parent company and its subsidiary as a 'sale' for the purposes of a Canadian taxing statute. In another Canadian case the Privy Council came to the conclusion that a valid covenant in restraint of trade is violated if the covenantor acquires a 'controlling' interest in a competing company, and Farwell J held that an industrial and provident society and a company which succeeds to its assets may be separate entities 'in law', but 'in substance and in truth exactly the same thing' for the purposes of the application of a trust fund.

There are even cases where, despite *Salomon v Salomon & Co*, a company was treated as the trading agent either of its parent company or of its controlling shareholder, though, of course, the Courts were prevented by the strait-jacket of the *Salomon* decision from holding the latter liable for debts contracted by the company as his agent.

---

1 [1939] 3 All ER 991

But even outside the immediate scope of application of the *Salomon* rule the 'corporate entity' metaphor continues to hold its tyrannical sway. Indeed, in many cases it is a matter of guesswork whether the Court will allow the parties to 'draw the veil' or force them to lift it. It is not, of course, as if the superannuated conflict between the 'realists' and the believers in the fictitious nature of corporate personality had anything to do with this. The need for lifting the veil must be obvious to the realists even more than those who, like the present writer, have never been convinced by the reasoning of Maitland or Gierke. Why should a parent company be unable to deduct its subsidiary's trading losses as a revenue expense from its taxable income? Why should it be unable to claim an insurance interest in the latter's property? On the other hand, why should the Canadian Revenue authorities not be 'entitled, in the absence of fraud or improper conduct, to disregard the separate legal existence' of two very closely associated companies in connection with the fixing of depreciation allowances? And is it tolerable that business men should be able to rid themselves of their liabilities, just because when assigning assets belonging to a company which is a 'sham simulacrum and a cloak' they fail to act as shareholders or directors rather than individuals? Or that a business is no longer treated as that of an insured person for the purposes of a motor policy because it has been 'converted' into a company controlled by him? Or that the limitation of liability under the Merchant Shipping Act cannot be claimed by a shipowning company because the guilty vessel happens to belong to a subsidiary?

Enough has been said to prove that the surfeit of companies introduces into many branches of the law an element of caprice incompatible with the certainty which is the life-blood of commercial law. The metaphysical separation between a man in his individual capacity and his capacity as a one-man-company can be used to defraud his creditors who are exposed to grave injury owing to the timidity of the Courts and of the Companies Act. Sometimes, as shown by the cases concerning insurable interest and the shipowner's limitation of liability, 'corporate entity' works like a boomerang and hits the man who was trying to use it.

What can be done? How is it possible to check the one-man-company and other abuses of company law for purposes which it was never meant to serve? Is it conceivable that *Salomon's* case can be abrogated by legislation? Could the interests of outside creditors be protected by a general clause under which the persons owning a controlling interest in a company would be liable for its debts? Or could there be a provision according to which a company would be deemed to act as agent for the owners of controlling interests? The difficulty of defining a controlling interest might not be insurmountable, as shown by the precedent of income tax law. Nevertheless, there may be objections to such a course. The definition of a controlling interest might either be framed in very general terms and thus leave a wide scope to the discretion of the Courts, or it might be as strict as that of income tax legislation. In the former case the present uncertainty, though mitigated, would continue to exist, in the latter case the present hardships would not be removed in marginal situations.

Moreover, as shown by the above random examples, it is not just a question of overruling the *Salomon* case. The clash between 'law' and 'truth and substance' occurs not only to the detriment of the company's creditors. The incongruity of the present situation permeates the whole of legal business life — revenue law no less than insurance, shipping, and carriage by land. A 'general clause' might have to be even more general than the one suggested above. It might have to ordain that a company and the owners of the controlling interests must be treated as one for all legal purposes. The unforeseeable consequences of such a sweeping

provision are likely to deter the legislature from adopting it. It is, however, not
easy to see why company law should not be able to lift the veil of corporate entity,
at least in extreme cases, for the benefit of the creditors, if revenue law has been
able to achieve this in the interests of the Treasury. A limited general clause
should be seriously considered.

Perhaps a remedy can be found in a different direction as well. Instead of, or
in addition to, altering the legal consequences of company formation, one might
make the formation of companies more difficult and more expensive, and thus
reduce the number of companies and especially of small companies. By doing so,
Parliament might go some way towards restoring to the limited company its
original function, and to the partnership its proper place in business life.

At the present moment, it is almost unbelievably easy and even more
unbelievably cheap to form a company in this country.

. . .

SOURCE 45
Pickering, The Company as a Separate Legal Entity
[1968] 31 MLR 481

This is a good general survey, with the following amusing catalogue.

Under English company law the company is a separate legal entity. Yet, although
this is a fundamental concept, it has proved extremely intractable to define and
to describe satisfactorily. The difficulties experienced by the courts from time to
time in separating the company as a legal entity from its members are evidenced
by the remarkable range of judicial expletives or, in Younger LJ's phrase, 'term[s]
of polite invective,' which they have used on appropriate occasions to describe
corporations, including, for example, 'a mere nominee,' 'a mere fraud,' an
'agent,' 'a trustee,' a 'mere device,' 'a myth and a fiction,' 'a pretended
association,' a 'bubble,' an 'unreal' procedure, 'a cloak,' 'an alias,' 'a name,' 'an
artificial legal thing,' 'a legal abstraction,' 'mere machinery,' 'a metaphysical
conception,' 'a sham or bogus,' 'an abstract conception,' 'a simulacrum,' 'a
cloak,' a 'mere alter ego,' 'an abstract being,' a 'creature,' 'a screen,' and even
'black sheep.' In *Re Bugle Press Ltd*,[1] Harman LJ added 'a hollow sham' and an
'elementary... device,' going on to elaborate in more picturesque language:
'... the transferee company was nothing but a little hut...' whose legal
existence could be likened to 'the walls of Jericho' — 'The minority shareholder
has nothing to knock down, he has only to shout and the walls of Jericho fall flat.'
The apparent need to resort to such terms indicates an unexpected degree of
uncertainty on the part of the courts on some occasions when dealing with the
separate existence of the company.

SOURCE 46
Halpern, Trebilcock, Turnbull, An Economic Analysis of Limited Liability
(1980) 30 University of Toronto LJ 117

A sophisticated analysis of the economic efficiency of limited as opposed to
unlimited liability regimes, which concludes as follows:

We now attempt to derive some implications from the foregoing analysis for the
form of an efficient liability regime for corporations.

First, in the case of large, widely held companies, a limited liability regime, as

---

1 [1961] Ch 270; [1960] 3 All ER 791

a general rule, is the most efficient regime. By skewing the distribution of business risks amongst different shareholders, an unlimited liability regime would create a significant measure of uncertainty in the valuation of securities and threaten the existence of organized securities markets, thus inducing costly attempts by creditors and owners to transact around the regime. The case for a limited liability regime for this class of company is very compelling. The attenuated nature of the moral hazard factor in widely held companies does not create a strong countervailing consideration.

Second, in the case of small, tightly held companies, a limited liability regime will, in many cases, create incentives for owners to exploit a moral hazard and transfer uncompensated business risks to creditors, thus inducing costly attempts by creditors to reduce these risks. An unlimited liability regime for this class of enterprise (perhaps the 'private company', recognized by many corporation statutes with respect to financial disclosure and securities regulation exemptions, having fewer than, say, fifty shareholders, restrictions on share transfers, and no right to make public offerings) would seem to be the most efficient regime. The availability of an organized securities market is not, of course, a major countervailing factor with this class of company.

A major effect of adopting an unlimited liability regime in this context would be to shift to the corporation and its owners the onus of proposing contractual arrangements to creditors which limit the liability of the owners (where these are desired). Requiring explicit negotiation of such arrangements is likely to improve information flows to creditors about allocation of risks and sharpen the focus of creditors' incentives to monitor a corporation's activities. We acknowledge that the case for an unlimited liability regime for this class of company is not as compelling as the case for limited liability for large, widely held companies, given that in the former case, with fewer parties involved, most creditors and owners can contract around either regime at low cost, thus making the choice of liability regime relatively inconsequential. We also recognize that difficulties may be associated with attempting to distinguish by law small from large corporations for the purpose of applying different liability regimes, and that the distinction may induce some perverse and wasteful incentive effects as firms seek to manipulate internal structures to ensure compliance with the requirements of the preferred regime. However, our empirical intuition remains that, on balance, an unlimited liability regime is the most efficient regime for small, closely held companies.

Third, in cases where, as a general rule, a limited liability regime is the most efficient regime (large, widely held corporations, in our analysis), there is a case for a limited number of exceptions to the regime where some form of unlimited liability seems desirable. These exceptions might embrace the following classes of case:

A. MISREPRESENTATION

An exception is called for in the case of misrepresentations to creditors as to the legal status of a firm or its financial affairs . . . Here the party responsible for the misrepresentation should be personally liable for corporate debts induced by the misrepresentation, but, in addition, as we elaborate below, the directors of the corporation might be made personally liable (subject to offsetting insurance or compensation arrangements) to strengthen management incentives to have this form of behaviour monitored by corporate officers and employees.

B. THE INVOLUNTARY CREDITOR

In cases such as *Walkovsky v Carlton*,[1] transactions costs are such that a firm can transfer uncompensated business risks to this class of creditor. *Rockwell Developments Ltd v Newtonbrook Plaza Ltd*,[2] where a firm unilaterally imposed costs on another party through unmeritorious legal proceedings, involved similar considerations. Again, it can be argued that the directors of the company should be personally liable to this class of creditor. In the large, widely held corporation where this exception would apply, such a rule would minimize the information costs that owners would face in monitoring each other's wealth, would reduce creditors' transaction costs in enforcing claims, and would focus incentives to adopt cost-justified avoidance precautions on that body of persons (the directors) in such a class of corporation best able to respond to those incentives.

C. THE EMPLOYEE

Amongst corporate creditors, employees, as a class, probably face the most severe informational disabilities, have the least ability to diversify risk of business failure, and may have the strongest equity argument (in terms of relative capacity to absorb losses). The proposition is not universally true, as some employees will possess both superior information on corporate finances and high job mobility (eg corporate executives and professional employees), while some trade creditors may be afflicted with similar disabilities to those of the less informed, less mobile corporate employees. However, fashioning a rule that clearly differentiates these situations is likely to be difficult, and present rules governing the liability of directors for limited amounts of unpaid wages of 'employees' in the Canada Business Corporation Act may represent defensible approximations of optimal rules.

The net effect of these proposals would seem to be to obviate the need for the elaborate veil-piercing, subrogation, and consolidation rules in corporate bankruptcies advocated by Landers. In the case of small, tightly held corporations, the unlimited liability regime which we have proposed would seem responsive to many of the parent-subsidiary and affiliated company problems with which he is concerned. In the case of large, widely held companies, involuntary creditors and employees, under our proposals, receive special protection. Other creditors, prejudiced by intra-group transactions induced by moral hazard considerations, would have to rely on the misrepresentation exception. This exception is necessarily a much more limited response to creditor problems than the unlimited liability regime proposed for small, closely held corporations because any substantial move in the direction of unlimited liability in the case of large, widely held companies will engender the kind of costs that have led us generally to reject such a regime in this case. Our proposals would also contemplate as unnecessary and undesirable many of the provisions in the federal Bankruptcy Act and the new Bankruptcy Bill with respect to 'reviewable transactions' and the liability of corporate 'agents'. The operational uncertainty (and consequent costs) associated with these provisions would be reduced under the relatively straightforward rules that we have proposed.

---

1 (1966) 223 NE 2d 6
2 (1972) 30 OR (2nd) 199 (Ont CA)

SOURCE 47
Hamilton, The Corporate Entity
[1971] 49 Texas LR 979

A refreshingly robust article which stresses analysis of the facts of the cases rather than the retreat to fictions and metaphors.

...

The notion that a corporation is a fictional person or legal entity distinct from its shareholders also appears in early American decisions. In the Dartmouth College cases,[1] Mr. Chief Justice Marshall echoed Lord Coke in defining a corporation as 'an artificial being, invisible, intangible, and existing only in contemplation of law.' Similar definitions became increasingly popular with the courts during the wave of great industrial expansion in the latter part of the nineteenth century. Of course, many of these decisions tended to protect corporations, thereby encouraging industrial expansion. In the modern era, the 'legal person' approach has come under increasingly serious criticism from legal writers and thinkers. The starting point for this criticism is a fundamental truth about corporations that cannot be blinked — that flesh-and-blood people underlie every corporation and are essential to everything a corporation does. Some individual must decide what the corporation is to do; some individual must actually do the required act on behalf of the corporation, because manifestly a 'legal person' has no arms, legs, mouth, or eyes; some individual will ultimately reap any profits earned by the corporation; and some person must ultimately bear any loss. Realistically, a corporation is simply a device by which individuals conduct a business and other individuals share in the profit or loss.

...

A Proposed Solution

Without attempting to make an exhaustive list of considerations that appear to bear on the above cases, the following four general principles appear to have wide application when disregard of corporate form is genuinely presented:

1. *Notions of Simple Justice and Fairness* — Courts are likely to avoid answers that lead to results that are unfair or inconsistent with the court's view of policy. An insurance company that writes a policy covering an injury caused by a corporate agent is unlikely to receive much judicial sympathy when it seeks to argue that fortuitously the injured person was the sole shareholder of the corporation and therefore the company should not be liable on the policy. Similarly, a court is unlikely to allow a party to a contract to defend on the ground that a concession was obtained not only by the other party, as the contract required, but by a wholly owned subsidiary of the other party, or that a person should be free of a merger clause in an agreement merely because at the last minute the contract was entered into by his wholly-owned corporation. These notions of fairness and justice often have little or nothing to do with corporation law; rather, they belong to the substantive law of torts or contracts or insurance, or what have you. This again emphasizes the ends to which analysis should be directed.

2. *Desire to Retain Reasonable Procedures and Avoid Substantive Tangles* — The Unemployment Compensation Act contains a procedure by which successor organizations may assume the experience rating of the predecessor upon compliance with certain statutory requirements. The proper method of determining whether a successor is in fact entitled to an experience rating is under

---

1 17 US (4 Wheat) 518, 636 (1819)

that Act, not in a suit in which the parties argue about 'alter egos' and cite cases having nothing to do with experience ratings. Similarly, a holding that shareholders cannot treat their land as land owned by the corporation for purposes of measuring condemnation damages to the over-all tract avoids impossible problems of allocation of proceeds when there is not absolute identity of interest between the shareholdings and land ownership. Similarly, to allow shareholders to sue directly on corporate obligations may create multiple litigation when there is more than one shareholder.

3. Desire to Protect Potential Creditors and Minority Shareholders — Potential creditors and minority shareholders who have substantial interests in the corporation may be unrepresented in litigation. Certainly, a dominant shareholder should not be permitted to recover personally a corporate asset unless the court is convinced that all creditors and minority shareholders are protected. On the other hand, if there is such assurance, there is little point in requiring a new suit to be brought merely because the sole shareholder rather than the corporation was named as plaintiff. For the same reason there should be no objection to treating a conveyance by all the shareholders as the conveyance of the corporation if no creditors will be injured thereby.

4. Election of Corporateness — Some of the above cases may be explained by a judicial predilection against allowing a shareholder who elected to form a corporation to argue that the corporation does not really exist when it suits his purpose to do so. On the other hand, the court's holding in the Haitian concession case[1] that acquisition of the concession by plaintiff's subsidiary corporation is the same as acquisition by the plaintiff is not entirely consistent with this principle.

VI. CONCLUSION

Perhaps any conclusion to the foregoing analysis is unnecessary because there should be little mystery about the nature of a corporation. Whether or not it should be deemed a separate 'legal entity' or 'legal person' should depend on the question to be resolved. A corporation may be an entity for some purposes and not for others. In such circumstances, to argue that a corporation is an entity, and therefore that certain results follow, is to put the cart before the horse. Analysis, in other words, should be directed not to the nature of corporateness but to the substantive policies underlying the issues.

---

1 285 F 2d 726 (5th Circuit) (1960)

Chapter 3

FORMATION OF THE COMPANY

PART I: REGISTRATION

Types of Companies

Companies registered under the Companies Act can be limited or unlimited and, if limited, limited by shares or guarantee (s 1(1), (2)). Company limited by guarantee is the form of organisation for a non-profit making group of people who have come together to further common purposes of a public, cultural, scientific or other intellectual or political kind. With a company limited by shares, people associate together so that *their money* may be pooled and exploited; in the case of a company limited by guarantee, the essential link is the sharing of a particular purpose and a wish to further that purpose. Here, money is raised by annual subscriptions and other appropriate outside sources (eg collections, appeals). Companies limited by guarantee are exempt from the requirement that 'limited' be part of their name, provided that the conditions laid down for this exemption are complied with (ss 30, 31).

With an unlimited company there is no limit to the liability of the shareholders for the debts of the company. In the case of the company limited by shares, the limit of the liability is set by the nominal ('par') value of the share. In the case of a company limited by guarantee, the liability is limited to the amount ('guarantee') stated to be the amount which all members will be required to contribute in the event of the company being wound up and being unable to pay its debts in full (s 2(4); see Companies (Tables A–F) Regulations 1985, SI 1985/805, Tables B, C, E). It is now no longer possible to have a company limited by guarantee and with a share capital, (s 1(4), of the Companies Act 1985).

A further important distinction is that between public and private companies. The regime established by the Companies Act is that any company registered is a private company unless the requirements for registration as a public company are fulfilled (ss 1(3), 3(1): statement in the memorandum; ss 11, 101, 117, 118: minimum issued and paid-up share capital; ss 25(1), (2), 27(1), (4): name of company; s 282(1): at least two directors. Public companies must have a minimum of two members, private companies need only one (ss 1(1), 3A).

The distinction between private and public companies is mainly significant in connection with the raising and maintenance of capital — only public companies may invite the public to subscribe for shares (see Part III, the Flotation of Public Companies, at p 174). See also s 13(6), (7) (certificate of incorporation); note also effect on allotment of shares, ss 101–104; disclosure of interest in shares, ss 198, 199; restrictions on distribution of assets, s 264.

Some principles of company law have, by their nature, developed in relation to either public or private companies. Thus, the principles as to the truthfulness and accuracy of the prospectus inviting the public to subscribe for shares, are relevant only to public companies. Likewise, principles governing the winding up of companies on the ground that this is just and equitable, derive from partnership and apply to small (invariably private) companies (see pp 561ff) and principles governing the application and interpretation of provisions restricting the transfer of shares relate almost exclusively to private companies.

Procedure for Registration

Application must be made on the prescribed forms to the Registrar of Companies submitting the proposed constitution of the company (the memorandum and articles of association). See ss 2, 3, 7, 8, 10. If all necessary requirements have been completed, registration follows and a certificate of registration will be issued, ss 12, 13.

Company Name

The company's name must comply with ss 25–27 of the Companies Act 1985 (CA), ss 2–3 of the Business Names Act 1985, and any Regulations made by the Secretary of State under CA, s 29 (Company and Business Names Regulations 1981, SI 1981/1685, as amended by the Company and Business Names (Amendment) Regulations 1992 (SI 1992/1196). The Registrar of Companies has a discretion as to the name of the company (Sources 48 and 49). The name can be changed (CA, s 28) and will have to be where it is misleading (CA, s 32). Principles of the common law, in particular as to the tort of passing off, also govern the choice of name (Sources 50 and 51).

SOURCE 48
The King *v* Registrar of Companies, ex parte Bowen
[1914] 3 KB 1161

Application was made to the Registrar of Companies to register the memorandum and articles of association of a proposed company under the Companies Act, 1908. The name of the company was 'The United Dental Service, Limited.' The objects of the company, stated in the memorandum, included: 'To carry on the practice, profession, or business of practitioners in dentistry in all its branches.' The memorandum and articles were signed by seven persons who were all members of a society called 'The Incorporated Dental Society, Limited,' the members of which were all unregistered practitioners in dentistry.

The Registrar refused to register the company unless the memorandum provided that the work of the company should be undertaken only by means of duly qualified dental practitioners, that is, dental practitioners registered under the Dentists Act, 1878 or the title of the company was amended so as not to include the word 'dental,' 'dentist,' or any similar or equivalent word.

LORD READING CJ: . . . In my opinion the question turns in the main, although not entirely, in view of the arguments addressed to us, upon whether the use of these words, 'The United Dental Service,' would amount to an offence under the Dentists Act, 1878. In other words, whether the use of those words is a description implying that the persons who are intending to practise under that name are persons 'specially qualified to practise dentistry'; that is, whether those words mean that the persons who are ready to perform that service are, or may be, persons who hold a licence, diploma, degree, or whatever the term may be which is used, implying that such persons are entitled to be registered under the Act for the reason that they hold such licence, &c.

Does the use of those words amount to an offence under the Dentists Act, 1878? In my opinion it does not.

. . .

I think these words, 'United Dental Service,' imply a description of the acts to be performed, and do not imply that the persons who will perform them are persons specially qualified under the statute of 1878. The Registrar of Companies would be entitled, if the use of the proposed name would be an offence under the statute (either under this or any other statute), to refuse to register the company with that name; but, having arrived at the conclusion that that would not be the effect of the use of the words 'United Dental Service,' I hold that the Registrar was wrong in refusing registration upon that ground.

Then it is said by the Solicitor-General that it is not necessary to go so far as that; that although the words may not imply by their use sufficient to constitute an offence under the Act, yet they are calculated to mislead persons notwithstanding that they would not be held in a criminal prosecution to imply a particular meaning; that the distinction may be a fine one but is plain enough; and that if there is even reasonable doubt, that is, a reasonable possibility, that persons might be misled into thinking that, if they attended at the premises of this company, the operation, or service, or attendance, would be performed by persons specifically qualified under the Act, then that is sufficient ground for refusal to register. I dissent from that proposition. I do not think that the Registrar has any discretion to consider whether, when the name is presented to him with a memorandum and articles of association, it is calculated to deceive the public. The Registrar has a discretion or a duty under s 2 of the Companies Act 1908 [now s 1, CA 1985], not to register an association which is not formed for a lawful purpose.

. . .

If he came to the conclusion that the phrase used in the name of the company implied in the circumstances that an offence under the statute would be committed, he would be right in refusing registration. I am far from saying that he has no discretion at all if the association is formed for a lawful purpose. For instance, I think if the name presented to him for registration contained scandalous or obscene words he would be perfectly justified in refusing registration. But I cannot think it is open to him, who has not, as it seems to me, the power to hold a judicial inquiry upon evidence properly given, to come to a conclusion that the words are calculated to deceive.

. . .

It seems to me that the Registrar cannot take upon himself to determine that the mere use of the word 'Dental' in the name of the company, and attached to 'Service,' may be calculated to mislead, or does mislead, the public into the belief that the business will be carried on by persons specially qualified under this Act. For these reasons I am of opinion that this rule must be made absolute.

SOURCE 49
R *v* Registrar of Companies, ex parte Attorney-General
[1991] BCLC 476

ACKNER LJ: . . . The Attorney General applies to quash the incorporation and registration by the Registrar of Companies nearly a year ago, that is on 18 December 1979, of Lindi St Claire (Personal Services) Ltd as a limited company under the provisions of the Companies Acts 1948 to 1976.

The grounds of the application, to state them quite briefly, are these. In certifying the incorporation of a company and in registering the same the Registrar of Companies acted ultra vires or misdirected himself or otherwise erred in law, in particular as to the proper construction and application of s 1(1) of the Companies Act 1948 [now s 1, CA 1985] in that the company was not formed for any lawful purpose but, on the contrary, was formed expressly with the primary object of carrying on the business of prostitution, such being an unlawful purpose involving the commission of acts which are immoral and contrary to public policy.

. . .

Now as to the facts, these come within a very short compass and they amount to the following. A firm of certified accountants, Gilson Clipp & Co, on 16 August 1979 wrote to the Registrar of Companies at Companies House, Crown Way, Maindy, Cardiff pointing out that they had received a letter from the Inland Revenue Policy Division, who stated that they considered prostitution to be a trade which is fully taxable, and that they, the certified accountants, saw no reason why their client should not be able to organise her business by way of a limited company. They asked whether the name 'Prostitute Ltd' was available for registration as a limited company, pointing out the main object of the company would be that of organising the services of a prostitute.

The registrar did not like that name and did not accept it, nor did he accept another name 'Hookers Ltd' which was offered. But subsequently two further names were offered, 'Lindi St Claire (Personal Services) Ltd' and 'Lindi St Claire (French Lessons) Ltd', and it was the former which he registered.

The memorandum of association said in terms that the first of the objects of the company was 'To carry on the business of prostitution'.

The only director of the company is Lindi St Claire, Miss St Claire describing herself specifically as 'Prostitute'. The other person who owns also one share is a Miss Duggan, who is referred to as 'the cashier'.

Leave having been obtained to apply for judicial review, Miss St Claire wrote in these terms:

> 'I would like to say that prostitution is not at all unlawful, as you have stated, and I feel it is most unfair of you to take this view, especially when I am paying income tax on my earnings from prostitution to the government Inland Revenue.
>
> Furthermore, I feel it is most unfair of you to imply that I have acted wrongly, as I was most explicit to all concerned about the sole trade of the company to be that of prostitution and nothing more. If my company should not be deemed valid, then it should have not been granted in the first place by the Board of Trade. It is most unfair of the government to allow me to go ahead with my company one moment, then quash it the next.'

In regard to that paragraph Miss St Claire is perfectly right that she was most explicit to all concerned as to the trade of the company, and in that paragraph she confirms that it was the sole trade of the company. Mr Simon Brown on behalf of the Attorney General, concedes that, if the company should not be deemed valid, then it should not have been registered in the first place by the Board of Trade, and therefore the issue with which we are concerned is the validity of the registration.

That takes us to s 1(1) of the Companies Act 1948, and I need only read that subsection:

'Any seven or more persons, or, where the company to be formed will be a private company, any two or more persons, associated for any lawful purpose may, by subscribing their names to a memorandum of association and otherwise complying with the requirements of this Act in respect of registration, form an incorporated company, with or without limited liability.'

It is well settled that a contract which is made upon a sexually immoral consideration or for a sexually immoral purpose is against public policy and is illegal and unenforceable. The fact that it does not involve or may not involve the commission of a criminal offence in no way prevents the contract being illegal, being against public policy and therefore being unenforceable. Here, as the documents clearly indicate, the association is for the purpose of carrying on a trade which involves illegal contracts because the purpose is a sexually immoral purpose and as such against public policy.

Mr Simon Brown submits that if that is the position, as indeed it clearly is on the authorities, then the association of the two or more persons cannot be for 'any lawful purpose'.

To my mind this must follow. It is implicit in the speeches in the *Bowman* case to which I have just made reference. In my judgment, the contention of the Attorney General is a valid one and I would order that the registration be therefore quashed.

SOURCE 50

La Société Anonyme des Anciens Etablissements Panhard et Levassor *v* Panhard Levassor Motor Company Limited

(Chancery Division 1901) [1901] 2 Ch 513; 70 LJ Ch 738

FARWELL J: This appears to me to be a plain case. The plaintiffs are a well-known firm of motor-car manufacturers in Paris. Their reputation has extended to England for several years. Although prior to this action they had no agency and did not sell directly in England, they sold indirectly in the sense that their cars were bought and imported into England, both by the British Motor Company Limited, and by private individuals, so that England was one of their markets. The difficulty about England was that there were certain English patents, and the great majority of the cars formerly made by the plaintiffs could not be imported into England without the licence of the patentees. In many cases those licences were obtained, and the plaintiffs got the benefit of the English market, although they only got it indirectly in the way I have mentioned.

The defendants have registered a company in England under the name of the Panhard Levassor Motor Company, Limited. The seven signatories are joined as defendants. There is absolutely no sort of excuse or justification for taking the name 'Panhard Levassor.' It is said that their object is not so much to annex the benefit of the plaintiffs' reputation, as it is to shut out the plaintiffs from England, and prevent them interfering with some other company which is not a party to this action. With that I have nothing to do. I judge the case as I have it before me, and I find seven persons signing the memorandum of a company with a capital of £100 divided into 100 shares of £1 each, with seven signatories with one share apiece, and therefore an actual paid or possibly unpaid capital of £7, for I do not know whether it has been paid or not. . . . this court would certainly interfere to protect a foreign trader who has a market in England, . . . from having the benefit of his name annexed by a trader in England who assumes that name without any sort of justification.

The only part of the case which has caused me a little difficulty is the claim against the seven signatories to the memorandum, who are the directors and sole shareholders of the company. The allegation is that they have fraudulently and wrongfully, and with intent to injure the plaintiffs in their said business, conspired together to form, and have formed, and procured the defendant company to be registered. Now, as I hold that the defendant company has the fraudulent intention of annexing the benefit of the plaintiffs' name, it follows that the persons who have formed that company and caused it to be registered are guilty in the eye of this Court of a fraudulent conspiracy to carry into effect that which the company, an entity without body or soul, was attempted to do, and are liable in damages accordingly. It would certainly be exceedingly unfortunate if the Court were to hold that a limited company with a very small nominal capital can be formed for the purpose of trying to do unlawful, fraudulent and illegal acts, and that no one except the incorporated body is liable.

In my opinion, the injunction which I grant against the company involves a similar injunction against the signatories who have caused the company to be registered, and who remain the only directors and members of the company. . . .

SOURCE 51
Ewing *v* Buttercup Margarine Company Limited
(Chancery Division 1917) [1917] 2 Ch 1; 86 LJ Ch 441

ASTBURY J: . . . The ground of interference by the Court in these name cases is that the use of the defendant company's name, or intended name, is calculated to deceive, and 'so to divert business from the plaintiff to the defendant,' or 'to occasion a confusion between the two businesses': *Kerly on Trade Marks*, 4th edn, p 548. The text-book rightly adds that 'calculated to deceive' is not to be limited to the date of the proceedings, but the Court will have regard to the way in which the business may be carried on in the future, and to its not being carried on precisely as carried on at the date of the proceedings.

If the name, although not actually used by the plaintiff for the particular kind of goods to which the defendant has applied, or is proposing to apply it, is so identified with the name that the defendant uses that it may induce the belief that his goods are those of the plaintiff, or secondly that his business is an extension of, or otherwise connected with, the plaintiff's business, then the Court can grant relief.

In *Hendriks v Montagu*[1] James LJ said: 'All the Court requires is to be satisfied that the names are so similar as to be calculated to produce confusion between the two companies — so calculated to do it that when it is drawn to the attention of those adopting the name complained of that that would be the result, it is not honest for them to persevere in their intention, though originally the intention might not have been otherwise than honest'; and Cotton LJ said that in the particular case before him the evidence was: 'That what the defendants will do, if they are not restrained, will cause confusion and will induce people, or be the means of inducing people, who desire to insure in this long-established society of the plaintiff's, to insure in the defendants' office instead.'

Now in the present case I have to decide, as a fact, whether on the evidence before me the use of the name 'Buttercup Margarine Company Limited,' is calculated to deceive by diverting customers or potential customers, from the

---

1 (1881) 17 Ch D 638; 50 LJ Ch 456

plaintiff; or to occasion such a confusion between the two businesses as has been referred to in the various authorities.

Prima facie the defendants will deal with a set of people altogether different from the plaintiff's customers. As wholesalers they will sell to shops, whereas the plaintiff's customers only purchase from shops. But a company that sells margarine under the title of the 'Buttercup Margarine Company Limited,' need not be surprised if the natural result follows that its margarine comes to be so identified with its name that retail shops carrying on business in the districts served by the plaintiff's shops may honestly offer the defendant company's margarine for sale, as the Buttercup Margarine Company's margarine or, shortly, 'Buttercup Margarine.' In these circumstances there is a reasonable possibility of the plaintiff's customers in those districts believing that the 'Buttercup' margarine they have known in the past can now be obtained at other shops than 'The Buttercup Dairy Company.'

Further, I think that other confusion may arise. It is not an unknown thing for a dairy company selling butter substitutes to manufacture some of the products which it sells. For instance, the Maypole Dairy Company carry on business as manufacturers of margarine under the name of the Maypole Margarine Works, Limited, and just as that company's Maypole margarine can be purchased from the Maypole Dairy Company, so people may come to suppose that the plaintiff's 'Buttercup' margarine can be bought from the Buttercup Margarine Company.

Thirdly, although this is perhaps further off, the plaintiff largely deals with foreign vendors of margarine. It is possible that the defendant company may deal with the same firms for the purpose of purchasing the constituents from which they will make their product. It is possible that confusion may arise in that respect, and that in certain events the plaintiff might suffer in credit, or otherwise from that confusion which would be caused entirely by the similarity of the two names.

For these reasons I think the plaintiff has made out a prima facie case that he will be, or may be, damaged within the meaning of the authorities if the defendant company is allowed to commence trading and to continue trading in its present name.

Astbury J's decision was confirmed by the Court of Appeal.

Section 349(1) and (4) lays down requirements with regard to the statement of the company's name on business letters, instruments of payment (eg cheques, bills of exchange etc). How strictly is this section to be interpreted? It seems that the equitable doctrine of estoppel can save the defendant officer from personal liability (*Durham Fancy Goods Ltd v Michael Jackson (Fancy Goods) Ltd*, discussed in *Lindholst & Co A/S v Fowler* (Source 52), but not the equitable doctrine of rectification (*Blum v OCP Repartition SA* [1988] BCLC 170, applied in *Rafsanjan Pistachio v Reiss* [1990] BCLC 352). The officer of the company who signed the payment instrument is in a dilemma. His case depends on showing that the company is liable as the party to the contract in respect of which the payment is made and that he is not a party. Since he is not a party, he has no locus standi to claim rectification. How accurately does the name have to be mentioned? In *Blum v OCP Repartition SA* the mismention was the absence of the word 'limited'. Given the somewhat more lenient approach adopted in *Jenice Ltd v Dan* (Source 53), Blum's case may establish the principle that the omission of 'limited' (and, therefore, presumably 'plc' or 'public limited company') is a fatal mistake owing to the fact that the precise status of the author of the document is obscured.

SOURCE 52
Lindholst & Co A/S *v* Fowler
[1988] BCLC 166

SIR JOHN DONALDSON MR: . . . The background is quite simply this. The four bills of exchange were drawn to cover instalments of the price of equipment supplied by the plaintiffs for the poultry processing plant under a written contract concluded in July 1983. The parties to the contract were expressed to be on the one hand the plaintiffs and on the other Corby Chicken Co. The contract itself was signed by Mr Fowler as 'Managing Director'.

Under art II, which deals with price and payment, the total price is set out. Payment is dealt with as follows:

> 'The contract amount will be paid as follows: 20 per cent of contract amount being £80676.20 as deposit, to be paid on shipping advice, less £10,000.00 already paid. 80 per cent of contract amount being £322704.80 plus 10 per cent interest of the amount outstanding at any time, divided into ten . . . semiannual drafts, 1st draft due 6 months after shipment date *duly accepted by Corby Chicken Co*. Goods to be released to Corby Chicken Co against above mentioned accepted drafts.' (My emphasis).

The plaintiffs alleged in the statement of claim that the bills of exchange were intended to be accepted and were accepted on behalf of Corby Chicken Co Ltd. Mr Fowler agrees with that, and goes further: he says that the entire contract was with Corby Chicken Co Ltd. That being so, prima facie the only party who could be liable on the bill is Corby Chicken Co Ltd.

But it is at this point that the plaintiffs refer to s 349(4) of the Companies Act 1985 which, in substance, reproduces s 108 of the Companies Act 1948, and, indeed, can trace its ancestry back to the Joint Stock Companies Act 1856.
. . .

Mr Fowler accepts that, as a consequence of that section, he is prima facie personally liable to the plaintiffs. But, he says, this is an exceptional case in which he should not be held liable because of the principles of estoppel, which I applied as a trial judge in *Durham Fancy Goods Ltd v Michael Jackson (Fancy Goods) Ltd* [1968] 2 All ER 987, [1968] 2 QB 839. There what happened was that the drawers of the bill of exchange specified on the bill the words of acceptance which they required. It is put in this way ([1968] 2 All ER 987 at 991, [1968] 2 QB 839 at 848):

> 'Against this background, the plaintiffs did not, as one would have expected, send the bill to Jacksons without words of acceptance, but instead inscribed words of acceptance including a name which was deceptively similar to, but not the same as, that of Jacksons. In saying that the name was deceptively similar, I intend only to state what is an obvious fact and wish to emphasise that no deception was intended by the plaintiffs. The plaintiffs thereby implied that acceptance of the bill in that form would be, or would be accepted by them as, a regular acceptance of the bill. Such an acceptance would not, of course, have involved Mr Jackson in personal liability. In these circumstances it would be inequitable that the plaintiffs should be allowed to enforce the statutory liability of Mr Jackson without first giving him an opportunity of regularising the acceptance by inscribing the correct name of Jacksons on the bill and that it is now too late to do. Accordingly the plaintiffs are unable to enforce the statutory liability, although it continues to exist and would have been available to other holders, who were unaffected by the equitable defence.'

It is said on this appeal that that is precisely the position here. The plaintiffs knew perfectly well that they were dealing with Corby Chicken Co Ltd. They themselves prepared the contract with Corby Chicken Co Ltd using the form of words 'Corby Chicken Co' without adding 'Ltd'. It was they who put forward the bills of exchange addressed to 'Corby Chicken Co', again omitting the word 'Ltd'. It is said by counsel for Mr Fowler that, under art II which I have quoted, the obligation on the buyers was then duly to procure that bills were 'duly accepted by Corby Chicken Co', and that the only form of acceptance which complied with this contract was one by Corby Chicken Co.

For my part I am quite unable to accept that. Once it is admitted that the contract was with Corby Chicken Ltd, the obligation under art II was to accept in a proper form for Coby Chicken Co Ltd as prescribed by the statute. What occurred was not a compliance with art II.

Furthermore, I am quite unable to apply the doctrine of estoppel which I applied in *Durham Fancy Goods* to this case because, whereas in *Durham Fancy Goods* the form of words for acceptance was prescribed by the plaintiffs and they were estopped by what they had prescribed, in this case the form of words for acceptance was not prescribed by the plaintiffs or by the contract. The plaintiffs simply but forward bills of exchange addressed by the Corby Chicken Co, which both they and the defendants knew meant Corby Chicken Co Ltd, and it was for the two defendants to accept that bill in the proper form as required by the statute.

With some slight regret, but with no hesitation or doubt, I would dismiss the appeal.

SOURCE 53
Jenice Ltd *v* Dan
[1993] BCLC 1349

R TITHERIDGE QC. This matter raises an interesting question. There are five actions brought against the same defendant, Mr Joseph Saloman Dan, and they are all brought in respect of cheques signed by the defendant, and clearly intended to be signed, on behalf of a company of which he was a director Primekeen Ltd (P-R-I-M-E-K-E-E-N).

. . .

By letter dated 11 February, the plaintiffs' then solicitors received notice under s 98 of the Insolvency Act 1986 concerning a proposed creditor's voluntary liquidation. Each of the cheques bore the name 'PRIMKEEN LIMITED' printed upon them, in the ordinary way in which cheques now have the account holder's name printed by the bank, and PRIMKEEN LIMITED was spelt P-R-I-M-K-E-E-N, and, as I have made clear already, the registered name of the company was in fact PRIMEKEEN, with an 'e' in the middle.

[The judge then referred to s 349 and continued:]

On behalf of the plaintiffs, counsel submits that the matter is very simple and is in effect decided by well-established and binding authority. He says that none of these cheques, bore the name of the company, that, I interpret, in the words of the statute, none of these cheques had the company name mentioned on the cheques, and the authorities upon which he relies I shall come to in a moment.

On behalf of the defendant, the submission is again the case is simple, but not surprisingly for a very different reason. It is simple because the name of the company is mentioned, it is simply mis-spelt. And such error as there is, the error caused by the mis-spelling or possibly a typographical error, is de minimis, and if one looks at the purpose of the legislation, the purpose is clearly to ensure that people dealing with companies know both that they are dealing with a limited company and know the identity of the particular limited company with which they are dealing. In effect, the object of the legislation is to avoid confusion and in this case there is no confusion at all, there is simply a misspelling based on a typographical error.

Free of authority, I do not hesitate to say that I find the arguments for the defendant the more cogent and the more attractive. There is, in my judgment, in principle, a distinction to be drawn between a misdescription which may mislead (although authority clearly shows that it does not have to) and a spelling or typographical error which in the circumstances of a particular case cannot possibly mislead.

. . .

The next case upon which the plaintiffs rely is a case decided by Donaldson J in 1968. That is the case of *Durham Fancy Good Ltd v Michael Jackson (Fancy Goods) Ltd* [1968] 2 All ER 987, [1968] 2 QB 839. There, the correct name of the company was Michael Jackson (Fancy Goods) Ltd, but the bill was drawn addressed to 'M. Jackson' in brackets '(Fancy Goods Limited)' and inscribed the words of acceptance:

> 'Accepted payable . . . For and on behalf of M. Jackson (Fancy Goods) Ltd, Manchester.'

Donaldson J held that 'M' was not an acceptable abbreviation for 'Michael', and that, accordingly, the second defendant to the action, who was the director and secretary of the company, had committed a criminal offence under what was then s 108 of the Companies Act 1948, but that that liability could not be enforced because of estoppel. The learned judge said ([1968] 2 All ER 987 at 189, [1968] 2 QB 839 at 845):

> 'Counsel for Mr Jackson submits that there was sufficient compliance with the section in the present case because (a) the bill made it clear that the acceptors were a limited company and (b) there was no confusion as to their identity. In support of the first of these submissions he relied upon *Penrose v Martyr* (1858) EB & E 499 at 503 in which Crompton J stated that the purpose of the corresponding statutory provision "was to prevent persons from being deceived into the belief that they had a security with the unlimited liability of common law, when they had but the security of a company limited" and upon the judgment of Scrutton J in *Stacey & Co Ltd v Wallis* (1912) 106 LT 544 affirming this view and deciding that "Ltd" was an acceptable abbreviation for "Limited". Unfortunately for Mr Jackson, the second submission is unsupported by authority. Indeed it is contrary to the tenor of the decision of Denman J and the Court of Appeal in *Atkins v Wardle* (1889) 58 LJQB 377.'

Interestingly, *Atkins* with an 's', another example of mis-spelling.

> 'There, the drawer of the bill was a shareholder in the "South Shields Salt Water Baths Company (Limited)" but he drew on "Salt Water Baths Company (Limited), South Shields" and the directors accepted on behalf of "South Shields Salt Water Bath Company" which was equally incorrect. No question of confusion as to identity or as to the status of the drawers as a limited liability company could have arisen. Nevertheless the directors were

held to be personally liable. Lord Esher MR pointing out that the statute did not require the misdescription to be material.'

Stopping there it is clear to me that I am bound by the authority of *Atkin v Wardle*, reinforced as it is by the decision of Donaldson J, that the fact that the misdescription is not material is of no importance at all, and that I entirely accept. However, just looking at the case of *Durham Fancy Goods Ltd v Michael Jackson (Fancy Goods) Ltd*, I can and do distinguish it from the present case. There, as Donaldson J held 'M' was not an acceptable abbreviation of 'Michael', and what in my judgment would be a comparable case to the present, would be a case where, as I put to Mr Staddon in the course of his interesting argument, the word 'Michael' was there but had been mis-spelt, M-I-C-H-E-A-L instead of M-I-C-H-A-E-L; or, for the sake of illustration, a case where the name was there, but instead of two of the letters being placed in the wrong order, one of them had been omitted. To that Mr Staddon said, 'Well, that's right. In the plaintiff's submission, that would not be compliance with the Act but in any case I distinguish it.' Myself, I find that situation indistinguishable, and it is a different situation, in my judgment, from the situation that in fact arose in that case.

Looking at the matter in principle, if Mr Staddon's submission is right, it means this; that if, perhaps because of pressure of time, a company director of a company like Michael Jackson (Fancy Goods) Ltd, writes out an order mis-spelling the name of the company in one of the ways I have indicated, he is, in the absence of payment for the goods by the company, personally liable for the order and has committed a criminal offence. And I look again at the words of the Act, and I ask: In those circumstances, is that a case, where an error of that sort is made, a mis-spelling, which not only causes no confusion but is incapable of causing confusion, where it can properly be said that the company's name is not mentioned? And for these purposes I shall assume that in the illustrations I have given, legible characters are used. But that poses another and perhaps interesting academic question: Suppose the error is not in fact a mis-spelling at all, but in writing the word 'Michael', the 'a' or the 'e' (or perhaps both of them) become illegible or subject to confusion, is that a breach of the Act? I shall leave that interesting question, but I shall simply observe that this is a section which imposes a criminal liability. True, there is a great deal of difference between a criminal offence committed by inadvertence, which may be an offence of strict liability, and a criminal offence committed deliberately and perhaps with some fraudulent intent, and there are all sorts of variations between, but sitting in a criminal court I should find it extremely difficult to say that somebody respons-ible for an understandable and simple and common spelling error, were guilty of a criminal offence on the basis that, because of the spelling error, the court could be satisfied so that it was true, that the company name was not mentioned in the document.

In my judgment I can also distinguish the *Atkin* case, because that was not a case of a mis-spelling, that also was a case of the omission of a word or words or, as to the original addressee, the wrong order of words. I derive support for my view upon the words of Denman J in that case and, more importantly, to the case to which I have already referred several times, and to which I shall come, *Penrose v Martyr*. But at all events, I have reached the stage now when I can and do distinguish both the *Atkins* case and the *Durham Fancy Goods* case.

I come now to the next case upon which the plaintiffs rely, which is the case of *Hendon v Alderman* (1973) 117 Sol Jo 631. There, the name of the company was 'L. & R. Agencies Limited' and the director signed a cheque for the company, writing the name 'L.R. Agencies Limited', missing out the ampersand. This is the case of the missing E that I am now considering, that was the case of the missing ampersand. That was decided by MacKenna J and it is interesting to note that the cheque had the printed words put there by the bank, in accordance with what by then had become standard practice. And the bank had not copied the company's name correctly and, as the learned judge observed, had omitted the ampersand which connected the L & R. MacKenna J said that it would not be consistent with earlier authorities if he were to hold that a description was sufficient which totally omitted a connecting ampersand; 'L.R. Agencies' was not the same thing as 'L. & R. Agencies'. The omission of a word seemed a worse defect than its transposition or abbreviation, and 'transposition' I take to be a reference to the *Atkin* case and 'abbreviation' to the *Durham Fancy Goods* case. The report of the learned judge's judgment goes on:

> 'Section 108(1)(c) of the Companies Act 1948, which required that every company shall have its name mentioned in legible characters in cheques purported to be signed by or on behalf of the company, had not been complied with and as the cheque had not been duly paid, each of the defendants was liable to the plaintiff.'

It is perfectly clear that the judgment of MacKenna J proceeded on analogy with the *Atkin* and the *Durham Fancy Goods* case and related to the omission of a word, and although at first sight it might appear that there is little difference between the error in that case and the error in the present case, I find that there is a difference, and in my judgment a mis-spelling, by the omission of a letter in the middle of a word, is not to be equated with the omission of a whole word.

I entirely accept, on authority which is binding upon me, that a strict construction has to be given to the statutory provision, but a strict construction does not require any court to reach a nonsensical conclusion, and in my judgment the conclusion that the plaintiffs invite me to reach is nonsensical. For, in truth, no ordinary person, looking at what has happened in this case, would say, in the words of the section, that the company's name is not mentioned. It is mentioned and it is mis-spelt and, as I have observed, in circumstances that do not lead to any of the vices against which the statutory provisions were directed.

. . .

On behalf of the defendants it is strongly urged that the de minimis principle should apply. That may be right, but I am not going to base my judgment on the application of de minimis principle, although, as I make clear, I think that the argument has some force. What is important, and it does not seem to me that it matters whether one says that the de minimis principle is being applied or not, is to have regard to the actual words of the Act. Putting the matter in its simplest possible terms, as I have indicated, the question is: In the circumstances of this particular case, has the company, PRIMEKEEN, had its name mentioned in legible characters on these cheques? And in my judgment it has, despite a spelling or typographical error.

It follows that upon this issue I give judgment for the defendant.

PART II: PROMOTERS

The relationship between the promoter and company is a fiduciary one (cf partner and partner, director and company) see *Erlanger v New Sombrero*

Phosphate Company[1] (Source 54). The reason for this is simple, the promoter has a great deal of power over the newly formed company (see *Gluckstein v Barnes*,[2] Source 55). Does this explain the great reluctance of English law to provide an effective means for the enforcement, by and against the company, of pre-incorporation contracts (see pp 209ff)?

Nowadays, it is very rare for a company to be formed from conception as a public company. It will generally start off life as a private company dependent on the money provided by the promoter and by lenders. Later, if successful and in need of further capital, it can be converted into a public company with capital solicited from the public — 'flotation' (see Part III, the Flotation of Public Companies, p 174).

Who is a promoter? This is a question of fact. Who took the appropriate steps for the formation of the company? Professionals (accountants, lawyers) who prepare the necessary documents and reports are not *thereby* promoters. See *Twycross v Grant*;[3] *Emma Silver Mining Company v Lewis*;[4] *Lydney v Bird*[5] (Sources 56, 57 and 58).

Where the promoter is in breach of his duty (eg he makes a profit in the sale of his property to the company without the latter's informed consent), the company may rescind the transaction. See *Erlanger v New Sombrero Phosphate Company* (Source 54). Informed consent may necessitate disclosure beyond the Board of Directors. See *Lagunas Nitrate v Lagunas Nitrate Syndicate*[6] (Source 59). In certain circumstances, the company may be able to claim the secret profit from the promotor. See *Gluckstein v Barnes* (Source 55).

SOURCE 54
Erlanger v New Sombrero Phosphate Company
(House of Lords 1878) (1878) 3 App Ca 1218; 48 LJ Ch 73

LORD PENZANCE: My Lords, I will state to your Lordships my view of the circumstances under which the purchase now sought to be set aside was originally made.

What happened was this: The syndicate had bought the property in question, and it is probable that they bought it with the intention of getting up a company which should buy it of them at an increased price. Baron Erlanger, who acted for the syndicate, took steps for that purpose within a few days of the purchase, and there is no proof that any steps were even considered, much less adopted, for dealing with the property in any other way. No time was lost in carrying this intention into effect. The solicitor of the syndicate is set to work — he prepares articles of association and a prospectus. The articles provide that five gentlemen by name shall be the first directors of the company, and that any two of them shall be a quorum to bind the company. They also provide that without any farther authority from the shareholders, these five directors or any two of them may sanction and accept, on the part of the company, a certain contract bearing even date with the articles for the purchase by the company of the property in

---

1 (1878) 3 App Ca 1218; 48 LJ Ch 73
2 [1900] AC 240; 69 LJ Ch 385
3 (1877) 2 CPD 469; 46 LJ CP 636
4 (1879) 4 CPD 396; 40 LT 749
5 (1886) 33 Ch D 85; 55 LJ Ch 875
6 (1899) 2 Ch 392; 68 LJ Ch 699

question. This contract had been prepared by the syndicate themselves, and was on the face of it a contract between Evans as the vendor, and Pavy, on behalf of the future company, as vendee. Both Evans and Pavy were persons who had no interest in the property, and were the nominees of the syndicate, and remunerated by them for their trouble. In this contract the syndicate fixed their own price at which the future company was to buy, this price being in round numbers double what they had given for it some days before.

The articles of association were therefore so drawn by the solicitor for the syndicate, that the syndicate had it in their power to select, and did select, the five persons, any two of whom were to become the acting agents of the company for the acceptance or rejection of this bargain, by which the syndicate were to obtain for the property double what they had given for it.

...

The agents, then, who were to have the power of binding the company to the purchase in question, having been thus selected by the syndicate, and the articles of association having been signed by seven persons, all of whom it was admitted were connected with Baron Erlanger or other members of the syndicate, some of them being clerks of these persons, the next step was to hold a meeting of the directors. . . . It was attended by Sir Thomas Dakin, Admiral Macdonald, and Evans. It was also attended by Mr Westall, the solicitor of the syndicate, and himself (on his own part or that of his friends) a member of the syndicate. His interest in and services for the syndicate had been farther secured by the promise of a special fee of £500.

These three directors, without examination of Mr Chatteris' accounts, without any report from any competent person as to the then condition of the island, or the cost of raising and shipping the phosphate of lime, and, without any inquiry into facts or figures, proceeded at once, under the auspices of the vendors' solicitor, to adopt and ratify the proposed purchase of the island on behalf of the company, which had been completely formed and registered only eight days previously, and which became thereby bound to pay for the property double the sum which had been settled shortly before by the Vice-Chancellor as its true and marketable value.

Can a contract so obtained to be allowed to stand? The bare statement of the facts is, I think, sufficient to condemn it. From that statement I invite your Lordships to draw two conclusions: first, that the company never had an opportunity of exercising, though independent directors, a fair and independent judgment upon the subject of this purchase; and, secondly, that this result was *brought about by the conduct* and contrivance of the vendors themselves. It was the vendors, in their character of promoters, who had the power and the opportunity of creating and forming the company in such a manner that with adequate disclosures of fact, and independent judgment on the company's behalf might have been formed. But instead of so doing they used that power and opportunity for the advancement of their own interests. Placed in this position of unfair advantage over the company which they were about to create, they were, as it seems to me, bound according to the principles constantly acted upon in the Courts of Equity, if they wished to make a valid contract of sale to the company, to nominate independent directors and fully disclose the material facts. The obligation rests upon them to shew they have not made use of the position which they occupied to benefit themselves; but I find no proof in the case that they have discharged that obligation.

...

A contract of sale effected under such circumstances is, I conceive, upon principles of equity liable to be set aside.

The principles of equity to which I refer have been illustrated in a variety of relations, none of them perhaps precisely similar to that of the present parties, but all resting on the same basis, and one which is strictly applicable to the present case. The relations of principal and agent, trustee and *cestui que trust,* parent and child, guardian and ward, priest and penitent, all furnish instances in which the Courts of Equity have given protection and relief against the pressure of unfair advantage resulting from the relation and mutual position of the parties, whether in matters of contract or gift; and this relation and position of unfair advantage once made apparent, the Courts have always cast upon him who holds that position, the burden of shewing that he has not used it to his own benefit.

I have no difficulty, therefore, in asking your Lordships to assent to the proposition of the Lord Chancellor, that if, within a proper time after the completion of this purchase, a bill had been filed by the company, the purchase must have been set aside.

. . .

LORD CAIRNS LC: . . . My Lords, I stop at this point for the purpose of saying that I think it to be clear that the syndicate in entering into this contract acted on behalf of themselves alone, and did not at that time act in, or occupy, any fiduciary position whatever. It may well be that the prevailing idea in their mind was, not to retain or work the island, but to sell it again at an increase of price, and very possibly, to promote or get up a company to purchase the island from them; but they were, as it seems to me, after their purchase was made, perfectly free to do with the island whatever they liked; to use it as they liked, and to sell it how, and to whom, and for what price they liked. The part of the case of the Respondents which, as an alternative, sought to make the Appellants account for the profit which they made on the re-sale of the property to the Respondents, on an allegation that the Appellants acted in a fiduciary position at the time they made the contract of 30 August 1871, is not, as I think, capable of being supported, and this, as I understand, was the view of all the Judges in the Courts below.

. . .

I cannot but regard a meeting at which two of the principal directors did not and could not attend, at which one who did attend and take part in the deliberations was at once a person buying and selling, where the legal adviser present and assisting was virtually another vendor, and where the two remaining directors are not shewn to have had the means of exercising, or to have exercised, any intelligent judgment on the subject, as little else than a mockery and a delusion.

I have said nothing, my Lords, as to the provision that two directors should be a quorum. That is a provision which, in my opinion, could not be held to remedy defects such as I have pointed out as going to the entire constitution of the board.

I cannot, therefore, my Lords, entertain any doubt that if, within a proper time after the completion of this purchase, a bill had been filed by the company impeaching it on the grounds that I have stated, the purchase must have been set aside.

The part of the case which, however, has given me the most anxiety is the question whether, having regard to what was made known at the time that the company was formed, and to what became known, and to what also might farther have become known, shortly after it was formed, and having regard, farther, to the very peculiar nature of the property which had been purchased, and to the impossibility of restoring the parties to their original position, relief can or ought now, consistently with the principles of equity, to be given to those who seek to impeach the contract. On this question I have entertained, and still continue to entertain, considerable doubt, or more than doubt. The case has, however, been twice argued most elaborately and ably, and all of your Lordships are, I believe, of opinion that the company has not lost the right, which undoubtedly it had, to set aside the sale. I do not therefore think it necessary to do more than express generally the grounds of the doubts which on this part of the case I have felt.

. . . looking to the very peculiar nature of the property, and the utter impossibility of restoring the property, and the commercial undertaking connected with it, to the vendors in the state in which it was when the company took possession of it, looking to the amount of notice which the company had by the prospectus, and to the knowledge which they might have obtained by pursuing the inquiries which the prospectus ought to have suggested, I should be of opinion that it would be contrary to the principles of equity to give to the company the relief which, at an earlier period, they might have obtained.

The House of Lords was unanimous that, in circumstances such as these, the contract could be rescinded, and with the exception of Lord Cairns LC — who held that since the company had delayed too long before taking proceedings and as the property could not be restored, the right to rescind had been lost — that on the facts of the case the company had validly exercised its right of rescission.

SOURCE 55
Gluckstein *v* Barnes
(House of Lords 1900) [1900] AC 240; 69 LJ Ch 385

This was a summons by the liquidator of Olympia Ltd to recover secret profits made by the promoters in the sale of property to the company.

. . . in addition to the £40,000 profit which the prospectus stated, the syndicate realized more than £20,000 profit, being the difference between the sum they gave for the debentures and mortgage and the sum they received, as holders of the charges, from the liquidator of the National Agricultural Hall Company. Of this profit the appellant, Lyons, Hart and Hartley received £6341 . . . and in 1897, Olympia Limited having gone into liquidation, the respondent took out a summons against the appellant . . . The summons was dismissed by Wright J, but the Court of Appeal (Lindley, Rigby and Collins LJJ) reversed his decision and ordered the appellant to pay £6341 with interest.

EARL OF HALSBURY LC: My Lords, in this case the simple question is whether four persons, of whom the appellant is one, can be permitted to retain the sums which they have obtained from the company of which they were directors by the fraudulent pretence that they had paid £20,000 more than in truth they had paid for property which they, as a syndicate, had bought by subscription among themselves, and then sold to themselves as directors of the company. If this is an accurate account of what has been done by these four persons, of course so gross a transaction cannot be permitted to stand. That that is the real nature of it I now proceed to shew.

In the year 1892 the freehold grounds and buildings known as 'Olympia' were the property of a company which in that year was being wound up. That company had issued debentures to the extent of £100,000 as a first charge and a mortgage as a second charge for £10,000. The four persons in question knew that the property would have to be sold, and the combined to buy it in order that they might resell it to a company to be formed by themselves. The combination, which called itself the Freehold Syndicate, but which, perhaps, the common law would have described by a less high-sounding title, proceeded to buy up so far as they could the incumbrances on the property called 'Olympia.' They expended £27,000 in buying debentures. These, of course, were very much depreciated in value, and they gave £500 for the mortgage of £10,000. As soon as this transaction had been completed they, partners in it, proceeded to form a company, and it was of course necessary that the company should be willing to help, and accordingly the four persons in question were made by the articles of association the first directors.

The property was sold on 8 February by the chief clerk of North J for £140,000 and the syndicate purchased nominally for that sum, but, by reason of the arrangement to which I have referred, that sum was less by £20,734 6s. 1d. than what they appeared to give. On 29 March they completed as directors the purchase of the property for £180,000, and they as directors paid to themselves as members of the syndicate £171,000 in cash and £9000 in fully paid-up shares — in all £180,000.

The prospectus by which money was to be obtained from the public disclosed the supposed profit which the vendors were making of £40,000, while in truth their profit was £60,734. 6s. 1d., and it is this undisclosed profit of £20,000, and the right to retain it, which is now in question.

My Lords, I am wholly unable to understand any claim that these directors, vendors, syndicate, associates, have to retain this money. I entirely agree with the Master of the Rolls that the essence of this scheme was to form a company. It was essential that this should be done, and that they should be directors of it, who would purchase. The company should have been informed of what was being done and consulted whether they would have allowed this profit. I think the Master of the Rolls is absolutely right in saying that the duty to disclose is imposed by the plainest dictates of common honesty as well as by well-settled principles of common law.

Then it is said there is the alternative suggested upon the agreement that the syndicate might sell to a company or to some other purchaser. In the first place, I do not believe they ever intended to sell to anybody else than a company. An individual purchaser might ask inconvenient questions, and if they or any one of them had stated as an inducement to an individual purchaser that £140,000 was given for the property, when in fact £20,000 less had been given, it is a great error to suppose that the law is not strong enough to reach such a statement; but as I say, I do not believe it was ever intended to get an individual purchaser, even if such an intention would have had any operation. When they did afterwards sell to a company, they took very good care there should be no one who could ask questions. They were to be sellers to themselves as buyers, and it was a necessary provision to the plan that they were both to be sellers and buyers, and as buyers to get the money to pay for the purchase from the pockets of deluded shareholders.

My Lords, I decline to discuss the question of disclosure to the company. It is too absurd to suggest that a disclosure to the parties to this transaction is a disclosure to the company of which these directors were the proper guardians and trustees. They were there by the terms of the agreement to do the work of the syndicate, that is to say, to cheat the shareholders; and this, forsooth, is to be treated as a disclosure to the company, when they were really there to hoodwink the shareholders, and so far from protecting them, were to obtain from them the money, the produce of their nefarious plans.

I do not discuss either the sum sued for, or why Gluckstein alone is sued. The whole sum has been obtained by a very gross fraud, and all who were parties to it are responsible to make good what they have obtained and withheld from the shareholders.

I move your Lordships that the appeal be dismissed with costs.

LORD MACNAGHTEN: . . . the only fault to be found with the learned judges of the Court of Appeal, if I may venture to criticise their judgment at all, is that they have treated the defences put forward on Mr Gluckstein's behalf with too much ceremony. For my part, I cannot see any ingenuity or any novelty in the trick which Mr Gluckstein and his associates practised on the persons whom they invited to take shares in Olympia Limited. It is the old story. It has been done over and over again.

These gentlemen set about forming a company to pay them a handsome sum for taking off their hands a property which they had contracted to buy with that end in view. They bring the company into existence by means of the usual machinery. They appoint themselves sole guardians and protectors of this creature of theirs, half-fledged and just struggling into life, bound hand and foot while yet unborn by contracts tending to their private advantage, and so fashioned by its makers that it could only act by their hands and only see through their eyes. They issue a prospectus representing that they had agreed to purchase the property for a sum largely in excess of the amount which they had, in fact, to pay. On the faith of this prospectus they collect subscriptions from a confiding and credulous public. And then comes the last act. Secretly, and therefore dishonestly, they put into their own pockets the difference between the real and the pretended price. After a brief career the company is ordered to be wound up. In the course of the liquidation the trick is discovered. Mr Gluckstein is called upon to make good a portion of the sum which he and his associates had misappropriated. Why Mr Gluckstein alone was selected for attack I do not know any more than I know why he was only asked to pay back a fraction of the money improperly withdrawn from the coffers of the company.

However that may be, Mr Gluckstein defends his conduct, or, rather I should say, resists the demand, . . . In the first place, he says that he was not in a fiduciary position towards Olympia Limited, before the company was formed. Well, for some purposes he was not. For others he was. A good deal might be said on the point. But to my mind the point is immaterial, for it is not necessary to go back beyond the formation of the company.

In the second place, he says, that if he was in a fiduciary position he did in fact make a proper disclosure. With all deference to the learned counsel for the appellant, that seems to me to be absurd. 'Disclosure' is not the most appropriate word to use when a person who plays many parts announces to himself in one character what he has done and is doing in another. To talk of disclosure to the thing called the company, when as yet there were no shareholders, is a mere farce. To the intended shareholders there was no disclosure at all. On them was practised an elaborate system of deception.

The third ground of defence was that the only remedy was rescission. That defence, in the circumstances of the present case, seems to me to be as contrary to common sense as it is to authority. The point was settled more than sixty years ago by the decision in *Hichens v Congreve*,[1] and, so far as I know, that case has never been questioned.

---

1 (1831) 4 Sim 420; 58 ER 157

SOURCE 56
Twycross *v* Grant
(Common Pleas 1877) (1877) 2 CPD 469; 46 LJ CP 636

This was an action by a shareholder for damages against the promoters of the company. The company had failed and the shares subscribed for were worthless. The prospectus had failed to disclose two contracts entered into by the promoters and found by the jury to be material. Although there was no proven connection between the failure to disclose the contracts and the failure of the company, the defendants were held liable to compensate the plaintiff under the provisions of s 38 of the Companies Act 1867, which deemed fraudulent on the part of the promoters 'any prospectus or notice not specifying . . . the dates and the names of the parties to any contract entered into by the company or the promoters, directors, or trustees thereof before the issue of such prospectus or notice . . .'.

> COCKBURN CJ: . . . But were the defendants promoters at the time of issuing? It is contended that, even if promoters in the outset, they ceased to be so the moment the company was constituted and the governing body, the directors, were appointed. This connection was mainly founded on a provision of the 7 & 8 Vict. c. 110, s 3, which says that promoters shall continue to be such till the complete registration of the company, at which time directors would be appointed. But that Act, which had reference to a system of registration widely differing from the present, has been repealed, and there is now no statutory limitation to the functions of a promoter. The question as to when one who in the outset was a promoter of a company continues or ceases to be so, becomes, therefore, as it seems to me, one of fact. A promoter, I apprehended is one who undertakes to form a company with reference to a given project and to set it going, and who takes the necessary steps to accomplish that purpose. That the defendants were the promoters of the company from the beginning can admit of no doubt. They framed the scheme; they not only provisionally formed the company, but were, in fact, to the end its creditors; they found the directors, and qualified them; they prepared the prospectus; they paid for printing and advertising, and the expenses incidental to bringing the undertaking before the world. In all these respects the directors were passive; without saying that they were in a legal sense the agents of the defendants, they were certainly their instruments. All the things I have just referred to were done with a view to the formation of the company, and so long as the work of formation continues, those who carry on that work must, I think, retain the character of promoters. Of course, if a governing body, in the shape of directors, has once been formed, and they take, as I need not say they may, what remains to be done in the way of forming the company, into their own hands, the functions of the promoter are at an end. But, so long as the promoters are permitted by the directors to carry on the work of formation, the latter remaining passive, so long, I think, would a jury be warranted in finding that what was done by them was done as promoters. Here again, therefore, I see no reason for disturbing the verdict.

SOURCE 57
Emma Silver Mining Company *v* **Lewis**
(Common Pleas 1877) (1879) 4 CPD 396; 40 LT 749

LINDLEY J, delivered the judgment of the Court (Lord Coleridge CJ, Denman and Lindley JJ). There was abundant evidence to shew, and indeed it was in our opinion clearly proved:

1. That the defendants knew that Park came over here to sell the mine to a company, to be got up by himself and such persons as he could induce to assist him.

2. That the defendants were prepared to assist, and did assist, Park in his endeavours to sell the mine here to a company to be formed for the express purpose of purchasing it.

3. That the defendants had been metal brokers to the former owners of the mine at a commission of $2\frac{1}{2}$ per cent, and that there was an understanding between the defendants and Park that he should, if he could, procure them to be appointed the metal brokers of the new company at the usual English commission of 1 per cent.

4. That there was first an understanding, and secondly a verbal promise, that the defendants should be liberally remunerated by Park for their services and for their loss of commission.

5. That this remuneration was in some shape or other to come out of the purchase-money to be paid by the company.

6. That the defendants left Park to fix the price of the mine, to get up the company, and to manage all details with the company, and trusted him to protect their interests.

7. That Park, Grant, and others accordingly procured the plaintiff company to be formed, and procured it to buy the mine for £1,000,000, of which £500,000 was to be paid in cash, and £500,000 in paid-up shares of the company.

8. That the defendants became metal brokers to the new company on the terms of being paid the usual English commission of 1 per cent, and allowed themselves to be referred to in the prospectus of the plaintiff company for information concerning the mine; and, so far as such reference might induce people to take shares, the defendants themselves indirectly assisted in procuring shares to be taken.

9. That the defendants knew more of the mine and of its doubtful value, and of the grounds for distrusting Silliman's report in its favour, than they chose to disclose; and Park was aware of this, and promised the defendants liberal remuneration to insure silence on their part, even when referred to for information.

10. That the defendants, when referred to, were studiously careful to preserve that silence which was essential, or, at least, conducive to floating the company.

11. That pursuant to the above understanding and verbal promise, Park gave the defendants 250 fully paid-up shares of the company out of the shares given to him by the company for the mine; and Park entered into an agreement with the defendants respecting the disposal of the shares, so as not to injure the sale of other shares held by himself and others who had assisted him in forming the company.

12. That all these facts (except the appointment of the defendants to be metal brokers at the usual commission of 1 per cent and the reference to the defendants for information) were studiously concealed from the plaintiff company.

Under these circumstances the jury found the defendants to be promoters of the company, and to be liable to restore to the company the value of the 250 shares obtained by them.

The Common Pleas Division upheld the direction of the trial judge who left to the jury the question whether the defendants were promoters. The jury answered this in the affirmative and the defendants were ordered to account for their secret profits.

SOURCE 58
Lydney and Wigpool Iron Ore Company *v* Bird
(Court of Appeal 1886) (1886) 33 Ch D 85; 55 LJ Ch 875

LINDLEY LJ: . . . James Bird in fact procured the formation of the company. He suggested its formation, he took an active part in the preparation of its prospectus and memorandum and articles of association, in the appointment of two of its first directors, in the appointment of its secretary, and he procured his own firm to be engaged to conduct the sales of the company at a large commission. He fixed the purchase-money at £100,000 and stipulated for the payment of £10,800 to his own firm, and he procured the payment of that sum by the company, and he was himself a director when the last instalments of it were made. He was in truth the person who fastened the contract to pay £100,000 on the company without disclosing the fact that his firm were to get £10,800 out of the purchase-money.

The evidence when sifted shews clearly and conclusively that though the Allaways had not agreed to sell at £90,000, viz, £85,000 plus £5,000 for promotion expenses, they were prepared to do so, and that it was James Bird who ultimately settled that the nominal purchase-money was to be £100,000 of which he was to have £10,800. . . .

Having arrived at these conclusions of fact the legal principles applicable to them do not present any real difficulty. It is not correct to say that James Bird was the agent of the company when it did not exist, nor is it much less objectionable to talk of his being in a fiduciary relation to the company before the company had any existence. Moreover, to say that James Bird was a promoter of the company and therefore liable to account to it, as calculated to mislead; for the word 'promoter' is ambiguous, and it is necessary to ascertain in each case what the so-called promoter really did before his legal liabilities can be accurately ascertained. In every case it is better to look at the facts and ascertain and describe them as they are. In the present case James Bird procured the company to be formed and to be managed in such a way as to transfer from the moneys of the company to himself the sum of £10,800 without informing the company of that fact. The company were told that they had to pay £100,000 for the property, but they did not know that of that sum £10,800 was to go into the pocket of the man who had got the company up and who had in fact increased the purchase-money in order to get that £10,800. Under these circumstances he cannot retain the sum so got. Although not an agent of the company nor a trustee for it before its formation, the old familiar principles of the law of agency and of trusteeship have been extended, and very properly extended, to meet such cases; and using the word 'promoter' to describe a person acting as James Bird did, it is perfectly well settled that a promoter of a company is accountable to it for all moneys secretly obtained by him from it just as if the relationship of principal and agent or of trustee and *cestui que trust* had really existed between them and the company when the money was so obtained.

SOURCE 59

Lagunas Nitrate Company *v* Lagunas Nitrate Syndicate

(Court of Appeal 1899) [1899] 2 Ch 392; 68 LJ Ch 699

LINDLEY MR: . . . The first principle is that in equity the promoters of a company stand in a fiduciary relation to it, and to those persons whom they induce to become shareholders in it, and cannot in equity bind the company by any contract with themselves without fully and fairly disclosing to the company all material facts which the company ought to know. *Erlanger v New Sombrero Phosphate Co*[1] is the leading authority in support of this general proposition.

The second principle is that a company when registered is a corporation capable by its directors of binding itself by a contract with themselves as promoters if all material facts are disclosed. *Salomon v Salomon & Co*[2] is the leading authority for this principle.

The third principle is that the directors of a company acting within their powers, and with reasonable care, and honestly in the interest of the company, are not personally liable for losses which the company may suffer by reason of their mistakes or errors in judgment. *Overend, Gurney & Co v Gibb*[3] is the leading authority on this head.

A fourth principle, not confined to companies, but extending to them, is that a contract can be set aside in equity on proof that one party induced the other to enter into it by misrepresentations of material facts, although such mis-representations may not have been fraudulent.

A fifth principle is that a voidable contract cannot be rescinded or set aside after the position of the parties has been changed, so that they cannot be restored to their former position. Fraud may exclude the application of this principle, but I know of no other exception. With these preliminary observations I proceed to examine the facts of this case.

The Lagunas Nitrate Company was promoted and formed by the directors of another company called the Lagunas Nitrate Syndicate, in order to buy property belonging to that company. The memorandum and articles of association of the syndicate shew that in promoting and forming the nitrate company the directors of the syndicate were acting within, and not beyond, their powers as such directors. The syndicate therefore, as a company, may be properly described, and ought to be regarded as, the promoter, by their directors, of the nitrate company. The syndicate is therefore responsible for the acts and omissions of its directors in promoting and forming the nitrate company. . . .

The decision in *Erlanger v New Sombrero Phosphate Co* on which the appellants mainly rely, and which is one of the most valuable decisions on the duties of promoters to the companies which they bring into existence, does not warrant the conclusion that the contract between the two companies can be treated as no contract at all, and as a piece of paper not binding the nitrate company either at law or in equity. Nor is it possible after the decision in *Salomon's Case* to treat that contract as so opposed to the Companies Acts as to be ultra vires the nitrate company, or to be void upon the ground that there were not in truth two parties capable of contracting with one another. If the syndicate brought an action against the nitrate company for a breach of the agreement, the nitrate company could not successfully defend itself by a plea of non est factum, or by a mere

---

1 (1878) 3 App Ca 1218; 48 LJ Ch 73 (see p 163)

2 (1897) AC 22; 66 LJ Ch 35 (see p 91)

3 (1872) LR 5 HL 480; 42 LJ Ch 67

denial of the existence of any agreement. If the agreement can be set aside, it must be upon some other ground.

The first ground relied upon is the formation of the nitrate company itself without an independent body of directors. Notwithstanding all that has been said in *Erlanger v New Sombrero Phosphate Co* about the duties of the promoters of a company to furnish it with an independent board of directors, that decision does not require or indeed justify the conclusion that if a company is avowedly formed with a board of directors who are not independent, but who are stated to be the intended vendors, or the agents of the intended vendors, of property to the company, the company can set aside an agreement entered into by them for the purchase of such property simply because they are not an independent board. What vitiated the agreement in *Erlanger's Case* were the concealment of the fact that two out of the three managing directors were agents of the vendors and promoters, and the untrue statement that a provisional contract had been entered into by the directors, whilst, in fact, it had only been framed by the promoters and adopted by three directors, two of whom were not known to be their agents, and the third of whom knew nothing about the matter. In the present case there is no secrecy or concealment of the true position of the first directors, and no untrue statement as to what they did for the company. In the face of the memorandum and articles of association it is impossible to treat the nitrate company or the members thereof as ignorant of the real truth as to the position of its directors.

After *Salomon's Case* I think it impossible to hold that it is the duty of the promoters of a company to provide it with an independent board of directors, if the real truth is disclosed to those who are induced by the promoters to join the company. Treating promoters of companies as in a fiduciary relation to them, and as having a power of appointing trustees (namely, directors), I cannot treat companies or their shareholders as so many cestuis que trust under disability, nor even as cestuis que trust for whom trustees are appointed without their consent. No one need join a company unless he likes, and if a person knows that if he becomes a member he will find as directors persons who, in his opinion, ought not to be directors, he should not join the company. If he does, he has no right to redress on the ground that improper persons were appointed trustees. *Volenti non fit injuria* applies in such a case to the members of the company, and *Salomon's Case* shews that the company in its corporate capacity is in this respect in no better position. On these grounds the nitrate company is not, in my opinion, entitled to relief against the syndicate or its directors on the ground that they did wrong in creating the nitrate company with such provisions as are contained in the instruments by which it was created, and which govern its existence. The principles on which *Salomon's Case* was decided by the House of Lords are quite consistent with those on which *Erlanger v New Sombrero Phosphate Co* was decided, but are quite inconsistent with such an extension of those principles as would be necessary to give the nitrate company relief against those who formed it, on the ground that they formed it with an objectionable constitution.

Lindley MR went on to hold that the prospectus was seriously misleading. In view of the fact, however, that there was no fraud on the part of the syndicate and that it was impossible to restore the parties to their former positions, the right to rescind was lost. Collins LJ agreed with Lindley MR, but Rigby LJ dissented on the ground that the company had not lost the right to rescind the contract.

PART III: THE FLOTATION OF PUBLIC COMPANIES

The Different Regimes

Public companies seeking to raise money from the public will offer shares or debentures (together often described as 'securities') and may opt for one of three regulatory regimes, each having as a major role the protection of the investing public. In the first place the company may seek to have the newly issued securities admitted to the Official List of securities to be quoted and traded on the International Stock Exchange (ISE). This regime has been the subject of European Community harmonisation under which the ISE is the competent authority for the purposes of the EC Harmonisation Listing Directives, with authority to make rules regarding the listing of shares on the ISE (Financial Services Act 1986, s 142(6)). Secondly, the company may seek a listing for the securities on the Alternative Investment Market (AIM) which began operating on 19 June 1995 and which will supersede the Unlisted Securities Market (USM) which was established in 1980 and where the conditions for the listing of shares was far less stringent than those of The Stock Exchange. Finally, the company may not seek any listing for the securities.

In each of these cases, the company and others who may be involved in the issue of securities (eg the issuing house which may be handling the issue on behalf of the company or any experts whose opinions are disclosed to the investing public with a view to making the investment attractive) are subject to the principles of the common law developed largely in the 19th century. These principles had, by the end of that century, proved to be inadequate for the proper protection of the investing public and statutory and quasi-statutory regimes have increasingly supplemented the common law.

At present there are two statutory regimes, Part IV of the Financial Services Act for shares which are admitted to the Official List of The Stock Exchange and ss 56–71 (including Sch 3) of the Companies Act 1985 for all other issues (including the USM and, presumably, the AIM). Part V of the FSA 1986, which closely resembles Pt IV, was originally intended to replace these Companies Act provisions, but is now expected to be repealed without being brought into force. The Treasury has consulted ('Revised Implementation of the EC Prospectus Directive, Consultation Document', July 1994) with a view to enacting legislation to implement the EC Prospectus Directive (89/298/EC). This legislation will establish the appropriate regime in place of the provisions of the Companies Act.[1]

The current statutory regimes prescribe (as, undoubtedly, will any successor regimes) the information that must be disclosed (FSA 1986, ss 144, 146–147; CA 1985, s 56, Sch 3) and the basis for compensation for any investor who suffers loss when acting on misleading or inadequate information (FSA 1986, ss 150–152; CA 1985, ss 67–68). In addition, there is the all-important quasi-statutory regime, the Listing Rules ('The Yellow Book', latest edition, 1 December 1993, as amended) drawn up by the ISE under the powers delegated to it by s 142 of the FSA, setting out the disclosure and other

---

1 Such legislation, the Public Offers of Securities Regulations 1995 (SI 1995/1537) came into force on 19 June 1995 (see preface at pp v ff)

requirements for companies seeking to have their securities admitted to the Official List (Source 60). The ISE has also issued rules for the admission of securities to the USM and the AIM.

Types of Flotation

A company may raise money from its shareholders by inviting them to subscribe for further securities in proportion to their existing holdings. This offer may be designed for acceptance *only* by existing shareholders (a 'restricted rights offer') or as one which allows any shareholder to pass the invitation on to anyone else (including outsiders) for acceptance (a 'rights offer').

Alternatively, the company may invite the public at large to subscribe for securities. This is a 'public offer' and can either be made directly by the company or — now almost always the case — by an issuing house, to whom the entire issue is allotted by the company. The issuing house then takes responsibility for the preparation of the documentation and all other steps necessary for the flotation.

The company may, in addition, allot the entire issue to an issuing house to be placed with the issuing house's clients ('a placing'). This is not a public offer, but shares issued by this method may be accepted by The Stock Exchange for listing provided that the special conditions laid down by the Listing Rules have been followed.

The method of issue is, generally, renounceable letter of allotment or renounceable letter of right. The former is for public issue, the latter for a rights issue. When the company has decided which subscribers are to have shares and how many in each case, the renounceable letters are issued to each subscriber in respect of the number of shares subscribed. Subscribers may then be registered as shareholders or sell the rights by 'renouncing' the letters in favour of the purchaser, who, in turn, may be registered as a shareholder or sell the rights. If, in a Rights Issue, the company does not want outsiders to gain membership of the company, the issue can be done by non-renounceable letters of right. This will then not be a public issue.

The Legal Requirements

For public issues of shares which are to be listed on The Stock Exchange, the Stock Exchange Listing Particulars must be complied with. Where the shares are not to be so listed, any document advertising the securities for subscription or purchase is defined as a prospectus (s 744) and must comply with the provisions of the Companies Act 1985, s 56, Sch 3.

When an investor has acquired an unconditional right to be included in the company's register of members, the securities in question are said to be allotted (CA 1985, s 738). A company proposing to allot equity securities (as defined by CA 1985, s 94) must ensure compliance with the existing shareholders' pre-emption rights under the provisions of ss 89–94. These rights may be disapplied (s 95). In accordance with the Listing Rules (para 9.20), any authorisation by existing shareholders under this disapplication provision will last for 15 months only. In order to exercise the company's power to allot securities, the directors must be authorised under the provisions of s 80 or s 80A. No allotment may be made unless a minimum subscription has been received (s 83). Further, the entire issue must be subscribed unless the prospectus permits otherwise (s 84). In the event of the minimum subscription being not achieved, any money received by the company must be returned within 40 days and, if not done so within 48 days, the directors are jointly and severally liable in respect of these payments (s 84).

Commission may be paid to underwriters of the issue (ie those agreeing to subscribe) provided the conditions laid down by s 97 are complied with. Aside from this, no commissions may be paid or discounts allowed (s 98). Shares allotted must be paid up at least to the extent of one-quarter of the nominal value and the entire amount of any premium (s 101). Shares cannot be issued at a discount, but do not have to be issued at a premium, where it would otherwise be possible to do so (see Chapter 10, Part II and the extracts from *Ooregum Gold Mining Company v Roper* [1892] AC 125 and *Hilder v Dexter* [1902] AC 474).

Within one month of a successful allotment, the company must make certain returns to the Registrar of Companies (s 88).

At present, an issue of shares in exchange for other shares is not 'an offer to the public for subscription or purchase' and therefore does not fall within the prospectus requirements (*Government Stocks and Other Securities Investments Ltd v Christopher,*[1] Source 61 at p 187).

The offer may also not qualify as a public offer because it is restricted to a particular group, eg existing shareholders (ss 59, 60 of the Companies Act 1985, *Government Stocks v Christopher,* Source 61). Prospectuses must be registered with the Registrar of Companies on or before publication (s 64). Unlike the Listing Particulars, prospectuses do not have to be 'pre-vetted'. A powerful argument can be made for pre-vetting of prospectuses (Gower, *Review of Investor Protection,* HMSO, 1984, Cmnd 9125 (Source 62)).

Where the company allots the securities to an issuing house with a view to all or any of them being offered for sale to the public, the investing public is protected. If the shares are to be listed on The Stock Exchange, Listing Particulars will have to be filed; if not, any document by which the shares are offered to the public is deemed to be a prospectus issued by the company, s 58.

As competent authority, the ISE is also empowered to suspend or discontinue a listing of shares. This power derives from the EC Directive designed to 'co-ordinate the conditions for the admission of securities to official Stock Exchange listing' (Council Directive EC/79/279). While this Directive has as one of its purposes the protection of investors, there is no obligation on The Stock Exchange to advise shareholders or, *a fortiori,* other interested parties of the proposed suspension. Similarly, shareholders do not have any locus standi to challenge a decision to suspend or discontinue a share listing, only the company may do this (*R v Stock Exchange, ex parte Else,* Source 64).

---

1 [1956] 1 WLR 237; [1956] 1 All ER 490

Defective or Misleading Prospectuses and Listing Particulars

Where the public issue is of unlisted shares, investors have two statutory remedies. If the prospectus omits required information in breach of s 56 and Sch 3, an action for breach of statutory duty is available (*Re South of England Natural Gas Company*,[1] Source 64). If the prospectus contains a misrepresentation, an action is available against the directors, promoters, experts and anyone else who authorised the issue of the prospectus to *subscribers* (ie as opposed to *purchasers*, see *Peek v Gurney*, Source 65 and CA 1985, ss 67–69).

The remedies for investors where the listing particulars are defective or misleading are contained in ss 146 and 150 of the Financial Services Act 1986 and are available to purchasers as well as subscribers and in respect of omissions as well as misrepresentations. The principles of the common law which govern misrepresentations on which, in theory, an investor may base a claim, have been largely replaced by the statutory remedies, a process which is continued by the new statutory regime of the Financial Services Act. The basic principle of causation will remain — the loss suffered must have been caused by the misrepresentation, although it does not seem that it will be necessary for the investor to have actually read the prospectus or listing particulars (FSA 1986, ss 150, 166).

In the highly unlikely circumstances of an investor wishing to sue the *company*, a common law action may be maintained although there are substantial obstacles. The company will have to be shown to be vicariously liable, or to be liable for the acts of its alter ego (see pp 281ff). The plaintiff will no longer have to cease being a member of the company, whether it is an action based on misrepresentation or breach of contract (as was the case before the repeal of *Houldsworth v City of Glasgow Bank*,[2] (CA 1985, s 111A, as inserted by s 131 of the CA 1989).

An action may also be attempted under s 2 of the Misrepresentation Act 1967. Note, however, that the person who made the misrepresentation must be the other party to the contract which the plaintiff was induced to enter into. Does the defective prospectus constitute a contract (perhaps a collateral contract (?) see *Wedderburn* [1959] CLJ 58) between the company and the investor? Note, that like the statutory remedy provided by the Companies Act and the Financial Services Act, the burden of proof is shifted to the defendant to show that the misrepresentation was not negligent.

For the antecedents to the present statutory regime, for the common law principles which denied liability to purchasers (as opposed to subscribers) and denied liability for negligent (as opposed to fraudulent) misrepresentation, see *Peek v Gurney*[3] (Source 65) recently applied in *Al Nakib Investments Ltd v Longcroft*,[4] and *Derry v Peak*[5] (Source 66).

---

1 [1911] 1 Ch 573; 80 LJ Ch 358
2 (1880) 5 App Ca 317; 42 LT 194
3 (1873) LR 6 HL 377; 43 LJ Ch 19 (see p 200)
4 [1990] BCC 518; [1991] BCLC 7
5 (1889) 14 App Ca 337; 58 LJ Ch 864 (see p 202)

SOURCE 60
The Listing Rules
(London Stock Exchange, December 1993)

CHAPTER 6

CONTENTS OF LISTING PARTICULARS

Information required for the admission of shares or convertible debt securities to listing

A   the persons responsible for listing particulars, the auditors and other advisers
B   the shares for which application is being made
C   the issuer and its capital
D   the group's activities
E   the issuer's assets and liabilities, financial position and profits and losses
F   the management
G   the recent development and prospects of the group

The persons responsible for listing particulars, the auditors and other advisers

6.A.1   The name, home or business address and function of each of the persons giving the declaration set out in paragraph 6.A.3.

. . .

6.A.3   A declaration in the following form:

'The directors of [the issuer], whose names appear on page [   ], accept responsibility for the information contained in this document. To the best of the knowledge and belief of the directors (who have taken all reasonable care to ensure that such is the case) the information contained in this document is in accordance with the facts and does not omit anything likely to affect the import of such information.'

6.A.4   The names, addresses and qualifications of the auditors who have audited the issuer's annual accounts in accordance with national law for the last three financial years.

6.A.5   A statement that the annual accounts of the issuer for the last three financial years have been audited. If audit reports on any of those accounts have been refused by the auditors or contain qualifications, such refusal or such qualifications must be reproduced in full and the reasons given.

. . .

6.A.7   If auditors have resigned, have been removed or have not been re-appointed during the last three financial years and have deposited a statement with the issuer of circumstances which they believe should be brought to the attention of members and creditors of the issuer, details of such matters must be disclosed if material.

. . .

6.A.9　Where a statement or report attributed to a person as an expert is included in the listing particulars, a statement that it is included, in the form and context in which it is included, with the consent of that person, who has authorised the contents of that part of the listing particulars for the purposes of section 152(1)(e) of the FSA.

The shares of which application is being made

6.B.1　A statement that 'Application [has been] [will be] made to The International Stock Exchange of the United Kingdom and the Republic of Ireland Limited for [the shares] to be admitted to the Official List' setting out the relevant shares.

. . .

6.B.4　A statement of the resolutions, authorisations and approvals by virtue of which the shares have been or will be created and/or issued.

. . .

6.B.7　A summary of the rights attaching to the shares for which application is made, and in particular the extent of the voting rights, entitlement to share in the profits and, in the event of liquidation, in any surplus and any other special rights. Where there is or is to be more than one class of shares of the issuer in issue, like details must be given for each class.

. . .

6.B.11　Arrangements for transfer of the shares and (where permitted) any restrictions on their free transferability (for example, provisions requiring transfers to be approved).

. . .

6.B.15　The following information must be given concerning the terms and conditions of the issue and placing, public or private, of the securities in respect of which the application for admission is made where such issue or placing is being effected at the same time as admission or has been effected within the 12 months preceding admission:

(a) a statement of any right of pre-emption of shareholders exercisable in respect of the shares or of the disapplication of such right (and where applicable, a statement of the reasons for the disapplication of such right; in such cases, the directors' justification of the issue price where the issue is for cash; if the disapplication of the right of pre-emption is intended to benefit specific persons, the identity of those persons);

(b) the total amounts which have been or are being issued or placed and the number of shares offered, where applicable by category;

(c) if a public or private issue or placing has been or is being made simultaneously on the markets of two or more countries and if a tranche has been or is being reserved for certain of these, details of any such tranche;

(d)   (i) the issue price or offer or placing price, stating the nominal value or, in its absence, the accounting par value or the amount to be capitalised;

     (ii) the issue premium and the amount of any expenses specifically charged to any subscriber or purchaser; and

    (iii) the methods of payment of the price, particularly as regards the paying-up of shares which are not fully paid;

(e) the procedure for the exercise of any right of pre-emption, the transferability of subscription rights and the treatment of subscription rights not exercised;

(f) the period during which the issue or offer remained open or will remain open after publication of the listing particulars, and the names of the receiving agents;

. . .

(h)   (i) the names, addresses and descriptions of the persons underwriting or guaranteeing the issue for the issuer; and

     (ii) where not all of the isssue has been or is being underwritten or guaranteed, a statement of the portion not covered;

(i) a statement or estimate of the overall amount and/or of the amount per share of the charges relating to the issue payable by the issuer, stating the total remuneration of the financial intermediaries, including the underwriting commission or margin, guarantee commission, placing commission or selling agent's commission; and

(j) the estimated net proceeds accruing to the issuer from the issue and the intended application of such proceeds.

6.B.16   A description of the shares for which application is made and, in particular, the number of shares and nominal value per share or, in the absence of nominal value, the accounting par value or the total nominal value, the exact designation or class, and coupons attached.

6.B.17   If shares are to be marketed and no such shares have previously been sold to the public, a statement of the number of shares made available to the market (if any) and of their nominal value, or, if they have no nominal value, of their accounting par value, or a statement of the total nominal value and, where applicable, a statement of the minimum offer price.

. . .

6.B.20   If shares of the same class have not yet been admitted to listing but are dealt in on one or more other regulated, regularly operating, recognised open markets, an indication of such markets.

6.B.21   If during the period covered by the last financial year and the current financial year, there has occurred any public takeover offer by a third party in respect of the issuer's shares, or any public takeover offer by the issuer in respect of another company's shares, a statement to that effect and a statement of the price or exchange terms attaching to any such offers and the outcome thereof.

6.B.22   If, simultaneously or almost simultaneously with the issue of shares for which application is being made, shares of the same class are subscribed for or placed privately or if shares of other classes are created for public or private placing, details must be given of the nature of such operations and of the number and characteristics of the shares concerned.

6.B.23 Where the shares for which application is being made are offered by way of rights, or allotted by way of capitalisation of reserves or undistributed profits, to the holders of an existing listed security, the following information must be given:

    (a) (i) the pro rata entitlement;

         (ii) the last date on which transfers were or will be accepted for registration for participation in the issue;

      (iii) how the shares rank for dividend or interest;

      (iv) whether the shares rank pari passu with any existing listed securities;

       (v) the nature of the document of title (if any) and its proposed date of issue; and

      (vi) how any fractions will be treated;

    (b) in the case of a rights issue, how shares not taken up will be dealt with and the time in which the offer may be accepted; and

    (c) in the case of a capitalisation issue whether or not the documents of title (if any) are renounceable.

6.B.24 A statement whether the shares are in registered or bearer form.

6.B.25 In the case of bearer shares issued by a company incorporated or established in a member state other than the United Kingdom, where the definitive documents of title have not been or are not to be printed from engraved steel plates, a statement to this effect.

. . .

The issuer and its capital

6.C.1 The name, registered office and, if different, head office of the issuer.

6.C.2 The country of incorporation of the issuer.

6.C.3 The date of incorporation and the length of life of the issuer, except where indefinite.

6.C.4 The legislation under which the issuer operates and the legal form which it has adopted under that legislation.

6.C.5 A description of the issuer's principal objects and reference to the clause of the memorandum of association in which they are described.

6.C.6 The place of registration of the issuer and its registration number.

6.C.7   A statement that for a period of not less than 14 days at a named place in or near the City of London or such other place as the Exchange may determine, at the registered office of the issuer and at the offices of its paying agents in the United Kingdom (if any), the following documents (or copies thereof), where applicable, may be inspected:

(a) the memorandum and articles of association of the issuer;

(b) any trust deed of the issuer and any of its subsidiary undertakings;

(c) each document mentioned in paragraphs 6.C.20 (material contracts) and 6.F.12 (directors' service contracts) or, in the case of a contract not reduced into writing, a memorandum giving full particulars thereof;

. . .

(g) the audited accounts of the issuer or, in the case of a group, the consolidated audited accounts of the issuer and its subsidiary undertakings for each of the two financial years preceding the publication of the listing particulars, including, in the case of a company incorporated in the United Kingdom, all notes, reports or information required by the Companies Acts 1985 and 1989.

. . .

6.C.9   The amount of the issuer's authorised and issued capital and the amount of any capital agreed to be issued, the number and classes of the shares of which it is composed with details of their principal characteristics; if any part of the issued capital is still to be paid up, a statement of the number, or total nominal value, and the type of the shares not yet fully paid up, broken down, where applicable, according to the extent to which they have been paid up.

6.C.10   Where the issuer has authorised but unissued capital or is committed to increase the capital, an indication of:

(a) the amount of such authorised capital or capital increase and, where appropriate, the duration of the authorisation;

(b) the categories of persons having preferential subscription rights for such additional portions of capital; and

(c) the terms and arrangements for the share issue corresponding to such portions.

. . .

6.C.13   A summary of the provisions of the issuer's memorandum and articles of association regarding changes in the capital and in the respective rights of the various classes of shares.

6.C.14   A summary of the changes during the three preceding years in the amount of the issued capital of the issuer and, if material, the capital of any member of the group and/or the number and classes of shares of which it is composed. Intra group issued by wholly owned subsidiaries, pro rata issues by partly owned subsidiaries and changes in the capital structure of subsidiaries which have remained wholly owned throughout the period may be disregarded. Such summary must also state the price and terms of such issues, including particulars of any discounts or other special terms granted and (if not already fully paid) the dates when any instalments are payable with the amount of all calls or instalments in arrears. If there are no such issues, an appropriate negative statement must be made.

6.C.15 The names of the persons, so far as they are known to the issuer, who, directly or indirectly, jointly or severally, exercise or could exercise control over the issuer, and particulars of the proportion of the voting capital held by such persons. For these purposes, joint control means control exercised by two or more persons who have concluded an agreement which may lead to their adopting a common policy in respect of the issuer.

6.C.16 In so far as is known to the issuer, the name of any person other than a director who, directly or indirectly, is interested in 3% or more of the issuer's capital, together with the amount of each such person's interest or, if there are no such persons, an appropriate negative statement.

6.C.17 If the issuer has subsidiary undertakings or parent undertakings, a brief description of the group of undertakings and of the issuer's position within it stating, where the issuer is a subsidiary undertaking, the name of and number of shares in the issuer held (directly or indirectly) by each parent undertaking of the issuer.

. . .

6.C.19 The persons to whom any capital of any member of the group or of any of its subsidiary undertakings is under option, or agreed conditionally or unconditionally to be put under option, with particulars of the capital including the price and duration of the option and consideration for which the option was or will be granted, or an appropriate negative statement. Where options have been granted or agreed to be granted to all the holders of shares or debt securities, or of any class thereof, or to employees under an employees' share scheme, it will be sufficient, so far as the names are concerned, to record that fact without giving names.

6.C.20 A summary of the principal contents of each material contract (not being a contract entered into in the ordinary course of business) entered into by any member of the group within the two years immediately preceding the publication of the listing particulars, including particulars of dates, parties, terms and conditions, any consideration passing to or from the issuer or any other member of the group, unless such contracts have been available for inspection in the last two years in which case it will be sufficient to refer to them collectively as being available for inspection in accordance with paragraph 6.C.7(c).

6.C.21 The details of any payment or other benefit paid to or given to a promoter if and to the extent that disclosure of the same is required by the general law. In addition, if the Exchange so requires, details of the name of any promoter of any member of the group, including any director, the amount of any cash, securities or benefits paid, issued or given within the two years immediately preceding the date of publication of the listing particulars, or proposed to be paid, issued or given to any promoter and the consideration for such payment, issue or benefit.

6.C.22 Where the listing particulars are prepared in respect of shares issued in connection with any merger, division of a company, takeover offer, acquisition of an undertaking's assets and liabilities or transfer of assets:

(a) a statement of the aggregate value of the consideration for the transaction and how it was or is to be satisfied; and

(b) if the total emoluments receivable by the directors of the issuer will be varied in consequence of the transaction, full particulars of the variation; if there will be no variation, a statement to that effect.

The group's activities

6.D.1 A description of the group's principal activities, stating the main categories of products sold and/or services performed.

6.D.2 Information on any significant new products and/or activities.

6.D.3 A breakdown of net turnover during the last three financial years by categories of activity and into geographical markets in so far as such categories and markets differ substantially from one another, taking account of the manner in which the sale of products and the provision of services falling within the group's ordinary activities are organised.

6.D.4 The location, size and tenure of the group's principal establishments and summary information about land or buildings owned or leased. Any establishment which accounts for more than 10% of net turnover or production shall be considered a principal establishment.

6.D.5 Where the information given pursuant to paragraphs 6.D.1 to 6.D.4 has been influenced by exceptional factors, that fact must be mentioned.

6.D.6 Summary information regarding the extent to which the group is dependent, if at all, on patents or licences, industrial, commercial or financial contracts or new manufacturing processes, where such factors are of fundamental importance to the group's business or profitability.

6.D.7 Information concerning policy on the research and development of new products and processes over the past three financial years, where significant.

6.D.8 Information on any legal or arbitration proceedings (including any such proceedings which are pending or threatened of which the issuer is aware) which may have or have had in the recent past (covering at least the previous 12 months) a significant effect on the group's financial position or an appropriate negative statement.

6.D.9 Information on any interruptions in the group's business which may have or have had during the recent past (covering at least the previous 12 months) a significant effect on the group's financial position.

6.D.10 The average numbers employed and changes therein over the last three financial years (if such changes are material), with, if possible, a breakdown of persons employed by main categories of activity.

6.D.11 A description, with figures, of the main investments made, including interests such as shares, debt securities etc, in other undertakings over the last three financial years and during the current financial year.

6.D.12 Information concerning the principal investments (including new plant, factories, and research and development) being made, with the exception of interests being acquired in other undertakings, including:

(a) the geographical distribution of these investments (home and abroad); and

(b) the method of financing such investments (internal or external).

6.D.13 Information concerning the group's principal future investments (including new plant, factories, and research and development) (if any), with the exception of interests to be acquired in other undertakings, on which the issuer's directors have already made firm commitments.

6.D.14 In cases where two or more activities are carried on which are material, in terms of profits or losses, assets employed or any other factor, such figures and explanation as are necessary to demonstrate the relative importance of each such activity.

6.D.15 The principal place of business (if any) in the United Kingdom.

The management

6.F.1 The full name, home or business address and function in the group of each of the following persons and an indication of the principal activities performed by them outside the group where these are significant with respect to the group:

(a) directors of the issuer;

(b) partners with unlimited liability, in the case of a limited partnership with a share capital; and

(c) founders, if the issuer has been established for fewer than five years.

6.F.2 A description of other relevant business interests and activities of every such person as is mentioned in paragraph 6.F.1 and, if required by the Exchange, particulars of any former forename or surname of such persons.

6.F.3 The total aggregate of the remuneration paid and benefits in kind granted to the directors of the issuer by any member of the group during the last completed financial year under any description whatsoever.

6.F.4 In the case of an issuer which is a company subject to the Companies Act 1985, interests (distinguishing between beneficial and non-beneficial interests) relating to securities which:

(a) have been notified by each director to the issuer pursuant to section 324 or section 328 of the Companies Act 1985;

(b) are required pursuant to section 325 of that Act to be entered in the register referred to therein; or

(c) are interests of a connected person of a director which would, if the connected person were a director, be required to be disclosed under (a) or (b) above, and the existence of which is known to or could with reasonable diligence be ascertained by that director;

or an appropriate negative statement.

6.F.5 In the case of an issuer which is a company not subject to the Companies Act 1985, the interests of each director, including any connected person, the existence of which is known to, or could with reasonable diligence be ascertained by, that director whether or not held through another party, in the share capital of the issuer together with any options in respect of such capital.

6.F.6   All relevant particulars regarding the nature and extent of any interests of directors of the issuer in transactions which are or were unusual in their nature or conditions or significant to the business of the group, and which were effected by the issuer;

(a) during the current or immediately preceding financial year; or
(b) during an earlier year and remain in any respect outstanding or unperformed;

or an appropriate negative statement.

6.F.7   The total of any outstanding loans granted by any member of the group to the directors and also of any guarantees provided by any member of the group for their benefit.

6.F.8   Details of any schemes for involving the staff in the capital of any member of the group.

6.F.9   The full name and professional qualification (if any) of the secretary of the issuer.

6.F.10 Particulars of any arrangement under which a director of the issuer has waived or agreed to waive future emoluments together with particulars of waivers of such emoluments which occurred during the past financial year.

6.F.11 An estimate of the amounts payable to directors of the issuer, including proposed directors, by any member of the group for the current financial year under the arrangements in force at the date of the listing particulars.

6.F.12 Details of existing or proposed directors' service contracts (excluding contracts previously made available for inspection in accordance with paragraph 16.9 and not subsequently varied), such details to include the matters specified in paragraph 16.11, or an appropriate negative statement.

6.F.13 A summary of the provisions of the memorandum and articles of association of the issuer with regard to:

(a) any power enabling a director to vote on a proposal, arrangement, or contract in which he is materially interested;
(b) any power enabling the directors, in the absence of an independent quorum, to vote remuneration (including pension or other benefits) to themselves or any members of their body;
(c) borrowing powers exercisable by the directors and how such borrowing powers can be varied; and
(d) retirement or non-retirement of directors under an age limit.

SOURCE 61
Government Stocks and Other Securities Investments Ltd *v* Christopher
(Chancery Division 1956) [1956] 1 WLR 237; [1956] 1 All ER 490

A merger between two companies — Union Castle (in which the plaintiffs were shareholders and the defendants were the directors) and Clan — was proposed by the exchange of shares in the two companies for shares in a new company.

WYNN-PARRYJ: . . . This is a motion for interlocutory relief by way of injunction in an action brought by the plaintiff company on behalf of itself and all other shareholders and stockholders of Union-Castle other than the seven individual defendants who are the present directors of Union-Castle and other than Union-Castle itself. In substance what the plaintiff company seeks is a series of injunctions to prevent the defendants from taking any further step of any kind in connexion with an offer in writing dated 12 November 1955, made by the new company, to acquire the whole of each class of preference and ordinary shares and stock in the issued capitals of Union-Castle and Clan in exchange for preference and ordinary shares in the new company as set out in the circular. . . .

The plaintiff company then attacked the circular, alleging that it contained representations which are misleading, and omissions which had the effect of making what was stated misleading. I should say at once that Mr Lincoln for the plaintiff company, expressly disclaimed any suggestion that the individual defendants were acting otherwise than perfectly bona fide throughout the matter. I think that in order to understand and consider the attacks which the plaintiff company makes on the circular, I should first consider its nature. It is alleged by the plaintiff company that it is a prospectus to which section 38[1] of the Companies Act 1948, applies, and that as such it does not comply with the requirements of that Act. It is not disputed that if it is such a prospectus, it does in fact fail to comply with the requirements of the Act.

The word 'prospectus' is defined in section 455[2] of the Companies Act 1948. Subsection (1) of this section opens with the words: 'In this Act, unless the context otherwise requires, the following expressions have the meanings hereby assigned to them (that is to say) . . . "prospectus" means any prospectus, notice, circular, advertisement, or other invitation, offering to the public for subscription or purchase any shares or debentures of a company. . . .' It is argued that 'prospectus' in section 38 of the Companies Act 1948, has a wider meaning than in section 455, the reason put forward being that in subsection (3) reference is made to the issue of 'A form of application', and that there being nothing in the subsection to limit the issue of the form of application to an allotment and issue for cash, it must apply where the consideration is a consideration other than cash. This, it is said, constitutes a context requiring the word 'prospectus' to cover documents not included in the definition in section 455. I do not accept this view. Section 38 follows section 37, which appears under the heading 'prospectus.' There is no ground whatsoever for giving the word 'prospectus' in section 37 any more extended meaning than it has in section 455, and it would be strange if in the very next section 'prospectus' were to be found to have a wider meaning. I can see no need to attribute any other meaning to 'prospectus' in section 38 than that given in section 455. The reference in subsection (3) to a form of application

---

1 Now s 56 of the Companies Act 1985
2 Now s 744, ibid

means only a form of application in connexion with a prospectus offering shares for subscription or purchase.

It is clear that the circular does not involve an offer for the purchase of any shares. The shares in question are unissued shares of the new company, so they cannot be the subject of an offer for purchase (see *Re V. G. M. Holdings Ltd*).[1]

It becomes necessary, therefore, to consider the word 'subscription' in the definition of 'prospectus.' In my view the word means: taking or agreeing to take shares for cash. It imports that the person agreeing to take the shares puts himself under a liability to pay the nominal amount thereof in cash.

...

In Murray's Oxford Dictionary, one of the meanings attributed to 'subscription' is: 'A promise over one's signature to pay a sum of money for shares in an undertaking.' I can find no secondary meaning attributed to 'subscription' in the Companies Act 1948. On the contrary, paras 4, 5, 6 and 7 of Part I of Schedule 4 to the Act clearly require that 'subscription' and 'subscribe' involve the notion of payment in cash. The circular in this case does not invite subscription for shares for cash. For these reasons I am of opinion that the circular is not a prospectus within the meaning of that word as used in the Companies Act 1948. I would add that it would be somewhat strange if the circular were in fact a prospectus in view of the circumstance that the permission of the Board of Trade was obtained under section 13 of the Prevention of Fraud (Investments) Act 1939, on the basis that it was not a prospectus. I am further of opinion that the circular was not distributed to the public. I accept the proposition put forward by Sir Andrew Clark, namely, that the test is not who receives the circular, but who can accept the offer put forward. In this case it can only be persons legally or equitably interested as shareholders in the shares of Union-Castle or Clan. In the case of those who accept non-renounceable letters of allotment will be issued. In these circumstances the case appears to me to fall within section 55(2)[2] of the Companies Act 1948.

SOURCE 62
Gower, Review of Investor Protection
(pp 138–44)

[The Jenkins Committee] accepted that takeover offers and issues by prospectus were essentially variations of the same genus and suggested that they should be regulated broadly in the same way; their way, in effect, being to equate regulation of takeovers with an up-dated and more flexible legal regime for public issues. Among a number of recommendations regarding the latter, they suggested that documents offering securities for a consideration other than cash should be treated as prospectuses, that no allotment of shares offered to the public should be permitted after the expiry of three months from the first issue of a prospectus, that the Board of Trade should be empowered to amend Schedule 4 of the Companies Act by statutory instrument and to issue certifications of exemption in respect of prospectuses for unlisted securities, and that the Registrar of Companies should be empowered (subject to an appeal to the Court) to refuse to accept for registration a prospectus for unlisted securities if it did not set out the information required by the Act or did so 'in a manner likely to create a false impression on the mind of an unwary or inexperienced investor'. This last

---

1 [1942] Ch 235; 111 LJ Ch 145
2 Now ss 59–60 of the Companies Act 1985

recommendation was an attempt to fill the gap in pre-vetting of prospectuses, but was always regarded as hardly a practicable task for the Registrar to perform.

9.15 Under the Committee's recommendations, the same model would be followed for takeovers. The Board of Trade would have had power, by statutory instrument, to make regulations applicable to every takeover offer no matter by whom it was circulated and would have had a like power to grant exemptions. Circulars would have been treated as prospectuses and, as such, sent for registration to the Registrar who could reject them if they did not comply with the regulations or were liable to mislead. These proposals were, of course, made before the advent of the Code or the Panel. They assumed that the system for regulating issue prospectuses was, or would immediately be made, more effective and that the best solution was to bring takeovers into line with that system. No action has, however, been taken on these parts of the Jenkins Report and in the succeeding twenty years the regulation of takeovers has been transformed. Few people today, I think, would wish to scrap the City Code or the Panel. But the basic aims of the Committee, that like should be treated alike and that both types of prospectuses should be effectively scrutinised, still need to be achieved.

Pre-vetting of issue prospectuses
9.16 Pre-vetting of prospectuses for *listed* securities is already mandatory under the adopted E.E.C. Directives and will become mandatory under U.K. law when we implement them. This has been accepted without demur because The Stock Exchange already vets all prospectuses for securities which are to be listed and could continue to do so if nominated as the 'competent authority'. But the present proposals in the Draft Directive on public offer prospectuses propose to make pre-vetting mandatory in respect of all prospectuses even those for securities which are not to be listed. A determined rearguard action against this proposal has been mounted by a number of Member States, including the U.K. and Germany, the arguments which have been advanced by the U.K. being that there are, in the U.K., hardly any public issues of non-listed securities, and that the requirement would be wasteful and unnecessary. Since those countries where pre-vetting is already mandatory will not be precluded from continuing to make it mandatory and cannot be expected to care greatly what happens in the case of prospectuses addressed to investors in other countries and since the Commission is understandably anxious that the basic Directive shall be adopted as soon as possible, this rearguard action may succeed.

9.17 But whether it does or not, the U.K. arguments were unconvincing and, in so far as they depended upon the alleged paucity of unlisted public issues, are no longer being pursued. Nobody denies that there are a considerable number of companies which publish prospectuses in the U.K. relating to unlisted securities to be dealt in on the U.S.M. and that these prospectuses are vetted by The Stock Exchange and should be vetted. Nobody denies that some prospectuses are published in respect of public issues which are not admitted to either of The Stock Exchange's markets and that these escape any independent pre-vetting. Even if the numbers are relatively small, it is an unattractive argument to say that investors in them deserve less protection. But how few are these other prospectuses? Certainly few are published in the newspapers and that has led people to believe that the number is negligible. Since the securities are not to be listed, the prospectuses do not have to be so advertised and will not be if the sponsors of the issues have other channels of communication open to them. As no statistics seemingly were available, my Secretariat with the generous help of the C.S.I. and The Stock Exchange undertook some research at Companies House Cardiff. This

revealed the interesting, and rather surprising, results shown in the following
table:

Table	1978	1979	1980	1981	1982	Total
(a) Total no. of registered prospectuses	245	249	321	368	345	1528
(b) No. where securities not listed or on USM	72	81	112	94	94	453
(c) No. of (b) which were of securities of GB companies	41	48	58	46	38	231
(d) No. of (b) which were of securities of foreign companies	31	33	54	48	56	222

9.18 It will therefore be seen that over the 5 years no less than 29.6 per cent of
all registered prospectuses, i.e. the proportion of (b) to (a), related to securities
not listed or (in 1981 and 1982) admitted to the U.S.M. Even if one excludes
prospectuses of foreign companies, on the ground that some of them may have
been effectively regulated by authorities in their home countries, the proportion
is 17.7 per cent, i.e. the proportion of (c) to [(a) minus (d)]. These are very far
from insignificant figures. In the amount of money raised the proportion of non-
listed and non-U.S.M. prospectuses would, no doubt, be less. But although some
of the issues concerned were small, many were large — in millions of pounds
rather than thousands or hundreds. The issues were handled by a wide range of
sponsors — member firms of The Stock Exchange (when the Exchange would
have required a sight of the draft prospectus), accountants, licensed dealers and
members of recognised associations of dealers — or made directly by the
company itself without any declared professional sponsorship. It will be observed
that the number and proportion of such issues rose steadily until 1981 when, as
was to be expected, the opening of the U.S.M. led to a marked reduction in
respect of G.B. companies. But there are already signs that that downward trend
has been reversed because the tax incentives under the Government's Business
Expansion Scheme do not extend to investment in companies whose securities
are listed or admitted to the U.S.M.

9.19 One of the reasons for the unexpectedly large number proves to be that
some dealers sponsor issues and act as issuing house, underwriters, and market
makers — a potentially dangerous practice especially when the dealers are not
subject to any specific regulations in respect of these activities. Both the firms of
licensed dealers whose collapses precipitated this Review had done this with
unhappy results to their clients and others who invested in the issues. I was also
told by a solicitor in the Department that each of the five failed licensed dealers
whose affairs he had had to investigate in the last few years had sponsored such
issues, and that the prospectuses were such that in his view they would have not
passed the scrutiny of any reasonably skilled examiner.

9.20 The facts stated in the foregoing paragraphs seem to me to make out an
overwhelmingly strong case for the need for pre-vetting. However, I should refer
to some other arguments that have been made against it. The City Capital
Markets Committee, in their response, said: 'We do not think that an uncommitted and objective vetting agency can exercise a useful protective role, bearing
in mind that effective vetting involves a qualitative judgment'. This, on the face
of it, is a surprising observation because it appears to deny that the pre-vetting
role undertaken by The Stock Exchange performs any useful protective role —
unless perhaps they regard The Stock Exchange as not 'uncommitted and

objective'. But, surely, precisely what is needed, if a useful protective role is to be played, is the scrutiny, by an uncommitted and objective agency, of the documents submitted by the sponsors? The responsibility and reliability of the sponsors is equally if not more important — as the Committee stressed and as the Discussion Document recognised. But, precisely because the sponsors cannot take a wholly uncommitted and objective view, they should satisfy some agency that can. This is the role played by The Stock Exchange in relation to listed and U.S.M. issues and the role which some independent agency needs to play in the case of other public issues. There are, as I see it, two 'qualitative judgments' that might be made: (a) on the quality of the securities offered and (b) on the quality of the prospectus. The Stock Exchange may well try to judge both; as the securities are to be traded on its market it will naturally want to ensure that it is not selling a pup. But, in general, even it, when it vets the prospectus, is directing its attention only to (b) and that is all that any other agency can be expected to do. The House of Lords Select Committee on the European Communities, in its Report on the Draft Directive, pointed out that there are three possible levels of scrutiny:

> 'One form of scrutiny is to check that a document contains all the required statements . . . At the other extreme the statements are investigated . . . At an intermediate state investigation is made not as a routine but only if there is suspicion.'

They assumed that it would be carried out at the intermediate stage, as the Quotations Department of The Stock Exchange does with U.S.M. issues. To this I would add one observation. Vetting, at any level, should involve not only checking that all the required statements are made but that they are not made 'in a manner likely to create a false impression on the mind of an unwary or inexperienced investor'. To some extent a revised Schedule 4 could assist — at present it omits some of the most important information that such an investor needs to know. But not wholly: *how* statements are made is just as important as *what* statements are made, and this can be achieved only by pre-vetting.

9.21 The only other arguments that I have heard raised against pre-vetting are: (a) that if people know that their prospectus will be subjected to scrutiny prior to publication they will take less care in its preparation, relying on the scrutineers to correct their errors, (b) that those who subscribe will place exaggerated faith in the issue believing that the quality of the securities offered has received official endorsement and (c) that civil and criminal sanctions are more effective and economical restraints on false or inadequate disclosure than pre-vetting.

None of these arguments was made in any of the formal responses and I cannot believe that any has much force. The only evidence I know to support (a) is that some officials in the Department have gained the impression that those who submit circulars for their scrutiny sometimes seem to expect them to correct the authors' spelling mistakes and misprints. This, I suspect, is merely a facet of the general decline in standards of spelling and proof-reading. What must be certain is that knowledge that the prospectus will be pre-vetted is a deterrent against the graver danger of deliberate attempts to mislead or conceal. As for (b), the risk that subscribers will believe that the issue has received some sort of official blessing is equally inherent in the present statement that the prospectus 'has been delivered to the Registrar of Companies for registration' — a statement which, to most people, would imply that registration affords investors some meaningful protection — which in fact it does not. Argument (c) can hardly convince anyone with any knowledge of the cost of civil litigation in the U.K. or

of the problems it faces . . . . in relation to criminal prosecutions in this field. The
further arguments which are being advanced in Brussels are not against pre-
vetting in the U.K. as such, but against the need for a further Directive. These are:
first, that there will not be inter-State transactions in unlisted securities (which in
the light of the increasing internationalisation of the securities industry seems to
me to be an implausible assertion) and that therefore no Community action is
needed; and, secondly, that it would do more harm than good to harmonise a
requirement to pre-vet unless it was also practicable to harmonise the standards
of pre-vetting, which, in what is essentially a 'minimum standards' Directive, it is
not. The second argument may be more respectable, but, as I have said, it is not
an argument against pre-vetting in the U.K. if we can do it properly.

9.22 I am, therefore, of the opinion, even more firmly than I was when the
Discussion Document was written, that whether or not pre-vetting of all prospectuses becomes mandatory under E.E.C. law, it is high time that it was mandatory
under ours. By what body, then, is it to be undertaken? The House of Lords Select
Committee concluded that 'scrutiny should be carried out by The Stock
Exchange on behalf of' the competent authority, which they assumed would be
the Secretary of State. The Stock Exchange had objected to being nominated as
the competent authority but was apparently willing to act as agent for the
Department. But though that might be acceptable to The Stock Exchange I
cannot think that it would be acceptable to anyone else. A prospectus, prior to
publication, is a highly confidential document. It is reasonable that those
companies that have chosen to market their securities on The Stock Exchange
should submit drafts of prospectuses about them to the Quotations Department.
But it is wholly unreasonable and totally unacceptable that those that choose
another market should be asked to do so. Why, for example, should Granville &
Co Ltd, (formerly M. J. H. Nightingale & Co Ltd) when they launch a company
on their market, be expected to submit drafts of their prospectuses to their more
powerful rival? I think that the Committee's suggestion can have been made only
because they believed that U.S.M. issues were the only material examples of
public issues of unlisted securities.

9.23 Does this mean, then, that the vetting role will have to be undertaken by the
Department itself? I would be unhappy to think so — and so would the
Department. It is a task which would be wholly new to it and one which it is hardly
equipped to undertake. Though the number of prospectuses that it would have
to vet (assuming that those relating to the listed and U.S.M. issues continued to
be vetted by The Stock Exchange) might not exceed about 100 each year, it would
involve the scrutiny of prospectuses of both domestic and foreign companies and
would be a task which it would be expected to undertake with a rapidity and a
flexibility unusual in routine civil service channels. There would be a serious risk
that it would not be done well. And it would be somewhat ironical if, having just
relieved itself of the related task of vetting takeover documents except in a few
residual situations, it found itself saddled with another, even more onerous,
which it was less equipped to undertake and of which it totally lacked experience.
It would find the additional and novel burden not inconsiderable. Although the
pre-vetting of 100 prospectuses each year may appear to be less than 2 per week,
it would not work out like that. In some weeks there would be none; in others
there might be more than 10. Nor should it be assumed that it would merely
involve one scrutiny of each draft prospectus. In many cases the sponsors would
want to have discussions with the Department as the prospectus went through
various drafts and, in others, the Department would need to question the

sponsors about statements made in it. If there proved to be no alternative to the task being undertaken by the Governmental regulator that, in my view, would tip the scales in favour of that regulator being a self-standing Commission rather than the Department. The role is the primary task of the Securities Commissions in other countries and the one where the balance of advantages and disadvantages is weighted heavily in favour of a self-standing Commission.

Subsequent Surveillance

9.24 However, I do not wish to exaggerate what can be achieved by pre-vetting of prospectuses. Even the pre-vetting presently undertaken by The Stock Exchange cannot always prevent mis-statements occurring and when they do the legal sanctions imposed on the directors of the company concerned and on the sponsors of the issue assume importance as the ultimate remedy of damnified investors. At the most all that pre-vetting can ensure is that the law's and The Stock Exchange's requirements appear to have been complied with and that the prospectus taken as a whole gives a fair and sufficient picture of the company and its securities. Of importance at least equal to pre-vetting, and necessary corollaries of it, are subsequent continuing disclosure, and surveillance by The Exchange of the company under the listing agreement or general undertaking and of member-firms making a market in the securities. In the case of unlisted securities in which there is to be no market the most that can be done is to ensure that the prospectus makes this clear and in such a way that potential investors realise that they may not be able to liquidate their investments. In such cases it is likely that those who subscribe with their eyes thus opened will be doing so for sentimental, social or recreational reasons rather than as investors. But in a growing number of cases, the sponsors of the issue, even though a listing or admission to the U.S.M. is not to be sought, do make a market in the securities. Of these so-called 'over-the-counter' markets the best known is that of Messrs Granville & Co (formerly Nightingales) which at present provides a market for the securities of some twenty companies; but there are a number of others some of whom operate in quite a big way. One large firm of licensed dealers makes a market in the securities of fifteen companies and another in nine. While I have no reason to suppose that in most cases these markets are not properly conducted, this, at present, depends upon the integrity and efficiency of the firms and companies concerned and not on any regulations other than the Licensed Dealers (Conduct of Business) Rules when applicable. The dangers of this have already been stressed and are recognised by NASDIM and by some of those dealers who are not members of NASDIM, four of whom are founding 'The British Institute of Dealers in Securities' among the stated objectives of which are the formulation of rules relating to market-making by its members and of a standard 'listing' agreement applying to companies whose securities are marketed. It seems likely, however, that there will be still other market-makers who are not members of any self-regulatory agency and that there will be a further growth of over-the-counter markets on the approach of the end of the minimum 5-year period for which unlisted securities have to be held to reap the tax advantages of the Business Expansion Scheme; already a number of American stockbrokers plan to establish one. Hence there is clearly a need for more effective regulations here as well as in relation to vetting of the original prospectuses.

SOURCE 63
R *v* Stock Exchange, ex parte Else
(Court of Appeal) [1993] BCLC 834

SIR THOMAS BINGHAM: . . . In May 1988 the International Stock Exchange of the United Kingdom and the Republic of Ireland (which I shall for brevity call 'the Stock Exchange') suspended the listing of the company' shares because annual listing charges had not been paid. This omission was rectified and the listing was restored after one month's intermission.

On 28 June 1989 the listing of the company's shares was again suspended by the Stock Exchange. The immediate cause of this suspension was the arrest of the chairman of the company on suspicion of insider-dealing offences. (He was later prosecuted on a number of counts and, after the events giving rise to this appeal, acquitted.) The suspension of the listing continued, partly because of uncertainty concerning the chairman's position, partly because the Stock Exchange was concerned about possible failures to notify dealings in the company's shares and partly because the Stock Exchange was concerned about the adequacy of the financial information provided by the company and about its accounts. There were meetings between representatives of the company and the Stock Exchange concerning these matters, which were also raised in correspondence. It was made clear that the company wished the suspension to be ended, but it appears that in November 1990 the company's broker was told that the quotations department of the Stock Exchange had decided to take the matter of the listing of the company to the panel of the quotations committee with a recommendation that the listing be cancelled. The broker indicated that he would probably not attend the quotations panel but might appeal against any cancellation decision to the quotations committee. The case was duly referred to the panel, which on 23 November 1990 concluded that the listing should be cancelled.

. . .

The proceedings arise out of applications for judicial review made by three applicants. All of the applicants are shareholders in the company, having bought shares off-market during the period when the listing was suspended and before it was cancelled.

. . .

Before the judge an issue of European Community law arose on which the judge held it necessary to seek a ruling from the Court of Justice of the European Communities under art 177 of the EEC Treaty to enable him to give judgment. Although the applicants in the court below contended that the issue should be decided in their favour, they did not resist the course adopted by the judge if he was left in doubt on the issue, subject to settling appropriate questions. The Stock Exchange, on the other hand, contended below that the issue should be decided in their favour and opposed a reference. The judge having decided to refer, they appeal against his decision to do so. They continue to argue that the Community law issue should be resolved in their favour. As an authority responsible for regulating an important international market, they have further urged the practical importance of knowing where they stand as quickly as possible. The apparent cogency of that consideration has caused the hearing of this appeal, on the Community law issue, to be expedited. It has proved convenient also to consider an issue of domestic law closely related to the Community law issue. For the avoidance of doubt I should make clear that by 'domestic law' I mean, for present purposes, the law of England not including that part of it which derives directly from the law of the Community.

The issues

The central issues on this appeal are these. 1. Were the applicants as shareholders entitled to be notified of and given the opportunity to make representations (which should have been duly considered) about the committee's impending decision whether the company's listing should be cancelled (a) in Community law? (b) in domestic law? 2. Are the applicants as shareholders entitled to challenge the committee's decision to cancel the company's listing (a) in Community law? (b) in domestic law?

. . .

The directive was intended, as its long title makes plain, to co-ordinate the conditions for the admission of securities to official stock exchange listing. This was a step towards establishment of a common market in securities. In other member states, as here, conditions (imposed for the protection of investors) had to be met before a security was admitted to listing. There could be no truly common market so long as different conditions were imposed by the various members states. Still less could there be a truly common market if it was open to national authorities, under the guise of protecting investors, to make the admission of local securities to listing easier than that of foreign securities, the policy objectives to be achieved by co-ordinating the listing conditions in the various member states were outlined in the fifth recital to the directive: to provide equivalent protection for investors at Community level, because of the more uniform guarantees offered to investors in the various member states; to facilitate Community-wide listing of member state securities; and to enable member states to penetrate each other's securities markets so as to contribute to establishment of a European capital market. The directive applied to entities not covered by the second paragraph of art 58 of the Treaty and was acknowledged to go beyond art 54(3)(g), but was seen as directly affecting the establishment and functioning of the Common Market within the meaning of art 100.

The seventh recital to the directive is of such significance to this appeal as to justify verbatim quotation:

> 'Whereas there should be the possibility of a right to apply to the courts against decisions by the competent national authorities in respect of the application of this Directive, although such right to apply must not be allowed to restrict the discretion of these authorities.'

Co-ordination was in the first instance to be limited to establishing minimum conditions for the admission of securities to official stock exchange lists in member states, but issuers were to have no right to listing.

Section I of the directive contains general provisions. These prescribe minimum conditions to be satisfied by securities admitted to official listing in member states and minimum obligations to which issuers shall be subject. While member states may impose conditions and obligations more stringent than the minimum, they may not (generally speaking) discriminate in doing so. Member states may in accordance with applicable national rules require issuers of securities admitted to official listing to inform the public on a regular basis of their financial position and the general course of their business.

Section II of the directive concerns the authorities competent to admit securities to official listing and contains the provisions most central to this appeal. Member states are required to designate such competent authorities. It is common ground in this case that the Council of the Stock Exchange is so designated and that the committee on quotations is empowered to act on its behalf. Member states are to ensure that the competent authorities have such

powers as may be necessary for the exercise of their duties and, by para 3 of art
9:

> 'Without prejudice to the other powers conferred upon them, the com-
> petent authorities may reject an application for the admission of a security
> to official listing if, in their opinion, the issuer's situation is such that
> admission would be detrimental to investors' interests.'

This is supplemented by art 10:

> 'By way of derogation from Article 5, Member States may, solely in the
> interests of protecting the investors, give the competent authorities power to
> make the admission of a security to official listing subject to any special
> condition which the competent authorities consider appropriate and of
> which they have explicitly informed the applicant.'

Article 12 authorises competent authorities (in addition to any other sanction)
to publicise the fact that an issuer is failing to comply with its obligations. Article
13 requires an issuer whose securities are admitted to official listing to provide
the competent authorities with all the information they consider appropriate 'to
protect investors or ensure the smooth operation of the market' and, by para 2
of this article:

> 'Where protection of investors or the smooth operation of the market so
> requires, an issuer may be required by the competent authorities to publish
> such information in such a form and within such time limits as they consider
> appropriate. Should the issuer fail to comply with such requirement, the
> competent authorities may themselves publish such information after
> having heard the issuer.'

This section of the directive ends with arts 14, 15 and 16, which I quote in
full:

'Article 14

1. The competent authorities may decide to suspend the listing of a
security where the smooth operation of the market is, or may be, temporarily jeopardized or where protection of investors so requires.

2. The competent authorities may decide that the listing of the security be
discontinued where they are satisfied that, owing to special circumstances,
normal regular dealings in a security are no longer possible.

Article 15

1. Member States shall ensure decisions of the competent authorities
refusing the admission of a security to official listing or discontinuing such
a listing shall be subject to the right to apply to the courts.

2. An applicant shall be notified of a decision regarding his application
for admission to official listing within six months of receipt of the application or, should the competent authority require any further information
within that period, within six months of the applicant's supplying such
information.

3. Failure to give a decision within the time limit specified in paragraph
2 shall be deemed a rejection of the application. Such rejection shall give
rise to the right to apply to the courts provided for in paragraph 1.

Article 16

Where an application for admission to official listing relates to certificates representing shares, the application shall be considered only if the competent authorities are of the opinion that the issuer of the certificates is offering adequate safeguards for the protection of investors.'

...

At its request the court was referred to the proposal from the Commission, the opinion of the European Parliament and the opinion of the economic and social committee to which reference is made in the second, third and fourth recitals of the directive. These show, as one would expect, that the original draft of the directive was modified before its final adoption, but they throw no definitive light on the issue between the parties in this court. It is, however, of interest that the proposed directive contained no precursor of the seventh recital in the directive, although it did provide in art 10(2) that each member state should provide for a right of appeal to the courts against a decision to refuse an application for listing. The economic and social committee criticised that proposal, suggesting that a right of appeal should be provided against any decision of the competent authorities and not just against a decision to refuse an application for listing. The Parliament also felt that there should be greater rights of appeal against the decisions of the national authorities responsible for the admission of securities to quotation. It advised that there should be a right of administrative appeal against decisions to refuse listing, against decisions that information should be published, against decisions that listing be discontinued and against decisions by the competent authorities of their own motion to list a security (a power not in the event conferred by the directive itself). There was no suggestion that the right of appeal should be conferred on additional parties.

The parties to this appeal agree that the directive takes direct effect. We were told that the researches of counsel had unearthed no relevant authority on its construction.

The applicants' argument on the directive

On behalf of the applicants a long and detailed argument was advanced. I understood the essential steps in the argument to be these. (1) The directive is a measure intended to protect investors, including shareholders such as the applicants. (2) Shareholders such as the applicants are likely to suffer loss or prejudice if the public listing of the company in which they hold shares is cancelled. (3) Shareholders such as the applicants cannot effectively resist a potentially damaging cancellation unless they are notified of an impending decision, unless they are informed of the grounds on which the decision may be taken, unless they have the opportunity to make representations and unless the competent authority is bound to consider these representations before making a decision. (4) The seventh recital of the directive and art 15 impose no restriction upon the parties granted a right to apply to the courts. (5) In the light of (1) to (4) above the intention of art 15 is, or at any rate may be, to confer rights on shareholders such as the applicants to be notified of an impending decision whether a listing should be cancelled, to be informed of the grounds relied on and to be given an opportunity to make representations and, after the decision has been made, to challenge it. (6) The English court should accordingly seek a ruling from the Court of Justice on the correct construction of the directive, and the judge was right to refer.

Each of these steps calls for careful consideration.

The conditions which national authorities impose on admission to listing are imposed for the protection of investors. The body of investors includes existing shareholders. It also includes, very particularly in this context, potential future investors. In dealing with conditions imposed and obligations undertaken by companies whose securities are admitted to listing, the directive expressly recognises the responsibility of the competent authorities to protect the interests of investors, which must always be their overriding concern when exercising their powers. But the primary purpose of the directive is to co-ordinate the listing practice of competent authorities in the various member states with a view to establishing a common market in securities and not, in any direct way, to provide additional protection for investors.

I accept without question that shareholders such as the applicants are liable to suffer loss or prejudice if the public listing of a company in which they hold shares is cancelled. But so they may if the listing is suspended or, in a less obvious way, if an application for listing is refused. The applicants accept that the directive does not, in either of these situations, confer upon shareholders any right of recourse to the court.

I accept that in the ordinary way step (3) in the applicants' argument is likely to be factually correct.

I accept that the seventh recital of the directive and art 15 do not in express terms define the parties upon whom a right to apply to the courts is conferred. But several considerations compel me to what I regard as an inevitable conclusion that the right is conferred on a company or an issuer alone. (i) In the proposed directive the right provided for was one of appeal. While the Economic and Social Committee and the Parliament favoured a wider right of appeal, there is no suggestion that they or anyone envisaged any right other than a right of appeal. In any ordinary situation, a right of appeal is accorded to the party who has been the subject of an adverse decision. There is nothing to suggest that any party other than a company or issuer was seen as potentially the subject of any adverse decision or as having any right of appeal. (ii) The directive is concerned with relations between competent authorities (who are responsible for protecting the interests of investors) and companies or issuers. Nothing in the directive suggests that competent authorities may have direct relations with investors. (iii) Once it is accepted, as it must be, that the directive gives investors no right of recourse to the courts in respect of suspension and refusal of listing, it cannot rationally be construed as conferring such a right on investors in respect of cancellation.

I cannot accept the soundness of step (5). In addition to reasons already given, I see powerful further objections, particularly to the rights the applicants claim before a cancellation decision is made. (i) Such rights would in my view gravely restrict the discretion of the competent authorities, which the seventh recital indicates must not be allowed.

. . .

In the result, I feel able with complete confidence to reject the applicants' argument based on the directive. For reasons which I have tried to give, I do not share the doubts felt by the learned judge about the effect to be given to it. If I did, I would of course respect his exercise of discretion to refer, which would in any event have been the proper course. But taking the view I do, I do not find it necessary to seek a ruling on this question from the Court of Justice to enable me to give judgment. It follows that I would allow the appeal of the Stock Exchange on this point and quash the order made under art 177 of the Treaty.

Domestic Law

It was not suggested that the law of England, independently of Community law, permitted an affirmative answer to the question posed at 1(b) above. Nor, I think, was it argued that domestic law, independently of Community law, conferred a right on shareholders as envisaged by question 2(b).

LEGGATT LJ: It is the policy of the EEC Treaty to abolish restrictions on freedom of establishment. One way of furthering this policy is to co-ordinate safeguards for the protection of individuals by rendering the safeguards 'equivalent' throughout the Community. A series of directives has applied this principle to companies. But that does not detract from the distinction which English law recognises between a company and its members. The court cannot interfere with the internal management of a company acting within its powers. Although the court will interfere to prevent fraud on a minority of shareholders, it will not ordinarily recognise any independent right of action by an individual share-holder based on an allegation of damage to the value of his shareholding, whether caused by the directors or by third parties. Nothing in Community law departs from that principle unless the applicants' submission in the present case is correct that Council Directive (EEC) 79/279 accords to individual share-holders the right to apply to the court for the purpose of objecting to the discontinuance of the listing of the company of which they are members.

Community legislation about stock exchanges is mainly concerned with the listing of securities. Directive 79/279 has been followed by directives dealing with requirements for furnishing particulars of securities for which listing has been applied, and with information which must be published regularly by companies with listed shares. These directives are intended to protect investors as well as to facilitate access to the markets of the member states. By force of the Stock Exchange (Listing) Regulations 1984, SI 1984/716, these directives apply to the United Kingdom.

The scheme of the relevant Community legislation, and Directive 79/279 in particular, is to provide for the co-ordination of conditions for admission to listing by designating a competent authority in each member state to police the process. Ancillary provision is made for the suspension of listing and for discontinuance of listing. But although one of the main aims of controlling admission to listing is the protection of investors, the directive is concerned with the means of control by the competent authority rather than with conferring rights on investors so that they may look out for themselves.

SOURCE 64
Re South of England Natural Gas and Petroleum Company Limited
[1911] 1 Ch 573; 80 LJ Ch 358

The South of England Natural Gas and Petroleum Company was incorporated on 30 January 1909, with a capital of £20,000 divided into 10,000 preference shares of £1 each and 10,000 ordinary shares of £1 each. On 21 February 1910, a prospectus was issued marked 'For private circulation only,' but also containing a statement 'This prospectus has been filed with the Registrar of Joint Stock Companies.' It offered for subscription 7000 preference shares, 9900 ordinary shares, and £5000 debentures and stated that the minimum subscription upon which the directors might proceed to allotment was fifty shares. The prospectus was sent, it was stated, only to shareholders in certain gas companies in which Eaton, the promoter of the company, who undertook the distribution of the prospectus, was interested. The issue was not publicly advertised, and only 3000 copies were sent out. Only 200 shares were applied in consequence of this prospectus, and of these 180 were applied for by the directors of the company.

SWINFEN EADY J: This is a motion by the executors of a deceased shareholder asking that the register of members of the company may be rectified by removing their testator's name. The case made by the applicants is that their testator applied on the terms of a prospectus issued on 30 April 1910, which failed to comply with the Companies (Consolidation) Act 1908, section 81(*d*), in that it was a second offer for shares and did not state the amount offered for subscription and actually allotted on the first offer. On the other hand, it is urged that the first offer was not an offer within the meaning of section 81, because by the definition clause of the Act (section 285) a prospectus is defined as an offer of shares to the public, and the prospectus issued on 21 February did not offer shares to the public as it was marked 'For private circulation only' and was only issued to the shareholders in certain gas companies in which the promoter was interested. [His Lordship went through the evidence on this point, and proceeded.] I am satisfied that the first prospectus did offer shares to the public, and none the less because copies were sent only to shareholders in gas companies who were the most likely subscribers. It follows that the second prospectus contained a subsequent offer and did not comply with section 81(*d*).

Then the question is what is the remedy of the shareholder? Is he entitled to rescind his contract and have his money back? With regard to one of the matters required to be mentioned in the prospectus by section 81,[1] there are provisions in subsequent sections which entitle the allottee to rescind his contract. Section 81 requires the minimum of shares which must be applied for before the directors may proceed to allotment to be stated. Section 85, sub-section 4, provides that if the minimum is not reached the application money is to be returned and makes the directors liable for returning it. Then section 86 deals with the case of an allotment which is irregular within section 85. [His Lordship read that section.] In respect of that matter, therefore, there is an express provision enabling an allottee to rescind within a limited time for non-compliance with the statute. There is no provision of that kind in section 81, nor in any other section relating to the omissions relied on in this case. But the section does contemplate a liability in damages on the part of the 'directors and other persons responsible for the prospectus', for sub-section 6 exonerates such persons from liability if they can prove certain matters. That is equivalent to saying that they are liable if they cannot prove them. In my opinion the allottee is not entitled to rescind his contract because of any breach of the statutory requirements, which extend to such comparatively unimportant matters as the names and addresses of the company's auditors. His remedy is against the directors and other persons responsible for the prospectus.

SOURCE 65
Peek *v* Gurney
(House of Lords 1874) (1873) LR 6 HL 377; 43 LJ Ch 19

LORD CHELMSFORD: . . . The bill prayed in substance that the Respondents, the directors of the company called the *Overend & Gurney Company*, and the Respondents, the Messrs Gibb, the executors of a deceased director, might be decreed to make good to the Appellant or indemnify him against the loss which he had sustained by reason of his having become the purchaser of 2000 shares in the company, and having been, as he alleged, deceived and misled by a prospectus put forth by the Respondents and the deceased director, containing

---

1 See now s 56 of and Sch 3 to the Companies Act 1985

several misrepresentations and suppressions of material and important facts, with a view to deceive and mislead the public, and the Appellant as one of the public . . . The Master of the Rolls proceeded upon the principle, established by many decided cases, that an allottee, or purchaser of shares in a company, who seeks to divest himself of his shares upon the ground of having been induced to purchase them by misrepresentation, cannot be relieved if he has continued to hold the shares without objection after knowledge, or with the full means of knowledge, of the falsehood by which he has been drawn in to acquire them. These cases proceeded upon the ground of acquiescence, and on the application of a more general principle that an agreement induced by fraud is not absolutely void, but that it is entirely in the option of the person defrauded whether he will be bound by it or not. The suit in the present case is not for the rescission of the contract, but is founded upon the loss the Appellant has sustained, and may sustain, in consequence of his being bound by the contract he has entered into. It is a proceeding similar to an action at law for deceit; and the only amount of delay which could be a bar to relief is fixed by the Statute of Limitations, by analogy to which equity generally proceeds in questions of laches. . . . The last question to be considered is, whether the Appellant, who alleges that he purchased his shares upon the faith of the prospectus, has a remedy against the Respondents for the misrepresentations which it contains. The Appellant con-tends that the prospectus being addressed to the public for the purpose of inducing them to join the proposed company, any one of the public who is led by it to take shares, whether originally as an allottee, or by purchase of allotted shares upon the market, is entitled to relief against the persons who issued the prospectus. The Respondents on the other hand insist that the prospectus, not being an invitation to the public ultimately to become holders of shares, but to join the company at once by obtaining allotments of shares, those only who were drawn in by the misrepresentations in the prospectus to become allottees, can have a remedy against the Respondents.

There can be no doubt that the prospectus was issued with the object alleged by the Respondents. It is addressed from the temporary offices of the company for allotment and registration of shares. It states how much is to be paid upon application for shares, and how much upon allotment, and how and where the application for shares is to be made; and it gives the form of payment to the bankers and of the receipt to be given by them to the applicant for shares to be allotted.

But the learned counsel for the appellant, not denying the original purpose of the prospectus, contended, upon the authority of decided cases, that the prospectus, having reached the hands of the Appellant, and he, relying upon the truth of the statement it contained, having been induced to purchase shares, the Respondents were liable as for a misrepresentation made to him personally. . . . In all these cases the parties in one way or other are brought into direct communication; and in an action the misrepresentation would be properly alleged to have been made by the Defendant to the Plaintiff; but the purchaser of shares in the market upon the faith of a prospectus which he has not received from those who are answerable for it, cannot by action upon it so connect himself with them as to render them liable to him for the misrepresentations contained in it, as if it had been addressed personally to himself. I therefore think that the Appellant cannot make the Respondents responsible to him for the loss he has sustained by trusting to the prospectus issued by them inviting the public to apply for allotments of shares; and upon this ground only (being different from that on which the Master of the Rolls proceeded) I submit to your Lordships that the decree appealed from should be affirmed.

In *Andrews v Mockford*,[1] the plaintiff, having read the prospectus and having declined to subscribe for shares, later purchased shares in the same company on the strength of a telegram which was published in the newspaper and which purported to strengthen the claims made by the prospectus. The prospectus and the telegram were held to have made fraudulent misrepresentations and the defendants were held liable in damages to the plaintiff. Can this be distinguished from *Peek v Gurney*?

SOURCE 66
Derry *v* Peek
(House of Lords 1889) (1889) 14 App Ca 337; 58 LJ Ch 864

In February 1883 the appellants as directors of the company issued a prospectus containing the following paragraph:

'One great feature of this undertaking, to which considerable importance should be attached, is, that by the special Act of Parliament obtained, the company has the right to use steam or mechanical motive power, instead of horses, and it is fully expected that by means of this a considerable saving will result in the working expenses of the line as compared with other tramways worked by horses.'

Soon after the issue of the prospectus the respondent, relying, as he alleged, upon the representations in this paragraph and believing that the company had an absolute right to use steam and other mechanical power, applied for and obtained shares in the company.

The company proceeded to make tramways, but the Board of Trade refused to consent to the use of steam or mechanical power except on certain portions of the tramways.

In the result the company was wound up, and the respondent in 1885 brought an action of deceit against the appellants claiming damages for the fraudulent misrepresentations of the defendants whereby the plaintiff was induced to take shares in the company.

LORD HERSCHELL: My Lords, in the statement of claim in this action the respondent, who is the plaintiff, alleges that the appellants made in a prospectus issued by them certain statements which were untrue, that they well knew that the facts were not as stated in the prospectus, and made the representations fraudulently, and with the view to induce the plaintiff to take shares in the company.

'This action is one which is commonly called an action of deceit, a mere common law action.' This is the description of it given by Cotton LJ in delivering judgment. I think it important that it should be borne in mind that such an action differs essentially from one brought to obtain rescission of a contract on the ground of misrepresentation of a material fact. The principles which govern the two actions differ widely. Where rescission is claimed it is only necessary to prove that there was misrepresentation; then, however honestly it may have been made, however free from blame the person who made it, the contract, having been obtained by misrepresentation, cannot stand. In an action of deceit, on the contrary, it is not enough to establish misrepresentation alone; it is conceded on all hands that something more must be proved to cast liability upon the defendant, though it has been a matter of controversy what additional elements are requisite. . . .

---

1 [1896] 1 QB 372; 65 LJQB 302

Having now drawn attention, I believe, to all the cases having a material bearing upon the question under consideration, I proceed to state briefly the conclusions to which I have been led. I think the authorities establish the following propositions: First, in order to sustain an action of deceit, there must be proof of fraud, and nothing short of that will suffice. Secondly, fraud is proved when it is shown that a false representation has been made (1) knowingly, or (2) without belief in its truth, or (3) recklessly, careless whether it be true or false. Although I have treated the second and third as distinct cases, I think the third is but an instance of the second, for one who makes a statement under such circumstances can have no real belief in the truth of what he states. To prevent a false statement being fraudulent, there must, I think, always be an honest belief in its truth. And this probably covers the whole ground, for one who knowingly alleges that which is false, has obviously no such honest belief. Thirdly, if fraud be proved, the motive of the person guilty of it is immaterial. It matters not that there was no intention to cheat or injure the person to whom the statement was made.

In my opinion making a false statement through want of care falls far short of, and is a very different thing from, fraud, and the same may be said of a false representation honestly believed though on insufficient grounds.

. . .

At the same time I desire to say distinctly that when a false statement has been made the questions whether there were reasonable grounds for believing it, and what were the means of knowledge in the possession of the person making it, are most weighty matters for consideration. The ground upon which an alleged belief was founded is a most important test of its reality. I can conceive many cases where the fact that an alleged belief was destitute of all reasonable foundation would suffice of itself to convince the Court that it was not really entertained, and that the representation was a fraudulent one.

. . .

I have arrived with some reluctance at the conclusion to which I have felt myself compelled, for I think those who put before the public a prospectus to induce them to embark their money in a commercial enterprise ought to be vigilant to see that it contains such representations only as are in strict accordance with fact, and I should be very unwilling to give any countenance to the contrary idea. I think there is much to be said for the view that this moral duty ought to some extent to be converted into a legal obligation, and that the want of reasonable care to see that statements, made under such circumstances, are true, should be made an actionable wrong. But this is not a matter fit for discussion on the present occasion. If it is to be done the legislature must intervene and expressly give a right of action in respect of such a departure from duty. It ought not, I think, to be done by straining the law, and holding that to be fraudulent which the tribunal feels cannot properly be so described. I think mischief is likely to result from blurring the distinction between carelessness and fraud, and equally holding a man fraudulent whether his acts can or cannot be justly so designated.

It now remains for me to apply what I believe to be the law to the facts of the present case. The charge against the defendants is that they fraudulently represented that by the special Act of Parliament which the company had obtained they had a right to use steam or other mechanical power instead of horses. The test which I purpose employing is to inquire whether the defendants knowingly made a false statement in this respect, or whether, on the contrary, they honestly believed what they stated to be a true and fair representation of the facts. Before considering whether the charge of fraud is proved, I may say that I approach the case of all the defendants, except Wilde, with the inclination to scrutinise their conduct with severity. They most improperly received sums of money from the promoters, and this unquestionably lays them open to the suspicion of being ready to put before the public whatever was desired by those who were promoting the undertaking. But I think this must not be unduly pressed, and when I find that the statement impeached was concurred in by one whose conduct in the respect I have mentioned was free from blame, and who under no similar pressure, the case assumes, I think, a different complexion.

...

What conclusion ought to be drawn from the evidence? I think they were mistaken in supposing that the consent of the Board of Trade would follow as a matter of course because they had obtained their Act. It was absolutely in the discretion of the Board whether such consent should be given. The prospectus was therefore inaccurate. But that is not the question. If they believed that the consent of the Board of Trade was practically concluded by the passing of the Act, has the plaintiff made out, which it was for him to do, that they have been guilty of a fraudulent misrepresentation? I think not. I cannot hold it proved as to any one of them that he knowingly made a false statement, or one which he did not believe to be true, or was careless whether what he stated was true or false. In short, I think they honestly believed that what they asserted was true, and I am of opinion that the charge of fraud made against them has not been established.

Legislation followed swiftly. In 1890, the Directors' Liability Act was passed, providing a remedy for investors in the circumstances which gave rise to *Derry v Peek*. The legislation placed the onus on those responsible for the misleading statement to establish that the statement was not made negligently. This Act was later consolidated with the Companies Act and is now s 67 of the Companies Act 1985, and is the model for ss 150 and 166 of the Financial Services Act 1986.

NOTES AND QUESTIONS

1. *In certain instances the remedy of rescission is lost, eg liquidation of the company (which renders restitution impossible; the rights of third parties are now entrenched) or affirmation of the transaction.*

   In Re Cape Breton,[1] *the company purchased certain coal fields from a vendor who was acting as a trustee for a syndicate. One of the directors who approved the purchase was also an (undisclosed) member of the syndicate. The company paid substantially more for the coal fields than had the syndicate. Two years elapsed between the purchase and sale by the syndicate and a further two years until the liquidation of the company. Three years later, the contributories of the company voted to affirm the contract and the liquidator sold the coal fields at a substantial loss. An action to hold the director and member of the syndicate liable for the undisclosed profit failed.*

2. *Had the syndicate (or its members) been under a duty to acquire the coal fields for the company, at the time the syndicate purchased them (eg if at that time its members were already promoters or, a fortiori directors of the company), it would have been subject to the trustee remedy, to pass the property on to the company at the price at which it was acquired. Liquidation*

---

1 (1887) 12 App Ca 652; 57 LJ Ch 552

is no bar to this remedy and if the company is not in liquidation, it might choose between this remedy and rescinding the contract. This principle is particularly well expressed in the following quote (from Robinson v Randfontein Estates Gold Mining Co Ltd,[1] substituting 'promoter' for 'director').

> 'In any question as to the remedies available against a promoter who has sold his own property to the company, regard must be had to the relationship in which the promoter stood to the company when he acquired the property. If he was under no obligation at that time to acquire the property for the company instead of for himself, then his non-disclosure of the fact that the property was his own would entitle the company to repudiate the sale and restore the original position, but would not entitle it to retain the property at a price reduced by a deduction of the promoter's profit. When, however, the promoter's default extends further than non-disclosure, when a breach of duty attended the original acquisition, the company may, if it chooses retain the property purchased and also demand a refund of the profits.'

3. If the New Sombrero Phosphate Company had so chosen, could it have affirmed the transaction and called upon the syndicate to account for the secret profit?

4. If so, what would have been the considerations on which the decision, to rescind or affirm and call for an account of the profits, would have been based?

5. If not (and see the remarks of Lord Cairns especially in this regard) why was the company in Gluckstein v Barnes[2] entitled to call for an account of the profits? What is the precise distinction between this decision and Erlanger's[3] case?

6. The remuneration of promoters creates difficulties. When the promoter does his work, the company is, by definition, not yet in existence. There can, therefore, be no contract between the promoter and company. If a contract is made when the company comes into existence, it should be under seal (to cover the fact that the promoter's consideration is past).

   If the company refuses to enter into such a contract, would anyone be liable for the promoter's remuneration? See pp 206ff (pre-incorporation contracts). Would a provision in the company's articles of association providing for the remuneration be effective? (See Re English and Colonial Produce.[4])

---

1 1921 AD 168 (South African Sup Ct)
2 [1900] AC 240; 69 LJ Ch 385
3 (1878) 3 App Ca 1218; 48 LJ Ch 73
4 [1906] 2 Ch 435; 75 LJ Ch 831

Chapter 4

THE EXTERNAL RELATIONS OF THE COMPANY

A company must have a written constitution — the memorandum and articles of association (ss 1(1), 7, 8 of the Companies Act 1985). The memorandum must set out the company's objects (s 2(1) of the Companies Act 1985) and the articles will (almost invariably) prescribe the method of appointment, the qualifications, powers and duties of the company's agents insofar as these are not already laid down by statute and principles of the common law. (Table A, regs 75–112.)

By its very nature, a company cannot *itself* undertake the operations which lead to the legal consequences, by which it, as a legal person, will be bound. The company depends for these operations on the acts of its agents. Where a properly appointed agent, acting within the course and scope of his authority and in furtherance of the company's objects enters into a contract, the company is bound thereby and entitled to enforce it.

This chapter considers the legal consequences where:

(a) the transaction was entered into before the company was incorporated ('pre-incorporation contracts');
(b) the transaction was in furtherance of objects not expressed in the memorandum ('the ultra vires problem');
(c) the transaction carried out on behalf of the company was in furtherance of its expressed objects, but the relationship between it and the person who actually carried out the act, was defective ('the agency problem');
(d) a tort or crime was committed by the person while engaged on business on behalf of the company ('the criminal and tortious liability of the company').

PART I: PRE-INCORPORATION CONTRACTS

The Company is not Bound

At common law, contracts entered into before a company is formed, and expressed to be on behalf of the future company, are not binding on the company when the latter comes into existence. This rule applies even where the company purports to ratify or adopt the contract; at common law, adoption or ratification is only possible where done by a principal who or which was in existence at the time the transaction was performed (Sources 67 and 68).

SOURCE 67
Kelner *v* Baxter
(Court of Common Pleas 1866) (1866) LR 2 CP 174; 36 LJ CP 94

The plaintiff claimed payment for goods delivered to the defendants. One of
the defences was that the goods had been bought 'on behalf of a joint stock
company then proposed to be formed under the Joint Stock Companies Act
1862 and to be called the Gravesend Royal Alexandra Hotel Company
Limited . . . upon the terms that if the company, when registered, should
adopt the . . . contract and agree with the plaintiff to pay the agreed price of
the . . . goods, the goods should become the property of the company, and
the defendants . . . exonerated . . . from all further liability'. The agreement
was entered into on 27 January 1866. The company received its certificate of
incorporation on 20 February 1866. On 11 April 1866, the company
purported to ratify the contract. The company then collapsed and this action
was brought against the defendants.

At the trial before Erle CJ, evidence that it was not intended that the
defendants should not be personally liable, was rejected. Judgment was given
for the plaintiff. Source 68 and Source 71 are taken from the report of the
proceedings in which the defendants moved to enter a nonsuit on the
grounds that the agreement did not make them personally liable.

> ERLE CJ: . . . I agree that if the Gravesend Royal Alexandra Hotel Company had
> been an existing company at this time, the persons who signed the agreement
> would have signed as agents of the company. But, as there was no company in
> existence at the time, the agreement would be wholly inoperative unless it were
> held to be binding on the defendants personally. The cases referred to in the
> course of the argument fully bear out the proposition that, where a contract is
> signed by one who professes to be signing 'as agent,' but who has no principal
> existing at the time, and the contract would be altogether inoperative unless
> binding upon the person who signed it, he is bound thereby: and a stranger
> cannot by a subsequent ratification relieve him from that responsibility. When the
> company came afterwards into existence it was a totally new creature, having
> rights and obligations from that time, but no rights or obligations by reason of
> anything which might have been done before.

SOURCE 68
**Natal Land and Colonisation Company Limited (appellants) *v* Pauline Colliery
and Development Syndicate Limited (respondents)**
(Privy Council 1904) [1904] AC 120; 73 LJ PC 22

A contract was entered into between the appellant and one Mrs de Carrey in
terms of which she was entitled to ask for a lease of the coal mining rights on
the appellant's property. Mrs de Carrey assigned to one Louch 'in his capacity
as a provisional director of the Pauline Colliery and Development Syndicate
about to be registered . . .', all her interest under the contract. The appellant
agreed to the substitution of the respondent for Mrs de Carrey under the
agreement. Thereafter the respondent was registered. The respondent called
for the lease; the appellants averred that there was no contract between them.
The court below (the Supreme Court of Natal) decreed specific performance.
This was reversed on appeal to the Privy Council.

... The contract was made with Mrs de Carrey, and even if she can be treated as having made it on behalf either of the unincorporated syndicate, who were the promoters of the respondent company, or on behalf of the company itself when incorporated, it is clear that a company cannot by adoption or ratification obtain the benefit of a contract purporting to have been made on its behalf before the company came into existence. It is unnecessary to cite all the cases in which this has been decided from *Kelner v Baxter*[1] downwards. But the facts may shew that a new contract was made with the company after its incorporation on the terms of the old contract. The circumstances relied on for that purpose in the present case are not, in the opinion of their Lordships, necessarily referable to, and do not necessarily imply, a new contract with the respondents. But a conclusive reason which negatives any new contract is that Rycroft, by whose agency the new contract must be supposed to have been made, had no power or authority after 31 January 1898, to make such a contract on behalf of the appellants, and his want of authority was known to the solicitors acting for the respondents. He was not either the actual or the ostensible agent for that purpose of the appellants.

A Fresh Contract?

For the company to be bound, a fresh contract must be entered into between the company and the third party. This fresh contract may, but need not, lead to a novation of the contract (if any) between the promoter and the third party; simply to act on the original transaction in the belief that it constitutes a binding contract is insufficient for this purpose (Sources 69 and 70). An attempt was made in the 1973 Companies Bill to amend the law so as to provide for ratification of the pre-incorporation contract by the company on coming into existence (Sources 77 and 78). This bill, however, was never enacted (the government fell early in 1974). However, other jurisdictions have so provided, for example s 35 of the Companies Act of South Africa (Act 61 of 1973), which is as follows:

> 'Any contract made in writing by a person professing to act as agent or trustee for a company not yet incorporated shall be capable of being ratified or adopted by or otherwise made binding upon and enforceable by such company after it has been duly incorporated as if it had been duly incorporated at the time when the contract was made and such contract had been made without its authority: Provided that the memorandum on its registration contains as an object of such company the ratification or adoption of or the acquisition of rights and obligations in respect of such contract, and that two copies of such contract, one of which shall be certified by a notary public, have been lodged with the Registrar together with the lodgment for registration of the memorandum and articles of the company.'

For an attempt under the common law to provide for a similar result, see Sources 79 and 80.

---

1 (1866) LR 2 CP 174; 36 LJ CP 94

SOURCE 69

Re Northumberland Avenue Hotel Company

(Court of Appeal 1886) (1886) 33 Ch D 16; 2 TLR 636

COTTON LJ: The company was incorporated on 25 July 1882, and before that date, viz on 24 July, a contract in writing was entered into between a gentleman acting as agent for and on behalf of Mr Wallis, and another gentleman, who described himself as a trustee for the company, the company, in fact, having no existence at the time. That was a contract which was binding as between Mr Wallis and the other gentleman whom I have mentioned, and was a contract which provided that certain things should be done by the company. That contract in no way bound the company, because the company at that time was not formed. In fact it was not in terms a contract with the company, although it was a contract by a person who purported to act for the company that certain things should be done by the company. It is not contended that this contract was in any way binding on the company, nor is it disputed that the company after it was formed could not ratify the authority of the gentleman who purported to act as their trustee before they were incorporated, and who therefore could not have any authority to do so.

But it is said that we ought to hold that there was a contract entered into between the company and Wallis on the same terms (except so far as they were subsequently modified) as those contained in the contract of 24 July 1882. In my opinion that will not hold. It is very true that there were transactions between Wallis and the company in which the company acted on the terms of that contract entered into with Wallis by the person who said he was trustee for them. But why did the company do so? The company seem to have considered, or rather its directors seem to have considered, that the contract was a contract binding on the company. But the erroneous opinion that a contract entered into before the company came into existence was binding on the company, and the acting on that erroneous opinion, does not make a good contract between the company and Mr Wallis, and all the acts which occurred subsequently to the existence of the company were acts proceeding on the erroneous assumption that the contract of 24 July was binding on the company.

LOPES LJ: No doubt the company, after it came into existence, might have entered into a new contract upon the same terms as the agreement of 24 July 1882, and we are asked to infer such a contract from the conduct and transactions of the company after they came into existence. It seems to me impossible to infer such a contract, for it is clear to my mind that the company never intended to make any new contract, because they firmly believed that the contract of 24 July was in existence, and was a binding, valid contract. Everything that was done by them after their incorporation appears to me to be based upon the assumption that the contract of 24 July 1882 was an existing and binding contract.

SOURCE 70

Howard *v* Patent Ivory Manufacturing Company Ltd

(Chancery Division 1888) (1888) 38 Ch D 156; 57 LJ Ch 878

One Jordan entered into a contract with a company about to be formed (in the event the defendant company) to sell to its patents, leases and various other assets. The purchase money was £36,500, payable as to £6,500 in cash and as to £30,000 in fully paid-up shares. The company was then registered. At a meeting of the directors, at which Jordan, a director, was present, it was resolved that in consideration of Jordan accepting £3,000 in cash and £3,500 in debenture stock (instead of the originally agreed £6,500 in cash), the allotment of the fully paid shares should be proceeded with. The action was brought by one of the holders of the debenture stock issued pursuant to the varied agreement with Jordan, for the enforcement of that security.

> KAY J: . . . Now the case mainly relied upon, namely, *Re Northumberland Avenue Hotel Company*,[1] is certainly one of very considerable difficulty; but in order to ascertain whether it binds me here to hold that there was no contract, I must see whether the facts were the same. In the first place, I must observe that the question whether there was a contract between this company and Mr Jordan is a question, not of law, but of fact. Am I bound because in one case the Court, upon evidence before it, came to the conclusion as a matter of fact that there was no binding contract, to hold that in this case there was no such contract? The finding of a jury upon one set of facts does not bind a jury upon another set of facts; nor does the finding of any Court bind another Court where the facts are not the same.
>
> . . .
>
> Now, am I bound to find that there never was any contract as a result of the facts proved in the present case? Here there was passed in Mr Jordan's presence a resolution of the board of directors, to which he was a party, adopting this agreement. There was the conveyance by Mr Jordan of the leasehold property comprised in the agreement, and the seal of the company was affixed to it — clearly and obviously carrying out the contract between Mr Jordan and the company, which the company by that adoption seem to me distinctly to have made. There were no such facts as these in the case of *Re Northumberland Avenue Hotel Company*. Besides all that, I have here the payment of part of the price in debentures. That was a variation of the contract made by distinct agreement with Mr Jordan after the passing of a resolution for the issue of the debentures, contemporaneously with the deed by which Mr Jordan assigned part of the property to the company. After the winding-up the liquidator took an assignment of all the rest of the property of which he could possibly get an assignment, in pursuance of the very same arrangement. Now he comes to the Court and asks the Court to say that there never was a contract between the company and Mr Jordan. He says, 'True, I have taken from Mr Jordan everything I could possibly get from him: the company took an assignment of the leasehold premises which they have held ever since; I have treated all these as assets of the company, and I now turn round and say that there never was such an agreement.' Such a course of conduct would be, as I have characterized it during the argument, the most flagrant dishonesty.

Note

Despite the finding that there was a contract, only £1,000 of the £3,500 worth of debenture stock issued by the company could be recovered. The borrowing powers of the company were limited under the articles of association to £1,000, unless (which had not happened) extended by resolution of the general meeting of shareholders. Since all the debenture stockholders were directors they could not take advantage of the rule that outsiders who deal

---

1 (1886) 33 Ch D 16; 2 TLR 636 (see p 210)

with a company can assume that all internal regulations have been complied with (the 'Turquand Rule',[1] see pp 259ff).

The Rationale

The rationale behind the rule that the company is not bound by pre-incorporation contracts would appear to be the protection of the company and its innocent shareholders and creditors from fraudulent or oppressive schemes foisted upon a company specially created for the purpose (Source 71).

> **SOURCE 71**
> **Gluckstein *v* Barnes**
> **(For the facts, see 'Promoters', p 166.)**
> (House of Lords 1900) [1900] AC 240; 69 LJ Ch 385
>
> LORD MACNAGHTEN: Those gentlemen set about forming a company to pay them a handsome sum for taking off their hands a property which they had contracted to buy with that end in view. They bring the company into existence by means of the usual machinery. They appoint themselves sole guardians and protectors of this creature of theirs, half-fledged and just struggling into life, bound hand and foot while yet unborn by contracts tending to their private advantage, and so fashioned by its makers that it could only act by their hands and only see through their eyes. They issue a prospectus representing that they had agreed to purchase the property for a sum largely in excess of the amount which they had, in fact, to pay. On the faith of this prospectus they collect subscriptions from a confiding and credulous public.

Is There a Contract Between Promoter and Third Party?

A pre-incorporation contract might be valid as between promoter and third party where this was the intention of the parties to the transaction (Sources 72, 73, 74, 75).

> **SOURCE 72**
> **Kelner *v* Baxter**
> **(For the facts, see above.)**
> (Court of Common Pleas 1866) (1866) LR 2 CP 174; 36 LJ CP 94
>
> It was once, indeed, thought that an inchoate liability might be incurred on behalf of a proposed company, which would become binding on it when subsequently formed: but that notion was manifestly contrary to the principles upon which the law of contract is founded. There must be two parties to a contract; and the rights and obligations which it creates cannot be transferred by one of them to a third person who was not in a condition to be bound by it at the time it was made. The history of this company makes this construction to my mind perfectly clear. It was no doubt the notion of all the parties that success was certain: but the plaintiff parted with his stock upon the faith of the defendants' engagement that the price agreed on should be paid on the day named. It cannot be supposed that he for a moment contemplated that the payment was to be contingent on the formation of the company by 28 February. The paper expresses in terms a contract to buy. And it is a cardinal rule that no oral evidence

---

1 (1856) 6 E&B 327; 119 ER 886

shall be admitted to shew an intention different from that which appears on the face of the writing. I come, therefore, to the conclusion that the defendants, having no principal who was bound originally, or who could become so by a subsequent ratification, were themselves bound, and that the oral evidence offered is not admissible to contradict the written contract.

WILLES J: . . . Both upon principle and upon authority, therefore, it seems to me that the company never could be liable upon this contract: and, as was put by my Lord, construing this document ut res magis valeat quam pereat, we must assume that the parties contemplated that the persons signing it would be personally liable. Putting in the words 'on behalf of the Gravesend Royal Alexandra Hotel Company,' would operate no more than if a person should contract for a quantity of corn 'on behalf of my horses.'

BYLES J: . . . The true rule, however, is that stated by Mr Thesiger, viz. that persons who contract as agents are generally personally responsible where there is no other person who is responsible as principal. Suppose this company never came into existence at all, could it be doubted that these defendants must be held to have bound themselves personally? Then, was it contemplated that the liability was conditional only until the company should be formed? It is said that the contract was ratified by the company after it came into existence. There could, however, be no ratification. Omnis ratihabitio retrotrahitur, et mandato priori æquiparatur: but the ratification must be by an existing person, on whose behalf the contract might have been made at the time. That could not be so here: a subsequent ratification by the company could only be with the assent of the plaintiff; and then it would be a new contract.

SOURCE 73
Black *v* Smallwood
(High Court of Australia 1966) [1966] ALR 744; 39 ALJR 405

Action for specific performance of an alleged contract in terms of which the plaintiff sold land to a company. The purchaser was described as

'Western Suburbs Holdings Pty[1] Ltd
Robert Smallwood ⎫
                  ⎬ Directors'
J. Cooper   ⎭

In fact, at the time of the transaction, the company had not been registered.

BARWICK CJ, KITTO, TAYLOR and OWEN JJ: *Kelner v Baxter*[2] was cited as an authority for the proposition that there is a rule of law to the effect that where a person contracts on behalf of a non-existent principal he is himself liable on the contract. But we find it impossible to extract any such proposition from the decision. In that case it appeared from the contract itself that the defendants had no principal; they had purported to enter into a contract on behalf of the 'proposed Gravesend Royal Alexandra Hotel Company', and the fact that they had no principal was obvious to both parties. But it was not by reason of this fact alone that the defendants were held to be liable; the court proceeded to examine the written instrument in order to see if, in these circumstances, an intention should be imputed to the defendants to bind themselves personally, or, perhaps,

---

1 Abbreviated from proprietary (description in Australia for a private company)
2 (1866) LR 2 CP 174; 36 LJ CP 94

to put it in another way, whether, the intention being sufficiently clear that a binding contract was intended, there was anything in the writing inconsistent with the condition that the defendants should be bound personally. The decision was that, in the circumstances, the writing disclosed an intention that the defendants should be bound.

After quoting from the judgments of Erle CJ, and Willes and Byles JJ, they continued:

Understood literally this last proposition is, for reasons which will appear later, too wide but, nevertheless, it does not state as a proposition of law that a person purporting to contract on behalf of a non-existent principal is personally liable on the contract; the word 'generally' acknowledges that there are cases where he will not be bound. We should add that we fully agree with the observations of Fullagar J in *Summergreene v Parker*[1] concerning the basis of the decision in *Kelner v Baxter.* He said: 'I do not myself think that *Kelner v Baxter* or any of the cases cited affords any assistance in the present case. Where A, purporting to act as agent for a non-existent principal, purports to make a binding contract with B and the circumstances are such that B would suppose that a binding contract had been made, there must be a strong presumption that A has meant to bind himself personally. Where, as in *Kelner v Baxter*, the consideration on B's part has been fully executed in reliance on the existence of a contract binding on somebody, the presumption could, I should imagine, only be rebutted in very exceptional circumstances. But the fundamental question in every case must be what the parties intended or must be fairly understood to have intended. If they have expressed themselves in writing, the writing must be construed by the court. If they have expressed themselves orally, the effect of what they have said is a question of fact — a question for the jury, if there is a jury.' . . .

However in the present case the respondents did not contract, or purport to contract, on behalf of the non-existent company. They simply subscribed the name of the non-existent company and added their own signatures as directors in the belief that the company had been formed and that they were directors. The fact that their signatures appeared as part of the company's signature did not make them parties to the contract nor could, as was possible in *Kelner v Baxter*, an intention to be bound personally be imputed to them.

. . . It is, in our view, clear from the written instrument that the respondents in this case did not enter into any contract; they were not parties to the contract as agents or otherwise and there is no basis upon which they can be held liable upon it.

These reasons lead us to the respectful conclusion, not only that we should follow the decision in *Newborne v Sensolid (Great Britain) Ltd*,[2] but also that the decision in that case was correct. We would dismiss the appeal.

WINDEYER J: . . . I agree that this appeal must be dismissed. I have come to that conclusion without hesitation but with regret. The law requires it, but I do not think that it accords well with a belief that bargains should be kept.

If before the document sued upon was signed the registration of Western Suburbs Holdings Pty Ltd had been completed and it had emerged from the Registrar-General's office as a new-born entity in the law, no difficulty could have arisen. It could not then have been said that Smallwood and Cooper had contracted as agents on its behalf. It must have been said that it, not they, had

---

1 (1950) 8 CLR 304
2 [1954] 1 QB 45; [1953] 1 All ER 708 (see p 217)

made the contract. It, not they, would have been the purchaser entitled to a conveyance. Their putting the company's name to the document would have been purely in execution of its corporate act and their added signatures would have no more bound them personally to perform the contract than would the signatures of the directors or secretary of a company authenticating the affixing of its seal. There is a difference between a man's own acts and acts done for him by another man. The difficulty of the distinction in the case of a corporation is that a corporation must manifest its acts and intentions by the actions and declarations of human beings; and ambiguities and limitations of language make it difficult sometimes to express the distinction between acts done by a person as executant of the will of a corporation and acts done by a person as agent for a corporation, his principal. That the word 'agent' is in each case apt to describe the actor helps to disguise their different legal characters.

. . . In many cases courts have had to decide whether an agent had, in the particular case, incurred a personal liability on a contract in writing made by him on behalf of a principal. And these decisions have sometimes turned upon narrow differences in wording, which seem to be the progeny by miscegenation of early technical rules relating to the form of the execution of deeds to which Doctor Stoljar has referred in his work, *The Law of Agency* (1961), pp 251–255. But here that question does not really arise, for the document which the respondents signed does not purport to be a contract made by them as agents for the supposed company. They thought that the company existed and that they were in fact directors. It is therefore impossible to regard them as having used the name of the company as a mere pseudonym or firm name or as having intended to incur a personal liability. The reason for the formation of the company may have been to ensure that they would not be personally liable. It is however suggested that, notwithstanding the form of the document, a personal obligation to perform the contract has been imposed upon them by law, because at the time they inserted the name of the company as purchaser there was no such company in existence.

So far as this proposition is based upon *Kelner v Baxter*, it must fail. The facts of this case differ essentially from the facts of that.

. . . Doubtless in *Kelner v Baxter* both the plaintiff and the defendants expected that payment for the goods would be made from the funds of the company that was in process of being formed. That, however, was not a term of the contract. And when the goods were bought it was well-known to all concerned that the company had not yet been formed. The plaintiff, in his letter to the defendants offering to supply the goods, had referred to it as the 'proposed' company; and, as Asprey J has pointed out, the more ample report of the case in the *Law Journal* shows that the plaintiff was himself a participant in the project. The defendants were in fact the buyers of the goods. Their statement that they were buying on behalf of the proposed company was taken to mean, and could in the circumstances only mean, that they contracted to buy the goods with the intent and to the end that the company when formed might have the benefit of them. The words 'on behalf of' do not necessarily imply agency in the relevant legal sense, any more than does the word 'for' when a man says 'I am buying this for' someone whom he names. The words cannot be regarded as indicative of agency for a principal when it is known to the user of the words that there is no principal in existence. The defendants in *Kelner v Baxter* therefore contracted as principals. They were not substituted as principals. They were the principals. The contrast with this case is obvious. Here, instead of both parties knowing that the company was not in existence, they both, appellants and respondents, thought that it was.

SOURCE 74
Phonogram *v* Lane
(Court of Appeal 1981) [1982] QB 938; [1981] 3 All ER 182

The plaintiff advanced £6,000 to a company (Jelly Music Ltd) under an agreement with the defendant to provide part of the finance for a company to be formed (Fragile Management). The latter was never registered and this was an action against the defendant for recovery of the money.

DENNING MR: I will read the letter from Mr Rennie to Mr Lane of 4 July 1973. It is the subject matter of this action.

> Brian Lane, Esq,
> Fragile Ltd,
> 39 South Street,
> London W.1.
>
> Dear Brian,
> In regard to the contract now being completed between Phonogram Ltd and Fragile Management Ltd concerning recordings of a group consisting of Brian Chatton, John McBurnie and one other with a provisional title of 'Cheap Mean and Nasty' and further to our conversation this morning, I send you herewith our cheque for £6000 in anticipation of the contract signing, this being the initial payment for the initial LP called for in the contract. In the unlikely event that we fail to complete within, say, one month you will undertake to repay us the £6000. As per our telephone conversation the cheque has been made payable to Jelly Music Ltd. For good orders sake, Brian, I should be appreciative if you could sign the attached copy of this letter and return it to me so that I can keep our accounts people informed of what is happening.
> Yours sincerely,
> Roland G. Rennie
> Signed by . . . for and on behalf of Fragile Management Ltd.

That was signed by Mr Lane. So there is the written contract embodying the agreement between those concerned. An invoice was sent by Phonogram Ltd:

> *Invoice*
> To contract between Fragile Management
> and Phonogram Ltd.
> Re. 'Cheap Mean & Nasty'   6000.00
>   VAT   600.00
>   ─────────
>   £6600.00
> Initial Payment for first album as
> in contract.

The money was paid over. According to the accounts, it went into the account of Jelly Music Ltd, which was one of the subsidiaries of the Hemdale Group of which Mr Lane, with others, was a director.

The first question is whether, on the true construction of the contract, Mr Lane made himself personally liable. As I read the words of the contract — 'I send *you* herewith our cheque for £6000' and 'In the unlikely event that we fail to complete within, say, one month *you* will undertake to repay us the £6000' — the word 'you' referred to Mr Lane personally. The cheque was made out in favour of Jelly Music Ltd only as a matter of administrative convenience (as the judge found). It did not affect the fact that the agreement to repay was made by Brian

Lane: especially when it is realised that it was known to all concerned that Fragile Management Ltd had not been formed. So I would have construed the contract, without recourse to any other aids, as making Mr Lane personally liable.

. . .

OLIVER LJ: . . . The question I think in each case is what is the real intent as revealed by the contract? Does the contract purport to be one which is directly between the supposed principal and the other party, or does it purport to be one between the agent himself — albeit acting for a supposed principal — and the other party? In other words, what you have to look at is whether the agent intended himself to be a party to the contract. So in *Kelner v Baxter*,[1] where the correspondence was directed to the agents and referred to 'the proposed company' which everybody knew was not yet in existence, there really was no room for the suggestion that the purchasers were acting in any other capacity than personally. On the other hand, in *Newborne v Sensolid (Great Britain) Ltd*,[2] where the contract was on the company's notepaper, it was clearly intended to be a company's contract (nobody realising that it had not yet been registered) and it could not be said that the individual plaintiff's signature in the company's name could possibly have been intended to make him a party to the contract.

The case, in my judgment, does not rest on any narrow point as to the way in which the contract was actually signed. The result would have been exactly the same, in my judgment, as if the signature there had been accompanied by some such formula as 'for and on behalf of' or 'per pro.' The judgment of Parker J and the judgments in the Court of Appeal of Lord Goddard and Morris LJ show that the case turned on what the contract purported to do; and precisely the same applies I think in *Hollman v Pullin*,[3] where a contract, albeit signed by the plaintiff as chairman of the association, was clearly intended to be, and indeed only to be, a contract directly with the association by which the defendant's services were intended to be retained. The same again I think applies to the Australian case of *Black v Smallwood*.[4] The contract there on its face purported to be a contract between the vendor and the company as purchaser and nothing else, nobody then realising that the company had not been incorporated.

SOURCE 75
Newborne *v* Sensolid (Great Britain) Ltd
(Court of Appeal 1953) [1954] 1 QB 45; [1953] 1 All ER 708

A company, Leopold Newborne (London) Ltd, purported to sell tins of ham to the defendant. The defendant refused to take delivery. The company sued for breach of contract. When it was discovered that the company had been registered the day after the transaction was entered into, the plaintiff, the promoter and director of the company, continued the action in his own name. The sale note had been concluded as follows:

'Yours faithfully,
Leopold Newborne (London) Limited
[sgd] Leopold Newborne'

---

1 (1866) LR 2 CP 174; 36 LJ CP 94 (see p 212)
2 [1954] 1 QB 45; [1953] 1 All ER 708
3 (1884) Cab & Ell 254
4 [1966] ALR 744; (1966) 39 ALJR 405 (see p 213)

LORD GODDARD CJ (after discussing, *inter alia, Kelner v Baxter*)[1] . . . Those cases are well established and we are not departing in any way from the principle they lay down, but we cannot find the plaintiff purported to contract as agent or as principal. He was making the contract for the company, and, although counsel has argued that, in signing as he did, he must have signed as agent, for a company can only contract through an agent, that is not the true position. A company makes a contract. No doubt, it must do its physical acts through the directors, but their relationship is not the ordinary one of principal and agent. The company contracts and its contract is authenticated by the signature of one or more of the directors. This contract purports to be made by the company, not by Mr Newborne. He purports to be selling, not his goods, but the company's goods. The only person who has any contract here is the company, and Mr Newborne's signature is merely confirming the company's signature. The document is signed: 'Yours faithfully, Leopold Newborne (London) Ltd', and this signature underneath is that of the person authorised to sign on behalf of the company.

In my opinion, as the company were not in existence when the contract was signed, there never was a contract, and the plaintiff cannot come forward and say: 'It was my contract'. It seems to me, therefore, that the defendants can avail themselves of the defence which they pleaded and the appeal must be dismissed.

Reform

The first European Community Company Law Harmonisation Directive required all Member States to amend their law, insofar as this was necessary, to meet the following standard.

> 'If before a company being formed has acquired legal personality, action has been carried out in its name and the company does not assume the obligations arising from such action, the persons who acted shall, without limit, be jointly and severally liable therefor unless otherwise agreed' (Art 7, Dir 68/151/EEC).

The requisite legislation was first enacted, as s 9(2) of the European Communities Act 1972, consolidated as s 36(4) of the Companies Act 1985 and is now s 36C of the Companies Act 1985 (as substituted by s 130(1) of the Companies Act 1989). This section does not apply:

  (i) to companies not registered in the UK (*Rover International Ltd v Cannon Films Limited* [1987] BCLC 540, reversed on appeal, but not on this point [1989] 1 WLR 912);

 (ii) where the contract was purportedly made on behalf of a company which was believed (wrongly) to be in existence (*Cotronic (UK) Ltd v Dezonie* [1991] BCLC 721);

(iii) where the company is already in existence at the time of the transaction but was trading under another name (*Oshkosh B'Gosh v Dan Marbel* [1989] BCLC 507; *Badgerhill Properties Ltd v Cottrell* [1991] BCLC 805).

It applies where the company is not yet formed but, to the knowledge of the promoter and the third party is in the course of being formed (Source 76). Can a promoter take advantage of CA 1985, s 36C and enforce rights under a contract to which that section applies? This appears not yet to have been

---

1 (1866) LR 2 CP 174; 36 LJ CP 94

decided, but the affirmative would follow if, as the section appears to indicate, a contract comes into existence between promoter and third party.

SOURCE 76
Phonogram *v* Lane
(For the facts and reference, see p 216.)
[1982] QB 938; [1981] 3 All ER 182

DENNING MR: . . . Phonogram Ltd say that the law of England has been much altered by section 9(2) of the European Communities Act 1972. It says:

> 'Where a contract purports to be made by a company, or by a person as agent for a company, at a time when the company has not been formed, then subject to any agreement to the contrary the contract shall have effect as a contract entered into by the person purporting to act for the company or as agent for it, and he shall be personally liable on the contract accordingly.'

That seems to me to cover this very case. The contract purports to be made on behalf of Fragile Management Ltd, at a time when the company had not been formed. It purports to be made by Mr Lane on behalf of the company. So he is to be personally liable for it.

Mr Thompson, on behalf of Mr Lane, argued very skilfully that section 9(2) did not apply. First, he said: 'Look at the Directive under the European Community law which led to this section being introduced.' It is Council Directive of 9 March 1968 (68/151/EEC). In 1968 English was not one of the official languages of the European Community. So Mr Thompson referred us to the French text of article 7 of the Directive:

> 'Si des actes ont été accomplis au nom d'une société en formation, avant l'acquisition par celle-ci de la personnalité morale, et si la société ne reprend pas les engagements résultant de ces actes, les personnes qui les ont accompli en sont solidairement et indéfiniment responsables, sauf convention contraire.'

Mr Thompson says that, according to the French text, that Directive is limited to companies which are 'en formation,' that is companies which have already started to be formed.

Mr Thompson's submission is reinforced by passages from a French textbook — *Ripert et Roblot, Traité Elémentaire de Droit Commercial* (1970). As I read the passages at pp 601 and 604 of that treatise — interpreting the French as best I can — in the case of a French company or société there may be, recognised in law, a period of time while a company is in the course of formation when people have put their signatures to what I may call 'the articles of association.' That period is called the period when the société is 'en formation.' At p 604 a parallel is drawn with a baby at the time of gestation — between the time of conception and the time of birth — and a company when it is 'en formation.'

I reject Mr Thompson's submission. I do not think we should go by the French text of the Directive. It was drafted with regard to a different system of company law from that in this country. We should go by section 9(2) of our own statute, the European Communities Act 1972. Under article 189 of the EEC Treaty, directives are to be binding only in so far as the spirit and intent are concerned. Article 189 says:

'. . . A directive shall be binding, as to the result to be achieved, upon each member state to which it is addressed, but shall leave to the national authorities the choice of form and methods.'

Section 9(2) is in accordance with the spirit and intent of the Directive. We should go by our own statute, and not by the Directive (68/151/EEC).

That brings me to the second point. What does 'purports' mean in this context? Mr Thompson suggests that there must be a representation that the company is already in existence. I do not agree. A contract can purport to be made on behalf of a company, or by a company, even though that company is known by both parties not to be formed and that it is only about to be formed.

The third point made by Mr Thompson was that a company can be 'a person' within the second line of section 9(2). Mr Thompson says that Jelly Music Ltd was a 'person' which was purporting to contract on behalf of Fragile Management Ltd. I do not agree. Jelly Music Ltd were not entering into a contract, Mr Lane was purporting to do so. . . .

There is one further point on section 9(2) which I must mention. In the latest edition of *Cheshire and Fifoot's Law of Contract* (9th edn, 1976), after reciting section 9(2), it says, at p 462:

> 'How far it in fact does so will depend on the meaning given to the words 'subject to any agreement to the contrary' since it could be argued that words showing that A signs as agent express an agreement that he is not to be personally liable. If this were correct *Newborne v Sensolid (Great Britain) Ltd*[1] would still be decided the same way. But it may be suspected that the courts will try to give more content to the subsection.'

We certainly will. The words 'subject to any agreement to the contrary' mean — as Shaw LJ suggested in the course of the argument — 'unless otherwise agreed.' If there was an express agreement that the man who was signing was not to be liable, the section would not apply. But, unless there is a clear exclusion of personal liability, section 9(2) should be given its full effect. It means that in all cases such as the present, where a person purports to contract on behalf of a company not yet formed, then however he expresses his signature he himself is personally liable on the contract.

Despite changes in other jurisdictions,[2] there is, as yet, in the United Kingdom no change to the rule that a company is incapable of ratifying a pre-incorporation contract. A change of this kind was contemplated in the Companies Bill 1973, but that Bill never became law (Sources 77 and 78).

SOURCE 77
Companies Bill 1973

6. (1) Where a contract purports to have been made in the name or on behalf of a company at a time when the company has not been incorporated, the company may, after incorporation, ratify the contract to the same extent as if it had already been incorporated at that time and as if the contract had been entered into on its behalf by an agent acting without its authority.

---

1 [1954] 1 QB 45; [1953] 1 All ER 708

2 Section 81(2), (3) of the Model Australian Companies Act 1981; s 13 of the Ghana Companies Code 1963; s 35 of the South African Companies Act (re-enacting s 71 of the Companies Act 1926)

(2) Where a contract is ratified by virtue of this section, the person who purported to act for or on behalf of the company in making the contract shall not thereafter be under any greater liability than he would have been if he had entered into the contract on behalf of the company as an agent acting without its authority and after its incorporation; and section 9(2) of the European Communities Act 1972 (which imposes personal liability on such a person) shall have effect subject to the foregoing provision.

SOURCE 78
Report of the Company Law Committee
(Cmnd 1749 1962)

Pre-incorporation contracts

44. It frequently happens that a person engaged in forming a company has the company's notepaper printed and orders supplies thereon prior to the incorporation of the company. Under the present law, the company when formed cannot unilaterally adopt the resulting contracts, but must make a new contract with the parties concerned (*Kelner v Baxter*).[1] The unsatisfactory position of a person contracting with another acting on behalf of a company not yet formed is shown by a recent decision in *Newborne v Sensolid (Great Britain) Ltd*.[2] According to this case if the order was signed (as it normally would be), in the name of the company, the individual concerned adding his name as 'director', he cannot sue or be sued on the contract, which is a complete nullity. This may enable either the supplier or the company and those engaged in its formation, to refuse to honour their undertakings should a change in market conditions make it profitable for them to do so. We regard this as obviously undesirable. We also consider it anomalous that the enforceability of the contract should depend on subtle differences in the terminology employed; for example, if the order is signed not 'X and Co Ltd, X director' but 'X director as agent for X & Co Ltd', it appears that X can sue or be sued on the contract (*Kelner v Baxter*). We think that the Act should provide, as do some Commonwealth Acts, that a company may unilaterally adopt contracts which purport to be made on its behalf or in its name prior to incorporation and thereby become a party to the same extent as if the contract had been entered into after incorporation. We also think that, unless and until the company does so adopt such contracts, the persons who purported to act for the company should be entitled to sue and liable to be sued thereon.

The Trustee Escape Route?

UK courts have considered the notion that a contract might be entered into by a trustee for the benefit of the company about to be formed (Sources 79 and 80).

SOURCE 79
Re Empress Engineering
(Court of Appeal 1880) (1880) 16 Ch D 125; 43 LT 742

Under an agreement in terms of which the right of manufacturing a water motor was to be sold to one 'J. H. T. Cottier for and on behalf of a company

---

1 (1866) LR 2 CP 174; 36 LJ CP 94 (see p 208)
2 [1954] 1 QB 45; [1953] 1 All ER 708 (see p 217)

intended to be registered as a limited company and to be called the Empress Engineering Company', it was provided that 'the sum of sixty guineas shall be paid to Messrs Jones and Pride, solicitors, Liverpool, by the company, for the incorporation thereof . . .' At a meeting of the directors after the company was incorporated, the directors purported to ratify the agreement. Later in the same year, the company was compulsorily wound up. The claim by the solicitors failed.

> JESSEL MR: . . . The contract between the promoters and the so-called agent for the company of course was not a contract binding upon the company, for the company had then no existence, nor could it become binding on the company by ratification, because it has been decided, and, as it appears to me, well decided, that there cannot in law be an effectual ratification of a contract which could not have been made binding on the ratifier at the time it was made, because the ratifier was not then in existence. It does not follow from that that acts may not be done by the company after its formation which make a new contract to the same effect as the old one, but that stands on a different principle. I am of opinion, therefore, that there was no contract binding the company to pay this £63 to Messrs Jones & Pride.
>
> Supposing, however, that there was, it is then contended that a mere contract between two parties that one of them shall pay a certain sum to a third person not a party to the contract, will make that third person a *cestui que trust*. As a general rule that will not be so. A mere agreement between A. and B. that B. shall pay C. (an agreement to which C. is not a party either directly or indirectly) will not prevent A. and B. from coming to a new agreement the next day releasing the old one. If C. were a *cestui que trust* it would have that effect. I am far from saying that there may not be agreements which may make C. a *cestui que trust*.

SOURCE 80
Cumming *v* Quartzag Ltd
(Scottish Court of Session 1981) [1981] SLT 205

The plaintiffs ('pursuers') granted a lease of property to one John Milne, 'for and on behalf of a company to be incorporated under the Companies Act 1948 to be named Quartzag Limited . . .', to extract minerals. The company was thereafter incorporated. The company was referred to in the agreement as the 'second party' and no objection was raised when, after incorporation, it began to extract minerals from and set up plant and machinery on the leased premises. The plaintiffs also accepted payments of royalties from the defendants and throughout, treated the defendants as the tenant. In October 1976, the pursuers refused the request by the defendants to carry out further quarrying arrangements, alleging that the defendants had no right to be on the leased premises. It was found by the Sheriff that the defendants had no valid lease and were not entitled to extend or continue their operations. An appeal to the Second Division was dismissed.

> LORD JUSTICE CLERK (WHEATLEY) . . . The defenders relied on various cases to which we now refer. The facts in *Tanner v Christian*[1] were very different in that, in that case, although a person signed a deed 'for and on behalf of' a named person, the provisions in the deed indicated the intention that the agent should

---

1 4 EI & BI 591; 119 ER 217

be personally bound by all the provisions. That is not so in the present case where, as we have said, the obligations are to be on the company to be incorporated with two exceptions. *Morton's Trs v The Aged Christian Friend Society of Scotland*,[1] which the sheriff discusses in his note, is not in point since there was no question of agency there. We were further provided with the transcripts of two South African cases namely, *McCullogh v Fernwood Estate Ltd*[2] and *N.K.P. v Sentrale*.[3] In the former case the difficulty of a company obtaining the benefit of a contract made on its behalf before it came into existence was solved by deciding that the person who made the contract was acting individually, that is, as a principal, and not as an agent. He was said to have been a 'trustee' and not an agent. The latter case applied the same reasoning. In other words these cases decided that agents, as known in law, were to be treated as 'trustees' and principals in cases where a contract was made on behalf of a company to be incorporated after the agreement is made so that the contract would receive effect. They have no application to Scots law.

PART II: THE ULTRA VIRES PROBLEM

The principle of ultra vires — literally 'beyond the powers' — is in the most general sense designed to render void an act undertaken in contravention of statute. It was first applied to large statutory companies in the mid-nineteenth century to prevent them from acting beyond their objects as stated in the statute by which they were constituted. Any act that was ultra vires was legally void. These statutory companies often had wide powers to expropriate land (eg to carry out their object of building a railway line) and could accumulate substantial wealth and engage in a wide range of activities such as might threaten the livelihood of others (see eg *Colman v Eastern Counties Railway Company* (1846) 10 Beav 1, 50 ER 481; *Attorney General v Great Eastern Railway* (1880) 5 App Cas 473). Ultra vires, thus, was a mechanism through which these companies could be prevented from exceeding their powers.

By the decision of *Ashbury Railway Carriage Company v Riche* (see p 11) ultra vires was held applicable to registered companies. Given that the memorandum and articles of association (the constitution of a registered company) is registered and therefore open to inspection, in theory, anyone dealing with a company could know whether what the company was proposing to do was within the company's objects (and, therefore, valid) or beyond the objects (and, therefore, void). The combination of the doctrines of ultra vires and constructive notice (under which everyone dealing with a company was deemed to know what was contained in the company's registered documents) could have serious implications for commercial activities. The company might, for example, seek to escape from what turned out to be a bad bargain where the activity in question was beyond its objects (as in the *Ashbury* case). A number of legal principles were, however, developed to mitigate the effects of the ultra vires doctrine, namely:

---

1 (1899) 2 F (Ct of Sess) 82; 37 Sc LR 67
2 1920 AD 204 (South African Sup Ct)
3 1970 (3) SA 367 (AD)

(i) the objects clause included, by implication everything that was incidental to or consequential upon the company's expressed objects
(*Attorney-General v Great Eastern Railway* (1880) 5 App Cas 473);

(ii) the liberal construction of the company's objects clause so as to include
the activity in question (*New Finance & Mortgage Co Ltd* [1975] Ch 420;
Newstead v Frost [1980] 1 WLR 135);

(iii) as particular illustrations of (ii), liberal interpretation so as to bypass the
restricting 'main object' rule (*Re Kitson and Company Ltd* [1946] 1 All ER
435) and to uphold clauses in the company's constitution which gave
the directors wide freedom in deciding what the company should do (so
called 'subjective' clauses, *Bell Houses Ltd v City Wall Properties* [1966] 2
QB 656, Source 81);

(iv) granting relief to third parties who, having loaned money to the
company, were unaware that the loan was to be used for an ultra vires
purpose (*Young v David Payne* [1904] 2 Ch 608), although where the
lender knew of the ultra vires use or could be deemed to know by reason
of the constructive notice doctrine, the contract of loan was void (*Re Jon
Beauforte (London) Ltd* [1953] Ch 131, *Introductions Ltd v National
Provincial Bank Ltd* [1970] Ch 199;

(v) upholding gifts by the company in circumstances where the directors
believed this to be in the best interests of the company (*Evans v Brunner
Mond*, [1921] 1 Ch 359, Source 82), something which by definition,
could not apply where the company was ceasing or drastically reducing
its operations, (*Hutton v West Cork Railway Company* (1883) 23 Ch D 654,
Parke v Daily News Ltd [1962] Ch 927).

Decisions like *Evans v Brunner Mond* (Source 82) and *Bell Houses Ltd v City Wall
Properties* (Source 81) reduced the potency of ultra vires challenges by
accepting that the operations of a company are an internal matter for
decision by the board. The issues of the company's constitution thus became
questions of management power vis à vis the shareholders (see Chapter 6,
Part V). Here the internalising process has the effect of eliminating the ultra
vires challenge. In the more recent decisions of *Re Horseley & Weight Ltd* and
Rolled Steel Co v British Steel Corporation, (Source 86), we see a related
process:

(a) subjecting the allegedly ultra vires decision of the directors to challenge
from within as a matter of breach of duty to the company (and,
therefore, potentially ratifiable, *Re Horseley & Weight Ltd*, Source 85);

(b) vis à vis the third party treating the allegedly ultra vires decisions of the
board as valid and enforceable by the third party unless the latter was
implicated in the directors' breach of duty to the company (*Rolled Steel*,
Source 86).

This development in the legal principles away from the public, constitutional challenge of a company's actions towards the internal, private monitoring of the shareholders and the upholding of transactions vis à vis third
parties unless the latter participated in the breach of duty parallels the
statutory developments limiting and then eliminating the application of the
ultra vires doctrine to registered companies.

Ultra vires is not, however, dead and buried. It survives in public law as a means for controlling excessive acts by the administration. It still applies to organisations incorporated under other statutes, eg industrial and provident societies (*Halifax Building Society v Meridian Housing Association* [1994] 2 BCLC 540) and local authorities (*Hazell v Hammersmith & Fulham London BC* [1992] 2 AC 1). It is still employed as a means for checking illegal acts by companies (eg unauthorised reductions of capital, see eg *Simmons v Heffer*, Source 83 and *Aveling Barford v Perion*, Source 87), but it is no longer available as the instrument for a challenge to corporate activity on the ground that that activity is not provided for by the constitution.

SOURCE 81
Bell Houses Ltd *v* City Wall Properties
(Court of Appeal 1966) [1966] 2 QB 656; [1966] 2 All ER 674

The plaintiff introduced the defendant to a source of finance, the agreed procuration fee being £20,000. The defendant refused to pay on the grounds that the plaintiff, a development company, was not authorised by its objects, to carry out procuration contracts. Mocatta J dismissed the claim on the grounds that the contract was ultra vires the plaintiff and therefore void.

DANCKWERTS LJ: ... Clause 3 of the plaintiff company's memorandum of association contains the usual large number of sub-clauses, identified by the letters (a) to (u). It does not contain the provision sometimes inserted that all the sub-clauses are independent objects, or words to that effect. The following sub-clauses must be referred to:

'(a) To carry on the trade or business of general, civil and engineering contractors and in particular but without prejudice to the generality of the foregoing to construct, alter, enlarge, erect and maintain either by [the plaintiff company] or other parties, sewers, roads, streets, railways, sidings, tramways, electricity works, gas works, bridges, shops, reservoirs, factories, water-works, brick kilns and brick or tile works, timber yards, buildings, houses, offices and all other works, erections, plant, machinery and things of any description whatsoever either upon land acquired by [the plaintiff company] or upon other land and generally.

(b) To acquire by purchase, exchange or otherwise either for an estate in fee simple or for any interest or estate in land, whether in possession or in reversion and whether vested or contingent, any lands, tenements and premises of any tenure, whether subject or not to any charges or incumbrances and any easements or other rights in or over land and any concessions, patents, patent rights, licences, copyright, secret processes, machinery, plant, stock-in-trade and any other real or personal property and to hold or to sell, develop, let on rent, mortgage, charge or otherwise deal with all or any of such lands, tenements or premises and buildings erected thereon and all other such real and personal property.

(c) To carry on any other trade or business whatsoever which can, in the opinion of the board of directors, be advantageously carried on by [the plaintiff company] in connexion with or as ancillary to any of the above businesses or the general business of [the plaintiff company].

(m) To accept payment for any property or rights sold or otherwise disposed of or dealt with by [the plaintiff company].

(q) To sell, improve, manage, develop, turn to account, exchange, let on rent, royalty, share of profits or otherwise, grant licences, easements and other rights in or over, and in any other manner deal with or dispose of the undertaking and all or any of the property and assets for the time being of the company for such consideration as [the plaintiff company] may think fit.

(u) To do all such other things as are incidental or conducive to the above objects or any of them.'

. . .

As I have mentioned, it is also necessary to consider the effect of the words in clause 3(c) of the memorandum, 'in the opinion of the board of directors'. I think that it is plain that these words qualify the whole of that sub-clause. Counsel for the defendants contended that the opinion of the directors must not only be bona fide but also objective. Mocatta J, even went so far as to say that

'the mere fact that the board of directors of a company may be of opinion that an activity can be advantageously carried on by the company, even if the opinion be well-founded, will not per se make that activity *intra vires*.'

With all respect to the judge, if he is meaning to refer to the opinion required by the sub-clause, he is not quoting it correctly. The requirement of the sub-clause is that in the opinion of the board of directors the other trade or business can be advantageously carried on by the company in connection with or as ancillary to any of the above businesses or the general business of the company. If the judge means that the opinion of the directors has no effect at all, then I am afraid that I cannot agree with him. On the balance of the authorities it would appear that the opinion of the directors if bona fide can dispose of the matter; and why should it not decide the matter? The shareholders subscribe their money on the basis of the memorandum of association and if that confers the power on directors to decide whether in their opinion it is proper to undertake particular business in the circumstances specified, why should not their decision be binding? The shareholders by taking shares on the terms of the memorandum have agreed to it. It is a matter of internal management principally. Persons dealing with the plaintiff company in the course of trade or business are helped rather than hindered by a provision of this sort. In the result the judge appears to have completely disregarded this provision and to have dealt with the case on the basis that there was no real difference between sub-clause (c) and sub-clause (u).

. . .

In *Re Crown Bank*,[1] the company had been formed primarily for carrying on the business of banking, as a country bank, with an office in London. After a time it gave up its country office, ceased to do banking business and carried on in London land speculation, promoting a company in a foreign country and the business of investing in shares and securities. The objects of the company were expressed in very wide terms — North J, said . . . that they were

'So wide that it might be said to warrant the company in giving up banking business and embarking in a business with the object of establishing a line of balloons between the earth and moon.'

---

1 (1890) 44 Ch D 634; 59 LJ Ch 739

North J, on the petition of a shareholder made an order for the winding-up of the company. This was plainly a case where the company had abandoned its main objects and was attempting to carry on quite a different business.

In *Cotman v Brougham*[1] . . . a company called the Essequibo Rubber & Tobacco Estates Ltd, agreed to sub-underwrite twenty thousand shares in another company and 17,200 of those shares were allotted to it, on which there remained due and owing the sum of £14,456 for unpaid calls. These shares were transferred to a third company. All three companies were in liquidation, and the liquidator of the second company settled the transferee company on the A list of contributories and the Essequibo Co on the B list in respect of the shares. The liquidator of the Essequibo Co applied to have that company's name struck out of the B list, on the ground that the underwriting was *ultra vires* of the company. The company's memorandum had thirty clauses enabling the company to carry on almost any kind of business, and the objects clause concluded with a declaration that every sub-clause should be construed as a substantive clause and not limited or restricted by reference to any other sub-clause or by the name of the company and that none of such sub-clauses or the objects specified therein should be deemed subsidiary or auxiliary merely to the objects mentioned in the first sub-clause. It was held that the memorandum must be construed according to its literal meaning, and that the underwriting was *intra vires*. Both Lord Parker of Waddington and Lord Wrenbury criticised the long-standing practice of elaborating the objects of the company in a long series of sub-clauses containing, as Lord Wrenbury said: . . .

'paragraph after paragraph not specifying or delimiting the proposed trade or purpose, but confusing power with purpose and indicating every class of act which the corporation is to have power to do.'

This practice continues and I have heard it defended by eminent company lawyers on the ground that it satisfies nervous company directors that they have the ordinary powers which management of a company requires. I do not believe that anyone else, including those who have to deal with the company, usually pays much attention to the matter, unless someone wishes to wriggle out of some obligation.

SALMON LJ: Having regard to the view which I have formed on this part of the case, it is unnecessary to consider the interesting, important and difficult question which would arise were the contract *ultra vires*, namely whether, the plaintiff company having fully performed its part under the contract and the defendants having obtained all the benefit under the contract, the defendants could successfully take the point that the contract was *ultra vires* the plaintiff company and so avoid payment. It seems strange that third parties could take advantage of a doctrine, manifestly for the protection of the shareholders, in order to deprive the company of money which in justice should be paid to it by the third parties. In *Cotman v Brougham* Lord Parker of Waddington said:

' . . . the statement of the company's objects in its memorandum is intended to serve a double purpose. In the first place, it gives protection to subscribers, who learn from it the purposes to which their money can be applied. In the second place, it gives protection to persons who deal with the company, and who can infer from it the extent of the company's powers. The narrower the objects expressed in the memorandum the less is the

---

1 [1918] AC 514; 87 LJ Ch 379

subscriber's risk, but the wider such objects the greater is the security of those who transact business with the company.'

What Lord Parker of Waddington was contemplating was that third parties proposing to deal with the company could, by looking at the memorandum, have the security of knowing whether they could compel performance by the company of the contract in contemplation. I hardly think that he had in mind that third parties by looking at the memorandum should have the security of knowing that they might safely enter into a contract and promise to pay the company for services without any obligation to honour their contractual promise after they had received the services. The judge in effect came to the conclusion that the reasoning in *Ashbury Railway Carriage and Iron Company v Riche*[1] led to this strange result. I express no opinion on this point and leave it to be decided when it arises, for we have heard no argument on it.

I agree that this appeal should be allowed.

SOURCE 82
Evans *v* Brunner Mond & Co
[1921] 1 Ch 359; 90 LJ Ch 294

The plaintiff, a shareholder, was challenging the decision of the company to distribute to universities and scientific institutions, the sum of £100,000 in furtherance of scientific education. A resolution authorising this distribution had been passed by a substantial majority.

EVE J: . . . The question is whether such an application of the company's funds is within or without the power of the company. The defendants say that it is within an express power to be found in the company's memorandum of association. It has been argued that the clause which I am about to read is not really an object of the company properly stated in its memorandum but is only a power. No doubt for many years past a practice has obtained of mixing up objects and powers and inserting both in the memorandum, but for the purposes of to-day it is not necessary for me to distinguish between the two. Enough that I have the clause which I am about to read contained in the memorandum as one of the objects of the company. It is clause (s) of paragraph 3 of the memorandum, and it reads in this way: 'The doing of all such business and things as may be incidental or conducive to the attainment of the above objects, or any of them.' That clause again must be read with certain qualifications. You cannot pick out one of the objects enumerated under the letters (a) to (r) of paragraph 3, and having determined the particular act to be incidental or conducive to that object thereupon decide that the act is *intra vires*. The wide and general objects are to be construed as ancillary to the company's main purpose, and I apprehend that the act to be *intra vires* must be one which can fairly be regarded as incidental or conducive to the main or paramount purpose for which the company was formed. It is on these principles I propose to consider the questions raised upon this motion. It is beyond dispute that the paramount object for which this company was incorporated was the carrying on in all its branches of the trade or business of chemical manufacturers, and in order that any particular application of its funds can be justified under clause (s) of paragraph 3 it is essential that it should be established that it is an application incidental or conducive to the business of chemical manufacturers. The company accepts that position, and nothing has been urged on its behalf contrary to that principle. The plaintiff,

---

1 (1875) LR 7 HL 653; 44 LJ Exch 185 (see p 11)

who filed no evidence except a formal affidavit proving the facts, asserts that this proposed application of the company's funds is not incidental and will not be conducive to the company's main purpose or object on several grounds. In saying that I do not intend to convey that he denies that the company may not to some extent benefit thereby as chemical manufacturers. His contention is that it is the community at large that will really be benefited by the proposed expenditure, and that the company, as part of the community, may derive some distant, remote and more or less insignificant benefit but a benefit out of all proportion to the cost.

He puts his case against the validity of the proposal on these grounds. First, it is argued the object is too general, in that it is not confined to the particular branches of science calculated to promote the company's paramount purpose; scientific education, it has been pointed out, extends over a very wide area, and may include astronomy, geology and other matters having no very direct connection with the manufacture of chemicals; the resolution therefore empowers the directors to place funds at the disposal of donees who might utilise them for the advancement of branches of science in which the company is not very closely interested. In support of these arguments counsel relies strongly on the character of the possible donees. He points out that the Universities of Oxford and Cambridge, with their wide range of scientific training and education, might well apply any grant made to them for education and research work of too general a nature to lead to any direct benefit to the company and yet be acting within the exact terms of the resolution. But even if the money be appropriated for scientific education and work directly related to the company's main object it is argued that any benefit arising therefrom to the company is too remote; there is nothing that reserves to the company the services of men trained by the expenditure of this large sum, and the only benefit accruing to the company is that which it shares with the whole community from any advancement in scientific education and research: no direct benefit accrues to the company and no advantage preponderating over the advantage which every other member of the community receives. The plaintiff's argument therefore comes to this: either this money is capable of being applied for education which will in no way benefit the company, or, if applied for branches of science in which the company is directly interested, its expenditure will not secure to the company any advantage over its rivals in trade or any other members of the public, and if either proposition is established the proposed expenditure cannot properly be held to be conducive to the company's main purpose.

I confess I do feel some difficulty on these points. The furtherance of scientific education and research generally might certainly appear to sanction the application of this large fund in part to scientific education not necessarily useful or beneficial to the company, and in the absence of the evidence to which I am about to allude, I should have been disposed to think the terms of the resolution somewhat indefinite and wise and calculated to give rise to the suggestion that the advancement of science rather than the direct benefit of the company had dictated it. But it appears from the evidence of the chairman of the company, supported by the evidence of all the other directors, that the company is not aiming by this contribution at securing the education of scientific men as specialists in its business. What it desires is to encourage and assist men who will cultivate the scientific attitude of mind, and be prepared to devote their time and abilities to scientific study and research generally. According to the evidence that is the class of men for whom the company is constantly looking out, a class of men of which the supply is very inadequate but who when obtainable are readily capable of adapting themselves to the investigation research and scientific work of the company. It is not intended to impose on the universities and other institutions who may benefit under this grant any obligation to train men as specialists in the particular scientific work which the company undertakes. What is desired is to offer attractions to these who are prepared to take up science and to cultivate the scientific mind and scientific habits, and thereby to establish what one of the deponents speaks of as 'a reservoir of trained experts' from which the company will be able to select the right men to instruct in the particular branches of scientific investigation necessary for the purposes of the company. The evidence establishes this much, that the company is in constant need of a reserve of scientifically trained men for the purpose of its business — that the business cannot be maintained if the supply of such men is deficient — that a deficiency is almost inevitable unless substantial inducements are forthcoming to attract men to scientific study and research — that the best agencies for directing these studies are the well-equipped universities and scientific institutions, and that the interest of the company does not require that the education and training should necessarily be confined to scientific work of the nature of that in which the company is solely interested. These considerations dispose I think of the objection raised to the wide and general nature of the reference in the resolution to scientific education and research; it is not intended to limit the application of the money to the special branches of science affecting the company's business but to promote the training and education calculated to produce the class of men qualified to assist in maintaining the company's business.

SOURCE 83
Simmonds *v* Heffer
(Chancery Division 1983) [1983] BCLC 298

The League Against Cruel Sports Ltd, a company limited by guarantee, which had as its principal object, the prevention of cruelty to animals, made two separate gifts to the Labour Party to finance its campaign in the 1979 general election. The first for £50,000 was for general purposes, without restrictions on use; the second, of £30,000, was for the specific purpose of advertising the Labour Party's commitment to animal welfare. A member of the League brought these proceedings challenging the gifts as ultra vires.

MERVYN DAVIES J: . . . It is said that since it is an object or aim of the League to prevent cruelty to animals, and in particular cruelty resulting from hunting, it is within the powers of the League to translate that aim into action by paying out its funds to a political party that has, by its manifesto, given rise to the hope or expectation that cruelty to animals will be alleviated. I see considerable force in that argument. But I do not accept it. In deciding to give effect to its aims by the act of paying out money to the Labour Party General Election Campaign Committee for its general purposes the League also decided that the money paid out might be spent, not only on its own aims, but also on the aims of the Labour Party; those aims extend far beyond the League's aims. Thus, as to the £50,000, the payment is not a carrying out of the League's main aims or objects. The £30,000 is, I think, a horse of another colour. The memorandum in enabling the League to seek to prevent cruelty . . . authorises the League to spend its funds with that aim or object in view. Here the League, by its executive committee, decided to spend the £30,000, or rather, entrust the £30,000 to the Campaign Committee on the understanding that . . . Committee would, in the course of the election campaign include in its activities (1) advertising about animal welfare, (2) the production of leaflets on the same subject, and (3) publicising, in some constituencies, the animal commitment that appears in the manifesto. In paying out the £30,000 for those purposes it seems to me that the League was furthering the main objects. No doubt there are many ways of going about seeking to prevent cruelty to animals. The League, in deciding to entrust its funds to the Labour Party Committee in the way that it did, ie specifying the purposes for which the money could be used, seems to me to have acted consistently with its aims or objects. Accordingly I hold that the defendants are not accountable for a return of the £30,000.

. . .

There remains for consideration (o).[1] In this connection I was referred to *Evans v Brunner Mond.*[2] There a trading company decided to pay £100,000 to selected universities 'for the furtherance of scientific education and research'. The payment was regarded as justified by virtue of a provision in its memorandum whereby the company was enabled to do 'all such business and things as may be incidental or conducive to the attainment of the above objects or any of them' in that the payment was, on the evidence, conducive to the company's continued progress as a chemical manufacturer. So the payment was incidental to the company's main purpose. The payment was compatible with and not antagonistic to the company's main objects. I do not see that as the position here. My reading of (b) is that implicitly, payments may be made thereunder for the purpose of seeking to prevent cruelty, etc. There is also implicit a prohibition on the spending of money for purposes alien to the sense of (b), (c) and (d). Thus, as I have said, money may not be spent pursuant to (b) on the general purposes of the Labour Party. If (b) contains that implied prohibition then the prohibition is not, in my view, to be removed by calling in aid (o). The 'incidental' or 'conducive' power can only be used in the pursuit of, or to extend, an express authorised object. It was used in that way in the *Brunner Mond case.* Such a power may not be used to negative an implied prohibition in an express power. Accordingly I do not think that (o) helps the defendants. There is a further consideration that gives support to this view. Paragraph (g) indicates what subscriptions the League may make. One then looks at (o) which empowers the League 'to do all such other lawful things as are incidental or conducive in the attainment of any of the above objects'. If one pays the £50,000 pursuant to (o) it can hardly be said that the payment is incidental or conducive to the attainment of object (g) since (g) does not, as I have held, allow of the payment.

Accordingly the £50,000 is returnable to the League.

SOURCE 84
Re Halt Garage (1964) Limited
(Chancery Division 1982) [1982] 3 All ER 1016

These were proceedings by the liquidator under s 333(1) of the Companies Act 1948 (now s 212 of the Insolvency Act 1986) against the former directors of the company to recover remuneration paid to them by the company during the period prior to liquidation when the company was trading at a loss. It was submitted by the liquidator that the payments, although made in good faith, were ultra vires the company as being gratuitous payments and not being for the benefit of the company or to promote its prosperity.

---

1 The clause in the objects clause of the company which provided 'To do all such other lawful things as are incidental or conducive to the attainment of any of the above objects'
2 [1921] 1 Ch 359; 90 LJ Ch 294 (see p 228)

OLIVER J: The cases really divide into two groups: those such as *Hampson v Price's Patent Candle Co*,[1] *Hutton's case*,[2] *Henderson v Bank of Australasia*[3] and *Parke v Daily News*,[4] where the question was not so much that of the company's capacity to do a particular act as that of the extent to which a majority in general meeting could force a particular measure on a dissentient minority; and those such as *Lee, Behrens & Co*[5] itself, *Re W & M Roith Ltd*,[6] *Ridge Securities v IRC*[7] and the *Charterbridge case*,[8] where the question was as to the validity of an exercise of the powers, express or implied, by directors. Although the test of benefit to the company was applied in both groups of cases, I am not at all sure that the phrase 'benefit of the company' was being employed in quite the same sense in each.

In the latter group, where what was in question was whether an exercise of powers by directors was effective, the benefit regarded seems to have been that of the company as a corporate entity (see the phrase 'to promote the prosperity of the company') whereas in the former group it was, I think, used in the same sense as that in which it was used in the line of cases dealing with, for instance, the power of the majority to alter the articles of association. In *Allen v Gold Reefs of West Africa Ltd*[9] Lindley MR observed that such a power must —

'be exercised subject to those general principles of law and equity which are applicable to all powers conferred on majorities and enabling them to bind minorities. It must be exercised, not only in the manner required by law, but also bona fide for the benefit of the company as a whole . . . '

. . . counsel for the liquidators submits that since (at any rate during most of the material time) there were no profits available in the company for distribution and since directors' emoluments are always gratuities, except where payable under contract, and since the directors were shareholders as well, every payment to them constituted an illegal reduction of capital except to the extent to which it can be justified by the test of benefit to the company. One difficulty about that, even accepting the submission for the moment, is that if 'the benefit of the company' means, as Plowman J suggested in *Parke v Daily News*,[10] 'the benefit of the shareholders as a whole', it leads him nowhere.

I accept entirely the submission of counsel for the liquidator that a gratuitous payment out of the company's capital to a member, qua member, is unlawful and cannot stand, even if authorised by all the shareholders. What I find difficulty in accepting is that, assuming a sum to be genuinely paid to a director-shareholder as remuneration under an express power, it becomes an illegal return of capital to him, qua member, if it does not satisfy some further test of being paid for the benefit of the company as a corporate entity. If he genuinely receives the money as a reward for his directorship, the question whether the payment is beneficial to the company or not cannot, as I see it, alter the capacity in which he receives it: see, for instance, *Cyclists' Touring Club v Hopkinson*.[11]

Now, there is no presumption that directors' remuneration is payable only out

---

1 (1876) 45 LJ Ch 437; 34 LT 711
2 (1883) 23 Ch D 654; 52 LJ Ch 689
3 (1888) 40 Ch D 170; 48 LJ Ch 197
4 [1962] Ch 927; [1962] 2 All ER 929
5 [1932] 2 Ch 46; 48 TLR 248
6 [1967] 1 WLR 432; [1967] 1 All ER 427
7 [1964] 1 WLR 479; [1964] 1 All ER 275
8 [1970] Ch 62; [1969] 2 All ER 1185
9 [1900] 1 Ch 656; 69 LJ Ch 266
10 [1962] Ch 927; [1962] 2 All ER 929
11 [1910] 1 Ch 179; 79 LJ Ch 82

of divisible profits. That appears clearly from *Re Lundy Granite Co Ltd, Lewis's Case*,[1] where an alternative ground for the decision was that the company in general meeting had indeed sanctioned the payment of directors' remuneration out of capital, the company never having made any profits. James LJ said:

> '... independently of that construction, I think it would be mischievous, after four years' transactions that have been conducted honestly, there being no suggestion of fraud or concealment as against the directors — to open up transactions which had been submitted to the auditors and shareholders of the company who have passed the accounts, which were then submitted to the general meeting, and of which there was distinct notice given to everybody. It is true that the directors' fees appear in the accounts among a number of other items, but everything appears there. Shareholders, like other persons, must be supposed to read the accounts given to them of their own matters, and therefore there was distinct notice on the face of the reports that the directors' fees were paid, although no profits had been made ... It appears to me that it would be most mischievous to suggest that the company could have filed a bill under these circumstances to recover back the money, the payment of which they had assented to in that way. I am of opinion that creditors can be in no better position than the company itself would be in if it were a solvent company, and had raised this question with its directors.'

Mellish LJ said:

> 'The only question is whether that must necessarily be implied — whether it is so much the ordinary course, that directors should be paid only out of profits that that must necessarily be implied, and was intended, although it is not expressed. I am not aware that there is any such rule. If people want the services of directors, I presume directors are entitled to say, we will not serve unless we are paid for our services. If directors are appointed and act on that understanding, I do not see any reason why they should not be paid.'

Counsel for the liquidator does not go to the extent, in fact, of suggesting that when a company has fallen on bad times the directors must either close the business down immediately or go on trying to pull it round for nothing.

...

What I think counsel's submission comes to is this, that while the company has divisible profits remuneration may be paid on any scale which the shareholders are prepared to sanction within the limits of available profits, but that, as soon as there cease to be divisible profits, it can only lawfully be paid on a scale which the court, applying some objective standard of benefit to the company, considers to be reasonable. But assuming that the sum is bona fide voted to be paid as remuneration, it seems to me that the amount, whether it be mean or generous, must be a matter of management for the company to determine in accordance with its constitution which expressly authorises payment for directors' services. Shareholders are required to be honest but, as counsel for the respondents suggests, there is no requirement that they must be wise and it is not for the court to manage the company.

Counsel for the liquidator submits, however, that if this is right it leads to the bizarre result that a meeting of stupid or deranged but perfectly honest

---

1 [1872] 26 LT 673

shareholders can, like Bowen LJ's lunatic director, vote to themselves, qua directors, some perfectly outlandish sum by way of remuneration and that in a subsequent winding up the liquidator can do nothing to recover it. It seems to me, that the answer to this lies in the objective test which the court necessarily applies. It assumes human beings to be rational and to apply ordinary standards. In the postulated circumstances of a wholly unreasonable payment, that might, no doubt, be prima facie evidence of fraud, but it might also be evidence that what purported to be remuneration was not remuneration at all but a dressed-up gift to a shareholder out of capital, like the 'interest' payment in the *Ridge Securities case* which bore no relation to the principal sums advanced.

This, as it seems to me, is the real question in a case such as the present. . . . The real test must, I think, be whether the transaction in question was a genuine exercise of the power. The motive is more important than the label. Those who deal with a limited company do so on the basis that its affairs will be conducted in accordance with its constitution, one of the express incidents of which is that the directors may be paid remuneration. Subject to that, they are entitled to have the capital kept intact. They have to accept the shareholders' assessment of the scale of that remuneration, but they are entitled to assume that, whether liberal or illiberal, what is paid is genuinely remuneration and that the power is not used as a cloak for making payments out of capital to the shareholders as such.

In the event, the judge dismissed the liquidator's summons insofar as it attempted to recover remuneration paid to the working director, but upheld the summons in respect of the claim for the remuneration paid to the working director's wife.

'She had never held any office other than that of director and that she retained. . . . The fact is that however valuable and exacting may have been the services which [she] had rendered in the past, her continued directorship contributed nothing to the company's future, beyond the fact that she was and remained responsible as a director and was able to make up the necessary quorum for directors' meetings . . .'.

SOURCE 85
Re Horsley & Weight Ltd
(Court of Appeal 1982) [1982] Ch 442; [1982] 3 All ER 1045

Application by the liquidator under s 333(1) of the Companies Act 1948 (now s 212 of the Insolvency Act 1986) for a declaration that an insurance policy purchased by the company to provide a pension for a retiring director was ultra vires the company, a misfeasance on the part of the directors and that, as he (the director for whom the policy was purchased) had knowledge of the misfeasance, that the policy should be held by him on trust for the company. The application was dismissed by Oliver J in the court below and the Court of Appeal dismissed this appeal.

BUCKLEY LJ: Among the objects for which the company was established, set forth in clause 3 of its memorandum of association, is the following:

'(o) To grant pensions to employees and ex-employees and directors and ex-directors or other officers or ex-officers of the company, their widows, children and dependants, and to subscribe to benevolent and other funds for the benefit of any such persons and to subscribe to or assist in the promotion of any charitable benevolent or public purpose or object.'

Clause 3 contains the following paragraph, which has of recent years become regrettably common notwithstanding that it is often in some respects inappropriate, if not actually misleading:

> 'All the foregoing objects shall be read and construed as separate and distinct objects and the generality of such objects shall not be abridged or cut down by reference to any other object of the company.'

I shall use the expression 'separate objects clause' to describe any clause to this effect.

. . .

I will first consider the *ultra vires* point. The Companies Act 1948, section 2, requires the memorandum of association of a company incorporated under that Act to state the objects of the company. A company has no capacity to pursue any objects outside those which are so stated. It does not follow, however, that any act which is not expressly authorised by the memorandum is *ultra vires* the company. Anything reasonably incidental to the attainment or pursuit of any of the express objects of the company will, unless expressly prohibited, be within the implied powers of the company. It has now long been a common practice to set out in memoranda of association a great number and variety of 'objects' so called, some of which (for example, to borrow money, to promote the company's interests by advertising its products or services, or to do acts or things conducive or incidental to the company's objects) are by their very nature incapable of standing as independent objects which can be pursued in isolation as the sole activity of the company. Such 'objects' must, by reason of their very nature, be interpreted merely as powers incidental to the true objects of the company and must be so treated notwithstanding the presence of a separate objects clause: see *Re Introductions Ltd, Introductions Ltd v National Provincial Bank Ltd.*[1] Where there is no separate objects clause, some of the express 'objects' may on construction fall to be treated as no more than powers which are ancillary to the dominant or main objects of the company: see, for example, *Re German Date Coffee Co.*[2]

Ex hypothesi an implied power can only legitimately be used in a way which is ancillary or incidental to the pursuit of an authorised object of the company, for it is the practical need to imply the power in order to enable the company effectively to pursue its authorised objects which justifies the implication of the power. So an exercise of an implied power can only be *ultra vires* the company if it is ancillary or incidental to the pursuit of an authorised object. So also, in the case of express 'objects' which, on construction of the memorandum or by their very nature, are ancillary to the dominant or main objects of the company, an exercise of any such power can only be *intra vires* if it is in fact ancillary or incidental to the pursuit of some such dominant or main object.

On the other hand, the doing of an act which is expressed to be, and is capable of being, an independent object of the company cannot be *ultra vires*, for it is by definition something which the company is formed to do and so must be *intra vires*. I shall use the term 'substantive object' to describe such an object of a company.

The question, therefore, is whether clause 3(o) of the company's memorandum of association in the present case contains a substantive object or merely an ancillary power. Having regard to the presence of the separate objects clause, the former of these alternatives must be the case unless the subject matter of clause 3(o) is of its nature incapable of constituting a substantive object.

---

1 [1970] Ch 199; [1969] 1 All ER 887
2 (1882) 29 Ch D 169; 51 LJ Ch 564

We are not concerned here with whether the pension policy is a valid enforceable contract between the company and the insurers. It has been assumed in argument on both sides that this is the case. The question with which we are concerned is whether as between the company (now acting by its liquidator), and the respondent, the respondent can be made liable on the ground that he knowingly participated in an act of misfeasance by Mr Campbell-Dick and Mr Frank Horsley by expending the company's money in a way which was *ultra vires* the company, or which, if not *ultra vires* the company, was nevertheless a misfeasance which was incapable of ratification by Mr Campbell-Dick and Mr Frank Horsley as the only shareholders.

Counsel for the liquidator, relying principally on the judgment of Eve J in *Re Lee, Behrens & Co Ltd*[1] submits that, properly construed, paragraph (o) should be read as conferring merely an ancillary power. In that case the directors of a company procured that the company should enter into a deed of covenant to pay to the widow of a former director a life annuity. The company subsequently went into liquidation and the annuitant lodged a proof in the winding up for the capitalised value of the annuity. The liquidator rejected the proof on, among other grounds, the ground that the deed was *ultra vires* the company. Eve J held that, although the company's memorandum contained an express power to pension widows of ex-employees of the company, this did not extend to pensioning widows of ex-directors. Accordingly, the transaction in question had to be justified, if at all, under an implied power to pension widows of ex-directors. . . .

TEMPLEMAN LJ: The findings of the judge are sufficient to support the suspicion that the company could not afford to pay out £10,000 for the benefit of Mr Horsley senior, but this suspicion is largely based on hindsight. The accounts show that business was expanding, that there were no discernible cash flow problems and that past profits were sufficient to absorb half of the payment for the pension, leaving the other half to be absorbed in the future. There seemed to be every indication that with the profits anticipated, and the possibility of reducing directors' salaries if necessary, the remainder of the payment for the pension could be absorbed by the company. In these circumstances it is difficult to convict the directors of negligence. It is impossible to convict them of gross negligence amounting to misfeasance because the allegation was never clearly levied, the directors were not even accused by the receiver and did not give evidence, and the judge therefore made no sufficient finding.

I would dismiss the appeal on the grounds that the payment was *intra vires* the company and on the ground that misfeasance by the directors was not proved.

SOURCE 86
Rolled Steel Products (Holdings) Ltd *v* British Steel Corporation
(Court of Appeal 1984) [1986] Ch 246; [1985] 3 All ER 52

The objects of the plaintiff company authorised it to 'lend or advance money or give credit to such persons, firms or companies and on such terms as may seem expedient, and . . . to give guarantees or become security for any such persons, firms or companies'.

A complicated series of transactions between the plaintiff, the defendant and a third company formed by the majority shareholders of the plaintiff resulted in a guarantee being given by the plaintiff to secure a debt owing by

---

1 [1932] 2 Ch 46; 48 TLR 248

the third company to the defendant. This action was one for a declaration that the guarantee and the debenture issued to secure it were void as being ultra vires the plaintiff.

SLADE LJ:

(5) *The ultra vires point*

For many years, the phrase *ultra vires* has from time to time been used by company lawyers in two senses. Primarily it is used to describe acts which are beyond the capacity of a company. As is pointed out by the editors of *Gore-Browne on Companies* (43rd edn) para 3–1, the phrase is also sometimes used to describe acts which are not beyond the capacity of the company but simply beyond the authority of either the board of directors or a majority of the shareholders.

In many instances, the sense in which the phrase is being used is far from clear. However, I think it plain that paragraphs 11 and 13 of the statement of claim in this case, in alleging that each of the guarantee and the debenture was '*ultra vires* and void', were intended to allege that their execution was beyond the *corporate capacity* of R.S.P. on the grounds that they were executed not for the purposes or benefit of R.S.P. but for the purposes or benefit of Mr Shenkman.

Subject to a point relating to the true construction of the words 'as may seem expedient' in clause 3(K) of the memorandum of association, there is no doubt that these two transactions fell within *the letter* of clauses 3(K) and (L) of the memorandum. Accordingly, two important points of principle which arise in the present context may be expressed thus: Is a transaction which falls within the letter of the powers conferred on a company incorporated under the Companies Acts, but is effected for a purpose not authorised by its memorandum of association, properly to be regarded as being beyond the corporate capacity of the company? Apart from section 9(1) of the European Communities Act 1972, is such a transaction capable of conferring rights on a third party dealing with the company and, if so, in what circumstances?

The legal personality of a company incorporated under the Companies Acts exists only for the purpose of its incorporation, as defined in the objects clause, which have to be set out in its memorandum of association in the manner required by section 2(1)(c) of the Companies Act 1948. It does not, however, follow that any act is beyond its capacity unless expressly authorised by its objects clause. Any such company is treated as having implied powers to do any act which is reasonably incidental to the attainment or pursuit of any of its express objects, unless such act is expressly prohibited by the memorandum: see *Re Horsley & Weight Ltd*[1] per Buckley LJ. Strictly, therefore, it is not essential for the memorandum to insert any reference at all to mere powers, as distinct from objects. Indeed, in *Cotman v Brougham*,[2] Lord Wrenbury deprecated the widespread practice of introducing what should properly be called mere powers in memoranda, as opposed to articles of association, though he confessed that, when a junior at the Bar, he himself had had to yield to it after 'a vain struggle'.

The statutory requirement that the objects of a company shall be specified in the memorandum marks one important difference between objects and powers. In my judgment, however, whether a particular transaction, carried out in purported exercise of an express or implied power contained in a company's

---

1 [1982] Ch 442; [1982] 3 All ER 1045 (see p 234)
2 [1918] AC 514; 87 LJ Ch 379

memorandum of association, is within the capacity of the company must still depend on the true construction of that memorandum.

Correctly, therefore, in my opinion, counsel for the defendants' (Mr Heyman QC) argument has focussed attention in the present context on the words of the memorandum of R.S.P. His first submission has been that the guarantee was *intra vires* R.S.P. as a matter of corporate capacity because the provisions of clause 3(K) of the memorandum of R.S.P., read together with the closing words of that clause, set out a separate independent object, which R.S.P. was capable of carrying on as such, and that the execution of the guarantee fell within that provision.

If this submission as to the construction of clause 3(K) were well founded, I think the suggested conclusion would follow and that, while the relevant transactions might have involved breaches of duty on the part of the directors of R.S.P., there would be no possible question of their having been beyond its corporate capacity. For the recent decision of this court in *Re Horsley & Weight Ltd* has made clear, if this was not clear before, that:

> 'the doing of an act which is expressed (by the company's memorandum) to be, and is capable of being, an independent object of the company cannot be *ultra vires*, for it is by definition something which the company is formed to do and so must be *intra vires*.'

Furthermore, I think this decision also shows that this same principle applies whether or not the transaction in question is of a gratuitous nature:

> 'The objects of a company do not need to be commercial; they can be charitable or philanthropic; indeed they can be whatever the original incorporators wish, provided that they are legal. Nor is there any reason why a company should not part with its fund gratuitously or for non-commercial reasons if to do so is within its declared objects.'

In the light of the observations of Buckley LJ in that case, of Pennycuick J in *Charterbridge Corporation Ltd v Lloyds Bank Ltd*,[1] and of Oliver J in *Re Halt Garage (1964) Ltd*,[2] the three tests of *ultra vires* suggested by Eve J in an often-cited passage in his judgment in *Re Lee, Behrens & Co Ltd*,[3] should, in my opinion, now be recognised as being of no assistance, and indeed positively misleading, when the relevant question is whether a particular gratuitous transaction is within a company's corporate capacity. To this extent, the tests should, I think, be finally laid to rest, though they may well be helpful in considering whether or not in any given case directors have abused the powers vested in them by the company.

The question whether clause 3(K) of R.S.P.'s memorandum contains a separate independent object of the company is purely one of construction of that memorandum. The decision of the House of Lords in *Cotman v Brougham* requires that, in answering it, full force must be given, so far as possible, to the provision at the end of clause 3 of the memorandum, which directs that each sub-clause shall be construed independently of the other sub-clauses. I accept counsel's submission for the defendants that clause 3(K) must be treated as containing a substantive object unless either (i) the subject matter of this sub-paragraph is by its nature incapable of constituting a substantive object (as was the power to borrow in *Re Introductions Ltd, Introductions Ltd v National Provincial Bank Ltd* [1969] 1 All ER 887, [1970] Ch 199), or (ii) the wording of the memorandum shows expressly or by implication that the sub-clause was intended

1 [1970] Ch 62; [1969] 2 All ER 1185
2 [1982] 3 All ER 1016 (see p 231)
3 [1932] 2 Ch 46; 48 TLR 248

merely to constitute an ancillary power only: see, for example, the observations of Buckley J in the latter case at first instance ([1968] 2 All ER 1221 at 1224).

Counsel has submitted, and I agree, that there is no reason in principle why a company should not be formed for the specific purpose, inter alia, of giving guarantees, whether gratuitous or otherwise, rather unusual though such an object might be.

Attention, however, has to be directed to the particular wording of clause 3(K). The authority to give guarantees and become security conferred by the second limb of the sub-clause is not an unrestricted authority. It is merely an authority to give guarantees or become security for 'any such persons, firms or companies'. The six words just quoted echo the words of the first limb of the sub-clause, which authorise the company to —

> 'lend and advance money or give credit to such persons, firms or companies and on such terms as may seem expedient, and in particular to customers of and others having dealings with the Company . . . '

The phrase 'as may seem expedient' necessarily implies that there is some criterion by which expediency is to be tested. The only possible criterion, in my opinion, can only mean 'as may seem expedient for the furtherance of the objects of the company'. The references in clause 3(K) to the giving of credit and to customers of and persons having dealings with the company, make it additionally clear that the sub-clause in its context was intended to comprise merely a series of ancillary powers. It follows that, in my opinion, the power to give guarantees and become security, which are the relevant powers in the present case, are not to be construed as independent objects of R.S.P. and the judge was right in so holding. Correspondingly, I think he was right to reject the defendants' argument that the relevant transactions were intra vires R.S.P., in so far as that argument was based on the hypothesis that the powers conferred by clause 3(K) were independent objects of R.S.P.

What, then, is the position if (as I have concluded) the power to give guarantees and to become security are to be regarded as mere powers ancillary to the objects of R.S.P.? Even on this footing, R.S.P., in executing the guarantee and the debenture, was performing acts of a nature which, at least seemingly, it was expressly authorised by clause 3(K) and (L) of its memorandum to perform. The particular exercises of these powers were, on the face of them, well *capable of falling within the objects of R.S.P.*

The judge, as I have read his judgment, accepted that these transactions were capable of falling within the scope of the wording of the powers conferred on R.S.P. by its memorandum. Nevertheless, he considered that there is a general principle of company law that a transaction, which ostensibly falls within the scope of the wording of a company's memorandum but is in fact entered into for some purpose not authorised by that memorandum, will be *ultra vires* the company in what he called the 'wider sense', and will confer rights on another party only if he can show that he dealt with the company in good faith and did not have notice that the transaction was entered into for an unauthorised purpose (see [1982] 3 All ER 1057 at 1077, [1982] Ch 478 at 499). It was primarily on the basis of this principle that the judge ultimately held the defendants in the present case liable to restore the moneys which they had received.

As Lord Selborne said in *Ashbury Railway Carriage and Iron Co (Ltd) v Riche* (1875) LR 7 HL 653 at 693:

'. . . a statutory corporation created by Act of Parliament for a particular purpose, is limited, as to all its powers, by the purposes of its incorporation as defined in that Act.'

Strict logic might therefore appear to require that any act purported to be done by a company in purported exercise of powers ancillary to its objects conferred on it by its memorandum of association, whether express or implied, (eg a power to borrow) would necessarily, and in every case, be beyond its capacity and therefore wholly void if such act was in fact performed for purposes other than those of its incorporation. However, the practical difficulties resulting from such a conclusion for persons dealing with a company carrying on a business authorised by its memorandum, would be intolerable. As Buckley J put it, in regard to a power to borrow, *Re David Payne & Co Ltd.*[1]

'A corporation, every time it wants to borrow, cannot be called upon by the lender to expose all its affairs, so that the lender can say, "Before I lend you anything, I must investigate how you carry on your business, and I must know why you want the money, and how to apply it, and when you do have it I must see you apply it in the right way". It is perfectly impossible to work out such a principle.'

The *David Payne* decision, in my opinion, indicates the proper alternative approach. In that case, the company concerned had express power under its memorandum of association 'to borrow and raise money for the purposes of the company business'. It borrowed money and issued a debenture to secure the loan. Its liquidator claimed that the debenture was *ultra vires* and void because there was evidence that the borrowing had not in fact been made for the purposes of the company's business. Buckley J in his judgment considered the force of the phrase 'for the purposes of the company's business'. He asked the question:

'Is it a condition attached to the exercise of the power that the money should be borrowed for the purposes of the business or is that a matter to be determined as between the shareholders and the directors?'

In the course of answering this question he said:

'A corporation cannot do anything except for the purposes of its business, borrowing or anything else; everything else is beyond its power and is *ultra vires*. So that the words "for the purposes of the company's business" are a mere expression of that which would be involved if there were no such words.'

This passage has been frequently echoed in later cases and, perhaps not surprisingly, has on occasions been read as referring to the capacity of the company. However, I think that, in using the phrase *ultra vires* in this particular context, Buckley J can only have meant '*ultra vires* the directors'. This, in my opinion, is made clear by what followed. He accepted that, if the phrase 'for the purpose of the company's business' was a condition attached to the exercise of the power, a loan would be *ultra vires* and void if the condition had not been complied with. He did not, however, regard it as such a condition; in his view it did no more than state the obvious. In these circumstances, his conclusion was as follows:

---

1 [1904] 2 Ch 608; 73 LJ Ch 849

'If this borrowing was made, as it appears to me at present it was made, for a purpose illegitimate so far as the borrowing company was concerned, that may very well be a matter on which rights may arise as between the shareholders and directors of that company. It may have been a wrongful act on the part of the directors. But I do not think that a person who lends to the company is by any words such as these required to investigate whether the money borrowed is borrowed for a proper purpose or an improper purpose. The borrowing being effected, and the money passing to the company, the subsequent application of the money is a matter in which the directors may have acted wrongly; but that does not affect the principal act, which is the borrowing of the money.'

In these circumstances, he held that the defendants:

'who have paid this money and taken this debenture without notice that the money was going to be applied as it was are not affected by anything arising in regard to that.'

...

Vaughan Williams LJ and Cozens-Hardy LJ expressly approved the manner in which Buckley J had approached the problem. Vaughan Williams LJ expressly, and the other members of the court implicitly, rejected the borrower's first argument that, since the debenture was not issued to raise money for the purposes of the company, it was *ultra vires* altogether 'in the sense that nothing could make it right'. All three members of the court considered that the plaintiff company could succeed if, but only if, it showed that, at the time of the loan, the lending company knew that the money was going to be applied by the borrowers for an improper purpose and that this had not been proved.

The one crucially important point to which Buckley J and the Court of Appeal in *David Payne* did not expressly advert is the basis upon which the lenders would have lost their security if they had known of the improper purpose for which the moneys lent were going to be applied. The basis is, in my opinion, this. The directors of the borrowing company in fact had no authority from the company to take the loan and grant the debenture because these transactions were not effected for the purposes of the company. Nevertheless, as a general rule, a company incorporated under the Companies Acts holds out its directors as having ostensible authority to do on its behalf anything which its memorandum of association, expressly or by implication, gives the company the capacity to do. In *David Payne* the company's memorandum gave it the capacity to borrow. As a matter of construction of the company's memorandum, the court was not prepared to construe the words 'for the purposes of the company's business' as limiting its corporate capacity, but construed them simply as limiting the authority of the directors. In the absence of notice to the contrary, the lenders would thus have been entitled to assume, on the authority of the principle in *Turquand's case*,[1] and on more general principles of the law of agency, that the directors of the borrowing company were acting properly and regularly in the internal management of its affairs and were borrowing for the purposes of the company's business: see for example *Re Hampshire Land*,[2] a decision of Vaughan Williams J which was cited in the *David Payne* case; see also *Bowstead on Agency* (14th edn), pp 241–2 and the cases there cited. However, a party dealing with a company cannot rely on the ostensible authority of its directors to enter

---

1 (1856) 6 E&B 327; 119 ER 886
2 [1896] 2 Ch 743

into a particular transaction, if it knows they in fact have no such authority because it is being entered into for improper purposes. Neither the rule in *Turquand's case* nor more general principles of the law of agency will avail him in such circumstances (see *Bowstead on Agency* (14th edn), p 243). The various passages in the judgments in both courts in the *David Payne* case which refer to the extent of the lender's obligation (if any) to inquire as to the purposes for which the loan is to be used, in my opinion, are not directed at all to the corporate capacity of the borrowing company; they are directed to the right of the lender to rely on the ostensible authority of the borrower's directors.

In *Re Introductions Ltd*,[1] the Court of Appeal again had to consider the validity of debentures granted by a company as security for a loan. The company under clause (N) of its memorandum of association had a general ancillary power to borrow money and to issue debentures to secure its repayment. But this power was not an independent object of the company. As Harman LJ put it: 'borrowing is not an end in itself and must be for some purpose of the company'. The power was not expressed in terms to be exercisable only 'for the purposes of the company' but, following the reasoning of Buckley J in *Re David Payne Ltd* the court held that the words necessarily had to be implied. The company had borrowed money from a bank and granted debentures to secure the loan. But the only business carried on by it was that of pig-breeding, which was a purpose not authorised by its memorandum of association. On the liquidation of the company, a question arose as to the validity of the debentures. Harman LJ, who gave the leading judgment, after deciding that the power to borrow conferred by the memorandum was a mere ancillary power not an independent object, proceeded to cite the following passage from the speech of Lord Parker of Waddington in *Cotman v Brougham*.

'A person who deals with a company is entitled to assume that a company can do everything which it is expressly authorised to do by its memorandum of association, and need not investigate the equities between the company and its shareholders.'

This passage, it will be seen, closely echoes some of the language used by Buckley J in his judgment in the *David Payne case* and is, I think, an expression of the rule in *Turquand's case* and the more general principles of agency to which I have already referred.

Harman LJ went on to say this:

'I would agree that, if the bank did not know what the purpose of the borrowing was, *it need not inquire* (the emphasis is mine) but it did know and I can find nothing in *Cotman v Brougham* to protect it notwithstanding that knowledge.'

The words 'it need not inquire', in my opinion, make it clear that Harman LJ did not regard the borrowing as having been beyond the *capacity* of the company. However, he then went on to point out that the *David Payne* decision shows that the protection afforded by the principle stated by Lord Parker affords no protection to a lender who knows that the money is intended to be misapplied. The absence of any express provision in the company's memorandum of association requiring the loan to be applied for the purposes of the company, in his judgment, did not improve the bank's position, since such a provision would fall to be implied anyway. He concluded . . . 'This borrowing was not for a

---

1 [1970] Ch 199; [1969] 1 All ER 887

legitimate purpose of the company; the bank knew it and *therefore* (the emphasis is mine) cannot rely on its debentures.'

[The judge then discussed *Charterbridge Corporation v Lloyds Bank Ltd* and *Re Halt Garage* and approved of both and then concluded:]

My conclusion from these authorities on these questions of principle may be summarised as follows:

(1) The basic rule is that a company incorporated under the Companies Acts only has the capacity to do those acts which fall within its objects as set out in its memorandum of association or are reasonably incidental to the attainment or pursuit of those objects. Ultimately, therefore, the question whether a particular transaction is within or outside its capacity must depend on the true construction of the memorandum.

(2) Nevertheless, if a particular act (such as each of the transactions of 22 January 1969 in the present case) is of a category which, on the true construction of the company's memorandum, is *capable* of being performed as reasonably incidental to the attainment or pursuit of its objects, it will not be rendered *ultra vires* the company merely because in a particular instance its directors, in performing the act in its name, are in truth doing so for purposes other than those set out in its memorandum. Subject to any express restrictions on the relevant power which may be contained in the memorandum, the state of mind or knowledge of the persons managing the company's affairs or of the persons dealing with it is irrelevant in considering questions of corporate capacity.

(3) While due regard must be paid to any express conditions attached to or limitations on powers contained in a company's memorandum (eg a power to borrow only up to a specified amount), the court will not ordinarily construe a statement in a memorandum that a particular power is exercisable 'for the purposes of the company' as a condition limiting the company's corporate capacity to exercise the power; it will regard it as simply imposing a limit on the authority of the directors: see the *David Payne case*.

(4) At least in default of the unanimous consent of all the shareholders (as to which see below), the directors of a company will not have *actual* authority from the company to exercise any express or implied power other than for the purposes of the company as set out in its memorandum of association.

(5) A company holds out its directors as having *ostensible* authority to bind the company to any transaction which falls within the powers expressly or impliedly conferred on it by its memorandum of association. Unless he is put on notice to the contrary, a person dealing in good faith with a company which is carrying on an *intra vires* business is entitled to assume that its directors are properly exercising such powers for the purposes of the company as set out in its memorandum. Correspondingly, such a person in such circumstances can hold the company to any transaction of this nature.

(6) If, however, a person dealing with a company is on notice that the directors are exercising the relevant power for purposes other than the purposes of the company, he cannot rely on the ostensible authority of the directors and, on ordinary principles of agency, cannot hold the company to the transaction.

In the present case I construe the words 'as may seem expedient' in clause 3(K) of R.S.P.'s memorandum not as limiting the corporate capacity of R.S.P. but as simply imposing a limit on the authority of its directors. To adapt the wording of Harman LJ in the *Introductions case* following the *David Payne* decision, the guarantee and *pro tanto* the debenture were not executed for a legitimate purpose of R.S.P.; Colvilles and B.S.C. knew it and, therefore, cannot rely on the guarantee and *pro tanto* the debenture. All this results from the ordinary law of agency, not from the corporate powers of R.S.P. The relevant transactions in the present case, in my opinion, were not beyond its corporate capacity.

[It was held, however, that BSC had knowledge of the abuse of power by the directors of R.S.P. and was therefore accountable as a constructive trustee.]

BROWNE-WILKINSON LJ: . . . In my judgment, much of the confusion that has crept into the law flows from the use of the phrase 'ultra vires' in different senses in different contexts. The reconciliation of the authorities can only be achieved if one first defines the sense in which one is using the words 'ultra vires'. Because the literal translation of the words is 'beyond the powers', there are many cases in which the words have been applied to transactions which, although within the capacity of the company, are carried out otherwise than through the correct exercise of the powers of the company by its officers; indeed, that is the sense in which the judge seems to have used the words in this case. For reasons which will appear, in my judgment, the use of the phrase 'ultra vires' should be restricted to those cases where the transaction is beyond the capacity of the company and therefore wholly void.

A company, being an artificial person, has no capacity to do anything outside the objects specified in its memorandum of association. If the transaction is outside the objects, in law it is wholly void. But the objects of a company and the powers conferred on a company to carry out those objects are two different things: see *Cotman v Brougham* [1918] AC 514 esp at 520, 522, [1918–19] All ER Rep 265 esp at 268, 269 per Lord Parker and Lord Wrenbury. If the concept that a company cannot do anything which is not authorised by law had been pursued with ruthless logic, the result might have been reached that a company could not (ie had no capacity) to do anything otherwise than in *due* exercise of its powers. But such ruthless logic has not been pursued and it is clear that a transaction falling within the objects of the company is capable of conferring rights on third parties even though the transaction was an abuse of the powers of the company: see eg *Re David Payne & Co Ltd, Young v David Payne & Co Ltd* [1904] 2 Ch 608. It is therefore established that a company has capacity to carry out a transaction which falls within its objects even though carried out by the wrongful exercise of its powers.

In my judgment, for this purpose the position of a company is analogous to that of a human being who has fiduciary powers. If two trustees convey trust property in breach of trust, the conveyance is not void. As human beings they have the capacity to transfer the legal estate: their capacity to transfer flows from their status as human beings not from the powers conferred on them as trustees. Even if their powers under the trust instrument did not authorise the convey-ance, the legal estate will vest in the transferee. Beneficiaries under the trust would be entitled, if they learnt in time, to restrain the execution of such conveyance in excess of the powers of the trustees. If the beneficiaries only discovered the position after the conveyance, the transferee, if he took with notice, would be personally liable as a constructive trustee and the property conveyed could be recovered: but the conveyance would not be a nullity. So in the case of a limited company, if a transaction falls within the objects of the company (and is therefore within its capacity) it is effective to vest rights in a third party even if the transaction was carried out in excess or abuse of the powers of the company. If the members of the company learn of what is proposed in time, they will be able to restrain such transaction; if they only discover the facts later, their remedy lies against those who have wrongly caused the company to act in excess or abuse of the company's powers. If a third party has received the company's property with notice of the excess or abuse of powers, such third party will be personally liable as a constructive trustee and the company will be able to recover the property: see *Belmont Finance Corp v Williams Furniture Ltd (No 2)* [1980] 1 All ER 393.

However, the analogy between companies and trustees is not complete. As an artificial person, a company can only act by duly authorised agents. Apart from questions of ostensible authority, directors like any other agents can only bind the company by acts done in accordance with the formal requirements of their agency, eg by resolution of the board at a properly constituted meeting. Acts done otherwise than in accordance with these formal requirements will not be the acts of the company. However, the principles of ostensible authority apply to the acts of directors acting as agents of the company and the rule in *Royal British Bank v Turquand* (1856) 6 E & B 327, [1843–60] All ER Rep 435 establishes that a third party dealing in good faith with directors is entitled to assume that the internal steps requisite for the formal validity of the directors' acts have been duly carried through. If, however, the third party has actual or constructive notice that such steps had not been taken, he will not be able to rely on any ostensible authority of the directors and their acts, being in excess of their actual authority, will not be the acts of the company.

The critical distinction is, therefore, between acts done in excess of the capacity of the company on the one hand and acts done in excess or abuse of the powers of the company on the other. If the transaction is beyond the capacity of the company it is in any event a nullity and wholly void; whether or not the third party had notice of the invalidity, property transferred or money paid under such a transaction will be recoverable from the third party. If, on the other hand, the transaction (although in excess or abuse of powers) is within the capacity of the company, the position of the third party depends on whether or not he had notice that the transaction was in excess or abuse of the powers of the company. As between the shareholders and the directors, for most purposes it makes no practical difference whether the transaction is beyond the capacity of the company or merely in excess or abuse of its power: in either event the shareholders will be able to restrain the carrying out of the transaction or hold liable those who have carried it out. Only if the question of ratification by all the shareholders arises will it be material to consider whether the transaction is beyond the capacity of the company since it is established that, although all the shareholders can ratify a transaction within the company's capacity, they cannot ratify a transaction falling outside its objects.

In this judgment I therefore use the words 'ultra vires' as covering only those transactions which the company has no capacity to carry out, ie those things the company cannot do at all as opposed to those things it cannot properly do.

The two badges of a transaction which is ultra vires in that sense are (1) that the transaction is wholly void and (consequentially) (2) that it is irrelevant whether or not the third party had notice. It is therefore in this sense that the transactions in *Re David Payne & Co Ltd* [1904] 2 Ch 608 and *Charterbridge Corp Ltd v Lloyds Bank Ltd* [1969] 2 All ER 1185, [1970] Ch 62 were held not to be ultra vires. The distinction between the capacity of the company and abuse of powers was also drawn by Oliver J in *Re Halt Garage (1964) Ltd* [1982] 3 All ER 1016 at 1034. I consider the reasoning of the decision in *Re Lee Behrens & Co Ltd* [1932] 2 Ch 46, [1932] All ER Rep 889 to be wrong for the reasons given by Pennycuick J in the *Charterbridge* case [1969] 2 All ER 1185 at 1190–1191, [1970] Ch 62 at 70–71: the decision itself can only be justified (if at all) on the footing that the widow who was granted a pension had notice of the impropriety of the grant. The only other case which, at first sight, is difficult to reconcile with my views is *Re Introductions Ltd, Introductions Ltd v National Provincial Bank Ltd* [1968] 2 All ER 1221; *affd* [1969] 1 All ER 887, [1970] Ch 199, CA, which I will consider later.

For these reasons, in considering a claim based on ultra vires, the first step must be to determine what are the objects (as opposed to the powers) of a company. Not all activities mentioned in the objects clause are necessarily objects in the strict sense: some of them may only be capable of existing as, or on their true construction are, ancillary powers: see *Cotman v Brougham* [1918] AC 514, [1918–19] All ER Rep 265 and *Re Introductions Ltd*. And this may be the position even if the memorandum of association contains the usual 'separate objects' clause: such a clause is not capable of elevating into an object of the company that which is in essence a power: see *Re Introductions Ltd*.

If, on construction of the objects clause, the transactions fall within the objects (as opposed to the powers), it will not be ultra vires since the company has the capacity to enter into the transaction. If the objects clause contains provisions (whether objects or powers) which show that a transaction of the kind in question is within the capacity of the company, that transaction will not be ultra vires. Sometimes the drafting of the memorandum and articles may be such that they put third parties on notice of the fact that certain things can only properly be done subject to certain conditions being satisfied. If the third party is put on notice in this way, he will not be able to rely on any exercise of the power which he knew or ought to have discovered did not comply with such conditions. But a provision that a power can be exercised only 'for the purposes of the company's business' does not require a third party to satisfy himself that the power is in fact being exercised for that purpose.

In my judgment, the propositions in the last two paragraphs accord with the decisions in *Re David Payne & Co Ltd* [1904] 2 Ch 608 and *Charterbridge Corp Ltd v Lloyds Bank Ltd* [1969] 2 All ER 1185, [1970] Ch 62. As Slade LJ has pointed out, in the *David Payne* case the objects clause of the company stated expressly that the power to borrow was 'for the purposes of the company's business'; yet the borrowing (which was not in fact for the purpose of the company's business) was held not to be ultra vires. Buckley J plainly treated the provision as a power not an object (see [1904] 2 Ch 608 at 612). Vaughan Williams LJ held that the fact that the validity of the debenture depended on whether or not the lender had knowledge of the impropriety showed that the transaction was not ultra vires. Moreover, it was held that, knowledge being a necessary requirement to render the loan unenforceable, the lender was not put on inquiry whether the money was being borrowed for the purposes of the company's business, notwithstanding that the power to borrow was expressly limited to borrowing for those purposes (see [1904] 2 Ch 608 at 615). That case, therefore, is clear authority for two propositions: (1) that where there is a power to borrow for the purposes of the company's business (even if contained in the objects clause) and the borrowing is made otherwise than for those purposes, the borrowing is not void as being ultra vires; and (2) a third party is not put on notice by an express requirement that the power is only exercisable for the purposes of the company's business.

The main difficulty in reconciling the authorities is *Re Introductions Ltd* [1969] 1 All ER 887, [1970] Ch 199. In my judgment, however, the decision in that case accords with the views I have expressed. The bank seeking to enforce the debenture had actual knowledge that the company was going to use the borrowed moneys for a purpose (pig breeding) which was wholly outside its main objects. The provision relating to borrowing in the memorandum of association was construed as being an ancillary power to borrow for the purposes of the company's business. Accordingly, the lender had actual notice of all the facts necessary to appreciate that the borrowing was in excess of the powers, ie an abuse of powers. It is to be noted that in the Court of Appeal judgments the transaction is nowhere categorised as ultra vires and void. Indeed, as Slade LJ has pointed out, the Court of Appeal held that the liability of the bank depended on the fact that it had notice. Buckley J at first instance described the borrowing as being ultra vires: but, in my judgment, this was merely an unguarded use of language since he also regarded the bank's knowledge of the facts as being a crucial element rendering the debenture unenforceable (see [1968] 2 All ER 1221 at 1225). In my judgment, *Re Introductions Ltd* is not a decision relating to ultra vires in the strict sense: it is an example of a case in which a third party has entered into a transaction with a company with actual notice that the transaction was an abuse of power and accordingly could not enforce the transaction against the company.

I summarise my conclusions as follows. (1) To be ultra vires, a transaction has to be outside the capacity of the company, not merely in excess or abuse of the powers of the company. (2) The question whether a transaction is outside the capacity of the company depends solely on whether, on the true construction of its memorandum of association, the transaction is capable of falling within the objects of the company as opposed to being a proper exercise of the powers of the company. (3) Notwithstanding the fact that the provision authorising the company to enter into the particular transaction is found in the objects clause and there is a provision requiring each paragraph to be construed as a separate object, such provision may be merely a power (and not an object) if either it is incapable of existing as a separate object or it can only be construed as a power ancillary to the other objects in the strict sense. (4) If a transaction falls within the objects (and therefore the capacity) of the company, it is not ultra vires the company and accordingly it is not absolutely void. (5) If a company enters into a transaction which is intra vires (as being within its capacity) but in excess or abuse of its powers, such transaction will be set aside at the instance of the shareholders. (6) A third party, who has notice (actual or constructive) that a transaction, although intra vires the company, was entered into in excess or abuse of the powers of the company, cannot enforce such transaction against the company and will be accountable as constructive trustee for any money or property of the company received by the third party. (7) The fact that a power is expressly or impliedly limited so as to be exercisable only 'for the purposes of the company's business' (or other words to that effect), does not put a third party on inquiry whether the power is being so exercised, ie such provision does not give him constructive notice of excess or abuse of such power.

Applying those principles to the present case, in my judgment, no question of ultra vires arises. For the reasons given both by the judge and by Slade LJ the provisions of clause 3(K) of the memorandum of association of R.S.P. do not constitute a separate object but can only be construed as a power. R.S.P. had the capacity to enter into the transactions involving the giving of guarantees and could properly have done so if they had been expedient in the interests of R.S.P.'s business. If B.S.C. had known no more than that R.S.P. was purporting to give the guarantee as being expedient for R.S.P.'s business, the transaction would have been unimpeachable as against B.S.C.

But, as the judge and Slade LJ have demonstrated, B.S.C. had actual knowledge of facts which showed that the giving of the guarantee and the debenture was an abuse of powers by the directors of R.S.P. since the transaction was not even considered to be for the benefit of R.S.P. The borrowing by R.S.P. from B.S.C. of the £401,118 was formally invalid since such borrowing was not approved by a quorate board meeting of R.S.P. and the defence based on the rule in *Turquand's* case (1856) 6 E & B 327, [1843–60] All ER 435 was neither pleaded or established. B.S.C. had constructive knowledge of this formal invalidity. Accordingly, B.S.C. and the receiver are accountable as constructive trustees for all the moneys of R.S.P. received by them with such notice.

SOURCE 87
Aveling Barford Ltd v Perion Ltd
[1989] BCLC 626

The plaintiff company, all of whose shares were owned or controlled by Dr Lee, sold a piece of land to the defendant company (also controlled by Dr Lee) for £350,000. A few months later the defendant sold the land for £1,150,000. There was also evidence that immediately after the sale to the defendant, the land was worth £650,000. The plaintiff company was solvent at the time of the sale but its accumulated deficits on its profit and loss account prevented any distributions of dividends among its shareholders. Judgment in default of defence was granted in an action by the plaintiff for compensation against the defendant on the basis that the latter was accountable as a constructive trustee for the proceeds of sale of the property. These were proceedings to set aside that judgment, and to succeed in such proceedings it had to be shown that the defendant had an arguable defence.

HOFFMANN J . . . counsel for the defendant, submitted that whether or not the sale to Perion was a breach of fiduciary duty by Dr Lee, it cannot be challenged by the company because it was unanimously approved by the shareholders. This approval was both informal and formal. Informal approval was given at the time of the sale by virtue of the fact that Dr Lee owned or controlled the entire issued share capital. Formally, a sale at £750,000 was approved when the 1987 accounts were adopted at the company's annual general meeting. For the purposes of this motion I shall assume that shareholder consent was given in both these ways.

The general rule is that any act which falls within the express or implied powers of a company conferred by its memorandum of association, whether or not a breach of duty on the part of the directors, will be binding on the company if it is approved or subsequently ratified by the shareholders: see *Rolled Steel Products (Holdings) Ltd v British Steel Corp* [1984] BCLC 466 at 507, [1985] 3 All ER 52 at 85, [1986] Ch 246 at 296. But this rule is subject to exceptions created by the general law and one such exception is that a company cannot without the leave of the court or the adoption of a special procedure return its capital to its shareholders. It follows that a transaction which amounts to an unauthorised return of capital is ultra vires and cannot be validated by shareholder ratification or approval. Whether or not the transaction is a distribution to shareholders does not depend exclusively on what the parties choose to call it. The court looks at the substance rather than the outward appearance. Thus in *Ridge Securities Ltd v IRC* [1964] 1 All ER 275, [1964] 1 WLR 479 Pennycuick J was concerned with a tax avoidance scheme by a solvent company which involved the grant of a debenture to its parent under which very large and uncommercial sums were payable, purportedly as interest. He said that the 'interest' payments were ultra vires because they were dressed-up gifts of capital to the parent company ([1964] 1 All ER 275 at 288, [1964] 1 WLR 479 at 495):

'A company can only lawfully deal with its assets in furtherance of its objects. The corporators may take assets out of the company by way of dividend, or, with the leave of the court, by way of reduction of capital, or in a winding up.

They may of course acquire them for full consideration. They cannot take assets out of the company by way of voluntary disposition, however described, and if they attempt to do so, the disposition is ultra vires the company.'

That case was followed by Oliver J in *Re Halt Garage (1964) Ltd* [1982] 3 All ER 1016. In that case the liquidator of the company challenged payments of £30 a week purporting to be director's remuneration to a director and shareholder who had rendered no services to the company. Oliver J decided that so far as the payments exceeded £10 a week, which he considered to be the maximum remuneration reasonably payable to someone who merely held the office of director, they were dressed-up returns of capital to a shareholder and therefore ultra vires. The test, said the learned judge, was —

[The judge quoted the passage beginning 'whether the transaction in question . . .' and ending 'shareholders as such', see p 234, and continued:]

This did not mean that the payments need to have been made fraudulently or in bad faith: 'bona fides (in the sense of absence of fraudulent intention) and genuineness are [not] necessarily the same thing.' Applying his test, the learned judge said that no challenge could be made to the payments made at a time when the company had enough distributable reserves to have made equivalent payments by way of dividend. But thereafter —

'the sums paid to [the director] were so out of proportion to any possible value attributable to her holding of office that the court is entitled to treat them as not being genuine payments of remuneration at all but dressed-up dividends out of capital, like the dressed-up payments of "interest" in the *Ridge Securities case*.'

(See [1982] 3 All ER 1016 at 1042.) So it seems to me in this case that looking at the matter objectively, the sale to Perion was not a genuine exercise of the company's power under its memorandum to sell its assets. It was a sale at a gross undervalue for the purpose of enabling a profit to be realised by an entity controlled and put forward by its sole beneficial shareholder. This was as much a dressed-up distribution as the payment of excessive interest in *Ridge Securities* or excessive remuneration in *Halt Garage*. The company had at the time no distributable reserves and the sale was therefore ultra vires and incapable of validation by the approval or ratification of the shareholder. The fact that the distribution was to Perion rather than to Dr Lee or his other entities which actually held the shares in Aveling Barford is in my judgment irrelevant.

Counsel for the defendants relied on a passage in the judgment of Slade LJ in *Rolled Steel Products (Holdings) Ltd v British Corp* [1984] BCLC 466 at 507, [1985] 3 All ER 52 at 85, [1986] Ch 246 at 296:

[The judge quoted the passage beginning ' . . . if a particular act . . . is of a category . . .' and ending 'questions of corporate capacity', see p 243, and continued:]

Counsel for the defendants says that this was an act within the terms of the memorandum. It may have been a sale at an undervalue, but it was certainly a sale: a conveyance in exchange for a payment in money. It was not a sham. The terms of the transaction were in no way different from those appearing on the face of the documents. The purpose for which it was done was therefore irrelevant. Counsel submits that the test for the genuineness of the transaction proposed by Oliver J in *Re Halt Garage* admits by the back door all the questions about the motives, state of mind and knowledge of the company's directors which the Court of Appeal appeared to have expelled by the front door in the *Rolled Steel* case.

It is clear however that Slade LJ excepted from his general principle cases which he described as involving a 'fraud on creditors' (see [1984] BCLC 466 at 508, [1985] 3 All ER 52 at 86, [1986] Ch 246 at 296). As an example of such a case, he cited *Re Halt Garage*. Counsel for the defendants said that frauds on creditors meant transactions entered into when the company was insolvent. In this case Aveling Barford was not at the relevant time insolvent. But I do not think that the phrase was intended to have such a narrow meaning. The rule that capital may not be returned to shareholders is a rule for the protection of creditors and the evasion of that rule falls within what I think Slade LJ had in mind when he spoke of a fraud on creditors. There is certainly nothing in his judgment to suggest that he disapproved of the actual decisions in *Re Halt Garage* or *Ridge Securities*. As for the transaction not being a sham, I accept that it was in law a sale. The false dressing it wore was that of a sale at arms' length or at market value. It was the fact that it was known and intended to be a sale at an undervalue which made it an unlawful distribution.

It follows that in my judgment even on the view of the facts most favourable to Perion, it has no arguable defence and the motion to set aside the judgment must be dismissed.

Reform of the Doctrine of Ultra Vires

In 1972, the European Communities Act was passed as the constitutional instrument by which the UK acceded to the European Communities. Section 9 of this Act amended UK company law to comply with the terms of the First European Community Company Law Harmonisation Directive (see below) passed in 1968. Part of this Directive dealt with the protection of third parties in their dealings with companies (Source 88). This amendment was very close to what had been recommended by the Company Law Committee of 1962 ('the Jenkins Committee'), but was less radical than the recommendation of the Committee on Company Law Amendment ('the Cohen Committee') in 1945 (Sources 89 and 90). A recent report by Professor Daniel Prentice for the Department of Trade and Industry recommended the abolition of the doctrine of ultra vires (Source 91).

Section 9(1) of the European Communities Act 1972 reappeared in the 1985 consolidation as s 35 of the Companies Act. The Prentice Report was acted upon in the 1989 Companies Act, s 108(1) of which caused there to be substituted for s 35, new ss 35, 35A and 35B. The effect of these new provisions was to abolish the principle of ultra vires in relation to registered companies and to eliminate some of the issues of principle which had been left unresolved by the original implementation of the Directive. Note also the effect of s 110 of the Companies Act 1989 in introducing the new s 3A and substituting the new s 4 of the CA 1985.

To what extent do the changes introduced by the Companies Act 1989 deal with the problems raised in *International Sales and Agencies v Marcus* (Source 92) and *TCB Ltd v Gray* (Source 93)?

SOURCE 88
European Community Directive
68/151/EEC

Article 9

1. Acts done by the organs of the company shall be binding upon it even if those acts are not within the objects of the company, unless such acts exceed the powers that the law confers or allows to be conferred on those organs. However, Member States may provide that the company shall not be bound where such acts are outside the objects of the company if it proves that the third party knew that the act was outside those objects or could not in view of the circumstances be unaware thereof; disclosure of the statutes shall not of itself be sufficient proof thereof.

2. The limits on the powers of the organs of the company, arising under the statutes or from a decision by the competent bodies, may never be relied on as against third parties, even if they have been disclosed.

3. If the national laws provide that authority to represent a company may, in derogation from the law governing the subject, be conferred by the statutes on one person or on several persons acting jointly, that law may provide that such provision in the statutes may be relied on as against third parties on condition that it relates to the general power of representation.

SOURCE 89
Report of the Company Law Committee 1962 ('Jenkins Committee')

42. We recommend that:

(a) a contract entered into between a company and another party (including a shareholder contracting otherwise than in his capacity as a shareholder) contracting with the company in good faith should not be held valid as against the other party on the ground that it was beyond the powers of the company: he should not, however, be allowed to enforce the contract without submitting to perform his part of it so far as it is unperformed;

(b) in entering into any such contract the other party should be entitled to assume without investigation that the company is in fact possessed of the necessary power; and should not by reason of his omission so to investigate be deemed not to have acted in good faith, or be deprived of his right to enforce the contract on the ground that at the time of entering into it he had constructive notice of any limitations on the powers of the company, or on the powers of any director or other person to act on the company's behalf, imposed by its memorandum or articles of association;

(c) the other party should not be deprived of his right to enforce the contract on the ground that he had actual knowledge of the contents of the memorandum and articles at the time of entering into the contract if he honestly and reasonably failed to appreciate that they had the effect of precluding the company (or any director or other person on its behalf) from entering into the contract in question;

(d) there should be no change in the position of a company in relation to *ultra vires* contracts entered into by it.

SOURCE 90
Report of the Company Law Amendment Committee 1945 ('Cohen Committee')

The memorandum of a company defines its objects and a company's objects are limited to those expressly mentioned and such as are ancillary to the expressed objects. A contract made by the directors upon a matter not within the ambit of the company's objects is *ultra vires* the company, and, therefore, beyond the powers of the directors. This principle is intended to protect both those who deal with the company, and its shareholders.

12. Doctrine of *ultra vires*. — Had memoranda of association closely followed the forms in the First Schedule to the Act, this protection might have been real, but, partly with a view to obviating the necessity of applying to the Court for confirmation of an alteration of objects, a practice has grown up of drafting memoranda of association very widely and at great length so as to enable the company to engage in any form of activity in which it might conceivably at some later date wish to engage and so as to confer on it all ancillary powers which it might conceivably require in connection with such activities. In consequence the doctrine of *ultra vires* is an illusory protection for the shareholders and yet may be a pitfall for third parties dealing with the company. For example, if a company which has not taken powers to carry on a taxi-cab service, nevertheless does so, third persons who have sold the taxi-cabs to the company or who have been employed to drive them, may have no legal right to recover payment from the company. We consider that, as now applied to companies, the *ultra vires* doctrine serves no positive purpose but is, on the other hand, a cause of unnecessary prolixity and vexation. We think that every company, whether incorporated before or after the passing of a new Companies Act, should, notwithstanding anything omitted from its memorandum of association, have as regards third parties the same powers as an individual. Existing provisions in memoranda as regards the powers of companies and any like provisions introduced into memoranda in future should operate solely as a contract between a company and its shareholders as to the powers exercisable by the directors. In our view it would then be a sufficient safeguard if such provisions were alterable by special resolution without the necessity of obtaining the sanction of the Court, subject in cases where debentures have been issued before the coming into force of a new Act, to the consent of the debenture-holders by extraordinary resolution passed at a meeting held under the provisions contained in the trust deed or (in the absence of such provisions) convened by the Court.

SOURCE 91
Reform of the Ultra Vires Rule
(DTI, Prentice 1987)

50. It is proposed that:

(i) a company should have the capacity to do any act whatsoever;

(ii) a third party dealing with a company should not be affected by the contents of any document merely because it is registered with the registrar of companies or with the company (this could be made subject to appropriate exceptions);

(iii) a company should be bound by the acts of its board or of an individual director;

(iv) a third party should be under no obligation to determine the scope of the authority of a company's board or an individual director, or the contents of a company's articles or memorandum (this should extend to documents which have to be registered under section 380 of the Companies Act 1985);

(v) a third party who has actual knowledge that a board or an individual director do not possess authority to enter into a transaction on behalf of the company should not be allowed to enforce it against the company but the company should be free to ratify it. The same result should obtain where a third party has actual knowledge that the transaction falls outside the company's objects but in this case ratification should be by special resolution;

(vi) knowledge in this context will require understanding and it will only be knowledge of the individual entering into the particular transaction which will be relevant;

(vii) the proposal in (v) should be modified where a third party is an officer or director of the company and in this situation constructive knowledge should be sufficient to render the transaction unenforceable and for this purpose constructive knowledge should mean the type of knowledge which may reasonably be expected of a person carrying out the functions of that director or officer of that company.

SOURCE 92
International Sales and Agencies *v* Marcus
(Queen's Bench Division 1982) [1982] 3 All ER 551; [1982] 2 CMLR 46

The company was suing to recover £30,000 which had been paid to the defendants at the instance of one Munsey, who ran the plaintiff company before he died. The circumstances leading up to the payment were that the defendant had made a loan of £30,000 to a Mr Fancy, who prior to his death, had owned all but one share in the plaintiff company.

LAWSON J: . . . I now turn to the question raised by the amended defence, which is whether the defendants' liability to the plaintiffs to account for the moneys they knowingly received in breach of trust is affected by the provisions of section 9(1) of the European Communities Act 1972. This Act was passed to give effect in England to EEC Council Directive 68/151 of 9 March 1968. Section 9(1) of the 1972 Act reads as follows:

'In favour of a person dealing with a company in good faith, any transaction decided on by the directors shall be deemed to be one which it is within the capacity of the company to enter into, and the power of the directors to bind the company shall be deemed to be free of any limitation under the memorandum or articles of association; and a party to a transaction so decided on shall not be bound to enquire as to the capacity of the company to enter into it or as to any such limitation on the powers of the directors, and shall be presumed to have acted in good faith unless the contrary is proved.'

It is to be observed that the section (indeed the Act in which it is set) does not in fact reproduce, first, the statement of purposes which precedes the text of the actual articles in the directive; second, the heading of Section II of the directive (this is the section of the directive which contains article 9, which is the ancestor of section 9(1) of the 1972 Act) is: 'Validity of obligations entered into by a company'; third, there is an important qualification in the first paragraph of article 9 of the directive (which broadly corresponds with section 9(1) of the 1972 Act) which appears in the second paragraph of article 9. The introductory words of Directive 68/151 make it clear that what the directive is concerned with is the obligations of companies. For example, one of the recitals provides:

> 'Whereas the co-ordination of national provisions concerning disclosure, the validity of obligations entered into by, and the nullity of, such companies is of special importance . . . [and further on:] whereas the protection of third parties must be ensured by provisions which restrict to the greatest possible extent the grounds, on which obligations entered into in the name of the company are not valid . . .'

In my judgment, those passages and the heading of Section II of the directive are reflected effectively in the words: 'In favour of a person dealing with a company in good faith, any transaction decided on . . .' This is directed at transactions with companies which obviously will result in the companies being under obligations which before the enactment of the 1972 Act they might have been able to avoid by the application of the old *ultra vires* doctrine. The other passage in the directive which is not reflected in section 9(1) relates to the state of mind of the person dealing with the company. The second paragraph of article 9(1) reads:

> 'However, Member States may provide that the company shall not be bound where such acts are outside the objects of the company, if it proves that the third party knew that the act was outside those objects . . . [and it goes on:] or could not in view of the circumstances have been unaware of it . . .'

Whilst article 9(1) reflects, if it proves that the third party knew the act was outside those objects, it does not directly reflect or reflect in so many words, the alternative, 'or could not in view of the circumstances have been unaware of it'. Which seems to me very close to turning a blind eye. In my judgment I am entitled to look at the Council's directive as an aid to the interpretation of section 9(1) of the 1972 Act. I conclude, first, that section 9(1) relates only to legal obligations of the company under transactions with third parties, whether or not they be within or without its powers; second, that section 9(1) is designed to give relief to innocent third parties entering into transactions with companies against the operation in England of the old *ultra vires* doctrine; third, that the test of lack of good faith in somebody entering into obligations with a company will be found either in proof of his actual knowledge that the transaction was *ultra vires* the company or where it can be shown that such a person could not in view of all the circumstances, have been unaware that he was party to a transaction *ultra vires*.

It seems to me, so far as the amended defence is concerned, I have to ask a number of questions. First, does section 9(1) of the 1972 Act at all affect the principles of constructive trust in relation to the recipients of companies' moneys knowingly paid in breach of trust, as happened, I find, in this case? Second, if the answer to the first question be No, then there is no need to go any further; but, if the answer to the first question were Yes, one must then answer a number of further questions and these, in my judgment, are: were the defendants in this case '*dealing*' with the plaintiff companies (I emphasise the word 'dealing'); if so were the 'handouts', the result of these dealings, decided on by the directors of the plaintiff companies, to use the terms of section 9(1). Third, if so, has it been proved by the plaintiffs in this action that the defendants were not acting in good faith in relation to the 'handouts' which they received.

The onus of proof is on the defendants in relation to dealing with the companies in relation to the decision of the directors, but it is on the plaintiffs in relation to the absence of good faith. The first question: does section 9(1) of the 1972 Act affect the application of the principles of constructive trust in cases like the present? In my judgment, the answer to this question is No. Constructive trust situations may or may not arise in an *ultra vires* context. The basic principles governing the two doctrines are, I find, quite different. I am satisfied that section 9(1) of the 1972 Act was designed to deal not with the operation of the doctrine of constructive trust, but only with the effect of the doctrines of *ultra vires*. In my judgment, in the light of the EEC Council's directive, this conclusion is a plain one.

In the absence of any decided cases on the point (although I have referred to the text books, particularly Goff and Jones *The Law of Restitution* (2nd edn, 1978) and *Gower's Principles of Modern Company Law* (4th edn, 1979), which discuss this section) it is necessary for me to consider the further questions which would arise if my judgment that section 9(1) of the 1972 Act has no effect on the application of the doctrines and principles of constructive trusts. I may be wrong. So I ask whether the defendants in this case were dealing with the plaintiff companies. In my judgment, the answer to this is No. The payments here did not arise from dealings with the plaintiff companies; they arose clearly from dealings with Mr Munsey. Although the companies' cheques and moneys were used by Mr Munsey, they were used by him as a vehicle for his generosity to the defendants. Mr Marcus conceded that the plaintiff companies had no obligations to him in relation to the debt of Aziz Fancy's estate to the second defendants for £30,000 arising out of the April 1973 transaction.

Should I be wrong in my last conclusion, I have to answer the question whether these dealings were decided on by the plaintiffs' directors. In my judgment, although at the material times there were two other directors of the first plaintiffs (Mrs Fancy and Ismat Fancy) and three other directors of the second plaintiffs (the two Fancys and Mr Day), it is clear on the evidence that Mr Munsey was the sole effective director to whom all actual authority to act for the companies was effectively delegated. I conclude therefore that these dealings, if they were in fact dealings with the companies, were in fact decided on by the directors within the terms of section 9(1) of the 1972 Act.

The last question relating to the application of section 9(1) is whether the plaintiffs have proved that the defendants did not act in good faith as that expression in the 1972 Act is to be construed. My earlier findings are that the defendants had actual knowledge that the payments to them were in breach of duty and trust and were *ultra vires* the companies (and according to Mr Marcus's evidence, for example, he said specifically that he knew that company directors must not give away a company's money); alternatively, at the lowest, that the defendants could not in all the circumstances have been unaware of the unlawful nature of the payments that they received.

So, the final question on liability is whether, assuming Mr Munsey's dealings with the defendants were *ultra vires*, the plaintiffs, they being, through Mr Munsey, parties to the transactions, are disentitled to recover in this action. Counsel for the defendants relies on *Sinclair v Brougham*.[1] He cited extensively from speeches in that case. Counsel for the plaintiffs also referred me to important parts of the speech of Lord Parker in that case, to a passage in the speech of Lord Wright in *Fibrosa Spolka Akcynja v Fairbairn Lawson Combe Barbour Ltd*,[2] and finally to Goff and Jones *The Law of Restitution* (2nd edn, 1978) pp 363–4 and the authorities there referred to. My conclusion is that on my finding that

1 [1914] AC 398; 83 LJ Ch 465
2 [1943] AC 32

Mr Munsey handed out the plaintiffs' moneys to the defendant without any obligation on his or their parts, the defendants gave no consideration for these moneys and received the moneys with notice that they were the companies' moneys paid over in breach of trust in order to implement Mr Munsey's assurance of 'using his best endeavours' to help an old friend, the decided cases in no way preclude the plaintiffs from recovery at common law or in equity. I base my conclusion, primarily, on my finding of the accountability of the defendants as constructive trustees, but I would reach the same conclusion if the plaintiffs' claims were based solely on the defendants' receipt (in the circumstances I find here) of the moneys paid *ultra vires.*

SOURCE 93
TCB Ltd *v* Gray
(Chancery Division) [1986] 1 All ER 587

The defendant guaranteed a debenture granted by a company (Link) to the plaintiff to secure a loan. The debenture was not signed by the directors as required by Link's articles of association. The defendant resisted payment under the guarantee on this basis *inter alia.*

BROWNE-WILKINSON VC . . .

The debenture granted by Link

It will be recalled that counsel's second line of defence for the defendant was that the guarantee given by the defendant was invalidated or discharged by the failure of TCB to obtain a valid debenture from one of the principal debtors, Link.

The articles of Link incorporate clause 113 of Table A, which provides:

> 'The Directors shall provide for the safe custody of the Seal which shall only be used by the authority of the Directors or a Committee of the Directors authorised by the Directors in that behalf, and every instrument to which the Seal shall be affixed shall be signed by a Director and shall be countersigned by the Secretary or by a second Director or by some other person appointed by the Directors for the purpose.'

The debenture was not signed by any director of Link, but by an attorney for a director. There is no power in the articles of Link for a director to act by an attorney. Therefore, says counsel for the defendant, on the principle delegatus no potest delegare the seal was not affixed in accordance with the requirements of the articles: accordingly the debenture is not the act of Link.

Apart from s 9(1) of the European Communities Act 1972, there would be much force in these submissions. But in my judgment that section provides a complete answer. Under the old law, a person dealing with a corporation was required to look at the company's memorandum and articles to satisfy himself that the transaction was within the corporate capacity of the company and was to be carried through in accordance with the requirements of its articles. The rigour of those requirements was only tempered to the extent that the rule in *Royal British Bank v Turquand* (1856) 6 E & B 327, [1843–60] All ER Rep 435 allowed third parties to assume that acts of internal management had been properly carried out.

It has been generally assumed that the old law has to a large extent been swept away by s 9(1) of the 1972 Act, which provides as follows:

> 'In favour of a person dealing with a company in good faith, any transaction

decided on by the directors shall be deemed to be one which it is within the capacity of the company to enter into, and the power of the directors to bind the company shall be deemed to be free of any limitation under the memorandum or articles of association; and a party to a transaction so decided on shall not be bound to enquire as to the capacity of the company to enter into it or as to any such limitation on the powers of the directors, and shall be presumed to have acted in good faith unless the contrary is proved.'

Section 9(1) was passed to bring the law of England into line with art 9 of EEC Council Directive 68/151. In approaching the construction of the section, it is in my judgment relevant to note that the manifest purpose of both the directive and the section is to enable people to deal with a company in good faith without being adversely affected by any limits on the company's capacity or its rules for internal management. Given good faith, a third party is able to deal with a company through its 'organs' (as the directive describes them) or directors. Section 9(1) achieves this in two ways. First, it 'deems' all transactions to be authorised. Second, it 'deems' that the directors can bind the company without limitations. The second part of the section reinforces this by expressly abolishing the old doctrine of constructive notice of the contents of a company's memorandum and articles. It being the obvious purpose of the section to obviate the commercial inconvenience and frequent injustice caused by the old law, I approach the construction of the section with a great reluctance to construe it in such a way as to reintroduce, through the back door, any requirement that a third party acting in good faith must still investigate the regulating documents of a company.

Counsel for the defendant, whilst accepting that TCB had no actual or imputed knowledge of any irregularity in the execution of the debenture, at first submitted that TCB did not act 'in good faith' within the meaning of the section since TCB was put on inquiry by the unusual manner in which the debenture had been executed. He said that TCB should have looked at the articles and would then have discovered the irregularity. Accordingly, he submitted, they were not acting 'in good faith'. On further consideration counsel abandoned this argument, to my mind rightly. The last words of the second part of the subsection expressly provide that good faith is to be presumed; the second part further provides that the person dealing with the company is *not* bound to inquire as to limitations on the powers of directors. In my judgment it is impossible to establish lack of 'good faith' within the meaning of the section solely by alleging that inquiries ought to have been made which the second part of the subsection says need not be made.

The next submission of counsel for the defendant was that, in order for the section to apply at all, the first requirement is that there must be a transaction by the company. Since Link never sealed the debenture in the only way authorised by the articles, there was here no transaction by Link at all: the debenture was not the act of Link. If this argument is right, it drives a coach and horses through the section: in every dealing with the company the third party would have to look at its articles to ensure that the company was binding itself in an authorised manner. In my judgment the section does not have that effect. The section is dealing with purported actions by a company which, having regard to its internal documents, may be a nullity eg acts outside its corporate capacity. In such a case under the old law the purported act of the company would not be the act of the company at all. Yet the first part of s 9(1) of the 1972 Act 'deems' it so to be. Similarly a document under seal by the company executed otherwise than in accordance with its articles was not, under the old law, the act of the company; but s 9(1) deems it so to be since the powers of the directors are deemed to be free from limitations, ie as to the manner of affixing the company's seal. In my judgment, s 9(1) applies to transactions which a company purports to enter into and deems them to be validly entered into.

Counsel for the defendant also submitted that art 113 (regulating the way in which Link can seal documents) is not a 'limitation' on the powers of directors to bind the company but a mandatory direction as to the only way in which the company can bind itself. I reject this submission also. Link has either actual or (under s 9(1)) deemed capacity to enter into the debenture. Being an artificial person, Link can only enter into the debenture by its agents, the directors. Any provision in the articles as to the manner in which the directors can act as agents for the company is a limitation on their power to bind the company and as such falls within the first part of s 9(1).

Finally, counsel for the defendant submitted that in order to rely on the section it has to be shown that the debenture was a transaction 'decided on by the Directors'. I agree. Then, says counsel for the defendant, the evidence shows that the directors of Link never did decide to enter into this debenture.

The facts as I find them are that on completion of the loan there was handed to TCB a minute of a board meeting of Link held on 25 January 1982. That minute records that there were present the defendant, Mr Pond, Mr Green and Mr Rowan. Paragraph 2 of the minute, after reciting the proposal to grant the debenture, continued:

> 'It was therefore resolved that the facility be accepted and the Form of Debenture in favour of TCB be executed under the Common Seal of the Company in the presence of Messrs. Rowan (as attorney for Mr. Gray) and Mr. Green.'

Paragraph 5 of the minute provided as follows:

> 'It was further resolved that Messrs Rowan and Green be authorised to deliver the said Debenture to TCB and that they may be also empowered to execute any other documents required by TCB to complete the security documentation.'

The minutes are signed by Mr Rowan 'as attorney for V. Gray'. The evidence clearly established that no such meeting of the directors of Link ever took place. But in fact all the directors of Link individually had decided to grant the debenture, although not at a meeting at which they were all present.

It has to be borne in mind on this aspect of the case that I have to determine whether a valid debenture was granted by Link. In my judgment Link, having put forward the minutes of the meeting of 25 January as one of the completion documents on the basis of which TCB made the loan, could not be heard to challenge the validity of that minute by denying that such meeting ever took place. Therefore the minute stands as irrefutable evidence against Link that the grant of the debenture was a 'transaction decided on by the Directors'. Accordingly the necessary basis for s 9(1) of the 1972 Act to apply as between Link and TCB exists. It follows that the debenture was valid, and the defendant's second line of defence also fails.

PART III: THE TURQUAND RULE AND AGENCY PRINCIPLES

Companies cannot act except through the medium of human beings. Such human beings may be appointed to a particular office in the company, for example managing director, director or secretary. Alternatively, someone may be specifically authorised by the company to carry out a particular task. The anticipated end result is a contract by which the company and a third party are bound. What, however, is to be the outcome where the company denies that it is bound, on the ground, either that the person acting or purporting to act on its behalf lacked authority or that the proper procedure laid down by the company's constitution for entering into such a contract were not fulfilled? (It may be that the latter is but an example of the former.) We need to ask the following:

1. *If the company alleges that the person lacked authority*

(a) Was the person who purported to act on behalf of the company appointed or elected to a particular office in the company? (Sources 94, 96, 98, 99.)
(b) If so,
   (i) What authority is usually carried by such an office ('usual authority') (Sources 94, 96 — director; 98 — chairman; 99 — secretary)
   (ii) Was the usual authority supplemented in any way? (Source 98?)
   (iii) Was the usual authority diminished in any way?
(c) If not, was he represented as having a particular office? (Sources 95, 97, 98.)
(d) If so, repeat (b)(i). [(b)(ii) and (iii) cannot arise.] (Sources 95 — director, secretary; 97 — managing director; 98 — managing director.)
(e) If so, was the third party reasonably misled by this representation? (Sources 95, 97, 98.)

2. *If it is alleged that the proper procedure was not complied with*

(a) What has been omitted?
(b) Should the third party have been suspicious (assuming him to be a reasonable person)? (Contrast, say Source 95 with Source 96.)
   [whether he does or does not know that something is missing will be a factor — but not a conclusive factor — in deciding whether he should have been suspicious. If he did know it is more likely that a court would say that he should have been suspicious than if he did not know.]
[(c) If not, could he have known that something was missing by reason of the fact that knowledge of that requirement *and* its omission were available to him by reference to public documents?]

The last question — 2(c) — is in square brackets because it refers to the doctrine of constructive notice and is, therefore, no longer applicable *insofar as section 35 applies*. The information might have been contained in a special resolution, for example. That doctrine is a negative doctrine only, ie the third party cannot claim, by virtue of the doctrine to 'know' what he is deemed to know and, therefore to have been misled by the representation by which he would have been misled had he actually known (Source 96).

SOURCE 94
Royal British Bank *v* Turquand
(Queen's Bench affirmed Exchequer Chamber) (1856) 6 E&B 327;
119 ER 886

An action for the return of £2,000 borrowed from the plaintiff by the joint stock company of which the defendant was the official manager. The defence was based on Rule 50 of the company's Deed of Settlement:

> 'That the Board of Directors may borrow on mortgage, bond or bill in the name of, and if necessary under the common seal of, the Company such sum or sums of money as shall from time to time, by a resolution passed at a general meeting of the Company, be authorized to be borrowed: provided that the total amount of the sum or sums of money so borrowed shall not at any time exceed two thirds of the total amount on the instalments on the capital of the Company paid up or called for, and actually due and payable at the time of, the passing of such resolution.'

Averred by the defendant that no resolution, as required, had been passed.

> LORD CAMPBELL CJ (Queen's Bench): No illegality appears on the face of the bond or condition. A good plea, therefore, must allege facts to establish illegality, as was done in *Collins v Blantern*[1] and *Paxton v Popham*.[2] But this plea makes no charge of fraud against the plaintiffs, and states no facts from which fraud can be inferred: it shows no immorality nor breach of common law or statute law. It alleges that, as between the directors and the shareholders, the directors exceeded their authority in executing the bond, but without adding that this was known to the plaintiffs, or that it was to the prejudice of the shareholders. Looking to the business to be carried on by this Company, it might well be presumed that opening such an account and carrying on such dealings with a banking house as are described in the condition would be within the authority of the directors, and would be for the benefit of the shareholders. A mere excess of authority by the directors, we think, of itself would not amount to a defence. The bond being under the seal of the Company, the gist of the defence must be illegality. If the directors had exceeded their authority to the prejudice of the shareholders by executing the bond, and this had been known to the obligees, illegality, we think, would have been shown. The obligors in executing, and the obligees in accepting, the bond might be considered as combining together to injure the shareholders; the two parties would have been in *pari delicto*: and the action could not have been maintained. In such circumstances *potior est conditio defendentis*. But without the *scienter*, and without prejudice to the shareholders or any others whatsoever, illegality is not established against the obligees. If no illegality is shown as against the party with whom the directors contract under the seal of the Company, excess of authority is a matter only between the directors and the shareholders.

---

1 2 Wils KB 341; 95 ER 847
2 10 East 366; 103 ER 814

Looking to the resolution of the general meeting of shareholders set out in the replication, there seems ground for contending that rule 50 in the deed of settlement was substantially complied with, and that the directors may be considered as having had authority to execute the bond: but, at all events, we think that the bond cannot be rendered illegal and void from any irregularity in the proceedings of the Company, nor even by an excess of authority, the plaintiffs having acted with good faith, and the shareholders not being prejudiced. The plaintiffs have bonâ fide advanced their money for the use of the Company, giving credit to the representations of the directors that they had authority to execute the bond; and the money which they advanced, and which they now seek to recover, must be taken to have been applied in the business of the Company and for the benefit of the shareholders. If the plaintiffs must be presumed to have had notice of the contents of the registered deed of settlement, there is nothing there to show that the directors might not have had authority to execute the bond as they asserted.

JERVIS CJ (Exchequer Chamber): The deed allow the directors to borrow on bond such sum or sums of money as shall from time to time, by a resolution passed at a general meeting of the Company, be authorized to be borrowed: and the replication shows a resolution, passed at a general meeting, authorizing the directors to borrow on bond such sums for such periods and at such rates of interest as they might deem expedient, in accordance with the deed of settlement and the Act of Parliament; but the resolution does not otherwise define the amount to be borrowed. That seems to me enough. If that be so, the other question does not arise. But whether it be so or not we need not decide; for it seems to us that the plea, whether we consider it as a confession and avoidance or a special *Non est factum*, does not raise any objection to this advance as against the Company. We may now take for granted that the dealings with these companies are not like dealings with other partnerships, and that the parties dealing with them are bound to read the statute and the deed of settlement. But they are not bound to do more. And the party here, on reading the deed of settlement, would find, not a prohibition from borrowing, but a permission to do so on certain conditions. Finding that the authority might be made complete by a resolution, he would have a right to infer the fact of a resolution authorizing that which on the face of the document appeared to be legitimately done.

SOURCE 95
Mahony v East Holyford Gold Mining Company Ltd
(House of Lords 1875) (1875) LR 7 HL 869; 33 LT 383

The plaintiff, the public officer of a bank, was appealing against an order upholding the claim of the liquidator of the company to repayment of all money paid by the bank on cheques drawn on behalf of the company. The bank had acted on instructions to honour cheques signed by any two of three named directors. The instructions were signed by someone who described himself as the secretary. In fact the directors and secretary had never been appointed.

LORD CAIRNS: Under these circumstances it becomes necessary to consider how far the bankers were justified in paying the cheques. They were informed by Wall, who was attending at the only office of the company as its secretary, and was acting as such, that a resolution of the board had been passed authorizing cheques to be signed by two of the three directors, McNally, Wadge, and Hoare, and countersigned by the secretary. Undoubtedly McNally, Wadge, and Hoare, were acting as directors of the company; undoubtedly no person else was professing or claiming to act as directors; and undoubtedly it was necessary that some persons should act as directors of the company, or the business of the company could not be carried on. Undoubtedly McKenna, Murphy, Hughes, and Tully, were aware that Wadge, Hoare, and McNally were acting as directors, for they were acting as clerks under them, and they made no opposition to McNally, Wadge, and Hoare so acting. It appears to me that under these circumstances the bankers were justified in accepting the statement of Wall, who, as acting secretary of the company, was clearly the proper person to make the communication that McNally, Wadge, and Hoare, were the directors, and would sign the cheques. It is suggested that they might have inquired into the accuracy of Wall's statements. But suppose they had inquired, and that Wall had shown them a resolution appointing these persons as directors, the document so shown might have been false or spurious, just as Wall's letter is said to have been false, and the bankers could have no certainty of the truth of what was stated to them unless they had themselves attended the meetings of the directors, and heard what was done there — a course which I need hardly say it would be impossible for men of business to take. It appears to me that this is exactly such a case as section 85 of the articles of association is meant to meet. There is no regular appointment of directors, and the persons so acting may perhaps have been disqualified; but the acts done by them are to be taken as being as valid as if they had been duly appointed and qualified.

LORD HATHERLEY: It is a point of very great importance that those who are concerned in joint stock companies and those who deal with them should be aware of what is essential to the due performance of their duties, both as customers or dealers with the company, and as persons forming the company, and dealing with the outside world respectively. On the one hand, it is settled by a series of decisions, of which *Ernest v Nicholls*[1] is one and *Royal British Bank v Turquand*[2] a later one, that those who deal with joint stock companies are bound to take notice of that which I may call the external position of the company. Every joint stock company has its memorandum and articles of association; every joint stock company, or nearly every one, I imagine (unless it adopts the form provided by the statute, and that comes to the same thing) has its partnership deed under which it acts. Those articles of association and that partnership deed are open to all who are minded to have any dealings whatsoever with the company, and those who so deal with them must be affected with notice of all that is contained in those two documents.

After that, the company entering upon its business and dealing with persons external to it, is supposed on its part to have all those powers and authorities which, by its articles of association and by its deed, it appears to possess; and all that the directors do with reference to what I may call the indoor management of their own concern, is a thing known to them and known to them only; subject to this observation, that no person dealing with them has a right to suppose that anything has been or can be done that is not permitted by the articles of association or by the deed. For instance, a person dealing with such a company as this, a mining company, could not attempt to set up any right upon a policy of insurance as having been granted to him by the directors of the company, or to found a claim upon any other matter which is not a matter contained in their articles of association. He must be taken to have perfect knowledge that they had

1 (1857) 6 HLC 401; 10 ER 1351
2 (1856) 6 E&B 327; 119 ER 886 (see p 260)

no power to do anything of that kind, and therefore nothing can be of any avail to him that is contrary to the articles of association, with which he must be taken to be acquainted.

This being the case, a banker dealing with a company must be taken to be acquainted with the manner in which, under the articles of association, the moneys of the company may be drawn out of his bank for the purposes of the company. My noble and learned friend on the woolsack has read those articles by which, in this case, the bankers were informed that cheques might be drawn upon the bank by three directors of the company. And the bankers must also be taken to have had knowledge, from the articles, of the duties of the directors, and the mode in which the directors were to be appointed. But, after that, when there are persons conducting the affairs of the company in a manner which appears to be perfectly consonant with the articles of association, then those so dealing with them, externally, are not to be affected by any irregularities which may take place in the internal management of the company. They are entitled to presume that that of which only they can have knowledge, namely, the external acts, are rightly done, when those external acts purport to be performed in the mode in which they ought to be performed. For instance, when a cheque is signed by three directors, they are entitled to assume that those directors are persons properly appointed for the purpose of performing that function, and have properly performed the function for which they have been appointed. Of course, the case is open to any observation arising from gross negligence or fraud. I pass that by as not entering into the consideration of the question at the present time. Outside persons when they find that there is an act done by a company, will, of course, be bound in the exercise of ordinary care and precaution to know whether or not that company is actually carrying on and transacting business, or whether it is a company which has been stopped and wound up, and which has parted with its assets, and the like. All those ordinary inquiries which mercantile men would, in the course of their business make, I apprehend, would have to be made on the part of the persons dealing with the company.

But what do the bankers find in the case now before us? They find on the face of the deed how the directors are to be appointed; they find that the first directors are to be appointed by the majority of the first seven persons (that is to say, by four of them) who signed the articles of association, they find, both by the articles of association and by the second prospectus which was issued (the prospectus which was issued before the articles were signed could, of course, have no effect upon the company, which was not then formed, but a second one was issued very shortly afterwards in July, after the incorporation of the company and the registration of the articles of association), that the place of business was fixed at 12, Grafton Street. That was an external fact with which they might well acquaint themselves. They might well have been justified in entertaining doubts as to whether they should transact business with the company if they had found it carrying on business in any other place, supposing they had not been made acquainted with any change of abode. But they go to No 12, Grafton Street, and they find there an office, and they find there a person acting as secretary, who is the same person as the person described as the secretary in the second prospectus, issued after the company was formed. They find there certain persons in constant attendance, namely, six out of seven persons who signed the articles of association. I believe all the seven were at one time or another in attendance, but six were there constantly. And one of the witnesses says (I need not turn to his evidence for this purpose), that Mr Hoare and another person, as to whom they were informed that they were the directors, were there acting as directors. Finding then a certain number of persons acting as directors, who had been represented to them to be directors, and finding four other persons who might well have elected them to be directors (having the authority and the power to do so), on the spot daily, sitting by and seeing them performing those directorial functions, what conclusion could they come to but that those directors had been duly appointed? And, my Lords, I apprehend we are quite justified in holding that clause 85 of the articles of association covers any defect there might have been in that appointment.

Then the bankers get a notice from a person who calls himself the secretary, and who says he gives them a Resolution under the authority of which, and according to the form there stated, the cheques are to be drawn. I pass by altogether, as really immaterial in the inquiry, the circumstance that a fraud may have been intended on the part of the company in the way in which the letter was expressed. That could have no effect upon the bankers; the jury found by the verdict that the bankers acted entirely in good faith upon the representations contained in that letter. It has been noticed that that letter does not mention, in words, that the resolution was passed by a vote of the board of directors. But the subject matter of it was the drawing of cheques; the mode of providing for the drawing of cheques is treated of in the articles, and it is there laid down that that duty is to be performed by the directors. The bankers were furnished with the names of three so called 'directors,' who sent their signatures in order that the bankers might have an opportunity of verifying the signatures upon any cheques that might be drawn. If the bankers went there and found the secretary sitting there, as the evidence tells us he did all day long from ten till six, and performing the duties of a secretary, and if they found some of these other gentlemen sitting there appearing to be performing the duties of directors, and if they saw those four other gentlemen who might have appointed them as directors sitting there also, witnessing them performing the duties of directors, I must ask what more could be required on the part of those who were dealing with the company, and who had obtained all the external information they could upon the subject. If we are not now to hold that the bankers are to be protected in honouring the drafts of these three persons, who, they were informed, were authorized to draw cheques, I do not know how any person, dealing with a company, can be safe against being bound to inquire into all the minute transactions which may have taken place indoors.

SOURCE 96
JC Houghton & Co *v* Nothard, Lowe & Wills Ltd
(Court of Appeal, affirmed House of Lords 1927) [1927] 1 KB 246 affirmed [1928] AC 1

The plaintiffs, fruit sellers, entered into an agreement with one Maurice Lowe, apparently acting on behalf of the defendant, that the plaintiff should advance sums of money to the defendant in consideration of the right to sell, on commission, fruit imported by the defendant and also that the plaintiff should be entitled to retain the defendant's fruit as security. The articles of association of the defendant company provided that the board of directors had very wide powers of delegation. The defendant repudiated the agreement on the ground that Maurice Lowe was not authorised to negotiate such an agreement. The plaintiff sued for the balance owing on the advance; the defendant counterclaimed for the sums received by the plaintiffs as the proceeds for the sale of the defendant's fruit. The Court of Appeal upheld an appeal against the decision of Wright J who had held the agreement binding. The House of Lords dismissed a further appeal.

SARGANT LJ (Court of Appeal): In this case it is quite clear that neither Mr Maurice Lowe, as a director, nor Mr Prescott, as the secretary of the defendant company, had any authority to make any such contract on behalf of the company as that alleged in paragraph 1 of the statement of claim. The management of the business of the company was in the usual course and under the express provisions of article 71 of Table A, in the hands of the directors, that is of the board of directors; and there had been no delegation to Mr Maurice Lowe or to the secretary of the power of the board to enter into a contract of this character. The entrusting to Mr Maurice Lowe and his brother of the duties in connection with the selling of the produce of the defendant company obviously did not include the formation of a contract, under which the produce of the company should be charged by way of collateral security to secure a series of advances made and to be made to another company, however closely associated in business with the defendant company. The decision of Wright J in favour of the plaintiffs is founded not on actual authority, but on a wholly different ground — namely, the title of the plaintiffs in the circumstances to assume that such an authority had been given, and to act on that assumption. . . .

Turning now to a more minute examination of the judgment of Wright J, the steps by which he arrives at the conclusion that the defendant company were bound as towards the plaintiffs are as follows. In the first place he finds that Mr Maurice Lowe contracted with Mr Dart, not only on behalf of the Preserving Co, but on behalf of the defendant company, and that this contract was affirmed on behalf of the defendant company by their secretary's letter of 22 July 1922. In the next place he relies on the fact that under the articles of association of the defendant company (both as incorporating Table A and under a special article 28) their board of directors might have delegated their power to enter into such a contract to any person, including a single director or their secretary. And, thirdly, he draws the conclusion that, although this power to delegate was unknown to Mr Dart or to any one else acting for the plaintiffs, yet Mr Dart and the plaintiffs were entitled to treat this as a matter of internal management only and to assume that Mr Maurice Lowe and the secretary in fact possessed the power to bind the defendant company. . . .

Next as to the power to delegate which is contained in the articles of association. In a case like this where that power of delegation had not been exercised, and where admittedly Mr Dart and the plaintiff firm had no knowledge of the existence of that power and did not rely on it, I cannot for myself see how they can subsequently make use of this unknown power so as to validate the transaction. They could rely on the fact of delegation, had it been a fact, whether known to them or not. They might rely on their knowledge of the power of delegation, had they known of it, as part of the circumstances entitling them to infer that there had been a delegation and to act on that inference, though it were in fact a mistaken one. But it is quite another thing to say that the plaintiffs are entitled now to rely on the supposed exercise of a power which was never in fact exercised and of the existence of which they were in ignorance at the date when they contracted. No case was cited to us in which a binding obligation has been constructed out of so curious a combination; and I cannot see any principle on which an obligation could be so constructed.

But even if Mr Dart, and through him the plaintiffs, had been aware of the power of delegation in the articles of the defendant company, this would not in my judgment have entitled him or them to assume that this power had been exercised in favour of a director, secretary or other officer of the company so as to validate the contract now in question. The learned judge, indeed, has said that this follows from a well recognized line of cases, refers as an example to the case of *Re Fireproof Doors Ltd*[1], and holds that the plaintiffs were entitled to assume that anything necessary to delegate any of the functions of the board to one director or two directors had been done as a matter of internal management. But, in my opinion, this is to carry the doctrine of presumed power far beyond anything that has hitherto been decided, and to place limited companies, without any sufficient reason for so doing, at the mercy of any servant or agent who should purport to contract on their behalf. On this view, not only a director of a limited company with articles founded on Table A, but a secretary or any subordinate officer might be treated by a third party acting in good faith as capable of binding the company by any sort of contract, however exceptional, on the ground that a power of making such a contract might conceivably have been entrusted to him.

Cases where the question has been as to the exact formalities observed when the seal of a company has been affixed, such as *Royal British Bank v Turquand*[2] or *County of Gloucester Bank v Rudry Merthyr Colliery Co*,[3] are quite distinguishable from the present case. *Re Fireproof Doors Ltd*, tends rather against than in favour of the plaintiffs, since if a single director has as towards third parties the authority now contended for, the whole of the elaborate investigation of the facts in that case was entirely unnecessary. Perhaps the nearest approach to the present case is to be found in *Biggerstaff v Rowatt's Wharf Ltd*.[4] But there the agent whose authority was relied on had been acting to the knowledge of the company as a managing director, and the act done was one within the ordinary ambit of the powers of a managing director in the transaction of the company's affairs. It is I think clear that the transaction there would not have been supported had it not been in this ordinary course, or had the agent been acting merely as one of the ordinary directors of the company. I know of no case in which an ordinary director, acting without authority in fact, has been held capable of binding a company by a contract with a third party, merely on the ground that that third party assumed that the director had been given authority by the board to make the contract. A limitation of the right to make such an assumption is expressed in Buckley on the Companies Acts (10th edn), p 175, in the following concise words: 'And the principle does not apply to the case where an agent of the company has done something beyond any authority which was given to him or which he was held out as having.'

SOURCE 97
Freeman & Lockyer *v* Buckhurst Park Properties Ltd
(Court of Appeal 1964) [1964] 2 QB 480; [1964] 1 All ER 630

The plaintiffs, a firm of architects and surveyors, were engaged by one K, acting as the defendant's managing director to prepare an appeal against a refusal of permission. The claim for fees was met by the defence that K was not the company's managing director and not authorised to engage the plaintiffs. There was provision in the company's articles for the appointment of a managing director, but K had not been appointed although he acted as such to the knowledge of the board. The plaintiffs neither examined the

---

1 [1916] 2 Ch 142; 85 LJ Ch 444
2 (1856) 6 E&B 327; 119 ER 886 (see p 260)
3 [1895] 1 Ch 629
4 [1896] 2 Ch 93; 65 LJ Ch 536

defendant's articles, nor enquired whether K was, in fact, the managing director. The county court upheld the plaintiffs' claim and the Court of Appeal dismissed the appeal.

> WILLMER LJ: . . . a company can act only through its officers, and the powers of its officers are limited by its articles of association. It is well established that all persons dealing with a company are affected with notice of its memorandum and articles of association, which are public documents open to inspection by all; see *Mahoney v East Holyford Mining Co.*[1] However, by the rule in *Royal British Bank v Turquand*,[2] re-affirmed in *Mahony's case*, it was also established, in the words of Lord Hatherley in the latter case,

> [see p 263, '. . . that, when there are . . . internal management of the company.']

> Thus in *Biggerstaff v Rowatt's Wharf Ltd*,[3] where the articles of association conferred power to appoint a managing director, the company was held bound by the act of a person who purported to contract as its managing director, though he had never been formally appointed as such. Lopes LJ, in a passage cited by the judge in the present case said that:

> > 'A company is bound by the acts of persons who take upon themselves, with the knowledge of the directors, to act for the company, provided such persons act within the limits of their apparent authority; and strangers dealing bona fide with such persons, have a right to assume that they have been duly appointed.'

> In the same case Lindley LJ, said:

> > 'The persons dealing with him [the apparent managing director] must look to the articles, and see that the managing director might have power to do what he purports to do, and that is enough for a person dealing with him bona fide.'

> I take the lord justice to mean, not that persons dealing with the supposed managing director must actually look at the articles, but that, being affected with notice of them, they must have regard thereto. Consequently, if in that case the articles of association had conferred no power to appoint a managing director, the plaintiffs could not have been heard to say that the person with whom they contracted had been held out by the company as its managing director.
> A similar case was that of *British Thomson-Houston Co Ltd v Federated European Bank Ltd*.[4] . . . There was nothing to show that the plaintiffs in fact knew of the articles of association of the defendant company; nevertheless, the company was held bound by a guarantee given to the plaintiffs by the chairman of the board, one N. Pal, and signed in the following form: 'Federated European Bank Ltd (signed) N. Pal'. Again in *Clay Hill Brick and Tile Co Ltd v Rawlings*[5] a company was held bound by the act of its chairman, who acted as managing director, though never appointed as such, in receiving cheques from a customer in payment for goods supplied by the company. These, it will be seen, were all cases in which not only did the articles of association confer power on the directors to delegate, but

---

1 (1875) LR 7 HL 869; 33 LT 383 (see p 261)
2 (1856) 6 E&B 327; 119 ER 886 (see p 260)
3 [1896] 2 Ch 93; 65 LJ Ch 536
4 [1932] 2 KB 176; 101 LJKB 690
5 159 LT 482; [1938] 4 All ER 100

the person purporting to act for the company was acting within the scope of what would normally be expected to be within the authority of one in his position.

It has been submitted on behalf of the defendant company, however, that where, as here, the person contracting with someone purporting to act on behalf of a company has in fact no knowledge of its articles of association, and has made no inquiries with regard thereto, he cannot rely on any power of delegation contained therein when there has been no actual delegation. In such a case, it has been argued, the rule in *Turquand's Case* has no application, and there can be no room for any presumption that the power of delegation has been properly and regularly exercised. In support of this submission reliance is placed on the decision of this court in *J C Houghton & Co v Nothard, Lowe and Wills Ltd*,[1] especially on the judgment of Sargant LJ, which was followed in this court in *Kreditbank Cassel GmbH v Schenkers Ltd*,[2] and also by Slade J, in *Rama Corpn Ltd v Proved Tin and General Investments Ltd*.[3] If *Houghton's Case* does establish the broad proposition contended for, it would, I agree, be difficult to reconcile it with the authorities to which I have previously referred, especially with the decision of this court in *British Thomson-Houston Co Ltd v Federated European Bank Ltd*. This was a difficulty which was clearly felt by Slade J, in *Rama's Case*. He made no secret of the fact that he thought the decisions of this court were conflicting; he accordingly based his judgment on the decision in *Houghton's Case* and refused to follow that of *British Thomson-Houston Co Ltd v Federated European Bank Ltd*.

Though I have no doubt that *Rama's Case* was rightly decided on its own facts, I cannot agree with the view expressed by Slade J, that the previous decisions of this court were conflicting. I do not think that, when properly understood, the cases relied on by the defendant company here are in conflict with the decision in the *British Thomson-Houston Case* or with the principles which I have already stated. If I correctly understand them, the cases relied on by the defendant company deal with a much narrower point. They were all cases of most unusual transactions, which would not be within what would ordinarily be expected to be the scope of the authority of the officer purporting to act on behalf of the company. Thus in *Houghton's Case* a director purported to make on behalf of his company an agreement with the plaintiffs whereby the plaintiffs were to sell on commission goods imported by the defendant company on terms that the plaintiffs should retain the proceeds of sale as security for a debt due from another company. In the *Kreditbank Case* a branch manager of a company carrying on business as forwarding agents purported to draw bills of exchange on behalf of his company, which he subsequently endorsed on their behalf. In *Rama's Case* a director of the defendant company purported to make an agreement with a director of the plaintiff company whereby the two companies were to join in subscribing to a fund to be used for financing the sale of goods produced by a third company, the defendant company being responsible for administering the fund and accounting to the plaintiffs. Thus in none of these cases were the plaintiffs in a position to allege that the person with whom they contracted was acting within the scope of such authority as one in his position would be expected to possess. There was accordingly no ground for saying that the officer in question was in fact being held out by the company as having authority to perform the act relied on. The plaintiffs indeed had nothing to go on beyond the fact that in each case power to do the acts relied on might, under the articles of association, have been delegated to the person with whom they

1 [1928] AC 1; [1927] 1 KB 246 (see p 264)
2 [1927] 1 KB 826; 96 LJKB 501
3 [1952] 2 QB 147; [1952] 1 All ER 554

contracted. But in none of the cases did the plaintiffs have any knowledge of the articles of association.

In the circumstances the three decisions relied on by the defendant company are to my mind no more than illustrations of the well established principle that a party who seeks to set up an estoppel must show that he in fact relied on the representation that he alleges, be it a representation in words or a representation by conduct.

DIPLOCK LJ: It is necessary at the outset to distinguish between an 'actual' authority of an agent on the one hand, and an 'apparent' or 'ostensible' authority on the other. Actual authority and apparent authority are quite independent of one another. Generally they co-exist and coincide, but either may exist without the other and their respective scopes may be different. As I shall endeavour to show, it is on the apparent authority of the agent that the contractor normally relies in the ordinary course of business when entering into contracts.

An 'actual' authority is a legal relationship between principal and agent created by a consensual agreement to which they alone are parties. Its scope is to be ascertained by applying ordinary principles of construction of contracts, including any proper implications from the express words used, the usages of the trade, or the course of business between the parties. To this agreement the contractor is a stranger; he may be totally ignorant of the existence of any authority on the part of the agent. Nevertheless, if the agent does enter into a contract pursuant to the 'actual' authority, it does create contractual rights and liabilities between the principal and the contractor. It may be that this rule relating to 'undisclosed principals', which is peculiar to English law, can be rationalised as avoiding circuity of action, for the principal could in equity compel the agent to lend his name in an action to enforce the contract against the contractor, and would at common law be liable to indemnify the agent in respect of the performance of the obligations assumed by the agent under the contract.

An 'apparent' or 'ostensible' authority, on the other hand, is a legal relationship between the principal and the contractor created by a representation, made by the principal to the contractor, intended to be and in fact acted on by the contractor, that the agent has authority to enter on behalf of the principal into a contract of a kind within the scope of the 'apparent' authority, so as to render the principal liable to perform any obligations imposed on him by such contract. To the relationship so created the agent is a stranger. He need not be (although he generally is) aware of the existence of the representation. The representation, when acted on by the contractor by entering into a contract with the agent, operates as an estoppel, preventing the principal from asserting that he is not bound by the contract. It is irrelevant whether the agent had actual authority to enter into the contract.

In ordinary business dealings the contractor at the time of entering into the contract can in the nature of things hardly ever rely on the 'actual' authority of the agent. His information as to the authority must be derived either from the principal or from the agent or from both, for they alone know what the agent's actual authority is. All that the contractor can know is what they tell him, which may or may not be true. In the ultimate analysis he relies either on the representation of the principal, ie, apparent authority, or on the representation of the agent, ie, warranty of authority. The representation which creates 'apparent' authority may take a variety of forms of which the commonest is representation by conduct, ie, by permitting the agent to act in some way in the conduct of the principal's business with other persons. By so doing the principal represents to anyone who becomes aware that the agent is so acting that the agent has authority to enter on behalf of the principal into contracts with other persons of the kind which an agent so acting in the conduct of his principal's business has normally 'actual' authority to enter into.

In applying the law, as I have endeavoured to summarise it, to the case where the principal is not a natural person, but a fictitious person, viz, a corporation, two further factors arising from the legal characteristics of a corporation have to be borne in mind. The first is that the capacity of a corporation is limited by its constitution, ie, in the case of a company incorporated under the Companies Act, by its memorandum and articles of association; the second is that a corporation cannot do any act, and that includes making a representation, except through its agent. Under the doctrine of *ultra vires* the limitation of the capacity of a corporation by its constitution to do any acts is absolute. This affects the rules as to the 'apparent' authority of an agent of a corporation in two ways. First, no representation can operate to estop the corporation from denying the authority of the agent to do on behalf of the corporation an act which the corporation is not permitted by its constitution to do itself. Secondly, since the conferring of actual authority on an agent is itself an act of the corporation, the capacity to do which is regulated by its constitution, the corporation cannot be estopped from denying that it has conferred on a particular agent authority to do acts which, by its constitution, it is incapable of delegating to that particular agent. To recognise that these are direct consequences of the doctrine of *ultra vires* is, I think, preferable to saying that a contractor who enters into a contract with a corporation has constructive notice of its constitution, for the expression 'constructive notice' tends to disguise that constructive notice is not a positive, but a negative doctrine, like that of estoppel of which it forms a part. It operates to prevent the contractor from saying that he did not know that the constitution of the corporation rendered a particular act or a particular delegation of authority *ultra vires* the corporation. It does not entitle him to say that he relied on some unusual provision in the constitution of the corporation, if he did not in fact so rely.

The second characteristic of a corporation, viz, that unlike a natural person it can only make a representation through an agent, has the consequence that, in order to create an estoppel between the corporation and the contractor, the representation as to the authority of the agent which creates his 'apparent' authority must be made by some person or persons who have 'actual' authority from the corporation to make the representation. Such 'actual' authority may be conferred by the constitution of the corporation itself, as, for example, in the case of a company, on the board of directors, or it may be conferred by those who under its constitution have the powers of management on some other person to whom the constitution permits them to delegate authority to make representations of this kind. It follows that, where the agent on whose 'apparent' authority the contractor relies has no 'actual' authority from the corporation to enter into a particular kind of contract with the contractor on behalf of the corporation, the contractor cannot rely on the agent's own representation as to his actual authority. He can rely only on a representation by a person or persons who have actual authority to manage or conduct that part of the business of the corporation to which the contract relates. The commonest form of representation by a principal creating an 'apparent' authority if an agent is by conduct, viz, by permitting the agent to act in the management or conduct of the principal's business. Thus, if in the case of a company the board of directors who have 'actual' authority under the memorandum and articles of association to manage the company's business permit the agent to act in the management or conduct of the company's business, they thereby represent to all persons dealing with such agent that he has authority to enter on behalf of the corporation into contracts of a kind which an agent authorised to do acts of the kind which he is in fact permitted to do normally enters into in the ordinary course of such business. The making of such a representation is itself an act of management of the company's business. Prima facie it falls within the 'actual' authority of the board of directors, and unless the memorandum or articles of the company either make such a contract ultra vires the company or prohibit the delegation of such authority to the agent, the company is estopped from denying to anyone who has entered into a contract with the agent in reliance on such 'apparent' authority that the agent had authority to contract on behalf of the company.

If the foregoing analysis of the relevant law is correct, it can be summarized by stating four conditions which must be fulfilled to entitle a contractor to enforce against a company a contract entered into on behalf of the company by an agent who had no actual authority to do so. It must be shown: (a) that a representation that the agent had authority to enter on behalf of the company into a contract of the kind sought to be enforced was made to the contractor; (b) that such representation was made by a person or persons who had 'actual' authority to manage the business of the company either generally or in respect of those matters to which the contract relates; (c) that he (the contractor) was induced by such representation to enter into the contract, ie, that he in fact relied on it; and (d) that under its memorandum or articles of association the company was not deprived of the capacity either to enter into a contract of the kind sought to be enforced or to delegate authority to enter into a contract of that kind to the agent.

The confusion which, I venture to think, has sometimes crept into the cases is, in my view, due to a failure to distinguish between these four separate conditions, and in particular to keep steadfastly in mind (first) that the only 'actual' authority which is relevant is that of the persons making the representation relied on, and (second) that the memorandum and articles of association of the company are always relevant (whether they are in fact known to the contractor or not) to the questions (i) whether condition (b) is fulfilled, and (ii) whether condition (d) is fulfilled, and (but only if they are in fact known to the contractor) may be relevant (c) as part of the representation on which the contractor relied.

In each of the relevant cases the representation relied on as creating the 'apparent' authority of the agent was by conduct in permitting the agent to act in the management and conduct of part of the business of the company. Except in *Mahony v East Holyford Mining Co Ltd*, the conduct relied on was that of the board of directors in so permitting the agent to act. As they had, in each case, by the articles of association of the company full 'actual' authority to manage its business, they had 'actual' authority to make representations in connection with the management of its business, including representations as to who were agents authorised to enter into contracts on the company's behalf. The agent himself had no 'actual' authority to enter into the contract, because there had not been compliance with the formalities prescribed by the articles for conferring it on him. In *British Thomson-Houston Co Ltd v Federated European Bank Ltd*, where a guarantee was executed by a single director, it was contended that a provision in the articles, requiring a guarantee to be executed by two directors, deprived the company of capacity to delegate to a single director authority to execute a guarantee on behalf of the company, ie, that condition (d) ante was not fulfilled; but it was held that other provisions in the articles empowered the board to delegate the power of executing guarantees to one of their number, and this defence accordingly failed.

In *Mahony's Case* no board of directors or secretary had in fact been appointed, and it was the conduct of those who, under the constitution of the company, were entitled to appoint them which was relied on as a representation that certain persons were directors and secretary. Since they had 'actual' authority to appoint these officers, they had 'actual' authority to make representations who the officers were. In both these cases the constitution of the company, whether it had been seen by the contractor or not, was relevant in order to determine whether the persons whose representations by conduct was relied on as creating the 'apparent' authority of the agent had 'actual' authority to make the representations on behalf of the company. In *Mahony's Case*, if the persons in question had not been persons who would normally be supposed to have such authority by someone who did not in fact know the constitution of the company, it may well be that the contractor would not have succeeded in proving condition (c), viz, that he relied on the representations made by those persons, unless he proved that he did in fact know the constitution of the company. This, I think, accounts for the passages in the speeches of Lord Chelmsford and Lord Hatherley which are cited by Slade J, in *Rama Corpn v Proved Tin and General Investments Ltd*.

The cases where the contractor's claim failed, viz, *J C Houghton & Co v Nothard, Lowe and Wills Ltd*; *Kreditbank Cassel GmbH v Schenkers, Ltd*; and the *Rama Corpn Case* were all cases where the contract sought to be enforced was not one which a person occupying the position in relation to the company's business, which the contractor knew that the agent occupied, would normally be authorised to enter into on behalf of the company. The conduct of the board of directors in permitting the agent to occupy that position, on which the contractor relied, thus did not of itself amount to a representation that the agent had authority to enter into the contract sought to be enforced, ie, condition (a) was not fulfilled. The contractor, however, in each of these three cases sought to rely on a provision of the articles, giving to the board power to delegate wide authority to the agent, as entitling the contractor to treat the conduct of the board as a representation that the agent had had delegated to him wider powers than those normally exercised by persons occupying the position in relation to the company's business which the agent was in fact permitted by the board to occupy. Since this would involve proving that the representation on which he in fact relied as inducing him to enter into the contract comprised the articles of association of the company as well as the conduct of the new board, it would be necessary for him to establish, first, that he knew the contents of the articles (ie, that condition (c) was fulfilled in respect of any representation contained in the articles) and, secondly, that the conduct of the board in the light of that knowledge would be understood by a reasonable man as a representation that the agent had authority to enter into the contract sought to be enforced, ie, that condition (a) was fulfilled. The need to establish both these things was pointed out by Sargant LJ, in *Houghton's Case*, in a judgment which was concurred in by Atkin LJ; but his observations, as I read them, are directed only to a case where the contract sought to be enforced is not a contract of a kind which a person occupying the position which the agent was permitted by the board to occupy would normally be authorised to enter into on behalf of the company.

I find some confirmation for this view of Sargant LJ's judgment in the dictum of Atkin LJ, in the *Kreditbank Cassel Case*, another case of an 'abnormal' contract.

SOURCE 98

Hely-Hutchinson *v* Brayhead Ltd

(Queen's Bench Division affirmed on different grounds, Court of Appeal 1966) [1968] 1 QB 549; [1967] 3 All ER 98

The plaintiff advanced money to the defendant, as well as guaranteeing other loans made to the defendant. Undertakings indemnifying the plaintiff against any loss he might suffer as a result of the loan and guarantee, were given on the notepaper of the defendant and signed by one Richards as chairman. Richards acted as, but was never appointed managing director of the defendant. The plaintiff, who was a non-executive director of the defendant, sued to recover his loan and money paid out under the guarantee.

ROSKILL J: The right starting point is to deal with the question of ostensible or apparent authority. Counsel for the plaintiff did not put ostensible or apparent authority in the forefront of his argument. He claimed first that there was here implied authority in Mr Richards by virtue of the position which he occupied as chairman of directors and de facto managing director. It is convenient to say at this point that although, as one would expect, the articles of association of Brayhead contain power to appoint a managing director . . . , no formal appointment of a managing director was ever made. I have no doubt at all, however, on the evidence to which I have listened and from what I have read in the documents, that Mr Richards was at all times in the position of a managing director and was running Brayhead as if he were its managing director, and that he was at all times its chief executive in addition to being chairman. The question to what extent there may be implied authority in a chairman or managing director acting as such as distinct from express authority, so as to bind a company to acts done by him in the course of his duties as chairman or managing director or chief executive is one of considerable difficulty and one on which there appears to be little or no relevant authority. The conception of implied authority in such a person as distinct from express authority is not easy having regard to the cases on this branch of the law on ostensible or apparent authority. It was urged by counsel for the plaintiff that, as Mr Richards was both chairman and de facto managing director, there was for that reason alone implied authority in him to do what he did. I have some difficulty in accepting that. I would not be prepared to hold that there is implied authority in a chairman of a company, merely by reason of his office, to do what Mr Richards did in this particular case in signing C.23 and C.26. I do not think that mere status, derived from the holding of a particular office such as chairman or managing director or chief executive, of itself implies an authority which would not otherwise exist. There may be cases where such an implication can be made, but I do not propose to decide this issue on this point because I am quite satisfied for the reasons which I shall endeavour to give in a moment, that there was ostensible or apparent authority in Mr Richards to do what he did. I think that for a large number of reasons.

The set-up in Brayhead is easy to envisage. It was an industrial holding company with a large number of subsidiaries. Its directors were in the main — not all, but in the main — working directors, each in charge of a section of the holding company's subsidiaries. One would look after electronics, another engineering, and so on. They would all come back to Mr Richards for advice and, which is more important, for decision from time to time on matters concerning their own particular group. The final decision, and most especially on any matter concerning finance, was Mr Richards' and nobody else's. Sometimes, I daresay, the directors persuaded him to take or to refrain from taking a particular step; no doubt, like any wise chief executive, he sought and obtained advice before he made up his mind; but in all these cases the final decision, I am quite satisfied, rested with him and with nobody else. If one goes through the minutes and documents which have been put before me, one can see repeated examples of Mr Richards acting in this way. Sometimes, of course, the matter would come back to the board for formal ratification after he had committed Brayhead, perhaps technically without express authority. On other occasions, of which there are a number of examples in the minutes, he plainly committed Brayhead and then, as it were, reported the matter afterwards. There is a striking example of this, as counsel for the plaintiff pointed out in cross-examining Mr Richards, in connexion with a Mr Short and his company. It is worth noting that in connexion with the agreement to advance £150,000 to Perdio and the taking over of the Kleinwort Benson acceptance credits there is no reference that I can find until a much later date, 19 May 1965, to Mr Richards having reported this or obtained formal authority to enter into these commitments. More important, perhaps, in this connexion is what is revealed by one of the early documents, that Mr Richards, acting for Brayhead, varied the agreement of January 1965, by a document signed by him 'A. J. Richards. A director duly authorised for and on behalf of Brayhead Limited'. This came to the notice of Brayhead's then solicitors who wrote a letter to Mr Bond saying it would be necessary for the directors to ratify the signing of that document and enclosing a draft minute for this purpose. That minute, I am told by Mr Bond, was never in fact signed. I can understand that sort of thing happening in a busy office, but the importance of the point is not that the minute was not signed, but that the whole incident is illustrative of the sort of thing which Mr Richards was doing. It is just what one would expect a busy man in his position to do. I have no doubt that the board knew that he was doing this sort of thing all the time and that whenever he thought it was necessary he assumed, or purported to assume, authority to bind Brayhead and that the board allowed him to do it and acquiesced in his doing it. That is not to say, adopting the phrase used yesterday by counsel for the defendants, that all the directors were 'Yes men', I am sure that they were nothing of the kind. Mr Richards was a forceful personality, he knew his own mind and, as I said earlier in his judgment, he is a man of financial acumen. He quite clearly was allowed by Brayhead to hold himself out as having ostensible or apparent authority to enter into commitments of the kind which he entered into, or purported to enter into, when he signed C.23, C.24, C.25 and C.26. As I have already said, the defendants have not sought to say that the commitments in C.24 and C.25 were entered into without authority.

It seems plain on the cases that if Lord Suirdale were a 'third party', as it is sometimes called, or an outside party, or a 'stranger' in relation to these transactions he would prima facie be entitled to rely on the rule in *Royal British Bank v Turquand.*[1] I would respectfully borrow the statement of that rule from the language which Lord Simonds in turn borrowed from 5 Halsbury's Laws of England (2nd edn) p 423, para 69 in his speech in *Morris v Kanssen,*[2] a case to which I shall refer in a moment. His Lordship said this:

'The so-called rule in *Turquand's Case* is, I think, correctly stated in 5 Halsbury's Laws of England (2nd edn) p 423: "But persons contracting with a company and dealing in good faith may assume that acts within its constitution and powers have been properly and duly performed, and are

1 (1856) 6 E&B 327; 119 ER 886 (see p 260)
2 [1946] AC 459; [1946] 1 All ER 586

not bound to inquire whether acts of internal management have been regular".'

. . .

What is first contended in answer to those arguments is that the plaintiff was a director of Brayhead, and, as a director of Brayhead (even though there would vis à vis a true third party be ostensible or apparent authority) the plaintiff cannot take advantage of the rule in *Turquand's Case* because he is not, for the purposes of that rule, a 'stranger', or an 'outsider', or a 'third party', whichever phrase one chooses to use. Counsel for the defendants, naturally, based this branch of his argument on the decision of the House of Lords, to which I have already referred, in *Morris v Kanssen*. The complex facts of that case are summarised in the headnote, which I will not stop to read. Suffice it to say that Mr Morris, the appellant, had thought that he was a director of a company when he was not a director and he thought that he had acquired certain shares in that company, having along with other purported directors purported to allot them to himself. He sought to rely on the rule in *Turquand's Case* for the purpose of establishing rights against the respondent, Kanssen. Lord Simonds, who delivered the leading speech, rejected the argument — the argument appears previously to have been rejected in the Court of Appeal in the judgment of Lord Greene MR. After stressing that Morris had been himself acting as a director in the allotment and issue of the shares to himself and others and that he was at all times the officer and agent of the company for that purpose, Lord Simonds said:

> 'What then is the position of the director or acting director who claims to hold the company to a transaction which the company had not, though it might have, authorised? Your lordships have not in this case to consider what the result might be if such a director had not himself purported to act on behalf of the company in the unauthorised transaction. For here Morris was himself purporting to act on behalf of the company in a transaction in which he had no authority. Can he then say that he was entitled to assume that all was in order? My lords, the old question comes into my mind, "*Quis custodiet ipsos custodes?*".'

Later Lord Simonds said:

> 'Admit — as, to my mind, one must admit — that a director is not for the purpose of the rule in the same position as a stranger; then it is as immaterial how long he has been a director, as it is whether he is an idle or diligent director, or a robust or sick director.'

It must be observed in relation to the passages which I have just read that Morris, the alleged director, in doing what he did, had been acting for and on behalf of the company. As I read Lord Simonds' speech it was the fact that he had been acting for and on behalf of the company which disentitled him later to turn round as allottee of the shares and seek to take advantage of the rule in *Turquand's Case* in his own favour.

. . .

The plaintiff did not act on behalf of Brayhead in relation to the allegedly unauthorised transaction. But leading counsel for the defendants and, in his admirable argument following his learned leader, their junior counsel said it was enough to exclude the operation of the rule in *Turquand's Case*, that the plaintiff was a party to the transaction and was a director of Brayhead, even though he did not act for Brayhead. With the utmost respect to that argument and the skill with which it was advanced by both counsel for the defendants, I find nothing in these cases which compels me to go so far as they have invited me to go. In some cases — and of course *Morris's Case* is one and *Howard's Case*[1] is another — a director is quite plainly anything but a 'stranger', or an 'outsider', or a 'third party', but I do not think that the mere fact that a director of a company makes a contract with that company in a capacity other than that of a director, automatically affects him in the capacity in which he is contracting with constructive knowledge of such disabilities and limitations as he might be deemed to know were he also acting for the company in the transaction in question. As counsel for the plaintiff said in the course of his reply, to extend this doctrine in the way suggested would have very far-reaching ramifications on ordinary day-to-day business transactions and would, or might, involve very often considerable enquiry before a contract could be signed what the respective position and authority was of a particular individual by whom it was proposed that a contract should be signed. I regard the decisions in *Morris v Kanssen* and in *Howard's Case* as decisions where, on the facts of those particular cases, the rights sought to be enforced by the plaintiffs concerned arose from acts done by them as directors which were so closely interwoven with their duties and acts as directors as to make it impossible for the directors involved to say that they were not for all purposes to be treated as possessed of knowledge of the limitations on their powers as directors. In the present case Brayhead's agreement with the plaintiff had nothing to do with his duties and obligations as a director of Brayhead. What he was doing was to agree to advance money to an associated company of Brayhead of which he was chairman and managing director against a guarantee and indemnity from Brayhead, who were expected to become the parent company of that associated company. He was acting, as I think, otherwise than in his capacity as a director of Brayhead in making that agreement. He was acting as an individual, for it was he who was going to advance the money in consideration of the agreement into which Mr Richards was purporting to enter on behalf of Brayhead. He was going to be the other contracting party. I think therefore that this argument fails.

Counsel for the defendants then submitted that, even assuming that he was wrong on the point which I have just decided, this transaction was an 'unusual' transaction for the purposes of the exceptions to the rule in *Turquand's Case*. He put the argument in two ways: first he said that it was not the sort of transaction into which one would expect a managing director to enter in the circumstances with somebody who was, in fact, also a director of the same company; and, secondly, he sought to say that it was 'unusual' by reason of the provisions of article 99 of Brayhead's articles of association. I should emphasise that this argument is independent of his principal submission based on article 99. I will deal with these points first because I can take them briefly. Counsel relied in particular on the well-known decision of the Court of Appeal in *J C Houghton & Co v Nothard Lowe and Wills Ltd*,[2] a case considered by the Court of Appeal in *Freeman's Case*,[3] to which I have already referred. If one attempts to look at this through the eyes of an ordinary businessman, I cannot see anything in the least unusual in this transaction. The loan was being made by the plaintiff. The parent company (as it was hoped Brayhead would become in relation to Perdio) was going to give a guarantee and an indemnity. Brayhead itself had already made a very large investment in Perdio: it had lent money, it had accepted obligations under the acceptance credits, and it was obviously going to assist towards helping Brayhead's investment in Perdio if Perdio could be kept afloat a little longer with

---

1 (1866) 1 Ch App 561
2 [1928] AC 1; [1927] 1 KB 246 (see p 264)
3 [1964] 2 QB 480; [1964] 1 All ER 630 (see p 266)

the aid of the plaintiff's money, particularly as Brayhead itself might be going to put in further money. Therefore, as between 'usual' and 'unusual' transactions, I see no reason for thinking there was anything 'unusual' in the transaction in the sense in which that adjective has been used in the cases. Nor do I think that the fact that the agreements were or may have been contracts in which the plaintiff was 'interested' within the meaning of article 99 of Brayhead's articles of association makes that which was not commercially an 'unusual' transaction 'unusual' in the sense to which I have just referred.

This decision was affirmed by the Court of Appeal but on the ground that Richards was *actually* authorised and not on the ground that he was being held out by the company as its managing director. It was therefore not necessary for the Court of Appeal to deal with the question whether an 'insider' can rely on the Turquand presumption. For a cogent criticism of the Court of Appeal's approach, see *Nock* [1967] 30 MLR 705.

SOURCE 99
Panorama Developments (Guildford) Ltd *v* Fidelis Furnishing Fabrics (Ltd)
(Court of Appeal 1971) [1971] 2 QB 711; [1971] 2 All ER 1028

The secretary of the defendant company hired cars from the plaintiff, ostensibly for the use of the defendant, but in fact for himself. The defendant refused to pay for the hire. The county court upheld the plaintiff's claim and the Court of Appeal dismissed the appeal.

LORD DENNING MR: Mr Hames' second point is this: he says that the company is not bound by the letters which were signed by Mr Bayne as 'Company Secretary.' He says that, on the authorities, a company secretary fulfils a very humble role: and that he has no authority to make any contracts or representations on behalf of the company. He refers to *Barnett, Hoares & Co v South London Tramways Co*,[1] where Lord Esher MR said:

> 'A secretary is a mere servant; his position is that he is to do what he is told, and no person can assume that he has any authority to represent anything at all; . . .'

Those words were approved by Lord Macnaghten in *George Whitechurch Ltd v Cavanagh*.[2] They are supported by the decision in *Ruben v Great Fingall Consolidated*.[3] They are referred to in some of the textbooks as authoritative.

But times have changed. A company secretary is a much more important person nowadays than he was in 1887. He is an officer of the company with extensive duties and responsibilities. This appears not only in the modern Companies Acts, but also by the role which he plays in the day-to-day business of companies. He is no longer a mere clerk. He regularly makes representations on behalf of the company and enters into contracts on its behalf which come within the day-to-day running of the company's business. So much so that he may be regarded as held out as having authority to do such things on behalf of the company. He is certainly entitled to sign contracts connected with the administrative side of a company's affairs, such as employing staff, and ordering cars,

---

1 (1887) 18 QBD 815
2 [1902] AC 117; 71 LJKB 400
3 [1906] AC 439; 75 LJKB 843

and so forth. All such matters now come within the ostensible authority of a company's secretary.

SOURCE 100
First Energy *v* Hungarian International Bank
(Court of Appeal) [1993] BCLC 1409

The plaintiff sought financial facilities from the defendant. A facility letter was sent to the plaintiff and the plaintiff followed the instruction of signing both copies and returning them to the defendant in the expectation of receiving one back signed by the defendant. According to the letter, the offer was one to be made by the plaintiff and on y on receipt of a signed copy of the letter from the defendant could the contract to provide the facilities be established. The plaintiff never received a signed copy of the facility letter. Nor were any of the documentation or security arrangements as outlined in the letter ever put in place. Nevertheless, funding was arranged for the plaintiff's first project ('the Wisbech project') and when the plaintiff sought further funding for three more projects, it received a letter in the following terms from the senior manager of the Manchester branch (Jamison), with whom the plaintiff (represented by Croft) had been dealing throughout the negotiations.

> 'Further to our telephone conversation earlier today, I am pleased to attach herewith three hire purchase agreements, one for each of the contracts recently concluded by First Energy.
>
> You will see that I have indicated in pencil how the documents should be completed and I would be obliged if you would arrange for the directors of First Energy to sign and have witnessed as appropriate.
>
> In order to complete our transaction we shall require an invoice similar to that which was provided in respect of CMB Wisbech (copy attached). In each case the amount invoiced should be the cash price as shown on the HP agreement, plus VAT again as shown on the HP agreement, less deposit equal to the amount of VAT leaving the net amount due the same as the cash price. Our invoice should be accompanied by the appropriate supporting invoices from First Energy suppliers.
>
> On receipt of the above we will be in a position to release funds of £616,151.43 which is approximately £30,000 in excess of the total installation costs.
>
> I trust you will find the documentation self explanatory and look forward to being of further assistance.'

It was quite clear from the outset that the general manager, although clearly of considerable significance in the hierarchy of the defendant was not authorised to sign facility letters. In this action, however, the plaintiff submitted that it relied on the general manager's authority to convey the offer of a facility on behalf of the defendant. This submission was upheld both before the trial judge and by the Court of Appeal.

STEYN LJ: . . .

Ostensible authority
   In order for a plea of apparent authority to succeed it is necessary for First Energy to establish not only that HIB through its appropriate organs held out Mr Jamison as having such authority but also that First Energy relied on that fact in entering into the transaction. In context the letter was calculated to convey to

First Energy that Mr Jamison had obtained the approval of the transaction at the appropriate level at head office. The evidence of Mr Croft was that he relied on that fact. That evidence was supported by the inherent probabilities. The judge found that the element of reliance was established. And the appellants do not challenge the judge's finding that the element of reliance was established.

The appellants' challenge was to the judge's finding that HIB had held out Mr Jamison to be HIB's agent for the purpose of conveying to First Energy approval of the offer contained in the letter of 2 August. It is common ground that a plea of apparent authority can only be based on a holding out, or representation, as to authority of the agent by the principal sought to be held bound by the particular act. Our law does not recognise, in the context of apparent authority, the idea of a self-authorising agent: see *Armagas Ltd v Mundogas* SA [1986] 2 All ER 385, [1986] AC 717.

It is possible to narrow down the issue of ostensible authority, which arises in the present case. A principal may clothe an agent with apparent authority in more than one way. The present case falls into a category, which, in *Armagas Ltd v Mundogas* SA [1986] 2 All ER 385 at 389, [1986] AC 717 at 777, was described by Lord Keith as follows:

> 'In the commonly encountered case, the ostensible authority is general in character, arising when the principal has placed the agent in a position which in the outside world is generally regarded as carrying authority to enter into transactions of the kind in question.'

This type of apparent authority is often described as the usual authority of an agent. But it is important to remember that the idea of usual authority is used in two senses. First, it sometimes means that the agent had implied actual authority to perform acts necessarily incidental to the performance of the agency. Secondly, it sometimes means that the principal's conduct in clothing the agent with the trappings of authority was such as to induce a third party to rely on the existence of the agency. The issue in the present case is one of usual authority in the second sense.

. . .

[I]n *Soplex Wholesale Supplies Ltd v Egyptian International Foreign Trade Co, The Raffaella* [1985] 2 Lloyd's Rep 36

. . .

Browne-Wilkinson LJ analysed the matter in some detail. He said (at 42–43):

> 'I have so far ignored the representation made by Mr Booth that "in London one signature is sufficient". Mr Stamler submitted that a principal cannot be held liable as a result of the agent holding himself out as possessing an authority he does not in fact possess: he relied on remarks to that effect in the *Freeman & Lockyer* case at p 505, *Attorney General for Ceylon v Silva*, [1953] 1 Lloyd's Rep 563; [1953] AC 461 at pp 571 and 479, *The British Bank of The Middle East* case (sup) and *Armagas Ltd v Mundogas SA*, [1985] 1 Lloyd's Rep 1. As at present advised, I am not satisfied that the principle to be derived from those cases is as wide as Mr Stamler suggests; they were all cases or dicta dealing with the position where the agent had neither authority to enter into the transaction nor authority to make representations on behalf of the principal. It is obviously correct that an agent who has no actual, or apparent authority either (a) to enter into a transaction or (b) to make representations as to the transaction cannot hold himself out as having authority to enter into the transaction so as to affect the principal's position. But, suppose a company confers actual or apparent

authority on X to make representations and X erroneously represents to a third party that Y has authority to enter into a transaction; why should not such a representation be relied upon as part of the holding out of Y by the company? By parity of reasoning, if a company confers actual or apparent authority on A to make representations on the company's behalf but no actual authority on A to enter into the specific transaction, why should a representation made by A as to his authority not be capable of being relief on as one of the acts of holding out? There is substantial authority that it can be: see *British Thomson-Houston Co Ltd v Federated European Bank Ltd*, [1932] 2 KB 176, especially at p 182 (where the only holding out was an erroneous representation by the agent that he was managing director); and the *Freeman & Lockyer* case per Lord Justice Pearson at p 499; *Hely-Hutchinson v Brayhead Ltd*, [1968] 1 QB 549 per Lord Denning, MR at p 593A–D. If, as I am inclined to think an agent with authority to make representations can make a representation that he has authority to enter into a transaction, then the Judge was entitled to hold, as he did, that Mr Booth, as the representative of Refson in charge of the transaction, had implied or apparent authority to make the representation that only one signature was required and that this representation was a relevant consideration in deciding whether Refson had held out Mr Booth as having authority to sign the undertaking. However, since it is not necessary to decide this point for the purposes of this appeal, I express no concluded view on it.'

Miss Arden said that the authorities referred to by Browne-Wilkinson LJ are in the line of company law cases of which the decision in *Royal British Bank v Turquand* (1856) E & B 327, [1843–60] All ER Rep 435, is the classic illustration. That may be right. But in my view those authorities are not irrelevant to the question before us. This line of authority reveals a tension between two conflicting principles. The first is that the shareholders of a company should be protected against hasty and ill-considered transactions entered into by the company. The second is that third parties who deal with companies in good faith ought to be protected. The *Royal British Bank v Turquand* line of cases represents an intensely pragmatic and serviceable resolution of the competing considerations in particular situations. Leaving aside cases which focused specifically on the impact of the public document of a company, I regard this line of authority as throwing light on the approach we ought to adopt.

It seems to me that the law recognises that in modern commerce an agent who has no apparent authority to conclude a particular transaction may sometimes be clothed with apparent authority to make representations of fact. The level at which such apparent authority could be found to exist may vary and generalisation will be unhelpful. But let me take the concrete example of a company secretary. In *Panorama Developments (Guildford) Ltd v Fidelis Furnishing Fabrics Ltd* [1971] 3 All ER 16, [1971] 2 QB 711 it was recognised that the managerial functions of a company secretary are today far greater than they once were. Mr Ponting was HIB's company secretary. He attended negotiations in July. If he had been asked for a resolution of the board of directors of HIB approving the transaction, and if he had in error sent a document purporting to be such a resolution, it is surely possible, depending on the evidence, that he might have acted within his apparent authority by virtue of his position as company secretary. That would be so despite the fact that he plainly had no apparent authority to sanction the transaction. My reason for this tentative view is that a company secretary is known to be the employee specifically charged with keeping the minutes of board meetings.

Miss Arden accepted that if the managing director of HIB had confirmed that the transaction had been approved by HIB a case of ostensible authority could be made out. While HIB did not in fact have a general manager, Miss Arden was prepared to accept that the same would generally be true of a general manager. Confining myself strictly to a situation of a merchant bank or a trading bank, such as HIB, I take the view that it would be unrealistic to assert the contrary. And the reason is that in accordance with the general understanding in commerce the managing director and general manager of such a bank is clothed with a general actual or apparent authority to convey such information. It would be absurd to suggest that the third party should seek information from the board of directors as a whole. But Miss Arden submitted that as senior manager in Manchester Mr Jamison was in a different position.

In agreement with the judge I have come to the conclusion, on the particular facts of this case, that Mr Jamison's position as senior manager in Manchester was such that he was clothed with ostensible authority to communicate that head office approval had been given for the facility set out in the 2 August letter. Although his status was below that of a managing director or general manager, it was nevertheless considerable. And, in the circumstances of this case, the idea that First Energy should have checked with the managing director in London whether HIB had approved the transaction seems unreal. This factor is, of course, not decisive, but it is relevant to the ultimate decision.

Having come to a conclusion, on the application of what I regard as orthodox principles of law, that the judge was entitled and indeed right to find as a matter of fact that ostensible authority to communicate head office approval of the transaction had been established, I return to the place where I started. In my judgment a decision that Mr Jamison did not have apparent authority to communicate head office approval would defeat the reasonable expectations of the parties. And it would fly in the face of the way in which in practice negotiations are conducted between trading banks and trading customers who seek commercial loans. I would reject this ground of appeal.

For these reasons, and for the reasons given by the judge in his careful judgment, I would dismiss the appeal.

PART IV: THE TORTIOUS AND CRIMINAL LIABILITY OF THE COMPANY

A company will be vicariously liable for the torts of its employees. It is no defence on the part of the company to say that the commission of a tortious act could never be within the company's objects and that, therefore the act was ultra vires and void (Source 101). But vicarious liability is insufficient as a basis for holding a company liable where *actual* fault is a requirement. For this purpose, the organic theory or alter ego doctrine was developed. If the act in question has been performed by someone sufficiently closely associated with the company, that person's fault will be attributed to the company *as the company's* fault.

The development of the organic theory as the basis for a company's liability in tort led to the phenomenon of the company's criminal liability, something which can never depend on vicarious responsibility (Sources 102, 103, 104).

SOURCE 101

Campbell *v* Paddington Corporation

(King's Bench Division 1911) [1911] 1 KB 869

The plaintiff let her balcony to someone who wanted to view the funeral procession of the King. The defendant unlawfully created a stand in front of the plaintiff's premises blocking the view as a result of which she had to release the person from his contract with her.

> AVORY J: Three objections are taken to this verdict. First, it is said that the defendants, the mayor, aldermen and councillors of the metropolitan borough of Paddington, being a corporation, are not liable because the borough council had no legal right to do what they did, and therefore the corporation cannot be sued. This stand was erected in pursuance of a formal resolution of the borough council. To say that, because the borough council had no legal right to erect it, therefore the corporation cannot be sued, is to say that no corporation can ever be sued for any tort or wrong. The only way in which this corporation can act is by its council, and the resolution of the council is the authentic act of the corporation. If the view of the defendants were correct no company could ever be sued if the directors of the company after resolution did an act which the company by its memorandum of association had no power to do. That would be absurd. The first objection therefore fails, and the defendants are liable to be sued . . .

SOURCE 102

Lennard's Carrying Company Ltd *v* Asiatic Petroleum Co Ltd

(House of Lords 1915) [1915] AC 705; 84 LJKB 1281

John Lennard was the active director of a company which managed the appellant company (of which he was also a director). As a result of unseaworthiness, a ship chartered by the appellant owners sank with the loss of cargo. The respondents brought an action for damages for the loss of the cargo and the appellants sought to rely on s 502 of the Merchant Shipping Act 1894, in terms of which it was exempt from liability for loss unless the loss was caused by its actual fault. It was established that Mr Lennard was at fault as he ought to have known of the unseaworthiness of the ship.

> VISCOUNT HALDANE LC: . . . Now, my Lords, did what happened take place without the actual fault or privity of the owners of the ship who were the appellants? My Lords, a corporation is an abstraction. It has no mind of its own any more than it has a body of its own; its active and directing will must consequently be sought in the person of somebody who for some purposes may be called an agent, but who is really the directing mind and will of the corporation, the very ego and centre of the personality of the corporation. That person may be under the direction of the shareholders in general meeting; that person may be the board of directors itself, or it may be, and in some companies it is so, that that person has an authority co-ordinate with the board of directors given to him under the articles of association, and is appointed by the general meeting of the company, and can only be removed by the general meeting of the company. My Lords, whatever is not known about Mr Lennard's position, this is known for certain, Mr Lennard took the active part in the management of this ship on behalf of the owners, and Mr Lennard, as I have said, was registered as the person designated for this purpose in the ship's register. Mr Lennard therefore was the natural person to come on behalf of the owners and give full

evidence not only about the events of which I have spoken, and which related to the seaworthiness of the ship, but about his own position and as to whether or not he was the life and soul of the company. For if Mr Lennard was the directing mind of the company, then his action must, unless a corporation is not to be liable at all, have been an action which was the action of the company itself within the meaning of section 502. It has not been contended at the Bar, and it could not have been successfully contended, that section 502 is so worded as to exempt a corporation altogether which happens to be the owner of a ship, merely because it happens to be a corporation. It must be upon the true construction of that section in such a case as the present one that the fault or privity is the fault or privity of somebody who is not merely a servant or agent for whom the company is liable upon the footing *respondeat superior*, but somebody for whom the company is liable because his action is the very action of the company itself. It is not enough that the fault should be the fault of a servant in order to exonerate the owner, the fault must also be one which is not the fault of the owner, or a fault to which the owner is privy; and I take the view that when anybody sets up that section to excuse himself from the normal consequences of the maximum *respondeat superior* the burden lies upon him to do so.

SOURCE 103
Tesco Supermarkets Ltd *v* Nattrass
(House of Lords 1972) [1972] AC 153; [1971] 2 All ER 127

The appellant supermarket had been convicted of an offence under the Trade Descriptions Act for selling a product at a price higher than the advertised sale price. The store had sold out its sale items of that product and the shelves had been restocked by an assistant with the regular priced items. The manager of the store — who was in sole charge of that branch — was unaware of the fact that the sale priced items were sold out and the shelves restocked with regular priced items. Under the statute, it was a defence to the charge if it could be established that the accused had taken all reasonable steps and exercised all due diligence to avoid the commission of the offence and that the offence was committed by 'another person'. The House of Lords upheld the appeal. The mind (and fault) of the branch manager was not that of the appellant and the appellant had established that they had taken all reasonable steps to ensure that branch managers were issued with proper instructions.

LORD REID: . . . I must start by considering the nature of the personality which by a fiction the law attributes to a corporation. A living person has a mind which can have knowledge or intention or be negligent and he has hands to carry out his intentions. A corporation has none of these: it must act through living persons, though not always one or the same person. Then the person who acts is not speaking or acting for the company. He is acting as the company and his mind which directs his acts is the mind of the company. There is no question of the company being vicariously liable. He is not acting as a servant, representative, agent or delegate. He is an embodiment of the company or, one could say, he hears and speaks through the persona of the company, within his appropriate sphere, and his mind is the mind of the company. If it is a guilty mind then that guilt is the guilt of the company. It must be a question of law whether, once the facts have been ascertained, a person in doing particular things is to be regarded as the company or merely as the company's servant or agent. In that case any liability of the company can only be a statutory or vicarious liability.

In *Lennard's Carrying Co Ltd v Asiatic Petroleum Co Ltd*[1] the question was whether damage had occurred without the 'actual fault or privity' of the owner of a ship. The owners were a company. The fault was that of the registered managing owner who managed the ship on behalf of the owners and it was held that the company could not dissociate itself from him so as to say that there was no actual fault or privity on the part of the company. Viscount Haldane LC said:

> 'For if Mr Lennard was the directing mind of the company, then his action must, unless a corporation is not to be liable at all, have been an action which was the action of the company itself within the meaning of section 502 . . . It must be upon the true construction of that section in such a case as the present one that the fault or privity is the fault or privity of somebody who is not merely a servant or agent for whom the company is liable upon the footing *respondeat superior*, but somebody for whom the company is liable because his action is the very action of the company itself.'

Reference is frequently made to the judgment of Denning LJ in *H L Bolton (Engineering) Co Ltd v T J Graham & Sons Ltd.*[2] He said:

> 'A company may in many ways be likened to a human body. It has a brain and nerve centre which controls what it does. It also has hands which hold the tools and act in accordance with directions from the centre. Some of the people in the company are mere servants and agents who are nothing more than hands to do the work and cannot be said to represent the mind or will. Others are directors and managers who represent the directing mind and will of the company, and control what it does. The state of mind of these managers is the state of mind of the company and is treated by the law as such.'

In that case the directors of the company only met once a year: they left the management of the business to others, and it was the intention of those managers which was imputed to the company. I think that was right. There have been attempts to apply Lord Denning's words to all servants of a company whose work is brain work, or who exercise some managerial discretion under the direction of superior officers of the company. I do not think that Lord Denning intended to refer to them. He only referred to those who 'represent the directing mind and will of the company, and control what it does.'

I think that is right for this reason. Normally the board of directors, the managing director and perhaps other superior officers of a company carry out the functions of management and speak and act as the company. Their subordinates do not. They carry out orders from above and it can make no difference that they are given some measure of discretion. But the board of directors may delegate some part of their functions of management giving to their delegate full discretion to act independently of instructions from them. I see no difficulty in holding that they have thereby put such a delegate in their place so that within the scope of the delegation he can act as the company. It may not always be easy to draw the line but there are cases in which the line must be drawn. *Lennard's Case* was one of them.

In some cases the phrase alter ego has been used. I think it is misleading. When

---

1 [1915] AC 705; 84 LJKB 1281 (see p 282)
2 [1957] 1 QB 159; [1956] 3 All ER 624

dealing with a company the word alter is I think misleading. The person who speaks and acts as the company is not alter. He is identified with the company. And when dealing with an individual no other individual can be his alter ego. The other individual can be a servant, agent, delegate or representative but I know of neither principle nor authority which warrants the confusion (in the literal or original sense) of two separate individuals.

. . .

What good purpose could be served by making an employer criminally responsible for the misdeeds of some of his servants but not for those of others? It is sometimes argued — it was argued in the present case — that making an employer criminally responsible, even when he has done all that he could to prevent an offence, affords some additional protection to the public because this will induce him to do more. But if he has done all he can how can he do more? I think that what lies behind this argument is a suspicion that magistrates too readily accept evidence that an employer has done all he can to prevent offences. But if magistrates were to accept as sufficient a paper scheme and perfunctory efforts to enforce it they would not be doing their duty — that would not be 'due diligence' on the part of the employer.

Then it is said that this would involve discrimination in favour of a large employer like the appellants against a small shopkeeper. But that is not so. Mr Clement was the 'opposite number' of the small shopkeeper and he was liable to prosecution in this case. The purpose of this Act must have been to penalise those at fault, not those who were in no way to blame.

The Divisional Court decided this case on a theory of delegation. In that they were following some earlier authorities. But they gave far too wide a meaning to delegation. I have said that a board of directors can delegate part of their functions of management so as to make their delegate an embodiment of the company within the sphere of the delegation. But here the board never delegated any part of their functions. They set up a chain of command through regional and district supervisors, but they remained in control. The shop managers had to obey their general directions and also take orders from their superiors. The acts or omissions of shop managers were not acts of the company itself.

SOURCE 104
El Ajou *v* Dollar Land Holdings plc
(Court of Appeal) [1994] 1 BCLC 464

NOURSE LJ
Introduction

Of the questions that remain in dispute in this case, the most important is whether, for the purposes of establishing a company's liability under the knowing receipt head of constructive trust, the knowledge of one of its directors can be treated as having been the knowledge of the company. That is essentially a question of company law. There are or have been other questions on tracing and constructive trust.

The company is the first defendant, Dollar Land Holdings plc (DLH). The director is Mr Sylvain Ferdman, who was the chairman and one of the three directors of DLH between June 1985 and June 1987. The party who seeks to recover against DLH in constructive trust is the plaintiff, Abdul Ghani El Ajou. He has put his claim at £1.3m. On 12 June 1992, after a trial extending over some 11 days, Millett J delivered a reserved judgment dismissing the plaintiff's action. He held that the plaintiff had an equitable right to trace the money into the hands of DLH, but that Mr Ferdman's knowledge of their fraudulent misapplication could not be treated as having been the knowledge of DLH, either on the ground of his having been its directing mind and will or on the ground of his having been its agent in the transaction. The judge found that another person closely concerned with the affairs of DLH, Mr William Stern, did not have the requisite knowledge of the misapplication.

. . .

Mr Ferdman is a Swiss national, resident in Geneva. He worked for many years for the Bank of International Credit in Geneva. In 1972 he left the bank and set up his own company, Société d'Administration et de Financement SA (SAFI), through which he acted as a fiduciary agent. SAFI was originally owned jointly by Mr Ferdman and an old-established Swiss cantonal bank of good reputation, but in 1982 Mr Ferdman became its sole proprietor. SAFI acted as a fiduciary agent for clients who did not wish their identities to be disclosed. Two of its clients were a Mr Singer and a Mr Goldhar, who were associates of the Canadians. Mr Ferdman was accustomed to accept funds from clients without questioning their origin, and to act for clients who were anxious to conceal their identity. He regarded the need to preserve his clients' anonymity as paramount — without it he would have had no business — and to this end he was willing on occasion to present himself or SAFI as a beneficial owner and to make false statements to that effect.

. . .

Knowledge

It having been established that DLH received assets representing proceeds of the fraud, I come to the question of knowledge. By the end of the hearing there could have been no doubt that Mr Ferdman himself had the requisite knowledge. The judge said of him (at 759):

> 'He freely admitted that he knew that the persons who were providing the money for the Nine Elms project were the persons who had been behind the fraud in Amsterdam; and that by 7 April 1986, when he signed the letter to Yulara, he knew (or assumed) that the money which he would be receiving into the Keristal no 2 account was part of the proceeds of the fraud.'

Thus arises the most important question remaining in dispute, which is whether Mr Ferdman's knowledge can be treated as having been the knowledge of DLH. The plaintiff contends that it can and ought to be, first, on the ground that Mr Ferdman was, in relation to DLH's receipt of the assets representing the moneys fraudulently misapplied, its directing mind and will; secondly and alternatively, on the ground that he was its agent in the transaction. Because a company's directing mind and will are often the mind and will of one or more of its directors and because a director is for many purposes an agent of the company, there is a danger of confusion between the two grounds on which the plaintiff relies. But they are, as the judge made clear, quite separate. The plaintiff can succeed on either. The convenient course is to deal with the law and the facts in regard to each of them in turn.

Directing mind and will

This doctrine, sometimes known as the alter ego doctrine, has been developed, with no divergence of approach, in both criminal and civil jurisdictions, the authorities in each being cited indifferently in the other. A company having no mind or will of its own, the need for it arises because the criminal law often requires mens rea as a constituent of the crime, and the civil law intention or knowledge as an ingredient of the cause of action or defence. In the oft-quoted words of Viscount Haldane LC in *Lennard's Carrying Co Ltd v Asiatic Petroleum Co Ltd* [1915] AC 705 at 713:

> 'My Lords, a corporation is an abstraction. It has no mind of its own any more than it has a body of its own; its active and directing will must consequently be sought in the person of somebody who for some purposes may be called an agent, but who is really the directing mind and will of the corporation, the very ego and centre of the personality of the corporation.'

The doctrine attributes to the company the mind and will of the natural person or persons who manage and control its actions. At that point, in the words of Millett J ([1993] BCLC 735 at 760):

> 'Their minds are its mind; their intention its intention; their knowledge its knowledge.'

It is important to emphasise that management and control is not something to be considered generally or in the round. It is necessary to identify the natural person or persons having management and control in relation to the act or omission in point. This was well put by Eveleigh J in delivering the judgment of the Criminal Division of this court in *R v Andrews Weatherfoil Ltd* [1972] 1 All ER 65 at 70, [1972] 1 WLR 118 at 125:

> 'It is necessary to establish whether the natural person or persons in question have the status and authority which in law makes their acts in the matter under consideration the acts of the company so that the natural person is to be treated as the company itself.'

Decided cases show that, in regard to the requisite status and authority, the formal position, as regulated by the company's articles of association, service contracts and so forth, though highly relevant, may not be decisive. Here Millett J adopted a pragmatic approach. In my view he was right to do so, although it has led me, with diffidence, to a conclusion different from his own.

DLH contends that its directing mind and will in relation to its receipt of the assets representing the moneys fraudulently misapplied were either the mind and will of Mr Stern alone or of Mr Stern and the Americans together. They were not the mind and will of Mr Ferdman. The judge's acceptance of this contention is expressed ([1993] BCLC 735 at 760):

> 'In 1986 [DHL's] directors were all officers of SAFI, but they were merely nominee directors representing the interests of the Americans. Mr Ferdman was a non-executive director. His only executive responsibilities were to act as a fiduciary agent, represent the interests of the Americans, and ensure that the necessary corporate documentation was in order. The witnesses agreed that, in the early days of DLH, Mr Ferdman played a bigger role than he did [later]; but I do not think that that was due to any change in his role. He was always responsible for the formal paper work, but not for the business. As the business expanded, so his relative importance diminished. Even in 1986, he played no part in business decisions. These were taken by Mr Stern in consultation with the Americans. In my judgment, Mr Ferdman's position as chairman and non-executive director of DLH was insufficient by itself to constitute his knowledge ipso facto the knowledge of DLH. It has not been alleged, still less established, that the other two officers of SAFI, who with Mr Ferdman constituted the board of DLH in 1986,

shared Mr Ferdman's knowledge of the source of the Canadians' money, but
in my judgment it would make no difference if they did. Like Mr Ferdman,
they were merely nominee directors with non-executive responsibility. They
had no authority to take business decisions. In relation to its business affairs
in 1986, neither Mr Ferdman alone nor the board as a whole can realistically
be regarded as the directing mind and will of DLH.'

In disagreeing with the judge on this question, I start from the position that the
transactions to be considered are those by which DLH received assets representing the moneys fraudulently misapplied.

. . .

The crucial considerations are that Mr Ferdman made all the arrangements for
the receipt and disbursement of the £270,000 and the £1,030,000; that it was he
who signed the letter of 20 March to Roth; that it was he who, on 25 March,
copied that letter to Mr D'Albis; that it was he who signed and despatched the
letter of 7 April to Yulara; that it was he who, on 6 May, signed the agreement with
Yulara; and that it was those steps that caused DLH to become involved in the
project and enabled it later to acquire the assets representing the moneys
fraudulently misapplied.

Each of the steps taken by Mr Ferdman was taken without the authority of a
resolution of the board of DLH. That demonstrates that as between Mr Ferdman
on the one hand and Mr Favre and Mr Jaton on the other it was Mr Ferdman who
had the de facto management and control of the transactions. It may be that that
state of affairs involved some breach of the directors' duties to DLH. But that
would not enable DLH to say that Mr Favre and Mr Jaton were parties to its
directing mind and will in any relevant respect. Mr Tager[1] sought to show that
they did perform duties as directors of DLH. No doubt they did. But there is no
real evidence that they had any responsibility for the transactions in question. In
my view the directing mind and will of DLH in relation to the relevant
transactions between March and June 1986 were the mind and will of Mr
Ferdman and none other. That means that DLH had the requisite knowledge at
that time.

Next, I must consider whether the plaintiff's right to recover is affected by Mr
Ferdman's having ceased to be a director of DLH in June 1987. This question is
of significance only in relation to the £1,030,000. It has no bearing on the
£270,000. Millett J, having repeated his view that, in regard to the £1,030,000, the
relevant transaction was the acquisition by DLH of Yulara's interest in the joint
venture on 16 March 1988, continued (at 762):

'By then Mr Ferdman had ceased to be a director of DLH for nine months,
and he had nothing at all to do with the transaction. Even if, contrary to my
judgment, Mr Ferdman's knowledge should be attributed to DLH in 1986,
it would be quite wrong to treat DLH as still possessing that knowledge in
1988. As Megarry V-C pointed out in *Re Montagu's Settlement Trust* [1992] 4
All ER 308 at 329, [1987] Ch 264 at 284, a natural person should not be said
to have knowledge of a fact that he once knew if at the time in question he
has genuinely forgotten all about it. In my judgment, where the knowledge
of a director is attributed to a company, but is not actually imparted to it, the
company should not be treated as continuing to possess that knowledge
after the director in question has died or left its service. In such circumstances, the company can properly be said to have "lost its memory".'

---

1 Counsel for the defendant

While I might agree with the judge that the knowledge of a director, who had known of a misapplication of trust moneys at the time of their misapplication but had genuinely forgotten all about it by the time that they were received by the company, could not be attributed to the company, I am unable to see how that can assist DLH here. The steps that caused DLH to become involved in the project and enabled it later to acquire the asset representing the £1,030,000 were all taken between March and June 1986. Moreover, although the judge held that the plaintiff was bound to treat the £1,030,000 as represented by Yulara's interest in the project, he found that that sum had been paid into Grangewoods' client account on 29 May 1986 and had thereafter been wholly disbursed as directed by DLH, £745,000 approximately in satisfaction of the purchase price (at 749). In the circumstances, DLH having had the requisite knowledge at the time that it became involved in the project and when the £1,030,000 was disbursed as it directed, it would in my view be unrealistic to hold that it ceased to have that knowledge simply because the mind and will that had been the source of it played no part in the receipt of the asset itself. I am therefore of the opinion that DLH is on this ground liable to the plaintiff in constructive trust.

HOFFMANN LJ: . . .

(b) *The 'directing mind and will' theory*

The phrase 'directing mind and will' comes from a well-known passage in the judgment of Viscount Haldane LC in *Lennard's Carrying Co Ltd v Asiatic Petroleum Co Ltd* [1915] AC 705 which distinguishes between someone who is 'merely a servant or agent' and someone whose action (or knowledge) is that of the company itself. Despite their familiarity, it is worth quoting the terms in which Viscount Haldane said that the directing mind could be identified (at 713):

> 'That person may be under the direction of the shareholders in general meeting; that person may be the board of directors itself, or it may be, and in some companies it is so, that that person has an authority co-ordinate with the board of directors given to him under the articles of association, and is appointed by the general meeting of the company and can only be removed by the general meeting of the company. My Lords, whatever is not known about Mr Lennard's position, this is known for certain, Mr Lennard took the active part in the management of this ship on behalf of the owners, and Mr Lennard, as I have said, was registered as the person designated for this purpose in the ship's register.'

Viscount Haldane therefore regarded the identification of the directing mind as primarily a *constitutional* question, depending in the first instance upon the powers entrusted to a person by the articles of association. The last sentence about Mr Lennard's position shows that the position as reflected in the articles may have to be supplemented by looking at the actual exercise of the company's powers. A person held out by the company as having plenary authority or in whose exercise of such authority the company acquiesces, may be treated as its directing mind.

It is well known that Viscount Haldane derived the concept of the 'directing mind' from German law (see *Gower Principles of Modern Company Law* (5th edn, 1992) p 194, n 36) which distinguishes between the agents and organs of the company. A German company with limited liability (GmbH) is required by law to appoint one or more directors (Geschäftsführer). They are the company's organs and for legal purposes represent the company. The knowledge of any one director, however obtained, is the knowledge of the company (Scholz, *Commentary on the GmbH Law* (7th edn, 1986), s 35). English law has never taken the view that the knowledge of a director ipso facto imputed to the company: *Powles v Page* (1846) 3 CB 16, 136 ER 7; *Re Carew's Estate Act* (1862) 31 Beav 39, 54 ER 1051. Unlike the German Geschäftsführer, an English director may as an individual have no powers whatever. But English law shares the view of German law that whether a person is an organ or not depends upon the extent of the powers which in law he has express or implied authority to exercise on behalf of the company.

Millett J did not accept that Mr Ferdman was the directing mind and will of DLH because he exercised no independent judgment. As a fiduciary he acted entirely upon the directions of the American beneficial owners and their consultant Mr Stern. All that he did was to sign the necessary documents and ensure that the company's paper work was in order. This involved seeing that decisions which had really been taken by the Americans and Mr Stern were duly minuted as decisions of the board made in Switzerland.

But neither the Americans nor Mr Stern held any position under the constitution of the company. Nor were they held out as doing so. They signed no documents on behalf of the company and carried on no business in its name. As a holding company, DLH had no independent business of its own. It entered into various transactions and on those occasions the persons who acted on its behalf were the board or one or more of the directors.

It seems to me that if the criterion is whether the candidate for being the 'directing mind and will' was exercising independent judgment, as opposed to acting upon off-stage instructions, not even the board of directors acting collectively would in this case have qualified. It also did what it was told. But Mr Tager was inclined to concede that the board, acting as a board, could properly be regarded as the directing mind and will. It was certainly held out in certain quarters as such. DLH claimed non-resident status from the Inland Revenue on the ground that its 'central management and control' was situated in Switzerland.

The authorities show clearly that different persons may for different purposes satisfy the requirements of being the company's directing mind and will. Therefore the question in my judgment is whether in relation to the Yulara transaction, Mr Ferdman as an individual exercised powers on behalf of the company which so identified him. It seems to me that Mr Ferdman was clearly regarded as being in a different position from the other directors. They were associates of his who came and went. SAFI charged for their services at a substantially lower rate. It was Mr Ferdman who claimed in the published accounts of DLH to be its ultimate beneficial owner. In my view, however, the most significant fact is that Mr Ferdman signed the agreement with Yulara on behalf of DLH. There was no board resolution authorising him to do so. Of course we know that in fact he signed at the request of Mr Stern, whom he knew to be clothed with authority from the Americans. But so far as the constitution of DLH was concerned, he committed the company to the transaction as an autonomous act which the company adopted by performing the agreement. I would therefore hold, respectfully differing from the judge, that this was sufficient to justify Mr Ferdman being treated, in relation to the Yulara transaction, as the company's directing mind and will. Nor do I think it matters that by the time DLH acquired Yulara's interest in the Nine Elms project on 16 March 1988, Mr Ferdman had ceased to be a director. Once his knowledge is treated as being the knowledge of the company in relation to a given transaction, I think that the company continues to be affected with that knowledge for any subsequent stages of the same transaction. So, for example, if (contrary to the judge's finding) the £1,030,000 sent by Yulara on 29 May 1986 had been received beneficially by DLH as a loan, but Mr Ferdman had resigned or died a week earlier, I do not think that the DLH could have said that it received the money without imputed knowledge of the fraud. And in my judgment the subsequent acquisition of Yulara's interest was sufficiently connected with the original investment to be affected by the same knowledge.

I would therefore allow the appeal. I do not regard this as an unsatisfactory outcome. If the persons beneficially interested in a company prefer for tax or other reasons to allow that company to be for all legal purposes run by off-shore fiduciaries, they must accept that it may incur liabilities by reason of the acts or knowledge of those fiduciaries.

NOTES AND QUESTIONS

1. *In addition to being bound under contract or by reason of s 36 of the Companies Act 1985, a promoter may also be liable for damages for breach of warranty of authority.*[1]

2. *For contracts made by public companies between registration and the issue of the certificate of incorporation, see s 117(7) and (8).*

3. *What is the effect of the following:*

    (a) *the promoter acquires an option on terms that the rights contained therein may be assigned to the company when formed and that the option shall lapse at a specific date if not exercised?*

    (b) *the promoter enters into a contract with a third party as 'trustee' for a prospective company subject to being released from liability upon the company entering into a new contract with the third party on the terms of the earlier contract?*

4. *Can a third party obtain an order for specific performance against a promoter by relying on s 36?*

5. *In* A L Underwood Ltd v Bank of Liverpool,[2] *it was held that the bank at which a director of a company kept his private bank account was put on enquiry if he paid cheques made out in favour of the company into his private account. Similarly, in* B Ligget (Liverpool) Ltd v Barclay's Bank Ltd[3] *a bank was held liable where, contrary to instructions, it honoured cheques signed by one director only.*

6. *The rationale of the* Turquand[4] *presumption was, according to Lord Simmonds in* Morris v Kanssen[5] *that '. . . the wheels of business will not go smoothly unless it may be assumed that that is in order which appears to be in order'. How far is it necessary to rely on the* Turquand *presumption in this regard?*[6] *Consider the following extract from Campbell, 'Contracts With Companies' [1960] 76 LQR 115 at p 117:*

---

1 See *Bowstead on Agency* (15th edn Reynolds, 1985) pp 457–469
2 [1924] 1 KB 775; 93 LJKB 690
3 [1928] 1 KB 48; 97 LJKB 1
4 [1856] 6 E&B 327; 119 ER 886 (see p 260)
5 [1946] AC 459; [1946] 1 All ER 586
6 See the very useful discussion of the *Turquand* Rule by *Nock* (1966) 30 Conveyancer (NS) 123

'The rule operates as a modification of the doctrine of constructive notice in cases of usual or ostensible authority. The effect of that doctrine is to negative usual or ostensible authority which is at variance with the provisions of the articles. The officials of the company cannot be assumed to have greater authority than the articles permit. But here the Turquand rule comes into play. The outsider can succeed on the basis of the usual or ostensible authority of the agent unless it exceeds not merely his actual but also his potential authority under the articles.

But the rule may also be applicable where the agent had no usual or ostensible authority. In this case the outsider must have actual knowledge of the articles, as he is not relying on any independent appearance of authority. He sees from the articles that in certain circumstances the person who purports to have power to make the contract on behalf of the company could have that power. If the circumstances are such that they relate entirely to the indoor management of the company, he is entitled to enter into the transaction on the assumption that the necessary power has been granted. It is presumed in his favour, as against the company, that the internal acts necessary to give validity to the transaction have been duly and regularly performed. Whether the rule is to be applied in this extended fashion is discussed below.

The rule is such that it can operate only in favour of the person dealing with the company and cannot be invoked by the company itself. In this respect it is the converse of the doctrine of constructive notice. Where the agent has exceeded his actual authority the indoor management rule provides a means whereby the outsider may be able to hold the company to the contract. If, however, the outsider wishes to avoid liability on the ground of the lack of authority in the agent, the appropriate course for the company, if it wishes to sustain the transaction, is to ratify the contract.

The rule is not confined to cases where the potential authority arises under the provisions in the public documents. It is equally applicable, for example, where authority has been conditionally or provisionally conferred under a power of attorney given by the company or under a resolution of a general meeting or of the board of directors.'

7. What is the relevance of knowledge of the articles? Consider the following extract from Montrose, 'The Apparent Authority of an Agent of a Company' (1965) Malaya LR 253, at p 262:

'One can state in the following manner the propositions established by the Buckhurst Case[1] with regard to the operation of knowledge or absence of knowledge of provisions in articles conferring powers to delegate authority. (i) Knowledge of such provision at the time of the transaction is not required (a) for the purpose of rejecting a contractor's claim by virtue of the negative doctrine of constructive notice of Ernest v Nicholls[2] (b) for the purpose of allowing a contractor's claim by virtue of the Rule in Turquand's Case.[3] (ii) Knowledge of such provisions (a) is not required for the purpose of accepting a contractor's claim based on apparent authority existing apart from the articles, (b) is required for the purpose of accepting a contractor's claim based on apparent authority where no such authority exists apart from the articles. With regard to the fourth proposition it should be noted that knowledge of the provision is not by itself enough. Not only must there be 'reliance on' the knowledge, the knowledge is but 'part of the circumstances' which may constitute apparent authority. Those circumstances should indicate that it is usual for the person with whom the contractor has dealt to have the authority on which the contractor relies. If the circumstances are

1 [1964] 2 QB 480; [1964] 1 All ER 630 (see p 266)
2 (1857) 6 HLC 401; 10 ER 1351
3 (1856) 6 E&B 327; 119 ER 886 (see p 260)

such that there could not usually be authority then mere knowledge of the provision in the articles would be inadequate.

8. *In* British Bank of the Middle East v Sun Life Assurance Company of Canada (UK) Ltd,[1] *it was held that where a branch manager has no actual authority to sign an undertaking on behalf of his company, in that the undertaking is unrelated to the company's business, he can not, by 'confirming' the authority of a similarly unauthorised under-manager, clothe the under-manager with an ostensible authority so as to bind the company. The decision in* Freeman & Lockyer v Buckhurst Park Properties Ltd[2] *was applied, it being held that condition (2) of Diplock LJ's four conditions was not satisfied (p 271).*

---

1 [1983] BCLC 78
2 [1964] 2 QB 480; [1904] 1 All ER 030

Chapter 5

THE INTERNAL RELATIONS OF THE COMPANY

PART I: A CONTRACT INTER SE?

Here we are concerned principally with the relationship between the share-holders and the company. The company, having legal personality, can enter into contracts, and, in terms of s 14 of the Companies Act 1985, the memorandum and articles of association represent a contract between the company and each member. Were the association in question to be other than a company and unincorporated, it would be unable to enter into contracts. The legal relationships arising within such an association would be between the members — probably a contract between each member and each other member on the basis of the rules of the association. This prompts the question whether there is not, within a company, in addition to the contracts between the company and each member, a further contract between each shareholder and each other shareholder on the basis of the memorandum and articles of association. Is there, to use a common shorthand, a contract between the members inter se? (See Sources 105, 106, 107, 108, 109, 110.)

> **SOURCE 105**
> **Welton v Saffery**
> (House of Lords 1897) [1987] AC 299; 66 LJ Ch 362

The appellant was the holder of shares which had been issued at a discount and was placed on the list of contributories in the winding up in respect of the unpaid part of the full nominal value of the shares. He contended that there was a contract between himself and the other shareholders under which his liability was restricted to the discounted value of the shares. The appeal was dismissed (Lord Herschell dissenting).

> LORD HALSBURY LC: . . . My Lords, in respect of the liability to pay up the shares so far as it is necessary to satisfy creditors and the cost of winding-up, I believe no doubt exists in the minds of any of your Lordships. Since the *Ooregum Case*[1] [p 755] in this House it would be impossible to contend that that question is not covered by authority. But it is said that, where the only object in making a call is to settle the rights of the shareholders inter se, the law laid down in the *Ooregum Case* does not conclude the question.
>
> My Lords, I am unable to accede to that view. I think the legislature, in permitting the existence of a company limited by shares and with limited liability, created a machinery which makes it impossible by any expedient, either by company or shareholder, to act otherwise than in pursuance of the provisions of the statute. Whether for the purpose of settling the rights inter se, or for the purpose of satisfying creditors, it appears to me that the statute enforces upon company and shareholder alike conformity to the rule laid down, that a share for

---

1 [1892] AC 125; 61 LJ Ch 337

a fixed amount shall make the person agreeing to take that share liable for that amount. I think that is the decision in the *Ooregum Case*, and though I am aware that a different view has been suggested where the question is not the payment of the debts of the company, but the settlement of the rights of the shareholders inter se, I am unable to see how this artificial creature, limited within its sphere of action by the statute under which it is created, can do anything contrary to the provisions of the statute. It is not a question for what purpose it is done. Dealing with it as I think it must be dealt with, as an artificial creation, it can only act as a company or as shareholder in either of those characters within the fetters created by the Act of Parliament.

It is said, and I think justly said, that people have been invited to take shares under an article of association which expressly provided that shares might be issued at a discount. It is, I think, hard for persons who have relied upon that assurance to find out that the article which authorized the issue of the shares at a discount was *ultra vires* of the company, because it is in conflict with the memorandum of association which by the statute itself must determine the rights in that respect; but not the less on that account must one insist that the statute must be obeyed. If one were to suppose that the whole 6000 original shareholders or persons who became shareholders by purchase in the market were to have agreed that these shares should only be regarded as having 10s. due upon them, each of them might perhaps against himself establish some contract by which the person agreeing with him in his individual capacity might have rights, but it would not be in his capacity as shareholder — it would be in his capacity as individual. The liquidator can only recognise shareholders, and their relation to the company of which they are shareholders must be regulated by the Act of Parliament.

The right to have a call made where it is necessary to adjust the rights between the different shareholders themselves appears to me not less imperative than if only the creditors were in question. The supposed bar to such a proceeding is the agreement not to ask more than 10s. per share upon the discount shares; but the whole question goes back to the same point. If the legislature has prohibited that, there is no such agreement. The directors have no power to make such an article. The company quâ company have no power to agree to such an article, and those who have taken shares and paid for them in pursuance of the Act of Parliament, I think, have a right to have the shares paid up which the Act of Parliament has enacted shall be liable to that payment.

LORD HERSCHELL (dissenting): . . . Section 16 of the Act of 1862[1] provides that the articles of association, when registered, shall bind the company and the members thereof to the same extent as if each member had signed his name and affixed his seal thereto, and there were in such articles contained a covenant on the part of himself, his heirs, executors, and administrators to conform to all the regulations contained in such articles, subject to the provisions of this Act. The articles thus become in effect a contract under seal by each member of the company, and regulate his rights. They cannot, of course, diminish or affect any liability created by the express terms of the statute; but, as I have said, the statute does not purport to settle the rights of the members inter se, it leaves these to be determined by the articles (or the articles and memorandum together), which are the social contract regulating those rights.

I think it was intended to permit perfect freedom in this respect. It is quite true that the articles constitute a contract between each member and the company,

---

1 Now s 14 of the Companies Act 1985

and that there is no contract in terms between the individual members of the company; but the articles do not any the less, in my opinion, regulate their rights inter se. Such rights can only be enforced by or against a member through the company, or through the liquidator representing the company; but I think that no member has, as between himself and another member, any right beyond that which the contract with the company gives.

SOURCE 106
Wood *v* Odessa Waterworks Company
(Chancery Division 1889) (1889) 42 Ch D 636; 58 LJ Ch 628

The articles of association provided:

'101. The directors may, with the sanction of the company at the ordinary general meeting, declare a dividend to be paid to the members in proportion to their shares, subject, however, to the provision contained in article 105 of these presents, and the next succeeding article.'

The general meeting approved a resolution that dividends be paid by way of a distribution of bonds (debentures). This was an action to restrain the company from acting on this resolution.

STIRLING J: ... The question, simply, is whether it is within the power of a majority of the shareholders to insist against the will of a minority that the profits which have been actually earned shall be divided, not by the payment of cash, but by the issue of debenture-bonds of the company bearing interest at £5 per cent and repayable at par by an annual drawing extending over thirty years. It is to be inferred from the terms in which the bonds are offered for subscription that the company cannot issue them in the open market except at a discount of at least £10 per cent. Now the rights of the shareholders in respect of a division of the profits of the company are governed by the provisions in the articles of association. By section 16[1] of the Companies Act 1862 (25 & 26 Vict. c. 89), the articles of association 'bind the company and the members thereof to the same extent as if each member had subscribed his name and affixed his seal thereto, and there were in such articles contained a covenant on the part of himself, his heirs, executors, and administrators, to conform to all the regulations contained in such articles, subject to the provisions of this Act. Section 50[2] of the Act provides the means for altering the regulations of the company contained in the articles of association by passing a special resolution, but no such resolution has in this case been passed or attempted to be passed; and the question is, whether this is a matter as to which the majority of the shareholders can bind those shareholders who dissent. The articles of association constitute a contract not merely between the shareholders and the company, but between each individual shareholder and every other; and the question which I have just stated must, in my opinion, be answered in the negative if there be in the articles a contract between the shareholders as to a division of profits, and the provisions of that contract have not been followed. That appears to have been distinctly laid down with reference to the very matter in question by the Earl of Selborne in the case of the *Oakbank Oil Company v Crum*,[3] where his Lordship said: 'It appears to me that directors and general meetings of companies of this sort can have no powers

1 Now s 14 of the Companies Act 1985
2 Now s 9 of the Companies Act 1985
3 (1882) 8 App Ca 65; 48 LT 537

by implication except such as are incident to, or properly to be inferred from, the powers expressed in the memorandum and articles of association. Their powers are entirely created by the law and by the contract founded upon the law which enables such companies to be constituted. Therefore I think the word "may" means, that if the directors get the assent of a general meeting they may declare a dividend; but that is not to be any kind of dividend, it is to be dividend of that kind which the clause contemplates.' That then brings me to consider whether that which is proposed to be done in the present case is in accordance with the articles of association of the company.

The injunction was granted.

SOURCE 107
Borland's Trustee *v* Steel Brothers & Co Ltd
(Chancery Division 1901) [1901] 1 Ch 279; 70 LJ Ch 51

The articles of association provided that on any manager or assistant ceasing to be such, or on his death or bankruptcy, he must, on receiving certain notice, transfer his shares.

FARWELL J: . . . It is said that the provisions of these articles compel a man at any time during the continuance of this company to sell his shares to particular persons at a particular price to be ascertained in the manner prescribed in the articles. Two arguments have been founded on that. It is said, first of all, that such provisions are repugnant to absolute ownership. It is said, further, that they tend to perpetuity. They are likened to the case of a settlor or testator who settles or gives a sum of money subject to executory limitations which are to arise in the future, interpreting the articles as if they provided that if at any time hereafter, during centuries to come, the company should desire the shares of a particular person, not being a manager or assistant, he must sell them. To my mind that is applying to company law a principle which is wholly inapplicable thereto. It is the first time that any such suggestion has been made, and it rests, I think, on a misconception of what a share in a company really is. A share, according to the plaintiff's argument, is a sum of money which is dealt with in a particular manner by what are called for the purpose of argument executory limitations. To my mind it is nothing of the sort. A share is the interest of a shareholder in the company measured by a sum of money, for the purpose of liability in the first place, and of interest in the second, but also consisting of a series of mutual covenants entered into by all the shareholders inter se in accordance with section 16 of the Companies Act, 1862. The contract contained in the articles of association is one of the original incidents of the share. A share is not a sum of money settled in the way suggested, but is an interest measured by a sum of money and made up of various rights contained in the contract, including the right to a sum of money of a more or less amount.

   . . .

Then it is said that this is contrary to the rule against perpetuity. Now, in my opinion the rule against perpetuity has no application whatever to personal contracts.

   . . .

I have said that these articles are nothing more or less than a personal contract between Mr Borland and the other shareholders in the company under section 16 of the Companies Act 1862. Mr Borland was one of the original shareholders, and he and his trustee in bankruptcy are bound by his own contract. I do not know that I am concerned to consider the case of other shareholders who come in afterwards; but if I am, the answer so far as they are concerned is that each of them on coming in executes a deed of transfer which, in the terms in which it is executed, makes him liable to all the provisions of the original articles. Mr Borland cannot be heard to say there is any repugnancy or perpetuity in the convenant he has entered into, and his trustee in bankruptcy stands in no better position.

Declaration, that the provision in the articles was not binding, refused.

SOURCE 108
Salmon *v* Quin & Axtens Limited
(Court of Appeal 1909) [1909] AC 442; 78 LJ Ch 506

For the relevant provisions of the articles, see p 414.

FARWELL LJ: . . . it appears to me to be plain that this is a contract by which the business of the company shall be managed by the board. The articles, by section 16 of the Act of 1862, are made equivalent to the deed of covenant signed by all the shareholders. The Act does not say with whom that convenant is entered into, and there have no doubt been varying statements by learned judges, some of them saying it is with the company, some of them saying it is both with the company and with the shareholders. Stirling J in *Wood v Odessa Waterworks Co*[1] says: 'The articles of association constitute a contract not merely between the shareholders and the company, but between each individual shareholder and every other.' I think that that is accurate subject to this observation, that it may well be that the Court would not enforce the covenant as between individual shareholders in most cases. Now the general power of the board to manage here is qualified by the stipulation which follows, that it is to be subject to the provisions of these articles. I therefore turn to article 80, [p 415] and I find this provision to which these general powers of management are made subject: . . . In the present case Mr Salmon did so dissent according to the terms of that article, and therefore the veto therein provided came into operation. That was met by the company being called together by a requisition of seven shareholders and by passing general resolutions for the acquisition of this property and the letting of the vacant premises. It is said that those resolutions are of no effect, and I am of opinion that that contention is right. I base my opinion on the words of article 75, 'subject, nevertheless, to the provisions of any Acts of Parliament or of these articles,' . . . these resolutions are absolutely inconsistent with article 80; in truth this is an attempt to alter the terms of the contract between the parties by a simple resolution instead of by a special resolution. The articles forming this contract, under which the business of the company shall be managed by the board, contain a most usual and proper requirement, because a business does require a head to look after it, and a head that shall not be interfered with unnecessarily. Then in order to oust the directors a special resolution would be required.

Appeal upheld; injunction granted.

---

1 (1889) 42 Ch D 636; 58 LJ Ch 628 (see p 297)

SOURCE 109

London Sack and Bag Co Ltd *v* Dixon and Lugton Ltd

(Court of Appeal 1943) [1943] 2 All ER 763

SCOTT LJ: By writ issued on 8 June 1943, the respondent company (to whom I will refer as the buyers) brought an action against the appellant company (to whom I will refer as the sellers). The dispute arose out of a contract for the sale of 5,000 used cotton flour bags. The contract was made by a letter dated 18 May 1943, from the buyers to the sellers, and a letter and telegram both dated 20 May 1943, from the sellers to the buyers. The price was 2s per bag payable in advance. The buyers paid the £500, but on delivery complained that the goods were not up to description and claimed to get their money back with interest and damages. There was no arbitration clause in that written contract — either set out in the letters or printed on the back or expressly incorporated in it in any way, as is so usual with contracts made by members of commercial associations. But the sellers none the less took out a summons under the Arbitration Act 1889, section 4, to stay the action relying on the contention that there was a written submission within the Act for the following reasons. (i) Both companies, the sellers allege, are members of the United Kingdom Jute Goods Association Ltd, a company incorporated in 1909; (ii) that company has rules binding on all members, rule 1 of which provides that:

> '. . . all disputes arising out of transactions connected with the trade . . . shall be referred to arbitration . . . '

(iii) a sale of used cotton flour bags is, as proved by an affidavit, a transaction connected with the jute trade.

. . .

His [counsel for the appellants] second contention was a roundabout one. He submitted that section 20 creates a contract between the members of a company inter se, and cited the chief cases dealing with that topic such as *Hickman v Kent or Romney Marsh Sheepbreeders' Assocn;*[1] *Welson v Saffery;*[2] *Wood v Odessa Waterworks Co*[3] and *Borland's Trustee v Steel Bros & Co Ltd.*[4]

, I am not satisfied that he has interpreted those decisions correctly. It may well be, even as between ordinary members of a company who are also in the nominal way shareholders, that section 20 adjusts their legal relations inter se in the same way as a contract in a single document would if signed by all; and yet the statutory result may not be to constitute a contract between them about rights of action created entirely outside the company relationship, such as trading transactions between members. I notice that Halsbury's Laws of England Hailsham edn, Vol 5, p 142, para 256, says this:

> 'While the articles regulate the rights of the members, inter se, they do not it would seem constitute a contract between the members, inter se, but only a contract between the company and its members, and, therefore, the rights and liabilities of members as members under the articles can only be enforced by or against the members through the company.'

The importance of that paragraph is that any doubt about the written submission being quite clearly established is, in my view, a sufficient reason for the judge's

---

1 [1915] 1 Ch 881; 84 LJ Ch 688 (see p 303)
2 [1897] AC 299; 66 LJ Ch 362 (see p 295)
3 (1889) 42 Ch D 636; 58 LJ Ch 628 (see p 297)
4 [1901] 1 Ch 279; 70 LJ Ch 51 (see p 298)

exercising his discretion against a stay: and a fortiori a reason for our not disagreeing with him.

There is an even stronger point against allowing the appeal. Even if the cases which counsel for the appellants cited amounted to the enunciation of a clear rule that, as between shareholding members — ie, ordinary members of a company having a capital interest in the company by reason of their shares — there is a written contract for what may be called the purposes of company law, it does not in the least follow that the rule applies to extrinsic purposes such as individual trading. But in the present case that objection may be pushed even further. The two companies parties to this litigation are not ordinary members of the company at all; they are only members in the same sense that members of a proprietary club who have no shares in the company owning the club, are given certain rights of members, eg, to frequent the club for meals, or golf, or reading. I cannot think that the principle of the cases cited to us can be extended to such members as these two companies are. Their directors are required to hold a share in order to represent them, but no trusts are recognised by the articles; and I do not think the cases in question have any bearing on the issue we have to decide. I am not satisfied that it is possible to spell a written submission out of the memorandum and articles of association and the rules, even with the help of the Companies Act 1929, section 20.

SOURCE 110
Rayfield *v* Hands
(Chancery Division 1960) [1960] Ch 1; [1958] 2 All ER 194

The articles of the company provided:

'11. Every member who intends to transfer shares shall inform the directors who will take the said shares equally between them at a fair value but subject to the above no person shall hold more than 1,000 shares in the capital of the company.'

The plaintiff gave notice to the directors of his intention to transfer his shares, but the defendant directors denied any obligation to take them. The company does not appear to have been a party to the litigation.

VAISEY J: . . . The next and most difficult point taken by the defendants as to which it would appear that there is no very clear judicial authority, is that article 11, as part of the company's articles of association, does not do what it looks like doing, that is, to create a contractual relationship between the plaintiff as shareholder and vendor and the defendants as directors and purchasers. This depends on section 20(1) of the Companies Act 1948.[1]

. . .

In the 12th edition of *Buckley on the Companies Acts* at p 52 allusion is made to the 'large number of apparently conflicting judicial decisions and dicta as to the exact nature of the contractual relations established by the memorandum and articles both as between the company and the members and as between the members inter se,' and it is further expressly pointed out that there are decisions or dicta both to the effect that the articles do, and also to the effect that they do not, constitute a contract between the members inter se.

The variety of the judicial views on the matter is not I think overstated here. Gore-Browne's *Handbook on Joint Stock Companies*, 41st edn, at p 45, states the

---

1 Now s 14 of the Companies Act 1985

effect of section 20 in these words: '[It] is to create an obligation binding alike on the members in their dealings with the company, on the company in its dealings with the members as members, and on the members in their dealings with one another as members . . . and even a member cannot enforce provisions for his benefit in some other capacity than that of member: for example he cannot assert a right to be appointed solicitor, secretary, or director by reason of provisions contained only in the articles.'

In Palmer's *Company Precedents*, 16th edn, Part I, at p 458, the matter is discussed on general lines, and the effect of some of the cases is summarised, and the following quotation is cited from the speech of Lord Herschell in *Welton v Saffery*[1]: 'It is quite true that the articles constitute a contract between each member and the company, and that there is no contract in terms between the individual members of the company; but the articles do not any the less, in my opinion, regulate their rights inter se.' I find that statement somewhat cryptic.

In Halsbury's *Laws of England*, 3rd edn, vol 6, at p 129, under the sub-heading of 'Memorandum and Articles,' there is a paragraph in these words: 'While the articles regulate the rights of the members, inter se, they do not, it would seem, constitute a contract between the members, inter se, but only a contract between the company and its members, and, therefore, the rights and liabilities of members as members under the articles can only be enforced by or against the members through the company.' I will consider this proposition later on.

Now the question arises at the outset whether the terms of article 11 relate to the rights of members inter se (that being the expression found in so many of the cases), or whether the relationship is between a member as such and directors as such. I may dispose of this point very briefly by saying that, in my judgment, the relationship here is between the plaintiff as a member and the defendants not as directors but as members.

In *Re Leicester Club and Country Racecourse Co*,[2] Pearson J, referring to the directors of a company said that they 'continue members of the company, and I prefer to call them working members of the company,' and on the same page he also said: 'directors cannot divest themselves of their character of members of the company. From first to last, . . . they are doing their work in the capacity of members, and working members of the company . . .' I am of opinion, therefore, that this is in words a contract or quasi-contract between members, and not between members and directors.

I have now to deal with the point for which there is considerable support in the cases, that the notional signing and sealing of the articles creates a contractual relation between the company on the one hand and the corporators (members) on the other, so that no relief can be obtained in the absence of the company as a party to the suit.

. . .

The case of the plaintiff may also be said to rest upon the well-known decision of *Carlill v Carbolic Smoke Ball Co*,[3] to which I need not refer except to say that it seems to me to be relevant here. To the like effect is *Clarke v Earl of Dunraven*[4] upon which the plaintiff here also relied.

In general discussions on the effect of section 20 to be found in the cases, I have, of course, considered the dissentient speech of Lord Herschell in *Welton v Saffery*, and the comprehensive review of the earlier authorities by Astbury J in

---

1 [1897] AC 299; 66 LJ Ch 362 (see p 296)
2 (1885) 30 Ch D 629
3 (1893) 1 QB 256
4 [1897] AC 59

Hickman v Kent and Romney Marsh Sheepbreeders' Association.[1] Among the numerous dicta in the judgment in that case, one which seems to me to be helpful and convincing is the one which reads as follows: 'the articles of association are simply a contract as between the shareholders inter se in respect of their rights as shareholders. They are the deed of partnership by which the shareholders agree inter se.'

I will make an appropriate declaration of the plaintiff's rights, or will order the defendants to give effect to them, and if necessary there must be an inquiry to ascertain the fair value of the shares.

PART II: THE CAPACITY OF THE MEMBERS

The contract between the company and the shareholders gives rise to mutual rights and obligations but these lie in favour of and against the shareholder *in his capacity as a member* of the company (Sources 111 and 112). This distinction has, however, proved to be very elusive and has been the subject of much academic study (Source 113).

SOURCE 111
Hickman *v* Kent or Romney Marsh Sheepbreeders' Association
(Chancery Division 1915) [1915] 1 Ch 881; 84 LJ Ch 688

Article 49: Whenever any difference arises between the association and any of the members touching the true intent or construction or the incidents or consequences of these presents or of the statutes, ... every such difference shall be referred to the decision of an arbitrator...

A dispute arose between the plaintiff — a member of the defendant company — and the defendant company. The plaintiff issued a writ seeking, inter alia, an injunction to restrain the defendant from taking any steps to expel him. The defendant issued a summons asking that the action be stayed and the dispute referred to arbitration.

ASTBURY J: . . . The principal authorities in support of the view that the articles do not constitute a contract between the company and its members are *Pritchard's Case*,[2] *Melhado v Porto Alegre Ry Co*[3] *Eley v Positive Life Assurance Co*,[4] and *Browne v La Trinidad.*[5]

In *Pritchard's Case* the articles of association of a mining company provided that the company should immediately after incorporation enter into an agreement with De Thierry the vendor for the purchase of the mine for £2000 and 3200 fully-paid shares. The articles were signed by the vendor and six other persons, and the directors allotted the 3200 shares to the vendor or his nominees, but no further agreement was made with him. It was held, affirming the decision of Wickens V-C, that the articles of association did not constitute a contract in writing between the vendor and the company within section 25 of the Companies Act, 1867 (30 & 31 Vict. c. 131), and that the shares could not therefore be

---

1 [1915] 1 Ch 881; 84 LJ Ch 688
2 (1873) LR 8 Ch 956; 42 LJ Ch 768
3 (1874) LR 9 CP 503
4 (1876) 1 ExD 88; 45 LJ Exch 451
5 (1888) 37 Ch D 1; 57 LJ Ch 292

considered as fully paid. Mellish LJ in giving judgment said (1): 'I am of opinion that the articles of association cannot be considered as a contract in writing between De Thierry and the company for the sale of the mine to them. It may, no doubt, be the case, if no other contract was entered into, and if De Thierry signed these articles and they were acted upon, that a Court of Equity would hold that as between him and the company — from their acting upon it — there was a binding contract; but in themselves the articles of association are simply a contract as between the shareholders inter se in respect of their rights as shareholders. They are the deed of partnership by which the shareholders agree inter se.'

In *Melhado v Porto Alegre Ry Co* the articles of association of a joint stock company provided that the company should defray such expenses incurred in its establishment as the directors should consider might be deemed and treated as preliminary expenses to an amount not exceeding £2000. The plaintiffs, who were promoters of the company, had incurred preliminary expenses in its establishment, but it was held that no action for these expenses would lie at the suit of the plaintiffs against the company under the articles. Lord Coleridge CJ said: 'The action is brought on a clause in the articles of association, by which the directors are authorised to pay certain expenses if they should consider them to be properly deemed preliminary expenses. The declaration avers that all conditions were performed necessary to entitle the plaintiffs to be paid their expenses which, if the directors had thought proper to pay them, the articles would have justified them in paying. The question, therefore, is whether an action will lie for the payment of these expenses, in pursuance of the articles of association, to which the plaintiffs were not parties. I have come to the conclusion that no such action will lie — I must say somewhat reluctantly, because, though I wish to express no opinion on the merits of this particular case, having no materials for forming such an opinion, it does seem just, in general, if a company takes the benefit of the work and expenditure by which its existence has been rendered possible, and voluntarily comes into existence on the terms that it shall be liable to pay for such work and expenditure, that a cause of action should be given. I can find, however, no legal principle upon which such an action can be maintained. It appears to me that there is no contract between the plaintiffs and the defendants. The doctrine of ratification is inapplicable, for the reasons given in the judgments in *Kelner v Baxter*,'[1] Mellor J said: 'The plaintiffs were not in any way parties to the articles of association, and there was not, therefore, any express contract to pay them,' Brett J said: 'There is no contract, in my judgment, of any sort upon which they can sue, and unless there be a contract of some sort between them and the company, I do not see that they can have any cause of action. No contract made with them before the existence of the company can be ratified by the company for the reasons pointed out in the case of *Kelner v Baxter*, with which I fully agree.'

In *Eley v Positive Life Assurance Co* the articles of association contained a clause in which it was stated that the plaintiff, a solicitor, should be the solicitor to the company and transact its legal business. The articles were registered and the company incorporated, and eleven months later the plaintiff became a member. The plaintiff was not appointed solicitor by any resolution of the directors, nor by any instrument bearing the seal of the company, but he acted as such for a time. Subsequently the company ceased to employ him and he brought an action for breach of contract against the company for not employing him as its solicitor.

---

1 (1866) LR 2 CP 174; 36 LJCP 94

The first count of the declaration stated that it was agreed by and between the plaintiff and the defendants that the plaintiff should be employed by the defendants as, and appointed by them to the office of, solicitor of the company. During the argument it was contended that the contract declared on was not the contract purported to be contained in the articles. Amphlett B said: 'The articles, taken by themselves, are simply a contract between the shareholders inter se, and cannot, in my opinion, give a right of action to a person like the plaintiff, not a party to the articles, although named therein. If authority were wanted for this proposition, the cases cited in the argument, *Pritchard's Case* and *Melhado v Porto Alegre Ry Co*, are, in my opinion, quite conclusive on the subject.' Subsequently he said: 'For these reasons, I think that there was no contract at all between the plaintiff and the company to the effect stated in the declaration.' Cleasby B confined his judgment to the last points raised in the case and said: 'I am of opinion that clause 118 of the articles cannot by itself be taken to operate as a contract between the solicitor and the company.' Kelly CB said: 'I forbear to pronounce any opinion as to whether these articles, with the fact of the subsequent employment, constitute a contract on the terms contained in them, because, were I to so hold, there would be a difficult question behind, whether it was not *ultra vires* for the directors to attempt to bind the company to employ a solicitor to transact, for all his life, all the legal business of the company. Passing by this, I come to consider the objection raised under section 4 of the Statute of Frauds. I do not see how any one can doubt that this agreement was not to be performed within a year. It was for the life of the plaintiff, subject to a defeasance on the possibility of his being guilty of some misconduct. But, assuming, as I think we must, that this was not to be performed in a year, the question arises, whether there is any memorandum or note in writing of it signed by the defendants. The signatures affixed to the articles were alio intuitu, and it can hardly be suggested that the directors had any idea that, in signing the articles, they were signing a note of this contract.'

This case went to the Court of Appeal and Lord Cairns LC said: 'I wish to say, in the first place, that in my opinion a contract of the kind suggested to exist in this case ought not to receive any particular favour from that Court. The statement is that Baylis was endeavouring to form a joint stock insurance company upon a new principle, and applied to the plaintiff to make advances to meet the expenses of getting up the company, and it was arranged between them that in the event of the company being formed the plaintiff should be appointed permanent solicitor to the company. That is to say, a bargain is made between a professional man and Baylis which, so far as the case is concerned, does not appear to have been communicated to those who were invited to join the company, that if the former will advance money for the formation of the company, he shall be appointed permanent solicitor, and the company shall be obliged to employ him as their professional adviser. When the articles are prepared, they are so by the plaintiff, and in them he inserts a clause which no doubt informs those who signed the articles of the arrangement, but does not appear to have been brought to the notice of those who joined from receiving circulars. This, I repeat, is not a proceeding which the Court would encourage in any way. I also wish to reserve my judgment as to whether a clause of this kind is obnoxious to the principles by which the Courts are governed in deciding on questions of public policy.' Then a little lower down he said: 'This case was first rested on article 118. Articles of association, as is well known, follow the memorandum, which states the objects of the company, while the articles state the arrangement between the members. They are an agreement inter socios, and in that view, if the introductory words are applied to article 118, it becomes a covenant between the parties to it that they will employ the plaintiff. Now, so far as that is concerned, it is res inter alios acta, the plaintiff is no party to it. No doubt he thought that by inserting it he was making his employment safe as against the company; but his relying on that view of the law does not alter the legal effect of the articles. This article is either a stipulation which would bind the members, or else a mandate to the directors. In either case it is a matter between the directors and shareholders, and not between them and the plaintiff.'

In *Browne v La Trinidad* before the formation of the company an agreement was entered into between B and a person as trustee for the intended company, by which it was stipulated (inter alia) that B should be a director and should not be removable till after 1888. Clause 6 of the articles provided that the directors should adopt and carry into effect the agreement with or without modification, and that subject to such modification (if any) the provisions of the agreement should be construed as part of the articles. The agreement was acted upon, but no contract adopting it was entered into between the plaintiff and the company. It was held that treating the agreement as embodied in the articles, still there was no contract between B and the company that he should not be removed from being a director, the articles being only a contract between the members inter se, and not between the company and B. Cotton LJ towards the end of his judgment said: 'Assuming that an unlimited power is given to the meeting by article 91, ought we, having regard to the contract entered into by the memorandum of 24 November 1884, and article 6, to interfere by injunction to restrain the company in general meeting from acting under that power? I do not give any opinion upon the question how far the Court would have interfered by injunction in order specifically to enforce an agreement between the company and the plaintiff that he should be an irremovable director. That point raises questions upon which I should not like to give any opinion without having them fully discussed. In my opinion we ought not to interfere in the present case, because there is no such contract between the plaintiff and the company. The memorandum of agreement of 24 November 1884, is in no way a contract between the plaintiff and the company. It is said that it was adopted and incorporated into the articles, but I cannot accede to that. The company by its directors acted upon the agreement, but that does not make it binding on the company. Then is it incorporated into the articles in such a way as to entitle the plaintiff to say I have such a contract between me and the company as can be enforced by a Court of law, and as I might enforce in equity by way of specific performance? That point is clearly settled, I think, by *Eley v Positive Life Assurance Co*. There two of the members of the Court of first instance held, and the other member did not express dissent, that the articles are merely a contract between the shareholders inter se, and that though a person in whose favour a stipulation is made in the articles may afterwards have shares allotted to him, he does not by that means become in the same position as if he had entered into a contract with the company.' Lindley LJ said: 'Having regard to the construction put upon section 16 of the Companies Act of 1862 in the case of *Eley v Positive Life Assurance Co* and subsequent cases, it must be taken as settled that the contract upon which he relies is not a contract upon which he can maintain any action, either on the common law side or the equity side. There might have been some difficulty in arriving at that conclusion if it had not been for the authorities, because it happens that this gentleman has had shares allotted to him, and is therefore a member of the company. Having regard to the terms of section 16, there would be some force, or at all events some plausibility, in the argument that, being a member, the contract which is referred to in the articles has become binding between the company and him. Of course that argument is open to this difficulty that there could be no contract between him and the company until the shares were allotted to him, and it would be remarkable that, upon the shares being allotted to him, a contract between him and the company, as to a matter not connected with the holding of shares, should arise.'

Now in these four cases the article relied upon purported to give specific contractual rights to persons in some capacity other than that of shareholder, and in none of them were members seeking to enforce or protect rights given to them as members, in common with the other corporators. The actual decisions amount to this. An outsider to whom rights purport to be given by the articles in his capacity as such outsider, whether he is or subsequently becomes a member, cannot sue on those articles treating them as contracts between himself and the company to enforce those rights. Those rights are not part of the general regulations of the company applicable alike to all shareholders and can only exist by virtue of some contract between such person and the company, and the subsequent allotment of shares to an outsider in whose favour such an article is inserted does not enable him to sue the company on such an article to enforce rights which are res inter alios acta and not part of the general rights of the corporators as such.

. . .

It seems clear from other authorities that a company is entitled as against its members to enforce and restrain breaches of its regulations. See, for example, *MacDougall v Gardiner*[1] and *Pender v Lushington.*[2]

. . .

It is also clear from many authorities that shareholders as against their company can enforce and restrain breaches of its regulations, and in many of these cases judicial expressions of opinion appear, which, in my judgment, it is impossible to disregard.

[Here Astbury J discussed, inter alia, *Wood v Odessa Waterworks*[3] (p 297); *Salmon v Quin & Axtens Ltd*[4] (p 299) and *Welton v Saffery*[5] (p 295) and continued:]

In all these last mentioned cases the respective articles sought to be enforced related to the rights and obligations of the members generally as such and not to rights of the character dealt with in the four authorities first above referred to.

It is difficult to reconcile these two classes of decisions and the judicial opinions therein expressed, but I think this much is clear, first, that no article can constitute a contract between the company and a third person; secondly, that no right merely purporting to be given by an article to a person, whether a member or not, in a capacity other than that of a member, as, for instance, as solicitor, promoter, director, can be enforced against the company; and, thirdly, that articles regulating the rights and obligations of the members generally as such do create rights and obligations between them and the company respectively.

. . .

In the present case, the plaintiff's action is, in substance, to enforce his rights as a member under the articles against the association. Article 49 is a general article applying to all the members as such, and, apart from technicalities, it would seem reasonable that the plaintiff ought not to be allowed in the absence of any evidence filed by him to proceed with an action to enforce his rights under

---

1 (1875) 1 Ch D 13; 45 LJ Ch 27
2 (1877) 6 Ch D 70; 46 LJ Ch 317 (see p 314)
3 (1889) 42 Ch D 636; 58 LJ Ch 628
4 [1909] AC 442; 78 LJ Ch 506
5 [1897] AC 299; 66 LJ Ch 362

the articles, seeing that the action is a breach of his obligation under article 49 to submit his disputes with the association to arbitration . . .

SOURCE 112
Beattie *v* E & F Beattie Ltd
(Court of Appeal 1938) [1938] Ch 708; [1938] 3 All ER 214

The Articles and association of the company provided:

'Whenever any doubt, difference, or dispute shall arise between any members of the company, or between the company and any member or members . . . the members of the company respectively, shall not take proceedings at law in respect of such doubt, difference, or dispute, but the same shall be referred to two arbitrators or their umpire. . . .'

SIR WILFRED GREENE MR: . . . The company is a private company, and the action is brought by the plaintiff. . . . She alleged that the defendant, Ernest Beattie, had paid to himself and to Edward Beattie certain sums by way of remuneration which, under the regulations of the company, he was not entitled to pay. There is no allegation of any bad faith or anything of that kind in respect of the payments. They are merely payments of remuneration which are said not to have been justified.

. . . Ernest Beattie applied under section 4 of the Arbitration Act to have that part of the action stayed pursuant to an arbitration clause contained in the articles of association. . . .

As I have said, Mr Ernest Beattie is, and was at all material times, a director of the company and it is against him, in his capacity as director, that these claims were made. It is as a director in charge of the company's funds that he is responsible for their proper application, in accordance with the regulations which govern the company. It is in that capacity, therefore, that the action is brought against him.

The claim which the plaintiff is seeking to enforce in the action — I am now only dealing with the new matter which it is sought to introduce — is, and must be, in a representative action of this character, a claim of the company itself, because a minority shareholder suing in a representative action is suing to enforce rights of the company. The reason the action takes that form is that the minority shareholder is not in a position to see that the action is brought in the name of the company itself to enforce the company's rights. Nevertheless, the action is, in reality, an action to enforce the rights of the company and of nobody else. The essence of the claim is that the plaintiff is seeking to enforce the company's right to recover from Mr Ernest Beattie moneys of the company, which, as it is alleged, have been paid away by him. The company, of course, is a necessary defendant because the order, if an order is made, will be an order for payment to the company, the moneys being the company's moneys. . . .

Mr Cleveland-Stevens[1] says: Here is a member — namely, Mr Ernest Beattie. Here is an article which provides that a dispute between the company and a member shall be referred to arbitration. It covers, among other others, a dispute relating to an act or default of a director. And he says that what he is seeking in the present case to do is to enforce that right as a member under that article and not any right as a director; that he has a right, and all other members have a right, when they find the company disputing with a director, to insist on that dispute being referred to arbitration. Mr Cleveland-Stevens says that the case must be

---

1 Counsel for the defendant (Mr Beattie)

treated as though the circumstance that the appellant happens to be a director is immaterial. He says that it is quite immaterial that the member who is demanding arbitration is himself the member attacked.

In my judgment, that argument is based on an incorrect view both as to the effect of the article and as to the effect of section 20 of the Companies Act. The question as to the precise effect of section 20 has been the subject of considerable controversy in the past, and it may very well be that there will be considerable controversy about it in the future. But it appears to me that this much, at any rate, is good law: that the contractual force given to the articles of association by the section is limited to such provisions of the articles as apply to the relationship of the members in their capacity as members.

I do not think, in saying that, that I am in any way departing from or extending (and it certainly is not my intention to depart from or extend) certain observations of Astbury J in the well-known case of *Hickman v Kent or Romney Marsh Sheep-Breeders' Association*.[1] In that case Astbury J made a careful review of all the decisions, and he expressed his conclusions with regard to them in this way. He referred to *Eley v Positive Life Assurance Co Ltd*,[2] and certain other cases, and pointed out that those decisions amounted to this: 'An outsider to whom rights purport to be given by the articles in his capacity as such outsider, whether he is or subsequently becomes a member, cannot sue on those articles treating them as contracts between himself and the company to enforce those rights. Those rights are not part of the general regulations of the company applicable alike to all shareholders and can only exist by virtue of some contract between such person and the company.' Then, again, he said: 'no right merely purporting to be given by an article to a person, whether a member or not, in a capacity other than that of a member, as, for instance, as solicitor, promoter, director, can be enforced against the company.'

With those two statements I respectfully agree. They are statements with regard to the true construction and operation of section 20, and they have the result in the present case of preventing that section from giving contractual force to the article as between the company and its directors as such.

It is to be observed that the real matter which is here being litigated is a dispute between the company and the appellant in his capacity as a director, and when the appellant, relying on this clause, seeks to have that dispute referred to arbitration, it is that dispute and none other which he is seeking to have referred, and by seeking to have it referred he is not, in my judgment, seeking to enforce a right which is common to himself and all other members. He is seeking to enforce a quite different right. I will explain what I mean. Let me assume that this article on its true construction entitles any member of the company to say to the company, when it is in dispute with a director: You, the company, are bound by your contract with me in the articles to refer this dispute to arbitration, and I call upon you so to do.' That is the right, and the only right in this respect, which is common to all the members, under this article. If that were the right which the appellant was seeking to exercise, there might be something to be said for that argument, but, with all respect to the able argument of Mr Cleveland-Stevens, it appears to me that that is not at all the right which the appellant is seeking to enforce. He is not seeking to enforce a right to call on the company to arbitrate a dispute which is only accidentally a dispute with himself. He is asking, as a disputant, to have the dispute to which he is a party referred. That is sufficient to differentiate it from the right which is common to all the other members of the

---

1 [1915] 1 Ch 881; 84 LJ Ch 688 (see p 303)
2 (1876) 1 Ex D 88; 45 LJ Exch 451

company under this article, which I have tried to define. That right is one which a member might find very great difficulty in enforcing in the Courts, because it concerns a matter relating to the internal management of the company, with which the Courts will not, in general, interfere.

But quite apart from that consideration, the two rights are, in my judgment, perfectly distinct and quite different — the general right of a member as a member and the right which the appellant as a party to the dispute is seeking to enforce. Indeed, Mr Cleveland-Stevens agrees that his argument really amounted to saying that the present application is in essence the same as proceedings brought by Mr Ernest Beattie, as a shareholder, to restrain the company from litigating and to obtain a mandatory order on the company to go to arbitration. But that is a very different thing from what he is now seeking since his claim, as I have said, is to insist on a reference of his own dispute.

SOURCE 113
Wedderburn, Shareholders' Rights and the Rule in Foss *v* Harbottle[1]

In *Edwards v Halliwell*[2] Jenkins LJ considered that anything which according to the articles ought to be done by special majority fell outside the rule; otherwise, 'a company which, by its directors, had broken its own regulations by doing something without a special resolution which could only be done validly by a special resolution, could assert that it alone was the proper plaintiff in any consequent action, and the effect would be to allow a company acting in breach of its articles to do *de facto* by ordinary resolution that which according to its own regulations could only be done by special resolution. That exception exactly fits the present case.' There a trade union had purported to increase subscriptions by ordinary majority of delegates when the rules demanded a two-thirds majority of the members.

Of the other cases said to produce the same rule in regard to companies, the critical decision is *Quin and Axtens Ltd v Salmon*.[3] In this case, the Rule in *Foss v Harbottle* was swept aside during the argument in the Court of Appeal, was never raised again by any of the eminent judges or counsel who took part in the case, and was something, moreover, which might have assisted the losing party. By the articles of association of a registered company, the management of the business of the company was delegated to the directors; but article 80 provided that no resolution of the directors upon a number of matters, including acquisition and letting of premises, should be valid unless notice had been given 'to each of the managing directors' (A and S), and neither had dissented. S had dissented from such a decision of the directors; but subsequently a simple majority of share-holders passed a resolution purporting to confirm that decision. It was held that S had the right, in an action brought on behalf of himself and all other shareholders except the defendants, to obtain an injunction restraining the company and its directors from these acts which were inconsistent with the provisions of the articles. The judgments are concerned mainly with the principle, discussed above, that shareholders cannot interfere with the exercise of functions delegated to directors; but they also establish that S had the right to prevent this attempt to 'alter the terms of the contract between the parties by a simple resolution instead of by a special resolution.' The contract referred to was the one which always arises from a company's articles of association, by virtue of

---

1 (1843) 2 Hare 461; 67 ER 189
2 [1950] 2 All ER 1064; [1950] WN 537
3 [1909] AC 442; 78 LJ Ch 506

section 20 of the Companies Act 1948, and its predecessors. That section says, 'Subject to the provisions of this Act, the memorandum and articles shall, when registered, bind the company and the members thereof to the same extent as if they respectively had been signed and sealed by each member, and contained covenants on the part of each member to observe all the provisions of the memorandum and of the articles.'

At first sight, the effect of this section appears to be a contract only between the members *inter se*. Such a contract may, indeed, be one result of the section, 'subject to this observation, that it may well be that the court would not enforce the covenant as between individual shareholders in most cases.' On the other hand, it is now abundantly clear that the articles constitute a contract between the *company and each member, in his capacity as member.* The law is clear 'first that no article can constitute a contract between the company and a third person; secondly, that no right merely purporting to be given by an article to a person, whether a member or not, in a capacity other than that of a member, as, for instance, as solicitor, promoter, director, can be enforced against the company; thirdly, that articles regulating the rights and obligations of the members generally as such do create rights and obligations between them and the company respectively.' To be comprehensive, it is necessary to add that the articles can be treated as evidence of the terms of an informal contract made between company and 'outsider'; if that is the case that contract will usually incorporate, along with the terms of the articles, the implied agreement inherent in the articles to the effect that changes in the terms can at any time be produced by special resolution changing the articles. That term as to alteration is also, of course, implied in the contract constituted by the articles — the 'contract under section 20' defined by Astbury J in the passage cited above. The contract under section 20 is, in other words, subject to section 10 of the Act. But it is a binding contract, nevertheless, and in *Salmon's case*, discussed above, it would appear that S was doing no more than compel the company to observe that contract. It is a commonplace of company law that 'a member can, by injunction, restrain the company from acting in contravention of its articles.' If that is right, what has become of the Rule in *Foss v Harbottle*, or, at any rate, of the 'internal interference' rule? In *MacDougall v Gardiner*,[1] where a poll was refused at a meeting, and in many other cases, breaches of the articles occurred, but because the majority either could, or did, ratify them, no minority action lay. There is, in fact, a clash between the outmoded rule against internal interference and the simple principle that contracts are enforceable.

PART III: CONFLICTING RIGHTS

Companies are, in general, subject to the will of the majority of the shareholders as expressed in their votes at the general meeting. In some cases this majority will has to be gainsaid, where, for example, the issue is one of the management of the company and the shareholders had agreed that the company's management should be the prerogative of the directors (see pp 410ff); likewise, where the majority is attempting to perpetrate a fraud (pp 540ff). Where, however, it is neither a question of management nor an attempted fraud, a clash may arise between the will of the majority and the

---

1 (1876) 1 Ch D 13; 45 LJ Ch 27

rights of an individual shareholder conferred by the articles or even between a majority shareholder and significant outside interests. How is such a clash resolved? (Sources 114, 115 and 116.)

SOURCE 114
Charter Oil Co Ltd *v* Beaumont
(British Columbia Court of Appeal 1967) [1968] 65 DLR (3d) 112

The articles of association provided:

'38. The annual general meetings shall be called ordinary meetings; all other general meetings shall be called extraordinary.

40. Not less than fourteen days' notice of a general meeting at which a special resolution is to be proposed, and not less than seven days' notice of any other general meeting (exclusive of the day on which the notice is given), specifying the place, the day, and the hour of meeting, and, in case of special business, the general nature of that business, shall be given in manner hereinafter mentioned, or in such other manner (if any) as may be prescribed by ordinary resolution, whether previous notice thereof has been given or not, to such persons as are, under the regulations of the Company, entitled to receive such notices from the Company, but the non-receipt of the notice by any member shall not invalidate the proceedings at any general meeting.

41. All business shall be deemed special that is transacted at any extraordinary meeting and all that is transacted at any ordinary meeting with the exception of sanctioning a dividend, the consideration of the accounts, balance sheets, and the ordinary report of the directors and auditors, the election of directors and other officers, and the fixing of the remuneration of the auditors.

59. Until otherwise determined by a general meeting, the number of the directors shall be not less than two nor more than ten, and the number and names of the first directors may be determined in writing by a majority of the subscribers of the Memorandum of Association, and until so determined the subscribers of the Memorandum shall for all purposes be deemed to be the directors of the Company.

61. The business of the Company shall be managed by the directors, who may pay all expenses incurred in getting up and registering the Company, and may exercise all such powers of the Company as are not, by the 'Companies Act', or any statutory modifications thereof for the time being in force, or by these articles required to be exercised by the Company in general meeting, subject nevertheless to any regulation of these articles, to the provisions of the said Act, and to such regulations, being not inconsistent with the aforesaid regulations or provisions, as may be prescribed by ordinary resolution, whether previous notice thereof has been given or not; but no regulation made by ordinary resolution shall invalidate any prior act of the directors which would have been valid if that regulation had not been made.

76. The Company may from time to time increase or reduce the number of directors by ordinary resolution, whether previous notice thereof has been given or not.

77. Any casual vacancy occurring in the Board of Directors may be filled up by the directors.

78. The directors shall have the power at any time, and from time to time, to appoint a person as an additional director.'

These were proceedings to restrain the defendants from acting on a resolution passed at an extraordinary general meeting increasing the number of directors to 15 and filling the vacancies with the nominees of the defendants. No notice of this resolution had been given.

> ROBERTSON JA: . . . Counsel for the appellants submits that article 59 fixes the maximum and minimum numbers of directors; that article 76 authorizes the numbers so fixed to be changed by ordinary resolution without notice, and authorizes nothing more; that the power to name additional directors to fill positions created by the increase in the authorized number is an inherent power and does not flow from article 76; that notice of intention to appoint additional directors is required under article 40; that the notice of the meeting on 25 August 1967, did not state that this business was to be transacted; and that consequently the appointment of the named persons was invalid. Counsel for the respondents submits that article 76 confers a power to fill positions created by an increase in the authorized number made under that article.
>
> . . .
>
> If article 76 is construed as authorizing the appointment of named directors without notice at an extraordinary general meeting, there may be far-reaching and serious results. For example, a meeting is called for some expressed purpose that arouses little support and no opposition. Only 10 per cent of the shares are represented at the meeting, but this constitutes a quorum under article 42. Shareholders representing 5.1 per cent of the shares see their opportunity, increase the authorized number of directors by more than 100 per cent and elect additional directors to fill all the positions so created. The Company now has a board with an entirely different complexion from that of the board that was elected at the last annual general meeting. Before the other shareholders can correct the situation under article 79, or otherwise, havoc can be wrought in the Company's affairs.
>
> I do not think that the subscribers of the Company's articles can have intended that the safeguard of notice afforded by article 40 should not apply in the vitally important matter of electing directors at an extraordinary general meeting, that is, at any meeting other than the annual general meeting. I think that the whole tenor of the articles is against such a construction.
>
> . . .
>
> In his argument Mr Maguire[1] said something to the effect that to grant an injunction here would interfere with the right of his clients, who hold more than 50 per cent of the shares in the Company, to manage the Company. I must reject this submission for the reasons stated in *Salmon v Quin & Axtens Ltd.*[2]

[Here the judge quoted the passage extracted on pp 415–416 below beginning with 'The case is, in my view, entirely governed . . .' and ending 'should be managed by the board of directors' and continued:]

> With great respect to the learned Judge, I would allow the appeal and grant an injunction, until the trial of the action or further order, enjoining the respondents and each of them from taking any steps to implement the resolution in question.

---

1 Counsel for the defendants
2 [1909] AC 442; 78 LJ Ch 506

SOURCE 115
Pender *v* Lushington
(Chancery Division 1875) (1877) 6 Ch D 70; 46 LJ Ch 317

The articles of association of the company provided:

> Article 56: No member holding less than ten shares is entitled to a vote, and every member holding at least that number of shares shall have one vote for every complete number of ten shares, with the limit that no shareholder shall be entitled to more than 100 votes in all.

JESSELL MR: This is a motion by Mr J Pender, on behalf of himself and all shareholders who voted with him against an amendment, and the Direct United States Cable Company Limited, as plaintiffs, against E H Lushington and other gentlemen as defendants, in substance to obtain the opinion of the Court that certain votes at a general meeting on behalf of the plaintiff were improperly rejected by the chairman.

> . . .

In all cases of this kind, where men exercise their rights of property, they exercise their rights from some motive adequate or inadequate, and I have always considered the law to be that those who have the rights of property are entitled to exercise them, whatever their motives may be for such exercise — that is as regards a court of law as distinguished from a court of morality or conscience, if such a court exists.

> . . .

I am confirmed in that view by the case of *Menier v Hooper's Telegraph Works*,[1] where Lord Justice Mellish observes: 'I am of opinion that, although it may be quite true that the shareholders of a company may vote as they please, and for the purpose of their own interests, yet that the majority of shareholders cannot sell the assets of the company and keep the consideration.' In other words, he admits that a man may be actuated in giving his vote by interests entirely adverse to the interests of the company as a whole. He may think it more for his particular interest that a certain course may be taken which may be in the opinion of others very adverse to the interests of the company as a whole, but he cannot be restrained from giving his vote in what way he pleases because he is influenced by that motive. There is, if I may say so, no obligation on a shareholder of a company to give his vote merely with a view to what other persons may consider the interests of the company at large. He has a right, if he thinks fit, to give his vote from motives or promptings of what he considers his own individual interest.

> . . . I am only bound to decide whether or not these people were entitled to vote. . . .

It is admitted that the votes tendered were the votes of persons on the register of shareholders.

That being so, their votes were rejected on this ground: It was said that the persons who gave the votes were trustees for other persons, and that these other persons, the *cestuis que trust* of those trustees, were also either holders in their own name or as *cestuis que trust* of other shares, amounting in the whole to more than 1000 shares, so that if all the shares to which the persons were entitled had been registered in one name, that person could not have given more than 100 votes, section 56 of the articles saying, that every member holding at least ten shares shall have one vote for every complete number of ten shares, with this limit, that no shareholder shall be entitled to more than 100 votes in all.

------

1 (1874) LR 9 Ch 250; 43 LJ Ch 330 (see p 541)

Now the argument is, that the words 'every member' mean, not a man registered on the list of shareholders, but any person beneficially entitled to shares, because if not carried to that extent I do not understand the argument at all. If it means that a man may hold 1000 shares beneficially, or that a man may disunite his shares, then there is no reason why he should be disqualified because he has one share in his own name or ten shares in his own name. Therefore the argument must go the whole length that any one man entitled beneficially to more than 1000 shares is not entitled to put them in the name of two or more persons as trustees for him, so as to allow those two or more persons to exercise the power of voting under the articles. It must go to that extent. But, taking even the restricted view, and reading the words 'every member' to mean only a person whose name is on the register, then it means this, that any man whose name is registered as a holder of shares cannot, if he is the *cestui que trust* of other shares, give together with his trustee more votes than if all the shares were registered in his own name. . . .

It appears to me that it is plain from reading these articles alone that the articles meant to refer to a registered member,

. . .

The result appears to me to be manifest, that the company has no right whatever to enter into the question of the beneficial ownership of the shares. Any such suggestion is quite inadmissible, and therefore it is clear that the chairman had no right to inquire who was the beneficial owner of the shares, and the votes in question ought to have been admitted as good votes independently of any inquiry as to whether the parties tendering them were or were not, and to what extent, trustees for other persons beneficially entitled to the shares.

SOURCE 116
Standard Chartered Bank Ltd *v* Walker
(Chancery Division) [1992] BCLC 603

VINELOTT J: The principal applications which are before me are applications by two banks, the Standard Chartered Bank (SCB) and TSB Bank plc (TSB). They are the plaintiffs in two separate actions, the defendants to both actions being Mr George Walker and Birdcage Walk Ltd, the latter a company incorporated in Hong Kong.

An extraordinary general meeting of a well-known company, Brent Walker plc, which of course has been long associated with Mr Walker, is due to take place at 10 am tomorrow. Mr Walker and Birdcage Walk are the beneficial owners of substantial blocks of ordinary and preference shares in Brent Walker. Mr Walker is the registered holder of 1.4m ordinary shares. Birdcage Walk is the registered holder of and beneficially entitled to 4.9m ordinary shares and 3.9m preference shares. It is not clear whether Mr Walker or Birdcage Walk is beneficially entitled to the shares registered in his name. The preference shares carry votes on certain resolutions at the extraordinary general meeting equal to four-fifteenths of the votes on the ordinary shares. The votes capable of being exercised at the extraordinary general meeting in respect of these shares amount, as I understand it, to between 5–10% of the votes capable of being cast at the extraordinary general meeting. That percentage may be critical.

In this application, SCB and TSB seek either a mandatory injunction requiring the defendants to vote in favour or a negative injunction restricting them from voting against resolutions to be proposed at that meeting. The effect of the resolutions if passed will be first to confirm a proposal for reconstructing Brent

Walker and its indebtedness and, secondly, to remove Mr Walker and a colleague, Mr Hemingway, from their offices as non-executive directors.

The resolutions are linked in this way. The banks, who propose this reconstruction and the liabilities to which exceed the likely realisable assets of Brent Walker, are not willing to go ahead with the reconstruction arrangements unless Mr Walker and Mr Hemingway are removed.

. . .

It is no doubt only in an extreme case that the court will interfere by injunction with the exercise by a shareholder — debtor with his own property — the voting right attached to his own shares. However, I have come to the conclusion that in this case the banks have shown that a vote against the restructuring facilities would cross that boundary. It is said that if the restructuring proposals do not go through there may be a chance that the banks will think again and provide something more favourable to the shareholders. That is flatly inconsistent with the evidence and I see no justification whatever for taking such an optimistic view. The banks have not only been holding their hands; they have been providing finance for the company and the restructuring proposals have already been delayed until the eleventh hour. The period during which the financing will endure comes to an end at the end of January. I see no reason to doubt Lord Kindersley's judgment that if the vote is not in favour of restructuring it will be the end of the company and that the shareholders and bondholders will then have no prospect of receiving anything.

It is suggested in the evidence that another company, Lonrho plc, might be interested in a rescue and that the shareholders should be given an opportunity of compelling the bank to look at proposals by Lonrho. The answer to that is that there is no offer by Lonrho either on the table or in prospect.

It was said by Mr Oliver that the shares are worthless anyway. The answer to that is that unless the restructuring proposals prove abortive they will have some hope value. I understand that they now trade at 10p a share. The plaintiff banks want to keep alive such hope as there may be. As I have said, I think the circumstances in which the court will interfere in a case of this sort are very rare indeed. To my mind, opposing or in any way obstructing the reconstruction proposals would be so pointlessly harmful that whatever motive inspired it would amount to the wilful dissipation of assets which the court has jurisdiction, consistently with the Mareva principles, to prevent.

There is an added feature in this case. Each of the plaintiff banks has a charge on other shares which they are in a position to vote. The security they have over their shares will be destroyed along with any prospect of executing a judgment against shares beneficially owned by the defendants. Mr Oliver said that the proposition that a creditor with a security over shares should be entitled to prevent a defendant from voting shares over which he has no security in order to preserve the value of the shares over which he has security is an extravagant one.

I do not think it is an extravagant proposition. It is a very unusual situation, but the situation is that the shares over which the security exists cannot be preserved except in a way which also preserves the other shares. But the aim is, quoad those shares, to ensure that the debtor does not act in a way which is destructive of the security he has given to the creditor. However that jurisdiction is described, whether it is waste or brought under some other head, I myself feel no doubt that the courts of equity do have jurisdiction to restrain conduct which would destroy property over which a debtor has given a charge in appropriate, and no doubt rare, circumstances.

PART IV: THE EFFECT OF STATUTE

A further qualification to the contract established by the memorandum and articles of association lies in the fact that legislation, especially the Companies Act, may prescribe a course of conduct which differs from that laid down in the contract. The contract may have to be read subject to certain statutory provisions (Sources 117, 118 and 119).

SOURCE 117
Re Greene Deceased
(Chancery Division 1949) [1949] Ch 333; [1949] 1 All ER 167

The articles of the company provided that:

> 'upon the death of any... director if such director leaves a wife him surviving,.... the share or shares of such deceased director shall, notwithstanding any provision or direction made by such director in his lifetime as to the disposition of such share or shares upon his death to the contrary, be deemed to have passed upon the death of such director to such deceased director's wife and such wife shall be the only person recognized by the Company as having any title to the share or shares and shall forthwith be registered as the holder of such share or shares in place of such deceased director.'

A director died intestate and his widow was registered as a shareholder in his place under the provisions of this regulation. These were proceedings in the administration of the estate of the intestate to determine whether his shares were part of his estate.

> HARMAN J: . . . Is it competent to a company by an article in this form to by-pass, so to speak, the personal representatives of a deceased holder of shares and to put them direct into the name of his widow? In my judgment, it is not. Such an article is contrary to section 63 of the Companies Act 1929.[1]
>
> I believe that the primary object of a section in this form, which first appeared in the Companies Act 1928, was to scotch the then prevalent practice of providing for the oral transfer of shares to the great detriment of the Revenue, but in my judgment it applies to this or a similar case, for no proper instrument of transfer has been delivered, nor has the right to the shares been transmitted to the widow by operation of law. In my judgment, therefore, the registration of the widow was wrong and the register ought to be rectified accordingly by registering the shares in the joint names of the personal representatives, who are the plaintiff and the first defendant.
>
> . . .
>
> Thirdly the widow seeks to rest her claim in contract and she points first to section 20 of the Companies Act 1929, whereby the articles constitute a contract between the members. The answer to this is that such a contract could only be enforced by or through the company (*Welton v Saffery*[2]), and an article which is, as I have held, *ultra vires* the company clearly cannot be so enforced.

---

1 Now s 183 of the Companies Act 1985
2 [1807] AC 200; 66 LJ Ch 362 (see p 295)

SOURCE 118
Bushell *v* Faith
(House of Lords 1970) [1970] AC 1099; [1970] 1 All ER 53

LORD UPJOHN: . . . Mr Faith was a director but his conduct as such displeased his sisters who requisitioned a general meeting of the company which was held on 22 November 1968, when a resolution was proposed as an ordinary resolution to remove him from his office as director. On a show of hands the resolution was passed, as the sisters voted for the resolution; so the brother demanded a poll and the whole issue is how votes should be counted upon the poll having regard to special article 9 of the company's articles of association.

The company adopted Table A in the First Schedule to the Companies Act 1948, with variations which are immaterial for present purposes. The relevant articles of Table A are:

'2. Without prejudice to any special rights previously conferred on the holders of any existing shares or class of shares, any share in the company may be issued with such preferred, deferred or other special rights or such restrictions, whether in regard to dividend, voting, return of capital or otherwise as the company may from time to time by ordinary resolution determine.

62. Subject to any rights or restrictions for the time being attached to any class or classes of shares, on a show of hands every member present in person shall have one vote, and on a poll every member shall have one vote for each share of which he is the holder.'

Special article 9 is as follows:

'In the event of a resolution being proposed at any general meeting of the company for the removal from office of any director, any shares held by that director shall on a poll in respect of such resolution carry the right to three votes per share and regulation 62 of Part 1 of Table A shall be construed accordingly.'

Article 96 of Table A, which empowers a company to remove a director by ordinary resolution is excluded by the articles of the company so that the appellant relies on the mandatory terms of section 184(1) of the Companies Act 1948[1] . . .

It is not in doubt that the requirements of subsection (2) have been satisfied. So the whole question is whether special article 9 is valid and applicable, in which case the resolution was rejected by 300 votes to 200, or whether that article must be treated as over-ridden by section 184 and therefore void, in which case the resolution was passed by 200 votes to 100. . . .

The appellant argues that special article 9 is directed to frustrating the whole object and purpose of section 184 so that it can never operate when there is such a special article and the director in fact becomes irremovable. So she argues that, having regard to the clear words 'notwithstanding anything in its articles' in section 184, special article 9 must be rejected and treated as void. The learned judge, Ungoed-Thomas J, so held. He said: 'It would make a mockery of the law if the courts were to hold that in such a case a director was to be irremovable.' And later he concluded his judgment by saying: 'A resolution under article 9 is therefore not in my view an ordinary resolution within section 184. The plaintiff succeeds in the application.'

---

1 Section 303 of the Companies Act 1985

The brother appealed, and the Court of Appeal (Harman, Russell and Karminski LJJ) allowed the appeal. Harman LJ did so on the simple ground that the Act of 1948 did not prevent certain shares or classes of shares having special voting rights attached to them and on certain occasions. He could find nothing in the Act of 1948 which prohibited the giving of special voting rights to the shares of a director who finds his position attacked. Russell LJ in his judgment gave substantially the same reasons for allowing the appeal and he supported his judgment by reference to a number of recent precedents particularly those to be found in *Palmer's Company Precedents*, (17th edn 1956), but, with all respect to the learned Lord Justice, I do not think these precedents which, so far as relevant, are comparatively new can be said to have the settled assent and approbation of the profession, so as to render them any real guide for the purposes of a judgment; especially when I note the much more cautious approach by the learned editors of the *Encyclopedia of Forms and Precedents*, (4th edn 1966), vol 5, p 428, where in reference to a form somewhat similar to special article 9 they say in a footnote:

> 'The validity of such a provision as this in relation to a resolution to remove a director from office remains to be tested in the courts.'

My Lords, when construing an Act of Parliament it is a canon of construction that its provisions must be construed in the light of the mischief which the Act was designed to meet. In this case the mischief was well known; it was a common practice, especially in the case of private companies, to provide in the articles that a director should be irremovable or only removable by an extraordinary resolution; in the former case the articles would have to be altered by special resolution before the director could be removed and of course in either case a three-quarters majority would be required. In many cases this would be impossible, so the Act provided that notwithstanding anything in the articles an ordinary resolution would suffice to remove a director. That was the mischief which the section set out to remedy; to make a director removable by virtue of an ordinary resolution instead of an extraordinary resolution or making it necessary to alter the articles.

An ordinary resolution is not defined nor used in the body of the Act of 1948 though the phrase occurs in some of the articles of Table A in the First Schedule to the Act. But its meaning is, in my opinion, clear. An ordinary resolution is in the first place passed by a bare majority on a show of hands by the members entitled to vote who are present personally or by proxy and on such a vote each member has one vote regardless of his shareholding. If a poll is demanded then for an ordinary resolution still only a bare majority of votes is required. But whether a share or class of shares has any vote upon the matter and, if so, what is its voting power upon the resolution in question depends entirely upon the voting rights attached to that share or class of shares by the articles of association.

I venture to think that Ungoed-Thomas J overlooked the importance of article 2 of Table A which gives to the company a completely unfettered right to attach to any share or class of shares special voting rights upon a poll or to restrict those rights as the company may think fit. Thus, it is commonplace that a company may and frequently does preclude preference shareholders from voting unless their dividends are in arrear or their class rights are directly affected. It is equally commonplace that particular shares may be issued with specially loaded voting rights which ensure that in all resolutions put before the shareholders in general meeting the holder of those particular shares can always be sure of carrying the day, aye or no, as the holder pleases.

Mr Dillon, for the appellant, felt, quite rightly, constrained to admit that if an article provided that Mr Faith's shares should, on every occasion when a resolution was for consideration by a general meeting of the company, carry three votes such a provision would be valid on all such occasions including any occasion when the general meeting was considering a resolution for his removal under section 184.

My Lords, I cannot see any difference between that case and the present case where special voting rights are conferred only when there is a resolution for the removal of a director under section 184. Each case is an exercise of the unfettered right of the company under article 2 whereby

> 'any share in the company may be issued with such . . . special rights . . . in regard to . . . voting . . . as the company may from time to time by ordinary resolution determine.'

Parliament has never sought to fetter the right of the company to issue a share with such rights or restrictions as it may think fit. There is no fetter which compels the company to make the voting rights or restrictions of general application and it seems to me clear that such rights or restrictions can be attached to special circumstances and to particular types of resolution. This makes no mockery of section 184; all that Parliament was seeking to do thereby was to make an ordinary resolution sufficient to recover a director. Had Parliament desired to go further and enact that every share entitled to vote should be deprived of its special rights under the articles it should have said so in plain terms by making the vote on a poll one vote one share. Then, what about shares which had no voting rights under the articles? Should not Parliament give them a vote when considering this completely artificial form of ordinary resolution? Suppose there had here been some preference shares in the name of Mr Faith's wife, which under the articles had in the circumstances no vote; why in justice should her voice be excluded from consideration in this artificial vote?

I only raise this purely hypothetical case to show the great difficulty of trying to do justice by legislation in a matter which has always been left to the corporators themselves to decide.

I agree entirely with the judgment of the Court of Appeal, and would dismiss this appeal.

LORD MORRIS OF BORTH-Y-GEST [dissenting]: My Lords, it is provided by section 184(1) that a company may by ordinary resolution remove a director before the expiration of his period of office. The company may do so notwithstanding anything to the contrary in its articles. So if an article provided that a director was irremovable he could nevertheless be removed if an ordinary resolution to that effect was passed. So also if an article provided that a director could only be removed by a resolution carried by a majority greater than a simple majority he would nevertheless be removed if a resolution was passed by a simple majority.

Some shares may, however, carry a greater voting power than others. On a resolution to remove a director shares will therefore carry the voting power that they possess. But this does not, in my view, warrant a device such as article 9 introduces. Its unconcealed effect is to make a director irremovable. If the question is posed whether the shares of the respondent possess any added voting weight the answer must be that they possess none whatsoever beyond, if valid, an ad hoc weight for the special purpose of circumventing section 184. If article 9 were writ large it would set out that a director is not to be removed against his will and that in order to achieve this and to thwart the express provision of section 184 the voting power of any director threatened with removal is to be deemed to be greater than it actually is. The learned judge thought that to sanction this would be to make a mockery of the law. I think so also.

I would allow the appeal.

SOURCE 119
Russell *v* Northern Bank Development Corp
(House of Lords) [1992] BCLC 1016

The shareholding in Tyrone Brick Ltd (TBL) consisted of 20 shares each for the plaintiff and three other individual shareholders (all four being the directors) and 120 for the defendant company. The three individual shareholders other than the plaintiff were also defendants to this action. The five shareholders and TBL entered into a shareholders' agreement in the following terms:

'WHEREAS:

1. The Corporation and the Executives (hereinafter collectively called "the Shareholders") are the holders of the entire issued share capital of the Company.

2. The shareholders have agreed to regulate the relationship between them with regard to the management and control of the Company so long as they shall remain shareholders of the Company.

NOW THIS AGREEMENT WITNESSETH AS FOLLOWS:

1. The terms of this Agreement shall have precedence between the shareholders over the Articles of Association and the parties agree to do, execute and perform such further acts, deeds, resolutions, consents, documents and things as may be necessary to give effect to this clause. Where the Articles of Association are silent on any matter, the provisions of this Agreement shall operate between the parties. Where there is conflict between the provisions of this Agreement and the Articles of Association the parties hereto shall cooperate where necessary to have the Articles amended from time to time to take account of the provisions of this Agreement and any subsequent consequential changes. Where this Agreement requires any future action to be taken by the Board of Directors or by the members of the company the shareholders as such shareholders or as the parties entitled to nominate the Board of Directors of the Company will co-operate and do all such things as are necessary to implement such future action.

2. The provisions of this Agreement shall not be amended without the written consent of each of the parties hereto.

3. No further share capital shall be created or issued in the Company or the rights attaching to the shares already in issue in any way altered (save as is herein set out) or any Share Transfer of the existing Shares permitted, save in the following manner, without the written consent of each of the parties hereto.

Article 131 of the Companies (Northern Ireland) Order 1986 (SI 1986/1032), which corresponds to s 121 of the CA 1985 was in force at the relevant time and TBL's articles of association included the following provision:

'The company may from time to time by ordinary resolution increase the share capital by such sum, to be divided into sharers of such amount as the resolution shall prescribe.'

LORD JAUNCEY: . . . The issue between the parties in this House was whether art 3 of the agreement constituted an unlawful and invalid fetter on the statutory power of TBL to increase its share capital or whether it was no more than an agreement between the shareholders as to their manner of voting in a given situation. Both parties accepted the long-established principle that 'a company cannot forgo its right to alter its articles' (*Southern Foundries (1926) Ltd v Shirlaw* [1940] 2 All ER 445 at 468, [1940] AC 701 at 739 per Lord Porter), a principle that was earlier stated in *Allen v Gold Reefs of West Africa Ltd* [1900] 1 Ch 656 at 671, [1900–3] All ER Rep 746 at 749 per Lindley MR:

> ' . . . the company is empowered by the statute to alter the regulations contained in its articles from time to time by special resolutions (ss 50 and 51); and any regulation or article purporting to deprive the company of this power is invalid on the ground that it is contrary to the statute: *Walker v London Tramways Co* ((1879) 12 Ch D 705).'

Murray J and MacDermont LJ both considered that this principle applied also to the right of a company to alter its memorandum and I agree that this must be the case. Mr McCartney QC for the appellant advanced a number of arguments to the effect that the agreement in no way contravened the above principle inasmuch as it was merely an agreement between shareholders outside the scope of company legislation which in no way fettered the statutory power of TBL to alter its memorandum and articles. Mr Girvan QC, on the other hand, submitted that the agreement was not only a voting arrangement between shareholders inter se but was tantamount to an article of association which constituted a restriction on the power of TBL to alter its share capital.

My Lords, while a provision in a company's articles which restricts its statutory power to alter those articles is invalid an agreement dehors the articles between shareholders as to how they shall exercise their voting rights on a resolution to alter the articles is not necessarily so. In *Welton v Saffery* [1897] AC 299 at 331, [1895–9] All ER Rep 567 at 585, which concerned an ultra vires provision in the articles of association authorising the company to issue shares at a discount, Lord Davey said:

> 'Of course, individual shareholders may deal with their own interests by contract in such way as they may think fit. But such contracts, whether made by all or some only of the shareholders, would create personal obligations, or an exceptio personalis against themselves only, and would not become a regulation of the company, or be binding on the transferees of the parties to it, or upon new or non-assenting shareholders. There is no suggestion here of any such private agreement outside the machinery of the Companies Acts.'

I understand Lord Davey there to be accepting that shareholders may lawfully agree inter se to exercise their voting rights in a manner which, if it were dictated by the articles, and were thereby binding on the company, would be unlawful.

I turn to examine the agreement in more detail. It appears from the narrative clauses that the agreement was intended to regulate the relationship between the shareholders with regard to the management and control of TBL. Clause 1 provides that the terms of the agreement was intended to regulate the relationship between the shareholders with regard to the management and control of TBL. Clause 1 provides that the terms of the agreement shall have precedence *between the shareholders* over the articles of association. It further provides that where there is a conflict between the provisions of the agreement and the articles parties shall co-operate where necessary to have the articles amended to take account of the provisions of the agreement. It further provides that no further share capital shall be created or issued in TBL without the written consent of the parties to the agreement. TBL was incorporated under a previous name on 13 July 1979 and the agreement was executed on 14 December of that year. Since that date no attempt has been made to amend the articles for the purposes of clause 1, but I do not find that in anyway surprising because clause 3 affects only existing shareholders and does not purport to bind other persons who may at some future date become shareholders in TBL by allotment or transfer. Clause 3 at least so far as shareholders are concerned constitutes an agreement collateral to the provisions of reg 44 of Table A and is, as MacDermott LJ has concluded, neither in substitution for nor in conflict with that regulation.

However, it must be remembered that the agreement was executed not only by the shareholders but also by TBL. In *Bushell v Faith* [1969] 1 All ER 1002, [1969] 2 Ch 438 one of the articles of a private company provided that in the event of a resolution being proposed at a general meeting of the company for the removal of a director any share held by him should carry three votes per share. The issued capital of the company was equally divided between three persons and an attempt by two shareholders to remove the third from the office of director failed because his 300 votes outnumbered the 200 of the two other shareholders. It was held that the article in question was not invalidated by s 184 of the Companies Act 1948, which empowered a company by ordinary resolution to remove a director. Russell LJ said ([1969] 1 All ER 1002 at 1006, [1969] 2 Ch 438 at 447–448):

'Counsel for the plaintiff argued by reference to s 10, and the well-known proposition that a company cannot by its articles or otherwise deprive itself of the power by special resolution to alter its articles or any of them; but the point is the same one. An article purporting to do this is ineffective; but a provision as to voting rights which has the effect of making a special resolution incapable of being passed if a particular shareholder or group of shareholders exercises his or their voting rights against a proposed altera-tion is not such a provision. An article in terms providing that no alteration shall be made without the consent of "X" is contrary to s 10 and ineffective, but the provision as to voting rights that I have mentioned is wholly different, and it does not serve to say that it can have the same result.'

Both parties sought to derive comfort from this dictum. Mr McCartney relied on it as demonstrating that a provision as to the exercise of voting rights, even although it had the effect of preventing a resolution being passed, was never-theless valid. Mr Girvan argued that the effect of clause 3 was the same as that of an article containing a provision that 'No alteration should be made without the consent of X'.

I do not doubt that if clause 3 had been embodied in the articles of association so as to be binding on all persons who were or might become shareholders in TBL it would have been invalid but it was, of course, not so embodied. To my mind the significant part of this dictum for the purposes of this appeal is the words 'articles or otherwise' occurring in the first sentence thereof. These words appear to recognise that it is not only fetters on the power to alter articles of association imposed by the statutory framework of a company which are obnoxious.

Turning back to clause 3 of the agreement it appears to me that its purpose was twofold. The shareholders agreed only to exercise their voting powers in relation to the creation or issue of shares in TBL if they and TBL agreed in writing. This agreement is purely personal to the shareholders who executed it and as I have already remarked does not purport to bind future shareholders. It is, in my view, just such a private agreement as was envisaged by Lord Davey in *Welton v Saffery*. TBL on the other hand agreed that its capital would not be increased without the consent of each of the shareholders. This was a clear undertaking by TBL in a formal agreement not to exercise its statutory power for a period which could, certainly on one view of construction, last for as long as any one of the parties to the agreement remained a shareholder and long after the control of TBL had passed to shareholders, who were not party to the agreement. As such an undertaking it is, in my view, as obnoxious as if it had been contained in the articles of association and therefore is unenforceable as being contrary to the provisions of art 131 of the Companies (Northern Ireland) Order 1986. TBL's undertaking is, however, independent of and severable from that of the share-holders and there is no reason why the latter should not be enforceable by the shareholders inter se as a personal agreement which in no way fetters TBL in the exercise of its statutory powers. I would therefore allow the appeal.

It only remains to consider the relief which would be afforded to the appellant. He stated in evidence that he had no objection to the proposed resolutions in themselves but that he wished to establish the validity of clause 3 and was concerned that if further capital were issued he might in future be faced with a rights issue without the necessary cash to make it up with the result that his position might be weakened in relation to other shareholders. In these circum-stances it would be inappropriate to grant him the injunction sought in his writ. In my view the proper order would be a declaration as to the validity of clause 3 of the agreement as between the shareholders.

PART V: REMEDIES

The remedies available where the contract is breached include specific performance and injunction (see eg *Pender v Lushington*[1] and *Rayfield v Hands*[2]). There may be some doubt whether damages is an appropriate remedy and rectification is excluded (Sources 120, 121 and 122).

SOURCE 120
Moffatt *v* Farquhar
(Chancery Division 1878) (1878) 7 Ch D 591

'58: That if five or more proprietors present at any general meeting of proprietors, and qualified to vote at a ballot as herein is mentioned, shall, either before or after the voting, by shew of hands, demand that the votes thereupon be ascertained and taken by ballot, then the same shall be done accordingly, and in the case of such ballot every proprietor holding twenty shares in the company shall have one vote, and one additional vote in respect of each complete number of twenty shares (beyond the first twenty) held by him in the company, but no shareholder shall have more than twenty votes on the whole.'

MALINS VC: . . . It appears that in the year 1875 differences of opinion arose between some of the shareholders in this way: The company being one of unlimited liability, and every shareholder being consequently liable for every farthing he has in the world, it seems to have occurred to Mr Moffatt and some other shareholders that it would be very desirable to turn this company into one

---

1 (1877) 6 Ch D 70; 46 LJ Ch 317 (see p 314)
2 [1960] Ch 1; [1958] 2 All ER 194 (see p 301)

of limited liability, under the powers contained in the Companies Act 1862. . . . Mr Moffatt finding that he had only twenty votes for his 3031 shares . . . it occurred to Mr Moffatt that [he was] not properly represented upon any division of opinion, and that by selling his shares, or transferring them to trustees for themselves, the power of voting might be increased. Accordingly Mr Moffatt sold to Mr Roger Eykyn, a gentleman well known to be of the highest respectability, a stockbroker, and formerly a member of Parliament, to whom it was impossible that any objection could be raised, 400 shares. It was suggested that this was not a bonâ fide sale, but a transfer by way of trust; but Mr Eykyn was examined as a witness and swore that he desired to be a member of the company, and that he was ready to pay the money for the shares. I am bound, therefore, to take this as a bonâ fide sale of 400 shares at the price of £8 per share. Upon this sale taking place there was the usual notice given to the directors that Mr Moffatt was desirous of transferring these shares to Mr Eykyn, and he also gave them notice that he was desirous of transferring 400 other shares to Mr R Moffatt. The result of the evidence given by Mr R Moffatt is to shew that he was not to pay for them, but to hold the shares in trust for his uncle, the plaintiff; therefore I have a transfer of 400 shares for value at the full market price, and a transfer of 400 shares voluntarily to a trustee for the plaintiff, Mr Moffatt.

. . .

The question therefore raised, and the only question that I have to decide, is, what is the power of the directors in vetoing or forbidding the transfer of the shares? . . .

The only power which is given by that section to the directors of objecting to the transfer is as to the person of the transferee. If the person or persons proposed shall be approved of, then a transfer of the shares is to take place. In my opinion therefore, it is perfectly clear there can be no justification for refusing the transfer unless they have an objection to the person of the transferee. That they should have such a power seems reasonable; because, this being a limited company, and it being very desirable that they should have respectable men and solvent men as members, and persons who would be able to pay the calls which should be made, it is reasonable that they should have the power of objecting to the person, and not have introduced among them insolvent persons, or, it might be, if you like, disagreeable persons who would throw them into confusion; and therefore the directors have the power of objecting to the person. Certainly, there is, in my opinion, no other power of objecting to the transfer, and if, therefore, a proper transferee is proposed, I take it to be perfectly clear that the proprietor has a right to transfer his shares to whatsoever he likes, and the board has no right whatever to inquire into what the object of that transfer is.

. . . This right of transfer is a right of property; and if the directors have an arbitrary power, from any fancy they choose to take up, to say there shall be no transfer, that is an annihilation of property. . . . the objection raised by these directors to this transfer was without justification, and I am bound, therefore, to order that the transfers to Mr Roger Eykyn and Mr Robert Moffatt, in pursuance of the notice of 29 November 1875, be made. . . .

Another very important question is raised whether there should be an inquiry as to damages. I do not know whether it is desired to press that. I should strongly desire that the litigation should stop here as far as I am concerned.

[The case was again mentioned. An offer to waive the inquiry was made on conditions, which were not accepted, and the Vice-Chancellor then directed an inquiry as to damages.]

SOURCE 121
Scott *v* Frank F Scott (London) Ltd
[1940] Ch 794; [1940] 3 All ER 508

LUXMOORE LJ: On 14 March 1939, the plaintiff, who is the widow and sole executrix of the will of the late Frank Stanley Scott, instituted this action against a private company incorporated under the Companies Acts 1908 to 1917, with the name of Frank F. Scott (London) Ltd, and her two brothers-in-law, Stuart Arthur Scott and Reginald Scott. The relief claimed was a declaration that upon the true construction of the articles of association of the company and in the events that have happened the plaintiff is entitled to be placed upon the company's register of members in respect of 100 ordinary shares in the company which were registered in the name of her husband at his death. The plaintiff further claimed to have the company's register of members rectified by the insertion therein of her name as the holder of the shares in question, and certain other relief to which it is immaterial to refer. The defendants challenged the plaintiff's right to be registered as the holder of the said shares and claimed that on the true construction of the articles of association the plaintiff, as the executrix of the late Frank Stanley Scott, was bound to offer those shares to the defendants, Stuart Arthur Scott and Reginald Scott. The defendants also asserted that if, contrary to their contention, the Court should hold that on the true construction of the articles of association the plaintiff was not bound to offer the shares in question to the two personal defendants they were entitled to have the articles of association of the company rectified so as to provide in effect that all ordinary shares of a deceased member should be offered by his executors or administrators forthwith after his death to the principal shareholders, that is, in the existing circumstances, the personal defendants; and the defendants counter-claimed for a declaration in accordance with the construction for which they contended and for rectification of the articles of association in the manner indicated, if the Court should not accept their contention as to construction.

[The court decided the question of construction in favour of the plaintiff.]

The next question which falls to be considered is whether the defendants are entitled to have the articles of association rectified in the manner claimed by them. . . .

It seems to us that there is no room in the case of a company incorporated under the appropriate statute or statutes for the application to either the memorandum or articles of association of the principles upon which a Court of Equity permits rectification of documents whether inter partes or not. The memorandum and articles of association of any company which it is proposed to incorporate must be signed by the requisite number of persons who desire its incorporation and must comply with the statutory requirements in respect of registration.

. . .

It is not until all these requirements have been satisfied that the company comes into being and the certificate of its incorporation is issued, and the memorandum and articles become binding upon the company and its members . . . It is quite true that in the case of the rectification of a document, such as a deed inter partes, or a deed poll, the order for rectification does not order an alteration of the document; it merely directs that it be made to accord with the form in which it ought originally to have been executed. This cannot be the case with regard to the memorandum and articles of association of a company, for it is the document in its actual form that is delivered to the Registrar and is retained and registered by him, and it is that form and no other that constitutes the charter of the company and becomes binding on it and its members. The legal entity only comes into existence as a corporate body, distinct from the subscribers to the memorandum and articles registered, upon registration.

...

Further the effect of registration of the memorandum and articles of a company under section 14 of the 1929 Act is to bind the company (which, as already stated, only comes into existence after the registration is effected) and the members thereof to the same extent and in the same manner as if they had respectively been signed and sealed by each member and contained covenants on the part of each member, his heirs, executors and administrators to observe all the provisions of the memorandum and of the articles subject to the provisions of the Act. It seems plain that this section does not admit of any rectification of the memorandum and articles apart from alterations under the express powers of the Act, for the only contract is a statutory contract in which the Company is included by reference to the registered documents and to no other documents.

SOURCE 122
Bratton Seymour Service Co *v* Oxborough
(Court of Appeal) [1992] BCLC 693

DILLON LJ. This is an appeal by Mr Oxborough, who is the defendant in the action, against an order made by his Honour Judge O'Malley on 11 July 1990 in the Yeovil County Court whereby he adjudged and declared —

> 'that the Defendant is, by virtue of his membership of the Plaintiff Company [which is a company called Bratton Seymour Service Co Ltd], under an obligation to pay such reasonable contribution, determined by the Company, towards the expenses reasonably incurred of maintaining both the utility and the amenity areas of the Bratton House development, provided that the element of such contribution attributable to utility expenditure does not exceed the amount that would be due in respect thereof under the covenant in the conveyance to him of his property.'

The form of the declaration distinguishes between the utility and the amenity areas of the Bratton House development and the reason for that will become apparent. The judge granted that declaration because he held that he was entitled to imply such an obligation as a term of the articles of association of the company.

...

I see insuperable difficulties in the way of any such implication into the articles of association of the company. It is said, 'Oh, the articles constitute a contract between the company and its members, and so you can imply any term into such a contract as you can imply any term into any other contract in order to give business efficacy'. But the articles of association of a company differ very considerably from a normal contract. They are a document which has statutory force. If a company, limited by shares, chooses to have articles of association instead of merely relying on Table A, then those articles have to be registered. These articles were registered when the company was incorporated. The articles thus registered are one of the statutory documents of the company open for inspection by anyone minded to deal with the company or to take shares in the company. It is thus a consequence, as was held by this court in *Scott v Frank F Scott (London) Ltd* [1940] 3 All ER 508, [1940] Ch 794, that the court has no jurisdiction to rectify the articles of association of a company, even if those articles do not accord with what is proved to have been the concurrent intention of the signatories of the memorandum at the moment of signature.

It is because of the statutory force of the articles, when registered, that that conclusion was reached. The articles, if not in accordance with the intention of the subscribers, have to be altered by the statutory procedure of a special resolution if the appropriate majority of the members agree to such an alteration. There is the further restriction that the company cannot, by an alteration of its articles, impose an extra burden of contribution on a member who does not vote in favour of the alteration. That was introduced into company law by way of clarification in the Companies Act 1928 and is now to be found in s 16(2) of the Companies Act 1985. Of course, Mr Asprey, appearing for the company in this court, does not seek to rely on alteration of the articles. He says that he can get round that difficulty by implication into the original articles at the time the company was incorporated. But there is nothing in the articles to give any hint of any contribution by the members to the maintenance of the utilities or the amenity areas or anything else. He has to reach his implication by taking into account surrounding circumstances not apparent from the articles themselves or from the memorandum.

On the facts, what was in issue in *Scott v Scott Ltd* was whether the executor of a deceased member of a company was bound to offer the deceased member's shares in the company to the other members at par. It was said that the common intention of the subscribers was that if one of the subscribers died the others should be entitled to acquire his shares at par. When one died his widow and sole executrix claimed, by virtue not of any special provision in the articles but of her ownership of the shares in the absence of any provision to the contrary in the articles, to be registered in the share register of the company as the owner of her deceased husband's shares in the company. This court held that she was so entitled, and held also, affirming in this respect the decision of the judge at first instance, that the court had no jurisdiction to rectify the articles of association, even if they did not accord with what was proved to have been the concurrent intention of the signatories at the moment of signature.

The argument advanced in the present case of an implied term necessary to give business efficacy to the scheme which the subscribers had formed would, it would seem, have been open to the respondents in *Scott v Frank F Scott (London) Ltd* but their counsel, Mr Charles Harman KC, and Mr Winterbotham, apparently did not think of that easy way round their difficulties and they argued instead for the court's right to rectify the articles to bring in a provision obliging the executrix to offer the deceased's shares to the other shareholders at par. I do not need to quote specifically from the judgment of the court delivered by Luxmore LJ. To my mind it is wholly inconsistent with that judgment that there should be any such power in the court to imply a term into the articles of association, such as Mr Asprey has contended for, which arises from the surrounding circumstances not apparent from the terms of the memorandum and articles themselves. In particular, it does not in the least appear from the memorandum and articles themselves that the purchasers of the various parts of the property are going to enter into covenants to contribute to the cost of the utilities but not covenants to contribute to the maintenance of the amenity areas; nor does it appear from the memorandum and articles that there was no intention to form some members' club to run the amenity areas for the benefit of those residents and others who wished to take advantage of the tennis courts and swimming pools.

There is the further point in relation to Mr Oxborough that his conveyance came subsequent to the incorporation of the company, and so at the time of the incorporation of the company it would have been perfectly possible that terms might have been negotiated in his conveyance which did put a contractual obligation on him to contribute to the development company a due proportion, whatever it may have been, of the cost of maintaining the amenity areas. The percentages also that are fixed for contribution to the upkeep of the utilities must make it highly doubtful whether contribution to the upkeep of the amenities was intended to be per shareholding in the company rather than by some other means related to user.

In these circumstances, with all respect to the learned judge, I am wholly unable to agree that there is any term to be implied into the articles of association of this company. I would therefore allow this appeal.

SIR CHRISTOPHER SLADE. A careful prospective shareholder in a private limited company, such as the plaintiff company in the present case, may wish to know, before he subscribes for his shares, to what potential financial liabilities in relation to the company he will be exposed. For this purpose he will be entitled to direct his attention to the memorandum and articles of association of the company as registered. Their form will, in this context be crucial. As has already been pointed out, they will constitute a form of contract between himself and the company of a special nature having statutory operation. The decision in *Scott v Frank F Scott (London) Ltd* [1940] 3 All ER 508, [1940] Ch 794 to which Dillon LJ had referred, shows that this form of contract has some special incidents, in particular because it is incapable of rectification.

To quote some words from the judgment of Jenkins LJ in *Holmes v Keyes* [1958] 2 All ER 129 at 138, [1959] Ch 199 at 215, I accept Mr Asprey's submission that:

> '. . . the articles of association of the company should be regarded as a business document and should be construed so as to give them reasonable business efficacy, where a construction tending to that result is admissible on the language of the articles, in preference to a result which would or might prove unworkable.'

Mr Asprey, however, has had to accept that the language of the articles of association of the company in the present case, if read on its own without extrinsic evidence, cannot be said to impose on the shareholders the financial obligations which the judge held to have been imposed on them by the articles. He has therefore been driven to rely on extrinsic evidence for this purpose.

I accept that, in construing the articles of association of a company, evidence of surrounding circumstances may be admissible for the limited purpose of identifying persons, places or other subject matter referred to therein. Mr Asprey, however, has not invoked extrinsic evidence of surrounding circumstances in the present case for that limited purpose. He has sought to invoke it for the purpose of imposing additional financial obligations on the members far beyond those which the language of the articles of association of the company, read fairly on its own, would impose on them, because, he says, such an implication is required to give the articles business efficacy. No authority has been cited to us which begins to support the proposition that extrinsic evidence is admissible for that wide purpose in construing the statutory contract created by the articles of association of a company. In my judgment, the admission of such evidence for such purpose would be quite contrary to the principles governing this type of statutory contract. If it were to be admissible, this would place the potential shareholders in a limited company, who wished to ascertain their potential obligations to the company, in an intolerable position. They are in my judgment entitled to rely on the meaning of the language of the memorandum and articles of association, as such meaning appears from the language used.

For these short reasons, I would agree that this appeal must be allowed.

PART VI: ALTERATION OF THE CONTRACT

The procedure for the alteration of the memorandum is stricter than for the articles (compare ss 4–6 with s 9). It may have been thought that these provisions give the only method for the alteration of the company's constitution, but see *Cane v Jones*[1] (p 385).

The power to alter the articles is expressly made subject to other provisions in the Companies Act, among which should be noted ss 125 and 461(3). Section 125 (which originated in the Companies Act 1980) put an end to a long standing uncertainty as to whether special rights attached to a separate class of shares in the articles could be altered simply by altering the articles or whether any special procedure laid down by the articles for the alteration of class rights had to be followed or whether (where there was no such special procedure) the special rights were unalterable (see Chapter 9, especially at pp 634 ff).

At least from 1900 it has also been clear that the power to alter the articles has been subject to equitable principles (Sources 123, 124, 125 and 126).

SOURCE 123
Allen *v* Gold Reefs of West Africa Ltd
(Court of Appeal 1900) [1900] 1 Ch 656; 69 LJ Ch 266

The articles of the company originally provided:

> '29: that the company shall have a first and paramount lien for all debts, obligations, and liabilities of any member to or towards the company upon all shares (not being fully paid) held by such member. . . .'

LINDLEY MR: . . . The directors, . . . desired to extend the lien and power of sale and power to refuse to register transfers to Zuccani's[2] fully paid-up shares. I say, to his shares, for he was the only person entitled to fully paid-up shares from whom any calls were due. Accordingly steps were taken to pass a special resolution to alter article 29 by striking out the words 'not being fully paid,' and a resolution to that effect was passed.

. . .

The facts above stated raise the following very important question, namely, (1) Whether a limited company, registered with articles conferring no lien on its fully paid-up shares, can by special resolution alter those articles by imposing a lien on such shares? (2) Whether, if it can, the lien so imposed can be made to apply to debts owing by fully paid-up shareholders to the company at the time of the alteration of the articles? (3) Whether, if it can, fully paid-up shares allotted to vendors of property to the company are in any different position from other fully paid-up shares issued by the company? (4) Whether, assuming the altered articles

---

1 [1980] 1 WLR 1451; [1981] 1 All ER 533
2 The shareholder subsequently died and his executors included Allen

to be valid and to be binding on the general body of the holders of fully paid-up shares in the company, there are any special circumstances in this particular case to exclude the fully paid-up shares held by Zuccani from the operation of the altered articles?

... the company is empowered by the statute to alter the regulations contained in its articles from time to time by special resolutions (sections 50 and 51), and any regulation or article purporting to deprive the company of this power is invalid on the ground that it is contrary to the statute: *Walker v London Tramways Co.*[1]

The power thus conferred on companies to alter the regulations contained in their articles is limited only by the provisions contained in the statute and the conditions contained in the company's memorandum of association. Wide, however, as the language of section 50 is, the power conferred by it must, like all other powers, be exercised subject to those general principles of law and equity which are applicable to all powers conferred on majorities and enabling them to bind minorities. It must be exercised, not only in the manner required by law, but also bonâ fide for the benefit of the company as a whole, and it must not be exceeded. These conditions are always implied, and are seldom, if ever, expressed But if they are complied with I can discover no ground for judicially putting any other restrictions on the power conferred by the section than those contained in it. How shares shall be transferred, and whether the company shall have any lien on them, are clearly matters of regulation properly prescribed by a company's articles of association. . . . Speaking, therefore, generally, and without reference to any particular case, the section clearly authorizes a limited company, formed with articles which confer no lien on fully paid-up shares, and which allow them to be transferred without any fetter, to alter those articles by special resolution, and to impose a lien and restrictions on the registry of transfers of those shares by members indebted to the company.

But then comes the question whether this can be done so as to impose a lien or restriction in respect of a debt contracted before and existing at the time when the articles are altered. Again, speaking generally, I am of opinion that the articles can be so altered, and that, if they are altered bonâ fide for the benefit of the company, they will be valid and binding as altered on the existing holders of paid-up shares, whether such holders are indebted or not indebted to the company when the alteration is made. But, as will be seen presently, it does not by any means follow that the altered article may not be inapplicable to some particular fully paid-up shareholder. He may have special rights against the company, which do not invalidate the resolution to alter the articles, but which may exempt him from the operation of the articles as altered.

The conclusion thus arrived at is based on the language of section 50,[2] which, as I have said already, the Court, in my opinion, is not at liberty to restrict. This conclusion, moreover, is in conformity with such authorities as there are on the subject. *Andrews v Gas Meter Co*[3] is an authority that, under section 50 of the Companies Act 1862, a company's articles can be altered so as to authorize the issue of preference shares taking priority over existing shares, although no power to issue preference shares was conferred by the memorandum of association or by the original articles. The answer to the argument that the company could not alter existing rights is that, within the limits set by the statute and the memorandum of association, the rights of shareholders in limited companies, so

---

1 (1879) 12 Ch D 705; 49 LJ Ch 23
2 Now s 9 of the Companies Act 1985
3 [1897] 1 Ch D 361; 66 LJ Ch 246

far as they depend only on the regulations of the company, are subject to alterations by section 50 of the Act.

But, although the regulations contained in a company's articles of association are revocable by special resolution, a special contract may be made with the company in the terms of or embodying one or more of the articles, and the question will then arise whether an alteration of the articles so embodied is consistent or inconsistent with the real bargain between the parties. A company cannot break its contracts by altering its articles, but, when dealing with contracts referring to revocable articles, and especially with contracts between a member of the company and the company respecting his shares, care must be taken not to assume that the contract involves as one of its terms an article which is not to be altered.

I take it to be clear that an application for an allotment of shares on the terms of the company's articles does not exclude the power to alter them nor the application of them, when altered, to the shares so applied for and allotted. To exclude that power or the application of an altered article to particular shares, some clear and distinct agreement for that exclusion must be shewn, or some circumstances must be proved conferring a legal or equitable right on the shareholder to be treated by the company differently from the other share-holders.

. . .

After carefully considering the whole case, and endeavouring in vain to discover grounds for holding that there was some special bargain differentiating Zuccani's shares from others, I have come to the conclusion that the appeal from the decision of the learned judge, so far as it relates to the lien created by the altered articles, must be allowed. His decision as to the forfeiture having, however, been affirmed, each party should be left to pay his own costs.

SOURCE 124
Peter's American Delicacy Company Limited *v* Heath
(High Court of Australia 1938) (1939) 61 CLR 457

The plaintiffs sought a declaration that the resolutions whereby the shareholders purported to alter the articles were not validly passed, and an injunction restraining the company and its directors from acting upon those resolutions or making any distribution of the assets of the company inconsistent with article 120 as it stood at the date of the extraordinary general meeting above mentioned.

The grounds upon which the declaration and the injunction were sought in the statement of claim as originally drafted were in substance: (i) that the resolutions were passed solely for the purpose of benefiting fully paid share-holders to the disadvantage of partly paid shareholders and not in the interests of or for the benefit of the company, or the body of shareholders; and (ii) that 'the members of the company at all material times holding only partly paid shares were only a small minority of the shareholders and the plaintiffs charge and it is the fact that the fully paid shareholders used their majority voting power to pass the said resolutions to benefit themselves at the expense of the partly paid-up shareholders.'

. . .

Article 120 was headed 'Capitalization of Profits' and was in the following terms: 120. Notwithstanding anything in any other article contained the whole or any part of the undivided profits including amounts at credit of reserve or any other fund may with the sanction of the company in general meeting be converted into capital of the company by distributing the same amongst the holders of shares as a special dividend or bonus by issuing partly or fully paid-up shares in respect thereof to the holders of such shares in proportion to the shares held by them in the company.

DIXON CJ: . . . The articles, as they existed, contained clauses providing that the profits of the company should be divisible among the shareholders in proportion to the capital paid up on the shares held by them respectively; that a general meeting might declare a dividend to be paid to the members according to their rights and interests in the profits; that a general meeting might increase the capital by the creation of new shares; and that such a meeting might determine that the new shares should be offered to the members in proportion to the capital held by them or make any other provision as to the issue and allotment of such shares (articles 108, 110, 111, 34 and 36).

The articles contained no provision as to the division of a surplus in a winding up. But they contained a clause (article 120) specifically dealing with capitalization, and the purpose of the alterations was to overcome the effects which this clause produced. The meaning of the clause has been disputed, but I think that it clearly means that with the sanction of a general meeting undistributed profits might be capitalized by making a ratable distribution among the members of shares paid up in full or in part out of such profits. The article means that the ratable distribution shall be in proportion with the shares held by the members, not with the capital paid up thereon, and that the amount paid up on the bonus shares should be uniform and should not vary with the amount paid up on the existing shares of the respective members.

The issued capital of the company was in fact divided into fully paid and contributing shares. About three-fourths of the shares were paid up in full, and about one-fourth were paid up to one-third only of their amount. . . . as the articles stood, accumulations of profit, if distributed as a cash dividend or under the older indirect procedure for capitalization, would be distributed according to one proportion, viz, according to capital paid up; if distributed directly as shares, according to another proportion, viz, according to capital subscribed; and if distributed as upon a reconstruction through a liquidator, according to still a third method, viz, by first equalizing paid-up capital and then distributing according to shares held.

. . .

After taking much advice the directors determined to deal with the question by proposing alterations of the articles which would enable a direct distribution of shares according to the amount of capital paid up by the respective shareholders upon their shares. The alterations designed to effect this result were proposed as special resolutions at an extraordinary general meeting of the company on 14 September 1937. The notice summoning the meeting stated that resolutions would be proposed for the necessary increase of capital and for authorizing the directors to carry out the proposed transaction and, also, if the resolutions altering the articles increasing the capital and approving of the transaction were passed, for the capitalization under the new articles of the profits arising from the sale of the goodwill. At the meeting the special resolutions were passed by the requisite majority. No poll was demanded. The remaining resolutions were then also carried.

. . .

The power of altering the articles of the company is now derived from section 20 of the Companies Act 1936 (NSW), which is a general statutory provision. The section in terms empowers a company by special resolution to alter or add to its articles. No limitations or restrictions on the power are expressed, except that it is made subject to the provisions of the Act and the conditions contained in the memorandum of association. The section goes on to enact that any alteration or addition should be as valid as if originally contained in the articles.

The conditions expressed by the section itself make it clear that no alteration of the articles can validly operate to destroy or prejudice rights which the statute confers upon members of a company or which are lawfully fixed under provisions of the memorandum. But the power of altering articles of association now conferred by statute had its analogue, if not its source, in clauses found in deeds of settlement by which a specified majority of the members of companies constituted or regulated by such instruments were empowered to alter or add to their provisions. The mala-fide use or abuse of such powers would naturally fall under the jurisdiction of courts of equity, and from the time of the Act of 1856 (19 & 20 Vict. c. 47, secs. 33, 34 and 35), which included the statutory authority to alter articles of association, it has never been conceded that the power is unrestrained. It is one thing, however, to say that such a power is not unlimited or uncontrolled and another to define the grounds upon which an ostensible exercise of the power should be considered invalid. At first an attempt was made to distinguish between matters which went to the foundation of a company's structure and matters which related only to the conduct and management of its affairs. Thus, in the course of his now overruled judgment in *Hutton v Scarborough Cliff Hotel Co Ltd*[1] Kindersley VC said: 'The question is whether the power given to a general meeting, by special resolution, to modify the regulations of the company is unlimited: clearly there must be some limit to the power; otherwise they might alter not only such as relate to the management of the company, but they might alter the very constitution and nature of the company.' But the distinction was found untenable. It is the province of the memorandum of association to fix the constitution and nature of the company, and the power of altering the articles is subject to whatever restrictions it may contain. But no article as such could be made unalterable. It may be altered notwithstanding that it is expressed to be fundamental or part of the constitution of the company or unalterable, and a company cannot contract itself out of the power. In spite of what is said in *British Murac Syndicate Ltd v Alperton Rubber Co Ltd*,[2] the better opinion still appears to be that the fact that to alter an article involves a breach of contract can be no more than an evidentiary consideration and does not in itself make the alteration invalid: See *Buckley on the Companies Acts*, (10th edn 1924), pp 24, 25; (11th edn 1930) pp 18, 19; *Law Quarterly Review*, vol 31, p 359. After the abandonment of the distinction between, on the one hand, matters of administration and management admittedly subject to the power of alteration and, on the other, matters going to the constitution of the company and said therefore to be outside the power, the courts sought for a limitation in the more general doctrine that a power must be exercised bona fide for the end for which the power is designed. Primarily a share in a company is a piece of property conferring rights in relation to distributions of income and of capital. In many respects the proprietary rights are defined by the articles of association, and it is easy to see that a power of alteration might be used for the aggrandisement of a majority at the expense of a minority. For example, if there were no check upon the use of the power, it is conceivable that a three-fourths majority might adopt an article by which the shares which they alone held would participate, to the exclusion of the shares, in the surplus assets in winding up or even in distributions of profit by way of dividend. Again, authority might be obtained

---

1 (1865) 2 Dr & Sm 521; 13 CT 57
2 [1915] 2 Ch 186; 84 LJ Ch 665 (see also p 358)

under an alteration so as to convert the assets or operations of a company into a source of profit not of the company but of persons forming part of or favoured by the majority. It has seemed incredible that alterations of such a nature could be made by the exercise of the power. But reliance upon the general doctrine that powers shall be exercised bona fide and for no bye or sinister purpose brings its own difficulties. The power of alteration is not fiduciary. The shareholders are not trustees for one another, and, unlike directors, they occupy no fiduciary position and are under no fiduciary duties. They vote in respect of their shares, which are property, and the right to vote is attached to the share itself as an incident of property to be enjoyed and exercised for the owner's personal advantage. No doubt the exercise of the right affects the interests of others too, and it may be that an analogy may be found in other powers which though given to protect the donee's own interests affect the property rights of others, as, for instance, does a mortgagee's power of sale. Some such analogy probably gave rise to the suggestion made in *Buckley on the Companies Acts* (10th edn 1924), p 26; (11th edn 1930), p 21 that the limitation on the power is that the alteration must not be such as to sacrifice the interests of the minority to those of a majority without any reasonable prospect of advantage to the company as a whole: Compare the expression in *Kennedy v De Trafford*.[1]

Apart altogether from altering articles of association, the voting strength of a majority of shareholders may be used in matters of management and administration to obtain for themselves advantages which otherwise would enure for the benefit of all the members of the company, and in some circumstances such an attempt on the part of the majority to secure advantages to the prejudice of the minority conflicts with ordinary notions of fair dealing and honesty. Often when this is done the thing attempted will be found by its nature to fall outside the power of the members in general meeting and even outside the corporate powers of the company. But this is not necessarily the case, and a thing not of its own nature *ultra vires* may be invalidated by the effect which it produces or is intended to produce in benefiting some shareholders at the expense of others or individuals at the expense of the company. The ground upon which the invalidity is placed is fraud, but what amounts to fraud has not been made the subject of definition; possibly under the influence of the tradition that 'the court has never ventured to lay down, as a general proposition, what shall constitute fraud' (per Lord Eldon, *Mortlock v Buller*).[2]

An example of a misuse of power on the part of shareholders constituting a majority in the administration of a company's affairs is the unjustifiable refusal to allow an action to be maintained in the name of the company to redress a wrong done to it by one of themselves. 'The cases in which the minority can maintain such an action are,' says Lord Davey in *Burland v Earle*,[3] 'confined to those in which the acts complained of are of a fraudulent character or beyond the powers of the company. A similar example is where the majority are endeavouring directly or indirectly to appropriate to themselves money, property, or advantages which belong to the company, or in which the other shareholders are entitled to participate.' In *Dominion Cotton Mills Co Ltd v Amoyot*[4] Lord Macnaghten reduces the rule to a brief statement of general application: 'The principles applicable to cases where a dissentient minority of shareholders in a company seek redress against the action of the majority of their associates are well settled . . . In order

---

1 [1896] 1 Ch 762
2 (1804) 10 Ves & Jun 292; 32 ER 857
3 [1902] AC 83; 71 LJPC 1
4 [1912] AC 546; 81 LJPC 233

to succeed it is incumbent on the minority either to show that the action of the majority is *ultra vires* or to prove that the majority have abused their powers and are depriving the minority of their rights.' In *Cook v Deeks*[1] resolutions were in question which disclaimed on behalf of a company any interest in a contract made by persons who were directors of the company and who formed the majority of shareholders passing the resolutions. They were in fact constructive trustees of the benefit of the contract for the company, because they had made the contract in breach of their fiduciary duty as directors. Lord Buckmaster in giving the reasons of the Privy Council said: 'If, as their Lordships find on the facts, the contract in question was entered into under such circumstances that the directors could not retain the benefit of it for themselves, then it belonged in equity to the company and ought to have been dealt with as an asset of the company. Even supposing it be not *ultra vires* of a company to make a present to its directors, it appears quite certain that directors holding a majority of votes would not be permitted to make a present to themselves. This would be to allow a majority to oppress the minority . . . In the same way, if directors have acquired for themselves property or rights which they must be regarded as holding on behalf of the company, a resolution that the rights of the company should be disregarded in the matter would amount to forfeiting the interest and property of the minority of shareholders in favour of the majority, and that by the votes of those who are interested in securing the property for themselves. Such use of voting power has never been sanctioned by the courts'.

In these formulations of general principle there is an assumption that vested in the company or in the majority of shareholders, as the case may be, is an independent title to property, to rights or to remedies, and the ground of the court's intervention is that by the course adopted by the majority, the company or the minority will be deprived of the enjoyment of that to which they are so entitled. The conduct of the majority is then given some dyslogistic description such as 'fraudulent,' 'abuse of powers' or 'oppression.' A chief purpose of articles of association is to regulate the rights of shareholders *inter se*, and their relations to the profits and surplus assets of the company are governed by the provisions of the articles. A power to alter articles of association is necessarily a power to alter the rights of shareholders *inter se*, including their mutual rights in respect of profits and surplus assets. It is therefore evident that some difficulty must arise in applying to resolutions for the alteration of articles a statement of principle which assumes the independent existence of rights which should not be impaired or destroyed. Prima facie rights altogether dependent upon articles of association are not enduring and indefeasible but are liable to modification or destruction; that is, if and when it is resolved by a three-fourths majority that the articles should be altered. To attempt to distinguish between alterations which deserve the epithet fraudulent or oppressive or unjust and those deserving no moral censure without explaining the considerations upon which the distinction depends, is to leave the whole question to general notions of fairness and propriety. In *Sidebottom v Kershaw, Leese & Co Ltd*[2]), after expressing the opinion that a regularly passed resolution for the alteration of articles could be held bad only on the ground of mala fides, Eve J referred to the question what is meant by mala fides in this connection and said: 'Speaking for myself, I do not think the solution of that question is assisted by these of such phrases as "the ordinary principles of justice," "just and equitable" or "oppressive." ' To base the application of these descriptions to a particular resolution upon the fact that it

---

1 [1916] 1 AC 554; 85 LJPC 161
2 [1920] 1 Ch 154; 89 LJ Ch 113

involves a modification or defeasance of rights of a valuable or important nature, is in effect to go back to the discarded distinction between articles affecting the constitution and those affecting the administration of the company or to a distinction very like it. To base the application of the epithets upon the circumstance that the majority obtain a benefit by the change seems to involve some departure from the principle that the vote attached to a share is an incident of property which may be used as the shareholder's interests may dictate.

The considerations which I have mentioned all arise in attempting to discover and fasten upon some element the presence of which will always vitiate a resolution for the alteration of articles of association. But, whatever may constitute bad faith, it is evident that, if a resolution is regularly passed with the single aim of advancing the interests of a company considered as a corporate whole, it must fall within the scope of the statutory power to alter the articles and could never be condemned as mala fides. A positive test was therefore available, conformity with which necessarily spelt validity. When the rejection of the doctrine of *Hutton v Scarborough Cliff Hotel Co Ltd* was made final by *Andrews v Gas Meter Co*,[1] compliance with this positive test was declared to be all that was demanded, that is, besides consistency with the provisions of the statute and of the memorandum of association.

In *Allen v Gold Reefs of West Africa Ltd*[2] a majority of the Court of Appeal upheld as valid an amendment of a company's articles which had the effect of extending to the paid-up shares of members a lien which under the previous article was confined to partly paid shares. The lien secured all debts, obligations and liabilities of a member to the company and as a result of other provisions contained in the articles was enforceable by forfeiture of the shares. The occasion for adopting the amendment was the failure of the executors of a member who died holding a large number of vendor's fully paid shares and a smaller number of partly paid shares either to register themselves as shareholders or to pay the calls, the assets being insufficient. Lindley MR said that, wide as the statutory power of alteration was, it must, like all other powers, be exercised subject to those general principles of law and equity which are applicable to all powers conferred on majorities and enabling them to bind minorities. 'It must be exercised not only in the manner required by law, but also bona fide for the benefit of the company as a whole, and it must not be exceeded'. For the decision it was enough to say that an alteration which was made 'bona fide for the benefit of the company as a whole' could not be invalid. And Lindley MR went on to say that if these conditions were complied with he could discover no ground for judicially putting any other restrictions on the power. But, as in literal terms it was expressed as a positive requirement which must be fulfilled and not merely negatived as a test compliance with which was enough, Lord Lindley's statement was taken in some subsequent cases as formulating the issue on which validity or invalidity depended absolutely, viz, whether 'the power had been exercised bona fide for the benefit of the company as a whole.' Vaughan-Williams LJ, who dissented, did so on the ground 'that the resolution was not passed in good faith, being really passed merely to defeat the existing rights of an individual shareholder'. He took good faith as the test and added that an alteration involving oppression of the shareholder would not be made in good faith. But the opening words of his judgment show that he regarded these standards as the same as those formulated by Lindley MR. Nevertheless, not only have the latter's words been sometimes received as embodying an exclusive and conclusive test,

1 [1897] 1 Ch D 361; 66 LJ Ch 246
2 [1900] 1 Ch 656; 69 LJ Ch 266 (see p 330)

but through repetition they tended to become almost a formula. Their meaning was sometimes questioned but more often assumed. In *Brown v British Abrasive Wheel Co Ltd*[1] Astbury J appears to have read the words as distinguishing into separate matters the good faith of the alteration and its tendency to benefit the company as a whole. The company in that case was faced with liquidation unless it could obtain further capital, which a majority holding ninety-eight per cent of the shares was ready to supply, provided the remaining two per cent of the share capital was placed under the same control. An alteration of the articles was proposed by which a transfer of the shares might be compelled at a value fixed by a method prescribed by the existing articles for the case of compulsory sale. Astbury J, after quoting the statement of Lindley MR, said: 'The question therefore is whether the enforcement of the proposed alteration on the minority is within the ordinary principles of justice and whether it is for the benefit of the company as a whole'. Stating the issue in this way, he concluded that to expropriate a minority was unjust and for the benefit not of the company but of the majority. But shortly afterwards, in *Sidebottom v Kershaw, Leese & Co Ltd*, an alteration was upheld as valid by the Court of Appeal though it provided for the expropriation at a value of the shares of any member carrying on business in direct competition with that of the company or being a director of another company so doing. Lord Sterndale MR and Warrington LJ, as he then was, both made it clear that in their opinion Astbury J in *Brown v British Abrasive Wheel Co Ltd* had been wrong in treating bona fides and benefit of the company as separate conceptions, and the justification, if any, for his decision lay in a finding of fact that the majority had acted entirely for their own benefit. But the members of the Court of Appeal relied upon the same passage from the judgment of Lindley MR, which Eve J restated in the form of a question: 'Was the resolution adopted, or was the resolution made for the benefit of the company or for the benefit of some section of the company, without reference to the benefit of the company as a whole?' Yet within a few months of the decision of the Court of Appeal Peterson J decided the validity of an alteration of articles as upon an issue whether in fact it could 'properly be said to be for the benefit of the company' (*Dafen Tinplate Co Ltd v Llanelly Steel Co (1907) Ltd*[2]). The article adopted, though apparently not directed against any shareholder in particular, conferred an arbitrary power to compel the transfer of shares exercisable without cause and upon grounds unspecified and not expressly limited. But, whatever may be said as to the validity of such a provision, it could not depend on the opinion of the court that as an alteration it did or it did not operate for the benefit of the company considered as a whole. The view taken by Peterson J was corrected by the Court of Appeal in *Shuttleworth v Cox Brothers & Co (Maidenhead) Ltd*,[3] where the validity of an alteration was upheld which provided that any one of a board of directors appointed for life should lose office if his fellow-directors requested in writing that he should resign. The alteration was directed at a particular director whose conduct had not been satisfactory. The words of Lindley MR, 'exercised bona fide for the benefit of the company' (*Allen v Gold Reefs of West Africa Ltd*), were again interpreted as stating one condition only, a condition which Scrutton LJ understood 'as meaning that the shareholders must act honestly having regard to and endeavouring to act for the benefit of the company'. Bankes LJ, after saying that the test is whether the alteration was, in the opinion of the shareholders, for the benefit of the company, continued: 'By what criterion is the court to ascertain

---

1 [1919] 1 Ch 290; 88 LJ Ch 143
2 [1920] 2 Ch 124; 89 LJ Ch 346
3 [1927] 2 KB 9; 96 LJ KB 104 (see p 341)

the opinion of the shareholders upon this question? The alteration may be so oppressive as to cast suspicion on the honesty of the persons responsible for it, or so extravagant that no reasonable men could really consider it for the benefit of the company'. Atkin LJ (as he then was) made a significant but very natural remark: 'But neither this court nor any other court should consider itself fettered by the form of words, as if it were a phrase in an Act of Parliament which must be accepted and construed as it stands. We must study what its real meaning is by the light of the principles which were being laid down by the Master of the Rolls when he used the phrase'. In *British Equitable Assurance Co Ltd v Bailey*[1] Lord Lindley said: 'Of course, the powers of altering by-laws, like other powers, must be exercised bona fide, and having regard to the purposes for which they are created, and to the rights of persons affected by them.' I imagine that in *Allen v Gold Reefs of West Africa Ltd* Lord Lindley meant no more.

If no restraint were laid upon the power of altering articles of association, it would be possible for a shareholder controlling the necessary voting power so to mould the regulations of a company that its operations would be conducted or its property used so that he would profit either in some other capacity than that of member of the company or, if as member, in a special and peculiar way inconsistent with conceptions of honesty so widely held or professed that departure from them is described, without further analysis, as fraud. For example, it would be possible to adopt articles requiring that the company should supply him with goods below cost or pay him ninety-nine per cent of its profits for some real or imaginary services or submit to his own determination the question whether he was liable to account to the company for secret profits as a director.

The chief reason for denying an unlimited effect to widely expressed powers such as that of altering a company's articles is the fear or knowledge that an apparently regular exercise of the power may in truth be but a means of securing some personal or particular gain, whether pecuniary or otherwise, which does not fairly arise out of the subjects dealt with by the power and is outside and even inconsistent with the contemplated objects of the power. It is to exclude the purpose of securing such ulterior special and particular advantages that Lord Lindley used the phrase 'bona fide for the benefit of the company as a whole.' The reference to 'benefit as a whole' is but a very general expression negativing purposes foreign to the company's operations, affairs and organizations. But unfortunately, as appears from the foregoing discussion, the use of the phrase has tended to cause misapprehension. If the challenged alteration relates to an article which does or may affect an individual, as, for instance, a director appointed for life or a shareholder whom it is desired to expropriate, or to an article affecting the mutual rights and liabilities *inter se* of shareholders or different classes or descriptions of shareholders, the very subject matter involves a conflict of interests and advantages. To say that the shareholders forming the majority must consider the advantage of the company as a whole in relation to such a question seems inappropriate, if not meaningless, and at all events starts an impossible inquiry. The 'company as a whole' is a corporate entity consisting of all the shareholders. If the proposal put forward is for a revision of any of the articles regulating the rights *inter se* of shareholders or classes of shareholders, the primary question must be how conflicting interests are to be adjusted, and the adjustment is left by law to the determination of those whose interests conflict, subject, however, to the condition that the existing provision can be altered only

---

1 [1906] AC 35; 75 LJ Ch 73

by a three-fourths majority. Whether the matter be voting rights, the basis of distributing profits, the basis of dividing surplus assets on a winding up, preferential rights in relation to profits or to surplus assets, or any other question affecting mutual interests, it is apparent that though the subject matter is among the most conspicuous of those governed by articles and therefore of those to which the statutory power is directed, yet it involves little if anything more than the redetermination of the rights and interests of those to whom the power is committed. No-one supposes that in voting each shareholder is to assume an inhuman altruism and consider only the intangible notion of the benefit of the vague abstraction called by Lord Robertson in *Baily's case* 'the company as an institution.' An investigation of the thoughts and motives of each shareholder voting with the majority would be an impossible proceeding. When the purpose of a resolution is spoken of, a phrase is used which refers rather to some characteristic implicit in the resolution in virtue of the circumstances or of some larger transaction of which it formed a part or step. It is not far removed from what Lord Sumner called 'one of those so-called intentions which the law imputes . . . the legal construction put on something done in fact' (*Inland Revenue Commissioners v Blott*).[1] But, when the very question to be determined is a conflict of interests, unless the subject matter is held outside the power, the purpose of the resolution, as distinguished from the motives of the individuals, often must be to resolve the conflict in favour of one and against the other interest.

In my opinion it was within the scope and purpose of the power of alteration for a three-fourths majority to decide the basis of distributing shares issued for the purpose of capitalizing accumulated profits or profits arising from the sale of goodwill, and in voting for the resolution shareholders were not bound to disregard their own interests. I am far from saying that the resolution for the alteration of the articles would have been bad if the existing articles had been uniform and clear in requiring that, however the 'capitalization' was effected, the basis of distribution should be the number of shares respectively subscribed for by members. But the facts of the case were that by one method, the older indirect method, a capitalization might have been effected which would mean a distribution according to capital paid up. Doubts were felt about the propriety of adopting this course, and doubts were agitated as to the meaning of the article providing for the direct method. If there were no capitalization, the accumulated profits would not be distributed in proportion with capital subscribed. In these circumstances the holders of partly paid shares had no 'right' to receive the profits in proportion with capital paid up. As the articles stood they were entitled only to receive shares in that proportion if and when issued by way of direct capitalization. That event would never be likely to occur; for the holders of fully paid shares were perfectly entitled to prevent it and would no doubt do so. In these circumstances it appears to me that the resolution involved no oppression, no appropriation of an unjust or reprehensible nature and did not imply any purpose outside the scope of the power.

---

1 [1921] 2 AC 171

SOURCE 125
Shuttleworth v Cox Brothers & Co (Maidenhead) Ltd
(Court of Appeal 1927) [1927] 2 KB 9; 96 LJ KB 104

The articles of association provided:

'22: The office of a director shall be vacated:
(a) If he become bankrupt or insolvent or compound with his creditors;
(b) if he become of unsound mind or be found a lunatic;
(c) if he be convicted of an indictable offence;
(d) If he cease to hold the necessary share qualification or do not obtain the same within one month from the date of his appointment;
(e) if he absent himself from the meetings of directors for a period of six calendar months without special leave of absence from the other directors;
(f) if he give the directors one calendar month's notice in writing that he resigns his office.'

The following special resolution was passed:

'That the following paragraph be added to article 22 of the articles of association of the company after paragraph (f) of the said article — "(g) if he be requested in writing by all the other directors to resign his office." '

BANKES LJ: This is a cross-appeal by the plaintiff in an action brought by him to challenge the validity of a resolution of the shareholders in a company, the effect of which was to deprive him of his position as a permanent director of the company.
. . .
At the trial the jury were also asked to consider the plaintiff's complaint that he had been wrongfully deprived of his position of permanent director. He contended that the alteration of article 22 was invalid and that the amendment was not bona fide for the benefit of the company as a whole. He also contended that it amounted to a breach of a contract to be implied from the articles that he should be a permanent director of the company as long as he should live unless he became disqualified from any of the causes specified in article 22 as it originally stood. In this case the contract, if any, derives its force and effect from the articles themselves, which may be altered. It is therefore not an absolute but a conditional contract; and the question of the plaintiff's rights under it depends, as do the other questions raised, upon whether the alteration of article 22 was validly made.

The power to alter articles of association is conferred by section 13 of the Companies (Consolidation) Act 1908, which provides that, 'Subject to the provisions of this Act and to the conditions contained in its memorandum, a company may by special resolution alter or add to its articles.' The memorandum of this company contains nothing in terms controlling the power conferred by that section of altering or adding to the articles; but it is well established that the Courts assert some control over the exercise of that power by a company, and the test applied by the Courts in deciding whether the power has been properly exercised was laid down by Lindley MR in *Allen v Gold Reefs of West Africa Ltd*[1] . . . the first thing to be considered is whether, in formulating the test I have mentioned Lindley MR had in mind two separate and distinct matters; first, bona fides, the state of mind of the persons whose act is complained of, and secondly, whether the alteration is for the benefit of the company, apart altogether from

---

1 [1900] 1 Ch 656; 69 LJ Ch 266 (see p 330)

the state of mind of those who procured it. In my opinion this view of the test has been negatived by this Court in *Sidebottom's case*.[1] So the test is whether the alteration of the articles was in the opinion of the shareholders for the benefit of the company. By what criterion is the Court to ascertain the opinion of the shareholders upon this question? The alteration may be so oppressive as to cast suspicion on the honesty of the persons responsible for it, or so extravagant that no reasonable men could really consider it for the benefit of the company. In such cases the Court is, I think, entitled to treat the conduct of shareholders as it does the verdict of a jury, and to say that the alteration of a company's articles shall not stand if it is such that no reasonable men could consider it for the benefit of the company. Or, if the facts should raise the question, the Court may be able to apply another test — namely, whether or not the action of the shareholders is capable of being considered for the benefit of the company. I cannot agree with what seems to have been the view of Peterson J in *Dafen Tinplate Co v Llanelly Steel Co*,[2] that whenever the Court and the shareholders may differ in opinion upon what is for the benefit of the company, the view of the Court must prevail. In the present case it seems to me impossible to say that the action of these defendants was either incapable of being for the benefit of the company or such that no reasonable men could consider it for the benefit of the company. It is idle to say that their action was directed against the plaintiff, because the more outrageous the conduct of a director the more certain it is that his removal will be bona fide for the benefit of the company, and the more certainly will the efforts of the shareholders, acting bona fide and for the benefit of the company, be directed against him, because it is necessary to protect the company against such conduct for the future. For these reasons I am of opinion that this appeal must be dismissed.

SCRUTTON LJ: . . . it must be taken that there was no evidence of malice, and so there still remains a finding that the action of the shareholders was for the benefit of the company. That would apparently conclude this case but for one point which Mr Porter raised — namely, that article 22 in its original form constituted a contract between the company and the plaintiff, that he should be a permanent director for life, except in the events specified in that article, a contract which could not be varied without the consent of both parties; and that the plaintiff never consented to the article in its altered form. That argument would be sound if he could show a contract outside the articles; for then an alteration of the articles would not affect the contract. A good example of that principle is *Nelson v James Nelson & Sons*.[3] There the articles of association of a company empowered the directors to appoint a managing director and to revoke his appointment. They appointed by a separate document in writing a managing director for a specified term. During the term they tried to use the articles to revoke the appointment. The Court held that the contract being outside the articles could not be altered without the consent of both parties. But if a contract is contained in the articles it must be, as the articles themselves are, subject to alteration in accordance with the power given by section 13 of the Companies (Consolidation) Act 1908. Consequently the plaintiff's contract, if any, is not a contract constituting him a permanent director unconditionally, but is a contract constituting him a permanent director subject to the power of terminating his appointment in

---

1 [1920] 1 Ch 154; 89 LJ Ch 113
2 [1920] 2 Ch 124; 89 LJ Ch 346
3 [1914] 2 KB 770; 83 LJ KB 823 (see p 350)

accordance with the articles or any modification of the articles sanctioned by the Companies Act. So far, therefore, the appeal fails.

Then Mr Porter advanced an argument based on an expression of Peterson J in *Dafen Tinplate Co v Llanelly Steel Co.* He contended that the question is not what the shareholders think, but what the Court thinks is for the benefit of the company — I suppose he would treat the verdict of the jury in the same way — that the Court must be satisfied that the alteration of the articles is genuinely for the benefit of the company, and that in this case the Court on the materials before it ought to be of opinion that this alteration was not genuinely for the benefit of the company and ought therefore to reject the honest opinion of the shareholders and the equally honest opinion of the jury and declare that the alteration is invalid. To adopt that view would be to make the Court the manager of the affairs of innumerable companies instead of the shareholders themselves. I think it is a mistaken view, based on a misunderstanding of an expression used by Lindley MR in *Allen's case* and by Lord Sterndale MR in *Sidebottom's case.*

SOURCE 126
Greenhalgh *v* Arderne Cinemas Ltd
(Court of Appeal 1051) [1951] Ch 286; [1950] 2 All ER 1120

The articles of association of the company provided:

'(a) No shares in the company shall be transferred to a person not a member of the company so long as any member of the company may be willing to purchase such shares at a fair value to be ascertained in accordance with sub-cl. (b) hereof.
(b) If any member desires to sell or transfer his shares or any of them, he shall notify his desire to the directors by sending them a notice in writing (hereinafter called a "transfer notice") to the effect that he desires to sell or transfer such shares. . . .'

There had been a series of actions in relation to the affairs of the Arderne company which had left the plaintiff with a strong sense of grievance. In April 1948, the defendant Mallard opened negotiations with the third defendant Sol Sheckman (hereinafter called 'the purchaser') for the sale of a controlling interest in the company to the purchaser. By agreements of 4 June 1948, the defendant Mallard agreed to sell or procure the sale of the purchaser of 85,815 fully paid ordinary shares at 6s. a share in the Arderne company. At the same time the purchaser obtained the control of the Tegarn company.

In order to give effect to these agreements an extraordinary meeting of the Arderne company was held on 30 June 1948. At that meeting the following special resolution was passed: 'That the articles of association of the company be altered by adding at the end of article 10 the following additional clause: "Notwithstanding the foregoing provisions of this article any member may with the sanction of an ordinary resolution passed at any general meeting of the company transfer his shares or any of them to any person named in such resolution as the proposed transferee, and the directors shall be bound to register any transfer which has been so sanctioned".' That resolution was followed by an ordinary resolution sanctioning the transfer by the defendant Mallard of 500 shares to the purchaser.

EVERSHED MR: . . . Mr Jennings says, the validity of a special resolution depends upon the fact that those who passed it did so in good faith and for the benefit of the company as a whole. The cases to which Mr Jennings referred are *Sidebottom v Kershaw, Leese & Co Ltd.*[1] Peterson J's decision in *Dafen Tinplate Co Ltd v Llanelly Steel Co (1907) Ltd,*[2] and, finally, *Shuttleworth v Cox Brothers & Co (Maidenhead) Ltd.*[3] Certain principles, I think, can be safely stated as emerging from those authorities. In the first place, I think it is now plain that 'bona fide for the benefit of the company as a whole' means not two things but one thing. It means that the shareholder must proceed upon what, in this honest opinion, is for the benefit of the company as a whole. The second thing is that the phrase, 'the company as a whole', does not (at any rate in such a case as the present) mean the company as a commercial entity, distinct from the corporators: it means the corporators as a general body. That is to say, the case may be taken of an individual hypothetical member and it may be asked whether what is proposed is, in the honest opinion of those who voted in its favour, for that person's benefit.

I think that the matter can, in practice, be more accurately and precisely stated by looking at the converse and by saying that a special resolution of this kind would be liable to be impeached if the effect of it were to discriminate between the majority shareholders and the minority shareholders, so as to give to the former an advantage of which the latter were deprived.

. . . I felt at one time sympathy for the plaintiff's argument, because, after all, as the articles stood he could have said: 'Before you go selling to the purchaser you have to offer your shares to the existing shareholders, and that will enable me, if I feel so disposed, to buy, in effect, the whole of the shareholding of the Arderne company'. I think that the answer is that when a man comes into a company, he is not entitled to assume that the articles will always remain in a particular form; and that, so long as the proposed alteration does not unfairly discriminate in the way which I have indicated, it is not an objection, provided that the resolution is passed bona fide, that the right to tender for the majority holding of shares would be lost by the lifting of the restriction. I do not think that it can be said that that is such a discrimination as falls within the scope of the principle which I have stated.

PART VII: THE EFFECT OF THE ALTERATION

The fact that an alteration of the articles may constitute or give rise to a breach of contract between the company and a third party is not a ground for restraining the alteration (Source 127).

SOURCE 127
Southern Foundries (1926) Ltd *v* Shirlaw
(House of Lords 1940) [1940] AC 701; [1940] 2 All ER 445

The Southern Foundries (1926) Ltd (hereinafter called the 'Southern'), by an agreement dated 21 December 1933, appointed the respondent, Mr Shirlaw, who was then a director of the company, to be managing director for ten years from 1 December 1933. Article 91 of the Southern's articles of association provided that a managing director shall, 'subject to the provisions of any contract between him and the company be subject to the same provision as to resignation or removal as the other directors of the company, and if he cease to hold the office

---

1 [1920] 1 Ch 154; 89 LJ Ch 113
2 [1920] 2 Ch 124; 89 LJ Ch 346
3 [1927] 2 KB 9; 96 LJ KB 104 (see p 341)

of director he shall ipso facto and immediately cease to be a managing director.'
Article 105 gave the Southern power to remove a director before the expiration
of his period of office. In 1935 the second defendants, Federated Foundries Ltd
(hereinafter called 'Federated'), formed to take over the shares of a number of
other companies, including Southern, acquired all the shares of Southern. By a
special resolution passed on 17 April 1936, the existing articles of Southern were
cancelled and new articles adopted, which, by article 8, empowered Federated by
an instrument subscribed by two directors and the secretary to remove any
director of Southern.

. . .

. . . an instrument duly signed by two directors and the secretary of Federated,
was delivered to Southern, removing the plaintiff from the office of director, and
Southern thereupon treated him as ceasing to be managing director.

Mr Shirlaw thereupon commenced proceedings, claiming damages as against
Southern for their wrongful repudiation of the contract, and as against Federated
for wrongly procuring, causing, and inducing Southern's breach of contract.

VISCOUNT MAUGHAM (dissenting): . . . The new article clearly put it in the
power of Federated to remove the respondent from his office as a director
whenever it seemed to Federated desirable so to do. Directors of the other
companies were in the same position. There is no suggestion, however, that this
article was aimed in any way at the respondent, or that it was unreasonable from
the point of view of an amalgamation of the interests of the eleven companies.
Nor is it pleaded in the action that the adoption of the articles was a breach of
the contract of 21 December 1933, and counsel for the respondent disclaimed at
the Bar any intention to set up such an argument. It must therefore be accepted
that the articles of Southern were lawfully and properly changed without a breach
of the contract with the respondent.

. . . In my view it would be unwarrantable in this case to imply a term that the
articles of Southern should not be altered, however essential it was in the interests
of the company, merely because such an alteration might possibly at some future
date lead to the termination of the respondent's position as a director. The right
of a company under section 10 of the Companies Act 1929, to alter its articles is
statutory. It is conferred in the widest terms, and is, I think, subject only to the
implied qualification that it must be exercised in good faith for the benefit of the
company: *Allen v Gold Reefs of West Africa*;[1] but the alteration may not excuse a
breach of contract for which the company may be liable in damages: *Baily v British
Equitable Assurance Co.*[2]

The right to alter the articles being inherent, if it is desired by a contract to give
an employee or a third person a right of action if there should be an alteration
of the articles which causes damages to him, I think it is very desirable to express
such a term in clear language. Such a prohibition cannot be implied without very
strong reasons: see *Swabey v Port Darwin Gold Mining*;[3] *Re Argus Life Assurance Co*;[4]
Baily v British Equitable Assurance Co.

In my opinion it would have been a breach of the negative term properly
understood for Southern to have removed the respondent under article 105 from
his position as director during the ten years; but I am also of opinion that it was

---

1 [1900] 1 Ch 656; 69 LJ Ch 266 (see p 330)
2 [1906] AC 35; 75 LJ Ch 73
3 (1889) 1 Meg 385
4 (1888) 39 Ch D 571

not a breach of any implied term in the agreement for Southern to alter its articles as was done and to include in the altered articles the new article 8.

   . . .

My Lords, the question which remains is whether the act of Federated, under article 8 of the articles of Southern, in removing the respondent from his office of director of that company by an instrument in writing signed by two directors and the secretary of Federated was a breach by Southern of its agreement with the respondent or a repudiation of that agreement. It was the act of Federated which had the effect of removing the respondent from his directorship. After the new articles had been adopted Southern was powerless to prevent that act. Southern indeed was completely controlled by Federated, who held beneficially every share in Southern as in all the other associated companies. With all respect to those who think otherwise, I cannot understand the suggestion that Federated were acting as agents or, which is the same thing, as mandatories, of Southern in that matter, since Southern had not and indeed never had any power or influence whatever over Federated. It held not a single share in Federated. It was Federated who held the shares in Southern. Nor was there any contractual relation between Federated and Southern which might have enabled Southern to object to the act of Federated under article 8.

   . . .

My Lords, in my opinion, it has not been established in this case that Southern has committed any breach of the agreement or has repudiated the agreement, and the action therefore fails.

LORD ATKIN: I feel no doubt that the true construction of the agreement is that the company agreed to employ the respondent and the respondent agreed to serve the company as managing director for the period of ten years. It was by the constitution of the company a condition of holding such office that the holder should continue to be a director: and such continuance depended upon the terms of the articles regulating the office of director. It was not disputed, and I take it to be clear law, that the company's articles so regulating the office of director could be altered from time to time: and therefore the continuance in office of the managing director under the agreement depended upon the provisions of the articles from time to time. Thus the contract of employment for the term of ten years was dependent upon the managing director continuing to be a director. This continuance of the directorship was a concurrent condition. The arrangement between the parties appears to me to be exactly described by the words of Cockburn CJ in *Stirling v Maitland*;[1] 'If a party enters into an arrangement which can only take effect by the continuance of an existing state of circumstances'; and in such a state of things the Lord Chief Justice said: 'I look on the law to be that . . . there is an implied engagement on his part that he shall do nothing of his own motion to put an end to that state of circumstances, under which alone the arrangement can be operative.' That proposition in my opinion is well established law.

LORD WRIGHT: [In] *Allen v Gold Reefs of West Africa* . . . it was held that a company, by altering its articles under which there was no lien on fully paid shares so that the altered articles did impose such a lien, could enforce that lien against a shareholder indebted to the company. The members' rights depended on the articles, which were altered in good faith by the company under its statutory powers. But Lindley MR observed: 'It does not . . . follow that the

---

1 (1864) 5 B&S 840; 122 ER 1043

altered article may not be inapplicable to some particular fully paid up shareholder. He may have special rights against the company, which do not invalidate the resolution to alter the articles, but which may exempt him from the operation of the articles, as altered.' Later, he considers the case of a special contract made with a company in the terms of or embodying one or more of the articles, and adds that this may raise the question whether in such a case an alteration of the articles so embodied is consistent or inconsistent with the real bargain between the parties. He points out that 'a company cannot break its contracts by altering its articles.' The Master of the Rolls is emphasizing the distinction between power or capacity and right. Romer LJ said that the shares became bound by the company's alteration of its articles unless he [the shareholder] could show some special bargain with the company or some special obligation incurred towards him by the company in respect of his fully paid up shares. This he failed to do. The alteration must, of course, be made in good faith.

In *Baily v British Equitable Assurance Co* the question did not relate to articles of association but to by-laws of the insurance company. The Court of Appeal treated the by-laws as comparable to articles of association and the question as being whether the alteration of the by-laws which prejudiced the rights of policy holders as regards sharing in profits, was effective against them under the principles laid down in *Allen*'s case. Cozens Hardy LJ in delivering the opinion of the Court, said: 'It would be dangerous to hold that in a contract of loan or a contract of service ... there is any greater power of variation of the rights and liabilities of the parties than would exist if, instead of the company, the contracting party had been an individual. A company cannot, by altering its articles, justify a breach of contract.' This expression of opinion with which I agree is very pertinent to this case. That case went to this House which reversed the decision of the Court of Appeal on the ground that no special contract existed, *British Equitable Assurance Co v Baily*, but did not question the principle stated by the Court of Appeal.

In *Nelson v James & Sons Ltd*,[1] the plaintiff was appointed managing director of the defendant company under an agreement which provided that he was to hold the office so long as he should remain a director of the company and should perform his duties efficiently. The appointment was made under articles of association which empowered the directors to appoint the managing director for such period as they deemed fit, 'and might revoke the appointment.' The Court of Appeal held that the directors' power was in effect to appoint for a fixed time, and that this power was inconsistent with a power in the board to revoke the appointment at any time. As Swinfen Eady LJ said: 'the power to appoint and the power to revoke the appointment are in the board, but the power to revoke is to be subject to the terms of the contract for the time being between the managing director and the company.' Hence when the directors dismissed the plaintiff without just cause, while still fulfilling the conditions of his contract, he was held entitled to recover damages for wrongful dismissal against the company.
. . .

Apart from Government interference or the like, the contract can only rightfully be dissolved by the will of the parties who entered into it. That will may be evinced by the conditions, express or implied, which were originally agreed to, and by action in accordance with them, or by a subsequent agreement to rescind the contract. But nothing of the sort can be shown by the appellants. They have to justify the determination of the contract, or the case will be one of

---

1 [1914] 2 KB 770; 83 LJ KB 823 (see p 350)

breach or repudiation. If their only justification is the action of Federated Foundries, that in my opinion is no defence. The alteration of the articles did not constitute a breach of contract by the appellant company as against the respondent, but his removal the following year did, and entitled him to damages.

In my opinion the appellant company fail in their defence and the appeal should be dismissed.

PART VIII: THE ARTICLES AND THE RELATIONSHIP BETWEEN THE COMPANY AND ITS DIRECTORS

The relationship between a director and his or her company is governed by several different sources and principles of law. First, there are many relevant statutory provisions, some are concerned with eligibility (eg s 291, the share qualification; s 293, the age limit; the Company Directors Disqualification Act, passim), some with the removal of the director (ss 303–304, p 379, above), and a whole Part (Part X, ss 311–346) with the enforcement of fair dealing by the director (the subject matter of Chapter 7, below). Secondly, there are many regulations in the typical articles of association (eg their powers, appointment, retirement etc, see regs 70–98 of the present Table A). Thirdly, the director may be treated as the company itself (the alter ego doctrine) usually for the purpose of attributing liability to the company, where otherwise this would not be possible (pp 281 ff). Fourthly, the board of directors is frequently treated as an independent organ of the company either to assist in establishing the company's liability under the alter ego doctrine or to emphasise its status vis à vis the shareholders. This is the way in which Sargant J expressed this principle in *British Murac Syndicate Ltd v Alperton Rubber Co Ltd*:[1]

> . . . I now turn to the second objection, namely, that the contract under which the plaintiff syndicate is to have the right of appointing two directors is in the nature of a contract of service, and accordingly is one which, on the ordinary principles relating to that class of contracts, the court will not specifically enforce so as to compel one person to accept another as his servant. I feel great doubt whether the relation between a company and a director is in the nature of a contract of service within the meaning of that doctrine. It appears quite clearly from *Automatic Self-Cleansing Filter Co v Cunninghame*[2] that directors may have rights and powers and duties under the constitution of the company independently of a majority of the shareholders, that is to say, that to some extent at least they may occupy an independent position . . .

It is also clear, despite the apparent independence of the directors, that the relationship between a director and his or her company is contractual. In many instances this will be by way of an express contract independent of (extrinsic to) the articles (see Sources 128 and 129); in other instances the appointment may be by way of resolution of the board of directors or statement in the articles without reference to any extrinsic contract (Sources

---

1 [1915] 2 Ch 186; 84 LJ Ch 665
2 [1906] 2 Ch 34; 75 LJ Ch 437 (see p 413)

130, 131 and 132). Where there is no extrinsic contract governing all aspects of the relationship between company and director, terms of this relationship may have to be inferred, more likely than not from the articles (which cannot themselves be the terms because of the rule that such terms can only confer rights on members in their capacity as such — see pp 303ff and Source 132).

In the light of these authorities, would Shuttleworth have been successful in a claim for compensation for unfair dismissal (see *Shuttleworth v Cox Brothers*, p 341)?

SOURCE 128
Shindler *v* Northern Raincoat Co Ltd
(Queen's Bench Division 1960) [1960] 1 WLR 1038; [1960] 2 All ER 239

The defendant company entered into an agreement with the plaintiff to employ the plaintiff as the defendant's managing director for 10 years. The defendant purported to dismiss the plaintiff within one year, by exercising its rights under the articles of association to remove the plaintiff as a director.

> DIPLOCK J: . . . The articles of association of the Northern Raincoat Co incorporated by article (1) the articles set out in Table A of the Companies Act 1929, and among the articles so incorporated was article 68 about managing directors which is in the following terms:
>
> The directors may from time to time appoint one or more of their body to the office of managing director or manager for such term and at such remuneration (whether by way of salary, or commission, or participation in profits, or partly in one way and partly in another) as they may think fit, and a director so appointed shall not, while holding that office, be subject to retirement by rotation, or taken into account in determining the rotation or retirement of directors; but this appointment shall be subject to determination ipso facto if he ceases from any cause to be a director, or if the company in general meeting resolve that his tenure of the office of managing director or manager be determined.' Since on 21 November 1958, the plaintiff was removed from office as a director and thus ipso facto ceased to be managing director, and his tenure of office was determined by the company in general meeting, the defendants contend that as a matter of law he was not wrongfully dismissed and he had no claim in this connection.
>
> . . .
>
> The argument for the defendants on this matter, which gains some support from the cases I have referred to and from *Nelson v Nelson (James) & Son Ltd*,[1] must, I think, be put thus: where a company's articles of association include article 68, the directors have no power to appoint a managing director on terms which purport to exclude the company's right to terminate his office and his appointment as managing director ipso facto upon his ceasing to be a director, or by resolution in general meeting to resolve that his tenure of office as managing director be determined. That argument can be put in alternative ways, either that an agreement for a fixed term which does not incorporate the right of the company set out in article 68 is ultra vires, or else that an agreement for a fixed term must be subject to the implied term, that it is terminable in either of the circumstances set out at the end of article 68.

---

1 [1914] 2 KB 770; 83 LJ KB 823 (see p 350)

It seems to me that this point is concluded against the defendants by the decision of the House of Lords in *Southern Foundries v Shirlaw*.[1] That case was somewhat complicated, and gave rise to a division of opinion in the House of Lords. Two of their Lordships who were most familiar with the chancery side came to one conclusion, and three of their Lordships who were perhaps more familiar with the common law side came to another. There are some references in subsequent cases in the Chancery Division which suggest that it is difficult to ascertain what *Southern Foundries v Shirlaw* determined. It does, however, seem to me that all five of their Lordships in the *Southern Foundries* case were agreed upon one principle of law which is vital to the defendants' contention in this case. That principle of law is that laid down in the case of *Stirling v Maitland*,[2] where Cockburn LJ said: 'if a party enters into an arrangement which can only take effect by the continuance of a certain existing set of circumstances, there is an implied engagement on his part that he shall do nothing of his own motion to put an end to that state of circumstances under which alone the arrangement can be operative.' Applying that respectable principle to this case, there is an implied engagement on the part of the company that it will do nothing of its own motion to put an end to the state of circumstances which enables the plaintiff to continue as managing director: that is to say, an undertaking that it will not revoke his appointment as a director and will not resolve that his tenure of office be determined.

Plaintiff's claim upheld.

SOURCE 129
Nelson *v* James Nelson & Sons Ltd
(Court of Appeal 1914) [1914] 2 KB 770; 83 LJ KB 823

LORD READING CJ: This is an appeal by the defendants against a judgment of Scrutton J in favour of the plaintiff for £15,000, which was the amount of the damages awarded by the verdict of the jury.

The argument which has been addressed to us turns upon the meaning of certain words, 'and may revoke such appointment,' in article 85(B) of the articles of association of the defendant company. The question therefore is a short one.

It is clear upon the facts that, unless the directors were entitled under those words of article 85(B) to revoke the appointment of the plaintiff as managing director, they had no ground whatever in law for putting an end to the agreement with him. Indeed it is not suggested that the directors had any such right apart from that article. The contention is that under article 85(B) the directors of the company, to whom the company had delegated its powers in this respect, were entitled to appoint a managing director or managing directors and to revoke any such appointment; that the effect of the article is that the directors could not make an appointment without reserving to themselves the right also to revoke the appointment, and that if they purported to make an appointment for a period of years without reserving to themselves the power of revocation they were acting *ultra vires*. The contention, put in another way, is that in any agreement for the appointment of a managing director into which the directors enter a clause must be implied giving them the right to revoke the appointment. Those are the alternative ways of putting the proposition which has been argued before us.

The material words of the articles, under the heading 'Power of Directors,' are

---

1 [1940] AC 701; [1940] 2 All ER 445 (see p 344)
2 (1864) 5 B&S 840; 122 ER 1043

as follows: Article 84 provides that 'the business of the company shall be managed by the board'; and article 85 provides that 'without restricting the generality of the foregoing powers, the board may do the following things: (A) Establish local boards, local managing committees, or local agencies in the United Kingdom or abroad, and appoint any persons to be members thereof, with such powers and authorities under such regulations, for such period, and at such remuneration as they may deem fit, and may from time to time revoke any such appointment. (B) Appoint from time to time any one or more of their number to be managing director or managing directors on such terms as to remuneration . . . and with such powers and authorities, and for such period as they deem fit, and may revoke such appointment.'

The directors had entered into an agreement which may be described as one for the efficient business life of the plaintiff, subject to certain contingencies for which provision is made in the agreement. That is to say, subject to the contingencies specified in the agreement there was no power expressly reserved to the directors to determine the appointment at any time. The agreement reserved to the plaintiff the right to resign his office at any time by giving six calendar months' written notice, but there was no corresponding right reserved to the directors to determine the agreement. So long as the plaintiff remained a director of the company and retained his due qualification and efficiently performed the duties of his office, and well and faithfully served the company and attended to its business affairs, and so long as the company was not wound up and so long as he did not infringe the requirements of clause 7 as to his interest in other businesses, he was entitled to continue to serve the company and to be paid his salary at the rate of £3000 a year.

The appeal was dismissed.

SOURCE 130
Read *v* Astoria Garage (Streatham) Ltd
[1952] Ch 637; [1952] 2 All ER 292

The company adopted as their articles of association Table A of Schedule 1 to the Companies Act 1929, with certain modifications. Article 68 of Table A provides:[1] 'The directors may from time to time appoint one or more of their body to the office of managing director or manager for such term and at such remuner-ation . . . as they may think fit, and a director so appointed shall not, while holding that office, be subject to retirement by rotation, or taken into account in determining the rotation or retirement of directors; but his appointment shall be subject to determination ipso facto if he ceases for any cause to be a director, or if the company in general meeting resolve that his tenure of the office of managing director or manager be determined.'

JENKINS LJ: . . . There remains the second point — the claim in respect of the alleged wrongful dismissal of the plaintiff from his office of managing director. There is no record anywhere of any terms on which the plaintiff was appointed managing director beyond the minute of resolution No 4 which was passed at the first meeting of the directors by which the plaintiff was appointed managing director at a salary of £7 a week from 1 February 1932, and the articles of association of the company. The company's articles adopted Table A, with certain modifications. Amongst the articles of Table A adopted was article No 68. [His Lordship read the article.]

---

1 See now, reg 84 Companies (Tables A–F) Regulations 1085

It is argued by Mr Harold Brown for the plaintiff that, notwithstanding the provisions of article 68, there was a contract between the plaintiff and the defendant company in the nature of a contract of general hiring — a plain contract of employment, one of the terms of which was that the plaintiff's employment should not be determined by the defendant company except by reasonable notice. The judge came to the conclusion that the terms of the plaintiff's appointment were not such as to entitle him to any notice in the event of the company choosing under article 68 to resolve in general meeting that his tenure of office as managing director be determined, and, in my judgment, the judge was clearly right.

. . .

The directors purported by a resolution of the board to appoint him managing director. In my view, it is really clear beyond argument that the directors must be taken to have been making that appointment with reference to the provisions of article 68 of Table A — it was only under that article that they could make the appointment. Accordingly, in my view, the resolution, containing as it did no other special terms beyond the fixing of the remuneration of £7 a week, and containing nothing whatever amplifying, or inconsistent with, the provisions of article 68, must be taken to have been an appointment of the plaintiff as managing director on the terms of article 68, and accordingly it was an appointment upon terms, inter alia, that it should be subject to termination if the company in general meeting resolved that the plaintiff's tenure of the office of managing director be determined.

Mr Harold Brown said alternatively that even if the appointment made by the resolution of the board must be taken as in effect incorporating the provisions of article 68, nevertheless the provisions of the article as so incorporated must be held to be subject to an implied term that the plaintiff's employment could not be determined without reasonable notice. For my part, I see no ground for implying any such term; indeed, to imply one really comes back to saying over again that the appointment was not on the terms of article 68, but on some other and different terms, including a term as to reasonable notice. I see no ground for implying any such term in the absence of any contract outside the article and the resolution, and in the absence, moreover, of any provision about it at all in the resolution itself.

We were referred to various authorities on this topic which, in one form or another, has been fairly often before the courts. The first was the well-known case of *Nelson v James Nelson & Sons Ltd.*[1] In that case the headnote is: 'The articles of association of the defendant company provided that the board of directors might appoint one of their number to be managing director for such period as they deemed fit, and might revoke the appointment. The board appointed the plaintiff to be managing director upon the terms of an agreement which provided that he should hold the office so long as he should remain a director of the company and retain his due qualification and efficiently perform the duties of the office. Subsequently, while the plaintiff was still fulfilling the conditions of the agreement, the board revoked the appointment. The plaintiff sued the company for damages for breach of agreement: — *Held*, that the articles of association did not empower the board to revoke the appointment at will, or otherwise than in accordance with the terms of agreement under which the plaintiff was appointed managing director, and that the plaintiff was entitled to recover damages against the company.'

---

1 [1914] 2 KB 770; 83 LJ KB 823 (see p 350)

It is to be observed that this was a case in which there was an actual agreement with the plaintiff that he should be managing director for a period which was inconsistent with the unfettered exercise by the directors of their power under the articles to revoke the appointment of a managing director; and it seems to me that this is a vital distinction from the present case; in which there is no vestige of any contract beyond the minute of the resolution making the appointment and the article by reference to which, in my view, the appointment was made. The learned judge[1] referred in the course of his judgment to a passage in the judgment of Swinfen Eady LJ in the *Nelson case* in which he drew a distinction between a case like the one there under consideration, where the directors were seeking to exercise a power to revoke an appointment, and a case where the appointment of a managing director is, as in the present case, made subject to a power for the company to deal with it in general meeting; and the Lord Justice, after referring to that kind of article, continued: 'With an article in that form it is manifest that the directors can only appoint a managing director subject to the right of the company in general meeting to resolve at any time that his tenure of the office of managing director is to be determined. That, however, is not the article which we have to construe.'

It will be seen that the learned Lord Justice was there recognizing that where a company in general meeting reserves the right to determine the appointment of a managing director, the directors cannot by the appointment of a managing director for some fixed term, override that power in the company. At all events, I think it is plain that where there is an article in that form, a managing director, whose appointment is determined by the company in general meeting in exercise of that power, cannot claim to have been wrongfully dismissed unless he can show that an agreement has been entered into between himself and the company, the terms of which are inconsistent with the exercise by the company of the power conferred on it by the article to determine a managing director's appointment in general meeting. In the present case, as I have said before, there is no evidence of the existence of any such contract.

. . .

In my view, on the facts of this case, the position was simply that the plaintiff was appointed to be managing director in accordance with article 68 of the 1929 Table A with such tenure of office as was provided for by that article, and had no special right to receive any particular notice of the termination of his employment in the event of the company deciding to determine it and doing so by a resolution in a general meeting. Accordingly, in my view, the learned judge came to a right conclusion on the plaintiff's second claim; and in the result the appeal fails on both points, and should be dismissed.

SOURCE 131
Re Richmond Gate Property Co Ltd
[1965] 1 WLR 335; [1964] 3 All ER 936

Richmond Gate Property Co Ltd was incorporated on 19 January 1962, and by its articles of association Table A of the Companies Act 1948, was adopted in so far as it was not specifically excluded by or in conflict with the company's articles. By article 9 of the company's articles Herbert Leslie Brock Walker (hereinafter called 'the applicant'), one of the two subscribers to the memorandum of association, was appointed joint managing director with one Derek Gordon Clancy, both to hold office for life.

---

1 Harman J in the court below

. . .

The applicant was not employed in any other capacity than as managing director, and the only mention of remuneration in that capacity was in article 108 of Table A,[1] which had been incorporated into the company's articles as above, but at no time did the directors determine his remuneration pursuant to that article, or otherwise.

PLOWMAN J: The effect of article 9 of the articles, coupled with article 108 in Table A, coupled with the fact that Walker was a member of the company, in my judgment, is that a contract exists between himself and the company for payment to him of remuneration as managing director, and that remuneration depends on article 108 of Table A and is to be such amount 'as the directors may determine'; in other words, the managing director is at the mercy of the board, he gets what they determine to pay him, and if they do not determine to pay him anything he does not get anything. That is his contract with the company, and those are the terms on which he accepts office.

Since there is an express contract with the company in regard to the payment of remuneration it seems to me that any question of quantum meruit is automatically excluded.

. . .

In the present case there was an express contract which relates to payment of remuneration, and the only question with which I am concerned is: according to the terms of that express contract, is any sum payable for remuneration? When one finds that the express contract is that the remuneration payable is such sum as the directors may determine that the managing director shall have, and that the directors have not determined that any sum is to be payable to the managing director, it seems to me to follow as a necessary consequence that no remuneration can be claimed.

SOURCE 132
Re New British Iron Company, ex parte Beckwith
[1898] 1 Ch 324

The articles of association included the following provision:

'62: The remuneration of the board shall be an annual sum of £1000 to be paid out of the funds of the company, which sum shall be divided in such manner as the board from time to time determine.'

WRIGHT J: Article 62 fixes the remuneration of the directors at the annual sum of £1000. That article is not in itself a contract between the company and the directors; it is only part of the contract constituted by the articles of association between the members of the company inter se. But where on the footing of that article the directors are employed by the company and accept office the terms of article 62 are embodied in and form part of the contract between the company and the directors. Under the article as thus embodied the directors obtain a contractual right to an annual sum of £1000 as remuneration.

NOTES AND QUESTIONS

1. *In* Clarke v Dunraven,[2] *the appellant (Clarke) and respondent (Dunraven) entered a yacht race, each independently of the other agreeing to be*

---

1 See now, reg 84 Companies (Tables A–F) Regulations 1985
2 [1897] AC 59

bound by the rules of the Yacht Club Association. One of these rules provided that if any entrant broke any of the rules, he would be liable for all damages which resulted. The appellant did, without any fault, break one of the rules as a result of which he caused the respondent's yacht to sink. Under statute (the Merchant Shipping Act 1894), the appellant's liability was limited, but the respondent alleged a contract with the appellant in terms of which the appellant agreed to be responsible for all damages in the event of breaking any rule governing the yacht race. The House of Lords upheld the decision of the Court of Appeal holding the appellant liable in full for the loss suffered by the respondent. Lord Herschell said:

'*I cannot entertain any doubt that there was a contractual relation between the parties to this litigation. The effect of their entering for the race, and undertaking to be bound by these rules to the knowledge of each other, is sufficient, I think, where those rules indicate a liability on the part of the one to the other to create a contractual obligation to discharge the liability.*'

2. *What is the ratio of* Borlands Trustee v Steel Brothers?[1]
3. *Using the facts* Borland's Trustee v Steel Brothers *how could you reconstitute the litigation in order to test the proposition that there were contracts between Borland and each other shareholder?*
4. *How would you distinguish* London Sack & Bag[2] *and* Rayfield v Hands?[3]
5. *What is the significance of the company not being a party to the litigation in* Rayfield v Hands?
6. *If the correct explanation of* Quin & Axtens[4] *is the member's right to enforce the contract established by the articles, would the result in* Eley v Positive Life Assurance Company[5] *(p 304) have been different if the plaintiff had asserted a 'member's right to have the articles enforced' rather than a right to be the company's solicitor? If so, could any member have asserted this right in order that Eley should remain the company's solicitor? How does Sir Wilfred Greene MR deal with this in* Beattie's case?[6]
7. *One problem there might be said to be with* Rayfield v Hands[7] *is that the obligation to take transfer of the shares was imposed by the articles on the directors (ie it was an 'outsider' obligation). Consider (i) how Vaisey J dealt with this problem and (ii) whether it could be approached on the basis that corresponding to the general members' right to enforce the articles there is a general members' obligation to do whatever is necessary to facilitate the upholding of the articles (compare the rule in* Stirling v Maitland,[8] *as described and applied by Diplock J in* Shindler v Northern Raincoat Company Limited).[9]

---

1 [1901] 1 Ch 279; 70 LJ Ch 51 (see p 298)
2 [1943] 2 All ER 764 (see p 300)
3 [1960] Ch 1; [1958] 2 All ER 194 (see p 301)
4 [1909] AC 442; 78 LJ Ch 506
5 (1876) 1 Ex D 88; 45 LJ Exch 451
6 [1938] Ch 708; [1938] 3 All ER 214 (see p 308)
7 [1960] Ch 1; [1958] 2 All ER 194 (see p 301)
8 (1864) 5 B&S 840; 122 ER 1043
9 [1960] 1 WLR 1038; [1960] 2 All ER 239 (see p 349)

8. The question of when the articles will and will not be enforceable is closely tied in with the application of the rule in Foss v Harbottle.[1] Following Wedderburn's seminal study (see Source 113 at p 310) there have been numerous attempts to resolve this conundrum, see Goldberge [1972] 35 MLR 362; Smith [1978] 41 MLR 147; Prentice [1980] 1 Company Lawyer 179; Wedderburn (again) [1981] 44 MLR 202; Gregory [1982] 45 MLR 524; Baxter [1983] CLJ 96; Goldberge (again) [1985] 48 MLR 158; Drury [1986] CLJ 219.

9. Other shareholders' rights upheld against the wishes of the majority have been the right to a share certificate (Burdett v Standard Exploration),[2] the right to the payment of a dividend as against the issue of debentures (Wood v Odessa Waterworks Company,[3] p 297), the right to have notice of forfeiture issued in compliance with the articles (Johnson v Lyttle's Agency[4]) and (more controversially) the right to have the articles enforced (Quin & Axtens Ltd v Salmon).[5]

10. There are, on the other hand, many instances of the will of the majority being upheld at the expense of the individual shareholder's right. This is most likely to be described as the application of the rule in Foss v Harbottle,[6] a particularly good illustration of which is McDougall v Gardiner[7]. Contrast McDougall's case with Pender v Lushington[8] (p 314). Are these two cases reconcilable? What is the wrong which is the subject matter of each dispute? Who is the victim of the wrong in each case?

11. In Bushell v Faith,[9] of course, the House of Lords held there to be no conflict between the statutory provision and the relevant regulation in the articles. In the South African case of Swerdlow v Cohen,[10] where the statutory provisions (s 220(1)(a) of the South African Companies Act 1973) was virtually indistinguishable from s 184 of the Companies Act 1948 (now s 303 of the Companies Act 1985), the relevant regulation in the articles was:

'. . . questions arising at any meeting of members shall be decided by a majority of votes, provided that if and for so long as Arnold Swerdlow, Stanley Ernest Cohen and Karl Bahr or any of them shall be members no resolution shall be of any force or effect unless they or those of them who are members of the company are in favour of the resolution . . .'

The court distinguished Bushell v Faith, on the ground that there the regulation conferred weighted voting rights, whereas in Swerdlow a blocking mechanism was achieved simply by voting (irrespective of the quantity of votes recorded) or, indeed, of abstaining from voting. The regulation in question

---

1 (1843) 2 Hare 461; 67 ER 189
2 (1899) 16 TLR 112
3 (1889) 42 Ch D 636; 58 LJ Ch 628
4 (1877) 5 Ch D 687; 46 LJ Ch 786
5 [1909] AC 442; 78 LJ Ch 506
6 (1843) 2 Hare 461; 67 ER 189
7 (1876) 1 Ch D 13; 45 LJ Ch 27
8 (1877) 6 Ch D 70; 46 LJ Ch 317
9 [1970] AC 1099; [1970] 1 All ER 53
10 1977 (3) SA 1050

was not unlawful, simply ineffective in the case of a resolution to dismiss a director (because of the statutory provision).

12. *Section 9 confers a power on the company to alter its articles under specified conditions. It has also been held that the company cannot contract out of this power* (Shirlaw v Southern Foundries,[1] *(p 344)). Any attempt by the articles to confer a more (or less) onerous regime for the alteration of the articles would, therefore, be in conflict with section 9. In the light of this, consider* Cane v Jones[2] *(p 385).*

13. *The approach of the court to the alteration of the articles should be considered as part of a broader inquiry, namely the principle of majority rule (as long ago as 1812 Lord Eldon said in* Carlen v Drury[3] *that the court was 'not to be required on every occasion to take the management of every playhouse and brewhouse in the Kingdom'). Only twice has the English court upheld an objection to the alteration of the articles on the bona fide for the benefit of the company principle. In* Brown v British Abrasive Wheel Company[4] *in 1919 and* Dafen Tinplate v Llanelly Steel[5] *in 1920, the principle was divided into a subjective element (whether the majority was bona fide) and an objective element (whether the alteration was for the benefit of the company). This separation was specifically disapproved in* Shuttleworth v Cox Brothers[6] *(p 341) and despite a heroic attempt by Evershed MR in* Greenhalgh v Arderne Cinemas Limited[7] *(p 343) to make the test a more objective one, the result of that case and the extreme difficulty of applying that test where the dispute is essentially an internecine fight between two factions, emphasises the extreme difficulty faced by the minority.*

14. *Coincidentally, between* Brown's case *and* Dafen's case, *in* Sidebottom v Kershaw, Leese and Company Ltd,[8] *in 1920, the Court of Appeal upheld an alteration of the articles despite a challenge on the bona fide principle. In* Sidebottom, *like* Brown *and* Dafen, *the proposed alteration was the insertion of a regulation providing a power to expropriate shareholders, in* Brown *because the majority 98 per cent shareholder wanted all the shares before pumping much needed further capital into the company and in the other two because the company wanted to expel shareholders whose business competed with the company.*

15. *The issue of expropriation of shareholders is, of course, a separate one from that of the alteration of the articles, although the cases discussed above show how closely these issues can be linked. Expulsion was the issue in* Gaiman v National Association of Mental Health,[9] *where the Council of the defendant association (a company limited by guarantee) voted to expel a whole class of members (scientologists, because, in the words of the association's chairman, of 'the threat that Scientology posed to the association*

1 [1940] AC 701; [1940] 2 All ER 445 (p 344)
2 [1980] 1 WLR 1451; [1981] 1 All ER 533
3 (1812) 1 V&B 154; 35 ER 61
4 [1919] 1 Ch 290; 88 LJ Ch 143
5 [1920] 2 Ch 124; 89 LJ Ch 346
6 [1927] 2 KB 9; 96 LJ KB 104
7 [1951] Ch 286; [1950] 2 All ER 1120
8 [1920] 1 Ch 154; 89 LJ Ch 113
9 [1971] 1 Ch 317; [1970] 2 All ER 362

and all that it stood for') under powers already conferred by the articles. Megarry J upheld the expulsion resolution on the ground that the council acted in the bona fide belief that the expulsion was in the best interests of the association.

16. *Megarry J also doubted whether, as a separate matter, the principles of natural justice applied to a proposed expulsion, where the expelling association was a registered company as opposed to the more usual case of an unincorporated association — a members' club or a trade union for example. Even there, however, support can be found for the strict application of the contract (the rules of the association) (see* McClean v Workers' Union;[1] *compare* Lee v Showmen's Guild of Great Britain).[2]

17. *A decision which may be seen as standing against the tide of support for majority rule in companies is* Clemens v Clemens[3] *(p 475). The issue there, however, was not alteration of the articles but the powers of the directors to issue shares.*

18. Shirlaw v Southern Foundries Ltd[4] *must be taken to have cast doubt on* British Murac Syndicate Ltd v Alperton Rubber Ltd,[5] *where the plaintiff applied successfully for an injunction to stop the defendant from effecting an alteration to its articles. The defendant was proposing to delete a regulation which declared the right of the plaintiff to appoint two directors to the defendant's board. This, of course, would only have conferred an outsider right but it was supported by an extrinsic contract. It is arguable that while the power to alter the articles cannot be enjoined, the company might be prevented from acting on the altered article. It is clear that where the company acts on its articles (whether original or altered) in such a way as to breach a contract, it is liable in respect of that breach (Source 128 at p 349). If damages is an inadequate remedy, the argument would proceed, the court ought to award specific performance or an injunction.*

19. *If* Shirlaw's *case and* British Murac *can be reconciled in this way, what obstacles, if any, would have been faced (a) by* British Murac, *and (b) by* Shirlaw *in attempting to enforce their respective contracts?*

---

1 [1929] 1 Ch 602
2 [1952] 2 QB 329; [1952] 1 All ER 1175
3 [1976] 2 All ER 268
4 [1940] AC 701; [1940] 2 All ER 445
5 [1915] 2 Ch 186; 84 LJ Ch 665

Chapter 6

STRUCTURE AND MANAGEMENT OF THE COMPANY

PART I: INTRODUCTION

In this chapter, as in the previous chapter, we are principally concerned with the internal workings of the company. In the previous chapter, we looked at the relationship between the company and its members, a relationship which is constituted by the memorandum and articles of association as well as by relevant statutory provisions. Here, too, the company's constitution and relevant statutory provisions are central to our concern, but less in order to learn of the respective rights and duties of the parties and more to understand what are the elements which make up the typical company and to understand how these elements relate, one to the other.

These elements — or organs, the managing director, the board of directors, the general meeting of shareholders and, possibly, the secretary — are the structure of the company. How they relate to each other tells how the company is managed.

There are obvious overlaps between this and the last chapter. The status and power of directors and managing directors pose contractual as well as management problems (fiduciary, as well, for that matter: see Chapter 7) and the material on the contractual relationship between directors and company, considered at the end of the previous chapter, leads naturally on to the structural questions which we discuss in this chapter.

Problems of structure and management are not, however, questions whose discussion is only within the framework of the distillation, reconciliation and application of legal principles. To the question, what is a company?, there are other significant answers apart from stating what are the different elements of a company and the principles in terms of which they interrelate. Another answer is contained in the debate among the rival theories as to the nature of corporate personality, largely a philosophical inquiry which was touched upon in Chapter 1. Yet another answer derives from the perspective of the operation of the company in its industrial and commercial context. Here, where the focus is likely to be on large national and multinational companies, the alternative form for the question, what is a company?, could be, whose interests does and should a company serve?

PART II: THE COMPOSITION OF THE BOARD OF DIRECTORS

The mechanics for the appointment and retirement of the directors are generally provided for in the company's articles and the Companies Act 1985.

The typical UK company structure with the model Table A articles (which, of course, are not mandatory; the precise Regulations are a matter for the incorporators and are subject to subsequent alteration) provide for the annual retirement (at the AGM) of one-third of the directors, who will (or some of whom will) commonly be re-elected (Table A, regs 73–78). The annual retirement provision does not apply to directors appointed to executive office, such as managing directorships (reg 84). Directors may be appointed or co-opted between AGMs to fill a vacancy (reg 79). Directors may be represented by alternates (Table A, regs 65–69).

Under the Companies Act 1985, s 303, directors can be removed by ordinary resolution, notwithstanding anything to the contrary in the articles (see *Bushell v Faith*, p 318; see also, Table A, reg 81). If two or more directors are appointed at the same meeting, there must be separate resolutions for each nominee unless this has otherwise been agreed by a resolution to which there are not dissenters (s 292). In certain circumstances, persons over 70 years old cannot be appointed as directors (ss 293–294).

The board of directors will almost invariably undertake the management of the company (Table A, reg 70). The role of the shareholders is to appoint and to remove the directors but not to manage the company unless there is fraud in the board, or in extremely rare circumstances where the articles clearly empower the shareholders to manage or partly manage the company, or where the board is impotent or non-existent.

It is not, however, only people appointed or elected in accordance with the appropriate procedure who will be regarded by the law as directors. In addition, the law recognises the categories of 'de facto' and 'shadow' directors. Both are treated by the law (generally for the purpose of ascribing liability either to the 'director' or to the company) as directors although not appointed as such. The former describes someone who has openly assumed or been represented as a director (see, eg *Mahony v East Holyford Gold Mining Co*, p 261 and *Morris v Kanssen*, p 274); the latter describes someone who has manipulated the operations of the board through the person or persons actually appointed to the board — the latter are sometimes referred to as nominee directors (see the Companies Act 1985, ss 305(7), 317(8), 318(6), 319(7), 320(3), 322B(3), 323(4), 324(6), 325(6), 330(5), 741(2); and the Insolvency Act 1986, ss 213, 214, 251, *Re A Company, ex parte Copp (No 005009/1987)* [1989] [BCLC] 13, p 665).

There is another dimension to the issue of the composition of the board, ie should the board consist solely of shareholder representatives or is there a case for wider representation of, say, employees and consumers? If we consider such deviations from the traditional model, we must be aware of the ways in which this will alter the relationship between the board and the general meeting of shareholders (see Source 133).

Here, too, we see the growing influence of the European Communities on English company law. Germany has long imposed on companies above a certain size, the legal requirement that there be two boards of directors — the supervisory board and the management board — and that at least one-third of the members of the supervisory board (which in turn appoints the management board) be elected from amongst the employees of the company.

Other European countries have followed this pattern, as has the European Communities in two draft instruments which it is at present attempting to persuade the Member States to adopt — the draft statute for a European Company and the Draft Fifth Directive on the harmonisation of Company Law both of which incorporate board models which include employee representation. Strong opposition from the UK government has prevented any progress on either of these measures.

Shareholders and creditors argue that their interests are not adequately protected by the increasingly independent management. Very real differences arise as to strategy in the management of companies and in policies as to the distribution of the company's assets (see Part IV: 'Competing Claims to Management', p 410, *Evans v Brunner Mond*,[1] p 228 and *Parke v Daily News*[2]). As the informal split between executive and non-executive directors gains greater recognition, non-executive directors are sometimes looked to, to provide this protection for shareholders (see Sources 134 and 135).

SOURCE 133
Report of the Committee of Inquiry on Industrial Democracy ('Bullock Report') (Cmnd 6706)
CHAPTER 3

The pressures for change
1. One of the earliest uses of the term 'industrial democracy' was by Sidney and Beatrice Webb in 1897, as the title of their book on the structure and functions of trade unions. Since then there has been a shift of emphasis in the use of the term. With changes in the structure of the economy and the nature of society since World War II, it has come to focus increasingly on the need to involve employees to a greater extent in company decision-making.

. . .

Industrial and economic changes
2. The last 20 years have seen the growth of the giant industrial enterprise, and the concentration of economic power in the hands of fewer and fewer such companies. For example, in 1953 the 100 largest manufacturing enterprises in the UK accounted for 25 per cent of the total net output; in 1971 the corresponding figure was 40 per cent. There has been a growing recognition of the influence of such companies on many aspects of people's lives at home as well as at work. As companies have grown in size and complexity, they have also tended to become remote from the communities in which they operate and from the people whom they employ. Major decisions about the nature of a company's or plant's organisation, affecting closely the future of the local community or the jobs of the employees, may often be taken far away from the site by the directors of a parent or holding company, sometimes by the management of a parent company overseas.

3. The power and complexity of the industrial enterprise and the remoteness of decision-making have led to demands for large companies to be more responsive

---

1 (1921) 1 Ch 359; 90 LJ Ch 294
2 [1962] Ch 927; [1962] 2 All ER 929

to the needs of society in general and of their employees in particular. Industry has come under pressure to consider the wider effects of the decisions it takes in pursuit of profitability, and companies now explicitly or implicitly accept that they have responsibilities not just to shareholders, but also to employees, customers, creditors, suppliers, the local community and to society at large. The Confederation of British Industry (CBI), has accepted the special duty of companies to take into account the interests of employees and argued strongly that companies should develop effective systems of employee participation to channel the energies and abilities of its workforce to constructive ends:

> 'The responsibilities of the board to its employees are today different from but no less important than those which it must accept to its shareholders. It might be said that they are even more important, at least in the short term, as failure to achieve satisfactory working relationships with employees can put a board in a position where it will have great difficulty in fulfilling its obligations to its shareholders.'

This is, of course, partly a recognition of the reality of the increased and increasing influence of employees, through their trade unions, on company decision-making, but it is also an acceptance of the principle that a socially responsible company in a democratic society cannot operate without taking account of the interests of its employees.

4. At the same time, the effect of the 'managerial revolution' in large companies has been to concentrate power in the hands of boards of directors. Although in theory, and in law, directors are appointed by shareholders, the shareholders are too numerous to act effectively as a body, and have largely acquiesced in effective control by the board of directors. It is only when there is a financial crisis or dissension within the board that shareholders are called upon to exercise power and take decisions. Except in such circumstances the members of the board are free to run the company and secure the appointment of the directors they wish.

5. During recent decades the directors and senior executives of large companies have as a result of the speed of technological change and rapid fluctuations in the economic climate become increasingly aware of the need to be more responsive to change, if they are to remain profitable. They are faced more often with important investment decisions about the introduction of new technology, the re-equipment of a plant or the transfer of production to a new locality. Often their decisions closely affect the lives of thousands of employees, and in such cases it becomes increasingly difficult for employers to deny the right of these employees, not only to have their interests taken into account by management, but also to have an opportunity for active involvement in the decision-making process. Such responses on the part of companies may in part be a recognition of social responsibility or of democratic principles, but they are also evidence of the practical reality that if a company neglects to make provision for such involvement, employees are now in a position, through the strengthening of trade union organisation and power, to resist the implementation of changes that threaten their livelihood and security. Such resistance may appear shortsighted, but it is understandable that individual workers or groups may interpret the universally accepted goal of full employment as meaning job security for themselves. The EEC Green Paper, *Employee participation and company structure*, has pointed out that there is a potential contradiction between the needs of companies to respond to change quickly and the need to involve employees in those changes, because of the inherent and understandable reluctance of

employees to accept changes which seem to threaten their work and livelihood. But the Green Paper goes on to argue that, in the long term, conflicts between unions and management and frustrations arising from failure to involve the employees in such changes from the outset are liable to prove much more damaging than any delays and inconvenience caused by the participation of employees in the decision-making process.

6. More recently a recognition, shared by Government, management and trade unions, of the urgent need for British industry to be more responsive to change if there is to be any hope of reversing the relative decline of this country's industrial performance, has led to the development of a tripartite industrial strategy. This is founded on the assumption that Britain's industrial problems can only be successfully remedied by concerted action to improve the performance of industry. The strategy takes account of the trends in size and concentration mentioned earlier and aims to develop effective mechanisms for ensuring that the plans of large companies are in harmony with national needs and objectives. Trade union involvement is seen as fundamental to the strategy, not simply because such involvement is necessary to forestall negative resistance to change, but also because employees through their trade unions have a positive role to play in combating industrial stagnation and in stimulating much needed changes in industrial structure and performance. This tripartite industrial strategy is likely to act as a catalyst to the further development of joint regulation of forward planning decisions at company level.

Social changes
7. New concepts of the role of employees in decision-making at company level are not just reactions to economic trends. They also derive from social changes which have taken place since the war, especially rising standards of education and higher standards of living. The significance of the educational developments is not just that more people have received a basic education; it is the nature of that education which has changed. There is now less concentration on formal authoritarian teaching methods and more encouragement to children to adopt independent and questioning approaches in order to develop individual initiative and ability. It is only since World War II that we have seen the end of the deferential society, in which working people rarely aspired to positions of power or authority in local or national life. The coming of age of democracy in our society is a process that inevitably affects the whole of people's lives; it cannot be excluded from the workplace. The parallel increase in standards of living has also been important. Most people now live in more comfortable homes and have more money and leisure to enjoy them. They have come to expect a higher and rising standard of material comfort and are therefore naturally less tolerant of low standards, discomfort, boredom and lack of proper provisions for safety and health in their working environment, as well as less prepared to accept the prospect of redundancy and unemployment. The EEC Green Paper quoted above recognised these social changes in Western Europe in the following paragraph:

> 'Furthermore, the current economic situation, with its reduced possibilities for growth, has emphasised the need for mechanisms which will adequately ensure the pursuit of goals other than economic growth, such as the improvement of the quality of life and working conditions, the protection of the environment and the interests of the consumer. The pursuit of such goals can probably be secured only by the existence of decision-making

processes in enterprises which have a broader, more democratic base than such processes often have at present.'

8. The effect of those social changes has been an increasing desire among employees to control their working environment and to have a say in decisions which affect their working lives. They have become less prepared to accept unquestioningly unilateral decisions by management, and have shown a readiness to challenge a decision if it seems to have ignored their point of view or to affect them adversely. Traditional management prerogatives have therefore come under attack, and the modern manager has had to develop a style of participative management, which has recognised the necessity and the benefits of involving employees in decision-making, rather than imposing decisions upon them without consultation.

...

Developments in Europe

13. Another fact which has had considerable influence on the debate has been the experience of Britain's neighbours in Europe. As part of a general movement to involve employees more effectively in decision-making, some eight countries in Western Europe now have schemes of one kind or another in operation which secure or at least make possible the representation of employees on company boards. It is now 25 years since *Mitbestimmung* (co-determination) was introduced in the Federal Republic of Germany. This year has seen further steps to increase the proportion of employee representatives on the supervisory boards of companies employing more than 2,000 people. In Sweden, 1976 has also seen confirmation of the three-year experiment in putting employee representatives on company boards. The fact that the West German and Swedish economies, despite differences between the social philosophies of the two countries, have been among the most successful in the world — not least in avoiding the industrial conflict which has cost Britain so dear — has not escaped notice.

14. As long ago as 1972 the EEC Commission published draft proposals for a Fifth Directive on company law, proposing employee representation on the supervisory boards of all companies in the Community with over 500 employees. The Directive is being revised in an attempt to find a more flexible approach which can accommodate more easily the various systems of company law in the nine member states. To help this, the Commission published at the end of 1975 the Green Paper, the discussions and comments on which are to be the basis of a revised Fifth Directive. During 1975 the Commission also published its amended proposals for a European Company Statute, which will permit the creation of 'European Companies'. These will have to meet certain requirements regarding employee participation, including the establishment of a European Works Council and the representation of employees on a supervisory board of the Company. Thus, even without the current interest in board level representation in the United Kingdom, the British Government as a member of the EEC would have found itself involved in the debate about its merits and demerits.

Conclusion

15. Our conclusion from the foregoing discussions are two-fold. First, we believe that there is a widespread recognition in this country of what the EEC Green Paper has called 'the democratic imperative' for employee participation, described in that document as follows: 'those who will be substantially affected by decisions made by social and political institutions must be involved in the making of those decisions'. We believe this is an important agreed basis on which the

debate on the extent and method of participation can take place. Second, there is already a great deal of participation through the trade unions, particularly at local level in collective bargaining and at national level through discussions between the TUC and the Government and in such tripartite institutions as the National Economic Development Council. The concern of this Committee has been to consider how these existing forms of participation can best be complemented, extended and developed, in response to the pressures for change documented in this chapter.

CHAPTER 6

. . .

The interests of consumers
42. Two main concerns were expressed in evidence to us on behalf of consumers. The first was that there would be a conspiracy at board level between the representatives of capital and labour to pursue the twin aims of higher profits and wages without due regard to the consumer. As the National Consumer Council (NCC) commented in their written evidence:

> 'We cannot but fear that if labour and capital were locked together into one organisational combine the push for security would become strongly underpinned and the tendency to monopolistic limitation of new entrants to a trade enhanced. Since the interests of consumers are served best by competition (even with all its weaknesses), such tendency would not be to their advantage.'

43. The second source of concern was that the introduction of parity representation on the lines proposed by the TUC and the extension of trade union power involved could only reduce the efficiency of companies, making for higher prices and poorer service to the consumer. The NCC emphasised the importance of efficiency to the consumer as follows:

> 'The more efficiency, the better the prospects of consumers getting goods and services which are better value for money — reasonably priced, safer, more durable, more reliable, better serviced and delivered on time.'

The NCC concluded by opposing employee representation on the board, but it added that if the concept was accepted then the interests of consumers should also be specifically represented.

44. Others took the view that the interests of consumers would be furthered, not damaged, by the introduction of employee representation on the boards of companies, because of the positive influence this would have on productivity, efficiency and the avoidance of wasteful confrontation. Given our persuasion that board level representation will have a positive impact on efficiency, we naturally incline to the view that such developments will enhance rather than damage consumer interests. Moreover, fears of adverse effects on consumer interests appear to be based at least partly on a misunderstanding of how boards reach decisions and how companies operate. We do not believe that boards representing labour and capital could, even if they wanted, pursue profit without regard to the interests of consumers. The constraints of competition in the marketplace, however imperfect, oblige companies which by definition depend absolutely for their existence on customers for the goods or services they produce, to be constantly aware of and responsive to the needs and preferences of consumers.

These constraints will not change simply because the composition of the board is altered. The economic relationship between the company and its customers remains constant. Whatever interests or instinct to 'exploit the market' a company may have, the addition of employee representatives to its board will not enhance its capability of so doing.

45. A separate question is whether the predisposition of companies to act contrary to the interests of consumers may be increased or decreased by representation of employees on company boards. The NCC foresees a greater propensity to anti-consumer behaviour, operating for example through the monopolistic or at least oligopolistic powers of large companies to raise prices or to limit new entrants to a trade or industry. Assuming that such powers exist, and that they are not fully used by companies with their present boards of directors, we may still ask why boards of directors including employee representatives would be more inclined than existing boards to make use of them. The NCC gives as the reason an increased 'push for security'. In contrast to this hypothesis of a conspiracy by the representatives of capital and labour to exploit the consumer, some British trade unionists have asserted that employee representation on boards will lead to monopolistic or anti-consumer policies being modified or abandoned, because they will be subject to the scrutiny of people in closer touch with the interests of consumers in general than the predominantly middle-class group of existing directors of large companies. We find both arguments speculative and therefore unconvincing.

46. We do not accept the view put forward by the NCC that if there was to be employee representation on company boards (to which it was opposed in principle) then there must also be representation of consumer interests. We do not agree that there is a need for the latter, partly because we do not accept the thesis that board level representation of employees will damage the consumer interests. Consumer interests must continue to be protected, as they are now, against the actions of industrial enterprises, but the way to do this is through legislation and through the existing consumer organisations, rather than by involving consumers in the running of companies. The involvement of employees and shareholders in a company is different in kind from that of consumers. Furthermore, we see serious practical difficulties in achieving satisfactory representation of consumers on boards. Generally speaking there is no recognisable consumer constituency equivalent to that of employers and shareholders and therefore no way in which a guardian of consumer interests could be appointed to the board through representative machinery. . . .

47. There are other ways as well in which the consumer interest is protected. The Monopolies Commission, for example, exists to ensure that the abuses of a monopoly position, where one company dominates and in consequence can manipulate a market, are curbed. Recent years have seen the growth of the consumer movement, reflected in the establishment of bodies like the NCC itself, to identify and represent the consumer interest, and in the increasing amount of legislation like the Fair Trading Act 1973 and Consumer Credit Act 1974 to protect various aspects of the consumer interest. We are not saying that such protection is perfect. Our point is that none of these forms of protection will be affected by employee representation on boards. The many different pressures within the economy which require companies to take into account the interests of consumers will continue to exist. In our view, the effect on consumers of employee representation on company boards will be marginal. For this reason, and because of the problems mentioned above, we do not recommend that the

law should provide for consumer representation on boards of directors in the private sector.

. . .

CHAPTER 8

The implications of employee representation for the structure and function of company boards

. . .

7. We believe that the introduction into the United Kingdom of a two-tier board on the West German model would impose on companies a measure of inflexibility which would be detrimental to their efficient management. It is important to understand that the West German system of two-tier boards was developed during the last century, in response to demands that the shareholders should supervise more closely the work of management and long before employee representation was introduced. West German companies have therefore grown and developed in this century within the legal framework of a two-tier board system, and when employee representation was introduced, the supervisory board was the obvious place for it. In contrast as we have seen, United Kingdom law has largely left it to companies to define for themselves the role of their boards in relation to management. This has enabled them to draw up their own rules about where the job of the board ends and the job of management begins. It has meant that the distinction between the functions of supervision and management has remained fluid, responsive to the changing circumstances within the enterprise. It has also meant that no two companies have developed exactly the same method of operation or organisation. In our view, therefore, an attempt to impose the rigidity of the statutory two-tier system on British companies at the present stage in their development could be damaging to their efficiency and could restrict their ability in the future to alter their structures at top level to meet new demands on their business. If such a statutory system were introduced, companies would be required to adopt a form of board structure and to maintain a separation of functions at top level which might bear no resemblance to the way in which they had developed their organisation over a period of years. One of two consequences could ensue. Either companies would conform to the new system with considerable disruption to their management structure, or alternatively and more likely in our view, the system would be inoperable.

. . .

10. . . . We recognise that whatever system is devised, management will play the central role in the formulation and implementation of policy, and that boards will be very largely reliant on the advice they receive from senior executives. But we hope that employees through their representation on the board will have the opportunity to join in setting the framework of policy within which management operate and to influence decisions on major questions concerning investment, rationalisation, expansion and the like. We are not convinced that they will have this opportunity if their right to representation is on a board which is limited in the extent to which it can intervene in company policy or supervise the activities of management. The effect of the introduction of a statutory two-tier system in this country could be to enshrine in the law the dominance of management to the detriment of the interests of both employees and shareholders.

. . .

16. We propose that company law should, specify certain areas, where the right to take a final decision would rest with the board of directors. The board could not delegate authority for decisions in these areas to senior management. The shareholders' meeting would however, retain a right to approve or reject the board's proposals in certain specified circumstances. We list below the seven areas in which we think responsibility should be reserved to the board. For the rest of the report we shall refer to these areas as the 'attributed functions of the board'.

. . .

18. The list of attributed functions is in two parts. The first part is concerned with the relationship between on the one hand the board and senior management and on the other the board and shareholders. These are the functions, which cannot be delegated to management, and in respect of which the board will have the exclusive right to submit a resolution for consideration at the shareholders' meeting:

    (a) winding-up of the company;
    (b) changes in the memorandum and articles of association;
    (c) recommendations to shareholders on the payment of dividends;
    (d) changes in the capital structure of a company (eg as regards the relationship between the board and the shareholders, a reduction or increase in the authorised share capital; as regards the relationship between the board and senior management, the issue of securities on a take-over or merger);
    (e) disposal of a substantial part of the undertaking.

The second part of the list is concerned solely with the relationship between the board and senior management. These functions place the *responsibility* for decisions with the board of directors:

    (f) the allocation or disposition of resources to the extent not covered in (c) to (e) above (although, of course, here the board may delegate to management);
    (g) the appointment, removal, control and remuneration of management, whether members of the board or not, in their capacity as executives or employees.

19. We would not propose any alteration to the present position as regards the company's dealings with third parties: inasmuch as any transaction entered into by a managing director, for example, on behalf of a company without requisite board authority, would normally bind the company vis-à-vis third parties under company law as it is now, especially in the light of the amendments made in the European Communities Act 1972.[1] The remedy and sanction would, of course, be the liability to dismissal of those who exceeded their powers.

. . .

The board and senior management
21. In many respects the relationship between the board and senior management will be largely unaffected by the legal changes which we are proposing. The main change relates to the attributed functions of the board. Where company law specifies that on a certain matter ultimate responsibility lies with the board, management will not be able to take action unilaterally. This does not mean that either at the request of the board itself or on their own initiative, management

---

1 See now s 35 of the Companies Act 1985

will not be able to carry out the detailed work on the consideration of options and the formulation of policy in these areas. But they will be required to refer the matter to the board for a final decision.

. . .

The board and the shareholders

. . .

26. . . . We are proposing considerable changes in the legal rights of shareholders, though it will be argued below that in practice the changes may not be as great as they seem. They are necessary because, if our proposals are adopted, the new concept of a partnership between capital and labour in the control of companies will supersede the idea that a company and its shareholders (ie its 'owners' or 'members') are one and the same thing. The purpose of changing the powers of shareholders is to ensure that the board which has employee representatives on it cannot, in matters which are important to both employees and shareholders, be unilaterally overruled by shareholders. The power of individual shareholders to sell their shares remains, of course, unaffected and constitutes the normal recourse to shareholders who dislike the way a company is being run.

27. Our proposal in paragraph 18 for attributing to the board a number of functions affects the present powers of shareholders in five important areas: changing the company's constitution (ie its memorandum and articles of association), winding-up, changes in the company's capital structure, the fixing of dividends, and the disposal of a substantial part of the undertaking. These are all matters of central importance to the interests of shareholders as investors in the company: they concern the objectives and organisation of the enterprise and the long term value of the shareholders' holding in it. At present, as a general rule, in all these matters the shareholders not only retain ultimate control by approving or rejecting proposals put to them by the board but also the power of initiative by requisitioning an extraordinary general meeting pursuant to section 132 of the Companies Act 1948.[1] These are also issues, however, which closely affect the interests of employees and which are directly related to their future employment and pay prospects. It would be undesirable in our view to put employee representatives on a board which could not have a decisive influence on these matters, or which could find its policy changed by the passing of a resolution at the shareholders' meeting, which was not supported by the board.

28. We have suggested an approach therefore which distributes the power to take decisions in these areas between the board and the shareholders' meeting. The exclusive right to convene a meeting for the purpose of considering resolutions in these areas should belong to the board, but the shareholders' meeting should retain the right to decide whether to pass the resolutions or not. Thus, in the case of voluntary winding-up the present power of shareholders holding 10 per cent or more of the voting capital, under section 132[1] of the Companies Act 1948, to convene a general meeting for the purposes of considering a resolution to wind-up the company would be removed. Again, in fixing dividends the shareholders' power would lie in the right to reject a proposal put to it by the board, not to fix the dividend itself. The approval of the shareholders, where it is given, would however have to command the same majority as is required under the existing

---

1 See now s 368 of the Companies Act 1985

law (eg three-quarters majority of those voting in the case of a special resolution concerning a change in the company's constitution or to put the company into liquidation). A proposal to dispose of a substantial part of the undertaking does not in law (and in the absence of a specific restriction in the company's constitution), require the approval of the company in general meeting although, as the Jenkins Committee Report notes, it is standard practice among well-conducted companies to obtain the consent of the shareholders to such a disposal. We therefore consider that no change is necessary in law or practice.

29. In practice these changes will not be as great as they may seem. The law amended on the lines outlined above will more closely reflect current practice in large companies. We noted in Chapter 7 that the shareholders' meeting was most commonly a reactive and passive body, rarely acting of its own accord without or against the advice of the board of directors. There are few cases of shareholders initiating action in such important areas as a change in the company's constitution; and even if a resolution is duly proposed at an annual general meeting, it is even rarer for it to be carried against the advice of the board. On the payment of dividends it is most unusual for a shareholders' meeting to have the power to increase the amount of dividend proposed by the board. Most companies include in their articles of association a provision similar to regulation 114 of Table A[1] that 'the company in general meeting may declare dividends, but no dividend shall exceed the amount recommended by the directors'. Essentially therefore our proposals will have the effect of bringing the law into line with reality, rather than reducing any real power or valuable rights that shareholders possess. At the same time they will ensure that in the unusual case the shareholders cannot propose a change of policy in these areas without the approval of the board.

. . .

31. . . . We think that the right of shareholders to ratify or validate an act done, for example, by one or more directors who exceeds the powers delegated to them, or which needs approval by the company (eg payment of compensation for loss of office) should be modified. These are important powers and it seems to us illogical that once employee representatives are on the board they should remain solely with the shareholders' meeting. We therefore propose that in this case approval by both the board and the shareholders' meeting should be required. In other respects we see no need to make changes in the shareholders' legal rights. In particular, we think that the power to impose borrowing limits on the board, to appoint auditors and to require a Department of Trade investigation of a company's affairs, all of which are important means by which the shareholders can check on the activities of the board, should remain vested in the shareholders.

. . .

34. In framing our proposals we have tried to strike a balance between those who believe that the board should be the supreme organ of the company with the power to overrule the shareholders' meeting in all important matters, and those who champion the rights of the company's owners to retain control over the purposes for which their investment is used. We have recognised the need to adjust the relationship between the board and the shareholders in order to ensure that employee representatives on the board have a real say in decision-making on fundamental questions like winding-up and changes in the company's constitution. We have acknowledged that it would be illogical and frustrating to

---

1 Now reg 102 of Companies (Tables A–F) Regulations 1985

the true objective of industrial democracy to put employees on the board and then allow the shareholders the power to retain control of all major decisions.

Legal duties and liabilities of directors

. . .

36. First, we think it is important that there should be a clear statement of the basic duties of directors in statute law. We realise that this will not clarify all the complexities and ambiguities in the case law and that specific points will continue to be tested in the courts. But we believe that there must be one place where a director, and particularly the new employee representative, can see a statement of the basic duties he owes to the company as a result of his membership of the board. We would not want, however, the complex job of codification to hold up progress on the introduction of board level representation.

37. Second, we are agreed in principle that all directors should have the same legal duties and liabilities. We believe that to create two standards of directors owing different or separate duties would not be conducive to the development of cooperation between employee and shareholder representatives on the board, nor ultimately to the efficient management of the company. Nor, judging by the unanimity of the many company managements who gave evidence to us on this point, would it strengthen their confidence in the effects on companies of board level representation. However we do recognise the TUC's concern that the employee representatives should not be put under impossible obligations which could cut them off from their constituents, or force them to pay sole regard to the interests of shareholders. We therefore propose that there should be some changes in the law regarding directors' duties to ensure that the employee representatives are able to carry out their normal and reasonable functions as representatives of the workforce.

38. The most important change, and it is a change which should be made whether employee representatives are put on the board or not, should be in the duty of directors to act in the best interests of the company, which, as we said in Chapter 7, has been defined in the courts as meaning the interests of share-holders, present and future. We recommend that all directors should continue to be required to act in the best interests of the company, but that in doing so they should take into account the interests of the company's employees as well as its shareholders. A number of formulations have been proposed to amend the law in this way — in the Companies Bill 1973, in the Industrial Democracy Bill 1975, and most recently in a Conservative amendment to the Companies Bill 1976. The formulation in the Companies Bill 1973 was:

> 'The matters to which the directors of a company are entitled to have regard in exercising their powers shall include the interests of the company's employees generally as well as the interests of its members' (ie the shareholders).

The Industrial Democracy Bill's provision (repeated in the proposed amendment to the Companies Bill 1976) was slightly different:

> 'The matters to which the directors . . . of a company shall have regard in exercising their powers shall include the interests of the company's workers generally as well as the interests of its shareholders.'

We prefer the second formula because it places a clear obligation on directors, (ie directors 'shall have regard') whereas the 1973 Bill merely entitles, but does not require, directors to take into account the interests of the employees.[1] We think it important that the members of a parent or holding company board should also be able to look beyond the interests of the company, to those of its subsidiaries. We recommend therefore that directors of a company should be entitled to take into account the interests of the employees and shareholders, present and future, of subsidiaries and sub-subsidiaries of that company. It is for consideration whether the directors of a subsidiary company should be able to have regard to the interests of the shareholders and employees of the holding company and of its other subsidiaries.

SOURCE 134
Report of the Committee on the Financial Aspects of Corporate Governance ('Cadbury Report') (1 December 1992)

Board Effectiveness

4.1   Every public company should be headed by an effective board which can both lead and control the business. Within the context of the UK unitary board system, this means a board made up of a combination of executive directors, with their intimate knowledge of the business, and of outside, non-executive directors, who can bring a broader view to the company's activities, under a chairman who accepts the duties and responsibilities which the post entails.

4.2   Tests of board effectiveness include the way in which the members of the board as a whole work together under the chairman, whose role in corporate governance is fundamental, and their collective ability to provide both the leadership and the checks and balances which effective govern-ance demands. Shareholders are responsible for electing board members and it is in their interests to see that the boards of their companies are properly constituted and not dominated by any one individual.

4.3   All directors are equally responsible in law for the board's actions and decisions. Certain directors may have particular responsibilities, as execu-tive or non-executive directors, for which they are accountable to the board. Regardless of specific duties undertaken by individual directors, however, it is for the board collectively to ensure that it is meeting its obligations.

4.4   Whilst it is the board as a whole which is the final authority, executive and non-executive directors are likely to contribute in different ways to its work. Non-executive directors have two particularly important contributions to make to the governance process as a consequence of their independence from executive responsibility. Neither is in conflict with the unitary nature of the board.

4.5   The first is in reviewing the performance of the board and of the executive. Non-executive directors should address this aspect of their responsibilities carefully and should ensure that the chairman is aware of their views. If the chairman is also the chief executive, board members should look to a senior non-executive director, who might be the deputy chairman, as the person to whom they should address any concerns about the combined office of chairman/chief executive and its consequences for the effectiveness of the

---

1 See now s 309 of the Companies Act 1985

board. A number of companies have recognised that role and some have done so formally in their Articles.

4.6 The second is in taking the lead where potential conflicts of interest arise. An important aspect of effective corporate governance is the recognition that the specific interests of the executive management and the wider interests of the company may at times diverge, for example over takeovers, boardroom succession, or directors' pay. Independent non-executive directors, whose interests are less directly affected, are well-placed to help to resolve such situations.

The Chairman

4.7 The chairman's role in securing good corporate governance is crucial. Chairmen are primarily responsible for the working of the board, for its balance of membership subject to board and shareholders' approval, for ensuring that all relevant issues are on the agenda, and for ensuring that all directors, executive and non-executive alike, are enabled and encouraged to play their full part in its activities. Chairmen should be able to stand sufficiently back from the day-to-day running of the business to ensure that their boards are in full control of the company's affairs and alert to their obligations to their shareholders.

4.8 It is for chairmen to make certain that their non-executive directors receive timely, relevant information tailored to their needs, that they are properly briefed on the issues arising at board meetings, and that they make an effective contribution as board members in practice. It is equally for chairmen to ensure that executive directors look beyond their executive duties and accept their full share of the responsibilities of governance.

4.9 Given the importance and particular nature of the chairman's role, it should in principle be separate from that of the chief executive. If the two roles are combined in one person, it represents a considerable concentration of power. **We recommend**, therefore, that there should be a clearly accepted division of responsibilities at the head of a company, which will ensure a balance of power and authority, such that no one individual has unfettered powers of decision. Where the chairman is also the chief executive, it is essential that there should be a strong and independent element on the board.

Non-Executive Directors

4.10 The Committee believes that the calibre of the non-executive members of the board is of special importance in setting and maintaining standards of corporate governance. The emphasis in this report on the control function of non-executive directors is a consequence of our remit and should not in any way detract from the primary and positive contribution which they are expected to make, as equal board members, to the leadership of the company.

4.11 Non-executive directors should bring an independent judgement to bear on issues of strategy, performance, resources, including key appointments, and standards of conduct. **We recommend** that the calibre and number of non-executive directors on a board should be such that their views will carry significant weight in the board's decisions. To meet our recommendations on the composition of sub-committees of the board, all boards will require a minimum of three non-executive directors, one of whom may be the chairman of the company provided he or she is not also its executive head. Additionally, two of the three should be independent in the terms set out in the next paragraph.

4.12 An essential quality which non-executive directors should bring to the board's deliberations is that of independence of judgement. **We recommend** that the majority of non-executives on a board should be independent of the company. This means that apart from their directors' fees and shareholdings, they should be independent of management and free from any business or other relationship which could materially interfere with the exercise of their independent judgment. It is for the board to decide in particular cases whether this definition is met. Information about the relevant interests of directors should be disclosed in the Directors' Report.

4.13 On fees, there is a balance to be struck between recognising the value of the contribution made by non-executive directors and not undermining their independence. The demands which are now being made on conscientious non-executive directors are significant and their fees should reflect the time which they devote to the company's affairs. There is, therefore, a case for paying for additional responsibilities taken on, for example, by chairmen of board committees. In order to safeguard their independent position, we regard it as good practice for non-executive directors not to participate in share option schemes and for their service as non-executive directors not to be pensionable by the company.

4.14 Non-executive directors lack the inside knowledge of the company of the executive directors, but have the same right of access to information as they do. Their effectiveness turns to a considerable extent on the quality of the information which they receive and on the use which they make of it. Boards should regularly review the form and the extent of the information which is provided to all directors.

4.15 Given the importance of their distinctive contribution, non-executive directors should be selected with the same impartiality and care as senior executives. **We recommend** that their appointment should be a matter for the board as a whole and that there should be a formal selection process, which will reinforce the independence of non-executive directors and make it evident that they have been appointed on merit and not through any form of patronage. We regard it as good practice for a nomination committee (dealt with below) to carry out the selection process and to make proposals to the board.

4.16 Companies have to be able to bring about changes in the composition of their boards to maintain their vitality. Non-executive directors may lose something of their independent edge, if they remain on a board too long. Furthermore, the make-up of a board needs to change in line with new challenges. **We recommend**, therefore, that non-executive directors should be appointed for specified terms. Their Letter of Appointment should set out their duties, term of office, remuneration and its review. Reappointment should not be automatic, but a conscious decision by the board and the director concerned.

4.17 Our emphasis on the qualities to be looked for in non-executive directors, combined with the greater demands now being made on them, raises the question of whether the supply of non-executive directors will be adequate to meet the demand. When companies encourage their executive directors to accept appointment on the boards of other companies, the companies and the individuals concerned all gain. A policy of promoting this kind of appointment will increase the pool of potential non-executive directors, particularly if the divisional directors of larger companies are considered for non-executive posts, as well as their main board colleagues.

THE CODE OF BEST PRACTICE

1   The Board of Directors

1.1   The board should meet regularly, retain full and effective control over the company and monitor the executive management.

1.2   There should be a clearly accepted division of responsibilities at the head of a company, which will ensure a balance of power and authority, such that no one individual has unfettered powers of decision. Where the chairman is also the chief executive, it is essential that there should be a strong and independent element on the board, with a recognised senior member.

1.3   The board should include non-executive directors of sufficient calibre and number for their views to carry significant weight in the board's decisions.

1.4   The board should have a formal schedule of matters specifically reserved to it for decision to ensure that the direction and control of the company is firmly in its hands.

1.5   There should be an agreed procedure for directors in the furtherance of their duties to take independent professional advice if necessary, at the company's expense.

1.6   All directors should have access to the advice and services of the company secretary, who is responsible to the board for ensuring that board procedures are followed and that applicable rules and regulations are complied with. Any question of the removal of the company secretary should be a matter for the board as a whole.

2   Non-Executive Directors

2.1   Non-executive directors should bring an independent judgment to bear on issues of strategy, performance, resources, including key appointments, and standards of conduct.

2.2   The majority should be independent of management and free from any business or other relationship which could materially interfere with the exercise of their independent judgement, apart from their fees and shareholding. Their fees should reflect the time which they commit to the company.

2.3   Non-executive directors should be appointed for specified terms and reappointment should not be automatic.

2.4   Non-executive directors should be selected through a formal process and both this process and their appointment should be a matter for the board as a whole.

3   Executive Directors

3.1   Directors' service contracts should not exceed three years without shareholders' approval.

3.2   There should be full and clear disclosure of directors' total emoluments and those of the chairman and highest-paid UK director, including pension contributions and stock options. Separate figures should be given for salary

and performance-related elements and the basis on which performance is
measured should be explained.

3.3 Executive directors' pay should be subject to the recommendations of a
remuneration committee made up wholly or mainly of non-executive
directors.

4   Reporting and Controls

4.1 It is the board's duty to present a balanced and understandable assessment
of the company's position.

4.2 The board should ensure that an objective and professional relationship is
maintained with the auditors.

4.3 The board should establish an audit committee of at least three non-
executive directors with written terms of reference which deal clearly with
its authority and duties.

4.4 The directors should explain their responsibility for preparing the accounts
next to a statement by the auditors about their reporting responsibilities.

4.5 The directors should report on the effectiveness of the company's system of
internal control.

4.6 The directors should report that the business is a going concern, with
supporting assumptions or qualifications as necessary.

SOURCE 135
**Boyle, Company Law and the Non-Executive Director — the USA and Britain
Compared**
[1978] 27 ICLQ 487

. . . the American experience . . . consists largely of various studies of the way big
corporations are run at top level. The shortcomings that have been exposed have
had two general consequences. Firstly, various proposals have been made for
reform in the relationship between the executive and the non-executive element
on the board. The general effect of this would be to strengthen the independence and access to information of the non-executive members of the board, so
that they would be better equipped to monitor the performance of the
management. A second consequence, but one also considerably influenced by
the collapse of some major corporations in circumstances where grave abuses
were exposed, is that the organisation and composition of the board room has
also been changing — at least to the extent that it has become not only
fashionable but standard practice to set up 'audit committees' controlled by the
non-executive directors.

. . .

The non-executive director in Britain
A study of a sample of widely read books on 'management in big business'
(published or re-published in the 1960s) reveals a surprising omission (like the
dog that failed to bark in the night!). There is no discussion of the board of
directors or of the role of non-executive directors. Moreover, these terms do not
even rate an entry in any index. I am referring to books as profound at the level
of theory as Theo Nichols, *Ownership, Control and Ideology*, as slick and well turned
as Anthony Jay's *Management and Machiavelli*, and as well known as James
Burnham's *The Managerial Revolution*, or as informative as Christopher Tugend-
hat's, *The Multinationals*. There is, of course, much talk of managers and
management, shareholders and entrepreneurs, capitalists, corporate bureaucrats
and investors, but none, or very little, of the functioning of the boardroom and

the differing roles of executive and non-executive directors. These works are written *not* by lawyers and accountants, but by economists, politicians, specialists in management and social scientists interested in business organisations. Not for them the complexities of group structures or the legal niceties as to responsibility of the 'main board' of the holding company. Such questions are left to the company lawyer and the accountant as the technicians — or maintenance engineers — of the corporate machine. These writers have learnt Berle and Means' lesson (as to the divorce of ownership from control) all too well; for them only the managers count. Their autonomy is taken for granted.

A very different vision is that of Alex Rubner in *The Ensnared Shareholder*. He brings to bear an altogether sharper eye, if one with a narrower band of vision. His experience is that of a financial journalist and a business consultant. He holds aloft the banner of shareholders' rights in their most extensive form. Once you talk in any thoroughgoing way of shareholders' rights (or of ways of re-establishing the control of shareholders as the true proprietors of the corporate enterprise), then you can no longer ignore the function of the board (and of the roles of differing types of director). Rubner's index has, indeed, an entry for 'directors' with a long list of subheadings. Some of these turn out to be somewhat unflattering references to the non-executive director (eg 'guinea-pigs,' 'honorary,' and 'ornamental'). All these items refer to a passage (in a chapter entitled 'The Genus of Company Directors') under the heading 'a mixed bag'! Some of his remarks are worth quoting because, though undoubtedly jaundiced, harsh and rather sweeping, they reflect a dissatisfaction with the traditional type of non-executive director among many informed investors:

> 'When scrutinizing the composition of the boards one must perforce conclude that many of the members are not to be taken seriously. The appointment of 'guinea-pig directors' originated in Britain, where nobles, drawing fees in guineas, lent their names to corporations; in order to dupe the public, to whom the presence on the board of a member of the aristocracy symbolized business acumen and/or respectable management. The credulity of the public has declined, and aristocrats only have limited publicity value nowadays. Television personalities and sportsmen (and the present writer would add, some well known politicians) are now grilled for director-tasks, for which they often have no competence.'

Rubner later refers to other avenues to the boardroom of which he likewise disapproves:

> 'Some people are appointed to boards because they are being kicked upstairs for incompetence in the lower managerial echelons. As a sop to their pride deposed managers of companies, which have been taken over, are not infrequently offered a guinea-pig membership.'

He also gives examples of other types of board member, who while not purely ornamental, are not 'determining decision-makers.' For example, on the boards of many British insurance companies 'are representatives of some of their large clients — courtesy appointments. . . '. Banks are frequently appointed, he says, as directors 'to endow the client firms with prestige and to act as silent watch dogs; they are not meant to bark.' Again, 'when a group of independent companies have a community of interest — say, a steel supplier, a car manufacturer and a car hiring business — it is sometimes politic to have interlocking directors on the board.' Finally, he refers to executive directors or professional men who for reasons of expediency play a passive role:

'When a corporation is dominated by one person whose power is undisputed, departmental representatives are frequently invited to sit on the
board — they are expected to speak only on their subject and to listen to the
boss expounding policy. A similar arrangement prevails when specialists are
given directorships; this is so particularly with accountants and lawyers.'

This is of course a highly partial account even of what went on in the past. It
could never have been true of the best run companies in the hands of highly
skilled, professional management. A household name in manufacturing or
distribution hardly needs to impress the investing public with such tawdry
'ornaments', or to appoint compliant 'yes men.' However, there have been less
successful companies whose spectacular collapse in recent years bears witness to
the fact that Rubner's observations are not without foundation, even if they are
somewhat exaggerated. It is what has been disclosed (eg in the Department of
Trade reports on such cases) that has belatedly encouraged a movement to
strengthen the role of the non-executive director. One way of doing this is by
linking this function to that of the auditor through the mechanism of an audit
committee. As in the United States and Canada, this has been influenced by the
need to redress the balance of power which was seen to favour management at
the expense of the auditors. This will also be, ultimately, at the expense of the
shareholders and creditors and, indeed, of the company's employees, who would
be without a job in the event of financial disaster.

The arrival of the audit committee
We have seen that audit committees have now become standard practice in North
America for publicly held corporations. The New York Stock Exchange has made
it a requirement that all companies listed on the 'big board' must establish audit
committees by the deadline of 30 June 1978. The Securities Exchange Commission (which first mooted the idea of an audit committee nearly 40 years ago) set
its seal of approval on this development by describing it as 'an effective and
constructive response to the need for more effective corporate measures against
questionable payments.' However, those who advocate the audit would give it a
much broader and more positive aim than this. One should note that the New
York Stock Exchange is in any event riding with the tide. A recent survey has
shown that the proportion of American publicly held corporations having audit
committees grew from just over 70 per cent in 1973 to just over 90 per cent in
1976. In Canada the matter has not been left to trends in corporate fashion or
Stock Exchange requirements. In Ontario the Lawrence Committee proposed
the audit committee as a legal requirement for public companies as long ago as
1967. This became the law in Ontario in 1970, then spread to other provinces,
and is now part of the Canada Business Corporation Act 1975 (which governs
federally created corporations). In the Canadian legislation, though there are
differences of detail, all the legislation requires that the audit committee consist
of a *majority* of non-executive directors. It requires that such a committee must
review the annual financial statements before these are considered or approved
by the full board of directors. The New York Stock Exchange rules does not
define the audit committee's precise function — but it does demand that it be
composed of directors *wholly independent of management.*
    In both Canada and the United States the spur to these developments (as we
have seen) has been an atmosphere of growing public unrest brought about by
a number of spectacular business failures. In Canada, the collapse of the Atlantic
Acceptance Corporation led to a Royal Commission. When this eventually

reported in 1969 it proposed numerous changes in corporation law, one of which was to make audit committees compulsory. In the United States another influential development was the growing amount of successful and widely publicised litigation against auditors. This has been accompanied by a growing chorus of condemnation of the accounting profession's failure from (among other sources), the Securities Exchange Commission which was *itself* in turn the target of public strictures in the financial press and elsewhere.

The audit committee in Britain

It is obvious that similar disasters have overtaken great public companies in Britain as well. As Sir Brandon Rhys Williams put it, in attempting (unsuccessfully) to introduce the 'audit committee' at the Committee Stage of what is now the 1976 Companies Act:

> 'There is a serious weakness in British Company Law. The supervisory elements in the joint-stock company do not have enough strength. Therefore the curative function which should be carried out within the joint-stock company at the start of its troubles, if it is going into a bad patch, is largely ineffective. We find that companies allow problems to become worse over a period of years before recognising that they have a serious problem. When the shareholders, the public, the Government or management, recognise that there is a grave problem to be tackled, all too often it is too late. As a result there are dreadful disclosures in the newspapers and shocks for the economy when companies suddenly collapse like a tree which has rotted from the inside but given no sign on the outside that it is losing its health.'

> . . .

The audit committee is seen as having an obvious advantage for executive directors as well. It is said that it will mean that the whole audit function in a company will be given the increased attention it deserves. The audit committee can, it is said, direct the operation of the *internal* audit team, as well as monitoring the quality and competence of the company's own internal accounting and financial controls more closely than the main board could ever do. The argument supposes, plausibly enough, that the energy and expertise of most of the main board's executive directors are absorbed with other non-financial managerial tasks (eg production, marketing, planning future growth, handling industrial relations, supervising the recruitment and training of management personnel). So engaged are they in the myriad day-to-day problems within their sphere, that it may well be that many executive directors have little interest in the financial statements that come before the board; they are probably not trained in accounting and may fail to understand the finer points of accounting or other disclosure requirements. All this they leave to the finance director (or the chief internal accountant) and their team (unless, of course, their own operating budget is affected!).

The gain for the non-executive director is clearly that he is at least given a distinct and significant role to perform. The audit committee will clearly strengthen his position — particularly on boards dominated by one or two very powerful, not to say overbearing, individuals (*e.g.* the chairman and the managing director). Mr Simon Coles, Manager of the Research Department of Touche Ross & Co., after summarising the critical contents of certain DTI reports (on London and Counties Securities, Hartley Baird, the Lowson Group, and Roadships Ltd) makes this pertinent observation:

> 'These few examples illustrate common themes in the history of business failures and scandals — a company dominated by one individual; a rapid

growth outstripping a company's managerial and accounting resources; poor
internal controls; and auditors either too overworked or too weak to do an
adequate audit. Of course it can be argued that such examples are isolated
instances, and that the vast majority of directors and auditors do a perfectly
adequate and conscientious job, and there is no reason to think that this is
not so. But it is the exceptions that get the publicity, that catch the public's
eye and damage the credibility of published financial information.'

Clearly firms of accountants (and the shareholders to whom they must answer)
have as genuine a stake in the credibility of published financial information as do
the Treasury and the British public in the credibility of the currency.

PART III: COMPANY MANAGEMENT: THE BASICS

Management requires the taking of decisions, usually by organs and often in
meetings. For this purpose, the Companies Act 1985 and the company's
articles of association (usually Table A or very close to Table A) provide a wide
apparatus of administrative procedures and institutions. Sometimes the Act
defers to the Articles (see, eg ss 370(1), 372(2) and sometimes it overrides
them (ss 368(1), 369(1), 372(5)).

The general body of shareholders must hold certain meetings and may
hold others (ss 366–368, 371, Table A, regs 36–37). Notice of meetings must
be given (ss 369, 370(2), Table A, regs 38–39, 111–116), as must notice of
resolutions (ss 376–377, 379). A quorum must be present (s 370(4), Table A,
regs 40–41) and the shareholders' voting rights (ss 370(6), 374, regs 50,
54–59), rights to vote by proxy (s 372, regs 60–62) and right to call for a poll
(s 373, regs 46, 48–49, 51–52) are all specified. Indeed, these are all matters
of the contract between company and member and will in appropriate cases
be enforced (eg *Pender v Lushington*[1]. Adjournments of meeting are provided
for (s 379, regs 41, 45) as is the chairing of the meetings (s 370(5), regs 42, 43,
47, 50). Decisions are taken by way of resolution s 378, reg 53), which in
appropriate cases require publicity s 380). Minutes must be kept (s 382(1),
reg 100) and may be inspected (s 383, reg 100).

Aside from these general provisions, a number of sections provide for
meetings in specific circumstances and may prescribe additional or alternative procedures (eg reduction of capital, ss 135–138, or the making of
compromises or arrangements, ss 425–427).

Directors, too, are expected to hold meetings and to pass resolutions, but,
while Table A makes it clear that overall management is in the hands of the
directors (reg 70, see pp 410–425), it is assumed that they will regulate their
own affairs. The Act lays down no mandatory requirements for directors'
meetings and decisions and minimal provisions are laid down by the Table A
articles (regs 88–93).

Table A recognises that resolutions of the board may be agreed in writing
without the need for a meeting, but there must be unanimous agreement for
this absence of formality (Table A, reg 93). Aside from this informal control

---

1 (1877) 6 Ch D 70; 46 LJ Ch 317 (see p 314)

where the board is unanimous, the actions of the directors are subject to such contractual and institutional constraints and liberties as are laid down in the articles and outside agreements, as well as being subject to general common law principles such as adequate notice, proper information and so on. One general principle may be that agreed informality is one thing (permissible), while ignoring minorities is another (impermissible).

The materials in this section explore: (i) permissible informality through the unanimity of the shareholders (Sources 136–141); (ii) the adequacy of notice for forthcoming meetings (Sources 142–146); (iii) holding meetings where the quorum is unavailable (Sources 147–149); and (iv) the conduct of meetings where the facilities are inadequate (Source 150).

Unanimity of Shareholders and Procedural Informality

It is clear from the authorities in this section that the common law has favoured informality (ie deviation from the procedure laid down by the Companies Act 1985) where there has been unanimous agreement by the shareholders. This principle has now become formalised by the enactment of provisions which allow for the dispensing of certain hitherto sacred procedures (eg the holding of AGMs, see s 366A) and the passing of resolutions in writing rather than at meetings (see ss 379A and the sections therein referred to, and ss 381A–381C).

> **SOURCE 136**
> **Re Oxted Motor Co**
> [1921] 3 KB 32; 90 LJKB 1145

The only two directors and shareholders of the company resolved that the company, being unable to pay its debts, should be voluntarily wound up. The Companies Act prescribed an extraordinary resolution for this purpose (s 182 of the 1908 Act; now s 572(1)). The procedure laid down for the passing of an extraordinary resolution (s 69 of the 1908 Act; now s 378(1)) was not complied with.

> LUSH J: . . . There is no doubt that no notice had been given before the shareholders met intimating an intention to propose the resolution to wind up the company as an extraordinary resolution. It is contended that unless the notice contemplated by that section has been given a resolution is invalid as an extraordinary resolution; and it is said that notwithstanding that all the shareholders in the company were present and were dealing with a matter which was intra vires, and notwithstanding that there was no fraud, still the resolution was invalid on that account. In my opinion that contention is not well founded. It would be an extraordinary result it after all the shareholders of a company have been present at a meeting and passed a resolution to wind up the company, afterwards any one else could impeach that resolution on the ground that the shareholders had not had notice of intention to propose the resolution as an extraordinary resolution and that therefore the requirements of section 69 had not been complied with. In my opinion the shareholders are entitled to waive the formality of notice. *Re Express Engineering Works*[1] is an authority in support of the

1 [1920] 1 Ch 466; 89 LJ Ch 379

view that the statutory requirements as to notice can be waived. It is true that in that case the resolution was not a resolution to wind up the company, but a resolution to issue certain debentures. What happened there was this: all the shareholders of the company — there were only five — met as directors at a board meeting, and afterwards in their capacity of shareholders passed the resolution to issue the debentures without any notice having been given for the calling of a general meeting of the shareholders, as required by section 67 of the Companies (Consolidation) Act 1908. The company was afterwards wound up, and it was contended by the liquidator that as the requirements of the statute had not been complied with the resolution to issue the debentures was invalid. The Court of Appeal held, affirming Astbury J, that the requirements of the statute were intended for the protection of the shareholders, and that if the resolution was in a matter intra vires the members of the company, and there was no fraud, the shareholders were able to waive all formalities as regards notice and that the resolution that had been passed was just as valid as if there had been the requisite notice. Warrington LJ said: 'It happened that these five directors were the only shareholders of the company, and it is admitted that the five, acting together as shareholders, could have issued these debentures. As directors they could not, but as shareholders acting together they could have made the agreement in question. It was competent to them to waive all formalities as regards notice of meetings, etc, and to resolve themselves into a meeting of shareholders and unanimously pass the resolution in question.' If that is true in the case of a resolution to issue debentures it seems to me that it is equally true in the case of a resolution to wind up a company voluntarily, such as the resolution in the present case.

SOURCE 137
Parker & Cooper Limited *v* Reading
[1926] Ch 975; 96 LJ Ch 23

The plaintiff company (in liquidation) challenged a number of transactions, including the issue of a debenture to the defendant, on the grounds of procedural irregularity. It was accepted by the court that no meeting had been held to resolve in favour of issuing the debenture and that the company's seal had been improperly affixed to the document and that the people purporting to act as the directors of the company were, in fact, not so appointed.

ASTBURY J: . . . The debenture was issued with the assent of every shareholder, and the question is whether the plaintiffs, or rather the liquidator, ought to succeed in obtaining a declaration that the debenture and the resolution authorizing it were inoperative and invalid, so that the creditors may get the advantage of the defendant Reading's £1750 and deprive him of the security on which he made that advance. . . .

In *Re George Newman & Co*[1] the chairman of a company in which substantially all the shares were held by himself and his family, purchased on behalf of the company the right to a building agreement to be obtained from certain commissioners. The commissioners objected to the company as tenant, and proposed to substitute the chairman, who thereupon sold the benefit of the agreement to the company at an advance of £10,000 of which £7000 was spent upon commissions and otherwise in order to obtain the agreement from the commissioners, and £3000 was applied by the chairman to his own use. A further sum of £3500 was spent by the chairman out of the company's assets upon his

---

1 [1985] 1 Ch 674; 64 LJ Ch 407

private house. These payments were made out of money borrowed by the company for the purpose of its business; they were sanctioned by resolutions of the directors, 'and were approved of by all the shareholders.' The articles contained no power to make presents to directors. Upon a summons taken out by the liquidator against the chairman it was held that he was not liable for the £7000, but was liable for the £3000 and the £3500, first, because the shareholders for the time being had no power to authorize the making of presents to directors out of money borrowed by the company; secondly, because if there had been such power it could be exercised only at a 'general meeting.' Lindley LJ, delivering the judgment of Lord Halsbury, A.L. Smith LJ and himself, said: 'When the facts are understood both these sums were in truth presents by the directors out of the company's assets to [the chairman] with the consent of the other shareholders who were of age; and the question is whether these presents can be treated as valid against the liquidator on the winding up of the company, which is hopelessly insolvent and which was largely in debt when these presents were made. Vaughan Williams J has held that they are unimpeachable, and he referred to . . . *Re British Seamless Paper Box Co*[1] as supporting his view. But that case is very unlike this. The directors there had allotted shares to some of themselves as fully paid up. The shares were, in fact, allotted in consideration of some patents taken over by the company; and an agreement to issue the shares as paid up was registered. The transaction, therefore, was *intra vires*, and it was taken to be so both by counsel and by the Court. Further, the transaction was perfectly honest throughout, and it was sanctioned by a general meeting of the company, which then consisted of only the directors and one other person, who assented to what was done. More than a year afterwards shares were issued to other people, and, the company being ultimately wound up, the liquidator sought to recover the nominal value of the shares, treating them, in fact, as not paid up. The Court held that this could not be done, because the transaction (being *intra vires*) was honest and was sanctioned by all the members of the company at the time. But in this case the presents made by the directors to . . . their chairman, were made out of money borrowed by the company for the purposes of its business; and this money the directors had no right to apply in making presents to one of themselves. The transaction was a breach of trust by the whole of them; and even if all the shareholders could have sanctioned it, they never did so in such a way as to bind the company. It is true that this company was a small one, and is what is called a private company; but its corporate capacity cannot be ignored. Those who form such companies obtain great advantages, but accompanied by some disadvantages. A registered company cannot do anything which all its members think expedient, and which, apart from the law relating to incorporated companies, they might lawfully do. An incorporated company's assets are its property and not the property of the shareholders for the time being; and, if the directors misapply those assets by applying them to purposes for which they cannot be lawfully applied by the company itself, the company can make them liable for such misapplication as soon as any one properly sets the company in motion.' Later on he said: 'Directors have no right to be paid for their services, and cannot pay themselves or each other, or make presents to themselves out of the company's assets, unless authorized so to do by the instrument which regulates the company or by the shareholders at a properly convened meeting. The shareholders at a meeting duly convened for the purpose, can, if they think proper, remunerate directors for their trouble or

---

1 (1881) 17 Ch D 407, 50 LJ Ch 497

make presents to them for their services out of assets properly divisible amongst the shareholders themselves. . . . But to make presents . . . out of money borrowed by the company is a very different matter. Such money cannot be lawfully divided amongst the shareholders themselves, nor can it be given away by them for nothing to their directors so as to bind the company in its corporate capacity. But even if the shareholders in general meeting could have sanctioned the making of these presents, no general meeting to consider the subject was ever held. It may be true, and probably is true, that a meeting, if held, would have done anything which [the chairman] desired; but this is pure speculation, and the liquidator, as representing the company in its corporate capacity, is entitled to insist upon and to have the benefit of the fact that even if a general meeting could have sanctioned what was done, such sanction was never obtained. Individual assents given separately may preclude those who give them from complaining of what they have sanctioned; but for the purpose of binding a company in its corporate capacity individual assents given separately are not equivalent to the assent of a meeting. The company is entitled to the protection afforded by a duly convened meeting, and by a resolution properly considered and carried and duly recorded. The articles of this company, wide as they are, do not authorize such presents as those impeached by the liquidator.'

Now all Lindley LJ's statements, both with regard to *Re British Seamless Paper Box Co* and *Re George Newman & Co* then before him, are made with reference to the particular facts which he states. It is quite true that in reciting the facts of the former case he states that the transaction was sanctioned by a general meeting, but he does not in any way rely on that fact. The plaintiffs suggest that this was the whole point of his decision. But what he really means is that where a transaction is *intra vires* the company and honest the sanction of all the members of the company, however expressed, is sufficient to validate it, especially if it is a transaction entered into for the benefit of the company itself.

In *Re Express Engineering Works*,[1] a syndicate of five persons formed a private company, in which they were the sole shareholders, and sold to it for £15,000 in debentures of the company property which they had, a few days before, acquired for £7000. The contract for the sale and the issue of the debentures was carried out at a meeting of the five, who there and then appointed themselves directors. This meeting was described in the minutes as a board meeting. At a subsequent meeting the company's seal was affixed to the debentures. The articles provided that no director should vote in respect of any contract or arrangement in which he might be interested. On the liquidator claiming a declaration that the issue of the debentures was invalid, it was held, there being no suggestion of fraud, that the company was bound in a matter *intra vires* by the unanimous agreement of its members. Although the meeting was styled a directors' meeting, all the five shareholders were present, and they might well have turned it into a general meeting and transacted the same business. In these circumstances the issue of the debentures was not invalid. Lord Sterndale MR, who was referred to *Re George Newman & Co* in the same way that I have been, said: 'There were, however, two differences between that case and the present one. First, the transaction there was *ultra vires*, and, secondly, in that case there never was a meeting of the corporators. In the present case these five persons were all the corporators of the company and they did all meet, and did all agree that these debentures should be issued. Therefore it seems that the case came within the meaning of what was said by Lord Davey in *Salomon v Salomon & Co*:[2] "I think it an inevitable inference

---

1 [1920] 1 Ch 466; 89 LJ Ch 379
2 [1897] AC 22; 66 LJ Ch 35 (see p 91)

from the circumstances of the case that every member of the company assented to the purchase, and the company is bound in a matter intra vires by the unanimous agreement of its members."

. . .

It was said here that the meeting was a directors' meeting, but it might well be considered a general meeting of the company, for although it was referred to in the minutes as a board meeting, yet if the five persons present had said, "We will now constitute this a general meeting", it would have been within their powers to do so, and it appears to me that that was in fact what they did.' Warrington and Younger LJJ said the same thing.

All three judges no doubt refer to the fact that there had been a meeting. But I cannot think that they came to their decision because the five shareholders happened to meet together in one room or one place, as distinct from agreeing to the transaction inter se in such manner as they thought fit.

. . .

Now the view I take of both these decisions is that where the transaction is *intra vires* and honest, and especially if it is for the benefit of the company, it cannot be upset if the assent of all the corporators is given to it. I do not think it matters in the least whether that assent is given at different times or simultaneously.

SOURCE 138
Cane *v* Jones
[1980] 1 WLR 1451; [1981] 1 All ER 533

The articles of association of the company provided that the chairman should be elected by the directors, that he should have a casting vote at board meetings, that he should preside at general meetings, at which, also, he was to have a casting vote. The shareholding of the company was divided equally between two sides of a family (Harold Jones and his daughter, the plaintiff Gillian Cane on the one hand, Percy Jones and his children Ronald and Heather on the other). An agreement was entered into in 1967 between the two factions, in terms of which it was agreed that the chairman would no longer have a casting vote. What was the effect of this agreement?

MICHAEL WHEELER QC, sitting as a deputy judge: Now as to the arguments about the effect of the 1967 agreement. Mr Weaver[1] contends that it operated as an alteration of the articles on what was conveniently called in argument 'the *Duomatic* principle' based on *Re Duomatic Ltd*[2] . . . and the principle is, I think conveniently summarised in a short passage in the judgment in that case of Buckley J where he says:

'. . . I proceed upon the basis that where it can be shown that all shareholders who have a right to attend and vote at a general meeting of the company assent to some matter which a general meeting of the company could carry into effect, that assent is as binding as a resolution in general meeting would be.'

Applying that principle to the present case, Mr Weaver says that the agreement of all the shareholders embodied in the 1967 agreement had the effect, so far as requisite, of overriding the articles. In other words, it operated to deprive the chairman for the time being of the right to sue his casting vote, except, perhaps, in

1 Counsel for the plaintiff
2 [1969] 2 Ch 365; [1969] 1 All ER 161

so far as an independent chairman contemplated by clause (1) might need to do. I should add here that it is quite clear that Percy, who was actually chairman of the company at the time, was well aware of the terms of the 1967 agreement.

For the first and third defendants, Mr Potts[1] has two answers to Mr Weaver's argument. First, that on its true interpretation in relation to a special or extraordinary resolution the *Duomatic* principle only applies if there has been (i) a resolution, and (ii) a meeting; and that here he says, with some truth, there was neither a resolution nor a meeting of the four shareholders. Secondly, he stresses that the agreement does not in terms purport to alter the articles at all: it rests, he says, solely in contract and Gillian, not being a party, cannot take either the benefit or the burden of the agreement.

On the first of these two arguments, Mr Potts helpfully reminded me of the line of cases in which the effect of the unanimous consent of the corporators has been considered, starting with *Baroness Wenlock v River Dee Co.*[2] I do not propose to refer to all these cases in detail but, for the record, I will list them. The other cases are *Re George Newman & Co,*[3] *Re Express Engineering Works Ltd,*[4] *Re Oxted Motor Co Ltd,*[5] *Parker and Cooper Ltd v Reading,*[6] *Re Pearce Duff & Co Ltd,*[7] *Re Duomatic Ltd* to which I have already referred, and finally a decision of Slade J in *Re Moorgate Mercantile Holdings Ltd.*[8]

Mr Potts pointed out — correctly — that of these cases only three were concerned with special or extraordinary resolutions, namely, *Re Pearce Duff & Co Ltd*, *Re Moorgate Mercantile Holdings Ltd* (both of which were concerned with special resolutions) and *Re Oxted Motor Co Ltd*, which was concerned with an extraordinary resolution. All the rest were concerned with matters which, if capable of ratification at all, could have been validated by ordinary resolutions.

Mr Potts's starting point is section 10 of the Companies Act 1948, which provides for the alteration of articles by special resolution; and from that he goes on to section 141, mentioning subsections (1) and (2) and including the particular proviso, laying down how special and extraordinary resolutions are to be passed.

Here the judgment sets out ss 10 and 141(1) and (2) of the 1948 Act — see now ss 9 and 378(1), (2), (3).

Thus, says Mr Potts, you can only alter the articles by special resolution. That is his first argument. Secondly, that a special resolution must be passed at a meeting; thirdly, that here there was neither a resolution nor a meeting. *Re Pearce Duff & Co Ltd* he says, does not help Mr Weaver because in that case there had been a resolution and a meeting: and all that was later cured by the unanimous, but separate, consents of the shareholders was a defect in the consent to short notice under the proviso to section 141(2). *Re Moorgate Mercantile Holdings Ltd* was concerned with the extent to which, if at all, a resolution which is to be proposed as a special resolution could be amended at the meeting, and its relevance for present purposes lies solely in the fact that Slade J referred to *Re Pearce Duff & Co Ltd* and to *Re Duomatic Ltd* and also to section 143(4) of the Act to which I too shall refer in a moment, and stated that the proposition which he had laid down earlier in his judgment for the amendment of special resolutions might be

---

1 Counsel for the defendant
2 (1883) 36 Ch D 675
3 [1895] 1 Ch 674; 64 LJ Ch 407
4 [1920] 1 Ch 466; 89 LJ Ch 379
5 [1921] 3 KB 32; 90 LJKB 1145 (see p 381)
6 [1926] Ch 975; 96 LJ Ch 23 (see p 382)
7 [1960] 1 WLR 1014; [1960] 3 All ER 222
8 [1980] 1 WLR 227; [1980] 2 All ER 40

subject to modification where the members unanimously agreed to waive the requirements of notice.

Re Oxted Motor Co Ltd was a case of an extraordinary resolution for voluntary winding up. There were only two shareholders, who were also the two directors. They met and passed a resolution that the company be wound up and they signed a minute to that effect; but no notice to propose the resolution as an extraordinary resolution had ever been given. The Divisional Court of the Queen's Bench Division upheld the resolution on the ground that it was competent for the shareholders of the company acting together to waive the formalities required by what is now section 141(1) of the Act of 1948. In *Re Pearce Duff & Co Ltd*, which was a petition to confirm a reduction of capital, Buckley J, after referring to *Re Oxted Motor Co Ltd* and also to *Parker and Cooper Ltd v Reading* as showing that in certain circumstances all the corporators, if they agree, can bind the company, continued:

> 'Those cases, I think, relate to a rather different subject matter from that which I have to consider, because, as I see it, I have to consider not whether these resolutions bound the company as special resolutions but whether any shareholder could now say that the resolutions were not properly passed as valid special resolutions. Having regard to the 100 per cent consent which has been obtained to the resolutions being treated as valid and to the fact that the petition has been presented upon that footing, I do not think that this court ought to hear any of the shareholders to say that those resolutions were not validly passed. In those circumstances, I think, the case being a rather exceptional one, that I am entitled to regard this special resolution as sufficient basis for the reduction which the court is asked to confirm; and accordingly, subject to being satisfied on the evidence as to excess of wants, I will confirm the reduction.'

It is with very great diffidence that I venture to criticise the reasoning of so distinguished a judge in a short extempore judgment delivered, I notice, on the last Monday of the 1960 Trinity term. But with great respect to Buckley J the problem he was faced with surely was not whether any shareholder could *object* that the resolutions had not been passed as valid special resolutions, but whether as a matter of law they *had* been validly so passed: because unless he had before him a validly passed special resolution he had no jurisdiction to confirm the desired reduction of capital: see section 66(2) and section 67(1) of the Act of 1948.[1] I do not think, therefore, that I can regard the decision in *Re Pearce Duff & Co Ltd* as concluding the point which I have to consider.

The first of Mr Potts's two arguments — namely that there must be a 'resolution' and a 'meeting' — does not appear to have been raised in any of the three reported cases which were concerned with special or extraordinary resolutions. But it is not an argument to which I would readily accede because in my judgment it would create a wholly artificial and unnecessary distinction between those powers which can, and those which cannot, be validly exercised by all the corporators acting together.

For my part I venture to differ from Mr Potts on the first limb of his argument, namely that articles can *only* be altered by special resolution. In my judgment, section 10 of the Act is merely laying down a procedure whereby *some only* of the shareholders can validly alter the articles: and if, as I believe to be the case, it is a basic principle of company law that all the corporators, acting together, can do

---

1 Now ss 135(3), 136(1)

anything which is intra vires the company, then I see nothing in section 10 to undermine this principle. I accept that the principle requires all the corporators to 'act together': but with regard to this I respectfully adopt what Astbury J said in *Parker and Cooper Ltd v Reading*:

> 'Now the view I take of both these decisions [those were *Re Express Engineering Works Ltd* and *Re George Newman & Co*] is that where the transaction is intra vires and honest, and especially if it is for the benefit of the company, it cannot be upset if the assent of all the corporators is given to it. I do not think it matters in the least whether that assent is given at different times or simultaneously.'

> . . .

I should add that the evidence in the case before me is that the 1967 agreement was signed by 'the two sides,' if I may call them that, separately, and that they did not meet together, however informally, for the purpose of signing the document. But it is clear beyond doubt that the agreement did represent a meeting of minds which is, after all, the essence of a meeting and the passing of a resolution.

Some light is also, I think, thrown on the problem by section 143(4) of the Act of 1948.[1] Section 143[2] deals with the forwarding to the Registrar of Companies of copies of every resolution or agreement to which the section applies:

> . . .

Paragraph (c) thus appears to recognise that you can have a resolution, at least, which has been agreed to by all the members and is as effective as a special or extraordinary resolution would have been: but, as Mr Potts was quick to point out, paragraph (c) says nothing about 'agreements' in contrast to paragraph (d) which refers to resolutions or agreements which have been agreed to by all the members of some class of shareholders.

Section 380(4) of the 1985 Act, which replaces s 143(4) of the 1948 Act, does, in fact, in paragraph (c) refer to 'resolutions or agreements'.

> . . .

> I cannot regard this difference in drafting between paragraphs (c) and (d) of section 143(4) as fatal to the basic argument. It may be, as Mr Weaver suggested, that a document which is framed as an agreement can be treated as a 'resolution' for the purposes of paragraph (c). I should add in passing that a copy of the 1967 agreement was never, as far as I am aware, sent to the Registrar of Companies for registration. It may be that there is a gap in the registration requirements of section 143. But be that as it may, the fact that the 1967 agreement was drafted as an agreement and not as a resolution, and that the four signatories did not sign in each other's presence does not in my view prevent that agreement overriding pro tanto — and so far as necessary — the articles of the company; in my judgment Mr Potts's first argument fails and unless he can show that the 1967 agreement has been superseded, the chairman of the company has no casting vote at board or general meetings.

> In view of my conclusion on Mr Potts's first argument, it is not strictly necessary to consider his second argument that the 1967 agreement does not purport to alter the articles and that its force and effect rest solely in contract so as to preclude Gillian from relying upon it since she did not sign it.

The informality principality in general and its application to the case where

---

1 Now s 380(4)
2 Now s 380

a special resolution is required, in particular, have been subject to academic analysis and criticism. Consider the following extracts:

SOURCE 139
Report of the Company Law Committee ('Jenkins Report')
(Cmnd 1749, 1962)

Resolutions
460. The Act requires some powers of a company to be exercised 'by the company in general meeting' (eg alteration of share capital, section 61), some by special resolution (eg alteration of articles, section 10) and others by ordinary resolution (eg the removal of a director, section 184). We do not support the view that the Act should be amended to provide generally for voting on such resolutions by postal ballot. Where there is any possibility of there being a difference of opinion between members about such matters we think there should be a meeting at which it may be discussed. Where the members who are entitled to vote are unanimous, however, we see no need for a meeting. Section 143(4) appears to recognise that a resolution agreed to by all the members may be equivalent to a special resolution although the definition of special resolution in section 141 seems to require it to be passed at a general meeting. We think that the position should be clarified and that there should be an express provision in the Act that a resolution in writing signed by or on behalf of all those who would have been entitled to vote upon it at a general meeting shall be equivalent to a special or ordinary resolution (as the case may require) passed by the appropriate majority at a general meeting convened by the appropriate notice.
461. There is wide agreement that the Act should no longer provide for extraordinary resolutions and we think that a special resolution should be required in all those cases in which an extraordinary resolution is now required under the Act.

SOURCE 140
Beuthin, The Principle of Unanimous Consent
[1974] 91 South African Law Journal 2, pp 8–13

The Privy Council in *EBM Co Ltd v Dominion Bank*[1] deliberately avoided expressing any view as to the correctness of the decision in *Parker & Cooper Ltd*[2] or as to the validity of the general principle itself, while in 1962 the Jenkins Company Law Committee recommended that the prevailing uncertainty should be clarified by legislation. It does not, perhaps, seem unreasonable to permit existing members by their unanimous assent to put themselves in a position where they will be precluded 'from complaining of what they have sanctioned', but, as G K Morse points out,[3] to permit the corporate will to be formulated and expressed by such an informal resolution will not only deprive the members of the undoubted advantages of having a particular motion ventilated in open discussion and debate, but it will also open the door to possible intrigue and improper pressure. In the absence of a carefully framed notice of meeting and of any assembly of the shareholders, there may be a great temptation to put the motion informally to individual members with a slightly different emphasis, or in a slightly different form, perhaps also advancing somewhat different reasons, in

1 [1937] 3 All ER 555
2 [1926] Ch 975; 96 LJ Ch 23 (see p 382)
3 'Formality in Company Affairs' (1971) 121 NLJ 379, 380

order that the motion may be presented to each individual shareholder in the manner best designed to secure his approval. It would also make it possible for a 'dictator' director to exert the maximum pressure on each member in private with the object of extracting an assent from him at a time when he might be unable to gain courage and determination from the sympathy for his point of view that he might have found in a general meeting. Experience has shown that when members of a company are actually gathered in general meeting, a motion which may at first appear uncontroversial and destined to be approved *nem con* will often be lost after a debate initiated by the most tentative inquiry 'on a point of information, Mr Chairman'.

However, while there may be no deep-rooted objection to allowing the existing members to avoid the procedural rules and to bind themselves merely by their unanimous assent, it does not follow that it is equally unobjectionable to permit them in the same manner to formulate and express the corporate will so as to bind also those members of the public who become members only after the unanimous assent has been obtained. In this regard it seems important to distinguish between those cases in which the juristic acts assented to unanimously by the members have, as it were, already run their full course, and those where the real effects of what was assented to continue to live on, operating also in the future to the possible prejudice of others — and particularly new members and existing preference shareholders. In drawing this distinction, Morse has pointed out that prior to the decision of Buckley J in *Re Duomatic Ltd*[1] the cases in which the principle had been upheld had generally been cases in which the allegedly invalid act had already been carried through to completion — the money had been paid out, or the shares or debentures had been issued. In such cases, where the only persons affected by the juristic act in question have consented, and where what has been done is reflected in the accounting records, it may well be unnecessary and unduly legalistic to insist upon adherence to the prescribed formalities. But in the other type of case, if there has been no notice of meeting, or any record of any proceedings or minute recording the assent, and not even a written resolution in existence, this is likely to make it very difficult for any new member to become aware even of the fact that something had previously been assented to. Furthermore, a preferent shareholder who may have no right to receive notice of or to attend and vote at a general meeting will find that an informal unanimous assent can effectively deprive him of yet another possible opportunity of protecting his interests, viz the chance of discovering that a meeting is being convened. If he were to discover that a meeting was being convened, it might be possible for him to arrange for his point of view to be brought to the attention of the assembled members, or perhaps to discover something about the company's affairs which might assist him in deciding whether to hold on to his shares or to dispose of them. In this latter type of case the court should be slow to recognize the unanimous assent as a valid act of the company, for this may be to disregard the real, if not immediately obvious, interests of others which the formalities were also designed to protect.

In those cases in which the law will permit the principle to operate, the question whether a member who has once given his assent is able to retract would seem to depend upon the rationale of the principle. There has been some suggestion that the principle is based upon estoppel, and on this basis it may be possible for any member to withdraw his assent at any time before an act is done in reliance upon the unanimous assent. However, the true rationale is probably

---

1 [1969] 2 Ch 365; [1969] 1 All ER 161

not that of estoppel but simply that unanimous assent is only another method of passing a valid resolution of the company — one which does not require compliance with the procedure prescribed in the articles of association. If this is so, then it is suggested that the oral assent or vote is validly cast once it has been communicated to the person charged with taking the assents and that it cannot thereafter be withdrawn. Should any point of disagreement arise, for instance, as to the precise wording of the motion, it should be noticed that the chairman will not be entitled to exercise the discretion which he will generally have in the case of a formal resolution. In the case of the signing of a written resolution it is suggested that the vote is irrevocably cast once the signature has been appended and the written document returned to the officer from whom it was received.

The remaining question to be considered is whether the principle of unanimous assent can ever have any application in the case of special resolutions. In England the question is probably still an open one. So far as *Re Oxted Motor Co Ltd*[1] is concerned, the judgment of the court is simply that the resolution which had been passed was an extraordinary resolution in spite of the fact that no proper notice of the meeting had been given. A meeting of shareholders had in fact been held, and the resolution still required to be registered as such. Article 5 in Table A Part II of the First Schedule of the English Companies Act[2] seems to imply some legislative approval of at least a written unanimous assent, but the article is expressly made '[s]ubject to the provisions of the Act', and, bearing in mind the provisions of the English section 141(2),[3] which suggest that a special resolution may be passed only at a meeting, this may have the effect of conferring a power to pass informally only ordinary resolutions. Furthermore, although it may also just be possible to read into the provisions of section 143(4)(c)[4] the implication that special resolutions, too, should be exercisable by way of an informal unanimous assent of all the members, it does not seem likely that the legislature would have been content simply to leave this matter to a somewhat doubtful implication — particularly as it had gone to the lengths in the proviso to section 141(2) of expressly prescribing certain circumstances in which one of the formalities for the passing of a special resolution could be dispensed with. Finally, it may be noted that the provisions of sub-section (3) of section 9[5] of the European Communities Act do not take the matter much further. In requiring the registrar to give 'official notification' by publication in the *Gazette* of the issue or receipt by him of certain documents, the subsection refers, *inter alia*, simply to 'any document making or evidencing an alteration in the memorandum or articles of association of a company'.

SOURCE 141
Sealy (Comment on Cane *v* Jones[6])
[1981] CLJ 224, 226

The possibility that a company's articles can be altered without proper formalities, and without registration under section 143 of the Companies Act 1948, although supported by the cases and tacitly accepted by section 143(4),[7] must give rise to some disquiet. Suppose that one of the parties to the 1967 agreement

1 [1921] 3 KB 32; 90 LJKB 1145 (see p 381)
2 See now reg 53 of the Companies (Tables A–F) Regulations 1985
3 See now s 378(2) of the Companies Act 1985
4 See now s 380(4)(c) of the Companies Act 1985
5 See now s 711 of the Companies Act 1985
6 [1980] 1 WLR 1451; [1981] 1 All ER 533 (see p 385)
7 See now s 711 of the Companies Act 1985

had transferred his shares to a stranger who took without notice of that agreement, and that the remaining shareholders had then sought to enforce the agreement *against* him. He surely ought not to be bound by so covert a constitutional change. Enforcement by the *company* would now be precluded by the terms of section 9(4)[1] of the European Communities Act 1972, and probably in any case by estoppel; but neither argument would apply to the other shareholders as individuals, whom section 9(4), with the inept drafting so characteristic of that whole section, fails to mention. One wonders whether the indulgence understandably shown by the court to Mrs Cane in this case would be matched in a future case by a similar willingness to impose the burden of an undisclosed alteration of articles on an unsuspecting defendant?

Adequacy of Notice for Forthcoming Meetings

Directors' Meetings

Directors may regulate their own proceedings (ie, as to the number and frequency of meetings); any director may insist on the holding of a meeting and notice does not need to be given to any director who is absent from the UK. Questions will be decided by a majority, with the chairman having a second or casting vote (Table A, reg 88).

> **SOURCE 142**
> **La Compagnie De Mayville *v* Whitley**
> [1896] 1 Ch 788

A director, S, who did not attend a meeting of the board, issued a writ against the other directors in the name of the company asking for a declaration that resolutions passed at that meeting were void because the notice summoning that meeting failed to state the business to be transacted at it.

> LINDLEY LJ: This case involves one question which is of great importance to companies. The rest of the points are comparatively trifling. The great point is whether, when a directors' meeting is to be held, it is necessary to give a notice not only of the meeting, but of the business to be transacted at the meeting. I am not prepared to say as a matter of law that it is necessary. As a matter of prudence it is very often done, and it is a very wise thing to do it; but it strikes me, as it struck Lord Tenterden in *R v Pulsford*,[2] that there is an immense difference between meetings of shareholders or corporators and meetings of those whose business it is to attend to the transaction of the affairs of the company or corporation. It is not uncommon for directors conducting a company's business to meet on stated days without any previous notice being given either of the day or of what they are going to do. Being paid for their service — as they generally are, and as is the case in this company — it is their duty to go when there is any business to be done, and to attend to that business whatever it is; and I cannot now say for the first time that as a matter of law the business conducted at a directors' meeting is invalid if the directors have had no notice of the kind of business which is to come before them. Such a rule would be extremely embarrassing in the transaction of the business of companies.
>
> Lord Tenterden had the very point before him in regard to municipal

---

1 See now s 42 of the Companies Act 1985
2 8 B & C 350; 108 ER 1073

corporations in *R v Pulsford*. I need not refer to the facts, but the point was taken there that a notice was not given of the business to be transacted at a meeting of the managing body. Lord Tenterden says: 'In *R v Hill*[1] the election was by the body at large, which is a very different thing.' Then he goes on, a little lower down: 'The present is the case of an election by a select body, and we are of opinion that it was not necessary in the notice to them to state the purpose of the meeting. But although we are of that opinion in this case, we avoid giving any opinion as to an election by a corporate body at large. The difference between them is this: the select body are appointed to be aiding and assisting the mayor on all occasions concerning the city, when required so to do. It is, therefore, their duty to attend whenever the mayor gives them reasonable notice that their attendance is required; and we think they are not at liberty to say that they abstained from attending because they did not know the specific purpose for which the meeting was about to be holden. If, indeed, it had appeared to be usual in this borough to give a more precise notice, the case would have been very different; but nothing of that kind is suggested.' He decided, therefore, that the notice, though not stating the object of the meeting, was sufficient. The only other case, so far as I know, in which this point has ever been brought forward or considered, is the case of *Re Homer District Consolidated Gold Mines*.[2] The judgment of North J in that case no doubt contains a passage which goes to shew that he thought it was at all events an important point that the purpose for which the directors' meeting there was called was not stated; but when the case is examined you find that, whatever may be said about the necessity for the giving of any such notice, the decision is absolutely right. The case was this: Some shares had been applied for, and at a board meeting it was resolved that no allotment should be made until at least 14,000 preferences shares should have been applied for by approved applicants. Some time after this, some applications for shares having been made, two directors held a meeting with very short notice, the notices for a meeting at 2 pm not being posted till 11 am on the same day — a meeting held very irregularly in many respects — at which they rescind that resolution and proceed to allot shares. The persons to whom those shares are allotted come and say, 'It is a trick, and we require that allotment to be cancelled'; and it was cancelled accordingly. It was an attempt to capture shareholders — a trick which no judge could possibly countenance. In the course of dealing with that trick, North J says, amongst other things, 'What is more, it' (that is, the notice convening that meeting of the board) 'was expressed in such a way (I cannot help thinking intentionally so expressed) as not to give Witt and Simpson notice of what was to be done. On that notice at two o'clock, the two directors present knowing that one of the other two summoned could not be present till three, and not knowing whether the other could come, proceeded at once to rescind a resolution passed by the board two weeks before. In my opinion that was about as irregular as anything could be.' That the notice did not mention the business is only treated as one of the circumstances unfavourable to the validity of the resolutions, and we are asked to say now, for the first time as a matter of law, that a notice to the directors of a directors' meeting must state what the business is if it is anything more than routine business. If we did so, I think we should not be laying down sound law. Such a rule is not required for the honest transaction of business, and would be most disastrous.

---

1 [1825] 4 B & C 426; 107 ER 1118

2 (1888) 39 Ch D 546; 58 LJ Ch 134

SOURCE 143
Young *v* Ladies' Imperial Club Limited
[1920] 2 KB 523; 89 LJKB 563

The plaintiff was applying for an injunction to prevent the defendant club from expelling her in terms of a resolution passed to that effect by the executive committee. The grounds for the plaintiff's action were, first that one member of the executive committee had not been given notice of the meeting at which the motion for expulsion was discussed and voted upon, and, secondly, that the notice sent to all other members, gave insufficient information as to the proposed business.

> LORD STERNDALE MR: . . . The only point that we have to decide is whether the meeting of the executive committee, at which the lady's name was erased from the membership of the club, was a properly constituted meeting of the executive committee. . . .
>
> I cannot entertain any doubt that, with certain very limited exceptions where a special meeting of a committee or any other body has to be specially convened for a particular purpose, every member of that body ought to have notice of and a summons to the meeting. It seems to me that is quite clearly laid down in *Smyth v Darley*[1] where Lord Campbell says: 'The election' — and you may read 'expulsion' for 'election'; exactly the same principle applies — 'being by a definite body on a day of which, till summons, the electors had no notice, they were all entitled to be specially summoned, and, if there was any omission to summon any of them, unless they all happened to be present, or unless those not summoned were beyond summoning distance — as, for instance, abroad — there could not be a good electoral assembly.' And in the same way in *Portuguese Consolidated Copper Mines*[2] Lord Esher says this: 'I will assume that every point taken by Mr Rigby and Mr Buckley ought to be decided in their favour except one. That one is this, that according to their own argument it is necessary that all the directors should have had notice of the meeting of the 24th.' That was on general principles I think, and not any special provision in the articles that notice should be sent to every member. 'If they had not, then the meeting of the 24th was no valid meeting, and being an invalid meeting could not adjourn itself to the 26th.' Therefore as to the general principle, I think, there can be no question. If the absent member of the body is at such a distance that it is physically impossible for him to attend in obedience to a summons, then the convener of the meeting is excused from sending the notice to that member, and without any such notice to him the meeting of the body will be properly convened. I incline to think, but I do not express any very definite opinion, that the same exception would probably be held good where it was undoubted that a member of the body was so dangerously ill that it was impossible for him to be moved, even although he might not be at a distance; and in *Re Portuguese Consolidated Copper Mines* it is also, I think, decided that a person who ought to be summoned cannot dispense the convener of the meeting from summoning him by saying 'I shall not be able to come; you need not summon me.'
>
> . . .
>
> The circumstances to which that principle has to be applied in this case are these. The executive committee consisted of fourteen members, including the chairman, the vice-chairman, and twelve other members, and one of those

---

1 2 HLC 789; 9 ER 1293
2 (1889) 42 Ch D 160; 58 LJ Ch 813

members was the Duchess of Abercorn. It is undoubted that the Duchess of Abercorn was not summoned; she had no notice sent to her of the meeting. It is equally undoubted that the Duches of Abercorn was a member of the executive committee, and that has not been denied throughout the case. But the reason that was given for not summoning her was that she was really only a nominal member of the executive committee, and would not have attended if she had been summoned, and therefore it was unnecessary to send her notice. Even if it were proved that she would not have attended I should be of opinion that that would not have excused the convener of the meeting from summoning her, but in my opinion nothing of the kind is proved.

. . . To my mind it is not shown that she would never have attended, but, whether she would or whether she would not, in my opinion there is no ground whatever for not giving her the opportunity, and therefore no excuse for not summoning her.

If that be so this meeting is bad. It was an invalid meeting, quite incapable of acting under rule 42.

It was argued that to hold this would be dangerous because it might interfere with the internal management of clubs. In my opinion it would be far more dangerous to hold otherwise, because that would be leaving it to the discretion of the secretary or some other person to omit to summon people, because the secretary or the chairman of the committee thought they would not attend. That, to my mind, would be very dangerous indeed. But I do not think it matters really one way or the other, it is a pure point of law, and, in my opinion, it ought to be decided in the appellant's favour.

. . .

There is another point — namely, that the notice of the business to be transacted at the meeting was not sufficient. The notice was, 'To report on and discuss the matters concerning Mrs Young and Mrs Lawrence,' and therefore there is no reference to action under rule 42, and no reference to any possibility of a request to a member to resign, or the expulsion of a member.

. . . I quite agree with what has been said to the effect that one ought not to examine this agenda and these notices of meetings too particularly and too meticulously; if in substance they convey to the members of the committee what is going to be done, that is sufficient, although one might have thought it might have been better done. My inclination is to say that this is not sufficient, but I do not think it is necessary to decide it, because the meeting was in my opinion incapable of acting on the other ground which I have stated. But I have no doubt of this, that the defendants would be well advised in summoning meetings of this kind to make their notices more particular, and to give better notice to the members summoned of the kind of business that is going to be transacted. I can see no difficulty in framing such a notice without hurting anybody's feelings.

Shareholders' meetings

The requirement that notice of meetings and resolutions be given to all permitted to attend the meeting is statutory (ss 369, 370(2), 376–377, 379) and is usually repeated in the articles (regs 38–39, 111). Aside from this, there is the question how specific the notice has to be. There are two important principles, first that the notice should give sufficient description of the business of the meeting so as to enable the recipients to decide whether or not it is necessary to attend, and secondly, that where the directors are personally interested in the business such that a particular decision will be of benefit to them, this must be clearly disclosed. This latter principle derives from the common law and forms part of the wider duty of the directors to disclose their interest to the company. It has also been made statutory in certain events (ss 314(2), 426(2)).

SOURCE 144
Tiessen *v* Henderson
[1899] 1 Ch 861; 68 LJ Ch 353

The plaintiff was applying for an injunction to restrain the company from acting on certain resolutions approving a scheme for the reconstruction of the company. The application was based on the failure of the notice summoning the meeting to disclose the fact that certain of the directors stood to benefit substantially from the approval of the scheme.

KEKEWICH J: . . . Now, Mr Henderson was a very large shareholder in the Henderson Company, and he was likely to receive considerable benefit from the adoption of this scheme. It is said that it was well known, at any rate to a large number of the shareholders, that he occupied that position; and I think it must be taken to have been well known that the Henderson Company was largely interested in the reconstruction of the company — largely interested, that is to say, in the company, reconstructed or not reconstructed. I am not disposed, however, to attach much weight to the position of Mr Henderson. I think it would have been better, and made the matter clearer, if that position had been a little dwelt upon in the circular; but I do not think that point alone would be sufficient to justify me in saying that this circular was not thoroughly explicit so as to put the matter fairly before the shareholders.

But two other directors were distinctly interested. Mr Van Ryn had agreed to underwrite a certain number of the debentures. I will take it from his own affidavit. He says: 'I agreed to underwrite or guarantee the subscription of a portion of the debentures, and was to receive as commission or remuneration for so doing a call on certain shares of the new company in the same proportion as others who were willing to underwrite the debentures.' It seems that later he withdrew that offer, and there was no binding contract; but when the notice was issued he had made what he and ordinary persons call an agreement, although it may not be enforceable in a court of law, to underwrite the debentures and to receive a commission for the same, and that fact was not disclosed. Mr Schlesinger, another director, was still more largely interested, practically in the same way. He was a stockbroker, with clients largely interested in this company, and he busied himself on behalf of his clients. He says that he was to receive no benefit from it himself — that he only did it on behalf of his clients. It seems to me impossible to go into that. The man who really entered into the agreement by which he was to receive a large benefit, namely, a call on shares to the extent of 12,500, a fourth of the 50,000, was Mr Schlesinger, and how he was to distribute them among other people seems to me to be perfectly immaterial. He was the only man known to the directors — the only man known to those who were framing this reconstruction scheme. Who his clients were was not stated, and was not inquired into by any one. That is a fact which is left out again; and, therefore, the shareholder who receives this circular is told, no doubt, that there is to be a call on 50,000 shares for the managers and the issuing company, and another 50,000 for the guarantors; but he is not told that some of his own directors, the persons whom he is trusting to put the scheme before the meeting, are themselves largely interested in that scheme, and that they are to have a portion of the call on those shares. The shareholder must be regarded as a man of ordinary prudence. Treating it as a commercial matter, he has invested his money in this company; the company is in difficulties, and reconstruction is necessary, and what he has to consider when the notice and circular come to him is whether, on the whole, this is the best thing that can be done. He is either to vote himself in person or by proxy, or he is to leave it to the majority to decide. It seems to me impossible to exclude from the matters which he ought, as a prudent man, to consider, the question whether some of this directors should be remunerated by means of this call on shares. It is really the same thing which occurred in *Kaye v Croydon Tramways Co.*[1] There is a passage in Rigby LJ's judgment which I read as expressing in his own language his agreement with the language of the Master of the Rolls. 'I quite agree with what the Master of the Rolls has said, that no man of business would ever come to the conclusion what when a meeting was summoned for the purpose of sanctioning a sale from the company to a purchaser it was also intended at that meeting to do so different a thing as to sanction the payment of part of the consideration that was to proceed from the purchaser, not to the company, but to the directors of the company.' It seems to me that with a very slight change those words may be applied to this case. Why should any shareholder reading this circular think for a moment that two of his directors (I am excluding Mr Henderson) were to have a large proportion of the 50,000 shares on which there was to be a call in favour of the guarantors? He is told that the guarantors were the Henderson Company. He is not told that the guarantors were to be some of his own directors, and that they were to derive a personal benefit. Of course I am told, and with perfect honesty no doubt, that these gentlemen only wished to do the best for the company, that they were largely interested in it, and they thought it the best thing to do. True; but they did so for a commission, or for remuneration; and they were not prepared to do the best they could without being paid for it — neither Mr Schlesinger nor Mr Van Ryn; and those facts were not stated in the circular. If a meeting properly convened, and properly instructed as to the purpose for which it is convened, chooses to assent to this, there is no reason why it should not do so; but I think it ought to have the opportunity of considering the point. The man I am protecting is not the dissentient, but the absent shareholder — the man who is absent because, having received and with more or less care looked at this circular, he comes to the conclusion that on the whole he will not oppose the scheme, but leave it to the majority. I cannot tell whether he would have left it to the majority of the meeting to decide if he had known the real facts. He did not know the real facts; and, therefore, I think the resolution is not binding upon him.

SOURCE 145
Young *v* South African and Australian Exploration and Development Syndicate
[1896] 2 Ch 268; 65 LJ Ch 683

The meeting was called to approve the adoption of new articles of association. The notice convening the meeting referred to a place where the proposed articles could be read. One of the provisions gave substantially increased remuneration to the directors. At the meeting the new articles were not distributed or read out and the approving resolution was passed by nine votes of the twelve present. These were proceedings to restrain the company from calling a confirmatory meeting or from acting on the resolution.

---

1 [1898] 1 Ch 358, 67 LJ Ch 222

KEKEWICH J: . . . There was a notice of a special general meeting, and there was thereby given, in general terms, notice of the character of the business to be submitted to it. That seems to be sufficient within article 35 of Table A; and besides that, it was apparent on the face of the notice that the intention was to substitute new regulations, and the members of the company were told that they were at liberty to inspect a copy of the proposed regulations at the office of the solicitors of the company, whose address was given.

Now it is common knowledge that members of a company do not usually attend either ordinary or special meetings: they take no particular interest in them; and, as long as they have any confidence in the executive at all, they leave the management in the hands of the executive, and are quite prepared to support any reasonable proposal which the executive may make. So that often it would really be a waste of time and incurring useless expense to send to each shareholder a copy for himself of proposed new regulations or to read them through at a meeting. Perhaps it is not assuming too much to say that, as to some of the shareholders in this company, if they had read the proposed new regulations they would not have understood them or have discovered that they altered the remuneration of directors, or to what they pointed. I am satisfied myself that practically no real good would have been gained by sending the members notice of every one of the new regulations in that way. I think they had sufficient notice in a general way to bind them; and that is borne out by what happened at the meeting, for it is clear on the evidence that some of the members who attended had looked at the regulations. Questions were asked about them, and one amendment at all events with regard to the voting power was proposed and carried, and the proposed regulations were altered accordingly.

I think, therefore, that sufficient notice was given to satisfy the law, though it would have been better to have given the shareholders a short explanatory statement of what was proposed.

In fact the injunction was granted because one of the nine assenting voters was not registered.

SOURCE 146
Baillie _v_ Oriental Telephone and Electric Company Limited
[1915] 1 Ch 503; 84 LJ Ch 409

The meeting was called to approve modifications to the articles of a subsidiary company ('the Egyptian company') of the defendant, in terms of which the directors of the Egyptian company (also of the defendant) were given authorisation for greatly increased remuneration. In addition, shareholders were asked to approve the insertion of a regulation in the defendant's articles rendering any director free from having to account for any benefit derived from his position as a defendant. The chairman refused to answer any questions designed to elicit the precise nature of the directors' benefits received as directors of the Egyptian company. The resolutions were passed with the assistance of proxy votes. The plaintiff sued to restrain the directors from acting on the resolutions and for an account for all sums received as directors of the Egyptian company. At first instance, Astbury J refused the injunction on the authority of *Normandy v Ind Coope & Co.*[1] The plaintiff appealed to the Court of Appeal, who upheld the appeal.

> LORD COZENS-HARDY MR: . . . It is startling to be told that in this company a sum of upwards of £40,000 — I think it is £44,000 — has been received by these directors in respect of the Egyptian Company, and put into their pockets; and there is no hint of that in this circular. It suggests that these directors got very small remuneration in respect of the Japan Company, and that the shareholders really ought not to object to their having more; it suggests, by mentioning that, that that is the only material figure. I do not go so far as to say that the shareholders of the Oriental Company might not honestly agree, on full information with regard to the facts, to the directors retaining in the past, and keeping in the future, this large remuneration for their services, but I am very clear in my own mind that if any attempt is to be made by the directors to get the sanction of the shareholders it must be made on a fair and reasonably full statement of the facts upon which the directors are asking the shareholders to vote. This notice coupled with the circular, and I think also with the statements made by the chairman at the meeting, seems to me to be not frank, not open, not clear, and not in any way satisfactory. That being so, assuming that the notice is, by its suppression as well as by what it states, not satisfactory or, to use Lindley LJ's word, 'tricky,' what are the consequences? We are told that *Foss v Harbottle*[2] shows that such an action as this can only be brought against the directors in the name of the company, and the plaintiff suing on behalf of himself and all other shareholderrs cannot maintain the action at all. I think there is no foundation for that. The Court of Appeal in *Kaye v Croydon Tramways Co,*[3] which in all that is material is almost a replica of the present case, decided that in such a case the Court could say that when there was a special resolution passed by what was a 'tricky' notice it could not be supported. It is quite true that *Foss v Harbottle* was not cited there. I am sure there is nobody in Court who would venture to say that the very distinguished counsel who argued that case had never heard of *Foss v Harbottle* and were not perfectly familiar with the principle and with the cases in which *Foss v Harbottle* has been applied. I feel no difficulty in saying that special resolutions obtained by means of a notice which did not substantially put the shareholders in the position to know what they were voting about cannot be supported, and in so far as these special resolutions were passed on the faith and footing of such a notice the defendants cannot act upon them.

Holding Meetings Without A Quorum

Directors' Meetings

In the absence of any other determination by the directors, the quorum for directors' meetings is two directors (Table A, reg 89). If there is no quorum, those directors present may act only to fill any vacancies or for the calling of a general meeting of shareholders (reg 90). There are certain circumstances where directors may not vote, principally on decisions in which the director has a personal interest (reg 94, subject to reg 96). In such circumstances, neither can such director count towards the quorum for the meeting (reg 95).

---

1 [1908] 1 Ch 84; 77 LJ Ch 82
2 (1843) 2 Hare 461; 67 ER 189 (see p 532)
3 [1898] 1 Ch 358; 67 LJ Ch 222

SOURCE 147
Barron v Potter
[1914] 1 Ch 895; 83 LJ Ch 646

The plaintiff and the defendant were the only two directors of the company. The defendant was the chairman and as such had a casting vote at board meetings. The plaintiff, however, refused to attend board meetings with the defendant and summoned an extraordinary general meeting of the company with the purpose of removing the defendant as managing director and appointing other directors to the board. The defendant, in turn, summoned a meeting of the directors (ie himself and the plaintiff) and sent notice thereof to the plaintiff, but the plaintiff did not receive this notice until after the date. On two occasions, once as the plaintiff alighted from the train on arriving in London, and once just before the extraordinary general meeting, the defendant purported to put before the plaintiff resolutions for the appointment of additional directors to the company and purported to pass these by the exercise of his casting vote. The plaintiff only heard part of the defendant's proposals and reiterated his refusal to attend meetings with the defendant.

> WARRINGTON J: . . . What then took place is said to have been a directors' meeting at which a valid appointment was made of the three additional directors proposed by Mr Potter. The answer, in my opinion, is that there was no directors' meeting at all for the reason that Canon Barron to the knowledge of Mr Potter insisted all along that he would not attend any directors' meeting with Mr Potter or discuss the affairs of the company with him, and it is not enough that one of two directors should say 'This is a directors' meeting' while the other says it is not. Of course if directors are willing to hold a meeting they may do so under any circumstances, but one of them cannot be made to attend the board or to convert a casual meeting into a board meeting, and in the present case I do not see how the meeting in question can be treated as a board meeting. In my opinion therefore the true conclusion is that there was no board meeting, but that Canon Barron came with the deliberate intention of not attending a board meeting. If he had received the notice sent to him by Mr Potter summoning him to a board meeting different considerations might have arisen, but he had not received it and came with the fixed intention of not attending any such meeting. There was therefore no board meeting at which Canon Barron was present. Mr Potter was alone present, so that there was no quorum, and I must hold that the three additional directors named by him were not validly appointed.

Shareholder's Meetings

Under s 371 of the Companies Act 1985, a court may order the holding of a meeting where this would otherwise be impracticable. The history of this provision was recently discussed by Dillon LJ in Source 148:

SOURCE 148
Harman v BML Group
[1994] 2 BCLC 674

The wording of the section is wide. The sort of circumstances in which it was commonly invoked, so far as my experience goes, up until 1958, were where for instance a company with a large number of shareholders or members had failed to comply with the provisions of the articles as to the retirement of directors by rotation and thus by the operation of the rule in *Re Consolidated Nickel Mines Ltd* [1914] 1 Ch 883 suddenly found, contrary to its belief, that it had no directors and it was necessary to have directors appointed. Other circumstances would be where the company's share register and records of its membership had been destroyed by wartime bombing or in a fire, and a meeting was necessary to resurrect the membership of the company and carry out the necessary formalities until that could be done. Equally there could be a case where, under the articles, notices of meetings had to be given to overseas shareholders and there were hostilities in foreign parts which prevented that being done and that could have prevented meetings being validly convened. So other directions could be given by the court.

However, in 1958, Wynn-Parry J decided the case of *Re El Sombrero Ltd* [1958] 3 All ER 1, [1958] Ch 900. That was a case where there was a dispute between the majority shareholder, who held 900 shares of 1,000 shares in a private company, and two minority shareholders, who were the only directors and each only held 50 shares. It appeared that the two directors were happy with the situation and were not willing to attend a general meeting which might have involved their removal from office. They could prevent it de facto because the articles provided that two members had to be present in person or by proxy to constitute a quorum for a general meeting. Wynn-Parry J held that the general right to have a quorum of two members, whoever they might happen to be, could not be regarded as a class right attached to any particular shares and so could be overridden by the court directing a meeting to be held at which one shareholder would be a quorum.

SOURCE 149
Re Opera Photographic Ltd
(Chancery Division) [1989] BCLC 763

MORRIT J: . . . The company, the first respondent, was incorporated in November 1985. It has an authorised share capital of £1,000 divided into 1000 shares of £1 each, of which 100 have been issued, 51 to the applicant and 49 to the second respondent. The applicant and the second respondent are the only directors. The articles incorporate the relevant provisions of Table A, in consequence of which the necessary quorum for a meeting of members is two and for directors is also two. The company has traded profitably but the applicant and the second respondent have effectively fallen out.

On 22 November 1988 the applicant requisitioned the company to convene a meeting for the purpose of considering a resolution for the removal of the second respondent as a director. The second respondent declined to attend any relevant board meeting for that purpose so it was not possible for the company to convene the meeting. In consequence the applicant himself convened it on 16 December 1988 under the provisions of s 368(5) for 9 January 1989. On that date the second respondent did not attend. Accordingly there was no quorum and the meeting could not proceed to business.

The provisions of s 371 are as follows:

. . .

The provisions of the statutory predecessor of s 371(1) (s 135(1) of the Companies Act 1948) have been considered twice in reported cases. The first is *Re El Sombrero* [1958] 3 All ER 1, [1958] Ch 900, a decision of Wynn Parry J in which, as summarised by the headnote, he concluded that the question raised by the word 'impracticable' was merely whether in the particular circumstances of the case the desired meeting of the company could, as a practical matter, be conducted. Second, that that case was eminently one in which the court ought to exercise its discretion because otherwise it would be depriving the applicant of his statutory right under s 184(1) to remove the respondents as directors. The facts in that case were, for present purposes, merely that the applicant held 90% of the issued shares; the two respondents held the remaining 10% and were the only directors, and by seeking to absent themselves from any meetings that were convened effectively prevented the majority shareholder from exercising the rights attached to his 90% holding.

The section also came before the court in the subsequent case of *Re H & R Paul & Son Ltd* (1974) 118 Sol Jo 166. In that case there had been provisions for some form of takeover and the consequence had been that directors ceased to be qualified and amendments were proposed to the articles of association so that directors could be properly appointed. There had been a dissentient minority who did not like the takeover or the merger and who by absenting themselves from the meetings convened for the purpose of amending the articles and other purposes effectively frustrated anything being done. In his judgment Brightman J is reported as saying:

> 'The jurisdiction conferred by the section was discretionary and his Lordship was therefore not bound to make an order but to refuse B Ltd's application would deprive the majority shareholder of the right to alter the articles of association and confer on the minority a right of veto not commensurate with their shareholding. His Lordship did not accept that the quorum provisions should be regarded as a right vested in the minority to frustrate the wishes of the majority and he would therefore grant the relief sought.'

In this case counsel for the second respondent (Mr Instone), submits that there is no allegation of breach of duty against the second respondent; that the second respondent was acting within his rights; and that the company is what is conventionally described as a quasi partnership case in which each of the individuals had an equity of equal management participation. He submits that *Re El Sombrero* is of no assistance because in 1958 it was considered that 51% gave an absolute right to remove a director and, as he submits, that has been overtaken by events in the form of a decision of the House of Lords in *Ebrahimi v Westbourne Galleries Ltd* [1972] 2 All ER 492, [1973] AC 360 to the effect that the legal rights of the parties may be overlaid by equitable considerations arising out of the constitution and their agreement.

The plain fact of this matter is that deadlock exists between the two individuals which has to be resolved one way or another. It is either capable of being resolved by ordering a meeting, at which no doubt Mr Martin will be removed, and which will then no doubt result either in him exercising the preemption rights under the articles of selling his shares, or presenting a petition for the winding up of the company, or presenting a petition under s 459 based on unfair prejudice to him. If no order is made the deadlock will continue because no meetings can be conducted which are going effectively to manage or procure the management of this company, and if that persists for any length of time then no doubt one or other of the individuals will again be presenting a petition based on that deadlock in order to provide some form of resolution.

In the circumstances I do not think that the distinction which counsel for the second respondents seeks to draw is a valid one. The point still remains that the applicant, as the 51% shareholder, has the statutory right under the Companies Act 1985 to remove Mr Martin as a director. As Brightman J's decision in *Re H & R Paul* shows, the quorum provisions cannot be regarded as conferring on the second respondent some form of veto as being his entitlement. If he is, as no doubt he will be, removed if I make the order sought it may then well be that further proceedings will have to be undertaken by one side or another to procure the purchase of the other shares, but that seems to me to be inevitable in any event. It would be in those proceedings that the wrongfulness or otherwise of the conduct of either of the individuals would have to be determined in order to decide what order to make and what form the relief should be.

This issue has come before the court on at least three occasions since Morrit J's decision in *Re Opera*. All shared the feature of a breakdown in the working relationship of the shareholders and in each case a petition under s 459 had either been presented or threatened by one of the shareholders (see p 571). In *Re Sticky Fingers Restaurant Ltd* [1992] BCLC 84, Mervyn Davies J, also acceded to the application under s 371 for a meeting to be called (on that occasion to pass a resolution appointing two further directors), but owing to the fact that the respondent shareholder had already presented a s 459 petition, he made the order conditional in the following way:

'I think the right course to take is to accede to paras 1, 2 and 2a of the application . . . , but to qualify the order in this way. The order will provide that any director appointed pursuant to the order will be restrained from acting as such director, unless and until there is delivered to Mr Mitchell's[1] solicitors an undertaking signed by the director to the effect that, pending the outcome of the s 459 petition proceedings, he will not (a) at any meeting vote in such fashion as to dismiss Mr Mitchell from his directorship, or to exclude him from his rights and duties as such director, or to diminish such rights or duties in any way, and (b) interfere with Mr Mitchell's day to day conduct of the restaurant business so long as Mr Mitchell conducts such business as he has done in the past, and (c) vote to effect any alteration in the constitution or capital of the company.'

In *Re Whitchurch Insurance Consultants Ltd* [1993] BCLC 1359, however, Harman J disagreed with Mervyn Davies J as to the relevance of the presentation of the s 459 petition, and granted the order under s 371 without conditions, despite the fact that a s 459 petition had been presented. Finally, in *Harman v BML Group* [1994] 2 BCLC 674 (p 400), the Court of Appeal upheld an appeal against the order of the court below which had acceded to the application under s 371. In Harman's case, the appellant — who as the respondent had opposed the application — was the owner of all the shares of one class (the B shares). According to the articles, no shareholders' meeting was quorate without a representative from the shareholders of the B shares. The Court of Appeal held that to accede to the application of the two A shareholders for a meeting to be called would deprive the B shareholder of a right attached to his shares (cf *Cumbrian Newspaper Group v Cumberland & Westmorland Herald Newspaper & Printing Co* [1987] Ch 1, [1986] 23 All ER 816, p 629).

---

1 The respondent to the application

The Conduct of Meetings where the Facilities are Inadequate

SOURCE 150
Byng *v* London Life Association
(Court of Appeal) [1989] BCLC 400

The respondent organisation — a company limited by guarantee — called a members' meeting to consider a resolution to amend the memorandum of association to facilitate a merger between the respondent and another organisation. The meeting was scheduled to take place at a particular venue, but with increasing interest in the proceedings, the directors first arranged for overflow facilities with technological assistance so that people attending the meeting could be accommodated and participate in the meeting even if not at the main venue. As a further precautionary measure, a very much larger hall was reserved for the afternoon in case the morning facilities proved inadequate. The morning's proceedings were a disaster, with people in the overflow sections unable to register their presence, let alone partici-pate. The chairman decided to adjourn the meeting to the afternoon, despite protests from those who were unable to attend the afternoon proceedings at which the resolution was passed. The articles of the respondent association included the following provision:

> 'The Chairman may, with the consent of any meeting at which a quorum is present (and shall if so directed by the meeting) adjourn the meeting from time to time and from place to place, but no business shall be transacted at any adjourned meeting except business which might lawfully have been transacted at the meeting from which the adjournment took place. When a meeting is adjourned for thirty days or more, notice of the adjourned meeting shall be given as in the case of an original meeting. Save as aforesaid, it shall not be necessary to give any notice of an adjournment or of the business to be transacted at an adjourned meeting.'

The plaintiff (appellant) sought an order that the meeting was a nullity and that the resolution was not passed. The first question was whether or not the morning proceedings could be said to have been a meeting (so as to enable a valid adjournment to have been made).

> BROWNE-WILKINSON VC: . . . The first difficulty is to identify what, if anything, was the meeting. Was it the assembly of the members in the cinema alone (from which all those in the overflow rooms and foyer were excluded) or was it the conglomerate assembly of those in the cinema plus those in the overflow rooms and foyer?
>
> Counsel's first submission for the plaintiff under this head was made with a view to showing that the conglomerate assembly in the cinema, the overflow rooms and the foyer could not constitute a meeting. He submitted that for there to be a meeting at all everyone must be in the same place, face to face. If this submission were correct, even if the audio-visual links had worked perfectly, there would still have been no meeting at the Barbican on 19 October since all the members attending would not have been face to face but scattered between different rooms. In support of this submission counsel relied on the definition of the word 'meet' in the *Shorter Oxford English Dictionary*, viz 'To come face to face with or into the company of [another person]'. He also relies on the fact that the requirement in the Companies Act 1985, s 378 that an extraordinary resolution has to be passed at a general meeting has a long statutory history dating back to

times long before the invention of audio-visual links. This, he submits, shows that a meeting for the purpose of the Act requires that everyone shall be physically present in the same room or space.

I do not accept this submission. The rationale behind the requirement for meetings in the 1985 Act is that the members shall be able to attend in person so as to debate and vote on matters affecting the company. Until recently this could only be achieved by everyone being physically present in the same room face to face. Given modern technological advances, the same result can now be achieved without all the members coming face to face; without being physically in the same room they can be electronically in each other's presence so as to hear and be heard and to see and be seen. The fact that such a meeting could not have been foreseen at the time the first statutory requirements for meetings were laid down, does not require us to hold that such a meeting is not within the meaning of the word 'meeting' in the 1985 Act. Thus, communication by telephone has been held to be a 'telegraph' within the meaning of the Telegraph Acts 1863 and 1869, notwithstanding that the telephone had not been invented or contemplated when those acts were passed: see *A-G v Edison Telephone Co of London Ltd* (1880) 6 QBD 244.

I have no doubt therefore that, in cases where the original venue proves inadequate to accommodate all those wishing to attend, valid general meetings of a company can be properly held using overflow rooms provided, first, that all due steps are taken to direct to the overflow rooms those unable to get into the main meeting and, second, that there are adequate audio-visual links to enable those in all the rooms to see and hear what is going on in the other rooms. Were the law otherwise, with the present tendency towards companies with very large numbers of shareholders and corresponding uncertainty as to how many shareholders will attend meetings, the organisation of such meetings might prove to be impossible.

In the event, counsel for the defendants did not contend that the conglomerate assembly was a meeting of the company. He submitted that the assembly in the cinema was the meeting. I accept this submission. If there was a meeting at all it was the assembly in the cinema, that being the venue specified in the notice convening the meeting. Such meeting was incapable of proceeding to business, since all those members unable to get into the cinema were excluded. For the reasons I have given, if proper overflow facilities had in fact been provided, those in the overflow rooms and the foyer would not have been excluded from the meeting but would, electronically, have been present at it. But since the audio-visual links did not work, those in the overflow rooms and foyer were excluded and the meeting in the cinema was incapable of transacting any business.

Does the fact that the assembly in the cinema was incapable of conducting any business necessarily mean that it was not a 'meeting' at all? Counsel for the plaintiff submitted that it was an invalid meeting, a nullity. He said that, as in the case of a meeting of which proper notice has not been given or at which there is no quorum, where members are excluded from a meeting it is invalid and cannot be adjourned.

In my judgment the phrase 'invalid meeting', although useful as a shorthand description of a meeting at which no business can be validly transacted, is capable of giving rise to confusion. The fact that a meeting cannot pass a valid resolution in certain circumstances does not necessarily mean that there has been no meeting at all. Thus in many cases (including the present) the articles of a company provide that, in the event of there being no quorum present at a meeting, the meeting shall be adjourned for a fixed period. In such a case it is clear that the inquorate meeting was a meeting notwithstanding the fact that it could conduct no business.

In my judgment there is no absolute rule of law that a meeting from which members are wrongly excluded is a nullity. The meeting, as such, can conduct no business, but it is nevertheless a meeting. I can see no good reason why the law should shut its eyes to the reality that, in response to a notice convening them, certain members of the company have assembled together at what, in ordinary usage, would be called a meeting. What that meeting can validly do is quite another matter.

In the present case the sole question is whether Mr Dawson was, within art 17, the chairman of a general meeting of London Life. The answer to that question must depend on the meaning of the word 'meeting' in the articles of London Life. Article 15 provides:

> 'No business shall be transacted at any General Meeting unless a quorum is present when the meeting proceeds to business . . . '

Article 16 then provides:

> 'If within half an hour from the time appointed for the meeting a quorum is not present, the meeting, if convened on the requisition of Members, shall be dissolved. In any other case it shall stand adjourned to the same day in the next week, at the same time and place . . . '

These two articles therefore proceed on the basis that an inquorate meeting incapable of conducting any business is still a 'meeting' of London Life, capable of being adjourned. Similarly, under regs 40 and 41 of Table A in the Companies (Tables A to F) Regulations 1985, SI 1985/805, an inquorate meeting is treated as a meeting capable of adjournment. Therefore, the draftsman of the London Life articles and Parliament both plainly envisaged that the word 'meeting' covered an assembly which could conduct no business.

. . .

I can therefore see no reason why, as common sense suggests, the assembly at the cinema should not in law constitute a 'meeting' within the meaning of that word in the 1985 Act and the articles of London Life. It follows that I agree with Vinelott J that under art 17 Mr Dawson was the chairman of the meeting and had all the powers of the chairman.

[Mustill LJ disagreed on this point that the morning proceedings were not a nullity, but Woolf LJ agreed with Browne-Wilkinson VC. The next question was whether the chairman had the power to adjourn the meeting.]

BROWNE-WILKINSON VC: . . . In my judgment the position at common law is correctly set out in *John v Rees* and in the two following passages. The first is from *R v D'Oyly* (1840) 12 Ad & El 139 at 159, 113 ER 763 at 771:

> 'Setting aside the inconvenience that might arise if a majority of the parishioners could determine the point of adjournment, we think that the person who presides at the meeting is the proper individual to decide this. It is on him that it devolves, both to preserve order in the meeting, and to regulate the proceedings *so as to give all persons entitled a reasonable opportunity of voting.* He is to do the acts *necessary for those purposes* on his own responsibility, and subject to being called upon to answer for his conduct if he has done anything improperly.' (My emphasis).

The second passage is from Rogers *A Practical Arrangement of Ecclesiastical Law*

(1840) p 874 quoted in *John v Rees* [1969] 2 All ER 274 at 292, [1970] Ch 345 at 381. The passage says that a particular decision —

> 'by no means interferes with the right which every chairman has to make a bona fide adjournment, whilst a poll or other business is proceeding, if circumstances of violent interruption make it unsafe, or seriously difficult for the voters to tender their votes; nor of adjourning the place of polling, if the ordinary place used for that purpose be insufficient, or greatly inconvenient. In most of such cases, the question will turn upon the intention and effect of the adjournment, if the intention and effect were to interrupt and procrastinate the business, such an adjournment would be illegal; if, on the contrary, the intention and effect were to forward or facilitate it, *and no injurious effect were produced,* such an adjournment would, it is conceived, be generally supported.' (My emphasis).

In my judgment, were it not for art 18, Mr Dawson would at common law have had power to adjourn the meeting at the cinema since the inadequacy of the space available rendered it impossible for all those entitled to attend to take part in the debate and to vote. A motion for adjournment could not be put to the meeting as many who would be entitled to vote on the motion were excluded. Therefore, at common law it would have been the chairman's duty to regulate the proceedings so as to give all persons entitled a reasonable opportunity of debating and voting. This would have required him either to abandon the meeting or to adjourn it to a time and a place where the members could have a reasonable opportunity to debate or vote. I see no reason to hold that in all circumstances the meeting must be abandoned; in my judgment the chairman can, in a suitable case, merely adjourn such meeting.

What then is the effect of art 18 which expressly confers on the chairman power to adjourn but only with the consent of a quorate meeting?

. . .

In my judgment art 18 regulates the chairman's powers of adjournment to the extent that its machinery is effective to cover the contingencies which occur. Therefore if the circumstances are such that it is possible to discover whether or not the meeting agrees to an adjournment, art 18 lays down a comprehensive code. But if the circumstances are such that the wishes of the meeting cannot be validly ascertained, why should art 18 be read as impairing the fundamental common law duty of the chairman to regulate proceedings so as to enable those entitled to be present and to vote to be heard and to vote?

. . .

I do not find that any principle of construction requires me to hold that an express provision regulating adjournment when the views of the meeting can be ascertained necessarily precludes the existence of implied powers when consent of the meeting cannot be obtained. The *Salisbury Gold*[1] case lays down no such proposition. Accordingly, I reach the conclusion that in any circumstances where there is a meeting at which the view of the majority cannot be validly ascertained, the chairman has a residual common law power to adjourn 'so as to give all persons entitled a reasonable opportunity of voting' and, I would add, speaking at the meeting.

[Finally, was the power of adjournment validly exercised?]

---

1 *Salisbury Gold Mining Co v Hathorn* [1897] AC 268

BROWNE-WILKINSON VC: . . . The starting point is to consider the nature of the residual power to adjourn which in my judgment remains vested in the chairman. It was a residual power exercisable only when the machinery provided by the articles had broken down. This residual common law power is itself tightly circumscribed by reference to the objects for which it exists. I quote again from the passages which I have emphasised above in the quotations from *R v D'Oyly* and Mr Rogers's book. The power is to regulate proceedings 'so as to give all persons entitled a reasonable opportunity of voting'. The chairman must 'do the acts necessary for those purposes'. The power to adjourn is only validly exercised if 'no injurious effect were produced'. I would add that at a company meeting a member is entitled not only to vote but also to hear and be heard in the debate. Therefore it is the very purpose of the power to facilitate the presence of those entitled to debate and vote on a resolution at a meeting where such debate and voting is possible. To my mind, this is inconsistent with the view that the exercise of the power can only be impugned on the grounds of lack of good faith. In my judgment the chairman's decision must also be taken reasonably with a view to facilitating the purpose for which the power exists. Accordingly, the impact of the proposed adjournment on those seeking to attend the original meeting and the other members must be a central factor in considering the validity of the chairman's decision to adjourn.

The quotation from *Rogers* might suggest that if the chairman's decision proves in the event to have an adverse effect on the members, that will render the decision invalid. In my judgment that is not the correct test. The chairman's decision will not be declared invalid unless on the facts which he knew or ought to have known he failed to take into account all the relevant factors, took into account irrelevant factors or reached a conclusion which no reasonable chairman, properly directing himself as to his duties, could have reached, ie the test is the same as that applicable on judicial review in accordance with the principles of *Associated Provincial Picture Houses Ltd v Wednesbury Corp* [1947] 2 All ER 680, [1948] 1 KB 223. This was the approach adopted by Uthwatt J in *Second Consolidated Trust Ltd v Ceylon Amalgamated Tea and Rubber Estates Ltd* [1943] 2 All ER 567, where he held a chairman's decision invalid on the grounds that he had failed to take into account a relevant factor.

I turn then to consider the position confronting Mr Dawson at the Barbican cinema on the morning of 19 October. The principal factors were as follows: (1) the business before the meeting was to amend the memorandum of association but the meeting was also treated as being in the nature of a referendum to establish the attitude of the members to the proposed merger of a large part of the business of London Life with AMP, a matter of fundamental importance to the company and its members; (2) the last date by which the merger had to be approved was 31 March 1989 (I note that this fact is not mentioned in the judgment of Vinelott J and may well not have been brought to his attention); (3) the merger would be much easier to put into operation if completed on 31 January 1989 being the end of the accounting years of both London Life and AMP. To that end a date (5 December 1988) had been fixed for a hearing in court under the Insurance Companies Act 1982; (4) the meeting at the cinema was incapable of either debating or voting on the resolution to amend the memorandum of association; (5) there was a substantial 'ginger group' opposing the merger, at least until alternative courses had been considered; many of them were present at the Barbican; (6) there were repeated attempts from the floor and the overflow rooms to obtain an adjournment of the meeting sine die; (7) when the possibility of adjournment to the Café Royal in the afternoon was first suggested, there were objections from the floor that some members present in the cinema would not be able to attend such adjourned meeting; (8) there were present at the meeting a number of members who had come from a distance and might not be able to attend a further meeting on another date; (9) if the meeting were adjourned to the Café Royal on the same day, those present at the Barbican but unable to be present at the Café Royal in the afternoon would not only be unable to speak but also unable to vote. Under art 30, proxies have to be deposited 48 hours before any adjourned meeting; and (10) the chairman was advised by leading counsel that he could properly adjourn to the Café Royal in the afternoon.

Mr Dawson gave evidence of the factors which most persuaded him to adjourn to the Café Royal. These include all the factors mentioned above, except those which in my view were of central importance, viz (2), (6), (7) and (9). It would not be fair or sensible to find that, because he did not specifically mention that he took into account the desire of certain members for an adjournment sine die and their inability to be at the Café Royal in the afternoon, he did not have that well in mind; he was being bombarded with this information at the time he took his decision. But I can see nothing to suggest that he took into account the fact that there was no absolute necessity to obtain approval of the merger until 31 March 1989, a date more than five months away. Nor is there anything to suggest that he appreciated that those who could not be at the Café Royal would not only be unable to speak but would be unable to vote even by proxy.

It was suggested in argument that those whose other arrangements precluded them from attending the afternoon meeting at the Café Royal would probably not have been able to stay long enough to vote even if the Barbican meeting had proceeded in the ordinary way, since this would have lasted for a long time. This is a point which carried weight with the judge. But, to my mind, it has only a limited impact. First, it is a hypothesis, not a fact. Second, and more important, the purpose of members attending meetings is to enable them not only to vote but also to take part in the debate. Those present in the morning could in any event have been present and spoken in the debate if it had continued at the Barbican, even if they could not have waited until the vote was taken. By the adjournment to the Café Royal they were precluded from even taking part in the debate.

In these circumstances, in my judgment, Mr Dawson's decision to adjourn to the Café Royal in the same afternoon was not valid on the ground either that he failed to take into account relevant factors or that the decision was *Wednesbury* unreasonable. The legal advice tendered was in my judgment erroneous, probably because it failed to take account of the very limited ambit of the chairman's residual power to adjourn. Since such power is only exercisable for the purpose of giving the members a proper opportunity to debate and vote on the resolution, there must in my judgment be very special circumstances to justify a decision to adjourn the meeting to a time and place where, to the knowledge of the chairman, it could not be attended by a number of the members who had taken the trouble to attend the original meeting and could not even lodge a proxy vote. To overlook this factor is to leave out of account a matter of central importance. True it is that those who were available for the afternoon meeting would have been inconvenienced by an adjournment to another date or the convening of a wholly new meeting since they would either have to have attended at the fresh meeting or to have lodged proxies. But in my judgment this could not outweigh the central point that the form of the adjournment was such as undoubtedly to preclude certain members from taking any part in the meeting either by way of debate or by way of vote.

If the time factor had been such that the merger proposal could not have been carried through at all unless there was an immediate decision on the resolution before the meeting (ie if the merger had to be approved within a period which rendered impossible the convening of a further meeting on 21 days' notice or the adjournment of the original meeting for a sufficient period to allow proxies to be lodged) the matter might have been different. But in fact there was no compelling time factor in this case. True it is that expenditure would have to be incurred in calling a further meeting. But if, instead of adjourning to the detriment of certain members, the meeting at the Barbican had either been abandoned or adjourned sine die, 21 days' notice could have been given of a fresh meeting to be held, say, a month later, well before even the date fixed for the hearing in court. If such fresh meeting had been called, all the members would have had an opportunity to be present either in person or by proxy. There is no sign that Mr Dawson ever appreciated this factor or took it into account in reaching his decision.

Accordingly, although Mr Dawson acted in complete good faith, his decision to adjourn to the Café Royal on the same date was not one which, in my judgment, he could reasonably have reached if he had properly apprehended the restricted nature and purpose of his powers. Therefore in my judgment his decision was invalid.

PART IV: COMPETING CLAIMS TO MANAGEMENT

The typical company today with its three organs — shareholders, directors and managing director — evolved from the nineteenth-century model in which the directors were regarded as the agents of the shareholders (*Isle of Wight v Tahourdin*,[1] Source 151). The development of the board of directors as an independent organ probably dates from *Automatic Self-Cleansing Filter Syndicate Company Ltd v Cunninghame*[2] (Source 152). The office of managing director first made its appearance in the model articles annexed to the Companies (Consolidation) Act 1908 (First Schedule, Table A). It was soon established as an organ of the company by *Quin & Axtens v Salmon*[3] (Source 153) and *Lennards Carrying Company v Asiatic Petroleum*[4] (p 282).

Each of these organs is capable of being identified with the company — the *alter ego* doctrine — and, more importantly for the purposes of this section, each is entitled to certain powers of management in the company. The materials extracted below illustrate the principles in terms of which disputes between any two organs as to the right to manage, are resolved.

The organs are constituted and their powers described by the statute in the case of a statutory company (*Isle of Wight v Tahourdin*) and by the articles of association in the case of a registered company. The division of functions between the board of directors and the general meeting of shareholders was, until the 1985 Companies Act, usually governed by a provision identical or close to reg 80 of the model articles annexed to the 1948 Companies Act as

---

1 (1883) 25 Ch D 320; 53 LJ Ch 353 (see p 411)
2 [1906] 2 Ch 34; 75 LJ Ch 437 (see p 413)
3 [1909] 1 Ch 311, affd. [1909] AC 442, 78 LJ Ch 506 (see p 414)
4 [1915] AC 705; 84 LJKB 1281

Sch 1, Table A. This remains the relevant provision for companies registered prior to the coming into force of the 1985 Act and is as follows:

> 'The business of the company shall be managed by the directors who may pay all expenses incurred in promoting and registering the company, and may exercise all such powers of the company as are not, by the Act or by these regulations, required to be exercised by the company in general meeting, subject, never-theless, to any of these regulations, to the provisions of the Act and to such regulations, being not inconsistent with the aforesaid regulations or provisions, as may be prescribed by the company in general meeting; but no regulations made by the company in general meeting shall invalidate any prior act of the directors which would have been valid if that regulation had not been made.'

The relevant provision in the model articles annexed to the 1985 Act (reg 70) adopts most of its predecessor and clears up one question — any regulations prescribed in general meeting to govern the directors' actions must be by special and not ordinary resolution.

The modern principle in cases of competing claims by the board and the general meeting of shareholders, where both are functioning organs and where the dispute cannot be readily resolved by reference to the constituting documents, is, it is submitted, that the board prevails. The policy underlying the development of this principle can be seen below (*Quin & Axtens Ltd v Salmon*; *Scott v Scott*,[1] *Breckland Group Holdings Ltd v London & Suffolk Properties* [1989] BCLC 100, Sources 153, 154 and 155 respectively), although academic opinion is divided (Sources 159, 160, 161).

Where the board of directors is unable to act (eg deadlocked or cannot be summoned), its powers can be exercised by the shareholders (*Foster v Foster*,[2] *Re Argentum*,[3] *Alexander Ward v Samyang*,[4] Sources 156, 157, 158).

SOURCE 151
Isle of Wight *v* Tahourdin
(1883) 25 Ch D 320; 53 LJ Ch 353

The Isle of Wight Railway Company is a company incorporated by Act of Parliament and subject to the provisions of the Companies Clauses Act 1845. The special Act of the company did not contain anything as to removal of directors by the company.

On 20 October, 1883, the requisite number of shareholders under the power given by clause 70 of the Companies Clauses Act, sent a requisition to the directors to call an extraordinary meeting of the company for the following objects:

> '1. To appoint a committee to inquire into the working and general management of the company, and the means of reducing the working expenses. To empower such committee to consolidate all or any of the duties of secretary, general manager, accountant, and cashier, and to concentrate the offices in the Island, and to remove any of the officers or

---

1 [1943] 1 All ER 582; [1943] WN 16 (see p 416)
2 [1916] 1 Ch 532; 85 LJ Ch 305 (see p 421)
3 [1975] 1 WLR 186; [1975] 1 All ER 605 (see p 421)
4 [1975] 1 WLR 673, [1975] 2 Lloyd's Rep 1 (see p 423)

servants of the company and appoint others, and to authorize and require
the directors to carry out the recommendations of the committee.
2. To remove (if deemed necessary or expedient) any of the present
directors, and to elect directors to fill any vacancy in the board.'

KAY J: . . . The simple question is, would it or would it not be within the right of
a general meeting to empower a committee to do all these things? In my opinion
it clearly would not be. It would be to displace the directors, and to transfer to a
committee to be appointed the functions of the directors to a very considerable
extent. It seems to me that a general meeting has no power whatever to give any
authority of that kind to a committee. . . .

Therefore I ought to grant an injunction, and it will be simply an order to
prevent the meeting being held.

The Defendants appealed.

COTTON, LJ: We are of opinion that this injunction ought not to have been
granted. It is a very strong thing indeed to prevent shareholders from holding a
meeting of the company, when such a meeting is the only way in which they can
interfere, if the majority of them think that the course taken by the directors, in
a matter which is *intra vires* of the directors, is not for the benefit of the
company.

. . . Directors have great powers, and the Court refuses to interfere with their
management of the company's affairs if they keep within their powers, and if a
shareholder complains of the conduct of the directors while they keep within
their powers, the Court says to him, 'If you want to alter the management of the
affairs of the company go to a general meeting, and if they agree with you they
will pass a resolution obliging the directors to alter their course of proceeding.'

. . .

Then it is said that there is no power in the meeting of shareholders to elect
new directors, for that under the 89th section the power would be in the
remaining directors. The remaining directors would no doubt have that power if
there was a quorum left. But suppose the meeting were to remove so many
directors that a quorum was not left, what then follows? It has been argued that
in that case, there being no board which could act, there would be no power of
filling up the board so as to enable it to work. In my opinion that is utterly wrong.
A power is given by the section 89 to the remaining directors 'if they think proper
so to do,' to elect persons to fill up the vacancies. I do not see how it is possible
for a non-existent body to think proper to fill up vacancies. In such a case a
general meeting duly summoned for the purpose must have power to elect a new
board so as not to let the business of the company be at a dead lock. . . .

LINDLEY LJ: I am of the same opinion. It appears to me that this case is very
much more important than at first sight appears. It raises a question of the
utmost possible consequence as to the management of the railway and other
companies. We must bear in mind the decisions in *Foss v Harbottle*[1] and the line
of cases following it, in which this Court has constantly and consistently refused
to interfere on behalf of shareholders, until they have done the best they can to
set right the matters of which they complain, by calling general meetings. Bearing
in mind that line of decisions, what would be the position of the shareholders if
there were to be another line of decisions prohibiting meetings of the shareholders to consider their own affairs?

---

1 (1843) 2 Hare 461; 67 ER 189 (see p 532)

SOURCE 152

Automatic Self-Cleansing Filter Syndicate Company Ltd *v* Cunninghame

(Chancery Division, Court of Appeal 1908) [1906] 2 Ch 34; 75 LJ Ch 437

WARRINGTON J: The question I have to determine in this case is whether the shareholders of a company have power by a resolution passed by a simple majority of their number to order the directors to seal an agreement for the sale of the whole of the assets of the company notwithstanding that the directors may think that the sale is improvident, and that the terms on which it is to be carried out are not fit terms on which the company ought to carry out such a sale. To my mind this question depends upon the true construction of the articles. The only articles which are material are articles 96 and 97.

96. The management of the business and the control of the company shall be vested in the directors, who, in addition to the powers and authorities by these presents expressly conferred upon them, may exercise all such powers and do all such acts and things as may be exercised or done by the company, and are not hereby or by statute expressly directed or required to be exercised or done by the company in general meeting; but subject nevertheless to the provisions of the statutes and of these presents, and to such regulations, not being inconsistent with these presents, as may from time to time be made by extraordinary resolution, but no regulation shall invalidate any prior act of the directors which would have been valid if such regulation had not been made.

97. Without prejudice to the general powers conferred by the last preceding clause, and to the other powers and authorities conferred as aforesaid, it is hereby expressly declared that the directors shall be entrusted with the following powers, namely, power —

(1) To purchase or otherwise acquire for the company any property, letters patent, rights or privileges which the company is authorized to acquire, at such price, and generally on such terms and conditions, as they think fit; also to sell, lease, abandon, or otherwise deal with, any property, rights, or privileges to which the company may be entitled, on such terms and conditions as they may think fit.

(16) To enter into all such negotiations and contracts and rescind and vary all such contracts, and execute and do all such acts, deeds, and things in the name or on behalf of the company as they might consider expedient for or in relation to any of the matters aforesaid, or otherwise for the purpose of the company.

The effect of this resolution, if acted upon, would be to compel the directors to sell the whole of the assets of the company, not on such terms and conditions as they think fit, but upon such terms and conditions as a simple majority of the shareholders think fit. But it does not rest there. Article 96 provides that the management of the business and control of the company are to be vested in the directors. Now that article, which is for the protection of a minority of the shareholders, can only be altered by a special resolution, that is to say, by a resolution passed by a three-fourths majority, at a meeting called for the purpose, and confirmed at a subsequent meeting. If that provision could be revoked by a resolution of the shareholders passed by a simple majority. I can see no reason for the provision which is to be found in article 81 that the directors can only be removed by a special resolution. It seems to me that if a majority of the shareholders can, on a matter which is vested in the directors, overrule the discretion of the directors, there might just as well be no provision at all in the articles as to the removal of the directors by special resolution. Moreover, pressed to its logical conclusion, the result would be that when a majority of the shareholders disagree with the policy of the directors, though they cannot remove the directors except by special resolution, they might carry on the whole of the business of the company as they pleased, and thus, though not able to remove the directors, overrule every act which the board might otherwise do. It seems to me on the true construction of these articles that the management of the business and the control of the company are vested in the directors, and consequently that the control of the company as to any particular matter, or the management of any particular transaction or any particular part of the business of the company, can only be removed from the board by an alteration of the articles, such alteration, of course, requiring a special resolution.

. . .

COLLINS MR: This is an appeal from a decision of Warrington J, who has been asked by the plaintiffs, Mr McDiarmid and the company, for a declaration that the defendants, as directors of the company, are bound to carry into effect a resolution passed at a meeting of the shareholders in the company . . . if it is desired to alter the powers of the directors that must be done, not by a resolution carried by a majority at an ordinary meeting of the company, but by an extraordinary resolution. In these circumstances it seems to me that it is not competent for the majority of the shareholders at an ordinary meeting to affect or alter the mandate originally given to the directors, by the articles of association. It has been suggested that this is a mere question of principal and agent, and that it would be an absurd thing if a principal in appointing an agent should in effect appoint a dictator who is to manage him instead of his managing the agent. I think that the analogy does not strictly apply to this case. No doubt for some purposes directors are agents. For whom are they agents? You have, no doubt, in theory and law one entity, the company, which might be a principal, but you have to go behind that when you look to the particular position of directors. It is by the consensus of all the individuals in the company that these directors become agents and hold their rights as agents. It is not fair to say that a majority at a meeting is for the purposes of this case the principal so as to alter the mandate of the agent. The minority also must be taken into account. There are provisions by which the minority may be over-borne, but that can only be done by special machinery in the shape of special resolutions. Short of that the mandate which must be obeyed is not that of the majority — it is that of the whole entity made up of all the shareholders. If the mandate of the directors is to be altered, it can only be under the machinery of the memorandum and articles themselves.

COZENS-HARDY LJ: . . . it seems to me that the shareholders have by their express contract mutually stipulated that their common affairs should be managed by certain directors to be appointed by the shareholders in the manner described by other articles, such directors being liable to be removed only by special resolution. If you once get a stipulation of that kind in a contract made between the parties, what right is there to interfere with the contract, apart, of course, from any misconduct on the part of the directors? There is no such misconduct in the present case.

SOURCE 153
Salmon *v* Quin & Axtens Limited
(Court of Appeal 1909) [1909] 1 Ch 311 affd [1909] AC 422; 78 LJ Ch 506

The relevant provisions of the articles of association of the defendant company were as follows:

75. The business of the company shall be managed by the board, who may pay all expenses of or incident to the formation, registration, and advertising of the company, and the issue of its capital. The board may exercise all the powers of the company, subject, nevertheless, to the provisions of any Acts of Parliament or of these articles, and to such regulations (being not inconsistent with any such provisions of these articles) as may be prescribed by the company in general meeting, but no regulations made by the company in general meeting shall invalidate any prior act of the board which would have been valid if such regulations had not been made.

. . .

80. No resolution of a meeting of the directors having for its object the borrowing of money, the entering into any contract the subject-matter of which shall be of a value exceeding £1000, the acquisition by purchase, lease or otherwise, or the sale, leasing, letting, mortgaging or charging of any hereditaments or premises, the renewal or extension of any existing lease or tenancy or the acquisition of any reversionary lease, the opening of any additional shop or branch of the company's business, the carrying on of any business or class of business not then carried on by the company, the convening of an extraordinary general meeting of the company other than a meeting convened pursuant to a requisition of shareholders under section 13 of the Companies Act 1900, or any matter affecting the rights of either of them, the said William Raymond Axtens and Joseph Salmon, as holders of ordinary shares of the company shall be valid or binding unless not less than twenty-four hours' notice in writing by letter or telegram of the meeting specifying the business proposed to be transacted thereat, shall have been given to each of the managing directors, the said William Raymond Axtens and Joseph Salmon, and neither of them shall have dissented therefrom in writing before or at the meeting at which such resolution is put to the vote.

FARWELL LJ: . . . In the present case Mr Salmon did so dissent according to the terms of that article, and therefore the veto therein provided came into operation. That was met by the company being called together by a requisition of seven shareholders and by passing general resolutions for the acquisition of this property and the letting of the vacant premises. It is said that those resolutions are of no effect, and I am of opinion that the contention is right. I base my opinion on the words of article 75, 'subject, nevertheless, to the provisions of any Acts of Parliament or of these articles,' which I read to be 'subject, nevertheless, to article 80,' 'and to such regulations (being not inconsistent with any such provisions of these articles) as may be prescribed by the company in general meeting.' That is to say, 'subject also to such regulations not inconsistent with article 80 as may be prescribed by the company in general meeting.' But these resolutions are absolutely inconsistent with article 80; in truth this is an attempt to alter the terms of the contract between the parties by a simple resolution instead of by a special resolution. The articles forming this contract, under which the business of the company shall be managed by the board, contain a most usual and proper requirement, because a business does require a head to look after it, and a head that shall not be interfered with unnecessarily. Then in order to oust the directors a special resolution would be required. The case is, in my view, entirely governed, if not by the decision, at any rate by the reasoning of the Lords

Justices in *Automatic Self-Cleansing Filter Syndicate Co v Cunninghame*[1] and *Gramophone and Typewriter Ltd v Stanley*.[2] I will only refer to one passage in Buckley LJ's judgment in the latter case. He says: 'This Court decided not long since, in *Automatic Self-Cleansing Filter Syndicate Co v Cunninghame*, that even a resolution of a numerical majority at a general meeting of the company cannot impose its will upon the directors when the articles have confided to them the control of the company's affairs. The directors are not servants to obey directions given by the shareholders as individuals; they are not agents appointed by and bound to serve the shareholders as their principals. They are persons who may by the regulations be entrusted with the control of the business, and if so entrusted they can be dispossessed from that control only by the statutory majority which can alter the articles. Directors are not, I think, bound to comply with the directions even of all the corporators acting as individuals.' That appears to me to express the true view. Any other construction might, I think, be disastrous, because it might lead to an interference by a bare majority very inimical to the interests of the minority who had come into a company on the footing that the business should be managed by the board of directors.

SOURCE 154
Scott *v* Scott
(Chancery Division 1943) [1943] 1 All ER 582; [1943] WN 16

The following resolution — which the plaintiffs claimed was invalid — was passed at a general meeting of shareholders of the company.

That as from 13 March 1940, and until otherwise decided by the company in general meeting a weekly payment be made to each preference shareholder of a sum equivalent to $\frac{1}{52}$ of 15 per cent on the capital for the time being paid up on the preference shares held by him or her by way of advance (without interest) pending the declaration and payment of the dividend on the preference shares for the current year, such weekly payment to be deducted and retained by the company out of such dividend when declared and payable and in case the dividend shall be insufficient to permit of such deduction and retainer any deficiency to be repaid to the company by the shareholder within one calendar month after demand by the company.

LORD CLAUSON: . . . It appears to me quite clear from these articles, including, as they do, article 71, that one thing which is to be managed by the directors and with which the company may interfere only by removing the directors or by having an investigation under the statutory provisions, is the management of the business of the company.

The trade of this company is that of shipping butchers and contractors. I cannot see how the business of a company whose trade is that of shipping butchers and contractors, on, as I understand it, not an insubstantial but a large scale, can be managed without regard to finance, and it appears to me that a resolution of the company which directs the directors to make certain loans is a most obvious interference with the very root of that which is committed to the directors, namely, the management of the business. How can you manage a business without managing its finance; how can things be carried on if at any moment the company can interfere and say to the directors: You must not keep a balance at the bank, although you may have demands coming forward in a week

---

1 [1906] 2 Ch 34; 75 LJ Ch 437 (see p 413)
2 [1908] 2 KB 89; 77 LJKB 834

or two; you must let out that money on loan, because that will bring in more interest, or something of that kind? It is purely a matter of the management of the business. It may not be management in actual dealing in butchers' meat, but that is not the point; the point is that the business is to be managed by the directors. How the directors can manage the business if they are to be interfered with in such an ordinary financial matter as to how to deal temporarily with balances which are for the moment not required for the purpose of the business, I confess I cannot conceive.

It seems to me it is quite clear that this resolution, if it is not aimed at declaring an interim dividend, is aimed at interfering with the management of the business by the directors and, as such, it is in my view wholly inoperative, and the general meeting had no power to pass it.

It is suggested that somehow or other the resolution can be justified under the terms of article 71, because it is said that while the directors are authorised by that article to

> ' . . . exercise all such powers of the company, as are not, by the Act, or by these articles required to be exercised by the company in general meeting, subject, nevertheless, to any regulation of these articles, to the provisions of the Act and to such regulations, being not inconsistent with the aforesaid regulations or provisions, as may be prescribed by the company in general meeting . . .'

those words must be treated as limiting the power, the right and the duty — I would prefer to say 'duty' rather than 'right' — of the directors to manage the business of the company.

To begin with, I do not take the view that those limiting words 'subject nevertheless,' and so forth, have anything to do with the duty cast upon the directors in the first two lines of the article to manage the business of the company. However that may be, if I am wrong in that, and, if I ought to treat the duty cast upon them to manage the business as being 'subject to any regulation of these articles' — which of course it must necessarily be — 'to the provisions of the said Act' — which it must necessarily be — 'and to such regulations, being not inconsistent with the aforesaid regulations or provisions, as may be prescribed by the company in general meeting,' the question is whether the company, by prescribing this important regulation, if it be a regulation, are prescribing something which is inconsistent with the aforesaid regulations or provisions. One of the aforesaid regulations or provisions is this provision about the business of the company being managed by the directors, and I find the greatest difficulty in seeing how any resolution of the company in general meeting, controlling the directors in the management of the business, can possibly be justified under the terms of this article.

SOURCE 155
Breckland Group Holdings Ltd *v* London & Suffolk Properties
(Chancery Division) [1989] BCLC 100

HARMAN J: . . . [Breckland] seeks an injunction restraining Crompton and Mr Holmes from continuing in the name of London and Suffolk or from procuring London and Suffolk to continue an action in the Queen's Bench, 1988 L no 1951, secondly it seeks an injunction restraining London and Suffolk from purporting to take any further step in action no 1951 save with the leave of this court,

Breckland is a 49% shareholder in London and Suffolk. Crompton is a 51% shareholder in London and Suffolk. London and Suffolk has a board of directors and has a very carefully drawn shareholders' agreement expressly restricting the powers of the board in particular ways. In particular clause 3 of the shareholders' agreement provides for the constitution of the board and provides especially that Crompton shall have two non-executive directors on the board and Breckland shall be entitled to appoint one at all times. Provisions are made about the chairman of the board and so on. Then under clause 3.04 any decision of the company relating to some matters requires the affirmative vote of the share-holders, so that general meeting voting is fettered to some extent by that provision.

Clause 3.05 fetters the decisions of the board in a different manner. The shareholders agree that any decision of the board relating to some specified matters shall require approval by the affirmative vote or the consent in writing of one Crompton director and the Breckland director, thus essentially requiring that both the 49% and the 51% shareholder representative shall be in favour of the action before the board can validly decide to take it. Amongst the listed matters is (xiv), 'the institution of material legal proceedings . . . '

In fact on 8 July 1988 the proceedings called no 1951 were issued in the name of London and Suffolk. That action was in the Queen's Bench Division and was against six defendants. First is Mr Avery, who is the principal shareholder in Breckland and controls it, and so indirectly controls 49% of the shares in London and Suffolk; he is also, I am told, the managing director of London and Suffolk and charged with all the executive management of its business.

. . .

That action . . . was brought without any prior board resolution of any sort. It was brought under a very surprising document, which purports to be a decision of Crompton, providing that Mr Holmes, who is a director I think of Crompton and certainly the controlling shareholder in Crompton and thus indirectly the 51% shareholder in London and Suffolk, should have the conduct of the action and give instructions on behalf of London and Suffolk to solicitors. That plainly is not valid authorisation on behalf of London and Suffolk, . . .

There has been convened a board meeting to be held, I think, on 3 August 1988 at which I believe, but I am not sure I have seen any agenda, a resolution is likely to be proposed adopting and ratifying the action no 1951 which will, following *Danish Mercantile Co Ltd v Beaumont* [1951] 1 All ER 925, [1951] Ch 680, amount to complete ratification and the adoption from the beginning of the action. The action will become completely valid from square one if the board so decide. However, it is plain that that is a matter within clause 3.05 (xiv) in the shareholders' agreement, and again counsel for the defendants with his usual good sense never sought to take any bad point and simply conceded that that was 'the institution of material legal proceedings' and plainly within the negative requirements of that agreement.

Mr Avery is entitled to attend that board meeting and his affirmative vote or consent in writing is essential for it. It was suggested to me by counsel for the defendants that it could be said now that Mr Avery would be bound to vote in favour of the institution of these legal proceedings. I do not believe that is sound. Firstly, one cannot exercise fiduciary discretions and duties nunc pro tunc. They must be exercised in the light of all circumstances known to the relevant fiduciaries at the time when the decision comes to be made, and I do not know what the position will be on 3 August, and nor does counsel. So it cannot be right that one can now say of Mr Avery that he is bound to vote in favour.

Secondly, Mr Avery is undoubtedly a fiduciary and undoubtedly must consider the true interests of the company and not his own interests in exercising his vote at the board. None the less, it is impossible to be sure that there are not countervailing arguments which could show that it was not in the interests of the company to assume the Queen's Bench action no 1951 because of factors which are not explored before me. One cannot at the moment possibly say that it is a foregone conclusion which way Mr Avery should vote at the board meeting.

There has also been attempted to be convened, but I think counsel for the defendants again sensibly abandoned any real reliance on it, a general meeting of the company. He said really, I believe in the end, and I believe soundly in law, that he did not need to rely on the convening of the general meeting, given the constitution of London and Suffolk with a 51% shareholder one way and a 49% shareholder the other way, and no restriction in the shareholders' agreement on how they could vote on a matter like this so that they were free (see *North-West Transportation Co Ltd v Beatty* (1887) 12 App Cas 589) to vote in their own interests at the general meeting. One can plainly say that if and when a validly convened general meeting is held one can be sure of what the outcome will be. It would be an affirmative vote in favour of the wishes of Mr Holmes and Crompton. Thus, says counsel for the defendants, it does not really matter whether the board meeting will or will not come to a conclusion in favour of ratifying and adopting action no 1951 because it can be foreseen now that that action will be ratified and adopted at a general meeting when one is properly convened, if necessary, and since one can forecast with certainty the outcome the court is not in the business of making people jump through unnecessary hoops and therefore you will not wait for the outcome of a preordained meeting.

I believe that is sound argument so far as it goes. It omits the difficult point of law with which I am faced at 4.20 on a Friday evening: can a general meeting in circumstances of this sort pass a resolution to adopt 'material legal proceedings' when by the provisions of art 80 of the articles of association which govern this company (see the Companies Act 1948, Sch 1, Table A, reg 80) such a matter is within the remit of the board? It is not only placed within the remit of the board by the articles because of some drafting process. The shareholders' agreement points to the shareholders thinking it was a matter that the board ought to control and consider. What is more the shareholders' agreement points to it being accepted by both parties that consent of both parties to the institution of legal proceedings at a board meeting was a requirement for such valid institution.

[Harman J then quoted the passage from the judgment of Buckley LJ in *Gramophone and Typewriter Ltd v Stanley* [1908] 2 KB 89 at 105–106, quoted by Farwell LJ in *Salmon v Quin & Axtens Ltd* [1909] 1 Ch 311 (see p 416) and continued:]

Thus one has in my view observations which are not stated to be expressly overruling Neville J's decision[1] but are inevitably wholly in conflict with it. I would cite only briefly also the well-known decision in *John Shaw & Sons (Salford) Ltd v Shaw* [1935] 2 KB 113 at 134, [1935] All ER Rep 456 at 464, where Greer LJ observed:

'A company is an entity distinct alike from its shareholders and its directors. Some of its powers may, according to its articles, be exercised by directors, certain other powers may be reserved for the shareholders in general

---

1 *Marshall's Valve Gear Co Ltd v Manning Wardle & Co Ltd* [1909] 1 Ch 267 (see p 428)

meeting. If powers of management are vested in the directors, they and they alone can exercise these powers. The only way in which the general body of the shareholders can control the exercise of the powers vested by the articles in the directors is by altering their articles ... '

...

Thus, as it seems to me, there is little doubt that the law is that, where matters are confided by articles such as art 80 to the conduct of the business by the directors, it is not a matter where the general meeting can intervene. Counsel for the defendants sought to distinguish the cases by saying that in the cases which have been referred to the directors had come to one decision and the general meeting sought to overrule them and come to an opposite decision. In my belief that factor or distinction which undoubtedly exists is not a distinction which in law affects the principles which I have to try and apply. The principle, as I see it, is that art 80 confides the management of the business to the directors and in such a case it is not for the general meeting to interfere. It is a fortiori when the shareholders coming together have specifically resolved some matters be required to have their joint consent and have confided that matter particularly to the directors. That seems to me to reinforce the general proposition which I derive from the authorities cited.

Thus, as it seems to me, the action was, as is admitted, wrongly brought: it cannot at present be known whether the board will adopt it or ratify it on 3 August. If the board do not adopt it, a general meeting would have no power whatever to override that decision of the board and to adopt it for itself. Thus at the moment there can be no certainty whatever as to what would happen. It seems to me that in those circumstances I ought to restrain further steps in this action pending a decision whether the company will by its proper organ, that is the board, adopt it. It may do so. If so, it will be valid and ratified and adopted from its initiation.

In those circumstances as it seems to me I ought to say that until that matter is decided no further steps should be taken in action no 1951. I will not and I should not strike it out at present. The matter of striking out must await later resolution. It could not be right at present when there is a pending board meeting. But it is right to say that an unauthorised action should not be pursued, particularly not at the cost of the company whose funds may be being wrongly misapplied. Further, in my judgment, a party should not obtain an advantage out of action which is, by definition, wrongly constituted at present, over other parties by wrongfully, at present, taking the name of the company into his own hands and using it without authority. Thus, as it seems to me, a temporary stay on all further steps in action no 1951 ought to be imposed on the particular persons concerned, Crompton and Mr Holmes. The form of the order in the notice of motion in para 1, restraining them from continuing in the name of London and Suffolk to carry on the action seems to me a proper one which I ought to make.

An order restraining the company itself from purporting to take any further steps seems to me necessarily to follow. There is a relationship between the plaintiff and the company in that the plaintiff is a 49% shareholder of the company. It is plainly wrong that the company's affairs be conducted in a manner which is wholly unauthorised and a shareholder in my view has a right to bring an action to restrain the company from so conducting itself.

SOURCE 156
Foster *v* Foster
(Chancery Division 1916) [1916] 1 Ch 532; 85 LJ Ch 305

The plaintiff was claiming (inter alia) to have set aside resolutions of the general meeting of shareholders which removed him as the managing director of the company and appointed the defendant in his place.

PETERSON J: . . . Here I think it must be taken on the facts that all parties agree that a managing director ought to be appointed; there is a contest between the plaintiff and Mrs Foster, the two persons who hold the largest blocks of shares, as to which of them should occupy that position. They were apparently the only persons whom any shareholder contemplated as possible managing directors of the company. First one was appointed, then the two were jointly appointed, and the Mrs Foster insisted on the appointment of herself, and that was objected to by the plaintiff. Owing to the way in which the shareholding of the directors is distributed neither of them can be appointed. The plaintiff holds a minority of the votes on the board; Mrs Foster is in the position that she is unable to vote in support of her own appointment. From a business point of view it seems to me that there are only two persons who are possible managing directors, and the board has been reduced to the position that it is unable, owing to internal friction and faction, to appoint anybody as a managing director. In those circumstances I should apply the decision of Warrington J in *Barron v Potter*.[1] The learned judge says: 'If directors having certain powers are unable or unwilling to exercise them — are in fact a non-existent body for the purpose — there must be some power in the company to do itself that which under other circumstances would be otherwise done. The directors in the present case being unwilling' — in this case unable — 'to appoint additional directors under the power conferred on them by the articles, in my opinion, the company in general meeting has power to make the appointment. The company has passed a resolution for that purpose, and though a poll has been demanded no date or place has yet been fixed for taking it. The result therefore is that I must grant the relief asked.'

The result is that this question relating to the appointment of Mrs Foster as managing director is one with which the general meeting of the company can deal, and recourse must be had to a general meeting; and therefore, having regard to the authorities, I think that this part of the plaintiff's case also fails.

SOURCE 157
Re Argentum Reductions (UK)
(Chancery Division 1975) [1975] 1 WLR 186; [1975] 1 All ER 605

This was an application under the provisions of s 227 of the Companies Act 1948 (now s 127 of the Insolvency Act 1986) to obtain the leave of the court to enable the company, against which a winding-up petition had been filed, to pay certain debts. The application was made by the company and one shareholder and was opposed by another shareholder.

MEGARRY J: . . . The question is really one of authority, in that Mr Potts[2] contends that Mr Merriman[3] has no authority to make any application in the name of the company. Mr Potts' contention was simplicity itself. The company

---

1 [1914] 1 Ch 895; 83 LJ Ch 646 (see p 400)
2 Counsel for the respondent shareholder (opposing the application)
3 Counsel for the company and the applicant shareholder

has no managing director: the only two directors are in complete disagreement with each other: there has been no resolution of the directors that the company should apply under section 227: therefore nobody can have authorised the company to make any application under the section.

Mr Merriman's answer was that Mr McAllister was managing director of the company de facto, though not de jure, and that as such he was entitled to authorise an application in the name of the company. His tacit authority as de facto managing director clearly extended to the day-to-day running of the company's affairs: section 227 was now impeding that day-to-day running of the company's affairs: and his authority must be taken to extend to seeking in the name of the company to remove the impediment. He supported his contention by reference to Mrs AcAllister's position as majority shareholder, and said that as such she could authorise her husband to make the application in the company's name. Mr Potts had contended that no meeting of the company could be held since Mrs Jenkins would not attend any meeting and so there would not be the necessary quorum of two: but, said Mr Merriman, *Marshall's Valve Gear Co Ltd v Manning, Wardle & Co Ltd*[1] sufficiently answered that.

In that case, three of the four directors of the company refused to sanction certain legal proceedings by the company. The other director, who held a simple majority of the shares in the company, had commenced the action in the name of the company. Neville J dismissed a motion by the other three directors, brought in the name of the company, to strike out the company's name as plaintiff and to dismiss the action on the ground that the company's name had been used without authority. The judge, . . . observed that it would be useless to call a meeting of the company to ascertain the wishes of the shareholders, as the wishes of the majority were perfectly well known, and that, contract apart, the majority of shareholders had the ultimate control of the company's affairs, and were entitled to decide whether or not an action in the company's name should proceed. That in essence, it was contended, was the situation in the present case, where Mrs AcAllister, with her 48 shares, could always out-vote Mrs Jenkins, with her 47.

Mr Potts' reply was that *Marshall's* case was at best of highly doubtful authority. He referred me to the text and supporting authorities in *Buckley on the Companies Act* (13th edn 1957), p 860. Put shortly, this passage is to the effect that, apart from fraud, where the articles have (as they have in this case) confided the control of the company's affairs to the directors, the shareholders, even if unanimous, cannot give directions to the directors as to what they are to do, or overrule their decisions. The shareholders may, of course, alter the articles or remove the directors, provided this is done in the appropriate way; but while the directors are in the saddle, in the saddle they remain. It is another matter where there is fraud or mala fides in the directors: and a footnote suggests that *Marshall's* case . . . might be supported on this ground. In that case, I may say, the three opposing directors were personally interested in the patent which was the subject of the disputed legal proceedings.

Now there are ways in which the deadlock in the case before me might be resolved. The refusal of Mrs Jenkins to attend any company meeting might be met if a successful application were to be made under section 135, and the court ordered the holding of a meeting of the company, with a direction that one person present in person or by proxy should be deemed to constitute a meeting. Steps might be taken to remove Mr Jenkins as a director, or to appoint another

---

1 [1909] 1 Ch 267; 78 LJ Ch 46 (see p 428)

director. These matters would, however, take a little time, and here I am concerned with a company which is carrying on a business and has been struck by section 227, one of the usual consequences of which is that its bank account is frozen. If one accepts to the full that the shareholders cannot reverse a decision of the directors, or compel them to do what they do not want to do, one does not necessarily reach the conclusion that where the directors are in deadlock as to a course of action, the majority of the shareholders are powerless to come down on one side or the other. Nevertheless, there are deep waters here; one has only to look at *John Shaw & Sons (Salford) Ltd v Shaw*[1] . . . to see that.

. . .

Mr Potts contended that where the petition or winding up the company was brought by a contributory and not by a creditor, the only proper applicants under section 227 were either the company itself or else the other party to the transaction in question, or someone claiming a proprietary interest under him. Thus if the company sold property to a purchaser who then mortgaged it, Mr Potts accepted that the purchaser and the mortgagee could both apply under the section. But he contended that a shareholder in the company, as such, has no such right.

. . .

I cannot see why this should be so. To a shareholder, and not least to a majority shareholder, it may be a matter of great concern, as closely affecting the value of his shares, that certain transactions should be saved from being invalidated. True, the shareholder as such will usually be no party to the transaction, and so it can be said that his interest in validating it is not direct but only indirect: yet an indirect interest may be of great value and importance. Why should a person with an interest to protect, even if it is indirect, be driven from the court when neither the Act nor the rules give any indication that he should be excluded? Where the company is able to apply to the court but chooses not to do so, the question of the weight to be attached to an application made by a person with an indirect interest is another matter: I am here concerned only with the right to apply. Furthermore, I do not see why, in companies where there is a state of potential deadlock, it should be open to one of the factions, by making the potential deadlock actual, to render it impossible for an application to validate a disposition under section 227 to be made except by the other party to that disposition, or those claiming under him. Of course, if a shareholder has the locus standi to seek an order, the jurisdiction in a case of deadlock must be exercised with a proper care: but it is a very different matter to say that the shareholder cannot even apply.

Accordingly, in my judgment a shareholder has a sufficient locus standi to make an application under section 227 for the validation of dispositions.

SOURCE 158
Alexander Ward *v* Samyang
(House of Lords 1975) [1975] 1 WLR 673; [1975] 2 Lloyd's Rep 1

The plaintiff company (pursuers — the action took place in Scotland) brought its action at the instance of its two shareholders. It had no board of directors and had held no general meeting for several years. The defendant pleaded that the action was not properly authorised in view of the fact that the plaintiff company's articles (arguably) entrusted the decision whether the

---

1 [1935] 2 KB 113; 104 LJKB 549

company litigated to the directors. The defendant's plea was dismissed and
the House of Lords dismissed the defendant's appeal. Subsequent to the
bringing of the action, the plaintiff company went into liquidation and the
liquidator adopted the action against the defendant.

LORD HAILSHAM: . . . I begin by pointing out, not as a pure piece of pedantry,
but as bearing on my opinion on both parts of the case, that the ratification relied
on is not that of the liquidator, but that of the company acting by the liquidator.
The proceedings were ab initio in the name of the company. By the time he was
sisted and adopted the proceedings, the liquidator was authorised to act for the
company. It is not simply an exercise in semantics to point out that if there was
a ratification of the acts of Ward and Irons, it was a ratification by the company
acting through the liquidator, and not by the liquidator acting on his own behalf.
The question for consideration is whether the company could ratify through the
liquidator, and not whether the liquidator could ratify for the benefit of the
company.

Clearly, if and in so far as the company could ratify the acts of Ward and Irons,
the company has done so by adopting the proceedings, and, on the general
principle governing the law of ratification, 'Omnis ratihabitio retrotrahitur et
mandato priori aequiparatur,' the ratification dates back to the acts ratified, and
so to the time when the arrestments were laid, and the summons issued.

The appellants' counsel relied, however, basically on the contention that none
of these acts can be ratified by the company as, he urged, the second of the three
conditions laid down by Wright J in *Firth v Staines*[1] viz that 'at the time the act was
done the agent must have had a competent principal' had not been fulfilled,
because the respondent company had neither appointed directors nor held a
general meeting and so was incapable of instructing solicitors or other agents to
do the acts alleged to have been ratified. Thus, it was contended, the company
was not a competent principal within the meaning of the requirement.

With respect, however, this argument is a non sequitur which should only
become cogent if one adopted a false and question-begging meaning to the word
'competent'. In my opinion, at the relevant time the company was fully
competent either to lay arrestments or to raise proceedings in the Scottish courts.
The company could have done so either by appointing directors, or, as I think, by
authorising proceedings in general meeting, which in the absence of an effective
board, has a residual authority to use the company's powers. It had not taken, and
did not take, the steps necessary to give authority to perform the necessary
actions. But it was competent to have done so, and in my view it was therefore a
competent principal within the meaning of the second of Wright J's three
conditions. So far as regards the powers of general meeting in *Gower Modern
Company Law*, (3rd edn 1969), pp 136–137 it is stated:

> 'It seems that if for some reason the board cannot or will not exercise the
> powers vested in them, the general meeting may do so. On this ground,
> action by the general meeting has been held effective where there was a
> deadlock on the board, where an effective quorum could not be obtained,
> where the directors are disqualified from voting, or, more obviously, where
> the directors have purported to borrow in excess of the amount authorised
> by the articles. Moreover, although the general meeting cannot restrain the
> directors from conducting actions in the name of the company, it still seems
> to be the law (as laid down in *Marshall's Valve Gear Co v Manning, Wardle &*

1 [1897] 2 QB 70

Co)[1] that the general meeting can commence proceedings on behalf of the company if the directors fail to do so.'

Counsel attempted to draw a distinction between the cases supposed in this passage, where the directors were for some reason unable or unwilling to act, and the instant case where there were no directors. I see no difference in this distinction and this also would appear to be the opinion of Harman LJ in *Bamford v Bamford*,[2] though the question at issue there was very different.

In my view this part of the present case is indistinguishable from *Danish Mercantile Co Ltd v Beaumont*,[3] and appellants' counsel was only able to draw a distinction between that case and the present by pointing to the fact that that was a case of deadlock between directors, and not of absence of any directors. In my view, as I have said, that is a distinction without a relevant difference, and, if that case was rightly decided, which I consider it was, the appellants' case on this part of the argument falls to the ground.

LORD KILBRANDON: ... The ground for the proposition that there was no person capable of giving instructions on behalf of the company was then, and is now, that article 74 of the pursuers' articles of association provides:

> 'The business of the company shall be managed by the directors, who-
> ... may exercise all such powers of the company as are not by the [Hong Kong] Ordinance or by these articles required to be exercised by the company in general meeting';

the raising of the action being an act of management, and there being no directors with the power to manage, the company cannot have, in the words of the fourth plea-in-law, 'authorised the raising of the action.' That plea has now been deleted, and there has been substituted, 'The pursuers not being the company have no title to sue.' I do not think that anything turns on that amendment.

My Lords, I must say I have the gravest doubts as to the soundness of the proposition pleaded. I am not at all convinced that, the management of a company having been confided to the directors, and the instructing of actions at law being an act of management, then, if the company has for the time no directors, it cannot during that time take steps to recover its debts. I think the article probably means no more than this, that the directors, and no one else, are responsible for the management of the company, except in the matters specifically allotted to the company in general meeting. This is a term of the contract between the shareholders and the company. But it does not mean that no act of management, such as instructing the company's solicitor, can validly be performed without the personal and explicit authority of the directors themselves. In any case I have even graver doubts whether the validity of the company's act, resting as it must on a construction of the contract with the shareholders, can in such a matter be challenged by someone whose only relationship with the company is one of indebtedness.

---

1 [1909] 1 Ch 267; 78 LJ Ch 46 (see p 428)
2 [1970] Ch 212; [1969] 1 All ER 969
3 [1951] Ch 680, [1951] 1 All ER 925

SOURCE 159
Blackman
[1975] 92 SALJ at 290

... There would, it is said, be chaos if the members were allowed to 'interfere' with the directors' exercise of their powers of management: 'a business does require a head to look after it, and a head that shall not be interfered with unnecessarily' [Farwell LJ in *Quin & Axtens v Salmon*] But why should this be so? There would of course be chaos if *both* the general meeting *and* the board were empowered to manage the business of the company; but it has never been suggested that article 80 does this. What is suggested is that the members can control the directors' exercise of their powers of management. The delegation of powers, subject to overriding control does not inevitably lead to chaos. On the contrary, it is, by far, the most common form of delegation. Indeed, it is in this very form that the directors usually delegate their powers to the managing director. And it is surely the appropriate form of delegation where it is the fundamental interests of those delegating the power that are at stake.

SOURCE 160
Sullivan
[1977] 93 LQR 579–80

It may be objected that the conclusion reached is only of more than academic concern in the small unquoted company and that in larger companies the power relationship between directors and shareholders can be described solely in terms of organisational reality and business practice. It is the conventional wisdom that in a company of any size a split emerges between ownership and control, the numerous and scattered shareholders becoming no match for the well organised, tightly knit management. Such an analysis is uncritically adopted by Bullock:

> 'the effect of the "managerial revolution" in large companies had been to concentrate power in the hands of the board of directors. Although in theory and in law directors are appointed by shareholders, the shareholders are too numerous to act effectively as a body, and have largely acquiesced in effective control by the board of directors.'

Thus a right of intervention under article 80 becomes largely theoretical.

Such a view distorts a more complex reality. In the 1960s a lack of confidence in British management led to low share prices under-representing the value of assets. Certain financial entrepreneurs recognised the opportunities implicit in this state of affairs and set about acquiring diffused shareholdings until they were able to force a take-over. As two commentators graphically put it,

> 'A portfolio investment is suddenly converted into a subsidiary company and all the traditional rights of property dramatically revert to one owner.'

Thus it was that 'strong' managers found themselves running an operating subsidiary of a financial empire owned by 'weak' shareholders. In the late sixties and early seventies the frequency of these occurrences caused one writer to describe them as a shift from 'managerial to finance capitalism.' It must be stressed that we are not speaking of a take-over by outside commercial management. The threat to incumbent management came from within the company, with one or more activist shareholders acquiring a controlling position by such expedients as share 'warehousing' and 'concert parties.' Sections 26 and 27 of the

Companies Act 1976,[1] which require the notification to the company of any 5 per cent holding of a class of shares within five days of acquisition and the disclosure of any beneficial interests in its voting shares, together with any voting agreement, are a direct if belated legislative response to this trend. Nor is it necessary to go to the extent of gaining a 50 per cent holding and dismissing the board; as J. Slater, amongst others, demonstrated one could acquire substantially less leaving the board *in situ* and still have anxious attention paid to one's policy preferences. This phase of British capitalism is already of unlamented memory but the opportunity for responsible intervention in management matters should now be clear to the financial institutions, pension funds and insurance companies who hold 42 per cent of the shares in quoted British companies.

Objections to this position may be summarised as follows:

(i) The great majority of modern decisions which would seem to go together with economic and political trends. Consider: *Company Law and Commercial Reality*, pp 60–61 (Source 161).

(ii) The ability to dismiss a director is subject to serious qualifications, first the contract (see s 303(5) of the Companies Act 1985), secondly, inhibiting provisions in the articles of association (see *Bushell v Faith*,[2] p 318), thirdly, the power of a minority shareholder, who was also a director, to petition for the winding up of the company (see *Ebrahimi v Westbourne Galleries*,[3] p 566).

(iii) Even if it were correct that Art 80 of Table A of the 1948 Act allowed the general meeting to control the directors by ordinary majority, this is now no longer the case (see p 411).

(iv) The rule in *Foss v Harbottle* (p 532) was of no avail in the cases extracted and discussed above and anyway, goes to the ability of the shareholders to ratify *wrongs* done to the company. To say that the act of the board in defiance of the majority of the shareholders is a wrong, begs the question.

SOURCE 161
Sealy, Company Law and Commercial Reality

Perhaps the biggest misconception of all is about meetings. The idea that shareholder democracy is a practicable concept, or that it is a good solution to any problem, has been shown time and again to be fallacious; and yet the Acts continue to make stipulations for the sanctioning of decisions by general meeting, and the cry for more and more matters to be put to the members is raised whenever company law reform is mooted. Paradoxically, the law reform committees do seem to have been aware that they were chasing a phantom; the Cohen Committee admitted that the control exercised by shareholders was 'illusory', and the Jenkins Committee regarded it as only 'theoretically desirable': management had to be given a free hand. And yet, in their *recommendations*, the same committees fall into the familiar trap. Of course, in the real world outside, even those matters which are by law for the shareholders to decide upon do not actually get settled by meaningful discussion and voting in a representative,

---

1 See now, ss 198 ff of the Companies Act 1985
2 [1970] AC 1099; [1970] 1 All ER 53
3 [1973] AC 360; [1972] 2 All ER 492

democratic way: most small companies do not hold meetings at all, and what resolutions they do bother to record are faked after the event — or, rather, the non-event. Larger companies do hold meetings, but in practice they are wholly unrepresentative, for all sorts of reasons. All initiative is with the existing management. Shareholder apathy can be relied on to ensure that most individual shareholders will stay away; and those who bother to complete and return proxy forms rarely hear anything but the management's case on the issue before they do so. The institutional shareholders mainly proceed on the basis of leaving things be or, if there is a case to intervene, are likely to take action through their own channels, which may by-pass the democratic processes. So any idea that shareholder control can be made to work as a counter to managerial power is baseless, and has been shown to be false by every fieldwork study that has been undertaken, from those of Berle and Means in the 1930s to the present day.

Efforts to *strengthen* the members' power by legislative devices have proved in practice to be very easily by-passed; and yet the reformers and would-be reformers will not give up their nostalgic striving after a wholly unattainable ideal. A recent writer goes so far as to suggest that meetings on important matters should be held *twice*, so that members may have an interval to think over the directors' proposals before the ultimate vote. Would the turnout be twice as large, or half as large, I wonder?

The Acts of 1980 and 1981 show no sign that anyone has learned the lesson; they contain a considerable number of new provisions requiring a shareholders' vote, sometimes with a supermajority, and even at times lay down very specific detail about the timing and the conduct of the meeting. I complained in an earlier lecture that requirements like this were introduced by the legislators without sufficient concern for the burdens that were put on business in the form of expense and delay, and pointed out that as long ago as the 1930s the United States codes were *removing* procedural stipulations like this in the interest of keeping commence moving along. Now I raise the subject again because I believe also that it is folly to assume that companies *will* actually go through all these rituals, that they *do* all hold meetings today like the characters did in the *The Forsyte Saga*; and to believe that those companies which do hold meetings reach informed, representative, democratic decisions. The lawmakers are mesmerised by the congenial, but false, analogy with parliamentary democracy; their assumptions belong only in a dream-world.

Marshall's Valve Gear, which stands out against this trend, needs explaining. Marshall was the majority shareholder and the managing director of the plaintiff company, which had been incorporated to exploit a patent which he had invented. There were three other directors. The defendant company *in which these three other directors were interested* was alleged by Marshall to have infringed the patent but the board of directors — on which Marshall was in the minority — refused to authorise action by the plaintiff company. Marshall therefore caused the company to take action and Neville J held that as majority shareholder, he was entitled to do so.

One way of analysing *Marshall's* case, is as an exception to the Rule in *Foss v Harbottle*. The failure by the directors to authorise the action against the defendants to restrain the breach of the patent constituted a fraud on the company. The wrongdoers were in control of the company (to the extent that they controlled the litigation machinery) and their decision not to take action was based on self-interest and was clearly not in the interest of the company (consider the comments of Megarry J on this case, in *Re Argentum*[1]).

In *Shaw v Shaw,* on the other hand (which is frequently contrasted with *Marshall*'s case, the decision by the board that the company should litigate was upheld by the court despite a resolution by the shareholders to the contrary. Yet the distinction between these two cases is clear. In *Shaw v Shaw,* the decision to litigate was a management decision taken in the best interests of the company.

Against this attempt to explain *Marshall*'s case it may be argued that the action should have taken the form of a derivative action (p 534), with the majority shareholder as the (nominal) plaintiff, the plaintiff company as the (nominal) defendant and the defendant company and Marshall's co-board members as the real defendants. As to this, we may admit to defective procedure, but plead that the derivative action was still in a formative state (even in 1974, it could not be said to have been settled, see *Wallersteiner v Moir*,[2] p 542) and there was much to be gained, in a practical sense, in approving the form of the action.

NOTES AND QUESTIONS

1. *Consider the application (extension?) of the procedural informality principle (pp 381ff) in* Re Duo-matic[3] *and* Re Baily Hay.[4] *In the former, the articles of association required that a resolution be passed in general meeting to determine the directors' salaries. Although no meeting was held and no resolution passed, payments made to two directors were held justified in the circumstances where the only two directors and voting shareholders approved the accounts in which the remuneration was recorded. The fact that there was, in addition to these two directors and shareholders, a shareholder who held non-voting preference shares and who did not know of the remuneration, was irrelevant since he 'had no right to receive notice of or to attend and vote at a general meeting of the company', and therefore 'could be in no worse position if the matter were dealt with informally by agreement between all the shareholders having voting rights than he would be if the shareholders met together in a duly constituted general meeting'. The ignorance of this preference shareholder was, on the other hand, fatal to the payment of a sum to a director as remuneration for loss of office, since disclosure to and approval by the company was required under the provisions of s 191 of the CA 1948 (now s 312 of the CA 1985).*

   In Re Baily Hay *(above), an extraordinary general meeting was technically defective in that insufficient notice was given. A winding up resolution was passed at the meeting on the assenting votes of two shareholders. The other voting shareholders who attended the meeting abstained on the resolution. No one complained of the defect until years later. In rejecting an*

---

1 [1975] 1 WLR 186; [1975] 1 All ER 605 (see p 421)
2 [1974] 1 WLR 991; [1974] 3 All ER 217 (see p 542)
3 [1969] 2 Ch 365; [1969] 1 All ER 161
4 [1971] 3 All ER 693; [1971] 1 WLR 1357

application to have the winding up order set aside, Brightman J said (at pp 701; 1366-7 of citations)

'I consider that on the particular facts of this case all the corporators ought to be treated as having assented on 9 December 1965 [the date of the meeting] to the company being wound up on that day. In my judgment, the case falls within the principle of the decisions of the two cases I have mentioned [Re Express Engineering Works Ltd[1] and Parker & Cooper.Ltd v Reading[2]]. Admittedly three of the five corporators did not vote in favour of the resolution, but they undoubtedly suffered it to be passed with knowledge of their power to stop it. The true quality of the acts of such corporators on 9 December is not to be judged exclusively by reference to what they did or did not do on that day, but is also to be judged in the light of what they did and did not do thereafter.

What these corporators did and did not do after 9 December 1965 down to 10 December 1969, when they swore their affidavits disclosing this defence, points, in my view, to one conclusion only. The conclusion is that they outwardly accepted the resolution to wind up as decisively as if they had positively voted in favour of it. If the corporators attend a meeting without protest, stand by without protest while their fellow-members purport to pass a resolution, permit all persons concerned to act for years on the basis that that resolution was duly passed and rule their own conduct on the basis the resolution is an established fact, I think it is idle for them to contend that they did not assent to the purported resolution.'

2. *Why was Brightman J in* Re Baily Hay *so concerned to read the abstentions as affirmative votes? The relevant jurisdiction derived from* Re Express Engineering Works Ltd *and* Parker & Cooper v Reading, *and is expressed as follows in the former decision, namely, 'there being no suggestion of fraud, . . . the company was bound in a matter* intra vires *by the unanimous agreement of its members'. There would, thus, seem to be two requirements for invoking this jurisdiction, that the subject matter of the agreement should be honest and* intra vires *and that the agreement should be unanimous. The former is no more nor less than a general principle. But why should the agreement be unanimous? (Cf the rule in* Foss v Harbottle[3] *which asserts the competence of the* majority *of the members of cure non-fraudulent,* intra vires *defects, see p 532.) Should a distinction be drawn between (a) the existence of the meeting and knowledge of the business to be conducted (as to which there must be unanimity), and (b) the voting at the meeting (as to which there need not be unanimity)? The rationale for this jurisdiction is, surely, that all members know what is happening and can object if they wish.* Re Baily Hay *clearly satisfies this test (it is implicit in the dicta of Brightman J quoted above, that acquiescence is an alternative ratio for the decision). This rationale also serves to distinguish* EBM Co Ltd v Dominion Bank,[4] *where the action of the three principal shareholders in assenting to the granting of a security to the Bank was avoided because two other shareholders (wives of two principal shareholders and holding only one share each) were ignorant of it.*

---

1 [1920] 1 Ch 466; 89 LJ Ch 379
2 [1926] Ch 975; 96 LJ Ch 23 (see p 382)
3 (1843) 2 Hare 461; 67 ER 189 (see p 532)
4 [1937] 3 All ER 555

3. Re Oxted Motor Company Ltd[1] *applied the informality principle where the Companies Act prescribed an extraordinary resolution for the action in question (winding up). Can this principle be applied where the Act prescribes a special resolution?*

4. *Table A specifically provides for dispensing with having to give notice of board meetings to a director who is abroad (reg 88).*

5. *In Bentley-Stevens v Jones,[2] the plaintiff was seeking an injunction restraining the defendants (one of which was a company of which the plaintiff was a director and minority shareholder), from acting on a resolution passed at an extraordinary general meeting of the company removing the plaintiff as a director of the company. That extraordinary meeting had been summoned by the company's holding company ('Holdings') in terms of a resolution by the board of the holding company. The plaintiff was also a director of the holding company and had not received notice of the board meeting called for the purpose of summoning the general meeting of the defendant company.*

   'PLOWMAN J: . . . The plaintiff's case is first of all that proper notice of the board meeting of Holdings on Monday, 28 January 1974, was not given, with the consequence that the proceedings of that meeting, and everything that flowed from them, were invalid.

   Secondly, it was submitted on behalf of the plaintiff that even if sufficient notice of the meeting was given, a board meeting of the defendant company was necessary before an extraordinary general meeting of that company could be validly convened, and no such meeting was ever held, with the consequence that the extraordinary general meeting was not properly convened and its proceedings were therefore a nullity.

   . . . In my judgment, even assuming that the plaintiff's complaint of irregularities is correct, this is not a case in which an interlocutory injunction ought to be granted. I say that for the reason that the irregularities can all be cured by going through the proper processes and the ultimate result would inevitably be the same. In Browne v La Trinidad[3] Lindley LJ said: "I think it is most important that the court should hold fast to the rule upon which it has always acted, not to interfere for the purpose of forcing companies to conduct their business according to the strictest rules, where the irregularity complained of can be set right at any moment." It seems to me that the motion which is before me falls within the principle stated by Lindley LJ.'

6. *Is there an irreconcilable clash between the rule that unanimity is required to dispense with existing procedural requirements (pp 381ff) and the principle expressed by Lindley LJ, above?*

7. *Where the board is deadlocked and no meeting can be called (cf Barron v Potter,[4] above), there is authority for the proposition that the power of the directors reverts to the general meeting of shareholders which can meet and dismiss some directors and appoint others. In terms of s 371 of the Companies Act 1985, the court may order the calling of a meeting where it is otherwise impractical to do so, see Re El Sombrero.[5] Does this power extend to the*

1 [1921] 3 KB 32; 90 LJKB 1145 (see p 381)
2 [1974] 1 WLR 638; [1974] 2 All ER 653
3 (1888) 37 Ch D 1; 57 LJ Ch 292
4 [1914] 1 Ch 895; 83 LJ Ch 646 (see p 400)
5 [1958] Ch 900; [1958] 3 All ER 1

calling of a board meeting? Such deadlock may also lead to the exercise by the court of its just and equitable winding-up jurisdiction (see pp 561ff).

8. *Where the notice is specific as to the business to be transacted, it does not have to reveal all the details. Thus a notice describing the business as the election of directors does not have to specify how many directors will be elected or who the candidates for election are, see* Choppington Collieries Limited v Johnson & Others,[1] Betts & Co Limited v Macnaghten.[2]

9. *In* Normandy v Ind Coope & Co Limited,[3] *the company summoned a meeting by a notice which described the business as being '[t]o consider and, if thought fit, approve the draft new regulations which will be submitted to the meeting, . . .' and setting out a proposed resolution 'that such regulations be . . . adopted as the regulations of the company to the exclusion of all the existing regulations thereof'. The draft regulations were not circulated but the notice gave an address where they could be inspected 'without fee during the usual business hours'. The resolution was passed. The plaintiff, who did not attend the meeting, saw the new regulations for the first time when they were circulated with a notice summoning a second meeting to confirm the earlier resolution. He objected to those regulations which gave the directors wide powers to give pensions to retiring directors and which substantially increased the directors' remuneration and applied for an injunction to restrain the company from acting on the resolution. Kekewich J held that the first meeting was irregularly summoned on account of the failure to draw attention to the specific and important changes which the new articles would bring about in the powers of the directors, but he dismissed the claim. The rule in* Foss v Harbottle[4] *applied; only the company was empowered to bring the proceedings.*

   Normandy *is to be contrasted with* Baillie's[5] *case (p 398 which at first instance was decided on the authority of* Normandy, *but which was reversed on appeal).* Pennington, Company Law *(6th edn), p 658 considers* Normandy *'particularly harsh' and submits that* Baillie *is to be preferred otherwise ' . . . the rules which the court has devised to ensure that members have proper warning of the business to be transacted at meetings, would be valueless if members who controlled a majority of the votes at a general meeting wished to sustain a resolution of which inadequate notice was given, and which the minority have consequently not had a proper opportunity to consider'.*

10. *But are* Normandy *and* Baillie *in conflict? Consider the following propositions:*

    (i) *There is a common law principle that everyone entitled to attend a meeting is entitled to reasonable notice of it and its business (see pp 392ff and cf s 370(2) of the 1985 Act and reg 39 of Table A).*

---

1 [1944] 1 All ER 762
2 [1910] 1 Ch 430; 79 LJ Ch 207
3 [1908] 1 Ch 84; 77 LJ Ch 82
4 (1843) 2 Hare 461; 67 ER 189 (see p 532)
5 [1915] 1 Ch 503; 84 LJ Ch 409 (see p 398)

(ii) *This obligation is satisfied by reference in the notice to a publicly available document* (Young's[1] *case, p 397).*

(iii) Normandy *could therefore have been decided as it was, ie against the plaintiff in terms of (9) above and not by the application of the rule in* Foss v Harbottle.

(iv) *In* Baillie, *the principle covered by (8)* and *(9) was decisive — the crucial information was not available to the shareholders.*

(v) *The rule in* Foss v Harbottle *has no application and it is misleading to talk of* Baillie *as an example of an exception to this rule (cf* Wedderburn, 'Shareholders' Rights and the Rule in Foss v Harbottle', [1957] Cam LJ 194, [1958] Cam LJ 93 — *the only true exception is where the majority in control of the company are acting fraudulently. Note in this regard, the express forswearing of fraudulent behaviour on the part of the defendants by the plaintiff in* Tiessen v Henderson,[2] *p 396).*

(vi) *The rule in* Foss v Harbottle *applies in relation to transactions at meetings, not to the preparation for meetings; otherwise there would be a conflict with (i) above. Consider the dicta of Kekewich J in* Tiessen v Henderson:

'The man I am protecting is not the dissentient but the absent shareholder — the man who is absent because, having received and with more or less care looked at this circular, he comes to the conclusion that on the whole he will not oppose the scheme, but leave it to the majority. I cannot tell whether he would have left it to the majority of the meeting to decide if he had known the real facts. He did not know the real facts; and, therefore, I think the resolution is not binding upon him.'

(vii) *The rationale for the common law rule expressed in (i) above was well expressed by Megarry J in* John v Rees.[3]

'I also bear in mind the rule that, in general, a failure to give due notice of a meeting to even one member of a body who is entitled to attend invalidates the decisions of that body: see, eg Smyth v Darley,[4] concerning the election of an officer, and Young v Ladies' Imperial Club, Ltd[5] [p 394] where an expulsion was in issue. Here, no notice of the second meeting was given to a number of the members of the local Labour Party; and it is clear that this was due not to inadvertence or accident but to deliberation. It follows that the meeting was not validly constituted, and so its proceedings were void. In the words of Lord Campbell LC, in Smyth v Darley, "even a unanimous election by those who did attend would be void".

It may be that there are some who would decry the importance which the courts attach to the observance of the rules of natural justice. "When something is obvious," they may say, "why force everybody to go through the tiresome waste of time involved in framing charges and giving an opportunity to be heard? The result is obvious from the start." Those who take this view do not, I think, do themselves justice. As everybody who has anything to do with the law well knows,

---

1 [1896] 2 Ch 268; 65 LJ Ch 683
2 [1899] 1 Ch 861; 68 LJ Ch 353
3 1970 Ch 345; [1969] 2 All ER 274
4 2 IILC 789; 9 ER 1293
5 [1920] 2 KB 523; 89 LJKB 563

the path of the law is strewn with examples of open and shut cases which, somehow, were not; of unanswerable charges which, in the event, were completely answered; of inexplicable conduct which was fully explained; of fixed and unalterable determinations that, by discussion, suffered a change. Nor are those with any knowledge of human nature who pause to think for a moment likely to underestimate the feelings of resentment of those who find that a decision against them has been made without their being afforded any opportunity to influence the course of events.'

11. *If there is a rule in terms of 11(i) and (ii) above, is it part of the duty of the directors, in acting for the good of the company and in disclosing transactions in which they have an interest, to draw attention to provisions in the publicly available document referred to in the circular, which will benefit them? Here may be the proper sphere for the rule in* Foss v Harbottle, *to be applied where the directors are innocent or negligent (Pavlides v Jensen)[1] and not where they are fraudulent (Atwool v Merryweather).[2]*

12. *Why should notices convening shareholders' meetings have to be more informative and more specific than notices convening directors' meetings?*

13. Quin & Axtens v Salmon[3] *is a comparatively rare case of a conflict between the managing directorate and another organ as to a question of management and where that conflict falls to be resolved by reference to the articles. In* Holdsworth v Caddies,[4] *the managing director of the appellant company (and whose contract required him 'to perform the duties and exercise the powers in relation to the business of the company and the businesses (howsoever carried on) of its existing subsidiary companies . . . which may from time to time be assigned to or vested in him by the board of directors of the company') was refused damages for breach of contract where he was instructed to confine his duties to one small subsidiary. The instruction did not constitute a breach of contract. Like many others, this was a case which turned on the terms of the contract between the company and the managing director and reveals little of the comparative powers of the organs of managing director and board of directors.*

14. *Despite the substantial twentieth-century authority to the contrary, there is strong academic support in favour of the general meeting of shareholders as the strongest organ of the modern company. (See* Goldberge, *[1970] 33 MLR 177,* Blackman *[1975] 92 SALJ 286,* Sullivan *[1977] 93 LQR 569; for academic opinion to the contrary, see Sullivan op cit 573, n 23, 24.) Yet, apart from Sources 152, 154 and 155, the modern cases of* Shaw v Shaw[5] *and* Black White & Grey Cabs Limited v Fox[6] *strongly support the board of directors as the most powerful organ in a functioning company with all its organs. In the former decision, Slesser and Greer LJJ were, despite disagreement on other issues, in clear agreement that where the directors had authorised proceeding against certain of the company's directors, a vote by the majority of the shareholders to discontinue such litigation was null and void*

---

1 [1956] Ch 565; [1956] 2 All ER 518 (see p 440)
2 (1867) LR 5 Eq 464n; 37 LJ Ch 35 (see p 540)
3 [1909] Ch 311, affd [1909] AC 422; 78 LJ Ch 506 (see p 414)
4 [1955] 1 WLR 352; [1955] 1 All ER 725
5 [1935] 2 KB 113; 104 LJKB 549
6 [1969] NZLR 824

(see, in particular, pp 98 and 105–106). In the latter case, the New Zealand High Court held to be a nullity a resolution of the shareholders that all members of the company should be entitled to operate only one cab, whereas the directors had previously permitted two.

15. *The support for the general meeting of shareholders would seem to rest on the following:*

   (i) *the decision in* Marshall's Valve Gear v Manning Wardle;[1]

   (ii) *a close textual analysis of the relevant provisions of the articles of association;*

   (iii) *the rule in* Foss v Harbottle;[2]

   (iv) *the ability of the shareholders to dismiss a director by ordinary majority;*

   (v) *a belief that this was proper.*

---

1 [1909] 1 Ch 267, 78 LJ Ch 46
2 (1842) 2 Hare 461; 67 ER 189 (see p 532)

Chapter 7

DIRECTORS' DUTIES

PART I: INTRODUCTION

The relationship between shareholders and directors seems direct and obvious. Shareholders elect, generally from among themselves, a few to direct the operations of the company. This relationship thus seems to resemble that of principal and agent. Alternatively, in view of the fact that the directors are required to run the company in the best interests of those who have elected them, the relationship has some resemblance to that of trustee and beneficiary. The latter is all the more striking in view of the fact that the directors have control over the company's property which derives from the shareholders' own investment.

Yet, we saw in the last chapter the tensions there could be in the division of functions between the shareholders and directors within the company. We saw, too, the development of the board of directors from being the agent of the shareholders to the status of an independent organ alongside the shareholders. And now we confront the phenomenon that *in law* the relationship between shareholders and directors is anything but obvious. As we observed in an earlier chapter (pp 65ff), the veil of incorporation converts the relationships which we see, into legal forms which take account of the company's existence. Thus, there is not normally a legal relationship between shareholders and the directors but there are two separate relationships, one between the directors and the company, the other between the shareholders and the company.

We have already seen that the relationship between director and company can consist of, or indeed, be constituted by contractual provisions, which are either express or implied or a combination of both (pp 348ff). There is nothing strange in the idea of the company and the director enjoying and suffering contractual rights and duties vis à vis one another. Furthermore, the directors have control over the company's property, are expected to carry out its decisions and, in doing so, to behave diligently rather than negligently or fraudulently.

We can thus see that this relationship will also consist of principles derived from trusts, agency and torts. Indeed, the two major categories of directors' duties, fiduciary duties and duties of skill and care fall respectively into the separate areas first of equity built up of principles governing trusts and other fiduciary relationships, and, secondly, the common law consisting of principles of contract and tort.

It should also be mentioned that this relationship has increasingly become subject to statutory provisions. These occasionally reinforce existing principles of common law and equity (eg s 317 of the Companies Act 1985 requiring a director to disclose any interest he has in a contract involving the company), but mostly owe their existence to the inadequacies of the common law and

equity to handle the very complex world of modern commerce and corporations. And much of this statutory intervention is to prohibit a variety of
practices, usually on pain of criminal penalty (perhaps the best known of
these is the criminalising of insider trading, see ss 52–64 of the Criminal
Justice Act 1993). The relationship between director and company has,
therefore, also begun to absorb principles of criminal law.

This barrier between shareholders and directors has profound legal effects.
One consequence, that shareholders only *qua shareholders* enjoy a contractual
relationship with the company on the basis of the company's constitution, has
already been wrestled with (pp 303ff). In this area of company law — the
enforcement of directors' duties — this barrier is, if anything, even more
significant.

According to the legal analysis, directors derive their powers from the
company and owe their duties to the company. This places serious problems
before shareholders whose investments are threatened or diminished by the
acts of the directors. The directors' wrong will have been done to the
company, yet the shareholder will have suffered. This is the conundrum
which parades through company law as the rule of *Foss v Harbottle*[1] and its
exceptions and which binds together the problems of the enforcement of
directors' duties and the protection of minority shareholders.

PART II: TO WHOM ARE DIRECTORS' DUTIES OWED?

To Whom are the Duties Owed?

The orthodox position is that directors owe their duties to the company. This
applies both to the duties of care and skill as well as the fiduciary duties (see
Sources 162 and 163). There are a number of exceptions to this orthodox
principle, however. The circumstances may be such that a direct relationship
between directors and shareholders may have been established and where the
shareholders may be the beneficiaries of the directors' fiduciary duties
(Source 164). Thus, directors of a target company subject to a takeover bid
may be called upon to advise the shareholders whether to accept the offer
(Sources 165 and 166 and see ss 312–316 of the Companies Act 1985). A duty
on the part of the directors to the employees of the company is now
recognised by statute (s 309) and has also been accepted at common law
(Source 167).

SOURCE 162
Percival *v* Wright
(Chancery Division 1902) [1902] 2 Ch 421; 71 LJ Ch 846

This was an action to set aside a sale of shares in a limited company, on the
ground that the purchasers, being directors, ought to have informed their
vendor shareholders of certain pending negotiations for the sale of the company's undertaking. The shares of the company, which were in few hands and

---

1 (1843) 2 Hare 461; 67 ER 189 (see p 532)

were transferable only with the approval of the board of directors, had no market price and were not quoted on the Stock Exchange.

... the chairman of the company wrote to the plaintiffs' solicitors stating that ... he would take the shares at £12 5s.

On 20 October 1900, the plaintiffs' solicitors having taken a fresh valuation, replied that the plaintiffs were prepared to accept £12 10s. per share.

On 22 October 1900, the chairman wrote accepting that offer, and stating that the shares would be divided into three lots.

On 24 October 1900, the chairman wrote stating that eighty-five shares were to be transferred to himself and eighty-four shares apiece to two other named directors.

The transfers having been approved by the board, the transaction was completed.

The plaintiffs subsequently discovered that, prior to and during their own negotiations for sale, the chairman and the board were being approached by one Holden with a view to the purchase of the entire undertaking of the company, which Holden wished to resell at a profit to a new company. Various prices were successively suggested by Holden, all of which represented considerably over £12 10s. per share; but no firm offer was ever made which the board could lay before the shareholders, and the negotiations ultimately proved abortive. The Court was not in fact satisfied on the evidence that the board ever intended to sell.

SWINFEN EADY J: The position of the directors of a company has often been considered and explained by many eminent equity judges. In *Great Eastern Ry Co v Turner*[1] Lord Selborne LC points out the twofold position which directors fill. He says: 'The directors are the mere trustees or agents of the company — trustees of the company's money and property — agents in the transactions which they enter into on behalf of the company.' In *Re Forest of Dean Coal Mining Co*[2] Jessel MR says: 'Again, directors are called trustees. They are no doubt trustees of assets which have come into their hands, or which are under their control, but they are not trustees of a debt due to the company. The company is the creditor, and, as I said before, they are only the managing partners.' Again, in *Re Lands Allotment Co*,[3] Lindley LJ says: 'Although directors are not properly speaking trustees, yet they have always been considered and treated as trustees of money which comes to their hands or which is actually under their control; and ever since joint stock companies were invented directors have been held liable to make good moneys which they have misapplied upon the same footing as if they were trustees, and it has always been held that they are not entitled to the benefit of the old Statute of Limitations because they have committed breaches of trust, and are in respect of such moneys to be treated as trustees.'

It was from this point of view that *York and North Midland Rly Co v Hudson*[4] and *Parker v McKenna*[5] were decided. Directors must dispose of their company's shares on the best terms obtainable, and must not allot them to themselves or their friends at a lower price in order to obtain a personal benefit. They must act bonâ fide for the interests of the company.

The plaintiffs' contention in the present case goes far beyond this. It is urged that the directors hold a fiduciary position as trustees for the individual shareholders, and that, where negotiations for sale of the undertaking are on

1 (1872) LR 8 Ch App 149; 42 LJ Ch 83
2 (1878) 10 Ch D 450; 40 LT 287
3 [1894] 1 Ch 616; 63 LJ Ch 291
4 (1853) 15 Beav 485; 22 LJ Ch 529
5 (1874) 10 Ch App 96; 44 LJ Ch 425

foot, they are in the position of trustees for sale. The plaintiffs admitted that this fiduciary position did not stand in the way of any dealing between a director and a shareholder before the question of sale of the undertaking had arisen, but contended that as soon as that question arose the position was altered. No authority was cited for that proposition, and I am unable to adopt the view that any line should be drawn at that point. It is contended that a shareholder knows that the directors are managing the business of the company in the ordinary course of management, and impliedly releases them from any obligation to disclose any information so acquired. That is to say, a director purchasing shares need not disclose a large casual profit, the discovery of a new vein, or the prospect of a good dividend in the immediate future, and similarly a director selling shares need not disclose losses, these being merely incidents in the ordinary course of management. But it is urged that, as soon as negotiations for the sale of the undertaking are on foot, the position is altered. Why? The true rule is that a shareholder is fixed with knowledge of all the directors' powers, and has no more reason to assume that they are not negotiating a sale of the undertaking than to assume that they are not exercising any other power. It was strenuously urged that, though incorporation affected the relations of the shareholders to the external world, the company thereby becoming a distinct entity, the position of the shareholders inter se was not affected, and was the same as that of partners or shareholders in an unincorporated company. I am unable to adopt that view. I am therefore of opinion that the purchasing directors were under no obligation to disclose to their vendor shareholders the negotiations which ultimately proved abortive. The contrary view would place directors in a most invidious position, as they could not buy or sell shares without disclosing negotiations, a premature disclosure of which might well be against the best interests of the company. I am of opinion that directors are not in that position.

There is no question of unfair dealing in this case. The directors did not approach the shareholders with the view of obtaining their shares. The shareholders approached the directors, and named the price at which they were desirous of selling. The plaintiffs' case wholly fails, and must be dismissed with costs.

SOURCE 163
Pavlides *v* Jensen
(Chancery Division 1956) [1956] Ch 565; [1956] 2 All ER 518

The complaint of the plaintiff related to a sale of an asbestos mine in Cyprus, which was acquired by the company (according to the statement of claim) in 1936 for about £142,000 and was resold in 1947 for about £182,000 to Cyprus Asbestos Mines Ltd, in which the company held 25 per cent of the issued capital. This sale was carried through by the defendant directors, and was not submitted to the approval of the company in general meeting.

... the plaintiff alleged that the conduct of the defendant directors in effecting the sale was grossly negligent, in that it was a sale at a gross undervalue as the defendant directors well knew or ought to have known the true value of the mine (according to the plaintiff's allegations) having been 'somewhere in the neighbourhood of £1,000,000.'

...

DANCKWERTS J: It is contended on behalf of the defendants that the matters in respect of which the plaintiff complains, and in particular the question whether proceedings should be taken against the directors, is a matter of internal management of the company, with which, on the principle stated in *Foss v Harbottle*,[1] the court normally will not interfere. It is contended further on behalf of the defendants that the present case — based on negligence of directors — is not within the few recognized exceptions to the above-mentioned rule, namely, cases of *ultra vires*, illegality, or fraud (including fraudulent oppression of a minority by the majority of the shareholders). Further, it is said, the case is not a case where the control of the voting power is in the hands of the directors of the company whose actions are impugned; for they are not the shareholders; the shares are held by another company of which the defendant directors merely happen also to be among the directors.

For the plaintiff, it is contended that the above-mentioned exceptions are not exhaustive, and the court will grant relief wherever justice requires on any ground, and particularly where an otherwise helpless minority shareholder is in need of assistance by the court. As regards control, it is contended that, except for an immaterial period, the defendant directors, being a majority of the directors of Portland Tunnel Cement Co Ltd (the holders of the vast bulk of the shares of the company) were in a position to stifle any attempt to institute proceedings in the name of the company against them.

On the facts of the present case, the sale of the company's mine was not beyond the powers of the company, and it is not alleged to be *ultra vires*. There is no allegation of fraud on the part of the directors or appropriation of assets of the company by the majority shareholders in fraud of the minority. It was open to the company, on the resolution of a majority of the shareholders, to sell the mine at a price decided by the company in that manner, and it was open to the company by a vote of the majority to decide that, if the directors by their negligence or error of judgment had sold the company's mine at an undervalue, proceedings should not be taken by the company against the directors. Applying, therefore, the principles as stated by Lord Davey [in *Burland v Earle*, below, p 535], it is impossible to see how the present action can be maintained.

I have examined again all of the large number of authorities which were cited to me in the course of the arguments. Though there are to be found, in one or two instances, observations which at first sight might justify a more liberal view of the extent of minority shareholders' rights, when taken out of their context, I do not think any of the authorities justify any conclusion other than that which I have reached.

That really disposes of the matter, and it is not really necessary to consider whether, on the allegations contained in the re-amended statement of claim, the defendant directors can be said to have such control of the company as to require (in any appropriate case) the allowance of an action by a minority shareholder. The defendant directors are not in fact the holders of the shares, the voting power of which would settle the company's decision. I think that it must be admissible in certain cases to go behind the apparent ownership of the shares in order to discover whether a company is in fact controlled by wrongdoers — as, for instance, in the case where the shares were held by mere nominees, bound to vote as the owners required them to vote. In the present case, the shares are held by a company of which the defendant directors were, for the greater part of the material period, not only directors, but sufficient in number to out-vote the other directors, of the shareholding company. In this manner, it is said they could prevent the shareholding company passing any resolution which might result in proceedings being taken in the name of the company which is alleged to have

---

1 (1843) 2 Hare 461; 67 ER 189 (see p 532)

been injured against them. I suppose the shareholders of the shareholding company could in general meeting decide differently and disagree with the decision of the directors of that company. I am not satisfied that the defendant directors are in such control of the company as is necessary to justify an action by a minority shareholder, but I need not decide this question.

SOURCE 164
Allen *v* Hyatt
(Privy Council 1914) (1914) 30 TLR 444

... general and similar representations were made by the appellants to each of the respondents, to the effect that the former as directors wanted the options from the shareholders in order to deal on behalf of all the shareholders with the representatives of the Dominican Company; ... the appellants expected to realize the par value of the shares and the 7 per cent interest, and that all the shareholders, including themselves, were to share pro rata in the amount realized; ... the appellants did not inform the other shareholders that they were buying their shares on their own account, and that they had entered into a secret arrangement by which they kept concealed from the other shareholders the information which it was their duty, as directors, to disclose, and that the appellants were thereby guilty of fraud. Objections were taken on behalf of the appellants to the form of the proceedings. It was said that the directors were trustees, if at all, for the Lakeside Company, and that the latter ought to have been a party either as plaintiff or defendant, and that in its absence the respondents were not entitled to sue on behalf of themselves and the other shareholders.

    ...

The Court of Appeal took the ... view ... that although in other circumstances it might be that the fiduciary duty of the directors was a duty to the company and not to individual shareholders, yet in circumstances such as those of the case before them the directors became the agents in the transaction of the shareholders, when they took the options from them. They thought that the addition of the Lakeside Company as a party, if made, had been irregularly made, having regard to the real character of the action as one brought by a group of individual plaintiffs with what were substantially similar causes of action, and they struck out the name of the company from the record in affirming the judgment.

Arguments had been addressed to their Lordships both on the question of procedure and on the substantial issue whether the appellants were properly found to have put themselves in the circumstances in a fiduciary relation to the respondents. On the latter point their Lordships did not think it necessary to say more, so far as the questions of fact were concerned, than that, having heard the arguments and considered the evidence, they saw no ground for not accepting the concurrent findings of the three Courts which had already decided that issue. They agreed with the Court of Appeal in thinking that the respondents were entitled to treat the appellants as trustees for them, and, subject to the question of procedure, to ask for the relief they obtained.

The appellants appeared to have been under the impression that the directors of a company were entitled in all circumstances to act as though they owed no duty to individual shareholders. No doubt the duty of the directors was primarily one to the company itself. It might be that in circumstances such as those of

Percival v Wright[1] they could deal at arm's length with a shareholder. But the facts in the present case were widely different from those in *Percival v Wright*, and their Lordships thought that the directors must here be taken to have held themselves out to the individual shareholders as acting for them on the same footing as they were acting for the company itself, that was, as agents.

The appeal was dismissed.

SOURCE 165
Gething *v* Kilner
(Chancery Division 1972) [1972] 1 WLR 337; [1972] 1 All ER 1164

BRIGHTMAN J: This application relates to a takeover bid by Town Centre Securities Ltd (which I shall call 'Town Centre') for the issued stock of the Rochdale Canal Co (which I shall call 'Rochdale').

It raises an important and, as far as I am concerned, a novel question, which can be put shortly in this way: whether a shareholder in an offeree company who is dissatisfied with the manner in which an intended takeover is being conducted can, as it were, stop the takeover in mid-stream on the ground, in substance, that other shareholders are being misled into accepting the offer. No reported authorities were cited to me in argument.

. . .

The writ was issued on 5 November and claimed relief based on a breach of duty on the part of the Rochdale board and relief based on the existence of an alleged conspiracy between the Rochdale and Town Centre boards. The notice of motion seeks an injunction to restrain the Rochdale board from recommending the offer in any further way to the stockholders of Rochdale and also an injunction — and this is the principal relief sought — restraining Town Centre until judgment or further order from declaring or purporting to declare the offer unconditional.

The argument of Mr Arnold on behalf of the plaintiffs — with whom I have some sympathy — is this, that the directors of Rochdale had a duty towards the Rochdale stockholders to provide them with proper information. The Rochdale directors were in breach of that duty when they permitted the Town Centre offer to go out with their expressed recommendation, without disclosure of the contrary advice of Messrs Henry Cooke & Son. Town Centre was clearly implicated in that wrongful act on the part of the Rochdale board. Therefore Town Centre should be enjoined against declaring their offer unconditional, thus freeing any assenting stockholders of Rochdale from the assent which they have already given.

I accept that the directors of an offeree company have a duty towards their own shareholders, which in my view clearly includes a duty to be honest and a duty not to mislead. I also accept that a shareholder in an offeree company may be prejudiced if his co-shareholders are misled into accepting the offer. I express this view because as soon as the appropriate percentage of shareholders have been misled and have assented, the minority become subject under section 209 [see now s 429 of the CA 1985], to statutory powers of compulsory purchase. It therefore seems to me that a minority could complain if they were being wrongfully subjected to that power of compulsory purchase as a result of a breach of duty on the part of the board of the offeree company.

---

1 [1902] 2 Ch 421; 71 LJ Ch 846 (see p 438)

In the case before me, in my judgment, having considered the evidence as a whole, it is clear to me that the Rochdale board honestly believed that an offer of £200 for £100 of Rochdale's stock was advantageous and ought to be recommended to the stockholders; and on considering the figures before me it is also clear to me that a director could reasonably hold that belief.

In such circumstances it does not seem to me to be right that this court should interfere by way of interlocutory relief so as to prohibit the offeror company from declaring the offer unconditional if it so decides. The plaintiffs have other remedies if they do not wish to accept the Town Centre offer, if they wish to resile from an acceptance already given and if they are able to sustain that any wrong has been done. But I see no reason whatever on the facts of this case why the court should interfere with the conditional offer and the acceptances now subsisting between Town Centre and other Rochdale stockholders.

I appreciate that the plaintiffs may be disenchanted with the offer made by Town Centre and dissatisfied with the explanation given by Rochdale for recommending it. On the other hand there may be many stockholders not parties to this action who are perfectly satisfied with Town Centre's offer and I see no sufficient reason why their contract should be placed in peril in the absence of bad faith on the part of the two boards or conduct so unreasonable as to approach bad faith.

In those circumstances I decline to grant the relief sought by this motion.

SOURCE 166
Dawson International *v* Coats Paton
[1989] BCLC 233 (Outer House, Court of Session, Scotland); [1990] BCLC 560 (Inner House)

Dawson and Coats entered into negotiations for a takeover by Dawsons of Coats. A joint press announcement was made to the effect that the directors of Coats would recommend the Dawson's takeover bid. Subsequently, however, Viyella made a takeover offer for the shares in Coats and the directors of Coats recommended the Viyella bid to the Coats' shareholders. Dawson, which had no wish to be involved in a contested takeover bid, withdrew. It instituted these proceedings, inter alia, for breach of contract. The proceedings are reported at the preliminary stage of the motion by Coats that they be dismissed as disclosing no case in law (ie no cause of action) and should, therefore, not go ahead to inquiry by proof. Both courts agreed that the claim by Dawsons was sufficiently specific and relevant to go ahead.

LORD CULLEN (OUTER HOUSE): . . . I next consider the proposition that in regard to the disposal of their shares on a take-over the directors were under a fiduciary duty to the shareholders and accordingly obliged to act in such a way as to further their best interests. It is well recognised that directors owe fiduciary duties to the company. Thus the directors have the duty of fiduciaries with respect of the property and funds of the company. In terms of s 309 of the Companies Act 1985 when discharging their functions the directors are under a fiduciary duty to the company to have regard to, inter alia, the interests of members and employees. These fiduciary duties spring from the relationship of the directors to the company, of which they are its agents. I should observe that for the purposes of s 309 there appears to be no reason why 'members' should not be capable of applying to future as well as to present members of the company.

In contrast I see no good reason why it should be supposed that directors are, in general, under a fiduciary duty to shareholders, and in particular current shareholders with respect to the disposal of their shares in the most advantageous way. The directors are not normally the agents of the current shareholders. They are not normally entrusted with the management of their shares. The cases and other authorities to which I was referred do not seem to me to establish any such fiduciary duty. It is contrary to statements in the standard textbooks such as *Palmers Company Law* (23rd edn, 1982), para 64–02. The absence of such a duty is demonstrated by the remarkable case of *Percival v Wright* [1902] 2 Ch 421. I think it is important to emphasise that what I am being asked to consider is the alleged fiduciary duty of directors to current shareholders as sellers of their shares. This must not be confused with their duty to consider the interests of shareholders in the discharge of their duty to the company. What is in the interests of current shareholders who are sellers of their shares may not necessarily coincide with what is in the interests of the company. The creation of parallel duties could lead to conflict. Directors have but one master, the company. Further it does not seem to me to be relevant to the present question to build an argument on the rights, some of them very important rights, which shareholders have to take steps with a view to seeing that directors act in accordance with the constitution of the company and that their own interests are not unfairly prejudiced.

If on the other hand directors take it on themselves to give advice to current shareholders, the cases cited to me show clearly that they have a duty to advise in good faith and not fraudulently, and not to mislead whether deliberately or carelessly. If they fail to do so the affected shareholders may have a remedy, including the recovery of what is truly the personal loss sustained by them as a result. However, these cases do not, in my view, demonstrate a pre-existing fiduciary duty to the shareholders but a potential liability arising out of their words or actions which can be based on ordinary principles of law. This, I may say, appears to be a more satisfactory way of expressing the position of directors in this context than by talking of a so-called secondary fiduciary duty to the shareholders.

This brings me to comment on the use made in argument of the decision of the Court of Appeal in *Heron International Ltd v Lord Grade* [1983] BCLC 244. It is important to note that this case was concerned with the power of directors under art 29 of the articles of association, to decide who should be the purchaser and transferee when any shareholder desired to sell his shares. Lawton LJ said (at 264–265):

'In the present case, for example, the directors as a whole were under a duty to decide whether to sanction a sale by any director of voting shares to Bell. This duty to determine which person shall acquire and be registered as the holder of voting shares in ACC is a fiduciary power which the directors must exercise in the interests of the company and in the interests of the shareholders of the company. The fact that the directors as individuals held between them a majority of the voting shares did not authorise them to reflect their individual inclinations. The directors as directors had a duty to consider whether, in exercise of the fiduciary power vested in them by Art 29, they should agree to voting shares being transferred to Bell.'

The directors had accepted the Bell offer in respect of 53% of the voting shares held by them as individuals, as a result of which no other bid could be successful. It was held that in asserting that they would accept the Bell offer themselves irrespective of what advice should be given to other shareholders, they had ignored the fiduciary duties imposed by art 29. Accordingly it was a case in which the directors had allowed their personal inclinations to conflict with their duties as directors, with the effect of preventing the other shareholders from having the opportunity to accept or reject a rival bid. I understand Lawton LJ to mean that where it was decided by the directors that the company should be taken over, the duty to consider the interests of the company when exercising the power under art 29 resolved itself into a duty to have regard to the current shareholders (see [1983] BCLC 244 at 265). I do not consider that the case is authority for the proposition that directors may not on behalf of the company agree to recommend a bid and not to encourage or co-operate with an approach from another would-be bidder without being in breach of a fiduciary duty to the current shareholders.

SOURCE 167
Re Welfab Engineers Ltd
(Chancery Division) [1990] BCLC 633

These proceedings were taken out by the liquidators of the company (under what is now s 212 of the Insolvency Act 1986) against the former directors of the company. The company was insolvent and the directors were faced with three options, first to sell the land on which the business was carried on for £125,000, a course of action which almost certainly would entail the liquidation of the company and the loss of the business, secondly, the sale of the entire business, including the land for £110,000 and the company's debts so as to afford a reasonable opportunity for the continuation of the business and, finally, to ask the bank to appoint a receiver. The directors (the respondents to these proceedings) decided to take the second option. In the event, the business failed some months later.

> HOFFMANN J: . . . The view to which I have come after hearing the evidence of the respondents is that they never really considered the possibility of any deal which would not either allow the company to continue in business or involve the sale of the business as a going concern. If they had been unable to achieve either of these objects on reasonable terms, they would have invited the bank to appoint a receiver or, if the bank did not wish to do so, summoned a meeting of creditors. I do not think that they regarded it as their function to act as informal liquidators on a winding up of the business itself. It was for that reason that, having appreciated that the Bell & Webster offer[1] would not allow the business to continue, they decided to pursue it no further.
>
> . . .
>
> On this basis, I think that even on the assumption that the respondents should have undertaken the task of liquidating the business, there was not a great deal between the two offers. But there is, I think, a point of principle involved in the question of whether they should be judged on the footing that it was their duty to do so. The liquidators accept that, if they had decided to invite the appointment of a receiver, the chances of the creditors having done any better would have been minimal. The bank's correspondence shows that it was very conscious of the realities of the situation: the costs would have been high, the debts would have been difficult to collect, the equipment, stock and work in progress would have realised very little indeed. But counsel for the liquidators (Mr Parker) says that this is no answer. It only shows that the respondents could

---

1 To buy just the land (the first option)

have done worse. Having undertaken the task of realising the assets, they should have done so to the best advantage of creditors.

I do not think that this would be fair or realistic. In my view the respondents were entitled to take the view that, if the business could not be saved, its liquidation was not a task which they were required to undertake. If they had decided to invite a receiver or wind up the company, with all the consequences which that would have involved, they could not possibly have been criticised. I therefore consider that, in judging the propriety of the respondents' actions, they should be compared with the alternatives of receivership or liquidation. This seems to me in accordance with recent developments in insolvency law, such as the institution of administration, which are intended to encourage trying to save the business rather than destroy it. Of course directors are not entitled to sell the business to save their jobs and those of other employees on terms which would clearly leave the creditors in a worse position than on a liquidation. But I do not think that an honest attempt to save the business should be judged by a stricter standard. This is particularly so against the background of the pressures which must have been imposed on directors of companies like this by the widespread unemployment and industrial devastation in the Midlands at the time. And in my judgment, the respondents were completely honest and believed in good faith that they were entitled to enter into the Thermaspan deal.

I therefore consider that the respondents were not in breach of duty and that the summons must be dismissed. If I were wrong in this, I would consider that the respondents had acted honestly and reasonably and ought fairly to be excused from liability under s 727 of the Companies Act 1985.

PART III: BY WHAT STANDARDS ARE DIRECTORS TO BE JUDGED?

Directors' duties have generally been categorised as the duty of good faith and the duty of care and skill. The former derives from equitable principles and reflects the fact that directors, while not actually the owners of property belonging beneficially to others (as in the case of trustees), have control over property which does not belong to them. In theory, this property belongs in law *and equity* to the company. This duty is thus designed to ensure that the directors use this property for the benefit of the company and not for their own benefit. In principle, the duty is a strict one captured in the following dicta of Lord Cranworth LC in *Aberdeen Railway Company v Blaikie Brothers*[1] (where the House of Lords reversed a decree of the Scottish court and struck down a contract under which the company had agreed to purchase a large order of chairs from the firm of which chairman of the board of directors was a partner):

'A corporate body can only act by agents, and it is of course the duty of those agents so to act as best to promote the interests of the corporation whose affairs they are conducting. Such agents have duties to discharge of a fiduciary nature towards their principal. And it is a rule of universal application, that no one, having such duties to discharge, shall be allowed to enter into engagements in which he has, or can have, a personal interest conflicting, or which possibly may conflict, with the interests of those whom he is bound to protect.

1 (1854) 1 Macq 461

So strictly is this principle adhered to, that no question is allowed to be raised
as to the fairness or unfairness of a contract so entered into.'

This case and these dicta are still quoted and relied upon, but we should
observe two important qualifications to their apparently unremitting nature.
In the first place, the company's constitution reflects the agreement of the
incorporators and can include provisions which reduce the scope of this duty
(see, eg Table A, regs 85, 86 and Source 186 at p 513). Secondly, the duty of
good faith includes other powers enjoyed by the directors apart from the
power to use the company's property, for example, the powers to sanction or
refuse a transfer of the company's shares and the power to allot unissued
shares. In relation to both these powers, the court adopts a much more
benign attitude to the directors, establishing a very strong presumption that
directors act in good faith and for the benefit of the company (Source 172)
and if they have apparently not acted in good faith and for the benefit of the
company, then in some circumstances their actions may be ratified by the
shareholders (Source 173).

The latter duty — the duty of care and skill – derives from the common law
and seeks to ensure that directors act diligently in the performance of their
duties, ie reasonably and not unreasonably. In theory acting carelessly,
constitutes the tort of negligence for which the wrongdoing directors can be
made to compensate the victim, ie the company. In practice, however, as we
have already seen (see *Pavlides v Jensen*, Source 163) and as we shall observe
in the next chapter, there are substantial procedural problems with pursuing
such a claim. In addition, the courts established relatively low standards
against which to assess the conduct of directors, in particular laying down the
principle that directors are entitled to rely on the honesty and diligence of
those to whom work is delegated unless there is good reason to suspect
otherwise (Sources 168 and 169).

The common law has been supplemented by statute to try to ensure that
directors do not take advantage of their power and control over the
company's property (pp 477ff). In addition, statute gives the court power to
relieve directors of the consequences of breach of duty in certain circumstances and has also sought to outlaw provisions in the company's articles
which seek to exclude or limit the liability of directors for breach of their
duties (pp 506ff).

PART IV: THE COMMON LAW DUTY OF CARE AND SKILL

SOURCE 168
Dovey *v* Corey
(House of Lords 1901) [1901] AC 477; 70 LJ Ch 753

EARL OF HALSBURY LC: ... Mr John Cory was a director of the company, and
it is for his supposed misconduct in the management of the affairs of the
company that this liability was imposed upon him. It is alleged and proved that
certain losses have been sustained by the company, and the ground upon which
Mr John Cory is sought to be made liable is the very short and intelligible ground
that he was a party to false and fraudulent statements as to the position of the

company, and had had a share in causing those losses. The Court of Appeal have acquitted him of any knowledge of what was falsely stated, and Sir Robert Reid, in opening this appeal, stated to your Lordships that he did not intend, in arguing for Mr John Cory's liability, to impute to him any moral obliquity. Now, there is no doubt that there were balance-sheets laid before meetings of the shareholders which, to use the language of the articles of association, were not proper and which did not truly report as to the state and condition of the company, and did not comply with the requirements of the articles in question in respect of the particular sum which the directors recommended as dividend that it should be paid out of profits, but a greater sum was paid out as dividend than would have been paid if certain things had been taken into consideration, and therefore larger than should have been paid.

. . .

Dealing with the several heads of charge as they have been formulated in the judgment of Wright J, namely, negligence, breaches of trust in respect of advances made contrary to the said articles of association, and payment of dividends out of capital, I think each and all of them may be disposed of by the proposition that Mr Cory was not himself conscious of any one of these things being done, and that unless he can be made responsible for not knowing these things, and, as Wright J put it, he is shewn to have exhibited a complete neglect of the duties he had undertaken, the charges are not made out.

The charge of neglect appears to rest on the assertion that Mr Cory, like the other directors, did not attend to any details of business not brought before them by the general manager or the chairman, and the argument raises a serious question as to the responsibility of all persons holding positions like that of directors, how far they are called upon to distrust and be on their guard against the possibility of fraud being committed by their subordinates of every degree. It is obvious if there is such a duty it must render anything like an intelligent devolution of labour impossible. Was Mr Cory to turn himself into an auditor, a managing director, a chairman, and find out whether auditors, managing directors, and chairmen were all alike deceiving him? That the letters of the auditors were kept from him is clear. That he was assured that provision had been made for bad debts, and that he believed such assurances, is involved in the admission that he was guilty of no moral fraud; so that it comes to this, that he ought to have discovered a network of conspiracy and fraud by which he was surrounded, and found out that his own brother and the managing director (who have since been made criminally responsible for frauds connected with their respective offices) were inducing him to make representations as to the prospects of the concern and the dividends properly payable which have turned out to be improper and false. I cannot think that it can be expected of a director that he should be watching either the inferior officers of the bank or verifying the calculations of the auditors himself. The business of life could not go on if people could not trust those who are put into a position of trust for the express purpose of attending to details of management. If Mr Cory was deceived by his own officers — and the theory of his being free from moral fraud assumes under the circumstances that he was — there appears to me to be no case against him at all. The provision made for bad debts, it is well said, was inadequate; but those who assured him that it was adequate were the very persons who were to attend to that part of the business; and so of the rest. If the state and condition of the bank were what was represented, then no one will say that the sum paid in dividends was excessive.

Liquidator's appeal against the Court of Appeal's decision upholding Cory's appeal against the judgment of Wright J, dismissed.

SOURCE 169
Re City Equitable Fire Insurance Company Limited
[1925] Ch 407; 94 LJ Ch 445

The articles of association contained the following regulation (see, now, section 310 of the Companies Act 1985).

'Article 150: "The directors, ... shall be indemnified and secured harmless out of the assets and profits of the company from and against all actions, costs, charges, losses, damages and expenses which they or any of them ... shall or may incur or sustain by or by reason of any act done, concurred in or omitted in or about the execution of their duty, or supposed duty, in their respective offices or trusts, except such (if any) as they shall incur or sustain by or through their own wilful neglect or default respectively, ... "'

These were proceedings by the liquidator of City Equitable Fire Insurance Co Ltd ('the company') under s 215 of the Companies Act 1908 (now s 212 of the Insolvency Act 1986) against the directors. The chairman of the company (Beaven) had been adjudicated bankrupt and had been convicted for his frauds against the company. The general manager (Mansell) had been adjudicated bankrupt and acquitted of fraud. Large sums of the company's money had been paid over to Beaven and Mansell and were, therefore, lost to the company. In addition, the directors were alleged to have invested the company's funds in ventures which had failed and to have authorised the payment of dividends out of capital.

No fraud was alleged against any of the respondents, except Beaven. The allegation was (in the words of counsel for the liquidator):

'... purely one of negligence, and the common law principle applies — namely, that where a person undertakes an operation which requires a certain amount of skill, he will be responsible for damaging results from his not exercising the amount of skill which a reasonable person, who is competent to carry out that transaction, would make use of. For example, a person acting as a director of a large insurance company is bound to exercise the skill that a reasonable person, competent to act in that way, would exercise, and he is not entitled to say that he knew nothing about business; that he was not a businessman at all, and that he was there for some quite subsidiary purpose.

In the case of an insurance company the investment of the funds of the company is a most important matter, and we submit that the directors ought to ascertain from time to time what the investments are in which the funds under their control are invested, that they should provide some system for the care and custody of the investments which they hold, and that they ought to see that the investments are reasonably proper for the class of company of which they are directors.

Where directors take so little part in the management of the business of the company as to make it perfectly easy, without inquiry, for one of their number to dissipate the funds of the company then they ought to be liable for the consequences.'

ROMER J: It has sometimes been said that directors are trustees. If this means no more than that directors in the performance of their duties stand in a fiduciary relationship to the company, the statement is true enough. But if the statement is meant to be an indication by way of analogy of what those duties are, it appears to me to be wholly misleading. I can see but little resemblance between the duties of a director and the duties of a trustee of a will or of a marriage settlement. It is indeed impossible to describe the duty of directors in general terms, whether by way of analogy or otherwise. The position of a director of a company carrying on a small retail business is very different from that of a director of a railway company. The duties of a bank director may differ widely from those of an insurance director, and the duties of a director of one insurance company may differ from those of a director of another. In one company, for instance, matters may normally be attended to by the manager or other members of the staff that in another company are attended to by the directors themselves. The larger the business carried on by the company the more numerous, and the more important, the matters that must of necessity be left to the managers, the accountants and the rest of the staff. The manner in which the work of the company is to be distributed between the board of directors and the staff is in truth a business matter to be decided on business lines. To use the words of Lord Macnaghten in *Dovey v Cory*:[1] 'I do not think it desirable for any tribunal to do that which Parliament has abstained from doing — that is, to formulate precise rules for the guidance or embarrassment of business men in the conduct of business affairs. There never has been, and I think there never will be, much difficulty in dealing with any particular case on its own facts and circumstances; and, speaking for myself, I rather doubt the wisdom of attempting to do more.'

In order, therefore, to ascertain the duties that a person appointed to the board of an established company undertakes to perform, it is necessary to consider not only the nature of the company's business, but also the manner in which the work of the company is in fact distributed between the directors and the other officials of the company, provided always that this distribution is a reasonable one in the circumstances, and is not inconsistent with any express provisions of the articles of association. In discharging the duties of his position thus ascertained a director must, of course, act honestly; but he must also exercise some degree of both skill and diligence. To the question of what is the particular degree of skill and diligence required of him, the authorities do not, I think, give any very clear answer. It has been laid down that so long as a director acts honestly he cannot be made responsible in damages unless guilty of gross or culpable negligence in a business sense.

But as pointed out by Neville J in *In re Brazilian Rubber Plantations and Estates, Ltd*, one cannot say whether a man has been guilty of negligence, gross or otherwise, unless one can determine what is the extent of the duty which he is alleged to have neglected. For myself, I confess to feeling some difficulty in understanding the difference between negligence and gross negligence, except in so far as the expressions are used for the purpose of drawing a distinction between the duty that is owed in one case and the duty that is owed in another. If two men owe the same duty to a third person, and neglect to perform that duty, they are both guilty of negligence, and it is not altogether easy to understand how one can be guilty of gross negligence and the other of negligence only. But if it be said that of two men one is only liable to a third person for gross negligence, and the other is liable for mere negligence, this, I think, means no more than that the duties of the two men are different. The one owes a duty to take a greater degree of care than does the other. . . . If, therefore, a director is only liable for gross or culpable negligence, this means that he does not owe a duty to his company, to take all possible care. It is some degree of care less than that. The

---

1 [1901] AC 477; 70 LJ Ch 753 (see p 448)

care that he is bound to take has been described by Neville J in the case referred to above as 'reasonable care' to be measured by the care an ordinary man might be expected to take in the circumstances on his own behalf. In saying this Neville J was only following what was laid down in *Overend & Gurney Co v Gibb* as being the proper test to apply, namely: 'Whether or not the directors exceeded the powers entrusted to them, or whether if they did not so exceed their powers they were cognisant of circumstances of such a character, so plain, so manifest, and so simple of appreciation, that no men with any ordinary degree of prudence, acting on their own behalf, would have entered into such a transaction as they entered into?'

There are, in addition, one or two other general propositions that seem to be warranted by the reported cases: (1) A director need not exhibit in the performance of his duties a greater degree of skill than may reasonably be expected from a person of his knowledge and experience. A director of a life insurance company, for instance, does not guarantee that he has the skill of an actuary or of a physician. In the words of Lindley MR: 'If directors act within their powers, if they act with such care as is reasonably to be expected from them, having regard to their knowledge and experience, and if they act honestly for the benefit of the company they represent, they discharge both their equitable as well as their legal duty to the company': see *Lagunas Nitrate Co v Lagunas Syndicate*. It is perhaps only another way of stating the same proposition to say that directors are not liable for mere errors of judgment. (2) A director is not bound to give continuous attention to the affairs of his company. His duties are of an intermittent nature to be performed at periodical board meetings, and at meetings of any committee of the board upon which he happens to be placed. He is not, however, bound to attend all such meetings, though he ought to attend whenever, in the circumstances, he is reasonably able to do so. (3) In respect of all duties that, having regard to the exigencies of business, and the articles of association, may properly be left to some other official, a director is, in the absence of grounds for suspicion, justified in trusting that official to perform such duties honestly. In the judgment of the Court of Appeal in *In re National Bank of Wales, Ltd*, the following passage occurs in relation to a director who had been deceived by the manager, and managing director, as to matters within their own particular sphere of activity: 'Was it his duty to test the accuracy or completeness of what he was told by the general manager and the managing director? This is a question on which opinions may differ, but we are not prepared to say that he failed in his legal duty. Business cannot be carried on upon principles of distrust. Men in responsible positions must be trusted by those above them, as well as by those below them, until there is reason to distrust them. We agree that care and prudence do not involve distrust; but for a director acting honestly himself to be held legally liable for negligence, in trusting the officers under him not to conceal from him what they ought to report to him, appears to us to be laying too heavy a burden on honest business men.' That case went to the House of Lords, and is reported there under the name of *Dovey v Cory*. Lord Davey, in the course of his speech to the House, made the following observations: 'I think the respondent was bound to give his attention to and exercise his judgment as a man of business on the matters which were brought before the board at the meetings which he attended, and it is not proved that he did not do so. But I think he was entitled to rely upon the judgment, information and advice, of the chairman and general manager, as to whose integrity, skill and competence he had no reason for suspicion. I agree with what was said by Sir George Jessel in *Hallmark's Case*, and by Chitty J in *In re Denham & Co*, that directors are not bound to examine entries in the company's books. It was the duty of the general manager and (possibly) of the chairman to go carefully through the returns from the branches, and to bring before the board any matter requiring their consideration; but the respondent was not, in my opinion, guilty of negligence in not examining them for himself, notwithstanding that they were laid on the table of the board for reference.'

These are the general principles that I shall endeavour to apply in considering the question whether the directors of this company have been guilty of negligence. But in order to determine whether any such negligence, if established, renders the directors liable in damages, it is necessary to consider the provisions of art 150 of the company's articles of association [p 450].

. . .

I must now consider the question of the responsibility of the respondent directors for the overpayments to Mansell. Every payment made to him on account or in anticipation of commission was made by a cheque drawn in his favour signed, as required by the articles of association, by two directors and also by Mansell himself, or, in I think four instances, by the accountant Mr Lock.

. . . a director who signs a cheque that appears to be drawn for a legitimate purpose is not responsible for seeing that the money is in fact required for that purpose or that it is subsequently applied for that purpose, assuming, of course, that the cheque comes before him for signature in the regular way having regard to the usual practice of the company. If this were not so, the business of a large company could not be carried on. In the case of an insurance company, for instance, the cheques to be signed at the board meeting would often include cheques in payment of insurance claims. If a claim appears to have been examined into and passed by the manager or other proper official for the purpose, a director who signs the necessary cheque in payment of the claim (the cheque being brought before him in the customary way) cannot be expected to investigate the whole matter over again, for the purpose of satisfying himself that the claim is well founded. A director must of necessity trust to the officials of the company to perform properly and honestly the duties allocated to those officials. In many large companies — it was so in the case of the City Equitable — it is the duty of the manager to pay the salaries and wages of the staff. For that purpose cheques are drawn by the directors in his favour, the exact amounts required being calculated by him. So long as there is nothing suspicious about the amount, the directors are justified in trusting him to calculate it correctly, and to use the proceeds of the cheque for the purpose for which it was drawn. . . . I must consider the circumstances in which [a director] signed the cheques in question for the purpose of seeing whether there was anything that should have put him on inquiry, either by reason of the amounts for which the cheques were drawn, or of any irregularity in the method in which they were presented to him for payment. . . . Every director who signed a cheque at a directors' meeting would see from the slip and the counterfoil the purpose for which the cheque was required. He was, moreover, entitled to assume that the cheque had been passed by the general manager, the accountant and the secretary. He would therefore have done all that could reasonably be required of him as to satisfying himself both as to the purpose and as to the authority for signing the cheque.

. . .

It is the duty of each director to see that the company's moneys are from time to time in a proper state of investment, except in so far as the company's articles of association may justify him in delegating that duty to others. So far as the respondent directors, other than Mr Haig Thomas and Mr Grenside, are concerned, they were justified in delegating this general duty to the finance committee, and thought that they had done so. The position of Mr Thomas and

Mr Grenside was, however, very different. They knew that neither the board nor the finance committee were attending to the temporary investments and were content to leave the duty of doing so to Mr Bevan and Mr Mansell. In this they were wrong. Thinking, as they did, that the duty had not been delegated to the finance committee, they should have regarded it as being still reposed in the board as a whole. That Bevan and Mansell were persons enjoying the highest reputation is beside the mark. If the shareholders had desired to leave hundreds of thousands of pounds of the company's money under the sole control of Bevan, they would have done so. But the shareholders had preferred to have associated with Bevan a board of six or seven other directors, and it was not for these other directors to leave Bevan to discharge one of the most important of the duties that had been entrusted by the shareholders to the board as a whole, however reasonable and however safe it might have seemed to the directors to do so. Still less would it be permissible to leave the control of the company's temporary investments to the general manager. It is not any part of the functions of a manager of an insurance company to decide upon the method of investment of the company's cash resources. His advice and assistance will no doubt be sought. But the responsibility for the ultimate decision as to investment must rest with the directors or, when the articles permit, with a committee of the directors, and none the less that the investment is only a temporary one. In my judgment, Mr Haig Thomas and Mr Grenside were guilty of a breach of their duty as directors in failing to control and safeguard the moneys of the company that were not in a state of permanent investment.

   ...

I should have had to find them responsible for the loss occasioned by any and every temporary investment made by Bevan or Mansell. But this breach of duty on the part of Mr Thomas and Mr Grenside was due to nothing more than ignorance of what their duty was in the matter. It is clear that it never occurred to either of them that it was his duty to keep under his own control the matter of the temporary investments. But further than this, it is established to my satisfaction that each of them in fact honestly thought that he did not owe any such duty to the company. In these circumstances, unless I have arrived at a wrong conclusion as to the meaning of the expression 'wilful negligence or default,' both of them must be absolved by reason of the 150th article of association from liability for this breach to their duty.

SOURCE 170
Dorchester Finance Co Ltd *v* Stebbing
(Chancery Division) [1989] BCLC 498

This case was decided in 1977, but reported only in 1989.

The first plaintiff, Dorchester Finance Co Ltd, and the second plaintiff, Talbex Group Ltd, brought an action against Frederick Stebbing, Brian Hamilton and Howard Lewis Parsons, the first, second and third defendants respectively, alleging that the defendants had been negligent in the discharge of their duties as directors of Dorchester Finance Co Ltd and claiming damages.

FOSTER J: ...

The law
For the plaintiffs' three main submissions were made in regard to the duties of the directors. a) A director is required to exhibit in performance of his duties such a degree of skill as may reasonably be expected from a person with his

knowledge and experience. b) A director is required to take in the performance of his duties such care as an ordinary man might be expected to take on his own behalf. c) A director must exercise any power vested in him as such honesty, in good faith and in the interests of the company and reliance was placed on *Re City Equitable Fire Insurance Co Ltd* [1925] Ch 407, [1924] All ER Rep 485, *Re Sharpe* [1892] 1 Ch 154, and *Re Smith & Fawcett Ltd* [1942] 1 All ER 542, [1942] Ch 304.

For the first defendant it was submitted that mere negligence was insufficient and the court had to be satisfied that there had been crassa neglentia or gross negligence and reliance for this submission was placed on *Turquand v Marshall* (1869) LR 4 Ch App 376, *Overend & Gurney Co v Gibb* (1872) LR 5 HL 480, *Sheffield and South Yorkshire Permanent Building Society v Aizlewood* (1889) 44 Ch D, 412, *Re New Mashonaland Exploration Co* [1892] 3 Ch 577 and *Lagunas Nitrate Co v Lagunas Syndicate* [1899] 2 Ch 392. In none of those cases was there a suggestion of dishonesty or recklessness on the part of the directors. In those cases the directors were charged with what might be called errors of judgment. In the *New Mashonaland* case [1892] 3 Ch 577 at 586 Vaughan Williams J says:

> 'If I had arrived at the conclusion that that was done, I should have said that the director who advanced money on a security, without waiting for the security, could not have used any discretion or judgment at all. For to advance money on security without waiting for the security is so unbusiness-like an act that it cannot be called a mere error of judgment or an imprudent act.'

I find myself in agreement with Romer J in the *City Equitable* case [1925] Ch 407 at 427–428 where he says:

> 'For myself, I confess to feeling some difficulty in understanding the difference between negligence and gross negligence, except in so far as the expressions are used for the purpose of drawing a distinction between the duty that is owed in one case and the duty that is owed in another.'

I accept the plaintiff's three submissions as accurately stating the law applicable, and counsel for the first defendant conceded that I could take into account the fact that of the three directors two are chartered accountants and the third has considerable experience of accountancy.

The evidence

. . .

Stebbing . . . elected to give no evidence, as is his right, and his counsel therefore made the last speech. However, both Hamilton and Parsons were sworn in and made prepared statements. Both were then cross-examined by counsel for the plaintiffs.

. . .

Hamilton's evidence

Although he has no qualifications as an accountant he said that he trained as one and worked for some 14 years for the Ministry of Health on the audit of the books of regional hospital boards, and as a deputy finance officer of a regional hospital board controlling 12 hospitals. . . .

He admitted that he signed blank cheques as a director of Dorchester but could not remember how many. However, five cheques dated in August and September 1973 were produced to him and he admitted signing them in blank. In his statement he says this:

'As they required the additional signature of either Mr Stebbing or Mr Parsons, both chartered accountants, the former being chairman, the latter, from 1 April 1973, managing director of the Talbex Group, both of whom had substantial personal interests in seeing that Talbex prospered, I considered this to be a reasonable thing to do.'

He also relied on the fact that the accounts for the years ending 31 July 1972 and 1973 had received an unqualified certificate from the auditors. Apart from the signing of the blank cheques, he did not consider that he had acted in an improper manner as a non-executive director of Dorchester. It is fair to say that it was due to his efforts that the sorry state of affairs was revealed in December 1973 and January 1974. But he admitted that there had never been a board meeting of the directors of Dorchester, that he did not know whether Dorchester kept proper books of account or not, and he was not involved in the purpose of the various loans made by Dorchester. In his own words, 'I let Mr Stebbing have absolute control. He could dispose of money as he liked.'

Parsons' evidence

He became a chartered accountant in 1958 and in June 1967 became a partner with Stebbing and Mr Armstrong in the accountancy firm of Stebbing & Co. He was a director of Dorchester from 21 April 1972 until 21 February 1974 and a director of Talbex from 13 July 1972 until 21 February 1974.

. . .

In his statement he says this:

'As I was very rarely at head office, a secretary would sometimes ask me to sign cheques in blank so that payments could be made whilst I was away and this I willingly did, assuming that they were used to pay expenses.'

When shown the five cheques, he admitted that when he added his signature on all five in addition to Mr Hamilton's signature the cheques were still blank. In his statement he further says: 'I think that a non-executive Director is entitled to rely on the auditors as I see no point in having auditors in the first place', and adds:

'My Directorship of Dorchester, like Mr Hamilton's was purely non-executive. No board meetings were ever held, as is the case in the vast majority of wholly-owned subsidiaries in groups in this country. Under the circumstances I have outlined, I do not believe I have acted negligently.'

He admitted knowing that it was the intention of Dorchester to use the cash of Fielding but had no knowledge of the loans made by Dorchester and never took part in its business at all.

. . .

European Fabrics Ltd

In November 1971 Stebbing requested Hamilton to form a Channel Island Co and to administer its affairs for him. On 23 November 1971 European Fabrics Ltd (which I will call 'Fabrics') was duly incorporated in Guernsey and at all times during its subsistence Hamilton was a director of it. Fabrics had two other directors who were residents of the Island of Sark. So that although Fabrics was registered in Guernsey, it was resident for tax purposes in Sark which has no income tax. In a report by Stebbing dated 18 March 1974 he describes Fabrics thus: 'This is an investment dealing company controlled by myself.' In February 1972 Dorchester started to lend money to Fabrics for the purpose of investment dealing and by 31 July 1972 the company owed Dorchester some £210,000. There were no memoranda at all for the purpose of s 6 of the 1900 Act and no proper security was held by Dorchester to secure repayments of the loans. The only document to be found is a letter signed by Hamilton as a director of Fabrics and written to Stebbing & Co on 14 February 1972 in these terms:

> 'Please accept this letter as our irrevocable authority for you to act as agents of Dorchester Finance Company Limited and this Company in dealing with Sheppards and Chase, Stock Brokers, in the purchase and sale of Shares and securities on behalf of European Fabrics Limited. We hereby give you formal authority to register such Shares or securities in the nominee Company of Sheppards and Chase, and should Dorchester Finance Company Limited, who will make advances from time to time, require you by seven days' notice in writing to repay the balance due from European Fabrics Limited, this is our irrevocable authority for you to dispose of such Shares or securities at your discretion as are necessary to effect repayment of the balance of the account with Dorchester Finance Company Limited.'

However, to satisfy the auditors who were auditing the accounts of Dorchester for the year ending 31 July 1972, Stebbing asked Hamilton to sign a letter, which has Stebbing's reference on it, dated 5 September 1972, as director of Fabrics to Dorchester in these terms:

> 'We acknowledge receipt of your statement of account for £15,000 and confirm that the total balance due to your company as at the 31st July 1972 after adjusting the statement above amounted to £120,805.74. We confirm that against this balance you are holding securities registered in the nominee company of Shepherds & Chase as per copy list attached which are held to the order of Stebbing & Co, who have our written authority at your request to dispose of such securities as are necessary to repay your loan together with interest thereon at any time, subject to giving us 7 days' notice of repayment.'

A large number of fresh transactions were carried out by Fabrics during the year up to 31 July 1973 with the assistance of loans from Dorchester. As a result of a transfer of £5,193 to another account of Dorchester on 31 July 1973 Fabrics owed nothing to Dorchester. The borrowings from Dorchester by Fabrics between 7 August and 23 November 1973 amounted to no less than £108,530, though some repayments had been made. When the whole matter came to light in December 1973 and January 1974, it was discovered that Fabrics owed Dorchester £49,778. Since then there have been some small repayments of capital so that the amount of capital owing on 31 May 1977 was £48,144. Efforts were made by Dorchester's solicitors to seek repayments of this sum but in 1977 they received a certificate from Her Majesty's Greffier in Guernsey to say that Fabrics had been struck off the register on 28 July 1975 and had been dissolved. As Dorchester had no security and in any event the provisions of the 1900 Act had not been followed, that sum is a total loss to Dorchester. Hamilton in his evidence said that the board of directors of Fabrics had no knowledge of any of the transactions carried out through Fabrics and had never approved any of them. Stebbing acted on his own account.

Conclusion

For a chartered accountant and an experienced accountant to put forward the proposition that a non-executive director has no duties to perform I find quite alarming. It would be an argument which, if put forward by a director with no accounting experience, would involve total disregard of many sections of the

Companies Act 1948 (see in particular ss 176 to 204). The signing of blank cheques by Hamilton and Parsons was in my judgment negligent, as it allowed Stebbing to do as he pleased. Apart from that they not only failed to exhibit the necessary skill and care in the performance of their duties as directors, but also failed to perform any duty at all as directors of Dorchester. In the Companies Act 1948 the duties of a director whether executive or not are the same.

In the absence of any oral evidence by Stebbing, the documents must speak for themselves. They show clearly that Stebbing as a director of Dorchester failed to exercise any skill or care in the performance of his duty as a director and that he knowingly and recklessly misapplied the assets of Dorchester to the extent of nearly £400,000. His negligence can only be described as gross negligence and he also is liable for damages.

[The judge then referred to the plea in mitigation based on s 448 of the Companies Act 1948 [see now s 727 of the CA 1985] and continued:]

There are three requirements for relief: (i) that he acted honestly, (ii) that he acted reasonably, (iii) that he ought fairly to be excused. In my judgment, in the circumstances of this case, none of them can bring themselves within the requirements of (ii) and (iii) and Stebbing fails to bring himself within (i).

I have no hesitation in concluding that they should not be relieved under the provisions of this section.

SOURCE 171
Norman *v* Theodore Goddard
(Chancery Division) [1991] BCLC 1028

The plaintiff brought a claim against the partners of the defendant firm for compensation for money transferred to a partner of the defendant (Bingham) who stole the money from a trust company which he controlled. The defendants admitted the claim and brought third party proceedings against a director of the trust company (Quirk).

HOFFMANN J: . . . The principal issue in these proceedings is therefore whether Mr Quirk was liable to replace the money which Mr Bingham stole from LBI. As a director of LBI, Mr Quirk owed a duty to the company to act in good faith and with reasonable care. There is no suggestion that Mr Quirk acted otherwise than in good faith. The question is whether in all the circumstances he took reasonable care. The extent of the duty of care owed by a director has been discussed in a number of cases but I need mention only two principles which seem to me to emerge clearly from the authorities. First, a director performing active duties on behalf of the company need not exhibit a greater degree of skill than may reasonably be expected from a person undertaking those duties. A director who undertakes the management of the company's properties is expected to have reasonable skill in property management, but not in offshore tax avoidance. It may be that in considering what a director ought reasonably to have known or inferred, one should also take into account the knowledge, skill and experience which he actually had in addition to that which a person carrying out his functions should be expected to have. Miss Gloster QC, who appeared for Theodore Goddard, submitted that the test was accurately stated in s 214(4) of the Insolvency Act 1986:

'. . . the facts which a director of a company ought to know or ascertain, the conclusions which he ought to reach and the steps which he ought to take are those which would be known or ascertained, or reached or taken, by a reasonably diligent person having both — (*a*) the general knowledge, skill and experience that may reasonably be expected of a person carrying out the same functions as are carried out by that director in relation to the company, and (*b*) the general knowledge, skill and experience that that director has.'

I have not called for any argument on this point from Mr Edelman, who appears for Mr Quirk, because I am willing to assume that the test is as Miss Gloster QC submits. There is, however, a second relevant principle and that is, as Romer J said in *Re City Equitable Fire Insurance Co Ltd* [1925] 1 Ch 407 at 429, 'Business cannot be carried on upon principles of distrust' and men in responsible positions may be trusted until there is reason to distrust them.

. . .

LBI turned out to have rather a lot of spare money. It had previously maintained an account with the Shoreditch High Street branch of Barclays Bank, Mr Quirk found that it had a cash deposit of £240,000. This information was conveyed to Mr Quirk through Mr Collins, to whom Mr Bingham had asked the bank to send the statements, on 27 June. Mr Quirk discussed it with Mr Bingham when he had lunch with him at Thackeray's Restaurant in Tunbridge Wells on that or the following day. As I have said, I have not seen Mr Bingham, but it seems clear from the evidence of others that he gave at any rate non-experts in tax and offshore finance the impression of expertise in these matters. Mr Playfoot said that he appeared to be confident and knowledgeable. Mr Quirk said that he was a bulky man with a slow, deliberate, soft-spoken manner who never seemed to say anything except after grave consideration and whom one could not associate with anything ill-considered or even undignified. Within the practice of Theodore Goddard there seems to have been some friction between Mr Bingham and Mr Lloyd, the partner in Jersey, which the senior partner in London occasionally had to smooth over. To an outsider like Mr Quirk, however, Mr Bingham was the picture of the respectable member of a very eminent firm of city solicitors.

Mr Bingham said that LBI's cash could earn £20,000 a year if invested offshore. This could be arranged, he said, by transferring to Gibbon Ltd, which Mr Bingham said was a company regularly used by the Theodore Goddard trusts in Jersey for this purpose. . . .

Mr Quirk was closely cross-examined about this critical lunchtime conversation, when the decision to make deposits in Gibbon was taken. The money on deposit at Shoreditch had been earning $12\frac{1}{8}\%$. After corporation tax at 40%, this would produce £17,460 a year. £20,000 gross was 8.3%, so that assuming no tax, the advantage to LBI was about £2,500 a year. Had Mr Quirk made these calculations? Mr Quirk said that he and Mr Bingham had done so and that he was satisfied that LBI would gain an appreciable advantage. I have no reason to reject this evidence, even though no written calculations have survived from the lunch to support it. Mr Quirk was asked why he was content to accept so little detail about the precise terms of the deposit with Gibbon: what exactly would be the rate of interest and the terms of withdrawal. Mr Quirk said that once satisfied that the deposit as described by Mr Bingham was advantageous and that the money would be available when required, he saw no need to obtain further detail. The money would be in the hands of Theodore Goddard, who held themselves out as experienced fund managers, expert in offshore investment. He felt that he could rely upon the security offered by their name and was sure that they would obtain the best terms available in the interests of the company.

Another question which it was suggested might have occurred to him was how the interest was going to be returned to LBI, an English company, without attracting corporation tax. Mr Quirk made no inquiry about this. He understood that in the short term the interest would be 'rolled up' by Gibbon, that is periodically added to capital. There had been talk about a company reorganisation of LBI to take it entirely offshore and Mr Quirk vaguely thought that might be connected with eventually recovering the interest tax free, but he admitted that he did not give much thought to the mechanics of tax avoidance. If Mr Bingham said that the income would accrue to LBI tax free, he was willing to take his word and not ask for explanations which he probably would not understand.

No doubt some people might have been more curious but Mr Quirk cannot in my judgment be regarded as having been negligent or naive. Mr Bingham had assured him on three critical points: first, that a deposit with Gibbon would be more profitable for the company than a deposit elsewhere; secondly, that the money would be available if needed for the company's property business and thirdly, that Gibbon was a company under the control of Theodore Goddard and therefore a safe investment. This information, if true, would in my view have formed a proper basis on which a director in the position of Mr Quirk could have decided to accept Mr Bingham's suggestion.

. . .

Given the position occupied by Mr Bingham, I think that Mr Quirk acted reasonably in accepting that the information was true without asking more questions or making independent inquiry. What independent inquiry ought Mr Quirk to have made? It was suggested that he should have consulted 'the trustees' on whose behalf he had been appointed a director. But the trustees were Theodore Goddard and there was Theodore Goddard, in the person of Mr Bingham, proposing the investment in Gibbon. Another suggestion was that he should have consulted his co-director Mr Somerville. But Mr Somerville was an employee of Theodore Goddard, apparently a subordinate of Mr Bingham. Does one check with an employed trust officer whether a senior partner in the firm is telling the truth? In my judgment that suggestion is unrealistic.

. . .

It was submitted that in transferring the money to Gibbon, Mr Quirk surrendered his discretion to Mr Bingham and acted merely as his unthinking instrument. This submission was the foundation for an argument that Mr Quirk should have attributed to him the dishonest state of mind of Mr Bingham, in accordance with a passage from the judgment of Mellish LJ in *Gray v Lewis, Parker v Lewis* (1873) 8 Ch App 1035 at 1056:

> 'If a person allows himself to be the mere nominee of, and acts for another person, he must be bound by the notice which that other person for whom he acts has of the nature of the transaction.'

This statement was followed by Ungoed-Thomas J in *Selangor United Rubber Estates Ltd v Cradock (No 3)* [1968] 2 All ER 1073, [1968] 1 WLR 1555. I think that there may be some dangers in taking this dictum of Mellish LJ as a comprehensive statement of all the conditions which must be present in order to attribute the state of mind of one person to another who acts on his behalf. I note that in both *Gray v Lewis* and *Selangor* there were also findings that the transaction was one which would have aroused suspicion in the mind of anyone who gave thought to what he was doing and this feature may well be an unstated premise in both cases. But I need not explore the question because in my view even the expressed conditions for the application of the principle are lacking. Mr Quirk did not allow himself to be the mere nominee of Mr Bingham. He described in evidence the way he saw his relationship to Mr Bingham as follows:

'I made it clear to Mr Bingham that I would have to rely on him for all non-property matters. The ideas on property matters would normally come from me but unless they were simple or urgent, I would normally discuss them with Mr Bingham before taking action. The ideas, in the creative sense, on tax or financial matters, I expected to come from Mr Bingham. They would of course be discussed with me and I would rely upon his advice. I discussed them with Mr Bingham himself and sometimes sought the advice of others. I was not abdicating responsibility but I relied on Mr Bingham for his advice, in respect of his being a partner in Theodore Goddard and his acting for the company as its solicitor and in respect of his acting as solicitor to the trustee shareholders'.

. . .

Miss Gloster QC submitted that there was no analogy between Mr Quirk's behaviour and that of the directors in *Re City Equitable Fire Insurance Co Ltd* [1925] Ch 407, [1924] All ER Rep 485, whom Romer J held to have been prima facie in breach of duty and whom he would have held liable if they had not been protected by a provision in the articles. The City Equitable was an insurance company and apart from underwriting, its principal business was the investment of funds. The board delegated control of investment to a finance committee of three directors, one of whom was the chairman of the company. The other two directors left the entire control of the funds for short-term investment to the chairman, who fraudulently advanced huge sums to a firm of stockbrokers in which he was a partner. Romer J found that the other two directors —

'did not ever seriously bring their minds to bear upon the question as to how and by whom the temporary investments were being made.'

(See [1925] Ch 407 at 466.)

Accordingly, the fact that the chairman was a person of the highest reputation whose integrity had never been doubted, did not prevent Romer J from saying that the two directors had been in breach of duty:

'If the shareholders had desired to leave hundreds of thousands of pounds of the company's money under the sole control of [the chairman] they would have done so . . . it was not for [the] other directors to leave [the chairman] to discharge one of the most important of the duties that had been entrusted by the shareholders to the board as a whole, however reasonable and however safe it might have seemed to the directors to do so.'

(See [1925] Ch 407 at 467.)

This was a case of complete abdication of the principal responsibility of the directors concerned and in my judgment is far removed from the specific decision which Mr Quirk made on advice to deposit money with Gibbon. There is also in my judgment no parallel with the other ground upon which Romer J would have held some directors in breach of duty, namely that they were content to approve the accounts without ever having seen a list of the company's assets. Miss Gloster QC also referred me to *Dorchester Finance Co Ltd v Stebbing* [1989] BCLC 498, in which two non-executive directors had signed blank cheques and left them for the third director to fill in as he pleased. They were reduced to arguing by way of defence that non-executive directors had no duties whatever and it is not surprising that they were held liable. This was, in my view, an extreme case which gives me little assistance.

. . .

I have already said that in my judgment Mr Quirk did not commit a breach of his duty of care as a director when he made the original decision in Thackeray's Restaurant to deposit LBI's spare cash with Gibbon. Was there anything in the later history which should have made him reconsider that decision and either stop sending money to Gibbon or try to recover what had been sent? I do not think there was. The incidents of the English Trust loan and the Allied Dunbar office had received explanations which I think he was entitled to accept. Nothing had been said to cast any doubt upon Mr Bingham's honesty until the telephone call from Mrs Stacey on 21 July 1986. There he felt that he was being called upon to take sides in a dispute between the partners of Theodore Goddard and Mr Bingham. Mrs Stacey was saying that her information about Gibbon contradicted that given by Mr Bingham. Mr Quirk had no way of knowing who was right and asked Mrs Stacey to write to him. There is some question about whether the matter was left on the footing that she would be in contact with him or he with her, but Mrs Stacey, if really concerned, could easily have gone back to Mr Quirk or spoken to Mr Playfoot. She never did either. Nor is there anything to suggest that action at this time would have succeeded in recovering the money.

In my judgment, therefore, Theodore Goddard has failed to establish the first necessary condition for claiming a contribution under the Civil Liability (Contribution) Act 1978 and the claim must be dismissed.

PART V: DIRECTORS' FIDUCIARY DUTIES

Directors must exercise their powers in good faith (bona fide) for the benefit of the company (compare the principle governing the power of shareholders to vote for an alteration of the articles, pp 330ff). The directors are generally given full management control over the company (see Table A, reg 70), for example with power to approve a transfer of shares (Source 172), to issue new shares (Sources 173, 174, 175 and 176), to cause the company to buy or sell assets and so on. These powers naturally include power over the company's property thus creating the possibility of the directors diverting to their own benefit, the company's assets (whether its tangible assets or its intangible assets such as opportunities). Dealings between a director and the company are thus subjected to stringent rules of disclosure and approval (Sources 177, 178, 179 and 180).

If directors do act in breach of this duty and expropriate the company's property, the company will usually be unable to take the appropriate proceedings for compensation or restitution because it will, generally, be controlled by the alleged wrongdoers. Thus, where directors are alleged to have expropriated the company's property, a special procedure allows the minority shareholders to bring proceedings on behalf of the company to recover the expropriated property, for example *Cook v Deeks, Atwool v Merryweather, Menier v Hooper's Telegraph, Wallersteiner v Moir* (Sources 185, 190, 191 and 192 at pp 511, 540, 541 and 542 respectively).

In the case of the misuse of power where there is no expropriation of the company's property, it seems that the majority of the shareholders may ratify the directors' breach of duty. The position where there was an expropriation of property is more complicated (contrast Sources 177 and 185 in this regard).

Directors' Discretion to Refuse an Application for a Transfer of Shares

SOURCE 172
Re Smith & Fawcett Ltd
(Court of Appeal 1942) [1942] Ch 304; [1942] 1 All ER 542

Article 10 of the articles of association provided: 'The directors may at any time in their absolute and uncontrolled discretion refuse to register any transfer of shares, and clause 19 of Table A shall be modified accordingly.' Fawcett by his will . . . appointed his wife and his son, Edwin Arthur Fawcett, the plaintiff, to be the executors and trustees thereof, and . . . bequeathed . . . 2000 shares in the company to his daughter, Alice Marjorie Fawcett, and 2001 shares to the plaintiff.
. . . Mrs Fawcett and the plaintiff, as executors of Joseph Fawcett, applied to Smith [the surviving director] that they should be registered as members of the company, and that the plaintiff should be appointed to be a director of the company. Smith, however, refused to consent to the registration or appointment, but offered to register 2001 shares and to buy 2000 of the shares at a price fixed by himself. In July 1940, Smith appointed the second defendant, his solicitor, J W Feather, to be a director of the company. Mrs Fawcett died on 11 April 1941. Some time afterwards the plaintiff again asked Smith to register him as a member of the company, but Smith, with the assent of Feather, refused. The plaintiff then applied to the court by way of motion that the register of members of the company might be rectified by inserting his name as the holder of the 4001 shares. Simonds J dismissed the motion. The plaintiff appealed.

LORD GREENE MR: The principles to be applied in cases where the articles of a company confer a discretion on directors with regard to the acceptance of transfers of shares are, for the present purposes, free from doubt. They must exercise their discretion bona fide in what they consider — not what a court may consider — is in the interests of the company, and not for any collateral purposes. They must have regard to those considerations, and those considerations only, which the articles on their true construction permit them to take into consideration, and in construing the relevant provisions in the articles it is to be borne in mind that one of the normal rights of a shareholder is the right to deal freely with his property and to transfer it to whomsoever he pleases. When it is said, as it has been said more than once, that regard must be had to this last consideration, it means, I apprehend, nothing more than that the shareholder has such a prima facie right, and that right is not to be cut down by uncertain language or doubtful implications. The right, if it is to be cut down, must be cut down with satisfactory clarity. It certainly does not mean that articles, if appropriately framed, cannot be allowed to cut down the right of transfer to any extent which the articles on their true construction permit. Another consideration which must be borne in mind is that this type of article is one which is for the most part confined to private companies. Private companies are in law separate entities just as much as are public companies, but from the business and personal point of view they are much more analogous to partnerships than to public corporations. Accordingly, it is to be expected that in the articles of such a company the control of the directors over the membership may be very strict indeed. There are, or may be, very good business reasons why those who bring such companies into existence should give them a constitution which confers on the directors powers of the widest description.

. . .

There is nothing, in my opinion, in principle or in authority to make it impossible to draft such a wide and comprehensive power to directors to refuse to transfer as to enable them to take into account any matter which they conceive to be in the interests of the company, and thereby to admit or not to admit a particular person and to allow or not to allow a particular transfer for reasons not personal to the transferee but bearing on the general interests of the company as a whole — such matters, for instance, as whether by their passing a particular transfer the transferee would obtain too great a weight in the councils of the company or might even perhaps obtain control. The question, therefore, simply is whether on the true construction of the particular article the directors are limited by anything except their bona fide view as to the interests of the company. In the present case the article is drafted in the widest possible terms, and I decline to write into that clear language any limitation other than a limitation, which is implicit by law, that a fiduciary power of this kind must be exercised bona fide in the interests of the company. Subject to that qualification, an article in this form appears to me to give the directors what it says, namely, an absolute and uncontrolled discretion.

That being my view on the question of law in this case, it only remains to consider the issue of fact which has been raised. It is said that on the evidence before us we ought to infer that the directors here were purporting to exercise their power to refuse a transfer not bona fide in the interests of the company but for some collateral purpose, namely, the desire of the leading director to acquire part of the shares for himself at an under-value. Speaking for myself, I strongly dislike being asked on affidavit evidence alone to draw inferences as to the bona fides or mala fides of the actors. If it is desired to charge a deponent with having given an account of his motives and his reasons which is not the true account, then the person on whom the burden of proof lies should take the ordinary and obvious course of requiring the deponent to submit himself to cross-examination. That does not mean that it is illegitimate in a proper case to draw inferences as to bona fides or mala fides in cases where there is on the face of the affidavit sufficient justification for doing so, but where the oath of the deponent is before the court, as it is here, and the only grounds on which the court is asked to disbelieve it are matters of inference, many of them of a doubtful character, I decline to give to those suggestions the weight which is desired. In the present case the principal director has sworn an affidavit which, if accepted, makes it clear that, whether rightly or wrongly, the directors have bona fide considered the interests of the company and come to the conclusion that it would be undesirable to register the transfer of the totality of these shares. Accordingly, on the evidence I am satisfied, as the learned judge was satisfied, that there is no ground shown here for saying that the directors' refusal has been due to anything but a bona fide consideration of the interests of the company as the directors see them.

Appeal dismissed.

The Exercise of the Power to Issue Shares

In 1980, UK company law was changed so as to provide *statutory* protection for existing shareholders against a misuse of the power to issue shares (see ss 80, 89–94 of the CA, 1985). Sources 173, 174, 175 and 176 explore the common law controls over directors exercising this power.

SOURCE 173
Hogg *v* Cramphorn Ltd
(Chancery Division 1963) [1967] Ch 254; [1966] 3 WLR 995

... Mr Baxter proposed to buy the whole of the issued share capital of the company at 25s. for each preference share and 50s. for each ordinary share. Mr Baxter had no experience of the particular kind of business carried on by the company. He gave Colonel Cramphorn an assurance that if he acquired control of the company it would be his intention to expand its business, but it appeared to Colonel Cramphorn that there would be a change in the nature of the company's trading. Colonel Cramphorn formed the view that the offer would unsettle the company's staff. Colonel Cramphorn reported the offer to the board on 3 April 1963. The board took legal advice, and a scheme was devised and put into operation under which the company entered into a trust deed, the other parties to which were the three personal defendants, for the benefit of employees. The trustees applied for allotment of the 5707 unissued preference shares on condition that there should be attached to them 10 votes per share on a poll. The board allotted those shares to the trustees at par with such special voting rights. The board made a loan to the trustees out of the company's funds of £5707 free of interest and not to be repaid until the termination of the scheme contained in the trust deed. The trustees utilised that loan to pay for the shares. The total of votes was thereby increased to 183,251, of which the directors and their supporters already controlled about 37,000, which added to the 57,070 votes purportedly conferred on the trustees amounted to about 94,000, more than half the total on which the directors could rely. Those steps were taken at a board meeting held on 18 April 1963, and together constituted a scheme avowedly formulated to meet the situation created by Mr Baxter's offer.

...

BUCKLEY J: I now turn to what has been the main matter of debate in this case, which is whether the allotment of the 5707 shares was an improper use by the directors of their discretionary and fiduciary power under article 10, to decide to whom these unissued shares should be allotted.

... It is also common ground that the directors were not actuated by any unworthy motives of personal advantage, but acted as they did in an honest belief that they were doing what was for the good of the company. Their honour is not in the least impugned, but it is said that the means which they adopted to attend their end were such as they could not properly adopt.

I am satisfied that Mr Baxter's offer, when it became known to the company's staff, had an unsettling effect upon them. I am also satisfied that the directors and the trustees of the trust deed genuinely considered that to give the staff through the trustees a sizeable, though indirect, voice in the affairs of the company would benefit both the staff and the company. I am sure that Colonel Cramphorn and also probably his fellow directors firmly believed that to keep the management of the company's affairs in the hands of the existing board would be more advantageous to the shareholders, the company's staff and its customers than if it were committed to a board selected by Mr Baxter. The steps which the board took were intended not only to ensure that if Mr Baxter succeeded in obtaining a shareholding which, as matters stood, would have been a controlling shareholding, he should not secure control of the company, but also, and perhaps primarily, to discourage Mr Baxter from proceeding with his bid at all.

... There is no doubt that the staff thoroughly appreciated and approved the board's action in establishing the trust. Mr Goulding says that the scheme was rightly regarded by the board as being in the interests of the shareholders, both on the ground that it tended to cement the loyalty of the staff and on the ground that it would be likely to prevent the displacement of an experienced management by an inexperienced one. On these grounds he contends that the establishment of the fund, the issue of the 5707 shares with special voting rights and the making of the interest-free loans to the trustees were justified as reasonably incidental to the favourable conduct of the company's business, and so *intra vires* not only the company but also the board.

Accepting as I do that the board acted in good faith and that they believed that the establishment of a trust would benefit the company, and that avoidance of the acquisition of control by Mr Baxter would also benefit the company, I must still remember that an essential element of the scheme, and indeed its primary purpose, was to ensure control of the company by the directors and those whom they could confidently regard as their supporters. Was such a manipulation of the voting position a legitimate act on the part of the directors?

Somewhat similar questions have been considered in the well-known cases of *Punt v Symons & Co Ltd*[1] and *Piercy v S Mills & Co Ltd*.[2] In *Punt v Symons & Co Ltd* the directors had issued shares with the object of creating a sufficient majority to enable them to pass a special resolution depriving other shareholders of special rights conferred on them by the company's articles. In *Piercy v S Mills & Co Ltd* the directors had issued shares with the object of creating a sufficient majority to enable them to resist the election of three additional directors, whose appointment would have put the two existing directors in a minority on the board. In each case the directors were held to have acted improperly. In *Punt v Symons & Co Ltd* Byrne J said:

> 'A power of the kind exercised by the directors in this case, is one which must be exercised for the benefit of the company: primarily it is given them for the purpose of enabling them to raise capital when required for the purposes of the company. There may be occasions when the directors may fairly and properly issue shares in the case of a company constituted like the present for other reasons. For instance, it would not be at all an unreasonable thing to create a sufficient number of shareholders to enable statutory powers to be exercised; but when I find a limited issue of shares to persons who are obviously meant and intended to secure the necessary statutory majority in a particular interest, I do not think that it is a fair and bona fide exercise of the power.'

In *Piercy v Mills & Co Ltd*, Peterson J, after citing *Fraser v Whalley*[3] and *Punt v Symons & Co Ltd* said:

> 'The basis of both cases is, as I understand, that directors are not entitled to use their powers of issuing shares merely for the purpose of maintaining their control or the control of themselves and their friends over the affairs of the company, or merely for the purpose of defeating the wishes of the existing majority of shareholders. That is, however, exactly what has happened in the present case. With the merits of the dispute as between the directors and the plaintiff I have no concern whatever. The plaintiff and his friends held a majority of the shares of the company, and they were entitled, so long as that majority remained, to have their views prevail in accordance with the regulations of the company; and it was not, in my opinion, open to the directors, for the purpose of converting a minority into a majority, and

---

1 [1903] 2 Ch 506; 72 LJ Ch 768
2 [1920] 1 Ch 77; 88 LJ Ch 509
3 (1864) 2 H&M 10; 71 ER 361

solely for the purpose of defeating the wishes of the existing majority, to issue the shares which are in dispute in the present action.'

With those observations I respectfully agree. Unless a majority in a company is acting oppressively towards the minority, this court should not and will not itself interfere with the exercise by the majority of its constitutional rights or embark upon an inquiry into the respective merits of the views held or policies favoured by the majority and the minority. Nor will this court permit directors to exercise powers, which have been delegated to them by the company in circumstances which put the directors in a fiduciary position when exercising those powers, in such a way as to interfere with the exercise by the majority of its consitutional rights; and in a case of this kind also, in my judgment, the court should not investigate the rival merits of the views or policies of the parties. Thus, in *Fraser v Whalley* Page Wood V-C said: 'I say nothing on the question whether the policy advocated by the directors, or that which I am told is to be pursued by Savin, is the more for the interest of the company,' and in *Piercy v S Mills & Co Ltd*, Peterson J said that he had no concern whatever with the merits of the dispute. It is not, in my judgment, open to the directors in such a case to say, 'We genuinely believe that what we seek to prevent the majority from doing will harm the company and therefore our act in arming ourselves or our party with sufficient shares to outvote the majority is a conscientious exercise of our powers under the articles, which should not be interfered with.'

Such a belief, even if well founded, would be irrelevant. A majority of shareholders in general meeting is entitled to pursue what course it chooses within the company's powers, however wrong-headed it may appear to others, provided the majority do not unfairly oppress other members of the company. These considerations lead me to the conclusion that the issue of the 5707 shares, with the special voting rights which the directors purported to attach to them, could not be justified by the view that the directors genuinely believed that it would benefit the company if they could command a majority of the votes in general meetings. The fact that, as I have held, the directors were mistaken in thinking that they could attach to these shares more than one vote each is irrelevant. The power to issue shares was a fiduciary power and if, as I think, it was exercised for an improper motive, the issue of these shares is liable to be set aside.

. . .

In these circumstances I propose to stand the action over for a specified period to enable the directors, if so advised, to convene a general meeting to consider such resolutions as may be submitted to it. I will consider what order I should make in the light of the proceedings at any such meeting. Mr Goulding will undertake that at any such meeting the trustees will not vote in respect of the 5707 shares, but I do not think there is any need for me to disenfranchise any other shares from voting at the meeting.

A meeting of shareholders was called and ratified all acts of the directors in connection with this scheme.

SOURCE 174
Teck Corporation *v* Millar
(British Columbia Supreme Court 1972) (1972) 33 DLR (3d) 288

BERGER J: . . . The law says that the directors of a company, in exercising their powers, must act bona fide in what they consider to be the best interests of the company. So the directors can issue shares when they decide that it is in the best interests of the company to do so. But their purpose must be one countenanced by the law. They cannot exercise their power for an extraneous purpose.

Earlier this year the plaintiff Teck Corporation Limited sought to gain control of Afton by acquiring a majority of the shares of the company. Teck alleges that on 1 June, the defendant directors signed a contract on behalf of the company, providing for the issuance of 1,167,437 shares to the defendant Canadian Exploration Ltd (Canex). Teck says that the directors were actuated by an improper purpose. They were not seeking to serve the best interest of the company. Their purpose, it is said, was to frustrate the attempt by the plaintiff to obtain control of the company, and the contract was a colourable device made for that purpose. That purpose was an extraneous one and, it is said, Canex knew of it. Therefore, the plaintiff says, the contract should be declared null and void. If the contract were declared null and void, the allotment of shares would fall with it.

. . .

There is no dispute that the directors had the power to manage the affairs of the company. Afton's articles of association contain the following provision regarding the powers and duties of the directors:

> 'POWERS AND DUTIES OF DIRECTORS
> The management of the business of the Company shall be vested in the directors, and the directors may exercise all such powers and do all such acts and things as the Company is, by its memorandum of association or otherwise, authorized to exercise and do, and are not hereby or by statute directed or required to be exercised or done by the Company in general meeting, but subject nevertheless to the provisions of the 'Companies Act' and of these regulations, and to any regulations not being inconsistent with these regulations from time to time made by the Company in general meeting; PROVIDED that no such regulation shall invalidate any prior act of the directors which would have been valid if such regulation had not been made.'

There is no dispute that under the articles of association the directors had the power to enter into the contract here, and no dispute that they had the power to allot shares pursuant to such a contract. The case alleged against them is that they were actuated by an improper purpose in the exercise of their powers.

The directors' power to manage the affairs of the company is complete. That is, a majority of shareholders, even if they pass a resolution at a general meeting, cannot dictate to the directors: *Automatic Self-Cleansing Filter Syndicate Co Ltd v Cunninghame.*[1] The directors are not the agents of the shareholders. Once given the power to manage the company, they can exercise the power according to their best judgment, until removed from office: *Gramophone & Typewriter Ltd v Stanley.*[2]

. . .

Counsel for Teck says the reasoning in *Hogg v Cramphorn Ltd,*[3] supra, is applicable in the case at bar. He says the defendant directors believed Teck would use its dominant position to compel Afton to give Teck the ultimate deal. They believed that under Teck's management the property would not be developed as profitably as it would under Placer's management. They also believed that the

---

1 [1906] 2 Ch 34; 75 LJ Ch 437 (see p 413)
2 [1908] 2 KB 89; 77 LJKB 834
3 [1967] Ch 254; [1966] 3 All ER 420 (see p 465)

value of Afton's shares, including their own, would decline, under Teck's management. Therefore, the argument goes, the defendant directors entered into the contract with Canex so that shares would be allotted under the contract to defeat Teck's majority. The case then is on all fours with *Hogg v Cramphorn Ltd.*

Counsel for Teck says that *Hogg v Cramphorn Ltd* offers an elaboration of the rule that directors may not issue shares for an improper purpose. If their purpose is merely to retain control, that is improper. So much may be taken for granted. Counsel then goes on to say that *Hogg v Cramphorn Ltd* lays it down that an allotment of shares, and any transaction connected with it, made for the purpose of defeating an attempt to secure a majority is improper, even if the directors genuinely consider that it would be deleterious to the company if those seeking a majority were to obtain control.

This, it seems to me, raises an issue of profound importance in company law. Lord Greene MR, expressed the general rule in this way in *Re Smith & Fawcett Ltd:*[1] 'They [the directors] must exercise their discretion bona fide in what they consider — not what a court may consider — is in the interests of the company, and not for any collateral purpose.' Yet, if *Hogg v Cramphorn Ltd*, supra, is right, directors may not allot shares to frustrate an attempt to obtain control of the company, even if they believe that it is in the best interests of the company to do so. This is inconsistent with the law as laid down in *Re Smith & Fawcett Ltd.* How can it be said that directors have the right to consider the interests of the company, and to exercise their powers accordingly, but that there is an exception when it comes to the power to issue shares, and that in the exercise of such power the directors cannot in any circumstances issue shares to defeat an attempt to gain control of the company? It seems to me this is what *Hogg v Cramphorn Ltd* says. If the general rule is to be infringed here, will it not be infringed elsewhere? If the directors, even when they believe they are serving the best interests of the company, cannot issue shares to defeat an attempt to obtain control, then presumably they cannot exercise any other of their powers to defeat the claims of the majority or, for that matter, to deprive the majority of the advantages of control. I do not think the power to issue shares can be segregated, on the basis that the rule in *Hogg v Cramphorn Ltd* applies only in a case of an allotment of shares.

Neither can it be distinguished on the footing that the power to issue shares affects the rights of the shareholders in some way that the exercise of other powers does not. The Court's jurisdiction to intervene is founded on the theory that if the directors' purpose is not to serve the interest of the company, but to serve their own interest or that of their friends or of a particular group of shareholders, they can be said to have abused their power. The impropriety lies in the directors' purpose. If their purpose is not to serve the company's interest, then it is an improper purpose. Impropriety depends upon proof that the directors were actuated by a collateral purpose, it does not depend upon the nature of any shareholders' rights that may be affected by the exercise of the directors' powers.

I am not prepared therefore to follow *Hogg v Cramphorn Ltd*, supra. I think that directors are entitled to consider the reputation, experience and policies of anyone seeking to take over the company. If they decide, on reasonable grounds, a take-over will cause substantial damage to the company's interests, they are

---

1 [1942] Ch 304; [1942] 1 All ER 542 (see p 463)

entitled to use their powers to protect the company. That is the test that ought to be applied in this case.

. . .

So how ought the Court go about unravelling the motives of the directors? The whole problem was, in my view, articulated in the most illuminating way in *Mills et al v Mills et al*[1] Latham CJ, said:

'It must, however, be recognized that as a general rule, though not invariably (as, for example, in the case of Birtchnell in this case), directors have an interest as shareholders in the company of which they are directors. Most sets of articles of association actually require the directors to have such an interest, and it is generally desired by shareholders that directors should have a substantial interest in the company so that their interests may be identified with those of the shareholders of the company. Ordinarily, therefore, in promoting the interests of the company, a director will also promote his own interests. I do not read the general phrases which are to be found in the authorities with reference to the obligations of directors to act solely in the interests of the company as meaning that they are prohibited from acting in any matter where their own interests are affected by what they do in their capacity as directors. Very many actions of directors who are shareholders, perhaps all of them, have a direct or indirect relation to their own interests. It would be ignoring realities and creating impossibilities in the administration of companies to require that directors should not advert to or consider in any way the effect of a particular decision upon their own interests as shareholders. A rule which laid down such a principle would paralyse the management of companies in many directions. Accordingly, the judicial observations which suggest that directors should consider only the interests of the company and never their own interests should not be pressed to a limit which would create a quite impossible position.'

Latham CJ, then referred to the difficulty facing directors when they have to choose between preference and ordinary shareholders:

'Directors are required to act not only in matters which affect the relations of the company to persons who are not members of the company but also in relation to matters which affect the rights of shareholders *inter se*. Where there are preference and ordinary shares a particular decision may be of such a character that it must necessarily affect adversely the interests of one class of shareholders and benefit the interests of another class. In such a case it is difficult to apply the test of acting in the interests of the company. The question which arises is sometimes not a question of the interests of the company at all, but a question of what is fair as between different classes of shareholders. Where such a case arises some other test than that of 'the interests of the company' must be applied, and the test must be applied with knowledge of the fact already mentioned that the law permits directors, and by virtue of provisions in articles of association often requires them, to hold shares, ordinary or preference as the case may be. A director who holds one or both classes of such shares is not, in my opinion, required by the law to live in an unreal region of detached altruism and to act in a vague mood of ideal abstraction from obvious facts which must be present to the mind of any honest and intelligent man when he exercises his powers as a director. It would be setting up an impossible standard to hold that, if an action of a

---

1 (1938) 60 CLR 150

director were affected in any degree by the fact that he was a preference or ordinary shareholder, his action was invalid and should be set aside. . . . The question is: What was 'the moving cause' of the action of the directors?'

Dixon J (as he then was), said:

'When the law makes the object, view or purpose of a man, or of a body of men, the test of the validity of their acts, it necessarily opens up the possibility of an almost infinite analysis of the fears and desires, proximate and remote, which, in truth, form the compound motives usually animating human conduct. But logically possible as such an analysis may seem, it would be impracticable to adopt it as a means of determining the validity of the resolutions arrived at by a body of directors, resolutions which otherwise are ostensibly within their powers. The application of the general equitable principle to the acts of directors managing the affairs of a company cannot be as nice as it is in the case of a trustee exercising a special power of appointment. It must, as it seems to me, take the substantial object the accomplishment of which formed the real ground of the board's action. If this is within the scope of the power, then the power has been validly exercised. But if, except for some ulterior and illegitimate object, the power would not have been exercised, that which has been attempted as an ostensible exercise of the power will be void, notwithstanding that the directors may incidentally bring about a result which is within the purpose of the power and which they consider desirable.'

So it is necessary, then, to disentangle the directors' primary motive or purpose from subsidiary ones. I do not think it is necessary to distinguish motive, purpose or object. The question is, what was it the directors had uppermost in their minds?

. . .

If I am wrong in rejecting *Hogg v Cramphorn Ltd*, it is not applicable here in any event. In *Hogg v Cramphorn Ltd* the primary purpose of the directors was to frustrate an attempt to obtain control of the company. In the case at bar the primary purpose of the directors was to make the best contract they could for Afton. I find that the primary purpose of the directors was to serve the best interests of the company. Their primary purpose was to see that the ultimate deal the company made was a deal with Placer, not Teck. They were not motivated by a desire to retain control of the company. They may have thought the issuance of shares under the contract with Canex would enable them, if they had Canex' support, to regain control from Teck. If they did, that was a subsidiary purpose. On any view of the law, therefore, no allegation of improper purpose can be sustained against the defendant directors.

SOURCE 175
Howard Smith Ltd *v* Ampol Petroleum Ltd
(Privy Council 1974) [1974] AC 821; [1974] 1 All ER 1126

The litigation arose out of a struggle for the takeover and control of Millers, the rival parties to which were Ampol on one side and Howard Smith on the other. Associated with Ampol was Bulkships Ltd, a substantial shareholder in Millers. Ampol had acquired, in May 1972, a large shareholding in Millers; this holding was 29.8 per cent of Millers' issued share capital; Ampol bought it for a price of $2.27 a share. Bulkships owned 25.1 per cent of Millers' issued share capital so that Ampol and Bulkships together had about 55 per cent, the remaining 45 per cent being held by outside shareholders. By the allotment, made on 6 July 1972, Howard Smith obtained 4,500,000 shares at $2.30 a share. The effect of this, if valid, would be that Ampol and Bulkships would no longer be the majority shareholders in the company.

1. The judge found, as their Lordships think it right to make clear at once, that the Millers' directors were not motivated by any purpose of personal gain or advantage, or by any desire to retain their position on the board. The judge said:

> 'I discard the suggestion that the directors of Millers allotted these shares to Howard Smith in order to gain some private advantage for themselves by way of retention of their seats on the board or by obtaining a higher price for their personal shareholding. Personal considerations of this nature were not to the forefront so far as any of these directors was concerned, and in this respect their integrity emerges unscathed from this contest.'

2. He then proceeded to consider the main issue which he formulated in accordance with the principle stated in the High Court of Australia by Dixon J in *Mills v Mills*.[1] This was to ascertain the substantial object the accomplishment of which formed the real ground of the board's action. The issue before him he considered to be whether the primary purpose of the majority of directors was to satisfy Millers' need for capital or whether their primary purpose was to destroy the majority holding of Ampol and Bulkships.

. . .

After hearing and considering the evidence of Messrs Taylor, Nicholl, Balhorn and Anderson, each asserting that his primary purpose in voting for the allotment on 6 July 1972, was to meet an urgent capital need of Millers, the judge found that he was unable to accept these assertions. He found that the primary purpose so far as the management team was concerned (this is *not* the directors, but the team headed by Mr Taylor which negotiated with Howard Smith) was to issue shares to Howard Smith so as to enable the Howard Smith takeover to proceed. As to the Millers' majority directors he said:

> 'They had found themselves enmeshed in a takeover struggle. The greater part, if not the whole, of their thinking in the critical days up to and including July 6 was directed to this takeover situation. It is unreal and unconvincing to hear them assert in the witness box that their dominant purpose was to obtain capital rather than to promote the Howard Smith's takeover offer, and I do not believe these assertions.
>
> The conclusion that I have reached is that the primary purpose of the four directors in voting in favour of this allotment was to reduce the proportionate combined shareholding of Ampol and Bulkships in order to induce Howard Smiths to proceed with its takeover offer. There was a majority bloc in the share register. Their intention was to destroy its character as a majority. The directors were, and had for some weeks been, concerned at the position of strength occupied by Ampol and Bulkships together. They were aware that in the light of the attitude of these two shareholders Howard Smiths could not be expected to proceed with its takeover offer that these directors regarded as attractive. They issued the shares so as to reduce the interest of these two shareholders to something significantly less than that of a majority. This was the immediate purpose.

---

1 (1938) 60 CLR 150

The ultimate purpose was to procure the continuation by Howard Smith's of the takeover offer made by that company.'

Their Lordships accept these findings.

The law

The directors, in deciding to issue shares, forming part of Millers' unissued capital, to Howard Smith, acted under clause 8 of the company's articles of association. This provides, subject to certain qualifications which have not been invoked, that the shares shall be under the control of the directors, who may allot or otherwise dispose of the same to such persons on such terms and conditions and either at a premium or otherwise and at such time as the directors may think fit. Thus, and this is not disputed, the issue was clearly *intra vires* the directors. But, *intra vires* though the issue may have been, the directors' power under this article is a fiduciary power: and it remains the case that an exercise of such a power though formally valid, may be attacked on the ground that it was not exercised for the purpose for which it was granted. It is at this point that the contentions of the parties diverge. The extreme argument on one side is that, for validity, what is required is bona fide exercise of the power in the interests of the company: that once it is found that the directors were not motivated by self-interest — ie by a desire to retain their control of the company or their positions on the board — the matter is concluded in their favour and that the court will not inquire into the validity of their reasons for making the issue. All decided cases, it was submitted, where an exercise of such a power as this has been found invalid, are cases where directors are found to have acted through self-interest of this kind.

On the other side, the main argument is that the purpose for which the power is conferred is to enable capital to be raised for the company, and that once it is found that the issue was not made for that purpose, invalidity follows.

. . .

In their Lordships' opinion it is necessary to start with a consideration of the power whose exercise is in question, in this case a power to issue shares. Having ascertained, on a fair view, the nature of this power, and having defined as can best be done in the light of modern conditions the, or some, limits within which it may be exercised, it is then necessary for the court, if a particular exercise of it is challenged, to examine the substantial purpose for which it was exercised, and to reach a conclusion whether that purpose was proper or not. In doing so it will necessarily give credit to the bona fide opinion of the directors, if such is found to exist, and will respect their judgment as to matters of management; having done this, the ultimate conclusion has to be as to the side of a fairly broad line on which the case falls.

> 'The application of the general equitable principle to the acts of directors managing the affairs of a company cannot be as nice as it is in the case of a trustee exercising a special power of appointment.' (*Mills v Mills*, per Dixon J)

The main stream of authority, in their Lordships' opinion, supports this approach. In *Punt v Symons & Co Ltd*[1] Byrne J expressly accepts that there may be reasons other than to raise capital for which shares may be issued. In the High Court case of *Harlowe's Nominees Pty Ltd v Woodside (Lakes Entrance) Oil Co NL*,[2] an

---

1 [1903] 2 Ch 506; 72 LJ Ch 768
2 (1968) 121 CLR 483

issue of shares was made to a large oil company in order, as was found, to secure the financial stability of the company. This was upheld as being within the power although it had the effect of defeating the attempt of the plaintiff to secure control by buying up the company's shares. The joint judgment of Barwick CJ, McTiernan J and Kitto J contains this passage.

> 'The principle is that although primarily the power is given to enable capital to be raised when required for the purposes of the company, there may be occasions when the directors may fairly and properly issue shares for other reasons, so long as those reasons relate to a purpose of benefiting the company as a whole, as distinguished from a purpose, for example, of maintaining control of the company in the hands of the directors them-selves or their friends. An inquiry as to whether additional capital was presently required is often most relevant to the ultimate question upon which the validity or invalidity of the issue depends; but that ultimate question must always be whether in truth the issue was made honestly in the interests of the company. Directors in whom are vested the right and the duty of deciding where the company's interests lie and how they are to be served may be concerned with a wide range of practical considerations, and their judgment, if exercised in good faith and not for irrelevant purposes, is not open to review in the courts. Thus in the present case it is not a matter for judicial concern, if it be the fact, that the allotment to Burmah would frustrate the ambitions of someone who was buying up shares as opportunity offered with a view to obtaining increased influence on the control of the company, or even that the directors realised that the allotment would have that result and found it agreeable to their personal wishes: ...
>
>   Their Lordships were referred to ... *Teck Corporation Ltd v Millar*[1] ... Berger J found ... [that t]heir [*sc.* the directors'] purpose was to obtain the best agreement they could while ... still in control. Their purpose was in that sense to defeat Teck. But, not to defeat Teck's attempt to obtain control, rather it was to foreclose Teck's opportunity of obtain-ing for itself the ultimate deal. That was ... no improper purpose.'

His [Berger J's] decision [*in Teck Corporation Ltd v Millar*] upholding the agreement with Canex on this basis appears to be in line with the English and Australian authorities to which reference has been made.

By contrast to the cases of *Harlowe*[2] and *Teck*,[3] the present case, on the evidence, does not, on the findings of the trial judge, involve any considerations of management, within the proper sphere of the directors. The purpose found by the judge is simply and solely to dilute the majority voting power held by Ampol and Bulkships so as to enable a then minority of shareholders to sell their shares more advantageously. So far as authority goes, an issue of shares purely for the purpose of creating voting power has repeatedly been condemned: *Fraser v Whalley*,[4] *Punt v Symons & Co Ltd; Piercy v S. Mills & Co Ltd*[5] ('merely for the purpose of defeating the wishes of the existing majority of shareholders') and *Hogg v Cramphorn Ltd.*[6] In the leading Australian case of *Mills v Mills*, it was

---

1 (1972) 33 DLR (3d) 288, 328
2 (1968) 121 CLR 483
3 (1972) 33 DLR (3d) 288 (see p 467)
4 (1864) 2 H&M 10; 71 ER 361
5 [1920] 1 Ch 77; 88 LJ Ch 509
6 [1967] Ch 254; [1966] 3 All ER 420 (see p 465)

accepted in the High Court that if the purpose of issuing shares was solely to alter the voting power the issue would be invalid. And, though the reported decisions, naturally enough, are expressed in terms of their own facts, there are clear considerations of principle which support the trend they establish. The constitution of a limited company normally provides for directors, with powers of management, and shareholders, with defined voting powers having power to appoint the directors, and to take, in general meeting, by majority vote, decisions on matters not reserved for management. Just as it is established that directors, within their management powers, may take decisions against the wishes of the majority of shareholders, and indeed that the majority of shareholders cannot control them in the exercise of these powers while they remain in office (*Automatic Self-Cleansing Filter Syndicate Co Ltd v Cunninghame*[1]) so it must be unconstitutional for directors to use their fiduciary powers over the shares in the company purely for the purpose of destroying an existing majority, or creating a new majority which did not previously exist. To do so is to interfere with the element of the company's constitution which is separate from and set against their powers. If there is added, moreover, to this immediate purpose, an ulterior purpose to enable an offer for shares to proceed which the existing majority was in a position to block, the departure from the legitimate use of the fiduciary power becomes not less, but all the greater. The right to dispose of shares at a given price is essentially an individual right to be exercised on individual decision and on which a majority, in the absence of oppression or similar impropriety, is entitled to prevail. Directors are of course entitled to offer advice, and bound to supply information, relevant to the making of such a decision, but to use their fiduciary power solely for the purpose of shifting the power to decide to whom and at what price shares are to be sold cannot be related to any purpose for which the power over the share capital was conferred upon them. That this is the position in law was in effect recognised by the majority directors themselves when they attempted to justify the issue as made primarily in order to obtain much needed capital for the company. And once this primary purpose was rejected, as it was by Street J, there is nothing legitimate left as a basis for their action, except honest behaviour. That is not, in itself, enough.

Their Lordships therefore agree entirely with the conclusion of Street J that the power to issue and allot shares was improperly exercised by the issue of shares to Howard Smith. It was not disputed that an action to set aside the allotment and for rectification of the register was properly brought by Ampol as plaintiff.

SOURCE 176
Clemens *v* Clemens Bros Ltd
(Chancery Division 1976) [1976] 2 All ER 268

FOSTER J: At present the plaintiff has 800 ordinary £1 shares (or 44.4 per cent) and Miss Clemens has 1000 ordinary shares (or 55.5 per cent). Each has 100 preference shares which carry a vote, so that the plaintiff has 900 votes (45 per cent) of the total votes and Miss Clemens has 1100 votes (55 per cent) out of the total number of 2000 votes. It is proposed that each of the four directors should be issued with 200 ordinary shares, a total of 800 shares, and the trustees of the employees' trust should be given 850. If those shares are issued, the shares will be increased from 2000 to 3650, and the effect of that is that the percentage of the votes will be as follows: the plaintiff 24.6575 per cent, Miss Clemens 30.1369 per cent, employees' trust 23.2876 per cent and each director 5.4795 per cent,

---

[1] [1906] 2 Ch 34; 75 LJ Ch 437 (see p 413)

making a total for the four directors of 21.9180 per cent. If the new shares are added together, totalling 1650, they have a percentage of 45.2056. This gives Miss Clemens and her fellow directors together an overall majority of some 52 per cent and, if the trustees join them, more than 75 per cent.

The new shares of £1 each were to be issued at a price of £19.50, a price which, as I have said, the company's chartered accountant had fixed. This was originally challenged as being too low by Mr Wilson, who put the value somewhat higher, but he agreed in cross-examination that the price of £19.50 was within the permitted tolerance of differences between experts. The 850 shares for the employees' trust were to be fully paid, as the company is permitted under section 54 of the Companies Act 1948 to lend the trustees the necessary money which would simply be returned to the company. So far as the 800 shares to be issued to the four directors are concerned, it was proposed that only £1 should be paid up, leaving £18.50 unpaid on each share.

What inferences can be drawn from these figures? Counsel for the defendants asked me to infer that the number of shares to be issued to each director was arrived at so that the directors could borrow to pay for the shares and, if they did, they could, if they were purchasing more than 5 per cent voting shares, set against their income the interest payable on the loans: see the Income and Corporation Taxes Act 1970, section 283(6), and the Finance Act 1974, Schedule 1, paragraphs 9 and 10.

There was no evidence to warrant such an inference and there was evidence that the company was not in need of liquid resources and that the directors did not intend to call up the £18.50 premium per share in the foreseeable future. Even if I accept this inference, I asked why the figure of 850 shares had been put forward for the employees' trust and was told that that figure would produce sufficient income for the long-serving employees, if the dividends remained the same. Counsel for the defendants then sought to refer to Mr Bennett's affidavit to establish the number of long-service employees, but this could hardly be an admission on his part, so that there was no evidence to show why that figure was suggested.

I for my part am driven to the conclusion that the figure of 850 was arrived at in order that the plaintiff's percentage of votes should be below 25 per cent. This is clearly shown, since there is no reason why the shares given to the employees' trust should have a vote and, if they were non-voting shares, the relative voting percentages would be the plaintiff 32.14 per cent, Miss Clemens 39.28 per cent and the four directors 28.56 per cent.

. . .

For the plaintiff it was submitted that the proposed resolutions were oppressive, since they resulted in her losing her right to veto a special or extraordinary resolution and greatly watered down her existing right to purchase Miss Clemens's shares under article 6. For the defendants it was submitted that if two shareholders both honestly hold differing opinions, the view of the majority must prevail and that shareholders in general meeting are entitled to consider their own interests and vote in any way they honestly believe proper in the interests of the company.

I think that one thing which emerges from the cases to which I have referred is that in such a case as the present Miss Clemens is not entitled to exercise her majority vote in whatever way she pleases. The difficulty is in finding a principle, and obviously expressions such as 'bona fide for the benefit of the company as a whole', 'fraud on a minority' and 'oppressive' do not assist in formulating a principle.

I have come to the conclusion that it would be unwise to try to produce a principle, since the circumstances of each case are infinitely varied. It would not, I think, assist to say more than that in my judgment Miss Clemens is not entitled as of right to exercise her votes as an ordinary shareholder in any way she pleases. To use the phrase of Lord Wilberforce, that right is 'subject ... to equitable considerations ... which may make it unjust ... to exercise [it] in a particular way'. Are there then any such considerations in this case?

Conclusion

I do not doubt that Miss Clemens is in favour of the resolutions and knows and understands their purport and effect; nor do I doubt that she genuinely would like to see the other directors have shares in the company and to see a trust set up for long service employees. But I cannot escape the conclusion that the resolutions have been framed so as to put into the hands of Miss Clemens and her fellow directors complete control of the company and to deprive the plaintiff of her existing rights as a shareholder with more than 25 per cent of the votes and greatly reduce her rights under article 6. They are specifically and carefully designed to ensure not only that the plaintiff can never get control of the company but to deprive her of what has been called her negative control. Whether I say that these proposals are oppressive to the plaintiff or that no one could honestly believe they are for her benefit matters not. A court of equity will in my judgment regard these conditions as sufficient to prevent the consequences arising from Miss Clemens using her legal right to vote in the way that she has and it would be right for a court of equity to prevent such consequences taking effect.

The Directors' Duty to Use the Company's Property for the Benefit of the Company

It is this duty which reflects the similarity in the relationships between director and company on the one hand, and that of trustee and beneficiary, on the other. Directors do not own (legally) the company's property (which in law is owned legally and beneficially by the company), but they do have control over it. Hence the introduction into company law of a number of trust law principles. The directors must not allow their duty to the company to come into conflict with their personal interests and they must not make any secret profits. If the company can be said to have given full and free consent to the acquisition by the directors of any profit which would otherwise belong to the company, the directors will be able to retain such profit. The difficulty in this case is to establish who gives this consent on behalf of the company.

SOURCE 177
Regal (Hastings) Ltd *v* Gulliver
(House of Lords 1942) [1967] 2 AC 134n; [1942] 1 All ER 378

The appellant company owned a cinema. As part of a scheme, it acquired 2,000 shares in a 'subsidiary' company, the other 3,000 being acquired by its directors and solicitor. The subsidiary acquired the leases of two other cinemas and all the shares in both companies were sold, yielding a profit on the shares in the subsidiary for its shareholders (ie the appellant company, its directors — now former directors). This action was initiated by the new shareholders of the appellant company to recover the profits made by the directors on the basis that those profits belonged to the appellant. The Court of Appeal dismissed an appeal against the decision of the trial court rejecting the claim. The House of Lords upheld the appeal against all the defendants except the former chairman of the directors and the solicitor. The chairman had taken his shares in the subsidiary as a trustee and the beneficiary owed no fiduciary duty to the appellant. The solicitor, too, owed no fiduciary duty to the appellant and had only taken the shares at the express request of the directors.

> LORD RUSSELL OF KILLOWEN: . . . We have to consider the question of the respondents' liability on the footing that, in taking up these shares in Amalgamated, they acted with bona fides, intending to act in the interest of Regal.
>
> Nevertheless, they may be liable to account for the profits which they have made, if, while standing in a fiduciary relationship to Regal, they have by reason and in course of that fiduciary relationship made a profit.
>
> . . .
>
> The rule of equity which insists on those, who by use of a fiduciary position make a profit, being liable to account for that profit, in no way depends on fraud, or absence of bona fides; or upon such questions or consideration as whether the profit would or should otherwise have gone to the plaintiff, or whether the profiteer was under a duty to obtain the source of the profit for the plaintiff, or whether he took a risk or acted as he did for the benefit of the plaintiff, or whether the plaintiff has in fact been damaged or benefited by his action. The liability arises from the mere fact of a profit having, in the stated circumstances, been made. The profiteer, however honest and well-intentioned, cannot escape the risk of being called upon to account.
>
> The leading case of *Keech v Sandford*[1] is an illustration of the strictness of this rule of equity in this regard, and of how far the rule is independent of these outside considerations. A lease of the profits of a market had been devised to a trustee for the benefit of an infant. A renewal on behalf of the infant was refused. It was absolutely unobtainable. The trustee, finding that it was impossible to get a renewal for the benefit of the infant, took a lease for his own benefit. Though his duty to obtain it for the infant was incapable of performance, nevertheless he was ordered to assign the lease to the infant, upon the bare ground that, if a trustee on the refusal to renew might have a lease for himself, few renewals would be made for the benefit of *cestuis que trust*. Lord King LC, said:
>
>> 'This may seem hard, that the trustee is the only person of all mankind who might not have the lease: but it is very proper that the rule should be strictly pursued, and not in the least relaxed . . .'
>
> One other case in equity may be referred to in this connection, viz, *Ex parte James*,[2] decided by Lord Eldon LC. That was a case of a purchase of a bankrupt's estate by the solicitor to the commission, and Lord Eldon LC, refers to the doctrine thus:
>
>> 'This doctrine as to purchases by trustees, assignees, and persons having a confidential character, stands much more upon general principles than upon the circumstances of any individual case. It rests upon this: that the purchase is not permitted in any case however honest the circumstances; the

---

1 (1726) Sel Cas T King 61; 25 ER 223
2 (1803) 8 Ves Jun 337; 32 ER 385

general interests of justice requiring it to be destroyed in every instance; as no court is equal to the examination and ascertainment of the truth in much the greater number of cases.'

. . .

It now remains to consider whether in acting as directors of Regal they stood in a fiduciary relationship to that company. Directors of a limited company are the creatures of statute and occupy a position peculiar to themselves. In some respects they resemble trustees, in others they do not. In some respects they resemble agents, in others they do not. In some respects they resemble managing partners, in others they do not. In *Re Forest of Dean Coal Mining Co*[1] a director was held not liable for omitting to recover promotion money which had been improperly paid on the formation of the company. He knew of the improper payment, but he was not appointed a director until a later date. It was held that, although a trustee of settled property which included a debt would be liable for neglecting to sue for it, a director of a company was not a trustee of debts due to the company and was not liable. I cite two passages from the judgment of Sir George Jessel MR:

'Directors have sometimes been called trustees, or commercial trustees, and sometimes they have been called managing partners, it does not matter what you call them so long as you understand what their true position is, which is that they are really commercial men managing a trading concern for the benefit of themselves and all other shareholders in it.'

Later, after pointing out that traders have a discretion whether they shall sue for a debt, which discretion is not vested in trustees of a debt under a settlement, he said:

'Again directors are called trustees. They are no doubt trustees of assets which have come to their hands, or which are under their control, but they are not trustees of a debt due to the company ... A director is the managing partner of the concern, and although a debt is due to the concern I do not think it right to call him a trustee of that debt which remains unpaid, though his liability in respect of it may in certain cases and in some respects be analogous to the liability of a trustee.'

The position of directors was considered by Kay J, in *Re Faure Electric Accumulator Co*.[2] That was a case where directors had applied the company's money in payment of an improper commission, and a claim was made for the loss thereby occasioned to the company. In referring to the liability of directors, the judge pointed out that directors were not trustees in the sense of trustees of a settlement, that the nearest analogy to their position would be that of a managing agent of a mercantile house with large powers, but that there was no analogy which was absolutely perfect; and he added:

'However, it is quite obvious that to apply to directors the strict rules of the Court of Chancery with respect to ordinary trustees might fetter their action to an extent which would be exceedingly disadvantageous to the companies they represent.'

1 (1878) 10 Ch D 450; 40 LT 287
2 (1888) 40 Ch D 141; 58 LJ Ch 48

In addition a passage from the judgment of Bowen LJ, in *Imperial Hydropathic Hotel Co v Hampson*[1] may be usefully recalled. He said:

'I should wish . . . to begin by remarking this, that when persons who are directors of a company are from time to time spoken of by judges as agents, trustees, or managing partners of the company, it is essential to recollect that such expressions are not used as exhaustive of the powers and responsibilities of those persons, but only as indicating useful points of view from which they may for the moment and for the particular purpose be considered — points of view at which for the moment they seem to be cutting the circle, or falling within the category of the suggested kind. It is not meant that they belong to the category, but that it is useful for the purpose of the moment to observe that they fall *pro tanto* within the principles which govern that particular class.'

These three cases, however, were not concerned with the question of directors making a profit; but that the equitable principle in this regard applies to directors is beyond doubt. In *Parker v McKenna*[2] a new issue of shares of a joint stock bank was offered to the existing shareholders at a premium. The directors arranged with one Stock to take, at a larger premium, the shares not taken up by the existing shareholders. Stock, being unable to fulfil his contract, requested the directors to relieve him of some. They did so, and made a profit. They were held accountable for the profit so made. Lord Cairns LC, said:

'The court will not enquire and is not in a position to ascertain, whether the bank has or has not lost by the acts of the directors. All the court has to do is to examine whether a profit has been made by an agent, without the knowledge of his principal, in the course and execution of his agency, and the court finds, in my opinion, that these agents in the course of their agency have made a profit, and for that profit they must, in my opinion, account to their principal.'

In the same case James LJ, stated his view in the following terms:

' . . . it appears to me very important that we should concur in laying down again and again the general principle that in this court no agent in the course of his agency, in the matter of his agency, can be allowed to make any profit without the knowledge of his principal; that the rule is an inflexible rule, and must be applied inexorably by this court, which is not entitled, in my judgment, to receive evidence, or suggestion, or argument, as to whether the principal did or did not suffer any injury in fact, by reason of the dealing of the agent; for the safety of mankind requires that no agent shall be able to put his principal to the danger of such an inquiry as that.'

In *Imperial Mercantile Credit Assocn v Coleman*,[3] one Coleman, a stockbroker and a director of a financial company, had contracted to place a large amount of railway debentures for a commission of 5 per cent. He proposed that his company should undertake to place them for a commission of $1\frac{1}{2}$ per cent. The 5 per cent commission was in due course paid to the director, who paid over the $1\frac{1}{2}$ per cent to the company. He was held liable to account for the $3\frac{1}{2}$ per cent by Malins V-C, who said:

---

1 (1882) 23 Ch D 1; 49 LT 150
2 (1874) 10 Ch App 96; 44 LJ Ch 425
3 (1873) LR 6 HL 189; 42 LJ Ch 644

'It is of the highest importance that it should be distinctly understood that it is the duty of directors of companies to use their best exertions for the benefit of those whose interests are committed to their charge, and that they are bound to disregard their own private interests whenever a regard to them conflicts with the proper discharge of such duty.'

His decree was reversed by Lord Hatherley on the ground that the transaction was protected under the company's articles of association. Your Lordships' House, however, thought that in the circumstances of the case the articles of association gave no protection, and restored the decree with unimportant variations. The liability was based on the view, which was not disputed by Lord Hatherley, that the director stood in a fiduciary relationship to the company. That relationship being established, he could not keep the profit which had been earned by the funds of the company being employed in taking up the debentures. The courts in Scotland have treated directors as standing in a fiduciary relationship towards their company and, applying the equitable principle, have made them accountable for profits accruing to them in the course and by reason of their directorships. It will be sufficient to refer to *Huntington Copper Co v Henderson*,[1] in which the Lord President cites with approval the following passage from the judgment of the Lord Ordinary:

'Whenever it can be shown that the trustee has so arranged matters as to obtain an advantage whether in money or money's worth to himself personally through the execution of his trust, he will not be permitted to retain, but be compelled to make it over to his constituent.'

In the result, I am of opinion that the directors standing in a fiduciary relationship to Regal in regard to the exercise of their powers as directors, and having obtained these shares by reason and only by reason of the fact that they were directors of Regal and in the course of the execution of that office, are accountable for the profits which they have made out of them. The equitable rule laid down in *Keech v Sandford* and *Ex parte James*, and similar authorities applies to them in full force. It was contended that these cases were distinguishable by reason of the fact that it was impossible for Regal to get the shares owing to lack of funds, and that the directors in taking the shares were really acting as members of the public. I cannot accept this argument. It was impossible for the *cestui que trust* in *Keech v Sandford* to obtain the lease, nevertheless the trustee was accountable. The suggestion that the directors were applying simply as members of the public is a travesty of the facts. They could, had they wished, have protected themselves by a resolution (either antecedent or subsequent) of the Regal shareholders in general meeting. In default of such approval, the liability to account must remain.

SOURCE 178
Industrial Development Consultants Ltd *v* Cooley
(Birmingham Assizes 1972) [1972] 1 WLR 443; [1972] 2 All ER 162

The defendant was employed by the plaintiff as its managing director with the specific intention of securing for the plaintiff a contract to build a depot for the Eastern Gas Board. Although he spared no effort, it seemed highly unlikely that the plaintiff would be given the contract. The defendant was invited by the Gas Board to work on the project, but not as the plaintiff's

---

1 (1877) 5 R (Ct of Sess) 1; 15 Sc LR 217 (Scot)

managing director. The defendant obtained his release from his position with
the plaintiff by misrepresenting that he was ill and he accepted the post with
the Gas Board without disclosing the manner in which he had obtained his
release.

ROSKILL J: ... The remarkable position then arises that if one applies the
equitable doctrine on which the plaintiffs rely to oblige the defendant to account,
they will receive a benefit which on Mr Smettom's[1] evidence at least it is unlikely
they would have got for themselves had the defendant complied with his duty to
them. On the other hand, if the defendant is not required to account he will have
made a large profit as a result of having deliberately put himself into a position
in which his duty to the plaintiffs who were employing him and his personal
interests conflicted. I leave out of account the fact that he dishonestly tricked Mr
Hicks[2] into releasing him on 16 June although counsel for the plaintiffs urged
that that was another reason why equity must compel him to disgorge his profit.
It is said that the plaintiffs' only remedy is to sue for damages either for breach
of contract or maybe for fraudulent misrepresentation. Counsel for the plaintiffs
has been at pains to disclaim any intention to claim damages for breach of
contract save on one basis only and he has disclaimed specifically any claim for
damages for fraudulent misrepresentation. Therefore, if the plaintiffs succeed
they will get a profit which they probably would not have got for themselves had
the defendant fulfilled his duty. If the defendant is allowed to keep that profit he
will have got something which he was able to get solely by reason of his breach of
fiduciary duty to the plaintiffs.

When one looks at the way the cases have gone over the centuries it is plain that
the question whether or not the benefit would have been obtained but for the
breach of trust has always been treated as irrelevant. I mentioned *Keech v
Sandford*[3] a few moments ago and this fact will also be found emphasised if one
looks at some of the speeches in *Regal (Hastings) Ltd v Gulliver*,[4] although it is true,
as was pointed out to me, that if one looks at some of the language used in the
speeches in *Regal* such phrases as 'he must account for any benefit which he
obtains in the course of and owing to his directorship' will be found.

In one sense the benefit in this case did not arise because of the defendant's
directorship; indeed, the defendant would not have got this work had he
remained a director. However, one must, as Lord Upjohn pointed out, look at the
passages in the speeches in *Regal* having regard to the facts of that case to which
those passages and those statements were directed. I think counsel for the
plaintiffs was right when he said that it is the basic principle which matters. It is
an overriding principle of equity that a man must not be allowed to put himself
in a position in which his fiduciary duty and his interests conflict. The variety of
cases where that can happen is infinite. The fact there has not previously been a
case precisely of this nature with precisely similar facts before the courts is of no
import. The facts of this case are, I think, exceptional and I hope unusual. They
seem to me plainly to come within this principle.

I think, although perhaps the expression is not entirely precise, counsel for the
plaintiffs put the point well when he said that what the defendant did in May,
June and July was to substitute himself as an individual for the company of which
he was managing director and to which he owed a fiduciary duty. It is on the

1 Of the Gas Board
2 Chairman of the plaintiff
3 (1726) Sel Cas T King 61; 25 ER 223
4 [1967] 2 AC 134n; [1942] 1 All ER 378 (see p 477)

ground which I have stated that I rest my conclusion in this case. Perhaps it is permissible to say that I have less reluctance in reaching that conclusion on the application of this basic principle of equity since I know that what happened was enabled to happen because a release was obtained by the defendant from a binding contractual obligation by the dishonest and untrue misrepresentations which were made to Mr Hicks on 16 June. In my judgment, therefore, an order for an account will be issued because the defendant made and will make his profit as a result of having allowed his interests and his duty to conflict.

I would only add that if I am wrong on this central question counsel for the plaintiffs did in the alternative advance a claim for damages — this was the only claim for damages advanced — for the plaintiffs' loss of the opportunity to get this contract. I mentioned earlier in this judgment the fact that Mr Lacey and Mr Smettom both said they would not — I think I can put it as high as this — have employed the plaintiffs because of their objection to this type of organisation. Therefore it cannot be said that it is anything like certain that the plaintiffs would ever have got this contract. I accept both those witnesses as witnesses of truth. On the other hand, there was always the possibility of the plaintiffs persuading the Eastern Gas Board to change their minds; and ironically enough, it would have been the defendant's duty to try and persuade them to change their minds. It is a curious position under which he whose duty it would have been to seek to persuade them to change their minds should not say that the plaintiffs suffered no loss because he would never have succeeded in persuading them to change their mind.

In the circumstances, while I do not put the chance of their being shifted from the stand they adopted very high, nonetheless, the opportunity was there and could not be taken because the plaintiffs never knew about it owing to the defendant's conduct. I do not put the chance very high. I cannot rate it, as I am dealing with liability only, at a greater than ten per cent chance. If I am wrong in making an order for account I should have given the plaintiffs as damages whatever would represent a ten per cent chance.

SOURCE 179
Canadian Aero Services Ltd *v* O'Malley
(Supreme Court of Canada 1972) [1973] 40 DLR (3d) 371

LASKIN J: This appeal arises out of a claim by the plaintiff-appellant (hereinafter referred to as Canaero) that the defendants had improperly taken the fruits of a corporate opportunity in which Canaero had a prior and continuing interest. The allegation against the defendants O'Malley and Zarzycki is that while directors or officers of Canaero they had devoted effort and planning in respect of the particular corporate opportunity as representatives of Canaero, but had subsequently wrongfully taken the benefit thereof in breach of a fiduciary duty to Canaero. The defendant Wells, who had been a director of Canaero but never an officer, was brought into the action as an associate of the other individual defendants in an alleged scheme to deprive Canaero of the corporate opportunity which it had been developing through O'Malley and Zarzycki; and the defendant Terra Surveys Limited was joined as the vehicle through which the individual defendants in fact obtained the benefit for which Canaero had been negotiating.

. . .

There are four issues that arise for consideration on the facts so far recited. There is, first, the determination of the relationship of O'Malley and Zarzycki to Canaero. Secondly, there is the duty or duties, if any, owed by them to Canaero by reason of the ascertained relationship. Thirdly, there is the question whether there has been any breach of duty, if any is owing, by reason of the conduct of O'Malley and Zarzycki in acting through Terra to secure the contract for the Guyana project; and, fourthly, there is the question of liability for breach of duty if established.

Like Grant J, the trial Judge, I do not think it matters whether O'Malley and Zarzycki were properly appointed as directors of Canaero or whether they did or did not act as directors. What is not in doubt is that they acted respectively as president and executive vice-president of Canaero for about two years prior to their resignations. To paraphrase the findings of the trial Judge in this respect, they acted in those positions and their remuneration and responsibilities verified their status as senior officers of Canaero. They were 'top management' and not mere employees whose duty to their employer, unless enlarged by contract, consisted only of respect for trade secrets and for confidentiality of customer lists. Theirs was a larger, more exacting duty which, unless modified by statute or by contract (and there is nothing of this sort here), was similar to that owed to a corporate employer by its directors. I adopt what is said on this point by Gower, *Principles of Modern Company Law* (3rd edn 1969) as follows:

> ' . . . these duties, except in so far as they depend on statutory provisions expressly limited to directors, are not so restricted but apply equally to any officials of the company who are authorised to act on its behalf, and in particular to those acting in a managerial capacity.'

. . .

It follows that O'Malley and Zarzycki stood in a fiduciary relationship to Canaero, which in its generality betokens loyalty, good faith and avoidance of a conflict of duty and self-interest. Descending from the generality, the fiduciary relationship goes at least this far: a director or a senior officer like O'Malley or Zarzycki is precluded from obtaining for himself, either secretly or without the approval of the company (which would have to be properly manifested upon full disclosure of the facts), any property or business advantage either belonging to the company or for which it has been negotiating; and especially is this so where the director or officer is a participant in the negotiations on behalf of the company.

An examination of the case law in this Court and in the Courts of other like jurisdictions on the fiduciary duties of directors and senior officers shows the pervasiveness of a strict ethic in this area of the law. In my opinion, this ethic disqualifies a director or senior officer from usurping for himself or diverting to another person or company with whom or with which he is associated a maturing business opportunity which his company is actively pursuing; he is also precluded from so acting even after his resignation where the resignation may fairly be said to have been prompted or influenced by a wish to acquire for himself the opportunity sought by the company, or where it was his position with the company rather than a fresh initiative that led him to the opportunity which he later acquired.

It is this fiduciary duty which is invoked by the appellant in this case and which is resisted by the respondents on the grounds that the duty as formulated is not nor should be part of our law and that, in any event, the facts of the present case do not fall within its scope.

This Court considered the issue of fiduciary duty of directors in *Zwicker v Stanbury et al*,[1] where it found apt for the purposes of that case certain general

---

1 [1954] 1 DLR 257

statements of law by Viscount Sankey and by Lord Russell of Killowen in *Regal (Hastings) Ltd v Gulliver et al.*[1] These statements reflecting basic principle which is not challenged in the present case, are represented in the following passage. Per Viscount Sankey:

> 'In my view, the respondents were in a fiduciary position and their liability to account does not depend upon proof of *mala fides.* The general rule of equity is that no one who has duties of a fiduciary nature to perform is allowed to enter into engagements in which he has or can have a personal interest conflicting with the interests of those whom he is bound to protect. If he holds any property so acquired as trustee, he is bound to account for it to his *cestui que trust.* The earlier cases are concerned with trusts of specific property: *Keech v Sandford*[2] per Lord King, LC. The rule, however, applies to agents, as, for example, solicitors and directors, when acting in a fiduciary capacity.

Per Lord Russell of Killowen:

[Laskin J quoted the passage beginning 'In the result . . .' and concluding '. . . liability to account must remain', p 481 and continued:]

I need not pause to consider whether on the facts in *Regal (Hastings) Ltd v Gulliver* the equitable principle was over-zealously applied; see, for example, *Gower,* op cit, at pp 535–7. What I would observe is that the principle, or, indeed, principles, as stated, grew out of older cases concerned with fiduciaries other than directors or managing officers of a modern corporation, and I do not therefore regard them as providing a rigid measure whose literal terms must be met in assessing succeeding cases. In my opinion, neither the conflict test, referred to by Viscount Sankey, nor the test of accountability for profits acquired by reason only of being directors and in the course of execution of the office, reflected in the passage quoted from Lord Russell of Killowen, should be considered as the exclusive touchstones of liability. In this, as in other branches of the law, new fact situations may require a reformulation of existing principle to maintain its vigour in the new setting.

The reaping of a profit by a person at a company's expense while a director thereof is, of course, an adequate ground upon which to hold the director accountable. Yet there may be situations where a profit must be disgorged, although not gained at the expense of the company, on the ground that a director must not be allowed to use his position as such to make a profit even if it was not open to the company, as for example, by reason of legal disability, to participate in the transaction. An analogous situation, albeit not involving a director, existed for all practical purposes in the case of *Boardman et al v Phipps,*[3] which also supports the view that liability to account does not depend on proof of an actual conflict of duty and self-interest. Another, quite recent, illustration of a liability to account where the company itself had failed to obtain a business contract and hence could not be regarded as having been deprived of a business opportunity is *Industrial Development Consultants Ltd v Cooley,*[4] a judgment of a Court of first instance. There, the managing director, who was allowed to resign his position on a false assertion of ill health, subsequently got the contract for himself. That case is thus also illustrative of the situation where a director's

---

1 [1967] 2 AC 134n; [1942] 1 All ER 378 (see p 477)
2 (1726) Sel Cas T King 61; 25 ER 223
3 [1967] 2 AC 46; [1966] 3 All ER 721
4 [1972] 1 WLR 443; [1972] 2 All ER 162 (see p 481)

resignation is prompted by a decision to obtain for himself the business contract denied to his company and where he does obtain it without disclosing his intention.

What these decisions indicate is an updating of the equitable principle whose roots lie in the general standards that I have already mentioned, namely, loyalty, good faith and avoidance of a conflict of duty and self-interest. Strict application against directors and senior management officials is simply recognition of the degree of control which their positions give them in corporate operations, a control which rises above day [by day] accountability to owning shareholders and which comes under some scrutiny only at annual general or at special meetings. It is a necessary supplement, in the public interest, of statutory regulation and accountability which themselves are, at one and the same time, an acknowledgment of the importance of the corporation in the life of the community and of the need to compel obedience by it and by its promoters, directors and managers to norms of exemplary behaviour.

. . .

In my opinion, the fiduciary duty upon O'Malley and Zarzycki, if it survived their departure from Canaero, would be reduced to an absurdity if it could be evaded merely because the Guyana project had been varied in some details when it became the subject of invited proposals, or merely because Zarzycki met the variations by appropriate changes in what he prepared for Canaero in 1965, and what he proposed for Terra in 1966. I do not regard it as necessary to look for substantial resemblances. Their presence would be a factor to be considered on the issue of breach of fiduciary duty but they are not a *sine qua non*. The cardinal fact is that the one project, the same project with Zarzycki had pursued for Canaero, was the subject of his Terra proposal. It was that business opportunity, in line with its general pursuits, which Canaero sought through O'Malley and Zarzycki. There is no suggestion that there had been such a change of objective as to make the project for which proposals were invited from Canaero, Terra and others a different one from that which Canaero had been developing with a view to obtaining the contract for itself.

. . .

Counsel for O'Malley and Zarzycki relied upon the judgment of this Court in *Peso Silver Mines Ltd (NPL) v Cropper*,[1] as representing an affirmation of what was said in *Regal (Hastings) Ltd v Gulliver* respecting the circumscription of liability to circumstances where the directors or senior officers had obtained the challenged benefit by reason only of the fact that they held those positions and in the course of execution of those offices. In urging this, he did not deny that leaving to capitalize on their positions would not necessarily immunize them, but he submitted that in the present case there was no special knowledge or information obtained from Canaero during their service with that company upon which O'Malley and Zarzycki had relied in reaching for the Guyana project on behalf of Terra.

There is a considerable gulf between the *Peso* case and the present one on the facts as found in each and on the issues that they respectively raise. In *Peso*, there was a finding of good faith in the rejection by its directors of an offer of mining claims because of its strained finances. The subsequent acquisition of those claims by the managing director and his associates, albeit without seeking shareholder approval, was held to be proper because the company's interest in them ceased. There is some analogy to *Burg v Horn*[2] because there was evidence

---

1 (1966) 58 DLR (2d) 1
2 (1967) 380 F 2nd 897

that Peso had received many offers of mining properties and, as in *Burg v Horn*, the acquisition of the particular claims out of which the litigation arose could not be said to be essential to the success of the company. Whether evidence was overlooked in *Peso* which would have led to the result reached in *Regal (Hastings) Ltd v Gulliver* (see the examination by Beck, 'The Saga of Peso Silver Mines: Corporate Opportunity Reconsidered', 49 Can Bar Rev 80 (1971), at p 101) has no bearing on the proper disposition of the present case. What is before this Court is not a situation where various opportunities were offered to a company which was open to all of them, but rather a case where it had devoted itself to originating and bringing to fruition a particular business deal which was ultimately captured by former senior officers who had been in charge of the matter for the company. Since Canaero had been invited to make a proposal on the Guyana project, there is no basis for contending that it could not, in any event, have obtained the contract or that there was an unwillingness to deal with it.

It is a mistake, in my opinion, to seek to encase the principle stated and applied in *Peso*, by adoption from *Regal (Hastings) Ltd v Gulliver*, in the straight-jacket of special knowledge acquired while acting as directors or senior officers, let alone limiting it to benefits acquired by reason of and during the holding of those offices. As in other cases in this developing branch of the law, the particular facts may determine the shape of the principle of decision without setting fixed limits to it. So it is in the present case. Accepting the facts found by the trial Judge, I find no obstructing considerations to the conclusion that O'Malley and Zarzycki continued, after their resignations, to be under a fiduciary duty to respect Canaero's priority, as against them and their instrument Terra, in seeking to capture the contract for the Guyana project. They entered the lists in the heat of the maturation of the project, known to them to be under active Government consideration when they resigned from Canaero and when they proposed to bid on behalf of Terra.

Appeal by Canaero upheld.

SOURCE 180
Guinness plc *v* Saunders
(House of Lords) [1990] BCLC 402

LORD TEMPLEMAN: ... Mr Ward admits receipt of £5.2m from Guinness and pleads an agreement by Guinness that he should be paid this sum for his advice and services in connection with the bid. Mr Ward admits that payment was not authorised by the board of directors of Guinness.

The articles of association of Guinness provide:

'REMUNERATION OF DIRECTORS

90. The Board shall fix the annual remuneration of the Directors provided that without the consent of the Company in General Meeting such remuneration (excluding any special remuneration payable under Article 91 and Article 92) shall not exceed the sum of £100,000 per annum ...

91. The Board may, in addition to the remuneration authorised in Article 90, grant special remuneration to any Director who serves on any Committee or who devotes special attention to the business of the Company or who otherwise performs services which in the opinion or the Board are outside the scope of the ordinary duties of a Director. Such special remuneration

may be made payable to such Director in addition to or in substitution for his ordinary remuneration as a Director, and may be made payable by a lump sum or by way of salary, or commission or participation in profits, or by any or all of those modes or otherwise as the Board may determine.'

Articles 90 and 91 of the articles of association of Guinness depart from the Table A articles recommended by statute, which reserve to a company in general meeting the right to determine the remuneration of the directors of the company. But by art 90 the annual remuneration which the directors may award themselves is limited and by art 91 special remuneration for an individual director can only be authorised by the board. A committee, which may consist of only two or, as in the present case, three members, however honest and conscientious, cannot assess impartially the value of its work or the value of the contribution of its individual members. A director may, as a condition of accepting appointment to a committee, or after he has accepted appointment, seek the agreement of the board to authorise payment for special work envisaged or carried out. The shareholders of Guinness run the risk that the board may be too generous to an individual director at the expense of the shareholders but the shareholders have, by art 91, chosen to run this risk and can protect themselves by the number, quality and impartiality of the members of the board who will consider whether an individual director deserves special reward. Under art 91 the shareholders of Guinness do not run the risk that a committee may value its own work and the contribution of its own members. Article 91 authorises the board, and only the board, to grant special remuneration to a director who serves on a committee.

. . .

Since, for the purposes of this application, Guinness concede that Mr Ward performed valuable services for Guinness in connection with the bid, counsel on behalf of Mr Ward submits that Mr Ward, if not entitled to remuneration pursuant to the articles, is, nevertheless, entitled to be awarded by the court a sum by way of quantum meruit or equitable allowance for his services. Counsel submits that the sum awarded by the court might amount to £5.2m or a substantial proportion of that sum; therefore Mr Ward should be allowed to retain the sum of £5.2m which he has received until, at the trial of the action, the court determines whether he acted with propriety and, if so, how much of the sum of £5.2m he should be permitted to retain; Mr Ward is anxious for an opportunity to prove at a trial that he acted with propriety throughout the bid. It is common ground that, for the purposes of this appeal, it must be assumed that Mr Ward and the other members of the committee acted in good faith and that the sum of £5.2m was a proper reward for the services rendered by Mr Ward to Guinness.

My Lords, the short answer to a quantum meruit claim based on an implied contract by Guinness to pay reasonable remuneration for services rendered is that there can be no contract by Guinness to pay special remuneration for the services of a director unless that contract is entered into by the board pursuant to art 91. The short answer to the claim for an equitable allowance is the equitable principle which forbids a trustee to make a profit out of his trust unless the trust instrument, in this case the articles of association of Guinness, so provides. The law cannot and equity will not amend the articles of Guinness. The court is not entitled to usurp the functions conferred on the board by the articles.

Snell's Principles of Equity (28th edn, 1982), first published in 1868, contained

the distilled wisdom of the author and subsequent editors, including Sir Robert
Megarry, on the law applicable to trusts and trustees. It is said (p 244):

> 'With certain exceptions, neither directly nor indirectly may a trustee make
> a profit from his trust ... The rule depends not on fraud or mala fides, but
> on the mere fact of a profit made.'

Palmer's Company Law (24th edn, 1987), first published in 1898, contains the
distilled wisdom of the authors and subsequent editors concerning the law
applicable to companies and directors. It is said (vol 1, pp 943–944,
para 63–13):

> 'Like other fiduciaries directors are required not to put themselves in a
> position where there is a conflict (actual or potential) between their
> personal interests and their duties to the company ... the position of a
> director, *vis-à-vis* the company, is that of an agent who may not himself
> contract with his principal, and ... is similar to that of a trustee who,
> however fair a proposal may be, is not allowed to let the position arise where
> his interest and that of the trust may conflict ... he is, like a trustee,
> disqualified from contracting with the company and for a good reason: the
> company is entitled to the collective wisdom of its directors, and if any
> director is interested in a contract, his interest may conflict with his duty,
> and the law always strives to prevent such a conflict from arising.'

The application of these principles to remuneration in the case of a trustee is
described by *Snell* p 252 as follows:

> 'As the result of the rule that a trustee cannot make a profit from his trust,
> trustees and executors are generally entitled to no allowance for their care
> and trouble. This rule is so strict that even if a trustee or executor has
> sacrificed much time to carrying on a business as directed by the trust, he
> will usually be allowed nothing as compensation for his personal trouble or
> loss of time.'

The application of these principles to remuneration in the case of a director is
described by *Palmer* p 902, para 60–38 as follows:

> 'Prima facie, directors of a company cannot claim remuneration, but the
> articles usually provide expressly for payment of it ... and where this is the
> case, the provision operates as an authority to the directors to pay
> remuneration out of the funds of the company; such remuneration is not
> restricted to payment out of profits.'

The following also appears (p 903, para 60–40):

> 'The articles will also usually authorise the payment by the directors to one
> of their number of extra remuneration for special services. Where such
> provision is made, it is a condition precedent to a director's claim for
> additional remuneration that the board of directors shall determine the
> method and amount of the extra payment; it is irrelevant that the director
> has performed substantial extra services and the payment of additional
> remuneration would be reasonable.'

So far as contract is concerned, Lord Cranworth LC in *Aberdeen Rly Co v Blaikie
Bros* (1854) 1 Macq 461 at 471–472, [1843–60] All ER Rep 249 at 252–253
considered:

'. . . the general question, whether a Director of a Railway Company is or is not precluded from dealing on behalf of the Company with himself, or with a firm in which he is a partner. The Directors are a body to whom is delegated the duty of managing the general affairs of the Company. A corporate body can only act by agents, and it is of course the duty of those agents so to act as best to promote the interests of the corporation whose affairs they are conducting. Such agents have duties to discharge of a fiduciary nature towards their principal. And it is a rule of universal application, that no one, having such duties to discharge, shall be allowed to enter into engagements in which he has, or can have, a personal interest conflicting, or which possibly may conflict, with the interests of those whom he is bound to protect. So strictly is this principle adhered to, that no question is allowed to be raised as to the fairness or unfairness of a contract so entered into. It obviously is, or may be, impossible to demonstrate how far in any particular case the terms of such a contract have been the best for the interest of the *cestui que* trust which it was possible to obtain. It may sometimes happen that the terms on which a trustee has dealt or attempted to deal with the estate or interest of those for whom he is a trustee have been as good as could have been obtained from any other person — they may even at the time have been better. But still so inflexible is the rule that no inquiry on that subject is permitted.'

So far as equity is concerned, Stuart V-C in *Barrett v Hartley* (1866) LR 2 Eq 789 at 796 said that there was a —

'very well established principle of this Court, that a trustee is not to exact anything for his services. For the Defendant it was contended, that although the payment was called a *bonus*, it was for important services rendered. No doubt the importance and benefit of the services can hardly be exaggerated. But a trustee who greatly benefits his *cestui que trust* by performing his duties, is not entitled to say to him that he will not give him his property, or proceed to execute the trust, unless he be paid a bonus.' (Stuart V-C's emphasis.)

In *Bray v Ford* [1896] AC 44, [1895–9] All ER Rep 1009 a solicitor who was a governor of a charitable college charged profit costs for his professional services under the mistaken belief that the memorandum of association allowed him to do so. Lord Watson said that the respondent was not —

'legally justified in charging and accepting payment of full professional remuneration in respect of services rendered by him to the college in his capacity of solicitor . . . the respondent was neither entitled to charge profit costs in respect of these services, nor to retain them when received by him. Such a breach of the law may be attended with perfect good faith, and it is, in my opinion, insufficient to justify a charge of moral obliquity, unless it is shewn to have been committed knowingly or with an improper motive.'

(See [1896] AC 44 at 48, [1895–9] All ER Rep 1009 at 1012.)
Lord Herschell said ([1896] AC 44 at 51–52, [1895–9] All ER Rep 1009 at 1011):

'It is an inflexible rule of a Court of Equity that a person in a fiduciary position, such as the respondent's, is not, unless otherwise expressly provided, entitled to make a profit; he is not allowed to put himself in a position where his interest and duty conflict. It does not appear to me that this rule is, as has been said, founded upon principles of morality. I regard it rather as based on the consideration that, human nature being what it is, there is danger, in such circumstances, of the person holding a fiduciary duty being swayed by interest rather than by duty, and thus prejudicing those whom he was bound to protect. It has, therefore, been deemed prejudicing those whom he was bound to protect. It has therefore, been deemed expedient to lay down this positive rule. But I am satisfied that it might be departed from in many cases, without any breach of morality, without any wrong being inflicted, and without any consciousness of wrongdoing.'

Equity forbids a trustee to make profit out of his trust. The articles of association of Guinness relax the strict rule of equity to the extent of enabling a director to make a profit provided that the board of directors contracts on behalf of Guinness for the payment of special remuneration or decides to award special remuneration. Mr Ward did not obtain a contract or a grant from the board of directors. Equity has no power to relax its own strict rule further than and inconsistently with the express relaxation contained in the articles of association. A shareholder is entitled to compliance with the articles. A director accepts office subject to and with the benefit of the provisions of the articles relating to directors. No one is obliged to accept appointment as a director. No director can be obliged to serve on a committee. A director of Guinness who contemplates or accepts service on a committee or has performed outstanding services for the company as a member of a committee or has performed outstanding services for the company as a member of a committee may apply to the board of directors for a contract or an award of special remuneration. A director who does not read the articles or a director who misconstrues the articles is nevertheless bound by the articles. Article 91 provides clearly enough for the authority of the board of directors to be obtained for the payment of special remuneration and the submissions made on behalf of Mr Ward, based on arts 2, 100(D) and 110, are more ingenious than plausible and more legalistic than convincing. At the board meeting held on 19 January 1986, Mr Ward was present but did not seek then or thereafter to obtain the necessary authority of the board of directors for payment of special remuneration. In these circumstances there are no grounds for equity to relax its rules further than the articles of association provide. Similarly, the law will not imply a contract between Guinness and Mr Ward for remuneration on a quantum meruit basis awarded by the court when the articles of association of Guinness stipulate that special remuneration for a director can only be awarded by the board.

It was submitted on behalf of Mr Ward that Guinness, by the committee consisting of Mr Saunders, Mr Ward and Mr Roux, entered into a voidable contract to pay remuneration to Mr Ward and that since Mr Ward performed the services he agreed to perform under this voidable contract there could be no restitutio in integrum and the contract cannot be avoided. This submission would enable a director to claim and retain remuneration under a contract which a committee purported to conclude with him, notwithstanding that the committee had no power to enter into the contract. The fact is that Guinness never did contract to pay anything to Mr Ward. The contract on which Mr Ward relies is not voidable but non-existent. In support of a quantum meruit claim, counsel for Mr Ward relied on the decision of Buckley J in *Re Duomatic Ltd* [1969] 1 All ER 161, [1969] 2 Ch 365. In that case a company sought and failed to recover remuneration received by a director when the shareholders or a voting majority of the shareholders had sanctioned or ratified the payment. In the present case there has been no such sanction or ratification either by the board of directors or by the shareholders. Mr Ward also relied on the decision in *Craven-Ellis v Canons Ltd* [1936] 2 All ER 1066, [1936] 2 KB 403. In that case the plaintiff was appointed managing director of a company by an agreement under the company's seal which also provided for his remuneration. By the articles of association each director was required to obtain qualification shares within two months of his appointment. Neither the plaintiff nor the other directors obtained their qualification shares within two months or at all and the agreement with the managing director was entered into after they had ceased to be directors. The plaintiff having done work for the company pursuant to the terms of the agreement was held to be entitled to the remuneration provided for in the agreement on the basis of a quantum meruit. In *Craven-Ellis's* case the plaintiff was not a director, there was no conflict between his claim to remuneration and the equitable doctrine which debars a director from profiting from his fiduciary duty, and there was no obstacle to the implication of a contract between the company and the plaintiff entitling the plaintiff to claim reasonable remuneration as of right by an action in law. Moreover, as in *Re Duomatic Ltd*, the agreement was sanctioned by all the directors, two of whom were beneficially entitled to the share capital of the company. In the present case Mr Ward was a director, there was a conflict between his interest and his duties, there could be no contract by Guinness for the payment of remuneration pursuant to art 91 unless the board made the contract on behalf of Guinness and there was no question of approval by directors or shareholders.

In support of a claim for an equitable allowance, reference was made to the decision of Wilberforce J in *Phipps v Boardman* [1964] 2 All ER 187, [1964] 1 WLR 993. His decision was upheld by the Court of Appeal (see [1965] 1 All ER 849, [1965] Ch 992) and ultimately by this House (see [1966] 3 All ER 721, [1967] 2 AC 46). In that case a trust estate included a minority holding in a private company which fell on lean times. The trustees declined to attempt to acquire a controlling interest in the company in order to improve its performance. The solicitor to the trust and one of the beneficiaries, with the knowledge and approval of the trustees, purchased the controlling interest from outside shareholders for themselves with the help of information about the shareholders acquired by the solicitor in the course of acting for the trust. The company's position was improved and the shares bought by the solicitor and the purchasing beneficiary were ultimately sold at a profit. A complaining beneficiary was held to be entitled to a share of the profits on the resale on the ground that the solicitor and the purchasing beneficiary were assisted in the original purchase by the information derived from the trust. The purchase of a controlling interest might have turned out badly and in that case the solicitor and the purchasing beneficiary would have made irrecoverable personal losses. In these circumstances it is not surprising that Wilberforce J decided that in calculating the undeserved profit which accrued to the trust estate there should be deducted a generous allowance for the work and trouble of the solicitor and purchasing beneficiary in acquiring the controlling shares and restoring the company to prosperity. *Phipps v Boardman* decides that in exceptional circumstances a court of equity may award remuneration to the trustee. Therefore, it is argued, a court of equity may award remuneration to a director. As at present advised, I am unable to envisage circumstances in which a court of equity would exercise a power to award remuneration to a director when the relevant articles of association confided that power to the board of directors. Certainly, the circumstances do not exist in the present case. It is in this respect that s 317 of the Companies Act 1985 is relevant. By that section:

'(1) It is the duty of a director of a company who is in any way, whether directly or indirectly, interested in a contract or proposed contract with the company to declare the nature of his interest at a meeting of the directors of the company ...

(7) A director who fails to comply with this section is liable to a fine ... '

In *Hely-Hutchinson v Brayhead Ltd* [1967] 3 All ER 98, 1 QB 549 the Court of Appeal held that s 317 renders a contract voidable by a company if the director does not declare his interest. Section 317 does not apply directly to the present case because there was no contract between Guinness and Mr Ward. But s 317 shows the importance which the legislature attaches to the principle that a company should be protected against a director who has a conflict of interest and duty. There is a fundamental objection to the admission of any claim by Mr Ward whether that claim be based on art 100(D), a quantum meruit, s 727 of the 1985 Act or the powers of a court of equity. The objection is that by the agreement with the committee, which is the foundation of Mr Ward's claim to any relief, he voluntarily involved himself in an irreconcilable conflict between his duty as a director and his personal interests. Both before and after 19 January 1986 Mr Ward owed a duty to tender to Guinness impartial and independent advice untainted by any possibility of personal gain. Yet by the agreement, which Mr Ward claims to have concluded with the committee and which may have been in contemplation by Mr Ward even before 19 January 1986, Mr Ward became entitled to a negotiating fee payable by Guinness if, and only if, Guinness acquired Distillers and, by the agreement, the amount of the negotiating fee depended on the price which Guinness ultimately offered to the shareholders of Distillers. If such an agreement had been concluded by the board of directors, it would have been binding on Guinness under art 91 but foolish in that the agreement perforce made Mr Ward's advice to Guinness suspect and leased. But at least the conflict would have been revealed to the board. As it was, the agreement was not made by the board and was not binding on Guinness. The agreement was made by the committee and ought not to have been made at all. By the agreement Mr Ward debarred himself from giving impartial and independent advice to Guinness. Mr Ward was a director of Guinness and in that capacity was able to negotiate his own agreement with the committee of which he was a member, and was able to discuss the bid by Guinness for Distillers with the other directors, to advise and participate in decisions on behalf of Guinness relevant to the bid (including a decision to increase the amount of the offer) and to procure the acquisition by Guinness of Distillers and thus to claim £5.2m from Guinness. I agree with my noble and learned friend Lord Goff that for the purposes of this appeal it must be assumed that Mr Ward acted in good faith, believing that his services were rendered under contract binding on the company, and that in that mistaken belief Mr Ward may have rendered services to Guinness of great value and contributed substantially to the enrichment of the shareholders of Guinness. Nevertheless, the failure of Mr Ward to realise that he could not properly use his position as director of Guinness to obtain a contingent negotiating fee of £5.2m from Guinness does not excuse him or enable him to defeat the rules of equity which prohibit a trustee from putting himself in a position in which his interests and duty conflict and which insist that a trustee or any other fiduciary shall not make a profit out of his trust.

Finally, judgment against Mr Ward on this application was resisted in reliance on s 727 of the 1985 Act. That section provides:

'(1) If in any proceedings for negligence, default, breach of duty or breach of trust against an officer of a company or a person employed by a company as auditor . . . it appears to the court hearing the case that that officer or person is or may be liable in respect of the negligence, default, breach of duty or breach of trust, but that he has acted honestly and reasonably, and that having regard to all the circumstances of the case (including those connected with his appointment) he ought fairly to be excused for the negligence, default, breach of duty or breach of trust, that court may relieve him, either wholly or partly, from his liability on such terms as it thinks fit
. . .'

Mr Ward requested the committee to pay him and received from the committee out of moneys belonging to Guinness the sum of £5.2m as a reward for his advice and services as a director. Mr Ward had no right to remuneration without the authority of the board. Thus the claim by Guinness for repayment is unanswerable. If Mr Ward acted honestly and reasonably and ought fairly to be excused for receiving £5.2m without the authority of the board, he cannot be excused from paying it back. By invoking s 727 as a defence to the claim by Guinness for repayment, Mr Ward seeks an order of the court which would entitle him to remuneration without the authority of the board. The order would be a breach of the articles which protect shareholders and govern directors and would be a breach of the principles of equity to which I have already referred.
    I would dismiss this appeal.

LORD GOFF: . . . What course has the action taken? Before Sir Nicholas Browne-Wilkinson V-C, judgment was given against Mr Ward on admissions, on the basis that he had received the money in breach of his fiduciary duty as a director of Guinness, by reason by his failure to disclosure his interest in the agreement under which he performed the services, as required by s 317(1) of the 1985 Act. In the Court of Appeal, Mr Ward's appeal against that decision was dismissed. It was said of him that he had 'succeeded in getting his hands on the company's money', and that the company had never ceased to own the money which he had been paid (see [1988] BCLC 607 at 613–614, [1988] 2 All ER 940 at 945–946). Accordingly, Mr Ward was constructive trustee of the money which he had received, and must pay it back. If he wished to make a claim for remuneration in respect of the services which he claimed to have rendered to Guinness, he must bring a separate action.
    . . .
It gradually became clear that counsel's criticisms of the decision of the courts below were well founded and that (quite apart from very serious difficulties arising on the construction of s 317) they were inconsistent with *Hely-Hutchinson v Brayhead Ltd* [1967] 3 All ER 98, [1968] 1 QB 549, a decision of an exceptional Court of Appeal consisting of Lord Denning MR, Lord Wilberforce and Lord Pearson. The decision in that case proceeded on the basis that the statutory duty of disclosure (then embodied in s 199 of the Companies Act 1948) did not of itself affect the validity of a contract. The section had however to be read with provisions in the articles of association, imposing a duty of disclosure on directors of the company. If a director enters into, or is interested in, a contract with the company, but fails to declare his interest, the effect is that, under the ordinary principles of law and equity, the contract may be voidable at the instance of the company, and in certain cases a director may be called on to account for profits made from the transaction (see [1967] 3 All ER 98 at 106, 109, [1968] 1 QB 549 at 589, 594 per Lord Wilberforce and Lord Pearson). Perhaps the matter is put

most clearly by Lord Pearson, who said ([1967] 3 All ER 98 at 109, [1968] 1 QB 549 at 595):

> 'It is not contended that s 199 in itself affects the contract. The section merely creates a statutory duty of disclosure and imposes a fine for non-compliance; but it has to be read in conjunction with art 99. The first sentence of that article is obscure. If a director makes or is interested in a contract with the company, but fails duly to declare his interest, what happens to the contract? Is it void, or is it voidable at the option of the company, or is it still binding on both parties, or what? The article supplies no answer to these questions. I think that the answer must be supplied by the general law, and the answer is that the contract is voidable at the option of the company, so that the company has a choice whether to affirm or avoid the contract, but the contract must be either totally affirmed or totally avoided and the right of avoidance will be lost if such time elapses or such events occur as to prevent rescission of the contract.'

On this basis I cannot see that a breach of s 317, which is not for present purposes significantly different from s 199 of the 1948 Act, had itself any effect on the contract between Mr Ward and Guinness. As a matter of general law, to the extent that there was failure by Mr Ward to comply with his duty of disclosure under the relevant article of Guinness's articles of association (art 100(A)), the contract (if any) between him and Guinness was no doubt voidable under the ordinary principles of the general law to which Lord Pearson refers. But it has long been the law that, as a condition of rescission of a voidable contract, the parties must be put in statu quo; for this purpose a court of equity can do what is practically just, even though it cannot restore the parties precisely to the state they were in before the contract. The most familiar statement of the law is perhaps that of Lord Blackburn in *Erlanger v New Sombrero Phosphate Co* (1878) 3 App Cas 1218 at 1278, [1874–80] All ER Rep 271 at 285–286 when he said:

> 'It is, I think, clear on principles of general justice, that as a condition to a rescission there must be a *restitutio in integrum*. The parties must be put in *statu quo* ... It is a doctrine which has often been acted upon both at law and in equity.'

However, on that basis Guinness could not simply claim to be entitled to the £5.2m received by Mr Ward. The contract had to be rescinded, and as a condition of the rescission Mr Ward had to be placed in statu quo. No doubt this could be done by a court of equity making a just allowance for the services he had rendered; but no such allowance has been considered, let alone made, in the present case.

Faced with these problems, counsel for Guinness was driven, in the last resort, to submit that *Hely-Hutchinson v Brayhead Ltd* was wrongly decided. I have to confess that I would hesitate long before holding that a decision of such a court was erroneous. Careful study of the decision, with the assistance of counsel, merely served to reinforce my natural expectation that the case was rightly decided.

This being so, it followed that the decisions of the courts below in the present case, founded as they were on a breach of s 317 of the 1985 Act by Mr Ward, were erroneous. In ordinary circumstances, this conclusion would have led to the appeal being allowed. But counsel for Guinness then sought to justify the judgment on the other grounds.

. . .

I understand it to be suggested that arts 90 and 91 provide (art 100 apart) not only a code of the circumstances in which a director of Guinness may receive recompense for services to the company, but an exclusive code. This is said to derive from the equitable doctrine whereby directors, though not trustees, are held to act in a fiduciary capacity, and as such are not entitled to receive remuneration for services rendered to the company except as provided under the articles of association, which are treated as equivalent to a trust deed constituting a trust. It was suggested that, if Mr Ward wishes to receive remuneration for the services he has rendered, his proper course is now to approach the board of directors and invite them to award him remuneration by the exercise of the power vested in them by art 91.

The leading authorities on the doctrine have been rehearsed in the opinion of my noble and learned friend Lord Templeman. These indeed demonstrate that the directors of a company, like other fiduciaries, must not put themselves in a position where there is a conflict between their personal interests and their duties as fiduciaries, and are for that reason precluded from contracting with the company for their services except in circumstances authorised by the articles of association. Similarly, just as trustees are not entitled, in the absence of an appropriate provision in the trust deed, to remuneration for their services as trustees, so directors are not entitled to remuneration for their services as directors except as provided by the articles of association.

Plainly, it would be inconsistent with this long-established principle to award remuneration in such circumstances as of right on the basis of a quantum meruit claim. But the principle does not altogether exclude the possibility that an equitable allowance might be made in respect of services rendered. That such an allowance may be made to a trustee for work performed by him for the benefit of the trust, even though he was not in the circumstances entitled to remuneration under the terms of the trust deed, is now well established. In *Phipps v Boardman* [1964] 2 All ER 187, [1964] 1 WLR 993 the solicitor to a trust and one of the beneficiaries were held accountable to another beneficiary for a proportion of the profits made by them from the sale of shares bought by them with the aid of information gained by the solicitor when acting for the trust. Wilberforce J directed that, when accounting for such profits, not merely should a deduction be made for expenditure which was necessary to enable the profit to be realised, but also a liberal allowance or credit should be made for their work and skill. His reasoning was ([1964] 2 All ER 187 at 208, [1964] 1 WLR 993 at 1018):

> 'Moreover, account must naturally be taken of the expenditure which was necessary to enable the profit to be realised. But, in addition to expenditure, should not the defendants be given an allowance or credit for their work and skill? This is a subject on which authority is scanty; but COHEN, J, in *Re Macadam, Dallow and Moscrop v Codd* ([1945] 2 All ER 664, [1946] Ch 73) gave his support to an allowance of this kind to trustees for their services in acting as directors of a company. It seems to me that this transaction, ie, the acquisition of a controlling interest in the company, was one of a special character calling for the exercise of a particular kind of professional skill. If Mr Boardman had not assumed the role of seeing it through, the beneficiaries would have had to employ (and would, had they been well advised, have employed) an expert to do it for them. If the trustees had come to the court asking for liberty to employ such a person, they would in all probability have been authorised to do so, and to remunerate the person in question. It seems to me that it would be inequitable now for the

beneficiaries to step in and take the profit without paying for the skill and labour which has produced it.'

Wilberforce J's decision, including his decision to make such an allowance, was later to be affirmed by the House of Lords (see [1966] 3 All ER 721, [1967] 2 AC 46).

It will be observed that the decision to make the allowance was founded on the simple proposition that 'it would be inequitable now for the beneficiaries to step in and take the profit without paying for the skill and labour which has produced it.' Ex hypothesi, such an allowance was not in the circumstances authorised by the terms of the trust deed; furthermore, it was held that there had not been full and proper disclosure by the two defendants to the successful plaintiff beneficiary. The inequity was found in the simple proposition that the beneficiaries were taking the profit although, if Mr Boardman (the solicitor) had not done the work, they would have had to employ an expert to do the work for them in order to earn that profit.

The decision has to be reconciled with the fundamental principle that a trustee is not entitled to remuneration for services rendered by him to the trust except as expressly provided in the trust deed. Strictly speaking, it is irreconcilable with the rule as so stated. It seems to me therefore that it can only be reconciled with it to the extent that the exercise of the equitable jurisdiction does not conflict with the policy underlying the rule. And, as I see it, such a conflict will only be avoided if the exercise of the jurisdiction is restricted to those cases where it cannot have the effect of encouraging trustees in any way to put themselves in a position where their interests conflict with their duties as trustees.

Not only was the equity underlying Mr Boardman's claim in *Phipps v Boardman* clear and, indeed, overwhelming; but the exercise of the jurisdiction to award an allowance in the unusual circumstances of that case could not provide any encouragement to trustees to put themselves in a position where their duties as trustees conflicted with their interests. The present case is, however, very different. Whether any such an allowance might ever be granted by a court of equity in the case of a director of a company, as opposed to a trustee, is a point which has yet to be decided; and I must reserve the question whether the jurisdiction could be exercised in such a case, which may be said to involve interference by the court in the administration of a company's affairs when the company is not being wound up. In any event, however, like my noble and learned friend Lord Templeman, I cannot see any possibility of such jurisdiction being exercised in the present case. I proceed, of course, on the basis that Mr Ward acted throughout in complete good faith. But the simple fact remains that, by agreeing to provide his services in return for a substantial fee the size of which was dependent on the amount of a successful bid by Guinness, Mr Ward was most plainly putting himself in a position in which his interests were in stark conflict with his duty as a director. Furthermore, for such services as he rendered, it is still open to the board of Guinness (if it thinks fit, having had a full opportunity to investigate the circumstances of the case) to award Mr Ward appropriate remuneration. In all the circumstances of the case, I cannot think that this is a case in which a court of equity (assuming that it has jurisdiction to do so in the case of the director of a company) would order the repayment of the £5.2m by Mr Ward to Guinness subject to a condition that an equitable allowance be made to Mr Ward for his services.

PART VI: DIRECTORS' STATUTORY DUTIES

The relationship between a director and his company is subject to substantial
statutory regulation. He is required to disclose any payments made to him in
connection with loss of office (Companies Act 1985, ss 312–315); he cannot
receive remuneration free of income tax (s 311); he is obliged to disclose any
interest he has in contracts with the company (although this disclosure can be
to the board of directors, s 317); his service contract is to be open for
inspection (s 318); if his contract of employment is to run for more than five
years, it must receive shareholder approval (s 319); there must be shareholder
approval for substantial property transactions involving directors (ss 320–322);
certain types of share dealings by a director and his family are prohibited
(s 323); his interest in the shareholding of his own company must be disclosed
(ss 324–329, Sch 13) and the circumstances in which the company can make
loans to the director are carefully circumscribed (ss 330–346).

Dealings by a director in the listed shares of his or other companies is also
now subject to criminal prosecution where he is in possession of confidential
information (Criminal Justice Act 1993, ss 52–64) and a model code for such
dealings is laid down by The Stock Exchange in the case of directors of listed
companies.

The manner in which the statutory duties complement the common law
has already been seen in *Guinness plc v Saunders* (Source 180). This is further
illustrated by Sources 181 and 182.

SOURCE 181
Nitan Carson Ltd *v* Hawthorne
(Queen's Bench Division) [1988] BCLC 298

HODGSON J.: ... I now turn to consider s 48 of the 1980 Act.[1] Mr Nelson's[2]
main contention has throughout been that the contract made in April 1983 was
illegal because it contravened s 48. Section 48 was a brand new section of the
1980 Act and it has, I think, never been considered by any court so far as the
detailed research of counsel can discover. It deals with substantial property
transactions involving directors. Section 48(1) reads:

> 'A company shall not enter into an arrangement — (*a*) whereby a director
> of the company ... is to acquire one or more non-cash assets of the
> requisite value from the company ... unless the arrangement is first
> approved by a resolution of the company in general meeting ...'

(I have left out the irrelevant words.) Plainly, there would not have been the
slightest difficulty in obtaining approval at the time, but, as I have said, I am sure
that Mr Nelson did not then know of the section at all.

By s 87(1) 'non-cash asset' means any property or interest in property other
than cash. A lease is undoubtedly an interest in property, so it is a 'non-cash asset'.

Section 48(2) is in these terms:

> 'For the purposes of this section, a non-cash asset is of the requisite value if at
> the time the arrangement in question is entered into its value is not less than

---

1 See now ss 320–322B of the Companies Act 1985
2 A director of the plaintiff company

£1,000 but, subject to that, exceeds £50,000 or 10 per cent of the amount of the company's relevant assets, and for those purposes the amount of the company's revelant assets is (*a*) except in a case falling within paragraph (*b*) below, the value of its net assets determined by reference to the accounts prepared and laid under section 1 of the 1976 Act in respect of the last preceding accounting reference period in respect of which such accounts were so laid; (*b*) where no accounts have been prepared and laid under that section before that time, the amount of its called-up share capital.'

That subsection is not easy to construe but, to make sense, I think that either the words 'whichever is the greater' or the words 'whichever is the lesser' have to be read into the subsection.

Section 48 is replaced by s 320 of the 1985 Act and, of this section, *Gore-Browne on Companies* (44th edn, 1986) vol 2, p 27.13, has this to say:

'Any contract by which a company sells to or buys from a director property of any sort, and any other property dealings between directors and their companies are subject to the general rules regarding directors' contracts already discussed. The provisions of s 320 of the Companies Act 1985 reinforce these general requirements and impose more onerous requirements than the articles would otherwise normally stipulate. Further, the scope of s 320 is wider than simply contracts between directors and their companies, and it applies to shadow directors and to persons connected with directors. The section applies to an arrangement for the acquisition from the company of one or more non-cash assets of the requisite value by a director of the company or its holding company or a person connected with such a director, and conversely, to an arrangement for the acquisition by a company of one or more such non-cash assets from such a director or connected person. To fall within the section, the value of the asset or assets must be more than £50,000 or 10 per cent of the company's asset value, subject in the latter case to a minimum of £1,000. The amount of a company's asset value is the value of its net assets as determined by reference to its last annual accounts prepared and laid under Part VII, or its called-up share capital if no such accounts have been prepared and laid at the relevant time. Any arrangement as described above is forbidden unless it is first approved by a resolution of the company in general meeting, and if the director or connected person is a director of its holding company or a person connected with such a director, by a resolution in general meeting of the holding company ... Any breach of the requirement of s 320(1) of general meeting sanction renders the arrangement and any transaction entered into in pursuance of it voidable at the instance of the company, except in the following circumstances ... (3) If the arrangement is within a reasonable time affirmed by the company in general meeting, and by a resolution in general meeting of its holding company if it involves a director of the holding company or a person connected with such a director.'

That passage, I think correctly, construes the section as including the words whichever is the lesser'. It is, however, of interest that in the Bill, according to *Gower's Principles of Modern Company Law* (4th edn, 1979), p 590, the actual words used were 'whichever is the greater'.

Mr Nelson submits that the value of this lease exceeds 10% of the net assets or £50,000, but has adduced no evidence as to what the value of the lease was or how the value of such a lease is calculated. Nor has he produced any accounts of the company although, certainly in 1981, there were such accounts. It seems to me to be clear that anyone who alleges that a non-cash asset exceeds the requisite value has to prove that fact. I have no idea how a monthly periodic lease is valued. No premium was agreed to be paid, and the obligation to pay the rent of £1,500 per month would presumably appear in Mrs Hawthorne's business accounts as a debt item. I cannot imagine that anyone could value a lease of this nature at over £50,000, and I have no idea whether its value, which I know not anyway, exceeds 10% of the net assets. Mr Nelson seeks to invoke s 48(2) (*b*) but he cannot, I think, do that in the absence of evidence as to the latest accounts and evidence as to the value of the lease.

In the absence of any evidence as to value it is, I think, impossible to hold that the April agreement contravenes the section.

I have already cited from *Gore-Browne* s 48(3) (*c*). That subsection seems to me to show clearly that a contract entered into contrary to s 48 is not illegal ab initio. It remains valid and binding until avoided at the instance of the company. . . . (I do not think the company has ever avoided the agreement).

. . .

Of the main submissions made on the Chancery issue part of this case, that only leaves Mr Nelson's contention that the agreement of April was contrary to the equitable principle laid down in *Aberdeen Rly Co v Blaikie Bros* (1854 1 Macq 461, [1843–60] All ER Rep 1281 and he has bombarded me with authority which, he submits, shows that Mrs Hawthorne was in breach of her fiduciary duty to the company in acting as she did.

So far as the *Aberdeen Rly Co case* was concerned, Mr Nelson seemed to have completely overlooked the waiver clause in reg 84(3) of the Table A of the 1948 Act, which had been incorporated into the articles of association of the company. So far as relevant, that regulation reads:

'. . . no director . . . shall be disqualified by his office from contracting with the company . . . as vendor, purchaser or otherwise, nor shall any such contract . . . be liable to be avoided, nor shall any director so contracting . . . be liable to account to the company for any profit realised by any such contract or arrangement by reason of such director holding that office or of the fiduciary relation thereby established.'

There was, therefore, nothing ex facie illegal with the contract made in April.

Mr Nelson also cited case after case, all designed to show that Mrs Hawthorne had acted in breach of her fiduciary duty. In every case there was an element of unconscionable behaviour, secret profit, deception or non-disclosure and none seemed to me to be in any way relevant to what happened in this case. I think it is really plain that, on my findings of fact, and I reach them all without doubt or hesitation, there can be no possible suggestion that Mrs Hawthorne was, at any time, in breach of her fiduciary duties. The company did not want to run the home (as was the case in *Peso Silver Mines Ltd v Cropper* (1966) 58 DLR (2d) 1); it was only too happy for Mrs Hawthorne to take the risk and, if she could, make the profit, and everyone was very happy with the arrangement until Mr Nelson's volte face.

SOURCE 182
Runciman *v* Walter Runciman plc
(Queen's Bench Division) [1992] BCLC 1084

SIMON BROWN J: . . . The 1976 service agreement provided so far as relevant:

(1) That the plaintiff's employment as executive chairman (until 31 December

1999) was terminable by the company upon three years' notice, and by the plaintiff on six months' notice.

. . .

By letter dated 1 July 1987 Mr Haley[1] wrote to the plaintiff on company writing paper as follows:

> '*Re service agreement*
>
> I am writing to advise you that (your 1976 agreement) is hereby amended so that the period of notice to be given by the company will be increased from three years to five years.'

. . .

The first two issues, as to whether there ever was any properly authorised agreement to increase the notice term and as to whether the plaintiff was required to declare an interest in this increase, require reference to the company's articles of association. Article 85 in particular is crucial:

> '85(1) A Director who is in any way, whether directly or indirectly, interested in a contract or proposed contract with the Company shall declare the nature of his interest at a meeting of the Directors in accordance with section 199 of the Act.
>
> (2) A Director shall not vote in respect of any contract or arrangement in which he is interested, and if he shall do so his vote shall not be counted . . .
>
> (3) A Director may hold any other office or place of profit under the Company (other than the office of Auditor) in conjunction with his office of Director for such period and on such terms (as to remuneration and otherwise) as the Directors may determine. No Director or intending Director shall be disqualified by his office from contracting with the Company, either with regard to his tenure of any such other office or place of profit, or as vendor, purchaser or otherwise. No such contract, and no contract or arrangement entered into by or on behalf of the Company, in which any Director is in any way interested, shall be liable to be avoided, nor shall any Director so contracting or being so interested by liable to account to the Company for any profit realised by any such contract or arrangement by reason of such Director holding that office or of the fiduciary relation thereby established.
>
> (4) A Director, notwithstanding his interest, may be counted in the quorum present at any meeting whereat he or any other Director is appointed to hold any such office or place of profit under the Company or whereat the terms of any such appointment are arranged, and he may vote on any such appointment or arrangement other than his own appointment or the arrangement of the terms thereof.'

. . .

Given that the relevant terms here were never decided at a directors' meeting, the critical question raised is, of course, this: did the directors as a body, ie all of them, determine that the plaintiff's notice term should be increased to five years? The plaintiff says Yes, the defendants No.

Let it be said at once that if the answer is indeed No, then the purported agreement is clearly void. Many are the authorities and extensive the academic commentary establishing that. Prominent amongst the cases are *Re Richmond Gate*

---

1 The then deputy chairman of the defendant company

Property Co Ltd [1964] 3 All ER 936, [1965] 1 WLR 335 and *Guinness plc v Saunders* [1990] BCLC 402, [1990] 2 AC 663.

[The judge then quoted the passage from Lord Templeman's speech in *Guinness plc v Saunders*, beginning 'Equity forbids a trustee . . .' and ending '. . . the articles of association provide', p 491 and continued:]

Was there then a failure here to determine the variation of the plaintiff's notice period in accordance with article 85(3)?

. . .

The articles say nothing as to how or when the directors are to arrive at their determination. In my judgment, therefore, provided only and always that by that time the term relied upon is sought to be enforced all the other directors can be shown to have concurred in the agreement of that term, it can then fairly and properly be said that they have indeed determined it as the article requires.

That directors, provided they act unanimously, can act informally appears clearly established — *Re Bonnelli's Telegraph Co, Collie's claim* (1871) LR 12 Eq 246 and *Charterhouse Investments Trust Ltd v Tempest Diesels Ltd* [1986] BCLC 1 so decide, the latter on the basis that informal acquiescence by other board members in an otherwise unauthorised agreement by one of their number binds the company. So in my judgment in the present case.

. . .

What really serves to distinguish *Guinness* from this case is not the different articles of association in play, not the different kind of remuneration in question, not (on this issue) the absence of knowledge on the part of the other members of the Guinness board, but rather that the decision there was taken by a committee so that the matter was never determined by the board as a whole whereas in the present case I have found that it was.

I pass to the defendants' second argument which centres on art 85(1). Section 199 of the Act (of 1948) there referred to, has been superseded by s 317 of the Companies Act 1985 — as recognised in *Guinness*, not for the present purposes significantly different. The argument here is that the plaintiff was required by art 85(1) to declare at a directors' meeting the nature of his interest in the relevant variations to his service agreement, that he failed to do so, and that accordingly the variations relied upon, both as to the period of notice and the fringe benefits (the salary increases, I repeat are not challenged in these proceedings), are voidable at the suit of the company, unenforceable by the plaintiff against it.

Once again there is ample authority for the proposition that non-compliance with a requirement such as that imposed here by art 85(1) leaves the contract voidable at the option of the company: see most notably *Hely-Hutchinson v Brayhead* [1967] 3 All ER 98, [1968] 1 QB 549 and *Guinness*.

. . .

Four particular questions are raised upon this part of the case. First, as to whether s 317 (and therefore art 85(1)) has any application to service contracts between a company and its own directors. Second, assuming it has, whether it applies to the variation of an existing contract. Third, again assuming it does, whether disclosure was made here by the plaintiff in conformity with the section. Fourth, assuming that the plaintiff was in breach of a duty to disclose, whether it is equitable to permit the defendants now to rescind.

. . .

Whatever may have been the strict legal requirements of the position, on the particular facts of this case I am perfectly satisfied that for the plaintiff to have made a specific declaration of interest before agreement of the variations here in question would have served no conceivable purpose. It would have been mere incantation. Any non-compliance with art 85(1) was accordingly wholly technical. Nothing could be less just than that the new owners of the company after take-over should now benefit from their adventitious discovery of such breach. To allow them to do so would be to sacrifice the plaintiff's legitimate interests on the altar of slavish adherence to ritualistic form.

To revert, however, to the questions. Does s 317 apply to service contracts? (Section 317 I propose to take as read rather than lengthen this judgment by its detailed recitation). The plaintiff argues not, on the footing that self-evidently an executive director is interested in his own service contract so that it could never be necessary for him to declare that interest at a meeting. Mr Elias prays in aid in this regard s 317(3) which permits a director in certain circumstances to give a general notice which is then deemed a sufficient declaration of interest for future purposes. True, Mr Elias accepts, that subsection has no direct application to this case but, the argument runs, it appears at least to suggest that the legislation is concerned with realities rather than form. Compelling although at first blush I confess to have found this argument, I have regretfully come to reject it. Not only is it inconsistent with the plain language of the section, but there is ample authority for the proposition that the mere obviousness of a director's interest in a particular contract is no reason for non-compliance with the requirements of the section. That, indeed, is implicit in decisions like *Hely-Hutchinson* and *Guinness* each of which concerned contracts directly between a director and his company, contracts respectively of guarantee and for services. True, the contracts there in issue were made without knowledge on the part of some at least of the board's members. But that consideration cannot logically affect the question whether or not a particular type of contract falls within the legislation. And s 317(5), referring as it does to other transactions or arrangements in which a director is interested (such as loans to directors), points to the same conclusion. Furthermore, as Mr Falconer points out, to exclude service contracts from the ambit of s 317 would involve ridiculous and pointless distinctions being drawn, (a) between the employed and the self-employed director; and (b) between benefits given to a director as part of his contract of employment and those given separately. Finally on this point the defendants drew my attention to *Foster v Foster* [1916] 1 Ch 532, [1916–1917] All ER Rep 856 a decision holding in terms that the statutory predecessor to s 317 applied to service contracts.

Does s 317 apply to variations? The plaintiffs' contention that it does not again on analysis relies heavily on the apparent absurdity of requiring a declaration of interest in regard to such an agreement. Why declare an interest in the variation of a contract which the company already knows is one in which the director is interested? In addition, submits Mr Elias, if s 317 was intended to cover variations it would have said so expressly, in the same way that sub-s (10 of s 318 expressly applies sub-ss (1) and (5) of that section to a variation of a contract of service as to the contract itself. But those arguments too must in my judgment fail. So far as the analogy with s 318 goes, I accept the defendants' submission that s 318(10) was necessary because s 318(1) and (5) deal specifically with contracts of service and a variation of such a contract, albeit a contract, might well not in itself be regarded as a contract of service. And I accept too the defendants' fundamental argument that a variation of contract is itself a contract and that to construe s 317 otherwise would lead to pointless debate about whether a given agreement constitutes a variation or a fresh contract. Looking moreover to the purpose of the legislation and the mischief against which it is directed, there will certainly be cases where it is as necessary for an interest to be declared in a variation of contract as in the making of the contract in the first place: take *Guinness* and suppose that the consideration for Ward's services had initially and in conformity with the articles been agreed at £5,000 and only later varied to the eventual figure of £5.2m.

[The judge accepted that there had been no formal disclosure, and continued:]

I remain profoundly reluctant to conclude that a director must solemnly declare an interest in his own service agreement, a contract which by its very nature involves his interest, before any variation is made concerning his salary or other terms of employment. Is there really, irrespective of the commonsense of the position, a statutory requirement for such formal declaration? I do not believe that the point is free from doubt. Lord Goff, for instance, spoke in *Guinness* of the 'very serious difficulties arising on the construction of s 317'. And when *Lee Panavision* got to the Court of Appeal, Dillon LJ ([1992] BCLC 22 at 33) similarly recognised the problems in the legislation and, wisely as I believe, declined counsel's urgent invitation to express a view on the construction and effect of art 85 in the light of s 317 despite blandishments that it was necessary to do so to resolve difficulties for all practitioners. Against that background it would surely be rash indeed for me needlessly to venture a definitive view upon this troublesome issue.

As stated, it is upon the fourth question that I have reached the clearest conclusion. It is at this point that Dillon LJ's comments on s 317 becomes most pertinent ([1992] BCLC 22 at 33):

'. . . if the judge was entitled to make the findings of non-disclosure and non-declaration of interests that he did, the position is that each of the directors has failed to disclose formally at the board meeting an interest common to all the directors and, ex hypothesi, already known to all the directors. I would hesitate to hold that such apparently technical non-declaration of an interest in breach of s 317 has the inevitable result, as to which the court has no discretion, that the second management agreement is fundamentally flawed and must be set aside if Lee Lighting chooses to ask sufficiently promptly that it be set aside.'

As it seems to me, the (assumed) non-declaration of the plaintiff's interest in the variations here in question was as purely technical as it could ever be. Whatever may be the suggested advantages of a strictly formal approach to the section, such as a record of the proceedings and a reduced risk of directors abusing their position, no such advantage would have accrued here. It is certainly not suggested in this case that the plaintiff or his fellow directors in any way abused their position. Rather the basis of Mr Falconer's case for holding the plaintiff unable to enforce his increased notice term is the contention that the strict rule should invariably be applied save only where the right of rescission must in law be regarded as lost — by acquiesence [*sic*], delay, the impossibility of making restitutio in integrum, or on some other similarly recognised ground. Here it is submitted that no such reason exists. In reality, submits Mr Falconer, there has been no delay and no acquiesence [*sic*]: it was not until after Avena's takeover that the new management and shareholders learned of the circumstances in which the service agreements came to be varied, and in particular of the plaintiff's failure to disclose his interest. In this context he draws my attention to the decision of the House of Lords in *Erlanger v New Sombrero Phosphate Co* (1878) 3 App Cas 1218 at 1279–1280, [1874–80] All ER rep 274 at 286 and Lord Blackburn's speech where, dealing with the question of laches by a corporation, he said:

'. . . it should be recollected that shareholders who seek to set aside a contract made by the governing body, have practically first to change that governing body, and must have time to do so.'

The force of that observation is plain. But it must be read in the context of this earlier passage in the speech:

'. . . I think, from the nature of the enquiry, it must always be a question more or less, depending upon the degree of diligence which might reasonably be required, and the degree of change which has occurred, whether the balance of justice or injustice is in favour of granting the remedy or withholding it. The determination of such a question must largely depend upon the turn of mind of those who have to decide, and must therefore be subject to uncertainty; but that, I think, is inherent in the nature of the enquiry.'

If then one poses the simple question: what does the balance of justice require in the present case, I am left in no doubt whatever as to the proper answer. The plain fact is that this plaintiff continued, from 1987 to 1990, to serve the company as its chairman understanding that his notice term had been increased to five years; that equally was the understanding of all his fellow directors; and Avena too, at the time of their take-over of the company, clearly understood that to be the position an understanding in their case derived from the company's explicit letter published earlier in opposition to the bid. To hold in these circumstances that what was at most a merely technical breach of statutory duty of disclosure should render that variation unenforceable would to my mind involve the most patent injustice.

I turn to the defendants' third argument, that the increase in the notice term should be set aside as having been made in breach of the directors' fiduciary duty, ie the duty of the plaintiff's fellow directors to exercise their powers bona fide in the interests of the company as a whole and for a proper corporate purpose.

The principles of law here in play are not in doubt. They are stated in *Palmer's Company Law* (25th edn) para 8.508 as follows:

'The duty imposed upon directors to act bona fide in the interests of the company is a subjective one. As Lord Greene, MR put it in *Re Smith and Fawcett Ltd* [1942] 1 All ER 542, [1942] Ch 304 directors must act "bona fide in what they consider — not what a Court may consider — is in the interests of the company." So long as the directors have correctly informed themselves as to how the company is defined in law (for this purpose, present and future shareholders), it is left to the directors in the exercise of their business judgment to decide how the interests of the company may best be promoted. The Courts will interfere only if no reasonable director could possibly have concluded that a particular course of action was in the interests of the company.'

In *Howard Smith Ltd v Ampol Petroleum Ltd* [1974] 1 All ER 1126 at 1134, [1974] AC 821 at 835 Lord Wilberforce put it thus:

'. . . it is then necessary for the Court, if a particular exercise of [power] is challenged, to examine the substantial purpose for which it was exercised, and to reach a conclusion whether that purpose was proper or not. In doing so it will necessarily give credit to the bona fide opinion of the directors, if such is found to exist, and will respect their judgment as to matters of management; having done this, the ultimate conclusion has to be as to the side of a fairly broad line on which the case falls.'

. . .

Given the accepted bona fides of the directors, and given that it is essentially for them and not the court to decide what is in the company's interests, I find it quite impossible to say that this board in 1987 reached a view of the matter which was simply not open to them. Mr Grant told me in terms that he thought it right to make no distinction between the four working directors, that it would have been invidious to have done so. Am I really to say that such a view was plainly wrong? On the contrary, in the context of this small and close knit executive team, the approach taken seems to me eminently understandable. As Mr Elias points out, the position is really not unlike that arising when salary increases are in question: merely because one particular director may have reached an age when his prospects of alternative employment have faded would hardly be a sufficient, let alone a compelling, reason for denying him an increase otherwise required to maintain his appropriate position in the overall salary scale. Yet on Mr Falconer's argument, if there were no risk of his leaving the company, it would be unnecessary and therefore impermissible, in breach of his fellow directors' fiduciary duty, to pay him his increase.

It follows from all this that in my judgment the plaintiff is entitled to rely upon his five-year notice term.

PART VII: RELEASE AND RATIFICATION

The fiduciary duty appears somewhat unremitting at times. In certain circumstances, however, the duty expires (Source 183). It is also important to remember that where the company, as the beneficiary of the profit, is able to give full and free approval to the acquisition by the directors of the profit, the directors may retain it. How is such ratification to be given? (Contrast the approaches in Source 182 with Sources 184 and 185).

The extent to which prior authority can be granted by the articles for the directors to retain such profits has already been alluded to, see Source 180 at p 487. If such authority is too extensive, it may fall foul of s 310 of the Companies Act 1985 (Source 186). A recent amendment to this section (by the Companies Act 1989) now permits the purchase and maintenance by the company of insurance protecting officers against their negligence. Finally, it should be pointed out that the court is given a discretion under s 727 of the Companies Act 1985 to absolve a director from the consequences of a breach of duty in certain circumstances. The reluctance of the court to exercise this discretion in cases of expropriation of the company's property or profits is obvious (Source 180, contrast Source 171 at p 458, where Hoffmann J made clear that he would have exercised this power had he found against the defendant, although note again that the opposite was the case in Source 170). The court has also held that s 727 is not available in the case of a decision under s 214 of the Insolvency Act 1986, that a director is liable to make a contribution to the assets of a company in insolvent liquidation (*Re Produce Marketing Consortium Ltd* [1989] BCLC 513; for the extract of the full proceedings, see p 72).

SOURCE 183
Island Export Finance Ltd *v* Umunna
(Queen's Bench Division 1985) [1986] BCLC 460

HUTCHISON J: The plaintiff company, Island Export Financing Ltd, is one of a considerable number of companies controlled by Mr Alan Lewis, an experienced, forceful and successful businessman. The second defendant, Benosi International Ltd, is a company controlled by the first defendant, Mr Umunna, a resident in the United Kingdom but a Nigerian by birth. Between the middle of 1975 and a date (precisely when is in issue) in 1977 Mr Umunna represented the plaintiff company, for much of the time as its managing director, in what was its sole activity, the pursuit of business in West Africa. One piece of business was brought to fruition: an order by the postal authorities in the Cameroons for 6,000 postal caller boxes. After he ceased to be employed by the plaintiff company Mr Umunna obtained for his own company, Benosi, two further orders for not dissimilar equipment from the same department in the Cameroons. The plaintiff's case is that in doing so he breached his fiduciary duty as a director of the plaintiff company and/or made improper use of the plaintiff company's confidential information, and accordingly he and Benosi must account for the profits derived from those two orders.

. . .

The plaintiff's case is based on the assertion that in approaching the Postal Department in the Cameroons and obtaining the two 1977 orders Mr Umunna was in breach of the fiduciary duty that he owed as a director of the plaintiff company. Counsel for the plaintiff began by referring me to *Regal (Hastings) Ltd v Gulliver.*[1] He relies in particular on passages in the speeches of Lord Russell and Lord Wright, to which he referred me but which I do not think I need cite. He contends (and counsel for the defendants does not dispute this) that the case is authority for the proposition that directors of a company are in a fiduciary position and their liability to account does not depend on proof of bad faith and arises quite irrespective of whether the company could itself have taken advantage of the opportunity of which the directors availed themselves, or of the question whether in the event the company benefited from what they did. The rule is a strict one, to the effect that where directors have obtained a benefit only by reason of the fact that they were directors and in the course of the execution of their office, they are accountable for any profits which they have made. In that case the fact was that the company had not the means itself to take up the shares the purchase of which by the directors gave rise to the claim against them, but this was held to be altogether irrelevant. Counsel for the defendants, of course, fully accepts the propositions for which that case is cited.

Counsel for the plaintiff seeks to extend the principle by means of the following submission. He contends that a director is liable to account to the company if he learns of an opportunity or business advantage whilst he is working for the company and by virtue of his fiduciary position, and then uses the opportunity or exploits the advantage for his own benefit either while he is still working for the company or after the termination of his appointment. However,

---

1 [1907] 2 AC 134n; [1942] 1 All ER 378 (see p 477)

he recognises a limitation which applies in those cases where the use of the opportunity occurs after termination of the appointment, conceding that in such cases the director is liable only if (a) he had such use or exploitation in contemplation whilst a director, or (b) the opportunity fairly belongs to the company, for example if the company was actively pursuing the opportunity through the director before termination.

In support of this extended principle counsel for the plaintiff relies on the decision of the Supreme Court of Canada in the case of *Canadian Aero Services Ltd v O'Malley*.[1]

Counsel for the defendants submitted that this decision does not accord with the law of England, which does not recognise any fiduciary duty after termination. He contended that there was no English authority which held that it did, suggesting that one of the cases relied on by counsel for the plaintiff, the decision of Roskill J in *Industrial Development Consultants Ltd v Cooley*,[2] was not in truth an authority for such a proposition because the breach of duty found really related to the actions of the defendant while still employed. In a sense, this is true, but the fact remains that the case is one in which the contract was obtained after the defendant had left the plaintiff's employment though (the judge found) as a result of work which he did while still the plaintiff's managing director. Essentially, the assertion of counsel for the defendants that there is no continuing fiduciary duty after termination of employment is based on the absence of any English case which positively asserts that there is such a duty: and certainly he has been unable to point to any case which asserts that there is not.

It seems to me that counsel's bold submission cannot be right, amounting as it does to the contention that a director, provided he *does* nothing contrary to his employers' interests while employed, may with impunity conceive the idea of resigning so that he may exploit some opportunity of the employers and, having resigned, proceed to exploit it for himself. Such a suggestion has only to be stated to be seen to be unsustainable, and in my judgment counsel for the plaintiff is right when he says that it conflicts with the dictum in one of the earliest cases in this line of authority, cited and relied on in the Can. Aero case, namely *Ex parte James*,[3] where Lord Eldon LC said, speaking of the fiduciary in that case (who was a solicitor purchasing at a sale):

> 'With respect to the question now put, whether I will permit *Jones* to give up the office of solicitor, and to bid, I cannot give that permission. If the principle is right, that the solicitor cannot buy, it would lead to all the mischief of acting up to the point of sale, getting all the information that may be useful to him, then discharging himself from the character of solicitor, and buying the property... On the other hand I do not deny, that those interested in the question may give the permission.'

...

It is, in my judgment, unnecessary in the present case that I should attempt definitively to state the limits of the rule as to accountability of directors. Since it is not necessary, it would be presumptuous of me to make the attempt. I return to the formulation of counsel for the plaintiff. It appears to me that, on the basis of the findings I have made, the plaintiff's claim fails for a variety of reasons. I would summarise them as follows: (a) The hope of obtaining further orders for postal caller boxes could not in any realistic sense be said to be 'a maturing business

---

1 (1973) 40 DLR (3d) 371 (see p 483)
2 [1972] 1 WLR 443; [1972] 2 All ER 162 (see p 481)
3 (1803) 8 Ves Jun 337; 32 ER 385

opportunity'. (b) Neither when Mr Umunna resigned nor when he succeeded in obtaining the two June 1977 orders was the plaintiff actively pursuing the matter. (c) It cannot in any true sense be said that, at the time he resigned, Mr Umunna had in contemplation the exploitation of the Cameroons postal box business. As I have already indicated, the highest that it can be put is that, if asked, he would undoubtedly have replied that that was a potential source of business which he might be minded to pursue. It was certainly not his motive for resigning, and it cannot possibly be said that his resignation was 'prompted or influenced by a wish to acquire for himself the opportunity sought by the company'.

SOURCE 184
North-West Transportation Co Ltd *v* Beatty
(Privy Council 1887) [1887] 12 App Ca 589; 56 LJPC 102

. . . The claim in the action is to set aside a sale made to the company by James Hughes Beatty, one of the directors, of a steamer called the United Empire, of which previously to such sale he was sole owner.

The general principles applicable to cases of this kind are well established. Unless some provision to the contrary is to be found in the charter or other instrument by which the company is incorporated, the resolution of a majority of the shareholders, duly convened, upon any question with which the company is legally competent to deal, is binding upon the minority, and consequently upon the company, and every shareholder has a perfect right to vote upon any such question, although he may have a personal interest in the subject-matter opposed to, or different from, the general or particular interests of the company.

On the other hand, a director of a company is precluded from dealing, on behalf of the company, with himself, and from entering into engagements in which he has a personal interest conflicting; or which possibly may conflict, with the interests of those whom he is bound by fiduciary duty to protect; and this rule is as applicable to the case of one of several directors as to a managing or sole director. Any such dealing or engagement may, however, be affirmed or adopted by the company, provided such affirmance or adoption is not brought about by unfair or improper means, and is not illegal or fraudulent or oppressive towards those shareholders who oppose it.

. . .

At a meeting of the directors held on 10 February 1883, and at which all the directors except the defendant William Beatty were present, it was resolved that a bye-law, which was read to the meeting, for the purchase of the United Empire should pass. It is unnecessary to refer in detail to the terms in which this bye-law was expressed; it is sufficient to state that, after reciting an agreement between the company and the defendant James Hughes Beatty, that the company should buy and the defendant should sell the steamer United Empire for the sum of $125,000, to be in part paid in cash and in part secured, as therein mentioned, it was enacted that the company should purchase the steamer from the defendant upon those terms, with various directions for giving effect to the terms of the contract.

The agreement recited in the bye-law was executed at the same meeting.

At a meeting of shareholders, held, as arranged, on 16 February 1883, the bye-law which had been enacted by the directors was read by the secretary, and, after being modified in its terms, with respect to the price, was adopted by a majority of votes.

. . .

At the shareholders' meeting of the 16th the voting was as follows:
For the confirmation of the bye-law:

	Votes
The defendant J H Beatty	291
The defendant J E Rose	5
The defendant R Laird	5
The defendant William Beatty	5
Total	306

Against the confirmation:

	Votes
John C Graham	39
F. L. Hankey	71
The plaintiff	120
The defendant John D Beatty	59
Total	289

It follows that the majority of votes in favour of the confirmation of the bye-law was due to the votes of the defendant J H Beatty.

It is clear upon the authorities that the contract entered into by the directors on 10 February could not have been enforced against the company at the instance of the defendant J H Beatty, but it is equally clear that it was within the competency of the shareholders at the meeting of 16 February to adopt or reject it. In form and in terms they adopted it by a majority of votes, and the vote of the majority must prevail, unless the adoption was brought about by unfair or improper means.

The only unfairness or impropriety which, consistently with the admitted and established facts, would be suggested, arises out of the fact that the defendant J H Beatty possessed a voting power as a shareholder which enabled him, and those who thought with him, to adopt the bye-law, and thereby either to ratify and adopt a voidable contract, into which he, as a director, and his co-directors had entered, or to make a similar contract, which latter seems to have been what was intended to be done by the resolution passed on 7 February.

It may be quite right that, in such a case, the opposing minority should be able, in a suit like this, to challenge the transaction, and to shew that it is an improper one, and to be freed from the objection that a suit with such an object can only be maintained by the company itself.

But the constitution of the company enabled the defendant J H Beatty to acquire this voting power; there was no limit upon the number of shares which a shareholder might hold, and for every share so held he was entitled to a vote; the charter itself recognised the defendant as a holder of 200 shares, one-third of the aggregate number; he had a perfect right to acquire further shares, and to exercise his voting power in such a manner as to secure the election of directors whose views upon policy agreed with his own, and to support those views at any shareholders' meeting; the acquisition of the United Empire was a pure question of policy, as to which it might be expected that there would be differences of opinion, and upon which the voice of the majority ought to prevail; to reject the votes of the defendant upon the question of the adoption of the bye-law would be to give effect to the views of the minority, and to disregard those of the majority.

Appeal upheld; claim to have the transaction set aside dismissed.

SOURCE 185
Cook v Deeks
(Privy Council 1916) [1916] 1 AC 544; 85 LJPC 161

Two questions of law arise out of this long history of fact. The first is whether, apart altogether from the subsequent resolutions, the [Toronto] company would have been at liberty to claim from the three defendants the benefit of the contract which they had obtained from the Canadian Pacific Railway Company; and the second, which only arises if the first be answered in the affirmative, whether in such event the majority of the shareholders of the company constituted by the three defendants could ratify and approve of what was done and thereby release all claim against the directors.

It is the latter question to which the Appellate Division of the Supreme Court of Ontario have given most consideration, but the former needs to be carefully examined in order to ascertain the circumstances upon which the latter question depends.

It cannot be properly answered by considering the abstract relationship of directors and companies; the real matter for determination is what, in the special circumstances of this case, was the relationship that existed between Messrs Deeks and Hinds and the company that they controlled. Now it appears plain that the entire management of the company, so far as obtaining and executing contracts in the east was concerned, was in their hands, and, indeed, it was in part this fact which was one of the causes of their disagreement with the plaintiff. The way they used this position is perfectly plain. They accelerated the work on the expiring contract of the company in order to stand well with the Canadian Pacific Railway when the next contract should be offered, and although Mr McLean was told that the acceleration was to enable the company to get the new contract, yet they never allowed the company to have any chances whatever of acquiring the benefit, and avoided letting their co-director have any knowledge of the matter. Their Lordships think that the statement of the trial judge upon this point is well founded when he said that 'it is hard to resist the inference that Mr Hinds was careful to avoid anything which would waken Mr Cook from his fancied security,' and again, that 'the sole and only object on the part of the defendants was to get rid of a business associate whom they deemed, and I think rightly deemed, unsatisfactory from a business standpoint.' In other words, they intentionally concealed all circumstances relating to their negotiations until a point had been reached when the whole arrangement had been concluded in their own favour and there was no longer any real chance that there could be any interference with their plans. This means that while entrusted with the conduct of the affairs of the company they deliberately designed to exclude, and used their influence and position to exclude, the company whose interest it was their first duty to protect.

. . .

It is quite right to point out the importance of avoiding the establishment of rules as to directors' duties which would impose upon them burdens so heavy and responsibilities so great that men of good position would hesitate to accept the office. But, on the other hand, men who assume the complete control of a company's business must remember that they are not at liberty to sacrifice the interests which they are bound to protect, and, while ostensibly acting for the company, divert in their own favour business which should properly belong to the company they represent.

Their Lordships think that, in the circumstances, the defendants T R Hinds and G S and G M Deeks were guilty of a distinct breach of duty in the course they took to secure the contract, and that they cannot retain the benefit of such contract for themselves, but must be regarded as holding it on behalf of the company.

There remains the more difficult consideration of whether this position can be made regular by resolutions of the company controlled by the votes of these three defendants. The Supreme Court have given this matter the most careful consideration, but their Lordships are unable to agree with the conclusion which they reached.

In their Lordships' opinion the Supreme Court has insufficiently recognized the distinction between two classes of case and has applied the principles applicable to the case of a director selling to his company property which was in equity as well as at law his own, and which he could dispose of as he thought fit, to the case of a director dealing with property which, though his own at law, in equity belonged to his company. The cases of *North-West Transportation Co v Beatty*[1] and *Burland v Earle*[2] both belonged to the former class. In each, directors had sold to the company property in which the company had no interest at law or in equity. If the company claimed any interest by reason of the transaction, it could only be by affirming the sale, in which case such sale, though initially voidable, would be validated by subsequent ratification. If the company refused to affirm the sale the transaction would be set aside and the parties restored to their former position, the directors getting the property and the company receiving back the purchase price. There would be no middle course. The company could not insist on retaining the property while paying less than the price agreed. This would be for the Court to make a new contract between the parties. It would be quite another thing if the director had originally acquired the property which he sold to his company under circumstances which made it in equity the property of the company. The distinction to which their Lordships have drawn attention is expressly recognized by Lord Davey in *Burland v Earle* and is the foundation of the judgment in *North-West Transportation Co v Beatty*, and is clearly explained in the case of *Jacobus Marler Estates v Marler*,[3] a case which has not hitherto appeared in any of the well-known reports.

If, as their Lordships find on the facts, the contract in question was entered into under such circumstances that the directors could not retain the benefit of it for themselves, then it belonged in equity to the company and ought to have been dealt with as an asset of the company. Even supposing it be not ultra vires of a company to make a present to its directors, it appears quite certain that directors holding a majority of votes would not be permitted to make a present to themselves. This would be to allow a majority to oppress the minority. To such circumstances the cases of *North-West Transportation Co v Beatty* and *Burland v Earle* have no application. In the same way, if directors have acquired for themselves property or rights which they must be regarded as holding on behalf of the company, a resolution that the rights of the company should be disregarded in the matter would amount to forfeiting the interest and property of the minority of shareholders in favour of the majority, and that by the votes of those who are interested in securing the property for themselves. Such use of voting power has never been sanctioned by the Courts, and, indeed, was expressly disapproved in the case of *Menier v Hooper's Telegraph Works*.[4]

If their Lordships took the view that, in the circumstances of this case, the

---

1 (1887) 12 App Ca 589; 56 LJPC 102 (see p 509)
2 [1902] AC 83; 71 LJPC 1 (see p 535)
3 (1913) 114 LT 640n; 85 LJPC 167n
4 (1874) 9 Ch App 350; 43 LJ Ch 330 (see p 541)

directors had exercised a discretion or decided on a matter of policy (the view which appears to have been entertained by the Supreme Court) different results would ensue, but this is not a conclusion which their Lordships are able to accept. It follows that the defendants must account to the Toronto Company for the profits which they have made out of the transaction.

SOURCE 186
Movitex Ltd *v* Bulfield
(Chancery Division) [1988] BCLC 104

VINELOTT J: . . . The main issues which arise in respect of this transaction (which I will call 'the first transaction') are first whether the direction given by Mr Bulfield to the vendors of the Edgware property to transfer that property to CRS was authorised by the board of directors of Movitex, which then comprised Mr Bulfield, Mr Perry and Mr Jack Dawes; second whether if it was so authorised CRS ought none the less to be ordered to convey the property to Movitex on appropriate terms on the ground that the directions were given by a board of directors of whom two had a personal interest in the transaction or, alternatively, that it was given without full disclosure of their interest having been made to Mr Dawes or that it was otherwise in breach of the fiduciary duties owed by Mr Bulfield and Mr Perry to Movitex.

. . .

As a result of the bank's insistence that Movitex reduce its overdraft from the sale of the Wembley property, Movitex sought alternative sources of finance but was unsuccessful. Eventually it was arranged that the property should be acquired by a newly formed company, CRS, of which Mr Bulfield was a director and that this company would lease the property to Movitex at a fair market rent. There was a dispute as to whether this arrangement had the consent of the Movitex board, in particular the assent of Mr Dawes a director of Movitex, and on this the judge concluded that 'the substitution of CRS for Movitex as the purchaser of the Edgware property on terms that CRS would grant Movitex a long lease at a rent equal to ten per cent of CRS's expenditure, was carried out with the authority of the Board . . .'

. . .

Articles 99 and 100 contain general provisions relating to the disclosure of an interest in and participation of a director in relation to transactions in which he has an interest. These articles have been subjected to detailed examination in the course of the argument, and I must, I think, set them out in full. Article 99 reads:

> 'No Director shall be disqualified by his office from contracting with the Company either as vendor, purchaser or otherwise, nor shall any such contract or any contract, matter or arrangement entered into by or on behalf of the Company in which any Director shall be in any way interested be avoided nor shall any Director so contracting or being so interested be liable to account to the Company for any profit realised by any such contract, matter or arrangement by reason of such Director holding that office or of the fiduciary relationship thereby established. The nature of a Director's interest must be declared by him at the meeting of the Directors at which the question of entering into the contract, matter or arrangement is first taken into consideration, or if the Director was not at the date of that meeting interested in the proposed contract, matter or arrangement at the next meeting of the Directors held after he became so interested, and in a case where the Director becomes interested in a contract, matter or

arrangement after it is made or arises at the first meeting of Directors held after he becomes so interested. A general notice to the Directors by a Director that he is a member of any specified firm or company and is to be regarded as interested in any contract, matter or arrangement which may after the date of the notice be made or arise with such firm or company shall (if such Director shall give the same at a meeting of the Directors or shall take reasonable steps to secure that the same is brought up and read at the next meeting of the Directors after it is given) be a sufficient declaration of interest in relation to such contract, matter or arrangement under this Article, and after such general notice it shall not be necessary to give any special notice relating to any particular contract, matter or arrangement with such firm or company.'

Article 100:

'A Director shall not as a Director vote in respect of any contract, matter or arrangement which he shall make with the Company or in which he is so interested as aforesaid and if he do so vote his vote shall not be counted nor shall he be counted in the quorum present upon a motion in respect of any such contract, matter or arrangement, but neither of these prohibitions shall apply
    . . .
(iv) to any contract or dealing in the subsidiary of the Company or with a corporation where the sole interest of a Director is that he is a director or other officer, member or creditor thereof.
    The question is whether this exception applies where, as here, the contract or dealing is between Movitex and a company of which a director is both a director and member, or whether it applies only if the director has one but not more than one of the characteristics, 'director or other officer, member or creditor'.

The judge construed this so as to provide that this exception permitted a director of Movitex to vote where his interest in the company with which Movitex was dealing was both as director and member.

Section 205
Section 205 provides that, subject to immaterial exceptions —

'any provision, whether contained in the articles of a company or in any contract with a company or otherwise, for exempting any officer of the company or any person (whether an officer of the company or not) employed by the company as auditor from, or indemnifying him against, any liability which by virtue of any rule of law would otherwise attach to him in respect of any negligence, default, breach of duty or breach of trust of which he may be guilty in relation to the company shall be void . . .'

The argument advanced on behalf of Movitex can be shortly summarised as follows. The self-dealing rule is founded on and exemplifies the wider principle that 'no one who has a duty to perform shall place himself in a situation to have his interests conflicting with that duty' (see *Broughton v Broughton* (1855) 5 De GM & G 160 at 164, 43 ER 831 at 833 per Lord Cranworth). To that should be added for completeness 'nor to have his duty to one conflicting with his duty to another' (see *Re Haslam & Hier-Evans* [1902] 1 Ch 765). So, it is said, the fiduciary owes a duty to the person whose interest he is bound to protect not to place himself in a position in which duty and interest or duty and duty are in conflict. If he does place himself in such a position in relation to a particular transaction, the beneficiary may have the transaction set aside or compel the fiduciary to account for any profit he has made or, if no profit has been realised but if restitution of the property is none the less impractical or inequitable, to make compensation. So, it is said, to the extent that a provision in the articles of a company permits a director to enter into a transaction in which one of their number has an interest or owes a duty to another the provision is one 'for exempting' the director from a liability which under the general law would otherwise attach to him in respect of a breach of his duty not to place himself in a position of conflict.

This argument, if sound, would have very startling consequences, for it would give rise to inconsistency between s 205 on the one hand and arts 78 and 84 of Table A, which correspond in their general purport though not in detail with arts 98 to 100 of Movitex's articles, on the other hand. Whether s 205 would then override or be overridden by arts 78 and 84 of Table A read in conjunction with s 8(2) of the 1948 Act, is a question which does not directly arise. The articles of Movitex exclude the regulations in Table A and arts 98 to 100 of Movitex's articles, though similar in their general purport to arts 78 and 84, cannot be said to be a mere repetition of them, but it would be at the lowest very paradoxical to find that s 205 conflicts with arts 78 and 84. The legislature in enacting the 1948 Act must have contemplated that the modifications of the self-dealing rule in arts 78 and 84 do not infringe s 205. Accordingly, if s 205 is fairly capable of a construction which avoids that conflict, that construction must clearly be preferred to one which does not.

This problem has attracted the attention of the authors and editors of some of the leading text books. The solution advanced by the editors of *Gore Browne on Companies* (43rd edn) is that a provision may, without infringing s 205, reduce or abrogate a duty owed by a director, provided it does not exempt the director from liability for breach of it. That solution fails, I think, to give effect to the words, 'for exempting', and leads to the absurd result that an article could, without infringing s 205, modify a director's duty to use reasonable skill and care in the conduct of the company's affairs and so avoid a liability for damages for breach of duty which would otherwise arise, a conclusion which seems to me manifestly in conflict with the purpose of the section.

Counsel for the defendants (Mr Stubbs QC) took me through a number of early cases in which the scope and effect of an article modifying a director's duty to a company and exempting him from breach of that duty has been considered by the courts and in particular the decision of Romer J and of the Court of Appeal in *Re City Equitable Fire Insurance Co Ltd* [1925] Ch 407, [1924] All ER Rep 485 and to the report of the Greene Committee which led to the inclusion of the Companies Act 1929 of s 152, the legislative predecessor of s 205. If I may say so without disrespect to counsel's very thorough argument, it does not follow that because the purpose of s 152 was to nullify articles similar to the article on which the directors successfully relied in the *City Equitable Fire Insurance* case that that section and s 205 should be construed as invalidating only an article in those or similar terms. A patch may be intentionally wider than the visible hole to which it is applied.

There is so far as the researches of counsel have been able to discover no guidance to be found in any reported case. Upjohn LJ, in summarising the self-dealing rule in *Boulting v Association of Cinematograph, Television and Allied Technicians* [1963] 1 All ER 716 at 729, [1963] 2 QB 606 at 636, observed that 'articles may validly permit directors to be present at board meetings and even to vote when proposed contracts in which they are interested are being discussed'.

However, the effectiveness of such an article was not in issue, and s 205 was not referred to.

I was at first inclined to find the solution to this conundrum in the principle, stressed by Upjohn LJ in the *Boulting* case, that there is no breach of the self-dealing rule if a trustee enters into a transaction in which he has a personal interest with the consent of his beneficiary (if of full age and capacity and so capable of giving consent or with the authority of the court given on behalf of any who are not so capable). The trustee, of course, must be able to show that he has made full disclosure and took no advantage of his position or of any information gained from it. The consent must be an informed consent freely given. If that condition is satisfied, the conflict between duty and interest is dissolved. The trustee is relieved from his duty to deal with the trust property for the benefit of the beneficiary to the extent that the beneficiary chooses freely and with full knowledge of the circumstances to concur in the transaction.

As I understand it, this is the ground which underlies the well-settled principle that a transaction entered into by a director on behalf of a company in which he has a personal interest is not liable to be avoided if the company was authorised by the company in general meeting to enter into it. The company in general meeting is for this purpose the beneficiary. The resolution in general meeting protects the director not because it operates to release him or absolve him from the consequences of a breach of the self-dealing rule but because, to the extent that the company in general meeting gives its informed consent to the transaction there is no breach, the conflict of duty and interest is avoided.

It is at first sight tempting to construe arts 78 and 84 and arts 98 to 100 as substituting the board, at least to the extent that there is a quorum of independent directors, for the purpose of giving the concurrence of the company. But this is not a satisfactory solution. There are two reasons. First the rule is that the company is entitled to the unbiased judgment of every one of its directors. If it is the duty of a director not to place himself in a position of conflict, the duty is just as much breached by an article which permits a director to do so, if he does not vote or is not counted in the quorum, as it is by an article which permits him to vote and to be counted in the quorum. Secondly even on that construction arts 78 and 84 and arts 98 to 100 would be invalid to the extent to which a director is in the cases specified entitled to vote and to be counted in the quorum on the resolution to enter into a transaction in which he has a personal interest. Indeed, one commentator has suggested that arts 78 and 84 are valid, save in this one respect.

The true solution is, I think, to be found in a passage in the judgment of Megarry V-C in *Tito v Waddell* (No 2) [1977] 3 All ER 129, [1977] Ch 106. The facts of that case were very complex. It is sufficient for present purposes to say that the resident commissioner of Ocean Island had statutory powers to grant mining leases over the land owned by the inhabitants. It was argued that in the exercise of that duty and the fixing of the royalty and other terms of the leases he owed a fiduciary duty to the owners and a duty, therefore, not to put himself in a position where the fiduciary duty (owed by him as servant of the Crown to the inhabitants) might conflict with the indirect interest of the Crown as a participant in the British Phosphate Commissioners, the body to which the leases were granted. It was argued in the alternative that in dealing with the owners of the land, he owed them a fiduciary duty to make full disclosure and to act fairly.

One issue was whether, assuming contrary to the decision of the Vice-Chancellor that the resident commissioner did have a fiduciary duty to the owners of the land, a breach of that duty would have been a breach of trust within s 19(2) of the Limitation Act 1939 and so subject to a six-year period of limitation. Section 19(1) was not in point since the resident commissioner did not himself receive any part of the royalty. It was argued that in so far as the resident commissioner owed a fiduciary duty bringing into operation either the self-dealing or the fair-dealing rule, breach of that duty was a breach of trust within s 19(2). The answer to this submission is given in a passage in the judgment of the Vice-Chancellor, which I think I should read in full. He said ([1977] 3 All ER 129 at 247–248, [1977] Ch 106 at 248–249):

'In this case, the question becomes one of whether a trustee as such can properly be said to be under a 'duty' not to purchase the trust property, and under a 'duty' not to purchase a beneficiary's interest in the trust property without making proper disclosure, and so on. If the answer is Yes, then of course there is much logical force in the contention that a breach of these duties is a breach of trust within the Limitation Act 1939, s 19(2), and so is subject to the six-years period of limitation. The problem is essentially one of classification. Now it is true that some textbooks set out the rules about self-dealing and fair-dealing as part of the duties and discretions of trustees. Snell's Equity does this, and there are others. Some books avoid any problems of classification by setting out the rules in a separate self-contained chapter: see leading counsel for the plaintiffs learned edition of Lewin on Trusts ((16th Edn, 1964) pp 693–706). But Halsbury's Laws of England includes both the self-dealing rule and the fair-dealing rule under the head of 'Disabilities of Trustees' and not 'Duties of Trustees'; and it is this that appears to me to be the true view. Snell (Equity (27th edn, 1973)), I think, is wrong. In my judgment, what equity does is to subject trustees to particular disabilities in cases falling within the self-dealing and fair dealing rules. I may add that Pomeroy's Equity Jurisprudence (3rd edn, 1905) discusses self-dealing, under Constructive Fraud, and fair dealing under Constructive Trusts, with no more than a cross reference to these passages under Duties of Express Trustees (vol 2, p 1752, vol 3, pp 2020, 2085). This way of regarding the matter is reinforced by considering those who fall within the scope of the fair-dealing rule. This applies, of course, not only to trustees, but also to many others, such as agents, solicitors and company directors. If a breach of the fair-dealing rule by a trustee were to be treated as a breach of trust to which the six-years period under the Limitation Act 1939 would apply, while a breach of the rule by one of the others were to be free from the six-years period, the result would indeed be anomalous. A possible line of escape from the anomaly would be to treat agents, solicitors and the rest as constructive trustees for this purpose, so that all would be subject to the six-years period; but I should be reluctant to resort to such an artificiality unless driven to it. Another aspect of the matter, producing the same result, is that the fair-dealing rule is essentially a rule of equity that certain persons (including trustees) are subject to certain consequences if they carry through certain transactions without, where appropriate, comply-ing with certain requirements. The rule seems to me to be a general rule of equity and not a specific part of the law of trusts which lays down the duties of a trustee. Trusteeship is merely one of the categories of relationship which brings a person within the rule. There are many things that a trustee may do or omit to do which will have consequences for him as a trustee without the act or omission amounting to a breach of trust. I do not think that it could be said that a trustee is under a duty as trustee not to become bankrupt, so that his bankruptcy will constitute a breach of trust; yet his bankruptcy may be a ground for removing him from his trusteeship.'

Looked at in the light of this analysis of the self-dealing rule, the explanation of the apparent conflict between s 205 and arts 78 and 84 becomes clear. The true principle is that if a director places himself in a position in which his duty to the company conflicts with his personal interest or his duty to another, the court will intervene to set aside the transaction without inquiring whether there was any breach of the director's duty to the company. That is an over-riding principle of equity. The shareholders of the company, in formulating the articles, can exclude or modify the application of this principle. In doing so they do not exempt the director from or from the consequences of a breach of a duty owed to the company.

In *Tito v Waddell* Megarry V-C suggested that the fair-dealing rule was similarly 'a rule of equity that certain persons (including trustees) are subject to certain consequences without, where appropriate, complying with certain rules'. In *Tito v Waddell* the question was whether, assuming that the resident commissioner owed a fiduciary duty to the landowners, a breach of that duty would have been properly categorised as a breach of trust for the purposes of s 19(2) of the Limitation Act 1939. It seems to me that it is one thing to say that a breach of the fair-dealing rule by a trustee in, for instance, purchasing a beneficiary's beneficial interest in trust property (or what is, I think, substantially the same thing, in purchasing the trust property with the consent of the beneficiary without making proper disclosure) is not a breach of trust and quite another to say that it involves no breach of duty. It seems to me that while such a breach may not be a breach of the trustee's primary duty to deal with the trust property in the interests of its beneficiaries and so not a breach of trust, the trustee in dealing with the beneficiary owes a duty to him to make full disclosure and to deal fairly with him, which is founded on the inequality in the relationship between the trustee and the beneficiary and the opportunity which the trustee had in the course of managing the trust property of acquiring knowledge relevant to its value which is denied to the beneficiary. Similarly if a director seeks the approval of the company in general meeting to the purchase by him of the company's property, he owes a duty to make full disclosure to the company. However, this question does not arise for decision, and I express no concluded opinion on it. In the instant case Mr Perry and Mr Bulfield as directors of Movitex owed a statutory duty of disclosure under s 199 of the 1948 Act and a duty of disclosure under art 99. Moreover, it is common ground that as directors of Movitex they owed a duty to promote the interests of Movitex and, where the interests of Movitex conflicted with their own, to prefer the interests of Movitex. Any purported modification of either duty would infringe s 205.

The remaining question is whether in relation to the first transaction Mr Bulfield or Mr Perry was in breach of either of these duties. As regards the first of these duties, the duty 'to declare the nature of his interest' must, I think, impose on a director the duty to disclose full information as to the nature of any transaction which it is proposed to enter into. The disclosure must be such that the other director or directors can see what his interest is and how far it goes.

On this question I can be brief. On 11 March 1969 Mr Dawes was told that CRS was in the process of being formed. Asked whether he knew that Mr Perry and Mr Bulfield were to be the directors, he said in a telling passage in his evidence that if he was not told he would have probed. Although he did not know or inquire into the proportions in which they owned the share capital, he thought it self-evident that they or their respective families would own all or substantially all of the issued shares. In my judgment he knew that Movitex had contracted to purchase the Edgware property and the difficulties that it had encountered in completing it. He satisfied himself that the rent and other proposed terms of the lease were fair and not more onerous than could have been obtained if other suitable premises had been found. No material information was withheld.

Moreover, viewed objectively, the transaction was to my mind plainly in the interest of Movitex. Movitex could not complete the purchase of the Edgware property. Although Mr Perry thought that when the time came when they would have to vacate the Wembley property Movitex could have struggled along in the inadequate premises occupied by subsidiaries, it would have survived with difficulty, and it would most probably not have found suitable other premises at less than the rent offered by CRS. In addition, it would have faced all the expense of adapting them.

PART VIII: DISQUALIFICATION OF DIRECTORS

Under the Company Directors Disqualification Act 1986 (CDDA), the court may grant an order prohibiting the respondent to the application from acting as a director for any period between 2 and 15 years. The CDDA consolidates the provisions which were formerly contained in the Companies Acts and has been the focus of increasing activity on the part of the Secretary of State for Trade and Industry. A large number of applications for disqualification has now been reported but the difficulty of these for the purpose of study is the emphasis (as would necessarily be the case) on the facts in each instance. Points of law have developed, however, especially in connection with the nature of the procedure and to ensure its fairness. Thus it has been held that it is not unfair to insist that the respondent file evidence against a disqualification by way of affidavit (as opposed to insisting on the giving of this evidence at the hearing of the application), it is permissible to use evidence obtained in the form of third party statements in investigations under the Companies Act 1985 (despite the hearsay nature of such evidence) and that, given their public interest nature, the proceedings do not have to be delayed until the outcome of civil proceedings against the respondent (*Re Rex Williams Leisure plc* [1994] 2 BCLC 555).

The offence of insider trading is an offence in connection with the management of a company for the purposes of an application for disqualification under s 2(1) of the CDDA. The appellant argued that his conduct was not undertaken in connection with the management of the company, but the Court of Appeal held that all that was required was that the act should have a factual connection with the management of the company (which insider trading did, *R v Goodman* [1994] 1 BCLC 349).

An application for disqualification on the ground that the respondent was a director of a company which became insolvent and is unfit to be a director (s 6 of the CDDA) must be made within two years of the company becoming insolvent (s 7(2) of the CDDA). Nevertheless, it has been held that leave will be given for such proceedings to be brought out of time if there is an arguable case that such an application will succeed and that there are no factors which will prejudice the respondent (eg length and reason for the delay, *Re Tasbian Ltd (No 3)* [1993] BCLC 297). It was decided in *Secretary of State v Langridge*

[1991] BCLC 543 that the 10 days' notice required under s 16 to be given to the person against whom the proceedings are to be presented, is directory and not mandatory. Thus, where the notice was not given, the proceedings were held not to be fatally irregular.

Under s 18 of the CDDA, a register of disqualification orders is maintained by the Secretary of State. Source 187 is designed to provide some idea of the facts and issues taken into account in a disqualification application.

SOURCE 187
Re Sevenoaks Stationers Ltd
(Court of Appeal) [1991] BCLC 325

DILLON LJ . . . Section 6(4) provides that the minimum period of disqualification is two years and the maximum period is 15 years. Section 9 provides that where it falls to a court to determine whether a person's conduct as a director of any particular company or companies makes him unfit to be concerned in the management of a company the court shall have regard in particular to the matters mentioned in Sch 1 of the Act. I abbreviate the section since nothing turns in this case on its wording.

It follows that the judge, if he is going to disqualify a person under s 6, has to be satisfied that that person's conduct in relation to the company or companies in question 'makes him unfit to be concerned in the management of a company.'

. . .

The main point urged for Mr Cruddas on this appeal was however that the period of seven years' suspension imposed by the judge was too long. In that regard this appeal has an importance beyond its own facts, since it is the first appeal against a disqualification order which has come to this court.

. . .

I found certain statistics produced by the Official Receiver somewhat disturbing, viz: in 1989, of 115 disqualification orders made in the High Court under s 6, only one, that against Mr Cruddas, imposed disqualification for more than five years, whereas of 123 such orders made in county courts 18 involved disqualification for more than five years. In the first six months of 1990, of 79 disqualification orders made in the High Court under s 6 only four imposed disqualification for more than five years whereas of 96 such orders made in county courts again 18 imposed disqualification for more than five years.

Under s 6 the court having jurisdiction to make a disqualification order is, where the company is in compulsory liquidation, the court by which the company is being wound up. That is likely to depend under s 117 of the Insolvency Act 1986, on where the petitioning creditor found it most convenient to present the petition for winding up. It seems surprising if it were the case that the applications for disqualification orders under s 6 made in the High Court should have been in significantly less serious cases than those made in the county courts.

I would for my part endorse the division of the potential 15-year disqualification period into three brackets, which was put forward by Mr Keenan for the Official Receiver to Harman J in the present case and has been put forward by Mr Charles for the Official Receiver in other cases, viz: (i) The top bracket of disqualification for periods over ten years should be reserved for particularly serious cases. These may include cases where a director who has already had one period of disqualification imposed on him falls to be disqualified yet again. (ii) The minimum bracket of two to five years' disqualification should be applied where, though disqualification is mandatory, the case is, relatively, not very serious. (iii) The middle bracket of disqualification for from six to ten years should apply for serious cases which do not merit the top bracket.

...

Over the five years from December 1981 to December 1986, Mr Cruddas was a director, as was a Mr Hooker, of no less than five trading companies which became insolvent and went into liquidation. Mr Cruddas is, as I have said, a chartered accountant. Mr Hooker's original occupation was, we are told, as a lorry driver. A three-year disqualification period was imposed on Mr Hooker by Mr Registrar Buckley before Mr Cruddas' case was heard by Harman J. The five companies were Hoo Paper Co Ltd (Hoo Paper), Hoo Waste Paper Co Ltd (Hoo Waste Paper), Sevenoaks Stationers Ltd (Sevenoaks Stationers), Rochester Paper Co Ltd (Rochester) and Sevenoaks Stationers (Retail) Ltd (Retail). The application for disqualification was made in the matter of Retail, but the court was required to consider the complaints of the Official Receiver as formulated in his report in respect of Mr Cruddas' conduct as a director of each of the five companies.

The total net deficiency of all five companies as regards creditors (disregarding lost share capital) comes to over £559,000 according to the statements of affairs prepared by directors. That involves an element of double-counting in that the deficiency in Sevenoaks Stationers duplicates to the extent of some £50,000, because of a guarantee, the net deficiency in Hoo Paper. But the evidence indicates that the net deficiency in Rochester could be up to £193,000 more than was allowed for in the statement of affairs. In effect Rochester restarted, albeit with a significant fresh paid up share capital, the business which had failed in the hands of Hoo Paper and Hoo Waste Paper, and Retail restarted the business which had failed in the hands of Sevenoaks Stationers.

...

The term 'Crown debts' has become a term of art on applications for the disqualification of directors under s 6 or under the legislation which preceded the 1986 Act. It denotes debts due from the company in question to the Crown in respect of PAYE national insurance contributions and VAT, but not debts due to the Crown in respect of other matters (such as development grants). The judgments at first instance of judges in the Chancery Division appear to show a considerable difference in approach to the significance of Crown debts, as so interpreted, in relation to the disqualification of directors. One of the matters we have to consider on this appeal is the correctness of the explanations of law in certain judgments, and the correctness of Harman J's assessment of the significance of the Crown debts in the present case.

It is beyond dispute that the purpose of s 6 is to protect the public, and in particular potential creditors of companies, from losing money through companies becoming insolvent when the directors of those companies are people unfit to be concerned in the management of a company.

The test laid down in s 6, apart from the requirement that the person concerned is or has been a director of a company which has become insolvent, is whether the person's conduct as a director of the company or companies in question 'makes him unfit to be concerned in the management of a company'. These are ordinary words of the English language and they should be simple to apply in most cases. It is important to hold to those words in each case.

The judges of the Chancery Division have, understandably, attempted in certain cases to give guidance as to what does or does not make a person unfit to be concerned in the management of a company. Thus in *Re Lo-Line Electric Motors Ltd* [1988] BCLC 698 at 703, [1988] 2 All ER 692 at 696, [1988] Ch 477 at 486 Browne-Wilkinson V-C said:

'Ordinary commercial misjudgment is in itself not sufficient to justify disqualification. In the normal case, the conduct complained of must display a lack of commercial probity, although I have no doubt in an extreme case of gross negligence or total incompetence disqualification could be appropriate.'

Then he said that the director in question —

'has been shown to have behaved in a commercially culpable manner in trading through limited companies when he knew them to be insolvent and in using the unpaid Crown debts to finance such trading.'

(See [1988] BCLC 698 at 709, [1988] 2 All ER 692 at 701, [1988] Ch 477 at 492.)

Such statements may be helpful in identifying particular circumstances in which a person would clearly be unfit. But there seems to have been a tendency, which I deplore, on the part of the Bar and possibly also on the part of the Official Receiver's Department, to treat the statements as judicial paraphrases of the words of the statute which fall to be construed as a matter of law in lieu of the words of the statute. The result is to obscure that the true question to be tried is a question of fact, what used to be pejoratively described in the Chancery Division as 'a jury question'.

. . .

In the present case, the allegations relied on against Mr Cruddas are helpfully and properly summarised, in relation to each of the five companies successively, in the report of the deputy Official Receiver, Mr Bennett. The volume of documents lodged in support of the application is such that without the summaries Mr Cruddas could not have known what was actually charged against him.

Slightly shortened the matters set out in the report as the matters by reference to which Mr Cruddas was unfit to be concerned in the management of a company were the following:

Retail
(a) Mr Cruddas failed to ensure that audited accounts were prepared and delivered to the Registrar of Companies.
(b) Mr Cruddas caused Retail to make a loan of £21,000 to Rochester when he knew or ought to have known that there was no prospect of repayment.
(c) Mr Cruddas misrepresented the position of Retail to a creditor who had presented a winding-up petition and committed Retail to payments by instalments to that creditor with which he knew or ought to have known Retail could not comply. I interject that this allegation was abandoned in the light of Mr Cruddas' unchallenged evidence that he had provided £10,000 out of his own money to pay off the winding-up petition, and had intended to pay future instalments out of his own money.
(d) Mr Cruddas failed to keep proper accounting records of Retail.
(e) Mr Cruddas failed to ensure that the statutory records of Retail were preserved for the prescribed period.
(f) Mr Cruddas caused Retail to trade whilst insolvent for at least 2 years from 31 December 1984 to 20 December 1986, during which period its deficiency increased by £100,000 and
(g) Mr Cruddas was responsible for causing Retail to retain £7000 of Crown debts.

Rochester

(a) Mr Cruddas failed to ensure that audited accounts were prepared and delivered to the Registrar of Companies.

(b) Mr Cruddas failed to ensure that the statutory records of Rochester were preserved for the prescribed period.

(c) Mr Cruddas caused Rochester to trade whilst insolvent from the time when draft accounts for the period to 30 November 1984 became available until the appointment of the provisional liquidator on the 25 September 1986 and

(d) Mr Cruddas was responsible for causing Rochester to retain £91,000 of Crown debts (particularly in respect of PAYE and national insurance contributions).

Sevenoaks Stationers

(a) Mr Cruddas was responsible for causing Sevenoaks Stationers to guarantee the indebtedness of Hoo Paper at a time when that company was clearly in severe financial difficulties.

(b) Mr Cruddas failed to ensure that audited accounts of Sevenoaks Stationers were prepared and delivered to the Registrar of Companies and

(c) Mr Cruddas was responsible for causing Sevenoaks Stationers to retain £2620 of Crown debts.

Hoo Waste Paper

(a) Mr Cruddas failed to ensure that audited accounts of Hoo Waste paper were prepared and delivered to the Registrar of Companies.

(b) Mr Cruddas caused Hoo Waste Paper to pay debts of Hoo Paper from August 1982 to early 1983 at a time when Mr Cruddas knew or ought to have known that Hoo Paper was insolvent and would not be able to repay the moneys.

(c) Mr Cruddas failed to ensure that annual returns were filed with the Registrar of Companies for Hoo Waste Paper and

(d) Mr Cruddas was responsible for causing Hoo Waste Paper to retain £14,572 of Crown debts and

Hoo Paper

(a) Mr Cruddas failed to ensure that audited accounts of Hoo Paper were prepared and delivered to the Registrar of Companies.

(b) Mr Cruddas was responsible for causing Hoo Paper to retain £1724.23 of Crown debts.

(c) Mr Cruddas failed to ensure that annual returns were filed with the Registrar of Companies for Hoo Paper and

(d) Mr Cruddas caused Hoo Paper to continue to trade whilst insolvent from May 1982, when cheques were being returned by the bank until 11 March 1983.

All these allegations were substantially proved against Mr Cruddas, except the allegation (c) in respect of Retail which was abandoned, as I have mentioned. They vary, however, considerably in gravity.

. . .

I turn next to the question of Crown debts. As to this the judge said ([1990] BCLC 668 at 671):

'In the circumstances I am faced with admitted deficiencies of a most serious character, including in particular Crown debts in total of an order of £120,000 which were left outstanding . . . It is, in my judgment, a badge of commercial immorality to cause moneys which have been taken under force of law from third parties (PAYE deductions, after all, are taken from wages which are owed to employees; under compulsion of law VAT is taken under compulsion of law from members of the public who purchase goods as an addition to the price of the goods) to be not paid over to the Crown.'

There have been differing views expressed by Chancery judges about the significance of Crown debts on a disqualification application and the phrase has tended to become something of a ritual incantation.

In some earlier cases, Harman J regarded such Crown debts as 'quasi-trust moneys'. That view has not however been followed by other judges, and the Official Receiver does not seek to resurrect it.

A different view was expressed by Hoffmann J in *Re Dawson Print Group Ltd* [1987] BCLC 601 at 604–605 where he said, in a passage with which I entirely agree:

'. . . but the fact is that, no doubt for good reasons, the Exchequer and the Commissioners of Customs and Excise have chosen to appoint traders to be tax collectors on their behalf with the attendant risk. That risk is, to some extent, compensated by the preference which they have on insolvency. There is, as yet, no obligation on traders to keep such moneys in a separate account as there might be if they were really trust moneys. They are simply a debt owed by the company to the Revenue or the Commissioners of Customs and Excise. I cannot accept that failure to pay these debts is regarded in the commercial world generally as such a breach of commercial morality that it requires in itself a conclusion that the directors concerned are unfit to be involved in the management of a company.'

The current consensus of the judges in the Chancery Division is, I apprehend, expressed in the following passage in the judgment of the Vice-Chancellor in *Re Lo-Line Electric Motors Ltd* [1988] BCLC 698 at 704–705, [1988] 2 All ER 692 at 697–698, [1988] Ch 477 at 487–488:

'The debts owed by the companies included substantial Crown debts, ie sums for which the company was liable to the Inland Revenue or Customs and Excise in respect of PAYE, national insurance and value added tax. There is a slight difference of judicial approach to Crown debts. In *Re Dawson Print Group Ltd* [1987] BCLC at 601 Hoffmann J, on the facts of that case, did not draw any distinction between a failure to pay Crown debts and the failure to pay other trading debts. However, in *Re Wedgecroft Ltd* (7 March 1986, unreported) Harman J treated Crown debts as "quasi-trust" moneys and the failure to pay them as being more morally culpable than failure to pay ordinary commercial debts. In *Re Stanford Services Ltd* [1987] BCLC 607 Vinelott J treated the failure to pay Crown debts as more serious than the failure to pay commercial debts. He described the Crown as an involuntary creditor and said (at 617): "The directors of a company ought to conduct its affairs in such a way that it can meet these liabilities when they fall due, not only because they are not moneys earned by its trading activities, which the company is entitled to treat as part of its cash flow (entitled that is in that the persons with whom it deals expect the company to do so) but, more importantly, because the directors ought not to use moneys which the company is currently liable to pay over to the Crown to finance its current trading activities. If they do so and if, in consequence, PAYE, national insurance contributions and VAT become overdue and, in a winding up, irrecoverable, the court may draw the inference that the directors were continuing to trade at a time when they ought to have known that the company was unable to meet its current and accruing liabilities, and were unjustifiably putting at risk moneys which ought to have been paid over to the Crown as part of the public revenues to finance trading activities which might or might not produce a profit. It is, I think, misleading (or at least unhelpful) to ask whether a failure to pay debts of this character would be generally regarded as a breach of commercial morality. A director who allows such a situation to arise is either in breach of his duty to keep himself properly informed, with reasonable accuracy, as to the company's current financial position . . . or is acting improperly in continuing to trade at the expense and jeopardy of moneys which he ought not to use to finance the company's current trade." I agree with those remarks and add this. Although the Crown debts are not strictly trust moneys, the failure to pay them over does not only prejudice the Crown, as creditor, but in the case of PAYE and national insurance may also have a prejudicial effect on the company's employees. The use of moneys obtained by compulsory deductions from wages for the financing of the company's business is to use moneys which morally, if not legally, belong either to the employees or to the Crown without the consent of either. I consider the use of the moneys which should have been paid to the Crown to finance continuation of an insolvent company's business more culpable than the failure to pay commercial debts.'

I would see validity in this if it were correct, as the Vice-Chancellor apparently thought, that failure to pay over to the Crown moneys deducted from the wages of employees might have a prejudicial effect on the employees.

. . .

The Official Receiver cannot, in my judgment, automatically treat non-payment of any Crown debt as evidence of unfitness of the directors. It is necessary to look more closely in each case to see what the significance, if any, of the non-payment of the Crown debt is.

Thus in the case of Hoo Paper, which had a deficiency of £74,591, a mere £1,724 of unpaid Crown debt, representing unpaid national insurance contributions which for some unexplained reason had not been included in the statement of affairs, does not appear to be significant at all. Again Sevenoaks Stationers had a deficiency of £79,948 and an unpaid Crown debt of £2620 for PAYE, but what is significant is not the Crown debt, but that the deficiency includes £70,000 on a guarantee which the directors caused Sevenoaks Stationers to give for the indebtedness of Hoo Paper at a time when that company was clearly in severe financial difficulties.

Much more significant, however, is the position in relation to Crown debts in Rochester and Retail. In Rochester unpaid Crown debts exceeded £90,000, but they were allowed to accumulate at a time when Rochester was to the directors' knowledge getting into ever greater difficulties, and when it was in fact insolvent. In Retail the unpaid Crown debts were only £7,000 but that was PAYE for years, and the company only had four employees. Moreover Retail had lent £21,000 to Rochester in early 1986 when Mr Cruddas knew or ought to have known that there was no prospect of repayment.

Mr Cruddas made a deliberate decision to pay only those creditors who pressed for payment. The obvious result was that the two companies traded, when in fact insolvent and known to be in difficulties at the expense of those creditors who, like the Crown, happened not to be pressing for payment. Such conduct on the part of a director can well, in my judgment, be relied on as a ground for saying that he is unfit to be concerned in the management of a company. But what is relevant in the Crown's position is not that the debt was a debt which arose from a compulsory deduction from employees' wages or a compulsory payment of VAT, but that the Crown was not pressing for payment, and the director was taking unfair advantage of that forbearance on the part of the Crown, and, instead of providing adequate working capital, was trading at the Crown's expense while the companies were in jeopardy. It would be equally unfair to trade in that way and in such circumstances at the expense of creditors other than the Crown. The Crown is the more exposed not from the nature of the debts but from the administrative problem it has in pressing for prompt payment as companies get into difficulties. As Peter Gibson J observed in *Re Bath Glass Ltd* [1988] BCLC 329 at 333 at the end of a paragraph, which I would generally approve without limiting it to Crown debts:

> 'Even if such conduct does not amount to wrongful trading within s 214, in my judgment it would still be conduct amounting to misconduct and so relevant to s 6. Whether in any particular case that misconduct, or the various matters of misconduct, proved to the satisfaction of the court, will justify a finding of unfitness will depend on all the circumstances of the case.'

Taking that view of the Crown debts in Rochester and Retail and adding to it (i) that there were never any audited accounts of any of the five companies, let alone registered accounts (ii) the inadequacy of the accounting records of Retail (iii) the loan by Retail to Rochester (iv) the payment of debts of Hoo Paper by Hoo Waste Paper (v) the guarantee given by Sevenoaks Stationers for liabilities of Hoo Paper (vi) the continued trading while insolvent and known to be in difficulties of Rochester and Retail and (vii) the extent of the deficiency in each company after a relatively short period of trading, I have no doubt at all that it is amply proved that Mr Cruddas is unfit to be concerned in the management of a company. His trouble is not dishonesty, but incompetence or negligence in a very marked degree and that is enough to render him unfit; I do not think it is necessary for incompetence to be 'total', as suggested by the Vice-Chancellor in *Re Lo-Line Electric Motors Ltd* [1988] BCLC 698, [1988] 2 All ER 692, [1988] Ch 477, to render a director unfit to take part in the management of a company.

If the judge had been entitled to take into account in the way he did the absence of proper accounting records for Rochester, Hoo Paper, Hoo Waste Paper and Sevenoaks Stationers, I would have regarded the case as in the middle bracket and would have hesitated to interfere with the period of seven years disqualification which the judge imposed, even taking into account the extent of Mr Cruddas' losses of his own money in the five companies, and the other factors of mitigation urged for Mr Cruddas. My only qualm would have been as to whether it was right that the period of disqualification of Mr Cruddas should be more than twice as long as that imposed by the Registrar on his co-director Mr Hooker.

As it is, however, the judge took into account matters which he was not entitled to take into account, and in particular the supposed failure to keep proper accounting records for the four companies in addition to Retail. Failure to keep proper accounting records is such a serious matter in the case of a director in the position of Mr Cruddas that the period of disqualification imposed on him must be reduced. In all the circumstances, I would reduce it to five years, and would allow this appeal to that extent.

NOTES AND QUESTIONS

1. *Is it significant in* Percival v Wright[1] *(Source 162 at p 438) that the shareholder approached the director, rather than the other way around?*

2. *If so, what would be the principle in such a case?*

3. *Is there any coherent principle or set of principles which would enable us to distinguish between when the directors owed their duties to the company and when to the shareholders?*

4. Percival v Wright *(Source 162) may seem morally offensive — someone relying on information not available to the other party, but is it not in line with the established principle of caveat emptor in the sale of goods?*

5. *Was it the duty of the directors in* Pavlides v Jensen[2] *(Source 163 at p 440) to cause the company to institute action against themselves for their alleged negligence? Is their failure to do this not a misapplication of the company's 'property' (see Source 193* Prudential v Newman Industries, *at p 545)?*

6. *If directors do, indeed, owe their duties to 'the company' what constitutes the company? Consider in this context the different possible constituent elements. Shareholders are an obvious element, but see* Evans v Brunner Mond[3] *(p 228) and* Re Saltdean Estates Ltd[4] *(p 801). What about employees?*

7. *How will s 214 of the Insolvency Act 1986 change the law as to directors' duty of skill and care (see* Re Produce Marketing Consortium, *p 72)?*

8. *Was the plaintiff in* Hely-Hutchinson v Brayhead Ltd[5] *(p 273) negligent? If so, should his claim have been dismissed?*

9. *Under s 3 of the Company Directors' Disqualification Act 1986, a person can be disqualified from being a company director if in persistent default in complying with the provisions of the Companies Acts 'requiring any return, account or other document to be filed with, delivered or sent, or notice of any matter to be given, to the registrar of companies'.*

10. *Should directors of companies (all or public limited companies?) be required to undertake some professional training and examination? (compare secretaries of public limited companies, s 286 of the CA 1985).*

11. *Who has the power to issue shares may not be clearly laid down by the constitution. This question has now been settled by statute (s 80).*

12. *If the directors have the power to issue shares, is there not a case for saying that if they decide that a takeover bid should be defeated in the interests of the company that decision should be respected? (Compare* Re Smith & Fawcett Ltd,[6] *(Source 172 at p 463) and see Sealy [1967] CLJ 33.)*

13. *Can* Hogg v Cramphorn[7] *(Source 173 at p 465) be distinguished from* Howard Smith v Ampol Petroleum[8] *(Source 175 at p 471) on the basis that in the one the majority was to remain the majority, whereas in the other the majority would be rendered the minority?*

1 [1902] 2 Ch 421; 71 LJ Ch 846 (see p 438)
2 [1956] Ch 565; [1956] 2 All ER 518 (see p 440)
3 [1921] 1 Ch 359; 90 LJ Ch 294
4 [1968] 1 WLR 1844; [1968] 3 All ER 829
5 [1968] 1 QB 549; [1967] 3 All ER 14
6 [1942] Ch 304; [1942] 1 All ER 542 (see p 463)
7 [1967] Ch 254; [1966] 3 All ER 14 (see p 465)
8 [1974] AC 821; [1974] 1 All ER 1126 (see p 471)

14. *If this is the explanation, what is the significance of the judgment of the Privy Council?*

15. *If this is the explanation, can* Clemens v Clemens[1] *(Source 176 at p 475) be brought within it? (Is not a reduction to below 25 per cent as significant as a reduction to below 50 per cent?)*

16. *Is the blanket rule of accountability as propounded by* Regal (Hastings)[2] *(Source 177 at p 477) and* Canadian Aero Services[3] *(Source 179 at p 483) salutary or bloody-minded?*

17. *What would have been the result in* Cooley[4] *(Source 178 at p 481) if, instead of lying to the chairman of IDC and the Gas Board, Cooley had told the truth and left IDC in breach of his contract? Would he still have been accountable for the profit, assuming he took up the same post?*

18. *If so, what would be the basis of this accountability?*

19. *If not, was he just being punished for telling lies?*

20. *Would the rule in* Regal *be an appropriate basis on which the company might recover profits made by a director or other insider or executive by dealing in the company's shares while in possession of confidential information? Is it relevant to this that it is unlawful for a company to deal in its own shares?*

21. Canadian Aero Services Limited[5] *(Source 179 at p 483) seems to suggest that if and when the company ratifies a breach of duty by a director or authorises a director to undertake what would otherwise be a breach of duty, the director interested should not vote as one of the ratifying shareholders. Is this reconcilable with* N W Transportation v Beatty[6] *(Source 184 at p 509)? Consider, in this connection, the judgments in Source 183 at p 507.*

22. *Is Lord Russell of Killowen correct when he says that the result in* Regal[7] *would have been different had there been a ratifying resolution?*

23. *Would he still be correct if one shareholder holding say 10 per cent of the shares would have voted against such a resolution?*

24. *If he is correct, how is* Regal *to be distinguished from* Cook v Deeks[8] *(Source 185 at p 511)?*

---

1 [1976] 2 All ER 268
2 [1967] 2 AC 134n; [1942] 1 All ER 378 (see p 477)
3 [1973] 40 DLR (3d) 371 (see p 483)
4 [1972] 1 WLR 443; [1972] 2 All ER 162 (see p 481)
5 (1973) 40 DLR (3d) 371
6 (1887) 12 App Ca 589; 56 LJPC 102
7 [1967] 2 AC 134n; [1942] 1 All ER 378
8 [1916] 1 AC 554; 85 LJPC 161

Chapter 8

THE PROTECTION OF MINORITY SHAREHOLDERS

PART I: INTRODUCTION

The Nature of Majority Rule

Majority rule is a fundamental principle in the governing and running of companies. How the majority is arrived at is sometimes a complex issue. The idea that each shareholder has one vote soon gives way in the typical company limited by shares to counting votes in accordance with the number of shares held (Companies Act 1985, s 373, Table A, regs 51, 52). There are, however, certain exceptions to the principle that a company limited by shares is run in accordance with the wishes of those who have the major investment stake.

(1) A company will, generally, be run by its directors and in a dispute between the directors and the majority of the shareholders, the court is likely to support the directors (pp 410ff). This, however, is likely to be only a temporary exception to the majority rule principle, because the majority may replace the board with other members who are more compliant to the wishes of the majority (s 303, although note that the dismissed directors' right to sue for breach of contract is preserved — s 303(5) — and this may seriously inhibit any dismissal).

(2) The company's constitution may give one or more shareholders enhanced voting rights. This will usually reflect the significance of the person whose idea or business represented the first major investment of the company. Alternatively, voting rights may be altered to meet particular contingencies (eg to resist dismissal as a director — see *Bushell v Faith*,[1] p 318).

(3) Shares may be issued with no voting rights.

(4) The constitution may structure voting rights so as to provide for one vote per share for say 1,000 shares, one vote per 10 shares for the next 1,000 and so on (in order to limit the influence of large shareholders). There are many examples of this in earlier cases (see eg *Moffat v Farquhar*,[2] and *Pender v Lushington*).[3]

Thus, while companies may be run contrary to the wishes of those holding the majority of the shares (the idea of the oppressed majority), in the main, it will be a minority that suffers where there is a dispute between shareholders as to the path to be followed by the company. At what point, if at all, does or should the law step in to prevent the company from acting in accordance with the wishes of the majority?

---

1 [1970] AC 1099, [1970] 1 All ER 53
2 (1878) 7 Ch D 591 (see p 324)
3 (1877) 6 Ch D 70 (see p 314)

The Procedural and Substantive Problems of the Minority

Certain points are clear. Thus, if the majority, through the directors, are planning to cause the company to act contrary to its objects clause, a minority shareholder can act against this (Companies Act 1985, s 35(2)). It is likely that an injunction will also be obtainable where the company is about to be conducted along some criminal path, although a distinction may need to be drawn between some proposed crimes where the court would not intervene and others where it would. What, however, where the company's proposed action is neither ultra vires nor criminal, but something which the minority is convinced is deeply flawed and a danger to the company's future? At this point, we need to observe the inherent procedural and substantive problems with which a minority shareholder in a company is faced. The substantive problem stems simply from the fact of being in the minority in circumstances where majority rule is the governing principle. Given that there will often be a wide range of potentially viable courses of action open to a company, the normal onus on a minority, successfully to oppose the plans of the majority is even heavier in the case of a dispute as to the right business course for a company. One person's anticipated disaster may easily be another's dream success.

The procedural problem stems from the form of any proposed litigation. The minority will, in general, be objecting to a course of action which, in law, will be taken by the company. Technically, therefore, the victim of any disaster will be the company and, thus, to satisfy the normal rules of civil procedure, the company must take the appropriate action to prevent the expected disaster. But how does a company litigate? At the instance of its majority through the directors!

So, in a nutshell, the problem for the minority is to convince the court that it is not simply in disagreement with the proposed course of action. The impending disaster must be observable by all, or at least, most, reasonable people. The issue must be beyond what might be described simply as a matter of business judgement. If this can be done, the procedural problem remains, although, as we shall see, the minority will be assisted to litigate on behalf of the company where the latter is under the control of those who are propelling the company to disaster.

It may help at this stage to broaden our vision to include the case of things having already gone wrong. There is, of course, an important difference between seeking to prevent what is believed to be a disastrous course of action, and seeking compensation for the consequences of a disastrous decision, but it is helpful to see where the court has drawn the line in the latter instance. If defendant directors have been held liable to compensate the company where the latter was directed along a particular course of action, a minority seeking to enjoin a similar course of action will at least have got a foot in the door of the court. The minority might have established a necessary, even if hardly a sufficient condition for a successful court action.

Another reason to view compensation and injunction cases at the same time is the close legal similarity between authorisation for future conduct and ratification of past conduct. Directors wanting the company to undertake a particular venture may seek the support of the shareholders. If the latter agree (probably by resolution) the directors will enjoy some (possibly total) protection if things go badly. If, without such an authorising resolution, the directors face the threat of litigation on account of the failure of the venture, they may seek to meet that threat by asking the shareholders to ratify their decision, in effect to ratify away the company's claim for compensation. And, in the case of both authorising and ratifying resolutions, the directors themselves, will vote *as shareholders*. Thus, they themselves will be assisting (quite possibly decisively) the authorising or ratifying of conduct which turns out to be, or which was, disastrous for the company. In both instances, the minority will face the same task of seeking to convince the court that the votes of the directors on the respective resolutions should be ignored, and to allow the wishes of the minority to prevail.

The Relevance of Directors' Duties

What are the principles on which the court will do this? We may start with quasi-certainties and ask whether directors who are proposing to act in breach of their duty to the company or who have acted in breach should be denied their voice. The answer is certainly no. We have seen examples in the previous chapter of directors' breach of duty being ratified (Source 173), being excused (Sources 163, 167, 168 — but not 170) and then, of course, we have left open the question of whether there has been a breach of duty or not (consider Sources 165, 167, 174 in the previous chapter). On the other hand, there have been breaches of duty which have led to successful suits against the directors (previous chapter, Sources 177 — where we were told that a ratifying resolution would have been sufficient to repel the suit — and 178, 179, 180 and 185 — where a ratifying resolution was or would have been useless).

The answer to this quest — insofar as there is an answer — is often revealed by the approach of the courts to the minority's procedural problem as outlined above. When the minority presents itself seeking a remedy, in effect, against the majority, the court is faced with the immediate issue of whether to allow the suit to proceed. It could be dismissed as inappropriate. If a wrong has been done to the company, the company should be the plaintiff. But this cannot always be the proper response, if only because the minority might have information of the proposed or past criminal expropriation of the company's property by the majority. The 'appropriate' proceedings would, to say the least, be highly unlikely in such circumstances.

Yet the principle — that the company should bring the action in respect of its own damage — remains fundamental. It enshrines the all-important majority rule principle and expresses a serious substantive point — a minority can engage in commercial blackmail and act out of other destructive motives and majority rule prevents this. Also, a vision has troubled the courts from time to time, if one shareholder can bring an action in respect of damage to the company, then why not many minority shareholders, leading to the spectre of a 'multiplicity' of suits all concerned with the same issue.

Majority rule not only expresses a fundamental principle, it prevents multiplicity of suits and enables the company to act informally (unconstitutionally) — something which business must be allowed to do from time to time. If all breaches of duty were to be actionable at the behest of the minority, the majority might, for example be prevented from acting quickly in the best interests of the company to ratify the holding of a meeting or to take a decision at shorter notice than permitted under the constitution. As we have seen (pp 381ff) the court encourages informal conduct on the part of the company, although there the informality is generally sanctioned by *all* the shareholders. Here, by definition, we are faced with a disagreement between the minority and the majority.

The Rule in Foss v Harbottle

Now to the legal principles. The principle that a wrong done to the company must be redressed by the company itself — that the company is the proper plaintiff — is enshrined in company law by the case of *Foss v Harbottle*.[1] Here it was alleged by the two plaintiffs that the directors of the company (the Victoria Park Company) had sold their own land to the company at a price in excess of its value. It was also alleged that the board of directors had not been properly constituted. The Vice-Chancellor upheld the defendants' demurrer (ie the plea that the suit was not well founded). The fundamental principle was expressed in the following terms:

> '... whilst the supreme governing body, the proprietors at a special general meeting assembled, retain the power of exercising the functions conferred upon them by the Act of Incorporation, it cannot be competent to individual corporators to sue in the manner proposed by the Plaintiffs on the present record. This in effect purports to be a suit by *cestui que trusts* complaining of a fraud committed or alleged to have been committed by persons in a fiduciary character. The complaint is that those trustees have sold lands to themselves, ostensibly for the benefit of the *cestui que trusts*. The proposition I have advanced is that, although the Act should prove to be voidable, the *cestui que trusts* may elect to confirm it. Now, who are the *cestui que trusts* in this case? The corporation, in a sense, is undoubtedly the *cestui que trust*; but the majority of the proprietors at a special general meeting assembled, independently of any general rules of law upon the subject, by the very terms of the incorporation in the present case, has power to bind the whole body, and every individual corporator must be taken to have come into the corporation upon the terms of being liable to be so bound. How then can this Court act in a suit constituted as this is, if it is to be assumed, for the purposes of the argument, that the powers of the body of the proprietors are still in existence, and may lawfully be exercised for a purpose like that I have suggested? Whilst the Court may be declaring the acts complained of to be void at the suit of the present Plaintiffs, who in fact may be the only proprietors who disapprove of them, the governing body of proprietors may defeat the decree by lawfully resolving upon the confirmation of the very acts which are the subject of the suit. The very fact that the governing body of proprietors assembled at the special general meeting may so bind even a reluctant minority is decisive to shew that the frame of this suit cannot be sustained whilst that body retains its functions. In order then that this suit may be sustained it must be shewn either that there is no such power as I have supposed remaining in the proprietors, or, at least, that all means have been resorted to and found ineffectual to set that body in motion.'

---

1 (1843) 2 Hare 461, 67 ER 189

It is significant to note that the Vice-Chancellor excepted from the principle cases where the body of shareholders did not have the power to ratify the wrong. He seemed there to be referring to the lack of constitutional power, but we shall observe that in the modern formulation (Source 193 at p 545), two of the exceptions to the rule in *Foss v Harbottle* are where the act in question is ultra vires (ie constitutional incapacity) or where it constitutes a fraud on the company (which nothing could empower). The Vice-Chancellor was also aware of the procedurally inhibiting effect of the principle that the company itself must sue and alluded to a general right for minority shareholders to present the company's suit where no other means was possible.

> '... Corporations like this, of a private nature, are in truth little more than private partnerships; and in cases which may easily be suggested it would be too much to hold that a society of private persons associated together in under-takings, which, though certainly beneficial to the public, are nevertheless matters of private property, are to be deprived of their civil rights, inter se, because, in order to make their common objects more attainable, the Crown or the Legislature may have conferred upon them the benefit of a corporate character. If a case should arise of injury to a corporation by some of its members, for which no adequate remedy remained, except that of a suit by individual corporators in their private characters, and asking in such character the protection of those rights to which in their corporate character they were entitled, I cannot but think that the principle so forcibly laid down by Lord Cottenham in *Wallworth v Holt*[1] (see also 17 Ves 320, per Lord Eldon) and other cases would apply, and the claims of justice would be found superior to any difficulties arising out of technical rules respecting the mode in which corporations are required to sue.'

The rule in *Foss v Harbottle* received strong support in *MacDougall v Gardiner* (1875) 1 Ch D 13, where the Court of Appeal upheld the decision of the chairman of the meeting, on a majority vote of the shareholders, to adjourn the meeting and to ignore the call by the plaintiff and other shareholders for the taking of a poll. This was an internal matter and, as an internal irregularity, was susceptible of cure by a majority vote. Even if this was a constitutional irregularity, it was a wrong to the company and

> '... it is the company, as a company, which has to determine whether it will make anything that is wrong to the company a subject-matter of litigation, or whether it will take steps itself to prevent the wrong from being done. If the majority of the company really are in favour of any particular shareholder who has been interfered with improperly, by misconduct of a director, by misconduct of a chairman, by miscarriage of a meeting or of certain shareholders at a particular date — if the company think that any shareholder has anything which ought to be made the subject of complaint, there is never any difficulty... in filing a bill in the name of the company, if the majority of the company desire it to be filed' (James LJ).

> ... if the thing complained of is a thing which in substance the majority of the company are entitled to do, or if something has been done irregularly which the majority of the company are entitled to do regularly, or if something has been done illegally which the majority of the company are entitled to do legally, there can be no use in having a litigation about it, the ultimate end of which is only that

a meeting has to be called, and then ultimately the majority gets its wishes' (Mellish LJ).

The further application of the rule in *Foss v Harbottle* can be seen from Sources 163, 188 and 193. The exceptions to the rule are enunciated in Source 189 and illustrated by Sources 190, 191 and 192. One of the exceptions appears to be where the shareholder asserts a personal right. This exception creates at least two acutely difficult problems. In the first place, were the shareholders in *MacDougall v Gardiner* not asserting a personal right (ie to call for a poll which was set out in the articles which constituted the contract between the company and the shareholders)? This should be contrasted with the approach in *Pender v Lushington*[1] (p 314). One way of attempting to distinguish these cases is to say that in *MacDougall*, the wrong was being done to the company (constitutional irregularity) and hence was subject to the majority rule principle, whereas in *Pender v Lushington*, the wrong was done by the company to the shareholder and was thus not a wrong to the company and therefore not susceptible to ratification. The problem then becomes one of distinguishing wrongs to the company from wrongs by the shareholder in breach of the latter's contract with the company.

The second problem is as to the civil litigation procedure to be adopted. If the action is by a shareholder against the company (eg *Pender v Lushington*), the action is by the shareholder as a proper plaintiff seeking redress of a wrong to the plaintiff. The company perpetrated the wrong and is, therefore, a proper defendant. The action is in representative form (Rules of the Supreme Court, Ord 15, r 12) so as to ensure that all shareholders are bound by the decision. All shareholders who share the plaintiff's position are represented by the plaintiff and all shareholders who are opposed to the plaintiff are represented by a representative shareholder defendant.

When, however, the action is one by minority shareholders bringing the action on behalf of the company, which the latter cannot bring owing to being controlled by the wrongdoers, the action looks identical — a shareholder plaintiff and the company as a defendant. Here, however, the plaintiff is only a nominal plaintiff seeking compensation for the company and the company is only a nominal defendant, put into that position because it must be a party to the proceedings but cannot be a plaintiff. Current usage now distinguishes between these very different actions by referring to that by the shareholder asserting his or her rights as a representative action and the company's action brought by a minority shareholder as a 'derivative action'. These and many related questions are discussed in what is still the leading article. Wedderburn, [1957] CLJ 194, [1958] CLJ 93.

Winding up the Company on the Just and Equitable Ground

The shareholder also has a right — derived from the common law of partnership — to petition for the winding up of the company on the grounds that this is just and equitable (s 122(1)(g) of the Insolvency Act 1986). These jurisdictions are considered in Sources 196, 197, 198 and 199.

---

1 (1877) 6 Ch D 70

The Minority Shareholder's Alternative Remedy

The development of the derivative action has clarified the procedure but much of the litigation on behalf of allegedly oppressed minority shareholders now takes place under statutory jurisdiction, the specially tailored remedy which is now contained in ss 459–461 of the Companies Act 1985 (illustrated in Sources 200–207).

PART II: THE RULE IN FLOSS *v* HARBOTTLE

SOURCE 188
Burland *v* Earle
(Privy Council 1902) [1902] AC 83; 71 LJPC 1

The action was commenced by the respondents on 7 December 1897. By their amended statement of claim they prayed for a declaration that the accumulation by the defendants of a surplus or reserve fund was *ultra vires*, and for an immediate division and distribution amongst the shareholders of all sums of money accumulated and retained as a reserve fund over and above the authorized capital stock of the company, and various other items of relief. Their Lordships will confine their attention to the points which have been discussed on these appeals. These are — (1) the formation of the rest or reserve fund; (2) the investment of it; (3) a claim by the respondents to treat Burland as a trustee of the plant and material of a certain insolvent company called the Burland Lithographic Company, which he purchased at a sale by auction and resold at an enhanced price to this company, and to make him account to the company accordingly for the profit made by the resale; (4) a question as to certain sums drawn as salaries by Burland and the appellant J H Burland.

    It is an elementary principle of the law relating to joint stock companies that the Court will not interfere with the internal management of companies acting within their powers, and in fact has no jurisdiction to do so. Again, it is clear law that in order to redress a wrong done to the company or to recover moneys or damages alleged to be due to the company, the action should primâ facie be brought by the company itself. These cardinal principles are laid down in the well-known cases of *Foss v Harbottle*[1] and *Mozley v Alston*,[2] and in numerous later cases which it is unnecessary to cite. But an exception is made to the second rule, where the persons against whom the relief is sought themselves hold and control the majority of the shares in the company, and will not permit an action to be brought in the name of the company. In that case the Courts allow the shareholders complaining to bring an action in their own names. This, however, is mere matter of procedure in order to give a remedy for a wrong which would otherwise escape redress, and it is obvious that in such an action the plaintiffs cannot have a larger right to relief than the company itself would have if it were plaintiff, and cannot complain of acts which are valid if done with the approval of the majority of the shareholders, or are capable of being confirmed by the majority. The cases in which the minority can maintain such an action are, therefore, confined to those in which the acts complained of are of a fraudulent character or beyond the powers of the company. A familiar example is where the majority are endeavouring directly or indirectly to appropriate to themselves

---

1 (1843) 2 Hare 461; 67 ER 189 (see p 532)
2 (1847) 1 Ph 90; 16 LJ Ch 217

money, property, or advantages which belong to the company, or in which the other shareholders are entitled to participate, as was alleged in the case of *Menier v Hooper's Telegraph Works*.[1] It should be added that no mere informality or irregularity which can be remedied by the majority will entitle the minority to sue, if the act when done regularly would be within the powers of the company and the intention of the majority of the shareholders is clear. This may be illustrated by the judgment of Mellish LJ in *MacDougall v Gardiner*.[2]

There is yet a third principle which is important for the decision of this case. Unless otherwise provided by the regulations of the company, a shareholder is not debarred from voting or using his voting power to carry a resolution by the circumstance of his having a particular interest in the subject-matter of the vote. This is shewn by the case before this Board of the *North-West Transportation Co Ltd v Beatty*.[3] In that case the resolution of a general meeting to purchase a vessel at the vendor's price was held to be valid, notwithstanding that the vendor himself held the majority of the shares in the company, and the resolution was carried by his votes against the minority who complained.

[The claims against the appellant were numerous, the following being taken as representative of the way the court dealt with them.]

> The next matter to which the appeal relates is the sale to the company by Burland of the lithographic plant, etc, of the Burland Lithographic Company. It appears that that company had been carrying on business in Montreal, and, having become insolvent, was wound up under the provisions of the Winding-up Act. Burland was interested in the company as a stockholder and a creditor. At the public sale by the liquidator on 10 May 1892, Burland bid for and purchased all the assets of the company in four lots. The price paid by him for lot 1 was $21,564, and he shortly afterwards sold the property comprised in that lot to the appellant company for $60,000. The property, together with some other plant purchased from another company, was subsequently sold to a company formed for the purpose at an enhanced price payable in shares, which were distributed as a bonus amongst the shareholders of the company.
>
> In these circumstances Burland has been ordered to pay to the company the sum of $38,436, being the amount of the profit realized by him on the resale. Both Courts have held that the resale was by Burland's advice and influence, and was made without disclosing to the company the price at which he had purchased. It was also held in the Court of Appeal that Burland had bought the property with the intention and for the purpose of reselling it to the company. It appears from the evidence of the respondent Earle, who was then the next largest shareholder to Burland and a director, that he was present at the sale and knew all about the transaction, and from the evidence of Gillelan that he knew what Burland had paid 'very shortly after.' There was evidence of two witnesses, Reinhold and Monk, that the price to the company was not unfair. But their Lordships do not think it necessary to pursue these topics, because they are of opinion that the relief prayed by the amended statement of claim, and granted in the Courts below, is altogether misconceived. There is no evidence whatever of any commission or mandate to Burland to purchase on behalf of the company, or that he was in any sense a trustee for the company of the purchased property. It may be that he had an intention in his own mind to resell it to the company; but it was an intention which he was at liberty to carry out or abandon at his own will.

---

1 (1874) 9 Ch App 350; 43 LJ Ch 330 (see p 541)
2 (1875) 1 Ch D 13; 45 LJ Ch 27 (see p 533)
3 (1887) 12 App Ca 589; 56 LJPC 102 (see p 509)

It may be also that a person of a more refined self-respect and a more generous regard for the company of which he was president would have been disposed to give the company the benefit of his purchase. But their Lordships have not to decide questions of that character. The sole question is whether he was under any legal obligation to do so. Let it be assumed that the company or the dissentient shareholders might by appropriate proceedings have at one time obtained a decree for rescission of the contract. But that is not the relief which they ask or could in the circumstances obtain in this suit. The case seems to their Lordships to be exactly that put by Lord Cairns in *Erlanger v New Sombrero Phosphate Co.*[1]

... There should be an order that the action be dismissed with costs in both Courts, so far as relates to (1) the questions of undrawn profits and the investment of the reserve fund; (2) the claim to the profits made by the appellant George B Burland from the sale to the company of the plant, machinery, and materials of the Burland Lithographic Company; (3) the claim against the appellant Jeffrey H Burland in respect of the sums drawn by him as salary since 28 May 1895; and (4) so far as any injunction was prayed against the defendants in the action, or any of them.

SOURCE 189
Edwards *v* Halliwell
(Court of Appeal 1950) [1950] 2 All ER 1064; [1950] WN 537

ASQUITH LJ: The main point in the appeal is whether Vaisey J, has rightly construed rule 19 of the rules of the union. The defendants contend that, even if he did rightly construe that provision, the plaintiffs are precluded, for other reasons, from obtaining the relief which they have been awarded. The only relevant part of rule 19 is the first five lines, which are:

> 'The regular contributions of employed members shall be as per tables (pp 115 and 116) and no alteration to same shall be made until a ballot vote of the members has been taken and a two-thirds majority obtained.'

In December 1943, a delegate meeting was held at which the delegates, without any ballot, let alone a ballot resulting in a two-thirds majority, purported to increase the regular contributions of employed members and also certain benefits payable to the members. The plaintiffs contend that that alteration in the contributions is a nullity because the condition precedent to its validity laid down in rule 19 had not been satisfied. They refused to pay the amount of the increase, and were threatened or actually visited with loss of their rights as union members, including that of eligibility for election to certain offices. In the action they claimed:

> 'A declaration that the alteration of the rules of the National Union of Vehicle Builders adopted at a delegate meeting in December 1943, is invalid in so far as it purports to alter the regular contributions of employed members.'

[His Lordship considered the rules of the union; held that, on construction of them, the alteration in December 1943, of the rates of contribution was invalid, and continued:]

> The other point relied on by the defendants was that, even if they were wrong on the point of construction, the court either could not, or should not, grant the plaintiffs the relief which they claim. Under this head counsel for the defendants

---

1 (1878) 3 App Ca 1218; 48 LJ Ch 73 (see p 163)

relied on the alleged principle that, when an action is brought by an individual in respect of a mere irregularity in a matter that is *intra vires* a trade union and concerns its internal management, the court will not as a rule intervene. For this purpose he conceded that a 'mere irregularity' meant something not involving fraud, oppression or unfairness. I confess I should have thought the action complained of here was strongly tinctured, not, indeed, with fraud, but with 'oppression' and 'unfairness.' Here were men who had a right not to have their contributions increased except after a ballot resulting in a two-thirds majority. This right was clearly violated. An unauthorised increase was sought to be extorted, and when they refused to pay, as they were entitled to do, severe penalties were imposed or threatened. To call this a mere informality or irregularity without any element of oppression or unfairness would be an abuse of language. When in circumstances such as I have described a remedy is sought by an individual, complaining of a particular act in breach of his rights and inflicting particular damage on him it seems to me the principle of *Foss v Harbottle*,[1] which has been so strongly relied upon by the defendants, does not apply either by way of barring the remedy or supporting the objection that the action is wrongly constituted because the union is not a plaintiff.

...

JENKINS LJ: I will pass to the argument based on the reluctance of the court to interfere with the domestic affairs of a company or association on the ground of mere irregularity in form in the conduct of those affairs, and the argument based on the more general proposition commonly called the rule in *Foss v Harbottle*. As to the contention that, even though the purported alteration of the tables of contributions was invalid, the court should not interfere because the omission to hold a ballot and obtain a two-thirds majority as required by rule 19 was a mere irregularity in point of form, in my judgment, that argument can be shortly dismissed by saying that this was not a matter of form. It was a matter of substance. The relevant part of rule 19, I conceive, was designed to protect members against increases in the rate of contributions unless those increases were agreed to by a particular majority of members on a vote obtained in a particular way — that is to say, a two-thirds majority on a ballot vote. It seems to me that the executive committee's disregard of that express provision in the rules was a wrong done to each individual member on a point of substance.

...

The rule in *Foss v Harbottle*, as I understand it, comes to no more than this. First, the proper plaintiff in an action in respect of a wrong alleged to be done to a company or association of persons is *prima facie* the company or the association of persons itself. Secondly, where the alleged wrong is a transaction which might be made binding on the company or association and on all its members by a simple majority of the members, no individual member of the company is allowed to maintain an action in respect of that matter for the simple reason that, if a mere majority of the members of the company or association is in favour of what has been done, then *cadit quæstio*. No wrong had been done to the company or association and there is nothing in respect of which anyone can sue. If, on the other hand, a simple majority of members of the company or association is against what has been done, then there is no valid reason why the company or association itself should not sue. In my judgment, it is implicit in the rule that the matter relied on as constituting the cause of action should be a cause of action properly belonging to the general body of corporators or members of the

---

1 (1843) 2 Hare 461; 67 ER 189 (see p 532)

company or association as opposed to a cause of action which some individual member can assert in his own right.

The cases falling within the general ambit of the rule are subject to certain exceptions. It has been noted in the course of argument that in cases where the act complained of is wholly *ultra vires* the company or association the rule has no application because there is no question of the transaction being confirmed by any majority. It has been further pointed out that where what has been done amounts to what is generally called in these cases a fraud on the minority and the wrongdoers are themselves in control of the company, the rule is relaxed in favour of the aggrieved minority who are allowed to bring what is known as a minority shareholders' action on behalf of themselves and all others. The reason for this is that, if they were denied that right, their grievance could never reach the court because the wrongdoers themselves, being in control, would not allow the company to sue. Those exceptions are not directly in point in this case, but they show, especially the last one, that the rule is not an inflexible rule and it will be relaxed where necessary in the interests of justice.

There is a further exception which seems to me to touch this case directly. That is the exception noted by Romer J, in *Cotter v National Union of Seamen*.[1] He pointed out that the rule did not prevent an individual member from suing if the matter in respect of which he was suing was one which could validly be done or sanctioned, not by a simple majority of the members of the company or association, but only by some special majority, as, for instance, in the case of a limited company under the Companies Act, a special resolution duly passed as such. As Romer J, pointed out, the reason for that exception is clear, because otherwise, if the rule were applied in its full rigour, a company which, by its directors, had broken its own regulations by doing something without a special resolution which could only be done validly by a special resolution could assert that it alone was the proper plaintiff in any consequent action and the effect would be to allow a company acting in breach of its articles to do *de facto* by ordinary resolution that which according to its own regulations could only be done by special resolution. That exception exactly fits the present case inasmuch as here the act complained of is something which could only have been validly done, not by a simple majority, but by a two-thirds majority obtained on a ballot vote. In my judgment, therefore, the reliance on the rule in *Foss v Harbottle* in the present case may be regarded as misconceived on that ground alone.

I would go further. In my judgment, this is a case of a kind which is not even within the general ambit of the rule. It is not a case where what is complained of is a wrong done to the union, a matter in respect of which the cause of action would primarily and properly belong to the union. It is a case in which certain members of a trade union complain that the union, acting through the delegate meeting and the executive council in breach of the rules by which the union and every member of the union are bound, has invaded the individual rights of the complainant members, who are entitled to maintain themselves in full membership with all the rights and privileges appertaining to that status so long as they pay contributions in accordance with the tables of contributions as they stood before the purported alterations of 1943, unless and until the scale of contributions is validly altered by the prescribed majority obtained on a ballot vote. Those rights, these members claim, have been invaded. The gist of the case is that the personal and individual rights of membership of each of them have been invaded by a purported, but invalid, alteration of the tables of contributions. In those

---

1 [1929] 2 Ch 58; 98 LJ Ch 323

circumstances, it seems to me the rule in *Foss v Harbottle* has no application at all, for the individual members who are suing sue, not in the right of the union, but in their own right to protect from invasion their own individual rights as members.

SOURCE 190
Atwool *v* Merryweather
[1867] LR 5 Eq 464n; 37 LJ Ch 35

In proceedings entitled *East Pant du United Lead Mining Co (Limited) v Merryweather*,[1] the Vice-Chancellor (Sir W Page Wood) held as follows:

In this case a numerous portion of the shareholders appear to have been of opinion that the mine mentioned in the pleadings has been improperly purchased; 600 shares have been allotted to the defendant, Merryweather, as part of the consideration for the purchase of this mine, and the bill seeks to set the whole transaction aside. But there does not seem to have been any regular authority for filing the bill on the part of the company; at any rate, there was no resolution to sanction the institution of the suit.

A general meeting of the shareholders has been held since the rising of the Court for the Vacation, for the purpose of ascertaining their opinion as to the prosecution of the suit. The majority of those present were in favour of proceeding with it, but upon a poll being demanded on an amendment, proposing that it should be discontinued, and the whole matter, including all questions as to costs, referred to the arbitration of a gentleman at Liverpool, the amendment was carried, but only by means of Merryweather's votes, in respect of his 600 shares. Without his votes there would have been a majority in favour of the original resolution to adopt the bill. The votes of the directors were equally divided; so that, in substance, a considerable body of shareholders were against the bill.

Then comes the question, has the company now sanctioned the suit? To decide that it has done so would be to discard Mr Merryweather's votes, and to do that would in effect be to decide now on this application the question at issue in the suit. But if I assume, as upon this motion I must assume, that Mr Merryweather was entitled to the 600 shares which he actually holds in the company, the further question occurs, has he a right to vote in respect of such shares upon a question in which he is personally interested? Now, as to the management of the company by the board, no director is entitled to vote as a director in respect of any contract in which he is interested; but the case is different when he acts as one of the whole body of shareholders. The shareholders of one company may have dealings with interests in other companies, and therefore it would be manifestly unfair to prevent an individual shareholder from voting as a shareholder in the affairs of the company. At a general meeting, therefore, Mr Merryweather's votes must be held to be good so long as he continues to hold his shares. Further than this the Court cannot be asked how to give an opinion, for to do so would be to decide the very question at issue in the cause.

A fresh bill was presented, this time in the name of the individual shareholder suing on behalf of himself and all other shareholders apart from the defendants.

SIR W PAGE WOOD VC: I think that, upon principle, a contract of this kind

---

1 (1864) 2 H&M 254; 71 ER 460

cannot stand, and that there is not such a defect in the constitution of the suit as would be fatal according to the authority of *Foss v Harbottle*.[1]

Looking at the facts as they come out, I am clearly of opinion that this arrangement, by which Merryweather was to have £4000 and Whitworth £3000, was concealed from everybody, and that Merryweather assisted in that concealment by allowing his name to appear as the sole vendor, and taking the purchase-money.

Upon such a transaction the Court will hold that the whole contract is a complete fraud.

...

With regard to the frame of the suit, a question of some nicety arises how far such relief can be given at the instance of a shareholder on behalf of himself and other shareholders on the ground that the transaction might be confirmed by the whole body if they thought fit, and that the case would fall within *Foss v Harbottle*, according to which the suit must be by the whole company. On the previous occasion, when it was desired to take proceedings to set aside this transaction, a gentleman took upon himself to file a bill in the name of the company. A motion was made to take that bill off the file, as the person filing the bill was not the solicitor of the company, and was not authorized to file the bill, and I ordered the bill to be taken off the file. There was a majority against setting aside this transaction. The number of votes for rescinding the transaction was 324, and 344 the other way. But Merryweather, in respect of the shares obtained by this sale, which I have held cannot stand, had 78 votes, and Whitworth 28, making altogether 106 out of the 344. If I were to hold that no bill could be filed by shareholders to get rid of the transaction on the ground of the doctrine of *Foss v Harbottle*, it would be simply impossible to set aside a fraud committed by a director under such circumstances, as the director obtaining so many shares by fraud would always be able to outvote everybody else. I held on a former occasion, and I adhere to that decision, that the Court must first be satisfied that the Plaintiffs were authorized to call themselves the company, the solicitor who put the bill upon the file having no retainer under the corporate seal.

SOURCE 191
Menier *v* Hooper's Telegraph Works
(Chancery Appeals 1874) (1874) 9 Ch App 350; 43 LJ Ch 330

JAMES LJ: The case made by the bill is very shortly this: the defendants, who have a majority of shares in the company, have made an arrangement by which they have dealt with matters affecting the whole company, the interest in which belongs to the minority as well as to the majority. They have dealt with them in consideration of their obtaining for themselves certain advantages. Hooper's Company have obtained certain advantages by dealing with something which was the property of the whole company. The minority of the shareholders say in effect that the majority has divided the assets of the company, more or less, between themselves, to the exclusion of the minority. I think it would be a shocking thing if that could be done, because if so the majority might divide the whole assets of the company, and pass a resolution that everything must be given to them, and that the minority should have nothing to do with it. Assuming the case to be as alleged by the bill, then the majority have put something into their pockets at the expense of the minority. If so, it appears to me that the minority have a right to

---

1 (1843) 2 Hare 461; 67 ER 189 (see p 532)

have their share of the benefits ascertained for them in the best way in which the Court can do it, and given to them.

It is said, however, that this is not the right form of suit, because, according to the principles laid down in *Foss v Harbottle*,[1] and other similar cases, the Court ought to be very slow indeed in allowing a shareholder to file a bill, where the company is the proper Plaintiff. This particular case seems to me precisely one of the exceptions referred to by Vice-Chancellor Wood in *Atwool v Merryweather*,[2] a case in which the majority were the Defendants, the wrong-doers, who were alleged to have put the minority's property into their pockets. In this case it is right and proper for a bill to be filed by one shareholder on behalf of himself and all the other shareholders.

Therefore the demurrer ought to be overruled.

SOURCE 192
Wallersteiner *v* Moir (No 2)
(Court of Appeal 1975) 2 QB 373; [1975] 1 All ER 849

Part II — Future Costs
1. *Mr Moir's anxiety as to future costs*
This case has brought to light a serious defect in the administration of justice. Mr Moir is a shareholder in a public company. He discovered that Dr Wallersteiner had been guilty of grave misconduct in the management of the company's affairs. He tried every known way to get an inquiry held. He applied many times to the Department of Trade and Industry to appoint an inspector: but that department put him off. They suggested that he had a remedy in the courts. He applied to the Ombudsman [see The Parliamentary Commissioner Act 1967], but he could do nothing. He raised the matter at shareholders' meetings, but was abruptly cut off. The only way in which he has been able to have his complaint investigated is by action in these courts. And here he has come to the end of his tether. He has fought this case for over 10 years on his own. He has expended all his financial resources on it and all his time and labour. He has received contributions from other shareholders but these are now exhausted. He has recovered judgment for over £250,000 against Dr Wallersteiner. It may be difficult to get the money out of Dr Wallersteiner, but if it is obtained, not a penny of it will go into Mr Moir's pocket. It will all go to benefit the companies Hartley Baird Ltd and H J Baldwin & Co Ltd. Yet the litigation is by no means finished. There is yet to be fought: (i) an inquiry into the damages suffered by Hartley Baird in respect of the £50,000 transaction; (ii) the remaining issues on the counterclaim on which Dr Waller-steiner seeks to put in a defence; and (iii) an appeal to the House of Lords, if leave is obtained. There is also (iv) the cost of enforcing the existing judgment against Dr Wallersteiner. He is in Germany and it may cost much time and expense to get anything out of him. Mr Moir tells us — and I have no doubt it is true — that he has no money left with which to pay the costs in further matters. He is fearful, too, that, if he should lose on them or any of them, he may be ordered to pay personally the costs of Dr Wallersteiner on them. Even if he wins all the way through, no part of it will redound to his own benefit. It will all go to the benefit of Hartley Baird and Baldwins. His few shares might appreciate a little in value, but that is all. In this situation he appeals to this court for help in respect of the future costs of this litigation. If no help is forthcoming, all his efforts will

---

1 (1843) 2 Hare 461; 67 ER 189 (see p 532)
2 [1867] LR 5 Eq 464n; 37 LJ Ch 35 (see p 540)

have been in vain. The delaying tactics of Dr Wallersteiner will have succeeded. Mr Moir will have to give up the struggle exhausted in mind, body and estate.

We felt the force of these points. So keenly indeed that we asked the Law Society to help. They instructed Mr Peter Webster as amicus curiae. He analysed the legal position in a most illuminating manner. We are much indebted to him. He took us through the three ways in which it was suggested that Mr Moir could be protected: (1) indemnity from the company; (2) legal aid; and (3) contingency fee. As the discussion proceeded, it appeared very necessary to be clear as to the nature of Mr Moir's counterclaim. He is a minority shareholder seeking to redress a wrong done to the company.

2. *The Derivative Action*

It is a fundamental principle of our law that a company is a legal person, with its own corporate identity, separate and distinct from the directors or shareholders, and with its own property rights and interests to which alone it is entitled. If it is defrauded by a wrongdoer, the company itself is the one person to sue for the damage. Such is the rule in *Foss v Harbottle*.[1] The rule is easy enough to apply when the company is defrauded by outsiders. The company itself is the only person who can sue. Likewise, when it is defrauded by insiders of a minor kind, once again the company is the only person who can sue. But suppose it is defrauded by insiders who control its affairs — by directors who hold a majority of the shares — who then can sue for damages? Those directors are themselves the wrongdoers. If a board meeting is held, they will not authorise the proceedings to be taken by the company against themselves. If a general meeting is called, they will vote down any suggestion that the company should sue them themselves. Yet the company is the one person who is damnified. It is the one person who should sue. In one way or another some means must be found for the company to sue. Otherwise the law would fail in its purpose. Injustice would be done without redress. In *Foss v Harbottle*, Sir James Wigram V-C saw the problem and suggested a solution. He thought that the company could sue 'in the name of some one whom the law has appointed to be its representative.' A suit could be brought

> 'by individual corporators in their private characters, and asking in such character the protection of those rights to which in their corporate character they were entitled, . . .'

This suggestion found its fulfilment in the *Merryweather*[2] case which came before Sir William Page Wood V-C on two occasions. It was accepted there that the minority shareholders might file a bill asking leave to use the name of the company. If they showed reasonable ground for charging the directors with fraud, the court would appoint the minority shareholders as representatives of the company to bring proceedings in the name of the company against the wrong doing directors. By that means the company would sue in its own name for the wrong done to it. That would be, however, a circuitous course, as Lord Hatherley LC said himself, at any rate in cases where the fraud could be proved on the initial application.

To avoid the circuity, Lord Hatherley LC held that the minority shareholders themselves could bring an action in their own names (but in truth on behalf of the company) against the wrong-doing directors for the damage done by them to the company, provided always that it was impossible to get the company itself to

---

1 (1843) 2 Hare 461, 67 ER 189 (see p 532)
2 [1867] LR 5 Eq 464n; 37 LJ Ch 35 (see p 540)

sue them. He ordered the fraudulent directors in that case to repay the sums to the company, be it noted, with interest. His decision was emphatically approved by this court in *Menier v Hooper's Telegraph*[1] and *Mason v Harris*.[2] The form of the action is always 'A. B. (a minority shareholder) on behalf of himself and all other shareholders of the company' against the wrongdoing directors and the company. That form of action was said by Lord Davey to be a 'mere matter of procedure in order to give a remedy for a wrong which otherwise would escape redress': see *Burland v Earle*.[3] Stripped of mere procedure, the principle is that, where the wrongdoers themselves control the company, an action can be brought on behalf of the company by the minority shareholders on the footing that they are its representatives to obtain redress on its behalf.

I am glad to find this principle well stated by Professor Gower in *Modern Company Law*, (3rd edn 1969), p 587, in words which I would gratefully adopt:

> 'Where such an action is allowed, the member is not really suing on his own behalf nor on behalf of the members generally, but on behalf of the company itself. Although . . . he will have to frame his action as a representative one on behalf of himself and all the members other than the wrongdoers, this gives a misleading impression of what really occurs. The plaintiff shareholder is not acting as a representative of the other shareholders, but as a representative of the company. . . . In the United States . . . this type of action has been given the distinctive name of a 'derivative action', recognising that its true nature is that the individual member sues on behalf of the company to enforce rights derived from it.'

As it happens in the present case the formula has been discarded. The counterclaim by Mr Moir was prepared by a careful, learned and skilful member of the bar, Mr William Stubbs. It is not headed 'on behalf of himself and all the other shareholders.' It is just headed 'Mr J. G. Moir, plaintiff on counterclaim.' The two companies were made parties by being added to the counterclaim. The prayer is: 'Mr Moir counterclaims for' several declarations of wrongs done to the two companies and orders on Dr Wallersteiner to pay specified sums to the two companies and that he do pay the costs of Mr Moir and the two companies. No objection has been taken to that form of proceeding. No suggestion has been made that it should be amended. Quite right. Let it stand as it is. It is in accord with principle. Mr Moir sues in his own name but in reality on behalf of the companies: just as an agent may contract in his own name but in reality on behalf of his principal.

3. Indemnity
Now that the principle is recognised, it has important consequences which have hitherto not been perceived. The first is that the minority shareholder, being an agent acting on behalf of the company, is entitled to be indemnified by the company against all costs and expenses reasonably incurred by him in the course of the agency. This indemnity does not arise out of a contract express or implied, but it arises on the plainest principles of equity. It is analogous to the indemnity to which a trustee is entitled from his *cestui que trust* who is *sui juris*: see *Hardoon v Belilios*[4] and *Re Richardson, Ex parte Governors of St. Thomas's Hospital*.[5] Seeing

---

1 (1874) 9 Ch App 350; 43 LJ Ch 330 (see p 541)
2 (1897) 11 Ch D 97; 48 LJ Ch 589
3 [1902] AC 83; 71 LJPC 1 (see p 535)
4 [1901] AC 118 (HL); 70 LJPC 9
5 [1911] 2 KB 705

that, if the action succeeds, the whole benefit will go to the company, it is only just that the minority shareholder should be indemnified against the costs he incurs on its behalf. If the action succeeds, the wrongdoing director will be ordered to pay the costs: but if they are not recovered from him, they should be paid by the company. And all the additional costs (over and above party and party costs) should be taxed on a common fund basis and paid by the company: see *Simpson and Miller v British Industries Trust Ltd.*[1] The solicitor will have a charge on the money recovered through his instrumentality: see section 73 of the Solicitors Act 1974.

But what if the action fails? Assuming that the minority shareholder had reasonable grounds for bringing the action — that it was a reasonable and prudent course to take in the interest of the company — he should not himself be liable to pay the costs of the other side, but the company itself should be liable, because he was acting for it and not for himself. In addition, he should himself be indemnified by the company in respect of his own costs even if the action fails. It is a well known maxim of the law that he who would take the benefit of a venture if it succeeds ought also to bear the burden if it fails. *Qui sentit commodum sentire debet et onus.* This indemnity should extend to his own costs taxed on a common fund basis.

In order to be entitled to this indemnity, the minority shareholder soon after issuing his writ should apply for the sanction of the court in somewhat the same way as a trustee does: see *Re Beddoe, Downes v Cottam.*[2] In a derivative action, I would suggest this procedure: the minority shareholder should apply ex parte to the master for directions, supported by an opinion of counsel as to whether there is a reasonable case or not. The master may then, if he thinks fit, straightaway approve the continuance of the proceedings until close of pleadings, or until after discovery or until trial (rather as a legal aid committee does). The master need not, however, decide it ex parte. He can, if he thinks fit, require notice to be given to one or two of the other minority shareholders — as representatives of the rest — so as to see if there is any reasonable objection. (In this very case another minority shareholder took this very point in letters to us). But this preliminary application should be simple and inexpensive. It should not be allowed to escalate into a minor trial. The mast should simply ask himself: is there a reasonable case for the minority shareholder to bring at the expense (eventually) of the company? If there is, let it go ahead.

SOURCE 193
Prudential Assurance Co Ltd *v* Newman Industries Ltd (No 2)
(Court of Appeal 1982) [1982] Ch 204; [1982] 1 All ER 354

CUMMING BRUCE, TEMPLEMAN, BRIGHTMAN LJJ: . . . A derivative action is an exception to the elementary principle that A cannot, as a general rule, bring an action against B to recover damages or secure other relief on behalf of C for an injury done by B to C. C is the proper plaintiff because C is the party injured, and, therefore, the person in whom the cause of action is vested. This is sometimes referred to as the rule in *Foss v Harbottle*[3] when applied to corporations, but it has a wider scope and is fundamental to any rational system of jurisprudence. The rule in *Foss v Harbottle* also embraces a related principle, that an individual shareholder cannot bring an action in the courts to complain of an

---

1 (1923) 39 TLR 286
2 [1893] 1 Ch 557
3 (1843) 2 Hare 461; 67 ER 189 (see p 532)

irregularity (as distinct from an illegality) in the conduct of the company's internal affairs if the irregularity is one which can be cured by a vote of the company in general meeting. We are not concerned with this aspect of the rule.

The classic definition of the rule in *Foss v Harbottle* is stated in the judgment of Jenkins LJ in *Edwards v Halliwell*[1] as follows. (1) The proper plaintiff in an action in respect of a wrong alleged to be done to a corporation is, prima facie, the corporation. (2) Where the alleged wrong is a transaction which might be made binding on the corporation and on all its members by a simple majority of the members, no individual member of the corporation is allowed to maintain an action in respect of that matter because, if the majority confirms the transaction, cadit quaestio; or, if the majority challenges the transaction, there is no valid reason why the company should not sue. (3) There is no room for the operation of the rule if the alleged wrong is *ultra vires* the corporation, because the majority of members cannot confirm the transaction. (4) There is also no room for the operation of the rule if the transaction complained of could be validly done or sanctioned only by a special resolution or the like, because a simple majority cannot confirm a transaction which requires the concurrence of a greater majority. (5) There is an exception to the rule where what has been done amounts to fraud and the wrongdoers are themselves in control of the company. In this case the rule is relaxed in favour of the aggrieved minority, who are allowed to bring a minority shareholders' action on behalf of themselves and all others. The reason for this is that, if they were denied that right, their grievance could never reach the court because the wrongdoers themselves, being in control, would not allow the company to sue.

By their summons issued on 10 May 1979, Mr Bartlett and Mr Laughton invoked the rule in *Foss v Harbottle*. After some $2\frac{1}{2}$ days of argument Vinelott J dismissed the summons on 18 June 1979, not on the ground that the plaintiffs were entitled to bring a derivative action but on the ground that it was more convenient to decide that issue after the action had been tried. For reasons which we explain later we have no doubt whatever that that was a wrong decision.

Although not a party to the summons of 10 May Newman supported it. Newman was represented by leading counsel, who made a forceful statement on day 1 to the effect that, although the action was brought for the benefit of Newman, 'it is the concern of the board that the company shall not be killed by kindness.' He added that not only was it the view of the board that the action was one which they did not wish to pursue on behalf of the company but that it was quite contrary to the interests of the company that the transaction should now be the subject of any rescission or criticism. He said: 'I am therefore concerned ... that this action ... shall not proceed — a fortiori ... it should be disposed of as quickly as possible.' This protest was repeated at the close of the plaintiffs' case on day 34, when counsel formally withdrew in order to avoid needless expense.

. . .

Observe what was being said on behalf of Newman to the judge: 'any advantage to the company which this action could procure is *vastly outweighed* by harm being inflicted upon it.' This was an apparently responsible statement made by eminent leading counsel on the instructions of persons said to be the independent members of the board. The judge does not refer to this statement in his judgment; he does not say that he did not believe it; he does not say that he regarded the independent members of the board as acting under the

---

1 [1950] 2 All ER 1064; [1950] WN 537 (see p 537)

influence of Mr Bartlett. He does not seem to have asked himself the all-important question: 'Ought I to be trying a derivative action?'

. . .

At the end of the day the judge found that a fraud had been committed by Mr Bartlett and Mr Laughton against Newman. The judge then addressed his mind to the question whether the right of a shareholder to sue in a case of fraud extended beyond a case of voting control by the wrongdoers. It was not pleaded, and could not be alleged, that Mr Bartlett and Mr Laughton had voting control. The conclusion reached by the judge was that a shareholder was entitled to prosecute an action on behalf of the company if 'the interests of justice do require that a minority action should be permitted'; and that this was established in the instant case because the judge was satisfied on the evidence as a whole:

> 'that there was no way in which Prudential could have ensured that the question whether proceedings should be brought by Newman would be fairly put to the shareholders or even that a full investigation would be made into all the circumstances surrounding the transaction including in particular Mr Cooper's valuation.'

. . .

It is commonly said that an exception to the rule in *Foss v Harbottle* arises if the corporation is 'controlled' by persons implicated in the fraud complained of, who will not permit the name of the company to be used as plaintiffs in the suit: see *Russell v Wakefield Waterworks Co*. But this proposition leaves two questions at large, first, what is meant by 'control,' which embraces a broad spectrum extending from an overall absolute majority of votes at one end, to a majority of votes at the other end made up of those likely to be cast by the delinquent plus those voting with him as a result of influence or apathy. Secondly, what course is to be taken by the court if, as happened in *Foss v Harbottle*, in the *East Pant Du case*[1] and in the instant case, but did *not* happen in *Atwool v Merryweather*, the court is confronted by a motion on the part of the delinquent or by the company, seeking to strike out the action? For at the time of the application the existence of the fraud is unproved. It is at this point that a dilemma emerges. If, upon such an application, the plaintiff can require the court to assume as a fact every allegation in the statement of claim, as in a true demurrer, the plaintiff will frequently be able to outmanoeuvre the primary purpose of the rule in *Foss v Harbottle* by alleging fraud and 'control' by the fraudster. If on the other hand the plaintiff has to prove fraud and 'control' before he can establish his title to prosecute his action, then the action may need to be fought to a conclusion before the court can decide whether or not the plaintiff should be permitted to prosecute it. In the latter case the purpose of the rule in *Foss v Harbottle* disappears. Either the fraud has not been proved, so *cadit quaestio*; or the fraud has been proved and the delinquent is accountable unless there is a valid decision of the board or a valid decision of the company in general meeting, reached without impropriety or unfairness, to condone the fraud.

. . . we have no doubt whatever that Vinelott J erred in dismissing the summons of 10 May 1979. He ought to have determined as a preliminary issue whether the plaintiffs were entitled to sue on behalf of Newman by bringing a derivative action. It cannot have been right to have subjected the company to a 30-day action (as it was then estimated to be) in order to enable him to decide whether the plaintiffs were entitled in law to subject the company to a 30-day

---

1 (1864) 2 H&M 254; 71 ER 460 (see p 540)

action. Such an approach defeats the whole purpose of the rule in *Foss v Harbottle* and sanctions the very mischief that the rule is designed to prevent. By the time a derivative action is concluded, the rule in *Foss v Harbottle* can have little, if any, role to play. Either the wrong is proved, thereby establishing conclusively the rights of the company; or the wrong is not proved, so *cadit quaestio*. In the present case a board, of which all the directors save one were disinterested, with the benefit of the Schroder-Harman report, had reached the conclusion before the start of the action that the prosecution of the action was likely to do more harm than good. That might prove a sound or unsound assessment, but it was the commercial assessment of an apparently independent board.

. . .

Whether in the events which have happened Newman (more exactly the disinterested body of shareholders) will feel that it has all been well worth while, or must lick its wounds and render no thanks to those who have interfered in its affairs, is not a question which we can answer. But we think it is within the bounds of possibility that if the preliminary issue had been argued, a judge might have reached the considered view that the prosecution of this great action should be left to the decision of the board or of a specially convened meeting of the shareholders, albeit less well informed than a judge after a 72-day action.

So much for the summons of 10 May. The second observation which we wish to make is merely a comment in Vinelott J's decision that there is an exception to the rule in *Foss v Harbottle* whenever the justice of the case so requires. We are not convinced that this is a practical test, particularly if it involves a full-dress trial before the test is applied. On the other hand we do not think that the right to bring a derivative action should be decided as a preliminary issue upon the hypothesis that all the allegations in the statement of claim of 'fraud' and 'control' are facts, as they would be on the trial of a preliminary point of law. In our view, whatever may be the properly defined boundaries of the exception to the rule, the plaintiff ought at least to be required before proceeding with his action to establish a prima facie case (i) that the company is entitled to the relief claimed, and (ii) that the action falls within the proper boundaries of the exception to the rule in *Foss v Harbottle*. On the later issue it may well be right for the judge trying the preliminary issue to grant a sufficient adjournment to enable a meeting of shareholders to be convened by the board, so that he can reach a conclusion in the light of the conduct of, and proceedings at, that meeting.

. . .

SOURCE 194
Smith *v* Croft
(Chancery Division 1987) [1986] 1 WLR 580; [1986] 2 All ER 551

WALTON J: This is a minority shareholders' action, claiming, putting it for present purposes extremely shortly, that its directors in whose hands under its articles of association the decision lies, have paid themselves out of the assets of the company wholly excessive remuneration. The defendants to the action are the present members of the board of the company concerned, certain companies to whom, in substance, the members of the board have from time to time directed their remuneration to be paid, or payment to which, having regard to their connection with the personal defendants, must be equated with such remuneration, and lastly, of course, the company itself.

In these proceedings, the plaintiffs, following a procedure suggested and sanctioned by the judgment of the Court of Appeal in *Wallersteiner v Moir (No 2)*,[1] applied ex parte to the master for an order that the company itself (on whose behalf ultimately the action is brought) should indemnify them against their own costs of the action and any costs which they might, if the action failed, be ordered to be paid by them, down to the conclusion of discovery and inspection of documents.

It is, of course, not for me to question the correctness of the decision of the Court of Appeal in *Wallersteiner v Moir*, but I may observe that the justice of an order which may throw upon a company which, in the event, is proved to have no cause of action whatsoever against the other defendants, who may prove to be completely blameless, the entire costs of an action which it did not wish to be prosecuted, is extremely difficult to comprehend. The real injustice of the situation lies in the encouragement which the Court of Appeal gave to the application for such an order being made at the commencement of the action, at a time when, of necessity, the plaintiffs believe that they have a good case, and will with hand on heart swear that they have, and before the completion of discovery and inspection, which may well show that their beliefs, though honestly enough held, are not in fact well-founded. It is to be observed that in *Wallersteiner v Moir* the application was made at a late stage in the proceedings, after Mr Moir (who was the plaintiff by counterclaim) has already substantially succeeded, but who had no powder and shot left to finish the battle. The manifest justice of such an order in favour of a person in such a position is plain enough.

I think that the matters of difficulty which arise in practice are as follows: (i) Should, in a normal case, the order be made ex parte? (ii) How much, if anything, relating to the evidence put before the court by the plaintiffs should be disclosed to the company? (iii) What is the proper test when deciding such an order should be made or not?

. . . the situation appears to me to become one very close to the situation in the old days when the Chancery Court was dealing with motions. Of course there is no room for a mini-trial, of course the court has no ability at this stage to decide the truth of the plaintiffs' allegations. What, however, it can and should do is to look at all the facts, firstly those which are common ground, then those alleged by the plaintiffs but denied by the company, and then those alleged by the company but denied by the plaintiffs, and make up its mind. The standard suggested by Buckley LJ was that of an independent board of directors exercising the standard of care which prudent businessmen would exercise in their own affairs. Would such an independent board consider that it ought to bring the action?

. . . the company, and all its shareholders, have benefited greatly from the efforts of the present board, even if the shareholders were to take the view that the directors had been extremely well paid for their efforts. Could it possibly be the view of an independent board of directors that this success should be jeopardised by the commencement of such an action as the present one which (a) in any event would have the effect of tying up an extremely large part of the time of the members of the board, when they might be required urgently elsewhere to deal with the monitoring of film production, which takes place all over the world? and (b) might well have the effect of causing the company to lose the services of its key executive? This would, indeed, be what was accurately described in *Prudential Assurance Co Ltd v Newman Industries Ltd (No 2)*[2] as killing the company by kindness.

---

1 [1975] 2 QB 373; [1975] 1 All ER 849 (see p 542)
2 [1982] Ch 204; [1982] 1 All ER 354 (see p 545)

This must be a matter of impression, but it seems to me that any well advised independent board would very probably come to the conclusion that the benefits to the company of retaining the services of the relevant executives far outweighed any long-term benefit to be obtained by pursuing any such action, even if wholly well-founded.

I wish, finally, on this aspect of the matter to observe that there has been no question of conducting a mini-trial here. Virtually everything is common ground from a purely factual point of view. In so far as it is not common ground it has all been thoroughly investigated by Peat Marwick Mitchell & Co, and they have found that there is nothing in it. If, in like circumstances, the question of the grant of an injunction had ever been raised under the old procedure, I cannot doubt for one second what the answer would have been.

But this is by no means the end of the matter. I have earlier referred to the position of W. T. Ltd. The question now is, is W. T. Ltd a genuinely independent shareholder or not? This is asserted by the defendants, but challenged by the plaintiffs. The position is that W. T. Ltd is the subsidiary of an extremely well-known, reputable, long established financial institution, which provides a range of merchant banking services, and which has over a period in excess of 25 years specialised in the provision of loan moneys, by way of loan or equity capital, to unquoted companies. The chairman has been an executive director of this company for more than 20 years, and he represents that company, and its subsidiaries, in this case of course W. T. Ltd, on the boards of a considerable number of companies. This is how the chairman comes to be on the board of the company, since W. T. Ltd has held its shares therein for some considerable time.

Of course the chairman is a party to these proceedings, not because it is alleged he has had anything in the nature of excessive remuneration, or anything of that nature, but because he has supported the other members of the board, this being equated with a conspiracy. Is this sufficient to brand W. T. Ltd a shareholder which is not independent? Before answering that question, it is, I think, essential to know why, in this particular instance W. T. Ltd is opposing the continuation of the present proceedings. If, for example, its sole reason for doing so was because an attack was being made on its chairman, then one might hesitate as to whether the reason for its opposition was grounded on reasons which, good, bad or indifferent, W. T. Ltd thought was genuinely in its own best interests as a company, or whether, on the other hand, it was motivated by purely personal considerations.

It is, I think, quite clear from the evidence on this point that W. T. Ltd does indeed support the executive directors throughout, but for the important reason that, in its view 'without them our investment would be valueless'. That is a view which W. T. Ltd or its holding company has formed, and, as I have already indicated, it appears to me an eminently reasonable and practical conclusion, obviously one taken in the best interests of W. T. Ltd itself.

In these circumstances, I see no reason whatsoever when considering whether a *Foss v Harbottle*[1] action has any real prospect of success not to take into account the views of by far the largest shareholder in the company. Accordingly, it appears to me quite clear that this is certainly an action which, even if it is allowed to proceed at all, should not be allowed to proceed against the express wish of the holders of the majority of the independently held shares at the expense of the company.

---

1 (1843) 2 Hare 461; 67 ER 189 (see p 532)

. . .

It therefore appears to me that in order to hold the balance as fairly as may be in the circumstances between plaintiffs and defendants, it will be incumbent on the plaintiffs applying for such an order to show that it is genuinely needed, ie that they do not have sufficient resources to finance the action in the meantime. If they have, I see no reason at all why this extra burden should be placed on the company. And in this connection I think the master ought to take a very broad view. The present action is as much for this benefit of Mr Hill's company as it is for the nominal plaintiffs, and I think the master ought to have taken their resources into consideration as well.

Naturally enough, no such evidence was in fact placed in front of the master, as nobody had been alerted to such a point, which, indeed, was first submitted to me by counsel for the ninth defendant, but which once submitted must be seen to be crystal clear. The master did only order the payment of 60 per cent of the taxed costs from time to time. In principle, I think he was right in this, because if an order is made for complete payment, then there will be no spur of any description on the plaintiffs to proceed with the action. I can envisage a case where the action might ultimately be dismissed for want of prosecution, and yet the company will have had to pay out vast sums in costs. Some spur is required: of course, the precise amount of the spur will as before depend upon the pecuniary situation of the plaintiffs. A spur of a mere 10 per cent to a genuinely poverty stricken individual may well be quite enough. To somebody merely hard up, much much more may be required. It must in the end all rest on the individual circumstances of each case.

To conclude therefore I allow the application of the defendants to set aside the order of Master Chamberlain of 28 March 1985, and allow the defendants' appeal from his order of 11 June 1985, and dismiss the plaintiffs' appeal from that order.

In subsequent proceedings (reported as *Smith v Croft (No 3)* at [1987] BCLC 355), the court struck out the plaintiff's statement of claim. The plaintiffs had alleged that the defendant directors had taken excessive remuneration from the company and had made unjustified payments to companies with which they were associated. The plaintiffs also alleged certain breaches of the sections of the Companies Act which prohibited help being given by a company in connection with the purchase of its shares. The court held that no prima facie case had been established in connection with the alleged excessive remuneration or the payments to associated companies. However, a prima facie case was established in connection with the breach of the Companies Act provision. Establishing a prima facie case was a minimum for a minority shareholders' action on behalf of the company. The plaintiffs' claim was struck out, however, because the action was opposed by a majority of shareholders who were independent of the defendants.

KNOX J: . . . I turn now to the question whether it is right for the court to have regard to the views of the majority inside a minority which is, I assume for this purpose, in a position to bring an action to recover on behalf of the company in respect of breaches of duty by persons with overall control.

The fourth defendant and the company claim that it is; the plaintiffs claim that it is not. On the plaintiffs' view of the matter all that the court is concerned with, in cases where the exception to the rule in *Foss v Harbottle* based on frauds on the minority applies, is the single question whether the defendants have control. The

issue is highlighted by the conflicting interpretations placed by the parties on
what the Court of Appeal said in *Prudential Assurance v Newman Industries (No 2).*
Immediately after the formulation of the two matters which in the Court of
Appeal's view a plaintiff ought at least to be required to show before proceeding
with a minority shareholder's action there comes the following sentence ([1982]
1 All ER 354 at 366, [1982] Ch 204 at 222):

> 'On the latter issue it may well be right for the judge trying the preliminary
> issue to grant a sufficient adjournment to enable a meeting of shareholders
> to be convened by the board, so that he can reach a conclusion in the light
> of the conduct of, and proceedings at, that meeting.'

Counsel for the plaintiffs submitted that the purpose of that adjournment was
to enable the courts to discern whether the defendants had control. I reject that
submission. In my judgment the concern of the Court of Appeal in making that
statement was to secure for the benefit of a judge deciding whether to allow a
minority shareholder's action on behalf of a company to go forward what was
described as the commercial assessment whether the prosecution of the action
was likely to do more harm than good or, as it was put originally by counsel for
Newman Industries, to kill the company by kindness (see [1982] 1 All ER 354 at
366, [1982] Ch 204 at 221). The whole tenor of the Court of Appeal's judgment
was directed at securing that a realistic assessment of the practical desirability of
the action going forward should be made and should be made by the organ that
had the power and ability to take decisions on behalf of the company. Also the
question of control pure and simple hardly admitted of any doubt in that
particular case.

Counsel for the plaintiffs submitted in the alternative that what the Court of
Appeal said was obiter. This I accept, but it was clearly a carefully considered
statement contrasting with the express acknowledgment that they had had little
argument on the proper boundaries of the exception to the rule in *Foss v
Harbottle* and were therefore not making any definitive statement on that subject,
and I propose to follow what I understand to be the true construction of this
statement albeit obiter, unless there is other authority binding on me the other
way.

As to that counsel for the plaintiffs submitted that no reported authority held
that in a case falling within the fraud on a minority exception to the rule in *Foss
v Harbottle* the court should go beyond seeing whether the wrongdoers are in
control and count heads to see what the other shareholders, ie those other than
the plaintiffs and the wrongdoers, think should be done. I accept that in many
reported cases the court has not gone on to the second stage. *Mason v Harris*
(1879) 11 Ch D 97 is one such case, and there are modern examples too, such as
Pavlides v Jensen [1956] 2 All ER 518, [1956] Ch 565 and *Daniels v Daniels* [1978]
2 All ER 89, [1978] Ch 406. But the fact that such an investigation was not
conducted is not conclusive that it could not be conducted, more especially in
the absence of any argument on this precise point. An investigation for
interlocutory purposes of the propriety of the exercise of voting power in
connection with the proposed prosecution of a minority shareholder's action was
conducted by Megarry V-C in *Estmanco (Kilner House) Ltd v Greater London Council*
[1982] 1 All ER 437, [1982] 1 WLR 2. In that case he permitted the action to
proceed, but counsel for the company (Mr Aldous QC) submitted that the
careful scrutiny to which the propriety of the shareholders' voting activities was
subjected is of itself an indication of the significance that the court in a proper
case will attach to it. This I accept. Another indication in the same direction is

Walton J's reaction in the earlier proceedings. He said this ([1986] 2 All ER 551 at 560, [1986] BCLC 207 at 218):

> 'This is, of course, not an application to strike out the action on the grounds that it cannot be justified as a minority shareholders' action, but quite clearly the same kind of considerations apply. If the majority of the independent shareholders do not wish the action to be continued, clearly the court will not sanction its continuance and certainly not at the expense of the company.'

I accept that this is only by way of obiter for that particular question was not argued at that stage or before Walton J, but it represents the reaction of a judge very experienced in this field. In my judgment the word 'control' was deliberately placed in inverted commas by the Court of Appeal in *Prudential Assurance Co Ltd v Newman Industries Ltd (No 2)* [1982] 1 All ER 354 at 362 [1982] Ch 204 at 219, because it was recognised that voting control by the defendants was not necessarily the sole subject of investigation. Ultimately the question which has to be answered in order to determine whether the rule in *Foss v Harbottle* applies to prevent a minority shareholder seeking relief as plaintiff for the benefit of the company is: 'Is the plaintiff being prevented improperly from bringing these proceedings on behalf of the company?' If it is an expression of the corporate will of the company by an appropriate independent organ that is preventing the plaintiff from prosecuting the action he is not improperly but properly prevented and so the answer to the question is No. The appropriate independent organ will vary according to the constitution of the company concerned and the identity of the defendants who will in most cases be disqualified from participating by voting in expressing the corporate will.

Finally on this aspect of the matter I remain unconvinced that a just result is achieved by a single minority shareholder having the right to involve the company in an action for recovery of compensation for the company if all the other minority shareholders are for disinterested reasons satisfied that the proceedings will be productive of more harm than good. If the argument of counsel for the plaintiffs is well founded, once control by the defendants is established the views of the rest of the minority as to the advisability of the prosecution of the suit are necessarily irrelevant. I find that hard to square with the concept of a form of pleading originally introduced on the ground of necessity alone in order to prevent a wrong going without redress.

I therefore conclude that it is proper to have regard to the views of independent shareholders. In this case it is common ground that there would be no useful purpose served by adjourning to enable a general meeting to be called. For all practical purposes it is quite clear how the votes would be cast, and that I described at the outset of this judgment. The questions therefore remain 'What is the test of independence' and 'Does Wren Trust pass it?'.

On the former, counsel for the plaintiffs submitted I should apply the test formulated in *Re Hellenic & General Trust Ltd* [1975] 3 All ER 382, [1976] 1 WLR 123 by analogy. That decision was concerned with a scheme of arrangement and was accepted by counsel not to be direct authority, but he suggested that the passage in the judgment of Templeman J provides appropriate guidance. He said ([1975] 3 All ER 382 at 385, [1976] 1 WLR 123 at 125):

> 'The question therefore is whether MIT, a wholly owned subsidiary of Hambros, formed part of the same class as the other ordinary shareholders. What is an appropriate class must depend on the circumstances but some general principles are to be found in the authorities. In *Sovereign Life*

Assurance Co v Dodd [1982] 2 QB 573 the Court of Appeal held that for the purposes of an arrangement affecting the policy-holders of an assurance company the holders of policies which had matured were creditors and were a different class from policy-holders whose policies had not matured. Lord Esher MR said ([1892] 2 QB 573 at 580): ". . . they must be divided into different classes . . . because the creditors composing the different classes have different interests; and, therefore, if we find a different state of facts existing among different creditors which may differently affect their minds and their judgment, they must be divided into different classes." Bowen LJ said ([1892] 2 QB 573 at 583): "It seems plain that we must give such a meaning to the term 'class' as will prevent the section being so worked as to result in confiscation and injustice, and that it must be confined to those persons whose rights are not so dissimilar as to make it impossible for them to consult together with a view to their common interest." Vendors consulting together with a view to their common interest in an offer made by a purchaser would look askance at the presence among them of a wholly owned subsidiary of the purchaser.'

Counsel for the fourth defendant (Mr Oliver QC), on the other hand, took me through a line of authority regarding the efficacy of resolutions passed by or with the help of votes whose validity was impugned. From *Allen v Gold Reefs of West Africa Ltd* [1900] 1 Ch 656, [1900-3] All ER Rep 746 onwards there has been applied a test whether the votes in question were exercised bona fide for the benefit of the company as a whole. The generality of the test has led to differences of judicial opinion on the result of applying it to a particular set of facts, notably in that particular case. That is further illustrated by the different results reached on not very dissimilar facts in *Brown v British Abrasive Wheel Co Ltd* [1919] 1 Ch 290 and *Sidebottom v Kershaw Leese & Co Ltd* [1920] 1 Ch 154. In my judgment in this case votes should be disregarded if, but only if, the court is satisfied either that the vote or its equivalent is actually cast with a view to supporting the defendants rather than securing benefit to the company, or that the situation of the person whose vote is considered is such that there is a substantial risk of that happening. The court should not substitute its own opinion but can, and in my view should, assess whether the decision-making process is vitiated by being or being likely to be directed to an improper purpose.

In general terms I would seek to apply the test applied by the Court of Appeal in *Allen v Gold Reefs of West Africa Ltd* but it seems to me possible to formulate a more particular one in the circumstances of this case. The analogy with schemes of arrangement and *Re Hellenic & General Trust Ltd* is a good deal less compelling. Moreover the application of such a test as I have indicated should prevent any risk of the danger that counsel for the plaintiffs relied on, of the resolution which prevents proceedings being brought on behalf of the company being itself treated as a fraud on the minority.

The question thus arises whether Wren Trust's decision, which is the equivalent of a vote, passes the test or is vitiated by being directed to an improper purpose.

. . .

Counsel for the plaintiffs (Mr Potts QC) relied on evidence that showed that Wren Trust has been described as an associate of the executive directors. I accept that there is evidence that Wren Trust sided with the executive directors in the boardroom tussle that resulted in Mr Garrett's resignation as a director of the company and could properly be described as associates in that context, and that there is evidence that Gresham Trust itself was involved in the share transactions leading up to Mr Garrett's resignation. I nevertheless remain firmly of the view that there is no sufficient evidence that in relation to the present question whether these proceedings should continue, Wren Trust has reached its conclusion on any grounds other than reasons genuinely thought to advance the company's interests. It is not for me to say whether the decision itself is right or wrong. It is for me to say whether the process by which it was reached can be impugned, and I hold that it cannot. Nor do I consider that in the circumstances there is shown to have been a substantial risk of Wren Trust's vote having been cast in order to support the defendants as opposed to securing the benefit of the company.

That conclusion means that I accede to the fourth defendant's and the company's motions and direct that the statement of claim be struck out. Before parting with the case I should like to say a further word about the procedure.

. . .

First, I consider there may well be a much stronger case for requiring a prospective plaintiff to have the onus of establishing that this case falls within the exceptions to the rule in *Foss v Harbottle* (1843) 2 Hare 461, 67 ER 189 or outside it altogether than there is for putting the same onus on him to show that the company would be likely to succeed if it brought the action. On the latter it might well be appropriate to apply the usual test under RSC Ord 18, r 19 and the inherent jurisdiction which puts the onus on the defendants to show the case is effectively unarguable.

Second, I consider it would be highly desirable for applications in respect of costs under *Wallersteiner v Moir (No 2)* [1975] 1 All ER 849, [1975] QB 373 procedure to be made at the same time as the plaintiff establishes whatever it is that he does have to establish. A great deal of expense has been caused in this case by the piecemeal way in which the matter has proceeded.

Third I believe that it would be helpful for there to be specific procedure laid down, whether by way of rules of court or practice direction I know not, for the initiation and prosecution of actions by minority shareholders to recover on behalf of a company.

SOURCE 195
Barrett *v* Duckett
(Court of Appeal) [1995] 1 BCLC 243

PETER GIBSON LJ: . . . on 13 November 1992 Christopher[1] petitioned in the Leicester County Court for the compulsory winding up of Travel. He did so on two grounds: one was that the company was insolvent and unable to pay its debts as they fell due; the other was on the just and equitable ground because of the deadlock position in which the company found itself. The petition has been advertised, but no creditor has appeared to support it. Mrs Barrett[2] opposes the petition. The petition has been transferred to the High Court on the order of Vinelott J.

An estimated statement of affairs at 29 October 1992 shows that Travel's assets at their book value exceed its liabilities by £46,743.

. . .

On 11 March 1993 this action was commenced by the issue of a specially indorsed writ. By the statement of claim Mrs Barrett states that she 'brings this

---

1 Christopher Duckett, one of the directors of Travel and a defendant in the reported proceedings
2 The plaintiff, a minority shareholder in Travel

action in a representative capacity on behalf of Travel and/or on behalf of herself' and 'is an oppressed minority shareholder and is entitled to bring this action to recover on behalf of Travel and/or on behalf of herself.' Relief is sought under the following heads:

(a) against Christopher, damages of at least £217,000, the moneys diverted into the Post Office Giro accounts;

(b) against Christopher and/or Janet,[1] who is alleged to be a de facto director of Travel, damages of at least £268,000 being as to £27,000 one year's pay to Janet and as to the remainder remuneration paid to Christopher between 1986/87 and 1990/91, no resolution having been passed by Travel for directors' remuneration;

(c) against Christopher, Janet and Coaches,[2] who are alleged to have entered into a conspiracy together; (1) damages of at least £308,000 (I have already referred to what Janet has said of this sum); (2) accounts and inquiries in respect of the transfer of assets (including confidential information) from Travel to Coaches; (3) declarations that the shares in Coaches are held for Travel and that the assets of Coaches are held for Travel;

...

On 9 June 1993 Christopher, Janet and Coaches issued their notices of motion to strike out the action or to stay it until after the hearing of the winding-up petition presented by Christopher. They did so on the basis that an alternative remedy to the derivative action existed and that Mrs Barrett is an inappropriate person to conduct such litigation on behalf of the company. Janet also applied under RSC Ord 18, r 19 to strike out the claims made against her as a de facto director. The judge rejected those claims, holding that the practical course was to list the action for hearing with the petition.

...

The general principles governing actions in respect of wrongs done to a company or irregularities in the conduct of its affairs are not in dispute:

1. The proper plaintiff is prima facie the company.

2. Where the wrong or irregularity might be made binding on the company by a simple majority of its members, no individual shareholder is allowed to maintain an action in respect of that matter.

3. There are however recognised exceptions, one of which is where the wrongdoer has control which is or would be exercised to prevent a proper action being brought against the wrongdoer: in such a case the shareholder may bring a derivative action (his rights being derived from the company) on behalf of the company.

4. When a challenge is made to the right claimed by a shareholder to bring a derivative action on behalf of the company, it is the duty of the court to decide as a preliminary issue the question whether or not the plaintiff should be allowed to sue in that capacity.

5. In taking that decision it is not enough for the court to say that there is no plain and obvious case for striking out; it is for the shareholder to establish to the satisfaction of the court that he should be allowed to sue on behalf of the company.

6. The shareholder will be allowed to sue on behalf of the company if he is bringing the action bona fide for the benefit of the company for wrongs to the company for which no other remedy is available. Conversely if the action is

---

1 Christopher's wife and, with Christopher, a director of Coaches

2 A company alleged to have been acquired to take transfer of assets from Travel (another company)

brought for an ulterior purpose or if another remedy is available, the court will not allow the derivative action to proceed.

Although Mrs Barrett is not a minority shareholder but a person holding the same number of shares as the other shareholder, Christopher, in the circumstances of this case she can be treated as being under the same disability as a minority shareholder in that as a practical matter it would not have been possible for her to set the company in motion to bring the action.

The debate before the judge and before us has largely turned on the applicability of the propositions in para 6 to the facts of the case, and because of their importance I will illustrate those propositions by reference to three authorities.

First on the necessity for the absence of an ulterior purpose, the words of Lawton LJ in *Nurcombe v Nurcombe* [1984] BCLC 557 at 562, [1985] 1 WLR 370 at 376 at apposite:

> 'It is pertinent to remember, however, that a minority shareholder's action in form is nothing more than a procedural device for enabling the court to do justice to a company controlled by miscreant directors or shareholders. Since the procedural device has evolved so that justice can be done for the benefit of the company, whoever comes forward to start the proceedings must be doing so for the benefit of the company and not for some other purpose. It follows that the court has to satisfy itself that the person coming forward is a proper person to do so.'

Second on the availability of alternative remedies, there are two authorities on the effect of liquidation in relation to a derivative action. In *Ferguson v Wallbridge* [1935] 3 DLR 66 at 83 Lord Blanesburgh delivering the judgment of the Privy Council said:

> 'in their Lordships' judgment, [the present action] could have been so maintained if the company were not in liquidation. *Cook v Deeks* ([1916] 1 AC 554) is clear authority for this. But could it be so maintained now that the company is assumed to be in liquidation? And the answer must again, as their Lordships think, be in the negative. The permissibility of the form of proceeding thus assumed, where the company concerned is a going concern, is an excellent illustration of the golden principle that procedure with its rules is the handmaid and not the mistress of justice. The form of action so authorised is necessitated by the fact that in the case of such a claim as was successfully made by the plaintiff in *Cook v Deeks* — and there is at least a family likeness between that case and this — justice would be denied to him if the mere possession of the company's seal in the hands of his opponents were to prevent the assertion at his instance of the corporate rights of the company as against them. But even in the case of a going company a minority shareholder is not entitled to proceed in a representative action if he is unable to show when challenged that he has exhausted every effort to secure the joinder of the company as plaintiff and has failed. But *cessante ratione legis, cessat lex ipsa*. So as soon as the company goes into liquidation the necessity for any such expedient in procedure disappears. Passing over the superficial difficulty that a company in compulsory liquidation cannot be proceeded against without the leave of the Court, the real complainants, the minority shareholders, are no longer at the mercy of the majority, wrongly retaining the property of the company by the strength of their votes. If the liquidator, acting at the behest of the majority, refuses when requested to take action in the name of the company against them, It

is open to any contributory to apply to the Court, [and then he refers to the Canadian statute and says:] and under s 234 of the Provincial Companies Act which corresponds to s 252 of the Imperial Statute (Companies Act, 1929 (Imp.), c. 23 [now s 112 of the Insolvency Act 1986], it is open to the Court, on cause shown, either to direct the liquidator to proceed in the company's name or on proper terms as to indemnity, and otherwise to give to the applicant leave to use the company's name as plaintiff in any action necessary to be brought for the vindication of the company's rights.'

That reasoning was applied by Walton J in *Fargro Ltd v Godfroy* [1986] BCLC 370, [1986] 1 WLR 1134. In that case a minority shareholder in a company which was deadlocked wished to bring a derivative action, alleging that the other shareholder and directors had diverted assets and opportunities belonging to the company to their own use. Before the writ was issued the company went into liquidation. When the plaintiff issued the writ, the defendants applied to strike out. The application succeeded. Walton J said ([1986] BCLC 370 at 372, [1986] 1 WLR 1134 at 1136):

'But once the company goes into liquidation the situation is completely changed, because one no longer has a board, or indeed a shareholders' meeting, which is in any sense in control of the activities of the company of any description, let alone its litigation. Here, what has happened is that the liquidator is now the person in whom that right is vested. Now, that being the case, the plaintiff can take a variety of courses. The plaintiff can ask the liquidator to bring the action in the name of the company. Doubtless, as in virtually all cases, the liquidator will require an indemnity from the persons who wish to set the company in motion against all the costs, including, of course, the costs of the defendants, which he may have to incur in bringing that action. The liquidator may ask for unreasonable terms or, on the other hand, the liquidator may be unwilling to bring the action, and under those circumstances it is always possible for the shareholders who wish the action to be brought to go to the court asking for an order either that the liquidator bring the action in the name of the company or, more usually, that they are given the right to bring the action in the name of the company, of course, against the usual type of indemnity, which will, if there is any difficulty about the matter, be settled by the court. And I think that this has been the practice and procedure for a very long time indeed.'

He then cited *Ferguson v Wallbridge* and commented ([1986] BCLC 370 at 374, [1986] 1 WLR 1134 at 1138):

'So there is clear authority in the Privy Council as to the vast distinction that there is between the position where the company is a going concern and the minority shareholders' action can be brought, and a case where when it goes into liquidation where there is no longer any necessity for bringing a minority shareholders' action. Because, subject if necessary to obtaining the directions of the court, which is in itself an excellent thing as acting as a filter against any totally wrong-headed action, the action can be brought directly in the name of the company as it should be so brought.'

In *Fargro Ltd v Godfroy* the liquidator had in fact agreed to bring the action, but it is clear from the reasoning of both Lord Blanesburgh and Walton J that even if the liquidator's views were unknown the derivative action would not be allowed to proceed. The obvious factual difference between *Fargro Ltd v Godfroy* and the present case is that Travel, unlike the company in *Fargro*, was not in liquidation at the time the derivative action was commenced. I shall return later to the question whether this difference is of crucial importance in the present case.

. . .

Mr Anthony Mann QC for Janet and Coaches and Mr Cayford for Christopher point out that the circumstances of the present case are unprecedented. In all the reported cases on derivative actions the wrongdoer has by his exercise of control over the company prevented proceedings being brought against him, whereas in the present case the alleged wrongdoer, by trying to put the company into liquidation, has attempted before the action commenced and is attempting to create a situation where the allegedly oppressed minority shareholder is no longer at the mercy of the controlling shareholder and director. In my judgment the court is entitled to view with suspicion and caution the actions of the alleged wrongdoer lest on their true interpretation they are no more than attempts to defeat or at least to defer judgment being obtained against him. But in the present case it is significant that Christopher's attempts to put the company into liquidation (i) came after a long period of deadlock during which he was frustrated in his attempt to put The Noakes or its proceeds into Travel to reduce the directors' loan account and the tax debt, (ii) followed advice from an insolvency practitioner in a well-known firm of accountants and (iii) preceded not only the commencement of the action but also any intimation that the action would be commenced.

Mr Guy for Mrs Barrett submitted that the judge was right to reject the contention that she had another available remedy through proceedings in the liquidation of Travel.

First he said that it was not certain that Travel would be wound up on Christopher's petition. But that ignores the fact that Mrs Barrett was given, but rejected, the opportunity to have Travel put into a creditors' voluntary liquidation, and whilst I accept that it is possible that the court in the exercise of its discretion would not on an opposed petition compulsorily wind up the company when the petitioner is the alleged wrongdoer, that possibility is only a live one because of her opposition. Even if she continued to oppose the petition, the court may be driven to accept that there is no alternative to a winding up, given the apparent insolvency and worsening financial position of Travel while further interest accrues to the Revenue and given the deadlock in the company.

Second, Mr Guy supported the judge's comment that there was no certainty that the liquidator would sue and that Mrs Barrett had no means of compelling him to sue. Mr Guy said that the liquidator need to incur the cost of applying to the court to sue. It is of course correct that the liquidator has a discretion. A liquidator in a compulsory liquidation can bring an action with the approval of either the liquidation committee or the court (see s 167(1) of the Insolvency Act 1986). If Mrs Barrett is aggrieved by the decision of such a liquidator, she can apply to the court under s 168(5) of the 1986 Act. In the case of a voluntary winding up, the liquidator is not obliged to obtain the sanction of the court or liquidation committee to bring any proceedings (see Sch 4, para 4 of the 1986 Act) and an aggrieved contributory has power to apply to the court under s 112(1) of the 1986 Act. But in any event it is apparent from the reasoning of Lord Blanesburgh in *Ferguson v Wallbridge* and of Walton J in *Fargro Ltd v Godfroy* that the fact that a liquidator has a discretion in relation to the bringing of an action is no answer to the objection based on the availability of an alternative remedy. No doubt the liquidator may be inhibited from pursuing claims by the shortage of available funds and may seek an indemnity from Mrs Barrett if she wants him to pursue claims which the assets available to him would not justify. But I see no injustice in that. On her own evidence she lacks the means to pursue this action further. As the company does have some money which might be used in litigating the claims, it is in my opinion manifest that it is better that the decision whether or not to use the money should be taken by an independent liquidator rather than by Mrs Barrett.

I therefore conclude that in the unusual circumstances of this case, the opportunity that Travel be put into liquidation which was offered and continues to be offered by Christopher can be said to provide an alternative remedy such as makes the derivative action inappropriate.

But the matter does not stop there. I turn to the second ground on which Mr Mann and Mr Crayford submit that this action should not be allowed to proceed, namely that Mrs Barrett has an ulterior motive which makes her an inappropriate person to bring these proceedings. On this the judge commented ([1995] 1 BCLC 73 at 82):

> 'No doubt there is ill-feeling between Mrs Barrett and Mr Duckett but that in itself cannot debar Mrs Barratt — were it to do so, most derivative actions would be frustrated.'

I see the force of that, but I am not persuaded that it is a sufficient answer to the point put against her in the light of the particular circumstances. Here I repeat what I have referred to as the salient features of this case. Personal rather than financial considerations would appear to be impelling her to pursue an action, in the outcome of which she would have no financial interest if the company were insolvent, and in preventing a winding up when that would provide the only practical means of obtaining some benefit from her shares if the company were in fact solvent.

I can well understand that Mrs Barrett is upset at what has occurred between Christopher and Carol and that she is indignant at the supplanting of Carol by Janet. But her partiality shows through all her evidence, and it is by her behaviour in relation to the claims against Carol, in contrast to the claims against Christopher and Janet, that I have become convinced that she is not pursuing this action bona fide on behalf of the company. If she had been, she would have had to sue Carol no less than Christopher in respect of diverted moneys. She claims that she did not sue Carol because Carol does not have any assets. But when Mr Guy was asked what assets Christopher had to make him worth suing, the first two items listed by Mr Guy were the jointly owned former matrimonial home in Gerrards Cross and the proceeds of The Noakes in each of which Carol retains her interest. Mr Guy sought to assure us that now that the decision had been made to sue Carol, the action would proceed against her. I am afraid that I simply do not believe that Mrs Barrett would pursue any claim against her daughter to the point of enforcing judgment: to my mind it is improbable in the extreme that she would force her daughter and grandchildren out of their home and I quite understand why she would not. Her failure to take the order making Carol a defendant any further speaks volumes. On the other hand I do not doubt that she would pursue the other defendants as far as she could, regardless of whether there is any real likelihood of recovery. This is not a satisfactory basis for an action on behalf of the company.

I am left in no doubt that this is an action which should not be allowed to proceed. Hoffmann LJ in giving leave to appeal said:

> 'As a matter of common sense, it seems arguable that the parties should not be subjected to lengthy and costly proceedings exacerbated by family hostilities when an independent liquidator might decide that the action could be settled on reasonable terms.'

I entirely agree with such argument. I hope that even now Mrs Barrett will agree to a voluntary winding up to save costs and that she will promptly give the liquidator the benefit of all the work that has been done in this case on her behalf to facilitate any proceedings which he may wish to pursue.

PART III: WINDING UP ON THE JUST AND EQUITABLE GROUND

SOURCE 196
Re Yenidje Tobacco Co Ltd
(Court of Appeal 1916) [1916] 2 Ch 426; 86 LJ Ch 1

LORD COZENS-HARDY MR: This is an appeal from a decision of Astbury J, who ordered this private company to be compulsorily wound up. I think it right to consider what is the precise position of a private company such as this and in what respects it can be fairly called a partnership in the guise of a private company.

In the present case there were two tobacco manufacturers, one Rothman and the other Weinberg. They were minded to amalgamate their business. They formed a private limited company, one certainly of a most peculiar kind. Under the constitution of that company they are the sole shareholders in the company; the only voting power is given to the 'A' shareholders, and although the holdings of the two members including 'B' shares and preference shares are unequal, one having a larger holding than the other, yet with regard to the only shares which give the power to voting, that is the 'A' shares, they each hold an equal number and consequently have equal voting rights. The articles of association provide that there shall be no casting vote, that one director shall form a quorum, and that in the event of any particular disagreement between the directors the matter in dispute shall be referred to arbitration;

. . .

In those circumstances, supposing it had been a private partnership, an ordinary partnership between two people having equal shares, and there being no other provision to terminate it, what would have been the position? I think it is quite clear under the law of partnership, as has been asserted in this Court for many years and is now laid down by the Partnership Act, that that state of things might be a ground for dissolution of the partnership for the reasons which are stated by Lord Lindley in his book on Partnership at p 657 in the passage which I will read, and which, I think, is quite justified by the authorities to which he refers: 'Refusal to meet on matters of business, continued quarrelling, and such a state of animosity as precludes all reasonable hope of reconciliation and friendly co-operation have been held sufficient to justify a dissolution. It is not necessary, in order to induce the Court to interfere, to show personal rudeness on the part of one partner to the other, or even any gross misconduct as a partner. All that is necessary is to satisfy the Court that it is impossible for the partners to place that confidence in each other which each has a right to expect, and that such impossibility has not been caused by the person seeking to take advantage of it.'

Now here we have this fact. Mr Rothman has commenced an action charging Mr Weinberg with fraud in obtaining the agreement under which he, Rothman, sold his business to the company.

. . .

The matter does not stop there. It is proved that these two directors are not on speaking terms, that the so-called meetings of the board of directors have been almost a farce or comedy, the directors will not speak to each other on the board, and some third person has to convey communications between them which ought to go directly from one to the other.

Is it possible to say that it is not just and equitable that that state of things should not be allowed to continue, and that the Court should not intervene and say this is not what the parties contemplated by the arrangement into which they entered? They assumed, and it is the foundation of the whole of the agreement that was made, that the two would act as reasonable men with reasonable courtesy and reasonable conduct in every way towards each other, and arbitration was only to be resorted to with regard to some particular dispute between the directors which could not be determined in any other way. Certainly, having regard to the fact that the only two directors will not speak to each other, and no business which deserves the name of business in the affairs of the company can be carried on, I think the company should not be allowed to continue. I have treated it as a partnership, and under the Partnership Act of course the application for a dissolution would take the form of an action; but this is not a partnership strictly, it is not a case in which it can be dissolved by action. But ought not precisely the same principles to apply to a case like this where in substance it is a partnership in the form or the guise of a private company? It is a private company, and there is no way to put an end to the state of things which now exists except by means of a compulsory order. It has been urged upon us that, although it is admitted that the 'just and equitable' clause is not to be limited to cases *ejusdem generis*, it has nevertheless been held, according to the authorities, not to apply except where the substratum of the company has gone or where there is a complete deadlock. Those are the two instances which are given, but I should be very sorry, so far as my individual opinion goes, to hold that they are strictly the limits of the 'just and equitable' clause as found in the Companies Act. I think that in a case like this we are bound to say that circumstances which would justify the winding up of a partnership between those two by action are circumstances which should induce the Court to exercise its jurisdiction under the just and equitable clause and to wind up the company.

Appeal against the winding-up order dismissed.

SOURCE 197
Re Cuthbert Cooper and Sons Limited
(Chancery Division 1937) [1937] Ch 392

SIMONDS J: The petition is to wind up a company called Cuthbert Cooper & Sons, Ltd. That company was incorporated in August 1913, it had a share capital of £10,000 divided into 10,000 shares of £1 each, and its main objects were to acquire and carry on the business of a boot-rivet and button-fastener manufacturer, formerly carried on under the style of Cuthbert Cooper & Sons. The company was formed by Mr Cuthbert Cooper and his two sons. They were the first directors — Mr Cuthbert Cooper the father, and his two elder sons, George Cooper and Charles Cooper. The share capital was originally allotted as to 5000 shares to the father, Cuthbert Cooper, and as to the remaining 5000 shares to his two elder sons equally.

The father's shares remained in his possession until his death. He died on 11 August 1930, having by his will, which was made in 1927 and proved shortly after his death, appointed as his executors his three younger sons, one of them also called Cuthbert Cooper, and the other two Stanley Cooper and Colin Cooper, to whom also he bequeathed his shareholding of 5000 shares in this company in equal shares.

It is necessary to look at the articles of association of the company to see what were the rights of the executors on the death of their father. The company was a private company which contained particularly stringent provisions with regard to the transfer and transmission of shares. Article 26 provided that the directors in their absolute uncontrollable discretion might decline to register any transfer of shares, including fully-paid shares, without assigning any reason therefor. That power of veto extended not only to transfers inter vivos, but also to the devolution of shares on the death of a holder to his executors, so that with regard to executors as well as to other transferees the directors had a power of absolute veto. The directors at all material times were the father and his two sons, and on the father's death the two sons remained as sole directors.

In the event of the directors refusing to register a transfer these courses were open to the executors of a deceased holder. They were in a position, if they thought fit, without being put on the register, to receive those very limited rights which the articles gave them — the rights to deceive dividends and rights in a winding up to such a return as their testator would have been entitled to, and I think no others. If they were not satisfied with that position, they were thrown back on the provisions of the articles which enabled them to transfer their shares which meant this. If they could find a member of the company who would purchase, they could sell. If they could not find such a member, they had to employ the somewhat elaborate machinery of the articles giving their sale notice in the ordinary way. I need not refer to it. If no member took up the notice, then they were in a position to sell to an outsider, but subject always to the qualification which the articles imposed that as to that person also the directors might exercise their veto. That was the position, as a matter of bargain entered into by their testator with those others, his sons, who had joined him in forming the company, in which the executors found themselves on the death of the testator.

It has been pressed on me in considering this case that I am to be guided by the principles which influence the Court in determining whether or not a partnership shall be wound up. I propose faithfully to follow that injunction, laid down as it is by the Court of Appeal in *Re Yenidje Tobacco Co Ltd*[1] and followed recently in *Re Davis & Collett Ltd*[2] by Crossman J. Whether it be a matter of articles of association or articles of partnership the rights of the parties are determined by those articles, and the question whether it is right for me applying here the principles of partnership to the question of dissolution to wind up this company or not largely depends on what are the contractual rights of the parties as determined by the articles of association in this case. Accordingly, when I come to consider the allegations which are made in the petition, I must be guided by what are the legal rights of the parties as determined by the bargain into which they entered.

. . . The first allegation, the first grievance under which the petitioners labour, and which is made a ground for asking me to exercise the jurisdiction of the Court and to say that it is just and equitable to wind up the company, is this, that the directors have consistently refused to register the petitioners as members. For the purpose of exercising this jurisdiction I am not going to assume that that discretion of the directors has been improperly exercised.

There is no evidence before this Court that it has been improperly exercised, and I should not be justified in assuming that it has been improperly exercised.

---

1 [1916] 2 Ch 426; 86 LJ Ch 1 (see p 561)
2 [1935] Ch 693; 104 LJ Ch 340

That is not a ground on which this Court can exercise its jurisdiction to wind up the company. I will neither assume that that discretion has been improperly exercised, nor will I assume that, if it was improperly exercised, the petitioners could not get the appropriate relief in the appropriate proceedings, which would either be by motion to rectify, or more properly, I think, since there would be disputed questions of fact, and perhaps an occasion for interrogatories or discovery, an action in the ordinary way in the Chancery Division. But, at least on a petition, I am not going to exercise my jurisdiction to wind up a company on that ground, on the footing that it is for that reason just and equitable.

As I have already said, paragraph (9) contains a number of allegations which do not appear to me to afford any ground whatever for winding-up this company. There is the suggestion, and again nothing more than the suggestion, that the petitioners, being relegated to their rights under the article of serving sale notices, may suffer because the dividends — it is the dividends which determine the price — have been reduced in the last year of the company's operations. It appears that the dividend has been reduced, but there is no allegation, much less proof, that the dividend has been unduly reduced to invade the rights of the petitioners.

In the view to which I have come on the facts of this case I hold that the petition is misconceived. I should be travelling altogether outside any case in which a winding-up has been decreed by the Court if, in circumstances such as these, I held that it was just and equitable to wind up the company. Accordingly I dismiss this petition, with costs.

SOURCE 198
Re Fildes Brothers Ltd
(Chancery Division 1970) [1970] 1 WLR 592; [1970] 1 All ER 923

MEGARRY J: This contributory's petition for a compulsory winding up order arises from an unhappy tale of two brothers and two companies. The petitioning contributory has been conveniently referred to by his first name, Brian, and the opposing contributory by his first name, Ian; and I shall adopt that usage. The two companies each carried on butchers' businesses, one wholesale and one retail, in the Manchester area; and each was a family company, the father being in effect the founder of both companies. For over a dozen years Brian, to some extent helped by Ian, ran the wholesale company, entitled J. H. Fildes & Sons Ltd; and at all material times since their mother's death in 1961, Brian and Ian held all the shares in the company equally between them, and they were the only two directors. The company fell upon hard times, however, and on 4 June 1969, it went into a creditors' voluntary liquidation.

The retail company, Fildes Bros. Ltd, is the one with which I am directly concerned. I shall call it 'the company.' This has at all material times been run by Ian, with a little intermittent assistance from Brian. Of the 1000 shares, each brother owns 499, and their wives own one each. The two brothers were at all material times the only directors of the company, and Ian is chairman of the company, with a casting vote both on the board and at meetings.

The petition is based upon a claim that it is just and equitable that the company should be compulsorily wound up. Brian's main complaints fall under three heads. First, Ian had opened a new bank account in his own name and was paying in and drawing out the company's money from it; and he had done this without consulting Brian.

. . .

Second, Brian complains that Ian will not employ him in the retail business. . . .

Third, Brian fears that Ian will run the company for his own benefit, taking all the profits by way of director's remuneration.

. . .

No authority has been cited to me in which the partnership concept has been applied to a company with one director who devotes nearly all his time to the company's business and another who does little more than attend the directors' meetings requisite to enable the company to continue in business. As I have already mentioned, Mr Settle[1] accepted that Brian had been somewhat of a sleeping partner in the company, just as Ian was somewhat of a sleeping partner (though less dormant) in the wholesale company. At the same time, the words 'just and equitable' are very wide in their scope, and I cannot say that they are incapable of embracing a case where one director is far more active in the company's affairs than the other.

I must, however, consider a further point. In *Re Cuthbert Cooper & Sons Ltd*[2] Simonds J made that Pennycuick J described in *Re K/9 Meat Supplies (Guildford) Ltd*[3] 'an extremely important extension' of the principle of the quasi-partnership cases. That extension was that in considering that principle, one must have regard to the contract between the parties as shown by the articles of association. Simonds J said:

> 'The question whether it is right for me applying here the principles of partnership to the question of dissolution to wind up this company or not largely depends on what are the contractual rights of the parties as determined by the articles of association in this case.'

(In parenthesis I may observe that the word 'largely' is omitted from the report of this case in [1937] 2 All ER 466, 468, and in the quotation from it in *Re K/9 Meat Supplies* case as reported in [1966] 3 All ER 320, 326. The reports of *Re Cuthbert Cooper & Sons Ltd* at (1937) 106 LJ Ch 250, 157 LT 546 and 53 TLR 549, however, all include the word, and I think its omission by the All England Reports must be a slip. In any case, the word seems to me to be properly included.)

In the present case, the articles do not have much bearing on what I have to decide: but as it is the contract between the parties which is of importance, then it seems to me that one must have regard not merely to what the articles say, but also to what the parties are shown to have agreed in any other manner. It cannot be just and equitable to allow one party to come to the court and require the court to make an order which disregards his contractual obligations. The same, I think, must apply to a settled and accepted course of conduct between the parties, whether or not case into the mould of a contract.

. . .

Accordingly, the question for me is whether, as matters stand today, what has been alleged in the petition and proved before me makes it just and equitable to wind up the company. Whatever grounds Ian may in the past have given Brian for the presentation of the petition, I have to decide the case in the light of the evidence now before me; and this includes the oral evidence of Ian and Brian. Mr Settle said that the court must decide this case largely on personalities. In that respect, I must say that I found Ian an impressive witness, frank, fair-minded and businesslike. Brian, on the other hand, was at times confused and not very lucid.

---

1 Counsel for the petitioner
2 [1937] Ch 392 (see p 562)
3 [1966] 1 WLR 1112; [1966] 3 All ER 320

In so far as their evidence conflicts, I prefer the evidence of Ian; and I think he will try to act honourably and properly in the management of this company. No doubt there will be differences of opinion about disputable matters; but taking the view of Ian and that I did, I do not think that he will act unfairly, especially now that he has acquired the knowledge of his duties towards his brother which this case has brought him.

Mr Settle very properly stressed that Ian's change of attitude was at the eleventh hour, and that he had given no hint of it before giving his evidence. It was, he said, a delayed repentance, with last minute concessions. I accept that, and the criticism of Ian that it implies. But I also accept Ian as a witness of sincerity: and if repentance is genuine, it is not nullified by being tardy. In my judgment, there is now no justifiable ground for Brian having such a lack of confidence in Ian as to support the making of a winding up order. Mr Settle accepts that this is not a case of deadlock, nor of exclusion; I have rejected the existence of the alleged agreement for sharing profits equally; Mr Settle accepts that the refusal to employ Brian is not enough per se, and in any case I have rejected it as having any weight; Mr Settle very properly says that he does not make too much of the bank episode; and I do not accept that Ian is proposing to run the company for his own benefit. Even if one goes outside the four corners of the petition, in the end Brian is left with complaints which in my judgment are wholly insufficient to support the petition. The petition must therefore be dismissed.

SOURCE 199
Ebrahimi v Westbourne Galleries Ltd
(House of Lords 1972) [1973] AC 360; [1972] 2 All ER 492

May 3. LORD WILBERFORCE: My Lords, the issue in this appeal is whether the respondent company Westbourne Galleries Ltd should be wound up by the court on the petition of the appellant who is one of the three shareholders, the personal respondents being the other two. The company . . . was formed in 1958 to take over a business founded by the second respondent (Mr Nazar). It is a fact of cardinal importance that since about 1945 the business had been carried on by the appellant and Mr Nazar as partners, equally sharing the management and the profits. When the company was formed, the signatories to its memorandum were the appellant and Mr Nazar and they were appointed its first directors. Of its issued share capital, 500 shares of £1 each were issued to each subscriber and it was found by the learned judge, after the point had been contested by Mr Nazar, that Mr Ebrahimi paid up his shares out of his own money. Soon after the company's formation the third respondent (Mr George Nazar) was made a director, and each of the two original shareholders transferred to him 100 shares, so that at all material times Mr Ebrahimi held 400 shares, Mr Nazar 400 and Mr George Nazar 200. The Nazars, father and son, thus had a majority of the votes in general meeting. Until the dispute all three gentlemen remained directors.

The company made good profits, all of which were distributed as directors' remuneration. No dividends have ever been paid, before or after the petition was presented.

On 12 August 1969, an ordinary resolution was passed by the company in general meeting, by the votes of Mr Nazar and Mr George Nazar, removing Mr Ebrahimi from the office of director, a resolution which was effective in law by virtue of section 184 of the Companies Act 1948 and article 96 of Part I of Table A. Shortly afterwards the appellant presented his petition to the court.

This petition was based in the first place upon section 210[1] of the Companies Act 1948, the relief sought under this section being an order that Mr Nazar and his son be ordered to purchase the appellant's shares in the company. In the alternative it sought an order for the winding up of the company. The petition contained allegations of oppression and misconduct against Mr Nazar which were fully explored at the hearing before Plowman J. The learned judge found that some were unfounded and others unproved and that such complaint as was made out did not amount to such a course of oppressive conduct as to justify an order under section 210. However, he made an order for the winding up of the company under the 'just and equitable' provision. I shall later specify the grounds on which he did so. The appellant did not appeal against the rejection of his case under section 210 and this House is not concerned with it. The company and the individual respondents appealed against the order for winding up and this was set aside by the Court of Appeal. The appellant now seeks to have it restored.

My Lords, the petition was brought under section 222(f) of the Companies Act 1948, which enables a winding up order to be made if 'the court is of the opinion that it is just and equitable that the company should be wound up.' This power has existed in our company law in unaltered form since the first major Act, the Companies Act 1862. Indeed, it antedates that statute since it existed in the Joint Stock Companies Winding Up Act 1848. For some 50 years, following a pronouncement by Lord Cottenham LC [*Ex parte Spackman*[2]] in 1849, the words 'just and equitable' were interpreted so as only to include matters *ejusdem generis* as the preceding clauses of the section, but there is now ample authority for discarding this limitation. There are two other restrictive interpretations which I mention to reject. First, there has been a tendency to create categories or headings under which cases must be brought if the clause is to apply. This is wrong. Illustrations may be used, but general words should remain general and not be reduced to the sum of particular instances. Secondly, it has been suggested, and urged upon us, that (assuming the petitioner is a shareholder and not a creditor) the words must be confined to such circumstances as affect him in his capacity as shareholder. I see no warrant for this either. No doubt, in order to present a petition, he must qualify as a shareholder, but I see no reason for preventing him from relying upon any circumstances of justice or equity which affect him in his relations with the company, or, in a case such as the present, with the other shareholders.

One other signpost is significant. The same words 'just and equitable' appear in the Partnership Act 1892, section 25, as a ground for dissolution of a partnership and no doubt the considerations which they reflect formed part of the common law of partnership before its codification. The importance of this is to provide a bridge between cases under section 222(f) of the Act of 1948 and the principles of equity developed in relation to partnerships.

The winding up order was made following a doctrine which has developed in the courts since the beginning of this century. As presented by the appellant, and in substance accepted by the learned judge, this was that in a case such as this the members of the company are in substance partners, or quasi-partners, and that a winding up may be ordered if such facts are shown as could justify a dissolution of partnership between them. The common use of the words 'just and equitable' in the company and partnership law supports this approach. Your Lordships were invited by the respondents' counsel to restate the principle on which this

---

1 The predecessor to s 459
2 (1849) 1 Mac & G 170; 41 ER 1228

provision ought to be used; it has not previously been considered by this House. The main line of his submission was to suggest that too great a use of the partnership analogy had been made; that a limited company, however small, essentially differs from a partnership; that in the case of a company, the rights of its members are governed by the articles of association which have contractual force; that the court has no power or at least ought not to dispense parties from observing their contracts; that, in particular, when one member has been excluded from the directorate, or management, under powers expressly conferred by the Companies Act and the articles, an order for winding up, whether on the partnership analogy or under the just and equitable provision, should not be made. Alternatively, it was argued that before the making of such an order could be considered the petitioner must show and prove that the exclusion was not made bona fide in the interests of the company.

. . . The foundation of it all lies in the words 'just and equitable' and, if there is any respect in which some of the cases may be open to criticism, it is that the courts may sometimes have been too timorous in giving them full force. The words are a recognition of the fact that a limited company is more than a mere legal entity, with a personality in law of its own: that there is room in company law for recognition of the fact that behind it, or amongst it, there are individuals, with rights, expectations and obligations inter se which are not necessarily submerged in the company structure. That structure is defined by the Companies Act and by the articles of association by which shareholders agree to be bound. In most companies and in most contexts, this definition is sufficient and exhaustive, equally so whether the company is large or small. The 'just and equitable' provision does not, as the respondents suggest, entitle one party to disregard the obligation he assumes by entering a company, nor the court to dispense him from it. It does, as equity always does, enable the court to subject the exercise of legal rights to equitable considerations; considerations, that is, of a personal character arising between one individual and another, which may make it unjust, or inequitable, to insist on legal rights, or to exercise them in a particular way.

It would be impossible, and wholly undesirable, to define the circumstances in which these considerations may arise. Certainly the fact that a company is a small one, or private company, is not enough. There are very many of these where the association is a purely commercial one, of which it can safely be said that the basis of association is adequately and exhaustively laid down in the articles. The superimposition of equitable considerations requires something more, which typically may include one, or probably more, of the following elements: (i) an association formed or continued on the basis of a personal relationship, involving mutual confidence — this element will often be found where a pre-existing partnership has been converted into a limited company; (ii) an agreement, or understanding, that all, or some (for there may be 'sleeping' members), of the shareholders shall participate in the conduct of the business; (iii) restriction upon the transfer of the members' interest in the company — so that if confidence is lost, or one member is removed from management, he cannot take out his stake and go elsewhere.

. . .

My Lords, this is an expulsion case, and I must briefly justify the application in such cases of the just and equitable clause. The question is, as always, whether it is equitable to allow one (or two) to make use of his legal rights to the prejudice of his associate(s). The law of companies recognises the right, in many ways, to remove a director from the board. Section 184 of the Companies Act 1948 confers this right upon the company in general meeting whatever the articles may say. Some articles may prescribe other methods: for example, a governing director may have the power to remove (compare *Re Wondoflex Textiles Pty Ltd*[1]). And quite apart from removal powers, there are normally provisions for retirement of directors by rotation so that their re-election can be opposed and defeated by a majority, or even by a casting vote. In all these ways a particular director-member may find himself no longer a director, through removal, or non-re-election: this situation he must normally accept, unless he undertakes the burden of proving fraud or mala fides. The just and equitable provision nevertheless come to his assistance if he can point to, and prove, some special underlying obligation of his fellow member(s) in good faith, or confidence, that so long as the business continues he shall be entitled to management participation, an obligation so basic that, if broken, the conclusion must be that the association must be dissolved. And the principles on which he may do so are those worked out by the courts in partnership cases where there has been exclusion from management (see *Const v Harris*[2]) even where under the partnership agreement there is a power of exclusion (see *Blisset v Daniel*;[3] *Lindley on Partnership*, 13th ed (1971), pp 331, 595).

I come to the facts of this case. It is apparent enough that a potential basis for a winding up order under the just and equitable clause existed. The appellant after a long association in partnership, during which he had an equal share in the management, joined in the formation of the company. The inference must be indisputable that he, and Mr Nazar, did so on the basis that the character of the association would, as a matter of personal relation and good faith, remain the same. He was removed from his directorship under a power valid in law. Did he establish a case which, if he had remained in a partnership with a term providing for expulsion, would have justified an order for dissolution? This was the essential question for the judge. Plowman J dealt with the issue in a brief paragraph in which he said:

'. . . while no doubt the petitioner was lawfully removed, in the sense that he ceased in law to be a director, it does not follow that in removing him the respondents did not do him a wrong. In my judgment, they did do him a wrong, in the sense that it was an abuse of power and a breach of the good faith which partners owe to each other to exclude one of them from all participation in the business upon which they have embarked on the basis that all should participate in its management. The main justification put forward for removing him was that he was perpetually complaining, but the faults were not all on one side and, in my judgment, this is not sufficient justification. For these reasons, in my judgment, the petitioner, therefore, has made out a case for a winding up order.'

Reading this in the context of the judgment, as a whole, which had dealt with the specific complaints of one side against the other, I take it as a finding that the respondents were not entitled, in justice and equity, to make use of their legal powers of expulsion and that, in accordance with the principles of such cases as *Blisset v Daniel*, the only just and equitable course was to dissolve the association. To my mind, two factors strongly support this. First, Mr Nazar made it perfectly clear that he did not regard Mr Ebrahimi as a partner, but did regard him as an employee. But there was no possible doubt as to Mr Ebrahimi's status throughout, so that Mr Nazar's refusal to recognise it amounted, in effect, to a

---

1 [1951] VLR 458
2 [1824] Turn & R 496; 37 ER 1191
3 (1853) 10 Hare 493; 68 ER 1022

repudiation of the relationship. Secondly, Mr Ebrahimi, through ceasing to be a director, lost his right to share in the profits through directors' remuneration, retaining only the chance of receiving dividends as a minority shareholder. It is true that an assurance was given in evidence that the previous practice (of not paying dividends) would not be continued, but the fact remains that Mr Ebrahimi was thenceforth at the mercy of the Messrs Nazar as to what he should receive out of the profits and when. He was, moreover, unable to dispose of his interest without the consent of the Nazars. All these matters lead only to the conclusion that the right course was to dissolve the association by winding up.

. . .

LORD CROSS (concurring): What the minority shareholder in cases of this sort really wants is not to have the company wound up — which may prove an unsatisfactory remedy — but to be paid a proper price for his shareholding. With this in mind Parliament provided by section 210 of the Companies Act 1948 that if a member of a company could show that the company's affairs were being conducted in a manner oppressive to some of the members including himself, that the facts proved would justify the making of a winding up order under the 'just and equitable' clause but that to wind up the company would unfairly prejudice the 'oppressed' members the court could (inter alia) make an order for the purchase of the shares of those members by other members or by the company. To give the court jurisdiction under this section the petitioner must show both that the conduct of the majority is 'oppressive' and also that it affects him in his capacity as a shareholder. Mr Ebrahimi was unable to establish either of these preconditions. But the jurisdiction to wind up under section 222 (f) continues to exist as an independent remedy and I have no doubt that the Court of Appeal was right in rejecting the submission of the respondents to the effect that a petitioner cannot obtain an order under that subsection any more than under section 210 unless he can show that his position as a shareholder has been worsened by the action of which he complains. The facts of this case are set out in detail in the judgment of Plowman J and I need not repeat them. The essence of the matter is that Mr Nazar and Mr Ebrahimi had been carrying on business as partners at will in equal shares; that the business was transferred to the company in which each had 40 per cent of the capital and Nazar's son George the remaining 20 per cent; that it was not contemplated that any dividends would be paid but was contemplated that the profits of the company should be distributed by way of director's fees; and that the result of Mr Ebrahimi's removal from the directorship was that instead of his having a share in the management of the business and an income of some £3,000 a year he was excluded from the management and deprived of any share in the profits save such dividend as might be paid on his shares if the Nazars thought fit to declare a dividend. The Court of Appeal held that Mr Ebrahimi could not obtain a winding up order under the 'just and equitable' clause unless he could show that the Nazars had not exercised the power to remove him from his directorship 'bona fide in the interests of the company' or that their ground for exercising the power were such that no reasonable man could think that the removal was in the interest of the company. With all respect to them I cannot agree that this is an appropriate test to apply. If one assumes that the company is going to remain in existence it may very well be that a reasonable man would say that it was in the interest of the company that Mr Ebrahimi should cease to be a director. 'These two men,' he might say, 'are hopelessly at loggerheads. If the business is to prosper one or other must go and the company is likely to do better without Mr Ebrahimi than without Mr Nazar.' But these considerations have not, to my mind, anything to do with the question whether in the circumstances it is right that the company should continue in existence if Mr Ebrahimi wishes it to be wound up. The argument upon which counsel for the respondent chiefly relied in support of the decision of the Court of Appeal was quite different. Mr Ebrahimi, he said, consented to the conversion of the partnership into a limited company. Even though he became, because George Nazar was taken in, only a minority shareholder he could have safeguarded his position by procuring the insertion in the articles of a provision 'weighting' the voting power of his shares on any question touching his retention of office as director: see *Bushell v Faith*.[1] He must, therefore, be taken to have accepted the risk that if he and Mr Nazar fell out he would be at Mr Nazar's mercy. There might be force in this argument if there was any evidence to show that the minds of the parties were directed to the point; but there is no such evidence and the probability is that no one gave a moment's thought to the change in relative strength of their respective positions brought about by the conversion of the partnership into a company. It was not suggested that Mr Ebrahimi had been guilty of any misconduct such as would justify one partner in expelling another under an expulsion clause contained in partnership articles. All that happened was that without one being more to blame than the other the two could not longer work together in harmony. Had no company been formed Mr Ebrahimi could have had the partnership wound up and though Mr Nazar and his son were entitled in law to oust him from his directorship and deprive him of his income they could only do so subject to Mr Ebrahimi's right to obtain equitable relief in the form of a winding up order under section 222 (*f*). I would, therefore, allow the appeal.

PART IV: THE ALTERNATIVE REMEDY

Restrictions on the winding-up remedy and difficulty with the rule in *Foss v Harbottle*[2] led to calls for a new minority shareholder remedy. The Cohen Committee,[3] which recognised the vulnerability of minority shareholders of a private company to oppression by the majority, gave two instances of oppressive conduct. First, the refusal of directors to register a transfer to outsiders of shares on the death of a shareholder, so that either the directors or some person approved by them, could acquire the shares at an under value; and secondly, the taking of excessive remuneration by directors.[4] The Report led to the introduction of s 210 of the Companies Act 1948 which allowed a member to petition the court for relief where the affairs of the company were being conducted in a manner *oppressive* to some part of the members. However, due to the drafting of the section and to judicial timidity, it lamentably failed to fulfil an effective role in protecting minorities. Against this background the Jenkins Committee (Source 200), recommended that the provision should be amended by replacing the requirement of 'oppression' with the term 'unfairly prejudicial', and by removal of the prerequisite that the remedy be linked to facts justifying a winding-up order on the 'just and

---

1 [1970] 1 All ER 53 (see p 318)
2 (1843) 2 Hare 461; 67 ER 189 (see p 532)
3 Report of the Committee on Company Law Amendment (Cmnd 6659 (1945))
4 Ibid at paras 58–60. The Committee noted at para 60 that these were only illustrations of a general problem

equitable' ground. This led to the enactment of s 75 of the Companies Act 1980 (now s 459 of the Companies Act 1985), as amended by the Companies Act 1989, Sch 19, para 11. The wide powers now conferred on the court to grant relief have been frequently used as a device to enforce the so-called 'legitimate expectations' of company members. While the concept of thwarted shareholder expectations is limited in widely held companies, nevertheless in small private companies, often termed quasi-partnerships, the concept has come to shape the scope of the provision.

SOURCE 200
Report of the Company Law Committee (The 'Jenkins Committee' 1962)
(Cmnd 1749)

204 In *Elder v Elder & Watson Ltd* 1952 SC 49, it was said by Lord Cooper (at p 55) with reference to the meaning of oppression in section 210 'the essence of the matter seems to be that the conduct complained of should at the lowest involve a visible departure from the standards of fair dealing, and a violation of the conditions of fair play on which every shareholder who entrusts his money to a company is entitled to rely'. This statement accords with our own view as to the intention underlying section 210 as originally framed, namely that it was meant to cover complaints not only to the effect that the affairs of the company were being conducted in a manner oppressive (in the narrower sense) to the members concerned but also to the effect that those affairs were being conducted in a manner unfairly prejudicial to the interests of those members. We think that the section should be amended to make this clear, and also to make it clear that it is to cover particular acts which are oppressive to or unfairly prejudice the interests of the complaining members as well as to courses of conduct having those effects.

205 As the Cohen Committee observed in paragraph 60 of their report, it is impossible to frame a recommendation to cover every case, and we do not propose to attempt to do so. But we may perhaps usefully mention as illustrative of the situations in which action under section 210 might be appropriate those in which directors appoint themselves to paid posts with the company at excessive rates of remuneration, thus depriving the complaining members of any dividend, or any adequate dividend, on their shares; or in which the directors, having power to do so under the articles, refuse to register personal representatives in respect of shares devolving upon them in that capacity, and by this expedient (coupled with the absorption of profits in payment of the directors' remuneration) force the personal representatives to sell their shares to the directors at an inadequate price. Other possibilities are the issue of shares to directors and others on advantageous terms; and the passing of non-cumulative preference dividends on shares held by the minority.

SOURCE 201
Re R A Noble & Sons (Clothing) Ltd
(Chancery Division 1983) [1983] BCLC 273

Although the possibility of petitioning the Companies Court for the winding up of the Company on the just and equitable ground had been adumbrated in Mr Bailey's solicitors' original letter before action of 20 February 1981, it was not until the end of the year, in a letter of 21 December, that they made a concrete threat to that effect. By that time they had been able to consider the accounts of the Company not only for the period ended 28 February 1979 but also for the year ended 29 February 1980, copies of the latter having been supplied to them at some time in or after July 1981. In any event, the letter of 21 December claimed that the accounts showed various irregularities and breaches of the Companies Act and accounting standards. Explanations were required in respect of ten specific matters. Mr Noble's solicitors replied on 5 January stating that they were seeking their clients' immediate instructions, but it appears that no explanations were given at that or any later stage.

In the result, on 14 July 1982, Anafield presented the petition which is now before the court. The respondents are the Company and Mr Noble. The relief sought is an order pursuant to section 75 of the 1980 Act for Mr Noble to purchase Anafield's shares in the Company at a price to be determined by an independent accountant on the basis that the Anafield and Mr Noble each own one-half of the issued share capital of the Company and, in the alternative, that an order be made for the winding up of the Company on the ground that it is just and equitable to do so. Anafield also seeks an order for costs against Mr Noble personally.

The principal complaints made in the petition are that Mr Bailey continually pressed Mr Noble to let him have details of the value of stock transferred by him to the Company, but that Mr Noble failed to supply any such valuation; that Mr Noble declined to execute the loan agreement on 10 September 1978; that Mr Noble never supplied Anafield with details of what he had contributed to the Company and the value of the assets so contributed; that Mr Noble failed to supply Mr Bailey with full information as to the financial state of the Company or with regular accounts and failed to invite Mr Bailey to attend meetings of the Company from time to time; that it was falsely asserted on Mr Noble's behalf that at the meeting on 10 September 1978 Mr Bailey had (a) agreed to reduce his stake in the Company to 49 per cent, and (b) had agreed that a meeting should be held formally to issue the shares and to complete the formalities, being a meeting which Mr Bailey had been too busy to attend; that in breach of the agreement between Mr Noble and Mr Bailey (a) Mr Noble caused 51 of the shares to be allotted to himself and only 49 to Anafield, and (b) that Mr Noble caused his wife and his son to be appointed directors in addition to himself and Mr Bailey, that remuneration had been voted to the other directors, but that nothing had ever been paid to Mr Bailey and that he was never informed of any meeting at which a resolution to appoint any directors was proposed, or indeed any meeting until March 1981; and that Mr Noble told Mr Bailey at their meeting in June 1980 that he fully understood Mr Bailey's desire to withdraw, that he would see his accountant and come back to Mr Bailey in the very near future, but that nothing further was heard from Mr Noble after that meeting. . . .

I was helpfully referred by counsel on both sides to various authorities on, first, section 222(*f*) of the 1948 Act, secondly, section 210 of the 1948 Act (the predecessor of section 75 of the 1980 Act) and, thirdly, section 75 itself.

As to section 222(*f*), the principles upon which the court should act in ordering a company to be wound up on the just and equitable ground have now been settled for more than a decade by the decision of the House of Lords in *Ebrahimi v Westbourne Galleries Ltd.*[1] Those principles are now very well known and I do not think it necessary to go into them in any detail. For the purposes of the present case it is enough for me to make two points. First, I am of the opinion that an order can be made in a case where a company embodies an association formed on the basis of a personal relationship involving mutual confidence and

---

1 [1973] AC 360; [1972] 2 All ER 429 (see p 566)

where there is an agreement or understanding that one of the shareholders shall participate in all major decisions relating to the company's affairs, even if not in the day-to-day conduct of the business. Secondly, it is unnecessary for the petitioner to show that the respondent has been guilty of some form of underhand conduct or that his own has been above reproach. In some cases he may even be able to obtain an order if his conduct has been more culpable than the respondent's. I do not need to explore that question in this case. It is enough for me to say that a petitioner can certainly obtain an order if he can show that it is the respondent's conduct which has been the substantial cause of the destruction of the mutual confidence involved in the personal relationship between them.

Although the authorities on section 210 of the 1948 Act are, and will continue to be, of importance in cases where relief is sought under section 75 of the 1980 Act, it is unnecessary for me to refer to any of them in this case. I merely desire respectfully to adopt the following observation of Slade J in *Re Bovey Hotel Ventures Ltd:*[1]

> 'For my own part, while I can think of many hypothetical cases that might fall within section 75 but would not fall within section 210, I can think of no hypothetical cases which, though giving rise to the court's jurisdiction under section 210, would not give rise to such jurisdiction under section 75.'

Re Bovey Hotel Ventures Ltd was the only authority to which I was referred on section 75. Before relief can be granted under that section it must be shown that the affairs of the company are being or have been conducted in a manner which is unfairly prejudicial to the interests of some part of the members (including at least the petitioner) or that any actual or proposed act or omission of the company (including an act or omission on its behalf) is or would be so prejudicial. In the *Bovey* case, Slade J said this in regard to unfairly prejudicial conduct:

> 'I do not think it necessary or appropriate in this judgment to attempt any comprehensive exposition of the situations which may give rise to the court's jurisdiction under section 75. Broadly, however, I would say this. Without prejudice to the generality of the wording of the section, which may cover many other situations, a member of a company will be able to bring himself within the section if he can show that the value of his shareholding in the company has been seriously diminished or at least seriously jeopardised by reason of a course of conduct on the part of those persons who have had de facto control of the company, which has been unfair to the member concerned. The test of unfairness must, I think, be an objective, not a subjective, one. In other words it is not necessary for the petitioner to show that the persons who have had de facto control of the company have acted as they did in the conscious knowledge that this was unfair to the petitioner or that they were acting in bad faith; the test, I think, is whether a reasonable bystander observing the consequences of their conduct, would regard it as having unfairly prejudiced the petitioner's interests.'

On the facts of that case, the learned judge found that the petitioner had been unfairly prejudiced. The case went to the Court of Appeal, but there was no appeal against that finding. Although the Court expressed the view that it was clear that the wife had been unfairly prejudiced, it was in the circumstances

---

1 (1981) 31 July (unreported)

unnecessary for them to deal with the general observations of Slade J to which I have referred.

   . . .

I have no doubt that sooner or later a case will emerge in which the particular facts will make it necessary for the court to make a closer examination of the relationship between section $222(f)$ and section 75 than I feel is necessary in the present case. In this case I have come to a clear view that it has not been established that the affairs of the Company are being or have been conducted in a manner which is unfairly prejudicial to the interests of Anafield, but that it has been established that it is just and equitable that the Company should be wound up.

As to winding up, I find that the Company did embody an association formed on the basis of a personal relationship between Mr Noble and Mr Bailey involving mutual confidence and that there was an implied agreement or an understanding that Anafield through Mr Bailey should participate in all major decisions relating to the Company's affairs. I find that Mr Noble was not guilty of underhand conduct, and I find that Mr Bailey's conduct was, by reason of his notable degree of disinterest and his decision to demand early repayment of the loans, not above reproach. Nevertheless I find that Mr Noble's conduct was the substantial cause of the destruction of the mutual confidence involved in the personal relationship between him and Mr Bailey. I should add that it is clear to me that the mutual confidence has been destroyed and cannot be repaired.

As to section 75, I certainly think that Mr Noble's conduct, inasmuch as it resulted in the exclusion of Mr Bailey from participation in all major decisions affecting the Company's affairs, could in other circumstances have amounted to conduct unfairly prejudicial to the interests of Anafield, even though the value of its shareholding in the Company may not have been seriously diminished or seriously jeopardised. I entirely agree with Slade J that section 75 cannot be limited to cases of that nature. On the other hand, I have acquitted Mr Noble of any form of underhand conduct. In particular, I acquit him of deliberately deceiving Mr Bailey as to the existence of the substantial overdraft on the Josy Fashions' account. I think that Mr Noble's attitude was that he just wanted to get on with the business without having to consult Mr Bailey about anything upon which he was not forced to consult him. But in all the circumstances of this case, including many to which I have not specifically referred, I do not think that it can be said that Mr Noble's conduct was unfairly prejudicial to the interests of Anafield. In my judgment, the crucial word on the facts of this case is 'unfairly'. It is at this point that Mr Bailey's disinterest becomes a decisive factor. In the end, and by reference to the test propounded by Slade J, I do not think that a reasonable bystander, observing the consequences of Mr Noble's conduct and judging it to have been prejudicial to the interests of Anafield, would regard it as having been unfair. I think he would say that Mr Bailey had partly brought it upon himself. That means that there is no case for relief under section 75.

I summarise the position as follows. Anafield (London) is entitled to judgment in the action in respect of the costs of the fitting out of the new shop at 20 Park Parade. I understand that there may be an agreement between the parties as to how the appropriate amount should be assessed. There may still be some debate as to interest. On the petition I decline to make an order under section 75, but I will if necessary make an order for the compulsory winding up of the Company on the ground that it is just and equitable to do so.

SOURCE 202
Re Bird Precision Bellows Ltd
(Chancery Division and Court of Appeal 1983) [1984] Ch 419; [1984] 3 All
ER 444

The petition[1] was presented on 12 October 1981. It alleged that the affairs of
the company had been and were being conducted in a manner unfairly
prejudicial to the petitioners as members. The basic ground of complaint was
that Mr Armstrong and Mr Nin had been wrongfully excluded from participation in the company's affairs. Pursuant to s 75(4)(d), the petition sought an
order that the respondents should purchase the shares of the petitioners at
the fair value thereof. In the alternative, it alleged that it was just and
equitable that the company should be wound up, but that allegation was soon
deleted by amendment.

The petition came on for a first hearing before Vinelott J on 23 November
1981, when it was ordered by consent that the respondents should jointly and
severally purchase the 7,800 shares in the company registered in the names of
the petitioners 'at such price as the court shall hereafter determine'.
Directions were given for the filing of evidence, discovery and inspection and
exchange of valuers' reports on the question of the appropriate purchase
price for the shares. The respondents were ordered to pay the petitioners'
costs of the petition to date.

The following remarks of Nourse J quoted here relate solely to the question
of valuing shares. On appeal, the Court of Appeal refused to interfere with
the judge's discretion on this issue.

> Although both ss 210 and 75 are silent on the point, it is axiomatic that a price
> fixed by the court must be fair. While that which is fair may often be generally
> predicated in regard to matters of common occurrence, it can never be
> conclusively judged in regard to a particular case until the facts are known. The
> general observations which I will presently attempt in relation to a valuation of
> shares by the court under s 75 are therefore subject to that important reserva-
> tion.
>
> Broadly speaking, shares in a small private company are acquired either by
> allotment on its incorporation or by transfer or devolution at some later date. In
> the first category it is a matter of common occurrence for a company to be
> incorporated in order to acquire an existing business or to start a new one, and
> in either event for it to be a vehicle for the conduct of a business carried on by
> two or more shareholders which they could, had they wished, have carried on in
> partnership together. Although it has been pointed out on the high authority to
> which I will soon refer that the description may be confusing, it is often
> convenient and it is certainly usual to describe that kind of company as a quasi
> partnership. In the second category, irrespective of the nature of the company, it
> is a matter of common occurrence for a shareholder to acquire shares from
> another at a price which is discounted because they represent a minority holding.
> It seems to me that some general observations can usefully be made in regard to
> each of these examples.
>
> As to the first, there is a well-known passage in the speech of Lord Wilberforce
> in *Ebrahimi v Westbourne Galleries Ltd* [1972] 2 All ER 492 at 500, [1973] AC 360
> at 379 where his Lordship, having observed that it is not enough that the

---

1 Under s 75 of the Companies Act 1980. See now s 459 of the Companies Act 1989

company is a small one, or a private company, identifies three typical elements, one, or probably more, of which will characterise the company as a quasi partnership. They are, firstly, an association formed or continued on the basis of a personal relationship involving mutual confidence, secondly, an agreement or understanding that all or some of the shareholders shall participate in the conduct of the business, and, thirdly, restrictions on share transfers. No doubt these three elements are the most familiar, and perhaps the most important, but they were not intended to be exhaustive. In my view there may be other typical and important elements, in particular the provision of capital by all or some of the participants.

I would expect that in a majority of cases where purchase orders are made under s 75 in relation to quasi partnerships the vendor is unwilling in the sense that the sale has been forced on him. Usually he will be a minority shareholder whose interests have been unfairly prejudiced by the manner in which the affairs of the company have been conducted by the majority. On the assumption that the unfair prejudice has made it no longer tolerable for him to retain his interest in the company, a sale of his shares will invariably be his only practical way out short of a winding up. In that kind of case it seems to me that it would not merely not be fair, but most unfair, that he should be bought out on the fictional basis applicable to a free election to sell his shares in accordance with the company's articles of association, or indeed on any other basis which involved a discounted price. In my judgment the correct course would be to fix the price pro rata according to the value of the shares as a whole and without any discount, as being the only fair method of compensating an unwilling vendor of the equivalent of a partnership share. Equally, if the order provided, as it did in *Re Jermyn Street Turkish Baths Ltd*, for the purchase of the shares of the delinquent majority, it would not merely not be fair, but most unfair, that they should receive a price which involved an element of premium.

Of the other, I would expect more rare, cases in which the court might make a purchase order in relation to a quasi partnership the arguments of counsel for the respondents require me to mention one. Suppose the case of a minority shareholder whose interests had been unfairly prejudiced by the conduct of the majority, but who had nevertheless so acted as to deserve his exclusion from the company. It is difficult to see how such a case could arise in practice, because one would expect acts and deserts of that kind to be inconsistent with the existence of the supposed conduct of the majority. Be that as it may, the consideration of that possibility has been forced on me by the agreement for the price to be determined by the court without any admission of unfairly prejudicial conduct on the part of the respondents. As will appear, counsel for the respondents submitted that the petitioners did act in such a way as to deserve their exclusion from the company. He further submitted that it would therefore be fair for them to be bought out on the basis which would have been applicable if they had made a free election to sell their shares pursuant to the articles, ie at a discount. Assuming at present that the respondents can establish the necessary factual basis, I think that the further submission of counsel for the respondents is correct. A shareholder who deserves his exclusion has, if you like, made a constructive election to sever his connection with the company and thus to sell his shares.

...

Next, I must consider the example from the second category of cases in which, broadly speaking, shares in a small private company are acquired. It is not of direct relevance for present purposes, but I mention it briefly in order finally to refute the suggestion that there is any rule of universal application to questions of this kind. In the case of the shareholder who acquires shares from another at a price which is discounted because they represent a minority it is to my mind self-evident that there cannot be any universal or even a general rule that he should be bought out under s 75 on a more favourable basis, even in a case where his predecessor has been a quasi partner in a quasi partnership. He might himself have acquired the shares purely for investment and played no part in the affairs of the company. In that event it might well be fair, I do not know, that he should be bought out on the same basis as he himself had bought, even though his interests had been unfairly prejudiced in the mean time. A fortiori, there could be no universal or even a general rule in a case where the company had never been a quasi partnership in the first place.

In summary, there is in my judgment no rule of universal application. On the other hand, there is a general rule in a case where the company is at the material time a quasi partnership and the purchase order is made in respect of the shares of a quasi partner. Although I have taken the case where there has in fact been unfairly prejudicial conduct on the part of the majority as being the state of affairs most likely to result in a purchase order, I am of the opinion that the same consequences ought usually to follow in a case like the present where there has been an agreement for the price to be determined by the court without any admission as to such conduct. It seems clear to me that, even without such conduct, that is in general the fair basis of valuation in a quasi partnership case, and that it should be applied in this case unless the respondents have established that the petitioners acted in such a way as to deserve their exclusion from the company.

SOURCE 203
Practice Direction (Companies Court: Contributory's Petition 1/90)
[1990] 1 WLR 490

1. Practitioners' attention is drawn to the undesirability of including as a matter of course a prayer for winding up as an alternative to an order under section 459 of the Companies Act 1985. It should be included only if that is the relief which the petitioner prefers or if it is considered that it may be the only relief to which he is entitled.

2. Whenever a prayer for winding up is included in a contributory's petition, the petition shall include a statement whether the petitioner consents or objects to an order under section 127 of the Insolvency Act 1986 in the standard form, and if he objects the affidavit in support shall contain a short statement of his reasons.

3. If the petitioner objects to a section 127 order in the standard form but consents to such an order in a modified form, the petition shall set out the form of order to which he consents, and the affidavit in support shall contain a short statement of his reasons for seeking the modification.

4. If the petition contains a statement that the petitioner consents to a section 127 order, whether in the standard or a modified form, but the petitioner changes his mind before the first hearing of the petition, he shall notify the respondents and may apply on notice to a judge for an order directing that no section 127 order or a modified order only (as the case may be) shall be made by the registrar, but validating dispositions made without notice of the order made by the judge.

5. If the petition contains a statement that the petitioner consents to a section 127 order, whether in the standard or a modified form, the registrar shall without

further inquiry make an order in such form at the first hearing unless an order to the contrary has been made by the judge in the meantime.

6. If the petition contains a statement that the petitioner objects to a section 127 order in the standard form, the company may apply (in cases of urgency ex parte) to the judge for an order.

Section 127 order
Standard form

'ORDER that notwithstanding the presentation of the said petition
(1) payments made into or out of the bank accounts of the company in the ordinary course of the business of the company and
(2) dispositions of the property of the company made in the ordinary course of its business for proper value

between the date of presentation of the petition and the date of judgment on the petition or further order in the meantime shall not be void by virtue of the provisions of section 127 of the Insolvency Act 1986 in the event of an order for the winding up of the company being made on the said petition.'

By direction of the Vice-Chancellor.

22 February 1990

SOURCE 204
Re A Company (No 00477 of 1986)
(Chancery Division 1986) [1986] BCLC 376

HOFFMANN J: This is a motion to strike out a petition under s 459 of the Companies Act 1985 as an abuse of the process of the court. There is also before the court an application for leave to re-amend the petition. Counsel for the company (Mr Crow) submits that the petition as it is proposed to be re-amended would still be demurrable and the matter has therefore been argued on the allegations made in the draft re-amended petition, which for the purposes of these applications must be assumed to be true.

These allegations are in substance a claim for damages for deceit and breach of contract. The petitioners are a husband and wife whom I shall call Mr and Mrs S. They say that until July 1985 they held all the issued share capital in a profitable company called A Ltd of which Mr S was managing director. In April 1985, they entered into negotiations with the respondent company, which I shall call O plc, a public company controlled by the personal respondents, whom I shall call Mr A and Mr B. The shares in O plc are not quoted but there can be dealings in the over-the-counter market when the market maker is able to match the bargain. At present there are said to be no prospects of any such dealings. The petitioners allege that Mr A and Mr B represented to them that O plc had 'substantial' funds on deposit in the bank which could be used to develop the business of A Ltd and that if the petitioners would sell their shares in A Ltd to O plc, that company would forthwith invest 'substantial sums' in its business. Mr and Mrs S would continue as directors of A Ltd, Mr S would be employed by A Ltd as managing director under a service contract and come onto the board of O plc and the association between the petitioners and the individual respondents would be one of 'partnership'. In reliance of these representations, the petitioners entered into a written agreement dated 18 July 1985 to sell their shares in A Ltd to O plc for an allotment of shares in that company treated as having a value of £100,000.

The petition then alleges that the representations made in April were false and fraudulent. O plc did not have any money deposited at the bank and no source of funds for investment in A Ltd. Instead it used A Ltd to supply goods and services on credit to another associated company known to be insolvent. As a result it is said that A Ltd has a £16,000 bad debt owing from the associated company, its assets have been sold off and it is no longer a going concern. The whole transaction is alleged to have been a fraudulent scheme to acquire A Ltd and strip its assets in an attempt to support the other company.

Then it is said that Mr S, in breach of his service contract, has been removed as managing director of A Ltd and asked to resign from the board of O plc. In any event, the present financial position of A Ltd is alleged to be such that it could not pay Mr S's salary. As a result of the dissipation of the assets of A Ltd and the cessation of its business, Mr and Mrs S say that they have lost, first, the benefit of Mr S's salary under his service agreement and second, the prospect of dividends from their shares in O plc, which are said to be worth little or nothing. They say that in September 1985 they offered to give them back in exchange for the return of their shares in A Ltd and compensation for their losses, but that this offer was refused.

The relief sought is an order that O plc or Mr A and Mr B be ordered to buy the petitioners' shares in O plc at a price which will be equivalent to the value attributed to the shares in A Ltd at the time of their sale in July 1985.

The principal ground for the application to strike out is that most of the matters of complaint (assuming them to be true) would constitute wrongs done to the petitioners in their capacity as defrauded vendors of the shares in A Ltd or to Mr S as a wrongfully dismissed employee of A Ltd, but they are not unfairly prejudicial to their interests as members of O plc. Section 459 of the Companies Act 1985 founds the jurisdiction of the court to grant a wide range of discretionary relief under s 461 on the ground that:

> '. . . the company's affairs are being or have been conducted in a manner which is unfairly prejudicial to the interests of some part of the members (including at least himself) . . .'

Counsel for the company submitted that the section must be limited to conduct which is unfairly prejudicial to the interests of the members as members. It cannot extend to conduct which is prejudicial to other interests of persons who happen to be members.

In principle I accept this proposition, as did Lord Granchester QC in *Re a company* [1983] 2 All ER 36, [1983] Ch 178. But its application must take into account that the interests of a member are not necessarily limited to his strict legal rights under the constitution of the company. The use of the word 'unfairly' in s 459, like the use of the words 'just and equitable' in s 517(1)(g), enables the court to have regard to wider equitable considerations. As Lord Wilberforce said of the latter words in *Ebrahimi v Westbourne Galleries* ([1972] 2 All ER 492 at 500, [1973] AC 360 at 379), they are a recognition of the fact that:

> '. . . a limited company is more than a mere legal entity, with a personality in law of its own: that there is room in company law for recognition of the fact that behind it, or amongst it, there are individuals, with rights, expectations and obligations inter se which are not necessarily submerged in the company structure.'

Thus in the case of the managing director of a large public company who is also the owner of a small holding in the company's shares, it is easy to see the distinction between his interests as a managing director employed under a service contract and his interests as a member. In the case of a small private company in which two or three members have invested their capital by subscribing for shares on the footing that dividends are unlikely but that each will earn his living by working for the company as a director, the distinction may be more elusive. The member's interests as a member who has ventured his capital in the company's business may include a legitimate expectation that he will continue to be employed as a director and his dismissal from that office and exclusion from the management of the company may therefore be unfairly prejudicial to his interests as a member.

I bear in mind that Lord Wilberforce added that in most companies and in most contexts, whether the company was large or small, the members' rights under the articles of association and the Companies Act could be treated as an exhaustive statement of his interests as a member. He mentioned various features typically present in cases in which further equitable considerations might arise: a personal relationship between shareholders involving mutual confidence, an agreement that some or all should participate in the management and restrictions on the transfer of shares which would prevent a member from realising his investment.

Counsel for the company submits that this is not a case in which one can look beyond the petitioner's interests as members of O plc as defined by the articles of association. O plc is not a small private company formed on the basis of mutual confidence with restrictions on the transfer of shares. It is a public company in which shares are freely transferable. Mr S's rights, if any, to be employed as managing director of A Ltd rest solely in contract and have nothing to do with his interests as a member of O plc. Accordingly those parts of the petition which are founded on the wrongful termination of Mr S's employment or conduct which affected the ability of A Ltd to pay his salary must be struck out and since these are the petitioners' main grounds of complaint, very little of substance would be left in the petition.

I think that there is much force in these submissions, but with some hesitation I have come to the conclusion that the parts of the petition based on prejudice to Mr S's position as managing director of A Ltd are not so plainly demurrable that they should be struck out. The petition alleges that the association between the petitioners and the individual respondent was to be one of 'partnership', that the petitioners were to take part in the management of the business by conducting the business of A Ltd as a subsidiary, and that although there is no legal restriction on transfer of shares in O plc, in practice there is no market in which they can be sold. Section 459 of the Companies Act 1985 operates within so potentially wide a frame of reference and gives the court so broad a discretion that I do not think that I can say that no evidence which the petitioners might bring in support of the petition could satisfy a court at the hearing that Mr S's employment as a director of A Ltd was not in all the circumstances part of his legitimate expectations as a member of O plc.

The other ground of complaint is that the respondents' conduct has adversely affected the value of the petitioners' shares in O plc. Counsel for the company conceded that the allegation in the draft re-amended petition which alleged that the shares had been made worthless by the respondents' conduct of the affairs of the company was capable of falling within s 459, notwithstanding that such conduct would affect the value of all the shares in O plc and not merely those of the petitioners. I think that this concession was rightly made because the particular circumstances of the petitioners or the basis upon which they had taken their shares might make such conduct unfair to them when it would not be unfair to other members. But counsel for the company submitted, again I think rightly, that the real complaint of the petitioners is not that the shares in O plc were valuable when acquired by the petitioners and have since been made worthless by the unfair conduct of the respondents; it is that the shares were worthless from the start and that the petitioners have been induced to part with their shares in A Ltd by fraudulent misrepresentations. These representations could have no effect upon the value of the shares in O plc but only upon the consideration which the petitioners were willing to give for them. Consequently, said counsel for the company, they could not be conduct unfairly prejudicial to the interests of the petitioners as members of O plc.

Again I think that there is much force in these submissions, and it may turn out that these paragraphs of the petition, even if fully made out, will not in themselves provide a basis for the exercise of the court's jurisdiction under s 459. But the facts which they allege may bear upon the unfairness or otherwise of other conduct alleged in the petition and I therefore do not think that I ought to strike them out.

SOURCE 205
Re Elgindata Ltd
(Chancery Division 1990) [1991] BCLC 959

The respondent and his wife, Mr and Mrs Purlow, were the two shareholders in Elgindata Ltd which was incorporated in 1982. The respondent was managing director of the company. In 1983 Elgindata Ltd entered into an agreement with a company controlled by the petitioner, Mr Rowland, under which Elgindata Ltd was granted a licence to manufacture and sell a calculator invented by the petitioner. A year later the petitioner invented and developed another specialist computing product which was also produced and marketed by Elgindata Ltd. The commercial success of these two products enabled the company's fortunes to prosper. In late 1986, as a result of the petitioner's threat to withdraw from the licensing agreement, the respondent was induced to allow the petitioner and his wife to acquire shares in the company. They were jointly allotted 33% of the share capital with an option to increase to 42.38% contingent upon Elgindata Ltd's shares being listed on The Stock Exchange, or upon a controlling interest in the company being offered to a third party. The petitioner was also appointed to the board as a non-executive director responsible for research and development. At this time he assumed a more pro-active role in the operations of Elgindata Ltd and soon became disillusioned with the respondent's management of the company. Confidence broke down and in November 1987 the petitioner resigned from the board. In December 1988 the respondent offered to purchase the shares held by the petitioner and his wife, but they failed to agree a price. The petitioner therefore commenced proceedings under s 459 of the Companies Act 1985 alleging that the respondent had conducted the affairs of the company in such a way that was unfairly prejudicial to his and his wife's interests. A number of allegations were made, in particular that the respondent had managed the company negligently.

WARNER J: . . . There is little authority on the extent to which negligent or incompetent management of a company's business may constitute conduct which is unfairly prejudicial to the interests of members for the purposes of s 459. Mr Chivers referred me to *Re Five Minute Car Wash Service Ltd* [1966] 1 All ER 242, [1966] 1 WLR 745, where Buckley J held that allegations that the chairman and managing director of a company had been unwise, inefficient and careless in the performance of his duties could not without more amount to allegations of oppressive conduct for the purposes of s 210 of the Companies Act 1948. Mr Chivers rightly conceded, however, that that authority afforded little guidance in a case under s 459, because the concept of oppressive conduct in s 210 was narrower than the concept of unfairly prejudicial conduct in s 459. Mr Nurse referred me to a paragraph in *Gore-Browne on Companies* (44th edn, 1986) vol 2, p 28.021 which reads as follows:

> 'Another aspect of the enforcement of directors' duties by means of a petition under section 459 which remains unclear is the directors' duty of care. It would seem that the Jenkins Committee intended that the reformed statutory remedy might be used in this regard, although the courts decided otherwise in the case of the old section 210.'

Then there is a reference to *Re Five Minute Car Wash Service Ltd*:

> 'Where serious mismanagement causes real economic harm to the company's business (and therefore to the value of the members interests) the general conceptual developments examined earlier should enable the courts to hold that unfair prejudice has been established. The terminology in section 459(1) (referring to "any actual or proposed act or omission of the company including an act or omission on its behalf" where this "is or would be so prejudicial") should be of assistance here. Once again, however, a petition in the case of a public listed company may present greater difficulty.'

Lastly I was referred, on this point also, to the judgment of Peter Gibson J in *Re Sam Weller & Sons Ltd* at the end of which (see [1990] BCLC 80 at 89, [1990] Ch 682 at 694) he said that he had no doubt that the court would ordinarily be very reluctant to accept that managerial decisions could amount to unfairly prejudicial conduct. The point for which that judgment is mainly authority is, of course, that conduct may be unfairly prejudicial to the interests of minority shareholders even if those responsible for that conduct may, as members of the company, have suffered the same or even greater prejudice. That point is relevant here.

I do not doubt that in an appropriate case it is open to the court to find that serious mismanagement of a company's business constitutes conduct that is unfairly prejudicial to the interests of minority shareholders. But I share Peter Gibson J's view that the court will normally be very reluctant to accept that managerial decisions can amount to unfairly prejudicial conduct.

Two considerations seem to me to be relevant. First, there will be cases where there is disagreement between petitioners and respondents as to whether a particular managerial decision was, as a matter of commercial judgment, the right one to make, or as to whether a particular proposal relating to the conduct of the company's business is commercially sound. I heard much evidence, including the expert evidence of Dr Rhodes, directed to issues of that kind arising from decisions made by Mr Purslow, or from decisions that it was said he should have made but did not make. In my view, it is not for the court to resolve such disagreements on a petition under s 459. Not only is a judge ill-qualified to do so, but there can be no unfairness to the petitioners in those in control of the company's affairs taking a different view from theirs on such matters.

Secondly, as was persuasively argued by Mr Chivers, a shareholder acquires shares in a company knowing that their value will depend in some measure on the competence of the management. He takes the risk that that management may prove not to be of the highest quality. Short of a breach by a director of his duty of skill and care (and no such breach on the part of either Mr Purslow or Mrs Purslow was alleged) there is prima facie no unfairness to a shareholder in the quality of the management turning out to be poor. It occurred to me during the argument that one example of a case where the court might none the less find that there was unfair prejudice to minority shareholders would be one where the majority shareholders, for reasons of their own, persisted in retaining in charge of the management of the company's business a member of their family who was demonstrably incompetent. That of course would be a very different case from this. Mr Rowland deliberately invested in a company controlled and managed by Mr Purslow, whom he had known for five years or so. Indeed, he did so, despite Mr Purslow's reluctance to have him as a shareholder in his company. Mr Nurse submitted that Mr Rowland had a right to expect a reasonable standard of general management from Mr Purslow. In my view, he had no such right. He took the risk that Mr Purslow's management of the company might not be up to the standard that he, Mr Rowland, had hoped and expected.

SOURCE 206
Re Posgate & Denby (Agencies) Ltd
(Chancery Division 1986) [1987] BCLC 8

The petitioner unsuccessfully argued that the exercise by the directors of powers contained in the company's articles of association and carried out in accordance with the statutory requirements, should be read as being subject to shareholder approval.

HOFFMANN J: In the absence of a breach of fiduciary duty, which is not here alleged, the equity shareholders plainly have no right under the articles to prevent the directors from exercising the company's power to sell its assets. But the concept of unfair prejudice which forms the basis of the jurisdiction under s 459 enables the court to take into account not only the rights of members under the company's constitution, but also their legitimate expectations arising from the agreements or understandings of the members inter se. There is an analogy in Lord Wilberforce's analysis of the concept of what is 'just and equitable' in *Ebrahimi v Westbourne Galleries Ltd* [1972] 2 All ER 492, [1973] AC 360. The common case of such expectations being superimposed on a member's rights under the articles is the corporate quasi-partnership, in which members frequently have expectations of participating in the management and profits of the company, which arise from the understandings on which the company was formed and which it may be unfair for the other members to ignore. The question is therefore whether the petitioner can be said to have had a legitimate expectation that in the circumstances which exist in this case, the board would not dispose of the syndicates without the approval of the holders of a majority of the equity shares.

Although the answer to this question must in each case depend on the particular facts, it is well to recall that in *Ebrahimi v Westbourne Galleries Ltd*, Lord Wilberforce said that in most cases the basis of the association would be 'adequately and exhaustively' laid down in the articles. The 'superimposition of equitable considerations' requires, he said, something more. This was said in the context of the 'just and equitable' ground for winding up, but in my judgment it is equally necessary for a shareholder who claims that it is 'unfair' within the meaning of s 459 for the board to exercise powers conferred by the articles to demonstrate some special circumstances which create a legitimate expectation that the board would not do so. Section 459 enables the court to give full effect to the terms and understandings on which the members of the company became associated but not to rewrite them.

In my judgment the matters relied on by counsel for the petitioner do not, singly or cumulatively, justify such an expectation. Each of them is expressly or impliedly contemplated by the articles which form the basis on which the petitioner took his shares, and which deny such a right to the equity shareholders. Firstly, the articles make it clear that although the equity shareholders are the persons principally interested in the profits and assets of the company, the whole of the conduct of the company's business is entrusted to the board and, with one immaterial exception, the equity shareholders are not to have a vote even on matters within the province of the company in general meeting. Secondly, the articles make it clear that conflicts of interest are not to inhibit the directors from taking part in board decisions. Thirdly, all decisions concerning the business of the company involve the risk that other decisions may turn out to have been better. The existence of such a risk cannot be a reason why it would be unfair not to seek the approval of the equity shareholders. In my judgment the articles make it impossible to superimpose an obligation of fairness requiring such approval even in the circumstances of this case. Accordingly there is no arguable basis for saying that it would be unfairly prejudicial to the petitioner if the proposed transaction were implemented without the approval of the equity shareholders. . . .

SOURCE 207
Re Saul D Harrison & Sons plc
(Court of Appeal 1994) [1995] 1 BCLC 14

HOFFMANN LJ (giving the first judgment at the invitation of Neill LJ): This is an appeal from an order of Vinelott J striking out as an abuse of process a contributory's petition from an order under s 459 of the Companies Act 1985 and to wind up on the just and equitable ground.

1. The company
The company was formed in 1947 to take over the business founded by the petitioner's great-grandfather in 1891 and subsequently carried on by four of his sons. Its original and until recently main business was the manufacture and sale of industrial cleaning and wiping cloths made from waste textiles. But it also sells Johnson & Johnson J-Cloths and wiping products made from paper and it sorts and sells second-hand clothing (mainly for export to Africa).

For many years the company owned a factory called the Stronghold Works in West Ham. In December 1989 London Regional Transport promoted a bill in Parliament for the extension of the Jubilee Line which included a power compulsorily to purchase the Stronghold Works. The company negotiated with London Regional Transport in advance of the passage of the bill, and in October 1990 it entered into an agreement to sell the Stronghold Works for £2,750,000 and at the same time bought new premises in Hackney for the same price. The move to Hackney was completed in October 1991.

In 1960 the company's shares were reorganised into three classes. There are 30 A shares, 174,300 B shares and 825,670 C shares. The A shares carry votes but no right to dividend. The B and C shares carry no votes but are entitled to a

dividend, with the B shareholders entitled to 10% before payment to the C
shareholders. For the purpose of avoiding estate duty, most of the C shares were
allotted to or in trust for the grandchildren of Saul Harrison's sons, including the
petitioner. But the A shares were allotted to the three surviving sons of the
founder, including the petitioner's grandfather Alfred. They have since devolved
upon the petitioner's aunt Marion and her second cousin Alan. The petitioner's
87,563 C shares represent 8.76% of the issued share capital of the company, all of
which is still held by or on trust for members of the family. At the time of the
hearing before Vinelott J the directors were Alan, his son Stephen and the
petitioner's first cousin David.

2. The allegations

The essence of the petitioner's complaint is that although the company has
substantial net assets, the prospects for its business have for some years been so
poor that by the time the petition was presented any reasonable board would
have closed it down and distributed the assets to the shareholders. Instead, the
directors have allowed the assets to be dissipated in losses in order to preserve
their own inflated salaries and perquisites. The petitioner relies in particular
upon the purchase of new premises in 1990. She says that any reasonable board
would have regarded the proposed compulsory purchase by London Regional
Transport as a golden opportunity to realise the company's principal asset and
cease trading. The decision to buy new premises to continue a loss-making trade
could not have been bona fide.

In addition to these central allegations the petition also complains that the
directors have caused the company to pay substantial salaries and benefits to their
wives for little or no consideration. The accounts are said to be deficient; first,
because the Stronghold Works were shown until sale at historic cost (£456,000)
when they were plainly worth a great deal more, and secondly, because proper
particulars of the directors' remuneration were not given. Finally, it is said that
the accounts for periods up to 31 March 1989 were qualified because the
directors did not keep proper accounting records.

On these grounds the petitioner says that the affairs of the company have been
conducted in a manner unfairly prejudicial to the C shareholders, including
herself, within the meaning of s 459 of the Companies Act 1985 and that it is just
and equitable that the company should be wound up.

3. 'Unfairly prejudicial' and 'just and equitable'

What must a petitioner show in order to justify an order under s 459 or an order
to wind up? The grounds for winding up are that it is 'just and equitable' to do
so. The grounds for an order under s 459 are that

> 'the company's affairs are being or have been conducted in a manner which
> is unfairly prejudicial to the interests of its members generally or of some
> part of its members (including at least [the petitioner]).'

If these grounds are made out, the court has a discretion to make such order as
it thinks fit for giving relief in respect of the matters complained of, including in
particular the relief sought in this case, which is an order that other members or
the company itself buy the petitioner's shares: see s 461(2)(d).

'Unfairly prejudicial' is deliberately imprecise language which was chosen by
Parliament because its earlier attempt in s 210 of the Companies Act 1948 to
provide a similar remedy had been too restrictively construed. The earlier section
had used the word 'oppressive', which the House of Lords in *Scottish Co-op
Wholesale Society Ltd v Meyer* [1958] 3 All ER 66, [1959] AC 324, [1958] 3 WLR 404

said meant 'burdensome, harsh and wrongful'. This gave rise to some uncertainty as to whether 'wrongful' required actual illegality or invasion of legal rights. The Jenkins Committee on Company Law, which reported in 1962, thought that it should not. To make this clear, it recommended the use of the term 'unfairly prejudicial', which Parliament somewhat tardily adopted in s 75 of the Companies Act 1980. This section is reproduced (with minor amendment) in the present s 459 of the Companies Act 1985.

Mr Purle, who appeared for the petitioner, said that the only test of unfairness was whether a reasonable bystander would think that the conduct in question was unfair. This is correct, so far as it goes, and has some support in the cases. Its merit is to emphasise that the court is applying an objective standard of fairness. But I do not think that it is the most illuminating way of putting the matter. For one thing, the standard of fairness must necessarily be laid down by the court. In explaining how the court sets about deciding what is fair in the context of company management, I do not think that it helps a great deal to add the reasonable company watcher to the already substantial cast of imaginary characters which the law uses to personify its standards of justice in different situations. An appeal to the views of an imaginary third party makes the concept seem more vague than it really is. It is more useful to examine the factors which the law actually takes into account in setting the standard.

In deciding what is fair or unfair for the purposes of s 459, it is important to have in mind that fairness is being used in the context of a commercial relationship. The articles of association are just what their name implies: the contractual terms which govern the relationships of the shareholders with the company and each other. They determine the powers of the board and the company in general meeting and everyone who becomes a member of a company is taken to have agreed to them. Since keeping promises and honouring agreements is probably the most important element of commercial fairness, the starting point in any case under s 459 will be to ask whether the conduct of which the shareholder complains was in accordance with the articles of association.

The answer to this question often turns on the fact that the powers which the shareholders have entrusted to the board are fiduciary powers, which must be exercised for the benefit of the company as a whole. If the board act for some ulterior purpose, they step outside the terms of the bargain between the shareholders and the company. As a matter of ordinary company law, this may or may not entitle the individual shareholder to a remedy. It depends upon whether he can bring himself within one of the exceptions to the rule in *Foss v Harbottle* (1843) 2 Hare 461. But the fact that the board are protected by the principle of majority rule does not necessarily prevent their conduct from being unfair within the meaning of s 459. Enabling the court in an appropriate case to outflank the rule in *Foss v Harbottle* was one of the purposes of the section. So in *Re a Company (No 00370 of 1987), ex p Glossop* [1988] BCLC 570, [1988] 1 WLR 1068, where the complaint was of a consistent refusal by the board to recommend payment of a dividend, Harman J said that such conduct could make it just and equitable to wind up the company. He did so by reference to the seminal judgment of Lord Wilberforce in *Howard Smith Ltd v Ampol Petroleum Ltd* [1974] 1 All ER 1126, [1974] AC 821 on the principles by which the court decides whether the board has acted within its fiduciary powers and said that on the facts alleged it was arguable that the board had exceeded them. This seems to me in principle the correct point at which to start the inquiry into both whether the conduct in question could justify a just and equitable winding up and also whether it is unfair for the purposes of s 459. It seems clear that but for a technical objection which was removed when the section was amended in 1989, Harman J would have allowed the petition to proceed on both grounds, as Peter Gibson J did before the amendment in *Re Sam Weller & Sons Ltd* [1990] BCLC 80, [1990] Ch 682. I should however add that while I respectfully think that Harman J was right in asking himself whether the board had abused its fiduciary powers, I would not necessarily subscribe to the theory of corporate hubris on which he decided that it arguably had.

Although one begins with the articles and the powers of the board, a finding that conduct was not in accordance with the articles does not necessarily mean that it was unfair, still less that the court will exercise its discretion to grant relief. There is often sound sense in the rule in *Foss v Harbottle* (1843) 2 Hare 461. In choosing the term 'unfairly prejudicial', the Jenkins Committee (para 204) equated it with Lord Cooper's understanding of 'oppression' in *Elder v Elder and Watson* 1952 SC 49:

> 'a visible departure from the standards of fair dealing and a violation of the conditions of fair play on which every shareholder who entrusts his money to a company is entitled to rely.'

So trivial or technical infringements of the articles were not intended to give rise to petitions under s 459.

Not only may conduct be technically unlawful without being unfair: it can also be unfair without being unlawful. In a commercial context, this may at first seem surprising. How can it be unfair to act in accordance with what the parties have agreed? As a general rule, it is not. But there are cases in which the letter of the articles does not fully reflect the understandings upon which the shareholders are associated. Lord Wilberforce drew attention to such cases in a celebrated passage of his judgment in *Ebrahimi v Westbourne Galleries Ltd* [1972] 2 All ER 492 at 500, [1973] AC 360 at 379, which discusses what seems to me the identical concept of injustice or unfairness which can form the basis of a just and equitable winding up:

> 'The words [just and equitable] are a recognition of the fact that a limited company is more than a mere judicial entity, with a personality in law of its own: that there is room in company law for recognition of the fact that behind it, or amongst it, there are individuals, with rights, expectations and obligations inter se which are not necessarily submerged in the company structure. That structure is defined by the Companies Act 1948 and by the articles of association by which the shareholders agree to be bound. In most companies and in most contexts, this definition is sufficient and exhaustive, equally so whether the company is large or small. The "just and equitable" provision does not, as the respondents suggest, entitle one party to disregard the obligation he assumes by entering a company, nor the court to dispense him from it. It does, as equity always does, enable the court to subject the exercise of legal rights to equitable considerations; considerations, that is, of a personal character arising between one individual and another, which may make it unjust, or inequitable, to insist on legal rights or to exercise them in a particular way.'

Thus the personal relationship between a shareholder and those who control the company may entitle him to say that it would in certain circumstances be unfair for them to exercise a power conferred by the articles upon the board or the company in general meeting. I have in the past ventured to borrow from public law the term 'legitimate expectation' to describe the correlative 'right' in the shareholder to which such a relationship may give rise. It often arises out of a fundamental understanding between the shareholders which formed the basis of their association but was not put into contractual form, such as an assumption that each of the parties who has ventured his capital will also participate in the management of the company and receive the return on his investment in the form of salary rather than dividend. These relationships need not always take the form of implied agreements with the shareholder concerned; they could enure for the benefit of a third party such as a joint venturer's widow. But in *Ebrahimi v Westbourne Galleries Ltd* ([1972] 2 All ER 492 at 500) Lord Wilberforce went on to say:

> 'It would be impossible, and wholly undesirable, to define the circumstances in which these considerations may arise. Certainly the fact that the company is a small one, or a private company, is not enough. There are very many of these where the association is a purely commercial one, of which it can safely be said that the basis of association is adequately and exhaustively laid down in the articles. The superimposition of equitable considerations requires something more . . .'

Thus in the absence of 'something more', there is no basis for a legitimate expectation that the board and the company in general meeting will not exercise whatever powers they are given by the articles of association.

In this case, as the judge emphasised, there is nothing more. The petitioner was given her shares in 1960 pursuant to a reorganisation of the share capital which vested the entire control of the company in the A shareholders and the board whom they appointed. This scheme is binding upon her and there are no special circumstances to modify its effects. Although the petition speaks of the petitioner having various 'legitimate expectations', no grounds are alleged for saying that her rights are not 'adequately and exhaustively' laid down by the articles. And in substance the alleged 'legitimate expectations' amount to no more than an expectation that the board would manage the company in accordance with their fiduciary obligations and the terms of the articles and the Companies Act.

Thus it seems to me that in this case one can be a good deal more precise than to ask in general terms, as Mr Purle suggested, whether a bystander would think that the board had been unfair. As there are no grounds for saying that it would be unfair for the board to act in accordance with the bargain between the petitioner and the company, the very minimum required to make out a case of unfairness is that the powers of management have been used for an unlawful purpose or the articles otherwise infringed. Hence the allegation in the petition that the board acted in bad faith, carrying on the business in order to provide themselves with salaries rather than because they genuinely thought that it was in the interests of the shareholders as a whole.

Mr Purle said that it was not necessary for this purpose that the petitioner should have to show that the board was motivated by self-interest. It would be sufficient that the decision to continue the business was irrational: one which no reasonable board of rational businessmen could have thought was in the interests of the company. There may be cases in which this distinction makes some sense but in this one it does not. If no rational board could honestly have thought that carrying on the business was in the interests of the company, the conclusion must inevitably follow that the board acted from some improper motive of their own. The petition recognises this and squarely alleges bad faith. In my judgment the claims for relief under s 459 and winding up stand or fall by whether this allegation can be made out. . . .

NOTES AND QUESTIONS

1. The scope for finding shareholder expectations which are supplementary to their strict legal rights contained either in the articles of association or in shareholder agreements, is obviously limited in public companies. This point was forcibly made by Vinelott J in Re Blue Arrow plc[1] who said:

> 'No doubt there are cases where a legitimate expectation may be inferred from arrangements outside the ambit of the formal constitution of the company, but it must be borne in mind that this is a public company, a listed company . . . Outside investors were entitled to assume that the whole of the constitution was contained in the articles, read, of course, together with the Companies Acts. There is in these circumstances no room for any legitimate expectation founded on some agreement or arrangement made between the directors and kept up their sleeves and not disclosed to those placing the shares with the public. . . .'

2. Following the recommendations of the *Lawrence Committee* (Interim Report of the Select Committee on Company Law, *Ontario, 1967*), and the *Dickerson Committee* (Proposals for a New Business Corporations Law for Canada, *Ottawa, 1971*), which described the rule in Foss v Harbottle as an 'infamous doctrine [which] should be relegated to legal limbo without compunction', Canada enacted a statutory derivative action. The Dickerson proposals were implemented by s 232 of the Canada Business Corporations Act 1974, which provides:

   '(1) Subject to subsection (2) a complainant may apply to a court for leave to bring an action in the name and on behalf of the corporation or any of its subsidiaries, or intervene in an action to which any such body corporate is a party, for the purpose of prosecuting, defending or discontinuing the action on behalf of the body corporate.

   (2) No action may be brought and no intervention in an action may be made under subsection (1) unless the court is satisfied that:

   (a) the complainant has given reasonable notice to the directors of the corporation or its subsidiary of his intention to apply to the court under subsection (1) if the directors of the corporation or its subsidiary do not bring, diligently prosecute or defend or discontinue the action;

   (b) the complainant is acting in good faith;

   (c) it appears to be in the interests of the corporation or its subsidiary that the action be brought, prosecuted, defended or discontinued.'

3. Should English law follow the Canadian model and adopt a statutory derivative action for remedying corporate wrongs, leaving s 459 purely as a provision for remedying abuses of a personal nature? (See Griggs and Lowry [1994] JBL 463.)

---

1 [1987] BCLC 585

Chapter 9

FINANCING THE COMPANY

PART I: SHARES AND DEBENTURES — A COMPARISON

A company can raise finance by the issue of shares or debentures, which together are described as 'securities'. They have much in common. Both are proper investments for trust funds (Trustee Investments Act 1961, Sch 1, Pt III.1 — as defined in Pt IV.4). Each can be listed on The Stock Exchange (Stock Exchange Admission of Securities to Listing 1984) and the public, when invited to advance finance to a company on the strength of an issue of shares or debentures, receives the same protection against any loss arising from misleading or inadequate information (see Chapter 3).

In the case of both debentures and fully paid shares (the vast majority of shares), disinvestment can be effected by transfer, using the simplified instrument of transfer form annexed to the Stock Transfer Act 1963. In the case of shares, there may be restrictions on transfer imposed by the articles of association (Sources 211, 212, 213, 214, 215).

The company is bound in contract to both shareholders (on the memorandum and articles of association — s 14 of the Companies Act, and Chapter 5) and debentureholders (on the terms of the debenture), but there are important differences. Debentureholders have a legally enforceable claim to the interest payable on the advance and a legally enforceable claim to the return of the advance. Shareholders are only entitled to a return on the investment (dividends) when this is declared and to the investment itself, only when the company is wound up or undergoes a capital reconstruction scheme which provides for a return of capital (Chapter 11).

The debentureholder is, in law, a creditor of, and therefore separate from, the company, whereas a shareholder is a member of and, therefore, within the company. In theory, at least, the latter's interest is not simply that of an investment, but includes participating in the running of the company. It will be on the basis of such distinctions, as well as the prevailing fiscal policy that the directors, when raising finance for the company, will decide whether to do it by way of shares or debentures (Source 208).

SOURCE 208
Cairncross & McCrae, Capital City
(1986) p 149

Companies quoted on the Exchange can, if their shareholders agree, raise extra money in one of two ways. They can go to their shareholders with a 'rights issue'. This is so called because the company offers its shareholders the right to buy more shares, generally at a cheaper price than the ruling market price. Or they can issue a debenture.

The choice between equity or loan capital (debentures) is determined by a number of factors. Sometimes it depends on tax legislation. Thus the 1965 Finance Act made it cheaper to raise loan capital than equity, because equity dividends had to be paid out of taxed profits whereas loan interest was paid before tax. Between the early 1970s and 1982, high long-term interest rates caused companies to shy away from borrowing by issuing loan stock. Instead they raised money almost exclusively by issuing more equity through rights issues. But when interest rates fell in 1982, the market re-opened, with several companies, banks and some foreign countries issuing loan stock.

The balance between equity and fixed interest capital is known as 'gearing'. A company is said to be 'highly geared' if it has a high ratio of fixed-interest capital to equity. Generally the more risky the business a company is involved in, the lower should be its gearing. A company which has a large amount of interest to be paid every year is more likely to be pushed into a loss in a bad year than one with a high proportion of equity capital on which it can reduce or if necessary pass its dividend.

PART II: SHARES

The Nature and Valuation of Shares

A share is more than an instrument giving rise to a contract on the basis of the memorandum and articles of association (the contractual aspects of share-holding are dealt with in Chapter 5). It is, itself, property capable of being transferred, subject to the restrictions, if any, contained in the contract. Its value depends upon a number of factors including the circumstances under which the valuation is made (Sources 209 and 210).

SOURCE 209
Commissioners of Inland Revenue v Crossman
[1937] AC 26; [1936] 1 All ER 762

The articles of association of the company contained substantial restrictions on the transfer of shares, namely:

Article 34(1) A male holder may at any time transfer any one or more of his said ordinary shares to any of his sons daughters or grandsons (being sons of sons) or brothers or nephews (being sons of brothers) and being of the age of 25 years at the least, and being in other respects in the opinion of the directors duly qualified for membership.
(2) A male holder may by his will or any codicil thereto appoint any one or more of his ordinary shares to any of his sons daughters or grandsons (being sons of sons) or brothers or nephews (being sons of brothers) and, being at the time of his death of the age of 25 years at the least; and any such appointee shall be entitled to a transfer of the shares from the legal personal representatives of the appointor, provided that the directors within three months after the death of the appointor signify their approval of the transferee.
(3) A male holder may by his will or any codicil thereto appoint any one or more of his ordinary shares to any of his sons daughters or grandsons (being sons of sons) or brothers or nephews (being sons of brothers) and who may at the time of his death be under the age of 25 years on the footing that the appointment is only to take effect as and when the appointee attains the age of 25 years, and may

in like manner make provision as to the application of the interim income arising from such shares for the benefit of the appointor's widow (if any) and any child or children or remoter issue or brother or nephew (being a son of a brother) of the appointor or some or one of them. And in default of and subject to any such provision such interim income shall be applied in such manner as the legal personal representatives of the appointor shall think fit for the benefit of any such person as aforesaid. Any such appointee shall on attaining the age of 25 years be entitled to a transfer of the shares from the legal personal representatives of the appointor, provided that the directors within three months after he becomes so entitled signify their approval of him as transferee.

. . .

Notice of Intention to Transfer. — (6) Except where the transfer is made pursuant to paragraphs 1, 2, 3 or 5 of this clause, a member proposing to transfer any ordinary share (hereinafter called 'the proposing transferor') shall give notice in writing (hereinafter called 'the transfer notice') to the company that he desires to transfer the same. Such notice shall constitute the company his agent for the sale of the share at par value to any member of the company holding any ordinary share or ordinary shares.

. . .

Company's Power. — (8) If the company shall, within the space of three months after being served with such notice, find a member holding an ordinary share or ordinary shares willing to purchase the share (hereinafter called 'the purchasing member') and shall give notice thereof to the proposing transferor, he shall be bound, upon payment of the par value to transfer the share to the purchasing member.

. . .

Default by Proposing Transferor. — (10) If in any case the proposing transferor, after having become bound as aforesaid, makes default in transferring the share, the company may receive the purchase-money and shall thereupon cause the name of the purchasing member to be entered in the register as the holder of the share, and shall hold the purchase-money in trust for the proposing transferor.

. . .

Default by Company. — (12) If the company shall not, within the space of three months after being served with the transfer notice, find a member holding an ordinary share or ordinary shares willing to purchase the shares and give notice in manner aforesaid, the proposing transferor shall, at any time within three calendar months afterwards, be at liberty (subject to paragraph 14 hereof) to sell and transfer the shares (or those not placed) to any person and at any price.

How Shares to be offered to Members. — (13) If, and so far as practicable, the shares comprised in a transfer notice shall be offered by the company to the members holding an ordinary share or ordinary shares in proportion as nearly as may be to the ordinary shares held by them respectively, and any shares not accepted in response to such offer, shall be offered to the remaining said members in the like proportion. Any share which it is impracticable thus to offer, may be offered to such member or members, whether a director or not, as the directors think fit.

General Power to Refuse Transfer. — (15) The directors may refuse to register any transfer of a share, (*a*) where the company has a lien on the share; (*b*) where, in the case of shares not fully paid up, it is not proved to their satisfaction that the proposed transferee is a responsible person; (*c*) where the directors are of an opinion that the proposed transferee is not a desirable person to admit to membership, and that without being bound to assign any reason for such opinion. But paragraphs (*b*) and (*c*) of this clause shall not apply where the proposed transferee is already a member holding more than 250 ordinary shares.

(16) The company may, by special resolution, repeal or alter any of the provisions of this clause, and the last preceding clause, but at the meetings to pass such special resolution, no member shall be entitled to be present or to vote, who is not a holder of an ordinary share or ordinary shares, and the quorum of each such meeting shall be members holding one-fifth at least of the issued ordinary shares.

In this case the court was faced with the problem of the valuation, for estate duty purposes, of shares in the company held by the estate of a deceased former member. The House of Lords decided by a majority of three to two that on the proper construction of s 7 of the Finance Act 1894, the shares were to be valued as though the restrictions on transfer did not apply.

> LORD RUSSELL (dissenting):[1] A share in a limited company is a property the nature of which has been accurately expounded by Farwell J, in *Borland's Trustee v Steel.*[2] It is the interest of a person in the company, that interest being composed of rights and obligations which are defined by the Companies Act and by the memorandum and articles of association of the company. A sale of a share is a sale of the interest so defined, and the subject matter of the sale is effectively vested in the purchaser by the entry of his name in the register of members. It may be that owing to provisions in the articles of association the subject matter of the sale cannot be effectively vested in the purchaser because the directors refuse to and cannot be compelled to register the purchaser as shareholder. The purchaser could then secure the benefit of the sale by the registered shareholder becoming a trustee for him of the rights with an indemnity in respect of the obligations. In the case of the sale of such a share, the risk of a refusal to register might well be reflected in a smaller price being obtainable than would have been obtained had there been no such risk. The share was property with that risk as one of its incidents.

SOURCE 210
Dean *v* Prince
[1954] Ch 409; [1954] 1 All ER 749

> EVERSHED MR: Three persons, all of whom were stated to be 'working men' and all of whom (save as to the late Mr Dean after his illness) were working directors, formed the defendant company shortly before the last war for the purpose of carrying on in Sheffield a light engineering business. The paid up capital of the company has consisted at all material times of 200 shares each of £1 and no more. Of these shares 140 were held by the late Mr Dean, and 30 each by the two individual defendants, Prince and Cowen.
>
>   . . .
>
> The late Mr Dean died on 6 November 1951, and the provisions of the special articles relating to transfers of shares in such an event, accordingly, came into operation. The relevant article is article 9 of the special articles, which was applicable to all cases of transfer and transmission of shares. The particular paragraph applicable in the circumstances of the case is paragraph (*g*) which is in the following terms: 'In the event of the death of any member his shares shall be purchased and taken by the directors at such price as is certified in writing by

---

1 The fact that he dissented is irrelevant as far as the extracted passage is concerned
2 [1901] 1 Ch 279; 70 LJ Ch 51 (see p 298)

the auditor to be in his opinion the fair value thereof at the date of death and in so certifying the auditor shall be considered to act as an expert and not as an arbitrator and accordingly the Arbitration Act 1889, shall not apply. Unless they otherwise agree the directors shall take such shares equally between them.'

. . .

The valuation which article 9(*g*) required to be made was in due course undertaken by Mr Jenkinson of the firm of W. G. Hawson, Wynn & Co, chartered accountants, the company's auditors.

. . .

Mrs Dean was dissatisfied with Mr Jenkinson's valuation, and she, accordingly, brought the present action, in which she has sought a declaration that she is not bound to transfer the shares at the valuation arrived at by Mr Jenkinson. Having regard to the form of the article it is not in doubt that, were it not for one circumstance, Mrs Dean could not have questioned the validity and conclusiveness of Mr Jenkinson's certificate, since no sort of imputation has been made, or could be made, of Mr Jenkinson's integrity. That one circumstance is this: Mr Jenkinson had (in the laudable hope of achieving agreement between Mrs Dean and the first two defendants) indicated in writing the method which he had adopted in arriving at his valuation, as follows: '3. In view of these trading results — and taking into account to some extent the difficult position in which the company would be placed if the amounts due to Mr and Mrs Dean had to be paid, it was clear that no value could be put on the shares on a normal going concern basis other than something purely nominal. It became necessary, therefore, to consider the only other basis which could apply, ie, break-up value. 7. The foregoing showed that to a third party the shares were unlikely to be worth more than £1400 and that it was by no means certain that that amount could be realized. To the parties who are under obligation to buy the shares it left out of account altogether one important factor, viz, that they could realize the break-up value only at the expense of losing their employment. To retain their employment, ie, considering the transaction on a going concern basis, they would be paying £7 for shares on which we could place no value. In view of this position it could be regarded as a matter of grave doubt whether a valuation of £7 a share did not substantially favour the seller.'

. . .

In the case of a private company carrying on a profitable business it is no doubt true that a sound and obvious basis of calculation would be in accordance with the expectation of profit for the future, particularly where the shares in question would constitute a majority holding. In my judgment, however, Mr Jenkinson rightly rejected any such basis of valuation in the present case; for a continued expectation of loss would produce necessarily a negative result; and I have already said that the change of fortune which occurred after Mr Jenkinson's valuation is, in my judgment, irrelevant. A calculation on the basis of profits (that is upon the basis of expected returns on the footing of the company continuing as a going concern) being out of the way, Mr Jenkinson, as I think, turned clearly to a break-up value as upon a forced sale as the only available alternative.

. . . (1) The effect of a valuation on the basis selected was plainly to depress greatly the value of the assets. It was made clear by Colonel Riddle, a valuer acting for Mr Jenkinson, in the written valuation supplied by him to Mr Jenkinson, and equally in his evidence in court, that his figure for the plant, furniture, machinery and so forth, namely, £1785 10s. 0d., was arrived at on the basis of their auction value, that is on being broken up and removed from the factory and in part, at any rate, sold for scrap. Colonel Riddle made it clear that he was not asked to consider any other basis, and further he said in evidence that a valuation 'in situ' would have been higher.

. . . (2) (And as a corollary to the above) Mr Jenkinson ignored the possibility of a gradual turning to account and disposal of the company's assets. (3) He ignored also in the same connexion the circumstances that a majority holding, even though not a three-fourths majority, would enable a buyer to control the method and speed of disposal. It is in this respect that to my mind the fact that the shares in question constituted a majority holding was relevant. I can well understand that a notional buyer of 30 of the shares in the company would find the proposed sale highly unattractive since, once in the company, he would be unable to get out and could not control in any way the conduct of the company's business. Finally: (4) Mr Jenkinson justified the basis selected by him 'on accountancy principles.'

. . .

In my judgment the relevant question cannot fairly be answered by a mere application of accountancy principles, by a mere arithmetical process. The question has to be answered in light of the general conditions affecting the light engineering business in Sheffield and all circumstances peculiar to the defendant company. As regards the former matter the evidence was, clearly, that the prospects of such business were generally, at the relevant time, good. As regards the latter matter it was, in my view, of great significance that of the company's four-storey factory premises, one floor was occupied by one Goodyear as tenant or licensee of the defendant company, and he was and is in the same line of business and said in evidence that he was and is interested in the company's plant, etc, and the company's business in the event of a sale. Mr Jenkinson did not, as is quite plain, make any inquiry of this Goodyear or of anyone else because he was not concerned to consider, as material to the 'asset content' of the company, the possibility of a sale of any of the assets 'in situ'.

. . .

In the result, therefore, Mrs Dean would in my judgment prima facie be entitled to the relief she claimed, and if the matter ended there I should for myself agree with Harman J in his conclusion. But there remains the special circumstance which I have mentioned above.

The 'special circumstances' were that the company had agreed to purchase the premises, on which its business was carried on, from Mrs Dean on very disadvantageous terms. For this reason, Evershed MR agreed with the other two members of the Court of Appeal (Denning LJ and Wynn-Parry J) that the appeal be allowed and the accountant's valuation upheld.

DENNING LJ: . . . In this case Harman J has upset the valuation on the ground that the auditor failed to take into account some factors and proceeded on wrong principles. I will take the points in order:
1. *The right to control the company.* Harman J said that the auditor should have taken into account the fact that the 140 shares were a majority holding and would give a purchaser the right to control the company. I do not think that the auditor was bound to take that factor into account. Test it this way: suppose it had been Prince who had died, leaving only 30 shares. Those 30 shares, being a minority holding, would fetch nothing in the open market. But does that mean that the other directors would be entitled to take his shares for nothing? Surely not. No matter which director it was who happened to die, his widow should be entitled to the same price per share, irrespective of whether her husband's holding was large or small. It seems to me that the fair thing to do would be to take the whole

200 shares of the company and see what they were worth, and then pay the widow a sum appropriate to her husband's holding. At any rate if the auditor was of opinion that that was a fair method, no one can say that he was wrong. The right way to see what the whole 200 shares were worth, would be to see what the business itself was worth: and that is what the auditor proceeded to do.

2. *Valuation of the business 'as a going concern.'* Harman J seems to have thought that the auditor should have valued the business as a going concern. I do not think that the auditor was bound to do any such thing. The business was a losing concern which had no goodwill: and it is fairly obvious that, as soon as Mrs Dean had sold the 140 shares to the other two directors — as she was bound to do — she would in all probability call in the moneys owing to herself and to her husband amounting to over £2000. The judge said that she was not likely to press for the moneys because that would be 'killing the goose that laid the eggs,' but he was wrong about this; because as soon as she sold the shares, she would have got rid of the goose and there was no reason why she should not press for the moneys. She was an executrix and the company's position was none too good. It had only £1200 in the bank to meet a demand for £2200. In these circumstances the auditor was of opinion that there was a strong probability of the company having to be wound up: and he rejected the going-concern basis. For myself, I should have thought he was clearly right, but at any rate no one can say that his opinion was wrong.

(3) *Valuation of the assets of the business.* Once the going-concern basis is rejected, the only possible way of valuing the business is to find out the value of the tangible assets. Harman J thought that the assets should have been valued as a whole in situ. It was quite likely, he said, that 'some one could have been found who would make a bid for the whole thing, lock, stock and barrel.' But the judge seems to have forgotten that no one would buy the assets in situ in this way unless he could also buy the premises; and the company had no saleable interest in the premises. In respect of part of the premises the company had only a monthly tenancy: in respect of the rest the company had only a contract for the purchase of the premises on paying £200 a year for 25 years. It had no right to assign this contract; and its interest was liable to be forfeited if it went into liquidation, either compulsory or voluntary; and the probability was, of course, that, if it sold all the assets, it would go into liquidation, and hence lose the premises. The company could, therefore, only sell the assets without the premises. That is how the auditor valued them and no one can say that he was wrong in so doing.

(4) *Valuation on a 'break-up' basis.* The auditor instructed the valuer, Colonel Riddle, to value the plant and machinery at the break-up value as loose chattels on a sale by auction. Harman J thought that that was a wrong basis because it was equivalent to a forced sale. I would have agreed with the judge if the business had been a profitable concern. The value of the tangible assets would then have been somewhere in the region of £4000 or £5000, being either the balance sheet figure of £4070 or Pressley's figure of £4835. But the business was not a profitable concern. It was a losing concern: and it is a well-known fact that a losing concern cannot realize the book value of its assets. There is an element to be taken into account which is sometimes spoken of as 'negative goodwill.' It comes about in this way: if a business is making a loss, that shows that its assets, regarded as an entity, are not a good investment. A purchaser will decline, therefore, to buy on that basis. He will only buy on a piece-meal basis, according to what the various assets taken individually are worth: and it is obvious that on a sale of assets piece-meal, the vendor will suffer heavy losses as compared with the book figures. The auditor was therefore quite justified in asking the vendor to value the assets as

loose chattels sold at an auction. At any rate, if he honestly formed that opinion, no one can say that he was wrong.

5. *The special purchaser.* Harman J thought that someone could have been found to buy the 140 shares who would use his majority holding to turn out the two directors, and reorganize the factory and put in his own business. In other words, that the shares would have a special attraction for some person (namely, the next-door neighbour) who wanted to put his own business into these premises. I am prepared to concede that the shares might realize an enhanced value on that account: but I do not think that it would be a fair price to ask the directors to pay. They were buying these shares — under a compulsory sale and purchase — on the assumption that they would continue in the business as working directors. It would be unfair to make them pay a price based on the assumption that they would be turned out. If the auditor never took that possibility into account, he cannot be blamed; for he was only asked to certify the fair value of the shares. The only fair value would be to take a hypothetical purchaser who was prepared to carry on the business if it was worth while so to do, or otherwise to put it into liquidation. At any rate if that was the auditor's opinion, no one can say that he was wrong.

I have covered, I think, all the grounds on which Harman J upset the valuation. I do not think they were good grounds. I would, therefore, allow the appeal and uphold the valuation.

Restrictions on the Transfer of Shares

Until the passing of the Companies Act 1980, it was a requirement that a private company contain some restriction on the transfer of its shares. This requirement was not further defined, but private companies tended to contain tight restrictions on the transfer of shares. This preserved the close partnership-type control over who might become members of the company (see Table A, Pt II, reg 3). Such restrictions — which are still permissible — are generally of two kinds, first a requirement that any shareholder wishing to dispose of his shares should be obliged to offer them first to existing shareholders, secondly a power for the directors to refuse to register a transfer of shares. The latter power could, especially when clothed by the protection given by the courts to directors who refused to give reasons for the exercise of this power, operate as a draconian control over the shareholder's property rights in his or her shares (see *Re Smith & Fawcett Ltd*[1] and *Re Cuthbert Cooper & Sons Ltd*[2] pp 463 and 562).

This is a difficult but very interesting issue to study. It is difficult because many of the cases depend on a close textual analysis of the particular provisions in the articles of association which impose the restrictions on transfer. It is interesting because it is the battleground for the clash of two fundamental legal concepts — the property rights of the shareholder on the one hand, and, on the other hand, the contractual obligations to abide by agreed restrictions on those rights.

It is dangerous to generalise where the cases are often decided on the nature of particular contractual provisions. Yet certain principles have emerged. First, the courts will, wherever possible, construe such provisions

---

1 [1942] Ch 304; [1942] 1 All ER 542 (see p 463)
2 [1937] Ch 392 (see p 562)

restrictively so as to favour the shareholder's property rights rather than the power to limit or prevent the transfer of the shares (Source 213). Secondly, directors must exercise their power of refusing a transfer in good faith in the interests of the company; while against this must be set the fact that directors do not have to state their reasons for refusing a transfer, the courts are sometimes astute at drawing inferences as to these reasons (Source 212).

Another common restriction on the transfer of shares is to require shareholders who wish to transfer their shares to offer those shares first to the existing shareholders (a right of pre-emption). Questions may arise as to whether shareholders are, in fact, wishing to transfer their shares (Sources 213 and 214).

SOURCE 211
Re Gresham Life Assurance Society, ex parte Penney
(Chancery Division and Court of Appeal 1872) (1873) 8 Ch App 446

The clause 17 of the deed of settlement was as follows: That subject to the provisions herein contained, and subject also to the provisions of the Joint Stock Companies Act, so long as the company shall be subject to the provisions of that Act, every shareholder shall be at liberty to sell and transfer his shares to any other person who shall already be a shareholder, or who shall have been approved of as such by the board of directors, and that no person not already a shareholder, or the executors or administrators, legatee or next of kin, of any shareholder shall be entitled to become the transferee of any share unless approved of by the board;

. . .

LORD ROMILLY MR said that the arguments addressed to him on behalf of the company amounted to this, that under clause 17 in the deed of settlement the directors were at liberty to refuse to register any transfer to any person not already a shareholder without giving any reason for their refusal. In his opinion the real meaning of the clause was, that when a shareholder had sold shares to any person not already a shareholder, and the name of the purchaser became known to the board, they might refuse to register it if they had any reasonable ground of objection to the purchaser; and the Court was the judge whether the objection was reasonable. If they had a reason for refusing to register the transfer they might refuse, and a slight reason might do; but they must give it. They could not refuse to register without any reason, out of caprice or from fraud. The board had given no reason why this transfer should not be registered, and he must take it that it was done capriciously. The application to rectify the register must be granted.

The matter then went to the Court of Appeal.

SIR W. M. JAMES LJ: In this case I feel compelled to come to a different conclusion from that of the Master of the Rolls. The clause in the deed of settlement appears to me very clear, which provides that no transfer shall be made to any person outside the company unless that person shall be approved of by the board of directors. No doubt the directors are in a fiduciary position both towards the company and towards every shareholder in it. It is very easy to conceive cases such as those cases to which we have been referred, in which this Court would interfere with any violation of the fiduciary duty so reposed in the directors. But in order to interfere upon that ground it must be made out that the directors have been acting from some improper motive, or arbitrarily and capriciously. That must be alleged and proved, and the person who has a right to allege and prove it is the shareholder who seeks to be removed from the list of shareholders and to substitute another person for himself. . . . it does not appear to me that this Court has any jurisdiction whatever to sit as a Court of Appeal from the deliberate decision of the board of directors, to whom, by the constitution of the company, the question of determining the eligibility or non-eligibility of new members is committed. . . . if it is said that wherever any shareholder has proposed to transfer his shares to some new member, the Court has a right to say to the directors, 'We will presume that your motives are arbitrary and capricious, or that your conduct is corrupt, unless you choose to tell us what your reasons were, and submit those reasons to our decision,' it would appear to me entirely altering the whole constitution of the company as provided by the articles. I cannot conceive that any director would choose to accept office, or exercise the power entrusted to him, if he were liable to be called upon to say what the particular reasons were or the particular motive was which influenced him in coming to the conclusion that any person was not eligible as a shareholder. I think, therefore, that these directors were well advised in not subjecting themselves to be cross-examined and interrogated as to what particular reasons they might have for personally objecting to this gentleman, and in confining themselves to saying, by their secretary, that the question was discussed at a board of the directors, that the propriety of the transfer to the particular transferee was the subject-matter for discussion, and having taken that into their consideration, they had arrived at the conclusion to which they had arrived. This conclusion, of course, in the absence of any suggestion to the contrary, or of any evidence to the contrary, we must take to be a bona fide conclusion on their part that, for some reason or other connected with the interests of the company, they did not think it fit to recognise that gentleman as a transferee. That gentleman was not then and is not up to the present moment in any relation of *cestui que trust* towards them, and therefore he has not right to complain, and the transferor has no right to complain unless he can induce us to believe that he could not find some other purchaser for those shares, either among the shareholders or outside the company, more agreeable to the directors, and who would give the same price. I am of opinion that we cannot sit as a Court of Appeal from the conclusion which the directors have arrived at if we are satisfied that the directors have done that which alone they could be compelled by mandamus to do, to take the matter into their consideration. It appears that they have taken the matter into their consideration, and there is nothing to shew that they have acted otherwise than honestly and fairly. I am of opinion, therefore, that the order of the Master of the Rolls ought to be discharged.

SOURCE 212
Re Bede Steam Shipping Company Limited
(Chancery Division and Court of Appeal 1917) [1917] 1 Ch 123; 86 LJ Ch 65

The company's articles provided as follows:

'The directors and managers may in their discretion and without assigning any reason therefor refuse to register the transfer of any share (not being a fully paid up share) to any person of whom they shall not approve as transferee and may decline to register the transfer of any fully paid up share or shares on certifying that in their opinion it is contrary to the interests of the company that the proposed transferee should be a member thereof.'

At first instance, Eve J held that the refusal by the directors to register a transfer of shares was not a proper exercise by the directors of the power vested in them by the articles and he ordered the proposed transfer to be registered. The company appealed:

LORD COZENS-HARDY MR: . . . What is the position of a shareholder in a company such as this? He has a property in his shares, a property which he is at liberty to dispose of, subject only to any express restriction which may be found in the articles of association of the company. If, for instance, to take a common case, the articles provide that before transferring to a stranger the shares shall be offered on certain terms to other shareholders, a man coming into that company takes subject to that restriction, and he cannot transfer to a stranger without having first made an offer of the shares to the shareholders. So, if there was a condition which is not common, but, I conceive, quite possible, that no transfer should be made to a married woman, that condition would, I think, be perfectly good. Subject to that right, the shareholder is at liberty to transfer a share as much as he is at liberty to sell a chair or table or any other property.

In the present case we are dealing with fully paid up shares where there is no question of escaping from liability to calls or anything of that kind. But it was at one time thought that where the directors had a power to object to a transfer that could not be exercised properly unless the directors stated the grounds of the decision at which they had arrived. In the case of *Ex parte Penney*[1] it was decided by the Court of Appeal (James LJ and Mellish LJ) that it was not necessary for directors to assign reasons, but the Court will presume that they did exercise their power honestly and rightly, unless it appears by the document itself or by a confession on their part or by some other circumstance that they have not done so.

. . .

Now in the present case we know the reasons for which the transfer was refused. It is stated in documents, it is stated in the evidence, to which I will call attention if need be. In this company there is to be found in article 22 an express right that the registered holder may transfer all his shares, subject only to the restrictions in the articles. Article 24 contains the restriction which is applicable to this case.

. . . in the present case there are very keen family disputes between the directors, two of whom take one view and the other, the transferor, another- . . . . Under those circumstances the learned judge has found as a fact, which seems to me to be abundantly clear, that in substance the opinion of the directors was clearly show. They said in effect that in the case of any transferor proposing to transfer one single share 'We shall decline to approve such transfer.' Is that an abuse of the power conferred by article 24, or is it not? In my opinion it is. You might just as well say 'We refuse to register any transfers from you because we do not approve of you splitting up your shares and therefore increasing the number of shareholders,' or anything of that kind. The illustration given by Chitty J in *Re Bell Brothers*[2] seems to me very much in point: 'If the reasons assigned are legitimate, the Court will not overrule the directors' decision merely because the Court itself would not have come to the same conclusion. But if they are not legitimate, as, for instance, if the directors state that they rejected the transfer because the transferor's object was to increase the voting power in respect of his shares by splitting them among his nominees, the Court would hold that the power had not been duly exercised.'

---

1 (1873) 8 Ch App 446 (see p 599)
2 (1891) 63 Ll 245

SCRUTTON LJ (dissenting): . . . Ordinarily speaking, every share of a share-holder is transferable without restrictions. It is his property, and the Court will protect the holder, but because it is not desirable in the interests of the company that unrestricted alienation should take place the practice has grown up of inserting certain restrictions on the power to transfer. Sometimes it is that the directors and managers may in their discretion refuse to register transfers of shares to a person of whom they do not approve. Sometimes a further restriction is added, as in the particular article we have now to construe. . . . I do not think there is any difference between the members of the Court as to the principle which is to be applied in dealing with any question which arises under that article. If the Court is to interfere, the applicant must satisfy the Court either that the directors have not honestly formed the opinion mentioned in the article, or that, though they have formed such an opinion, there are no reasonable grounds for the opinion. That latter view is expressed in some of the authorities by saying that they must not act arbitrarily or capriciously, which I take to be very much the same thing as the provision one is accustomed to in the case of juries, that if there are materials upon which a jury can come to a particular view reasonably, though the judge may have come to a different view he is bound by the opinion expressed by the jury. It is not enough in my own view that the Court should think that the opinion of the directors was wrong. It is not for the Court to decide that matter; it is for the directors to decide, provided there are grounds upon which they can reasonably express such an opinion. Now the learned judge below, who saw one of the directors, has found that these directors did form an honest opinion, and as far, therefore, as that branch of the principle is concerned there is no ground for interfering with their action. But, as I understand it, my brothers take the view that, though they formed an honest opinion, the matters they dealt with were such that they could not reasonably form the opinion, and that therefore they have exceeded the powers given them by the articles and the view of Eve J was right. . . . This company, not as far as its legal constitution was concerned but as far as actual members were concerned, had been almost entirely a family company, and is so common with many shipping companies, comprising the members of the family, the managers, the insurance brokers, and the man who supplies the stores. . . . Well, different things strike different minds in different ways. These two transfers apparently have excited no suspicion in my brothers' minds at all. All I can say is they arouse the liveliest suspicion in my own mind. I am possibly wrong, because my brother Warrington agrees with the Master of the Rolls, but I should have thought it was perfectly reasonable for the directors to approach these transfers in a state of the liveliest suspicion.
. . .

There is only one more matter I wish to mention. There are passages in the judgment of Chitty J in *Re Bell Brothers* which I think are contrary to the views which I have taken. Chitty J says: . . . 'I think that a power to approve a transferee is confined to the transferee personally. In the exercise of such a power the inquiry of the directors is confined to the transferee himself; the directors are not concerned in any way with his cestui que trust; they are not justified in extending their inquiry to the persons of the beneficiaries; and if they were at liberty to do so they would in most cases have to proceed on mere conjecture or surmise.' I am respectfully not able to agree with those two passages.

Take the instance which I have mentioned in the course of the argument. Supposing the directors have reason to believe that the transferee is a nominee of a person who has been trying to get control of the company — for example, of a German company trying to get control of an English company, and for that purpose putting forward a series of nominees unobjectionable in themselves, but who the directors have reason to believe are really nominees of a German agency; if Chitty J's view is right, the directors could not consider that matter at all; they could look at nothing but the proposed transferee and could not look at the power behind him. I respectfully disagree with that, and I think that Eve J disagreed with it too, because Eve J said: 'Nor are the pecuniary qualifications of the transferee the only elements to be considered; it is the duty of the directors to look at all the relevant circumstances in which the transferee is placed.' That is to say, they have to consider whether he may be acting for some other person, and whether the object of that other person is contrary to the interests of the company.

One other matter I wish to mention, and it is this: I think that Eve J, with great respect to him, has taken the view rather that it is his opinion which is important, that is to say, whether he thinks the directors were right rather than whether there were materials on which the directors could come to the view that they came to, for I find Eve J says, in dealing with what has happened, 'I cannot . . . construe that as a threat necessarily hostile to the company.' With great respect to the learned judge, that does not appear to me to be the question at all. It is not a question whether the judge thinks it must not necessarily be construed as a threat hostile to the company, but whether there is material on which such a view could reasonably be formed, though the learned judge disagreed with it.

For these reasons I am unable to assent to the judgments given by the other members of the Court, and the reason for which I dissent is this: that, it having been found that in the opinion of the directors it was contrary to the interests of the company that the proposed transferee should be a member of the company, and that that was an honest view, there appear to me to be materials upon which the directors could have taken that view, whether or not the members of this Court would have themselves taken it or not.

SOURCE 213
Re Swaledale Cleaners Limited
(Court of Appeal 1968) [1968] 1 WLR 1710; [1968] 3 All ER 619

Under the articles of association, the directors had an unfettered discretion to refuse to register any transfer of shares. The articles also repeated (in reg 19), the provisions of s 66(1) of the Companies Act 1929 (now s 183(5)), namely:

'If the directors refuse to register a transfer of any shares, they shall within two months after the date on which the transfer was lodged with the company send to the transferee notice of the refusal.'

HARMAN LJ: This is an appeal from Pennycuick J on a motion to rectify the register under the Companies Act 1948. He decided that the register ought to be rectified and the company appeals. This is one of these small private companies, carrying on a business as dry cleaners in Swaledale in Yorkshire. It has a capital of £10,000 which was divided among the members of the family. There was a Mr Henry Smart, who held 5000 shares; there was his brother, Major Smart, who held 4000 shares; and there were two smaller shareholders, one of them a Mrs Smart,[1] who held 500, and another the applicant, who himself held 500. The business has been going on for 20 years or more and no doubt it was a prosperous affair. Mr Henry Smart, the holder of the 5000 shares, died. His administrator has never been put on the register. Then more recently Mrs Smart[1] died. So that 5500

---

shares are in the hands of administrators not on the register. That left Major Smart as the only permanent director under the articles, and the applicant[1] as an elected director, being elected year by year, and also in later times secretary to the company.

The matter came to a head in August 1967. There was a meeting at that time, partly board meeting, partly general meeting. So far as the board meeting was concerned, the applicant retired by rotation and he was not re-elected. That left only Major Smart as a member of the board. That was not a quorum according to the articles of association, and, therefore, there was no effective board. Everything else that happened at that meeting was thus ineffective so far as it purported to be a board meeting. The applicant and Mrs Smart[2] presented transfers of the 5500 shares in their hands as administrators, but nothing effective could be done about it because there was not a competent board to consider the matter. There the matter seems to have gone temporarily asleep. So that you have this rather anomalous position that the company is in the hands of a minority shareholder and there is no effective board of directors.

That state of things continued to exist until December 1967. By that time there had been a four months' interval since the application had been made for the rectification of the register and no step taken to rectify it. It seems to me that by that time the natural right of a shareholder to have his name put on the register must exist — must prevail — unless there is some valid reason in the contract between the parties (ie the articles) why that should not be done. It is said here: oh, the directors have an absolute and uncontrolled discretion to refuse registration. If they have, it has never been exercised because there has never been an effective board meeting to consider it. It is well settled, and appears from a decision of Astbury J in *Re Hackney Pavilion Ltd* [3] that the refusal to register a transfer is a matter which needs a positive assertion by way of resolution. There had been none here when the motion was launched, so that at that date, it seems to me, the natural right of the would-be transferors was standing and had become as absolute as Astbury J held it to be in that case. But the difference here is that between the launching of the motion and the hearing Major Smart had appointed his wife an additional director, as he was empowered to do under the articles, and there had been a board meeting at which the registration was refused. The question here is, first, had there been unreasonable delay in refusing such a registration, and, secondly, if there had been such an unreasonable delay, had that delay destroyed the right to refuse?

As to unreasonable delay, I take the view of the judge (and it seems to me merely, if I may say so, common sense), that since there is an obligation on directors, who refuse to register a transfer, to inform the persons who are aggrieved within two months of such a refusal, the Act of 1948 clearly indicates that a reasonable time, other things being equal, within which directors must make up their minds either to accept the transfer or to refuse it must be the two months within which they must make an answer. Therefore, it seems to me that waiting four months without any decision at all was an unreasonable delay. But one must go one step further than that: one must say that that unreasonable delay has destroyed the right so that when, in December 1967, the new board purported to refuse, they were no longer in a position to exercise that discretion which, if they had acted promptly, undoubtedly would have been theirs, to

1 Mr Leslie Smart, the holder of 500 shares
2 Mrs Sybil Smart, administratrix of Mr Henry Smart
3 [1924] 1 Ch 276; 93 LJ Ch 193

consider and, if they thought fit in the interests of the company, to refuse registration of the transfers.

. . .

The judge firmly took the view, if you delay too long, you lose your rights, and that seems to me to be consonant with good sense. A shareholder prima facie has a transferable right of property in his shares and that can only be taken away from him by an express prohibition in the articles of association. Perhaps the best authority for that proposition is *Re Copal Varnish Co Ltd*,[1] decided by Eve J.

So here these administrators have in their hands two bundles of rights which consist of transferable shares, subject only to the limitation imposed by the articles. Those limitations, in my judgment, only give the directors a right to refuse if they exercise that right with reasonable promptitude — other things being equal, within the two months which the Act of 1948 now gives them in which to decide the question. They did not make any such decision here. At the time when the motion was launched there had been no refusal, and by that time, in my judgment, the right to register and transfer had become absolute and the subsequent meeting and refusal after the motion was launched was ineffective. I think that the judge was quite right and that the appeal ought to be dismissed.

SOURCE 214
Lyle & Scott *v* Scott's Trustees
[1959] AC 763; [1959] 2 All ER 661

By article 9 of the articles of association of Lyle & Scott Ltd 'no registered shareholder of more than one per centum of the issued ordinary share capital of the company shall, without the consent of the directors, be entitled to transfer any ordinary share for a nominal consideration or by way of security and no transfer of ordinary shares by such a shareholder shall take place for an onerous consideration so long as any other ordinary shareholder is willing to purchase the same at a price which shall be ascertained by agreement between the intending transferor and the directors and, failing agreement, at a price to be fixed by the auditor of the company. . . . Any such ordinary shareholder who is desirous of transferring his ordinary shares shall inform the secretary in writing of the number of ordinary shares which he desires to transfer. . . . '

By article 7 the directors might in their absolute discretion, without assigning any reason, decline to register any transfer of any share.

LORD REID: My Lords, in these two actions the pursuers and appellants are a private company whose articles of association contain provisions restricting the transfer of shares. The company carry on a knitwear and hosiery business in Hawick. In each case the defenders and respondents are shareholders of the company. On 6 November 1956, a firm of solicitors in Edinburgh, acting on behalf of a client then undisclosed but now known to be Mr Hugh Fraser, sent to all the shareholders letters offering to purchase their shares, the offer being conditional on acceptance by the holders of 75 per cent. of the ordinary shares.

Both respondents accepted the offer by completing and returning the form of acceptance sent to them and also completing a form of proxy. In the acceptance they agreed to sell their shares, authorised the use of the proxy, and agreed to deliver up their share certificates and to sign transfer deeds when called on in exchange for the price.

1 [1917] 2 Ch 349; 87 LJ Ch 132

On 31 December 1956, the appellants raised actions against the respondents and about ten other shareholders who had accepted the offer.

The appellants' case is that by reason of the provisions of the articles the respondents were not entitled to enter into these contracts for the sale of their shares.

I have come to the conclusion without difficulty that on their own admissions the respondents are in breach of article 9. The purpose of the article is plain: to prevent sales of shares to strangers so long as other members of the company are willing to buy them at a price prescribed by the article. And this is a perfectly legitimate restriction in a private company. But the respondents argue that, whatever may have been the intention, the terms of the article are such that it has only very limited application. They say that 'transfer' and 'transferring' only apply to a complete transfer of the ownership of shares by acceptance and registration of deeds of transfer, and that a shareholder who agrees to sell his shares is quite entitled to do so and to receive the price and vote as the purchaser wishes so long as he is not desirous of having a transfer registered.

I see no reason for reading the article in that limited way. Transferring a share involves a series of steps, first an agreement to sell, then the execution of a deed of transfer and finally the registration of the transfer. The word transfer can mean the whole of those steps. Moreover, the ordinary meaning of 'transfer' is simply to hand over or part with something, and a shareholder who agrees to sell is parting with something.

. . .

Whether the appellants are entitled to the remedy which they seek depends in the first place on whether the respondents are now 'desirous of transferring' their shares. They were certainly desirous of doing so when they made their contracts with Mr Fraser. It is said that, though they desired to transfer to him at £3, they never desired to transfer to the other shareholders under article 9. But the article does not say desirous of transferring in the manner which it provides. It simply says desirous of transferring and, if it is to be effective in ensuring that the other shareholders have an option to purchase, it must apply whenever a shareholder desires to sell to anyone. Then it is said that the respondents' desire to transfer has never been evinced by any overt act on which the appellants can found. But if the respondents' admitted actions were in breach of their obligations, I do not see that it matters whether or in what sense they were 'overt.' I would not hold a desire to transfer proved by some equivocal words or acts. But here it is impossible that the respondents could have done what they did unless they desired to transfer: there is no suggestion of any other reason why they should have contracted with Mr Fraser.

Another argument was that article 9 cannot be used as a compulsitor, that it is an avenue open to a shareholder who desires to sell his shares, but that he cannot be compelled to use it. That is true in a sense. No action can be taken against a shareholder who merely says that he wishes to sell or does something which shows that that is his intention. But, when he goes further and does something which is a breach of his obligations under the article, the position appears to me to be quite different. Unless some action can then be taken to assert the other shareholders' rights under the article there is a wrong without a remedy.

The respondents next maintained that, even if they were desirous of transferring their shares when they made these contracts, they are entitled to say that they are no longer desirous of doing so. They do not deny that they have received and intend to keep the price of the shares. But they say that at present neither they nor the purchaser intend transfers to be made. They appear to be waiting to see whether some change will be made in the appellant company which will result in transfers being accepted and registered. But, in my judgment, a person who has agreed to sell with a view to a transfer at some future date cannot be heard to say that he is not desirous of transferring the shares merely because it suits him and the purchaser to delay execution and presentation of the transfers.

One reason for not granting this remedy which appears to have weighed heavily with the learned judges of the Court of Session is that if it is granted the respondents will be unable to avoid a compulsory sale of their shares to other shareholders who are willing to buy them in terms of article 9. If that were so I would find this case much more difficult. It would seem unjust that a shareholder who in bona fide mistakes his rights should be compelled to sell his shares on terms which he cannot control, and I might find it difficult to read such a meaning into an article of this kind. But I think that that is not the meaning of article 9. That article requires a notice to be given by any shareholder who desires to sell his shares, but it does not make such a notice irrevocable. No doubt it becomes irrevocable when the procedure following on its results in a contract between the shareholder giving the notice and another shareholder who has made an offer for the shares, and I need not discuss the question of the exact stage at which such a contract emerges. But until that stage is reached it appears to me that it is open to the shareholder who gives the notice to withdraw it.

SOURCE 215
Safeguard Industrial Investments Ltd *v* National Westminster Bank Ltd
(Court of Appeal 1982) [1982] 1 WLR 589; [1982] 1 All ER 449

The defendant bank became the shareholder in M. Wright & Sons Ltd ('the company') in respect of shares of a deceased shareholder and for whose estate the defendant was the executor. According to a deed of family arrangement (made to supplement the deceased's will and to give effect to his expressed intentions), the shares were to go to Georgina and Michael. On the completion of the administration of the estate, the defendant held the shares as bare trustee for Georgina and Michael absolutely. Georgina and Michael did not, however, wish the shares to be transferred to them in view of the terms of the articles which imposed on shareholders intending to transfer shares, an obligation to offer the shares first to the members of the company. The plaintiff, a shareholder claimed that the defendant was obliged to offer the shares, of which it was bare trustee, to the members of the company.

OLIVER LJ: . . . I turn then to the articles themselves. Article 2 incorporates regulation 3 of Table A, Part II, which confers on the directors a discretion to refuse to register a transfer of shares. Article 8 gives a right to a member to transfer his shares to certain specified relatives or to trustees for them. Article 8(A) contains some special provisions relating to transfers of any shares held by Safeguard, which do not matter for present purposes.

The key article is article 7. I need not read the whole of the article, but I should read in full Clauses (A) and (B)(a) and (b). They are in the following terms:

'(A) The Preference Shares may be transferred without restriction except as provided by clause 3 of Part II of Table A.

(B) A member shall not be entitled to transfer an Ordinary Share except subject to clause 3 of Part II of Table A and in accordance with the following provisions: (a) An Ordinary Share may be transferred by a member or other person entitled to transfer to the other members in the proportions between them (if more than one) as nearly as may be to the number of

Ordinary Shares held by them respectively, but no Ordinary Share shall be transferred to a person who is not a member as long as any member is willing to purchase the same at the fair value. (b) Except where the transfer made is pursuant to article 8 hereof, in order to ascertain whether any member is willing to purchase an Ordinary Share, the proposing transferor shall give notice in writing (hereinafter called 'the Transfer notice') to the Company that he desires to transfer the same. Such notice shall constitute the Company his agent for the sale of such share to any member of the Company at the fair value . . .'

. . .

Those are the relevant articles and the learned judge held that, in the events which have happened and which I have already outlined, the bank came under no obligation to serve notice under article 7(B)(b).

Counsel for the plaintiff (the appellant before us) submits that the judge was wrong for a number of reasons. First, he says that the effect of the decision of the House of Lords in *Lyle & Scott Ltd v Scott's Trustees*[1] is that under articles of this sort members who achieve a position in which, whether voluntarily or by operation of law, they hold the shares registered in their names as bare trustees for a non-member are deemed to be persons who are desirous of transferring their shares even though the beneficiaries disclaim any desire to exercise their right to compel a transfer to them.

It is, counsel for the plaintiff submits, unnecessary, certainly in the case of the article with which this appeal is concerned, to demonstrate that the member has any actual desire to transfer. That is merely what, under the article, he is obliged to say in his notice. Once you find a member who is a 'proposing transferor' on the true construction of the article, he must then serve a notice saying that he desires to transfer, even though in fact that is the last thing that he wishes to do.

The question then is: is the bank, a proposing transferor? It says that it neither has proposed nor does propose to transfer. Counsel for the plaintiff says that that does not matter, because the *Lyle & Scott* case shows that, where the legal position is such that a person other than the member can require an immediate transfer to himself, then the member becomes a proposing transferor. If, of course, that is the effect of the *Lyle & Scott* case, then we must clearly follow it, but I confess that, for my part, I should require the most compulsive guidance before I allowed myself to be led to a conclusion which is, as this is in my judgment, so starkly at variance with any semblance of reality.

The judge analysed *Lyle & Scott Ltd v Scott's Trustees* — above — and continued.

. . . The unanimous decision, [in *Lyle & Scott*] which I am bound to say, for my part, I find scarcely a surprising one, was that, since they had entered into unconditional agreements to sell which obliged them to transfer when requested on payment of the price and since the price had been paid and the agreements remained uncancelled and unrepudiated, they could not be heard to say that they were anything other than desirous of transferring their shares. That is all that the case decided. But it is a thousand miles away from the position which obtains here and I find myself quite unable to read it as any sort of authority for the broader proposition contended for by counsel for the plaintiff. Viscount Simonds said '. . . it is not open to a shareholder, who has agreed to do a certain

1 [1959] AC 763; [1959] 2 All ER 661 (see p 605)

thing and is bound to do it, to deny that he is desirous of doing it.' What counsel for the plaintiff, in effect, seeks to do is to eliminate from that proposition the words 'who has agreed to do a certain thing' and treat it as establishing a simple equation: duty equals desire. I, for my part, am entirely unpersuaded that it is possible to extract such a proposition from the decision. Indeed, the speeches of all their Lordships emphasise the importance of the agreement into which the respondents had voluntarily entered and which they were, even at the hearing seeking to affirm. In my judgment, therefore, this court is not bound, or even persuasively urged, by that authority to the acceptance of counsel for the plaintiff's proposition and, authority apart, the proposition appears to me to be untenable.

I turn then to the alternative way in which he puts his case. The word 'transfer', he submits, where it is used in article 7(B), is a word which, although it embraces the execution of a deed of transfer or instrument of transfer and the registration of the transferee as a member, is not restricted to this. It is a word which is apt also to embrace any transaction or combination of circumstances producing the result that the whole beneficial interest previously vested in a member become vested in another person even though the legal title is not transferred at all.

There is an initial difficulty here, because the member who, on counsel for the plaintiff's proposition, is the proposing transferor, and is thus obliged to serve notice of desire to transfer, is the bank. But that member never had any beneficial interest. Counsel for the plaintiff meets this by this submission that, since what one is looking at is the equitable interest and not the transfer of the legal estate, the testator and the bank, which was the ultimate recipient of the legal title, fall, in effect, to be treated as one continuing person. The testator, by executing his will and leaving it unaltered until his death, evinced a desire to transfer the beneficial interest and that remained in suspense during the period of administration. When the administration was completed the beneficial interest formerly vested in the testator vested in the beneficiaries and the bank, as the same member as the testator, became bound to serve notice under the article. Alternatively, I think, counsel for the plaintiff really has to contend that the word 'member' does not mean necessarily the member holding shares on the register of the company but includes the owner of the whole equitable interest. . . . I agree with the judge's conclusion and I think that he rightly rejected this submission. Whatever may be said about the effect of an uncompleted agreement to sell shares, and it is unnecessary for the purposes of this appeal to express any concluded view about that, I find myself quite unable to construe the article in the instant case in a way which would make a person who involuntarily comes under an obligation to transfer, if called on, a 'proposing transferor'.

Appeal dismissed.

PART III: TYPES OF SHARES

A company can, by altering its articles if necessary, issue a class or classes of shares with different rights from those which have already been issued (Sources 216 and 217). Most commonly, where shares are divided into more than one class, there will be a class of ordinary shareholders and a class of preference shareholders. There will be three chief areas where the rights (known as 'class rights') attached to different classes of shares may differ — priority in the receipt of and the amount of the dividend, priority as to return of capital on a winding up or on a reduction of capital, and voting rights. Ultimately, the rights to which any class of shares will be entitled, will be based on a construction of the relevant articles or on the terms of issue of the shares.

To assist in this exercise of construction, a number of presumptions have been adopted. First, preferred dividends are presumed to be cumulative, that is if the stated preferred dividend is not declared in one year, it is to be carried forward to the next. Secondly, where a preferred right is expressed, it is prima facie exhaustive. Thus an expression of a preferred dividend excludes participation in other declared dividends (sometimes the expression used is non-participating) (Sources 218 and 219). Where a preference share is preferred only as to dividends, it will be presumed to be participating as to repayment of capital and vice versa. It may, therefore, be necessary to establish whether a particular fund belonging to the company is to be treated as profit (dividends) or capital (Sources 220, 221, 223).

Where a winding up occurs while cumulative dividends are still unpaid, the right of the preference shareholders to receive the arrears of unpaid dividends depends on the wording of the relevant articles or terms of issue. Here, we might discern a tendency on the part of the court to construe such provisions in favour of the preference shareholders (Sources 222 and 223).

SOURCE 216
Andrews v Gas Meter Co
(Court of Appeal 1897) [1897] 1 Ch D 361; 66 LJ Ch 246

LINDLEY LJ: The question raised by this appeal is whether certain preference shares issued by a limited company as long ago as 1865 were validly issued or not. . . .

The company's original capital as stated in its memorandum of association was '£60,000, divided into 600 shares of £100 each, every share being sub-divisible into fifths, with power to increase the capital as provided by the articles of association.' By the articles of association which accompanied the memorandum of association, and were registered with it, power was given to the company to increase the capital (article 27), and it was provided that any new capital should be considered as part of the original capital (article 28). The issue of preference shares was not contemplated or authorized. In 1865 the company desired to acquire additional works, and passed a special resolution under the powers conferred by the Companies Act 1862, sections 50 and 51, altering the articles and authorizing the issue of 100 shares of £100 each, fully paid, and bearing a preferential dividend of £5 per cent per annum. Those shares were accordingly issued to the vendors of the works referred to, and are the shares the validity of which is now in question. The company has been prosperous, and the ordinary shareholders have for years received a higher dividend than the preference shareholders. A considerable reserve has also been accumulated, and this action has been brought to determine the rights of the preference shareholders to this reserve fund. The learned judge has held that the creation of the preference shares was *ultra vires*, and that their holders never became and are not now shareholders in the company, and that they have none of the rights of shareholders, whether preference or ordinary. . . . we are of opinion that the second decision in *Hutton v Scarborough Cliff Hotel Co*[1] was wrong, and ought not to be followed, and that the decision appealed from must be reversed, and the resolutions thereby declared to be *ultra vires* must be declared *intra vires* and valid. If, by declining to follow the second decision in *Hutton v Scarborough Cliff Hotel Co*, we were disturbing titles or embarrassing trade or commerce we should treat it as one of those decisions which, though wrong, it would be mischievous to overrule. But such is not the case; and it is desirable, from all points of view, to remove from companies a fetter which ought never to have been imposed upon them, and which in practice has been got rid of by skilled draftsmen by the insertion of power to issue preference shares in the original articles of association or the memorandum of association itself. These devices will no longer be necessary.

SOURCE 217
White *v* Bristol Aeroplane Co
(Court of Appeal 1953) [1953] Ch 65; [1953] 1 All ER 40

SIR RAYMOND EVERSHED MR: The question raised in this appeal is whether, according to the proper construction of the memorandum and articles of association of the Bristol Aeroplane Co Ltd, to which I will refer hereafter as 'the company', the proposed distribution (by way of capitalisation of undistributed profits) of fully paid-up preference and ordinary shares requires (i) that a separate meeting of the existing preference stockholders should be summoned, and an extraordinary resolution in favour of the proposals passed thereat, and (ii) that the existing preference stockholders should be summoned to attend, and vote at, the general meeting of the company.

[His Lordship stated the existing capital position of the company and the effect of the proposals to increase the capital from £3,900,000 to £5,880,000, and continued:] It is, therefore, manifest that the ordinary stockholders, by obtaining between them the 660,000 preference shares of £1 each, or the equivalent amount of stock, will, on a matter which has solely to be debated by preference stockholders, have a majority over the existing preference stockholders, and it is also manifest that on a matter on which all the stockholders, preference and ordinary, debate together the new ordinary stock to be issued will swell the total number of votes that can be cast by ordinary stockholders, although it is fair to add that the proportion of votes which ordinary stockholders will have as against preference stockholders will be reduced from the present ratio of about eleven to one to the smaller ratio of about $7\frac{1}{2}$ to one.

It has been the contention of the representative of the preference stock-holders, who is the plaintiff in the action — a contention which was successful in the court below — that the proposal now made falls within the ambit of certain clauses in the articles which I will read, so as to give the preference stockholders the right to a separate meeting and to attendance at the general meeting of the company.

. . .

Article 68 bears the familiar heading: 'Modification of rights', and is as follows:

> 'Subject to the provisions of section 72 of the [Companies Act 1948][2] all or any of the rights or privileges attached to any class of shares forming part of the capital for the time being of the company may be affected, modified,

1 (1865) 2 Dr & Sm 521; 13 LT 57, where it had been held that the articles of a company could not be altered so as to confer the right to issue preference shares
2 Now s 127 of the Companies Act 1985

varied, dealt with, or abrogated in any manner with the sanction of an extraordinary resolution passed at a separate meeting of the members of that class. To any such separate meeting all the provisions of these articles as to general meetings shall . . . apply . . .'

I have no doubt, as I have already indicated, that, on a sufficient analysis, what is suggested in the present case will 'affect' the preference stockholders 'as a matter of business', but we are concerned with the question whether the rights of the preference stockholders are 'affected', not as a matter of business, but according to the meaning of the articles when construed according to the rules of construction and as a matter of law. I further think that, when regard is had to the fact that the word 'affected' was in the article in the *Mackenzie case*,[1] it would be wrong for this court now to say that its presence in this set of articles (and it may be, I dare say, that it has appeared in many others before and since *Mackenzie*) has so restrictive an effect on the ordinary shareholders in the company that separate meetings of preference stockholders and shareholders would have to be held whenever it could be shown that as a matter of business, on a close analysis, that which was proposed would, or might, affect in some degree the value of the preference shares or the way in which the rights conferred on them by the regulations of the company were to be enjoyed. The result is that, with all respect to the learned judge, I have come to the conclusion that the preference stockholders' claim in this case is not well-founded, or, perhaps, I should say, as this is an appeal by way of a motion, that the plaintiff has not satisfied me that any such interlocutory relief as he asks for on the motion ought to be granted to him. In those circumstances the appeal will be allowed.

SOURCE 218
Birch *v* Cropper
(House of Lords 1889) (1889) 14 App Ca 525; 59 LJ Ch 122

My Lords, the only question for determination in this case is upon what principle the balance of the proceeds of the realization of the assets of the Bridgewater Navigation Company remaining after satisfying all the liabilities of the company and returning to the shareholders the paid-up capital, is to be distributed as between the holders of the ordinary and preference shares of the company. The company was formed in 1872 for the purpose of acquiring the Bridgewater and other canals, with a capital of £500,000 divided into 500 shares of £1000 each. By resolution duly passed in September of that year, it was provided that the capital instead of being divided into shares of £1000 should be divided into 50,000 shares of £10 each, and should be increased to £1,300,000 consisting of 130,000 shares of that amount.

Prior to April 1880, 100,000 shares out of the capital of £1,300,000 had been issued as ordinary shares, upon which £2 10s. per share had then been paid; and on the 27th of that month it was resolved at an extraordinary meeting that the balance of the uncreated capital, viz £300,000, should be created, and that the 30,000 new shares should be issued as preference shares entitling the holder to a preferential dividend of 5 per cent. In pursuance of this resolution the shares were issued accordingly, and the additional capital of £300,000 was paid up. At the same time a call of £1 was made on the ordinary shares, raising the amount paid up on them to £3 10s. per share.

. . . after discharging all the debts and liabilities of the company there

---

1 [1916] 2 Ch 450; 85 LJ Ch 804 (see p 634)

remained in the hands of the liquidators a surplus of about £550,000. The question is how this surplus ought to be distributed amongst the ordinary and preference shareholders respectively?

The Court below has determined that the distribution ought to be made in proportion to the amounts respectively paid up on their shares, and your Lordships have to determine whether this is the correct principle to apply. It is contended on behalf of the appellant, who represents the ordinary shareholders, that they are entitled to the whole of the surplus; but failing this contention, it is insisted that the division ought to be made according to the capital subscribed and not to the amount paid up on the shares.

. . . The 85th article of association prescribes that the net profits of each year shall be divided pro ratâ upon the whole paid-up capital of the company and that the directors may declare a dividend to be payable thereout on the shares in proportion to the amounts paid up thereon. But this article is clearly inapplicable to the preference shareholders who do not share pro ratâ in the profits of the year. Their rights are determined by the resolution creating the new capital which provided that the new shares were to entitle the holders thereof to a dividend of 5 per cent per annum 'upon the amount of the time being called up thereon,' and taking precedence over all dividends on the ordinary shares. This clearly, by implication, excludes in the case of these shares the operation of article 85.

. . . The articles of association do not appear to me to afford the means of deciding this case upon any special grounds peculiar to this company. Their provisions are such as are commonly to be found regulating the distribution of profits in the case of joint stock companies. I think the determination of the question at issue must be arrived at upon principles wider and of more general application. In my opinion one consideration of essential importance, if an equitable distribution of the assets is to be attained, has been altogether lost sight of. The payment of £3 10s. per share was not the only contribution made by the ordinary shareholders to the assets of the company. They had each come under liability to pay the balance due on the shares held by them. Such a contribution might in many cases be just as valuable and tend just as effectually to the prosperity of the company as if they had actually paid the amount. I cannot think that this ought to be disregarded in estimating the respective rights and interests of members in the company and its property.

. . . The truth is that each member who has subscribed for a £10 share owns the same share in the company whether it be or be not paid up, and if he is so regarded for the purpose of meeting losses, I cannot see that it is equitable that he should be otherwise dealt with when we are considering to what share of the profit he is entitled. When the whole of the capital has been returned both classes of shareholders are on the same footing, equally members and holding equal shares in the company, and it appears to me that they ought to be treated as equally entitled to its property. It may be that the principle which I recommend your Lordships to adopt will not secure absolutely equal or equitable treatment in all cases, but I think that it will in general attain that end more nearly than any other which has been proposed.

I am therefore of opinion that the judgment appealed from should be reversed; and that it should be declared that the balance of the proceeds of sale ought to be divided amongst the holders of all the shares in the Bridgewater Navigation Company Limited, in proportion to the shares held by them respectively.

SOURCE 219
Re Isle of Thanet Electricity Supply Company
(Court of Appeal 1950) [1950] Ch 161; [1949] 2 All ER 1060

Article 3 of the articles of association provided:

> 'The issued preference shares shall confer on the holders the right to a fixed
> cumulative preferential dividend at the rate of 6 per cent per annum upon
> the amounts for the time being paid up or credited as paid up thereon
> respectively in priority to the ordinary shares, and the right to participate
> pari passu with the ordinary shares in the surplus profits which in respect of
> any year it shall be determined to distribute remaining after paying or
> providing for the said preferential dividend and a dividend for such year at
> the rate of 6 per cent per annum on the amounts for the time being paid up
> or credited as paid up on the ordinary shares, and the preference shares
> shall confer the right on a winding up of the company to repayment of
> capital together with arrears (if any) and whether earned or not of the
> preferential dividend to the date of the commencement of the winding up
> in priority to the ordinary shares.'

WYNN-PARRY J: This is an appeal from the judgment of Roxburgh J on an
originating summons which raises the question how the surplus property of the
company should be distributed as between the preference stockholders and the
ordinary stockholders of the company in its liquidation . . . I think that the effect
of *Re William Metcalfe & Sons Ltd*[1] can, stated shortly, be said to be that, in
questions between preference shareholders and ordinary shareholders as to the
right of the preference shareholders to share in what has been many times
described as surplus assets, the onus of showing that the preference shareholders
are not entitled to share in those surplus assets lies upon the ordinary
shareholders.

Since the matter was before Roxburgh J, the position has been materially
altered by the decision of the House of Lords in *Scottish Insurance Corporation Ltd
v Wilsons & Clyde Coal Co Ltd*.[2] For the purposes of the present case I do not think
that it is necessary to embark upon a detailed analysis of that case or the opinions
of the members of the House of Lords who heard it; but, as appears from the
head-note, the facts were that the colliery assets of a coalmining company had
been transferred to the National Coal Board under the Coal Industry Nationalisation Act 1946, and that in consequence it was the intention of the company to go
into voluntary liquidation. Meanwhile the company proposed to reduce its
capital by returning their capital to the holders of the preference stock, which
would be thereby extinguished. The reduction was opposed by certain preference stockholders on the ground, inter alia, that it deprived them of the right to
participate in the liquidation and the division of the company's surplus assets. It
was held by Viscount Maugham, Lord Simonds and Lord Normand, Lord Morton
of Henryton dissenting, 'that the proposed reduction was not unfair or inequitable and should be confirmed, because, even without it, the preference stockholders would not be entitled in a winding up to share in the surplus assets or to
receive more than a return of their paid-up capital. Accordingly, they could not
object to being paid, by means of the reduction, the amount which they would
receive in the proposed liquidation.'

For reasons which I shall endeavour to show, it appears to me that the effect of

1 [1933] Ch 142
2 [1949] AC 462; [1949] 1 All ER 1068

the decision of the majority in that case is not merely to remove the onus in cases such as this from the holders of ordinary shares, but to throw the onus upon the holders of preference shares; and it is for the holders of preference shares to satisfy the court that, on the true construction of the particular document, they are entitled to share in the surplus assets, at any rate in a case where a right to participate in surplus assets in a liquidation is conferred on the holders of preference shares.

Perhaps the point emerges most clearly from the speech of Lord Normand, where he quotes from the speech of Lord Haldane LC in *Will v United Lankat Plantations Co Ltd*.[1] Lord Normand said, quoting the Lord Chancellor: " 'Shares are not issued in the abstract and priorities then attached to them; the issue of shares and the attachment of priorities proceed *uno flatu*; and when you turn to the terms on which the shares are issued you expect to find all the rights as regards dividends specified in the terms of the issue.' With this opinion Earl Loreburn and Lord Atkinson agreed. My Lords, the *ratio decidendi* applies with equal force to priorities of participation in the company's property, and I see no ground on which it may be supposed that the declaration of rights as regards dividends is exhaustive, but the declaration of rights as regards property is not exhaustive. There is as good reason and it is equally easy to define exhaustively the one set of rights as the other. Sargant J in *Re National Telephone Co*[2] said: ' . . . it appears to me that the weight of authority is in favour of the view that, either with regard to dividend or with regard to the rights in a winding up, the express gift or attachment of preferential rights to preferential shares, on their creation, is, prima facie, a definition of the whole of their rights in that respect, and negatives any further or other right to which, but for the specified rights, they would have been entitled.' The decision of this House in *Will v United Lankat Plantations Co Ltd* had not been pronounced when Sargant J decided *Re National Telephone Co*, and his opinion reflects his construction of the judgment of the Court of Appeal."

In my view, it follows from what I have read that Lord Normand considered that the same principle applies to the construction of rights in a winding up as applies to the construction of dividend rights, and that he approved the extract from the judgment of Sargant J in *Re National Telephone Co Ltd*, which he cites. It is, therefore, I think, plain from consideration of what I have read from Lord Normand's speech that he takes the view, and expresses it, that the onus in such a case is this lies on the holders of preference shares.

I think that the same view is, in effect, expressed both by Viscount Maugham and by Lord Simonds, the other members of the majority. Viscount Maugham said: 'Much reliance is placed on behalf of the appellants on the case of *Re William Metcalfe & Sons Ltd*. I must say that in my opinion that case was wrongly decided; and it should be noted that it is expressly stated that the bulk of the sum of £21,000 there in dispute was attributable to accumulated profits. It seems to me difficult to reconcile that case with the decision of this House in *Will v United Lankat Plantations Co Ltd*, and impossible to reconcile it on sound grounds with the decision of *Re Bridgewater Navigation Co*.'[3] It appears to me from that statement of Viscount Maugham that he could not reconcile the decision in *Re William Metcalfe & Sons Ltd* with the decision of the House of Lords in *Will v United Lankat Plantations Co Ltd*, and that he was ranging himself on the same side

1 [1914] AC 11; 83 LJ Ch 195
2 [1914] 1 Ch 755; 83 LJ Ch 552
3 [1891] 2 Ch 317 (CA); 60 LJ Ch 415 (see p 617)

as Lord Normand in taking the view that the onus in such cases is upon the holders of preference shares.

Lord Simonds, having discussed the relevant words in the relevant article in that case, said: 'I do not ignore that in the same case' — that is *Will v United Lankat Plantations Co Ltd* — 'in the Court of Appeal and distinction between dividend and capital was expressly made by both Lord Cozens-Hardy MR and Farwell LJ, and that in *Re William Metcalfe & Sons Ltd*, Romer LJ reasserted it. But I share the difficulty, which Lord Keith has expressed in this case, in reconciling the reasoning that lies behind the judgment in *Will's case* and *Re William Metcalfe & Sons Ltd* respectively.' He proceeds: 'In *Collaroy Co Ltd v Giffard*[1] Astbury J, after reviewing the authorities, including his own earlier decision in *Re Fraser and Chalmers*,[2] said "But whether the considerations affecting them (scilicet capital and dividend preference respectively) are 'entirely different' is a question of some difficulty," and approved the proposition there urged by the ordinary shareholders that a fixed return of capital to shareholders in a winding up is just as artificial as a provision for a fixed dividend and that, if the latter is regarded as exhaustive, there is no prima facie reason why the former should not be similarly regarded.'

It was urged upon us that the true rule is to be found in the language of Lord Macnaghten in *Birch v Cropper*.[3] Mr Gray, on behalf of the preference stockholder, who in effect represents all the holders of preference stock, read a passage from Lord Macnaghten's speech which is as follows: 'Every person who becomes a member of a company limited by shares of equal amount becomes entitled to a proportionate part in the capital of the company, and, unless it be otherwise provided by the regulations of the company, entitled, as a necessary consequence, to the same proportionate part in all the property of the company, including its uncalled capital. He is liable in respect of all moneys unpaid on his shares to pay up every call that is duly made upon him. But he does not by such payment acquire any further or other interest in the capital of the company. His share in the capital is just what it was before. His liability to the company is diminished by the amount paid. His contribution is merged in the common fund. And that is all.'

That passage proceeds over the next three pages, ending with these words: 'There was an express bargain made as to their rights in respect of profits arising from the business of the company. But there was no bargain — no provision of any sort — affecting their rights as shareholders in the capital of the company.' So that, both at the beginning and at the end of the passage relied on, there is this vital qualification, that the rule which was stated by Lord Macnaghten only applies if the articles are silent as to any right in the preference shareholders to participate in surplus assets.

That rule, as it appears to me, is in no way impinged upon by the later cases, and in particular by the case of *Scottish Insurance Corporation Ltd v Wilsons & Clyde Coal Co Ltd*. And indeed Lord Simonds, in a passage which I shall read, brings the statement by Lord Macnaghten in *Birch v Cropper* into true perspective in the light of the subsequent authorities. He says: 'Finally on this part of the case I ought to deal with an observation made by Lord Macnaghten in *Birch v Cropper*, upon which counsel for the appellants relied. "They," he said, "[scilicet the preference shareholders] must be treated as having all the rights of shareholders, except so far as they renounced these rights on their admission to the company." But in my

---

1 [1928] Ch 144
2 [1919] 2 Ch 114
3 (1889) 14 App Ca 525; 59 LJ Ch 122 (see p 612)

opinion, Lord Macnaghten can have meant nothing more than that the rights of the parties depended on the bargain that they had made and that the terms of the bargain must be ascertained by a consideration of the articles of association and any other relevant document, a task which I have endeavoured in this case to discharge. I cannot think that Lord Macnaghten intended to introduce some new principle of construction and to lay down that preference shareholders are entitled to share in surplus assets unless they expressly and specifically renounce that right.'

Having regard to the view which I take of the opinions of the majority of the House of Lords in the *Scottish Insurance Corporation* case, it appears to me to be unnecessary to embark upon any review of the earlier authorities, all of which were considered in that case; and in my judgment the effect of the authorities as now in force is to establish the two principles for which Mr Christie contended: first, that, in construing an article which deals with rights to share in profits, that is, dividend rights, and rights to share in the company's property in a liquidation, the same principle is applicable; and, second, that the principle is that, where the article sets out the rights attached to a class of shares to participate in profits while the company is a going concern or to share in the property of the company in liquidation, prima facie, the rights so set out are in each case exhaustive.

With those considerations in mind I turn back to article 3 of the articles of association in this case. As regards the rights as to profits, the whole of the distributable profits are expressly dealt with. They are to be applied first in paying to the holders of the preference stock 'a fixed cumulative preferential dividend at the rate of 6 per cent per annum on the amounts for the time being paid up or credited as paid up thereon respectively in priority to the ordinary shares,' and, secondly, in paying a non-cumulative dividend at the rate of 6 per cent a year calculated on the same basis to the holders of the ordinary shares; and the balance is then distributable between the two classes of shares pari passu. Nothing could be more plainly exhaustive than that language. Then, as regards the rights in a winding-up, the holders of the preference shares are stated to be entitled to certain payments in priority to the ordinary shares. Those payments are, first of all, repayment of the capital paid up on the preference stock, and, second, any arrears of dividend whether earned or not. The question, then, is: is there anything to suggest that the language regarding the rights of the holders of the preference stock in a winding-up is not exhaustive? I can find nothing. The onus now, as I have said, is in my view on the holders of the preference stock to show that the provision is not exhaustive; and in my view that they have failed to discharge that onus.

EVERSHED MR (concurring): . . . I think, for myself, that during the sixty years which have passed since *Birch v Cropper* was before the House of Lords the view of the courts may have undergone some change in regard to the relative rights of preference and ordinary shareholders, and to the disadvantage of the preference shareholders, whose position has, in that interval of time, become somewhat more approximated to the role which Sir Horace Davey attempted to assign to them, but which Lord Macnaghten rejected in *Birch v Cropper*, namely, that of debentureholders.

SOURCE 220
Re Bridgewater Navigation Co
(Court of Appeal 1891) [1891] 2 Ch 317; 60 LJ Ch 415

LINDLEY LJ: The question raised by this appeal is, how a portion of the surplus assets of this company, remaining after payment of all its debts and liabilities and paid-up capital, ought to be divided between the ordinary and the preference shareholders.

The company was formed in 1872, with a nominal capital of £500,000, divided into 500 shares of £1000 each, which were afterwards altered into 50,000 shares of £10 each, and this capital was at the same time increased by the creation of 80,000 new shares of £10 each.

In 1874 a special resolution was passed, authorizing the creation of preference shares; and in 1880, 30,000 preference shares of £10 each were issued. The preference consisted of a preferential dividend of 5 per cent.

. . .

The House of Lords has already decided in *Birch v Cropper*[1] that the whole of this surplus does not belong to the ordinary shareholders as profit, and that, 'after adjusting the rights of the shareholders *inter se* (other than their rights in respect of the purchase-money),' the surplus in question ought to be divided between both classes of shareholders in proportion to their shares. There still, however, remain for determination two questions — namely, first, whether certain reserve funds are to be treated as undrawn profits and ought to be divided among the ordinary shareholders exclusively, or whether these reserve funds are to be treated as assets divisible amongst both classes of shareholders; and secondly, whether, in ascertaining the profits for the period between 31 December 1886, and 4 August 1887, the outstanding debts due to and from the company and the company's plant and machinery are to be estimated below their real amounts and values, as they always were when the company was a going concern, or whether these debts, etc. are to be taken at their actual ascertained amounts and values.

. . . The reserve funds are three in number, namely, £3500 standing to the credit of the canal and river improvement fund, £10,000 standing to the credit of the insurance fund, and £30,000 standing to the credit of the depreciation of steamers fund. None of these sums are actually set apart from the other assets of the company; they do not exist in the form of moneys carried to separate accounts and separately invested; the property representing them consists of the company's corporeal assets, and is mixed up with and not to be distinguished from other property of the same kind. On the other hand, it has been established beyond doubt that all these sums have been deducted from profits which the ordinary shareholders might have divided amongst themselves, but which it was considered judicious not to divide so long as the company was carrying on business. The sums in question are simply the undrawn profits of the ordinary shareholders.

. . .

It remains, however, to be considered whether these undrawn profits have been capitalized or so dealt with that they have become the property of both classes of shareholders instead of the property of the ordinary shareholders only. Carrying undrawn profits to a suspense account or to a reserve account does not necessarily change their character, still less their ownership; they remain the undrawn profits of those persons to whom they belonged, dedicated, no doubt, to certain purposes and applicable to those purposes, but not otherwise altered in their character or ownership. If the purposes for which such profits are set apart fail, or if the profits are not required for such purposes, they become divisible, not as capital, but as undrawn profits. When capital and profits belong to the same persons and in the same proportions, it becomes unimportant to

---

1 (1889) 14 App Ca 525; 59 LJ Ch 122 (see p 612)

distinguish the one from the other, and capitalization for convenience may be inferred from slight evidence. But when capital and profits belong to different persons, or to the same persons in different proportions, the effect of capitalizing profits is to change their ownership, and an intention to do this must be shewn before conversion of profits into capital can be properly inferred. Moreover, this is a matter on which a majority cannot bind a minority unless expressly empowered to do so by the constitution of the company, either as originally framed or as subsequently modified by some authority binding on all.

Held that all three reserve funds represented undrawn profits, uncapitalized, and, therefore, to which the preference shareholders had no rights, apart from the fixed dividend.

SOURCE 221
Dimbula Valley (Ceylon) Tea Co *v* Laurie
(Chancery Division 1961) [1961] Ch 353; [1961] 1 All ER 769

Article 5 of those articles was in the following terms:

'The 10,000 preference shares in the original capital shall confer on the holders the following rights: (a) The right to receive out of the profits of the company a cumulative preferential dividend at the rate of 6 per cent per annum on the amount for the time being paid up thereon, such dividend to commence as from 31 March 1896. (b) The right in the event of the company being wound up to be paid out of the surplus assets of the company the amount paid up in respect of such preference shares and all arrears (if any) or dividend thereon up to the date of the commencement of the winding up in priority to the other shareholders, and to participate in any further surplus assets of the company after payment of the amount paid up in respect of the other shares rateably with the other shareholders in proportion to the amount paid up on the said preference shares and the other shares respectively.

In 1946 the company adopted in place of the original articles of association a new set of articles of association, which included a capital-ization article which read: "140. The company in general meeting may at any time and from time to time on the recommendation of the board pass a resolution that any sum not required for payment or provision of any fixed preferential dividend and (A) for the time being standing to the credit of any reserve fund or reserve account of the company, including premiums received on the issue of any shares or debentures of the company, or any sum arising from any operation creating an excess of assets on capital account, or (B) being undivided net profits in the hands of the company, be capitalized, and that such sum be appropriated as capital to and amongst the shareholders who would have been entitled thereto if the same had been distributed by way of dividend in the shares and proportions in which they would have been so entitled, and in such manner as the resolution may direct . . . " '

BUCKLEY J: . . . First, it is clear that at any time before liquidation the ordinary shareholders, who control the voting at general meetings, could quite legit-imately extract by way of dividends on their ordinary shares the whole of the distributable but undistributed profits except to the extent that they might be required to pay accrued preference dividends. Secondly, assuming that article 140 of the new articles of association adopted in 1946 was validly adopted, it is clear that at any time before liquidation the ordinary shareholders could, under that article, capitalize for their own exclusive benefit the whole of such undistributed profits with the like exception. Even if, therefore, the preference shareholders were entitled to participate pari passu with the ordinary share-holders in any assets of the company remaining after paying creditors, costs and arrears of preference dividend and repaying paid-up capital, their expectations in this respect could not be said to be very great.

Considerations of this kind assisted the majority of the House of Lords in *Scottish Insurance Corporation Ltd v Wilsons & Clyde Coal Co Ltd*[1] to reach the conclusion on the construction of the relevant regulations in that case that the preference shareholders in the respondent company had no such right of participation.

But whether in the present case the preference shareholders have such a right depends upon the bargain between the members constituted by the company's memorandum and articles and depends upon the true interpretation of the original article 5 read in the context of the rest of the original articles of the company. The fact that the ordinary shareholders might be able to defeat the expectations of the preference shareholders to participate in a winding up in undistributed profits is not necessarily inconsistent with the preference share-holders having such a right.

In article 5(b) the expression 'surplus assets' is used twice. Where it first appears it must clearly mean property of the company remaining after the external liabilities of the company have been discharged and provision has been made for the costs of the winding up, but before any capital has been repaid to the preference shareholders or any arrears of preference dividend have been satisfied, and a priori before any capital has been repaid to the ordinary shareholders or any profits have been distributed to them. In other words, 'surplus assets' here means all the assets of the company remaining after creditors have been paid and the costs of winding up have been paid or provided for, but before any payment to members as such has been made or provided for. The article confers on the preference shareholders a right to certain preferential payments out of this fund; it then directs repayment thereout of the capital paid up on the other shares of the company, that is to say, the ordinary shares; finally it confers on the preference shareholders a right to 'participate in any further surplus assets of the company' rateably with the other shareholders. In this context I think that 'any further surplus assets' must mean that part of the fund of 'surplus assets' referred to earlier in the paragraph which remains after making thereout the specific payments referred to in the paragraph.

In *Re Bridgewater Navigation Co*[2] the question arose whether undistributed profits of the company were distributable in a winding up amongst the ordinary shareholders of the company only or amongst the preference and ordinary shareholders rateably. The company as originally constituted had only one class of shareholders.

. . . Subsequently the company created a class of preference shares whose right to participate in profits was limited to a preferential dividend at the rate of 5 per cent per annum.

In *Birch v Cropper*[3] the House of Lords had earlier decided that after adjusting the rights of the shareholders inter se the surplus assets of the company ought to be divided between the shareholders of both classes in proportion to their shares.

---

1 [1949] AC 462; [1949] 1 All ER 1068
2 [1891] 2 Ch 317 (CA); 60 LJ Ch 415 (see p 617)
3 (1889) 14 App Ca 525; 59 LJ Ch 122 (see p 612)

In *Re Bridgewater Navigation Co* both North J and the Court of Appeal took the view that that decision of the House of Lords had not decided the proper destination of the undistributed profits in question before them:

. . .

The Court of Appeal varied the order of North J, holding that the last-mentioned reserves also represented undistributed profits, which had not lost that character as a result of having been reserved for purposes for which in the event they were not required. The significant circumstances in the case was, in my judgment, that article 85 provided that the whole of the company's net profits of each year remaining after payment of the preference dividend should 'belong to and be divided among' the ordinary shareholders. The right of the preference shareholders to participate in the company's assets in a winding up necessarily took effect subject to this right of the ordinary shareholders.

By the articles of association which came under consideration in *Scottish Insurance Corporation Ltd v Wilsons & Clyde Coal Co Ltd* the right of the preference shareholders of the respondent company to participate in profits while the company was a going concern was limited to a cumulative preferential dividend at a stated rate, subject to which the residue of the profits was declared by article 128 to be 'divisible' amongst the ordinary shareholders. In a winding up the preference shareholders were given a preferential right to repayment of capital paid up on their shares but the articles were silent about what should happen to any assets remaining after that preferential right was satisfied. The majority of the House of Lords held as a matter of construction that the articles dealing with the preferential rights of the preference shareholders in a winding up contained an exhaustive statement of their rights to participate in the company's asset in a winding up. From that fact that their right to participate in profits while the company was a going concern was limited to their preferential dividend and that their right to participate in a winding up was restricted to repayment of the capital paid up on their shares, it would naturally follow that the profits of the company which were not required for payment of the preference dividend belonged at all times to the ordinary shareholders. Lord Maugham, Lord Simonds and Lord Normand, however, all seem to have reached the conclusion that the rights of the preference shareholders in a winding up were restricted to repayment of capital by the road of first holding that the profits so far as not required for payment of the preference dividend became appropriated to the ordinary shareholders and belonged to them while the company was still a going concern. In reaching this conclusion they were largely influenced by the circumstance that the articles gave the ordinary shareholders complete control of these profits until liquidation.

. . .

Having regard to the analysis which I have made of the language of paragraph (b) of article 5 I feel compelled to the view that in the present case the preference shareholders would be entitled to participate in a winding up rateably with the other shareholders in all the assets of the company which remain after paying creditors, costs and arrears of the preference dividend and after repaying all paid-up capital. I do not think that either the *Bridgewater case* or the *Wilsons & Clyde case* requires or enables me to reach another view. Indeed, I think that part of Lord Simonds' reasoning in the latter case strongly supports my view. He said: 'There is another somewhat general consideration which also, I think, deserves atten-tion. If the contrary view of articles 159 and 160 is the right one and the preference stockholders are entitled to a share in surplus assets, the question will still arise what those surplus assets are. For the profits, though undrawn, belong, subject to the payment of the preference dividend, to the ordinary stockholders and, in so far as surplus assets are attributable to undrawn profits, the preference stockholders have no right to them. This appears to follow from the decision of the Court of Appeal in *Re Bridgewater Navigation Company*, in which the judgment of the House of Lords in *Birch v Cropper* is worked out. This again is not decisive of the construction of particular articles, but I am unwilling to suppose that the parties intended a bargain which would involve an investigation of an artificial and elaborate character into the nature and origin of surplus assets.'

In a case like the present, in which it is clear that the preference shareholders are to participate to some extent in surplus assets, an investigation of the kind envisaged by Lord Simonds would be involved if the surplus assets had to be divided into two categories, namely, undistributed profits belonging to the ordinary shareholders and other surplus assets.

I consequently reach the conclusion that in the present case the right of the ordinary shareholders to the exclusive enjoyment of accumulated profits which are not required to pay the preference dividend depends upon appropriate resolutions being passed before liquidation begins and that in default of such resolutions such accumulated profits will form part of the fund of assets distributable under article 5(b).

SOURCE 222
Re E W Savory Ltd
(Chancery Division 1951) [1951] 2 All ER 1036; [1951] 2 TLR 1071

Adjourned Summons to determine, *inter alia*, (i) whether in the voluntary winding-up of E W Savory Ltd, the holders of the preference shares in the capital of the company (a) were entitled to arrears of the six per cent cumulative preferential dividend on their preference shares in priority to any repayment of capital to the holders of the ordinary shares, or (b) were not entitled to any such arrears;

WYNN PARRY J: . . . The relevant article is article 5b, which was adopted by special resolution of the company on 8 May 1931, and provides:

> 'The preference shares in the present capital shall confer on the holders the right to a fixed cumulative preferential dividend at the rate of £6 per cent per annum on the capital paid up thereon and shall rank both as regards dividends and capital in priority to all other shares, both present and future.'

In *Re Walter Symons Ltd*[1] the relevant provision was contained in clause 5 of the memorandum, and, so far as relevant, was as follows:

> 'The preference shares shall confer the right to a fixed cumulative preferential dividend at the rate of twelve per cent per annum on the capital for the time being paid up thereon . . . and shall rank both as regards dividends and capital in priority to the ordinary shares, but shall not confer the right to any further participation in profits or assets . . .'

Maugham J, held that, on the true construction of that provision, the preference shareholders were entitled in a liquidation, in priority to the holders of the ordinary shares, to payment of the arrears of the fixed cumulative preferential dividend and to repayment of capital. In the course of his judgment Maugham J, said:

---

1 [1934] Ch 308; 193 LJ Ch 136

'I think it is conceded, at any rate I think it is clear, that, but for the words 'and shall rank both as regards dividends and capital in priority to the ordinary shares,' the preference shareholders would not be entitled to claim in a winding-up payment of the arrears of fixed cumulative preferential dividend at the rate of twelve per cent. The question, therefore, is reduced to this: What is the true meaning of the words that I have last cited? To my mind, it is reasonably clear on construction that they refer to something which is to take place in the winding-up. Not only does that appear from the word 'rank,' but it also appears from the reference to capital, which of course would not be distributable if the company were a going concern . . . '

In *Re F de Jong & Co Ltd*[1] . . . the Court of Appeal had to consider an article in the following terms:

'The said preference shares shall carry the right to a fixed cumulative preferential dividend at the rate of six per cent per annum on the capital for the time being paid up thereon respectively, and shall have priority as to dividend and capital over the other shares in the capital for the time being, but shall not carry any further right to participate in the profits or assets.'

In the course of his judgment Morton LJ, having read the first part of the relevant article, said:

'That part of the sentence is perfectly clear. It is dealing with dividends payable out of the profits of the company, ie, dividends in the true and ordinary sense while the company is a going concern. It is to be noted that the word 'preferential' clearly shows that the dividend on those preference shares is to have priority over the dividend on the ordinary shares. The next part of the sentence is: . . . 'and all have priority as to dividend and capital over the other shares in the capital for the time being.' To what does that portion of the sentence refer? To my mind it refers to the rights in a winding up . . . '

Morton LJ, continues (ibid):

'I say that for three reasons. First, the provision as to having priority as to dividend must, I think, refer to a winding-up because the word 'preferential' has already established the priority of the preference shareholders as to dividend, while the company is a going concern. Secondly, the words 'priority as to capital' refer naturally to a distribution of the assets in the winding-up . . . The third reason is that one would expect to find, somewhere in the articles, provisions dealing, not only with the rights of the preference shareholders as to dividends while the company is a going concern, but also provisions as to what are to be the rights of the preference shareholders in a winding-up. Unless the passage which I have just read deals with those rights in a winding-up, there is no provision at all informing the preference shareholders what their rights in a winding-up are to be.'

In my view, the observations of Maugham J, and Morton LJ, in *Re Walter Symons Ltd*, and *Re F de Jong & Co Ltd*, respectively are of the greatest possible help in resolving the problem which I have before me. They are observations which were made on provisions which, in all material respects, were similar to the provision which I have to construe. As a matter of construction, Maugham J, and

---

Morton LJ, came to the conclusion that the twofold reference to the preferential nature of the dividend rights of the preference shareholders pointed almost of themselves conclusively to the result that the words 'shall rank both as regards dividends and capital' should be construed as referring to the time when the company has gone into liquidation.

. . . the preference shareholders in this case discharge the onus which is thrown on them by the decision of the Court of Appeal in *Re Isle of Thanet Electricity Supply Co Ltd,*[1] I, therefore, propose to declare that the holders of the preference shares are entitled to the arrears of the six per cent cumulative preferential dividend on their preference shares in priority to any repayment of capital to the shareholders of the ordinary shares.'

SOURCE 223
Re Wharfedale Brewery Co Ltd
(Chancery Division 1952) [1952] Ch 913; [1952] 2 All ER 635

(a) By a special resolution, passed and confirmed in 1896, it was resolved: 'That the capital of the company be increased to £50,000 by the creation of 2,000 new shares of £10 each, to be called preference shares, and to confer on the holders thereof the right to a fixed cumulative preferential dividend at the rate of 6 per cent per annum on the capital paid up thereon respectively, and such preference shares shall rank both as regards dividend and capital in priority to the other shares but shall not confer any further right to participate in profits or surplus assets.'

(b) By a special resolution, passed and confirmed in 1897, it was resolved: That the capital be increased from £50,000 to £80,000 by the creation of (1) 1,000 new ordinary shares of £10 each to rank *pari passu* with the original ordinary shares, and (2) 2,000 new preference shares of £10 each, 'and that such preference shares shall confer on the holders thereof the right to a fixed cumulative preferential dividend at the rate of £6 per cent per annum on the capital paid up thereon respectively, and shall rank, both as regards dividend and capital, in priority to the ordinary shares in the capital for the time being of the company, and *pari passu* in all respects with the 2,000 preference shares of £10 each created in 1896, but shall not confer any further right to participate in profits or surplus assets.'

On 24 January 1952, the company went into voluntary liquidation. At the date of the resolution for the winding up of the company the arrears of dividends on the preference shares amounted to over £112,000. At the date of the winding up there were profits available for distribution by way of dividend amounting to approximately £1,700. In April 1952, the liquidator had a surplus of £62,887, available for distribution, and he took out a summons to determine whether the preference shareholders were (a) entitled, in priority to any repayment of capital to the holders of the ordinary shares, to the full amount of the arrears of the 6 per cent cumulative preferential dividend on the preference shares, or (b) were entitled in priority as aforesaid only to arrears equivalent to the undistributed profits of the company earned before the commencement of the winding up.

WYNN PARRY J: . . . The capital originally consisted of one class of shares, but it was subsequently increased, and it was by the resolution for the first increase that part of the preference shares were created. There was a subsequent resolution increasing the capital by the creation of further preference shares, but the same

---

1 [1950] Ch 161; [1949] 2 All ER 1060 (see p 614)

rights were attached to these preference shares as to those created by the earlier resolutions. The resolutions provided that the preference shareholders should have the right to a fixed cumulative preferential dividend of 6 per cent per annum and should rank both as regards dividend and capital in priority to the other shares. It is agreed that, having regard to certain modern decisions, this provision should be read so that the preference shares should rank in a winding up both as regards dividend and capital in priority to the other shares. There is a conflict of authority on the point which I am called on to decide, namely, whether, under a provision in these terms, the preference shares are entitled to arrears of dividend, irrespective of whether or not profits were available to pay that dividend at the commencement of the liquidation.

The first case to which I have to refer is *Re W J Hall & Co Ltd.*[1] In that case the articles of association provided that, in the event of the company being wound up, the surplus divisible assets for the time being remaining 'after paying the liabilities of the company shall be applied first, in repaying the capital paid up on the said 500 preference shares or so many thereof as may be issued for the time being, and secondly, in paying the arrears (if any) of the 5 per cent preferential dividends thereon to the commencement of the winding up' and that the balance should belong to the ordinary shareholders. The accumulated profits at the commencement of the liquidation were less than the arrears of the preference dividend at that date. Two points were decided by Swinfen Eady J. First, he held that the preference shareholders were not entitled to claim arrears of dividend beyond the amount of the accumulated profits. Secondly, he held that arrears of dividend were payable whether declared or not. At the end of his judgment his Lordship says this: 'Reading the memorandum and articles together, I hold that the preference shareholders are entitled to the arrears on their 5 per cent dividends, whether declared or not, but so far only as profits are now available.'

It is difficult, with all respect to the learned judge, to see by what process of reasoning he arrived at that decision, because he was dealing with an article which provided that, in the event of the company being wound up, the surplus divisible assets should be applied *inter alia* in paying the arrears of the 5 per cent preferential dividend thereon. The surplus divisible assets represent no doubt a mixed fund, but a fund which for all purposes in a winding up must be treated as assets and not as partly assets and partly profits.

Turning back to the relevant resolution in this case, I am unable to discover any ground of distinction between the language used in this resolution which I have to consider and the material provisions in each of the three cases to which I have referred. As I have said, the effect of the modern authorities is that I must read this resolution as if after the words 'and such preference shares shall rank' there were inserted 'in a winding up,' the resolution continuing 'both as regards dividend and capital in priority to the other shares but shall not confer any further right to participate in profits or surplus assets.'

In my view, the word 'profits' there refers back to the phrase 'to confer on the holders thereof the right to a fixed cumulative preferential dividend at the rate of 6 per cent per annum on the capital paid up thereon, respectively' — that is, it refers back to the right of the preference shareholders while the company is a going concern. Similarly, the phrase 'surplus assets' refers to the provision which follows, which I have already read, beginning 'and such preference shares shall rank.'

---

1 [1909] 1 Ch 521; 78 LJ Ch 382

Thus in my judgment it is clear that on the true construction of these resolutions, when one comes to consider the position in a winding up, the fund, and the only fund, which is to be considered is the fund which constitutes the surplus assets, and it is that fund only the distribution of which falls to be considered.

Held, on the construction of the resolutions creating the preference shares that the latter were entitled to the entire fund.

PART IV: VOTING RIGHTS

A company may attach different voting rights (including no voting rights) to the shares it issues, but for a listing on The Stock Exchange, shares with restricted voting rights must be clearly designated (Source 224). Should a company be free to create shares with restricted voting rights? (Source 225). Voting rights attached only to certain shares will establish a separate class of such shares and where there are enhanced votes, the company will have to go through the special variation of rights procedure to reduce or eliminate such enhanced voting rights. Such rights will be treated as special rights even where they are not attached to particular shares, but operate where a particular percentage of shares is held (Source 226).

The articles of association will almost invariably make provision for proxy voting and also for a shareholder's right to call for a poll (Table A 1985, regs 54–63).

SOURCE 224
The Listing Rules
Chapter 13 Appendix 1

Non-voting shares
2. Where there are equity shares which do not carry voting rights, the words 'non-voting' must appear in the designation of such shares.

Restricted voting shares
3. Where there are equity shares with different voting rights, the designation of each class of shares, other than those with the most favourable voting rights, must include the words 'restricted voting' or 'limited voting'.

Preference shares
4. Where preference shares are listed, they must carry voting rights in at least the following circumstances:
   (a) when dividends on such shares are more than six months in arrears; and
   (b) on any resolution for the winding-up of the company.

SOURCE 225
Report of the Company Law Committee ('Jenkins Committee')
(1962)

NOTE OF DISSENT by Mr L Brown, Sir George Erskine and Professor L C B Gower

SHARES WITH RESTRICTED OR NO VOTING RIGHTS

. . .

2. In our opinion the growth of non-voting and restricted-voting shares (a) strikes at the basic principle on which our Company Law is based (paragraph 3 below), (b) is inconsistent with the principles underlying our Report and the Reports of earlier Company Law Committees (paragraphs 4, 5 and 6) and (c) is undesirable (paragraphs 7 et seq).

3. The business corporation is a device for enabling an expert body of directors to manage other people's property for them. Since these managers are looking after other people's money it is thought that they should not be totally free from any control or supervision and the obvious persons to exercise some control are the persons whose property is being managed. Hence the basic principle adopted by British Company Law (and, indeed, by the laws of most countries) is that ultimate control over the directors should be exercised by the shareholders. This control cannot be exercised in detail and from day-to-day, but shareholders retain the ultimate sanction in that it is they who 'hire and fire' the directorate.

When the directors own the majority of the equity they are free from outside control, but here they are managing what is, as to the major part, their own money. Hence the interests of the directors and the shareholders are unlikely to conflict, and self-interest should be a sufficient curb and spur (subject to certain legal rules to protect the minority against oppression). When, however, the directors have no financial stake in the prosperity of the company, or only a minority interest, the outside control operates.

4. Successive Company Law Amendment Committees have, in the words of our immediate predecessor, made it their major concern 'to find means of making it easier for shareholders to exercise a more effective general control over the management of their companies', in the belief that the result will be 'to strengthen the already high credit and reputation of British companies': Cohen Committee Report, paragraph 5. In pursuance of this aim the Cohen Committee recommended, among other reforms, what is now section 184 of the Companies Act 1948,[1] whereby the ultimate sanction vested in the shareholders (the right to dismiss the board) was greatly strengthened by enabling them to dismiss any director at any time by simple majority vote.

5. Many of our Committee's recommendations are expressly directed towards the same end of enhancing shareholder control. In particular, in Chapter III we recommend that certain activities should require the prior approval of resolutions in general meeting. These recommendations make sense only on the assumption that the general meeting will express the views of the majority of the equity shareholders and not merely the minority views of the directors themselves.

6. In recent years, however, control by shareholders has been stultified in two ways: firstly in a few cases by cross-holdings and circular-holdings within a group of companies, and secondly by non-voting equity shares. The first method has already received the attention of the legislature and an attempt has been made to control it by section 27[2] of the Act. In our discussion of this section in paragraphs 151–155 of Chapter IV we recognize that it is improper for directors to maintain themselves indefinitely in office, against the wishes of the other shareholders. We also recognize that section 27[2] does not go far enough in preventing this mischief and we reject an extension of the section with reluctance and only because of the complexity and arbitrary nature of the provisions which would be necessary.

---

1 Now s 303 of the Companies Act 1985
2 Now s 23 of the Companies Act 1985

Where the mischief can be easily prevented, for example by banning the exercise of votes on shares held on trust for the company, we recommend that this should be done: Chapter IV paragraphs 154 and 156(b).

The second method of maintaining control by the existing directors, by utilizing non-voting shares, is not as yet controlled in any way; it is only of recent years that it has become a major issue. Today non-voting shares are the simplest and most straightforward method whereby directors can render themselves irremovable without their own consent, notwithstanding that they only own or control a fraction of the equity. This is different from cross-holdings and circular-holdings which may have grown up for legitimate business reasons and with no intention of stultifying shareholder control and section 184.

7. It is said that shareholder control is ineffective because of the indifference of shareholders. Everyone would probably agree that shareholders are apathetic while all goes well. But, while all goes well, there is no reason why they should not be apathetic; their intervention is required only when things go ill. No doubt it is true that the small individual shareholder has little power even then, but, as we point out in paragraph 106, the institutional investor has considerable influence; and even non-institutional shareholders are collectively powerful so long as they have votes. It can hardly be doubted that the possibility that a take-over bidder will obtain control by acquiring these votes has caused directors to pay greater heed to the interests of shareholders.

8. It is also said that shareholder control is inefficient, since directors, as a class, know better what is good for business and for the shareholders than the shareholders themselves. In the normal case this is usually true. But if share-holder control is destroyed and nothing put in its place we have to go still further and say that business efficiency is best ensured by allowing the directors to function free from any outside control, except that of the Courts in the event of fraud or misfeasance, and by making themselves irremovable, without their own consent, however inefficient they may prove to be.

9. It is, admittedly, difficult to name actual examples where non-voting shares have already led to the prolongation of inefficient managements, but the development is relatively new and the testing time will come later. All one can say is that it appears to be generally agreed that take-over bids have on the whole served a useful economic purpose and led to a desirable re-deployment of resources, and that in most cases the new managers have proved more efficient than the old. We do not understand how one can at the same time favour take-overs bids and countenance non-voting shares which are designed to frustrate take-overs. Some recent take-overs have been made in the face of opposition by the existing board and would not have been possible had the board been entrenched through the use of non-voting shares. There may have been some cases where an efficient management has been able, thanks to non-voting shares, to protect itself against an inefficient or unscrupulous raider, but there is even less evidence of this. Efficient directors who have treated their shareholders fairly and frankly should have little to fear from a raider. In any case, it goes too far to allow them to protect themselves against this remote risk by converting them-selves into a self-perpetuating oligarchy.

10. The objections to non-voting shares are strongest in the case of publicly quoted companies, particularly with the current movement to encourage the spread of shareholdings amongst small private investors. Even here they may sometimes be justified (perhaps, for example, in the case of the television programme companies where the original subscribers for the voting shares and subsequent transferees have to be approved by the Independent Television Authority).

In the case of public companies, non-voting equity shares are banned by legislation in South Africa and India and in many Continental countries. For many years the New York Stock Exchange has refused to list non-voting shares. The Australian Associated Stock Exchanges have recently done likewise; see their Official List Requirements dated 26th June 1961. The Rules of the London Stock Exchange provide that quoted Preference Shares must be afforded reasonable voting rights but, despite this, the Exchange has hitherto refused to apply the same rule to Ordinary Shares although it has expressed its dislike of non-voting shares.

11. If the British Stock Exchanges were prepared to refuse quotations for new issues of non-voting shares it might still be unnecessary to impose legislative control. But, as it is, we think that legislation is called for to prevent the continued growth of such shares in the case of quoted companies. We would not think it necessary to provide for the compulsory enfranchisement of existing non-voting shares and, to avoid complications, we would be prepared to allow companies which already have non-voting shares to make further issues. The Stock Exchanges could be relied upon to ensure that this power was not abused, just as they would ensure that the legislative ban was not evaded by giving quotations for special types of securities designed to that end.

12. For these reasons we consider that the recommendations in paragraph 140 should be strengthened, and **we recommend:**

(a) **that all equity shareholders, whether or not they have votes, should be entitled to attend, in person or by proxy, and to speak at all general meetings of their company;**

(b) **that there should be a prohibition on the granting of a quotation for non-voting and restricted voting equity shares (save in exceptional circum-stances and subject to the approval of the Board of Trade) except as regards further issues of such shares for which a quotation had already been granted prior to the publication of our Report.**

SOURCE 226
Cumbrian Newspapers Group Ltd *v* Cumberland & Westmorland Herald Newspaper & Printing Co Ltd
(Chancery Division 1986) [1987] Ch 1; [1986] 2 All ER 816

SCOTT J: The plaintiff company, Cumbrian Newspapers Group Ltd is the holder of 10.67 per cent of the issued ordinary shares in the defendant company, Cumberland & Westmorland Herald Newspaper & Printing Co Ltd.

The plaintiff's share were issued to it in 1968. At the same time, and as part of the arrangement under which the shares were issued, the defendant adopted articles of association under which, inter alia, the plaintiff was granted, first, rights of pre-emption over the other ordinary shares in the defendant; secondly, rights in respect of unissued shares and, thirdly, the right, so long as it held not less than 10 per cent in nominal value of the issued ordinary shares of the defendant, to appoint a director of the defendant.

The board of directors of the defendants have made it known that they desire to convene an extraordinary general meeting of the shareholders of the defendant, and to put before the general meeting a special resolution designed to cancel the articles under which the plaintiff enjoys the special rights I have mentioned.

The plaintiff contends that the special rights which it enjoys under the articles in question are 'class rights' which cannot be varied or abrogated without its consent.

. . .

The defendant's articles adopt Table A.

Article 5 provides that:

'(a) Subject to any direction to the contrary by Special Resolution of the company and subject also to paragraph (b) of this article, no unissued shares in the capital of the company shall be issued to any person save

    (i) Cumberland Newspapers Ltd

    (ii) a person, who, on 28 day of August 1968 was entered on the register of members of the company

    (iii) persons who at the time of such issue are in the full time employment of the company

(b) Subject to any direction to the contrary by Special Resolution of the company in general meeting, all unissued Ordinary Shares shall, before issue, be offered to such persons as at the date of the offer are registered as holders of Ordinary Shares in proportion, as nearly as the circumstances admit, to the amount of the existing shares to which they are entitled.'

I need not read the rest of para (b).

This article 5 was obviously intended to give the plaintiff protection against its percentage of the issued share capital in the defendant being diluted by means of an issue of unissued ordinary shares. The protection is not, however, absolute. The provisions of the article are expressed to be 'subject to any direction to the contrary by special resolution'.

Article 7 provides that:

'The directors may in their absolute discretion and without assigning any reason therefore decline to register any transfer of any share whether or not it is a fully paid share not being a transfer to Cumberland Newspapers Ltd under the provisions of article 9.'

This article serves to ensure that if the plaintiff should exercise its rights of pre-emption over any shares, the directors cannot decline to register the transfer.

Article 8 authorises the transfer of shares (a) to other members; (b) to certain relatives of the transferor member; (c) to employees of the defendant, and (d) to certain defined family trusts.

Article 9 is the important pre-emption article. Except in the case of a transfer expressly authorised by article 8, article 9 imposes, in respect of all shares in the company, a restriction on the right to transfer unless, in accordance with a prescribed procedure, the shares are first offered to the plaintiff.

Finally, article 12 provides that:

'If and so long as Cumberland Newspapers Ltd shall be registered as the holder of not less than one tenth in nominal value of the issued Ordinary Share Capital of the company Cumberland Newspapers Ltd shall be entitled from time to time to nominate one person to be a director of the company.'

. . .

Section 125 is, in my judgment, intended to provide a comprehensive code setting out the manner in which 'rights attached to any class of shares . . .', whatever that phrase truly means, '. . . can be varied'.

I must decide, therefore, whether or not the plaintiff's rights under articles 5,

7, 9 and 12 are, for the purposes of section 125, rights attached to a class of shares. If they are, they can only be altered in the manner provided by the articles or, as the case might be, by the procedure described in sub-section (2). But if they are not rights attached to a class of shares, section 125 has no application to them.

The articles adopted by the defendant on 29 August 1968 contained no special article dealing with the alteration, either of the articles generally, or of articles 5, 7, 9 and 12, in particular; Table A was, however, incorporated, and article 4 of Table A contains provision for the variation or abrogation of class rights. The article contains this:

> 'If at any time the share capital is divided into different classes of shares, the rights attached to any class (unless otherwise provided by the terms of issue of the shares of that class) may, whether or not the company is being wound up, be varied with the consent in writing of the holders of three-fourths of the issued shares of that class or with the sanction of an Extraordinary Resolution passed a separate General Meeting of the holders of the shares of the class.'

The terms of this article underline the importance of the question whether or not the plaintiff's rights can properly be described as 'rights attached to any class' of shares. If the rights can be so described, both section 125 and article 4 of Table A apply. The effect would be that articles 5, 7, 9 and 12 could not be altered without the plaintiff's consent. But if the rights cannot be so described, then neither section 125 nor article 4 of Table A apply. The articles could therefore, it is said, be varied or cancelled by special resolution under the statutory authority granted by section 9. In effect, the plaintiff could be deprived of the rights which it enjoys under articles 5, 7, 9 and 12 by the other members of the company who do not enjoy such rights. Moreover, that would have been the position at all times since the adoption of the articles in August 1968.

I turn to the critical question: are the plaintiff's rights under articles 5, 7, 9 and 12, rights attached to a class of shares?

Rights or benefits which may be contained in articles can be divided into three different categories. First, there are rights or benefits which are annexed to particular shares. Classic examples of rights of this character are dividend rights and rights to participate in surplus assets on a winding up. If articles provide that particular shares carry particular rights not enjoyed by the holders of other shares, it is easy to conclude that the rights are 'attached to a class of shares', for the purpose both of section 125 and of article 4 of Table A. It is common ground that rights falling into this category are 'rights attached to a class of shares' for those purposes. Counsel for the defendant submitted at first that this category should be restricted to rights that were capable of being enjoyed by the holders for the time being of the shares in question. Such a restriction would exclude rights expressly attached to particular shares issued to some named individual, but expressed to determine upon transfer of the shares by the named individual. *Palmer's Company Precedents* (17th edn, 1956) Part I, at p 818, contains a form for the creation of a life governor's share in a company. Counsel for the defendant accepted that the rights attached to a share in accordance with this precedent would be 'rights attached to a class of shares'. He accepted, rightly in my judgment, that a provision for defeasance of rights on alienation of the share to which the rights were attached, would not of itself prevent the rights, pre-alienation, from being properly described as 'rights attached to a class of shares'. The plaintiff's rights under articles 5, 7, 9 and 12 cannot, however, be brought within this first category. The rights were not attached to any particular shares. In articles 5, 7 and 9, there is no reference to any current shareholding held by the plaintiff. The rights conferred on the plaintiff under article 12 are dependent on the plaintiff holding at least 10 per cent of the issued ordinary shares in the defendant. But the rights are not attached to any particular shares. Any ordinary shares in the defendant, if sufficient in number and held by the plaintiff, would entitle the plaintiff to exercise the rights.

A second category of rights or benefits which may be contained in articles (although it may be that neither 'rights' nor 'benefits' is an apt description), would cover rights or benefits conferred on individuals not in the capacity of members or shareholders of the company but, for ulterior reasons, connected with the administration of the company's affairs or the conduct of its business.

Eley v Positive Government Security Life Assurance Co Ltd,[1] was a case where the articles of the defendant company had included a provision that the plaintiff should be the company solicitor. The plaintiff sought to enforce that provision as a contract between himself and the company. He failed. The reasons why he failed are not here relevant, and I cite the case only to draw attention to an article which, on its terms, conferred a benefit on an individual but not in the capacity of member or shareholder of the company. It is, perhaps, obvious that rights or benefits in this category cannot be class rights. They cannot be described as 'rights attached to a class of shares.' The plaintiff in *Eley v Positive Government Security Life Assurance Co Ltd*, was not a shareholder at the time the articles were adopted. He became a shareholder some time thereafter. It is easy, therefore, to conclude that the article in question did not confer on him any right or benefit in his capacity as a member of the company. In a case where the individual had been issued with shares in the company at the same time and as part of the same broad arrangement under which the article in question had been adopted, the conclusion might not be so easy. But if, in all the circumstances, the right conclusion was still that the rights or benefits conferred by the article were not conferred on the beneficiary in the capacity of member or shareholder of the company, then the rights could not, in my view, be regarded as class rights. They would not be 'rights attached to any class of shares'.

In the defence in the present case, it is pleaded that the plaintiff's rights under articles 5, 7, 9 and 12:

> 'are privileges personal to the plaintiffs, whether or not they hold any shares in the defendant company.'

If this plea were well-founded, the rights would fall into this second category and would not be class rights. Counsel for the defendant did not, however, persist in this plea. In my judgment he was right not to do so. The evidence in this case has clearly established that the adoption by the defendant of articles 5, 7, 9 and 12, was inextricably connected with the issue to the plaintiff, and the plaintiff's acceptance, of the 280 ordinary £5 shares in the defendant. The purpose of the rights and privileges conferred on the plaintiff by those articles, was to enable the plaintiff, in its capacity as shareholder in the defendant, to obstruct an attempted take-over of the defendant. In my judgment, the plaintiff's rights under those articles do not fall within this second category.

That leaves the third category. This category would cover rights or benefits that, although not attached to any particular shares, were none the less conferred on the beneficiary in the capacity of member or shareholder of the company. The

---

1 (1876) 1 Ex D 88; 45 LJ Exch 451 (discussed at p 304)

rights of the plaintiff under articles 5, 7, 9 and 12 fall, in my judgment, into this category. Other examples can be found in reported cases.

In *Bushell v Faith*,[1] articles of association included a provision that on a resolution at a general meeting for the removal of any director from office, any shares held by that director should carry the right to three votes. The purpose of this provision was to prevent directors being removed from office by a simple majority of the members of the company. The validity of the article was upheld by the Court of Appeal and by the House of Lords; the reasons do not, for present purposes, matter. But the rights conferred by the article in question fall, in my view, firmly in this third category. They were not attached to any particular shares. On the other hand, they were conferred on the director/beneficiaries in their capacity as shareholders. The article created, in effect, two classes of shareholders, namely shareholders who were for the time being directors, on the one hand, and shareholders who were not for the time being directors, on the other hand.

The present case is, and *Bushell v Faith* was, concerned with rights conferred by articles. The other side of the coin is demonstrated by *Rayfield v Hands*.[2] That case was concerned with obligations imposed on members by the articles. The articles of the company included an article entitling every member to sell his shares to the directors of the company at a fair valuation. In effect, the members enjoyed 'put' options exercisable against the directors. Vaisey J held that the obligations imposed by the article on the directors for the time being were enforceable against them. He held that the obligations were imposed on the directors in their capacity as members of the company. It follows from his judgment that, as in *Bushell v Faith*, there were in effect two classes of shareholders in the company. There were shareholders who were not for the time being directors, and shareholders who were for the time being directors: the former had rights against the latter which the latter did not enjoy against the former. The two classes were identifiable not by reference to their respective ownership of particular shares, but by reference to the office held by the latter. But the rights of the former, and the obligations of the latter, required their respective ownership of shares in the company. Accordingly, as a matter of classification, the rights in question fall, in my view, into the third category.

In the present case, the rights conferred on the plaintiff under articles 5, 7, 9 and 12 were, as I have held, conferred on the plaintiff as a member or shareholder of the defendant. The rights would not be enforceable by the plaintiff otherwise than as the owner of ordinary shares in the defendant. If the plaintiff were to divest itself of all its ordinary shares in the defendant, it would not then, in my view, be in a position to enforce the rights in the articles. But the rights were not attached to any particular share or shares. Enforcement by the plaintiff of the rights granted under articles 5, 7 and 9, would require no more than ownership by the plaintiff of at least some shares in the defendant. Enforcement by the plaintiff of the rights granted under article 12, require the plaintiff to hold at least 10 per cent of the issued shares in the defendant. But any shares would do. It follows, in my judgment, that the plaintiff's rights under the articles in question fall squarely within this third category.

The extent to which the company could vary these special rights is shown in Source 229 at p 638.

---

1 [1970] AC 1099; [1970] 1 All ER 53 (see p 318)
2 [1960] Ch 1; [1958] 2 All ER 194 (see p 301)

PART V: VARIATION OF CLASS RIGHTS

A company may wish to vary the rights attached to one class of shares or it may act in such a way as to infringe the special rights of a class of shares. Prior to 1980, special rights could only be altered in accordance with a provision such as reg 4 of the 1948 Table A, which required that any alteration of class rights should be approved by a 75 per cent majority of the members of the class in question. A number of questions were posed with regard to the variation of class rights, many of which will remain unsolved in view of the enactment of a comprehensive code in 1980 for the required procedure (now s 125 of the Companies Act 1985).

Certain questions remain, chief of which, perhaps, is the identification of class rights. Unless the rights in question are class rights and new statutory protection cannot be invoked (Source 227; see also Sources 217 and 226 at pp 611 and 629, and *Re Saltdean Estate Ltd*[1] p 801). There might have been superficial compliance with the required procedure for the variation of rights attached to a class of shares, but an equitable principle — that votes cast for the variation at the class meeting should have been cast bona fide for the benefit of the *class* as a whole — can be invoked to invalidate the resolution (Source 228). The new code is intended to be a comprehensive one protecting special rights however they are attached to shares (Source 229).

It may be the case that the special rights are unalterable or virtually so (see s 125(5)), in which case the company may need to resort to the facility provided by s 425 in order to attempt to alter special class rights (see pp 810ff).

SOURCE 227
Re Mackenzie & Co
(Chancery Division 1916) [1916] 2 Ch 450; 85 LJ Ch 804

The above company was incorporated on 2 October 1900, to carry on the business of wine and spirit merchants. The capital was £200,000 divided into 10,000 shares of £20 each, of which 6000 were 4 per cent cumulative preference shares and 4000 were ordinary shares. The issued capital was 5300 preference and 1578 ordinary shares, all fully paid. This left 700 preference and 2422 ordinary shares unissued.

The memorandum provided as follows:

Clause 5. 'The capital of the company is £200,000 divided into 10,000 shares of £20 each, whereof 6000 are £4 per cent preference shares and 4000 are ordinary shares, with the respective rights and privileges specified in the articles of association registered herewith.'

The articles provided:

Article 62: 'The shares in the original capital of the company numbered 1 to 6000, both inclusive, shall be called £4 per cent cumulative preference shares, and the holders thereof shall be entitled to receive out of the profits of the company available for division among the members dividends at the rate of £4 per cent per annum on the nominal amount of the capital from time to time paid up or credited as paid up on the £4 per cent cumulative preference share held by them respectively, such dividend to be cumulative and to be payable half-yearly

---

1 [1968] 1 WLR 1844; [1968] 3 All ER 829

on 1 January and 1 July in each year, and to be a first charge on such profits upon a winding-up of the company.'

Article 64: 'All or any of the special rights, privileges and advantages attached to any class of shares may, with the sanction in writing of the holders of two-thirds of the issued shares of the class, but shall not without such sanction, be altered or modified, dealt with, or affected, in any manner whatsoever.'

By a special resolution unanimously passed and confirmed by the ordinary shareholders on 8 October and 5 November 1915, it was resolved that the capital of the company be reduced from £200,000 to £82,536 divided into 5300 4 per cent cumulative preference shares of £12 each and 1578 ordinary shares of £12 each and that such reduction be effected (1) by cancelling the unissued 700 preference and 2422 ordinary shares, (2) by cancelling capital that was lost or unrepresented by available assets to the extent of £5 per share upon each of the 5300 preference and 1578 ordinary shares, and (3) by returning to the holders of the 5300 preference and 1578 ordinary shares respectively paid up capital to the extent of £3 per share.

None of the preference shareholders attended or were represented at the first meeting, but letters written on behalf of those objecting to the scheme were read to the meeting before the resolution was submitted. The main grounds of objection were that having regard to article 64 their special rights could not be modified without the written sanction of the holders of two-thirds of the issued preference shares; . . .

On 28 February 1916, the company presented this petition to confirm the reduction.

At the hearing the petition was supported by the holders of 1947 preference shares. It was opposed by the holders of 1889 preference shares, ie, by the holders of more than one-third of the issued preference shares, on the ground that the requisite sanction of the preference shareholders under article 64 had not been obtained, that they had not been summoned to the meeting, and that the scheme was unfair to them.

ASTBURY J: The result of the memorandum and articles shortly is this. Subject to the right of the company to reduce its capital by the votes of the ordinary shareholders in any manner sanctioned by statute these preference shares are to be of the denomination of £20 each, and the only special right, privilege, or advantage attached to those shares is a cumulative 4 per cent preferential dividend on the nominal amount of capital from time to time paid up or credited as paid up thereon.

It is first contended that the company has no power to reduce its capital, if any of the preference shares are included in the reduction, without the consent of the holders of two-thirds of the issued shares of that class. I do not think that is the right construction of these articles. The fair and proper construction is that the special rights, privileges, and advantages of the preference shareholders are those, and those only, stated in article 62, which is confined to the right to a cumulative preferential dividend on the nominal amount of capital from time to time paid up or credited as paid up, and that is without prejudice to the right of the company, under article 59, to reduce its capital in any manner authorized by statute, provided that the reduction obtains the sanction of the Court.

. . .

The second objection is that the preference shareholders have not been summoned to the meetings at which the resolutions for reduction were passed, although it was admitted they had no right to vote at the meetings. Prior to the meetings, which were held on 8 October and 5 November last year, a circular dated 15 September was sent to every shareholder stating precisely what was proposed, and drawing the shareholders' attention to the fact that under the articles the preference shareholders had no vote at the extraordinary general meeting, but that the directors would be glad to hear whether they approved the scheme or not. In answer to that circular replies were received from every single preference shareholder. The holders of 1947 preference shares were in favour of the scheme, and the holders of 2210 preference shares against it, the remaining holders being neutral, whereas at this present hearing in Court the holders of 1947 preference shares support the scheme and the holders of 1889 preference shares oppose it. In the circumstances I think in the first place that there is no provision under the articles that the preference shareholders shall be summoned to a meeting at which they are not entitled to vote, and secondly, even if they were entitled to be summoned, the omission in the present case was immaterial, as each preference shareholder had a full statement laid before him of exactly what was proposed to be done at the meeting, their views were obtained accordingly, and they could have come to the meeting if so minded.

The reduction was confirmed.

SOURCE 228
Re Holders Investment Trust Ltd
(Chancery Division 1971) [1971] 1 WLR 583; [1971] 2 All ER 289

MEGARRY J: Unopposed petitions by a company for the confirmation of a reduction of capital are a commonplace of the Companies' Court; but an opposed petition such as the one I have before me is a comparative rarity. The company, Holders Investment Trust Ltd (which I shall call 'the company') was incorporated in 1933 and has an authorised capital of £2,275,000. What is in issue before me is a reduction of capital which is to be effected by cancelling 1,250,000 5 per cent cumulative redeemable preference shares of one pound each, redeemable at par on 31 July 1971, and allotting to the holders the same nominal amount of 6 per cent unsecured loan stock 1985/90. The preference shares are all issued and fully paid up, and confer the right on a winding up to repayment of capital and arrears of dividend in priority to any other class of shares, but no further right to participate in the profits or assets.

. . . The proposed reduction has been duly authorised by a special resolution of the company; and a separate class meeting of the preference shareholders also passed an extraordinary resolution approving the reduction. At that meeting, however, the trustees of the Lionel Barber Voluntary Settlement, who hold 95,000 of the preference shares, voted against the resolution; I shall call them the 'opposing trustees.' The trustees of another settlement, who hold 30,000 of the preference shares, were not in agreement as to how they should vote, and so did not vote. The resolution was carried by the requisite majority because nearly 90 per cent of the preference shares are vested in the trustees of three trusts set up by Mr William Hill, and they voted in favour of the resolution. These trustees (whom I shall call 'the supporting trustees') also hold some 52 per cent of the ordinary stock and shares. On the hearing of the petition, Mr Instone appeared for the company and Mr Drake for the opposing trustees.

Put briefly, Mr Drake's opposition to the confirmation of the reduction is twofold. First, he contends that the extraordinary resolution of the preference shareholders was not valid and effectual because the supporting trustees did not exercise their votes in the way that they ought to have done, namely, in the interests of the preference shareholders as a whole. Instead, being owners of much ordinary stock and many shares as well, they voted in such a way as to benefit the totality of the stocks and shares that they held. Secondly, Mr Drake contends that even if the extraordinary resolution was valid, the terms on which the reduction of capital is to be effected are not fair, in particular in that the increase in the rate of interest from 5 per cent to 6 per cent is not an adequate recompense for having the right of repayment or redemption postponed from 31 July 1971, until at earliest 31 October 1985, and at latest some unspecified date in 1990. I may say at the outset that it is common ground that the proposed reduction is not in accordance with the class rights of the preference shareholders.

. . .

Mr Instone put before me four propositions based on the authorities. Discarding what does not apply in this case, and putting the matter shortly, I think that three relevant propositions emerge. First, a reduction of capital which is not in accordance with the class rights is nevertheless regular if it is effectually sanctioned in accordance with the regulations of the company. Second, there is an effectual sanction to the modification of class rights if those holding a sufficient majority of the shares of that class vote in favour of the modification in the bona fide belief that they are acting in the interests of the general body of members of that class. Third, the burden of proof depends on whether or not there is any such sanction. If there is, the court will confirm the reduction unless the opposition proves that it is unfair; if there is not, the court will confirm the reduction only if it is proved to be fair. These propositions were based on *Carruth v Imperial Chemical Industries Ltd*,[1] when read in conjunction with *British America Nickel Corporation Ltd v M J O'Brien Ltd*[2] and *Shuttleworth v Cox Bros & Co (Maidenhead) Ltd*.[3] Whatever may be said about the precise formulation of the propositions, their substance was, I think, common ground between the parties. Accordingly, I must first consider the validity of the class resolution.

In the *British America Case*, Viscount Haldane, in speaking for a strong Board of the Judicial Committee, referred, at p 371 of the case, to

'a general principle, which is applicable to all authorities conferred on majorities of classes enabling them to bind minorities; namely, that the power given must be exercised for the purpose of benefiting the class as a whole, and not merely individual members only. . . . '

. . .

I have to determine whether the supporting trustees voted for the reduction in the bona fide belief that they were acting in the interests of the general body of members of that class. From first to last I can see no evidence that the trustees ever applied their minds to what under company law was the right question, or that they ever had the bona fide belief that is requisite for an effectual sanction of the reduction. Accordingly, in my judgment there has been no effectual sanction for the modification of class rights.

The judge went on to consider whether the reduction scheme was fair. Having concluded that the preference shareholders had not sanctioned the variation of their rights which the scheme would effect, Megarry J held that the onus on the question of fairness was on the company to establish that the scheme was fair. In the event, the company failed to discharge this onus and the application for reduction of capital was dismissed.

---

1 [1937] AC 707; [1937] 2 All ER 422
2 [1927] AC 369; 96 LJ PC 57
3 [1927] 2 KB 9; 96 LJ KB 104 (see p 341)

SOURCE 229
Cumbrian Newspapers Group Ltd *v* Cumberland & Westmorland Herald
Newspaper & Printing Co Ltd
(Chancery Division 1986) [1987] Ch 1; [1986] 2 All ER 816

For the facts, see p 629.

SCOTT J: . . . The question for decision is whether rights in this third category
are within the meaning of the phrase in section 125 and in article 4 of Table A,
'rights attached to a class of shares'.

    . . .

In my judgment, if it is right, as the defendant contends, that third category
rights are not 'rights attached to a class of shares', for the purpose of section 125,
it must follow that articles containing such rights can be altered by special
resolution pursuant to section 9. This conclusion is, I think, relevant to the
question whether the defendant's contention is right. It would, in my opinion, be
surprising and unsatisfactory if class rights contained in articles were to be at the
mercy of a special resolution majority at a general meeting, unless they were
rights attached to particular shares. If the articles of a particular company grant
special rights to a special class of members, it would be odd to find that members
not in that class could cancel the rights simply by means of a special resolution.

A number of considerations lead me to the conclusion that the purpose of
sections 125 and 127 of the 1985 Act, and of section 32 of the 1980 Act, was to
deal comprehensively with the manner in which class rights in companies having
a share capital could be varied or abrogated. They are as follows:

First, Chapter II of Part IV of the Act (which includes sections 125 to 129) is
headed 'Class rights'. The side note to section 125 reads 'Variation of class rights'.
The language seems to treat 'class rights' as synonymous with 'rights attached to
any class of shares', at any rate so far as companies with a share capital are
concerned.

Second, the use in section 17(2)(*b*) of the 1985 Act of the expression 'rights of
any class of members' in connection both with companies having a share capital
and with companies having no share capital, underlines the point that the
expression 'rights attached to any class of shares' in section 125, must have been
regarded by the legislature as synonymous with the former phrase, so far as
companies with a share capital were concerned.

Third, the evident intention of the legislature to protect 'rights attached to any
class of shares' against variation or abrogation by the mere alteration of articles,
would, if coupled with an intention to provide no such protection against
variation or abrogation of class rights of the third category, be anomalous and
arbitrary.

Fourth, if the variation or abrogation of third category rights are not dealt with
by section 125, then the conclusion would seem to follow that if the rights were
contained in the memorandum, the rights could not be varied or abrogated at
all. The enabling provisions of section 125 would obviously not apply, nor would
the enabling provisions of section 17. The terms of section 17, to my mind,
strongly suggest a legislative belief that section 125 would deal with the variation
or abrogation of any 'special rights of any class of member' contained in the
memorandum.

Fifth, the combination of the considerations thirdly and fourthly above-
mentioned, leads to a further point. What sense could there be in a result under
which third category rights contained in articles were more freely alterable than
'rights attached to any class of shares' contained therein, but under which third

category rights contained in the memorandum were less freely alterable than 'rights attached to any class of shares' contained in the memorandum? The distinction would not be merely anomalous; it would, to my mind, be perverse.

For these reasons I conclude that section 125 was intended by the legislature to cater for the variation or abrogation of any special rights given by the memorandum or articles of a company to any class of members, that is to say, not only rights falling into the first category I have described, but also rights falling into the third category. I must, therefore, construe section 125 so as to give effect to that legislative intention if the language of the section so permits. In my judgment, it does.

Subsection (1) refers to 'the rights attached to any class of shares in a company whose share capital is divided into shares of different classes'. In my judgment, if specific rights are given to certain members in their capacity as members or shareholders, then those members become a class. The shares those members hold for the time being, and without which they would not be members of the class, would represent, in my view, a 'class of shares' for the purposes of section 125. The class would include those shares of ownership of which for the time being entitled the members of the company to the rights in question. For the purposes of section 125, the share capital of a company is, in my judgment, divided into the shares of different classes, if shareholders, qua shareholders, enjoy different rights.

This construction of section 125 has the consequence that shares may come into or go out of a particular class on acquisition or disposal of the shares by a particular individual. I do not see any conceptual difficulty in this. Counsel for the defendant pointed out certain administrative difficulties that might follow, mainly regarding the details to be included in annual returns. These seem to me to be capable of administrative solution. I do not think they have any real weight on the question of construction of section 125.

In my judgment, a company which, by its articles, confers special rights on one or more of its members in the cpacity of member or shareholder thereby constitutes the shares for the time being held by that member or members, a class of shares for the purposes of section 125. The rights are class rights.

I have already expressed the opinion that the rights conferred on the plaintiff under articles 5, 7, 9 and 12, were conferred on the plaintiff as member or shareholder of the defendant. It follows that, in my judgment, the shares in the defendant for the time being held by the plaintiff constitute a class of shares for the purpose of variation or abrogation of those rights.

PART VI: SHARE REGISTERS

Every company must keep a register of its members containing the names and addresses of all its members, the date on which each was registered as a member and the date on which each ceased to be a member (CA 1985, s 352). The Companies Act also contains requirements as to location of the share register (s 353), entries in relation to share warrants (s 355), the right to inspect the register (s 356), the outlawing of any trust on the register (s 360, Table A, reg 5) and the court's power to rectify the register (s 359). *Re*

Swaledale Cleaners Ltd[1] and *Re Gresham Life Assurance, Ex Parte Penny*[2] are examples of the exercise of this power. It may be as important to be off the register as on it (see Sources 230, 231 and 232). The court has a discretion as to whether to exercise the power to rectify the share register.

Aside from cases where there is a dispute between a proposed transferee and the company, the court can also exercise this jurisdiction where there is a dispute between two claimants to the same shares (s 359(3), Source 233).

The fact that no trusts can be entered on the register may necessitate special procedures to protect equitable interests, where, for example shares are mortgaged by deposit of the share certificates. An equitable mortgagee might want to prevent the mortgagor from transferring the shares; equally, the mortgagor might have deposited the share certificates with a blank transfer form and might want to prevent the equitable mortgagee from registering himself as the owner. For this purpose, the Rules of the Supreme Court prescribe a procedure (Source 234).

SOURCE 230
Re Sussex Brick Company
(Court of Appeal 1904) [1904] 1 Ch 598; 73 LJ Ch 308

On 16 January 1901, William Belcher, the chairman and managing director of the Sussex Brick Company Limited, executed a transfer to George Bowman Browne and David G. H. Pollock of 5000 fully paid £1 shares in the company; and on 3 March 1903, he executed a transfer to them of 17,234 further fully paid £1 shares in the company. At the respective dates of the transfers Belcher was the duly registered holder of the shares. The company's articles of association contained a clause that 'The instrument of transfer of any share in the company shall be executed both by the transferor and transferee, and the transferor shall be deemed to remain a holder of such share until the name of the transferee is entered in the register-book in respect thereof.' Accordingly both transfers were executed by the transferees as well as by the transferor.

On 12 March 1903, Browne wrote to the company's secretary inclosing the transfer of the 17,234 shares and the certificate for those shares, with a request for a new certificate. On 14 March the secretary replied inclosing a receipt for that transfer, and stating that the transfer would be laid before the board, and that the new certificate would be ready about 28 March.

Between 14 and 21 March the secretary resigned, and at a board meeting on 21 March the directors appointed a new secretary. The transfer of the 17,234 shares was not submitted to the board at that meeting, the only resolution then passed being that appointing the new secretary. It was not until after the date of that meeting that the new secretary became aware of Browne's letter of 12 March and of the late secretary's reply of 14 March.

On 23 March the transfer books were closed.

On 27 March Browne wrote to the company's secretary inclosing the transfer and certificate of the 5000 shares, and also asking for a certificate of the 17,234 shares; and on 1 April the secretary replied acknowledging the receipt of the transfer and certificate, adding, 'As you are aware, the books have been closed until after the meeting to-morrow.'

On 2 April an extraordinary general meeting of the company was held at which

---

1 [1968] 1 WLR 1710; [1968] 3 All ER 619 (see p 603)
2 (1873) 8 Ch App 446 (see p 599)

special resolutions were passed for a voluntary winding-up and for the appointment of a liquidator, with a view to the reconstruction of the company with an increase of the capital.

On 25 April 1903, Messrs Browne and Pollock, being apparently under the impression that their transfers had been registered, served the liquidator with a notice, under section 161[1] of the Companies Act 1862, stating that they dissented from the resolutions, and requiring him either to abstain from carrying them into effect or to purchase their interest in the company at a price to be determined according to section 162.

In reply the liquidator reminded Messrs Browne and Pollock that their transfers had not been registered, so that their notice was invalid.

To enable them to rely upon their notice of dissent Messrs Browne and Pollock, together with Belcher, took out a summons under section 35[2] of the Companies Act 1862, against the liquidator for a declaration that the two transfers which had been deposited with the company for registration prior to 20 March and 4 April 1903, respectively ought to have stood registered on those dates, and for an order on the liquidator to rectify the register of members accordingly as and from those dates respectively by substituting the names of the transferees for that of the transferor.

Buckley J granted an order for rectification, but only as from the date of the order; the applicants appealed for the back-dating of the order.

VAUGHAN WILLIAMS LJ: I think that this appeal must be allowed. I propose to deal with this case as one in which there has been an unfortunate accident arising from very unnecessary delay in putting the names of these gentlemen, Messrs Browne and Pollock, upon the register. The section of the Act of 1862 one has first to consider is section 35, which is as follows: [His Lordship read the section, and proceeded:]

Now, in this case there can be no doubt but that the names of these gentlemen ought to have been on the register at a date earlier than the time of the holding of the meetings in relation to the reconstruction of this company. Under those circumstances, when one looks at *Nation's Case*,[3] which was a decision by Lord Romilly MR, there can be no doubt that that is an authority for the proposition that when it is right that an order for rectification should be made — whether the order be for rectification by taking a name off the register or by putting a name on — the Court may make an order, not only that the right name shall be put on or taken off, as the case may be, but that the register shall be treated as if the name had been on or off at the time it ought in fact to have been on or off.

. . .

I have only to add this, that I do not mean for a moment to suggest that any one is entitled to such an order *ex debito justitiae*; it is a matter in the discretion of the judge, and there might be cases in which the judge, although he considered such an order essential to completely establishing the rights of the applicant, might refuse to do so because he thought it would work injustice to other members of the company. If I thought here that such an order would work injustice to other persons, especially to persons who are not in any way bound by the mistake of the company, I should feel considerable hesitation in making the order; but in the present case there is no evidence before us that any injustice will be caused at all. It has been suggested that if we make the order asked for we shall invalidate the

1 Now s 110 of the Insolvency Act 1986
2 Now s 359 of the Companies Act 1985
3 (1866) 3 Eq 77

resolutions, because the meetings will not have been properly called; and other suggestions of a similar kind were made in the course of the argument. As the matter stands, we can do justice and prevent any wrong accruing to these two gentlemen, Messrs Browne and Pollock, without doing any injustice to any one else.

Under these circumstances I think that the order for rectification ought to be made as asked.

SOURCE 231
Re London, Hamburgh and Continental Exchange Bank — Ward and Henry's Case
(Chancery Appeals 1867) (1867) 2 Ch App 431

TURNER LJ: . . . This case of course depends mainly, if not wholly, upon the extent of the jurisdiction given to the Court by the 35th section of the Companies Act [now s 359], and the circumstances under which that jurisdiction ought to be exercised. . . . Now this much at least seems to me to be clear upon the section, that it rests in the discretion of the Court whether it will or will not exercise the jurisdiction thus given. There is not a word in the section rendering it imperative on the Court to exercise the jurisdiction. It must therefore, as it seems to me, depend upon the circumstances of each case whether the jurisdiction should be exercised or not; and my opinion is that, under the circumstances of this case, we ought not to exercise it. There is a question here whether Ward has not by his conduct released Stafford and adopted Henry as the purchaser of these shares; whether, in truth, Stafford or Henry is the equitable owner of these shares. There may, indeed, be a further question, whether enough may not have been done to release Stafford without enough having been done to adopt Henry; and beyond this, there is a suit actually pending between Stafford and Henry to determine to which of them these shares belong. What are the rights of these parties, and the equities between them, must, as it seems to me, depend upon facts and upon conduct which cannot be satisfactorily investigated under this summary jurisdiction. Upon this ground, therefore, I think that the order of the Master of the Rolls cannot be maintained, and that this summons ought to have been dismissed.

As, however, the question of the extent of jurisdiction given by this section was raised in the argument before us, I think it right to give my opinion upon it, although I much regret to say that my learned brother and I do not agree upon the point. It is not to be wondered at that different opinions should be formed upon the construction of a section worded as this section is. The question is, whether the jurisdiction given by it is general, applicable to all cases, or limited to cases in which there has been error, mistake, or default on the part of the company. Upon the best consideration I have been able to give to the subject, I am inclined to think that the jurisdiction is general, and not limited as suggested. The intention of the section, as I understand it, is to provide a summary means of dealing with cases which the Court in its discretion should think might be so dealt with. A large and wide discretion ought, I think, to be exercised by the Court in determining whether it will exercise the power given to it by the section, and it is, I think, too narrow a construction to hold that the section applies only where there is error, mistake, or default, on the part of the company.

CAIRNS LJ: . . . I think it clear that the object of these enactments was to secure a list or register which, supposing it to be fairly and properly kept by the company, in accordance with the authorities and documents of title furnished to them, would shew at any time who were the shareholders, entitled to the profits, and liable to contribute to the debts, of the company. Whether the register would be thus fairly and properly kept, would depend upon whether the company and its officers faithfully performed the duty thrown upon them by the Legislature; but, inasmuch as the mere imposition of penalties would not, necessarily, secure the performance of this duty, and, inasmuch as the rights of persons entering or leaving the company ought not to be prejudiced by its non-performance, it was further necessary to provide for the correction of errors in the register occasioned by the default of the company. This has been done by the 35th section, and this, in my opinion, is the scope and object of the 35th section; and by the 98th section, the power given by sect. 35 may be exercised, not only before a winding up of the company, but also for the purpose of settling a list of contributories upon a winding up.

That this is the object of the 35th section is, in my opinion, clear from various considerations. In the first place, the section, from its silence as to the execution and production of proper transfers, and as to the proof of a title to transfer, would appear to assume that all these forms have been gone through in a manner which ought to have been satisfactory to the company, and that nothing remains but the proper expression upon the register of their effect. In the next place, the act to be done under the powers of that section is the 'rectification' of the register, a term which of itself implies that the register, either in what is, or what is not upon it, is wrong: but the register cannot be wrong unless there has been a failure on the part of the company to comply with the directions in the Act as to the kind of register to be kept: for if the Act has been complied with, the register must be right and not wrong. Again, the section gives power to the Court, if it rectifies the register, to order costs and damages to be paid by the company, but not by any person other than the company against whom the motion may be directed. Further, the term 'rectification' implies that the register is to be placed in the state in which, either as regards the entry or omission of a name, it ought to have been at the time when the entry or omission should have been made; a retrospective operation having a material effect on the interests and property of the company, and one which it is hardly possible to suppose could take place unless the company, by its own act, had rendered itself subject to it.

If, on the other hand, we consider the construction which it is suggested might be put upon this section, namely, that under it the Court is to try a suit between vendor and purchaser, and to ascertain who, in equity, is really the owner of the shares, we are met by difficulties which appear to me to be insuperable. In the first place it is obvious that the result of this may be to shew, that at any one period the persons really liable to make good the unpaid capital of the company are persons wholly different from those held out upon the register to the world as the members of the company. Further, we must observe that an order under this section may be applied for from a Court of law, as well as from a Court of equity, nor is there any power in a Court of law to refuse to entertain the application. Again, the powers conferred by the section are wholly insufficient to enable even a Court of equity to do justice in the most ordinary case of a dispute between vendor and purchaser. No costs or damages can be given against the party to the contract who is in the wrong. No injunction can be granted to restrain a dealing with or alienation of the shares. No order can be made for the execution of a transfer; for payment of the stamp, and other expenses of it; for production of it to the company. Moreover, the utmost that the Court could do by an order in the nature of a decree for specific performance, would be to direct a transfer and registration as from the time of the decree, with damages for delay against the party in the wrong; whereas, under this section, the Court, as I have already observed, does not act personally against vendor or purchaser, but acts, and acts retrospectively, and by way of correcting an error upon the register, and puts the register in the form in which, at some antecedent period, it ought to have been.

SOURCE 232
Re National and Provincial Marine Insurance Company ex parte Parker
(Chancery Appeals 1867) (1867) 2 Ch App 685; 15 WR 1217

Heald, Mathwin, and Hoyle were respectively the registered owners of 500, 88, and 10 shares in the company. On 20 April 1867, each of them executed a transfer of his shares to Parker, in consideration of 5s. paid to them by him, and Parker executed the transfers at the same time. On 22 April the transfers by Heald and Mathwin were presented to the company for registration, and that by Hoyle was presented on the following day.

By the articles of association it was provided that shares might be transferred by deed executed by the transferor and transferee; that the transferor should remain the holder till the name of the transferee was entered on the register; and that on the transfer being executed and presented to the company, along with such evidence as to the title of the transferor, and of the execution of the transfer by him, as the board might require, the company should register the transferee as a member. It was also provided (clause 28) that the board might decline to register that transfer of any share made by a member indebted to the company; and (clause 29) that no transfer, unless with the previous consent of the board, should be made or registered after a call on such shares had been made, until the amount of such call, together with the amount of all overdue calls, if any, upon all other shares of the transferor, and the amount of all interest, if any, in respect of such overdue calls, should have been first paid to the company, and that notwithstanding the time appointed for payment of the calls should not have arrived; but the last-mentioned provision was not to apply to any transfer which might have been actually lodged at the office previously to the call being made.

On 23 April a call was made by the company. All previous calls had been paid by Heald, Mathwin, and Hoyle. The company (which had not been ordered to be wound up) having declined to register the transfers, Parker applied to the Court, under section 35 of the Companies Act 1862 [now s 359], to rectify the register as above-mentioned. . . . Heald and Hoyle admitted that their object in transferring the shares was to escape from further liability in respect of the shares, but they denied, and it was not contended by the company, that they intended to reserve to themselves any benefit in event of the shares becoming valuable.

The Master of the Rolls refused the application, holding that an inherent discretion was vested in the directors of a company, upon facts such as those of the present case becoming known to them, to refuse to register the transfers of shares, and that they were not compelled to register transfers solely effected for the purpose of evading liability.

SIR JOHN ROLT LJ: I am still inclined to think that the transfer of shares expressly to escape the liability of a shareholder, so far as it is right to express my opinion upon it in this case, does not necessarily vitiate the transfer; and I should not dispose of this case adversely to the Appellant upon any such ground.

I think, also, that probably Mr Roxburgh has been successful in shewing that the decision in *Ward and Henry's case*[1] does not determine that this is purely a

---

1 (1867) 2 Ch App 431 (see p 642)

discretionary jurisdiction which the Court is at liberty to exercise or not, as it thinks fit. But I think, so far as I find it necessary to form an opinion upon it, that if a very doubtful case were presented, and the Court thought that upon the whole a bill had better be filed, it would be entitled to say so under the 35th section, and that the difficulties arising from the delay pointed out by Mr Roxburgh would not be a sufficient reason to induce the Court to dispose of the matter upon an application such as this. I think the Court would have jurisdiction to say, 'Let a bill be filed, or take such other remedy as you think fit.' If that be not so, still I am by no means satisfied that Mr Parker is improperly omitted from this register. In determining that question I am at liberty to take into account every equitable consideration that bears upon it. Sitting here, and acting under this section, I am not bound to follow what a Court of law would do in such a case. On the contrary, I am not only at liberty, but bound, to take into consideration every principle that is entertained by Courts of equity applicable to any such subject.

. . . Now, the onus is upon Mr Heald, and those who are associated with him, to shew that the name of Mr Parker is improperly omitted, because the directors did not register these transfers made on 20 April. If, after the part he took on 17 April,[1] he asks me to say that it is just and equitable that this transfer should be made as against the directors, my opinion is that it is not just and equitable; and if this evidence, and no more, were before me, upon a bill filed by him to do what he is now asking the Court to do, I should not be disposed to give him the relief that he asks. No doubt this is a very important case, and one of very considerable difficulty, and if it is intended to make anything of it a bill must be filed. But as the case now stands I think it would not be just and equitable to compel the directors to accept these transfers. Therefore I think the decision of the Master of the Rolls is right, and this appeal must be dismissed, with costs.

SOURCE 233
Re Diamond Rock Boring Company Limited ex parte Shaw
(Queen's Bench Division 1877) [1877] 2 QBD 463; 25 WR 569

LORD COLERIDGE CJ (after stating the facts): It appears, therefore, that Smith was acting as agent for Sir E. Piers as well as for Mr Shaw, and the latter therefore having paid Smith as agent of Piers for the shares, and the transfer having been duly executed by both parties, Shaw had an undoubted legal right to the shares, and was entitled to be registered as the owner of them.

A question might arise, where one person claims to be put upon the register, and another person disputes his right, the company standing neutral, how far there can be said to have been a default in the company, — a question which might be of importance, and has been treated as important in some circumstances, but which I think is not important in this case. It might be otherwise if the company were taking an active part in the matter, but we are told that they desire to take no part, and submit themselves to the judgment of the Court. If it were necessary to determine the question, I should be inclined to think, although the transfer had been mutilated and could not be produced, that the company were in fault. The mere mutilation of the transfer, the purchaser being shewn to have a clear legal title, would not prevent his title from taking effect, and the company would be bound to register the purchaser in the place of the vendor.

. . . Now, applying the facts to section 35, we find there is a person whose name, without sufficient cause, has been omitted from the register. He applies to

---

1 He persuaded the directors not to make a call there and then

the Court for an order to rectify the register, the Court thinks the justice of the case requires that such an order should be made. It has been argued that because this was a matter in which the company was not in default, and because these are proceedings to which the company is only nominally a party, and not taking any real part in the litigation, the Court had no jurisdiction. The facts seem to bring the case within the words of the first part of the section, without having recourse to the second part, and all conditions necessary to give jurisdiction are fulfilled. But the section goes on to give jurisdiction to the Court to decide in any such proceeding any question of title, which there is here; and the question arises between two members, or alleged members: for whichever way you take it, Shaw is either a member or an alleged member, and Sir E. Piers is also a member or an alleged member; and it is also a question between two members or alleged members and the company: for Shaw demands, and Sir E. Piers resists, the rectification of the register by the company. Finally, the matter is put out of all question by the strength of the last clause: 'And generally the Court may in any such proceeding decide any question that it may be necessary or expedient to decide for the rectification of the register.'

If the case stood on the words of the Act alone, those words being the result of a course of legislation, the earlier Act of 1856 not having the later and more general powers which are added and supplied by the subsequent Act of 1857, and the two enactments being re-enacted together by section 35 of the Act of 1862 [now s 359], I should have thought that the jurisdiction of the Court was clear. But the point is not bare of authority, and there has been a great deal of discussion and several decisions on it. Two views have been entertained,

[The judge analysed the two views as expressed in *Ward and Henry's case*[1] (p 642) and continued:]

Looking at all the words of section 35, and giving them a reasonable construction, I think that the legislature intended to give the Court jurisdiction to make an order so as to decide questions of title, trusting to the discretion of the Court not to decide in this summary manner any intricate or difficult question of title; but that, if the Court think fit, they have jurisdiction to make the order in all cases.

SOURCE 234
Rules of the Supreme Court

Securities not in court: stop notice (O. 50, r. 11)
11. (1) Any person claiming to be beneficially entitled to an interest in any securities . . . other than securities in court, who wishes to be notified of any proposed transfer or payment of those securities may avail himself of the provisions of this rule.

(2) A person claiming to be so entitled must file in the Chancery Chambers or in a district registry —

(a) an affidavit identifying the securities in question and describing his interest therein by reference to the document under which it arises, and
(b) a notice in Form No. 80 in Appendix A (a stop notice) signed by the deponent to the affidavit and annexed to it, addressed to the Bank of England or, as the case may be, the body, state, territory or unit trust concerned,

---

1 (1867) 2 Ch App 431 (see p 642)

and must serve an office copy of the affidavit, and a copy of the notice sealed with the seal of Chancery Chambers or the district registry, on the Bank or other person or body, . . .

(3) There must be indorsed on the affidavit filed under this rule a note stating the address to which any such notice as is referred to in rule 12 is to be sent and, subject to paragraph (4), that address shall for the purposes of the rule be the address for service of the person on whose behalf the affidavit is filed.

(4) A person on whose behalf an affidavit under this rule is filed may change his address for service for the purpose of rule 12 by serving on the Bank of England, or other person or body, a notice to that effect, and, as from the date of service of such a notice the address stated therein shall for the purpose of that rule be the address for service of that person.

Effect of stop notice (O. 50, r. 12)
12. Where a stop notice has been served in accordance with rule 11, then, so long as the stop notice is in force, the Bank of England or other person or body on which it is served shall not register a transfer of the securities or take any other steps restrained by the stop notice until 14 days after sending notice thereof, by ordinary first class post, to the person on whose behalf the stop notice was filed, but shall not by reason only of that notice refuse to register a transfer, or to take any other step, after the expiry of that period.

. . .

Withdrawal, etc. of stop notice (O. 50, r. 14)
14. (1) The person on whose behalf a stop notice was filed may withdraw it by serving a request for its withdrawal on the Bank of England or other person or body on whom the notice was served.

(2) Such request must be signed by the person on whose behalf the notice was filed and his signature must be witnessed by a practising solicitor.

(3) The Court, on the application of any person claiming to be beneficially entitled to an interest in the securities to which a stop notice relates, may by order discharge the notice.

. . .

PART VII: SHARE CERTIFICATES

The certificate is prima facie evidence of the title to the shares of the person named in the certificate. The certificate will also be prima facie evidence of the amount paid up on the shares and the company will be estopped from denying the title of someone named in the certificate and the amount stated in the certificate as paid up on the shares. See s 185 of the Companies Act 1985, Table A, regs 6, 101.

Instead of certificates, a company may issue share warrants. These pass title simply by delivery (ie the warrants are made out to 'bearer' — anyone who holds them) and there is no need to complete a transfer form and undertake the transfer registration procedure through the company in order to transfer title to share warrants. See ss 188, 355 of the Companies Act 1985.

PART VIII: CALLS, FORFEITURE, SURRENDER

A call is a request by the company to the shareholders whose shares are unpaid or partly paid, for payment of the balance or part of the balance owing on the shares. If the shareholder fails to pay a call, his shares may be forfeited by the company. A surrender of shares is the voluntary giving up by the shareholder of his shares.

Forfeiture and surrender may result in the company acquiring its own shares and in the shareholder being released from payment of the full nominal value of the shares. They may, thus, be classed as operations which result in the reduction of the capital of the company (see pp 789ff) and therefore illegal. Forfeiture and surrender have, nevertheless, been accepted for a long time by the common law as not unlawful provided they are exercised only in consequence of the shareholder's failure to pay the call made on his shares (and, possibly, in the case of surrender, where the shares are fully paid) and are in accordance with the provisions of the articles. This is now recognised by the Companies Act 1985 (s 143(3)). For typical provisions in the articles, see Table A, regs 12–22.

Most shares nowadays are fully paid and problems of calls and forfeiture therefore rarely arise.

PART IX: LIENS AND PRIORITIES

A company may, by its articles of association assert a lien over its issued shares, whether partly or fully paid (see eg the facts of *Allen v Gold Reefs of West Africa*,[1] p 330). Difficult problems of priority arise where a shareholder mortgages his shares and the company asserts its lien (Source 235). A similar problem concerns the assertion by the company of its rights under the articles to refuse to register a transfer of shares as against a mortgagee attempting to enforce his rights against the mortgagor (Source 236).

SOURCE 235
Bradford Banking Company Limited *v* Briggs
(House of Lords 1886) (1886) 12 App Ca 29; 56 LJ Ch 364

LORD BLACKBURN: . . . The respondent company is a trading company limited by shares and incorporated under the Companies Act 1862, for the purpose of carrying on the business of a colliery. It has articles of association which exclude the regulations contained in the First Schedule Table A to the Companies Act 1862, and those articles of association were duly registered.

The Companies Act 1862, section 16 enacts that when registered the articles shall bind the company and the members thereof to the same extent as if each member had subscribed his name and affixed his seal thereto, and there were in such articles contained a covenant on the part of himself, his heirs, executors, and administrators to conform to all the regulations in such articles.

The only one of the articles of association which I think it material to notice is article 103, which is as follows: 'The company shall have a first and permanent

---

1 [1900] 1 Ch 656; 69 LJ Ch 266 (see p 330)

lien and charge, available at law and in equity, upon every share of every person who is the holder or one of several joint holders thereof, for all debts due from him, either alone or jointly with any other person, whether a shareholder or not in the company.'

John Faint Easby, a coal merchant, became a proprietor of a number of shares in the respondent company, and obtained certificates for them. This property in the shares was, by virtue of section 16 of the Act already quoted, I think, bound to the company as much as if he had (at the time he became holder of these shares) executed a covenant to the company in the same terms as article 103, but I do not think it was bound any further.

John Faint Easby filed a petition for liquidation on 31 December 1883, being then indebted to the company. He had been a customer of the respondent company, and owed them a considerable sum at that date. He still continued the registered holder of the shares, and, if there had been no more in the case, it is not now at least disputed that the respondent company would have had a first lien on the shares. But Easby was a customer of the Bradford Banking Company, the now appellants, and in November 1879 he deposited, amongst other things, the certificates of 120 shares in the respondent company, and the appellant company [gave notice to Briggs].

. . .

The points of law were argued on the admissions in the pleadings, and on admissions made by counsel at the bar and embodied in the judgment of Field J. The important admission, as far as regards Easby's shares, was that the account of John Faint Easby with the plaintiffs was closed in June 1881 (which involves an admission that all the advances in respect of which the plaintiffs sue were made before that date), and that all moneys owing by him to the defendants when the said account was so closed have since been paid.[1] This at once raised the question whether the plaintiffs, as pledgees of Easby's interest in the shares, had priority for advances over debts which were contracted after notice of that pledge, though the lien was claimed by virtue of a contract made at the very time when the shares were first acquired by Easby, and consequently before the shares could be pledged by Easby to the appellants or any one else.

. . .

As I understand it, the principle of *Hopkinson v Rolt*[2] is explained by Lord Campbell then Lord Chancellor, and it is this: The owner of property does not, by making a pledge or mortgage of it, cease to be owner of it any further than is necessary to give effect to the security which he has thus created. And if the security is, as that in *Hopkinson v Rolt* was, a security for present and also for future advances, the pledgee or mortgagee, though not bound to make fresh advances, may, if he pleases, do so, and will, if the property at the time of the further advance remains that of the pledgor, have the security of that property.

But the mortgagor (unless there is something to make it against conscience in him to do so) may cease to take further advances from the first mortgagee, and borrow money from anyone else ready to lend it on the security of that property remaining in him not already pledged to the first, subject to the priority of the first pledgee for advances made or begun to be made. The first mortgagee is entitled to act on the supposition that the pledgor who was owner of the whole property when he executed the first mortgage continued so, and that there has been no such second mortgage or pledge until he has notice of something to shew him that there has been such a second mortgage, but as soon as he is aware

---

1 Ie paid by Briggs to Easby by way of advance
2 (1861) 9 HLC 514; 34 LJ Ch 468

that the property on which he is entitled to rely has ceased so far to belong to the debtor, he cannot make a new advance in priority to that of which he has notice. As Lord Campbell says, 'the hardship upon the bankers from this view of the subject at once vanishes, when we consider that the security of the first mortgage is not impaired without notice of a second.' It seems to me to depend entirely on what I cannot but think a principle of justice, that a mortgagee who is entitled, but no bound, to give credit on the security of property belonging to the debtor, cannot give that credit after he has notice that the property has so far been parted with by the debtor.

The appellants held to have priority over the respondent's lien for all advances after notices of the deposit had been given by the appellant to the respondent.

SOURCE 236
Hawks v Mcarthur
(Chancery Division 1951) [1951] 1 All ER 22; [1951] 1 TLR 308

Articles 11, 12, 13 of the company's articles of association were as follows:

11. The directors may in their absolute discretion and without assigning any reason therefore or without specifying any grounds therefor, decline to register any transfer of shares (whether fully paid up or not) and no transfer shall be registered which if registered would make the number of members exceed the limit hereinbefore prescribed, and clause 19 of Table A shall be modified accordingly.

12. Save as in these presents otherwise provided no seven per cent cumulative preference shares or ordinary shares in the capital of the company shall be transferred unless and until the rights of pre-emption hereinafter conferred shall have been exhausted.

13. (*a*) Every member or other person entitled to the said cumulative preference shares or ordinary shares (hereinafter called 'the vendor') who intends to transfer such seven per cent cumulative preference shares or ordinary shares shall give notice in writing (hereinafter referred to as a 'transfer notice') to the board of directors of his intention. Such transfer notice shall specify the number and class of shares which the vendor desires to transfer and shall constitute the board his agent for the sale of the said shares in one or more lots at the discretion of the board to such members of the company as are hereinafter referred to at a price to be agreed upon by the vendor and such members of the company as are hereinafter referred to or in default of agreement at a price which the auditor or auditors of the company for the time being shall certify by writing under his or their hand to be in his or their opinion the fair selling value thereof as between a willing vendor and a willing purchaser. A transfer notice shall not be withdrawn except with the consent of the board. . . .

VAISEY J: The plaintiff is the holder of a charging order affecting five hundred ordinary shares of £1 each in a private company called W Lucas & Sons Ltd, which stand in the name of, and were originally the property of, the first defendant, Mr Theodore Hunter McArthur, who has not entered an appearance in these proceedings. He claims that that charging order operates on Mr McArthur's interest in those shares, which, he says, is a complete interest, both legal and equitable. The second and third defendants, Mr Roberts and Mr Fraser, claim that the beneficial interest in the shares in question has passed to them as a result of transfers executed in their favour by Mr McArthur in pursuance of certain agreements entered into between themselves and Mr McArthur prior to the execution of those transfers, and they allege that Mr McArthur had no interest in the shares at the date of the charging order on which the charge could operate.

. . .

There is, undoubtedly, a basic principle that a charging order only operates to charge the beneficial interest of the person against whom the order is made, and that it is not possible, for instance, to obtain an effective charging order over shares where the person against whom the order is made holds them as a bare trustee. The charging order affects only such interest, and so much of the property affected, as the person whose property is purported to be affected could himself validly charge.

. . .

I must now deal with the stringent provisions in the articles of the company for restricting the transfer of shares. Article 11 empowers the directors, in their absolute discretion, to decline to register any transfer of shares. By article 12 no share '. . . shall be transferred unless and until the rights of pre-emption hereinafter conferred shall have been exhausted.'

Article 13 contains an elaborate scheme for dealing with shares which are to be transferred or are proposed to be transferred. Among the requirements to be complied with is the following, viz, that, on receiving the transfer notice from the vendor, the board shall forthwith give notice of the intended transfer to all the members of the company stating inter alia the price of the shares to be sold (such price to be agreed by the vendor and members, or, in a default of agreement, to be fixed by the auditors), and invite each member to state in writing, within one month from the date of the transfer notice, whether he is willing to purchase any, and, if so, how many, of the shares. These requirements, however, were not complied with, having been either forgotten or overlooked.

The real question in this case, I think, is whether the alleged agreements (which, I think, I must consider to be the agreements between Mr McArthur and Mr Roberts and between Mr McArthur and Mr Fraser, respectively) operated so as to amount in equity to a transfer of the shares held by Mr McArthur, as to two hundred of them to Mr Roberts, and as to three hundred of them to Mr Fraser, or whether the failure or neglect to follow the code laid down by articles 11, 12 and 13 completely vitiates the whole transaction, so that the transfers are worthless and there has been a total failure of consideration for the moneys which were admittedly paid over by Mr Roberts and Mr Fraser to Mr McArthur.

. . .

The facts here are curious. Whether Mr Fraser and Mr Roberts thought they were doing something by agreement with the company, of which they were officers, or whether they thought they were doing something by agreement with Mr McArthur, I do not know. I think, probably, they thought that they were doing what they were doing under an agreement both with the company and with Mr McArthur. The one thing, however, which seems to me to be important is that they paid Mr MacArthur the money, and I cannot bring myself to suppose that they got nothing by their bargain and that the whole property in the shares remained in Mr McArthur, notwithstanding the transfers which had been executed and the money which he received. I should, however, have been content to come to the opposite conclusion because I think that there is something almost scandalous in the way in which Mr Roberts, Mr Fraser and Mr McArthur all seem to have disregarded the articles of association, by which they and the other members of the company were bound. I think it very regrettable that this muddle, for which the plaintiff was certainly not responsible — although he was a shareholder in the company — should have resulted in all the litigation which has led up to the judgment which I am now giving.

Admittedly, Mr McArthur is still the legal owner of the shares. Admittedly, the plaintiff's rights under this charging order are in the nature of equitable rights. And admittedly, the rights of Mr Roberts and Mr Fraser, if they have any rights, are also equitable rights. As I have come to the conclusion that Mr Roberts and Mr Fraser have some rights and that what they did was not a complete nullity, the question is whose rights should prevail. A not irrelevant circumstance is that the equitable rights of Mr Roberts and Mr Fraser precede the equities or quasi-equitable rights under the charging order. In my opinion, the rights of Mr Roberts and Mr Fraser had already accrued at the time the charging order was obtained, and I think, as between the merits (not moral merits, but legal merits) of the plaintiff and the defendants, the rights of the second and third defendants, Mr Roberts and Mr Fraser, must prevail over the claims of the plaintiff. As a result of my decision, the only thing I can do is to dismiss this summons. The result is, I suppose, to record my decision that the charging order is nothing but a charging order *nisi*. I propose, however, to dismiss the summons without costs, because I think that the trouble has arisen largely through the fault of Mr Roberts and Mr Fraser.

PART X: DEBENTURES

A debenture is, strictly speaking, the instrument which creates or acknowledges the debt arising out of the loan by the company. Nowadays, the loan transaction is almost invariably secured by a charge on the company's property and the instrument of debenture includes the charge. Furthermore, if, as again is nowadays common, finance is raised under an issue of debentures from more than a few lenders, it is convenient to constitute the lenders as beneficiaries under a trust, in terms of which the trustees hold the debt against the company for the benefit of the lenders. The legal relationships thus created are those between the trustees and the company (creditor and debtor) and between the trustees and the people who advance the finance (trustee and beneficiary). The trustees will be empowered to negotiate with the company to extend or otherwise vary the terms of the loan or charge, thereby greatly simplifying the relationship between lender and borrower. A company is not obliged to keep a register of debentureholders, but if it does, it should keep this at the place where it keeps its register of members (s 190(3) of the Companies Act 1985) (see Sources 237 and 238).

SOURCE 237
Levy *v* Abercorris Slate and Slab Company
(1883) 37 Ch D 260; 57 LJ Ch 202

CHITTY J: The Plaintiff in this case sues the Defendant company on an instrument set out in the statement of claim, and the company take a legal objection to the action, and say that the document in question is void under the Bills of Sale Act (1878) Amendment Act 1882, on two grounds, first, that it is one that requires registration and it has not been registered; and secondly, that it is not in the form prescribed by the schedule to the Act of 1882, and therefore void under section 9. In answer to these objections the Plaintiff alleges that the instrument in question is in effect a debenture, and therefore within the exception of section 17.

Now what is a 'debenture'? . . . My attention has been called to extracts from *Skeat's Etymological Dictionary* and *Blount's Law Dictionary* as to the derivation of the word 'debenture,' from which it appears that the term is a very old one and is derived from the Latin *debentur,* because it is said 'these receipts began with the words *debentur mihi'* . . . I do not accept Sir Arthur Watson's[1] definition that a debenture must be one of a series of instruments or issued *pari passu* with others.

I have myself known an instance of a single debenture payable to one individual. In my opinion a debenture means a document which either creates a debt or acknowledges it, and any document which fulfils either of these conditions is a 'debenture.' I cannot find any precise legal definition of the term, it is not either in law or commerce a strictly technical term, or what is called a term of art. It must be 'issued,' but 'issued' is not a technical term, it is a mercantile term well understood; 'issue' here means the delivery over by the company to the person who has the charge; as to what 'company' means I have already said it must be by 'an incorporated company,' and it must be secured on 'the goods, chattels and effects' of the company.

. . .

I may add this, that if the debentures had been actually issued in compliance with the agreement, it is clear that the section 17 would apply. I have here before me a document not in form the same as a debenture in the commonly accepted interpretation of the term, but its legal effect is the same, and it would be a strange interpretation to put upon this section to assume that it said that where the legal effect of two instruments was identical yet because there was some slight difference in form the one should be good and the other void. It is true that the document before me is not called a debenture, but that is no sufficient reason why it should not in effect be one; I cannot read it as Sir Arthur Watson wanted me to do, as a contract that it should not operate as a debenture; the parties had no such idea as this in their minds at the time, and I cannot impute such an intention to them. I think, therefore, that a mere agreement to issue what are called 'debentures' is not sufficient to prevent the agreement itself from operating as a debenture within the protection of section 17.

SOURCE 238
Knightsbridge Estates Trust Limited *v* Byrne
(House of Lords 1940) [1940] AC 613; [1940] 2 All ER 401

The plaintiffs mortgaged their property to the defendants to secure a loan. The loan was to be repaid by 80 equal half-yearly instalments. The plaintiffs wished to repay the loan sooner, but on the construction of the loan were not permitted to do so. Various equitable doctrines were unsuccessfully raised on behalf of the plaintiffs (that the loan was void as being perpetuitous, that the provisions of the loan were unreasonable as a clog on the equity of redemption); the loan was held to be a debenture within the meaning of s 74 of the Companies Act 1929 (now s 193) and, therefore not invalid simply by reason of being redeemable only on the expiration of a long period.

VISCOUNT MAUGHAM: . . . In the course of the able arguments for the appellants it became manifest that logically the first matter to be determined was

---

1 Counsel for the defendant

the third question above stated, namely, the question whether section 74[1] of the Companies Act 1929, applied. That section is in the following terms: 'A condition contained in any debentures or in any deed for securing any debentures, whether issued or executed before or after the commencement of this Act shall not be invalid by reason only that the debentures are thereby made irredeemable or redeemable only on the happening of a contingency, however remote, or on the expiration of a period, however long, any rule of equity to the contrary notwithstanding.'

Section 380[2] of the Act so far as relevant provides: 'In this Act, unless the context otherwise requires, the following expressions have the meanings thereby assigned to them (that is to say):

. . .

'Debenture' includes debenture stock, bonds and any other securities of a company whether constituting a charge on the assets of the company or not.'

If then the mortgage was a debenture within section 74 it was difficult to see how the appellants could succeed.

. . .

The position . . . is as follows: The substance of section 74 of the Companies Act, 1929, was first found in the Companies Act 1907, section 14, where it was prefaced by the words 'for removing doubts it is hereby declared that,' etc. There was no definition of the word 'debenture,' and there is strong ground for thinking that, whatever be the ambit of the word, it did not in that section include an ordinary mortgage of land. The consolidating Act of 1908, reproduced the provision of section 14 of the Companies Act 1907, omitting the introductory words. It was in the exact terms of the present section 74 of the Companies Act 1929. The definition clause (section 285) stated that ' "debenture" includes debenture stock,' which perhaps made it even clearer that 'debenture' did not include a mortgage of land in ordinary form. But the amending Act of 1928 contained the provision that at the end of the definition of 'debenture' in section 285 of the Companies Act 1908, 'there shall be added the words "bonds and any other securities of a company whether constituting a charge on the assets of the company or not." '

It is perhaps worth pointing out that the words 'unless the context otherwise requires,' which we find in the consolidating Act of 1929, are not to be found in the amending Act of 1928. I attribute little weight to this fact, for in my opinion some such words are to be implied in all statutes where the expressions which are interpreted by a definition clause are used in a number of sections with meanings sometimes of a wide and sometimes of an obviously limited character.

On the other hand I think due weight ought to be attributed to the words 'otherwise requires' in the Companies Act of 1929, and it is incumbent on those who contend that the definition does not apply to section 74 to show with reasonable clearness that the context does in fact require a more limited interpretation of the word 'debenture' than section 380 has assigned to it.

If we begin by asking what the word 'debenture' means, apart from any definition, the reply must be that it has no precise meaning. Chitty J observed in the case of *Levy v Abercorris Slate and Slab Co*,[3] that the word 'means a document which either creates a debt or acknowledges it, and any document which fulfils either of these conditions is a debenture.' An interesting extract from *Skeat's Etymological Dictionary* (1882) will be found in a footnote to the case (p 264). Sir

---

1 Now s 193 of the Companies Act 1985
2 Now s 744 of the Companies Act 1985
3 (1883) 37 Ch D 260; 57 LJ Ch 202 (see p 652)

Nathaniel Lindley had previously stated simply, 'What the correct meaning of "debenture" is I do not know': *British India Steam Navigation Co v Inland Revenue Commissioners.*[1] In *Lemon v Austin Friars Investment Trust Ltd,*[2] the same ignorance was professed in the Court of Appeal. Warrington LJ in particular, after observing that it had been said 'by a wiser man than himself' that it was impossible to give an exhaustive definition of the word 'debenture,' went on to remark that he did not propose to incur the reproach of venturing where wise men fear to tread. The text books are agreed at least in this that no accurate definition of the word can be found. I think it sufficient to cite *Buckley* on the point (11th edn, p 174). It is clear, therefore, that it was desirable to insert in any consolidation of the Companies Acts a definition of the word.

We must next ask ourselves whether there was any reason for limiting section 74 of the Act of 1929 to debentures of a series issued to a number of subscribers in one of the forms now in common use or in some such way. The reason for the section is explained in the note to the section in *Buckley,* (11th edn,) pp 154–5. Enormous sums had been borrowed by companies formed under the general Companies Act on debentures and debenture stock the principal of which was (in terms) either not repayable at all or only in certain specified events. Doubts had been expressed whether these restrictions on the right of redemption were valid . . . and it seemed desirable to remove these doubts by the Companies Act 1907. The equitable rule was based on the hypothesis that in a contract for a loan the borrower is not usually contracting on equal terms with the lender.

. . .

My Lords, loans made to limited companies on the security of their assets are in general very different from loans made to individuals. Companies may be wound up, in which event their debts have, if possible, to be paid, but they do not die. To the knowledge of both the company and the lender the loan is intended in most cases to be of the nature of a permanent investment. The former can only in the rarest of circumstances be at the mercy of the latter. There is no likelihood of oppression being exerted against the company. Considerations such as these make it manifest that clauses in debentures issued by companies making them irredeemable or redeemable only after long periods of time or on contingencies ought to be given validity. It may be conceded that the ground for excluding the rule in equity is stronger in the case of a series of debentures issued in one of the usual forms than in the case of mortgages of land to an individual; but some of the reasons still remain. It is difficult to see any real unfairness in a normal commercial agreement between a company and (for example) an insurance society for a loan to the former on the security of its real estate for a very prolonged term of years. Both parties may be equally desirous that the mortgage may have the quality of permanence. There is a great deal to be said in such a case for freedom of contract.

I do not think there is any strong argument for suggesting that section 74 of the Act of 1929, or any of its predecessors, ought by reason of its nature to be confined to what may be called ordinary debentures. As we have seen, some definition was certainly desirable, and the very wide terms used by the legislature in the Act of 1928 and reproduced in the consolidating Act of the following year seem to me to show that it was intended to give freedom of contract as regards the particular matter involved in section 74 in relation to any securities granted on loan by a company registered under the Companies Acts. It is contended that the context otherwise requires. I am unable to find any such context.

---

1 (1881) 7 QBD 165; 50 LJ QB 517
2 [1926] Ch 1; 95 LJ Ch 97

. . . All we can do is to see whether the interpretation clause in this case can reasonably be applied to section 74 without leading to any startling result and whether there is any context which requires us to reject some of the words of the definition. The fact that a particular section contains a provision relating to a particular kind of debenture does not assist us. We do not, for example, use the word 'man' in a restricted sense if we make a statement about white men. 'Man' has its ordinary meaning; it is the word 'white' which qualifies the statement and makes it applicable to only some men. So here section 74 itself applies only to debentures creating a charge. That is because the section applies only to debentures creating a charge capable of being redeemed. It is not a reason for holding a security of a company creating a mortgage of land is not a debenture within section 74. Finally, it should be noted that the mortgage with which we are concerned on the present appeal could without difficulty have been drafted in the form of an ordinary company debenture with a charge on its face followed by the provisions as to the instalments by which it is to be paid off, and if desired with the various conditions and provisos printed on the back.

For these reasons I am of opinion that the word 'debentures' in section 74 must be given the meaning attached to that word by section 380.

PART XI: TRADING IN SECURITIES — INSIDER DEALING

Insider dealing — trading in securities when in possession of information which is not public but which if made public would be likely to have a significant effect on the price of the securities traded — was first criminalised in the UK in 1980. This legislation was consolidated in 1985 as the Company Securities (Insider Dealing) Act. In 1989, the European Community enacted a Directive (89/592, OJ 1989 L334/30) co-ordinating regulations on insider dealing and this Directive was implemented in the UK by Pt V of the Criminal Justice Act 1993 (CJA). This new legislation came into force on 1 March 1994 replacing the Company Securities (Insider Dealing) Act 1985.

The offence is committed by someone who, when in possession of information as an insider (ie information which would, if made public, affect the price of certain securities):

(a) deals in those securities; or
(b) encourages another to deal in those securities; or
(c) discloses the information other than in the proper performance of employment functions (CJA, s 52).

The offence applies only to individuals and only where the dealing took place on a regulated market or where the person dealing relied on a professional intermediary or is himself or herself a professional intermediary. There are a number of defences (CJA, s 53) including:

(a) that the alleged offender did not expect the profitable outcome;
(b) that there was a reasonable belief that the information was public; and
(c) that he or she would have done what was done even without the information.

Dealing in securities is defined as acquiring or disposing of securities or 'procuring, directly or indirectly, an acquisition or disposal of the securities by any other person' (CJA, s 55(1)(b)). The information must relate to particular securities, it must be specific or precise, it must not have been made public and it must be such that, if made public, it would 'be likely to have a significant effect on the price of any securities' (CJA, s 56(1)). Section 58 describes a number of instances when information will be regarded as having been made public, but these are not exhaustive.

The maximum penalty is seven years in prison and a fine, and prosecutions may only be instituted with the consent of the Secretary of State or the Director of Public Prosecutions. If the alleged offence is one of dealing in securities, the alleged offender must be shown to have been within the UK when doing any act forming part of the offence, or it must be shown that the market on which the dealing took place was one regulated in the UK or, if a professional intermediary was involved, that professional intermediary must have been within the UK when doing anything by means of which the offence was alleged to have been committed (CJA, s 62(1)). If the alleged offence was one of encouraging another to deal, or of disclosing insider information, the alleged offender (or the alleged recipient of the encouragement or disclosure) must be shown to have been within the UK at the time of the encouraging or disclosing.

There has been a derisorily small number of prosecutions for alleged insider dealing offences since 1980. Unlike the United States, there is no statutory provision for civil liability for insider trading. Arguably, there are common law principles on the basis of which a successful suit could be brought for the recovery of profit made through insider dealing. Since directors — who are the most likely people to possess inside information — owe their duties to the company rather than to the shareholders, such suits would be limited to recovery by the company rather than individual shareholders and former shareholders. Ironically, it will have been the latter and not the former which will have suffered any loss as a result of the transaction in question.

Although both the old and the new legislation declare that a transaction in breach of the statute is not on that account to be treated as void and unenforceable (CJA, s 62(2)), the court might refuse to accede to the enforcement of a transaction at the behest of a party to the transaction and who possessed inside information at the time (*Chase Manhattan Equities Ltd v Goodman* [1991] BCLC 897 — Goodman was later disqualified under the Company Directors Disqualification Act on account of the insider dealing offence [1994] 1 BCLC 349).

NOTES AND QUESTIONS

1. *Should directors be required to give reasons for refusing to register a transfer of shares? See* Re Smith & Fawcett, *p 463.*
2. *What was the context in which the dispute in* Lyle & Scott[1] *arose? What was the eventual order in* Lyle & Scott?

---

1 [1959] AC 763; [1959] 2 All ER 661 (see p 605)

3. *In the recent case of* Theakston v London Trust,[1] *the plaintiff wanted to sell its shares but under the articles could insist on a registration of the transfer only if the proposed transfer was to an existing member (and other immaterial categories). An outsider wished to acquire the shares and it was agreed that an existing member would purchase the plaintiff's shares with the assistance of an interest free loan from the outsider. Other terms of the contract between the outsider and the purchasing member required the member to charge the shares as security for the loan, to vote in accordance with the directions of the outsider, to account to the outsider with respect to any distributions received. The loan was not repayable until the outsider had acquired the shares and a complicated machinery was built into the agreement to try to ensure that the outsider would become the shareholder in respect of the shares. This agreement was held not to be in breach of the articles and the purchasing member was successful in his motion to have the company's share register rectified to record him as the owner of the shares.*

4. *The court will, in a suitable case, imply a term in the articles to give them business efficacy. In* Tett v Phoenix Property and Investment Co Ltd,[2] *the articles prohibited a transfer to an outsider as long as any member of the company (or the wife, husband, parents or children of any member) was willing to purchase the shares. The articles failed, however, to provide any mechanism by which notice might be given to the members of the intended transfer. The Court of Appeal was willing to imply the following term into the articles:*

    > *'Before transferring any shares to any person not already a member of the company, the intending transferor shall first take reasonable steps to give all other members and their respective wives, husbands, parents and children (not being minors) a reasonable opportunity to make an offer to purchase the same at a fair value to be determined by the auditors in default of agreement.'*

5. *In* Re New Cedos [1994] 1 BCLC 797 *(actually decided in 1975) there was an interesting variation on the* Swaledale *decision (see Source 213 at p 603). The court decided as a matter of construction of the relevant regulations that the applicant was entitled to be registered as a member. As an alternative ground for this result, the court held that the directors could not be said to have validly exercised their power to refuse the transfer. Given the rotation and retirement provisions of the articles, the company had no validly appointed directors in the period following the request for the share transfer.*

6. *Where an offence has been committed under s 210 of the Companies Act 1985 or in the course of an investigation under ss 442 or 444 difficulty is experienced in obtaining information as to certain shares, the Secretary of State may subject any shares to the restrictions laid down by s 454. A company may apply for similar restrictions to be imposed in the conditions laid down by s 216. In proceedings, to lift such restrictions, the court may refuse to do so even where this affects an innocent third party purchaser of all*

---

1 [1984] BCLC 390
2 [1986] BCLC 149 (CA)

or some of the shares in question (Re Geers Gross plc *[1988] BCLC 140).*

The draconian nature of this jurisdiction has been recognised by the court, first in ordering a company which had obtained an ex parte order under s 454 to pay the costs when that order was discharged. The company (Lonrho) had sought the order after the service of a notice under s 212 seeking information regarding certain shares. That notice had been served on a foreign resident and had demanded the information by the following day (Re Lonrho plc (No 2) *[1989] BCLC 309). In subsequent proceedings the court refused to make an order under s 454 given the serious risk of prejudice to innocent third parties and in the circumstances of the respondent to the application giving an undertaking not to dispose of the shares pending a full investigation at an inter partes hearing* (Re Lonrho plc (No 3) *[1989] BCLC 480). In* Re Richard Group plc (*[1989] BCLC 566) the court expressed the view that an order under s 454 should not be made ex parte unless there is reason to believe that information about the shares is being deliberately withheld and that, if notified, the respondent would be likely to dispose of the shares.*

7. *One theme running through Sources 217 to 223 may be summed up (with apologies to Gilbert and Sullivan) as 'a preference shareholder's lot is not a happy one'. Consider this theme with reference also to the materials on variation of class rights (pp 634ff) and on reduction of capital (pp 789ff).*

8. White v Bristol Aeroplane Co[1] *(Source 217 at p 611) shows the vulnerability of preference shares to subsequent share issues (in* Andrews v Gas Meter Co,[2] *(Source 216 at p 610) it was the ordinary shareholders who were vulnerable to the issue of the preference shares). Are preference shareholders protected in this situation by the recently enacted pre-emption provisions (see ss 89–94 of the Companies Act 1985)?*

9. *Could* Dimbula Valley v Laurie[3] (Source 221 at p 619) *be analysed as imposing an onus on the preference shareholders to show that their rights were not exhausted?*

10. *Debentures can be issued to the public in the same way as shares can. In such a case, those who issue the debentures are required to comply with the requirements of the Public Offers of Securities Regulations 1995, SI 1995/1537 or the Financial Services Act 1986 as to prospectuses or listing particulars (pp 174ff).*

11. *Debentures can be irredeemable (s 193).*

12. *Debentures, unlike shares can be issued at a discount. If, however, they are convertible into shares, they cannot then be issued at a discount as this might be an evasion of the rule against the issue of shares at a discount,* Moseley v Koffyfontein.[4]

---

1 [1953] Ch 65; [1953] 1 All ER 40 (see p 611)
2 [1897] 1 Ch D 361; 66 LJ Ch 246 (see p 610)
3 [1961] Ch 353; [1961] 1 All ER 769 (see p 619)
4 [1904] 2 Ch 108

13. *If debentures are issued as part of a series they should all be expressed to rank*
    pari passu *to ensure equality among all lenders under the same instru-*
    ment.

14. *In* British America Nickel Corporation v O'Brien,[1] *the trust deed gave*
    power to 75 per cent of the debenture-holders to modify the rights of all
    debenture-holders. The Privy Council refused to sanction a scheme which had
    the approval of 75 per cent of debenture-holders where one only of the
    debenture-holders held 75 per cent and its approval had been separately
    negotiated by the company. According to Lord Haldane:

    'There is, however, a restriction of such powers when conferred on a majority of a
    special class in order to enable that majority to bind a minority. They must be exercised
    subject to a general principle, which is applicable to all authorities conferred on
    majorities of classes enabling them to bind minorities; namely that the power given
    must be exercised for the purpose of benefiting the class as a whole and not merely
    individual members only.'

---

1 [1927] AC 369; 96 LJ PC 57

Chapter 10

FLOATING CHARGES

PART I: THE DISTINCTION BETWEEN FIXED AND FLOATING CHARGES

Frequently, debentures issued by a company will be secured by a fixed and a floating charge. It is the latter which is unique to company borrowings and which we consider at length here. The distinction may not always be clear, although which charge it is may have important consequences (Sources 239, 240, 241, 242, 243).

> SOURCE 239
> **Re Yorkshire Woolcombers' Association**
> [1903] 2 Ch 284
>
> By a trust deed of 23 April 1900, the Yorkshire Woolcombers Association Limited, specifically mortgaged all its freehold and leasehold properties to trustees to secure its debenture stock, and, as beneficial owner, charged in favour of the trustees 'by way of floating security all its other property and assets both present and future, and its undertaking, but not including capital for the time being uncalled.' This deed contained (clause 21) the usual power enabling the association until the crystallization of the security 'to sell or specifically mortgage or charge, or otherwise deal with and dispose of, the property and assets expressed to be charged by way of floating security, or any part thereof, and to divide profits among the members of the company in as unfettered a manner as if these presents had not been executed.'

A receiver having been appointed subsequently in a debenture holder's action, it had to be established whether the charge in favour of the guarantor was or was not a floating charge. If it was a floating charge it required to be registered and, not having been registered, would be void as against the receiver.

> FARWELL J: (at first instance): . . . Now it is quite plain on the construction of the deed itself, that it was not intended to stop the company; the company was clearly intended to go on. These book debts are a considerable portion of the assets of the company, and at the date of the deed amounted to £71,000. If the assignment is to be treated as a specific mortgage or charge or disposition, then the company had no business to receive one single book debt after the date of it; but if, on the other hand, although not so called, the company was intended to go on receiving the book debts and to use them for the purpose of carrying on its business, then it contains the true elements of a floating security. It is of the essence of a charge of that kind that it remains dormant until the person in whose favour the charge is created intervenes. That appears to me to be the exact definition of the present assignment.
>
> . . .
>
> In my opinion this is, although the parties have chosen to call it a specific security, nothing more nor less than a floating security. But when one comes to

consider what 'specific security' means, in my opinion it is quite clear that anything which may take effect as a floating security is wholly inconsistent with, and is the antithesis of, a specific security. A specific security is that which is given on specific property. A charge on all book debts which may now be, or at any time hereafter become charged or assigned, leaving the mortgagor or assignor free to deal with them as he pleases until the mortgagee or assignee intervenes, is not a specific charge, and cannot be. The very essence of a specific charge is that the assignee takes possession, and is the person entitled to receive the book debts at once. So long as he licenses the mortgagor to go on receiving the book debts and carry on the business, it is within the exact definition of a floating security.

ROMER LJ (Court of Appeal, affirming Farwell J): . . . Under section 14 of the Companies Act 1900, for a charge to be a 'floating charge on the undertaking or property of the company' within the meaning of the words used in that section, it cannot, I think, be properly contended that it is essential that the charge must be on the whole undertaking, or on the whole property, of the company. The term 'floating' is one that until recently was a mere popular term. It certainly had no distinct legal meaning. It is not a legal term. It has recently been used in more than one statute; but when the Courts have to consider whether the charge is a floating one within the meaning of the term as used in the Acts of Parliament, and in particular within the meaning of the Companies Act 1900, one must, I think, deal with the question of substance to be answered according to the circumstance of each particular case. I certainly do not intend to attempt to give an exact definition of the term 'floating charge,' nor am I prepared to say that there will not be a floating charge within the meaning of the Act, which does not contain all the three characteristics that I am about to mention, but I certainly think that if a charge has the three characteristics that I am about to mention it is a floating charge. (1) If it is a charge on a class of assets of a company present and future; (2) if that class is one which, in the ordinary course of the business of the company, would be changing from time to time; and (3) if you find that by the charge it is contemplated that, until some future step is taken by or on behalf of those interested in the charge, the company may carry on its business in the ordinary way as far as concerns the particular class of assets I am dealing with.

In the present case those three characteristics do in my opinion distinguish the charge we have to consider. In the first place, the charge is one upon all the debts of the company present and future, not even limiting them (though I do not think it makes any difference) to the trade debts, present and future. In the second place, it obviously contemplates a class of asset which, in the ordinary course of the life of the company, must continually, and of necessity, change; and, thirdly, in the present case, if I look at the deed which created the charge here, to my mind it is clearly contemplated that until some step is taken by or on behalf of those who are to have the benefit of the charge, the company would be able to receive the debts due to the company in its ordinary course of business, and to deal with them for the ordinary purposes of the business. In the first place, in considering that question, it is important to consider that a charge of debts is not completed until notice is given to the debtors, and you find by this deed that by express provision it is contemplated that the trustees need not, unless they choose, give notice at all to the debtors, and more than that, there is an express provision that they cannot be compelled to do so, unless they have a request from those entitled to the charge — that is, the guarantors, or a majority of them. Then there is that further provision, to which my Lord has referred, that the trustees are not to be answerable for allowing the association to receive their debts, which I need not repeat. Treating this as a commercial document — as it is — what was the meaning of it? Did it not contemplate that until the trustees thought it necessary to intervene, the charge should not be perfected by notice being given to the debtors, and that the business should be carried on in the ordinary way in regard to these debts, and that a debtor might go and pay to the company a particular debt, and the company might receive it, and deal with the cash in the ordinary way in which it would be dealt with in the ordinary course of business? I think that certainly is what is contemplated by this deed, . . .

SOURCE 240
Re Brightlife Ltd
[1987] Ch 200; [1986] 3 All ER 673

HOFFMANN J: Brightlife Ltd ('Brightlife') is in creditors' voluntary liquidation. Its assets have realised about £40,000. It owes over £200,000 to Norandex Inc, an American company, secured by a debenture. It also owes over £70,000 to the Commissioners of Customs and Excise for VAT. The commissioners say that Norandex's debenture conferred only a *floating* charge and therefore the claim for VAT, being preferential, takes priority under section 614(2)(*b*) of the Companies Act 1985, which reads as follows:

> 'The preferential debts shall . . . so far as the assets of the company available for payment of general creditors are insufficient to meet them, have priority over the claims of holders of debentures under any floating charge created by the company, and be paid accordingly out of any property comprised in or subject to that charge.'

Norandex says that its debenture has priority because it created a *fixed* charge over most of the assets or, alternatively, because the floating charge over all the assets had become a fixed charge before the resolution for winding up.

I must first dispose of certain questions of construction. The debenture is dated 11 April 1983. It is expressed to secure all present and future indebtedness of Brightlife to Norandex. The charging clause is 3(A). Sub-clause (i) creates a 'first specific equitable charge' over freehold and leasehold property. Sub-clause (ii) charges:

> 'by way of first specific charge (a) all book debts and other debts now or at any time during the continuance of this security due or owing to Brightlife and the benefit of all securities and guarantees now or at any time held by Brightlife in relation thereto; (b) the goodwill and uncalled capital for the time being of Brightlife; and (c) the benefit of any licences for the time being in Brightlife.'

Sub-clause (iii) creates a floating charge over after acquired freehold and leasehold property and, 'the undertaking and all other property, assets and rights whatsoever present and future of Brightlife,' subject to a proviso which prohibits the creation of any other charges ranking in priority to or pari passu with the floating charge or the disposal of any assets subject to the floating charge contrary to the provisions of clause 5(ii). This important clause is quoted below. Clause 3(B) reads as follows:

> 'Norandex may at any time by notice to Brightlife convert the floating charge into a specific charge as regards any assets specified in the notice which Norandex shall consider to be in danger of being seized or sold under any form of distress or execution levied or threatened or to be otherwise in jeopardy and may appoint a receiver thereof.'

Clause 5 is a covenant by Brightlife that it:

> '(i) shall carry on and conduct its affairs in a proper and efficient manner;
> (ii) shall not without the prior consent in writing of Norandex sell transfer
> or otherwise dispose of the whole or, except in the ordinary course of
> business, any part of its undertaking property or assets (being in the
> aggregate substantial) or deal with its book or other debts or securities for
> money otherwise than in the ordinary course of getting in and realising the
> same which expression shall not authorise the selling, factoring or discount-
> ing by Brightlife of its book debts or other negotiable instruments held by
> it . . . (iv) shall furnish to Norandex: . . . (c) [each quarter] a statement of
> the book debts owing at the end of the relevant quarter, showing their
> amount and from whom they are owed and any other material information
> in the possession of Brightlife relating thereto . . .'

Clause 13 is a covenant for further assurance in the following terms:

> 'Brightlife shall execute and do all such assurances, acts and things as
> Norandex may reasonably require for perfecting or protecting the security
> created by these presents over the property hereby charged or any part
> thereof or for facilitating the realisation of such property and the exercise
> of all powers, authorities and discretions vested in Norandex . . . and shall in
> particular execute all transfers, conveyances, assignments and assurances of
> such property whether [to] Norandex or its nominees . . . which Norandex
> may think expedient and for the purposes of this Clause a certificate in
> writing by Norandex to the effect that any particular assurance, act or thing
> required by it is reasonably required shall be conclusive evidence of such
> fact.'

The first submission of the counsel for Norandex (Mr Sheldon) was that clause
3(A)(ii)(a) created, according to its terms, a 'first specific charge' over 'all book
debts and other debts'.

. . .

It is true that clause 5(ii) does not allow Brightlife to sell, factor or discount
debts without the written consent of Norandex. But a floating charge is consistent
with some restriction on the company's freedom to deal with its assets. For
example, floating charges commonly contain a prohibition on the creation of
other charges ranking prior to or pari passu with the floating charge. Such
dealings would otherwise be open to a company in the ordinary course of its
business. In this debenture, the significant feature is that Brightlife was free to
collect its debts and pay the proceeds into its bank account. Once in the account,
they would be outside the charge over debts and at the free disposal of the
company. In my judgment a right to deal in this way with the charged assets for
its own account is a badge of a floating charge and is inconsistent with a fixed
charge.

I was referred to *Siebe Gorman & Co Ltd v Barclays Bank Ltd*[1] and a recent
decision of the Irish Supreme Court in *Re Keenan Bros Ltd*,[2] in both of which
charges over book debts were held to be fixed and not floating. In the former
case, the debenture was in favour of a bank and not only prohibited the company
from selling or charging its book debts but required that they be paid into the
company's account with that bank. Slade J decided that as a matter of construc-

---

1 [1979] 2 Lloyd's Rep 142
2 [1986] BCLC 242

tion the bank would not have been obliged to allow the company to draw upon the account at a time when it still owed the bank money under the debenture. The company was not free to deal with the debts or their proceeds in the ordinary course of its business. Each debt as it accrued to the company could therefore properly be said to become subject to an equitable fixed charge. On the other hand, the judge said:

'. . . if I had accepted the premise that [the company] would have had the unrestricted right to deal with the proceeds of any of the relevant book debts paid into its account, so long as that account remained in credit, I would have been inclined to accept the conclusion that the charge on such book debts could be no more than a floating charge.'

Re Keenan Bros Ltd was an even stronger case than *Siebe Gorman & Co Ltd*. Again the debenture was in favour of a bank and this time the company was obliged to pay the proceeds of all debts into a designated account with the bank and 'not without the prior written consent of the bank in writing make any withdrawals or direct any payment from the said account'. Neither case is therefore of assistance or Norandex.

[Hoffmann J then dealt with the question as to whether the service of notice by the chargee had effected a crystallisation of the charge prior to winding up, see p 687.]

SOURCE 241
Re A Company ex parte Copp (No 005009 of 1987)
[1989] BCLC 13

The company had granted a debenture secured by a charge in favour of its bank lender. Clause 2 of the charge provided as follows:

'The Company as beneficial owner and to the intent that the security created shall rank as a continuing security hereby charges with the payment or discharge of all monies obligations and liabilities hereby covenanted to be paid or discharged . . . by way of specific charge all book debts and other debts now and from time to time due or owing to the Company.'

Clause 5 reads:

'With reference to the book debts and other debts hereby specifically charged the Company shall pay into the Company's account with the Bank all monies which it may receive in respect of such debts and shall not without the prior consent in writing of the Bank sell factor discount or otherwise charge or assign the same in favour of any other person or purport to do so and the Company shall if called upon to do so by the Bank from time to time execute legal assignments of such book debts and other debts to the Bank.'

A receiver was appointed under this charge and subsequently the company went into insolvent liquidation. There were insufficient assets to meet the claims of the bank and the liquidator applied for a declaration, inter alia, that the charge was a floating, not a fixed charge. The bank and the receiver opposed the application.

KNOX J: . . . The bank's claim to strike out the claim for a declaration which I have read is based on the proposition that this matter is covered by authority, and the authority relied on for this purpose is the decision of Slade J in *Siebe Gorman*

& Co Ltd v Barclays Bank Ltd [1979] 2 Lloyd's Rep 142. The headnote is not satisfactory in its rehearsal of the relevant passages in the debenture in that case and I take it from the statement of facts. On 5 January 1971 the debenture was executed by R H McDonald Ltd in favour of a bank as a corporate body. The relevant clauses were as follows. Clause 3 provided:

> 'The Company as beneficial owner hereby charges with the payment or discharge of all monies and liabilities hereby covenanted to be paid or discharged by the Company [and then I pass over (a), (b) and (c)] (d) by way of first fixed charge all books debts and other debts now and from time to time due or owing to the Company...'

Clause 5(c) provided:

> 'During the continuance of this security the Company... (c) shall pay into the Company's account with the Bank all monies which it may receive in respect of the book debts and other debts hereby charged and shall not without the prior consent of the bank in writing purport to charge or assign the same in favour of any other person and shall if called upon to do so by the bank execute a legal assignment of such book debts and other debts to the Bank.'

It will be seen that the debenture in this case follows closely, if not slavishly, the wording used in that particular case.

Slade J said this in the course of his judgment ([1979] 2 Lloyd's Rep 142 at 158):

> 'Before the decision of the House of Lords in *Tailby v Official Receiver* ((1888) 13 App Cas 523, [1886–90] All ER Rep 486) there was some doubt whether there could be an effective assignment of future book debts, because it was thought that an assignment in such terms might be so indefinite and uncertain that the Courts could not give effect to it. Any such doubts, however, were removed by this decision, which shows that it is undoubtedly competent for anyone to whom book debts may accrue in the future to create for good consideration an equitable charge upon those book debts, which will attach to them as soon as they come into existence. This much was common ground between the parties in the present case. [Counsel], however, on behalf of Siebe Gorman, strongly contended that, notwithstanding the wording of clause 3(d) of the debenture, referring to a first fixed charge on — "... all book debts ... now and from time to time due or owing to the Company..." the charge on the relevant bills could not be and was not more than a *floating* charge. He referred to the often cited passage from the judgment of Lord Justice Romer in *In re Yorkshire Woolcombers Association Ltd* ([1903] 2 Ch 284 at 295): "I certainly think that if a charge has the three characteristics that I am about to mention it is a floating charge. (1) If it is a charge on a class of assets of a company present and future; (2) if that class is one which, in the ordinary course of the business of the company, would be changing from time to time; and (3) if you find that by the charge it is contemplated that, until some future step is taken by or on behalf of those interested in the charge, the company may carry on its business in the ordinary way as far as concerns the particular class of assets I am dealing with."'

Then there is set out the argument which was submitted to him by counsel on behalf of Siebe Gorman (which was an assign of what were claimed to be book debts), and he said of that argument (at 158):

'[Counsel for Siebe Gorman] emphasised that, while according to the terms of clause 5(c) all the proceeds of future book debts would in the first instance have to go into the debtor's account with the bank, it must have been contemplated that R. H. McDonald Ltd would then be free immediately to draw out all those moneys for the ordinary purposes of its business, at least if such account was for the time being in credit. In regard to the latter point, if I had accepted the premise that R. H. McDonald Ltd would have had the unrestricted right to deal with the proceeds of any of the relevant book debts paid into its account, so long as that account remained in credit, I would have been inclined to accept the conclusion that the charge on such book debts could be no more than a floating charge.'

Then passing over two paragraphs he states his final conclusion on this aspect of the case as follows (at 159):

'In my judgment, however, it is perfectly possible in law for a mortgagor, by way of continuing security for future advances, to grant to a mortgagee a charge on future book debts in a form which creates in equity a specific charge on the proceeds of such debts as soon as they are received and consequently prevents the mortgagor from disposing of an unencumbered title to the subject matter of such charge without the mortgagee's consent, even before the mortgagee has taken steps to enforce its security . . . This in my judgment was the effect of the debenture in the present case. I see no reason why the Court should not give effect to the intention of the parties, as stated in clause 3(d), that the charge should be a first fixed charge on book debts. I do not accept the argument that the provisions of clause 5(c) negative the existence of a specific charge. All that they do, in my judgment, is to reinforce the specific charge given by clause 3. The mere fact that there may exist certain forms of dealing with book debts which are not specifically prohibited by clause 5(c) does not in my judgment turn the specific charge into a floating charge.'

That decision was followed by a decision of the Irish Supreme Court in *Re Keenan Bros Ltd* [1986] BCLC 242. I do not refer to that case in detail beyond mentioning that in that case it was specifically provided that the proceeds of the book debts should not be disposed of without the bank's consent.

Both that case and the *Siebe Gorman* decision were distinguished by Hoffmann J in *Re Brightlife Ltd* [1986] BCLC 418, [1986] 3 All ER 673, where he held that a credit balance in a company's bank account was not within a charge in a debenture of 'all book debts and other debts now or at any time during the continuance of this security due or owing to the company'. His decision, therefore, in relation to the effect of the charge is strictly obiter, but he did refer to the two authorities to which I have already referred. What he said is this

[The judge then quoted the passage beginning 'It is true that clause 5(ii) . . . ' and ending '. . . Neither case is therefore of assistance to Norandex', see pp 664–665 and continued:]

In that case, of course, Norandex (as appears by inference) was not a bank and the decision itself in *Re Brightlife* is plainly distinguishable from both the *Siebe Gorman* case itself, as Hoffmann J pointed out, and, therefore, also from this particular case. In my judgment, *Re Brightlife* is very far from expressing any doubt on the validity of the *Siebe Gorman* case and the distinction in that case turns on the absence of the fetter on dealing with the proceeds produced by the book debts which was found to exist by Slade J as a matter of the construction of the terms of the debenture in the *Siebe Gorman* case and was expressed in words explicitly in the Irish case of *Re Keenan Bros Ltd.*

Counsel for the liquidator (Mr Vos) submitted that there were two points of distinction between the *Siebe Gorman* case and the present one by way of postscript to his acceptance of the proposition that the present is very closely based on the document that was construed in the *Siebe Gorman* decision. The first point which he submitted was that eight years have rolled by since the *Siebe Gorman* decision and it would have been open to the parties to do what was in fact done in the *Keenan Bros* case, namely to put in express prohibitions against disposing of the book debts proceeds when received. He submitted that the absence of any such express provision, in the context of the well-known existence of the *Siebe Gorman* decision, was at least some ground for construing the particular turn of phrase which is used both in this case and in the *Siebe Gorman* debenture in a different way.

It seems to me that the indications are to the contrary effect, because this is a type of transaction in respect of which judicial precedent is a particularly valuable guide to the commercial adviser. It is one of the main justifications for the doctrine of precedent that the adviser can, if he can rely on precedent, give reliable advice to his clients and it is trite law that that is a particularly cogent consideration in regard to property transactions of one sort or another. The inference I draw from the very close correspondence between the phrases used in the *Siebe Gorman* case and those used in the document in the present case is that the parties intended to produce the same known result. I therefore see no strength in the first point of distinction between the two cases.

The second point of distinction was that at the time when the debenture was granted, whether one takes it on 20 May or, as I think would be more accurate, 29 May 1987, there was, in effect, an agreement between the bank and the company for the £300,000 overdraft limit to stay. In fact there were contemporaneous letters with regard to the first such agreement which made it clear that the overdraft remained repayable on demand on a day-to-day basis, but the existence of the overdraft limit was relied on by counsel for the liquidator as an indication that it was intended that the company should be able to deal with the proceeds of its book debts freely so long as the overdraft limit was not exceeded, and that this therefore, to use the language which I have quoted of my brethren, was a badge of a floating rather than a fixed charge.

There again, I do not find this submission at all compelling. I accept the submission that was made to me by counsel for the applicants (Mr Mann) that the overdraft limit arrangement, ephemeral and liable to instant determination as it was, does not negate the conclusion on construction that Slade J reached in relation to the charge in the *Siebe Gorman* case. It is true that there is no evidence one way or the other whether there was in the *Siebe Gorman* case, at the date of the debenture, a particular overdraft limit agreed to run. There plainly was, on the facts of that case, such an agreement after the debenture was granted, but the report does not make it clear what the position was at the date of the debenture. Nevertheless, I am persuaded by the submission of counsel for the applicants that, putting it at its highest, the arrangement with regard to an overdraft is a collateral arrangement to the debenture and not a matter which justifies giving the debenture itself as a matter of construction a different meaning from that which it would, but for the overdraft agreement, properly bear. In those circumstances, that does not seem to me, on the face of it, to provide an arguable defence to the claim advanced by the bank that the true construction of this document is covered by the authority of the *Siebe Gorman* case.

Finally on this aspect of the matter I should say that although, of course, the decision in *Siebe Gorman* is a decision of a judge at first instance and is therefore technically not absolutely binding on me, the views which I have expressed about the value of precedents in this particular class of work make it clear that it would be quite wrong for me, even if I thought (as I do not) that there was some error or flaw in the reasoning in the *Siebe Gorman* case, to decline to follow it.

The case went to trial on the other issues in respect of which a declaration was sought — both of interest to companies in insolvent liquidation — and is reported there as *Re M C Bacon* [1990] BCLC 324, [1991] Ch 127 (see Source 311).

SOURCE 242
Re New Bullas Trading Ltd
(Court of Appeal) [1994] 1 BCLC 485

NOURSE LJ: He who lends money to a trading company neither wishes nor expects it to become insolvent. Its prosperous trading is the best assurance of the return of his money with interest. But against an evil day he wants the best security the company can give him consistently with its ability to trade meanwhile. Hence the modern form of debenture, which, broadly speaking, gives the lender a fixed charge over assets that the company does not need to deal with in the ordinary course of its business and a floating charge over those that it does.

An asset peculiarly problematical in this context is a book debt of the company. There being usually no need to deal with it before collection, it is at that stage a natural subject of the fixed charge. But once collected, the proceeds being needed for the conduct of the business, it becomes a natural subject of the floating charge. While the company is a going concern, it is no less an advantage to the lender that the debt should be collected and the proceeds used in the business. But on insolvency, a crystallised floating charge on proceeds, which, in the event supposed, are all the more likely to have been dissipated, may be worthless; whereas a fixed charge enabling the lender to intercept payment to the company may be of real value.

. . .

In each of the previous authorities the draftsman treated book debts indivisibly, the question being to which form of charge they had, as such, been subjected. Here, for the first time in a reported case, the draftsman has deliberately and conscientiously set out to subject them to a fixed charge while they are uncollected and a floating charge on realisation. The essential question, as it has emerged in this court, is whether the law allows them to be treated in that fashion.

. . .

It is unnecessary to refer to the provisions of the bank's debenture, except to say that it included a charge on all book debts, both present and future, due or owing to the company, which was expressed to take effect as a first fixed mortgage by assignment; in other words, as a fixed charge.

The material provisions of 3i's debenture, to which I will refer simply as 'the debenture', are as follows. Clause 1 contains a covenant by the company to pay or discharge to 3i all moneys and liabilities at any time or times due or owing or incurred by the company to 3i. Clause 2 provides that their repayment or discharge shall be made on demand unless otherwise agreed in writing. Clause 3 contains a charge by the company of seven different categories of asset with the payment and discharge to 3i of all moneys and liabilities thereby covenanted to be paid and discharged and all other sums intended to be thereby secured. The assets charged include:

'FIFTH — THE book debts and other debts due or owing to the Company both present and future.'

Clause 4 provides:

'THE charges on the property and assets FIRST SECOND THIRD FOURTH and FIFTH described are created as fixed charges . . .'

. . .

The condition on which the outcome of this case mainly depends is condition 12, to which the marginal note is 'Book debts'. I set it out in full, adding numbers for the three parts into which para (A) is divided:

'During the continuance of this security the Company shall:

(A) [(i)] pay into a current account or a separate designated account (as 3i may require) of the Company with the Bank all moneys which it may receive in respect of the book debts and other debts hereby charged and (subject to any rights of the Bank in respect thereof) pay or otherwise deal with such moneys standing in such account in accordance with any directions from time to time given in writing by 3i; [(ii)] prior to any demand being made under condition 8 hereof or to the provisions of condition 9 hereof becoming operative in the absence of any directions from 3i any moneys received by the Company and paid into such account in respect of the book debts and other debts hereby charged shall upon such payment in stand released from the fixed charge on such debts here-inbefore by this Debenture created and shall stand subject to the floating charge hereinbefore by this Debenture created over the other property and assets of the Company; [(iii)] any such release shall in no respects derogate from the subsistence and continuance of the said fixed charge on all other book and other debts of the Company for the time being outstanding.

(B) if called upon to do so by 3i execute a legal assignment of such book debts and other debts to 3i in such terms as 3i may require and give notice thereof to the debtors from whom the debts are owing or incurred and take such other steps as 3i may require to perfect such legal assignment;

(C) deal with such book debts and other debts in accordance with any directions from time to time given in writing by 3i (subject to any rights of the Bank in respect thereof) and in default of and subject to any such directions deal with the same only in the ordinary course of getting in and realising the same (but not sell assign factor or discount the same in any way);

(D) permit the Bank to furnish directly to 3i from time to time upon request full statements and particulars of all the Company's accounts with the Bank and such other financial statements and information respecting the assets and liabilities of the Company as are from time to time available to the Bank.'

. . .

On 6 November 1991 the applicants, Mr Roger Murray Griffiths and Mr Andrew George Pearce, two partners in Ernst & Young, were appointed by the bank to be joint administrative receivers of the company. On 12 November 1991, pursuant to powers contained in the debenture, they were appointed by 3i to act in the like capacity. Those appointments brought into play s 40 of the Insolvency Act 1986.

. . .

When the administrative receivers were appointed, the amounts owing by the company to debenture holders were £1.136m to the bank, £100,000 to 3i and £37,500 to some former minority shareholders of the company, who, on 18 July 1989, had agreed to postpone their securities to those of the bank and 3i. Realisations of book debts have proved very successful. As at 20 January 1993, the debt owed to the bank had been discharged (save for a nominal amount of £37) and about £114,000 was owed to 3i. At that date the proceeds of realisations of book debts remaining in the administrative receivers' hands amounted to approximately £459,714 with some £104,000 (estimated to produce £26,000) remaining to be collected. The preferential debts had previously been estimated at £608,500, consisting of £253,000 owed to the Inland Revenue and the Department of Health and Social Security in respect of PAYE and national insurance contributions, £339,000 owed to the Customs and Excise in respect of VAT, £8,000 owed to the Department of Employment and £8,500 to 33 employees.

On these figures, it is clear that if the charge over book debts was created as a floating charge, the preferential debts will absorb all their proceeds and nothing will be left for 3i. Conversely, if it was created as a fixed charge, 3i will be paid in full and the amount available for the preferential creditors will be reduced accordingly. On neither footing will anything be left for unsecured creditors whose debts are not preferential.

Doubts having arisen as to whether the charge over book debts was, as created, a fixed or a floating charge, on 28 October 1992 the administrative receivers issued an originating application in the Companies Court for the determination of that question.

In this court there has been much common ground. It is agreed that the question depends on the intention of the parties, to be ascertained from the terms of the debenture; legal impossibility apart, that there are no considerations of public policy which prevented them from making whatever contract they chose; that it was possible for them to create a fixed equitable charge over future as well as present book debts; that their declared intention was to create such a charge; but that that intention was nevertheless defeated if the other provisions of the debenture are inconsistent with it.

Mr Sumption QC, for 3i, has made two main submissions, whose import can be summarised as follows: first, on the footing that condition 12 treated, or must be taken to have treated, book debts indivisibly, the charge created over them by the debenture was, as it was expressed to be, a fixed charge; secondly and in the alternative, the effect of condition 12 was to create a fixed charge over book debts while they were uncollected and a floating charge over their proceeds, there being no legal objection to their being treated in that fashion. It seems that in the court below it was the first of these submissions that was primarily, if not exclusively, relied on. Certainly it was by Knox J's rejection of it that the case was decided as it was. No trace of the second submission can be found in the judge's careful judgment. In this court it has assumed great prominence. Logically, as it seems to me, it deserves to be considered first.

The question depends in the first instance on the true construction of condition 12. In order to trace the fate, actual or potential, of one of the company's book debts, it is necessary to start with condition 12(C), whose effect, in the absence of any written directions by 3i, is to require the company to get in the debt in the ordinary course by demanding payment from the debtor in full.

On payment being made, condition 12(A)(i) requires it to be paid into a specified account of the company with the bank, where it must be paid or otherwise dealt with in accordance with any written directions given by 3i. Condition 12(A)(ii), which is in substance, though not in form, a proviso to condition 12(A)(i), then provides that, prior to crystallisation of the security under either of conditions 8 and 9 and in the absence of any written directions by 3i, the sum paid in shall be released from the fixed charge and become subject to the floating charge. Condition 12(A)(iii), in substance a further proviso, provides that the release of the sum paid in from the fixed charge shall not derogate from its continuation in relation to all other outstanding book debts of the company.

The judge held, and the parties are agreed, that when condition 12(A)(i) and (ii) are read together, it is seen that any directions given by 3i cannot have retrospective effect on any sums paid into the account beforehand. With that point out of the way, it is very clear, as Mr Henderson, for the Inland Revenue, accepts, that the parties intended to create a fixed charge over book debts while they were uncollected (and also, if there was any interval between collection and payment in, over the proceeds) and a floating charge over the proceeds once they had been paid into the specified account. So the decisive question is whether the law allowed the parties to make an agreement to that effect.

Mr Henderson has submitted that the distinction drawn between the book debts before collection and after realisation is unrealistic and artificial because a debt is worth nothing unless and until it is turned into money. He says that it is of the essence of a fixed charge that the asset is appropriated to the charge from the beginning and that it cannot be released from it without the consent of the chargee. He relies strongly on a passage in the judgment of Vaughan Williams LJ in *Re Yorkshire Woolcombers Association Ltd* [1903] 2 Ch 284 at 294, where he said:

> '... what you do require to make a specific security is that the security whenever it has once come into existence, and been identified or appropriated as a security, shall never thereafter at the will of the mortgagor cease to be a security.'

The short answer to these submissions is that here the asset does not cease to be subject to the fixed charge at the will of the company. It ceases to be such because both parties, not the company alone, have determined that if the proceeds of a book debt are paid into the specified account at a time when no directions have been given it shall thereupon be released. The matter is governed by a clear agreement of the parties. Unless there is some authority or principle of law which prevented them from agreeing what they have agreed, their agreement must prevail.

An equitable assignment, whether it takes effect as an out and out assignment or, as here, by way of charge, is a creature of exceptional versatility, malleable to the intention of its creators, adaptable to the subject matter assigned. Provided it is in writing, made for value and the intention is clear, it requires no formalities of expression; it may take effect over property real or personal, and over estates or interests legal or equitable, vested or contingent or, as in the case of future book debts, mere expectancies.

In *Tailby v Official Receiver* (1888) 13 App Cas 523, the case in which it was decided by the House of Lords that an equitable charge over future book debts could validly be created, Lord Macnaghten said (at 543):

> 'It has long been settled that future property, possibilities and expectancies

are assignable in equity for value. The mode or form of assignment is absolutely immaterial provided the intention of the parties is clear. To effectuate the intention an assignment for value, in terms present and immediate, has always been regarded in equity as a contract binding on the conscience of the assignor and so binding the subject-matter of the contract when it comes into existence, if it is of such a nature and so described as to be capable of being ascertained and identified.'

Having referred to the proposition that an assignment of future book debts not limited to a specified business was too vague to have any effect, and having found that it was unsupported by authority, Lord Macnaghten dealt with it as a matter of principle. He said (at 545):

'It was admitted by the learned counsel for the respondent, that a trader may assign his future book debts in a specified business. Why should the line be drawn there? Between men of full age and competent understanding ought there to be any limit to the freedom of contract but that imposed by positive law or dictated by considerations of morality or public policy? The limit proposed is purely arbitrary, and I think meaningless and unreasonable.'

These observations support the view that, just as it is open to contracting parties to provide for a fixed charge on future book debts, so it is open to them to provide that they shall be subject to a fixed charge while they are uncollected and a floating charge on realisation. No authority to the contrary has been cited and, the principle being as spacious as it has been expressed to be, no objection is on that account sustainable. For these reasons, I would accept Mr Sumption's second main submission and hold that the charge over book debts of the company, as created by the debenture, was, unless and until their proceeds were paid into the specified account, a valid fixed charge.

SOURCE 243
Report of the Review Committee on Insolvency Law and Practice ('Cork Report')
Definition of floating charge
1583. The increase in the burden of preferential debts which followed recent employment legislation has led the banks and other creditors to seek to increase the fixed and reduce the floating element of their security. There is already a growing tendency for the clearing banks to take fixed charges on the company's present and future book debts, which until a few years ago would have been included in the floating charge. If our proposals for a 10 per cent fund are adopted then, notwithstanding any reduction in the burden of preferential debts, it may be expected that this tendency will continue.

1584. It has been suggested in some quarters that it is possible to create a fixed security on present and future trading assets (cash balances, stock-in-trade, raw materials, book debts), which allows the company to deal with those assets for ordinary business purposes, yet which gives the creditor an automatic priority in certain circumstances (eg if the company goes into liquidation, or attempts to charge those assets, or suffers an execution in respect thereof). Such a charge would lead to the same injustices which our proposals are designed to remedy, but unless treated as if it were a floating charge it would circumvent them.

1585. It appears from a recent decision in England that a charge is a floating charge if it (i) extends or is capable of extending to future assets of the debtor and (ii) leaves the debtor free to deal with the assets comprised therein in the ordinary course of business without first obtaining the consent of the holder of the charge; but that a requirement that the creditor's consent to any dealing be first obtained, or a restriction on the debtor's right to deal freely, not with the assets themselves, but with their monetary proceeds, is sufficient to constitute the security a fixed charge. This effectively reproduces all the advantages of the floating charge (from the point of view of the creditor) with none of its disadvantages. Moreover, if as we propose the nature of a charge must be determined at the date of its creation, it would be all too easy to create a hybrid security with the best of both worlds if the law were left unchanged.

1586. We consider that a floating charge should be defined by statute to include any charge which (i) extends or is capable of extending to future assets of the debtor and (ii) leaves the debtor substantially free (with or without the consent of the creditor) to deal with assets comprised therein in the ordinary course of business; provided that for the purpose of determining whether the debtor is substantially free to deal with any assets as aforesaid, any restriction:

(a) on the creation of further charges or encumbrances on those assets; or
(b) on the disposal of book debts and other choses in action before they are paid or otherwise reduced to money; or
(c) on dealing with or disposing of the monetary proceeds of those assets; or
(d) requiring the prior consent of the creditor or any other person either generally or to any specified transaction or class of transaction

shall be disregarded. This would effect, as we intend, a statutory reversal of the decision in *Siebe Gorman v Barclays Bank*,[1] and a return to the more traditional approach.

---

1 (1979) 2 Lloyd's Rep 142

PART II: THE NATURE OF THE FLOATING CHARGE
(Sources 244, 245, 246, 247)

SOURCE 244
Governments Stock and Other Securities Investment Company Limited v Manila Railway Company Limited
(House of Lords 1902) [1897] AC 81; 66 LJ Ch 102

In 1888 the Manila Railway Company issued debentures of £100 each to secure £730,000. By each of the debentures the company agreed that they would on 1 January 1978, or on such earlier date as the principal moneys thereby secured should become payable, in accordance with the conditions indorsed thereon, pay the bearer £100, and in the meantime pay interest at the rate of £6 per cent per annum by equal half-yearly payments on 1 January and 1 July in each year. And the company thereby charged 'by way of floating security all its property whatsoever and wheresoever, both present and future, including its uncalled capital for the time being. This debenture is issued subject to the conditions indorsed hereon, and all persons may act accordingly.' Condition 2 indorsed on each of the debentures was as follows: 'Notwithstanding the said charge the company shall be at liberty in the course and for the purpose of its business to use, employ, sell, lease, exchange, or otherwise deal with any part of its property until default shall be made in payment of any interest hereby secured for the period of three calendar months after the same shall have become due, or until an order of some Court of competent jurisdiction shall have been made, or a special or extraordinary resolution shall have been duly passed for the winding-up of the said company.'

The company made default in payment of the interest that fell due upon the debentures on 1 January 1892.

By an indenture dated 1 March 1892, and made between the Manila Railway Company and the respondents, the Merchants Trust Limited, after reciting the issue of the debentures and the conditions of the same, and that all interest on the debentures had been paid up to 1 July 1891, inclusive, and further that the Manila Railway Company were about to issue mortgage bonds (hereinafter called the B Bonds) for the aggregate sum of £300,000 bearing interest at the rate of 6 per cent and that it had been agreed that the principal money and interest payable under the B bonds should be secured in manner thereinafter expressed, to the intent that, so far as regarded the property described in the schedule thereto, the charge securing the B bonds should rank in priority to the charge created by the existing debentures, the Manila Railway Company charged certain items of their property specified in a schedule thereto with payment of the B bonds, and undertook to execute a legal mortgage of the specified property to the Merchants Trust Limited, as trustees for the B bondholders. It was assumed for the purposes of the argument in the Courts below that the B bonds were issued after the expiration of three months from the time when the interest on the debentures payable on 1 January 1892, became due.

In an action brought in 1895 by the appellants as debenture-holders North J ordered that the Manila Railway Company should be restrained until judgment in the action or until further order from paying any interest out of the assets of the company to the holders of the B bonds. This order was discharged by the Court of Appeal.

LORD HALSBURY LC . . . Now, what is this instrument? It is a debenture upon which it is intended that money should be lent to a company which makes its money by trade, and I am asked to suppose that it was the intention of this condition that upon default being made in the additional period of grace given, from that moment the whole of the commercial conduct of this trading company was to come to an end. I entirely repudiate the idea that Mr Farwell[1] has suggested as to standing by and not interfering, and so on. The parties contemplated that the thing might go on and not be wrecked by mere lapse of time. That is the security which they had in their minds. The effect of Mr Farwell's construction would be not such a security as was agreed to. I must construe the document as it is; and looking at the document as it is, it appears to me that it would be so absolutely unworkable in its operation that I do not think the parties could have contemplated such a condition of things as this — that the moment the period of grace had elapsed, at that moment the power of the company to do anything with the property of the company ceased. How could that be the meaning? As a matter of business I should have thought it was impossible.

LORD MACNAGHTEN: My Lords, I also think the judgment of the Court of Appeal is quite right.

A floating security is an equitable charge on the assets for the time being of a going concern. It attaches to the subject charged in the varying conditions in which it happens to be from time to time. It is of the essence of such a charge that it remains dormant until the undertaking charged ceases to be a going concern, or until the person in whose favour the charge is created intervenes. His right to intervene may of course be suspended by agreement. But if there is no agreement for suspension, he may exercise his right whenever he pleases after default.

In the present case it was intended that the right of intervention on the part of the debenture-holders should be suspended for a time after default. That is what the second condition points to, and I do not think it was meant to do more. The condition, no doubt, is awkwardly expressed. If the condition had said, 'Notwithstanding the said charge the debenture-holders shall not be entitled to enforce their security' during the prescribed period of grace, there would have been no difficulty. What it does say is, 'notwithstanding the said charge' — that is, as I understand it, 'notwithstanding the right of the debenture-holders under the said charge' — the company shall be at liberty to carry on their business for the prescribed period unless there is a winding-up in the meantime. During the period of grace, or until there is a winding-up, the company are to be free to carry on their business: they are to carry it on as of right. When that period comes to an end, the charge will have its ordinary effect. Thenceforward so long as the default lasts the business will be carried on, not as of right, but by the sufferance of the debenture-holders and at their mercy. That, I think, is all that was meant.

Any other construction would obviously lead to consequences which it is impossible to suppose the parties could have intended. It is impossible to suppose that they could have meant that at the end of the period of grace the floating security should be turned into a fixed and binding charge, and that the business without being stopped should be allowed to drag on in a paralysed and helpless condition.

---

1 Counsel for the appellants (Governments Stock etc)

SOURCE 245
Evans *v* Rival Granite Quarries Limited
(Court of Appeal 1910) [1910] 2 KB 979; 26 TLR 509

. . . the defendant company, being indebted to one Lionel Phillips in the sum of
£13,000 executed an indenture (which Phillips also executed), which, after
reciting the fact of the debt and of a guarantee by Phillips of a bank overdraft to
the extent of £3000, and an agreement by the company to give security therefor,
witnessed as follows:

'1. The company hereby binds itself to pay to the said L. Phillips or his
representatives on demand the sum of £13,000 (being the aggregate
amount of the principal moneys due to him for advances as aforesaid) and
also such further sum or sums (if any) as the said L. Phillips or his
representatives shall pay in respect of his said guarantee of the bank
overdraft together with interest thereon from the date of the respective
advances or payments at the rate of £5 per cent per annum.

2. The company as beneficial owner hereby charges with such payments its
undertaking including the goodwill of its business and all its property and
assets whatsoever and wheresoever both present and future.

3. The said L. Phillips or his representatives may at any time after the
principal moneys hereby secured have become payable appoint by writing a
receiver (at a commission not exceeding 5 per cent on the gross amount of
all moneys received by him) to take possession of the property and assets
comprised in this security.'

. . .

The interest of Phillips in this security became in due course vested in one
Pitman, the claimant in the present case.

On 12 August 1908, the plaintiff brought an action in the county court against
the defendants to recover the rent of a cottage leased by him to the defendants.
On 30 August 1908, Pitman, who had become the transferee and holder of the
debenture above set out, demanded payment from the defendants of the £13,000
secured by the debenture, but took no further step to enforce his security. In
November 1908, the plaintiff recovered judgment for £86 1s 8d against the
defendants in the county court. The judgment not being satisfied, the plaintiff in
April 1909, obtained a garnishee order nisi against the banking account of the
defendants with the North and South Wales Bank. The debenture-holder gave
notice to the bank that he contested the right of the plaintiff to attach the
balance due from the bank to the defendants on their banking account and
demand payment thereof to himself; and he opposed an application by the
plaintiff in the county court that the garnishee order should be made absolute,
on the ground that as holder of the debenture he had priority over the plaintiff
as judgment creditor.

VAUGHAN WILLIAMS LJ: In this case there was an application in the county
court to make absolute a garnishee order nisi; the county court judge made it
absolute, and on appeal to the Divisional Court the order of the county court was
discharged. The question for our decision, therefore, is not what effect the
garnishee order absolute would have if made, but whether it ought to be made
at all. I have come to the conclusion that it ought to be made absolute.

The question necessarily depends upon the effect of the debenture itself,
which gives the debenture-holder from the moment of its execution a floating
charge over the company's assets, and we have to say what was the effect of giving
this floating charge. On the one hand it is said, that, when a creditor has a
floating charge, it gives him such rights over the company's assets that, if an

execution were put in upon the company's goods and chattels, it could not be enforced and ought to be stopped. The execution creditor, on the other hand, while not denying that a debenture of this kind gives some immediate rights to the debenture-holder, nor that the latter might immediately upon execution being put in bring an action asking for effect to be given to his equitable rights, contends that while it is true that the debenture-holder gets an equity by the mere execution of the instrument, yet that this is one of those instruments of charge in which it is contemplated and intended by all parties that after the actual issue of the debenture the company shall be able to carry on its business and to deal with the property which is the subject of the debenture for the purposes of its business; that it shall have power to sell its goods, power to vary its assets from day to day; in short, the power and right to manage its business without any interference from the debenture-holder that might prevent in any way the carrying on of its business effectively. It is said that, although in one sense the debenture-holder gets an immediate equity or charge on the assets of the company, it was not intended that he should exercise it by enforcing his security so long as he allowed the company to carry on its business in the ordinary way.

. . .

What clearly happened in the present case was that there was part payment by the company, the execution debtors, on account of their debt made whilst they were still carrying on business and with the view of enabling them to continue to carry it on. It is true that the payments of instalments of their debt by the defendants were made under pressure of the execution that had been levied by the sheriff; but does that fact by itself bring into force the debenture-holder's security? Does it determine the licence to the company to carry on their business in the ordinary way so as to make the company's property the property of the debenture-holder, and to enable him to say that the instalments are being paid with his money? That is what must be made out in order to enable the debenture-holder to succeed in his claim, and it has not been made out to my satisfaction.

Vaughan Williams LJ then discussed *Robson v Smith*,[1] as to which he said:

'Under the circumstances of the present case it seems to me that there is authority for saying that, whatever the ultimate result may be, it is impossible, if that decision is right, to say that an execution may not be enforced so long as the debenture-holders have not got a receiver appointed or have not done something in regard to the licence to the company to continue carrying on its business.

. . . In this particular case *Evans v Rival Granite*[2] the debenture-holder, not having chosen to do anything or to interfere in any way, cannot come forward and intervene in this execution by opposing the making of the garnishee order absolute, and cannot by so doing prevent the payment of the creditors of the company; he has indeed attempted to do exactly that which Romer J [in *Robson v Smith*] pointed out the holder of such a debenture could not do. . . . In my opinion nothing has happened in the present case to prevent the execution creditor from obtaining a garnishee order absolute, for although it may be that to-morrow there will be a receiver, at present there is nothing of the sort.'

---

1 [1895] 2 Ch 118; 64 LJ Ch 457
2 [1910] 2 KB 979; 26 TLR 509

BUCKLEY LJ: . . . The nature of a floating security has been discussed and described in *Re Florence Land and Public Works Co;*[1] *Simultaneous Colour Printing Syndicate v Foweraker;*[2] *Governments Stock Investment Co v Manila Rly Co;*[3] *Illingworth v Houldsworth,*[4] and other cases. The outcome of the decisions may be thus summarized. A floating security is not a future security; it is a present security; which presently affects all the assets of the company expressed to be included in it. On the other hand, it is not a specific security; the holder cannot affirm that the assets are specifically mortgaged to him. The assets are mortgaged in such a way that the mortgagor can deal with them without the concurrence of the mortgagee. A floating security is not a specific mortgage of the assets, plus a licence to the mortgagor to dispose of them in the course of his business, but is a floating mortgage applying to every item comprised in the security, but not specifically affecting any item until some event occurs or some act on the part of the mortgagee is done which causes it to crystallize into a fixed security.

PART III: CRYSTALLISATION

Can a floating charge crystallise automatically, without the intervention of the debenture-holder, if the charge itself so provides? Consider the following Sources (246, 247, 248) and those immediately above (244, 245).

SOURCE 246
Davey & Co *v* Williamson & Sons Limited
(Queen's Bench Division 1898) [1898] 2 QB 194; 67 LJQB 699

LORD RUSSELL OF KILLOWEN CJ: . . . The defendant company (a trading company) in January 1894, being duly authorized to do so, issued £3000 first mortgage debentures in sixty debentures of £50 each, and six of these were held by Richards, the claimant. They were made a charge on all the property of the company, real and personal, present and future, . . . By the 3rd condition indorsed on the debentures, it was provided that until the moneys thereby secured should become payable the debentures should be a floating security, and it was stipulated that the company should not before payment of such debentures create any charge to the prejudice of the debenture-holders without their sanction, and, finally, that no part of the property subject to the floating security of such debentures should be dealt with except in the ordinary course of the business of the company.

. . .

. . . This is an appeal from the decision of His Honour Judge Paterson on an interpleader issue in which the question was whether the rights of the claimant, claiming for himself and the other holders of debentures of the defendant company (the judgment debtors), to certain goods seized under a writ of fi. fa. by the sheriff prevailed over the rights of the plaintiffs, who were the execution creditors.

The learned county court judge held that they did not, and apparently on two grounds — (1) that the rights of the debenture-holders had not become 'crystallized,' the debentures not having become due, and no receiver for the

---

1 (1878) 10 Ch D 530; 48 LJ Ch 137
2 [1910] 1 KB 771; 70 LJ KB 453
3 [1897] AC 81; 66 LJ Ch 102 (see p 675)
4 [1904] AC 355; 73 LJ Ch 739

debenture-holders having been appointed; and (2) that seizure of the company's goods under execution was a dealing with such goods in the ordinary course of business, and did not contravene any rights of the debenture-holders, whose securities were, in his judgment, subject to the risk of such seizure.

. . .

In this state of things the question is, Do the rights of the debenture-holders prevail against those of the executor creditor? It may seem hard upon the execution creditors that they should not be able to realize their judgment for their debt incurred in supplying trade goods for the purposes of the company's business, and that they should be met by claims of debenture-holders of which they had no knowledge or public means of knowledge, and that such debenture-holders should be allowed to claim as theirs goods in the apparent control of the company, and upon which possibly, or indeed probably, credit had been given to them. But these are matters which concern the judgment and action of Parliament. We must determine the rights of litigants in conformity with what we believe to be the law. In our judgment, the rights of the debenture-holders do in this case prevail against the execution creditors. We cannot assent to the view of the learned county court judge that a seizure under an execution on a judgment against the company is a dealing by the company in the ordinary course of business within the 3rd condition indorsed on the debentures, so as to be within the authority given to the company by the terms of the debentures. It is not in the ordinary course of business that the debts of a going business firm or company shall be liquidated by seizure of their assets under legal process. Nor can the transaction be properly described as a dealing by the company at all. It is a compulsory legal process directed against the company — not a dealing by them.

The second ground on which the learned county court judge proceeded was that the rights of the debenture-holders had not 'crystallized,' or, in other words, that the moneys secured by the debentures had not become payable. As to this, it is in the first place to be observed that although this is so, yet by reason of the clause of the trust deed, previously set out, the security constituted by that deed had become enforceable by reason of the fact that an execution had been sued out against the company. But apart from this, the sheriff can only realize the judgment against the goods of the judgment debtor. Here the goods seized are validly charged with the payment of the amount of the debentures, and it is admitted that that charge far exceeds the value of the goods in question. The rights of the execution creditors are subject, not only to the legal, but also to the equitable rights of the debenture-holders. The sheriff cannot merely by seizing affect the rights of third persons to which property was subject when in the hands of the debtor, unless, indeed, such third persons have debarred themselves from the assertion of such rights.

SOURCE 247
Re Manurewa Transport Limited
(Supreme Court, New Zealand, 1971) [1971] NZLR 909

SPEIGHT J: . . . The dispute arises because G. E. D. Labrum (whom I will call Labrum Senior) had a mortgage debenture by way of a floating charge over all the company's assets and William Gill & Sons Ltd (which I will call Gills) had an instrument by way of security over a specific chattel, namely a Commer truck. [This debenture was duly registered.]

In the course of conducting its carrying business the company had a number of vehicles. One of these was this Commer truck and in September 1969 it was placed in the hands of William Gill & Sons Ltd, which is a motor garage firm, for repairs. The company had a current account with Gills which was at the time in debt. The amount of work required to be done on the truck was substantial, namely in the area of $2500. The work was carried out by Gills but before completion of the work and certainly before allowing the company to remove it, Gills insisted on obtaining security for their current account which, because of the repair work, had increased to $3653.

. . .

The instrument by way of security between the company and Gills was executed on 17 September 1969 and registered in the Chattels Register of the Supreme Court at Auckland on 23 September 1969. The company became progressively further in debt and on 15 April 1970 a Mr Bridgman, a chartered accountant, was appointed receiver by Bruce Properties Ltd, under its debenture.

. . .

The present contest is as to priority. In particular, the question arises as to whether Gills' security, though later in date of execution and registration, being specific in relation to the Commer (which realised more than enough to pay Gills), takes priority over Labrum Senior's earlier floating debenture.

Section 102 of the Companies Act 1955 provides for the registration of charges created by companies and subs (12) says:

'Except as provided in subsection (2) of section 4 of the Chattels Transfer Act 1924, registration of any instrument under this Part of this Act shall not in itself constitute notice to any person of the contents of that instrument.'

Section 4(2) of the Chattels Transfer Act 1924 in its turn provides:

'(Save as provided in subsection (3) hereof,) all persons shall be deemed to have notice of a security granted wholly or partly upon chattels by a company registered under (the Companies Act 1955) ((or by a society registered under the Industrial and Provident Societies Act 1908)), and of the contents of such security, so far as it relates to chattels, immediately upon the registration of such security in the manner provided by the said (Companies Act 1955) ((or the said Industrial and Provident Societies Act 1908, as the case may be)).'

The debenture in question provided, inter alia, as follows.

1. This debenture shall operate as a floating charge and the charge hereby created shall rank as a second charge upon the assets undertaking and goodwill of the company including book debts and uncalled capital present and future (including reserve capital if any) of the company to the intent that until the security hereby made shall become or attach as a fixed charge as hereinafter mentioned the company may in the ordinary course of business deal with any part of its assets otherwise than is hereby expressly restricted but the company shall not be at liberty to create any mortgage or other charge upon the said property and assets or any part thereof either in priority to or ranking pari passu with the charge hereby created except with the prior written consent of the lender.

13. The moneys hereby secured shall immediately become due and payable and the charge hereby created shall immediately attach and become affixed:

'(i) If the company mortgages charges or encumbers or attempts to mortgage charge or encumber any of its property or assets contrary to the provisions hereof without the prior written consent of the lender.'

Speight J decided that under the provisions of the Chattels Transfer Act, Gills had constructive notice of the provision in the debenture prohibiting the charging of any assets. The judge also offered an alternative basis for finding in favour of the debenture holder.

> However, there is another ground which in my view defeats Gills' security and that is that this floating charge had in fact crystallized prior to the completion and certainly prior to the registration of Gills' instrument by way of security. Most text book writers, with the exception of Professor Pennington in his 1967 text book *Company Law,* say that crystallization does not take place until the debenture holders intervene. In my respectful view this is erroneous and is so shown by an examination of the case which is usually quoted as authority for the proposition, namely *Evans v Rival Granite Quarries Ltd.*[1] Passages to the effect mentioned, namely that the debenture holder must intervene may be found in the judgment of Vaughan Williams LJ and Fletcher Moulton LJ. But it will be seen by an examination of the debenture which is set out in full in the report, that it was a much simpler document than the one I am here concerned with. In addition the question of crystallization then only arose in relation to a demand by the debenture holder for payment which was not an act which under the terms of the debenture there crystallized it. I find authority for the view I take that crystallization may, in certain circumstances, be self-generated or at least debtor-generated from the judgment of Buckley LJ ... There the learned Lord Justice reviewed a number of cases which had been cited on behalf of the debenture holders, and in particular, he approved *Davey & Co v Williamson & Sons.*[2] Because of the terms of the debenture in that case, the suing out of an execution by a third party against the property of the company was one of the conditions expressed to crystallize the debenture and Buckley LJ says:

>> 'One of those events was the suing out of an execution against the property of the company, and that event had happened; it resulted therefore, that the authority of the company to carry on business was at an end, and it could no longer deal with the property comprised in the security as though the security were not in existence. The floating charge had become a specific security on all the assets of the company; it was specific as between the execution creditor and the debenture holders, and the latter succeeded in their claim to the goods.'

Now, if one turns to that authority, it will be found that Lord Russell CJ delivering the judgment of himself and Mathew J dealt with an argument that crystallization had not taken place in respect of a debenture because the debenture holders had not taken the step of appointing a receiver. But the debenture had provided that part of the charge should be a floating charge and that the company could carry on its business until the happening of one or more of certain events upon which the security thereby constituted became enforceable. Execution had been attempted by a third party and this was sufficient reason in the judgment of the

---

1 [1910] 2 KB 979; 26 TLR 509 (see p 677)
2 [1898] 2 QB 194; 67 LJQB 699 (see p 679)

Lord Chief Justice to say that the charge had crystallized and the debenture holder had priority over the execution creditor.

I have followed through and can find no authority which undermines this.

SOURCE 248
The Queen in Right of British Columbia *v* Consolidated Churchill Copper Corpn Ltd
(British Columbia Supreme Court, Canada 1978) [1979] 90 DLR (3d) 357

BERGER J: In this case there are competing claims by the Province under the Mineral Royalties Act 1974 (BC), c. 54, and by the defendant Brameda Resources Limited under a debenture.

The Province has a lien against the defendant Consolidated Churchill Copper Corporation Ltd (the 'company'). The Province relies on section 10(1) of the Act, which says:

'10(1) Royalty payable but not paid in accordance with this Act forms a lien and charge in favour of the Crown in right of the Province on all property owned by the producer who is liable to pay the royalty, and has *priority over all other claims, except claims secured by registered liens, charges, or encumbrances on such property.*'

(The italics are mine.) The issue is whether Brameda's security under the debenture had crystallized by the time royalty became payable under the Act. The critical date is 15 April 1975. That is the date when the Province's lien attached.

. . .

If Brameda's security crystallized prior to 15 April, then Brameda's claim will take priority. If Brameda's security did not crystallize prior to 15 April then the Province's claim will take priority. A statutory lien has priority over a floating charge that has not crystallized:

. . .

The original debenture contains a covenant to repay. To secure repayment the debenture grants a 'fixed and specific mortgage' against the company's real property. There follows provision for a floating charge, which reads:

'As further security for such payment and a due performance of the said obligations and covenants, the Company hereby charges to and in favour of the Banks . . . as and by way of a first floating charge its undertaking and all its other property and assets for the time being, real and personal, moveable and immoveable of whatsoever nature and kind, both present and future . . . which the Company may be possessed of or entitled to or which may hereafter be acquired by the Company provided that *such floating charge shall in no way hinder or prevent the Company (except as hereinafter provided) until the security hereby constituted shall have become enforceable from selling, alienating, assigning, leasing, mortgaging, charging, pledging or otherwise disposing of or dealing with the subject matter of such floating charge in the ordinary course of its business* and for the purpose of carrying on the same, save and except only that the Company shall not, and the Company hereby covenants that it will not make, give or create any mortgage, pledge, charge, assignment or any other security, whether fixed or floating, upon the subject matter of such charge, or any part thereof, ranking in priority to or pari passu with such floating charge unless the same be given to or in favour of the Banks to secure loans required for the usual purposes of Company's business.'

(The italics are mine.) The mortgage on the real property is a fixed and specific charge. The mortgage on the inventory is a floating and general charge. The issue in this case relates to the floating charge. Did it crystallize, and, if so, when?

The debenture (condition 4) provides that 'the security hereby constituted shall become enforceable' in the event of any default in payment of principal or interest. The debenture goes on to provide (condition 6):

'6. *If the security hereby constituted shall become enforceable the Banks may, by instrument in writing* (of which due notice shall be given to the Company as soon as practicable after such appointment), *appoint any person or persons,* whether an officer or officers or employee or employees of the Banks or either of them or not, *to be a receiver or receivers of the property and assets hereby charged* and may remove any receiver or receivers so appointed and appoint another or others in his or their stead.'

(The italics are mine.)

In 1971 Churchill's mine went out of production. On 19 April 1972, the banks assigned their interest in the debentures to Brameda. Churchill has been in default ever since 19 April 1972, by reason of its failure to make payments on the loans secured by the debentures. The floating charge thereupon became 'enforceable' under the debenture. The question is whether it crystallized at any time from 19 April 1972, until 15 April 1975, when the Province's lien attached.

. . .

This brings me to Mr Cumming's[1] third argument. He says that in any event there was no need for intervention by Brameda. He relies on the provision in the debenture that on default the security was to become enforceable. Such a clause, it is said, is sufficient to bring about crystallization on default. No intervention is required. Crystallization occurred, so to speak, by operation of law. This proposition, like virtually all others in this field, is derived from the *Evans case.*[2] In that case, Buckley LJ said at p 1000:

'. . . it is a mortgage presently affecting all the items expressed to be included in it, but not specifically affecting any item till the happening of the event which causes the security to crystallize as regards all the items. This crystallization may be brought about in various ways. A receiver may be appointed, or the company may go into liquidation and a liquidator be appointed, or any event may happen which is defined as bringing to an end the licence to the company to carry on business.'

Thus, it is said the company's licence to carry on business can be terminated and the floating charge transformed into a fixed security on all the company's assets upon default without more. On the strength of this passage, Speight J, in *Re Manurewa Transport Ltd,*[3] held that it was not essential in every case that there should be intervention by the debenture-holder [p 680].

. . .

Speight J relied upon what was said by Buckley LJ in the *Evans case* at p 1000. But what Buckley LJ there said was *dicta.* All that had to be decided in that case was whether the debenture-holder could intervene so as to prevent the money in the company's bank account being paid to the execution creditor. I have already

---

1 Counsel for Brameda
2 [1910] 2 KB 979; 26 TLR 509 (see p 677)
3 [1971] NZLR 909 (see p 680)

indicated that the *ratio* of the judgment was that the debenture-holder could not allow the company to carry on business and yet prevent the execution creditor attaching the company's bank balance.

[Berger J analysed the judgments of Buckley and Vaughan Williams LJJ in *Evans v Rival Granite* (p 677) and continued:]

It was only Buckley LJ who took the view (in *obiter*) that a floating charge might crystallize without intervention.

The question before the Court in the *Evans case* was fundamentally the same question as in the case at bar. Can a debenture-holder allow the company to carry on business and yet insist, when another creditor (here the Province) makes a claim, that the floating charge has already crystallized? Brameda is seeking to undermine the footings upon which the law relating to debentures has been erected: you may terminate the company's licence to carry on business, or you may not. But you cannot seek to do both at the same time.

Of course this business of analyzing and dissecting these early judgments can be taken too far. I have referred to what Lord Macnaghten said in the *Manila Railway case*.[1] Yet in *Illingworth v Houldsworth*,[2] he said, at p 358:

'A specific charge, I think, is one that without more fastens on ascertained and definite property or property capable of being ascertained and defined; a floating charge, on the other hand, is ambulatory and shifting in its nature, hovering over and so to speak floating with the property which it is intended to affect until some event occurs or some act is done which causes it to settle and fasten on the subject of the charge within its reach and grasp.'

It may be said that the words 'until some event occurs or some act is done' are consistent with the argument in support of self-generating crystallization. But no authority has gone as far as Brameda urges the Court to go in the case at bar. In *Davey & Co v Williamson & Sons Ltd*,[3] which Speight J, cited in the *Manurewa case*, supra, the debenture provided that the floating charge crystallized if an execution were made, and in the *Manurewa case* itself it provided that the floating charge crystallized if an attempt were made to mortgage any of the assets covered by the debenture, the latter being a usual clause, according to Yorston and Brown, *Company Law*, 3rd edn, at p 240. Neither case is authority for the proposition that crystallization occurs on default of payment. In fact, in *Edward Nelson & Co Ltd v Faber & Co*,[4] this very argument was advanced in a case where the debenture provided that from and after default the debenture was to become enforceable. Joyce J held that:

'... such a debenture as this ... does not cease to be a floating security ... until the company has been wound up, or stops business, or a receiver has been appointed at the instance of the debenture-holders and it follows that, even after the interest payable on such debentures has been in arrears for the time specified, the company can deal with the property in the ordinary course of business until the company has been wound up, or stops business, or a receiver has been appointed.'

---

1 [1897] AC 81; 66 LJ Ch 102 (see p 675)
2 [1904] AC 355; 73 LJ Ch 739
3 [1898] 2 QB 194; 67 LJQB 699 (see p 679)
4 [1903] 2 KB 367; 72 LJKB 771

Gower, *Modern Company Law,* supra, cites *Nelson & Co v Faber & Co* and *Evans case*
and concludes, at p 421:

> 'Default alone will not suffice to crystallize the charge, the debenture-
> holders must intervene to determine the licence to the company to deal
> with the property, normally by appointing a receiver or by applying to the
> Court to do so.'

But there has been no judgment rendered on the question in Canada. The
matter is one of first impression. So policy considerations should be placed on
the scales. These considerations weigh heavily against the adoption of the notion
of self-generating crystallization. In the case at bar there were numerous acts of
default, going back to 1972. Brameda did not, until 14 April 1975, take the
position that the floating charge had crystallized. If in truth it had crystallized
back in 1972, when Brameda acquired the banks' interest in the debenture,
Brameda did not treat the company thereafter as if its licence to carry on business
was at an end. Brameda sought to have it both ways: to attain priority over the
Province's lien without putting Churchill into receivership. This shows the
parlous state of affairs which would result if the concept of self-generating
crystallization were to be adopted. The requirements for filing by a receiver
under the Companies Act would be rendered a dead letter. The company would
not know where it stood; neither would the company's creditors. How is anyone
to know the true state of affairs between the debenture-holder and the company
unless there is an unequivocal act of intervention? How can it be said that the
default by the company terminated its licence to carry on business when in fact
it was allowed by Brameda to carry on business for three years thereafter? If the
argument were sound, the debenture-holder would be able to arrange the affairs
of the company in such a way as to render it immune from executions. The
debenture-holder would have all the advantages of allowing the company to
continue in business and all of the advantages of intervening at one and the same
time, to the prejudice of all other creditors. This contention was rejected in the
Evans case: see Vaughan Williams LJ and Fletcher Moulton LJ.

It is my view that neither in the older cases, nor in the recent cases, nor in the
exigencies of policy, is there any justification for the adoption of a concept of self-
generating crystallization. If there is any practical scope for such a theory it does
not extend to a case where the conduct of the debenture-holder is inconsistent
with the assertion of any such claim.

This brings me back to the wording of the floating charge in the case at bar. It says
that 'such floating charge shall in no way hinder or prevent the company . . . until
the security hereby constituted shall have become enforceable from . . . dealing
with the subject matter of such floating charge in the ordinary course of its
business'. Condition 6 of the debenture says:

> 'If the security hereby constituted shall become enforceable the Banks
> (Brameda) may by instrument in writing . . . appoint any person . . . to be a
> receiver . . . of the property and assets hereby charged.'

The point is that default by the company renders the floating charge enforceable.
To that extent, default is a hindrance to the company, ie, the debenture-holder
has the right to intervene when he pleases. But in order to terminate the
company's licence to carry on business, the debenture-holder must in fact
intervene. This is provided for by the very language of the debenture itself. While
the security may become *enforceable* on default, still the debenture-holder must
intervene to *enforce* his security before it crystallizes.

I hold that the floating charge never crystallized. The Province's lien under the

Mineral Royalties Act has priority over the debenture. The parties have agreed that, in the event I should hold that the security never crystallized, the sum of $260,000 paid into an account at the defendant bank to await the outcome of this action should be paid out to the Province in full settlement of its claim for royalty. The Province is entitled to judgment accordingly.

SOURCE 249
Re Brightlife Ltd
(Chancery Division 1986, Hoffmann J (for the facts see p 663)) [1987] Ch 200; [1986] 3 All ER 673

The argument counsel for the commissioners actually advanced before me was far more radical. He said that the events of crystallisation were fixed by law and not by the agreement of the parties. Those events were (1) winding up, (2) appointment of a receiver, and (3) ceasing to carry on business. These three events and only these three would cause crystallisation notwithstanding any agreement to the contrary. Their common features were that in each case the business of the company would cease, or at any rate cease to be conducted by the directors.

Counsel for the commissioners referred to a number of cases in support of this submission. First, there were cases in which it was held the crystallisation had taken place on one or other of the three events notwithstanding the absence of an express provision to that effect. For example, in *Re Crompton & Co Ltd*,[1] Warrington J held that a floating charge crystallised on a winding up for the purposes of reconstruction notwithstanding that event being excluded from a clause containing the events of default which made the loan immediately repayable. He described winding up as an event 'which by law independently of stipulation would make the debenture realisable'. It must be observed that Warrington J says 'independently of stipulation' and not 'notwithstanding any stipulation to the contrary'. In a later passage he says that:

> 'the parties . . . have not provided as a matter of bargaining that, notwithstanding the general law, the other events shall not crystallise the security.'

In my judgment, when Warrington J said that crystallisation on winding up was a matter of general law, he meant only that such a consequence was an implied term of a floating charge.

. . .

Secondly, counsel for the commissioners relied on a number of cases in which courts have rejected a submission that an event of default (not being one of his three) has caused an automatic crystallisation. The most famous of these is the decision of the House of Lords in *Governments Stock and Other Securities Investment Co Ltd v Manila Rly Co Ltd* [p 675]. Counsel said that these cases showed that such events could not as a matter of law cause crystallisation.

In my view, however, the speeches in the *Manila Rly case* make it clear that the House of Lords regarded the question as being one of construction alone. They give rise to a plain inference that a sufficiently explicit provision for automatic crystallisation on default would have been given effect. It is true that the commercial inconvenience of automatic crystallisation gives rise to a strong presumption that it was not intended by the parties. Very clear language will be required. But that does not mean that it is excluded by a rule of law.

---

1 [1914] 1 Ch 954

The nearest any judge in this country has come to asserting such a rule of law is in *Edward Nelson & Co Ltd v Faber & Co*,[1] where Joyce J, after citing various judicial descriptions of the standard characteristics of a floating charge, said:

'It follows, I think, from these and other cases that such a debenture as this in the present case does not cease to be a floating security... until the company has been wound up, or stops business, or a receiver has been appointed at the instance of the debenture-holders ...'

Taken by itself, that remark may appear to lend support to counsel for the commissioners' tripartite rule of law. But I think that a fair reading of the whole judgment shows that Joyce J also accepted that his enumeration was subject to contrary agreement.

Thirdly, counsel for the commissioners cited several authorities statements of the standard characteristics of a floating charge, particularly those of Lord Macnaghten in the *Manila Rly case* and *Illingworth v Houldsworth*[2] and Romer LJ in the latter case in the Court of Appeal, *Re Yorkshire Woolcombers' Association*.[3] For example, in the *Manily Rly case* Lord Macnaghten said that it was of the essence of a floating charge that it remained dormant 'until the undertaking charged ceases to be a going concern, or until the person in whose favour the charge is created intervenes'. Counsel for the commissioners said that this formulation appeared to rule out automatic crystallisation without any act on the part of the debenture holder. To this counsel for Norandex replied that he was not asserting automatic crystallisation: both of the notices on which he relied were acts of intervention by the party entitled to the charge.

There is force in this answer but in my judgment there is a more fundamental objection to the use counsel for the commissioners seeks to make of the authorities. In *Illingworth v Houldsworth* Lord Macnaghten was at pains to point out that he had not attempted in the *Manila Rly case* to propound a 'definition' of a floating charge. He had only offered a 'description'. In making this distinction, it seems to me that what Lord Macnaghten had in mind was that a floating charge, like many other legal concepts, was not susceptible of being defined by the enumeration of an exhaustive set of necessary and sufficient conditions. All that can be done is to enumerate its standard characteristics. It does not follow that the absence of one or more of those features or the presence of others will prevent the charge from being categorised as 'floating'. There are bound to be penumbral cases in which it may be difficult to say whether the degree of deviation from the standard case is enough to make it inappropriate to use such a term. But the rights and duties which the law may or may not categorise as a floating charge are wholly derived from the agreement of the parties, supplemented by the terms implied by law. It seems to me fallacious to argue that once the parties have agreed on some terms which are thought sufficient to identify the transaction as a floating charge, they are then precluded from agreeing to any other terms which are not present in the standard case.

Fourthly, counsel for the commissioners said that the courts should take a lead from Parliament, which in the Preferential Payments in Bankruptcy Amendment Act 1897 and subsequent company legislation apparently assumed that it need provide for only two possible events of crystallisation, namely the appointment of a receiver and a winding up. Even on counsel's own submission this means that Parliament failed to consider his third event, cessation of business. It is true that

---

1 [1903] 2 KB 367; 72 LJKB 771
2 [1904] AC 355; 73 LJ Ch 739
3 [1903] 2 Ch 284 (see p 661)

Re Woodroffes (Musical Instruments) Ltd was the first case in which a court expressly decided that cessation of business had crystallised a floating charge. But, as Nourse J pointed out, this had been generally assumed for about a century. Furthermore, if Parliament is to provide any guidance, it is of some interest that section 7(1)(*a*)(iv) of the Agricultural Credits Act 1928 creates a statutory floating charge which can be crystallised without appointment of a receiver or winding up by a notice not dissimilar from that given under clause 3(B) in this case. I therefore do not think that I can draw any inferences about the nature of a floating charge from the way in which it has been treated in legislation.

Fifthly, counsel for the commissioners said that public policy required restrictions on what the parties could stipulate as crystallising events. A winding up or the appointment of a receiver would have to be noted on the register. But a notice under clause 3(B) need not be registered and a provision for automatic crystallisation might take effect without the knowledge of either the company or the debenture-holder. The result might be prejudicial to third parties who gave credit to the company. Considerations of this kind impressed Berger J in the Canadian case of *R v Consolidated Churchill Copper Corpn Ltd*[1] where the concept of 'self-generating crystallisation' was rejected.

I do not think that it is open to the courts to restrict the contractual freedom of parties to a floating charge on such grounds. The floating charge was invented by Victorian lawyers to enable manufacturing and trading companies to raise loan capital on debentures. It could offer the security of a charge over the whole of the company's undertaking without inhibiting its ability to trade. But the mirror image of these advantages was the potential prejudice to the general body of creditors, who might know nothing of the floating charge but find that all the company's assets, including the very goods which they had just delivered on credit, had been swept up by the debenture holder. The public interest requires a balancing of the advantages to the economy of facilitating the borrowing of money against the possibility of injustice to unsecured creditors. These arguments for and against the floating charge are matters for Parliament rather than the courts and have been the subject of public debate in and out of Parliament for more than a century.

Parliament has responded, first, by restricting the rights of the holder of a floating charge and second, by requiring public notice of the existence and enforcement of the charge. For example, priority was given to preferential debts in 1897 and the Companies Act 1907 invalidated floating charges created within three months before the commencement of the winding up. This period has since been extended and is now one year. The registration of floating and other charges was introduced by the Companies Act 1900. The Companies Act 1907 required registration of the appointment of a receiver and the Companies Act 1929 required notice of such appointment to be given on the company's letters and invoices.

These limited and pragmatic interventions by the legislature make it in my judgment wholly inappropriate for the courts to impose additional restrictive rules on grounds of public policy. It is certainly not for a judge of first instance to proclaim a new head of public policy which no appellate court has even hinted at before. I would therefore respectfully prefer the decision of the New Zealand Supreme Court in *Re Manurewa Transport Ltd*,[2] recognising the validity of a provision for automatic crystallisation, to the contrary dicta in the Canadian case I have cited. For present purposes, however, it is not necessary to decide any

---

1 (1979) 90 DLR (3d) 357 (see p 683)
2 [1971] NZLR 909 (see p 680)

questions about automatic crystallisation. The notices under clauses 3(B) and 13 constitute intervention by the debenture-holder and there is in my judgement no conceptual reason why they should not crystallise the floating charge if the terms of the charge on their true construction have this effect.

SOURCE 250
Report of the Review Committee on Insolvency Law and Practice

Crystallisation
1570. Crystallisation is simply the metaphorical term for the conversion of a floating into a fixed security. A security must be either floating or fixed. The terms are mutually exclusive; the existence of one by definition excludes the other. It is necessary to distinguish between (i) the happening of an event which automatically crystallises the security and causes it to become fixed, even though no receiver has been appointed; and (ii) the existence of grounds which merely justify the debenture-holder or the Court in appointing a receiver and *thereby* crystallising the security.
1571. It is well settled that a floating charge crystallises:

  (a) on the company going into liquidation;
  (b) on the debenture-holder intervening by appointing or obtaining the appointment of a receiver or by taking possession of the assets subject to the charge; or
  (c) (probably) on the happening of an event defined in the debenture as a crystallising event.

1572. Although there is no conceptual difficulty in the automatic crystallisation of a floating charge in a specified event, without either a liquidation or receivership, the practical consequences are extremely inconvenient. The moment the charge crystallises, the company's powers of disposition cease — if the charge extends to the whole undertaking, the company cannot deal with its cash balances, pay any debt, or sell any stocks without the debenture-holder's consent. To avoid this, the Courts have been extremely reluctant to construe floating charges as providing for automatic crystallisation. Thus an express provision that a security shall float until default does not, as might be supposed, mean that it shall then crystallise; but only that thereafter (and not before) the debenture-holder may take steps to crystallise it by obtaining the appointment of a receiver.
1573. It is usually assumed that a floating charge will also crystallise automatically, without any express provision to that effect, on the company's ceasing to carry on business, or ceasing to be a going concern, or disposing of its whole undertaking with a view to the cessation of trading. There is, however, no express decision on the point, at least in England. It is uncertain whether a floating charge will automatically crystallise, without any express provision to this effect, on the appointment of a receiver under a different floating charge held by another debenture-holder; though this has been assumed in Australia.
1574. In Scotland, the floating charge is wholly a creature of statute. The Scots Act of 1972 provides for crystallisation upon the commencement of the winding up (section 1(2)) or upon the appointment of a receiver under *the same* floating charge (sections 13(7) and 14(7)). Automatic crystallisation, whether on the occurrence of an event specified in the charge, or on the cessation of the company's business without liquidation, or on the appointment of a receiver under a different floating charge, is thus unknown in Scotland.
1575. The possibility of automatic crystallisation puts at risk anyone who deals with a company which has given a floating charge. There is no provision for

registration of any notice of crystallisation. Particulars of the appointment of a receiver and of a winding up will, of course, have been filed with the Registrar of Companies. To guard against the possibility that crystallisation may have occurred without a receivership or winding up, it is necessary to obtain a statement from the debenture-holder that the charge has not crystallised. The common practice of obtaining a certificate of non-crystallisation from an officer of the company is not enough.

1576. In a Memorandum on Floating Charges submitted by the Land Law Committee of the Law Society to the Law Commission and the Department of Trade and Industry in June 1973, it was suggested that a system of registration of notices of crystallisation be introduced. If the law on crystallisation remains unaltered, this would be most desirable. But we consider that a more radical reform is necessary; it is the law on crystallisation which needs to be changed.

1577. It is highly inconvenient that a floating charge should crystallise in circumstances in which this is unknown to any of the parties. This can happen, for example, where a complicated borrowing limit has been exceeded and the charge provides that this shall crystallise the charge. It is equally inconvenient that a floating charge should automatically crystallise against the wishes of both parties, as may happen, for example, where there is a technical default which the debenture-holder is willing to ignore. Ideally, a document should be executed to de-fix and re-float the charge; but in practice this is not done.

1578. Automatic crystallisation, however, is not merely inconvenient. In Australia, where it has become firmly established, it has disclosed an unfortunate loophole in the statutory provisions which give priority to preferential creditors. This has been partially corrected by amending legislation, which defines the expression 'floating charge' for the purposes of the statutory provisions corresponding to section 94 of the Act of 1948 as including a charge which was 'a floating charge at the date of its creation which has since become a fixed or specific charge'. This is probably the test in England but it would be prudent to add a definition to both sections 94 and 319(5) of the Act of 1948 on the lines of the Australian legislation.

1579. The practical consequences of automatic crystallisation of a floating charge without a liquidation or receivership lead us to the conclusion that there is no place for it in a modern insolvency law. There are strong policy arguments against it; there is no need for it; the debenture-holder is sufficiently protected if he has the right to take steps to crystallise his security by appointing a receiver.

1580. Accordingly, we recommend that the circumstances in which a floating charge will crystallise should be specified by statute and limited to those so specified. We consider that a floating charge should crystallise:

(a) on the commencement of a winding up or liquidation of assets;
(b) on the appointment of an administrator;
(c) on the appointment of a receiver under the charge in question; or
(d) on the appointment of a receiver under any other floating charge on any assets or property of the company;

but not otherwise.

1581. This, however, is not enough to deal with the situation which arises from time to time where there are successive floating charges which have crystallised, and the first debenture-holder refuses or fails to appoint a receiver until the preferential debts have lost their priority against him by effluxion of time. This calls for an amendment to section 94 so that, where there are successive floating charges, preferential debts enjoy the same priority against each, and their priority is not affected by any delay on the part of one debenture-holder in appointing a receiver.

1582. Accordingly, we recommend that section 94 be amended so that:

> (a) the periods of time referred to in subsection (3) should be reckoned, not from the appointment of the receiver or the taking of possession, but from the date of the crystallisation of the charge (which may occur by reason of the appointment of a receiver under a different floating charge); and
>
> (b) the receiver should be bound to apply the assets comprised in the charge under which he was appointed in payment of preferential debts in priority, not only to the debt secured by the charge under which he was appointed, but also to any other debts to which the preferential debts have priority.

PART IV: COMPETITION BETWEEN FLOATING CHARGEES AND OTHER CLAIMS AGAINST THE COMPANY

Floating Charges and Subsequent Fixed Charges (Sources 251 and 252)

SOURCE 251
Wheatley *v* Silkstone and Haigh Moor Coal Company
(Chancery Division 1885, North J) (1885) 29 Ch D 715; 54 LJ Ch 778

The company had in 1878 borrowed £10,000, for which they gave debentures payable to bearer, and purporting to charge with the repayment the undertaking, lands, cottages, mines, works, plant, property, revenues, and effects, both present and future, of the company, to the intent that the debentures might rank equally as a first charge on the undertaking, lands, cottages, mines, works, plant, properties, and effects, both present and future, of the company. In 1879 they borrowed about £7200 on similar debentures. In 1881 the company borrowed from the Plaintiff, J. H. Wheatley, £4000, depositing with him the lease and muniments of title of the Allerton Bywater Collieries, and by an agreement in writing, dated 4 June 1881, charging the hereditaments and property comprised in the deeds, evidences, and writings so deposited with the payment to the Plaintiff of £4000 and interest; and the company agreed at any time at the request of the Plaintiff to execute a legal mortgage of the property. By way of further security the company gave the Plaintiff a debenture for £4000 which was to rank *pari passu* with certain other debentures of the company, as a first charge upon the property; but that debenture and the other already existing debentures were thereby declared to be subject to the mortgage.

The £4000 advanced by the Plaintiff was applied by the directors in payment of rent and wages, and for the general purposes of the company.

The company in 1882 went into voluntary liquidation; and the Plaintiff brought this action against the company, the directors, and certain holders of the previous debentures, and the liquidator, claiming for the £4000 and interest a first charge upon the hereditaments and property comprised in the deeds.

The question was whether the Plaintiff's equitable mortgage for £4000 had or had not priority over the £17,200 debentures.

NORTH J: . . . His Lordship . . . read the terms of one of the debentures for the £10,000, and proceeded:

If this is, as contended, a first charge upon everything mentioned in the debenture, it would cover everything that was then or might at any time become the property of the company. It would include every penny they had at the bank, every piece of property they had at the time, every sum they subsequently received in the course of carrying on the business of the company; and would give the debenture-holders the right to have all such moneys applied in satisfying them; and would prevent anybody who knew the circumstances from receiving any part of such money without being liable to repay it if called upon to do so. It seems to me impossible to say that such can be the meaning of the parties. In fact it has not been contended that the debenture is to receive this construction; but it seems to me that if the words 'first charge' are to have the meaning put upon them by Mr Buckley,[1] it would necessarily go the length that I have indicated.

It is, in my opinion, clear that what was intended was that the parties holding the debentures should have the right of coming forward when the money was payable to them and saying that they had a first charge upon the property belonging to the company at that time, prior to any other charge to be set up in the same way against it; that is to say, if the money became payable, not only by the period of the loan elapsing, but — I merely take this as an instance — by winding-up, it was to be a first charge as against the general creditors of the company. But I do not think the words 'first charge' can mean a charge which shall prevent any person whatever under any circumstances from receiving any part of the assets of the company, even if his claim arose in the proper and bonâ fide exercise of the power of carrying on the undertaking. That construction is one which I am bound to put on the document, not only because it seems to me impossible to say that the undertaking was to be tied up and stopped at once, but also from the decisions which have been arrived at by the Courts with regard to similar instruments. . . .

Now, those authorities furnish a very clear and intelligible principle to be followed. In this case I find that the debenture is intended to be a general floating security over all the property of the company, as it exists at the time when it is to be put in force; but it is not intended to prevent and has not the effect of in any way preventing the carrying on of the business in all or any of the ways in which it is carried on in the ordinary course; and, inasmuch as I find that in the ordinary course of business and for the purpose of the business this mortgage was made, it is a good mortgage upon and a good charge upon the property comprised in it, and is not subject to the claim created by the debentures. I find also that the first charge referred to in the debentures is fully satisfied by being the first charge against the general property of the company at the time when the claim under the debentures arises and can have effect given to it. There will be a declaration, therefore, that the charge of the Plaintiff is prior to the debentures.

SOURCE 252
English and Scottish Mercantile Investment Company Limited *v* Brunton
(Court of Appeal 1892) [1892] 2 QB 700; 62 LJQB 136

Appeal from a judgment of Charles J . . . on an interpleader issue. . . .

In pursuance of their powers the company,[2] prior to 26 February 1891, issued 200 'first mortgage debentures' of £100 each. In the form of debenture issued the company charged with the payment of the sum of £100, and interest as specified,

---

1 Counsel for a debenture-holder of the first issue
2 Not the plaintiff; the plaintiff made a loan to the company

its undertaking and all its property whatsoever and wheresoever, both present and future, and one of the conditions was:

'This debenture is one of a series of 200 debentures issued, or about to be issued, by the Corporation. The debentures of the said series are all to rank pari passu as a first charge on the property hereby charged, without any preference or priority one over another; and the charge hereby created is to be a floating security, but so that the Corporation is not to be at liberty to create any mortgage or charge in priority to the said debentures.'

Early in 1891, further money being required for the purposes of the undertaking, the company desired to borrow money on the security of certain insurance moneys, which were then coming due to them from the Sun Fire Office, upon a policy of insurance on premises of the company at West Drayton, on which there had recently been a fire.

The plaintiff made a loan to the company on the strength of this security.

Evidence was given that a debenture might, according to present usage, be in one of three forms: — First, it might simply be an acknowledgement of debt under seal; secondly — and this is the more common form — it might be an instrument not only acknowledging the debt, but charging the property of the company issuing it with repayment; thirdly, it might be an instrument acknowledging the debt, charging the property of the company with repayment, and further restricting the company from giving any prior charge. Mr Paine[1] had never, in fact, seen a debenture in the third form with the restrictive clause, and stated that he had no suspicion, after the interview of 25 February, that the plaintiffs' security could be interfered with; all he knew was that debentures existed. He did not require to see the form of debenture issued by the company, and made no further inquiry into its contents.

LORD ESHER MR: In this case the question is whether the plaintiffs are entitled to the full benefit of the mortgage which they have taken. At the time they took it, through the managing director of the Electrical Engineering Corporation Limited, there were in existence debentures issued by that company, and there were things stated in those debentures which, if the plaintiffs had known, would have prevented them in equity from saying that their mortgage could be enforced in priority to the debentures. If they had known what was in the debentures they would, in equity, have taken the mortgage with notice of prior charges on the subject-matter of it. It is admitted that the plaintiffs did not in fact know that there was that in the debentures which would prevent them, in equity, from having the full benefit of the mortgage which they took; but it is said that they had what in equity is termed 'constructive notice' of what was in the debentures. The doctrine of constructive notice is wholly equitable; it is not known to the common law. There is an inference of fact known to common lawyers which comes somewhat near to it. When a man has statements made to him, or has knowledge of facts, which do not expressly tell him of something which is against him, and he abstains from making further inquiry because he knows what the result would be — or, as the phrase is, he 'wilfully shuts his eyes' — then judges are in the habit of telling juries that they may infer that he did know what was against him. It is an inference of fact drawn because you cannot look into a man's mind, but you can infer from his conduct whether he is speaking truly or not when he says that he did not know of particular facts. There is no question of

---

1 Solicitor acting for the plaintiff

constructive notice or constructive knowledge involved in that inference; it is actual knowledge which is inferred. Constructive notice or knowledge, as I have said, is an equitable doctrine wholly; it is a doctrine not known to the common law, but it must now be dealt with and acknowledged by the Courts which administer the common law. It is, therefore, necessary for us to see how far the doctrine extends. . . .

. . . We were told that debentures which would not affect a subsequent mortgage of the company's property at all were exceptional; but I do not find that in the evidence. There are certainly a class of debentures issued by companies which would not affect the mortgage at all. The first class of debentures stated in the evidence given in the Court below would not; those in the second class would not affect the title to this mortgage, and those in the third class are the only ones which would so affect this title. I, therefore, think that Charles J was right in saying that the notice which the plaintiffs had was only notice of documents which might or might not affect their title to the mortgage. I have a strong opinion that, even if the false statement that the debentures did not affect the plaintiffs' title to the mortgage had never been made, the doctrine of constructive notice would not have applied. It is not, however, necessary to decide that question now; and I do not decide it. Here, these debentures being such as might or might not affect the plaintiffs' title to the mortgage, their solicitor asked if they did so affect it, and was told they did not. Therefore, within the very terms of the proposition laid down by Lord Lyndhurst, constructive notice of the contents of the debentures cannot be imposed in equity upon the plaintiffs. This appeal, therefore, fails.

Floating Charge and Subsequent Floating Charge (Sources 253 and 254)

SOURCE 253
Re Benjamin Cope & Sons Ltd
(Chancery Division 1914) [1914] 1 Ch 800; 83 LJ Ch 699

Benjamin Cope & Sons Limited, a company limited by shares and incorporated under the Companies Act 1862, in 1894 created a series of twenty debentures for £100 each. Each debenture was headed with the name of the company and the words 'Issue of Debentures for £2000.'
. . .
All the twenty debentures were issued, and they were all outstanding at the commencement of this action.

In 1904 the company created another series of twenty debentures of £100 each.

Each of these debentures was headed with the name of the company and the words 'Second Issue of Debentures for £2000.'
. . .
Clause 6 was as follows: 'This debenture is one of a second series of twenty debentures for £100 each, issued or intended to be issued by the company, and numbered or intended to be numbered 21 to 40 (inclusive), and all of such debentures, of this and the first series, shall rank *pari passu* without regard to the date of issue thereof.'

SARGANT J: . . . The company has created two separate series of debentures. The debentures of the first series were issued in 1894 and each of them was headed with the words 'Issue of Debentures for £2000.' After covenants for payment of principal and interest, and provisions as to notices, the debenture proceeds, in clause 5, to charge the principal and interest on the company's present and future property, 'subject to any mortgages now affecting or which may hereafter affect the same or any part thereof.' Then clause 6 says that the twenty debentures of the series are all to 'rank *pari passu* without regard to the date of issue thereof.' Clause 7 provides that, notwithstanding the charge, 'the company may, in the course of its business and for the purpose of carrying on the same, deal with its property as it may think fit, and in particular may sell and mortgage the same or any part thereof.'

Ten years afterwards, when all the debentures of the first issue were out-standing, the company created a second series of debentures, each of which was headed 'Second Issue of Debentures for £2000.' Clause 6 of each of these debentures stated that the debenture was 'one of a second series of twenty debentures for £100 each,' and that 'all of such debentures, of this and the first series, shall rank *pari passu* without regard to the date of issue thereof.' The rest of the clauses are in the same words as the debentures of the first series.

All the debentures of the first series and fourteen of those of the second series are outstanding, and the Master has certified that the fourteen rank *pari passu* with the debentures of the first series.

Whether this decision is right or wrong depends on the answers to be given to two questions, namely, (1) whether in general a company has power to create a second floating charge ranking *pari passu* with a first floating charge; and (2) whether in this particular case the words of the first debentures are sufficient to alter the general rule.

Floating charges appear to have originated through the Courts having recognized that companies may validly charge the whole of their undertaking and assets, and having given practical effect to such a charge. To treat such a security as constituting a specific charge on the property of the company at the date of the charge itself would paralyse the business of a company, since the assent of the chargee, or of the whole body of chargees, would then be necessary to any sale or other disposition of any part of the property of the company in the course of carrying on its business. And accordingly the Courts solved the problem by treating such a charge, not as being specific or fixed, but as being ambulatory and attaching to the property for the time being of the company at the time when the charge came to be enforced.

. . .

It would not have been incompatible with this solution of the problem that the company, while left at liberty to sell and deal with their assets in most ways, should have been precluded from making specific mortgages or charges of parts of their property in priority to, or competition with, the floating charge. And this view seemed to commend itself to Giffard LJ in *Re Panama, New Zealand, and Australian Royal Mail Co*,[1] and has been shewn to be a quite workable view by the not uncommon adoption of a well-known form of floating security which in terms prohibits specific mortgages or charges. But the law was definitely settled the other way in *Re Colonial Trusts Corporation*[2] and *Wheatley v Silkstone and Haigh Moor Coal Co*.[3]

Ever since those cases it has been generally recognized that a floating security can be displaced by a specific legal or equitable mortgage. But does it follow that it can be displaced by a subsequent floating charge in the absence of words in the

---

1 (1870) LR 5 Ch 318; 39 LJ Ch 482
2 (1879) 15 Ch D 465
3 (1885) 29 Ch D 715; 54 LJ Ch 778 (see p 692)

first charge authorizing such a displacement? Nothing in the reported cases has carried the matter so far, and in so laying down the law I should, I believe, be acting contrary to all professional and commercial views on the subject — and it must be remembered that these debentures are commercial instruments.

If the above view is true in the case of an ordinary floating charge, is there anything in the present case which prevents me from saying that the debentures of the first series are entitled to priority? I am not sure that the words here used are not more strongly in favour of the first debenture holders than those of the forms ordinarily in use. The word 'mortgage,' apparently in contradistinction to the word 'charge,' is used in both clause 5 and clause 7 of the debentures of the first series, and in the latter clause the mortgages and other dealings allowed to be made by the company must be 'in the course of its business and for the purpose of carrying on the same.' That was the sole object of the power, and I do not think that this second issue of debentures giving a floating charge fairly comes within the words of clause 7.

There are other indications in favour of the contention on behalf of the first debenture holders. The fact that the first debentures constitute a series which is limited to £2000 is destructive of the suggestion that any future debentures giving a floating charge can be put before, or be made to rank *pari passu* with, the debentures of the first series. And, generally speaking, it would in my view be as incompatible with the company's bargain with the first debenture holders to put their debentures behind or on the same footing as subsequent debentures giving a charge of the same character as if the debentures had constituted a specific charge and it were then attempted to create a subsequent specific charge ranking *pari passu* with them or in priority to them.

I hold, therefore, that the first debentures have priority over the second debentures.

SOURCE 254

Re Automatic Bottle Makers Limited
(Court of Appeal 1926) [1926] Ch 412; 95 LJ Ch 185

In January 1925, the company issued a series of debentures for an aggregate sum of £50,000 and executed a trust deed dated 15 January 1925, for securing the same, whereby the company created a specific mortgage in favour of the trustees upon certain freehold property and in addition a general charge on its undertaking and assets. The material clauses referring to this general charge were:

Clause 6: 'The company hereby charges in favour of the trustees its undertaking and its other assets for the time being both present and future with the payment of the debentures and the interest thereon and premiums and all other moneys intended to be hereby secured and such charge shall be a floating security and accordingly shall in no way hinder or prevent the company from selling alienating leasing paying dividends out of profits or otherwise disposing of or dealing with such assets in the ordinary course of its business and for the purposes of carrying on the same. Provided always that the company is not to be at liberty save as hereinafter provided or except in accordance with the provisions of these presents to create any mortgage or charge on such assets ranking *pari passu* with or in priority to the charge hereby created.'

Clause 7: 'The company shall be at liberty to create such mortgages charges or incumbrances as the company shall think proper upon such property and for such amounts and purposes as are next hereinafter mentioned (but not for any greater amounts or for any other purpose) that is to say. (*a*) Upon any lands or buildings and their appurtenances agreed to be acquired by the company after the date of these presents for such amounts not exceeding the cost thereof and for such purposes as the company shall think proper; or (*b*) Upon any undertaking hereafter to be acquired by the company or upon the securities or shares of any such undertaking for the purpose of acquiring any hereditaments fixed plant machinery or trade fittings or furniture or for the purpose of rebuilding or (with the consent of the trustees which shall not be unreasonably withheld) for the purpose of improving any buildings for the time being owned by the company or for the purpose of securing bank loans or overdrafts obtained for the purposes specified in this clause or any of such purposes. (*c*) By the deposit of any dock warrants bills of lading or other similar commercial documents or upon any raw materials or finished or partly finished products and stock for the purpose of raising moneys in the ordinary course of the business of the company.'

Purporting to act upon the liberty conferred by clause 7, subclause (*c*), the company executed a debenture on 11 August 1925, in favour of trustees for its bankers, Williams Deacons Bank Ltd, for the sum of £12,000 and interest. By that document the company charged with the said sum of £12,000 and interest all its dock warrants, bills of lading or other similar commercial documents, raw materials, finished and partly finished products and stock, both present and future, and by the conditions forming part of the debenture it was provided amongst other things as follows: 'This debenture is issued in pursuance of the power in that behalf given to the company by clause 7(*c*) of [the debentures above referred to] . . . to secure the sum of £12,000 and interest and is to be a first charge on the dock warrants bills of lading or other similar commercial documents raw materials finished and partly finished products and stock of the company both present and future and such charge is to rank in priority in all respects to the floating charge created by the trust deed[1] and to the debentures for the time being thereby constituted and secured and is to be a floating security.'

POLLOCK MR: . . . The question to be determined in this appeal is whether the company had the power to issue such a debenture in view of the restrictions imposed upon it by clauses 6 and 7 of the trust deed. It is a question of the right construction of the proviso to clause 6 and the terms of clause 7, and in particular its subclause.

Both debentures are floating securities: and it is argued that to issue another debenture similar in character to that prior in date is in effect to undermine and to destroy the benefit of the charge created by the earlier security, and that if successive debentures were issued of a like nature, all the property charged under the first debenture might be, piece by piece, removed. In support of this argument reliance is placed upon a decision given by Sargant LJ, as a judge of first instance, in *Re Benjamin Cope & Sons*,[2] where he decided that a company after making its bargain with the first debenture holders cannot give a charge over the same assets which puts later charges on a similar or a prior footing to those who already have their charge. There is no doubt force in this argument, but we have to consider the effect of the exception made in terms to clause 6 of the trust deed.

No doubt it was realized that in the course of carrying on its business, which the floating charge of 15 January 1925, was intended to enable it to do, the

---

1 Above referred to
2 [1914] 1 Ch 800; 83 LJ Ch 699 (see p 695)

company might find it necessary to raise money in particular transactions. Hence the exception to clause 6 and the provisions made in clause 7.

. . . The purpose of making a charge a floating security is to enable the company to carry on its business in its ordinary way: see *Illingworth v Houldsworth,*[1] and the powers of a trading company include the power to mortgage by deposit, and a mortgage to debenture holders does not prevent a valid charge from being given on a specific asset. In the present case it appears clear from the terms of clauses 6 and 7, and especially the opening lines of clause 7, that the company was to be free to create charges of any nature that it thought proper upon the classes of assets mentioned in subclause 7(*c*) for the purpose of raising moneys in the ordinary course of business. The Vice-Chancellor's judgment appears to hold this power to be limited to raising money upon, and in close relation to, the assets charged, and by a specific as opposed to a floating charge upon them. This interpretation would hamper the company's activities, and render it impossible to raise money, which may be as vital to its existence and continuance as the particular sale or purchase transaction in respect of which he thinks that a specific charge may be given: such as for the payment of wages or rent, the purchase of coal, or the payment for the electric current required to keep the furnaces and power in operation.

. . . The covering words in clause 7 give the company 'liberty to make such mortgages charges or incumbrances as the company shall think proper.' I cannot read these wide words as restricting their discretion to specific charges only as opposed to floating charges. The whole purpose of the exceptions in clauses 6 and 7 is to give latitude to the company to carry on its business, while the decision given restricts that latitude; and by restricting the exception to specific charges on specific goods, lays down a narrow course for the company to follow which would deprive it surely and increasingly of any means to raise finance for its source of power and primary needs.

. . .

The argument for the respondent appears to be based upon a reading of the decision of Sargant J already referred to, which it does not bear. There was not in that case an exception in respect of particular securities, but the charge was upon the same securities as those already subject to the earlier debenture.

SARGANT LJ: . . . Great stress has, however, been laid for the respondents on a decision of my own as a judge of first instance in *Re Benjamin Cope & Sons,* and it has been argued that that case decides that a general floating charge is necessarily incompatible with the subsequent creation under a special charging power of a floating charge to rank in priority to or *pari passu* with the earlier floating charge. I have examined that decision with great care, and have no reason to think that it was wrong, particularly in view of the fact that it appears to be in accord with an earlier decision of Vaughan-Williams J in *Smith v England and Scottish Mercantile Investment Trust,*[2] and not to have been questioned since. But the facts in that case were very different. There the original charge was on the whole undertaking and property for the time being of the company, and the reservation of a power to mortgage was in quite general terms; and it was held that such a power could not have been intended to authorize a competing charge upon the entirety of the property comprised in the earlier charge. Here the reservation of the power to mortgage is precise and specific in its terms, and extends only to certain particular classes of the property of the company.

---

1 [1904] AC 355; 73 LJ Ch 739
2 [1896] WN 86

Floating charge and set off (Sources 255 and 256)

SOURCE 255
George Barker (Transport) Ltd *v* Eynon
(Court of Appeal 1974) [1974] 1 WLR 462; [1974] 1 All ER 900

The plaintiffs, George Barker (Transport) Ltd, were transport contractors. On 23 August 1971, they agreed with a company, Alderley Meats (UK) Ltd, to carry a consignment of meat from the London docks to Gravesend and a condition of the contract was that the plaintiffs should have a general lien on the company's goods for any moneys owed to them by the company, which at that time amounted to over £3,000. They delivered part of the consignment before 31 August, when the defendant Philip Louis Eynon, was appointed receiver of the company. On 2 September, the remainder of the meat was unloaded from the ship into the plaintiffs' vehicles. On the same day they learned of the receiver's appointment and only agreed to deliver the meat on condition that it would be without prejudice to any lien they had on the goods and that they were paid the cost of carriage of £58.40. The plaintiffs sought a declaration that they had a lien on the meat for £3335.30 in respect of charges owed by the company. The defendant admitted liability only for £58.40. Mocatta J held that the plaintiffs' claim failed.

EDMUND DAVIES LJ: . . . It is common ground that all transport orders given by the company were accepted by the plaintiffs subject to the Conditions of Carriage of the Road Haulage Association Ltd (revised April 1967). Condition 13 thereof is in the following terms:

> 'General Lien. The carrier shall have a general lien against the owner of any goods for any moneys whatsoever due from such owner to the carrier. If any lien is not satisfied within a reasonable time the carrier may at his absolute discretion sell the goods as agents for the owner and apply the proceeds towards the moneys due and the expenses of the sale, and shall upon account to the trader for the balance remaining, if any, be discharged from all liability whatsoever in respect of the goods.'

The practice followed was for the company to pay the plaintiffs' charges between four and six weeks after delivery of the consignments. The last payment before the events later giving rise to this litigation was made on 5 August 1971, and this covered transport charges incurred down to June 23.

Unknown to the plaintiffs, on 5 February 1970, that is, before they started doing business with Alderley Meats (UK) Ltd, the company had by a mortgage debenture charged its property to Westminster Bank Ltd as a continuing security for the payment of all sums which at any time might become due to the bank as

> '. . . a floating security but so that the company is not to be at liberty to create any mortgage or charge in priority to or *pari passu* with the charge hereby created . . . or to deal with its book or other debts or securities for money otherwise than by getting in and realising the same in the ordinary course of business.'

The zeal of counsel, to whom the court is greatly indebted, led them to cite for our consideration some 32 reported decisions. At times we seemed in danger of never emerging from the thicket of authorities. And, when the receiver's counsel dilated upon the consternation which would be caused were we to reverse

Mocatta J, it seemed almost preferable never to emerge from its umbrageous depths. But emerge we must, and describe what we at least think we saw within, and what in the end it all seems to come to. That I now proceed to do.

1. *The company and its receiver*

The debenture deed of 5 February 1970, created a floating charge on certain property of the company. It allowed the company to deal with its assets in the ordinary course of business until the company became wound up or stopped business or, as here, a receiver was appointed at the instance of the debenture holder. It gave a licence to the company to carry on its business so long as it remained merely a floating security, and until that licence was terminated its property could be dealt with in the ordinary course of business just as freely as if the debenture had not been created. To the foregoing, Romer J added in *Robson v Smith*,[1] '. . . any such dealing with a particular property will be binding on the debenture holders, provided that the dealing be completed before the debentures cease to be merely a floating security.' In *Brunton v Electrical Engineering Corporation*,[2] where the debenture contained a clause that, 'the charge hereby created is to be a floating security, but so that the corporation is not to be at liberty to create any mortgage or charge in priority to the said debentures,' it was held that the debenture holders could not prevent the company's solicitor, employed by them in the usual course of business, from acquiring the ordinary solicitor's lien, which, being a right given by the general law, was not a 'charge,' or, at any rate, not a charge 'created' by the company, and that accordingly the lien could be asserted in priority to the debenture holders even after they had appointed a receiver.
. . .

One consequence of the receiver's appointment by the debenture holders was that the incomplete assignment constituted by the 1970 deed became converted into a completed equitable assignment to them of the assets charged and of the company's rights: *Biggerstaff v Rowatt's Wharf Ltd*;[3] *N. W. Robbie & Co Ltd v Witney Warehouse Co Ltd*.[4] Another was that, both by reason of clause 6 of the deed and under the ordinary law, the receiver became, on 31 August 1971, the agent of the company and not of the debenture holders. The company continued to deal with its assets under the receiver's direction and control. His duty being to carry on the business so as to preserve the goodwill, he must fulfil company trading contracts entered into before his appointment or render it liable in damages if he unwarrantably declined: see the authorities conveniently collected in *Buckley on the Companies Acts*, (13th edn 1957), p 244. And, as the assignment of the company's rights was subject to rights already given by the company to outside parties under ordinary trading contracts, neither the receiver nor the debenture holders were in any way relieved by the former's appointment from the obligations which by such pre-appointment contracts the company had under-taken. Most of the numerous authorities cited to us in support of this last proposition were cases in bankruptcy and turned to some extent . . . on the particular provisions of the Bankruptcy Act. But, as Mocatta J observed in *Handley Page Ltd v Customs and Excise Commissioners*,[5] there is no reason why the equitable assignees for whom the receiver acts should be in any better position than a

---

1 [1895] 2 Ch 118; 64 LJ Ch 457
2 [1892] 1 Ch 434; 61 LJ Ch 256
3 [1896] 2 Ch 93; 65 LJ Ch 536
4 [1963] 1 WLR 1324; [1963] 3 All ER 613 (see p 745)
5 [1970] 2 Lloyd's Rep 459

trustee in bankruptcy or a liquidator and *Rother Iron Works Ltd v Canterbury Precision Engineers Ltd*[1] . . . is authority for the proposition that they are not.

2. *The plaintiffs' contract*

I have already set out the terms of the transport contract made between the plaintiffs and the company on 23 August 1971, eight days before the appointment of the defendant as receiver. It had been entered into by the company in the ordinary course of business, and it was accordingly one which the company were perfectly free to enter into notwithstanding the 1970 debenture. And, as such, it remained in force notwithstanding the appointment of the reciver on 31 August: *Parsons v Sovereign Bank of Canada*.[2] Assuming that the proper interpretation of what occurred between the parties on 2 September was that the defendant sought to repudiate the transport contract of 23 August, it is nevertheless clear that the plaintiffs refused to accept that repudiation and insisted on fulfilling their part of the contract. This they were entitled to do.

. . .

In these circumstances, stress was laid by defendant's counsel on what Mocatta J described as the 'classic statement' of Romer J in *Robson v Smith*, that any dealing with company property in the ordinary course of business 'will be binding on the debenture holders, provided that the dealing be completed before the debentures cease to be merely a floating security.' On the grounds previously stated, Mr Phillips submits that the 'dealing' here with the company's 316 cartons had not been 'completed' before 31 August, in the sense that *no* lien, particular or general, had been acquired by them and he sought to distinguish the set off cases, ranging from *Collins v Jones*[3] to *Rother Iron Works Ltd v Canterbury Precision Engineers Ltd*, to which we were referred, on the ground that whenever a right to set off had been successfully claimed the right had already accrued.

Despite the length of this judgment, I have in its course by no means explored again all the paths up which counsel on one side or the other took us and, with all respect to them, I do not propose doing so. In his peroration Mr Phillips reminded us that the courts dislike general liens, which can unfairly favour one unsecured creditor out of the general body of such creditors, and ended by saying (and I quote his *ipsissima verba*),

> 'The consequences of a decision against the receiver in this case would involve a grave inroad on the security of debenture holders, an unnecessary complication of receiverships and windings up, a scramble for possession in the days immediately after the appointment of a receiver, and detriment to the general body of creditors.'

Well, we cannot say that nobody warned us. Nevertheless, at the end of the day, I have come to the conclusion that this case ultimately turns upon the question of whether the company could simply shrug off the contract it had entered into on 23 August 1971. Indeed, if the defendant is right, it would have been open to the receiver to require the plaintiffs to carry the 316 cartons of meat to Gravesend and, this having been done, he could then demand their delivery up without first paying even the £58.40 transport charge for that particular journey, leaving the plaintiffs merely to prove, with other unsecured creditors, for that and the rest of his much larger claims if a liquidation supervened. As Stamp LJ pointed out during counsel's submission, it is difficult to reconcile that state of

---

1 [1974] QB 1; [1973] 1 All ER 394
2 [1913] AC 160; 82 LJPC 60
3 (1830) 10 B&C 777; 109 ER 638

affairs with such decisions as *Parsons v Sovereign Bank of Canada* and *Rother Iron Works Ltd v Canterbury Precision Engineers*. My conclusion, in the light of those cases, is that the debenture holders could assert their position as assignees of the company's property and contractual rights in the meat only by themselves recognising and giving effect to the pre-appointment contractual rights of the plaintiffs. These included a general lien, and that became exercisable when the plaintiffs acquired actual possession on 2 September, and this nonetheless because three days earlier the defendant had been appointed receiver. I find myself therefore unable to accept as correct the 'vital factor' which Mocatta J regarded as distinguishing *Rother's case* from the present one. On the contrary, the two cases appear to call for the same approach and should, *mutatis mutandis*, have led to similar conclusions.

In the result, I would be for allowing this appeal and granting the relief sought by the plaintiffs.

STAMP LJ . . . In coming to my conclusion, I derive assistance from the decision of this court in *Rother Iron Works Ltd v Canterbury Precision Engineers Ltd*. There Rother was indebted to Canterbury in the sum of £124. Canterbury then agreed to purchase goods from Rother for £159. A bank holding a debenture constituting a charge similar to that in the instant case and covering the business and assets of Rother then appointed a receiver. Rother delivered the goods pursuant to the contract. Had there been no receiver appointed Canterbury could, as against Rother, have set off the antecedent debt against the price of the goods. The question was whether the antecedent debt could be set off notwithstanding that the price of the goods was a debt belonging to the debenture holder. It was held that the rights of the debenture holder under the contract were always subject to the right of Canterbury to set off the antecedent debt against the purchase price of the goods contracted to be sold. The debt of £159 never came into existence except subject to the right to set off. That which became subject to the debenture charge on the appointment of the receiver was not £159, but the net claim sustainable by Rother of £35.

So here the right to have the goods delivered under the contract of carriage was always subject to the right of the carriers, on carrying the goods to their destination, to withhold delivery under condition 13. In one particular the instant case is a stronger one than the *Rother Iron Works case*, because here the right claimed by the creditor [the carriers] was expressly conferred by the company by the contract which the creditor performed. In neither case could the debenture holder, as assignee, be in any better position than the assignor would have been had there been no assignment. I, too, would allow the appeal.

SOURCE 256
Business Computers Ltd *v* Anglo-African Leasing Ltd
(Chancery Division 1977) [1977] 1 WLR 578; [1977] 2 All ER 741

The plaintiff company, Business Computers Ltd, had obtained loans from banks secured by debentures. Its assets were about £1 million and when it became insolvent preferential creditors took £300,000 and the debenture holders £700,000 in part discharge. Trade and unsecured creditors were owed about £3 million. The defendant company, Anglo-African Leasing Ltd, was an unsecured creditor claiming more than £30,000 but admittedly owing the plaintiffs £10,587.50. The receiver for the plaintiff company sought payment of the debt with interest and the defendant company sought to set off their claim against the debt.

. . .

TEMPLEMAN J: . . . The background facts are simple and depressingly typical. The plaintiff company, Business Computers Ltd, known in these proceedings as B.C.L., manufactured computers and financed its operations at least partly by bank loans. The banks prudently required B.C.L. to secure the bank loans by debentures which created a floating charge over all the assets of B.C.L. By commercial misfortune or administrative ineptitude B.C.L. lurched into insolvency and the debenture holders appointed a receiver. B.C.L.'s assets are about £1 million. The Crown, the rating authorities and other preferential creditors take their fill of £300,000. The debenture holders take the rest, about £700,000, in part discharge of the bank loans consisting no doubt of capital and interest at the crippling rates of between 10 per cent and 20 per cent which banks assert they are compelled to charge all and sundry. The trade creditors who perforce extended some credit to B.C.L. in the ordinary course of business and the other unsecured creditors claiming in all some £3 millions will get nothing. The question whether in this day and age it is necessary or desirable to permit the Crown and the holders of future floating charges the totality of the priorities which can be exercised under the existing law is not the subject of debate in this court, though I am inclined to think that it is at least debatable elsewhere.

The claim of the defendants against B.C.L. arises out of a transaction. B.C.L. manufactured a computer for their own use, sold it to the defendants for 75 per cent of its capital cost, namely £42,886.80 and hire-purchased the computer back from the defendants under a hire purchase agreement whereby B.C.L. agreed to pay the defendants 36 monthly instalments of £1,477.20 on the 18th of each month.

B.C.L. paid 12 instalments but did not pay the instalment of £1,477.50 due on 18 May 1974, or any subsequent instalment. On 13 June 1974, the debenture holders appointed a receiver of B.C.L. and on 17 June, the defendants received notice of that appointment. By that date, 17 June 1974, a date more than 14 days after B.C.L. defaulted in payment of the May 1974 instalment due on 18 May the defendants were entitled under condition 12 of the hire purchase agreement to determine the hire purchase agreement and to pursue the remedies specified in condition 13. The defendants took no action on or before 17 June. On 31 July 1974, the receiver repudiated the hire purchase agreement and on 8 August 1974, the defendants accepted that repudiation. The defendants sold the computer for £2,750, and under condition 13 now claim a sum exceeding £32,000.

In these proceedings B.C.L. acting by the receiver seek payment of the debt of £10,587.50 and interest. The defendants resist payment on the grounds that they can set off their claim to £32,000 which exceeds the debt.

The debt and the claim originally lay between B.C.L. and the defendants. The debentures were an incomplete assignment to the debenture holders of the assets of B.C.L. That assignment became complete when the receiver was appointed on 13 June 1974, and effective against the defendants on 17 June, when the defendants received notice of the appointment of the receiver and thus notice of the assignment.

> 'A floating charge is ambulatory and hovers over the property until some event occurs which causes it to settle and crystallise into a specific charge . . . One of the events which causes crystallisation is the appointment of a receiver. . . . One consequence of the receiver's appointment by the debenture holders was that the incomplete assignment constituted by the [debenture] became converted into a completed equitable assignment to

them of the assets charged . . .' per Edmund Davies LJ in *George Barker (Transport) Ltd v Eynon.*[1]

The debt of £10,587.50 owed by the defendants became vested in the debenture holders while the claim of the defendants arising under the hire purchase agreement remained the sole liability of B.C.L. The debenture holders acquired the debt owed by the defendants to B.C.L. subject only to equities affecting the debt at the date of notice of the assignment. As between the debenture holders and the defendants the equitable assignment to the debenture holders of the debt owed by the defendants to B.C.L. was subject to the same rights of set off as the defendants possessed against B.C.L. at the date, namely 17 June 1974, when the defendants received notice of the assignment.

'Now an assignee of a chose in action . . . takes subject to all rights of set off and other defence which were available against the assignor, subject only to this exception, that after notice of an assignment of a chose in action the debtor cannot by payment or otherwise do anything to take away or diminish the rights of the assignee as they stood at the time of the notice . . . ' per James LJ in *Roxburghe v Cox.*[2]

And see also to the same effect Joyce J in *Edward Nelson & Co v Faber & Co.*[3]

By 17 June 1974, the defendants had acquired the right to sue for and recover the debt owed to them by B.C.L. namely the instalment of £1,477.50 due under the hire purchase agreement on 18 May. It is conceded that this can be set off against the debt of £10,587.50 due from the defendants to B.C.L. The two debts were mutual debts in respect of which a right to set off vested in the defendants prior to receiving notice of the assignment to the debenture holders; see *Hanak v Green.*[4] That right of set off remains exercisable against the debenture holders.

The balance of the defendants' present claim amounting to £30,000-odd was not however a debt owed by B.C.L. to the defendants on 17 June 1974, although at that date B.C.L. were in default under the hire purchase agreement because they had not paid the instalment due on 18 May. The defendants did not in reliance on that default determine the hire purchase agreement on or before 17 June 1974, and the position therefore on 17 June 1974, was that the defendants had a right to determine the agreement but the right might never be exercised. The receiver might adopt the hire purchase agreement and pay the instalment in arrear if, for example, he could sell B.C.L.'s business as a going concern. The defendants might choose not to determine but to attempt to enforce the agreement. In the event, the right of determination created by B.C.L.'s default in not paying the May 1974 instalment never was exercised. The defendants' right to damages under clause 13 could not arise until the agreement was determined under clause 12. Determination did not take place until the receiver repudiated the hire purchase agreement on 31 July, and the defendants accepted that repudiation on 8 August. The defendants are not now claiming £30,000 under a right which was vested in them on 17 June 1974. They claim £30,000 under a right which arose on 8 August, that is to say, after notice of the assignment. This right arose out of a contract which was entered into before the assignment. The

---

1 [1974] 1 WLR 462; [1974] 1 All ER 900 (see p 700)
2 (1881) 17 Ch D 520
3 [1903] 2 KB 367; 72 LJKB 771
4 [1958] 2 QB 9; [1958] 2 WLR 755

question is whether such a right can support a set off by the defendants against the assignee debenture holders.

Set off has been allowed against an assignee in a variety of circumstances. In *Biggerstaff v Rowatt's Wharf Ltd*[1] a debtor who became entitled to a liquidated claim against a company before a floating charge crystallised was allowed to set off the liquidated claim against the debt after the debenture crystallised. This decision does not assist the defendants because in the present case no claim liquidated or otherwise for £30,000 arose on or before 17 June when the defendants received notice that the debentures had crystallised.

. . .

I was referred to *N. W. Robbie & Co Ltd v Witney Warehouse Co Ltd*,[2] but this case only decided that a debtor cannot after notice of an assignment of his debt by his creditor improve his position as regards set off by acquiring debts incurred by the assignor creditor to a third party. I have already referred to *George Barker (Transport) Ltd v Eynon*, but that case only decided that if a receiver after his appointment took the benefit of a contract entered into before his appointment, he could not dispute a lien conferred by that contract but not exercised until after the appointment. The defendants in the present case cannot invoke this principle. The contracts under which the debt of £10,587.50 became payable were completed before the receiver was appointed, apart from the payment now sought against the defendants. I was also referred to *Rother Iron Works Ltd v Canterbury Precision Engineers Ltd.*[3] In that case, pursuant to a contract made before the appointment of a receiver, a debtor delivered goods to the company and the goods were accepted by the receiver. The debtor was allowed to set off the price of the goods against his debt to the company because the receiver could not take the benefit of the contract without the burden. He was not entitled to the debt and to the goods and to keep the purchase price. A similar point does not arise in the present case.

The result of the relevant authorities is that a debt which accrues due before notice of an assignment is received, whether or not it is payable before that date, or a debt which arises out of the same contract as that which gives rise to the assigned debt, or is closely connected with that contract, may be set off against the assignee. But a debt which is neither accrued nor connected may not be set off even though it arises from a contract made before the assignment. In the present case the claim for £30,000 did not accrue before 17 June 1974, when the defendants received notice of the appointment of the receiver and thus notice of the completed assignment of the debt of £10,587.50 to the debenture holders and there was no relevant connection between the transactions which gave rise to the claim and to the debt respectively.

. . . The defendants were never asked to pay and never refused to pay £10,587.50 until B.C.L. had defaulted on the May 1974 instalment and it became first probable and then certain that B.C.L. would become liable to pay but would not be able to pay the defendants over £30,000 on the hire purchase agreement. That inability is the fault of B.C.L. In my judgment it does not lie in the mouth of B.C.L. in these circumstances to complain that they have been kept out of £10,587.50 while they blandly admit that they have kept the defendants out of £30,000 and must continue to do so. Of course if there had been inexcusable delay by the defendants before 17 June 1974, or if the argument about set off were hopeless, different considerations might apply. But it is only after three days

1 [1896] 2 Ch 93; 65 LJ Ch 536
2 [1963] 1 WLR 1324; [1963] 3 All ER 613 (see p 745)
3 [1973] 2 WLR 281; [1973] 1 All ER 394

of argument and the consideration of a number of authorities that I have with some reluctance come to the conclusion that the defendants were liable to pay without themselves being paid. In these circumstances I am not prepared to punish the defendants for withholding payment. In my judgment justice does not require me to listen to the complaint of B.C.L. about being kept out of their money, and in this respect the debenture holders who take from B.C.L. the benefit of the defendants' debt without submitting to set off are in no better position. I am not disposed to award any interest.

Floating Charges and Judgment Creditors (Sources 245, 257 and 258)

SOURCE 257
Norton *v* Yates
[1906] 1 KB 112; 75 LJKB 252

This was an interpleader issue which raised the question of priority between debenture-holders of a limited company with the usual floating security and a judgment creditor who had obtained and served a garnishee order nisi in respect of a debt due to the company two days before a receiver in a debenture-holders' action was appointed.

On 17 January 1905, Yates & Co obtained judgment against the company for £529 4s. 2d. and on the same day they obtained and served on Henry Tate & Sons Ltd, a garnishee order nisi for a debt of £434 13s. 10d. owing by that firm to the company.

On 19 January, one B. T. Norton was appointed receiver and manager of the company in a debenture-holders' action; the fact of the above judgment against the company being made one of the grounds for the appointment. Notice of this appointment was forthwith served on Yates & Co by letter, which was received by them on 20 January, on which day the garnishee order nisi was made absolute.

On 9 February, in consequence of the claim by the receiver to the garnished debt, Henry Tate & Sons Ltd, were ordered to pay the amount of £434 13s. 10d. into Court, to abide further order. This amount, with other debts that had also been garnished, was paid into Court.

WARRINGTON J: . . . The first question is, what is the effect of the garnishee order? It is, perhaps, easier to say what its effect is not, than to say positively what it is, and for present purposes it will be enough for me to say what its effect is not. That question arose in *Re Combined Weighing and Advertising Machine Co*,[1] though the main point was whether the judgment creditor under a garnishee order became a creditor of the garnishee; in other words, did the order operate as an assignment of the debt by way of security or otherwise so that the garnishor could to that extent stand in the place of the original creditor, and become a creditor of the garnishee? The Court of Appeal held that the garnishor was not a creditor of the garnishee; or in other words, that the garnishee order did not amount to an assignment, either absolutely or by way of security. I think that perhaps Bowen LJ puts the effect of the garnishee order in the way which is of most use for the purpose of the present case. At p 105 he says, after referring to the mode in which a garnishee order is obtained and the object of it: 'There cannot be said to be any equitable debt. There is no assignment in equity, and I cannot see that there is any legal debt. There is an order of a Court of Common Law that a sum equal to

---

1 (1889) 43 Ch D 99; LJ Ch 26

the original debt shall be paid by the garnishee to the judgment creditor, or as an alternative that execution may issue; but I think that the relation which is created by that section and the orders made under it does not create a debt at all; it creates an attachment of a portion of the debt, and in case of non-payment confers the right of issuing execution and nothing more.'

. . .

The rights of the garnishor, therefore, are subject to such rights and equities as affected the garnished debt in the hands of the company: and it is, now, therefore, necessary to consider what, in this case, is the right or equity to which that debt was subject, when the garnishee order nisi was obtained. That turns upon the question. What is the true effect of the debenture? The debenture is a floating security. That is not all: it is a floating security subject to the particular incidents which are expressed in the conditions, and therefore one has not to decide what is the meaning of the expression 'floating security' taken by itself, but what is the meaning of 'floating security' in this document.

[The judge then quoted with approval, the judgments of Lord Macnaghten in *Governments Stock and Other Securities Investment Co v Manila Ry Co*[1] (p 675) and Romer LJ in *Re Yorkshire Woolcombers' Association*[2] (p 661) and continued:]

The receiver here was appointed on 19 January, and it seems to me that when the receiver was appointed, his appointment operated on everything which was the property of the company at the moment of his appointment. As I have already said, this debt, though bound by the garnishee order, was still the property of the company, and therefore the receiver became entitled to receive this debt, subject to such rights as the garnishee might have. But in my judgment the garnishee had no right as against the debenture-holders, because, by virtue of the charge which existed at the date when the garnishee order had been obtained, the debenture-holders had obtained from the Court an order which gave somebody, not the garnishee, the right to receive this debt, namely, the receiver for the debenture-holders. It is said that there is authority to the contrary to be found in *Robson v Smith*;[3] but in my opinion *Robson v Smith* is not an authority to the contrary at all, and for this reason: I have held that the reason why the receiver becomes entitled to this debt is that the property in the debt had not been transferred to the garnishor, but remained in the company subject only to such rights as the garnishee order gave. In *Robson v Smith* the point that arose was a different one, because there the judgment creditor had obtained from the garnishee the payment of the debt. Nothing had been done by the debenture-holders there in order to obtain the appointment of a receiver. All that they had done was to give notice to the debtors of the company to pay the debt to them, and what Romer LJ held was that that notice was of no effect. No receiver had been appointed, nor had anything been done to make the dormant charge under the debentures into an active charge, and the debt in question had, by payment, been discharged, and therefore, ceased to be the property of the company. That, it seems to me, is really the *ratio decidendi* of *Robson v Smith*. It does not apply to the present case at all, nor is it, in my opinion, in any way, either from the reasons given by the learned judge or his judgment, an authority which helps the judgment creditor.

---

1 [1897] AC 81; 66 LJ Ch 102 (see p 675)
2 [1903] 2 Ch 284 (see p 661)
3 [1895] 2 Ch 118; 64 LJ Ch 457

...

The result is, in my opinion, that the receiver for the debenture-holders is entitled to receive the moneys paid into Court under the judgment under the garnishee order.

SOURCE 258
Cairney *v* Back
(King's Bench 1906) [1906] 2 KB 746; 75 LJKB 1014

WALTON J: . . . This is an interpleader issue, and the parties to it are practically the plaintiff Cairney on the one hand and the defendant Back on the other. The plaintiff is the holder of a debenture of the Consolidated Mines Limited, dated 27 January 1906. The defendant was secretary of the company from April 1905, until June 1906. On 15 June 1906, the defendant obtained judgment against the company for £96 1s. 4d. for arrears of salary and costs amounting to £2 2s., and on the same date he obtained a garnishee order nisi upon the Commercial Bank of Scotland, with whom the Consolidated Mines Limited, had an account which was in credit to an amount exceeding £98 3s. 4d.

The garnishee order nisi was, as I have said, made on 15 June. Notice of it was given to Cairney on 18 June. On 25 June the order nisi was made absolute. On 29 June a receiver was appointed of the assets and property of the company on behalf of the plaintiff under the powers contained in his debenture. What are the rights of the parties under these circumstances?

. . . It is contended on behalf of the defendant in the present case that since *Robson v Smith*[1] shews that, if the bank had paid the money to the defendant under the garnishee order absolute they could not be called upon to pay it over again to the plaintiff, it makes no difference, an order for payment having been made, that the money has not in fact been paid. I do not think that *Robson v Smith* establishes that proposition. All that it decides is that if the garnishee has paid the garnishor under the order he cannot be made to pay the debt over again, even if the payment to the garnishor was made with notice of the debenture-holder's claim. I do not think that the decision in *Robson v Smith* applies to the facts of this case. The question here is as to equities between the debenture-holder and the garnishor. It is contended that the effect of the order absolute as against the debt is much the same as an execution levied on chattels; but even supposing that a garnishee order absolute can be said to be analogous to the seizure of chattels under a fi. fa., putting the garnishor in possession of the debt in the same way that a seizure under a fi. fa. puts the sheriff in possession of the chattels, I am afraid that that will not assist the defendant, because it was held in *Davey v Williamson*[2] that, even as against the sheriff who has seized goods under a fi. fa., the title of a debenture-holder prevailed, although the rights of the debenture-holder had not 'crystallized,' as it is termed, that is, the time for payment had not arrived. For these reasons I have come to the conclusion that the rights of the plaintiff Cairney under his debenture must prevail over the rights of the defendant Back under the garnishee order absolute.

---

1 [1895] 2 Ch 118; 64 LJ Ch 457
2 [1898] 2 QB 194; 67 LJQB 699 (see p 679)

Floating Charge and Creditor Who has Retained Title to Goods Supplied

It is becoming increasingly common for suppliers of goods to try to protect themselves against defaulting purchasers by writing into the contract a clause in terms of which the title to the goods supplied remains with the supplier until the goods are paid for. In some instances the courts have upheld the suppliers' rights under such clauses, but not in others. In the latter, the suppliers have been defeated where the clause was construed as amounting to a charge which was void as against the liquidator for want of registration (Sources 259, 260, 261).

SOURCE 259
Clough Mill Ltd *v* Geoffrey Martin
(Court of Appeal 1985) [1985] 1 WLR 111; [1984] 3 All ER 982

The appellants supplied yarn to a company under a contract incorporating the following clause:

> However, the ownership of the material shall remain with the Seller, which reserves the right to dispose of the material until payment in full for all the material has been received by it in accordance with the terms of this contract or until such time as the Buyer sells the material to its customers by way of bona-fide sale at full market value.
>
> If such payment is overdue in whole or in part the Seller may (without prejudice to any of its other rights) recover or re-sell the material or any of it and may enter upon the Buyer's premises by its servants or agents for that purpose.
>
> Such payments shall become due immediately upon the commencement of any act or proceeding in which the Buyer's solvency is involved.
>
> If any of the material is incorporated in or used as material for other goods before such payment the property in the whole of such goods shall be and remain with the Seller until such payment has been made, or the other goods have been sold as aforesaid, and all the Seller's rights hereunder in the material shall extend to those other goods.

The defendant was appointed as receiver to the company and refused permission to the appellants to repossess unused yarn, despite the fact that money was still owing in respect of the yarn supplied. The receiver asserted that the clause on which the appellant relied was a charge and, therefore, invalid for want of registration under s 95 of the Companies Act 1948 (now s 395 of the Companies Act 1985).

> ROBERT GOFF LJ: ... There has been a spate of decisions in recent years concerning these so-called Romalpa clauses. But it is of great importance to bear in mind that these cases have been concerned with different clauses, very often in materially different terms, that different cases have raised different questions for decision and that the decision in any particular case may have depended on how the matter was presented to the court, and in particular may have depended on a material concession by counsel. So this is a field in which we have to be particularly careful in reading each decision in the light of the facts and issues before the court in question. So, for example, the original Romalpa case,

Aluminium Industrie Vaassen BV v Romalpa Aluminium Ltd[1] was concerned with the question whether sellers of aluminium foil under contracts containing a Romalpa clause could trace their title into money which was the proceeds of sale by the buyers of aluminium foil supplied by the sellers. That question (which was answered in the affirmative) was considered on the basis that, as was admitted by the buyers, title to the foil itself had been retained by the sellers and that the buyers became bailees of the foil on delivery to them. By contrast, the question in the present case is whether, under condition 12, the appellants did indeed retain their title to the yarn or (as the judge held) thereby became chargees of the yarn, a point which did not fall for decision in the *Romalpa case*. Again, in *Re Bond Worth Ltd*[2] a case on which the judge in the present case placed particular reliance, Slade J had to consider, in relation to facts of considerable complexity, a clause which provided not simply that 'the ownership' in the goods should be retained by the sellers, but that 'equitable and beneficial ownership' should remain with the sellers until full payment had been received or until prior resale, in which case their 'beneficial entitlement' should attach to the proceeds of sale. In that case, therefore, it was never suggested that the sellers retained the legal title to the goods; the only two possibilities were the creation of a trust or of a charge, and Slade J held that it was a charge which had been created. Finally, in *Borden (UK) Ltd v Scottish Timber Products Ltd*[3] the question at issue was whether, under a contract of sale of resin containing a Romalpa clause, the sellers could trace their title into chipboard in which resin supplied by the sellers had been incorporated during its manufacture by the buyers. This court held that they could not do so, the manufacture of the chipboard having amalgamated the resin and other ingredients into a new product by an irreversible process, so that the resin ceased to exist and the title in it must also have ceased to exist. However, in that case Templeman LJ made certain observations about the general effect of the Romalpa clause in the contract then before the court which have been of assistance to me in considering the question in the present case.

I approach that question as follows. We have to construe condition 12 as a whole, and in its contractual context; but it is convenient to start with the opening sentence of the condition, on which the appellants particularly rely. In that sentence, it is provided:

> '. . . the ownership of the material shall remain with the Seller, which reserves the right to dispose of the material until payment in full for all the material has been received by it in accordance with the terms of this contract or until such time as the Buyer sells the material to its customers by way of bona-fide sale at full market value.'

Now there are various points to notice about this sentence. The first is that what is reserved by the seller is the ownership of the material, the material being the material supplied under the particular contract (see condition 1(a)(ii)). Prima facie, in a commercial document such as this, ownership means, quite simply, the property in the goods. The second point is that the reservation of the right to dispose of the material is expressed to be until a certain event, viz until payment in full for all the material received by the buyer or until resale by the buyer. This shows the purpose for which the right of disposal is reserved, which is to provide the seller with security for any unpaid and overdue purchase price payable under the contract. It is obvious from the third sentence that the

---

1 [1976] 1 WLR 676; [1976] 2 All ER 552
2 [1980] Ch 228; [1979] 3 All ER 919
3 [1981] Ch 25; [1979] 3 All ER 961

possibility of insolvency is a matter which is particularly in contemplation. It also appears from the first sentence that the buyer has power to sell the material to his customers; and we know from the fourth sentence that it is also contemplated that the buyer has power to consume the material in the manufacture of goods, mixing it with other material in the process, the function of the last sentence being to provide for the rights of the seller in, and in respect of, any such manufactured goods. The second sentence empowers the seller to recover or resell the material or any of it, and to enter on the buyer's premises for that purpose.

The submission of counsel for the appellants as to the nature of the appellants' retention of title under the first sentence of the condition was extremely simple. Under the Sale of Goods Act 1979 a seller of goods is fully entitled, after delivery of the goods to the buyer, to retain title in the goods until he has been paid: see section 19(1) of that Act. That is precisely what the appellants have done by condition 12. The appellants' title did not derive from the contract; on the contrary, it was simply retained by them, though under the contract power was conferred on the buyers both to sell the goods and to use them in manufacturing other goods. As the buyers never acquired any title to the unused yarn in question, they could not charge the yarn to the appellants. So the appellants were, quite simply, the owners of the yarn; and there was no question of there being any charge on the yarn in their favour, which was void if unregistered.

This attractively simple approach was challenged by counsel for the receiver. He submitted, first of all, that, if the first sentence of condition 12 is read literally, as counsel for the appellants suggested it should be read, the buyers can only have had possession of the yarn in a fiduciary capacity, whether as bailees or as fiduciary agents. But, he said, the power conferred on the buyers under the contract, not merely to sell the material but also to mix it with other materials in the manufacture of goods, was inconsistent with the existence of any fiduciary capacity in the buyers, or indeed with the appellants' unqualified ownership of the yarn. In support of this submission, he relied in particular on a proposition derived from the judgment of Slade J in *Re Bond Worth Ltd*, when he said:

'. . . where an alleged trustee has the right to mix tangible assets or moneys with his own other assets or moneys and to deal with them as he pleases, this is incompatible with the existence of a *presently* subsisting fiduciary relationship in regard to such particular assets or moneys.' (Slade J's emphasis.)

Now this is a submission which I am unable to accept. In every case, we have to look at the relevant documents and other communications which have passed between the parties, and to consider them in the light of relevant surrounding circumstances, in order to ascertain the rights and duties of the parties *inter se*, always paying particular regard to the practical effect of any conclusion concerning the nature of those rights and duties. In performing this task, concepts such as bailment and fiduciary duty must not be allowed to be our masters, but must rather be regarded as the tools of our trade. I for my part can see nothing objectionable in an agreement between parties under which A, the owner of goods, gives possession of those goods to B, at the same time conferring on B a power of sale and a power to consume the goods in manufacture, though A will remain the owner of the goods until they are either sold or consumed. I do not see why the relationship between A and B, pending sale or consumption, should not be the relationship of bailor and bailee, even though A has no right to trace the property in his goods into the proceeds of sale. If that is what the parties have agreed should happen, I can see no reason why the law should not give effect to that intention. I am happy to find that both Staughton and Peter Gibson JJ have adopted a similar approach in the recently reported cases of *Hendy Lennox (Industrial Engines) Ltd v Grahame Puttick Ltd*[1] and *Re Andrabell Ltd*.[2]

Even so, it is necessary to examine counsel for the appellants' construction in a little more detail. If, under this condition, retention of title applied only to goods not yet paid for, I can see that his construction could be given effect to without any problem. But the difficulty with the present condition is that the retention of title applies to material, delivered and retained by the buyer, until payment in full for *all* the material delivered under the contract has been received by the seller. The effect is therefore that the seller may retain his title in material still held by the buyer, even if part of that material has been paid for. Furthermore, if in such circumstances the seller decides to exercise his rights and resell the material, questions can arise concerning (1) whether account must be taken of the part payment already received in deciding how much the seller should be entitled to sell and (2) whether, if he does resell, he is accountable to the buyer either in respect of the part payment already received, or in respect of any profit made on the resale by reason of a rise in the market value of the material.

...

There is another possible solution to this problem. This is that the seller should be held to retain the title to the material as trustee, on trust to sell the goods and apply the proceeds of sale, first in discharge of the outstanding balance of the purchase price, and then as to any surplus on trust for the buyer.

...

To me, the answer to these questions lies in giving effect to the condition in accordance with its terms, and on that approach I can discern no intention to create a trust. The condition provides that the seller retains his ownership in the material. He therefore remains owner; but, during the subsistence of the contract, he can only exercise his powers as owner consistently with the terms, express and implied, of the contract. On that basis, in my judgment, he can during the subsistence of the contract only resell such amount of the material as is needed to discharge the balance of the outstanding purchase price; and, if he sells more, he is accountable to the buyer for the surplus. However, once the contract has been determined, as it will be if the buyer repudiates the contract and the seller accepts the repudiation, the seller will have his rights as owner (including, of course, his right to sell the goods) uninhibited by any contractual restrictions; though any part of the purchase price received by him and attributable to the material so resold will be recoverable by the buyer on the ground of failure of consideration, subject to any set-off arising from a cross-claim by the seller for damages for the buyer's repudiation.

... In the course of his argument counsel for the receiver prayed in aid another proposition culled from the judgment of Slade J in *Re Bond Worth Ltd* when he said:

> 'In my judgment, any contract which, by way of security for payment of a debt, confers an interest in property defeasible or destructible on payment of such debt, or appropriates such property for the discharge of the debt, must necessarily be regarded as creating a mortgage or charge, as the case may be. The existence of the equity of redemption is quite inconsistent with the existence of a bare trustee-beneficiary relationship.'

1 [1984] 1 WLR 485; [1984] 2 All ER 152
2 [1984] 3 All ER 107, [1984] BCLC 522

However, so far as the retention of title in unused materials is concerned, I see no difficulty in distinguishing the present case from that envisaged by Slade J. Under the first sentence of the condition, the buyer does not, by way of security, *confer* on the seller an interest in property defeasible on the payment of the debt so secured. On the contrary, the seller *retains* the legal property in the material.

There is however one further point which I must consider. Counsel for the receiver relied, in support of his argument, on the fourth sentence of the condition. It will be remembered that this reads as follows:

> 'If any of the material is incorporated in or used as material for other goods before such payment the property in the whole of such goods shall be and remain with the Seller until such payment has been made, or the other goods have been sold as aforesaid, and all the Seller's rights hereunder in the material shall extend to those other goods.'

The submission of counsel for the receiver was that the effect of this provision is to confer on the seller an interest in the buyer's property and so must have been to create a charge; and he further submitted that, having regard to the evident intention that the seller's rights in goods in which the material provided by him has been incorporated shall be the same as his rights in unused material, the seller's rights in unused material should likewise be construed as creating a charge.

Now it is no doubt true that, where A's material is lawfully used by B to create new goods, whether or not B incorporates other material of his own, the property in the new goods will generally vest in B, at least where the goods are not reducible to the original materials (see 2 Bl Com (17th edn) pp 404–405). But it is difficult to see why, if the parties agree that the property in the goods shall vest in A, that agreement should not be given effect to. On this analysis, under the fourth sentence of the condition as under the first, the buyer does not *confer* on the seller an interest in property defeasible on the payment of the debt; on the contrary, when the new goods come into existence the property in them ipso facto vests in the seller, and he thereafter retains his ownership in them, in the same way and on the same terms as he retains his ownership in the unused material. However, in considering the fourth sentence, we have to take into account not only the possibility that the buyer may have paid part of the price for the material, but also that he will have borne the cost of manufacture of the new goods, and may also have provided other materials for incorporation into those goods; and the condition is silent, not only about repaying such part of the price for the material as has already been paid by the buyer, but also about any allowance to be made by the seller to the buyer for the cost of manufacture of the new goods, or for any other material incorporated by the buyer into the new goods. Now, no injustice need arise from the exercise of the seller's power to resell such goods provided that, having applied the price received from the resale in satisfaction of the outstanding balance of the price owed to him by the buyer, he is bound to account for the remainder to the buyer. But the difficulty of construing the fourth sentence as simply giving rise to a retention by the seller of title to the new goods is that it would lead to the result that, on the determination of the contract under which the original material was sold to the buyer, the ownership of the seller in the new goods would be retained by the seller uninhibited by any terms of the contract, which had then ceased to apply; and I find it impossible to believe that it was the intention of the parties that the seller would thereby gain the windfall of the full value of the new product, deriving as it may well do not merely from the labour of the buyer but also from materials that were his, without any duty to account to him for any surplus of the proceeds of sale above the outstanding balance of the price due by him to the seller. It follows that the fourth sentence must be read as creating either a trust or a charge. In my judgment, however, it cannot have been intended to create a trust. Those who insert Romalpa clauses in their contracts of sale must be aware that other suppliers might do the same; and the prospect of two lots of material, supplied by different sellers, each subject to a Romalpa clause which vests in the seller the legal title in a product manufactured from both lots of material, is not at all sensible. Accordingly, consistent with the approach of Vinelott J to a similar provision in *Re Peachdart Ltd*,[1] I have come to the conclusion that, although it does indeed do violence to the language of the fourth sentence of the condition, that sentence must be read as giving rise to a charge on the new goods in favour of the seller.

. . .

I recognise that, on the view which I have formed of the retention of title in the first sentence of condition 12 in this case, its effect is very similar to that of a charge on goods created by the buyer in favour of the seller. But the simple fact is that under the first sentence of the condition the buyer does not in fact confer a charge on his goods in favour of the seller: on the contrary, the seller retains his title in his goods, for the purpose of providing himself with security. I can see no reason in law why a seller of goods should not adopt this course, and, if the relevant contractual term is effective to achieve that result, I can see no reason why the law should not give effect to it in accordance with its terms. We were treated in argument to what I understand to be the common form appeal to the merits in cases of this kind, counsel for the appellants describing the unfortunate plight of suppliers of goods to manufacturers who, if in a poor financial position, are kept going by the suppliers for the benefit of debenture holders, usually banks, and counsel for the receiver describing the difficulties of liquidators grappling with incomprehensible Romalpa clauses. I sympathise with both; though I am tempted to observe that the mechanism of the floating charge, on which secured creditors are content to rely, is perhaps as much open to criticism as the mechanism of the retention of title clause, at which they now express their dismay. Be that as it may, my conclusion in the present case derives not from sympathy, but from an analysis of the clause.

SOURCE 260
Specialist Plant Services Ltd *v* Braithwaite Ltd
(Court of Appeal 1987) [1987] BCLC 1

The plaintiff repaired machinery belonging to the company on terms which included the following:

1(a) Property in goods and materials supplied hereunder or utilised by the Company [and that in this context is the first plaintiff] in performing the Contract between the Company and the Customer will pass to the Customer when (a) the said goods and materials and all work done hereunder and (b) all other goods and materials and all other work done the subject of any other contract between the Company and the customer which, at the time of payment of the full price due hereunder, have been delivered or has been carried out by the Company but not paid in full, have been paid for in full.
(b) Further, it is hereby agreed that if the said goods and materials or any part thereof supplied hereunder in any way whatsoever become a constituent of

---

1 [1984] Ch 131; [1983] 3 All ER 204

another article or other articles the Company shall be given the ownership of this (these) new article(s) as surety of the full payment of what the customer owes the Company. To this end the Company and the customer now agree that the ownership of the article(s) in question, whether finished or not, are to be transferred to the Company and that this transfer of ownership will be considered to have taken place through and at the moment of the single operation or event by which the goods and materials or any part thereof are connected into the new article or articles, or are mixed with or become a constituent of such article or articles. Until the moment of full payment of what the customer owes the Company the customer shall keep the article(s) in question for the Company in the capacity of fiduciary owner and, if required, shall store this (these) article(s) in such a way that it (they) can be recognised as such. Nevertheless the customer will be entitled to sell this (these) article(s) to a third party within the framework of the normal carrying on of his business and to deliver it (them) on condition that, if the Company so requires, the customer, so long as he has not fully discharged his debt to the Company, shall hand over to the Company the claim he has against his purchaser emanating from this transaction.

(c) The word 'article' or 'articles' contained in Clause (b) above shall mean and include and be deemed to mean and include any building or part thereof, any structure of whatever description or part thereof, any machinery or part thereof, or any other object, goods or article of whatever description.

The company went into receivership and the question was whether this clause conferred a proprietary interest in the goods repaired on the plaintiff.

> The grounds of appeal are several, but in the event it has become necessary to consider one only of them, because it was accepted that, if this court were to find that there was no triable issue, no serious point of law, to be determined on this question, that would dispose of this whole appeal. That single question is whether or not, under the conditions of trade to which I have already referred, the plaintiffs did in fact retain any proprietary interest in the machines in question such as to entitle them to the injunction which they claimed and which they were granted, or whether in particular the effect of clause (b) of those conditions was to create a charge which required to be registered under section 95 of the Companies Act 1948, or the equivalent section under the new consolidating Act of 1985; because, if that charge required to be registered and was not registered (as is conceded), then it was void; the plaintiffs had no proprietary interest in the machine or the torque divider and they were not entitled to the injunction which they claimed and which they were granted. In the result, in fact, the receiver paid the money into court. The machine was then sold and the real purpose of this appeal is to have the money which is now in court released for the general purposes of the receivership.
>
> It is accepted (very sensibly, if I may say so) that in the light of the opening words of clause (b), 'If the said goods and materials or any part thereof supplied hereunder ... become a constituent of another article or other articles', it is clause (b) that applies in this case and not clause (a), which is clearly by its terms confined to dealing with goods which have not been incorporated in some other article or articles.
>
> I have already read clause (b). There is no necessity to read it again. On its face it seems clearly to indicate that it is a clause by way of security, because it uses the express words 'the Company shall be given the ownership of this (these) new article(s) as surety of the full payment of what the customer owes the Company',

and that seems to me to make it clear that this was a clause creating security for moneys due.

. . .

We have been referred to a number of cases, because these retention of title clauses are becoming increasingly popular at the moment. I need not refer to all of them. I refer, first, to the case of *Re Bond Worth*[1] which was a case of carpet manufacturers purchasing fibre which was spun and then woven into the carpets; and the question was the retention of the ownership of the yarn by the suppliers of the yarn. Slade J said:

'In my judgment, any contract which, by way of security for the payment of a debt, confers an interest in property defeasible or destructible on payment of such debt, or appropriates such property for the discharge of the debt, must necessarily be regarded as creating a mortgage or charge, as the case may be. The existence of the equity of redemption is quite inconsistent with the existence of a bare trustee-beneficiary relationship.'

I would, with respect, wholly agree with those words. Then the judge went on to deal with the case of *Re George Inglefield Ltd*[2] when he says:

'The fact that all the characteristics of a mortgage or charge are to be found present in the retention of title clause is borne out by a passage from the judgment of Romer LJ in *Re George Inglefield Ltd.* There he summarised the essential characteristics of a mortgage as follows: "In a transaction of sale the vendor is not entitled to get back the subject-matter of the sale by returning to the purchaser the money that has passed between them. In the case of a mortgage or charge, the mortgagor is entitled, until he has been foreclosed, to get back the subject-matter of the mortgage or charge by returning to the mortgagee the money that has passed between them. The second essential difference is that if the mortgagee realizes the subject-matter of the mortgage for a sum more than sufficient to repay him, with interest and the costs, the money that has passed between him and the mortgagor he has to account to the mortgagor for the surplus. If the purchaser sells the subject-matter of the purchase, and realizes a profit, of course he has not got to account to the vendor for the profit. Thirdly, if the mortgagee realizes the mortgage property for a sum that is insufficient to repay him the money that he has paid to the mortgagor, together with interest and costs, then the mortgagee is entitled to recover from the mortgagor the balance of the money, either because there is a covenant by the mortgagor to repay the money advanced by the mortgagee, or because of the existence of the simple contract debt which is created by the mere fact of the advance having been made".'

It is sufficient if I say that in my judgment the provisions of clause (b) contain all the indicia which Romer LJ said were the indicia of a mortgage or charge.

Re Peachdart Ltd,[3] is another case of a retention of title clause about which I need say no more than that it supports the interpretation which Slade J put on a similar clause in *Re Bond Worth*. Finally, we were also referred to the case in this court of *Clough Mill Ltd v Martin*.[4] The facts in that case were that there was some unused yarn to which a retention of title clause applied. The yarn had not been

---

1 [1980] Ch 228; [1979] 3 All ER 919
2 [1933] Ch 1; 101 LJ Ch 360
3 [1984] Ch 131; [1983] 3 All ER 204
4 [1985] 1 WLR 111; [1984] 3 All ER 982 (see p 710)

incorporated in any other product, and since there is no reason why a retention of title clause cannot be made to say that property shall not pass until payment is made, the clause apparently caused no problems. The only matter which concerned the court was that there was a second part of the same clause dealing with what happened if material had been incorporated in other goods, and an argument was put before the Court of Appeal by counsel in that case that the effect of that second part should have been to persuade the court to adopt a different construction for the first part of the clause in relation to unused yarn (which had not been incorporated), than the ordinary literal meaning of the clause would require it to do. That argument failed, and it seems to me that we need not here be concerned with the case of *Clough Mill,* save only to say that, in so far as the court there construed the second half of the clause in question, its construction did not in any way detract from the argument put by counsel for the defendant even though it may not expressly have supported it. That argument is (as will be apparent from what I have already said) that clause 1(b) creates a charge which is void for lack of registration. [This argument was accepted.]

SOURCE 261
Report of the Review Committee on Insolvency Law and Practice ('Cork Report')

1590. The law, therefore, accords to the parties to a contract for the sale of goods complete freedom in their selection of the moment at which the property in the goods passes from seller to buyer. A contract for the sale of goods may provide that the property in the goods shall not pass to the buyer until the purchase price has been paid in full. A contractual provision to this effect is conveniently described as a reservation of title clause.

1591. In the ordinary course of trade goods are often supplied to manufacturers or dealers on the basis that, before payment for them has been made, they will either be used in the production of other goods or sold on. Frequently, therefore, a simple condition reserving title in the goods the subject-matter of the sale has coupled with it more elaborate provisions designed to give the seller an interest in property other than those goods. In considering reservation of title, it is necessary to examine both the property which a person who would otherwise be an unsecured creditor is seeking to withdraw from the estate of the insolvent and the claims which that person is seeking to protect.

1592. In broad terms, the property sought to be withdrawn from the estate can be divided into the following categories:

 (a) the specific goods the subject-matter of the contract of the sale which have not been paid for;
 (b) all other goods supplied by the unpaid vendor, even if those other goods have been paid for;
 (c) the right to sue the sub-purchaser for the price due under any onward sale of the goods;
 (d) the cash proceeds arising from an onward sale;
 (e) new products into which the goods the subject-matter of the original contract have been incorporated or infused in the course of some manufacturing or assembly process;
 (f) the right to sue a purchaser of the new products for the price due under any contract of sale; and
 (g) the cash proceeds arising from a sale of new products.

1593. The claims sought to be protected can be summarised as follows:

(a) the price of the goods themselves;
(b) the outstanding balance of account owing to the unpaid vendor arising from a series of transactions between the two parties under which one has supplied goods to the other; and
(c) all sums owing by the purchaser to the seller on any account whatsoever.

1594. It will be plain that there is scope for a wide variety of reservation of title clauses and a large number have been drawn to our attention deriving from many different trades and ranging from the short and simple to the extremely complex.

The security context
1595. It is important to set reservation of title clauses in context. A basic principle of insolvency law is that the estate of the insolvent should be divided among the creditors *pari passu*. However, freedom of contract inevitably leads creditors or prospective creditors to seek to put themselves in a position *vis-à-vis* a debtor or prospective debtor which is better than that of an unsecured creditor ranking for a rateable proportion of the insolvent debtor's estate.
1596. This is done, in the main, by obtaining direct rights against an asset of the debtor and preventing that asset falling into the estate to be administered when the debtor becomes insolvent. All types of property can be made the subject-matter of a trust. Goods can be prevented from passing into the ownership of the debtor by way of reservation of title under a contract for the sale of goods, by leasing and by hire purchase. A property interest can be retained by means of a lien, provided that possession of the property has been retained, actually or constructively.
1597. Moreover, and most importantly a security interest can be obtained by means of a mortgage, charge, or other enforceable encumbrance. In this last category there feature, as regards insolvent companies, floating charges which enable the debtor company to carry on business in the ordinary course, dealing with the assets the subject-matter of the charge accordingly, but on the basis that insolvency causes a crystallisation of the charge and withdraws the property the subject-matter of the charge from the unencumbered estate of the insolvent company.
1598. All these methods of improving the position of the creditor from that of an unsecured creditor fall to be considered together. It would, for example, be shortsighted to consider reservation of title without observing the close analogy between its extended form — a purported retention of an interest in goods the subject-matter of a sale and in all property deriving directly or indirectly from those goods by way of security for all sums due from the purchaser to the seller on any account whatsoever — and a floating charge. Where a seller is in a position, *vis-à-vis* his buyer, to demand reservation of title he may equally be in a position to demand the protection of a charge. A clause purporting to operate by way of reservation may be interpreted by the courts as constituting a charge or as partly reserving title and partly constituting a charge.

. . .

1618. In summary, therefore, it is possible as the law now stands to obtain protection against the insolvency of a purchaser of goods by means of a reservation of title clause where the goods or chattels sold remain in the possession of the purchaser intact in the form sold, or where proceeds of sale in respect of an onward sale of the goods in that form are separately identifiable in his possession. The protection may well extend beyond the price of the goods themselves to other sums due from the purchaser to the supplier, possibly to sums due on any account whatsoever. On the other hand, the preservation of a property interest in the goods supplied after they become mixed with other goods or consumed in some process of manufacture, is far more difficult and may be impossible. In such a case the appropriate course for the creditor to adopt is to obtain a charge in his favour, either fixed or floating, both requiring registration under section 95 [now s 395].

General considerations

1619. The supplier of goods is able to protect himself by adopting reservation of title clauses. No similar protection is available to the supplier of consumables or of services. Fuel supplied to heat furnaces, or fodder supplied for livestock, disappears on consumption and paint applied to the fabric of a factory becomes attached to the realty; the supplier on credit is necessarily left with an unsecured claim in the insolvency of the customer. The canteen operator, the contractor who cleans the factory, the pensions consultant, all extend credit with no means of protection similar to that of the supplier of goods. It is their concern that the estate of an insolvent customer is maximised, since it is only from a dividend out of the estate that any recovery in the event of the customer's insolvency is possible.
. . .

Consultees' submissions and our recommendations

1624. Many who submitted evidence to us referred to the experience on the Continent of Europe. They argued that the wide use of reservation of title clauses there had virtually emasculated insolvency procedures as an effective remedy for unsecured creditors. There was nothing left in the estate for the unsecured creditors and the liquidator or his equivalent had nothing to administer.

1625. We recognise that the use of reservation of title clauses on the Continent is widespread and that in certain jurisdictions, particularly West Germany, the recoveries achieved by unsecured creditors in insolvencies are low. We do not think, however, that the Continental experience affords useful guidance in any consideration of the reform of our law. The Continental jurisdictions do not recognise the floating charge and their respective laws governing the sale of goods, the creation of trusts, equitable charges and liens are all substantially different from ours. Unfortunately, as we have indicated above, reservation of title and insolvency are highly technical areas and comparisons of experience in different jurisdictions are, in our view, superficial and misleading.

. . .

1627. Before we turn to the principal submissions which have been made to us on the subject of reservation of title, it is necessary to deal with one aspect of a large number of the submissions which we received. This was a cry for certainty. Consultee after consultee has put to us, either on the basis of an imaginative flair for a complicated example or from the experience of a difficult commercial case, a series of illustrations of commercial circumstances in which the position regarding the competing claims of supplier, debenture-holder, liquidator and others, in respect of goods supplied under a reservation of title clause is confused and unclear. The common refrain has been that there must be certainty, since otherwise there will be interminable and expensive litigation resolving a host of nice and difficult points.

1628. We believe that certainty is unobtainable except, perhaps by enactment covering the whole area of credit sales and security interests, and even that is doubtful and in any case is beyond our terms of reference. It necessarily follows from the wide variety of clauses imposing reservation of title which can be employed, the many different commercial circumstances in which goods can be supplied and used, and the present illogical and complex law relating to security in respect of goods, that perplexing and difficult problems will constantly arise. Nothing that we propose in relation to insolvency law can prevent this.

1629. In the main we believe, from the experience of the years following the *Romalpa*[1] decision, that the contesting parties will be able to negotiate their way to a commercial settlement without incurring the expense of litigating abstruse legal points. Where the parties cannot agree a settlement litigation must follow, but we cannot devise a comprehensive code which will provide a clear and certain solution to all the ingenious problems which have been raised in evidence to us.

1630. The principal submission made to us on the interaction of reservation of title clauses and insolvency was that all reservation of title clauses should be void in insolvency. The arguments adduced in favour of this submission may be summarised as follows.

1631. In the first place it was said to be misleading to those dealing with a company and extending credit to it that raw materials, stock in trade, work in progress and book debts apparently owned by it could, in the event of insolvency, be removed from it. This was similar to the misleading impression which could be given by an individual trader and led to the development of the reputed ownership provisions of the Bankruptcy Act. These provisions allowed the trustee to include in the bankrupt's estate goods apparently within his possession, order or disposition, notwithstanding that a legal title or interest was vested in a third party. Further, it was argued, anything which tends to a reduction in the estate of the insolvent available for the general body of unsecured creditors is undesirable.

1632. Secondly, it was suggested that it was in the interests of society and of employees that, whoever might be entitled to the proceeds arising from the sale or transfer of a business of an insolvent debtor, the business itself should be kept intact and made available for continuation by a third party. The seizure of goods sold to the insolvent on reservation of title terms would make much more difficult the task of a receiver seeking to maintain the business and rehabilitate it or sell it as a going concern.

1633. For the reasons set out in Chapter 23, we consider that the reputed ownership rule should be abrogated. So we do not find the analogy with that rule persuasive. But, more importantly, it seems to us that a reservation of title clause is in substance a means whereby a supplier obtains protection similar to that obtained by a formal security. It would be anomalous for us to countenance the continuation of security in its ordinary form of fixed or floating charge, but to deny the continuation of the quasi-security of the reservation of title clause. It is true that fixed and floating charges over goods fall to be registered whether the purchaser is an individual or a company, and this constitutes a difference from the reservation of title clause. Registration is a point to which we turn below, but generally, looking at insolvency law in the round, there is no sense and no logic in striking down one form of security but allowing others to remain.

1634. An additional consideration telling, in our view, powerfully against blanket avoidance of reservation of title clauses in insolvency is that in many cases where a company is in receivership, the effect of such a law would be primarily to benefit the owner of the floating charge. It would not greatly enhance the position of the

---

1 [1976] 1 WLR 676; [1976] 2 All ER 552

unsecured creditors even when regard is had to our proposals giving them a ten per cent stake in the realisations from the floating charge. It would be the receiver who would turn to the supplier and say, 'This company is insolvent. You cannot reclaim these goods. I will now sell them for the benefit of the debenture-holder'. Suppliers have opted for reservation of title clauses precisely because they seek to avoid the unfairness which results when they supply goods on credit, a floating charge crystallises, and a receiver then takes the goods and realises them for the benefit of the debenture-holder leaving the supplier with nothing. It seems to us that suppliers are entitled, in such circumstances, to take steps to protect themselves and that it would be wrong to deny them the protection they seek.

. . .

1637. There has been a wide unanimity of view among those who submitted evidence to us that, if practicable, some form of disclosure should be required. English law has always proceeded on the basis that freedom of contract should not be curtailed more than necessary, but that the parties having exercised that freedom may, in society's and other parties' interests, be obliged to disclose what they have done.

1638. The difficulty in requiring disclosure of the use of reservation of title clauses flows from the multitude of transactions involved. Clearly it would be a physical impossibility for a register to be kept recording the use of a reservation of title clause in every contract for the sale of goods. We believe, however, that the difficulties of registration can be exaggerated. The essence of the matter is that there should be shown against the name of the purchaser first the name of the supplier imposing reservation of title, secondly a generic description of the types or classes of goods being and to be supplied, and thirdly the maximum amount which at any one time can be secured by the reservation of title. Article 9 of the Uniform Commercial Code of the United States of America has introduced in all the States of the United States with the exception of Louisiana the practice of notice filing, which in our view could be adopted and tailored for use in this country and forms a helpful precedent.

1639. We have concluded that the absence of any provisions requiring disclosure of reservation of title clauses is unsatisfactory and should be remedied as soon as possible. We recognise that there will be formidable technical difficulties in drafting an effective provision, given the insistence of English law on categorising commercial contracts in the highly technical way to which we have referred. Nevertheless, substantial progress would be made — having regard to the ordinary course of business in most industries in this country — if a simple law were introduced applying both to insolvent companies and insolvent individuals and stating that where goods had been delivered pursuant to a contract for the sale of goods any clause reserving title to the goods themselves or any other property deriving directly or indirectly and wholly or in part from the goods, and not constituting or having effect as a charge or other encumbrance, should in the absence of due registration be void as against a liquidator, trustee, administrator or any other creditor.

1644. The second further submission concerns the nature and extent of the money claim for which a reservation of title clause may be used. It has been submitted that the interest of the seller under an effective and duly registered reservation of title clause should be limited to the price outstanding for the goods the subject-matter of the contract containing the clause.

1645. We agree with this submission. A reservation of title clause of the type in the *Romalpa case*, purporting to secure all sums outstanding from the purchaser to the supplier on whatever account, resembles an all-monies debenture granted to a bank. We believe that if a supplier seeks to secure the payment of monies in excess of the price outstanding for the goods he should do so by means of a charge, whether fixed or floating, and should accept the qualifications which we are proposing as regards the rights and powers of owners of fixed and floating charges. By restricting the protection of a reservation of title clause to the outstanding balance of the price due for the goods themselves the law will force sellers requiring wider protection to seek to obtain a charge.

PART V: REGISTRATION OF FLOATING CHARGES

Failure to Register

Failure to register a floating charge within the prescribed time renders the charge void as against the liquidator or a subsequent chargee, but the debt remains valid (CA 1985, s 395). Negligent chargees have sought to escape this consequence by asserting that their security was not a floating charge or other charge requiring registration, but another form of unregistrable security. See the *Yorkshire Woolcombers' Association*[1] and, below, Sources 263, 264, 265.

SOURCE 262
Re Kent and Sussex Sawmills Limited
(Chancery Division 1946, Wynn Parry J) [1947] Ch 177; [1946] 2 All ER 638

On 6 June 1944, the company entered into a contract with the Ministry of Fuel and Power[2] for the supply to the Ministry by the company of 30,000 tons of cut logs. The company approached their bankers, Westminster Bank Ltd, the respondents, for overdraft facilities in connexion with the carrying out of the contract. The bank was agreeable to provide those facilities on the terms that the company should write a letter to the Ministry of Fuel and Power, which it did under date 18 September 1944. The letter was addressed to the Ministry of Fuel and Power and after referring to the particular contract proceeded as follows: 'With reference to the above-mentioned contract, we hereby authorize you to remit all moneys due thereunder direct to this Company's account at Westminster Bank Ltd, Crowborough, whose receipt shall be your sufficient discharge. These instructions are to be regarded as irrevocable unless the said bank should consent to their cancellation in writing, and are intended to cover any extension of the contract in excess of 30,000 tons if such should occur.'
 ... On 12 February 1946, the company went into a creditors' voluntary liquidation. £30,000 then remained owing to the company under the two contracts while the company's overdraft with the bank at that date amounted to £83,674.

WYNN PARRY J: This summons comes before me, in which the liquidator asks for a declaration that the two letters[3] of authority constitute charges on the book debts of the company under section 79(2)(*e*) of the Companies Act 1929, and that, not having been registered under that section — as is admitted — they are void as against the applicant the liquidator.

---

1 [1903] 2 Ch 284 (see p 661)
2 Overshadowed somewhat by other events on that day — the D Day landings in Europe!
3 There was a second in substantially similar form

. . . That leaves the . . . point for consideration, namely, whether the transaction evidenced by the two letters of 18 September 1944, and 4 June 1945, respectively, amounted to an out-and-out assignment in each case of the whole of the company's beneficial interest in the proceeds of their respective contracts or whether in each case nothing more was effected than the hypothecation of the respective book debts by the company to the bank by way of security.

It is clear from the authorities that it is the duty of the court to come to a conclusion on what is the substance of the matter and for the sake of convenience I shall test this matter by reference solely to the language of the letter of 18 September 1944. On behalf of the liquidator, Mr Strangman, as his first point submitted that the proper conclusion is that in this letter there can be found no assignment at all, in which case *cadit quaestio.*

. . . I have to consider the effect . . . of the second paragraph, which opens with these words: 'These instructions are to be regarded as irrevocable unless the said bank should consent to their cancellation in writing.'

. . .

Effect must be given to those words and in my judgment the proper way of construing this letter, looking at it as a whole, is to bear in mind and never to lose sight of the circumstance that the relationship of the two parties in question, the company and the bank, was that of borrower and lender and that this letter was brought into existence in connexion with a proposed transaction of borrowing by the company and lending by the bank. So regarded, I think the opening words of the second paragraph fall naturally into the picture and that they must be regarded as having been introduced for the protection of the bank. But once that is admitted, it throws light upon the whole of the letter and serves to underline what is obviously equally the intention of the first paragraph, namely, to provide protection for the bank. . . . and to lead to the conclusion that I must treat this letter as amounting to an equitable assignment.

That, however, does not conclude the matter because I have then to investigate the question whether that assignment on its true construction is an out-and-out assignment of the whole of the benefit accruing or to accrue to the company under the contract or whether it is no more than an assignment by way of security. Here, again, I think the truth is to be found by bearing in mind the relationship between the parties. Prima facie, at any rate when one has to look at a document brought into existence between a borrower and a lender in connexion with a transaction of borrowing and lending, one must approach the consideration of that document with the expectation of discovering that the document is intended to be given by the borrower to the lender in order to secure repayment of a proposed indebtedness of the borrower to the lender.

Mr Buckley for the bank, however, has submitted, in a very attractive argument, that the true view of this matter, particularly when one regards the effect of payments made to a bank on behalf of a customer, is that this letter amounts to a sale by the company to the bank of the whole of the company's interest in the moneys due or to become due under a contract. He points out that the ultimate test of whether this can be said to amount to a security is that one must be able to discover on the face of the letter, either in express words or by necessary implication, an equity of redemption in the company and that, properly read, this letter discloses neither expressly nor by implication any such equity of redemption. As I say, I approach this matter more in the expectation of finding that the parties have brought into existence a document consistent with their relations of borrower and lender rather than finding that notwithstanding those relations they brought into existence a document in which their relationship changed to that of vendor and purchaser. In my judgment, by implication an equity of redemption is to be discovered in the language of the second paragraph. I can see no commercial business reason for the introduction of those words: 'These instructions are to be regarded as irrevocable unless the said bank should consent to their cancellation' except upon the basis that the parties did deliberately contemplate that circumstances might arise in which it might become desirable that a cancellation of the instructions should be given by the bank; but the existence of that previous paragraph appears to me to operate strongly to lead to the conclusion that there was nothing in the nature of a sale.

. . .

For these reasons I propose to declare in answer to question 1 of the summons that the two letters of authority which I have read constitute charges on the book debts of the company under section 79(2)(*e*) of the Companies Act 1929, and not having been registered under that section are void as against the appellant.

SOURCE 263
Re Molton Finance Ltd
(Court of Appeal 1968) [1968] Ch 325; [1967] 3 All ER 843

LORD DENNING MR: Early in 1965 a firm of stockbrokers, Victor Levett & Co, members of the London Stock Exchange, lent a sum of £15,000 to Theo Garvin Ltd, or to its subsidiary company, Molton Finance Ltd. They took as security some documents. Unfortunately the charge which they created was not registered within the 21 days required by section 95 of the Companies Act 1948 [now s 395]. On 9 July 1965, both companies went into liquidation. So the charge is void under the section. But it is contended here today, as it was before the judge, that nevertheless the stockbrokers have a lien on the documents as a separate and independent right apart from the charge which has been avoided.

. . .

In support of that argument, they rely on a passage in Halsbury's Laws of England, (3rd edn, vol 24 1958), p 143, which says: 'Where an equitable mortgage is created by deposit of title deeds, the mortgagee has a legal lien on the deeds deposited.' There is no authority cited in Halsbury for that proposition, but Mr Albery in his argument before us has sought to find support for it. He starts with the observations of Lord Eldon LC in *Ex parte Whitbread*[1] and goes on to the observations of the same judge in *Ex parte Kensington*;[2] followed by *Barnard v Bywater*,[3] before Giffard V-C, and *Re the General Provident Assurance Co*[4] before Malins V-C.

We have looked into all those authorities, and I must say I think they have no application here. It seems to me that when an equitable mortgage or charge is created by deposit of title deeds, there is an implied contract that the mortgagee or chargee may retain the deeds until he is paid. This implied contract is part and parcel of the equitable mortgage or charge. It is not a separate legal or common law lien. It has no independent existence apart from the equitable mortgage or charge. When the mortgage or charge is avoided for non-registration, then everything which is ancillary to it is avoided also. So this contractual right of retention is avoided too. It seems to me quite impossible to suppose that a separate lien is preserved after the charge has been avoided. In the course of the

---

1 (1812) 19 Ves 209; 34 ER 496
2 (1813) 2 V&B 79; 35 ER 249
3 (1868) 17 WR 71
4 (1869) 17 WR 514

argument Diplock LJ put this point to Mr Albery:[1] take a legal mortgage which has not been registered and is avoided for non-registration. Could the mortgagee claim to have a lien on the deeds? Mr Albery hesitated to go as far as to say he had a lien. He suggested that an equitable mortgagee might be in a better position than a legal mortgagee. That would be a strange result, so strange that it cannot be right. I am quite clearly of opinion that there is no separate or independent lien distinct from the charge itself. When the charge itself is avoided by the statute, it follows inexorably that the ancillary right of retention has also gone.

I am afraid, therefore, that the stockbrokers cannot retain these deeds. The liquidator has avoided the charge. He is entitled to have the deeds delivered up.

SOURCE 264
Re Wallis & Simmonds (Builders) Ltd
(Chancery Division 1974) [1974] 1 WLR 391; [1974] 1 All ER 561

TEMPLEMAN J: The title deeds to a property in London Road, Portsmouth, owned by Wallis & Simmonds (Builders) Ltd, ('the Wallis Co'), were deposited with the solicitors acting for W. E. Pinhorn (Builders) Ltd, ('the Pinhorn Co'), as security for £10,000. If, by that deposit of title deeds, the Wallis Co created a charge on the London Road property, then that charge was registrable under section 95 of the Companies Act 1948 and, not having been registered, is now void against the liquidator of the Wallis Co. The liquidator, Mr Michael Gordon Victor Radford, is the applicant in the present summons and appears by Mr McCulloch to argue that the Pinhorn Co cannot any way rely on the deposit of title deeds. Mr Nourse, who appears on behalf of the Pinhorn Co, the respondents to the summons, submits that the deposit of title deeds only created a lien on the documents; that the lien is not registrable, was at all times effective, and enabled the Pinhorn Co to retain the title deeds with all the nuisance value which that entails. In the alternative, he submits that if the deposit of the title deeds resulted in a charge on the London Road property, that charge was not created by the Wallis Co but took effect by operation of law and is not registrable under section 95 which only applies to a charge created by a company.

. . . Counsel agreed that as a general rule a deposit of title deeds to secure a debt operates as an equitable charge on the land of which the title deeds are the flag and indicia of title and ownership. Thus, in *Coote on Mortgages* (9th edn 1927), vol 1, p 86, there is this passage:

> 'A deposit of title deeds by the owner of freeholds or leaseholds with his creditor for the purpose of securing either a debt antecedently due, or a sum of money advanced at the time of the deposit, operates as an equitable mortgage or charge, by virtue of which the depositee acquires, not merely the right of holding the deeds until the debt is paid, but also an equitable interest in the land itself. A mere delivery of the deeds will have this operation without any express agreement, whether in writing or oral, as to the conditions or purpose of the delivery, as the court would infer the intent and agreement to create a security from the relation of debtor and creditor subsisting between the parties, unless the contrary were shown; and the delivery will be sufficient part performance of such agreement to take the case out of the statute . . .'

---

1 Counsel for the stockbrokers

Of course, the reference there to 'the statute' is a reference to section 40 of the Law of Property Act 1925.

There is a similar statement in *Halsbury's Laws of England*, (3rd edn, vol 27, 1959), p 168, and in particular it is said:

> 'A mere deposit of title deeds upon an advance, with intent to create a security thereon, but without a word passing, gives an equitable lien, so that, as between a debtor and creditor, the fact of possession of the title deeds raises the presumption that they were deposited by way of security . . .' and it is also stated [ibid.] that a deposit '. . . lets in evidence of an intention to create a charge which would otherwise be inadmissible, and raises a presumption of charge which throws upon the debtor the burden of rebutting it.'

Section 95(1) of the Companies Act 1948 [now s 395] renders a charge to which the section applies:

> '. . . so far as any security on the company's property or undertaking is conferred thereby . . . void against the liquidator and any creditor of the company, unless the prescribed particulars of the charge together with the instrument, if any, by which the charge is created or evidenced, are delivered to or received by the registrar of companies for registration in manner required by this Act within 21 days after the date of its creation, . . .'

and the section applies, inter alia, to a charge on land, wherever situate, or any interest therein. There was no registration in the present case, and it follows that if the Wallis Co created an equitable charge on the land, then that charge is void.

If the charge is void, the Pinhorn Co cannot claim that they have a separate lien which enables them to retain the title deeds and to exercise such power and control as the mere possession of the documents will give them; the charge and the lien will stand or fall together. That is made clear by the decision of the Court of Appeal in *Re Molton Finance Ltd.*[1]

. . .

There being, in my judgment, a charge, I must turn to Mr Nourse's[2] third alternative submission. He says that even if there is a charge it is not registrable because it was not created by the Wallis Co. He says it was created by law.

He relied on *London and Cheshire Insurance Co Ltd v Laplagrene Property Co Ltd.*[3] It was a case which had several complications. Brightman J decided that an unpaid vendor's lien was the creature of the law; that it did not depend on contract but on the fact that the vendor had a right to specific performance of his contract and that, accordingly, it was not registrable under section 95. Brightman J deals with the point:

> 'In a powerful argument, Mr Lightman, for the chargees, submitted that the unpaid vendor's lien was "created" by the purchaser; that it was therefore registrable if the purchaser were a company to which section 95 applied; that it would be consistent with the policy of the Act to treat such a lien as registrable, since the policy was that any person dealing with the company

1 [1968] Ch 325; [1967] 3 All ER 843 (see p 725)
2 Counsel for the depositee
3 [1971] Ch 499; [1971] 1 All ER 766

should know what charges existed; and that there is no decided case which precludes my holding that such a lien is registrable under section 95.'

Brightman J said:

'If the field had been completely open, I might have been more tempted to accept Mr Lightman's submission. But the enactment in question has been in force since the Companies Act 1908, and no one has suggested to me that it is the practice for a vendor to register an unpaid vendor's lien merely because he is selling to a company. If such a lien is registrable, the time for registration would expire 21 days after the exchange of contracts for sale, because it is at that date that the lien is *created*; it is not *created* on completion because the purchase price is unpaid, but is *discharged* on completion to the extent that the purchase money is paid: . . . In most cases, the 21-day period would expire well before completion because contracts for sale of land are not usually completed in three weeks. It would be a profound inconvenience, therefore, if every vendor to a company were compelled as a matter of course to register an unpaid vendor's lien on the exchange of contracts, on the off chance that circumstances might arise in the future which would render it desirable for the vendor to be able to rely on an unpaid vendor's lien. For my part, I am content to rely on the dictum of Harman LJ in the *Capital Finance*[1] case that an unpaid vendor's lien is the creature of the law; and that it does not depend upon contract, but upon the fact that the vendor has a right to specific performance of his contract. This was also the view expressed by Lawrence J in *In re Beirnstein*[2] "There is, in my opinion, an essential distinction between a mortgage and a vendor's lien: the former is a security upon real or personal property for the payment of a debt, or for the performance of an engagement, created by contract between the parties; whereas the latter is a charge arising by operation of law."'

Mr Nourse says that it is quite clear that Brightman J only rejected the argument that an unpaid vendor's lien was registrable because of the inconvenience that would be caused, but that logically there can be no distinction between an unpaid vendor's lien created by the law and held by the judge not to be registrable, and a charge created as a result of the presumption of law in the present instance. But in my judgment this is a contractual lien — it is said to be a contractual lien — and that makes all the difference. It is also a contractual charge; true it is that the charge arises by presumption, but it does not arise by operation of law. What the court does is to say: 'We shall not compel the parties to write down in so many words what the effect of the deposit of title deeds is; we shall simply assume that when they contract, and although they probably do not know the consequences, the person who takes the title deeds contracts not only to retain them but also to have an equitable charge on the land.' The presumption reads into the contract the charge which is implied. If that is right, the charge was created by the company and is therefore registrable under section 95. No such shorthand appears to be employed in the case of an unpaid vendor's lien, where the parties are directing their minds to something entirely different; but where, as here, there is a security for a loan and unless something is said and done the security consists of a lien and also the charge, then it seems to me that the charge, at any rate for the purposes of section 95, is created by the company

---

1 [1969] 1 Ch 261; [1968] 3 All ER 625
2 [1925] 1 Ch 12

and is therefore registrable. If I may turn round the inconvenience argument given by Brightman J in the *London and Cheshire case,* far from its being a profound inconvenience if the charge in the present case were registrable, it would be profoundly inconvenient if it were not, because the object of the section is to give information of incumbrances on the property of a company. If the company could deposit title deeds and create a charge which would not be registrable, then the mischief at which the section is aimed could be largely and easily avoided.

    . . . I conclude that the £10,000 was secured by an equitable charge on the land created by the Wallis Co. It is agreed that in those circumstances the charge must be void under section 95 and that the lien has no separate existence.

The Effect of the Registrar's Certificate (Sources 265 and 266)

SOURCE 265

Re Mechanisations (Eaglescliffe) Ltd
(Chancery Division 1964) [1966] Ch 20; [1964] 3 All ER 840

Two legal charges granted by the company to the National Benzole Company were registered under the provisions of s 95[1] of the Companies Act 1948 and a certificate of registration issued under section 98(2)[2] of that Act. The certificate, however, failed to reflect accurately the amount of money secured by the charges in that it omitted to include the fact that the charges were also to cover interest on the money advanced.

BUCKLEY J: . . . I can understand that an argument might be founded on sections 95 and 98 on the following lines. Section 95 requires certain particulars to be given to the registrar. Those particulars are obviously intended to be accurate particulars. Section 95 ought, therefore, to be read and construed as a section requiring the company to deliver in an accurate and complete form the particulars prescribed. Section 98(2) says that, when the registration has been effected and the registrar has issued his certificate, that certificate 'shall be conclusive evidence' that the requirements as to registration have been complied with: that is to say, it shall be conclusive evidence that the particulars delivered to the registrar are accurate particulars. That conclusive quality of the certificate is binding upon the mortgagee, who, therefore, cannot be heard to say that any of the particulars are inaccurate. If, therefore, the particulars state that the amount secured by the mortgage is something less than in fact the mortgage secures, the mortgagees are precluded by the effect of section 98(2) and the registrar's certificate from asserting that in fact they have got a security of as wide an extent as they have and are precluded from saying they are secured creditors for any greater amount than that stated in the particulars. But if that is true with regard to the amount specified in the particulars it must be equally true, it seems to me, of every other part of the particulars; and I think that the authority shows that that is not the true view of the operation of the section.

    I was referred to a decision of the Court of Appeal in *National Provincial and Union Bank of England v Charnley.*[3] In that case a company had created a charge over certain leasehold property and certain movable chattels. The form in which the charge was expressed was this. The company 'demised' to the mortgagees the

---

1 Now s 395 of the Companies Act 1985
2 Now s 401(2) of the Companies Act 1985
3 [1924] 1 KB 431; 93 LJKB 241

leasehold property with all the movable 'plant used in or about the premises' for a long term of years. The charge was duly submitted for registration. In the particulars of the charge which were submitted to the registrar the instrument was described as a mortgage of the leasehold premises, no mention being made of the chattels. The registrar entered the description of the instrument in the register in similar terms, identifying it by date, but omitting any mention of any charge on the chattels. Subsequently a judgment creditor sought to levy execution on the chattels. The mortgagees, the bank, claimed the goods in question, under their mortgage. The question, therefore, was whether in these circumstances the mortgagees were entitled to claim to be secured creditors with a charge upon the chattels notwithstanding that they were not referred to either in the particulars submitted to the registrar or in the register of charges. The court first of all held that upon its true construction the document in question did create a charge on the chattels notwithstanding that the word 'demise' was not a very apt method of attempting to charge chattels, and it then went on to consider the effect of the history of the registration of the charge.

Bankes LJ, after saying that the mortgage must be regarded as one indivisible transaction and that it could not be treated as distinct and separate charges of the leaseholds and the chattels, said:

> 'It is not disputed, as I understand it, that the object of the legislature in requiring delivery to the registrar of the instrument as well as the particulars is to enable him to form an independent judgment in reference to what he ought to put on the register before he in fact registers it, and if he is entitled to do that, being only human, he may make a mistake, and if he makes a mistake and enters on the register something different from what the particulars really justify, the unfortunate person carrying in those particulars will, according to [the submission of counsel] find himself possessed of a void instrument, because the register, which, as I understand [counsel's] argument, is the conclusive document, does not contain true particulars of the instrument.'

Then he says that he agrees with the judgments in an earlier case *Re Yolland, Husson & Birkett Ltd*,[1] and he goes on to say: 'I think the object' — that is to say the object of the provisions of the Act relating to the operation of the registrar's certificate:

> 'is to protect the grantee of the charge, and, as between him and the general body of creditors or prospective creditors, the registrar is appointed as the tribunal to decide what shall be put upon the register, and when it has been put there his certificate to that effect is conclusive evidence that all the requirements of the section have been complied with.'

Then he refers to the circumstances of the particular case and says:

> 'It is quite true that there is an omission, because the property mortgaged or charged included chattels as well as land and fixtures; but when once the registrar has given his certificate that the registration was complete, and that the mortgage or charge was created by an instrument, identifying it, in my opinion you have to go to the instrument to see what was actually charged, there being nothing in the statute which says that when once registration has taken place the register shall be the evidence of the extent of the charge. All that the statute requires is satisfaction on the part of the appointed

---

1 [1908] 1 Ch 152; 77 LJ Ch 43

official that the preliminaries have been complied with, and, when once he certifies that, the parties are entitled to ask the court to say that what it has to look at in order to determine their rights is the instrument creating the mortgage or charge.'

Scrutton LJ dealt with the matter in these terms:

'The result of the legislation as it appears to me is that if the document sent in for registration does contain a charge on particular property, even if the company sending it in has misstated that charge, or the registrar considering it judicially has misunderstood it, when once the certificate has been given the grantees are safe. Though one can see that this may cause great hardship to a person who gives credit to the company in reliance on a defective register, one can also see that equal hardship would be caused to secured creditors if their security was to be upset for reasons connected with the action of persons over whom they had no control.'

Atkins LJ, the third member of the court said:

'There may well be a question whether all the strict requirements of that section as to registration were complied with in respect of the particulars and the form of the register, for neither the particulars nor the register contain any reference to the charge upon the chattels, and anybody examining the register would be led to assume that the charge only covered the hereditaments. But that does not determine the question, because of the provisions of subsection (5). It appears to me to be the true view that when once such a certificate has been given by the registrar in respect to a particular specified document which in fact creates a mortgage or charge, it is conclusive that the mortgage or charge so created is properly registered, even though the particulars put forward by the person applying for registration are incomplete, and the entry in the register by the registrar is defective. That I think follows from *Re Yolland, Husson & Birkett.'*

The condition contained in section 95(1) has nothing to do with the entry in the register: it is that the prescribed particulars, together with the instrument creating the charge, shall have been delivered to the registrar: once that has been done the condition contemplated by the subsection has been satisfied. The effect of section 98(2) appears to me to be that when the registrar gives his certificate it is to be evidence in fact not only that he, the registrar, has entered the particulars in the register of charges, but also that the steps preliminary thereto have been carried out, that is to say that the prescribed particulars have been presented to him. If the prescribed particulars have been presented to him, then it follows that the charge is not avoided, and the effect of the certificate is to put it out of anybody's power to say that the prescribed particulars have not been presented to him and, therefore, where a certificate has been given the charge cannot be void under section 95(1).

In order to discover the terms and effect of the charge (as was pointed out in the passages I have read from the judgments in *National Provincial and Union Bank of England v Charnley*) one must look at the document creating the charge and not at the register. It is from that document that one will discover what moneys are secured and what is the total amount secured by the charge.

It is perhaps just worth noticing that section 98(2) does not say that the certificate shall be conclusive evidence that the amount thereby stated to be secured by the charge is in fact the amount secured by the charge: it is only conclusive evidence that the requirements as to registration have been complied with; and although no doubt the legislature contemplated that when particulars are submitted to the registrar they will be accurate and that when the registrar makes entries in the register he will have checked the accuracy of such particulars against the instrument which he has for that purpose, the legislature has not made accuracy in that respect a condition of the validity of the charge. As was pointed out by Scrutton LJ in the passage I read from his judgment, this may in certain circumstances cause hardship if there is any inaccuracy. But the Lord Justice does not seem to have thought that any such inaccuracy could in any way affect the validity of the charge itself, once the process of registration has gone through and the registrar has given his certificate.

For these reasons it seems to me that in the present case the mortgagees are entitled to rely upon their principal mortgage and their further charges as conferring upon them a valid security for the full amounts due under those documents according to their tenor, and I think, therefore, that the application fails.

The application was by the liquidator for a declaration that the charges were void against him as to the amount secured in excess of that stated in the Registrar's certificate.

SOURCE 266
Re C L Nye Ltd
[1971] 1 Ch 442; [1970] 3 All ER 1061

The company was granted a loan and overdraft facilities by a bank and gave security over its premises in respect therefor. The bank's solicitor failed to file the particulars of the charge for registration within the requisite 3-week period. Some months later, he inserted a later date as the date on which the charge was created, and on the strength of that, the charge was duly registered. The company went into liquidation shortly afterwards; the Registrar issued a certificate under s 98(2)[1] as to due compliance with the requirements for registration of the change. This was an appeal by the liquidator against the refusal by the judge below for a declaration that the charge was void against him for want of registration.

> HARMAN LJ [after discussing *Charnley's* case[2] and *Re Mechanisations*[3] continued] In *Re Eric Holmes (Property) Ltd*[4] Pennycuick J held that even though the particulars delivered to the registrar with the application incorrectly stated the date of the charge, the certificate once granted was conclusive evidence that the Act had been complied with.
>
> That last case is exactly in point here but of course is not binding upon us. The judge [below] merely said that the case bore a superficial resemblance to the present but I confess I do not follow him in that particular.
>
> In the *Eric Holmes case* Mr Slade appeared for the liquidator and argued in the same sense as he argues here, namely, that while the certificate is conclusive as to the correctness of its contents it is not conclusive as to the date of its creation and that *Charnley's case* was thus distinguishable. This argument was based in part at least on the view that where there is an instrument creating the charge which is

---

1 Now s 401(2) of the Companies Act 1985
2 [1924] 1 KB 431; 93 LJKB 241
3 [1966] Ch 20; [1964] 3 All ER 840 (see p 729)
4 [1965] Ch 1052; [1965] 2 All ER 333

available to the registrar he can check the correctness of the particulars, but he has no such means where the date of the creation is concerned. This argument does not survive the test where the charge is created without any instrument at all and therefore none can be delivered to the registrar. In my judgment the certificate must be conclusive and not merely conclusive in part as the liquidators argue. The whole point of creating the register under section 95 is to give security to persons relying on the certificate. If it were possible to go behind the certificate and show that the date of the creation of the charge made it out of time, no lender on the faith of the charge could be secure and sure that it would not thereafter be attacked by somebody who could successfully prove that there was in fact an interval of more than 21 days between the charge's creation and its registration. This would be disastrous in my opinion and is not a view to be taken unless the language positively compels it. I find no such compulsion and see no reason why the word 'conclusive' should not mean what it says. The legislature in 1900 imposed on limited liability companies the obligation to disclose the charges they created. This was to the great advantage of the unsecured creditors but a limit was put to that advantage by giving a responsible official the right to judge whether all the prescribed particulars were in order. Once he has done this, in order they are, even though the company has misstated them or the registrar has taken a wrong view.

Mr Slade's argument was that it was a condition precedent to the registration of a charge by the registrar that the particulars should have been delivered to him in time and that if that were not done he had no jurisdiction and the registration was a mere nullity. I cannot accept this view. The duty to register the prescribed particulars is put on the registrar; the date of the creation of the charge is one of the particulars he is required to enter and if he is not in a position to investigate the matter further but acts on the particulars furnished by the applicant company that is the end of the matter. *Charnley's case* is indistinguishable from the present. The certificate is no less conclusive as to date than as to amount and to hold otherwise would frustrate the whole purpose of the legislature.

As to the maxim on which the judge decided the case, namely, that no man may take advantage of his own wrong I refer to *Re London Celluloid Co*[1] in which I find the following passage from Bowen LJ's judgment:

> 'The maxim that no man can take advantage of his own wrong must be carefully considered, and expressed in more precise terms, before it can be safely applied. It means that a man cannot enforce against another a right arising from his own breach of contract or breach of duty. The observations of Baron Bramwell in *Hooper v Lane*[2] on this subject are very instructive.'

Then Bowen LJ inquires 'What is the wrong here?' and he goes on in the middle of p 206:

> 'To return to the maxim that a man cannot take advantage of his own wrong, we can see the point where it ceases to be applicable. Construing the maxim as I have said, the first question is, has the right to demand payment in cash been acquired through the breach of contract in question? Was it through non-registration of the contract that the liability to pay in cash arose? In my opinion it was not.'

---

1 (1888) 39 Ch D 190; 57 LJ Ch 843
2 (1856) 6 HLC 443; 10 ER 1368

The wrong here must be that the bank has got a priority against unsecured creditors by giving a misleading statement to the registrar. Who then are those creditors? They can be none other than persons who gave credit to the company between the end of April 1964, when the charge should have been registered and 3 July when it was registered. After the latter date no one was misled. There is no evidence in this case that there were any such creditors and I cannot in these circumstances see that any case has been proved. I would therefore hold that the liquidators have not been on this ground, any more than on the others which I have discussed, entitled to the relief which they ask.

I would allow the appeal.

RUSSELL LJ: At the outset I will assume without deciding (a) that a charge on the property was created at latest on 9 March; (b) that the solicitor, Mr Bland, was acting exclusively for the chargee bank and (c) that no relevantly new or different charge was created on 29 June when the legal estate in the property became vested in the company. We thus have a situation in which the 21 days referred to in section 95 of the Companies Act 1948, had elapsed by 1 April.

. . .

It seems to me that section 98(2) should be taken as meaning what it says. There is good reason for this. Section 95 puts into a charge by a company a weakness; this weakness limits a chargee of the company in dealing with his charge; it is to be expected that the group of sections should not sterilise a chargee of a company in dealing with his charge; it is therefore to be expected that the group of sections should provide in absolute terms for a marketable security, which cannot be achieved unless the certificate of the registrar is in every respect conclusive and unassailable. Moreover it is to be noticed that until recently registration under the Companies Act 1948, was equivalent (for purposes of priority) to registration under the Land Charges Act 1925. This seems to me to make it improbable in the highest degree that registration under the Companies Act (with a certificate) should be regarded as a nullity in any circumstances; as against the company (as distinct from the liquidator) the priority depends upon registration initially under the Land Charges Act.

It may well be that if a chargee fraudulently deceives the registrar, a creditor personally damaged by the fraud can take proceedings in personam. This was hinted at in the *Charnley case*. But this could only relate, in a case such as the present, if there had been fraud, to someone who had extended credit between 1 April 1964, and the date of registration. As to this there is no evidence.

It was also suggested that this is a case for rectification under section 101 of the Act [now s 404] by deleting the whole registration. In my judgment this is not available under section 101. Under that section the court may rectify an omission by adding, or rectify a misstatement by correcting. It cannot delete a whole registration. The authority which says that a note of payment off of a charge may be deleted is nothing to the contrary. Indeed the lack of ability under section 101 to expunge a registration of a charge is strong support for the contrary view to that advanced by the liquidator.

I turn last to the ground upon which Plowman J in fact decided the case against the bank. This was that the bank (through the solicitor) put the wrong date on the charge, and that if the correct date had been put on it, 9 March, the registrar would not have registered the charge nor of course issued a certificate.

His view was that the law, according to Broom's maxim, forbade a man to make a profit from his own wrong, and that the application of this maxim prevented the bank from relying on the statutory provision that made the certificate of the registrar conclusive evidence that there had been no error and nothing wrong. The liquidator was prepared to support this view on the footing that the relevant wrong must involve a breach of duty. But I ask myself: What was the duty of which the bank (through its solicitor) was in breach? If it was the statutory duty to produce accurate particulars in time, this seems to me to be exactly the matter that the certificate was designed to override, as I have already indicated. What then was the duty to the liquidators and other creditors? It might be said that there was a duty not wilfully to set out to deceive the registrar. But that was not this case. I am unable to accept that there was a duty not to make an honest mistake — even an ill-informed honest mistake. Moreover the application of the maxim to this case seems to me to run counter to the decision of this court in the *Charnley* case. In that case, though the registrar had the means available to him to ascertain by careful inspection of the document of charge that the particulars submitted by the chargee were incorrect in omitting reference to movable chattels (as indeed so had a creditor), there can be no doubt that the omission from the registration and certificate of the registrar were directly attributable to the careless error of the chargee. But that made no difference to the outcome, or to the effective conclusive validity of the certificate. Plowman J considered that *Charnley's case* did not touch the present point. In this I respectfully consider that he erred.

Accordingly in my judgment the certificate of the registrar demonstrates that in law (contrary to the facts and law which I am prepared, without deciding, to assume) the bank has a valid security against the liquidator, and the appeal should be allowed.

SOURCE 267
Power v Sharp Investments
[1994] 1 BCLC 111

SIR CHRISTOPHER SLADE: . . . According to the evidence of Sharp's solicitor, Sharp, which had already made substantial advances to Shoe Lace, subsequently advanced to Shoe Lace £300,000 on 3 April, £50,000 in May, £75,000 in June and £11,500 on 16 July 1990.

At last, on 24 July 1990, the debenture was executed, signed by Mr Nolan on behalf of Shoe Lace and by Mr Nugent, a director of Sharp, on its behalf.

. . .

On 3 September 1990, at a meeting of the directors of Shoe Lace, it was resolved that they should 'immediately attempt to dispose of the assets of the company in the most efficient manner in order to generate cash to meet the claims of all creditors'. At that meeting Mr Nolan resigned as a director of Shoe Lace with immediate effect. On 4 September 1990, a petition was presented for its compulsory winding up. It was served at the company's trading address on the same day and was duly served on its registered office on 11 September 1990.

On 13 September 1990, Shoe Lace entered into a 'Sale of Business Agreement' (the sale agreement) whereby it sold the retail part of its business, together with stock, fixtures, fittings and equipment to Shoe Hut Ltd, described by the judge as 'another Channel Island company'. The consideration for the purchase was £211,000 of which £41,000 was expressed to be allocated to the immovable property and £5,000 to the goodwill. On completion of the sale agreement, on 13 September 1990, Shoe Hut Ltd paid direct to Sharp the sum of £180,710 in recognition of the rights asserted by Sharp as debenture holder. The balance was retained by Shoe Hut Ltd in respect of part of a stock of shoes to which a third party, named EF Clasters Ltd, claimed title.

On 20 November 1990, Shoe Lace was compulsorily wound up. On the next day, Mr D J Power was appointed its liquidator. He instituted proceedings against Sharp and Mr Mahtani seeking, inter alia, a declaration that the debenture was invalid.

. . .

Another significant issue raised by the liquidator's claim was an assertion that the debenture was a wrongful preference, in that it purported to create Sharp a secured creditor of Shoe Lace in prejudice to the position of all other creditors of Shoe Lace. The judge, however, found it unnecessary to decide these other issues because the principal ground upon which the liquidator founded his application was that the floating charge created by the debenture was invalidated by s 245 of the Insolvency Act (the 1986 Act).

. . .

In the present case the winding up commenced on 4 September 1990, the date of presentation of the petition (s 129(2) of the 1986 Act).

The judge held, and it is now common ground, that in the present case:

(1) the floating charge created by the debenture dated 24 July 1990 was created within a period of merely two months before 'the onset of insolvency' (4 September 1990);

(2) this floating charge was therefore created at 'a relevant time';

(3) at the date of creation, Shoe Lace was 'unable to pay its debts' within the meaning of s 123 of the 1986 Act;

(4) the floating charge was therefore invalid, except to the extent of 'the value of so much of the consideration for the creation of the charge as consists of money paid . . . to the company at the same time as, or after, the creation of the charge'.

In the circumstances, the judge said that the only real issue was whether any of the payments alleged to have been made by Sharp between early April and 16 July 1990 could be said to have been made 'at the same time as' the execution of the debenture. He held that none of these payments could be so described. He concluded ([1992] BCLC 636 at 640):

> 'For the purpose of obtaining an interim payment, the applicant must show a case of a strength justifying judgment under RSC Ord 14. This is subject to RSC Ord 14A, which enables the court to decide a question of law if it appears suitable for determination without full trial and such determination will finally dispose of an issue in the case. I think that the construction of s 245 is something which can be decided without a full trial of the liquidator's summons and that the determination will finally dispose of the question of the validity of the floating charge because it means that even on the respondent's own evidence, the charge must be invalid. . . .'

. . . it is submitted that the judge erred in concluding that none of the payments alleged to have been made by Sharp to Shoe Lace between early April and 16 July 1990 can be said to have been made 'at the same time' as the execution of the debenture, within the meaning of s 245 of the 1996[1] Act. Since the debenture was not executed until 24 July 1990, the judge's conclusion would, at first sight, appear difficult to challenge. As he recognised, however, two earlier authorities demonstrate or suggest that a bare reference to the calendar may not necessarily provide the right answer to this crucial question of time. Since these two earlier cases formed the sheet anchor of Mr Briggs's argument on his first

---

1 [*sic*], clearly 1986

ground of appeal, I think it will be necessary to review in some detail both the decisions themselves and their legislative background.

A predecessor of s 245, namely s 212 of the Companies (Consolidation) Act 1908 (the 1908 Act) provided:

> 'Where a company is being wound up, a floating charge on the undertaking or property of the company created within three months of the commencement of the winding up shall, unless it is proved that the company immediately after the creation of the charge was solvent, be invalid, except to the amount of any cash paid to the company at the time of or subsequently to the creation of, and in consideration for, the charge . . .'

The purpose of this provision was described by Parker J in *Re Orleans Motor Co Ltd* [1911] 2 Ch 41 at 45 as being —

> 'to prevent companies on their last legs from creating floating charges to secure past debts or for moneys which do not go to swell their assets and become available for creditors.'

It had to be read and applied alongside another provision in the 1908 Act which was designed (broadly) to prevent persons claiming to be secured creditors of a company on its liquidation unless other creditors had been given the opportunity to acquire notice of the relevant charge by its registration. Section 93 of the 1908 Act provided that a charge created by a company and falling within various specified descriptions, including a floating charge, should, so far as any security on the company's property or undertaking was thereby conferred, be void against the liquidator and any creditor of the company unless the prescribed particulars of the charge were registered within 21 days after the date of its creation.

In *Re Jackson & Bassford Ltd* [1906] 2 Ch 467 at 476–477, Buckley J drew an important distinction between two classes of case, namely (a) an agreement to give security which was 'so expressed as to create a present equitable right to a security' and was thus registrable; (b) an agreement to give security which was so expressed as to be 'merely an agreement that in some future circumstances a security shall in the future be created', (which would not require registration).

As to class (a), it should be observed that in equity a floating charge is created by a contract evidenced in writing and for valuable consideration to execute, when required, a formal mortgage by way of floating charge: (see 32 Halsbury's Laws of England (4th edn) paras 437 and 439). If the floating charge relates to a limited company's property or undertaking, it is registrable.

In *re Columbian Fireproofing Co Ltd* [1910] 1 Ch 758, the directors of a company on 25 November 1909 accepted an offer by S to advance £1,000 upon the security of all the property of the company and passed a resolution that a debenture to be prepared by S should be executed at the next board meeting. S, relying on the resolution, then paid £350, and on 2 December 1909 a further £350 to the company on account of the £1,000. At the next board meeting, on 6 December 1909, the debenture was duly executed. S then paid the balance of £300 to the company and registered the debenture on 23 December 1909. The company went into liquidation in January 1910 and the liquidator disputed the validity of the debenture. His counsel, in the course of argument, referred to *Re Jackson & Bassford Ltd*. He submitted, in effect that the debenture holder was on the horns of a dilemma. Either the resolution of 25 November created a present equitable charge, in which case, not having been registered within the due time, it was void against the liquidator under s 93 of the 1908 Act. Alternatively, if that resolution merely constituted an agreement that at some future time a charge would be given, then the two sums of £350 were advanced not 'at the time of' but before the creation of the security. Neville J, in giving judgment, by necessary inference rejected the submission that the resolution created a present equitable charge. He expressly held that the whole £1,000 was advanced 'at the time of the creation of the charge'. He said ([1910] 1 Ch 758 at 765):

> 'I think whether any particular payment comes within these words must always be a question of fact depending upon the circumstances of the particular case. The word "time" in this connection must always be to some extent indefinite, for the creation of the security and the payment of the money cannot be simultaneous.'

He went on to say:

> 'I think that a payment made on account of the consideration for the security, in anticipation of its creation and in reliance on a promise to execute it, although made some days before its execution, is made at the time of its creation within the meaning of the section.'

The Court of Appeal ([1910] 2 Ch 120) endorsed Neville J's judgment without qualification, both as to the point based on s 93 of the 1908 Act and as to that based on s 212. In the latter context, Cozens Hardy MR said this (at 123):

> 'It was conceded by counsel for the appellant that the word "at" does not mean contemporaneously with or immediately in exchange for the security or at the same moment as the security itself is created. It is a question of fact under all the circumstances of the case.'

Farwell LJ said (at 122):

> 'In my opinion it would be disastrous if we were to strain the words of a provision like this in order to invalidate bona fide honest transactions carried out in accordance with the usual course of business. It is plain to my mind that any cash paid to the company "at the time" cannot mean on the stroke of the clock or even within the same twenty-four hours. As Neville J has justly remarked, it is not a question of the clock: it is a question of what are the circumstances of each particular case.'

The *Columbian Fireproofing* case was one where the formal instrument was executed within 11 days from the date of the agreement and was registered 17 days after that. In some later cases, however, the delay has been much greater. In *Re F & E Stanton Ltd* [1929] 1 Ch 180, moneys were advanced in reliance on a promise to execute debentures creating a floating charge on the company's property by way of security. No less than 54 days elapsed after the first advance, and 5 days after the last advance, before the debentures were actually executed on 20 January 1926. The company went into liquidation on 25 January 1926. Maugham J, in giving judgment, referred to *Re Columbian Fireproofing Co Ltd* and cited the second of the passages from Neville J's judgment quoted above. He continued ([1929] 1 Ch 180 at 193–194):

> 'I have not a doubt here, as I have already said, that the payments were made on account of the consideration and in anticipation of its creation and in reliance on a promise to execute, and the real difficulty is whether the lapse of time which took place between that promise and between the payments made in reliance on that promise and the actual date of the issue of the debentures is so long that I ought to hold that the exception in the section does not apply. In that matter I have two other cases which seem to help me to some extent. One is an Irish case of *Re Olderfleet Shipbuilding Co* ([1922]

1 IR 26), and the other is an unreported case of *Re Nathan, Hope & Son Ltd*, where the judgment of Romer J was delivered on June 5, 1924. I have had the advantage of reading a shorthand note of the judgment in that case. In both of those cases there was a substantial delay between the dates of the payment in reliance on the promise to issue the debentures and the date upon which the debentures were secured, and, in fact in the case before Romer J, there was a delay of not less than sixty-seven days after the first advance and fifteen days after the last advance, before the issue of the debentures. In the present case the delay is serious, but not so serious as that . . . Now I am myself strongly of opinion that the exception in s 212 in regard to cash advances at the time will not avail the debenture holder if the delay in the issue of the debenture is one which he has himself procured or suggested, or if the delay is one in which he has in any true sense acquiesced. I am not thinking of a delay such as would ordinarily be necessary for the passing of the resolution and the consideration of the form of the debenture and its actual execution, because the four or five days necessary in most cases to do those things is clearly not a delay which, according to the authority of the first case I have mentioned, the *Columbian Fireproofing* case ([1910] 1 Ch 758 at 765), would be sufficient to invalidate the debentures if the cash had been or was being paid. But I think a delay greater than that requires explanation. In the present case I think there is sufficient explanation in the circumstances which I have mentioned, and I come to the conclusion as a fact that the delay was not acquiesced in by either [of the debenture holders].'

Maugham J concluded that, as a matter of fact, the sums in question were paid, within the true meaning of s 212 of the 1908 Act, 'at the time of the creation of the charge and in consideration for the charge'.

In the present case, Hoffmann J expressed his conclusions thus ([1992] BCLC 636 at 638–639):

'There is no authority upon the meaning of "at the same time as" in s 245. The degree of contemporaneity which such words connote must depend upon the context . . . In s 245, the context is commercial and regulatory. For example, it forms part of a scheme which includes the requirement that particulars of a floating charge must be delivered to the registrar of companies within 21 days of its creation. The question, I think, is whether a businessman having knowledge of the kind of time limits imposed by the Insolvency and Companies Acts and using ordinary language would say that the payments had been made at the same time as the execution of the debenture. In my judgment no businessman would use such language of the payments made in this case. He would say (taking the respondent's evidence at face value) that the parties had agreed in March that a debenture should be granted, that a number of payments were made in consideration of that promise, but that for one reason or another, they did not get round to executing the debenture until afterwards. The respondent's solicitor Mr Pugh says that it was not executed earlier because Mr Nolan, who was a director of both Sharp and Shoe Lace, was dilatory. He thought that as Shoe Lace had agreed to grant the debenture, there was no urgency about its execution. In other words, he had not read s 245.'

Later in this judgment, after reference to the authorities, the judge said (at 640):

'I mention these cases but I derive no principle from them except that stated by the Court of Appeal in *Columbian Fireproofing*, namely that the question is one of fact, or more precisely, whether the language of the statute appropriately describes the facts of the particular case. So far as the language of s 245 of the Insolvency Act 1986 differs from that of the 1908 Act, I think that the words "at the same time as" only emphasise that contemporaneity is an objective matter. If I am wrong about this and need to look at the reasons for the delay, it seems to me that Sharp (through Mr Nolan) acquiesced in the delay by Shoe Lace (through Mr Nolan) in executing the debenture.'

Mr Briggs submitted that Hoffmann J erred in his approach to the problem, and in his conclusion. The new wording in s 245 of the 1986 Act 'at the same time as, or after the creation of a charge' is not, in his submission, materially different from the old wording 'the amount of any cash paid to the company at the time of or subsequently to the creation of . . . the charge' which appeared in s 212 of the 1908 Act and much more recently in s 322(1) of the Companies Act 1948 ('the 1948 Act'); thus, he said, the new wording does not represent an 'emphasis on [objective] contemporaneity'. The judge, it was said, was wrong to take the relevant test as being how an informed businessman would view the matter. The correct starting point in construing the relevant wording is to prevent a valid charge being given to secure a past debt in respect of which there has been no promise to give a charge and which does not go to swell the company's assets. With this purpose in mind, the court must look at the real substance of the transaction, and if the payment is, in Neville J's words made —

'on account of the consideration for the security, in anticipation of its creation and in reliance on a promise to execute it, although made some days before its execution,'

it is made 'at the same time as the creation of the charge' within the meaning of s 245(2)(a) of the 1986 Act (see [1910] 1 Ch 758 at 765). Mr Briggs naturally relied strongly on the decisions of Neville J and the Court of Appeal in the *Colombian Fireproofing* case. He also referred us to a recent decision in *Re Fairway Magazines Ltd, Fairbairn v Hartigan* [1993] BCLC 643 where Mummery J, to whom the decision of Hoffmann J in the present case had been cited, expressed the view that 'although the language of s 245(2)(a) is different from the earlier provisions, the approach to be adopted is that adopted in the earlier cases'.

Hoffmann J, as has already appeared, stated in his judgment that, if he were wrong about the construction of the words 'at the same time as' in s 245 and (in the light of Maugham J's judgment in *Re F & E Stanton Ltd*) it was necessary to look at the reasons for the delay, Sharp (through Mr Nolan) had acquiesced in the delay by Shoe Lace (through Mr Nolan) in executing the debenture.

Mr Briggs sought leave to adduce to this court in evidence an affidavit sworn by Mr Mahtani on 18 February 1993 (which we read de bene esse), the gist of which was that Mr Nolan had no authority from Mr Mahtani or his brothers as effective controllers of Sharp, to delay the execution of the debenture or to permit Sharp to advance moneys before its execution. In broad terms, Mr Briggs submitted that the court should not adopt a strict construction of s 245 which would make it more difficult for companies to emerge from financial difficulties by raising money on security; that the sums in question in the present case, when advanced, were new money which swelled Shoe Lace's assets and became available for its creditors; that since they were paid with the intention that the payment and the creation of the charge would be simultaneous, they must be treated as having been paid 'at the same time as or after the creation of the charge' within s 245; and that if there was any delay in implementing that intention, the delay was on the facts excusable.

Since the relevant wording of s 245 of the 1986 Act is different from that of its statutory predecessors, such as s 212 of the 1908 Act and s 322 of the 1948 Act, it is common ground that decisions relating to the wording of those predecessors are not binding on this court on this appeal. Nevertheless, I for my part can see little or no material difference between the words 'at the time of or subsequently to the creation of . . .' in the old section and the words 'at the same time as, or after the creation of the charge' in the new section. If, therefore, the approach to the problem adopted by Neville J and the Court of Appeal in *Columbian Fireproofing* was correct in relation to the earlier sections, I could see no sufficient reason for declining to follow it in applying s 245.

In my judgment, however, with all due respect, that approach was wrong. As has been seen, it was based on the proposition that a 'payment made on account of the consideration for the security, in anticipation of its creation and in reliance on a promise to execute it . . . is made at the time of its creation within the meaning of the section'. As Hoffmann J observed, the proposition appears to treat the question whether the advance was in consideration for the charge as determinative of whether it was made 'at the time of the charge'. In my judgment, this cannot be correct. The words 'at the time of, or subsequently to the creation of . . . the charge' in s 212 of the 1908 Act (just as the words 'at the same time as, or after, the creation of the charge' in s 245 of the 1986 Act) were clearly included by the legislature for the purpose of excluding from the exemption the amount of moneys paid to the company before the creation of the charge, even though they were paid in consideration for the charge; on any other construction these words would have been mere surplusage. Though the distinction was brought to their attention in argument, both courts in *Columbian Fireproofing*, in my judgment, failed to pay due regard to the crucially important distinction between the two classes of case mentioned by Buckley J in *Re Jackson & Bassford* [1906] 2 Ch 467. In a case where the promise to execute a debenture creates a present equitable right to a security, and moneys are advanced in reliance on it, the delay between the advances and the execution of the formal instrument of charge is immaterial; the charge has already been created and is immediately registrable, so that other creditors of the company will have had the opportunity to learn of its existence; the temporal requirements of the relevant exemptions contained in s 212 of the 1908 Act and s 245 of the 1986 Act will be satisfied. In a case where the promise to execute a debenture does not create any such present equitable right, the situation is quite different. In that situation the existence of the promise is, in my judgment, irrelevant for the purpose of applying s 245 of the 1986 Act and also the statutory provisions governing the registration of charges. In the latter situation, I do not, for my part, see how the relevant temporal requirements of the exemption contained in s 212 of the 1908 Act or s 245 of the 1986 Act can be satisfied if the making of the advance precedes the formal execution of the debenture by any time whatsoever, unless the interval is so short that it can be regarded as de minimis — for example a 'coffee-break'.

Maugham J in *Stanton* recognised that the requirements relating to time and consideration imposed by s 212 of the 1908 Act were separate requirements. In the passage from his judgment quoted above, however, he appears to have considered that a debenture holder could avail himself of the statutory exemption relating to cash advances, even though they were made before the execution of the debenture, if either (a) the delay in such execution was no more than 'would ordinarily be necessary for the passing of the resolution and the consideration of the form of the debenture and its actual execution,' or (b) the delay was not one which the debenture holder had himself procured or suggested or in which he had in any true sense acquiesced. (See [1929] 1 Ch 180 at 193.)

As to (b), Hoffmann J commented ([1992] BCLC 636 at 640):

'I find this reasoning puzzling because the section makes no distinction between excusable and inexcusable delay. It simply says that the advance must have been made at the time of the creation of the charge and I do not see how the answer to this question can be affected by whether the reasons for delay were good or bad. It is always open to the lender not to lend until the charge has actually been executed.'

I entirely agree with these comments. Extraneous factors such as these cannot affect the application of the statutory test. For these reasons I would refuse the application to admit in evidence the affidavit of Mr Mahtani sworn on 18 February 1993 referred to above, on which we have not yet formally adjudicated.

As to (a) above, the relevant interval of time, according to the wording of s 245(2)(a) of the 1986 Act and its predecessor sections, is the interval between the payment of the money and the 'creation of the charge'. In a case where no presently existing charge has been created by any agreement or company resolution preceding the execution of the formal debenture, then, in my judgment, no moneys paid before the execution of the debenture will qualify for the exemption under the subsection, unless the interval between payment and execution is so short that it can be regarded as minimal and payment and execution can be regarded as contemporaneous. This is a somewhat more rigorous (and possibly somewhat more certain) test than the test of 'the businessman' applied by the judge. However, as he commented, it is always open to the lender not to lend until the charge has actually been executed; this must be the prudent course.

In the present case it is not asserted that a charge was created by the resolution passed by Sharp's board of directors or that the four sums paid in April, May, June and 16 July 1990 were secured by any charge at the time when they were advanced. If they were secured at all, they can have been secured only by the debenture itself when it was executed on 24 July 1990. I have no hesitation in agreeing with the judge that these payments cannot be treated as having been made 'at the same time as . . . ' the execution of the debenture.

In the context of this first ground of appeal, I have thought it right to deal in detail with the *Columbian Fireproofing* and *Stanton* cases because they are decisions of high authority on which Mr Briggs's submissions were largely founded, and also to highlight what seems to me the importance in this context of the statutory provisions for registration of charges to which little reference has been made in earlier decisions. I would add that, if Sharp's contentions were well-founded, it would follow that in respect of the advances made by it between April and July 1990 it could claim priority over any unsecured creditors who had advanced moneys to Shoe Lace during that period, but, presumably, would have had no opportunity to learn of the existence of the floating charge until it was registered on 13 August 1990.

NOTES AND QUESTIONS

1. *Why may it be important to establish whether a charge is fixed or floating? How did the issue arise in Sources 239–242? Consider the following factors:*

    (a) *the position of preferential creditors;*

    (b) *the effect of subsequent charges (see Sources 251 and 255);*

    (c) *the power which the company has over the property charged (contrast Sources 239, 240, 241, 242);*

    (d) *the difficulty of establishing that the floating charge has crystallised (consider Sources 244, 245, 246, 247).*

2. *The fixed charge over book debts has become very common since first established in* Siebe Gorman *([1979] 2 Lloyd's Rep 142) and consolidated in* Re Keenan Bros *([1986] BCLC 242). It is a standard part of the security required by banks and other big lenders and follows the legislation (see Insolvency Act 1986, ss 40, 175) so as to put the lender as far as possible in a superior position to preferential creditors in the event of the insolvency of the borrower. Note also* Northern Bank v Ross *[1991] BCLC 504, where the fixed charge over book debts was held to cover that part of the bank account which was made up of cheques and credit card payments of book debts, but that part of the account which consisted simply of cash was not so covered. In* Atlantic Medical Ltd *[1993] BCLC 386 a charge was held to be a fixed charge even though it consisted in part of future assets (rents and other money due from sub-lessees under future agreements with the lessee/ borrower). Thus while a typical floating charge is expressed to comprise of the borrower's present and future assets, the fact that the charge is constituted by future assets does not preclude it from being a fixed charge. In* Re G E Tunbridge Ltd *[1995] 1 BCLC 34, however, where the relevant clause in the debenture provided:*

    'The Chargor, as beneficial owner hereby charges to the Lender as security for the payment of the Chargor's monetary liabilities and the performance of its other obligations to the Lender from time to time:- (a) by way of Fixed Charge, the Fixed Assets and the proceeds and products thereof (and in the case of the assets described in Part I of the First Schedule, such charge shall be by way of legal mortgage);'

    and Pt I of the first Schedule referred to read:

    '2. All other assets (not being Floating Assets) now owned or hereafter acquired by the Chargor or in which it now has or in the future acquires an interest.'

    the court held that the charge in question was a floating charge and not a fixed charge. According to Sir Mervyn Davies J, the parties contemplated a charge over assets present and future which the borrower was free to deal with in the normal course of business.

3. *Professor Pennington has argued ([1960] 23 MLR 630) that there are two possible explanations for the floating charge — a fixed charge plus a licence; alternatively, a charge that hovers over the assets and only attaches when it crystallises. In the light of Sources 244 and 245, which is the favoured theory in English Law? Consider Sources 246–250 ('Crystallisation') and consider the advantages and disadvantages of each theory.*

4. *Should debenture-holders be allowed to bargain for and have enforced as part of their contractual rights, an automatic crystallisation clause?*

5. *If the answer to 4 above is yes, should such a clause be registrable? (See Source 252* English & Scottish Mercantile Investments v Brunton.[1]*)*

6. *There has been much recent academic debate on the validity of automatic crystallisation clauses, see Farrar [1976] 40 Conv 397; Boyle [1979] JBL 231; McLaughlin (1972) New Zealand LJ 300; Gough,* Company Charges; *Goode,* Legal Problems of Credit and Security. *In addition, there has been recent support for such clauses in Australia, see* Deputy Federal Commission v Horsburgh[2] *and* Re Obie Pty Ltd (No. 2).[3]

   Does the following extract from Goode op cit, p 36, offer a reasonable compromise?

   'A question much canvassed is whether an automatic crystallisation clause is "valid". I have put the word "valid" in quotation marks because it seems to me that it conceals the real issue, which is not whether chargor and chargee are free to agree upon the circumstances in which the chargor's management powers are to come to an end (clearly they can reach any agreement they like on this point) but what is the effect of crystallisation on third parties who are not aware of its having occurred. In other words, it is for the parties to the charge, and for them alone, to decide in what circumstances the security interest created by the charge is to attach so as to be enforceable against the debtor company in regard to specific assets; but whether the attached security interests prevail over a third party is a question not of validity but of priority, a point forcefully made by Dr W. J. Gough in his excellent book on company charges [p 104]. Unfortunately much of the argument directed against the validity of the automatic crystallisation clause fails to separate the issues of attachment and priority. It is assumed that to give effect to the wishes of the parties as to the events that are to cause the security interest to attach will as a necessary consequence result in the crystallised charge having priority over a subsequent fixed charge. But this is to confuse relations between chargor and chargee with relations between the chargee and third parties. More specifically, it confuses the debtor company's actual authority to dispose of its assets, which may be terminated at any time in accordance with the agreement between the parties, with the debtor's apparent authority to deal with its assets, which may continue notwithstanding that its actual authority has come to an end and the charge has thus crystallised. Once this point is appreciated, much of the ground for criticism of the automatic crystallisation clause falls away.'

7. *What light does* Governments Stock etc *(Source 244, p 675) throw on the question of automatic crystallisation?*

8. *In order to avoid the effects of the predecessor sections to ss 40 and 175 of the Insolvency Act 1986 (which give preferential creditors a superior claim to that of floating chargeholders out of the assets which comprise the floating charge), floating charges often provided for crystallisation 'by notice', ie by a notice given to the borrower and stating that by that notice the charge crystallised. It was held (eg in* Re Woodroffe's (Musical Instruments) Ltd *[1986] Ch 366, [1985] 2 All ER 908 and* Re Brightlife Ltd, *above, p 663) where such a notice was served, that since the charge had crystallised prior to the appointment of a receiver (or the winding up of the company) the preferential*

---

1 [1892] 2 QB 700; 62 LJQB 136 (p 693)

2 (1984) 83 ATC 823

3 (1984) 2 ACLC 69

creditor was not entitled to priority in respect of the floating charge assets. These sections only applied where the crystallisation of the floating charge was caused by the appointment of a receiver or the winding up of the company. This interpretation of the sections was however reversed by the Insolvency Act 1986 (see the definition of floating charge, s 251, and the insertion in s 40 of the words 'a charge which, as created, was').

9. *Part IV of the Companies Act 1989 (which is not yet in force but which, when brought into force, will set out a new code for registration of charges) gives the Secretary of State power to make regulations prescribing the notice that will have to be given to the Registrar of Companies (when a charge is registered) in relation to 'the occurrence of such events as may be prescribed affecting the nature of the security under a floating charge . . .' — Companies Act 1989, s 100, which will insert s 410 into the Companies Act 1985). Will this power enable the Secretary of State to eliminate automatic crystallisation?*

10. *What effect, if any, is achieved by a restrictive clause?*

11. *Do you agree with Professor Farrar ([1976] Conv 40) that since such restrictive clauses are now so common, any subsequent chargee should assume that the previous charge prohibits the creation of a subsequent charge without the consent of the prior chargee? (Goode and Gough disagree.)*

12. *What are the respective rationes of* Benjamin Cope[1] *(Source 253) and* Automatic Bottle Makers[2] *(Source 254)?*

13. *Are they reconcilable?*

14. *Do* Wheatley v Silkstone Collieries[3] *(Source 251) and* Re Automatic Bottle Makers *illustrate the same principle?*

15. *Should the question at issue — the power of the company to create subsequent charges — be purely a matter of contract or should the existence of one floating charge necessarily preclude the company from creating further floating (and fixed?) charges?*

16. *In* Robbie v Witney Warehouses[4] *the plaintiff supplied goods to the value of £95 to the defendant before a receiver was appointed under a charge given by the plaintiff to its bank. After the appointment (and therefore the crystallisation of the charge) a further £1,250 worth of goods were supplied by the plaintiff (with the receiver's permission) to the defendant. Prior to the appointment of the receiver, the plaintiffs had purchased goods to the value of £850 from a company (a subsidiary of the same parent company as the defendant), which after the appointment of the receiver assigned its claim of £850 against the plaintiff to the defendant. The defendant sought to set off the assigned debt against the plaintiff's claim for £1,345 (£95 and £1,250). The set off was disallowed because the effect of the crystallisation of the charge was to assign the claim of the plaintiff against the defendant to the* debenture-holder, *whereas the claim of the defendant was against the* plaintiff. *There was therefore an absence of the mutuality between the claims, as required by set off.*

---

1 [1914] 1 Ch 800; 83 LJ Ch 699 (p 695)
2 [1926] Ch 412; 95 LJ Ch 185 (p 697)
3 (1885) 29 Ch D 715; 54 LJ Ch 778
4 [1963] 1 WLR 1324; [1963] 3 All ER 613

17. What is the distinction between Robbie's case and the Rother Iron[1] case? *[outlined at p 703]*

18. Could the debenture-holder in Evans v Rival Granite *(Source 245)*, have secured the crystallisation of the charge after the judgment in the case?

19. If so, who would have had priority as between the judgment creditor and the debenture-holder?

20. If not, can Evans v Rival Granite be reconciled with Norton v Yates[2] *(Source 257) and* Cairney v Back[3] *(Source 258)?*

21. The number of cases in which the issue has arisen whether a retention of title clause is or is not a floating charge (and, therefore void for want of registration against a receiver or liquidator) has grown rapidly. Compaq Computer Ltd v Abercorn Group Ltd *[1993] BCLC 602,* Modelboard Ltd v Outer Box Ltd *[1993] BCLC 623,* Stroud v John Laing Construction Ltd *[1994] 2 BCLC 276,* Ian Chisholm Textiles Ltd v Griffiths *[1994] 2 BCLC 291 and* Re Highway Foods International *[1995] 1 BCLC 209 were all cases of sale and supply of goods in which the supplier retained title but in all of which the clause was held to be a charge void for want of registration.*

22. In Re Highway Foods International *([1995] 1 BCLC 209), however, the supplier was more fortunate than the suppliers in the other cases. The goods supplied were then sold on to sub-purchasers (where the contract of sub-purchase was also subject to a reservation of title provision) and, inasmuch as these goods were in their original form and not yet paid for, the original supplier retained its proprietary interest in the goods. The original supplier was, therefore, entitled as against the receivers of the purchaser to the sum of money paid by the sub-purchaser in respect of the goods supplied under the sub-sale which were in their original form and which had not been paid for at the date the receivers were appointed to the purchasers.*

23. In Re Curtain Dream plc *[1990] BCLC 925, a complex arrangement under which finance was supplied to Curtain by Churchill backed by a trading arrangement between lender and borrower under which goods were invoiced by Curtain to Churchill and re-invoiced by Churchill to Curtain (in the latter case with a retention of title provision in favour of Churchill), the retention of title was held to be security for the loan (and therefore registrable as a charge and, therefore void for want of registration as against the receivers appointed to Curtain). The parties clearly intended the retention of title provision to act as security for the loan and not as part of a sale and resale agreement. In* Lovell Construction Ltd v Independent Estates plc *[1994] 1 BCLC 31, on the other hand, where Lovell had undertaken to do certain construction work for Independent and the parties had entered into an agreement in terms of which money would be placed in an escrow account to be paid over to Lovell when the work was completed, that agreement was held to be machinery for payment and not a charge securing payment. It was not, therefore, registrable and Lovell was entitled to the money as against the liquidator of the insolvent Independent.*

---

1 [1973] 2 WLR 281; [1973] 1 All ER 394
2 [1906] 1 KB 112; 75 LJKB 252 (p 707)
3 [1906] 2 KB 746; 75 LJKB 1014 (p 709)

24. *In* Re ELS Ltd, *[1994] 1 BCLC 743, a local authority sought to exercise its powers to distrain against the assets belonging to the company for rate arrears. The court held, however, that the local authority's power to levy distress ended with the appointment of the receiver under a floating charge granted by the company to its bank lender because the appointment of the receiver effected an assignment of the goods subject to the charge to the debenture holder and such goods, therefore, no longer belonged to the company.*

25. *Even if the subsequent chargee knows that there is a previous charge, he, she or it is not bound if the prior charge is not registered* (Monolithic Building).[1]

26. *Certain charges are not registrable, either because they do not fall within those listed in CA 1985, s 396 or because they were not created by the company but arose by operation of law* (Brunton v Electrical Engineering[2] — *a solicitor's lien* — and London & Cheshire Insurance v Laplagrene[3] — *vendor's unpaid lien*).

27. *The assertion that the security was an unpaid vendor's lien failed where a charge was bargained for and obtained, but not registered. During the 21-day period permitted for registration, the change was valid and as such swallowed up the unpaid vendor's lien* (Capital Finance v Stokes).[4]

28. *Where, however, the charge bargained for was void* ab initio *(ie it could never have been validly registered), the unpaid vendor's lien did not disappear* (Burston v Speirway).[5]

29. *Some liens, which are liens* ab initio *and not adjuncts to charges are registrable, see* Re Welsh Irish Ferries Ltd.[6]

30. *Does C. L. Nye[7] (Source 266) suggest that in the light of the more stringent attitude now being taken to late registrants and to applications for late registrations of charges, a chargee who has failed to register his charge within the statutory period, is best advised to falsify the date of the creation of the charge?*

31. *CA 1985 has always made provision for an application to be made to court for late registration of a charge (see CA 1985, s 404). The exercise of this power must not cause any prejudice to the creditors or the shareholders of the company. Thus, while it is quite common for the court to exercise its discretion under s 404, it invariably grants the order for late registration subject to a proviso protecting any rights in the property (over which the charge when registered would extend) acquired by any person between the date of the creation of the charge and the date of actual registration. Whether the company is close to insolvent liquidation is a factor which the court will take into account in deciding whether to accede to an application for late registration. Another factor is: whose fault was it that the charge was not*

---

1 [1915] 1 Ch 643; 84 LJ Ch 441
2 [1892] 1 Ch 434; 61 LJ Ch 256
3 [1971] Ch 499; [1971] 1 All ER 766
4 [1969] 1 Ch 261; [1968] 3 All ER 625
5 [1974] 1 WLR 1648; [1974] 3 All ER 735
6 [1986] Ch 471; [1985] 3 WLR 610
7 [1971] 1 Ch 442; [1970] 3 All ER 1061 (p 732)

registered in time. Both these issues were considered by Hoffmann J in Re Braemar Investments Ltd *[1988] BCLC 556, where he said:*

> 'Counsel for the liquidator's second ground was that by the time of the registrar's order[1] the company was crippled by the two Mareva injunctions and plainly no longer a going concern. Although the proprietary interests of the unsecured creditors in its property had not yet technically crystallised, it was inevitable that they would. Liquidation was imminent. Counsel relied on the decision of the Court of Appeal in Re Resinoid and Mica Products Ltd *(1967)* [1982] 3 All ER 677, [1983] Ch 132, which was followed in Victoria Housing Estates Ltd v Ashpurton Estates Ltd,[2] to which I have referred. In Re Resinoid and Mica Products Ltd *the company and the chargees failed to register the charge because the solicitors on each side left it to the other to do so. It should have been registered by 22 February 1965. The mortgage debt was repayable by instalments and within a very short time the company was in default. The chargees nevertheless took no steps to protect their position. After 20 months of inactivity, the chargees received a notice convening a meeting of creditors with a view to a winding up. At that stage they applied for an extension of time to register, which came before Mr Registrar Berkeley on the day before the creditors' meeting was due to be held. In the exercise of his discretion, he refused to extend the time and that decision was affirmed by the Court of Appeal. Lord Denning MR said ([1982] 3 All ER 677 at 679, [1983] Ch 132 at 133–134):*
>
> > "As long ago as 1935 Clauson J said in Re L H Charles & Co Ltd *[1935] WN 15 that, before extending the time, his practice was to require evidence that the company was solvent and no winding up of the company was impending. No such evidence could be adduced here. There was a period from February 1965 to October 1966, that is 20 months, when nothing was done. The application for extension was only made when the winding up was imminent. That is far too late."*
>
> Counsel for the liquidator submitted that the effect of Lord Denning MR's remarks was that, as a general rule, an application for extension when winding up is imminent should be refused. I do not think that Lord Denning MR was intending to lay down such a rule. His statement that the application was far too late was, in my view, made in the context of the facts of the cause before him. In Victoria Housing Estates Ltd v Ashpurton Estates Ltd *Lord Brightman treated* Re Resinoid and Mica Products Ltd *only as authority for the proposition that the imminence of liquidation was a relevant factor. It was a ground on which the registrar had been entitled to exercise his discretion against the applicant. It does not suggest that he should regularly or even ordinarily do so. There are a number of cases in which orders have been made when liquidation was imminent and there is nothing in* Victoria Housing Estates Ltd v Ashpurton Estates Ltd *to suggest that they involved an improper exercise of the discretion. As a matter of strict law an application to extend time is not too late if the registration can be effected before the liquidation actually commences. The court may as a matter of discretion on particular facts decide that it is too late at an earlier date, but the overriding question must be whether it would be just and equitable to grant leave. On the facts of this case I think that the applicants, through no fault of their own, were only just in time. But they were, nevertheless, in time. When the application was made liquidation may well have appeared to be a likely short-term outcome. It is worth observing, however, that in giving their consent the company's solicitors wrote on 4 November saying that they were doing so —*

---

1 The application comes before the Registrar in the first instance and his decision can be appealed to the judge
2 [1982] 3 All ER 665, [1983] Ch 10

"With a view to maintaining the good relationship between our respective clients in the immediate future and for the long term . . ."

Unlike the Resinoid *case, no notice of a meeting of creditors had been sent out and it certainly could not be said that it was only the prospect of forthcoming liquidation which had alerted the applicants to the necessity for an extension of time.*

Taking all the circumstances into account, therefore, I do not think that the imminence of liquidation was a ground on which the application should have been refused and the motion is therefore dismissed.'

32. *In* Re Chantry House Developments plc *[1990] BCLC 813, the court acceded to an application for late registration, but in view of the fact that this would have the effect of reducing the dividend of the unsecured creditors from 9p to 3p in the £1 in the event of the liquidation of the company, the court attached a condition to the order to the effect that the applicant had to inform all the creditors so as to enable them to make an application to court to discharge the order.*

33. *Part IV of the Companies Act 1989 will, when enacted, provide an entirely new code for registration of charges with important changes to issues such as the certificate of registration and applications for late registration of charges.*

34. *In certain circumstances where a charge given by a company which subsequently goes into administration or liquidation has the effect of preferring the creditor to whom the charge was granted as against the company's other creditors, that charge can be set aside (see Insolvency Act 1986, ss 239, 245, and Source 267 at p 735).*

Chapter 11

CAPITAL AND CAPITAL RECONSTRUCTION

PART I: INTRODUCTION

Every company limited by shares is required to state in its memorandum the amount of share capital with which it is to be registered and the division of that amount into shares of a fixed amount (Companies Act 1985, s 2(5)). The amount — the nominal capital — is the maximum which the company might issue in exchange for cash or other consideration. The amount actually issued is called the issued or allotted capital and is further described as 'fully paid', 'partly paid' or 'unpaid' depending on the extent to which the consideration in respect of which it was issued passes to the company. A public limited company must have a minimum allotted share capital of £50,000 (ss 117(2), 118(1)). Since the coming into operation of the Companies (Single Member Private Limited Companies) Regulations 1992, SI 1992/1699 one person may now form a private company (CA 1985, s 3A). Thus the minimum capital required for a private company is one 1p share.

A company may divide its share capital into different classes by ascribing different rights to different shares or to shareholders holding specific or a specific number of shares. Where shares are divided into different classes, there are strict rules as to the alteration of such rights (pp 634ff).

A company may alter its share capital in four ways. It may increase the amount of its nominal capital (s 121(2)(a)); it may alter the manner of the division of its existing share capital (s 121(2)(b), (c), (d)); it may cancel shares which have neither been allotted nor agreed to be allotted (s 121(2)(e)); it may reduce its share capital. The first three of these are straightforward and depend simply on a decision of the company itself; the fourth — reduction of its share capital — may involve diminution of its resources to the detriment of creditors and possibly dissenting shareholders and is therefore subject to a strict regime. This is sometimes expressed as the rule that the company's capital must be maintained.

The issue of shares by a company is thus a means by which the company raises money to enable it to carry out its purposes (another method is by borrowing — longer term borrowing usually being described as debentures). This close relationship between the raising of capital and the company's purposes led to the labelling of any misuse by the company of its capital (especially reduction thereof without complying with the procedure laid down by the Companies Act) as ultra vires, although Lord Cairns had counselled against this confusion in *Ashbury Railway Carriage Company v Riche*[1] (p 11). Misuse of capital is more appropriately described as 'illegal' as

---

1 (1875) LR 7 HL 653; 44 LJ Exch 185

it cannot be corrected simply by the insertion of an appropriate clause in the company's memorandum (Source 268).

Matters of capital maintenance raise other general company law questions. There is an overlap between cases on capital and cases which illustrate questions about the enforcement of directors' duties. The directors might sanction dealings which are to their advantage but which represent a misapplication of the company's funds such as to constitute an unlawful reduction of capital. Alternatively, they might in ignorance rely on advice received from their executive staff or outside professional advisers which, if acted upon, would also represent a misapplication of the company's funds. In the former case there would be a breach of the directors' fiduciary duty, in the latter, possibly a breach of the duty of care and skill (Chapter 7).

SOURCE 268
Horrwitz, Company Law Reform and the Ultra Vires Doctrine
[1946] 62 LQR 69–73

Share Capital and the Ultra Vires Doctrine
The decision in the *Ashbury Case*,[1] which established the *ultra vires* doctrine for companies registered under the Companies Acts, was exclusively based on the fact that the objects of the company had to be stated in its memorandum of association and that the conditions contained in the memorandum could not be altered. In quoting section 8 of the Companies Act 1862, Lord Hatherley was the only one of the five Law Lords who took part in that decision who mentioned that in the case of a limited company the capital of the company had to be stated in the memorandum in addition to the objects. But he did not draw any conclusions from that fact. He remarked:

> 'The legislature said . . . You must state the amount of the capital which you are about to invest in it, and you must state the objects for which you are associated, so that the persons dealing with you will know that they are dealing with persons who can only devote their *means* to a given class of objects, and who are prohibited from devoting their *means* to any other purpose.
>
> I think that the Legislature had in view distinctly the object of protecting outside dealers and contractors with this limited company from the *funds* of the company being applied, or from a contract being entered into by the company, for any other object whatsoever than those specified in the memorandum of association which the Legislature thought should remain for ever unchanged.'

It seems clear, from the above, that the *ultra vires* doctrine, as originally expounded in the *Ashbury Case*, applies to all transactions and to all the assets of a company and is not qualified by, nor limited to, a company's share capital.

The first deviation from this original and true form of the *ultra vires* doctrine appears to have been made in *Flitcroft's case*.[2] There the directors had paid dividends based on accounts showing a fictitious profit. This was not the first case in which dividends had been paid out of capital. Previously, the doctrine that dividends must not be paid out of capital had been founded on the ground that any repayment of capital to shareholders, unless made by way of capital reduction

---

1 (1875) LR 7 HL 653; 44 LJ Exch 185
2 (1882) 12 Ch D 519; 52 LJ Ch 217

with the sanction of the Court, was contrary to the constitution of a limited company and a violation of general principles of the Act. In *Flitcroft's Case* this reasoning was intermingled with the *ultra vires* doctrine.

> 'A limited company', said Jessel MR, 'by its memorandum of association declares that its capital is to be applied for the purposes of its business. It cannot reduce its capital except in the manner and with the safeguards provided by statute, and looking at the Act 40 & 41 Vict c 26 (the Companies Act 1877), it clearly is against the intention of the Legislature that any portion of the capital should be returned to the shareholders without the statutory conditions being complied with'.

And Cotton LJ, erroneously identifying assets and share capital, remarked:

> 'The assets of a company are to be dealt with only for the purposes of its business. The application of the capital in paying dividends was therefore a misapplication.'

Having been once misquoted in *Flitcroft's case* the *ultra vires* doctrine became frequently misquoted in later cases dealing with similar problems. In *Guinness v Land Corporation of Ireland*[1] the memorandum of association stated that the share capital was divided into A and B shares. The articles provided that the capital of the B shares should be applied for making up a dividend of 5 per cent per annum of the A shares, if necessary. This was held to be invalid. Chitty J reasoned as follows:

> 'I say you are bound to state your objects and your capital where your company is one of limited liability and the general law with regard to all corporations steps in and says that no corporation can apply its capital to any objects except those for which it is incorporated.'

Cotton LJ said in the same case:

> 'The Act requires the memorandum to state the objects of the company and the amount of capital with which the company proposes to be registered'. (He then quotes section 38 of the Companies Act 1862, which provided that, in the event of a company limited by shares being wound up no contribution should be required from any member 'exceeding the amount if any unpaid on the shares in respect of which he is liable as a present or past member.') ... 'From that it follows that whatever has been paid by a member cannot be returned to him. In my opinion it also follows that what is described in the memorandum as the capital cannot be diverted from the objects of the society.'

Bowen LJ, in the same case, suggested that the capital- and the object-clause in the memorandum of association had to be read together:

> 'It seems to me that the collocation of the two things, the compulsory statement of the objects of the company in the first place, and the compulsory statement of the capital in the second place, produces at once the legal obligation that the company shall devote to those objects alone the capital which is subscribed, and I think that the other sections of the Act are based upon the assumption that this is so.'

---

1 (1882) 22 Ch D 349; 52 LJ Ch 177

In *Trevor v Whitworth*[1] Lord Macnaghten remarked:

> 'The Act of 1862 requires that the objects ... be stated in its memorandum. ... Further, every limited company is required to state in its memorandum the amount of capital with which it proposes to be registered. ... That is equivalent to a declaration that the capital is to be devoted to the objects of the company.'

A few weeks afterwards, the law was summed up by Stirling J in *Leeds Estate, Building and Investment Co v Shepherd*,[2] also a dividend case, as follows:

> 'It is now settled by decisions of the House of Lords and Court of Appeal that the capital of a company formed under the Act of 1862 can be legally applied only for the purposes specified in the articles of association.'

All the aforesaid cases dealt with the question whether assets representing share capital could be validly paid over to shareholders. It was held that they could not. The soundness of those holdings is beyond doubt. There is further no doubt that, if the *ultra vires* doctrine, as pronounced in the *Ashbury case*, applies to all assets of a limited company, it thereby applies automatically to capital assets which form part of the total assets of a company. The intricacy of the problem, however, lies in the fact that not all payments to shareholders can be considered invalid. And the question arises whether the *ultra vires* doctrine is a suitable means of determining which payments are valid and which are not.

If 'paying dividend is not the object of the company', as Cotton LJ said in *Lee v Neuchatel Asphalte Company*,[3] — and there will be hardly any company where the paying of dividends is included in the objects as stated in the memorandum of association — it would appear to follow from the *Ashbury case* that paying dividends were 'ultra vires' the company. This, of course, would be absurd. Cotton LJ evaded this absurdity by quoting the *ultra vires* doctrine in the form that

> 'capital assets of the company are not to be applied for any purpose not within the objects of the company.'

This distinction between capital assets and other assets, however, is not to be found in the *Ashbury case* and is, it is submitted, foreign to the *ultra vires* doctrine. In *Tomkinson v South Eastern Rly*[4] it was held by Kay J that a subscription of £1,000 by a railway company to the Imperial Institute was *ultra vires* the company, although the payment was to be made out of profits available for dividends. It would appear, therefore, that the *ultra vires* doctrine is not restricted to assets representing share capital, but applies, as Lord Hatherly said in the *Ashbury case*, to all the 'means' or 'funds' of the company. If it were otherwise, we would arrive at the odd result that the *ultra vires* doctrine was applicable to all assets of unlimited companies, which have no fixed share capital, but was restricted in its application to *capital* assets in the case of a limited company.

Actually, the doctrine that 'dividends must not be paid out of capital' has nothing to do with the *ultra vires* doctrine whatsoever. Any trading company has for its object the making of gain and, consequently, the dividing of this gain among its members. That is self-understood and need not be stated in the memorandum of association. When the Act requires that a company has to state

---

1 (1888) 12 App Ca 409; 57 LJ Ch 28
2 (1887) 36 Ch D 787; 57 LJ Ch 46
3 (1889) 41 Ch D 1; 58 LJ Ch 408
4 (1887) 35 Ch D 675; 56 LJ Ch 932

its 'objects', it thereby requires that the company shall state the specific means by which it intends to achieve this general aim, the making of profits. The object clause in the memorandum of association defines the proposed external transactions of a company. It does not deal, as a rule, with the internal relations between the company and its members. Those relations are usually regulated by the articles of association. It is difficult to see, therefore, how the object clause can be of any assistance in determining what is divisible among shareholders and what not.

It is submitted, with all respect, that no indication is to be found in the Companies Act 1862, nor in any subsequent Act, that the object- and the capital-clause in the memorandum of association are to be read as one. The statement of the objects of the company in the memorandum of association is one thing, the statement of the share capital in the memorandum is another thing.

From the fact that the *objects* have to be stated in the memorandum and that the object clause cannot be altered it follows that the 'funds', that is *all the assets* of the company, cannot be applied, and that no contract can be entered into by the company, for any other object than those specified in the memorandum of association.

From the fact that the *share capital* has to be stated in the memorandum of association, in connection with the further facts that the shareholders' liability is limited to the amount unpaid on their shares, and that the share capital cannot be reduced without the sanction of the Court, it follows that *assets representing share capital* must not be returned to shareholders. This rule is in no way related to the entirely separate rule concerning *ultra vires* activities. Any clause in the memorandum authorizing the division of such assets among shareholders would be illegal, any clause in the memorandum authorizing the division of other assets would be superfluous.

If the above quoted cases are scrutinized, it will be found that, when all the reasoning that a company's 'capital' is to be applied for the purposes of its business is ignored, those cases will still stand unimpaired. Their true *ratio decidendi* is the basic principle that, whatever the objects of a company are, assets representing share capital must not be paid over to shareholders unless the statutory provisions regarding the reduction of share capital are complied with. The irrelevancy of the object clause in this respect is clearly shown by Lord Macnaghten's famous *dictum* in *Trevor v Whitworth* [see p 762]:

> 'It seems to me that if a power to purchase its own shares were found in the memorandum of association of a limited company, it would necessarily be void.'

SOURCE 269
Ooregum Gold Mining Company of India *v* Roper
(House of Lords 1892) [1892] AC 125; 61 LJ Ch 337

The operations of the company were not, in the first instance, successful, and a winding-up order was obtained. An application was subsequently made to the Court for an order to stay the winding-up, with a view to the introduction of fresh capital and a resumption of mining operations, and an order was made accordingly. In pursuance of this policy an extraordinary general meeting of the company was summoned in 1885, at which it was resolved that the capital should be increased by the issue of 120,000 preference shares of £1 each, to be credited in the capital and books of the company as having the sum of 15s. per share paid thereon, such preference shares carrying the right to a non-cumulative preference dividend up to 10 per cent on the nominal amount of such preference capital out of the profits of the undertaking each year, and to equal participation (share per share) with the ordinary shares in such further profits as should remain for distribution each year after the payment of the above 10 per cent preference dividend. The special resolution so passed was duly confirmed. At this time the market value of the ordinary shares was only 2s. 6d. per share.

Upwards of 100,000 of these preference shares were allotted, with 15s. credited as paid thereon. Prior to the actual allotment an agreement was entered into between the company, of the one part, and an agent or trustee for the several persons whose names were entered in the schedule thereto, of the other part, whereby, after reciting the agreement to issue the shares at a discount of 15s. per share, and that 1s. had been paid on allotment, it was agreed that the shares to be allotted should be held as shares on which 16s. per share had been paid, and should be subject and liable to further payment of 4s. per share, and no more, and the company thereby undertook to cause the agreement to be registered at the Joint Stock Registration Office, pursuant to the Companies Act 1867, before the issue of the shares. The agreement was duly filed accordingly. The capital raised by means of the issue of the preference shares sufficed to discharge the obligations of the company, to extricate it from its difficulties, and to give it a new start. Gold to a considerable amount was shortly afterwards raised from the mines, and the company has since been prosperous, the market value of the ordinary shares having risen to about 40s.

In February 1889 the Respondent, George Roper, purchased on the Stock Exchange and paid for ten fully paid-up ordinary shares in the company. On 15 July following on behalf of himself and the other ordinary shareholders Roper brought this action against the company and Wallroth (as an original allottee of the preference shares and as representing the other original allottees) to have it declared that the issue by the company of the 120,000 preferred shares, at a discount of 15s. per share, was *ultra vires*, and to have the register rectified accordingly and other consequent relief granted. The statement of claim contained the allegation that the company had in 1889 issued debentures to the amount of £20,000, which were charged on all the property of the company, and which were then outstanding. It further alleged as follows: 'The defendant company had no power to issue the said preferred shares at a discount, and the entry of the preferred shares in the register book as fully paid-up should be rectified. The said preferred shares are now quoted on the Stock Exchange at a premium, and if the said entry is rectified the ordinary shares will benefit thereby, and the 15s. unpaid on the preferred shares will be available for paying off the said debentures as and when they fall due.'

North J upon the authority of *Re Almada and Tirito Company*[1] without argument made an order declaring that the issue of the preferred shares of £1 each at a discount of 15s. per share was beyond the powers of the company, and that the said shares so far as the same were held by Wallroth or by original allottees represented by him were held subject to the liability of the holders to pay to the company in cash so much of the £1 per share as had not been paid on the same; and ordering that the company do rectify the register in accordance with the above declaration. This order was affirmed by the Court of Appeal without argument. Against these orders appeals were brought by the company and by Wallroth.

LORD HALSBURY LC: My Lords, the question in this case has been more or less in debate since 1883, when Chitty J decided that a company limited by shares was

---

1 (1888) 38 Ch D 415

not prohibited by law from issuing its shares at a discount. That decision was overruled, though in a different case, by the Court of Appeal in 1888, and it has now come to your Lordships for final determination.

My Lords, the whole structure of a limited company owes its existence to the Act of Parliament, and it is to the Act of Parliament one must refer to see what are its powers, and within what limits it is free to act. Now, confining myself for the moment to the Act of 1862, it makes one of the conditions of the limitation of liability that the memorandum of association shall contain the amount of capital with which the company proposes to be registered, divided into shares of a *certain fixed amount.* It seems to me that the system thus created by which the shareholder's liability is to be limited by the amount unpaid upon his shares, renders it impossible for the company to depart from that requirement, and by any expedient to arrange with their shareholders that they shall not be liable for the amount unpaid on the shares, although the amount of those shares has been, in accordance with the Act of Parliament, fixed at a certain sum of money. It is manifest that if the company could do so the provision in question would operate nothing.

I observe in the argument it has been sought to draw a distinction between the nominal capital and the capital which is assumed to be the real capital. I can find no authority for such a distinction. The capital is fixed and certain, and every creditor of the company is entitled to look to that capital as his security.

SOURCE 270
Re Wragg Limited
(Chancery Division and Court of Appeal) [1897] 1 Ch 796; 66 LJ Ch 419

This was a summons taken out by the official receiver, as the liquidator in the winding-up of the above-named company, in substance for a declaration that certain shares in that company held by Messrs E. J. Wragg & J. B. Martin and registered in their names as fully paid up were not fully paid up, and for an order that Messrs Wragg & Martin should forthwith pay the amounts unpaid thereon.

For many years prior to 1894 Messrs Wragg & Martin carried on business together as omnibus and coach proprietors, livery-stable keepers and job-masters in Whitechapel, and elsewhere in London; and they were the owners of certain freehold and leasehold property, and a considerable number of horses and carriages, and a quantity of harness, stock-in-trade, plant and effects.

In 1894 they determined to convert their business into a private limited company, and with that intent they formed such a company to buy the goodwill, stock-in-trade, and property of their business at a price which they fixed at £46,300, to be payable in cash, debentures, and fully paid-up shares as hereinafter stated.

. . .

VAUGHAN WILLIAMS J: . . . Going back to the principles I have already pointed out, I may say that in the *Eddystone case*[1] absence of any real consideration was not only found as a fact by the Court, but practically appears upon the face of the contract; and that case is very different from the present case, in which substantial property of great value passed under the contract. The question which I have to decide is whether, in a case where there is a real contract, and real consideration is transferred against fully paid shares, the Court will go behind the

1 [1893] 3 Ch 9; 62 LJ Ch 742

contract, and say that the consideration transferred is a sham to the extent that the price given exceeds what the vendor and the company must have known to be the value of the property transferred.

. . . At all events, it seems to me that in a case where there is substantial property transferred and a price appears in the contract, and that contract has been acted on and the property parted with, where you cannot rescind the contract and restore the parties to their pre-contract position, you ought not to say that there was no consideration unless it is proved, and proved beyond all reasonable doubt, that the shares thus issued as fully paid were issued as a gift or a bonus to the vendors. The learned counsel who prepared the summons seems to have been impressed with that himself, and he seeks to allege it in the summons by saying that these fully paid shares were issued for promotion money. There is no evidence of that; and when one considers what was likely to actuate these very persons who were making the contract, and not leaving out of consideration their personal identity, it is clear they had nothing to do but to fix whatever price they thought right, and that price of course would be accepted. There was no need to allocate the price in the way in which it is done in this contract, and so doing would in no way assist the directors in carrying out any dishonest purpose, or in cloaking any gift, or in cloaking the payment of any promotion money. Under those circumstances it seems to me that it is a wrong inference to draw that this was either a gift or promotion money. I do not believe it in fact. If I am asked why the vendors, who had it in their power to sell without more this property for £46,300, allocated it in the way in which they did allocate it in the contract, I say the inference I draw is that they did it for the purpose of adjustment of the price amongst themselves. It is said that these directors might have gone into the witness-box and explained this if they chose, and it is said that they did not, and they have not, and they are not entitled, it is true, to ask the Court to draw the same inference that it might have drawn if they had gone into the witness-box and given satisfactory evidence; but, on the other hand, the official receiver is not entitled to say, because these respondents have not gone into the witness-box, 'Be good enough to draw an inference that the issue of this excess, as it is called, of £11,000 of shares was an issue of bonus shares, or an issue of shares to cover promotion money, or for some other illegal purpose.' The official receiver is not entitled to ask me to draw that inference from the mere absence of the respondents from the witness-box unless the evidence already makes out such a case as to entitle me to go behind the contract at all. Primâ facie, I am not entitled to go behind the contract. The contract on the face of it is a perfectly unimpeachable contract, and it is for the official receiver to shew that he is entitled to go behind it before he can place any such reliance upon the absence of these people from the witness-box, and it seems to me under those circumstances that I ought not to draw the inference that I am invited to draw.

I think, therefore, that the official receiver has failed to make out in fact in the present case that the consideration was to the extent, as has been contended, or to any extent, a sham. I think there was a real contract for sale at £46,300 and that the only way of getting out of this is either to succeed in maintaining the argument that there could be no contract between the vendors and the company in this case because of the identity of the vendors and the shareholders, or if you do not do that, the only other way that you can do it is to shew that, as to this £11,000, the consideration is a sham or a colourable consideration. I myself think that these people in law were independent contracting parties.

LINDLEY LJ (CA): . . . As regards the value of the property which a company can take from a shareholder in satisfaction of his liability to pay the amount of his shares, there has been some difference of opinion. But it was ultimately decided by the Court of Appeal that, unless the agreement pursuant to which shares were to be paid for in property or services could be impeached for fraud, the value of the property or services could not be inquired into. In other words, the value at which the company is content to accept the property must be treated as its value as between itself and the shareholder whose liability is discharged by its means.

I understand the law to be as follows. The liability of a shareholder to pay the company the amount of his shares is a statutory liability, and is declared to be a specialty debt (Companies Act 1862, section 16), and a short form of action is given for its recovery (section 70). But specialty debts, like other debts, can be discharged in more ways than one — eg, by payment, set-off, accord and satisfaction, and release — and, subject to the qualifications introduced by the doctrine of *ultra vires*, or, in other words, the limited capacity of statutory corporations, any mode of discharging a specialty debt is available to a share-holder as to any other specialty debtor. It is, however, obviously beyond the power of a limited company to release a shareholder from his obligation without payment in money or money's worth. It cannot give fully paid-up shares for nothing and preclude itself from requiring payment of them in money or money's worth: *Re Eddystone Marine Insurance Co*; nor can a company deprive itself of its right to future payment in cash by agreeing to accept future payments in some other way. It cannot substitute an action for the breach of a special agreement for a statutory action for non-payment of calls: see *Pellatt's case*.[1]

. . .

From this it follows that shares in limited companies cannot be issued at a discount. By our law the payment by a debtor to his creditor of a less sum than is due does not discharge the debt; and this technical doctrine has also been invoked in aid of the law which prevents the shares of a limited company from being issued at a discount. But this technical doctrine, though often sufficient to decide a particular case, will not suffice as a basis for the wider rule or principle that a company cannot effectually release a shareholder from his statutory obligation to pay in money or money's worth the amount of his shares. That shares cannot be issued at a discount was finally settled in the case of the *Ooregum Gold Mining Co of India v Roper*,[2] the judgments in which are strongly relied upon by the appellant in this case. It has, however, never yet been decided that a limited company cannot buy property or pay for services at any price it thinks proper, and pay for them in fully paid-up shares. Provided a limited company does so honestly and not colourably, and provided that it has not been so imposed upon as to be entitled to be relieved from its bargain, it appears to be settled by *Pell's case*[3] and the others to which I have referred, of which *Anderson's case*[4] is the most striking, that agreements by limited companies to pay for property or services in paid-up shares are valid and binding on the companies and their creditors. The Legislature in 1867 appears to me to have distinctly recognized such to be the law, but to have required in order to make such agreements binding that they shall be registered before the shares are issued.

Appeal dismissed.

---

1 (1867) LR 2 Ch 527; 36 LJ Ch 613
2 [1892] AC 125; 61 LJ Ch 337 (see p 755)
3 (1869) LR 5 Ch App 11; 39 LJ Ch 120
4 (1877) 7 Ch D 75

SOURCE 271
Hilder *v* Dexter
(House of Lords 1902) [1902] AC 474; 71 LJ Ch 781

The United Gold Coast Mining Properties, Limited, was incorporated on 17 December 1900, with a capital of £200,000, divided into 200,000 shares of £1 each. In January 1901, the directors determined to issue 33,333 shares, or one-sixth of their nominal capital. They did so by offering the shares, not to the public, but to fourteen persons, of whom the appellant Hilder was one, and who were invited to apply for the shares. Hilder applied for and was allotted 6975 shares upon the following terms:

> 'For each share allotted in accordance with this application a subscriber shall have the option during the period of one year from 3 January 1901, of taking up at par a further ordinary share of £1 in the initial capital of the company, and in the event of such last-mentioned share being taken up under such option, a further option during the period of two years from and after the said 3 January 1901, of taking up at par a further ordinary share of £1 in the initial capital of the company.'

For these shares Hilder paid £6975. The rest of the 33,333 shares were allotted upon the same terms to the other thirteen applicants. In July 1901, the £1 shares were selling at about £2 17s. 6d., and Hilder gave the company notice that he elected to take up further shares under his agreement with the company. The respondent, a shareholder, having brought an action against Hilder, the company, and the directors, Byrne J, holding the case governed by *Burrows v Matabele Gold Reefs and Estates Co Ltd*,[1] granted an injunction restraining the company and directors from carrying out the agreement. This decision was affirmed by the Court of Appeal (Rigby, Collins, and Romer LJJ) on the same ground.

LORD DAVEY: . . . I am not aware of any law which obliges a company to issue its shares above par because they are saleable at a premium in the market. It depends on the circumstances of each case whether it will be prudent or even possible to do so, and it is a question for the directors to decide. But the point which, in my opinion, is alone material for the present purpose is that the benefit to the shareholder from being able to sell his shares at a premium is not obtained by him at the expense of the company's capital. The prohibited application of the shares may be direct by allotting them as fully or partly paid up to the person underwriting the shares, or by allotting them in some other way with the intention that they shall ultimately find their way to such person or be applied in payment of his commission.

My Lords, it may be that in some particular case a contract such as that which your Lordships have before you would be open to impeachment as improvident, or an abuse, or in excess of the powers of management committed to the directors. In this case the question is as to the powers of the company itself, and not as to the due exercise of the directors' powers. I have come to the conclusion from a consideration of the language of section 8, subsection 2, that the prohibition therein contained extends only to the application, direct or indirect, of the company's capital in payment of a commission by the company, and the transaction impeached in this case is not within it.[2] It is satisfactory to find that the conclusion to which I have come will not have the effect of extending the

---

1 [1901] 2 Ch 23
2 Now ss 97, 98 of the Companies Act 1985

prohibition to transactions which were legitimate before the Act, and not, so far as I am aware, open to objection on any other ground.

I am of opinion that the appeal should be allowed.

PART II: MAINTENANCE OF CAPITAL

General

The original view of the company's capital as a guarantee fund for creditors — that the money subscribed in exchange for the issue of shares should be retained *in specie* to be used, if necessary to pay the debts which the company could not — is probably due to early unease about the limited liability of the shareholders. This rule has always been seen as resting on three sub-rules, that the shares might not be issued at a discount (ie in exchange for a consideration less than the nominal or par value of the shares issued), that the company may not purchase its own shares and that dividends may only be declared where the company had sufficient profits out of which the dividends might be paid.

In time these rules required supplementing and modifying. The practice of the company's funds being used to assist in the purchase of its shares made its appearance in the early part of the twentieth century and had to be outlawed as tending to the same mischief as the purchase by the company of its own shares. Equally significant was the relaxation of the rule that the capital subscribed had to be retained *in specie*. This rule seemed to collide with and give way to the important company law proposition that company decisions were to be made by the directors and not the courts; this was of especial significance in the matter of the declaration of dividends.

Prohibition of the Issue of Shares at a Discount

This is now a statutory provision (CA 1985, s 100). Prior to 1980, however, its source was a decision of the House of Lords (Source 269), as an interpretation of the statutory framework for a company limited by shares. On the other hand, the courts would not under the common law, except in extreme cases, set aside the allotment of shares for a consideration other than cash and of an apparently lesser value than the shares allotted (Source 270); nor is the company obliged to issue shares at a price higher than the nominal value (ie including a premium) where the prosperity of the company would enable the company to do so (Source 271).

Prohibition Against the Company Purchasing Its Own Shares

This too was a common law rule which derives from the framework within which a company limited by shares is registered (Source 272). Certain exceptions have always been accepted — forfeiture of shares for non-payment of calls (Table A regs 19–22), also surrender of fully paid shares (see Source 272). This rule has now been made statutory (s 143), supplemented by amendments first introduced by the Companies Act 1981 (now ss 144–150; 159–181 of the Companies Act 1985).

SOURCE 272
Trevor *v* Whitworth
(House of Lords 1887) (1888) 12 App Ca 409; 57 LJ Ch 28

The memorandum did not authorize the company to purchase its own shares.

. . .

Article 179. Any share may be purchased by the company from any person willing to sell it, and at such price, not exceeding the then marketable value thereof, as the board think reasonable.

Article 181. Shares so purchased may at the discretion of the board be sold or disposed of by them or be absolutely extinguished, as they deem most advantageous for the company.

The company having in 1884 gone into liquidation.

. . . a claim was made against the company by the respondents, as executors of Whitworth a deceased shareholder, for the balance of the price of Whitworth's shares sold by the executors to the company in 1880, and not wholly paid for. The circumstances under which the purchase in question and other purchases by the company of its own shares were effected are stated in the judgments.

A summons having been taken out by the appellants, the official liquidators, to determine whether the claim ought to be allowed, the Vice-Chancellor of the county palatine made an order declaring that, without prejudice to any claim by the claimants against any persons other than the liquidators and the company, the claim against the company ought not to be allowed.

The Court of Appeal (Cotton, Bowen and Fry LJJ) reversed this decision and allowed the claim. Against this decision the liquidators now appealed. The only question material to this report being the general question, whether such a company can purchase its own shares, the arguments on the other points are omitted.

. . .

LORD HERSCHELL: I pass now to the main question in this case, which is one of great and general importance, whether the company had power to purchase the shares. The result of the judgment in the Court below is certainly somewhat startling. The creditors of the company which is being wound up, who have a right to look to the paid-up capital as the fund out of which their debts are to be discharged, find coming into competition with them persons who, in respect only of their having been, and having ceased to be, shareholders in the company, claim that the company shall pay to them a part of that capital. The memorandum of association, it is admitted, does not authorize the purchase by the company of its own shares. It states, as the objects for which the company is established, the acquiring certain manufacturing businesses and the undertaking and carrying on the businesses so acquired, and any other business and transaction which the company consider to be in any way auxiliary thereto, or proper to be carried on in connection therewith.

It cannot be questioned, since the case of *Ashbury Railway Carriage and Iron Company v Riche*,[1] that a company cannot employ its funds for the purpose of any transactions which do not come within the objects specified in the memorandum, and that a company cannot by its articles of association extend its power in this respect. These propositions are not and could not be impeached in the judgments of the Court of Appeal, but it is said to be settled by authority, that although a company could not under such a memorandum as the present, by

---

1 (1875) LR 7 HL 653; 44 LJ Exch 185 (p 11)

articles authorize a trafficking in its own shares, it might authorize the board to buy its shares 'whenever they thought it desirable for the purposes of the company,' or 'in cases where it was incidental to the legitimate objects of the company that it should do so.' The former is Lord Justice Cotton's expression; the latter that of Lord Justice Bowen.

I will first consider the question apart from authority, and then examine the decisions relied on.

The Companies Act 1862 requires (section 8) that in the case of a company where the liability of the shareholders is limited, the memorandum shall contain the amount of the capital with which the company proposes to be registered, divided into shares of a certain fixed amount; and provides (section 12) that such a company may increase its capital and divide it into shares of larger amount than the existing shares, or convert its paid-up shares into stock, but that 'save as aforesaid, no alteration shall be made by any company in the conditions contained in its memorandum of association.'

What is the meaning of the distinction thus drawn between a company without limit on the liability of its members and a company where the liability is limited, but, in the latter case, to assure to those dealing with the company that the whole of the subscribed capital, unless diminished by expenditure upon the objects defined by the memorandum, shall remain available for the discharge of its liabilities? The capital may, no doubt, be diminished by expenditure upon and reasonably incidental to all the objects specified. A part of it may be lost in carrying on the business operations authorized. Of this all persons trusting the company are aware, and take the risk. But I think they have a right to rely, and were intended by the Legislature to have a right to rely, on the capital remaining undiminished by any expenditure outside these limits, or by the return of any part of it to the shareholders.

Experience appears to have shewn that circumstances might occur in which a reduction of the capital would be expedient. Accordingly, by the Act of 1867 provision was made enabling a company under strictly defined conditions to reduce its capital. Nothing can be stronger than these carefully-worded provisions to shew how inconsistent with the very constitution of a joint stock company, with limited liability, the right to reduce its capital was considered to be.

. . .

If the claim under consideration can be supported, the result would seem to be this, that the whole of the shareholders, with the exception of those holding seven individual shares, might now be claiming payment of the sums paid upon their shares as against the creditors, who had a right to look to the moneys subscribed as the source out of which the company's liabilities to them were to be met. And the stringent precautions to prevent the reduction of the capital of a limited company, without due notice and judicial sanction, would be idle if the company might purchase its own shares wholesale, and so effect the desired result.

. . .

It is urged that the views I have expressed are inconsistent with the forfeiture and surrender of shares in a company. I do not think so. The forfeiture of shares is distinctly recognized by the Companies Act, and by the articles contained in the schedule, which in the absence of other provisions regulate the management of a limited liability company. It does not involve any payment by the company, and it presumably exonerates from future liability those who have shewn themselves unable to contribute what is due from them to the capital of the company. Surrender no doubt stands on a different footing. But it also does not involve any payment out of the funds of the company. If the surrender were made in consideration of any such payment it would be neither more nor less than a sale, and open to the same objections. If it were accepted in a case when the company were in a position to forfeit the shares, the transaction would seem to me perfectly valid.

. . .

LORD WATSON: . . . One of the main objects contemplated by the legislature, in restricting the power of limited companies to reduce the amount of their capital as set forth in the memorandum, is to protect the interests of the outside public who may become their creditors. In my opinion the effect of these statutory restrictions is to prohibit every transaction between a company and a share-holder, by means of which the money already paid to the company in respect of his shares is returned to him, unless the Court has sanctioned the transaction. Paid-up capital may be diminished or lost in the course of the company's trading; that is a result which no legislation can prevent; but persons who deal with, and give credit to a limited company, naturally rely upon the fact that the company is trading with a certain amount of capital already paid, as well as upon the responsibility of its members for the capital remaining at call; and they are entitled to assume that no part of the capital which has been paid into the coffers of the company has been subsequently paid out, except in the legitimate course of its business.

The Rule Against a Company Assisting in the Purchase of its Shares

This rule was statutory in origin, passed on the recommendation of the Company Law Reform Committee 1926 (Source 273). Initially, the approach was to make the giving of financial assistance by the company, illegal, but this led to the absurd result that the company might not be able to recover money advanced for the illegal activity of assisting in the purchase of its own shares because it was party to the illegal transaction!

This was corrected by showing that the company was only an involuntary party and that those who had caused the company to enter into this illegal transaction (usually its directors or shadow directors) were liable in an action by the company to recover the money advanced for this purpose (Source 274). Observe the close connection between the principle of the main-tenance of the company's capital and the remedies available against directors for breach of their duties to the company.

One question with which the court has recently had to wrestle is whether there is a breach of this prohibition where the company enters into a bona fide commercial transaction, a part of which consists of a company giving assistance in the purchase of its shares (Sources 275, 276, 277). Section 54 of the Companies Act 1948 (now repealed) provided,

'Subject as provided in this section, it shall not be lawful for a company to give, whether directly or indirectly, and whether by means of a loan, guarantee, the provision of security or otherwise, any financial assistance for the purpose of or in connection with a purchase or subscription made or to be made by any person of or for any shares in the company, or, where the company is a subsidiary company, in its holding company . . .'

SOURCE 273
Report of the Company Law Amendment Committee 1925–6
('The Greene Report')

Company Providing Money for the Purchase of its own Shares
30. A practice has made its appearance in recent years which we consider to be highly improper. A syndicate agrees to purchase from the existing shareholders sufficient shares to control a company, the purchase money is provided by a temporary loan from a bank for a day or two, the syndicate's nominees are appointed directors in place of the old board and immediately proceed to lend to the syndicate out of the company's funds (often without security) the money required to pay off the bank. Thus in effect the company provides money for the purchase of its own shares. This is a typical example although there are, of course, many variations. Such an arrangement appears to us to offend against the spirit if not the letter of the law which prohibits a company from trafficking in its own shares and the practice is open to the gravest abuses.

Recommendation
31. We recommend that companies should be prohibited from directly or indirectly providing any financial assistance in connection with a purchase (made or to be made) of their own shares by third persons, whether such assistance takes the form of loan, guarantee, provision of security, or otherwise. This should not apply in the case of companies whose ordinary business includes the lending of money, to money lent in the ordinary course of such business, or to schemes by which a company puts up money in the hands of trustees for purchasing shares of the company to be held for the benefit of employees or to loans direct to employees for the same purpose.

SOURCE 274
Selangor United Rubber Estates Ltd *v* Cradock (No 3)
(Chancery Division 1968) [1968] 1 WLR 1555; [1968] 2 All ER 1073.

An agent acting for Cradock made a bid for all the shares in the plaintiff company. It was accepted by 79 per cent of the shareholders, the purchase price being £195,000, which amount was obtained by Cradock from the District Bank. The plaintiff company's cash account of £325,000 was transferred to the District Bank and loaned through an intermediary to Cradock who used it to repay the loan of £195,000.

. . .

UNGOED-THOMAS J: It was submitted that, in so far as the plaintiff's claim is founded on payment of its moneys as means of giving financial assistance for the purchase of stock in the plaintiff, the payment was unlawful and the plaintiff's claim fails. This submission does not affect the plaintiff's claim with regard to the £42,000 but it does affect claims made by the plaintiff with regard to the £232,500 (including the £195,000 claimed against Contanglo) and the £207,500, in so far as these claims are based on breach of trust and on constructive trusteeship.

Of course, if the plaintiff does not establish the breach of trust or requisite constructive trusteeship, there is no need to rely on the defence of illegality against a claim founded on them. So this defence goes on the assumption that, in the case of the directors, breach of trust or fiduciary duty and, in the case of the other defendants, constructive trusteeship, is established.

Section 54 of the Companies Act 1948, provides that '(1) . . . it shall not be lawful for a company to give . . . any financial assistance for the purpose of . . . a purchase . . . made or to be made by any person of or for any shares in the company.'

It is not disputed by the plaintiff that if a contract or 'consensual arrangement' is illegal ex facie, or made for an illegal purpose, then the court will not assist in enforcing the contract or 'consensual arrangement' (whether, eg, by specific performance, money judgment, or damages) or to recover property (including money) passed in pursuance of it. But the plaintiff contends that such refusal of the court to assist is limited to cases of contract or 'consensual arrangement' and does not extend in particular to claims based on breach of trust.

The ambit, within which such consequences of the illegality operate, has by no means been clearly defined. This amply appeared from the arguments before me. The usual field of its operation is certainly contract; but then contract is the field which gives most scope for its operation.

The principle governing such consequences of illegality is not, however, just a twig of any particular branch of the law, but is rooted deeply in public policy — that the courts are not to be instruments for aiding illegality. The policy is not that the courts are not to be instruments for aiding illegality in contract, but may be instruments for aiding illegality in other branches of the law. It is in accordance with this substantial public policy nature of the courts' refusal of aid to illegality that such illegality is not treated as a matter of pleading, or a matter merely as between the parties, but as a matter of which the court will, of its own initiative, take cognisance irrespective of pleadings or wishes of the parties.

The objection to aiding illegality is thus not limited in its origin in public policy to any particular form of action.

. . .

In *Steen v Law*[1] directors of a company, incorporated in New South Wales, lent the company's funds which the directors had to give financial assistance to purchase the company's shares. The liquidator of the company claimed that there had thus been a breach of a New South Wales section, which, so far as material, was in the terms of section 54 of the Act of 1948; and that the directors had thereby committed a breach of their fiduciary duty to the company and should reimburse the company the sums so illegally applied. It was not contended that the directors were absolved from accounting by reason of the illegality of the loan by the company. Such illegality was clearly before the Privy Council and, if available against such a claim, provided a complete answer to it. Yet the point was neither taken by the defendants nor by the Privy Council; and it seems to me for the very good reason that the company was not relying for its claim on the unlawful loan and the relationship of creditor and debtor thereby created, but upon the misapplication by the directors of the company's moneys by way of the unlawful loan. That is the position with regard to the plaintiff's claim in our case. It was founding its claim, as in our case, not on a wrong done by it as a party to the unlawful loan, but as a wrong done to it by parties owing a fiduciary duty to it. The courts were being invited, as in our case, not to aid illegality but to condemn it. If this were not so, the courts would give redress to companies against directors for misapplication and breach of fiduciary duty which did not involve the company in illegality, but no redress if they were so serious as to involve the company in illegality.

I appreciate that, in the ordinary case of a claim by a beneficiary against a trustee for an illegal breach of trust, the beneficiary is not a party to the illegality;

---

1 [1964] AC 287; [1963] 3 All ER 770

but that, when directors act for a company in an illegal transaction with a stranger, the company is itself a party to that transaction and therefore to the illegality. The company, therefore, could not rely on that transaction as 'the source of civil rights' and, therefore, for example, it could not successfully sue the stranger with regard to rights which it was claimed that the transaction conferred. If, however, property had passed under the illegal transaction, it is common ground that the right which the holding of that property conferred would be good against all the world, since the court would not assist the only party which had a better title, namely the party from whom it passed under the illegal transaction, to recover it. The right of the holder would be assisted by the courts, because it would be a right established by the holding, without having to rely on any right claimed to be conferred by the illegal transaction — and nonetheless because it was in pursuance of the illegal transaction, to which the holder was a party, that the holding in fact arose: (see particularly *Singh v Ali,*[1] and *Chettiar v Chettiar*[2]). In a claim based on an illegal breach of trust the claimant does not rely on a right conferred or created by that breach. On the very contrary, he relies on a right breached by the breach, as the very words 'breach of trust' indicate. It is only on the footing that there is a breach of trust that the defence of illegality becomes relevant. So it is assumed, for present purposes, that there is a breach of trust against the plaintiff by those who are directors and by those who are claimed to be constructive trustees. The constructive trustees are, it is true, parties with the plaintiff company itself to the transaction which is illegal. The plaintiff's claim, however, for breach of trust is not made by it as a party to that transaction, or in reliance on any right which that transaction is alleged to confer, but against the directors and constructive trustees for perpetrating that transaction and making the plaintiff company party to it in breach of trust owing to the plaintiff company. The breach of trust includes the making of the plaintiff a party to the illegal transaction. So it seems to me clear on analysis that the plaintiff is not precluded from relying on breach of trust by a party to an illegal transaction, to which the plaintiff itself is a party, when the breach includes the making of the plaintiff a party to that very transaction. Those who proved to be constructive trustees, sharing the responsibility with the directors for the breach of trust, share the liability too.

The result is that the plaintiff in this case would not, by reason of illegality, be prevented from being reimbursed money paid by it unlawfully under a transaction to which it is a party. But this does not mean that this would nullify the ordinary operation of illegality with regard to companies and parties outside the company, and not being or treated as being a trustee to it. But it would prevent such operation shielding those whose position or conduct makes them responsible as owing a fiduciary duty or as constructive trustee.

In the course of the argument *Victor Battery Co Ltd v Curry's Ltd*[3] was considered at length, with its implications for this case. It does not seem to me, on the views which I have taken on the different questions of law which have arisen, that the *Victor Battery case* affects my conclusions. But as that case has been relied on in various ways in the course of the hearing, and as it may conceivably be material to matters which have to be considered at the close of this judgment, it may assist the parties, as well as showing a proper and grateful appreciation of the very able argument addressed to me, if I deal with it.

---

1 [1960] AC 167; [1960] 1 All ER 269
2 [1962] AC 294; [1962] 1 All ER 494
3 [1946] Ch 242; [1946] 1 All ER 519

In that case the plaintiff company issued a debenture to secure a loan by another company to another person for the purchase of shares in the plaintiff company. The plaintiff company asked for a declaration that the debenture was invalid. It was decided: (1) that where a company gave by means of a security, which was a debenture, financial assistance for or in connection with the purchase of shares in the company, the debenture was a valid debenture, and (2) that even assuming that the debenture was an illegal contract, the plaintiff company was not a person for whose protection the illegality had been created, so that it was not relieved from the operation of the rule that a party to a transaction void for illegality cannot recover property transferred under it, which is in accordance with the maxim *in pari delicto potior est conditio defendentis*.

The Court of Appeal in *Essex Aero Ltd v Cross*[1] has since confirmed that a company within section 54 of the Act of 1948 is not a person for whose protection the illegality has been created. As a debenture creates a floating security, which confers a property interest in the property for the time being subject to the security, then it would be in accordance with well established law already referred to that the property interest should remain in the debenture holder despite the illegality. I am not concerned in this case with any question of the second ground of decision. But considerable criticism has been made of the first ground of decision (see *Dressy Frocks Pty Ltd v Bock*;[2] *E. H. Dey Pty Ltd v Dey*;[3] and see *Palmer on Company Law* (20th edn 1959, p 443). It is with this first ground of decision that I am concerned.

What was suggested in argument was that if the debenture in the *Victor Battery case*, being 'security' within section 54, was valid, then the loans to Woodstock and to Burden were valid, since 'loan' and 'security' are treated together on the same footing in section 54, ie, in the provision that it shall not be lawful for a company to give 'whether by means of a loan, guarantee, the provision of security or otherwise, any financial assistance . . .'

Roxburgh J said:

> 'The section provides, not that it shall not be lawful for a company to provide a security in order to give financial assistance, but that it shall not be lawful for a company by means of the provision of security to give any financial assistance. In my judgment, "security" prima facie means "valid security," although I do not say that it must mean that. Moreover, the words of the section are not "purport to give financial assistance" but "give financial assistance" and I cannot see how an invalid debenture could give any financial assistance.'

Thus it was insisted that the security must itself be the means of giving financial assistance and that an invalid security could not give financial assistance because, as I understand it, of its invalidity. It has been doubted (for example, in the Australian cases) whether an invalid security cannot give financial assistance. In a narrow strict sense, the security itself gives no financial assistance, in the narrow sense of payment, at all, but is security for the repayment of the financial assistance or payment that is given. But that is so however valid the security. The financial assistance for which the security is given is, therefore, what must be referred to in the section as giving 'by means of . . . the provision of security . . . financial assistance.' It is in that looser sense that the security is the means of giving financial assistance within the meaning of the section. And this is so

---

1 (1961) 17 November; Bar Library Transcript No 388
2 [1951] SR NSW 390
3 [1966] VR 464

even if 'security' is interpreted as the document by which this security is given and under which the payment is made. And, in that looser sense, its being the means of giving financial assistance does not depend upon its being valid, at any rate when the financial assistance is in fact given. Indeed, the greater the invalidity the greater the assistance, because the less the liability to repay.

I would very readily believe, as Roxburgh J has arrived at an opposite conclusion, that this reasoning is erroneous. But, assuming that it is erroneous, it nevertheless does not seem to me necessarily to follow from Roxburgh J's observations which I have quoted that a loan by a company of money as a part of a transaction by which that money is to purchase, and does purchase, shares in a company is a valid loan. Such a loan, unlike the debenture in the *Victor Battery case*, is a transfer of the purchase money of the shares, and the transfer is nonetheless effective because the loan is invalid. If such a loan is valid, then it seems to me that it can only be on the ground that the section itself establishes that, despite its declaring it unlawful for a company to give by means of a loan financial assistance for the purchase of shares in the company, yet the ordinary consequences of such illegality are not to follow. Statute, of course, could so provide expressly or by implication.

References in the *Victory Battery* judgment might be called in aid of such a conclusion. (1) That section 45 of the Companies Act 1929 (the predecessor of section 54 of the Act of 1948), unlike section 79 of the Act of 1929, does not indicate an intention to avoid the security. But section 79 (now replaced by section 95 of the Act of 1948) was not dealing with illegality, whose consequences are well established under the general law, but with registration of charges, where the consequences of non-registration were not provided by the general law and, therefore, had to be provided in the statute. (2) That the section does not indicate an intention to punish the lender. This is unless, be it added (as in our case) the lender is the company: so the lender in our case does not come within this observation. (3) That to destroy the security, which may be for very large amounts, is out of all proportion to the £100 fine imposed by section 54 of the Act of 1948. This is a common well-recognized consequence accepted by the courts in cases of transactions being made unlawful and participants being subjected to relatively light criminal punishment. That such provisions might prove a positive boon to the principal offenders has been similarly accepted on the well-accepted ground of public policy that the courts will not aid unlawful transactions but let the consequences fall where they lie. (4) That a person with 'knowledge of what the principal offender is doing' may suffer far more than the principal offender. This is subject to the same observation as in (3); and the lender would have the 'knowledge.' (5) The section was designed against the use of cash in shell companies to purchase the shares of those companies. That would, if the plaintiff establishes its allegations, place the defendants within the design of the section. If the section can be interpreted so as to exclude what is within this design and to exclude what is outside it, then effect can be given to the distinction, but no-one has suggested such an interpretation; and in its absence there appears no good reason for relying on it in some way to exclude the *Victor Battery case* any more than to include what, ex hypothesi, on interpretation is indistinguishable from it, namely the present case.

It is with hesitation and misgiving that I come to a conclusion different from that of Roxburgh J but I must state what I see, however faulty my sight.

For my part, I conclude that the loan by the plaintiff to Woodstock and the payment of the £207,500 by the plaintiff to Burden were made unlawful and avoided by section 54 of the Act of 1948. But for reasons already given, this conclusion does not, in my view, defeat the plaintiff's claims in this case.

SOURCE 275
Belmont Finance Corporation *v* Williams Furniture Ltd (No 2)
(Court of Appeal 1980) [1980] 1 All ER 393

The first defendant Williams owned all the shares in the second defendant company (City), which in turn owned all the shares in the plaintiff company. Mr James was the chairman of all three companies. Grosscurth was the controlling shareholder of Maximum and as Grosscurth and his associates were anxious to acquire the plaintiff and Mr James believed that an association with Grosscurth would be beneficial to the Williams group of companies, the following transaction was negotiated between James and Grosscurth. Maximum was sold to Belmont for £500,000 and Grosscurth and his associates bought the share capital of Belmont for £489,000. The first and second defendant invested further money in the plaintiff company. Grosscurth guaranteed that the profits of Maximum and its subsidiaries would not be less than £500,000 over the five years following the transaction. No independent valuation of the worth of Maximum was obtained but counsel's opinion was obtained to the effect that the transaction did not breach s 54 of the Companies Act 1948. The plaintiff went into insolvent liquidation and the receiver obtained a valuation of Maximum at the time of the transaction which suggested that Maximum was worth about £60,000 at the time. These were proceedings against the defendants as constructive trustees of money received in trust for Belmont and also for damages. One question was the legality of the transaction. Foster J upheld the transaction.

> BUCKLEY LJ: . . . The first question for consideration is whether the agreement did contravene section 54 of the 1948 Act. Only if the answer to that question is affirmative does the question whether the defendants or any of them are guilty of conspiracy arise, for it is the illegality of the agreement, if it be illegal, which constitutes the common intention of the parties to enter into the agreement a conspiracy at law.
>
> There is little judicial authority on the section. In *Re V. G. M. Holdings*[1] this court had to consider whether under the section in the form in which it stood in the Companies Act 1929, which did not contain the word 'subscription', the section covered a case where money which a company had provided had been used to assist a subscription for the company's own shares. Lord Greene MR said:
>
> > 'There could, I think, be no doubt that, if that question were answered in favour of the liquidator, the £15,980 was provided by the company by way of financial assistance, because whether a company provides the money by way of gift or by way of loan or by buying assets from the person who is purchasing the shares at a fraudulent overvalue, all those transactions, it seems to me, would fall within the phrase "financial assistance." '
>
> The transaction there in question was a fraudulent one. V. G. M. Holdings Ltd bought all the share capital of Century, which was worthless, from Vanbergen for £8,301 and Venbergen used the money to pay a call on shares which he held in V. G. M. The court, however, held that the transaction did not involve a purchase of V. G. M. shares and so was not within the section. In reliance on the reference by Lord Greene MR to a purchase at a fraudulent overvalue, it was suggested to

---

1 [1942] Ch 235; [1942] 1 All ER 224

us that the section does not apply to any case in which the company which is alleged to have given financial assistance got fair value for its money. I think that Lord Greene MR must be understood to have been speaking in the context of the facts of the case before him and not to have intended to attempt to put any limit on the scope of the section.

Our attention was also drawn to a South African case of *Gradwell (Pty) Ltd v Rostra Printers Ltd.*[1] The contract in that case was a little complicated, but the facts can be summarised as follows. Company A sold to company B all the shares in company C and a debt of £40,258 due from company C to company A. The price was £32,245. The contract was conditional on company B being able to borrow £30,000 on the security of company C's assets. That sum was to be applied in discharging an existing mortgage of company C's assets and in reducing company C's debt to company A. To the extent that the debt to company A was reduced, the cash so received by company A was to be treated as paid on account of the purchase price, that is to say, the price payable by company B was to be reduced by the amount that the debt to company A, which formed part of the subject-matter of the sale, was reduced. The statutory provision there under consideration was for present purposes identical with section 54(1) of the 1948 Act.

The case eventually came before the Appellate Division of the Supreme Court of South Africa. In the following passage Rostra is company A, Crowden is company B and 'the company' is company C. Schreiner JA, who delivered what was effectively the judgment of the court, said:

'We were pressed by counsel for Crowden with the importance of the purpose of the whole transaction. The purpose of Crowden and Rostra was inevitably that of the company, the actions of which were entirely controllable by Rostra. The purpose must be taken to have been to help Crowden to buy and Rostra to sell the company's shares. But this does not carry Crowden to success. Unless what was to be done would amount to giving of financial assistance within the meaning of the sub-section the purpose and the connection would not be important. Having money available the company could part with it in various ways that would enable the recipient to purchase the company's shares with the money. It could for instance buy an asset, not required for the purposes of its business, in order to provide the seller of the asset with money with which to buy the shares. It was contended on behalf of Crowden that this would be giving financial assistance. If the purchase of the asset were effected at a price known to be inflated, this would no doubt be the giving of financial assistance. It would indeed be equivalent to a gift and would clearly involve a reduction of the company's capital. It was one of the illustrations given by Lord Greene in *Re V. G. M. Holdings Ltd.* It is, I think, significant that the Master of the Rolls did not mention the case of the purchase of an asset at a fair price with the object of enabling the seller of the asset to buy the shares. But whatever may be the position in such a case the paying off of an existing debt seems to be decidedly more difficult to bring within the notion of giving financial assistance. The payer's assets and liabilities are put into a different form but the balance is unchanged. And the same applies to the financial position of the payee. Here the company would have no more and no less after the completion of the transaction than before. And the same would apply to

---

Rostra. The company would owe more to its mortgagee and correspondingly less to Rostra. The price to be paid by Crowden would be less by the
difference in the value of the assets to be acquired. Its financial position
would be unchanged — only its investment would be smaller. Where there
is an anticipation of the date when a debt becomes due and payable the
position may possibly be different, but where the debt is presently due and
payable and the debtor can have no answer to the creditor's demand for
payment, it would be straining the language to hold that by paying his debt
the debtor gives the creditor financial assistance.'

In that passage the learned judge reserves the question of what the effect
would be if company B were to purchase from company A an asset not required
for the purposes of its business but at a fair price.

Foster J treated as a proposition of law, accepted by counsel for Belmont, that
a company does not give financial assistance in connection with a purchase of its
own shares within the meaning of section 54 by reason only of its simultaneous
entry into a bona fide commercial transaction as a result of which it parts with
money or money's worth, which in turn is used to finance the purchase of its own
shares. He went on to find that the negotiations in the present case were at arm's
length and that on the one side Mr James genuinely believed that to buy the
capital of Maximum for £500,000 was a good commercial proposition for
Belmont and on the other side Mr Copeland honestly believed that in October
1963 the value of the capital of Maximum with Mr Grosscurth's guarantee of
Maximum's profits under clause 13(h) of the agreement secured on Renta-
home's share capital was not less than £500,000. On these findings he reached
the conclusion that the agreement was a bona fide commercial transaction, on
which ground he dismissed the action.

This reasoning assumes, as I understand it, that if the transaction under
consideration is genuinely regarded by the parties as a sound commercial
transaction negotiated at arm's length and capable of justification on purely
commercial grounds, it cannot offend against section 54. This is, I think, a
broader proposition than the proposition which the judge treated as having been
accepted by counsel for Belmont. If A Ltd buys from B a chattel or a commodity,
like a ship of merchandise, which A Ltd genuinely wants to acquire for its own
purposes, and does so having no other purpose in view, the fact that B thereafter
employs the proceeds of the sale in buying shares in A Ltd should not, I would
suppose, be held to offend against the section; but the position may be different
if A Ltd makes the purchase in order to put B in funds to buy shares in A Ltd. If
A Ltd buys something from B without regard to its own commercial interests, the
sole purpose of the transaction being to put B in funds to acquire shares in A Ltd,
this would, in my opinion, clearly contravene the section, even if the price paid
was a fair price for what is bought, and a fortiori that would be so if the sale to
A Ltd was at an inflated price. The sole purpose would be to enable (ie to assist)
B to pay for the shares. If A Ltd buys something from B at a fair price, which A
Ltd could readily realise on a resale if it wished to do so, but the purpose, or one
of the purposes, of the transaction is to put B in funds to acquire shares of A Ltd,
the fact that the price was fair might not, I think, prevent the transaction from
contravening the section, if it would otherwise do so, though A Ltd could very
probably recover no damages in civil proceedings, for it would have suffered no
damage. If the transaction is of a kind which A Ltd could in its own commercial
interests legitimately enter into, and the transaction is genuinely entered into by
A Ltd in its own commercial interests and not merely as a means of assisting B
financially to buy shares of A Ltd, the circumstance that A Ltd enters into the

transaction with B, partly with the object of putting B in funds to acquire its own shares or with the knowledge of B's intended use of the proceeds of sale, might, I think, involve no contravention of the section, but I do not wish to express a concluded opinion on that point.

The reasoning of the judge's judgment appears to me, with deference to him, to overlook the word 'only' in the suggested proposition of law.

[His Lordship then considered the judge's favourable assessment of Mr James as a witness and the failure of Mr James or any of his associates to obtain a valuation of Maximum and went on to consider an independent valuation made in July 1974 by Mr Howard Williams, a partner in Messrs Mann Judd & Co, a London firm of chartered accountants, who were instructed by Belmont's receiver as if to advise Belmont of a fair price to pay for the share capital of Maximum as at 3 October 1963. The valuation report of Messrs Mann Judd & Co valued the total issued share capital of Maximum as at 3 October 1963 at not more than the 'value of the underlying consolidated "tangible" assets of the company, that is, £60,069'. His Lordship then pointed out that Mr James had genuinely believed that the transaction was a good commercial proposition for Belmont without having any good grounds for that belief, and then continued:] After careful consideration I do not feel that we should be justified in disturbing the judge's finding that Mr James genuinely believed that the agreement was a good commercial proposition for Belmont. It was a belief which, on his view of the commercial aspects of the case, Mr James could have sincerely held.

In truth the purchase of the share capital of Maximum was not a commercial transaction in its own right so far as Mr James and his group of companies were concerned: it was part of the machinery by which City obtained £489,000 for the share capital of Belmont, £259,000 in cash and £230,000 by redemption of the redeemable preference shares subscribed in Belmont. It was not a transaction whereby Belmont acquired anything which Belmont genuinely needed or wanted for its own purposes: it was one which facilitated Mr Grosscurth's acquiring Belmont for his own purposes without effectively parting with Maximum. That the purpose of the sale of Maximum to Belmont was to enable Mr Grosscurth to pay £489,000 for Belmont was at all relevant times known to and recognised by Mr James and the members of his team as well as by Mr Copeland. There is no good reason disclosed by the evidence to suppose either that Mr Grosscurth and his associates could have sold Maximum to anyone else for £500,000 or that Belmont could have disposed of Maximum for £500,000 to anyone else at any time. The purchase of the share capital of Maximum may have been *intra vires* of Belmont (a matter which we have not been invited to consider), but it was certainly not a transaction in the ordinary course of Belmont's business or for the purposes of that business as it subsisted at the date of the agreement. It was an exceptional and artificial transaction and not in any sense an ordinary commercial transaction entered into for its own sake in the commercial interests of Belmont. It was part of a comparatively complex scheme for enabling Mr Grosscurth and his associates to acquire Belmont at no cash cost to themselves, the purchase price being found not from their own funds or by the realisation of any asset of theirs (for Maximum continued to be part of their group of companies) but out of Belmont's own resources. In these circumstances, in my judgment, the agreement would have contravened section 54 of the 1948 Act even if £500,000 was a fair price for Maximum. I think, however, that Mr Howard Williams's report and evidence clearly establish that £500,000 was in truth an inflated price. To the extent that it exceeded £60,000 or thereabouts it was speculative and depended on the continued availability of Mr Grosscurth to direct Maximum's affairs and his willingness to do so. The view that Belmont was buying Mr Grosscurth's services for a period of some five years or until Maximum had earned £500,000 gross profits is, in my view, untenable. As I remarked in the course of the argument, Belmont was not buying Grosscurth; Grosscurth was buying Belmont. The business of Cityfield, which was Maximum's main source of profit, was admittedly speculative and was financed by borrowing. Moreover, its profits as stated in its annual accounts were ascertained on a basis which Mr Copeland agreed was imprudent, though not improper, profits being brought into account before they were received. A considerable part of such profits had to be written off because the contracts on which they depended fell through. It is, in my judgment, manifest on the evidence, particularly that of Mr Howard Williams, that the existence of the warranty could not have added an amount anywhere near £440,000 to the saleable value of Maximum, if indeed it added anything.

It follows that in my judgment the agreement was unlawful, for it was a contract by Belmont to do an unlawful act, viz to provide financial assistance to Mr Grosscurth and his associates for the purpose of, or in connection with, the purchase of Belmont's own share capital.

SOURCE 276
Charterhouse Investments Trust Ltd *v* Tempest Diesels Ltd
(Chancery Division 1986) [1986] BCLC 1

HOFFMANN J: In this action the three plaintiff companies, members of the Charterhouse Group, claim an order for the specific performance of an agreement alleged to be constituted by a letter dated 20 August 1981 whereby the defendant, Tempest Diesels Ltd ('Tempest') agreed to surrender its tax losses for the years 1979 and 1980 to companies within the Charterhouse Group. In my judgment the action succeeds and the plaintiffs are entitled to specific performance.

. . .

The main defence argued for the defendant was that the agreement constituted by the surrender letter was unenforceable because it contravened section 54 of the Companies Act 1948. This section has been repealed by the Companies Act 1981 but the repeal did not take effect until 3 December 1981 and it was therefore in force at the time of the agreement, which in my judgment is the relevant time. Omitting immaterial words, it reads as follows:

'(1) . . . it shall not be lawful for a company to give, whether directly or indirectly, and whether by means of a loan, guarantee, the provision of security or otherwise, any financial assistance for the purpose of or in connection with a purchase or subscription made or to be made by any person of or for any shares in the company. . .'

Counsel for the defendant submits that the tax losses were valuable assets of Tempest and that their surrender could constitute the giving of financial assistance. He says that I should find that the sole or dominant purpose for the surrender of the tax losses was to facilitate the sale of the shares in Tempest by CIT to Mr Allam because the evidence shows clearly that without the surrender, CIT would either not have sold the shares or would only have sold them at a price substantially higher than £1. Once this is established as the only or main purpose of the transaction, the section is contravened whether or not the company received fair value for the surrender: see *Belmont Finance Corp v Williams Furniture Ltd (No 2)*[1] [above].

There are two elements in the commission of an offence under section 54. The first is the giving of financial assistance and the second is that it should have been given 'for the purposes of or in connection with', in this case, a purchase of shares. As Schreiner JA said in a passage in *Gradwell (Pty) Ltd v Rostra Printers Ltd*[2] . . . cited in the *Belmont case*:

> 'Unless what was to be done would amount to giving of financial assistance within the meaning of the sub-section the purpose and the connection would not be important.'

There is no definition of giving financial assistance in the section, although some examples are given. The words have no technical meaning and their frame of reference is in my judgment the language of ordinary commerce. One must examine the commercial realities of the transaction and decide whether it can properly be described as the giving of financial assistance by the company, bearing in mind that the section is a penal one and should not be strained to cover transactions which are not fairly within it.

The *Belmont case* shows that the sale of an asset by the company at a fair value can properly be described as giving financial assistance if the effect is to provide the purchaser of its shares with the cash needed to pay for them. It does not matter that the company's balance sheet is undisturbed in the sense that the cash paid out is replaced by an asset of equivalent value. In the case of a loan by a company to a creditworthy purchaser of its shares, the balance sheet is equally undisturbed but the loan plainly constitutes giving financial assistance. It follows that if the only or main purpose of such a transaction is to enable the purchaser to buy the shares, the section is contravened. But the *Belmont case* is of limited assistance in deciding whether or not an altogether different transaction amounts to giving financial assistance.

The need to look at the commercial realities means that one cannot consider the surrender letter in isolation. Although it constituted a collateral contract, it was in truth part of a composite transaction under which Tempest both received benefits and assumed burdens. It is necessary to look at this transaction as a whole and decide whether it constituted the giving of financial assistance by Tempest. This must involve a determination of where the net balance of financial advantage lay. I see no contradiction between this view and anything which was said in the *Belmont case*. In *Belmont* the company made cash available to the purchaser. This amounted to giving financial assistance and no less so because it was done without any net transfer of value by the company. On the facts of this case there is no question of cash being provided and the only way in which it can even plausibly be suggested that Tempest gave financial assistance as if it made a net transfer of value which reduced the price Mr Allam would have had to pay for the shares if the transaction as a whole had not taken place.

When one considers that the main feature of the transactions which preceded the sale of the shares to Mr Allam was the payment by CCI of £780,000 to Tempest for the purpose of enabling it to repay its overdraft and the bulk of its loan indebtedness, it may seem strange that it could possibly be said that Tempest was giving financial assistance rather than receiving it. But the £780,000 was paid in consideration of the allotment of 780,000 £1 shares in the company and section 53(2) of the Companies Act 1948 prohibits the issue of shares at a discount.

---

1 [1980] 1 All ER 393 (see p 770)
2 1959 (4) SA 419

Tempest must therefore be deemed to have given full value for the £780,000, notwithstanding that the allotted and original shares were immediately afterwards sold for £1. Thus far the law imposes a fiction on the commercial realities.

In addition to the share subscription moneys, Tempest derived substantial benefits from the principal agreement.

. . .

Against these benefits derived by Tempest, it undertook two burdens. The first was the covenant restraining it for two years from carrying on certain kinds of business. Mr Allam described this as a serious handicap to the ability of the company to expand its business and earn profits. He said that in a free negotiation he would have wanted £80,000 to enter into such a covenant. None of the prohibited businesses had previously been carried on by Tempest and Mr Fawcett's evidence was that with one minor exception, Tempest was not in a position to carry them on. I think that it is significant that throughout the negotiations over the terms of the principal agreement, which involved detailed consideration of suggested amendments to various clauses, nothing was said about the restraint clause being in any respect too wide or burdensome. Nor do I know what competition already faced the Charterhouse subsidiaries carrying on the relevant business. The covenant must be assumed to have been of some value to the Charterhouse Group simply because they asked for it, but there is no evidence on which I can find that its value was particularly substantial.

The other burden was the surrender of tax losses. Today it is clear that entitlement to those tax losses would be of substantial value to Tempest. Its profit record since Mr Allam assumed control has been so successful that it exhausted the benefit of its other tax losses at some stage towards the end of its 1983 accounting year. Retention of the tax losses in dispute would therefore eliminate a small charge to corporation tax for 1983 which would otherwise have been payable in September 1984 and would also eliminate a larger charge to corporation tax on the 1984 profits which will otherwise be payable in September 1985. Whether any further benefits could accrue depends on whether the company continues to be profitable.

The value of the tax losses in August 1981 is a very different matter. At that time its future was very uncertain. Mr Allam was confident that it could be made profitable, backed his confidence with money and personal initiative and has been justified by the events. But I do not think that any objective appraisal of the company's prospects in August 1981 could have assumed that he was bound to succeed. If the company failed and went into receivership or liquidation, the 1979–80 tax losses were worthless because it already had enough to cover any claim for stock relief claw-back. If the company recovered, the benefit of the tax losses would accrue only at an uncertain future date when it had exhausted its other losses and the day arrived for the payment of corporation tax (assuming that tax still to be in existence) on additional profits. There was no evidence that the losses could have been sold to a third party for ready money or of what they would have fetched if they were. Indeed, the whole question of the value of the losses at 20 August 1981 was left very much at large.

It will be seen that in the balance of benefits and burdens there are several on which, as it seems to me, the evidence does not enable me to put a precise or even a fairly imprecise value in money. I do not think it is necessary to do so. If I were required to express a view on the effect of the transaction as a whole, ignoring the effect of the £780,000 subscription, I would say that it clearly constituted financial assistance being given to Tempest for the purpose of putting it into a state in which Mr Allam would buy the shares for £1 and did not involve Tempest giving financial assistance to anyone. It is sufficient however for me to say that the defendant has failed to discharge the burden of proving that the transaction amounted to a giving of assistance.

SOURCE 277
Brady *v* Brady
(House of Lords 1988) [1988] 2 WLR 1308; [1988] 2 All ER 617

This case arose out of a complicated reconstruction of a family company ('Brady') run by two brothers and which ran a haulage business and a drinks business. The brothers were unable to work together and the scheme was designed to split the haulage and drinks businesses between the two brothers, Jack and Bob, with Jack taking the haulage business and Bob, the drinks business. It was decided not to liquidate the family company and the complicated scheme arose because of the necessity of creating two separate companies for each of the businesses. Motoreal Ltd and Actavista Ltd were incorporated, the former eventually owning the haulage business and the latter the drinks business. As the assets relating to the haulage business were greater than those relating to the drinks business, some adjustment was necessary to achieve an equal division of the family company between the two brothers. This was achieved by the issue of loan stock by Motoreal which was eventually transferred to Actavista, somewhat reduced by a set off arising through a claim by Brady on another company. The set off resulted from the fact that Brady had, in the course of the scheme become the wholly owned subsidiary of Motoreal to whom was therefore assigned Brady's claim against the other company. It was, therefore, indisputable that Brady had given assistance to Motoreal in the acquisition by Motoreal of the shares in Brady, but it was argued that this transaction was saved as an exception to the statutory prohibition.

> LORD OLIVER: . . . On the issue of whether the proposed transfers of assets by Brady and Athersmith are ultra vires and therefore void on that ground, the first essential is to consider the express objects of these companies as contained in their respective memoranda of association. Each of the companies has, as the final sub-clause of clause 3 of its memorandum, the usual form of *Cotman v Brougham*[1] declaration providing expressly that each sub-clause shall be construed as an independent object and not merely as subsidiary to objects mentioned in other sub-clauses. Sub-clauses (H), (J) and (U) of Brady's memorandum are respectively as follows:
>
> > '(H) To improve, manage, cultivate, develop, exchange, let on lease or otherwise, mortgage, charge, sell, dispose of, turn to account, grant rights and privileges in respect of, or otherwise deal with all or any part of the property and rights of the company. (J) To lend and advance money or give credit to such persons, firms or companies and on such terms as may seem expedient and in particular to customers of and others having dealings with the company, and to give guarantees or become security for any such persons, firms or companies. (U) To sell or otherwise dispose of the whole or any part of the business or property of the company, either together or in portions, for such consideration as the company may think fit, and in

---

1 [1918] AC 514; 87 LJ Ch 379

particular for shares, debentures, or securities of any company purchasing the same.'

Sub-clauses (e), (m) and (r) of Athersmith's memorandum, whilst not identical in terms, contained powers which are, for material purposes, indistinguishable. Similarly, in the case of each company the memorandum contains the usual sub-clause empowering the doing of 'such other things as are incidental or conducive' to the attainment of the company's objects.

  . . .

My Lords, there can, on the face of it, be no question but that the transfers were intended, as between the various companies concerned, not to be gratuitous, for it was inherent in the scheme as proposed that the transfer of assets which were to be applied in discharging Motoreal's indebtedness to Actavista on the loan stock was to be made only upon the terms of the creation of an equivalent indebtedness from Motoreal to Brady or Athersmith as the case may be.

  . . .

The question whether the proposed transfers of assets are ultra vires Brady and Athersmith can perhaps best be tested by postulating the following successive questions. First, does the express object enabling the company to dispose of its assets for such consideration as it thinks fit authorise a transfer in consideration of the promise of the transferee or of a third party to pay to the company the value of the assets transferred? The answer to that question must clearly be in the affirmative. Secondly, is this express object subject to some implied limitation excluding from the range of possible transferees or promisors either a company within the same group or a company which is the parent company of the transferor company? There can be no rational justification for any such implication and Mr Price has not contended that there is. Thirdly, if a promise of a parent or associated company is, in principle, an acceptable consideration, does it cease to be so because the promisor has, at the date of promise, no other assets than the shares which it holds in the promisee? For my part, I can see no reason why, purely as a matter of the vires of the transferor company, it should do so, though of course there may be very good reasons for saying, according to the circumstances, that to enter into a contract on these terms may be ill-advised. But that, at any rate at this stage of the inquiry, is not the question.

  . . .

My Lords, it follows from what I have said that if the appellants' claim is to be successfully resisted at all, it can only be only on the ground that the transaction proposed infringes the provisions of section 151 of the Act of 1985. Subsections (1) and (2) of section 151 provide:

'(1) Subject to the following provisions of this Chapter, where a person is acquiring or is proposing to acquire shares in a company, it is not lawful for the company or any of its subsidiaries to give financial assistance directly or indirectly for the purpose of that acquisition before or at the same time as the acquisition takes place. (2) Subject to those provisions, where a person has acquired shares in a company and any liability has been incurred (by that or any other person), for the purpose of that acquisition, it is not lawful for the company or any of its subsidiaries to give financial assistance directly or indirectly for the purpose of reducing or discharging the liability so incurred.'

The acquisition of the Brady shares by Motoreal has already taken place and has given rise to the issue of the loan stock to Actavista. The proposed transfer therefore falls within the provisions of subsection (2) and it is not in dispute that it does indeed constitute the provision of assistance by Brady to reduce Motoreal's liability incurred in the course of that acquisition. The appellants, however, rely upon the provisions of section 153(2) which is in the following terms:

> 'Section 151(2) does not prohibit a company from giving financial assistance if — (*a*) the company's principal purpose in giving the assistance is not to reduce or discharge any liability incurred by a person for the purpose of the acquisition of shares in the company or its holding company, or the reduction or discharge of any such liability is but an incidental part of some larger purpose of the company, and (*b*) the assistance is given in good faith in the interests of the company.'
>
> . . .

Where I part company both from the trial judge and from the Court of Appeal is on the question of whether paragraph (*a*) can, on any reasonable construction of the subsection, be said to have been satisfied. As O'Connor LJ observed, the section is not altogether easy to construe. It first appeared as part of section 42 of the Companies Act 1981 and it seems likely that it was introduced for the purpose of dispelling any doubts resulting from the query raised in *Belmont Finance Corporation Ltd v Williams Furniture Ltd (No 2)*[1] whether a transaction entered into partly with a genuine view to the commercial interests of the company and partly with a view to putting a purchaser of shares in the company in funds to complete his purchase was in breach of section 54 of the Companies Act 1948. The ambit of the operation of the section is, however, far from easy to discern, for the word 'purpose' is capable of several different shades of meaning. This much is clear, that paragraph (*a*) is contemplating two alternative situations. The first envisages a principal and, by implication, a subsidiary purpose. The inquiry here is whether the assistance given was principally in order to relieve the purchaser of shares in the company of his indebtedness resulting from the acquisition or whether it was principally for some other purpose — for instance, the acquisition from the purchaser of some asset which the company requires for its business. That is the situation envisaged by Buckley LJ in the course of his judgment in the *Belmont Finance case* as giving rise to doubts. That is not this case, for the purpose of the assistance here was simply and solely to reduce the indebtedness incurred by Motoreal on issuing the loan stock. The alternative situation is where it is not suggested that the financial assistance was intended to achieve any other object than the reduction or discharge of the indebtedness but where that result (ie the reduction or discharge) is merely incidental to some larger purpose of the company. Those last three words are important. What has to be sought is some larger overall corporate purpose in which the resultant reduction or discharge is merely incidental. The trial judge found Brady's larger purpose to be that of freeing itself from the deadlock and enabling it to function independently and this was echoed in the judgment of O'Connor LJ where he observed that the answer 'embraces avoiding liquidation, preserving its goodwill and the advantages of an established business.' Croom-Johnson LJ found the larger purpose in the reorganisation of the whole group. My Lords, I confess that I have not found the concept of a 'larger purpose' easy to grasp, but if the paragraph is to be given any meaning that does not in effect provide a blank cheque for avoiding the effective application of section 151 in every case, the concept must be narrower than that for which the appellants contend.

---

1 [1980] 1 All ER 393 (see p 770)

The matter can, perhaps, most easily be tested by reference to section 153(1)(*a*) where the same formula is used. Here the words are 'or the giving of the assistance for that purpose' (ie the acquisition of shares) 'is but an incidental part of some larger purpose of the company.' The words 'larger purpose' must here have the same meaning as the same words in subsection (2)(*a*). In applying subsection (1)(*a*) one has, therefore, to look for some larger purpose in the giving of financial assistance than the mere purpose of the acquisition of the shares and to ask whether the giving of assistance is a mere incident of that purpose. My Lords, 'purpose' is, in some contexts, a word of wide content but in construing it in the context of the fasciculus of sections regulating the provision of finance by a company in connection with the purchase of its own shares there has always to be borne in mind the mischief against which section 151 is aimed. In particular, if the section is not, effectively, to be deprived of any useful application, it is important to distinguish between a purpose and the person why a purpose is formed. The ultimate reason for forming the purpose of financing an acquisition may, and in most cases probably will, be more important to those making the decision than the immediate transaction itself. But 'larger' is not the same thing as 'more important' nor is 'reason' the same as 'purpose.' If one postulates the case of a bidder for control of a public company financing his bid from the company's own funds — the obvious mischief at which the section is aimed — the immediate purpose which it is sought to achieve is that of completing the purchase and vesting control of the company in the bidder. The reasons why that course is considered desirable may be many and varied. The company may have fallen on hard times so that a change of management is considered necessary to avert disaster. It may merely be thought, and no doubt would be thought by the purchaser and the directors whom he nominates once he has control, that the business of the company will be more profitable under his management than it was heretofore. These may be excellent reasons but they cannot, in my judgment, constitute a 'larger purpose' of which the provision of assistance is merely an incident. The purpose and the only purpose of the financial assistance is and remains that of enabling the shares to be acquired and the financial or commercial advantages flowing from the acquisition, whilst they may form the reason for forming the purpose of providing assistance, are a by-product of it rather than an independent purpose of which the assistance can properly be considered to be an incident.

Although the scheme was held to have contravened s 151, it was held to have been saved by virtue of the fact that it could be validly carried out under ss 155, 156 and 158.

Dividends May Be Paid Only Out of Profits

Here the courts moved right away from the earliest principles of capital maintenance. The declaration of dividends was seen by 1889 (in *Lee v Neuchatel Asphalte Company*)[1] to be a matter for the directors in the discharge of their managerial responsibilities. In the result a major gap developed between the legal principles and what came to be considered as good accounting practice.

The law laid down no requirement for the company to have to take account of the depreciation of its assets, even where depreciation was certain;

---

1 (1889) 41 Ch D 1; 58 LJ Ch 408

dividends might be declared so long as there was a surplus on the company's current trading account. Past years' trading losses did not have to be made good. In assessing whether a company had profits, account did not have to be taken of any losses in the company's fixed capital, even realized losses and only of its circulating assets in the current year (see Source 278). Capital gains revealed on a revaluation of assets might be treated as profits and enable dividends to be distributed (*Dimbula Valley (Ceylon) Tea Company Ltd v Laurie*);[1] although this practice was prohibited in Scotland (*Westburn Sugar Refineries Ltd v IRC*)[2] and, in England was made subject to the revaluation being carried out by a reputable person and in circumstances in which the revaluation would not be subject to short term fluctuations.

SOURCE 278
Ammonia Soda Company *v* Chamberlain
(Chancery Division and Court of Appeal 1918) [1918] 1 Ch 266; 87 LJ Ch 193

PETERSON J: . . . The plaintiffs in substance allege that the debit to profit and loss account, amounting to £19,028, or, after deducting the profits up to 31 July 1911, and return income tax, £12,960 18s. 3d., ought to have been made good out of profits before there were any profits available for dividend. The greater part (£13,722 15s. 7d. of this debit of £19,028 represented a depreciation of $2\frac{1}{2}$ per cent on buildings and $7\frac{1}{2}$ per cent on plant and machinery which had been written off as representing a diminution in value of these assets. The question is whether it is prohibited to utilize an increase in the value of the fixed assets for the purpose of wiping out this deficiency in the value of the capital assets. Sir Woodburn Kirby and Mr Gibson both expressed the view that it could not. Sir Woodburn's opinion was that it was contrary to all principles of commercial accountancy to write up the value of a fixed asset and apply the surplus so obtained to meet a deficit on trading, and Mr Gibson stated that such a course was absolutely wrong and 'illegal.' Sir Woodburn also accepted the proposition that it is a recognized and accepted principle of commercial accountancy that nothing should be taken into profit unless it is first realized. This, however, goes too far, for stock and book debts are habitually brought into profit and loss account before being realized, and probably Sir Woodburn intended to confine his statement to fixed assets. I am not satisfied that the proposition that it is contrary to all principles of commercial accountancy to utilize an increase in the value of a fixed asset for the purpose of getting rid of a debit which represents loss of paid-up capital is not too wide. It may be a precept of prudence and yet be far removed from the sphere of the categorical imperative. Assuming that a company ought to keep the value of its assets up to the amount of the liabilities and paid-up capital, or, in other words, to see that its paid-up capital is intact, why should it be absolutely precluded from stating the true value of its assets? If an agricultural company has land under which valuable coal measures are discovered, it is difficult to see why it should not be allowed to show in its balance-sheet the increased value of its lands. If it is necessary or proper that a company shall maintain its assets at the amount of its paid-up capital and liabilities, there would not appear to be anything illegitimate in showing that the assets are equal to the paid-up capital and liabilities. Nor for this purpose can it matter that the increased value is due to the fixed assets. The paid-up capital is represented by

---

1 [1961] Ch 353; [1961] 1 All ER 769
2 [1960] TR 105; (1960) 41 SLT 297

both fixed and circulating capital, and it seems somewhat arbitrary that circulating capital may be shown at its true value while fixed capital must not. Take the case of a depreciation fund. The effect is that the value of the assets as shown in the account is diminished by the amount of the depreciation fund. If the assets in fact increase in value to the extent of the depreciation fund, there is no rule which prohibits a company from wiping out the depreciation fund from the liabilities side of the account. In *Bond v Barrow Haematite Steel Co*[1] Farwell J held that if a sum is carried from profits to reserve account to meet an estimated deficiency of capital assets, and the assets subsequently increase in value to the necessary amount, the sum which has been carried to reserve account is not part of the capital, or, in other words, the subsequent increase in value may be utilized for the purpose of wiping out the previous estimated loss. To my mind it seems hardly logical to say that while this may be done in the case of an estimated loss it is necessarily illegitimate in the case of one which has been ascertained.

SWINFEN EADY LJ: . . . The Companies Acts do not impose any obligation upon a limited company, nor does the law require, that it shall not distribute as dividend the clear net profit of its trading unless its paid-up capital is intact or until it has been made good all losses incurred in previous years. Upon this point it is only necessary to refer to three decisions of the Court of Appeal and one in the House of Lords.

In *Lee v Neuchatel Asphalte Co*[2] Cotton LJ said: 'The plaintiff's second point is that the property of the company is not now sufficient to make good the share capital; that assets to provide for that share capital must be paid up before any dividend can be declared; and that if dividends are declared without that being done, that is to be treated as a return and a division of capital amongst the shareholders, and therefore illegal. In my opinion that is entirely wrong. It is a misapplication of the term "return of capital."' Later on he said: 'But if the Court sees that the directors and the company have acted fairly and reasonably in ascertaining whether this is a division of profit and not of capital, and then in what is really a matter of internal arrangement (if it is done honestly, and does not violate any of the provisions of the articles) the Court is very unwilling to interfere, and in my opinion ought not to interfere, with the discretion exercised by the directors, who have the management of the company or with the powers exercised by the company, within the articles.' Lindley LJ said: 'I may safely say that the Companies Acts do not require the capital to be made up if lost. They contain no provisions of the kind. There is not even any provision that if the capital is lost the company shall be wound up, and I think this omission is quite reasonable. The capital may be lost and yet the company may be a very thriving concern. As I pointed out in the course of the argument, and I repeat now, suppose a company is formed to start a daily newspaper; supposing it sinks £250,000 before the receipts from sales and advertisements equal the current expenses, and supposing it then goes on, is it to be said that the company must come to a stop, or that it cannot divide profits until it has replaced its £250,000 which has been sunk in building up a property which if put up for sale would perhaps not yield £10,000? That is a business matter left to business men.' Then later he said: 'Having shewn from the Acts (negatively, of course, because this is a negative proposition, and can only be proved by looking through the Acts) that the Acts do not require the capital to be made up if lost, I cannot find anything

---

1 [1902] 1 Ch 353; 71 LJ Ch 246
2 (1889) 41 Ch D 1; 58 LJ Ch 408

in them which precludes payment of dividends so long as the assets are of less value than the original capital.'

. . .

The next case was *Verner v General and Commercial Investment Trust.*[1] Lindley LJ, in delivering the judgment of himself and A. L. Smith LJ said: 'The law is much more accurately expressed by saying that dividends cannot be paid out of capital, than by saying that they can only be paid out of profits. The last expression leads to the inference that the capital must always be kept up and be represented by assets which, if sold, would produce it; and this is more than is required by law. Perhaps the shortest way of expressing the distinction which I am endeavouring to explain, is to say that fixed capital may be sunk and lost, and yet that the excess of current receipts over current payments may be divided, but that floating or circulating capital must be kept up, as otherwise it will enter into and form part of such excess, in which case to divide such excess without deducting the capital which forms part of it will be contrary to law.' Then later on he said: 'there is nothing in these Acts,' (ie, the Companies Acts 1867 and 1877) 'any more than in the Act of 1862, which prevents a company which has lost part of its capital from continuing to carry on business and declaring and paying dividends.' Kay LJ said that he did not know of any law to prevent income received from being divided, whether part of the capital is lost or not; and he added that 'it might be difficult to frame such a law, without unduly interfering with the liberty of commercial proceedings.'

. . .

The distinction between 'fixed' capital and 'circulating' capital is not to be found in any of the Companies Acts; it appears to have first found its way into the *Law Reports* in *Lee v Neuchatel Asphalte Co.*

. . .

What is fixed capital? That which a company retains, in the shape of assets upon which the subscribed capital has been expended, and which assets either themselves produce income, independent of any further action by the company, or being retained by the company are made use of to produce income or gain profits. A trust company formed to acquire and hold stocks, shares, and securities, and from time to time to divide the dividends and income arising therefrom, is an instance of the former. A manufacturing company acquiring or erecting works with machinery and plant is an instance of the latter. In these cases the capital is fixed in the sense of being invested in assets intended to be retained by the company more or less permanently and used in producing an income. What is circulating capital? It is a portion of the subscribed capital of the company intended to be used by being temporarily parted with and circulated in business, in the form of money, goods or other assets, and which, or the proceeds of which, are intended to return to the company with an increment, and are intended to be used again and again, and to always return with some accretion. Thus the capital with which a trader buys goods circulates; he parts with it, and with the goods bought by it, intending to receive it back again with profit arising from the resale of the goods. A banker lending money to a customer parts with his money, and thus circulates it, hoping and intending to receive it back with interest. He retains, more or less permanently, bank premises in which the money invested becomes fixed capital. It must not, however, be assumed that the division into which capital thus falls is permanent. The language is merely used to

---

1 [1894] Ch 239; 63 LJ Ch 456

describe the purpose to which it is for the time being appropriated. This purpose may be changed as often as considered desirable, and as the constitution of the bank may allow. Thus bank premises may be sold, and conversely the money used as circulating capital may be expended in acquiring bank premises. The terms 'fixed' and 'circulating' are merely terms convenient for describing the purpose to which the capital is for the time being devoted when considering its position in respect to the profits available for dividend. Thus when circulating capital is expended in buying goods which are sold at a profit, or in buying raw materials from which goods are manufactured and sold at a profit, the amount so expended must be charged against, or deducted from, receipts before the amount of any profits can be arrived at. This is quite a truism, but it is necessary to bear it in mind when you are considering what part of current receipts are available for division as profit.

WARRINGTON LJ: It has been asserted in this case, . . . that there is a . . . restriction . . . which would make it illegal for a company to pay dividends out of the profits of a current year, unless it first makes good deficiencies in paid-up capital occasioned by losses in previous years; or, to put the contention in a broader form, no dividends can properly be paid out of profits so long as there are losses previously incurred and not made good. In my opinion this alleged restriction has no foundation in law.

> . . .

I am, of course, far from saying that in all such cases dividends can properly be paid without making good the previous loss; the nature of the business and the amount of the loss may be such that no honest and reasonable man of business would think of paying dividends without providing for it. In such a case I apprehend the Court would take the view that a payment which no honest and reasonable man of business would think it right to make could not properly be made by directors.

We have no such case here. Even without taking credit for the appreciation of the land, I think the dividends paid were properly paid.

SOURCE 279
Re Cleveland Trust plc
(Chancery Division) [1991] BCLC 424

SCOTT J: . . . This is an application by the Cleveland Trust plc pursuant to s 359 of the Companies Act 1985 for the rectification of the register of members of the company.

At 20 December 1988 the issue share capital of the company was £91,318 divided into 365,272 ordinary shares of 25p each. On 20 December 1988 the board of directors resolved that, subject to the passing of the requisite resolutions at the extraordinary general meeting to be held later that day, there be a five-for-one bonus issue of fully paid shares in the company. The resolutions were duly passed at the extraordinary general meeting and the fully-paid bonus shares were accordingly issued. The bonus shares were entered on the register on 1 March 1989. The company now desires to rectify the register by, in effect, cancelling the bonus shares. The company contends that the bonus issue was a mistake and that, though the truth was not realised at the time, the company had no available funds by means of which the shares could be paid up. There are at present some 51 holders of bonus shares. All have been served with notice of this application. All bar four have consented to the rectification of the register that is sought. None of the four opposes the application or has taken any part in the proceedings.

...

The company has a wholly-owned subsidiary, Gunnergate Holdings Ltd (Gunnergate). Gunnergate in its turn has a wholly-owned subsidiary, McInnes Estates Ltd (McInnes). Each of the three companies has the same directors. McInnes is a property investment company. During the year ending 30 September 1988 McInnes sold the Marton Shopping Centre for a substantial sum which realised a capital profit of £1,132,177. In view of this profit, McInnes declared a dividend for the year of £1,214,000. At its annual general meeting held on 20 December 1988 it was resolved:

'... that a final dividend of £1,214,000 for the year ended 30th September 1988 be paid forthwith to the shareholders now on the register.'

'The shareholders' was a reference to Gunnergate. The £1,214,000 was accordingly paid to Gunnergate.

Gunnergate's accounts for its year to 30 September 1988 show a profit after taxation of £1,059,730. This was attributable entirely to the dividend received from McInnes. With a balance of £2,129 brought forward from the previous year, a total sum of £1,061,859 was shown as the credit balance on profit and loss account.

At the annual general meeting of Gunnergate held on 20 December 1988 it was resolved that:

'A net final dividend of £1,061,600 for the year to 30th September 1988 be paid to the shareholders on the register on 20th December 1988.'

'The shareholders' was a reference to Cleveland. The £1,061,600 was accordingly transferred to Cleveland.

Cleveland's annual general meeting, too, was held on 20 December 1988. Cleveland's balance sheet as at 30 September 1988 showed cash at bank of £1,045,485 and capital reserves of £1,221,306. The consolidated group profit and loss account for the year showed a profit for the year of £1,000,706 of which £926,767 was attributable to 'extraordinary items'. The capital profit arising from the sale of the Marton Shipping Centre was the source of the bulk of the £927,767.

The report of the directors of Cleveland referred to the group profit of £1,000,706 and announced that:

'It is proposed to capitalise part of the extraordinary profit by a bonus issue of five shares for every one held.'

...

The declaration of a £1,214,000 dividend by McInnes was an unfortunate mistake. The memorandum of association of McInnes provides, under para 3, for the objects of the company. Sub-paragraph (A) thereof starts by authorising McInnes's main business: 'To carry on business as a property investment company in all its branches ...' The second sentence of the sub-paragraph reads, however, as follows:

'If from time to time it shall be found necessary or advisable for the company to realise all or any of its property or assets, the company shall have power so to do, but any surpluses or deficiencies arising on or from such realisation shall be dealt with as capital surpluses not available for the payment of dividends or as capital deficiencies which shall be charged against capital account.'

. . .

1. *The McInnes dividend*

The circumstances to be taken into account in considering the effect in law of the declaration and payment of the £1,214,000 dividend are these.

The use for the purpose of paying a dividend of any part of the capital profit made on the sale of the Marton Shopping Centre was prohibited by para 3(A) of the memorandum of association. None the less, Gunnergate, the only shareholder of Cleveland, voted in favour of the dividend resolution at the annual general meeting and did so in the knowledge that without use of the capital profit McInnes had insufficient profit to frank the dividend. But Cleveland could have declared a dividend of £104,914 without using any part of the capital profit.

Mr Weaver QC submitted that in view of the prohibition in para 3(A) of the memorandum, Cleveland lacked the capacity to declare and pay the £1,214,000 dividend. He cited *Ashbury Rly Carriage and Iron Co Ltd v Riche* (1875) LR 7 HL 653 as authority for the proposition that the unanimous consent of all the corporators of a company does not suffice to give the company the corporate capacity to do an act that is outside the powers conferred on it by its constitution. Mr Charles accepted this proposition as an accurate statement of the law, and so do I. It would of course have been open to Cleveland, on following the procedure prescribed by s 4 of the Companies Act 1985, to have altered the objects clause of its memorandum by deleting therefrom the second sentence of para 3(A). If that had been done, there would have been no legal objection to the £1,214,000 dividend. But the s 4 procedure was not used. Paragraph 3(A) was not altered. The reflection that had the requisite procedure been adopted McInnes would have had power to declare the £1,214,000 dividend does not, in the events which actually happened, cure its incapacity to have done so (cf *Re Patent Invert Sugar Co* (1885) 31 Ch D 166).

McInnes's lack of corporate capacity in regard to the declaration and payment of the dividend does not, however, extend to the whole of the £1,214,000. As to £104,914 McInnes did have the corporate capacity to declare and pay a dividend.

The consequence of an ultra vires dividend payment was considered by the Court of Appeal in *Precision Dippings Ltd v Precision Dippings Marketing Ltd* [1985] BCLC 385, [1986] Ch 447. Dillon LJ said ([1985] BCLC 385 at 389, [1986] Ch 447 at 457):

'The payment of the dividend of £60,000 was therefore an ultra vires act by the company, just as if it had been paid out of capital or in any other circumstances in which under any of the other provisions of s 39 and the following sections there were not profits available for dividend. In those circumstances, can Marketing have any defence to the company's claim for repayment of the £60,000 with interest?'

Dillon LJ answered the question he had set by saying this ([1985] BCLC 385 at 390, [1986] Ch 447 at 457–458):

'I would put the position quite shortly. The payment of the £60,000 dividend to Marketing was an ultra vires act on the part of the company. Marketing when it received the money had notice of the facts and was a volunteer in the sense that it did not give valuable consideration for the money. Marketing accordingly held the £60,000 as a constructive trustee for the company: see *Rolled Steel Products (Holdings) Ltd v British Steel Corp* [1985] 3 All ER 52 at 87–88, 91, [1984] BCLC 466 at 509–510, 514 per Slade and Browne-Wilkinson LJJ.'

. . .

I am not satisfied that the constructive trust extends to the whole of the £1,214,000 dividend. As to £104,914 the payment of the dividend was within the power of the company.

. . .

But, on any footing, Gunnergate became constructive trustee in respect of £1,109,086, if not in respect of the whole £1,214,000.

2. *The Gunnergate dividend*

The impropriety of this dividend does not derive from any particular provision in the Gunnergate memorandum of association, but from the general law. Section 263 of the Companies Act 1985 provides, in sub-s (1) that:

'A company shall not make a distribution except out of profits available for the purpose.'

Subsection (2) defines 'distribution' as 'every description of distribution of a company's assets to its members, whether in cash or otherwise'. There then follow a number of exceptions, one of which is, 'Distribution by way of an issue of shares as fully- or partly-paid bonus shares'. Subsection (3) provides that:

'A company's profits available for distribution are its accumulated realised profits so far as not previously utilised by distribution or capitalisation less its accumulated realised losses.'

. . .

The directors of Gunnergate were also the directors of Cleveland. They knew, or ought to have known of the impropriety of the Gunnergate dividend. So, in my judgment, Cleveland held the dividend upon constructive trust for the repayment thereof to Gunnergate. There is here, unlike the McInnes dividend, no question of partial validity. In the absence of accounts which satisfy s 271, Gunnergate was not entitled to make any distribution by way of dividend at all (see s 270(5) and cf the *Precision Dippings* case [1985] BCLC 385, [1986] Ch 447.)

3. *The Cleveland bonus shares*

Cleveland's consolidated profit and loss account showed a profit for the financial year of £1,007,706 and, after payment of dividends of £50,225, retained profit of £957,481. There is no profit and loss account for Cleveland alone. But it is clear that without the Gunnergate dividend of £1,061,600 Cleveland would have had little, if any, profit for the year. Of course, if Gunnergate had not declared and paid the dividend, its investment value to Cleveland would have been enhanced by, presumably, the amount of the dividend. A revaluation of Gunnergate might, in that event, have led to an unrealised capital profit being shown in Cleveland's account. It would, I understand, have been possible for that profit to have been transferred to capital reserve and to have been utilised in issuing fully-paid bonus shares. That route was not, however, followed. Instead, the shareholders of Cleveland were asked to approve and did approve a bonus issue to be capitalised out of part of the balance standing to the credit of the profit and loss account. But the profit and loss account had been distorted by the inclusion therein of the Gunnergate dividend. Cleveland did not in truth have any profit out of which the bonus shares could be paid up.

. . .

Cleveland's power to issue fully- and partly-paid bonus shares derives from its articles of association. The articles incorporate Table A of the Companies Act 1948. Article 128 of Table A provides as follows:

> 'The Company in general meeting may, upon the recommendation of the directors, resolve that it is desirable to capitalise any part of the amount for the time being standing to the credit of the company's reserve accounts or to the credit of the profit and loss account or otherwise available for distribution, and accordingly that such sum be set free for distribution amongst the members who would have been entitled thereto if distributed by way of dividends and in the same proportions, on condition that the same be not paid in cash but be applied either in or towards paying up any amounts for the time being unpaid on any shares held by such members respectively, or paying up in full unissued shares or debentures of the company to be allotted and distributed, credited as fully paid up, to and amongst such members in the proportion aforesaid, or partly in the one way and partly in the other, and the directors shall give effect to such resolution.'

. . .

. . . the earmarking of the money in Cleveland's books to pay up the issued bonus shares was, in my judgment, a real transaction, not simply a notional one. The issue took place. Share certificates relating to the issued shares, describing them as fully paid, were sent to the shareholders. The constructive trust for repayment to Gunnergate of the amount of the dividend created, in my opinion, an equitable right in personam. It did not attach in rem to the balance standing to the credit of the profit and loss account. It may be that via some form of equitable tracing Gunnergate could trace the dividend into the bank account of Cleveland or could claim the benefit of the fully-paid bonus shares. But, if so, that could only be on the footing that the shares were, as they purported to be, fully paid.

The contract between the shareholders and Cleveland entitled each shareholder to be issued with fully-paid bonus shares. They were, in my opinion, issued with fully-paid bonus shares. The issue cannot, in my judgment, be avoided by treating the issue as an issue of shares on which nothing had been paid.

As to Mr Weaver QC's fourth point, I accept that the fundamental premise underlying the issue was that the capital profit deriving, via the intermediate dividends, from the sale of the shopping centre, would be the source of the capitalisation. But in fact this capital profit could not be the source of the capitalisation. Both the shareholders and the company were mistaken about this. Another way of putting the same point is that a fundamental premise underlying the bonus issue was that Cleveland had profits available for distribution sufficient in amount to pay up the bonus shares. The Cleveland accounts for the year to 30 September 1988 showed this to be so. But the accounts were wrong, and both the shareholders and the company were mistaken about this.

The issue and acceptance of the bonus shares involved, in my opinion, a relationship between Cleveland and the shareholders analogous to a contractual relationship. On the passing of the resolution of the extraordinary general meeting on 20 December 1988, the directors having already recommended the issue of the shares, each shareholder became entitled as against Cleveland to be issued with the appropriate number of bonus shares. It is well established that a declaration of dividend approved by the company in general meeting entitles each shareholder to recover the dividend as a debt from the company. Parity of reasoning applies, in my opinion, to declarations approving the issue of bonus shares. The relationship between company and shareholder vis-à-vis the declared dividend or the authorised bonus issue may not be strictly contractual but it is, in my opinion, sufficiently analogous for the principles of common law mistake to be as applicable to the bonus issue as to an ordinary contract.

PART III: INCREASE OF CAPITAL

This is a matter for the company. The principal question is, does the company's constitution allow for an increase of capital? Provided that the company's nominal capital has not been exceeded, the company can issue more shares. If the company has issued all its authorised shares, it may increase its authorised (nominal) capital by ordinary resolution in general meeting (CA 1985, s 121). Three important related issues, namely,

(a) who has the power to issue shares?,
(b) can shares be issued only for the purpose of raising more money?, and
(c) if the increase affects the rights of the existing shareholders, have they any redress?

are dealt with elsewhere (pp 464 and 609, respectively).

PART IV: REDUCTION OF CAPITAL

The Companies Act has, since 1867, contained a procedure for the reduction of the company's capital. In fact, it was on the strength of this provision that the House of Lords held illegal the practices of issuing shares at a discount and the company purchasing its own shares. Each of these practices constituted a reduction of the company's capital but was not in accordance with the procedure laid down (and which the House of Lords held to be exclusive).

The present procedure is in ss 135–141 of the Companies Act 1985. Two common law rules have been formulated alongside the statutory provisions but both would seem to be honoured more in the breach than in the observance. First, it was said in *British American Trustee Company v Couper*[1] (Source 280) that shareholders are to be treated as equally as possible. This is difficult to police (see the comments of Megarry J in *Holders Investment Trust Ltd*,[2] p 636). Secondly, it was said that the interests to be considered before sanctioning a reduction of a petitioning company's capital were the shareholders, the creditors and the public (see, however, Source 281).

A further question concerns the position of preference shareholders, who by reason of their usual priority right of return of capital on winding up, are vulnerable where there is a reduction of capital (Source 282). The reduction

---

1 [1894] AC 399; 63 LJ Ch 425
2 [1971] 1 WLR 583; [1971] 2 All ER 289 (p 636)

may constitute a variation of the preference shareholders' class rights, thereby generating the special variation of class rights procedure (pp 634ff; Sources 283 and 284). Creditors are generally protected, where necessary by the setting aside of a special reserve to take account of long-term commitments (Source 285, although contrast Source 286).

SOURCE 280
British American Trustee Company *v* Couper
(House of Lords 1894) [1894] AC 399; 63 LJ Ch 425

The company had carried on business in the United States, and a portion of its investments were in that country. These investments had been made on the advice of a committee of the board by the directors resident in America. Differences arose between the board of directors in England and the American committee as to the management of the business of the corporation, which rendered it impossible to carry on such business both in England and the United States with advantage. It was accordingly determined that the best course to be adopted was that the company should cease to carry on business in the United States, and it was arranged that the American investments should be made over to the American shareholders, subject to the payment of £11,000 to the corporation, and that the shares held by the American shareholders should be cancelled, thus reducing pro tanto the capital of the company. This arrangement was approved by the shareholders at two extraordinary general meetings. All the creditors of the company were either paid or assented to the arrangement. The interests of the shareholders alone had therefore to be considered. On the hearing of the petition, confirmation by the Court was opposed by one of their number. North J dismissed the petition with costs, and his decision was affirmed by the Court of Appeal.

LORD HERSCHELL LC: . . . Now, it can scarcely be denied that such a scheme as that under consideration, by which certain of the shareholders receive a part of the assets of the company equivalent to their shares therein, such shares being then cancelled, is a mode of effecting a reduction of the capital of the company.

   . . .

   My Lords, if all the shareholders of a company were of opinion that its capital should be reduced, and that this reduction would best be effected by paying off one shareholder and cancelling the shares held by him, I cannot see anything in the Acts of 1867 and 1877 which would render it incumbent on the Court to refuse to confirm such a resolution, or which shews that it would be *ultra vires* to do so.

   I do not see any danger in the conclusion that the Court has power to confirm such a scheme as that now in question, or any reason to doubt that this was the intention of the legislature. The interests of creditors are not involved, and I think it was the policy of the legislature to entrust the prescribed majority of the shareholders with the decision whether there should be a reduction of capital, and if so, how it should be carried into effect. The interests of the dissenting minority of the shareholders (if there be such) are properly safeguarded by this: that the decision of the majority can only prevail if it be confirmed by the Court. This is a complete answer to the argument, ably urged by Mr Romer at the Bar, that if all the shareholders of the same class were not dealt with in precisely the same fashion, the interests of the minority might be unjustly sacrificed to those of the majority.

There can be no doubt that any scheme which does not provide for uniform treatment of shareholders whose rights are similar, would be most narrowly scrutinised by the Court, and that no such scheme ought to be confirmed unless the Court be satisfied that it will not work unjustly or inequitably. But this is quite a different thing from saying that the Court has no power to sanction it.

LORD WATSON: . . . The company have practically no outside creditors; but their petition is opposed by the respondent, who owns shares of both classes. At the Bar of the House he did not maintain that under the scheme sought to be confirmed the shareholders of either class, whether they were bought out or continued to be members, would not each of them receive a fair and reasonable equivalent for his present interest in the company, and nothing more. He relied solely upon the plea that it is beyond the statutory jurisdiction of the Courts to sanction any scheme for the reduction of capital which does not deal in precisely the same way with each and every share belonging to the same class. If that be the law, it is manifest that in some cases the result might be unfortunate. Apart from the interest of creditors, the question whether each member shall have his shares proportionately reduced, or whether some members shall retain their shares unreduced, the shares of others being extinguished upon their receiving a just equivalent, is a purely domestic matter; and it might be greatly for the advantage of the company that the latter alternative should be adopted. Although every member of the company were agreed as to the desirability of taking that course, if the plea of the respondent be well founded the Court would have no power to assist them.

SOURCE 281
Ex Parte Westburn Sugar Refineries Ltd
(House of Lords 1951) [1951] AC 625; [1951] 1 All ER 881

LORD REID: My Lords, section 66, subsection 1(*c*), of the Companies Act 1948, authorizes a company, subject to confirmation by the court and if certain conditions have been satisfied, to 'pay off any paid-up share capital which is in excess of the wants of the company'. In this case the statutory conditions have been satisfied. The question is whether the court should confirm the reduction of capital proposed. The only unusual features of this case are that the appellants propose to pay off part of their share capital not with money but by transferring to the shareholders shares of another company, and that the value of the shares proposed to be so transferred greatly exceeds the amount by which the appellants' share capital is to be reduced. But there is nothing novel in paying off share capital otherwise than with money: it has long been recognized that this is not incompetent.

The real questions in this case are whether it is competent in a reduction of capital to pay off share capital by transferring assets whose value clearly exceeds the amount by which the share capital of the company is reduced; and if this is competent, whether it is proper in this case to allow it to be done. As regards competency 'the statute has not prescribed the manner in which the reduction is to be carried out, nor has it prohibited any method of effecting the object' (per Lord Herschell LC, in *British and American Trustee & Finance Corporation Ltd v Couper*[1]). And in the same case Lord Watson said: 'I do not find a single expression in the Act tending to indicate that the discretion of the court to grant

---

1 [1894] AC 399; 63 LJ Ch 425

or refuse such an application does not extend to every possible mode of reducing capital'.

The terms of the Act are as wide today as they were then. At first sight it may seem strange that the appellants' proposal should be competent; but once it has been recognized that paying off capital can be done otherwise than by payment of money, there cannot be any requirement of exact correspondence between the amount of capital paid off and the value of the assets used to pay it off, because in many cases it is impossible to make any exact valuation of such assets. So the most that could be required would be an approximate correspondence; but I can see no reason why it must be held that the statute has imposed any such vague or difficult limitation.

I therefore turn to the second question. Are the circumstances of this case such that the court ought to confirm the appellants' proposal? In effect what is proposed is to transfer to the shareholders assets which are valued in the appellants' sheet at sums which in total correspond exactly with the amount by which the share capital is to be reduced, but which may be worth rather more than three times the balance sheet values. I say 'may be' because the nature of most of these assets is such that any close estimate of their value is impossible.

What, then, is the duty of the court in considering a matter of this kind? In the first place the interest of creditors must be safeguarded; but here that has been done. Secondly the interests of shareholders may have to be considered: but in this case there has been no opposition by any shareholder at any time and it is difficult to see how there could be any prejudice to any single shareholder. And thirdly there is the public interest to consider: that this is a relevant consideration was clearly recognized by Lord Macnaghten in *Poole v National Bank of China Ltd.*[1] I would not be disposed, by attempting to define the public interest, to narrow in any way the discretion of the court in any future case. But in a case like the present I think that it is right to scrutinize the facts somewhat closely, having in mind the position of those who may in future form connexions with the company as creditors or shareholders. It appears to me to be proper to consider what assets the company will retain if the proposed reduction of capital is confirmed. In this case the assets to be distributed taken at their real value form only a comparatively small part of the total assets of the company. The value of the assets to be distributed has been estimated at £197,768, and the value of the assets to be retained by the company as shown in the balance sheet exceeds £1,400,000. It seems clear that the true value of these assets cannot be substantially less than that amount. The total capital of the company before reduction is £609,000 and liabilities to creditors and others did not exceed £500,000 at the time of the last balance sheet. In my opinion these facts are amply sufficient to remove any apprehension that the future conduct of the company may be adversely affected by confirmation of the present proposal.

It has been said that there are other matters concerning the public interest to be taken into account in this case. Lord Carmont took the view that there is or may be an ulterior object behind the present petition, namely to avoid in part the consequences of possible future legislation. The fact that the petitioners may have such an ulterior object may be a good reason for making quite certain that the existing law is complied with in every respect, but it cannot in my judgment be by itself a ground for dismissing the petition. The petition must be judged by the law as it exists today.

LORD RADCLIFFE: . . . Two reasons are advanced by Lord Carmont for his view.

---

1 [1907] AC 229; 76 LJ Ch 458

One is that on general grounds of public policy the court ought not to aid a company threatened with nationalization to 'eviscerate' itself by parting with valuable assets. My Lords, I do not think that the contingency of nationalization has any relevance to the public policy that Courts of Justice should support. If the reduction is objectionable on other grounds, it will not become the more acceptable because it may have been proposed in view of a pending measure of nationalization: conversely, the threat of nationalization cannot render improper what is otherwise unobjectionable. I pass, therefore, to the second, and, indeed, the main, reason which weighed with the learned judge. In his view it was essential for the company, which showed by its petition that the ground of the proposed reduction was that the share capital to be returned was in excess of its wants, to demonstrate to the court by how much its capital was in fact surplus; and, since the evidence presented to the court was deficient in this respect, a material fact had not been made out. Whether this conclusion would on any view have justified a dismissal of the petition, rather than its remitter for further inquiry, I do not think it necessary to discuss; for I think that the conclusion itself is based on a misunderstanding.

I cannot find any good reason why the court should be concerned to know what is the extent by which the company's capital is surplus to its requirements. If by that phrase, itself susceptible of ambiguity, is meant the extent by which the whole of the company's assets, at the best contemporary valuation that can be placed upon them, exceeds what is required for the future conduct of its business, precise information on this would do nothing to aid the task of the court. For it would throw no light on the sole thing which is here in question, how much of the paid-up share capital is to be returned as being surplus. Nor do I think that evidence of this kind is usually required in cases of this sort. In truth this, which is the real question, answers itself by the company's own resolution. When a company has come to employ in its business, as this company has, a volume of assets very much greater in value than the amount of its paid-up share capital, there is no obvious answer to the question how much of that capital it needs for future trading. It is a domestic matter, which the shareholders and their managers must decide among themselves, how much of the paid-up share capital the company can dispense with for the future. If the amount that they have decided upon works no injustice to creditors or to shareholders, I see no purpose which can be served by the court's insisting upon a precise figure of the company's wants or the striking of an exact balance between that figure and the total available resources in hand.

Appeal against the dismissal of the petition allowed.

SOURCE 282
Scottish Insurance Corporation Ltd *v* Wilsons & Clyde Co Ltd
(House of Lords 1949) [1949] AC 462; [1949] 1 All ER 1068

The articles of association of the respondent coal company included:

'128. Subject to the rights of members entitled to shares issued upon special conditions, and subject as hereinafter provided, the profits of the company, after setting aside any amount which may be carried to any reserve fund, written off for depreciation or otherwise, shall be applied in order of priority in manner following, viz: Firstly. To the payment of a cumulative preferential dividend at the rate of £7 per cent per annum on the capital for the time being paid up or credited as paid up on the preference shares (first issue). Secondly. To the payment of a cumulative preferential dividend at the rate of £7 per cent per annum on the capital for the time being paid up or credited as paid up on the preference shares (second issue), but only after satisfying the dividends payable on the said preference shares (first issue); and Thirdly. The residue shall be divisible among the holders of the ordinary shares in proportion to the amounts paid up or credited as paid up on the shares held by them respectively.

159. In the event of the company being wound up, the preference shares (first issue) shall rank before the other shares of the company on the property of the company, to the extent of repayment of the amounts called up and paid thereon.

160. In the event of the company being wound up, the preference shares (second issue) shall rank before the ordinary shares but after the said preference shares (first issue) on the property of the company to the extent of repayment of the amounts called up and paid thereon.'

LORD SIMONDS: My Lords, on 1 January 1947, the colliery assets of the respondent company, Wilsons & Clyde Coal Co Ltd, which I will call the respondents, were in terms of the Coal Industry Nationalization Act 1946, transferred to and vested in the National Coal Board, which was constituted under that Act. Thus the effective business of the respondents was brought to an end and it is their avowed intention in due course to go into voluntary liquidation. But this they will not do until the compensation payable to them under the Act has been assessed and paid. . . .

At an extraordinary general meeting held on 26 September 1947, the respondent company passed a special resolution for the reduction of its capital from £850,000 (consisting of £40,000 first preference stock, £10,000 second preference stock and 800,000 ordinary shares of £1 each, of which 675,000 had been issued and converted into £675,000 ordinary stock), to £462,500 divided into £337,500 ordinary stock and 125,000 ordinary shares of £1 each and for effecting such reduction by returning to the holders of the first and second preference stocks of £1 for each unit of stock held by them and extinguishing such stocks and by returning to the holders of the £675,000 ordinary stock capital to the extent of 10s. for each unit of such stock held by them. It appears that not all those who voted for the resolution were ordinary stockholders, nor did all the preference stockholders vote against it, nor do they all now oppose the reduction. I do not think that your Lordships can get any guidance from the way in which votes were given. . . . I do not entertain any doubt about this case. The court should in my opinion confirm the reduction upon which the respondents have resolved.

The Companies Act, 1929, no more than its predecessors, prescribes what is to guide the court in the exercise of its discretionary jurisdiction to confirm or to refuse to confirm a reduction of capital. But I agree with the learned Lord President that, important though its task is to see that the procedure, by which a reduction is carried through, is formally correct and that creditors are not prejudiced, it has the further duty of satisfying itself that the scheme is fair and equitable between the different classes of shareholders: see eg *British & American Trustee & Finance Corporation Ltd v Couper*.[1] But what is fair and equitable must depend upon the circumstances of each case and I propose, ignoring for the moment the particular factor introduced by the Coal Act, to consider the elements on which the appellants rely for saying that this reduction is not fair to them.

---

1 [1894] AC 399; 63 LJ Ch 425 (see p 790)

In the formal case which they have presented to the House the element of unfairness on which the appellants insist is that the reduction deprives them of their right to participate in the surplus assets of the company on liquidation and leaves the ordinary stockholders in sole possession of those assets. But in their argument both in the Court of Session and before your Lordships they have further relied on the fact that they have been deprived of a favourable 7 per cent investment which they cannot hope to replace and might have expected to continue to enjoy. They further contend that the deprivation of these rights, which would in any case have been an unmerited hardship, is rendered the more unfair because it is likely to be followed at an early date by liquidation of the company or, as it is less accurately expressed, because it is itself only a step in the liquidation of the company.

The first plea makes an assumption, viz, that the articles give the preference stockholders the right in a winding up to share in surplus assets, which I for the moment accept but will later examine. Making that assumption, I yet see no validity in the plea. The company has at a stroke been deprived of the enterprise and undertaking which it has built up over many years: it is irrelevant for this purpose that the stroke is delivered by an Act of Parliament which at the same time provides some compensation. Nor can it affect the rights of the parties that the only reason why there is money available for repayment of capital is that the company has no longer an undertaking to carry on. Year by year the 7 per cent preference dividend has been paid; of the balance of the profits some part has been distributed to the ordinary stockholders, the rest has been conserved in the business. If I ask whether year by year the directors were content to recommend, the company in general meeting to vote, a dividend which has left a margin of resources, in order that the preference stockholders might in addition to repayment of their capital share also in surplus assets, I think that directors and company alike would give an emphatic negative. And they would, I think, add that they have always had it in their power, and have it still, by making use of articles 139 or 141, to see that what they had saved for themselves they do not share with others.

. . .

Whether a man lends money to a company at 7 per cent or subscribes for its shares carrying a cumulative preferential dividend at that rate, I do not think that he can complain of unfairness if the company, being in a position lawfully to do so, proposes to pay him off. No doubt, if the company is content not to do so, he may get something that he can never have expected but, so long as the company can lawfully repay him, whether it be months or years before a contemplated liquidation, I see no ground for the court refusing its confirmation. To combat the suggestion that, so far as any benefit to the preference stockholders is concerned, the position is substantially the same whether they are now repaid their capital or full use is made of articles 139 and 141, it was urged that the incidence of income tax would be a sufficient deterrent of this alternative measure. I do not, however, consider that the court can properly have regard to such a consideration as this in determining what is fair between the parties. It might indeed be considered improper to do so if it drove the ordinary stockholders to a course less advantageous to themselves but no more advantageous to the preference stockholders.

It will be seen, my Lords, that, even making an assumption favourable to the appellants, I reject their first plea. But it is perhaps necessary, in case there should be a division of opinion which would make this a decisive issue, that I should shortly examine the assumption. It is clear from the authorities, and would be clear without them, that, subject to any relevant provision of the general law, the rights inter se of preference and ordinary shareholders must depend on the terms of the instrument which contains the bargain that they have made with the company and each other. This means, that there is a question of construction to be determined and undesirable though it may be that fine distinctions should be drawn in commercial documents such as articles of association of a company, your Lordships cannot decide that the articles here under review have a particular meaning, because to somewhat similar articles in such cases as *Re William Metcalfe & Sons Ltd*[1] that meaning has been judicially attributed. Reading the relevant articles, as a whole, I come to the conclusion that articles 159 and 160 are exhaustive of the rights of the preference stockholders in winding up. The whole tenor of the articles, as I have already pointed out, is to leave the ordinary stockholders masters of the situation. If there are 'surplus assets' it is because the ordinary stockholders have contrived that it should be so, and, though this is not decisive, in determining what the parties meant by their bargain, it is of some weight that it should be in the power of one class so to act that there will or will not be surplus assets.

There is another somewhat general consideration which also, I think, deserves attention. If the contrary view of articles 159 and 160 is the right one and the preference stockholders are entitled to a share in surplus assets, the question will still arise what those surplus assets are. For the profits though undrawn, belong, subject to the payment of the preference dividend, to the ordinary stockholders and, in so far as surplus assets are attributable to undrawn profits, the preference stockholders have no right to them. This appears to follow from the decision of the Court of Appeal in *Re Bridgewater Navigation Company*,[2] in which the judgment of the House of Lords in *Birch v Cropper*[3] is worked out. This again is not decisive of the construction of particular articles, but I am unwilling to suppose that the parties intended a bargain which would involve an investigation of an artificial and elaborate character into the nature and origin of surplus assets.

. . .

Finally on this part of the case I ought to deal with an observation made by Lord Macnaghten in *Birch v Cropper* upon which counsel for the appellants relied. 'They,' he said, '[sc. the preference shareholders] must be treated as having all the rights of shareholders, except so far as they renounced these rights on their admission to the company.' But in my opinion, Lord Macnaghten can have meant nothing more than that the rights of the parties depended on the bargain that they had made and that the terms of the bargain must be ascertained by a consideration of the articles of association and any other relevant document, a task which I have endeavoured in this case to discharge. I cannot think that Lord Macnaghten intended to introduce some new principle of construction and to lay down that preference shareholders are entitled to share in surplus assets unless they expressly and specifically renounce that right.

Appeal dismissed, reduction confirmed.

SOURCE 283
Re Old Silkstone Collieries Ltd
(Court of Appeal 1954) [1954] Ch 169; [1954] 1 All ER 68

The capital of the company consisted of first and second preference stock and ordinary shares. The preference stockholders were entitled to a preferred

1 [1933] Ch 142
2 [1891] 2 Ch 317; 60 LJ Ch 415 (see p 617)
3 (1889) 14 App Ca 525; 59 LJ Ch 122 (see p 612)

dividend and to priority of capital on a winding up. Arising out of the nationalisation of the coal industry, the company decided to reduce its capital stage by stage towards complete extinction.

The rights of these respective classes of stockholders had been varied from time to time. In July 1950, the first preference stockholders were entitled under the articles to a fixed cumulative preferential dividend of six per cent on the amount paid up (or credited as paid up) on the stock, but to no further right of participation in the company's profits, and upon a winding up to repayment of the capital paid up in priority to all other stockholders, but to no further participation in the surplus assets of the company. Their voting rights were strictly limited by the amended article 65, which was to the effect that they were not entitled to attend and vote at general meetings of the company unless the preferential dividend was in arrear to the extent there stated, or unless the business of the meeting included 'the consideration of a resolution directly and prejudicially affecting the special rights attached to' that stock.

The second preference stock carried the right to a 5 per cent non-cumulative preference dividend ranking after the preferential dividend on the first preference stock, but with a further right to participation in the profits of the company *pari passu* with the ordinary stockholders up to, but not beyond, a further 5 per cent on the paid up capital on the second preference stock. The second preference stockholders, like the first preference stockholders, were not entitled in a winding up to any participation in the surplus assets of the company beyond the amount required to repay the paid up capital on their stock, to which they were entitled in priority to the ordinary stockholders. Their voting rights were more extensive than those of the first preference stockholders, in that there was no limitation to their right to attend and vote at ordinary meetings of the company.

Article 6 of the articles of association provided: 'If at any time the capital of the company is divided into different classes of shares, the special rights attached to any class may either with the consent in writing of the holders of three-fourths of the issued shares of the class, or with the sanction of an extraordinary resolution passed at a separate general meeting of such holders (but not otherwise) be modified or abrogated.'

. . .

The then chairman thus expressed himself to all the stockholders:

'You will recollect that in my statement circulated on 1 May 1950, with the 1949 accounts, I stated it was the intention of the board to submit to stockholders a repayment of capital scheme. The company has substantial liquid funds which have accumulated from cash received for compensation in respect of stocks of stores, wagons, etc. Additionally, a substantial loan from the parent company to a wholly-owned subsidiary has been repaid. Your board has therefore decided to recommend that in the interests of the company and the stockholders the moneys for which the company has no present use shall be applied to the repayment of 10s. to the first preference stockholders and second participating preference stockholders for every £1 of such stock held by them.

Section 25 of the Coal Industry Nationalization Act 1946, provides for the adjustments of rights as between the holders of preference and ordinary stocks. It is your board's intention that any rights stockholders may have under section 25 shall be retained until the amount of compensation payable to the company is determined. Whilst the proposal to repay 10s. per

£1 of stock to both classes of preference stockholders is not strictly in accord with the rights of first preference stockholders under the company's articles of association, in that they are entitled to prior repayment of capital, your board draw attention to the fact that if the whole of the first preference stock was repaid, these stockholders would be deprived of any rights which they may have under section 25 as the stock would cease to exist. The funds which will be available for stockholders on determination of final compensation will be such that no prejudice can result to the priority rights of the first preference stockholders by the scheme now submitted. The proposals involve a payment of £198,780 which is available without resort to a claim for partial compensation by the parent company.'

Enclosed with that circular were notices of extraordinary general meetings first of the first preference stockholders, second of the second participating preference stockholders, and finally of the company. Since it was apprehended that the repayment was otherwise than in strict accordance with the stockholders' rights under the articles, the terms of article 6 made it necessary that the proposal should have the sanction of extraordinary resolutions duly passed at separate meetings of both classes of preference stockholders, and the provisions of article 65 made it necessary for the first as well as the second preference stockholders to attend the meeting of the company for reduction.

The resolution for reduction, which was to be submitted to the extraordinary general meeting of the whole company held on 23 August 1950 (all the stockholders, preference and ordinary, being treated as entitled to vote at it) took, so far as relevant, this form: 'That the capital of the company be reduced,' and then was set out the reduction scheme under which each class of preference stockholders suffered a 50 per cent reduction of the paid up capital. Then were followed the words: 'but so that notwithstanding such reduction of capital the holders of the said first preference stock, second participating preference stock and ordinary stock shall respectively remain entitled to claim the same adjustment of their interest as could have been claimed under section 25 of the Coal Industry Nationalization Act 1946, if the said reduction of capital had not taken effect.' That reduction of capital was duly confirmed by the court.

Slightly more than a year later the second stage in the gradual process of total liquidation was reached. The present chairman, who had become chairman on the death of the previous chairman, then sent to the stockholders a circular following in some respects closely the circular which had been sent by his predecessor. It was dated 21 September 1951, and opened thus: 'Further proposed part repayment of capital. You will recollect that following the authority of class meetings of first preference stockholders and second participating preference stockholders held on 22 August 1950, a repayment of 10s. to the first preference stockholders and second participating preference stockholders for every £1 of such stock held by them on 31 October 1950, was made on 1 November 1950.' Then he stated that the company has now received £100,000 Treasury Stock in part satisfaction of compensation.

'Your board has decided to recommend that in the interests of the company and the stockholders, the money for which the company has no present use shall be applied to the repayment of 5s. to the first preference stockholders and second participating preference stockholders for every 10s. of such stock held by them.' Then occurred this reflection of what had been said on the previous occasion. 'Section 25 of the Coal Industry Nationalization Act 1946, provides for the adjustment of rights as between the holders of preference and ordinary stocks. It is your board's intention that any rights stockholders may have under

could have been claimed under section 25 of the 1946 Act if the said reduction of capital had not taken effect.'

After the resolution of 1951 the holdings of the first preference stockholders had been reduced to 25 per cent of their original amount, but I read the proviso as stating that, notwithstanding that reduction, for the purposes of making their claim under section 25 and vis-à-vis the ordinary stockholders, they are entitled to present that claim on the footing that they hold four times the amount of the stock which at the material date they would in fact hold. Put in another way, it would be equivalent to saying that, for the purposes of such an application, they would be holders of first preference stock conferring the right of a fixed preferential cumulative dividend at the rate not of 6 per cent but of 24 per cent. What effect that would have, in the circumstances of the case, on the mind of the tribunal, which is given the task of deciding the question posed in section 25, it is not necessary to decide; but I find it impossible to reject the view that, by giving to them that special right or privilege, the preference stockholders have had created in their favour a special right (how valuable it is unnecessary to state) within the meaning of articles 6 and 65 of this company's articles of association.

. . .

One final point may be mentioned. It was said by Sir Andrew that, assuming everything else against him, still the effect of the last words in the resolution did not import any such permanence in their effect as to give any special right; in other words, that they merely said, in effect, that the rights of the preference stockholders would be as stated until such time as the company, in exercising its power *aliunde* in the articles, chose to put an end to them. I doubt whether that helps the company's argument, because so long as they remain, if I am right so far, these are special rights which can only be taken away under the articles by observing the restrictions of article 6; but I also think, as my brother Jenkins observed during the argument, that in its context the word 'remain' should fairly be construed as meaning 'should remain either until such time as the compensation or adjustment under the Act of 1946 has been paid or until the time for applying under the Act has expired.'

For those reasons, I am of opinion that the effect of these resolutions in 1950 and 1951 was to create special rights. If that view is correct, then, as Sir Andrew concedes, everything else follows, and the only course open to this court is to dismiss the petition.

Evershed MR also expressed the view that the scheme was not fair and equitable and should not be confirmed on that ground as well.

SOURCE 284
Re Saltdean Estate Co Ltd
(Chancery Division 1968) [1968] 1 WLR 1844; [1968] 3 All ER 829

The Saltdean Estate Co Ltd ('the company') was incorporated, in 1926, with an authorised share capital of £1000, divided into 1000 shares, all of one class, but, in consequence of an increase of capital, in 1932, the authorised capital was reorganised so as to consist of £12,500, divided into 20,000 preferred shares of 10s. each, and 50,000 shares of 1s. each. All the shares of each class had been issued, and were fully paid up. The company's principal objects were to carry on the business of a land and real estate company. Under article 8 of the articles of association, in order to 'affect, modify, deal with or abrogate in any manner' the rights and privileges attaching to any particular class of shares, an extraordinary resolution passed at a separate general meeting of the members of that class was necessary. The quorum required at any such meeting was members of the class holding or representing by proxy three-fourths of the capital paid up or credited as paid up on the issued shares of that class. Article 21, was in these terms

> 'For the purpose of providing a fund for the redemption of the debentures issued by the company, the directors shall set aside each year, until the whole of the said debentures have been redeemed, a sum of not less than $12\frac{1}{2}$ per cent of the cash receipts from the sales of freehold land during that year and subject thereto the net profits of the company which the directors shall determine to distribute by way of dividend in any year shall be applied, first, in payment of a dividend at the rate of 10 per cent per annum on the amounts paid up or credited as paid up on the preferred shares for the time being issued; secondly, in payment among the holders of the ordinary shares for the time being issued of a sum equivalent to the total sum paid by way of dividend to the holders of the preferred shares, and, thirdly, the balance of profits shall be divided as to 50 per cent among the holders of the preferred shares and 50 per cent among the holders of the ordinary shares for the time being issued.'

By article 24:

> 'If the company shall be wound up there shall first be paid to the holders of the preferred shares rateably the amounts paid up or credited as paid up thereon. The surplus assets (if any) shall be applied in repayment of the capital paid up or credited as paid up, on the ordinary shares at the commencement of the winding-up; and the excess (if any) shall be distributed among the members holding ordinary shares, in proportion to the number of ordinary shares held by them respectively at the commencement of the winding-up.'

Every share carried one vote on a poll at a general meeting, and consequently, the ordinary shareholders could carry an ordinary resolution, but not a special or extraordinary resolution against the holders of the preferred shares, if the latter all opposed it.

At an extraordinary general meeting of the company, held on 8 July 1968, a special resolution was passed to reduce the capital of the company to £2,500 divided into 50,000 ordinary shares of 1s. each, by repaying the full amount of the capital paid up on the preferred shares, together with a premium of 5s. per share. No separate meeting of the preferred shareholders had been convened to consider this proposed reduction, but the owner of all, or virtually of all, the ordinary shares approved it, and a large number of the preferred shares were held by the holder or holders of the ordinary shares.

The company's business had proved to be very profitable, and in the seven years ended 30 September 1966, the dividends distributed to the preferred shareholders in each year respectively were at the following rates per cent upon the amount paid up, viz: 200, 275, 125, 150, 50, 100 and 100 (gross). For the period from 1 October 1966, to 31 March 1968, a dividend of 100 per cent had been proposed, amounting to £10,000 (gross). At 31 March 1968, the amount standing to the credit of the company's revenue reserve was £324,924. If this amount were distributed the preferred shareholders would receive 1625 per cent on their capital.

. . .

BUCKLEY J: The evidence satisfies me that the sum of £15,000, proposed to be paid to or on account of the preferred shareholders upon the reduction of the company's capital, is not needed by the company. So far as it represents a return of paid up capital, that capital is in excess of the company's needs.

It has long been recognised that, at least in normal circumstances, where a company's capital is to be reduced by repaying paid up share capital, in the absence of agreement or the sanction of a class meeting to the contrary, that class of capital should first be repaid which would be returned first in a winding up of a company (see *Re Chatterley-Whitfield Collieries Ltd*,[1] per Lord Greene MR). In the present case the preferred shareholders are entitled to prior repayment of capital in a winding up and, consequently, if the company has more paid-up capital than it needs and wishes to repay some part of it, the first class of capital to be repaid should prima facie be the preferred shares.

. . .

First, it is said that the proposed cancellation of the preferred shares will constitute an abrogation of all the rights attached to those shares which cannot validly be effected without an extraordinary resolution of a class meeting of preferred shareholders under article 8 of the company's articles. In my judgment, that article has no application to a cancellation of shares on a reduction of capital which is in accord with the rights attached to the shares of the company. Unless this reduction can be shown to be unfair to the preferred shareholders on other grounds, it is in accordance with the right and liability to prior repayment of capital attached to their shares. The liability to prior repayment on a reduction of capital, corresponding to their right to prior return of capital in a winding up, is a liability of a kind of which Lord Greene MR, in the passage I have referred to, said that anyone has only himself to blame if he does not know it. It is part of the bargain between the shareholders and forms an integral part of the definition or delimitation of the bundle of rights which make up a preferred share. Giving effect to it does not involve the variation or abrogation of any right attached to such a share. Nor, in my judgment, has section 72 of the Companies Act 1948,[2] upon which the opponents place some reliance, any application to this case. That section relates to variation of rights attached to shares, not to cancellation of shares.

The opponents' main ground of complaint about the proposed reduction is that, as they contend, it is discriminatory. It will deprive the preferred shareholders of any opportunity of participating in the enjoyment not only of the future fruits of the company's prosperity but also of those which have already been garnered. It is said that the preferred shares of the company are not like preference shares with a limited interest in the profits of the company: as a class they carry a right to at least an equal share with the class of ordinary shares in the distributed profits. As regards participation in profits, they are, it is said, what are called 'equity' shares. This is true so far as it goes, but it should be noted that the profits which, under article 21, the preferred shareholders are entitled to share equally with the ordinary shareholders, are only those which the directors decide shall be distributed. Moreover, the preferred shareholders' only right, under article 24, in a winding up is a preferential right to repayment of paid-up capital.

Buckley J then analysed the articles of association and continued:

1 [1948] 2 All ER 593
2 See now s 127 of the Companies Act 1985

I, therefore, reach the conclusion that, on the true interpretation of the company's articles, if the company were now to be liquidated, all the undistributed profits would belong to the ordinary shareholders.

Reduction confirmed.

SOURCE 285
Re Lucania Temperance Billiard Halls (London) Ltd
(Chancery Division 1965) [1966] Ch 98; [1965] 3 All ER 879

The company, Lucania Temperance Billiard Halls (London) Ltd, carried on the business of operating billiard halls, mostly in the greater London area, and was the tenant of 29 leasehold properties in various places. Twenty-one of those leaseholds were held on terms significantly below current market rates and for periods long enough to give the leases an appreciable value; the remaining eight would not give rise to any significant claims from the landlords as creditors in the event of a winding up, since comparable rents could be secured from other tenants. The authorised capital of the company was £200,000 divided into 100,000 shares of £1 each denominated as ordinary shares and 100,000 shares of £1 each denominated as preference shares. All the ordinary shares and 70,000 of the preference shares had been issued. All the issued shares were fully paid.

On 1 October 1965, the company passed a resolution for the reduction of capital to £100,000, to be effected by cancelling the 30,000 unissued preference shares and by repaying and cancelling the 70,000 issued preference shares. The reduction, therefore, involved repayment to the preference shareholders of £70,000. The company had sufficient cash resources to cover its liabilities, apart from those under the leases of its various properties, as well as the amount proposed to be returned to the shareholders, with an adequate margin.

The company took out this summons seeking an order under section 67(3) of the Companies Act 1948,[1] that settlement of a list of creditors be dispensed with. . . .

BUCKLEY J: The practice usually followed hitherto, where a company owns a leasehold property, and a cash coverage, or a coverage in cash and trustee securities, is relied upon as affording the necessary special circumstance for the purposes of section 67(3), has been to insist upon that coverage extending to the whole of the rent to the end of the term of the lease, or where the coverage is insufficient for this and no acceptable guarantee is forthcoming, to insist upon the landlord's written consent to the reduction of capital being produced as well as his written agreement to postpone his claim to those of other existing creditors. Sometimes a bank guarantee of the debts of all creditors other than the landlord or landlords has been accepted, coupled with the written consent of the landlord or landlords to the reduction but without any agreement to postpone landlords' claims. Occasionally, and in special circumstances, a bank guarantee covering possible claims by landlords for a period of, say, ten years has been accepted without any consents or postponements on the part of any landlord. . . .

The evidence with regard to the company's leasehold properties is that of the 29 properties owned by the company 21 are held on terms as to rent or otherwise which are significantly below current market rates and for a period which is long enough to give the leases held by the company an appreciable value. It follows that if the company were to be wound up in the immediate future it would either

---

1 See now s 136(6) of the Companies Act 1985

be able to dispose of the residue of the respective terms for sums reflecting their varying values or, in cases where liquidation would operate to determine the leases, the lessors would benefit from the termination by being able to negotiate fresh leases on more favourable terms and in consequence would have no claims as creditors of the company by reason of such termination. The remaining eight properties are held either for periods which are too short to confer any premium value or at full current market rates, The surveyor whose affidavit is filed in support of the application, however, deposes to the fact that he is satisfied that in no case is the company paying a rent which is in excess of current market rates, so that in all these cases — that is, the eight properties — the lessors, though not benefiting from a hypothetical liquidation of the company, would not have any significant claims as creditors since they would be able to secure comparable rentals from other tenants.

Special circumstances to justify a direction under section 67(3) must, in my judgment, be such that the court is satisfied that so far as can be reasonably foreseen the relevant creditors will not be adversely affected by the reduction of capital. The circumstances must, I think, be such that broadly speaking the creditors affected will at least be no worse off than they would be if they were permitted to attend upon the application for confirmation of the reduction of capital and to object. In that case the court could only override a creditor's objection if the company secured payment of the creditor's debt or claim by appropriating a sufficient fund to satisfy the requirements of section 67(2)(*c*). If the debt were liquidated and admitted, the fund would have to be for the full amount of the debt. But a tenant's prospective liability to his landlord for rent and under lessee's covenants is not liquidated. The question is in what amount a landlord, as an objecting creditor, could insist upon an appropriation to secure payment of his claim.

... Mr Instone, for the company, says that if the company were to be put into liquidation, then, having regard to the beneficial nature of the majority of the leases and what I may call the neutral character of the rest, being neither beneficial nor onerous, the company's landlords would be in a position to prove only in very modest sums, if at all, in respect of future liabilities under the leases. A reduction of capital by repaying paid-up share capital is, he says, of the nature of a partial liquidation of the company, and he submits that the company's landlords can insist on no more favourable treatment in the one case than in the other. Therefore, he concludes, no provision for meeting potential claims by landlords need be insisted on in the present case as a condition of a direction under section 67(3) that section 67(2) shall not apply to any class of creditors of the company.

It seems to me that that argument ignores the fact that the company remains in possession of the leaseholds and, so far as I know, is likely to continue to do so for some years. There are no assignees whose performance of the tenants' obligations under the leases would relieve the company of any obligations they might otherwise be under by reason of covenants on the company's part. If the liquid resources of the company were now to be exhausted, or nearly exhausted, in paying or making provision for payment of the company's debts to creditors other than its landlords and in making a cash distribution to its shareholders, no liquid assets, or very few, would remain out of which the company could meet liabilities to its landlords accruing under the leases. This would, as it seems to me, clearly be prejudicial to the landlords.

A claim by a landlord against a tenant in respect of future rent or future breaches of covenant under a lease must, whether the tenant be the original lessee or an assignee of the term, be a claim the amount of which is not ascertained, for in either case the amount which will eventually accrue due to the landlord will depend on whether, and if so when, the tenant assigns the term to an assignee, and also, where the tenant is the original lessee, on the extent to which the obligations under the lease are discharged by any successor in title of his. Such a claim, therefore, falls within section 67(2)(c)(ii), which requires the court to fix the amount to be appropriated in respect of such a claim after the like inquiry and adjudication as if the company were being wound up by the court. If, in the present case, the company were being wound up by the court, landlords' claims would be capable of proof under section 316, a just estimate being made so far as possible to their value. If a company in winding up remains in possession of leaseholds with a view to realising its property to better advantage, the landlord may be able to demand payment of the rent in full as an expense of the winding-up, but otherwise he is restricted to his right of proof. It would not, I think, be right for the purposes of the notional winding-up referred to in section 67(2)(c) to treat the leaseholds of which the company is in possession as being retained for the convenience of the winding-up; although for a reason which I will explain in a minute it makes little difference whether the position is regarded in this way or not. In assessing the amount to be fixed under that sub-paragraph attention should, in my judgment, be fixed upon the amount for which any landlord could prove in the notional winding-up. This amount, however, would depend upon how long in fact the leasehold property remained in the possession of the company before it was assigned, surrendered or disclaimed. Down to that date the landlord could prove for all rent accrued. Upon the assignment of the lease he might also be able to prove, if the company were the original lessee or otherwise bound by covenant, for what Roxburgh J described in a passage I have read as the value of the lessee's covenants. But, since that value is one which takes into account the probability of an assignee duly discharging the tenant's obligations under the lease, it would, in my judgment, be clearly unfair to assume for the purposes of the notional liquidation that the liquidator had made, or would make, such an assignment; for there is no present prospect, so far as I am aware, of the company assigning any of its leaseholds and consequently no prospect of there being any assignees from whom the landlords can expect anything. An inquiry and adjudication under section 67(2)(c) should, in my judgment, accordingly proceed on the footing that the company will for an indefinite period remain in possession of the leaseholds, during which period the landlords will be entitled to prove for all rent accruing due. As the position is such that in a winding-up all admitted proofs will be met to the extent of 20s. in the pound, the result will be the same as if the leaseholds were retained in the notional liquidation for the convenience of the winding-up.

However, in this rather illusory state of affairs, in which the liquidator in a notional winding-up is to be treated as retaining leaseholds which no liquidator would normally be likely to retain longer than circumstances demanded, some recognition of reality must, in my opinion, be admitted in the exercise of the court's discretion under section 67(3). Where the term for which a leasehold is held is a long one, it should not, in my judgment, normally be necessary to insist on the full rent for the whole term being included in the amount of any coverage provided for the purpose of section 67(3). I think that ten years' rent should normally suffice to give a landlord adequate protection where the lease is not an onerous one. I say 'normally' because every case should be dealt with on its own facts. In the present case I consider that ten years' rent would be sufficient in respect of any of the company's leaseholds held for a term of which more than ten years remains outstanding.

SOURCE 286
Re Grosvenor Press plc
(Chancery Division 1985) [1985] 1 WLR 980 [1985] BCLC 286

This was an application for the reduction of the company's capital. The company had purchased a publishing and distribution business for £725,000, which it sold the same day at the same price to a subsidiary company. The price was left outstanding as a loan by the company to its subsidiary. The company, in consultation with its auditors decided that it was not possible to attribute any specific value to the business and that the outstanding sum of £725,000 should be written off. This resulted in a large deficit on the company's profit and loss account which in view of s 263(3) of the Companies Act 1985 greatly inhibited the declaration of dividends. This could be cured by a reduction of the company's capital but the question was what safeguards were necessary to protect creditors who would be put at risk by the greater flexibility of the company to declare dividends.

NOURSE J: . . . It is . . . made clear that the proposed reduction cannot be put forward, indeed that it is not put forward, as a cancellation of paid-up share capital which is lost. It is clear, first, as a simple matter of language, secondly, in principle and, thirdly, on authority that capital is not lost unless it is permanently lost:

. . . It is also clear that if capital is not permanently lost a cancellation of paid-up share capital will prejudice the interests of creditors. Accordingly, the company offered and the registrar accepted an undertaking for their protection.

. . .

On the basis of an undertaking . . . the registrar exercised the power conferred by section 67(3) of the Companies Act 1948 to dispense with the settlement of a list of creditors. He evidently took the view that the undertaking was an adequate protection for all those who would be creditors of the company (including contingent and prospective creditors) when the reduction took effect. I respectfully agree with that view. I should add that reductions of this kind, with undertakings substantially to the same effect, have been confirmed by the court in the past. The question which now arises is whether the undertaking ought to endure more permanently so as to safeguard the interests of future creditors and shareholders as well.

. . .

When the petition in *Re Jupiter House Investments (Cambridge) Ltd*[1] came before Harman J he took the view, with which I entirely and respectfully agree, that the loss had not been proved to be permanent. I need not go into detail. Although the facts were different, the impermanence of the loss was of much the same order as it is in the present case. It was possible that most or even all of it would be recovered. Eventually, after an adjournment of the hearing and the filing of further evidence, an undertaking was offered on the basis of which Harman J duly confirmed the reduction sought.

The undertaking was to set apart to a separate capital reserve the first £384,058 of the net sums recovered by the company (such net sums being then defined) and not without the leave of the court to distribute or part with the whole or any part of the sums so set apart to such separate capital reserve. In other words, the

1 [1985] 1 WLR 975

undertaking was to set apart a permanent capital reserve. Its effect was to safeguard the interests not only of existing creditors but of future creditors and shareholders as well. What I have to decide is whether a similar undertaking ought to be required in this case.

. . .

Under article 50 of its articles of association the company has power by special resolution to reduce its share capital and share premium account in any manner authorised by law. It is established by a series of decisions of the House of Lords starting in 1894 that the law authorises a company to reduce its capital in any manner and to any extent authorised by its articles of association and decided upon by the prescribed majority of its shareholders: see *Ex parte Westburn Sugar Refineries Ltd*[1] and the earlier cases there cited. Similarly, the court has jurisdiction to confirm any reduction so authorised and, subject to due observance of certain safeguards, it will usually do so.

In a conscientious argument Mr Richards, for the company, submitted, first, that in accordance with the principles so established the court has jurisdiction to confirm a reduction whose purpose is to eliminate a deficit on profit and loss account which results either (a) from a provision against the diminution in value of an asset which may not be permanent or (b) from a provision against a liability which, although likely to occur, may well not do so. (The present case falls within alternative (a), but alternative (b) is only the other side of the same coin.) There can be no doubt that that submission is correct. It is to be noted that sections 39(2) [now s 263(3)] and 40(2)(*c*) [now s 264(3)(*c*)] of the Act of 1980 expressly recognise that that is the case.

Secondly, Mr Richards submitted that, in the absence of special circumstances, the court will exercise its discretion to confirm such a reduction provided that certain normal requirements are satisfied. He accepted that the interests of existing creditors must be fully safeguarded, but he submitted that there is no general or usual requirement that the interests of future creditors and shareholders should be safeguarded, at all events by the provision of a permanent capital reserve.

In *Poole v National Bank of China Ltd*,[2] Lord Macnaghten recognised that the court might think that it ought to refuse its sanction to a reduction out of regard, as he put it, to the interests of those members of the public who might be induced to take shares in the company. This possibility was again recognised, although without comment or elaboration, by Lord Parker of Waddington in *Caldwell & Co Ltd v Caldwell*.[3] It was also recognised, and on that occasion extended to include the interests of future creditors as well, by the House of Lords in *Ex parte Westburn Sugar Refineries Ltd*, which appears to be the only case where there has been any discussion on the point. In that case the proposed reduction was by way of a return of capital to shareholders on the ground that it was in excess of the company's wants. Reasoned speeches were delivered by Lords Normand, Reid and Radcliffe, each of whom referred to the interests of future creditors and shareholders. Thus Lord Reid, in stating the duty of the court in considering a matter of this kind, said:

'And thirdly there is the public interest to consider: that this is a relevant consideration was clearly recognised by Lord Macnaghten in *Poole v National Bank of China Ltd*. I would not be disposed, by attempting to define the

1 [1951] AC 625; [1951] 1 All ER 881 (see p 791)
2 [1907] AC 229; 76 LJ Ch 458
3 [1916] WN 70; 1916 SC (HL) 120

public interest, to narrow in any way the discretion of the court in any future case. But in a case like the present I think that it is right to scrutinise the facts somewhat closely, having in mind the position of those who may in future form connections with the company as creditors or shareholders.'

Lord Radcliffe said:

'If the transaction is itself competent the court should only refuse its confirmation if what is proposed to be done is somehow unfair or inequitable; and the consideration of what is unfair or inequitable cannot well extend beyond consideration of the interests of creditors, shareholders and the general public, by which term is, I think, meant persons who may in the future have dealings with the company or may be minded to invest in its securities.'

All three of their Lordships commented on the proposals in that case, but in the main their observations do not give general assistance in deciding in what circumstances and in what manner the interests of future creditors and shareholders ought to be safeguarded. Their observations were mainly directed to an excess of wants case. However, Lord Radcliffe said:

'What are the actual circumstances of this case? The company is parting with these investments at the same value as they stand at in its books. If the reduction is effected, $45,192 (I ignore the funding loan for this purpose) disappears from one side of the balance sheet and the same amount from the other, in the form of issued share capital. There is nothing in this which, at first sight at all events, appears to threaten to confuse or mislead future traders or investors.'

And Lord Normand said:

'But in an arrangement in which assets are taken at balance sheet values there is the possibility that the scheme of reduction may be used as a means of defeating or injuring the rights of creditors or deceiving future investors. If the retained assets are entered in the company's balance sheet at a figure in excess of their real value, creditors may be prejudicially affected, and it may also be possible by adjustments in the balance sheet after the reduction takes effect to return paid up capital to shareholders.'

These remarks are of more general value. They emphasise that there should be no risk that the company's accounts will deceive future creditors and shareholders.

I respectfully agree with Lord Reid that it is not for the court in one case to narrow its discretion in any future case; and yet I am unable to see any ground, either in principle or on authority, for thinking that the court ought usually to require that a reserve be set aside indefinitely to safeguard the interests of future creditors and shareholders. Anyone who gives credit to or acquires shares in the company after the reduction takes effect is prima facie adequately protected by existing statutory safeguards. There are the provisions of section 69 of the Act of 1948, in particular subsection (2), which provides that the reduction shall take effect on, and not before, the registration of the order and the minute, and subsection (3), which provides for advertisement. Then there are the detailed requirements of section 149 of and Schedule 8 to the Act of 1948 as amended, which provide that a company's accounts shall give a true and fair view of the state of its affairs and of its profits or losses for each financial year. I do not think that it would be right for the court, except in special circumstances, to require a reserve to be set aside indefinitely. The statutory procedures which allow for its reduction demonstrate that there is no status of inviolability attaching to a company's capital. There is no purpose in being allowed to discard with one hand a loser which you must take back with the other.

I therefore accept Mr Richards' second submission. I accept that there may be cases in which special circumstances require some further safeguard for future creditors and shareholders . . . There are no special circumstances in this case.

PART V: RECONSTRUCTION, MERGER, TAKEOVER

The Companies Act provides two separate regimes to facilitate mergers between companies or the takeover by one company of another (ss 425–427, 428–430F). The first (ss 425–427) is designed to facilitate any major reconstruction and is used for a variety of purposes. Care is taken to ensure that all interests are represented before the scheme of reconstruction is approved and, where interests conflict, that they are treated separately (Source 287). The procedure is cumbersome involving two court orders, the first enabling the various meetings to be convened, the second approving the scheme, provided that all meetings have voted positively and that the court considers the scheme fair.

The Companies Act (ss 428ff) allows for a takeover bidder who has received 90 per cent or more acceptance of the bid, to acquire, compulsorily, the minority that has refused. In general, it is very unusual for the dissenting minority to invoke successfully, the provision which entitles it to resist expropriation (Source 288).

Under s 110 of the Insolvency Act 1986, there is provision for the takeover of one company by another, but this is rarely used. Those who dissent from the proposal are entitled to insist on being bought out at an agreed or an arbitrated price.

SOURCE 287
Re Hellenic & General Trust Ltd
(Chancery Division 1976) [1976] 1 WLR 123; [1975] 3 All ER 382

TEMPLEMAN J: This is an opposed petition for the sanction by the court under section 206 of the Companies Act 1948[1] of an arrangement relating to the ordinary shares of the company, Hellenic & General Trust Ltd.

The company carries on business as an investment trust. The ordinary shares of the company are held as to 53.01 per cent by Merchandise and Investment Trust Ltd (known as M.I.T.). All the shares of M.I.T. are held by Hambros Ltd and therfore M.I.T. is a wholly owned subsidiary of Hambros. The objectors, National Bank of Greece S.A., hold 13.95 per cent of the ordinary shares of the company proposed to be dealt with by the arrangement. By the arrangement the ordinary shares of the company will be cancelled. New ordinary shares will be issued to Hambros and the company will thus become, like M.I.T., a wholly owned subsidiary of Hambros. The former shareholders of the company will be paid by Hambros 48p per share for the loss of their former shares. The result is

---

1 Now s 425 of the Companies Act 1985

equivalent to a purchase by Hambros of the ordinary shares of the company at 48p per share.

. . .

In the present case the court, on the petition of the company, summoned a meeting of all the ordinary shareholders. A resolution agreeing to the arrangement was carried, some 91 per cent of the shareholders by value attending and voting. M.I.T., holding 53.01 per cent, voted in favour of the arrangement. The National Bank of Greece, the objectors, holding 13.95 per cent of the ordinary shares, voted against the arrangement. The arrangement was approved by 86.61 per cent in number and 84.67 per cent in value of those who attended and voted. The votes of M.I.T. were vital. If they had not attended and voted the requisite majority could not have been achieved against the opposition of the objectors. The objectors now pursue their opposition to the arrangement in this court. On their behalf Mr Wright puts forward four objections. The first objection goes to jurisdiction, and the other three concern the discretion of the court in sanctioning an arrangement and the proper principles for the exercise of that discretion.

The first objection put forward is that the necessary agreement by the appropriate class of members has not been obtained. The shareholders who were summoned to the meeting consisted, it is submitted, of two classes. First there were the outside shareholders, that it to say the shareholders other than M.I.T.: and secondly M.I.T., a subsidiary of Hambros. M.I.T. were a separate class and should have been exluded from the meeting of outside shareholders. Although section 206 provides that the court may order meetings, it is the responsibility of the petitioners to see that the class meetings are properly constituted, and if they fail then the necessary agreement is not obtained and the court has no jurisdiction to sanction the arrangement. Thus in *Re United Provident Assurance Company Ltd*[1] the court held that the holders of partly paid shares formed a different class from holders of fully paid shares. The objection was taken that there should have been separate meetings of the two classes, and Swinfen Eady J upheld the objection, saying: '. . . the objection that there have not been proper class meetings is fatal, and I cannot sanction the scheme.'

. . .

The question therefore is whether M.I.T., a wholly owned subsidiary of Hambros, formed part of the same class as the other ordinary shareholders. What is an appropriate class must depend upon the circumstances but some general principles are to be found in the authorities. In *Sovereign Life Assurance Co v Dodd*,[2] the Court of Appeal held that for the purposes of an arrangement affecting the policyholders of an assurance company the holders of policies which had matured were creditors and were a different class from policyholders whose policies had not matured. Lord Esher MR said:

'. . . they must be divided into different classes . . . because the creditors composing the different classes have different interests; and, therefore, if we find a different state of facts existing among different creditors which may differently affect their minds and their judgment, they must be divided into different classes.'

Bowen LJ said:

---

1 [1910] 2 Ch 477
2 [1892] 2 QB 573; 62 LJQB 19

'It seems plain that we must give such a meaning to the term "class" as will prevent the section being so worked as to result in confiscation and injustice, and that it must be confined to those persons whose rights are not so dissimilar as to make it impossible for them to consult together with a view to their common interest.'

Vendors consulting together with a view to their common interest in an offer made by a purchaser would look askance at the presence among them of a wholly owned subsidiary of the purchaser.

In the present case on analysis Hambros are acquiring the outside shares for 48p. So far as the M.I.T. shares are concerned it does not matter very much to Hambros whether they are acquired or not. If the shares are acquired a sum of money moves from parent to wholly owned subsidiary and shares move from the subsidiary to the parent. The overall financial position of the parent and the subsidiary remain the same. The shares and the money could remain or be moved to suit Hambros before or after the arrangement. From the point of M.I.T., provided M.I.T. is solvent, the directors of M.I.T. do not have to question whether the price is exactly right. Before and after the arrangement the directors of the parent and the subsidiary could have been made the same persons with the same outlook and the same judgment. Mr Heyman, on behalf of the petitioners, submitted that since the parent and subsidiary were separate corporations with separate directors, and since M.I.T. were ordinary shareholders in the company, it followed that M.I.T. had the same interests as the other shareholders. The directors of M.I.T. were under a duty to consider whether the arrangement was beneficial to the whole class of ordinary shareholders, and they were capable of forming an independent and unbiased judgment, irrespective of the interests of the parent company. This seems to me to be unreal, Hambros are purchasers making an offer. When the vendors meet to discuss and vote whether or not to accept the offer, it is incongruous that the loudest voice in theory and the most significant vote in practice should come from the wholly owned subsidiary of the purchaser. No one can be both a vendor and a purchaser and in my judgment, for the purpose of the class meetings in the present case, M.I.T. were in the camp of the purchaser. Of course this does not mean that M.I.T. should not have considered at a separate class meeting whether to accept the arrangement. But their consideration will be different from the considerations given to the matter by the other shareholders. Only M.I.T. could say, within limits, that what was good for Hambros must be good for M.I.T.

Accordingly I uphold the first objection, which is fatal to the arrangement. But in view of the careful arguments put forward by both sides I will consider the other objections which are raised by Mr Wright and which are material if the class meeting in the present case, contrary to my view, was properly constituted.

The second objection is founded on the analysis of the arrangement as an offer by Hambros to acquire the ordinary shares for 48p. Section 209[1] provides safeguards for minority shareholders in the event of a takeover bid and in a proper case provides machinery for a small minority of shareholders to be obliged to accept a takeover against their wishes. Thus section 209 provides that where a scheme or contract involving the transfer of shares in a company to another company has been approved by the holders of not less than nine-tenths in value of the shares whose transfer is involved (other than shares already held at the date of the offer by, or a nominee for, the transferee company or its subsidiary), the transferee company may give notice to any dissenting share-

---

1 Now s 428 of the Companies Act 1985

holder; and then, unless on an application made by the dissenting holder the court thinks fit to order otherwise, shall be entitled and bound to acquire those shares on the terms of the takeover bid. If the present arrangement had been carried out under section 209, M.I.T. as a subsidiary of Hambros would have been expressly forbidden to join in any approval for the purposes of section 209, and in any event the objectors could not have been obliged to sell because they hold 10 per cent of the ordinary shares of the company.

The fact that an arrangement under section 206 produces a result which is the same as a takeover under section 209 is not necessarily fatal. It is not always so unfair as to preclude the court from exercising its discretion in favour of the scheme. Thus in *Re National Bank Ltd*,[1] where a similar objection was taken, Plowman J considered the argument that the scheme in that case ought to be treated as a section 209 case needing a 90 per cent majority. He said:

> '. . . I cannot accede to that proposition. In the first place, it seems to me to involve imposing a limitation or qualification either on the generality of the word "arrangement" in section 206 or else on the discretion of the court under that section. The legislature has not seen fit to impose any such limitation in terms and I see no reason for implying any. Moreover, the two sections, sections 206 and 209, involve quite different considerations and different approaches. Under section 206 an arrangement can only be sanctioned if the question of its fairness has first of all been submitted to the court. Under section 209, on the other hand, the matter may never come to the court at all. If it does come to the court, then the onus is cast on the dissenting minority to demonstrate the unfairness of the scheme. There are, therefore, good reasons for requiring a smaller majority in favour of a scheme under section 206 than the majority which is required under section 209 if the minority is to be expropriated.'

Accepting that, the present proposals nevertheless seem to me to place the petitioners in an inescapable dilemma. They cannot succeed under section 209 because of the express provisions of that section and the size of the shareholding of the objectors. They can only succeed under section 206 by using the votes of their own subsidiary company, M.I.T., to secure the necessary majority. In these circumstances I agree with Mr Wright that the court should not in the exercise of its discretion authorise the acquisition of the shares of the objectors, the National Bank of Greece, against the wishes of the bank. The petitioners cannot succeed at all under section 209 and in my judgment they cannot fairly succeed under section 206.

Earlier authority appears to support that proposition. In *Re General Motor Cab Co Ltd*,[2] a company proposed to sell its assets and undertaking to a new company to be formed for that purpose and to compel shareholders to accept shares in the new company instead of their shares in the old company. The creditors were to be taken over by the new company. There was no provision for preserving the rights of dissentient shareholders. It was held by the Court of Appeal that the scheme was not a compromise or arrangement which could be sanctioned. That was admittedly a very strong case where the court came to the conclusion that what was being asked was not a compromise or arrangement at all, but it is significant that the court approached the application on the basis of it being something which if it had been a takeover bid would have required the rights of dissentient shareholders to be preserved.

1 [1966] 1 WLR 819; [1966] 1 All ER 1006
2 [1913] 1 Ch 377

Similarly in *Re Anglo-Continental Supply Co Ltd*,[1] the reconstruction of an existing company by winding up and sale of its entire undertaking and assets for shares in a new foreign company outside the scope of a reconstruction under the Companies (Consolidation) Act 1908 was effected as an arrangement under section 120 of that Act, the predecessor of the present section 206. But that was only done on terms that the rights of the dissentient minority were preserved in the same way as they would have been under a reconstruction.

Finally in *Re Bugle Press Ltd*,[2] where two majority shareholders formed a new company and propounded an arrangement simply for the purpose of enabling them to get the requisite majority under section 209, the court refused to have any truck with the proposals put forward. Lord Evershed MR said, . . . that the mechanism of the section had been admittedly invoked especially for the purpose and in order to enable the majority shareholders to expropriate the shares of their minority colleague. Counsel had argued that nevertheless

'. . . in the result, the case does fall within the strict language of the section and falling within it the consequences must follow. If that argument is right, it would enable by a device of this kind the 90 per cent majority of the shareholders always to get rid of a minority shareholder whom they did not happen to like. And that, as a matter of principle, would appear to be contrary to a fundamental principle of our law that prima facie, if a man has a legal right which is an absolute right, then he can do with it or not do with it what he will.'

Whereas in *Bugle Press* the motives of the applicants for the scheme were not particularly praiseworthy I hasten to say that in the present case the motives of the petitioners are entirely different, as will appear when I come to consider the details of the scheme. The petitioners are anxious that the ordinary shareholders should be offered the full net asset value of their shares which exceed the value of those shares on the open market. They are persisting with the scheme because they do not consider that it is fair to those shareholders who wish to accept the scheme that they should be frustrated by the opposition of the objectors. But the decision in *Re Bugle Press Ltd* fortifies me in thinking that where one has what is in effect a section 209 scheme then, putting it at its lowest, there must be a very high standard of proof on the part of the petitioner to justify obtaining by section 206 what could not be obtained by section 209, especially when there is the added element that section 206 itself only works with the help of a wholly owned subsidiary of the petitioners.

SOURCE 288
Re Grierson, Oldham and Adams Ltd
(Chancery Division 1966) [1968] Ch 17; [1967] 3 All ER 192

In September 1965, Holts made an offer through Lazard Brothers & Co Ltd, bankers, for the whole of the issued share capital of the company. The offer was announced to the press on 15 September, and on 27 September a circular was sent out in the usual way to all the company's shareholders.

---

1 [1922] 2 Ch 723; 91 LJ Ch 658
2 [1961] Ch 270; [1960] 3 All ER 791

Holts offer was accepted by more than 99 per cent of the shareholders in the company, but not by the applicants. Accordingly on 28 January 1966, Holts served a notice on each of the applicants pursuant to section 209(1)[1] of the Companies Act 1948, to the effect that they desired to acquire the applicants' shares and that unless the applicants applied to the court on or before 28 February 1966, and the court otherwise ordered, Holts would be entitled and bound to acquire their shares on the terms of the offer.

On 28 February 1966, the last available day, the applicants issued this originating summons, under section 209,[2] asking for an order declaring that Holts were neither entitled to nor bound to acquire their shares in the company, or any of them, on the terms of the scheme or contract dated 27 September 1965, notwithstanding that it had been approved by nine-tenths of the shareholders of the company. The summons further asked for an order that Holts should pay the costs of the application, and stated that the application was made under Order 96, r 8, of the Rules of the Supreme Court.

Evidence was given for the applicants that the market price of the ordinary shares had been substantially higher than the offer price of 6s. for a number of years.

. . . Evidence was also given by Mrs Freda Grace Letts, a chartered secretary, an associate of the Chartered Institute of Secretaries, who gave her opinion as an expert, after having examined the company's accounts, that the offer price was inadequate, in that (a) the amount allowed in respect of goodwill and future prospects was inadequate, particularly in view of the rising trend of profits, and the amount allowed for certain assets, being based on 1959 values, was also inadequate; (b) it is usual in takeover bids to find that the offer price is reasonably substantially in excess of the market price, whereas here the price was only very slightly above the market price and was made at a time when prices were temporarily depressed, owing to economic and political matters. It was suggested that had the accounts been published first it was probable that the market price would have risen; (c) the price offered for the ordinary shares was inadequate in relation to the price offered for the preference shares, since it was reasonable to assume that the good results for the year ended 31 March 1965, would have a greater effect on the price of the ordinary shares than on that of the preference shares; (d) statements by the directors of Holts seemed to suggest that substantial benefits would result to Holts from acquiring control of the company; and (e) taking all these factors into account the deponent, Mrs Letts, was of opinion that the offer price was inadequate and that an adequate price would be not less than 7s. a share, a price which had been exceeded during each of the last five years.

No evidence was called for the respondents.

PLOWMAN J: The first general observation is that the onus of proof here is fairly and squarely on the applicants, and indeed they accept that that is so. The onus of proof is on them to establish, if they can, that the offer was unfair. In *Re Hoare & Co Ltd*[3] Maugham J said:

'I have some hesitation in expressing my view as to when the court should think fit to order otherwise. I think however, the view of the legislature is

---

1 Now s 429 of the Companies Act 1985
2 Now s 430C of the Companies Act 1985
3 (1933) 150 LT 374

that where not less than nine-tenths of the shareholders in the transferor company approve the scheme or accept the offer, prima facie, at any rate, the offer must be taken to be a proper one, and in default of an application by the dissenting shareholders, which includes those who do not assent, the shares of the dissentients may be acquired on the original terms by the transferee company. Accordingly, I think it is manifest that the reasons for inducing the court to "order otherwise" are reasons which must be supplied by the dissentients who take the step of making an application to the court, and that the onus is on them of giving a reason why their shares should not be acquired by the transferee company.

One conclusion I draw from that fact is that the mere circumstance that the sale or exchange is compulsory is one which ought not to influence the court. It has been called an expropriation, but I do not regard that phrase as being very apt in the circumstances of the case. The other conclusion I draw is this, that again prima facie the court ought to regard the scheme as a fair one inasmuch as it seems to me impossible to suppose that the court, in the absence of very strong grounds, is to be entitled to set up its own view of the fairness of the scheme in opposition to so very large a majority of the shareholders who are concerned. Accordingly, without expressing a final opinion on the matter, because there may be special circumstances in special cases, I am unable to see that I have any right to order otherwise in such a case as I have before me, unless it is affirmatively established that, notwithstanding the views of a very large majority of shareholders the scheme is unfair. There may be other grounds, but I can see no other grounds available in the present case for the interference of the court.'

These remarks with regard to the onus of proof have been applied in later cases. I notice, for example, that at first instance in *Re Bugle Press Ltd*,[1] Buckley J, whose decision was upheld by the Court of Appeal, said:

'In the ordinary case of an offer under this section, where the 90 per cent majority who accept the offer are unconnected with the persons who are concerned with making the offer, the court pays the greatest attention to the views of that majority. In all commercial matters, where commercial people are much better able to judge of their own affairs than the court is able to do, the court is accustomed to pay the greatest attention to what commercial people who are concerned with the transaction in fact decide; and it has been recognised in the number of authorities to which I have been referred: *Re Hoare & Co*, a decision of Maugham J; *Re Press Caps Ltd*[2] and an unreported decision of Vaisey J given on 22 July 1959 in *Re Sussex Brick Co Ltd*[3] that where there is a large majority (and, of course, a 90 per cent majority is necessarily a large majority) of shareholders who are only concerned to see that they get what they consider to be a fair price for their shares, and who are in favour of accepting the offer, the burden is a heavy one on the dissentient shareholder to say that the offer is not one which he ought reasonably to have to accept.'

The second general observation which seems to me to be relevant is this: that since this is not a case of a purchase of assets, but of a purchase of shares, the market price on the Stock Exchange of those shares is cogent evidence of their

---

1 [1961] Ch 270; [1960] 3 All ER 791
2 [1949] Ch 434; [1949] 1 All ER 1013
3 [1961] Ch 289n; [1960] 2 WLR 665n

true value; not conclusive evidence, of course, but cogent evidence. In another case which was cited during the hearing, *Re Press Caps Ltd*, Wynn-Parry J, who was sitting as a member of the Court of Appeal, said:

'A valuation is only an expression of opinion. It may be made on one of a number of bases, but the final test of what is the value of a thing is what it will fetch if sold. In some cases a sale has to be made, as one knows who exercises the administrative jurisdiction of the Chancery Division, but if there exists a market, as, for instance, the Stock Exchange in the case of shares, in respect of which there is a quotation or in respect of which there is permission to deal, there may be no need to sell, and prima facie the Stock Exchange markings can be taken as a satisfactory indication of the value of the shares in question. For that reason alone it appears to me, with respect, that the view of Maugham J as to where the onus lies under the section is justified. It therefore follows that to succeed the applicants must go behind the Stock Exchange markings, and this undoubtedly is a heavy onus.'

And in this case it is a formidable onus that the applicants have set out to discharge, bearing in mind that not only was the offer price above the Stock Exchange price, but that over 99 per cent of the ordinary shareholders accepted the offer.

The third general observation which arises out of the arguments that have been put forward concerns the question whether the test of the fairness of the offer is fairness to the individual shareholder or fairness to the body of shareholders as a whole. In my judgment, the test of fairness is whether the offer is fair to the offerees as a body and not whether it is fair to a particular shareholder in the peculiar circumstances of his own case.

. . .

The other general observation, which arises from the *Sussex Brick case*, is that the fact that the applicants may be able to demonstrate that the scheme is open to criticism, or is capable of improvement, is not enough to discharge the onus of proof which lies upon them. Vaisey J said:

'I agree that certain criticisms set out in the applicant's affidavit show that a good case could be made out for the formulation of a better scheme, of a fairer scheme, of one which would be more attractive to the shareholders if they could have understood the implications of the criticisms. I have no doubt at all that a better scheme could have been evolved, but is that enough? Is it necessary to establish the validity of such an offer as put forward in the present case? Is there any point in the scheme on which a better view might have prevailed and rather more generous treatment might have been offered to persons whose shares are sought to be expropriated? A better and fairer offer might have been made, possibly, but I do not think that because a scheme is not 100 per cent fair or right there is the kind of unfairness with which Maugham J was dealing in the case to which I was referred. The mere finding of items, or details, in the scheme which are open to valid criticism, is not unfairness consistent with the spirit of that judgment.

A scheme must be obviously unfair, patently unfair, unfair to the meanest intelligence. It cannot be said that no scheme can be effective to bind a dissenting shareholder unless it complies to the extent of 100 per cent with the highest possible standards of fairness, equity and reason.'

Towards the end of his judgment Vaisey J said:

'It must be affirmatively established that, notwithstanding the view of the majority, the scheme is unfair, and that is a different thing from saying that it must be established that the scheme is not a very fair one or not a fair one: a scheme has to be shown affirmatively, patently, obviously and convincingly to be unfair.'

It is said that in the company's balance sheet the goodwill of the parent company is shown at a figure of £1 and that the freehold and leasehold properties have been valued either at 1959 values or at cost, part one way and part another; and it is said that those figures do not indicate the true value of either the goodwill or the fixed assets. There are a number of answers to that contention. First, as I indicated earlier, this is not a question of a purchase of assets, but a question of the purchase of shares. Secondly, the balance sheet does not purport to offer a current valuation of either the goodwill or of the fixed assets. It makes it perfectly plain what the basis is on which the properties are put in at those figures, so that anybody looking at the balance sheet with ordinary intelligence would know that £1 is not being put forward as representing the value of the goodwill and that £X, the figures in the balance sheet, are not being put forward as the current value of the assets in question. There is another point which Mr Instone mentioned, namely, that the balance sheet showed that the company had reserves totalling almost exactly the same amount as the amount of the issued ordinary share capital, which would give each ordinary share a net book value of twice its value, that is to say, each 2s. ordinary share would have a net book value of 4s. Mr Instone points out that the offer is 50 per cent in excess of that value of 4s., and 2s. a share represents something like an additional £380,000 which Holts are paying for the ordinary shares; it seems to me that that is a matter which has to be balanced against any question of undervaluation.

Then it is said that the price of 6s. a share does not reflect the advantages accruing to Holts by their obtaining complete control of the company. I agree with Mr Instone that that might possibly be used as an argument to justify paying a shareholder with a controlling interest a larger price for the shares than the price paid to minority holders. But, in my judgment, it is not unfair to offer a minority shareholder the value of what he possesses, ie, a minority shareholding. The same argument was put to the Court of Appeal in the *Press Caps case* to which I have been referred, and although the court did not find it necessary to pronounce conclusively upon that argument, it is quite clear that it did not find any favour with them.

I should add a word or two about the affidavit of Mrs Letts. She is a person who has some expert knowledge of share valuations. I think I have already covered a good many of the points which she makes in that affidavit in dealing with the points put forward by Mr Gurney-Champion. There are, perhaps, two points to which I should specifically refer. In paragraph 6(c), she says:

'The price offered for the ordinary shares would appear to be inadequate in relation to the price offered for the preference shares. If the prospects for the preference shares warranted a price of approximately 3s. in excess of the middle market price at the time that the offer was made, then it seems reasonable to assume that the ordinary shares warranted a price in excess of 3d. over the middle market price, particularly bearing in mind the good results for the year to 31 March 1965, which it is reasonable to assume would have had a much greater effect on the price of the ordinary shares than they would have had on the preference shares if the market had had an opportunity of reflecting these results before the bid was announced.'

In reply to that, Mr Instone says, 'Fair enough; that is fair comment. On the figures the preference shareholders were dealt with proportionately better than the ordinary shareholders.' But, Mr Instone says — and this is really the answer to the point — the question is not whether the preference shareholders were dealt with generously, but whether the ordinary shareholders were dealt with fairly. And whether the preference shareholders were dealt with over-generously I do not know. I do not know what considerations led to the offer being made to them at the figure at which it was made. But the mere fact they were dealt with generously, and that the ordinary shareholders were dealt with less generously or not generously at all, does not mean that the ordinary shareholders were not dealt with fairly.

The other point on Mrs Letts' affidavit is in paragraph 6(e) where, after referring to a number of matters, she says:

> 'Taking all these factors into account I am of the opinion that the offer price is inadequate and that an adequate price would be not less than 7s. an ordinary share, a price which the shares have exceeded in the market during each one of the last five years.'

Let us assume that by 'adequate price' she really means the same thing as a fair price; I have no doubt that that is her honest opinion, but the question of value is obviously one about which opinions may differ. Against her opinion I have to set off what seem to me to be the two overwhelming factors in this case, namely, that 99-plus per cent of the ordinary shareholders regarded this offer as a fair offer which they were prepared to accept and did accept and that in point of fact the offer to the ordinary shareholders was one which did exceed the Stock Exchange price. Of course, it is possible in cases like this to criticise figures, offers and balance sheets, and argue about matters of fairness and unfairness: but that is what makes the task of dissentients who come to the court under this section very difficult, one which, so far as the reported cases go, they have never succeeded in discharging; except in *Bugle Press*, which is quite a different case and one which really lies outside the scheme of section 209. Although I have sympathy, if I may say so, for the applicants, who naturally do not want to face a loss on their investment, I have no doubt in the end that they have failed like others before them to discharge this heavy onus of proof which lies upon them, and that being so, I am bound to dismiss this application.

This extract from *Re Grierson, Oldham & Adams* makes clear what a daunting task it is for the smaller than 10 per cent minority to resist the compulsory purchase of their shares under s 429 of the CA 1985. Yet two recent decisions (Sources 289 and 290) seem to suggest something of a change from previous decisions which, since the jurisdiction was first enacted (in the 1929 Companies Act), have been uniformly dismissive of the attempts by the minority to challenge the compulsory purchase.

SOURCE 289
Re Chez Nico (Restaurants) Ltd
(Chancery Division) [1992] BCLC 192

Browne-Wilkinson V–C, held that the letter by the largest shareholder of the company to the others to purchase their shares so as to transform the company from publicly owned to private status was not an offer and that the author was, therefore, not entitled to invoke the compulsory procedures of s 429. He continued:

5. *The exercise of the discretion*

I have already said that in my judgment the basic approach to the exercise of the court's discretion in these cases established in relation to the provisions of the 1929 and 1948 Acts is generally applicable to Pt XIII A of the 1985 Act. Perhaps the most basic principle is that stated by Maugham J in *Re Hoare & Co Ltd* (1933) 150 LT 374 dealing with a normal take-over bid, ie a bid by an outsider. He said this (at 375):

'I have some hesitation in expressing my view as to when the court should think fit to order otherwise. I think, however, the view of the Legislature is that where not less than nine-tenths of the shareholders in the transferor company approve the scheme or accept the offer, *prima facie*, at any rate, the offer must be taken to be a proper one, and in default of an application by the dissenting shareholders, which includes those who do not assent, the shares of the dissentients may be acquired on the original terms by the transferee company. Accordingly, I think it is manifest that the reasons for inducing the court to "order otherwise" are reasons which must be supplied by the dissentients who take the step of making an application to the court, and that the onus is on them of giving a reason why their shares should not be acquired by the transferee company... The other conclusion I draw is this, that again *prima facie* the court ought to regard the scheme as a fair one inasmuch as it seems to me impossible to suppose that the court, in the absence of very strong grounds, is to be entitled to set up its own view of the fairness of the scheme in opposition to so very large a majority of the shareholders who are concerned. Accordingly, without expressing a final opinion on the matter, because there may be special circumstances in special cases, I am unable to see that I have any right to order otherwise in such a case as I have before me, unless it is affirmatively established that, notwithstanding the views of a very large majority of shareholders that the scheme is unfair. There may be other grounds, but I see no other grounds available in the present case for the inference of the court.'

That approach has been repeatedly adopted in later decisions and is much relied upon in the present case by Mr Knott on behalf of Mr and Mrs Ladenis. But it is to be noted that *Re Hoare & Co Ltd* and the later cases to which I have been referred, bar one, relate to bids by outsiders. Moreover, Maugham J was careful to say that the approach was only a prima facie one. The decision of the Court of Appeal in *Re Bugle Press Ltd* [1960] 3 All ER 791, [1961] Ch 270 shows that it is not without exceptions. In that case two shareholders in Bugle (who together controlled 90% of the shares) incorporated another company, the X Co. Through the X Co they then made a bid for all the shares in Bugle which, not surprisingly, they as the majority accepted. X Co then claimed to be entitled to acquire the minority 10%. The Court of Appeal rejected this and Lord Evershed MR said ([1960] 3 All ER 791 at 794, [1961] Ch 270 at 284–285) that the approach in *Re Hoare & Co Ltd* was only applicable to a case where an outside party, not interested as a shareholder already, is the bidder.

In my judgment the approach in *Re Hoare & Co Ltd* cannot apply to a case where the bidder is already a director and shareholder in the target company and it is shown that the information made available to the assenting shareholders falls far short of what should have been provided. The fact that 90% of the shareholders have accepted the bid cannot carry decisive weight if it is shown that their acceptance was obtained in ignorance of facts of which they should have been informed.

In this case, Mr and Mrs Ladenis as the bidders well knew the financial position of the company was not at all the same as that disclosed by the audited accounts to May 1989, and the management accounts to November 1989, being all the information the outside shareholders had. The company which, according to those documents supplied to the shareholders, had traded at a loss down to May 1989 and was continuing to make a loss for the six months down to November 1989, was in fact trading profitably and, despite large increases in Mr and Mrs Ladenis's emoluments, was on course for a profit in the year ending May 1990. Moreover, the shareholders, had been provided with a valuation of a small holding of shares at 10p per share based on the figures to November 1989. It was not explained to me why this valuation was sent out in May 1990 based on the old figures. Moreover, the valuation does not purport to be advice as to the value of a holding in a bid situation where the bidder is a minority shareholder seeking to acquire a majority or 100% holding.

Mr Knott submitted that there was no legal requirement on Mr and Mrs Ladenis to make disclosure of the relevant circumstances. He relied first on *Percival v Wright* [1902] 2 Ch 421 as authority for the proposition that directors of a company owe no fiduciary duties to shareholders and that, even if they are acquiring shares in the company from a shareholder, owe no duty to disclose circumstances known to them which are relevant to the value of the shares.

The headnote in *Percival v Wright* reads as follows:

'The directors of a company are not trustees for individual shareholders, and may purchase their shares without disclosing pending negotiations for the sale of the company's undertaking.'

That proposition has long been regarded as established by *Percival v Wright*. As a result there have been suggestions, not acted upon, that the principle it is said to establish should be reversed by statute: the Cohen Committee's *Report on Company Law Amendment* (Cmnd 6659 (1945)) and the Jenkins Committee's *Report of the Company Law Committee* (Cmnd 1749 (1962)). But as the Court of Appeal of New Zealand have pointed out in *Coleman v Myers* [1977] 2 NZLR 225, it is very doubtful authority for the broad proposition contained in the headnote.

In *Percival v Wright* the plaintiffs wishing to sell their shares approached the board. The shares were eventually sold to three directors. The plaintiffs subsequently discovered that there had been negotiations (which came to nothing) to which the directors had been a party to sell the company at a price per share much higher than that paid for the shares by the directors. The plaintiffs were seeking to set aside the sale to the directors. When the case is carefully examined it is clear that the central points were conceded. It was conceded, first, that the directors would not have been bound to disclose a large casual profit or the discovery of a new deposit of ore and, secondly, that there was no unfair dealing or a purchase at an undervalue. The only decision was that in general the fiduciary duties of directors are owed to the company, not to the shareholders, and that on the concessions made there was nothing in the facts of that case to justify imposing any duty on the directors to the shareholders as opposed to the company. The actual decision does not bear out the headnote. Like the Court of Appeal in New Zealand, I consider the law to be that in general directors do not owe fiduciary duties to shareholders but owe them to the company: however, in certain special circumstances fiduciary duties, carrying with them a duty of disclosure, can arise which place directors in a fiduciary capacity vis-à-vis the shareholders. *Coleman v Myers* itself shows that where directors are purchasing shares in the company from outside shareholders such duty of disclosure may arise dependent on the circumstances of the case.

It is unnecessary for me to decide in the present case whether Mr and Mrs Ladenis were, under the general law, under a duty to disclose the true position to the shareholders since, as is accepted, the transaction fell within the City Code on Take-overs and Mergers. General principle 4 of the code says this:

'Shareholders must be given sufficient information and advice to enable them to reach a properly informed decision and must have sufficient time to do so. No relevant information should be withheld from them.'

The code requires the first approach on a take-over to be made to the board of the target company (r 1). Rule 3.1 provides as follows:

'The board of the offeree company must obtain competent independent advice on any offer, and the substance of such advice must be made known to its shareholders.'

Note 1 to that rule reads:

'Management buy outs and offers by controlling shareholders. The requirement for competent independent advice is of particular importance in cases where the offer is a management buy out or similar transaction, or is being made by the existing controlling shareholder or group of shareholders. In such cases it is particularly important that the independence of the adviser is beyond question.'

Rule 23.2 has the cross-heading 'The General Obligation as to Information', and reads as follows:

'Shareholders must be given sufficient information and advice to enable them to reach a properly informed decision as to the merits or demerits of an offer. Such information must be available to shareholders early enough to enable them to make a decision in good time. The obligation of an offeror in these respects towards the shareholders of the offeree company is no less than the offeror's obligation towards its own shareholders.'

For some reason that was not explained Mr and Mrs Ladenis's advisers did not alert them to the fact that the code applied, and the rules that I have read (and probably many others) were undoubtedly breached in the present case.

The code does not have the force of law. But in considering for the purposes of s 430C whether the court should exercise its discretion, in my judgment the code is a factor of great importance. One of the purposes of the code is to provide protection to the shareholders whose shares are the subject of a bid. Where, under the code, the bidder is himself under a duty to provide such information, substantial infringements of the provisions of the code as to disclosure in my judgment provides strong evidence that the offer is not fairly made: it certainly negatives any presumption that the offer is fair because 90% of the shareholders have accepted it: see *Re Lifecare International plc* [1990] BCLC 222. I am not suggesting that any infringement of the code (however small) will necessarily lead the court to exercise its discretion in favour of the non-assenting shareholder. But substantial failure by the bidder to comply with the code's provisions as to disclosure should, in my view, be a very major factor operating against the compulsory acquisition of the non-assenting shareholders' shares.

Mr Knott relied on the decision in *Re Evertite Locknuts (1938) Ltd* [1945] 1 All ER 401, [1945] Ch 220, where Vaisey J rejected an objection based on non-disclosure. Vaisey J said ([1945] 1 All ER 401 at 403, [1945] Ch 220 at 224):

'I have really no materials before me which will enable me to say either that any information with regard to that company was withheld, or as to whether, if so, it was withheld improperly. The difficulty I feel is that, if once it is conceded that a scheme of this kind can be upset merely for the reason that a shareholder is not given all the information which he might require or might expect from the directors of the transferor company, there would be no limit to the inquiry which would have to be set on foot as to the extent to which his demands for disclosure ought to be conceded. It may be — I do not say that it is — possible that the present applicant has some grievance against the directors of the Evertite Locknuts (1938) Ltd. But I am quite satisfied in my own mind that I should be going much further than MAUGHAM, J, was prepared to go in *Re Hoare & Co, Ltd* ((1933) 150 LT 374), if I said that it was not necessary for a dissentient shareholder, making an application under the Act, to establish unfairness, but that it would suffice if he merely said that he regarded himself, or was in fact, unprovided with all the materials upon which he could come to a just conclusion in regard to the acceptance or rejection of the offer.'

Whether or not that case was rightly decided, it dealt with a case where the bidder was an outsider and was not therefore necessarily in possession of the information which the target company could supply. Moreover, it was decided long before the introduction of the code. Here the bidders, Mr and Mrs Ladenis, were themselves the directors of the target company and, as such, under the code were bound to give all the relevant information. I cannot regard the decision in *Re Evertite Locknuts Ltd* as governing the present case.

SOURCE 290
Re Lifecare International plc
(Chancery Division) [1990] BCLC 222

The applicant, whose shares the takeover bidder (Tamaris) was seeking compulsorily to purchase under the provisions of s 428, was seeking an order (a) for discovery of documents relating to the recommendation by the board to the shareholders of the target company that the offer be accepted, and (b) for cross-examination.

HOFFMANN J: . . . It is well established that in an application such as this there is a heavy burden on the dissentient shareholder to satisfy the court that an offer which ex hypothesi has been accepted by over 90% of his fellow shareholders in the same class was in fact unfair. The court naturally starts with the assumption that the other shareholders are likely to know where their own interests lie as well as he. It seems to me, however, that the recommendation of the board, based on what is said to be independent advice, must play a significant part in determining the reaction of the shareholders to the offer. It is true that it is open to them to obtain advice of their own, and no doubt some of them do so, but one knows in practice many do not. If therefore the shareholder can demonstrate that the advice received by the board on the basis of which it made its recommendation was in some way flawed, he must thereby go some way towards discharging the burden on him. What the applicant seeks in this case is discovery limited to those documents relevant to the board's decision to recommend the offer.

Counsel who appears for Tamaris (Mr Cone) referred me to the decision of Roxburgh J in *Re Press Caps Ltd* [1948] 2 All ER 638, in which Roxburgh J took a very restricted view of the proper scope of discovery in an application such as this. First, he said that in all originating summons proceedings there was a burden on the applicant to show why there should be discovery at all. That position, while true at the time, has been changed by what is now RSC Ord 24, r 3 and 8, the effect of which is that discovery will ordinarily be ordered in originating summons' proceedings unless the court is satisfied that it is not necessary (see *Coni v Robertson* [1969] 2 All ER 609, [1969] 1 WLR 1007).

The second reason given by Roxburgh J was that there might be serious consequences if the holder of a small number of shares in the company could in a large number of cases become entitled by making an application of this kind to obtain what he called, 'an extensive investigation of the company's affairs'. That is a type of 'flood-gates' argument often used in terrorem, but should not, I think, discourage the court from applying the language of Ord 24, r 8. The question is, 'Am I satisfied in this case that discovery of the limited kind sought by the applicant is not necessary?' I am not so satisfied, because, in my view, the whole issue in the case is going to be whether the advice said to have been given to the board by Greg Middleton & Co Ltd was good advice or not, and I find it difficult to see how the judge hearing the summons could form a view on that matter without seeing the documents which reflect exactly what that advice was.

The documents in question are of course not the documents of Tamaris. They are the documents of Lifecare. But Tamaris now controls Lifecare, and there should not in practice be any difficulty about obtaining those documents for the purposes of discovery.

The next question is whether there should be cross-examination. Prima facie parties who have sworn affidavits are liable to be cross-examined on those affidavits, at any rate when the proceedings in question are of a final and not an interlocutory nature. That proposition is, I think, supported by *Comet Products UK Ltd v Hawkex Plastics Ltd* [1971] 1 All ER 1141, [1971] 2 QB 67. The effect of the usual practice is demonstrated by *Re Smith & Fawcett Ltd* [1942] 1 All ER 542, [1942] Ch 304, where Lord Greene MR said that he declined to make a finding of lack of good faith against a party who had sworn an affidavit in proceedings of a final nature, because no application had been made to cross-examine him.

In this case the registrar has given leave for both sides to adduce expert evidence, and the evidence which has already been sworn at any rate by Mr Clinton of Greg Middleton & Co Ltd is in the nature of expert evidence, because he says that he, presumably speaking as an expert corporate finance adviser, does not believe that the offer could have been structured in any other way. It seems to me that, for the judge in the hearing of the application to be able to decide the matter as between different experts, it will be advantageous for cross-examination to be allowed.

NOTES AND QUESTIONS

1. *The court will be astute to ensure no evasion of this rule by the issue of debentures at a discount — which is permissible — where those debentures can be converted into fully paid shares at a later date* (Mosely v Koffyfontein Mines Ltd[1]).

2. *On the other hand, consider the attitude of the court in relation to the issue of shares in consideration for the purchase of a business belonging to the original corporators (eg the facts in* Salomon's case,[2] *p 87 and Re Wragg,[3] Source 270). Does this not represent the issue of shares at a discount?*

---

1 [1904] 2 Ch 108
2 [1897] AC 22; 66 LJ Ch 35 (see pp 87ff)
3 [1897] 1 Ch 796; 66 LJ Ch 419 (see p 757)

(*Consider the provisions, introduced in 1980, now ss 99–115 of the Companies Act 1985.*)

3. *Is the issue of shares at a discount void or voidable (consider* Welton v Saffrey,[1] *p 296, and the* Ooregum *case, p 755)?*

4. *Would you, on the strength of* Hilder v Dexter[2] *(Source 271), advise a board of directors that it might issue shares at par even though the shares could attract a considerable premium? (Consider s 214 of the Insolvency Act 1986.)*

5. *Contrast the procedure which now enables a company to purchase its own shares (CA 1985, s 162 provides the basic power) with that which enables a company to reduce its capital (pp 789ff). Consider, in particular, the respective protections for dissenting shareholders and creditors who object to the proposed purchase and note the nature of s 164(5).*

6. *Advantages claimed for the company being able to purchase its own shares were that '[i]t may enable the company to buy out a dissident shareholder' and that '[i]t facilitates the retention of family control' (The Purchase by a Company of its Own Shares, Cmnd 7944, para 11(a),(b).)*

7. *Another of the advantages claimed for this facility was to enable the company 'to support the market for the shares if this is thought to be unduly depressed . . .' (The Purchase by a Company of its Own Shares, Cmnd 7944, para 11(j).) What potential abuses might this open up? Are they sufficiently guarded against?*

8. *An unlimited company was always able to purchase its shares and where fully paid shares devolved upon the company without the company having to pay anything for them (eg they might have been left to the company by the will of the deceased shareholder), the company was entitled to hold them, but only through a nominee.*

9. *This rule is further enforced by CA 1985, s 23, which forbids a subsidiary company from holding shares in its holding company.*

10. *Section 54 of the Companies Act 1948 was replaced by provisions in the Companies Act 1981, now consolidated as ss 151–158 of the Companies Act 1985. Consider the definition of 'financial assistance'. How would you treat the* Charterhouse *case[3] in the light of the new legislation?*

11. *In the light of:*
    (i) *the assertion by Mr James that he genuinely believed Maximum to be worth £500,000 (an assertion which was not challenged),*
    (ii) *the guarantee given by Grosscurth as to the profitability of Maximum and its subsidiaries over the five years following the transaction,*
    (iii) *counsel's opinion that the transaction was not a breach of section 54,*
    (iv) *Mr James's view that Grosscurth's association would be for the benefit of the group (including Belmont),*
    is the decision in the Belmont[4] *case supportable?*

12. *Would the* Belmont *transaction be legitimate under the new regime?*

---

1 [1897] AC 299; 66 LJ Ch 362 (see p 296)
2 [1902] AC 474; 71 LJ Ch 781 (see p 760)
3 [1086] BCLC 1 (see p 774)
4 [1980] 1 All ER 393 (see p 770)

13. *If the purchase price for Maximum had been £60,000 would the result in* Belmont *have been different?*

14. *For an example of an insolvent company teetering on the brink of liquidation being able to declare dividends out of 'profits' see* Quistclose Investments Ltd v Rolls Razor Ltd[1].

15. *In the Companies Act 1980, a new code was enacted to bring the legal provisions covering the payment of dividends into line with the best accounting practice. This code is now consolidated in Pt VIII of the CA 1985. Section 263(1) states the fundamental rule and defines distribution of dividend very widely so as to ensure that any unauthorised distribution comes within the legislative prohibition. The effect is to reverse the common law rules (a) that dividends can be declared without taking account of previous years' losses, and (b) that while unrealised profits may still be applied for paying up a bonus issue of shares, they cannot be used for the distribution of a dividend (see ss 263, 264, 275). A recent decision which explores common law principles and part of the new statutory code appears as Source 279.*

---

1 [1970] AC 567 (HL); [1968] 3 All ER 651

Chapter 12

COMPANIES IN DISTRESS

PART I: INTRODUCTION

When a company is unable to pay its debts in full as they fall due, it is said to be insolvent. This condition may lead to the termination of the company's life, a process called liquidation through which all the company's assets are realised and the proceeds distributed among the company's creditors in accordance with a well-established hierarchy. Liquidation may be unavoidable, but it is equally possible that the company may be facing a short-term crisis and that, given some assistance, either in the form of an injection of further funds or in its creditors exercising restraint in the recovery of their claims, the company will recover to a condition of solvency and be able to resume its place in the commercial world.

Given that the company is likely to be an employer, that it may be in the process of undertaking work in the provision of goods or services for its customers or clients and that its directors and shareholders would obviously prefer an opportunity for the recovery of the company's fortunes, the avoidance of liquidation, where this is a realistic option, has much to recommend it. The idea of rescuing insolvent companies is now widespread with most, if not all, capitalist countries possessing a statutory jurisdiction to facilitate such rescue. We can divide this chapter into three further sections: Corporate Rescue, Company Liquidation and the Insolvency Practitioner Profession.

PART II: CORPORATE RESCUE

Aside from the simple case of complete recovery, a company may be in the position where survival is possible if certain changes, more or less radical, are made to its operations, management or structure, or all of these. In certain circumstances the board of directors may be able to undertake such activities, but in the absence of appropriate assistance and where the directors are not up to the task, it may be necessary for the company to seek the refuge of legal principles and institutions which facilitate a rescue. In this category, we may consider the following:
– Receivership;
– Administration;
– Schemes of Arrangement;
– Corporate Voluntary Arrangements.

Receivership

This seems to have originated in the relationship of landlord and tenant and, with suitable extensions, was adopted by the commercial world in the nineteenth century through the relationship of debtor and creditor and in conjunction with the floating charge (Source 291). While a properly drafted debenture and floating charge would provide for the appointment of a receiver with full management powers, it has always been possible to apply to the court for the appointment of a receiver, although in this case the powers of the receiver will be those conferred by the court and not those conferred by the debenture and floating charge. The question may arise as to the power of such a receiver to effect the necessary reorganisation of the company to facilitate its survival (Source 292).

The powers of a receiver appointed under the provisions of a debenture were, until the passing of the Insolvency Act 1986, those set out in the debenture — usually very extensive. This, coupled with the fact that the receiver was accepted by the courts as being the agent of the company (not the debentureholder) by virtue of a contractual provision to this effect, has enabled the receiver to cause the company to break uneconomic contracts (Source 293), although not contracts which have conferred equitable rights on the third party (Source 294). The receiver clearly may have immense power and if the company to which a receiver has been appointed goes into liquidation, the liquidator may well have to defer to the receiver, if one has been appointed (or if one is appointed after the liquidation has begun, Source 295). This power must be exercised diligently and in good faith (Sources 296 and 297).

Part III of the Insolvency Act 1986 sets out a statutory structure for receivership without impairing any of its common law substance. What used to be called a receiver and manager is now an administrative receiver (s 29(2)) who cannot be removed except by order of the court (s 45). This statute now codifies the powers of an administrative receiver (s 42, Sch 1) and recognises the agency relationship between receiver and company (s 44). The administrative receiver has new statutory powers (ss 43, 47) and certain new statutory obligations (ss 46, 48, 49).

The administrative receiver will incur personal liability in respect of (a) contracts other than contracts of employment entered into, and (b) contracts of employment entered into or adopted during the receivership. Adoption of contracts of employment arises by operation of law if, after 14 days of the receivership have elapsed, the company, under the control and direction of the receiver, continues the employment of its employees (*Re Paramount Airways (No 3)* [1994] BCC 172, [1994] 2 BCLC 118). The administrative receiver is entitled to an indemnity against the company's assets in respect of any personal liability so incurred.

SOURCE 291
Gaskell *v* Gosling
(Court of Appeal) [1896] 1 QB 669, rev [1897] AC 575

RIGBY LJ (dissenting in the Court of Appeal):
    . . .

The plaintiffs in this action sued the defendant Francis Gosling for 488*l* 9*s* 3*d*, the balance of the price of goods alleged to have been sold and delivered between December 5, 1893, and January 31, 1895, to him and William Cunliffe Gosling, named as a defendant in the writ, but dead at the date of the writ.

It was not disputed that the goods were sold and delivered, and that the amount claimed remained due to the plaintiffs. The defendant Francis Gosling, however, denied that the goods were bought by him and the deceased William Cunliffe Gosling, or either of them; and the only issue in the action came to be whether he and the deceased, whose names had not appeared in the transactions and who were not alleged to have held themselves out as principals, or even to have been heard of by the plaintiffs, were nevertheless liable as undisclosed principals. The question whether they were principles or not was of course one of fact, but only in the sense that their liability or non-liability had to be ascertained by a consideration of the effect of documents and of admitted facts. The case was tried by the Lord Chief Justice without a jury; but, if there had been a jury, there would have been nothing to leave to them, as there were no facts in dispute.

The two Goslings were trustees of a deed of May 18, 1892, made between Poole and White, Limited, a company carrying on business as manufacturers and vendors of electrical appliances, of the one part, and the trustees of the other part. The effect in detail of this deed is dealt with hereafter; but it was a mortgage deed for securing the payment of a second series of debentures of the company, amounting altogether to 3000*l*. It was made subject to a similar mortgage trust deed for securing a first series of debentures, amounting to 7000*l*, taking priority over the second series. That deed was dated February 1, 1892. There were third debentures, amounting to 1000*l*, secured by a deed later in date than that securing the second series of debentures. The two Goslings were members with other partners of the banking firm of Goslings & Sharpe of Fleet Street, and the firm held all the second series of debentures as partnership property. Under a power in the trust deed of May 18, 1892, the trustees by writing dated July 22, 1892, appointed William John Kelly, the secretary of the company, receiver with very wide powers, and subject to a proviso, the effect of which will have to be considered later on, whereby it was made a term of the appointment that the receiver should forthwith open an account in his name as receiver at the bank of Messrs Goslings & Sharpe, that his receipts for moneys received by him as receiver should be countersigned by John Tryon that all moneys so received should on the day of receipt be paid to the said account, and that the bank should not honour any cheques drawn upon the account unless countersigned by the said John Tryon. John Tryon was a member of the firm of solicitors who acted for the trustees in the transactions of the debentures. He was also a man of some experience in the business of the company, being or having been its chairman, and he was interested at any rate as the holder of debentures of the third series in its commercial fortunes. William John Kelly accepted the appointment of receiver under the writing of July 22, 1892, was let into possession by the company, and on the 26th of the same month opened the account stipulated for with Messrs. Goslings & Sharpe, which was headed 'Poole and White, Limited. W. J. Kelly, Receiver.' The proviso with reference to the countersigning of cheques by Mr. Tryon was insisted upon up to September, 1893, after which time this limitation on the drawing power of the receiver was no longer enforced. The company's business was carried on by the receiver, and the banking account was continued, from July 26, 1892, down to September, 1892. On the 1st of that month a petition for the compulsory winding-up of the company was presented, and a compulsory wind-up order was made on the 11th, the winding up dating from the presentation of the petition. Notwithstanding the winding-up, the receiver assumed to continue the business as receiver until January or February, 1895, when the first debenture-holders or their trustees interfered, as they might have done at any time previously, and put an end to the carrying on of the business. The liquidator of the company never interfered at all. During the whole time the business was carried on as if for Poole and White, Limited, and all orders for goods, or at any rate all order to the plaintiffs, were signed 'Poole and White, Limited. W. J. Kelly, Receiver.' From time to time the receiver's account was charged by the banking firm with interest on the second debentures, the sums so charged amounting altogether to 484*l* 19*s.* The defendants' counsel gave evidence by correspondence that these charges were made by the authority of the receiver.

. . .

The trustees were mortgagees of the company, and it will be well to be consider some points on the law of mortgagor and mortgagee, having regard particularly to receivers and the position of a mortgagee in possession.

A mortgagor left in possession of the mortgaged property, whether real or personal, had a right to receive the income and apply it to his own use, without becoming liable to account to the mortgagee. If there was no receiver, the mortgagee could only make the income available for keeping down the interest on his security by entering into possession. This entry into possession by a mortgagee was always considered a strong assertion of his legal rights, since he did not come under any obligation to account to the mortgagor except in a suit for redemption. He was accordingly treated with exceptional severity in a suit for redemption and made to account, not only for what he actually received, but for what he might without wilful default have received. This was bad enough when there was only one mortgage; but the position became much worse when the mortgage was a second mortgage, since the second mortgagee could at any moment be turned out by the first, and for the sake of such a precarious possession it could seldom be worth while for a second mortgagee to incur the liabilities of a mortgagee in possession. Still greater were the risks and less desirable the possession when the mortgaged property consisted of or included, as it might do, property embarked in trade and subject to the vicissitudes of commercial business. It follows of course from the almost penal liabilities imposed upon a mortgagee in possession that Courts of Equity were very slow to decide that possession had been taken, and would not do so unless satisfied that the mortgagee in possession took the possession in his capacity of mortgagee without any reasonable ground for believing himself to hold in any other capacity: *Parkinson v Hanbury.* The Courts also favoured any means which would enable the mortgagee to obtain the advantages of possession without its drawbacks. Mortgagees began to insist upon the appointment by the mortgagor of a receiver to receive the income, keep down the interest on incumbrances, and hold the surplus, if any, for the mortgagor, and to stipulate often that the receiver should have extensive powers of management. Presently mortgagees stipulated that they themselves should in place of the mortgagor appoint the receiver to act as the mortgagor's agent. This made no difference in the receiver's position, and imposed no liability on the mortgagee appointing. Though it was the mortgagee who in fact appointed the receiver, yet in making the appointment the mortgagee acted, and it was the object of the parties that he should act, as agent for the mortgagor. Lord Cranworth, in *Jefferys v Dickson,* stated the doctrine of Courts of Equity on the subject to the effect following. The mortgagee, as agent of the mortgagor, appointed a person to receive the income, with directions to keep down the interest of the mortgage, and to account for the surplus to the mortgagor as his principal. These directions were supposed to emanate, not from the mortgagee, but from the mortgagor; and the receiver therefore, in the relation between himself and the mortgagor, stood in the position of a person appointed by an instrument to which the mortgagee was no party. Lord Cranworth, in the case referred to, was speaking of a mortgage of lands; but the same doctrine applies to all kinds of property, being founded, as it is, not upon any considerations peculiar to the law of real property, but upon the contract between the debtor who gives and the creditor who takes the security. Of course the mortgagor cannot of his own will revoke the appointment of a receiver, or that appointment would be useless. For valuable consideration he has committed the management of his property to an attorney whose appointment he cannot interfere with. The appointment so made will stand good against himself and all persons claiming through him, except incumbrancers having priority to the mortgagee who appoints the receiver. By degrees the forms of appointment of receivers became more complicated, and their powers of management more extensive, but the doctrine explained by Lord Cranworth in the case cited was consistently adhered to, and it remained true throughout that the receiver's appointment, and all directions and powers given and conferred upon him, were supposed to emanate from the mortgagor, and the mortgagee, though he might be the actual appointor, and might have stipulated for all the powers conferred upon the receiver, was in no other position, so far as responsibility was concerned, than if he had been altogether a stranger to the appointment.

. . .

It is essential now to arrive at a clear conclusion as to the position of the trustees under the deed of May 18, 1892. Their responsibilities (if any) arising from their appointment of a receiver can then be disposed of. At the date of the deed of May 18, 1892, the company were entitled to leasehold property in the King's Road, Camden Town, used for the purposes of their business and to other personal property, but, as appears from the recitals to the deed, the leasehold property except the last day of the term, and all the business and undertaking of the company, and all other the property, real and personal, both present and future, of the company other than its capital for the time being uncalled, had been conveyed to trustess for the purpose of securing payment of the moneys secured by the first series of debentures for 7000*l.*

. . .

Clause 13 is a clause of great importance. It enables the trustees on the security becoming enforceable (an event which had not arisen when the actual appointment of a receiver was made), or, among other events, on the trustees certifying that in their opinion the security given by the deed was endangered (a condition fulfilled on the appointment), by writing under their hands to appoint one or more person or persons receiver or receivers of the mortgaged premises, or any part thereof, and from time to time to remove any such receiver and appoint another in his place. Then follow the important, but common forms, words — 'and any person so appointed shall be the agent of the company, who alone shall be liable for his acts and defaults.' These words, unless their effect is in some way controlled, are decisive of the question whether by the appointment the trustees became principals of the receiver. They are inserted for the very purpose of preventing such a result. As appears from the statement hereinbefore contained, they express the usual intention in cases where a receiver is appointed by a mortgagee.

. . .

The above analysis of the position shews, in my opinion, that, at any rate, down to the date of the winding-up order, the trustees of the deed of May 18, 1892, had not taken a single step which would have even a tendency to make them responsible to creditors of the business or to the receiver.

Did then the winding up of the company make them for the first time principals? No evidence is suggested to any interference by them after the date of the winding-up order, unless the continuing of the banking account should amount to such an interference, which is shewn above not to be the case. They could, no doubt, have made void the appointment of the receiver or entered into possession. So also could trustees of the earlier deed in favour of the first series of debentures. Neither one nor the other set of trustees was under any obligation so to act, or could incur liability for omitting to do so. It has been already shewn that such interest as the trustees had in the moneys derived from carrying on the business could not make them liable as principals, having regard to the decisions in the House of Lords and Privy Council already dealt with. What, then, was the effect of the winding-up order? It could not give the company rights which it did not before possess; for instance, the right of revoking the appointment of the receiver, or withdrawing from his control and management any of the property committed to him, that being the property, first of all, of the debenture-holders, and only belonging to the company as to the equity of redemption expectant on the mortgages to them. But, even if there were any such right on the part of the company, its non-exercise could not make the trustees principals. No doubt the company was incapacitated by the winding-up order from carrying on business, and the receiver could not create debts which would be provable in the liquidation against the unmortgaged assets of the company — that is to say, the uncalled capital, if any there were. In other words, he could no longer pledge the credit of the company. But it seems that he could realize the trade assets and employ them in further trading so long as he was not stopped by the trustees for any of the debenture-holders. If he chose to buy goods for the purposes of the business, he might do so, and under the deed of May 18, 1892, had a right to be indemnified by applying any part of the mortgaged property, that is to say, any part of the company's property other than the uncalled capital, if any, in satisfaction of the debts so incurred. He is not a party to this action, and it would not be right to decide whether he was personally liable or not, though it might fairly be argued that he was personally liable, being in the position of a person professing to act for a principal who cannot himself be principal; but, if he paid the debts, he could recoup himself out of the assets, and, if he was unable to do so, and were made bankrupt, the trade creditors might ultimately be entitled to stand in his shoes against those assets. This, again, is a point which, however plain, ought not to be decided here, as the Court has no jurisdiction to decide it. The existence, however, of such a probability is a sufficient answer to the suggestion that the trade creditors must have a right against the defendants in this action, because otherwise they are without remedy. Such a conclusion, even if the want of any other remedy could be established, would not, as a matter of law, follow. On all the above grounds, the action of the plaintiffs, in my judgment, fails; and, if the case depended upon my judgment, the appeal ought to be allowed.

SOURCE 292
Re Newdigate Colliery Limited
[1912] 1 Ch 468

The company was incorporated in 1904, with a capital of £150,000, to work mines leased to it by the plaintiff. The company had since issued three series of debentures secured upon its undertaking and property present and future, including its uncalled capital, namely, £100,000 5 per cent first mortgage debentures, £11,500 7 per cent second mortgage debentures, and £20,000 5 per cent third mortgage debentures. In December 1911, the interest on the debentures was twelve months in arrear, and the plaintiff, who was the holder of a large number of the first mortgage debentures and of the whole of the third mortgage debentures, on January 8, 1912, commenced an ordinary debenture-holders' action on behalf of himself and the other first debenture-holders to enforce their security against the company and the representatives of the second debenture-holders. On January 20, 1912, he obtained an interlocutory order for the appointment of J. T. Browne as receiver and manager of the undertaking and property of the company. When he entered into possession of the colliery the receiver and manager found that in consequence of faults in the coal seams the output had dropped from 6000 to 4600 tons per week, the whole of which output would be required to satisfy the existing forward contracts, about eighty in number, which had been entered into by the company at a time when the price of coal was lower than it was at present. There was evidence that if the receiver and manager were to disregard these contracts he could sell the coal at an increased price of 1s. per ton more all round, and so realise an extra profit of 200*l* a week. There was also evidence that having regard to the possibility of a strike in the near future it was necessary to reserve some of the output for keeping the colliery pumped free from water during any such strike.

On January 21 1912, the plaintiff took out a summons asking that the receiver and manager might be at liberty to disregard the company's forward contracts for the sale of coal. The summons was heard in chambers by Eve J, who refused the application.

COZENS-HARDY MR: . . . The jurisdiction of the Court to appoint receivers is extremely old, but I believe the practice of appointing a manager is far more modern, and I think it has been settled that the Court will never appoint a person receiver and manager except with a view to a sale. The appointment is made by way of interlocutory order with a view to a sale, it is not a permanency.

. . .

If he elects to obtain the appointment of a receiver and manager of the business including the stock in trade and book debts, it is just as much the duty and the business of the receiver and manager to protect the goodwill and to guard against the destruction of the business or injury to the goodwill, as it is the duty of the receiver of mortgaged property, not being manager also, to take care that the property is preserved so far as it reasonably may be for the benefit of all whom it may concern the mortgagees and the mortgagor. There are really two separate properties comprised in a security of this kind — first, the property of which a receiver only is appointed, and secondly, the goodwill of the business of which a manager is appointed. Now it is said here that if an individual mortgagee had taken possession of this colliery he would not have been bound by the company's contracts; he would have taken possession of the unworked coal at his own risk as mortgagee in possession, or if a receiver had been appointed on his behalf the receiver would have sold the coal as he liked. The mortgagee would have said, 'I have nothing to do with the goodwill of this business, I have no charge upon it; I do not care whether it is damaged or not, and it does not concern me in the least'; but if he elects to have a manager appointed and takes upon himself through the manager the duty of carrying on the business, it is his duty to do nothing which will destroy, or prejudicially damage, the goodwill of the business at a time when it is not, and cannot be, apparent that the mortgagor may not have a real interest in the equity of redemption both of the colliery itself and of the business.

But we are asked to say, in circumstances which I think I can state in a sentence, that the receiver and manager has a wider right. This is a colliery in which there are forward contracts going to the end of this year, contracts entered into at a time when coal was at a lower price than it is now, which it is said will practically exhaust the full produce of the colliery. Coal has now risen considerably in price, and the colliery, apart from the business, would be no doubt more valuable if it could be worked without regard to these forward contracts, for a larger figure could be obtained for the coal. But if the mortgagee were allowed to abandon these forward contracts he would practically be discontinuing the company's business, because these contracts substantially take the whole of the output from the colliery. Is it fair, is it right, or is it reasonable that the mortgagee who has chosen not merely to act as mortgagee in possession of the colliery, but to take possession of the goodwill and book debts of the business also, should be entitled to say 'I will discontinue the business of which I have thought fit to appoint a manager, and I do it because I think there will not be any surplus coming to the mortgagor and because it will be an advantage, not in respect of the goodwill of the business, but in respect of my position as mortgagee of the colliery'? In my opinion that is not the true view. There may be circumstances in which the Court might hold on the application of the receiver and manager that it was desirable, or essential, for the purpose both of the colliery and the business that a certain amount of money should be raised, and might make an order in the presence of all parties, even at this early stage of the action, directing that it should be raised in advance of everybody, and repaid out of money realized by a sale of the coal; but I am not prepared to say that it can be right to do what we are asked to do here, namely, to make a general order allowing the receiver and manager to break these contracts simply because it would be very beneficial to the mortgagee that that should be done. I do not quite like the phrase 'break these contracts,' because it is not a question of breaking them. They are still subsisting, but it is impossible to suggest that the receiver and manager is under any liability to the persons who have entered into them. In my opinion they are not contracts with him; they are contracts made with the company, which is still a company, and has not yet been wound up. If he discharges the obligations of the company under the contracts he will be entitled to receive the money due from the other contracting parties to the company; but to say that he is under any personal liability with regard to the contracts and that he ought to be indemnified or relieved in respect of them is entirely to misunderstand the position of a receiver and manager.

I am anxious to deal with this matter in the general way in which it has been raised, namely, as an application that the receiver and manager may be at liberty to disregard practically all the contracts of this business and start entirely afresh. That is what it really comes to. To accede to such an application without the clearest possible evidence that there is, and can be, no possibility of the mortgagor ever having any substantial interest in the assets of this company would be very wrong. That was the view taken by the learned judge in the Court below. He said it was an entirely novel application for which no precedent could be found, and that it seemed to him, as it does to me, to be an application for leave for the receiver and manager to do something inconsistent with his duties, seeing that he was at least as much under an obligation to preserve the goodwill of this business from injury or destruction as to prevent the mine itself from being damaged by water or otherwise. What I have said will not in any way prevent the receiver and manager making a particular application under special circumstances dealing with a particular contract, but to ask for this general authority is altogether wrong.

. . .

SOURCE 293
Airline Airspares Ltd *v* Handley Page Ltd
[1970] 1 Ch 193

By an agreement, dated December 23, 1966, made between Keegan Aviation Ltd and Mr Thomas Denis Keegan (hereinafter jointly referred to as 'Keegan') and the first defendants, Handley Page Ltd, the first defendants agreed, inter alia, to pay to Keegan a commission of £500 in respect of every aircraft of a type known as 'Jetstream' sold by the first defendants. On September 11, 1968, Keegan assigned all rights and interests under that agreement to the plaintiffs, Airlines Airspares Ltd.

On October 28, 1968, the first defendants created a debenture to secure their indebtedness to Barclays Bank Ltd, and pursuant to the powers contained in the debenture Mr Kenneth Russell Cork, the second defendant, was appointed receiver and manager of the first defendants on August 7, 1969. Clause 8 of the debenture conferred upon the receiver the wide powers of sale of a mortgagee within the meeting of the Law of Property Act, 1925.

The receiver caused the first defendants, to form a subsidiary company, Handley Page Aircraft Ltd (hereinafter referred to as 'Aircraft') and by an agreement, dated August 15, 1969, the first defendants assigned to Aircraft such parts of the first defendants' undertaking, including goodwill and designs, as should constitute an economically viable business, which in practice meant the business in connection with 'Jetstream' aircraft. The receiver then intended and was proceeding to negotiate the sale of the shares of Aircraft to American interests, and at the same time informed Mr Keegan and Messrs Clifford Harris & Co, the plaintiffs' solicitors, that he was not willing to continue to comply with the contract made by the first defendants under which the plaintiffs would receive £500 in respect of each aircraft sold.

Accordingly, on August 29, 1969, the plaintiffs issued a writ against the first defendants and the receiver seeking an injunction to restrain them from selling, transferring or otherwise dealing with or entering into any contract for the sale of or completing any contract for sale of all or any of the shares in Aircraft, and a declaration that the plaintiffs were entitled under the agreement of December 23, 1966, and the assignment of September 11, 1968, to payment by the first defendants of £500 in respect of every 'Jetstream' aircraft sold by the first defendants or by Aircraft. On August 29, 1969, Graham J granted an ex parte injunction restraining this sale; and by this motion the plaintiffs moved to continue that injunction.

GRAHAM J: . . . Mr Lightman's[1] argument is as follows: — The first defendants are under an obligation, which is derived from an implied term of the contract and from general equitable principles, not to frustrate or put it out of their power to implement the agreement which the first defendants have entered into with the plaintiffs. In support of this proposition, he relies on *Southern Foundries (1926) Ltd v Shirlaw* [1940] AC 701; . . . Secondly, if it is said against the plaintiffs that

---

1 Counsel for the defendant (now Mr Justice Lightman)

the undertaking has already been transferred and that it is now too late and nothing can be done about it, that argument is unsound. It is unsound because in such circumstances the subsidiary will be treated by the court as the alter ego of the parent and the plaintiffs can obtain relief in respect of their contract against the parent and its subsidiary or either of them. Aircraft is at present admittedly a wholly owned subsidiary of the first defendants, and, as long as it remains so, the court can and will enforce the agreement against it. In this connection, he relies upon *Jones v Lipman* [1962] 1 WLR 832.

Thirdly, the defendants could only succeed if they could show that the receiver and manager appointed by a debenture holder is in a better position than the company, in that he can legitimately avoid a contractual obligation such as the present. Mr Lightman concedes that the receiver cannot be compelled to perform such a contract, but he contends that the receiver cannot legitimately frustrate the contract by a transfer to a subsidiary such as has been effected here. The onus is on the defendants to show that the receiver is in a better position than the company [the first defendants] and that the defendants can lawfully do what they have done. They have cited no authority which justifies such a contention. On the contrary, *In re Botibol, decd* [1947] 1 All ER 26 is against it, and it may properly be said here that the receiver has, by his actions, rendered himself liable in tort by inducing the first defendants to commit a breach of contract. There is, it is said, a clear distinction between declining to perform a contract, which the receiver is entitled to do, and frustrating the contract by his own act, which he is not entitled to do.

Mr Lindsay, on the other hand, argues that the plaintiffs' contentions are misconceived. First, says Mr Lindsay, this case is entirely different from *Jones v Lipman* [1962] 1 WLR 832. That was a case of specific performance of a contract to sell land where the first defendant had purported to frustrate the whole transaction by selling the land in question after the date of his contract with the plaintiffs to a company, the second defendant, which he had acquired purely for the purpose in question. The court held the whole transaction was a sham, that a decree of specific performance would be made against the first defendant, and that, as he controlled the second defendant, he was in a position to cause the contract to be completed. Here, says Mr Lindsay, there is no question of a sham transaction and the receiver is doing his best to realise the best price for those of the first defendant's assets which remain and are saleable, a course which is in the best interests of all the creditors, secured and unsecured.

Further, if, as in *Jones v Lipman*, the contract is of such a nature that specific performance is a nominal remedy, a plaintiff could expect to obtain it both against a parent and a subsidiary company, but if, as in the present case, breach of the contract normally only leads to damages — and it is accepted here that the receiver cannot be compelled to perform the contract — then the case of *Jones v Lipman* cannot have relevance.

Secondly, the defendants say that the plaintiffs are really trying, by their action, to get themselves placed in a preferential position over all other unsecured creditors, of which there are a large number. Yet, when the position is fairly examined, it will be seen that the plaintiffs are in no different position from any other unsecured creditor, in that they have an ordinary trading contract with the first defendants which the receiver can either adopt or decline. There is no evidence that the option granted by clause 2 of the agreement has been adopted by the plaintiffs and all the plaintiffs stand to receive under that agreement is £500 per aircraft sold. It would not be equitable for the receiver to prefer the plaintiffs to other unsecured creditors, and it is in the best interests of all such creditors that he should be able to sell that part of the first defendants' business which will constitute a viable unit in the way which will secure the highest price. If, in so doing, he does decline to take over the plaintiffs' contract, he may, of course, render the first defendants liable in damages and may also, to some extent, at any rate, damage their reputation as a trustworthy company which can be expected to honour its contracts. This, however, the defendants say, he is entitled to do, so long as the realisation of the net assets of the company [the first defendants] to the best advantage is not impaired. There may be cases where declining to adopt a contract of the company would so seriously impair the goodwill of the company that such realisation would be adversely affected, but that is not the case here. There is no evidence that it would so impair such realisation, nor that it would seriously damage the prospects of the first defendants' trading successfully in the future if they ever do so, and in fact the only goodwill of any real value, namely, that connected with the design, manufacture and prospects of sale of the 'Jetstream,' has been transferred to Aircraft. It is not suggested that the first defendants themselves are likely to do any active trading in the future.

Thirdly, it is said that to merit the grant of an injunction, the acts complained of must threaten an invasion of the plaintiffs' legal rights and the relief asked for must relate to those rights. Here, the relief asked for relates to the transfer of shares in Aircraft, and if that be so the plaintiffs must show that they have some legal rights in respect of the shares in question, and no such right has been shown. This argument seems to me to beg the real question the answer to which, in my judgment, determines the issue in this case. That question may be stated as follows: is a receiver and manager, appointed by debenture holders, in a stronger position, from the legal point of view, than the company itself, in respect of contracts between unsecured creditors and the company? Assuming that the company, on the authority of *Southern Foundries (1926) Ltd v Shirlaw* [1940] AC 701, cannot put it out of its own power to perform contracts it has entered into, can a receiver in effect do so on its behalf if, at the same time, he has made it clear that he is not going to adopt the contract anyway, and if, as is, in my judgment, the case here, the repudiation of the contract will not adversely affect the realisation of the assets or seriously affect the trading prospects of the company in question, if it is able to trade in the future?

Counsel, when I asked them, were not able to produce any authority which gave a direct answer to this question, but there is a helpful passage dealing generally with 'current contracts' in *Buckley on the Companies Acts*, 13th edn (1957), p 244. This passage, to my mind, makes it clear that, in the author's view, the answer to the question I have posed above must be 'yes.' I seems to me that it is common sense that it should be so, since otherwise almost any unsecured creditor would be able to improve his position and prevent the receiver from carrying out, or at any rate carrying out as sensibly and as equitably as possible, the purpose for which he was appointed. I therefore hold that the receiver, within the limitations which I have stated above, is in a better position than the company, qua current contracts, and that, in the present case, the receiver, in doing what he has done and is purporting to do, in connection with the transfer of Aircraft's shares, is not doing anything which the plaintiffs are entitled to prevent by this motion.

Further, having now heard the full argument and considered the defendants' evidence in Mr Cork's affidavit, which was, of course, not available on the ex parte motion, in my judgment the balance of convenience is in favour of refusing rather than of continuing the injunction. There are a number of obviously very important considerations from the point of view not only of the company but also of the public at large set out in paragraphs 7 to 13 of Mr Cork's affidavit which, in my judgment, tip the scales in favour of the defendants in this respect.

In the result, as already stated at the end of the hearing, I discharge the interim injunction against the defendants.

SOURCE 294
Freevale Ltd *v* Metrostore (Holdings) Ltd
[1984] 1 Ch 199

DONALD RATTEE QC: I have before me an appeal from Master Gowers from an order, made on 1 July 1983 in which he refused to make an order for specific performance under RSC, Ord 86, and instead gave leave to the defendants in the action to defend. The action is one by a company, Freevale Ltd, against two defendant companies, Metrostore (Holdings) Ltd and Metrostore (Hayes) Ltd, and is an action claiming specific performance of an agreement for the sale of land.

For present purposes, the material facts are set out in the statement of claim, and those facts, as alleged, are now admitted by a defence that has been put in on behalf of the defendants, so that there is no dispute between the parties as to the material facts. For present purposes, all I need say about the facts is that, as appears from the statement of claim, there was an agreement in writing of 4 February 1983 made between the two defendants of the one part and the plaintiff of the other, whereby the defendants agreed to sell and the plaintiff to buy three pieces of land at an aggregate price of £300,000.

  . . .

The master decided that the court would not, or perhaps might not, grant an order for specific performance against a company in receivership. Mr Lloyd, who appeared on behalf of the plaintiff, says that that decision was wrong. He says — and I do not think there is any dispute between the parties as to this — that but for this fact of receivership the relevant contract would have been subject to an order for specific performance at the behest of the plaintiff, because, like all other contracts for the sale of land, prima facie, damages are not an appropriate or satisfactory or sufficient remedy for breach. Mr Lloyd says that, a fortiori, damages are not an adequate remedy for breach of the contract in the present case, where, having regard to the fact of the receivership in relation to both the defendants, there is indeed real doubt as to how valuable, if at all, the right to damages against the companies would be having regard to their likely financial position.

Mr Hacker, who appears on behalf of the defendants, on the other hand, says that, because a receiver has been appointed of each of the defendant companies, the court will not order specific performance of the contract in the action brought by the plaintiff, and for that proposition he relies on two authorities. The first of those is *Airlines Airspares Ltd v Handley Page Ltd* [1970] Ch 193 [above pp 23 ff].

Now, the first thing to note about the facts of that case is that the contract concerned was not one of which the court would, apart from the receivership, grant specific performance. . . .

Graham J, after having set out the argument of the parties, really crystallises the question with which the court was concerned in that case, and gives his answer to it. He says,

  . . .

  'Counsel, when I asked them, were not able to produce any authority which
  gave a direct answer to this question, but there is a helpful passage dealing

generally with "current contracts" in *Buckley on the Companies Acts*, 13th edn (1957), p 244. This passage, to my mind, makes it clear that, in the author's view, the answer to the question I have posed above must be 'yes.' It seems to me that it is common sense that it should be so, since otherwise almost any unsecured creditor would be able to improve his position and prevent the receiver from carrying out, or at any rate carrying out as sensibly and as equitably as possible, the purpose for which he was appointed. I therefore hold that the receiver, within the limitations which I have stated above, is in a better position than the company, qua current contracts, and that, in the present case, the receiver, in doing what he has done and is purporting to do, in connection with the transfer of Aircraft's shares, is not doing anything which the plaintiffs are entitled to prevent by this motion.'

In my judgment, that decision of Graham J really affords me no help on the question which is raised by the present case, which is a totally different question. In my judgment, the real question raised in the present case is, 'Does the appointment out of court of a receiver in respect of a company vendor of land somehow destroy the equitable interest in the land which was vested in the purchaser prior to the appointment of the receiver by virtue of the subsisting valid contract for its sale and purchase, or does the appointment of a receiver alternatively somehow prevent the court perfecting that equitable interest by making an order for specific performance?'

As I say, in my judgment, Graham J's decision in the *Airlines Airspares Ltd* case [1970] Ch 193 really does not point the way to the correct answer to the question which I have just formulated. In his case, there was no contract for the sale of land whose enforcement the court was considering, and, as I have said, there was no doubt that the contract that the court was considering was not one which would have been subject to an order for specific performance whether or not there had been a receiver on the scene.

The second authority on which Mr Hacker relies is a Scottish case, *Macleod v Alexander Sutherland Ltd*, 1977 SLT (Notes) 44. Inevitably, having regard to the different legal terminology that unfortunately exists between the Scottish and the English jurisdictions, it is not, at all points, easy to follow the rather abbreviated report that appears in the Scots Law Times, but the report is comparatively short and I propose for the purpose of convenience to read it in full:

'In 1972 the pursuer sold the defenders an area of ground at Inverness on missives which provided inter alia that the defenders should perform certain specified building and construction work in relation to the ground. The work was never carried out. The pursuer raised an action seeking decree of implement and, failing implement, damages of £10,000.'

I intervene to say, as I understand it, a decree of implement is the equivalent of a decree of specific performance. The report goes on:

'The defenders were a company incorporated under the Companies Act, and a receiver was appointed to the company in June 1974 by creditors holding a floating charge secured over the company's entire assets. The receiver accordingly had complete control over the company's assets. The defenders had ceased to trade in the sense that they were no longer carrying on a building business. They did not employ anyone who could carry out the work, nor did they own the necessary materials. They averred that it was impossible for them to perform their obligations to the pursuer.

Section 17(4) of the Companies (Floating Charges and Receivers) (Scotland) Act 1972 provides that contracts undertaken by a company prior to the appointment of a receiver continue in force notwithstanding the appointment. Counsel for the pursuer submitted that it was no answer for a company which had undertaken contractual obligations to say that they no longer had the means of performing them. The defenders admitted that they were in breach of contract and were willing that decree should pass against them for payment of damages. The only question remaining at issue was whether the pursuer was entitled to decree of specific implement. In refusing decree of implement and granting decree for payment of damages the Lord Ordinary (Lord Stott) said: "It is plain that the defenders are not in a position to obtemper decree of specific implement through their directors as would normally be the position if the company were not in receivership."'

Now, again there is a certain difficulty of terminology, but I understand that that really is equivalent to saying it is plain that the defenders were not in a position to comply with a decree of specific performance through their directors.

. . .

The essence of the decision in that Scottish case, in my judgment, appears from the judgment of Lord Stott, the Lord Ordinary, in the passage where he says:

'Since ex hypothesi the responsibility for whatever is done is implement of the contract must in fact be done by the receiver it seems to me to be out of the question to pronounce a decree ostensibly against the company, which would in effect result in the receiver either incurring personal liability or in his bearing the responsibility for a contempt of court (whether his own or the company's).'

The facts, of course, in that case were that it was no longer physically possible for the company, which had become little more than a shell, it having ceased its business, to have complied with an order for specific performance to carry out the works required by the contract. The works could only have been carried out if the receiver, in exercise of his powers, had entered into some other obligations, contracts, be they what they may, but some other arrangements whereby he or the company could acquire the means with which to perform the company's obligations under the contract, and Lord Stott is saying, as I understand him in that passage I have just re-read, that, that being so, the decree for specific performance could only have been complied with at the cost of the receiver himself undertaking some personal liability, and that, not surprisingly, the court would not impose.

But those facts take the case, in my judgment, a long way from the problem I have to deal with in the present case. If an order for specific performance is made in the present case, there is no question of the receiver having to incur any personal liability as the only alternative to being in contempt of court. The land the subject of the contract remains in the companies. There is no difficulty, prima facie at any rate, in its being conveyed by the company acting through the receiver pursuant to an order for specific performance, if made.

. . .

Much more assistance, in my judgment, is to be derived from two authorities in the sphere of bankruptcy to which I was referred by Mr Lloyd on behalf of the plaintiff, and, indeed, by Mr Hacker on behalf of the defendants. The first of those is *Pearce v Bastable's Trustee in Bankruptcy* [1901] 2 Ch 122, where the headnote reads:

'Specific performance may be enforced against the trustee in bankruptcy of a vendor of property, and, if the property is leasehold, he cannot disclaim the contract without disclaiming the lease.'

In the course of his judgment, Cozens-Hardy J said, at p 125:

'It has been contended on his' — that is the trustee in bankruptcy's — 'behalf that the fact of the bankruptcy makes all the difference as regards the liability to specifically perform a contract. In support of that, *Holloway v York* (1877) 25 WR 627 has been referred to. The effect of that decision is correctly stated in *Dart's Vendors and Purchasers*, 6th edn (1888), p 1126 — that is to say, that specific performance cannot be decreed against the trustee in bankruptcy of the purchaser. That decision has no application to a case in which the vendor's trustee in bankruptcy is the defendant. If any authority is needed in support of this finding it is to be found in *Ex parte Rabbidge* (1878) 8 Ch D 367, 370 where James LJ said: "The result was that, upon the adjudication being made, the legal estate in the property vested in the trustee in the bankruptcy, subject to the equity of the purchaser under the contract. That equity gave him a right to have the property conveyed to him, upon payment of the purchase money to the person to whom the property belonged." And Cotton LJ said: "The trustee in the bankruptcy . . . had vested in him the estate of the bankrupt in the property. He was not in the fullest sense of the word a trustee of the property for the purchaser, because the whole of the purchase money had not been paid. But he took the legal estate in the property, subject to the equity of the purchaser under the contract, which gave the purchaser the right to say, 'Convey me the estate on my paying the purchase money.' " Anything more explicit on this part of the case could not well be imagined. All that the plaintiff asks the trustee to do is to execute the engrossment already approved and assign the property to him, and, the plaintiff disclaiming any right of proof against the bankrupt's estate, an order for such execution, and that the defendant is to pay the costs of the action, must be made.'

I appreciate, of course, that the court in that case was concerned with the position of a vendor's trustee in bankruptcy and not the receiver of a vendor company, and I, of course, appreciate that one important difference between those two situations is that the property of the bankrupt in the *Pearce* case [1901] 2 Ch 122, including the property subject to the contract of sale, vested in the trustee in bankruptcy, whereas the defendant companies' property in the present case is not vested in the receiver. But nonetheless, in my judgment, the approach which is adopted there by Cozens-Hardy J to determining the non-effect of bankruptcy on the equitable interest which a purchaser of land from a bankrupt had before the onset of bankruptcy, is certainly of assistance in considering the effect or non-effect of the appointment of a receiver of the vendor companies in the present case.

The other bankruptcy authority which arose, in fact, out of the same bankruptcy is in the Court of Appeal and is *In re Bastable, Ex parte the Trustee* [1901] 2 KB 518, and the headnote there reads:

'The trustee in a bankruptcy cannot, under section 55 of the Bankruptcy Act 1883, disclaim a contract entered into by the bankrupt for the sale of a lease unless he also disclaims the lease itself. Section 55 was intended to enable the trustee to get rid of an onerous property or contract, and it does not enable him to disclaim a contract merely because it would be more beneficial to the estate that the contract should not be carried out. The trustee cannot by a disclaimer take away from a purchaser of land from the bankrupt the equitable interest which vested in him under his contract.'

It is the latter sentence in the headnote which is obviously particularly relevant in the present case. The decision, so far as material, was that the trustee in bankruptcy of the bankrupt, who had prior to the bankruptcy contracted to sell land, could not by exercising his power of disclaimer destroy the equitable interest in the land of a purchaser under that contract. Now, of course, a receiver, as I say, is in a very different position. He does not have vested in him the property of the company, and perhaps more particularly, in considering the decision in *In re Bastable*, he does not have the power to disclaim. So, of course, the facts considered by the Court of Appeal were different, and the question was different, but nonetheless, in my judgment, the reasoning explained by Romer LJ in his judgment as to the effect of bankruptcy on the equitable interest of a purchaser from the bankrupt is extremely helpful in the situation with which I am confronted. In fact, the decision of the Court of Appeal was unanimous, but I think for present purposes the most help is to be derived from Romer LJ's judgment. I propose to read a passage from that judgment where his Lordship says, at p 527:

> 'It is in substance contended on behalf of the trustee' – that is the trustee in bankruptcy – 'that if a vendor of real estate, by contract entered into with a purchaser, becomes bankrupt, the trustee in the bankruptcy of the vendor, without disclaiming the land or the interest in the land which was the subject of the contract, can, by disclaiming the contract alone, put himself in the position of owner of the estate freed altogether from the purchaser's interest in the estate, leaving the purchaser only the remedy of proving in the bankruptcy for any loss he may have suffered by having his contract destroyed.'

Of course, that is in effect the position in which the defendants say that the purchaser plaintiff company is left in the present case, without even the need for any disclaimer. The defendants say the effect of the mere appointment of the receiver is that the plaintiff is left with what may well be a useless remedy in damages. Romer LJ goes on, at p 528:

> 'That would, indeed, be a serious contention if it could be maintained, because the result would be, that in every case in which an owner of real estate who had contracted to sell it subsequently became bankrupt, and after the contract of sale and before the bankruptcy the property had increased in value, the trustee in the bankruptcy would be able to deprive the purchaser of all interest in the estate and leave him merely the right to prove in the bankruptcy for any loss he might have incurred by the destruction of his contract, in which case he might possibly receive only an infinitesimal dividend upon the amount of his proof. It cannot, I think, be that such a result was ever intended by the Act.'

. . .

Quite apart from the fact that, as I say, the defendants' argument leads, in my judgment, to a situation of considerable injustice to a purchaser who finds himself at risk of, in effect, losing his contract if before completion the vendor company suffers the appointment of a receiver — quite apart from the fact that it leads to that injustice, in my judgment, the defendants' contention is not supported by an authority which has been referred to before me and is quite inconsistent, in my judgment, with the nature of the equitable interest of a purchaser of land.

In my judgment, the defendants in this case are in just the same position as the trustee in bankruptcy was in *In re Bastable* to whom Romer LJ referred as 'having no further interest in the property but an outstanding legal estate,' subject, of course, to the lien for the unpaid part of the purchase price. That being so, it seems to me quite clear that the court ought to perfect the interests of the purchaser by calling upon the companies to transfer that legal estate in perfection of the equitable interest already vested in the plaintiff.

So it follows that, in my judgment, the mere fact of receivership of the defendants affords no defence to a claim for specific performance. I do not overlook the fact that in this appeal I am only concerned with the question of whether leave should be given to the defendants to defend the claim; but the only point, as I say, that is raised as a possible defence is this legal effect of the appointment of a receiver. It is a pure point of law. It has been fully argued before me. I cannot see that anything is to be gained by anybody from some one or other party having to incur the expense of a further trial on the same point of law. In my judgment, the defence that is raised is sufficiently clearly unsustainable that the master should have refused leave to defend, and accordingly I would allow this appeal, and it now becomes necessary to consider the form of the order for specific performance that ought to be made.

SOURCE 295
Re Potters Oils
[1986] 1 WLR 201

HOFFMANN J: There is before the court a summons under section 371 of the Companies Act 1948, now section 494 of the Companies Act 1985, to fix the remuneration of the receiver of a mobile oil centrifuge who was appointed out of court under a power contained in a debenture. I am asked to disallow his remuneration and disbursements on the ground that in all the circumstances his appointment was unnecessary. Alternatively it is said that the amounts claimed for both remuneration and disbursements are excessive. I propose to dismiss the summons.

Potters Oils Ltd ('the company') carried on the business of maintaining and cleaning oil tanks and processing waste oil products. For this purpose it bought a highly specialised mobile plant from a French company called Guinard Centrifugation SA ('Guinard') for £250,000. This purchase was partly financed by a loan of £200,000 from Lloyds and Scottish Trust Ltd who are now called Lloyds Bowmaker Ltd ('LB'). In consideration of this loan the company executed a debenture dated 29 March 1983, by which repayment of the loan was secured by a fixed charge over the plant. Clause 6 of the debenture gave LB power:

'at any time after the loan or any part thereof shall have become payable to appoint by writing . . . a receiver of the property hereby charged upon such terms as to remuneration and otherwise as the debenture holder shall think fit . . .'

The receiver was to have power to take possession of and get in the property and to sell or concur in its sale. Clause 8 provided that the net proceeds of sale or realisation were to be applied by the receiver:

'first in payment of all costs charges and expenses of and incidental to the appointment of the receiver and the exercise by him of all or any of the powers aforesaid including the reasonable remuneration of the receiver not

exceeding a commission at the rate of five pounds per centum on the gross
amount received by him and all outgoings properly payable by him.'

The company took delivery of the plant in March 1983 and in order to perfect its
security, LB insisted upon and received an assurance from Guinard that title had
passed. Against this assurance the company was paid the £200,000 loan but
appears not to have paid the money over to Guinard. As a result Guinard issued
proceedings against the company on 10 November 1983, claiming payment of
the balance of the purchase price.

On 6 December 1983 a petition to wind up the company was presented by a
trade creditor. A winding up order was made on 23 January 1984. While the
petition was pending the company, on 13 January, delivered a defence in which
it alleged that on account of various defects of quality in the plant the sale
agreement with Guinard had according to its terms become null and void.

On 3 February 1984 Guinard obtained leave to continue its action against the
company. On 22 February 1984 Barry John Ward, a chartered accountant from
Worcester, was appointed liquidator. He found himself faced by some complicated and unusual litigation. The allegation that the sale agreement had become
null and void had caused some excitement in the French camp. It seemed to
offer the prospect of recovery of the plant itself instead of an unsecured claim
against an insolvent company. On 21 February Guinard issued a summons
seeking leave to amend its statement of claim to allege that the defence
constituted a repudiation of the contract which had been accepted and which
entitled Guinard to recovery of the plant. The summons also sought a summary
order for redelivery.

I must now turn to consider how the picture must have appeared at the time
to LB. It was owed about £186,000. It must have been surprised that Guinard had
not been paid the proceeds of a loan raised for the very purpose of buying the
plant. LB was also aware of the litigation over the plant and was no doubt also
concerned that Guinard was seeking a summary order for repossession of the
only asset over which it had a charge. The summons for delivery up was due to
be heard on 13 April. It is true that quite apart from the complications caused by
the existence of a proprietary interest in LB, Guinard's claim faced certain
obvious difficulties which is unnecessary to discuss in detail: see for example
Woodar Investment Development Ltd v Wimpey Construction UK Ltd [1980] 1 WLR 277.
Nevertheless the claim was being aggressively pursued and it would not be
surprising if LB felt apprehensive. Furthermore, Guinard was not the only
claimant to threaten the security. A company called T. Mat Engineering Ltd was
claiming to have retained title to a trailer to which part of the plant had been
attached.

On 15 March LB's in-house solicitor sent a telex to the liquidator's solicitors
notifying them of its charge over the plant and asking that it should be drawn to
the attention of the judge on the hearing of Guinard's summons. On 4 April the
liquidator's solicitors wrote to confirm that LB's 'alleged debenture' would be
mentioned to the judge, but added: 'However Lloyds Bowmaker Ltd must satisfy
the liquidator or the court that this is valid.' In these circumstances LB decided
to appoint a receiver to protect its interests and to assert a right to possession of
the plant in accordance with the debenture. By an instrument dated 6 April 1984
it appointed Mr M. C. Withall, a partner in Messrs Thornton Baker.

Mr Withall immediately instructed solicitors, Messrs David Elton and Wine-
man. They notified Guinard that they would appear by counsel on the hearing of
the summons on 13 April and apply for LB and the receiver to be joined as

defendants. For this purpose Mr Cowell, a senior legal assistant with LB hurriedly swore an affidavit on 12 April. In this affidavit he said that LB wished to be joined because it considered that its proprietary interest under the charge, antedating the alleged repudiation by the company, gave it a stronger defence than the company to Guinard's claim for possession. The joinder of the receiver was proposed on account of his right to possession under the debenture. At the very last moment, however, Guinard said that they had received the liquidator's evidence late and wanted an adjournment. As a result, there was no effective hearing on 13 April. On the company's undertaking not to dispose of the plant, the summons was adjourned, and LB decided to issue a summons to be joined which could be heard together with the adjourned hearing of Guinard's summons.

Also on 13 April Mr Withall's assistant Mr White spoke to the liquidator. Mr Ward. They discussed the question of selling the plant and Mr Ward said that no decision could be taken until Guinard's application had been heard. He also said that the value of the plant was in know-how which had been incorporated in patents filed by a former director of the company. The exact significance of this remark remains somewhat obscure but it was plainly not intended to be encouraging.

On 3 May Mr Withall wrote to Mr Ward saying that he had instructed agents to value the plant and assist him in marketing it in due course when the litigation was out of the way. The possibility of a joint sale by receiver and liquidator was also mentioned. This produced a sharp reply from Mr Ward dated 10 May. I must quote some passages in full:

> '. . . I am a little puzzled as to why you consider it necessary to instruct agents or for that matter why you consider you will be marketing the equipment in due course. It was, in my opinion, quite unnecessary for Lloyds Bowmaker to appoint a receiver because on the validation of their debenture they would have been paid amounts due anyway from the proceeds of sale. All that their action has achieved has been to increase the costs substantially to the detriment of the unsecured creditors. Finally you will recall that the equipment is effectively valueless without the appropriate technological know-how, which is the subject of a patent registered in the company's name. Any attempt to sell the equipment without that will, I feel, give rise to an action by myself against the debenture holder.'

The hostilities which might have been expected to follow this letter were temporarily suspended on account of the welcome appearance of an offer for the plant from a third party at a price of £345,000, which was much higher than either the liquidator or receiver had dared to hope. The liquidator then notified Guinard of the offer and said that he proposed to apply to the court for leave to sell. Guinard decided to make a counter-offer. After a series of bids by Guinard and the third party, the liquidator, with the consent of the receiver, sold the plant back to Guinard for £375,000. This was sufficient to pay off T. Mat Engineering Ltd for their trailer and leave more than enough to satisfy LB's claim under the debenture. But the liquidator has challenged the whole of the receiver's remuneration (£8,000 plus VAT) and his disbursements in respect of solicitor's fees (£5,162.71) and the services of the agents who valued the plant (£1,206.23). Hence the summons now before me seeking declarations under section 371 of the Companies Act 1948 that these sums are not to be paid out of the proceeds of sale of the plant.

I shall first consider the rights of the parties unmodified by statute. The liquidator concedes that the terms of the debenture are binding upon the company. The debenture gives LB an unfettered right to appoint a receiver at any time after the loan has become repayable. Mr Withall was appointed pursuant to this power. The debenture then gave him power to take possession of the plant and sell it or concur in its sale.

The liquidator says that the appointment of the receiver was unnecessary because he, the liquidator, was doing all that could be done to protect the interests of LB and the appointment of the receiver only caused duplication of effort and unnecessary expense. I think that there are two answers to this submission. The first is that LB was contractually entitled to appoint the receiver to protect its own interests. As between LB (by its receiver), and the company, the former had the prior right to possession of the plant. Since the liquidator was an officer of the court and already in possession, the receiver could not exercise his right to possession without the leave of the court. But he would be entitled to that leave as of right: see *In re Henry Pound, Son & Hutchins* (1889) 42 Ch D 402. It would be no answer that the property could be realised by the liquidator more cheaply and no less effectively. The debenture-holder is under no duty to refrain from exercising his rights merely because to exercise them may cause loss to the company or its unsecured creditors. He owes a duty of care to the company but this duty is qualified by being subordinated to the protection of his own interests. As Salmon LJ said in *Cuckmere Brick Co Ltd v Mutual Finance Ltd* [1971] Ch 949, 965H: 'If the mortgagee's interests, as he sees them, conflict with those of the mortgagor, the mortgagee can give preference to his own interests . . .'

A second answer is that in his case I think that LB was justified in thinking that its own interests would best be served by the appointment of a receiver to assert a right to possession of the plant. Mr Moss, for the liquidator, says that Guinard's claim for possession was bound to fail as against the company whether or not LB or its receiver could assert an independent right. I think that this is probably true, but there was no reason why LB should have taken any chance on the company's defences succeeding when it had a cast-iron defence of its own. To this Mr Moss says that the liquidator would have pleaded LB's right by way of *jus tertii* under section 8 of the Torts (Interference With Goods) Act 1977. It seems to me that such a plea would have led to the joinder of LB or the receiver or both of them pursuant to RSC, Ord 15, r 10A, and would therefore not have obviated the desirability, from LB's point of view, of having someone to protect its interests.

The liquidator says that it should have been clear to LB that they had identical interests in repelling the claims of Guinard and that he was quite capable of seeing off the French without any help or interference. I do not accept this submission. I think that it would be sufficient to say that LB was entitled to take a different view. But I also think that the liquidator's refusal to admit the validity of LB's debenture — for which he is not to be criticised — his telex telling LB that it would have to satisfy the court of the validity of the debenture and his threat to sue LB for patent infringement if it tried to sell the plant without his participation can only have confirmed LB's view that it needed to look after itself.

LB was therefore contractually entitled to appoint Mr Withall receiver 'upon such terms as to remuneration and otherwise as [LB] shall think fit.' The power to agree the receiver's remuneration, like other powers of the mortgagee, has no doubt to be exercised in good faith and with regard to the qualified duty of care to the company to which I have already referred. The receiver, as agent for the company, is also entitled to be indemnified out of the assets subject to his receivership for expenses properly incurred as such agent.

In my judgment there is no evidence to suggest that LB acted in bad faith or otherwise in breach of duty in fixing Mr Withall's remuneration. Nor do I think there was any impropriety or breach of duty on his part in instructing solicitors to participate in the litigation or agents to value the plant. Looked at from LB's point of view, this expenditure was reasonable.

The effect of section 371 of the Companies Act 1948 is to give the court power to interfere retrospectively with the contractual rights of the receiver and mortgagee. Section 371(1) provides that the court may, on the application of the liquidator:

> 'fix the amount to be paid by way of remuneration to any person who, under the powers contained in any instrument, has been appointed as receiver or manager of the property of the company.'

In its original form as section 309 of the Companies Act 1929 the power applied only to remuneration earned after the date of the order. In *In re Greycaine Ltd* [1946] Ch 269, 280, 281, Morton LJ said that retrospectivity would make it 'a penal section' conferring 'a remarkable power' to take away remuneration already earned. These considerations did not inhibit Parliament from adding subsection (2) to section 371 of the Act of 1948, making it clear that the power may be exercised in respect of any period before the date of the order and may require the receiver or his personal representatives to account for remuneration which he has already been paid or retained.

The scope of section 371 is, however, confined to the receiver's remuneration. It confers no jurisdiction to interfere with his right to indemnity for disbursements. This remains subject to the ordinary law of agency. As I have already held that there was no impropriety in the employment of the solicitors or agents, there is no basis for a challenge to their fees. I shall return later to the question of taxation of the solicitors' bill.

This leaves the question of whether I should exercise the power conferred by section 371 to fix the receiver's remuneration which is presently agreed between LB and the receiver at £8,000 plus VAT. I have not been referred to any authority which deals with the principles on which the power should be exercised. The section confers two separate discretions. The first is a discretion as to whether to interfere at all. The second, once the decision has been made to fix the remuneration, is a discretion as to the amount. Both appear to be entirely unfettered.

In exercising these discretions I bear in mind the following considerations. First, the exercise of the power involves interference with contractual rights in the interests of the unsecured creditors. As Andrew Clark KC said in argument in *In re Greycaine Ltd* [1946] Ch 269, 274, the mischief at which the section is aimed is that

> 'unsecured creditors may find themselves bound by an improvident bargain entered into by the directors and see the assets frittered away on the agent of the secured creditors.'

I respectfully adopt this description, which suggests to me that interference should be confined to cases in which the remuneration can clearly be seen as excessive rather than take the form of a routine taxation by the court of receivers' remuneration.

Secondly, the court is ill-equipped to conduct a detailed investigation of receivers' charges on an itemised basis. A judge could not do so without being expensively educated by expert evidence. Perhaps this is why neither counsel nor for that matter myself had any previous experience of an application under section 371. One may contrast the specialised experience available to the court in dealing with the taxation of solicitors' bills.

Thirdly, clause 8 of the debenture contemplates remuneration calculated as a percentage of the sum realised by the receiver and fixes a maximum which is on any view greater than the sum claimed. This is of course not in itself a reason for not interfering. The section was, as I have said, intended to give the court power to interfere with contractual rights. In this case, however, there is nothing to show that either a percentage calculation or the five per cent. maximum is unreasonable.

Guidance may be obtained from the fact that the fees of liquidators and trustees in bankruptcy are ordinarily calculated as a percentage of the moneys which pass through their hands. Thus under paragraph 8 of the Schedule to the Companies (Department of Trade and Industry) Fees Order 1984 (SI 1984/881 (L.10)) the official receiver as liquidator is entitled to charge a fee of five per cent. on sums in excess of £100,000 realised by him and paid into the insolvency services account and a higher percentage on sums less than £100,000. In addition, he is entitled to charge half these percentages on money distributed to creditors. Similar charges may be made by trustees in bankruptcy and voluntary liquidators.

It seems to me that the liquidator's case stands or falls by the proposition that the appointment of the receiver and his subsequent participation in the litigation and realisation of the plant were all unnecessary. Having rejected this argument as based upon a misapprehension about the extent of a mortgagee's powers, I can find no grounds upon which to exercise the power to fix remuneration under section 371. I therefore dismiss the summons.

I add a short postscript about the solicitors' bill. There was some discussion about whether the liquidator was entitled to have it taxed. This bill has been submitted in draft but not yet formally delivered. It was, I think, agreed that the liquidator could require it to be formally delivered and then apply for it to be taxed under section 71 of the Solicitors Act 1974. But this is not a matter before me upon the summons and I say no more about it.

SOURCE 296
Standard Chartered Bank Ltd *v* Walker
[1982] 1 WLR 1410

LORD DENNING MR: When a bank lends money to a private company, it usually insists on the overdraft being guaranteed by the directors personally. Especially when a husband and wife are the directors and shareholders of the company. Then, when the company crash and are unable to meet their liabilities, the bank puts in a receiver. He realises the assets of the company. But not enough to pay off the overdraft. The bank then comes down on the directors on the guarantee. Have they any defence? The directors here say that the assets were sold at a gross undervalue. How far does that give them any defence?

The directors here, the defendants, are Johnny Walker and his wife Gloria. They have been concerned with several private companies using the name 'Johnny Walker,' but nothing to do with whisky. We are here concerned with the latest one, Johnny Walker (Developments) Ltd. They carried on a very specialised business. They had a large workshop and warehouse in Gloucestershire. It was called Vortex Works at Tetbury. They bought huge metal presses and moulding machines second-hand and stored them there. They resold them to buyers all over the world. They did it on money borrowed from Standard Chartered Bank Ltd, the plaintiff. The bank insisted on a debenture. It was dated October 25, 1977. It gave the bank a fixed and floating charge on the assets of the company.

It gave the bank power to appoint a receiver who was to have power to take possession of the assets and to sell them. It contained an express provision:

> 'Any receiver or receivers so appointed shall be deemed to be the agent or agents of the company and the company shall be solely responsible for his or their acts or defaults and for his or their remuneration.'

The bank also insisted on a personal guarantee by Johnny Walker and his wife. It was dated December 12, 1978. It guaranteed the payment by the company of all their indebtedness to the bank provided that the total amount recoverable from Johnny Walker and his wife was not to exceed £75,000 together with interest thereon.

From 1978 onwards the business was badly hit by the slump in trade which was worldwide. In order to meet wages, rent and other expenses, the company incurred a large overdraft. At one time it was over £275,000. The bank pressed the company to reduce it. They took stringent measures. They cut down the staff greatly and reduced expenses on all sides. By April 1980 the overdraft had got down to £65,751. The bank urged its further reduction to £50,000. Johnny Walker constantly told them of his efforts. He told them of the sales he hoped to make. But, despite his efforts, the overdraft went somewhat higher. The bank thought of appointing a receiver. On September 1, 1980, Johnny Walker wrote:

> 'To put a receiver in at the moment, when the company has done so well in streamlining itself, "digging its heels" in and preparing to combat the recession, would mean, literally economic suicide . . . If common sense prevails and we are allowed to continue to trade, which I may add now is profitably so, it will not be long before we can reduce down within the £50,000 but it is going to take a little longer in time.'

Despite Johnny Walker's hopes, things got no better. They got rather worse. The overdraft came to over £80,000. So much so that on November 6, 1980, the bank appointed a receiver. He was Mr Heaford of the well known firm of chartered accountants, Touche Ross & Co of Bristol. John Walker saw Mr Heaford and asked if he could continue to trade through another of his companies. According to an affidavit of Mr Walker, the receiver said, 'As from now, Mr Walker, you are out of business. My instructions are to be out of here as quickly as possible,' and that he intended to hold an auction sale as quickly as possible.

The receiver instructed well-known auctioneers, Edward Rushton, Son & Kenyon. They examined the stock and estimated that at an action sale they might sell the whole of the stock for £90,000. They proposed to hold the auction on January 21, 1981. Johnny Walker afterwards thought this was too soon and asked for it to be postponed. It was then fixed for Wednesday, February 4, 1981, at the works at Tetbury. The auctioneers got to work preparing for the action. They numbered all the lots. They made up a catalogue containing a description of all the machines. They did some advertising.

On Wednesday, February 4, 1981, the auction was held. It was a disaster. Only about 70 persons attended — nearly all from places round about. Only one buyer from overseas — although the market for these machines was worldwide. It was a bitterly cold day. They had a few heating stoves, but these made such a noise that the auctioneer could not make himself heard. So they were turned off — and many prospective buyers left. The result in outline was that the stock only realised £42,864 and the expenses of realisation came to £42,718. That left hardly anything for the preferential creditors, who came to £37,139, and nothing at all for the bank whose debt was £88,432. So the result was a disaster for everyone.

The receiver had got enough to pay the expenses of the sale and so forth, but nothing for the preferential creditors, and nothing for the bank.

Soon afterwards, on April 8, 1981, the bank issued a writ against Johnny Walker and his wife as guarantors claiming the whole sum of £75,000 and interest at £30 a day. They issued a summons for judgment under RSC, Ord 14. The deputy registrar and the judge gave judgment in favour of the bank. Johnny Walker and his wife appeal to this court.

It is interesting to see that the only affidavit put in by the bank throughout was the formal affidavit under Order 14, which just said that in their belief the defendants were justly indebted in those sums. There were affidavits in answer. I will not go into all of them. Mr Johnny Walker set out his defence. The bank never replied to his affidavits. I will read a passage from one of his affidavits. He said:

> 'It is apparent from the affidavits referred to that the prices achieved at auction were much lower than could reasonably have been expected and, indeed, were less than half of the conservative valuation made by the auctioneer. There were many reasons for this. The main reasons are, in my opinion, that the auction was held at the wrong time of the year, that it was insufficiently advertised, that no notice was given to the prospective customers on my company's mailing list by direct mailing, that the viewing arrangements were inadequate and the attendance poor. . . . It will be apparent that the decision by the receiver to hold an auction quickly and without adequate publicity was taken by him as a result of an instruction received from the [bank]. . . . Messrs Touche Ross & Co of Bristol made a report to the [bank] on the financial affairs of [the company] on October 20, 1980. At about that time, I had a telephone conversation with Roger Bailey who was then the manager of the branch of the [bank] in Bristol. Mr Bailey told me during the conversation that the bank had already made provision to write off the entire . . . overdraft as a bad debt, that the [bank] had decided to appoint a receiver under its debenture and that the receiver would be instructed to sell off the stock of [the company] as quickly as possible so that the [bank] could recover quickly some of the loss incurred from writing off the overdraft of [the company].'

As I read that defence, it contains an allegation that the assets of the company were sold at a gross undervalue and that if reasonable care had been taken all the way through, they could have been realised at a much higher value, probably double, if not more — maybe up to £130,000. In which case, the company's debt would have been very much reduced. In consequence the guaranteed figure of £75,000 would have been reduced greatly. Such are the facts of the case.

We have had much discussion on the law. So far as mortgages are concerned the law is set out in *Cuckmere Brick Co Ltd v Mutual Finance Ltd* [1971] Ch 949. If a mortgagee enters into possession and realises a mortgaged property, it is his duty to use reasonable care to obtain the best possible price which the circumstances of the case permit. He owes this duty not only to himself, to clear off as much of the debt as he can, but also to the mortgagor so as to reduce the balance owing as much as possible, and also to the guarantor so that he is made liable for as little as possible on the guarantee. This duty is only a particular application of the general duty of care to your neighbour which was stated by Lord Atkin in *Donoghue v Stevenson* [1932] AC 562 and applied in many cases since: see *Dorset Yacht Co Ltd v Home Office* [1970] AC 1004 and *Anns v Merton London Borough Council* [1978] AC 728. The mortgagor and the guarantor are clearly in very close 'proximity' to those who conduct the sale. The duty of care is owing to them — if not to the general body of creditors of the mortgagor. There are several dicta to the effect that the mortgagee can choose his own time for the sale, but I do not think this means that he can sell at the worst possible time. It is at least arguable that, in choosing the time, he must exercise a reasonable degree of care.

So far as the receiver is concerned, the law is well stated by Rigby LJ in *Gaskell v Gosling* [1896] 1 QB 669, a dissenting judgment which was approved by the House of Lords [1897] AC 575. The receiver is the agent of the company, not of the debenture holder, the bank. He owes a duty to use reasonable care to obtain the best possible price which the circumstances of the case permit. He owes this duty not only to the company, of which he is the agent, to clear off as much of its indebtedness to the bank as possible, but he also owes a duty to the guarantor, because the guarantor is liable only to the same extent as the company. The more the overdraft is reduced, the better for the guarantor. It may be that the receiver can choose the time of sale within a considerable margin, but he should, I think, exercise a reasonable degree of care about it. The debenture holder, the bank, is not responsible for what the receiver does except in so far as it gives him directions or interferes with his conduct of the realisation. If it does so, then it too is under a duty to use reasonable care towards the company and the guarantor.

If it should appear that the mortgagee or the receiver have not used reasonable care to realise the assets to the best advantage, then the mortgagor, the company, and the guarantor are entitled in equity to an allowance. They should be given credit for the amount which the sale should have realised if reasonable care had been used. Their indebtedness is to be reduced accordingly.

The only doubt on those propositions is cast by two cases at first instance. The first is *Barclays Bank Ltd v Thienel* (1978) 122 SJ 472. It has not been fully reported, but we have been provided with a transcript of the judgment. That was a case of a mortgagee. The amount realised was only £6,500 to meet a debt of £11,000. The allegation on the part of the guarantor was that the sale was at a gross undervalue, and that there had been a want of care in the realisation. Thesiger J said that the guarantor could not rely on that want of care because of a very wide clause in the form of guarantee. But it seems to me that, if a clause in a guarantee makes the guarantor liable for a larger sum than the mortgagor, that clause is unenforceable. The guarantor is only under a secondary obligation to guarantee the debt of the principal debtor. If the principal debtor's debt is reduced for good reason, equally the guarantor's obligation is reduced. If there is a term in the contract to the contrary, it should be rejected as being repugnant or unreasonable: see *Gillespie Bros & Co Ltd v Roy Bowles Transport Ltd* [1973] QB 400 and the cases cited therein, at pp 415 and 416. But nowadays we do not have to look at those cases. The Unfair Contract Terms Act 1977 applies to this contract. The terms of a contract are only good in so far as they are fair and reasonable. So I would reject Thesiger J's reliance on the contract.

The second case is *Latchford v Beirne* [1981] 3 All ER 705. That was a case of a receiver. A debenture holder had put in a receiver. The receiver sold the property. Again the guarantor sought to say that there had been want of reasonable care in the disposal of the assets. Milmo J went so far as to say that there was no duty of care towards the guarantor. He said that there was no duty of care towards the creditor. He treated the guarantor as though he was simply a creditor. I cannot agree with that either. Clearly the guarantor's liability is dependent upon the company's. He is in a very special position. The amount of his liability depends entirely on the amount that the stock realises when sold with proper care. To my mind he is well within the test of 'proximity.' The receiver owes a duty not only to the company, but also to the guarantor, to exercise reasonable care in the disposal of the assets. I say nothing about creditors. We are not concerned with them today.

Neither counsel before us sought to support the decisions in those two cases. In so far as those decisions hold that the guarantor is liable for a larger amount than the principal debtor they are erroneous and should not be followed. I am afraid that those cases may have misled the bank in this case. That may be the reason why those who first advised the bank thought that they need only rely on their own formal affidavit, and that they did not have to worry about all the affidavits put in on behalf of Mr and Mrs Walker.

Putting those two cases on one side, it seems to me that on the facts of this case there are these triable issues. There is a triable issue as to whether or not the bank did interfere with the sale in such a way as to take away some of the receiver's discretion, not only by directing him to sell as quickly as possible, but also in regard to publicity and so forth. On reading the affidavit of Mr Walker it seems to me that, until there has been discovery, there is an arguable case for saying that the bank did interfere not only in the timing of the sale, but also in other respects. So the matter should be investigated to determine the liability of the bank. I will not go into whether or not the receiver would be liable for any negligence of the auctioneer; but there is certainly a triable issue as to whether or not the sale was conducted with the proper degree of care which is owed to all those interested in the proceeds of it. It is clear that it was a disastrous sale which realised far less than any of the experts had anticipated. There is a triable issue as to whether that was due to any fault in the arrangements for the sale.

Those are triable issues of fact which ought to go for trial. There should be unconditional leave to defend. That being given, it is for the advisers of Mr and Mrs Walker to consider whether they should put in a counterclaim and bring in other parties to their counterclaim — the receiver and the auctioneers. They should consider whether they should make an application to put in a counter-claim. It is undesirable that there should be a subsequent action brought by Mr and Mrs Walker against the receiver or the auctioneers separately. All should be dealt with in one action.

All I would say at the moment is that, in my opinion, the appeal should be allowed with unconditional leave to defend, and the defendants should take such steps on the pleadings and interlocutory matters as they are advised.

SOURCE 297
Downsview Nominees *v* First City Corporation
[1993] AC 295

The judgment of their Lordships was delivered by LORD TEMPLEMAN.

This appeal requires consideration of the duties, if any, which a first debenture holder and a receiver and manager appointed by a first debenture holder owe to a second debenture holder.

The mortgagor company, Glen Eden Motors Ltd, (formerly Glen Eden Fiat Centre (1975) Ltd and hereafter called 'GEM') carried on business as new and used motor vehicle dealers and held Fiat and Mazda franchises for the sale of their vehicles and spare parts. The principal shareholder and manager of the company was Mr Pedersen.

On 11 August 1975 GEM issued a first debenture ('the Westpac debenture') which eventually secured the principal sum of $230,000 in priority to a second debenture ('the FCC debenture'). That second debenture dated 18 September 1986 was made in favour of the first plaintiff, First City Corporation Ltd. Each debenture created a fixed charge over certain assets of the company and a floating charge over the remainder. Each debenture contained power for the debenture holder to appoint a receiver and manager, who was to be deemed to be the agent of the company and was authorised to perform any acts which the company could perform. For the six months' period to 30 September 1986 GEM traded at a loss. On 10 March 1987, the moneys secured by the second debenture having become due and payable, the first plaintiff appointed two chartered accountants, Messrs Chilcott and Chatfield, experienced in receiverships to be receivers and managers of GEM. The first plaintiff's receivers formed the provisional view that a sale of the assets of GEM would be necessary. They removed Mr Pedersen from his position as manager of GEM. Mr Pedersen consulted the second defendant, Mr Russell, who controlled the first defendant company, Downsview Nominees Ltd. On 23 March 1987 the Westpac debenture was assigned to the first defendant and the second defendant was appointed receiver and manager under that debenture. The second defendant took over the assets and management of GEM from the receivers and managers appointed by the first plaintiff and restored Mr Pedersen to the management of GEM. On 25 March 1987 the second defendant announced that it was his intention to trade the company out of its financial difficulties subject to a review in three months' time. On 27 March 1987 the solicitors for the first plaintiff wrote to the directors of the first defendant. The letter contained the following:

> 'Our client informs us that you as first debenture holder have now appointed a receiver of Glen Eden Motors Ltd. As a consequence our client's receivers Messrs Chilcott and Chatfield have temporarily withdrawn to permit your receiver [the second defendant] to take control of the company until such time as your debenture can be repaid in full. Our client informs us that it is your receiver's intention to attempt to trade the company out of its present difficulties. Our client considers that any such attempt is extremely unlikely to improve the situation and indeed is highly likely to result in damage to the shareholders of the company and to itself as subsequent debenture holder. To prevent any dispute developing our clients have instructed us to write to you and make the following offer on their behalf: our client will purchase your debenture at a price equivalent to all amounts outstanding and secured under your debenture at the date of settlement; or alternatively our client will sell to you its debenture for a price equivalent to all amounts secured and outstanding under its debenture at the date of settlement.'

The letter added that $721,621.69 was then outstanding under the FCC debenture.

. . .

On 30 September 1988 the first plaintiff assigned to the second plaintiff First City Finance Ltd the FCC debenture together with all its rights, titles and interests in the moneys payable thereunder and all rights, powers and remedies thereunder.

These proceedings were continued by the first plaintiff and by the second plaintiff.

. . .

Gault J made the following findings, at pp 749–753:

> '[The second defendant] said he took the view his responsibility was to the company to do the best possible job he could and that this would have been ultimately to the benefit of everyone, including [the first plaintiff]. I do not accept that that was his approach at the time. He resolved to acquire the debenture, appoint himself receiver and permit the company to trade on

under the same management, without taking the time to fully investigate the financial affairs of the company, the competence of its management or the basis upon which [the first plaintiff] was seeking to enforce its security. In my judgment his true motive was to involve himself in the affairs of [GEM] for the benefit of himself and his company while undertaking to assist Mr Pedersen and to "save" [GEM].

　　. . .

　　In pursuit of his own objectives [the second defendant] embarked upon a course having as its first objective disruption of the receivership under the [FCC] debenture. His intention in urgently acquiring the Westpac debenture and accepting appointment as receiver was not for the purpose of enforcing the security under the Westpac debenture but for the purpose of preventing the enforcement by the plaintiffs of the [FCC] debenture. Further . . . in conducting the correspondence with the solicitors for [the first plaintiff] in the months immediately following his appointment as receiver, he had no genuine intention of either agreeing to assign the Westpac debenture to [the first plaintiff], or of acquiring the [FCC] debenture. . . . In the circumstances I consider that [the second defendant] and [the first defendant] employed the powers under the Westpac debenture for their own purposes and not for their proper purposes. To use these powers as they did constituted a clear breach of each of their respective duties to the subsequent debenture holder. . . . I have no difficulty in reaching the conclusion that, taking office for the purposes he did and conducting his receivership in the manner I have outlined, constituted breach by [the second defendant] of his duty to the holder of the [FCC] debenture. While I consider his conduct fell below the required standard, even in the initial period, I find that after July 1987 his conduct can be described only as reckless. . . . The plaintiffs' claim for failure by [the first defendant] to assign the Westpac debenture had two separate bases. The first was on the refusal by [the first defendant] to accept [the first plaintiff's] offer to purchase the Westpac debenture when first made four days after [the first defendant] acquired the debenture. It follows from the finding I have made already, that had [the first defendant] acquired the debenture and exercised the powers under it for their proper purposes, the offer made on behalf of [the first plaintiff] would have been responded to . . . The response by [the second defendant] (for [the first defendant] and I believe for himself) simply underscores the finding I have already made, that both defendants employed the powers under the Westpac debenture in breach of the duty they had to the subsequent debenture holder.'

The judge, at pp 758–759, held that the plaintiffs were entitled to damages on the basis of the

'difference between the loss that would have been incurred had the first receivership of Chilcott & Chatfield been allowed to proceed unimpeded, and the loss actually incurred as it has emerged following the second receivership by those two accountants.'

In the result judgment was entered in favour of the plaintiffs against the first and second defendants for $554,566.33.

　　. . .

　　The Court of Appeal (Cooke P, Richardson and Casey JJ) in the judgment of the court delivered by Richardson J on 12 March 1990 accepted [1990] 3 NZLR 265, 273:

'that on the application of negligence principles a receiver and manager who elects to carry on the business of the company and to trade it out of receivership owes a duty of care to subsequent debenture holders to take reasonable care in dealing with the assets of the company.'

The Court of Appeal held that the second defendant was in breach of the duty of care to the first plaintiff and that the first defendant was not in breach.

. . .

The second defendant appealed against the decision of the Court of Appeal against him; the plaintiffs cross-appealed against the first and second defendants for the re-instatement of the orders made by Gault J.

When the appeal and cross-appeal came before the Board, it was apparent that the judgments of the courts below raised fundamental questions concerning the nature and extent of any liability by a mortgagee and by a receiver and manager to the mortgagor company or to a subsequent debenture holder for his actions. The statement of claim pleaded that the first and second defendants were in breach of a duty to exercise their powers for proper purposes, in breach of a duty to act honestly and in good faith and in breach of a duty to exercise reasonable care, skill and diligence. Gault J held [1989] 3 NZLR 710, 742, 744:

'the proposition that a receiver will not be liable in negligence so long as he acts honestly and in good faith no longer represents the law of New Zealand. . . .The authorities clearly indicate that on an application of negligence principles, a receiver owes a duty to the debenture holders to take reasonable care in dealing with the assets of the company.'

In the Court of Appeal [1990] 3 NZLR 265, 272, it was accepted by the court without any argument to the contrary by counsel that Gault J was correct in his conclusion

'that, if there were any duties on the part of [the first defendant] and [the second defendant] as receiver to a subsequent debenture they would have to be based in negligence.'

The defendants' case and the plaintiffs' case as presented to the Board did not challenge these conclusions. The Board however were considerably troubled by the approach of the courts below and on terms gave leave to the plaintiffs to raise the whole question of the foundation and extent of the duties owed by a first debenture holder and his receiver and manager to a subsequent debenture holder. An adjournment was granted so that both sides could reconsider the whole question and submit supplemental cases and arguments.

The first submission made on behalf of the first and second defendants is that they owed no duty to the first plaintiff because the first plaintiff was only a debenture holder and not a mortgagee. This submission is untenable.

A mortgage, whether legal or equitable, is security for repayment of a debt. The security may be constituted by a conveyance, assignment or demise or by a charge on any interest in real or personal property. An equitable mortgage is a contract which creates a charge on property but does not pass a legal estate to the creditor. Its operation is that of an executory assurance, which, as between the parties, and so far as equitable rights and remedies are concerned, is equivalent to an actual assurance, and is enforceable under the equitable jurisdiction of the court. All this is well settled law and is to be found in more detail in the textbooks on the subject and also in *Halsbury's Laws of England*, 4th edn, vol 32 (1980), p 187 paras 401 et seq. The security for a debt incurred by a company may take the form of a fixed charge on property or the form of a floating charge which becomes a fixed charge on the assets comprised in the security when the debt becomes due and payable. A security issued by a company is called a debenture but for present purposes there is no material difference between a mortgage, a charge and a debenture. Each creates a security for the repayment of a debt.

The second argument put forward on behalf of the first and second defendants is that though a mortgage owes certain duties to the mortgagor, he owes no duty to any subsequent encumbrancer; so the first and second defendants owed no duty to the first plaintiff. This argument also is untenable. The owner of property entering into a mortgage does not by entering into that mortgage cease to be the owner of that property any further than is necessary to give effect to the security he has created. The mortgagor can mortgage the property again and again. A second or subsequent mortgage is a complete security on the mortgagor's interests subject only to the rights of prior encumbrancers. If a first mortgagee commits a breach of his duties to the mortgagor, the damage inflicted by that breach of duty will be suffered by the second mortgagee, subsequent encumbrancers and the mortgagor, depending on the extent of the damage and the amount of each security. Thus if a first mortgagee in breach of duty sells property worth £500,000 for £300,000, he is liable at the suit of any subsequent encumbrancer or the mortgagor. Damages of £200,000 will be ordered to be taken into the accounts of the first mortgagee or paid into court or to the second mortgagee who, after satisfying, as far as he can, the amount of any debt outstanding under his mortgage will pay over any balance remaining to the next encumbrancer or to the mortgagor if there is no subsequent encumbrancer. In practice the encumbrancer who first suffers from the breach of duty by the first mortgagee and needs the damages payable by the first mortgagee to obtain repayment of his own debt will sue the first mortgagee. If the encumbrancers do not suffer because they have been able to obtain repayment of their debts without recourse to the damages, then it will be the mortgagor who will sue. In *Tomlin v Luce* (1889) 43 Ch D 191 the Court of Appeal held that the first mortgagees were answerable to the second mortgagees for the loss caused by a misstatement made by the auctioneer appointed by the first mortgagees to sell the property comprised in their security. The court directed that there should be an inquiry as to damages and that the first mortgagees should be allowed in their accounts the amount of their debt less the actual proceeds of sale from the property and the amount of the damages.

The next submission on behalf of the first and second defendants is that, even if a mortgagee owes certain duties to subsequent encumbrancers, a receiver and manager appointed by a mortgagee is not under any such duty where, as in the present case, the receiver and manager is deemed to act as agent for the mortgagor. The fallacy in the argument is the failure to appreciate that, when a receiver and manager exercises the powers of sale and management conferred on him by the mortgage, he is dealing with the security; he is not merely selling or dealing with the interests of the mortgagor. He is exercising the power of selling and dealing with the mortgaged property for the purpose of securing repayment of the debt owing to his mortgagee and must exercise his powers in good faith and for the purpose of obtaining repayment of the debt owing to his mortgagee. The receiver and manager owes these duties to the mortgagor and to all subsequent encumbrancers in whose favour the mortgaged property has been charged.

The next question is the nature and extent of the duties owed by a mortgagee and a receiver and manager respectively to subsequent encumbrancers and the mortgagor.

Several centuries ago equity evolved principles for the enforcement of mortgages and the protection of borrowers. The most basic principles were, first, that a mortgage is security for the repayment of a debt and, secondly, that a security for repayment of a debt is only a mortgage. From these principles flowed two rules, first, that powers conferred on a mortgagee must be exercised in good faith for the purpose of obtaining repayment and secondly that, subject to the first rule, powers conferred on a mortgagee may be exercised although the consequences may be disadvantageous to the borrower. These principles and rules apply also to a receiver and manager appointed by the mortgagee.

It does not follow that a receiver and manager must immediately upon appointment seize all the cash in the coffers of the company and sell all the company's assets or so much of the assets as he chooses and considers sufficient to complete the redemption of the mortgage. He is entitled, but not bound, to allow the company's business to be continued by himself or by the existing or other executives. The decisions of the receiver and manager whether to continue the business or close down the business and sell assets chosen by him cannot be impeached if those decisions are taken in good faith while protecting the interests of the debenture holder in recovering the moneys due under the debenture, even though the decisions of the receiver and manager may be disadvantageous for the company.

The nature of the duties owed by a receiver and manager appointed by a debenture holder were authoritatively defined by Jenkins LJ in a characteristically learned and comprehensive judgment in *In re B. Johnson & Co (Builders) Ltd* [1955] Ch 634, 661–663. Jenkins LJ said:

> 'the phrase "manager of the company," prima facie, according to the ordinary meaning of the words, connotes a person holding, whether de jure or de facto, a post in or with the company of a nature charging him with the duty of managing the affairs of the company for the company's benefit; whereas a receiver and manager for debenture holders is a person appointed by the debenture holders to whom the company has given powers of management pursuant to the contract of loan constituted by the debenture, and, as a condition of obtaining the loan, to enable him to preserve and realise the assets comprised in the security for the benefit of the debenture holders. The company gets the loan on terms that the lenders shall be entitled, for the purpose of making their security effective, to appoint a receiver with powers of sale and of management pending sale, and with full discretion as to the exercise and mode of exercising those powers. The primary duty of the receiver is to the debenture holders and not to the company. He is receiver and manager of the property of the company for the debenture holders, not manager of the company. The company is entitled to any surplus of assets remaining after the debenture debt has been discharged, and is entitled to proper accounts. But the whole purpose of the receiver and manager's appointment would obviously be stultified if the company could claim that a receiver and manager owes it any duty comparable to the duty owed to a company by its own directors or managers.
>
> In determining whether a receiver and manager for the debenture holders of a company has broken any duty owed by him to the company, regard must be had to the fact that he is a receiver and manager — that is to say, a receiver, with ancillary powers of management — for the debenture holders, and not simply a person appointed to manage the company's affairs for the benefit of the company. . . . The duties of a receiver and manager for debenture holders are widely different from those of a manager of the

company. He is under no obligation to carry on the company's business at the expense of the debenture holders. Therefore he commits no breach of duty to the company by refusing to do so, even though his discontinuance of the business may be detrimental from the company's point of view. Again, his power of sale is, in effect, that of a mortgagee, and he therefore commits no breach of duty to the company by a bona fide sale, even though he might have obtained a higher price and even though, from the point of view of the company, as distinct from the debenture holders, the terms might be regarded as disadvantageous.

In a word, in the absence of fraud or mala fides . . . the company cannot complain of any act or omission of the receiver and manager, provided that he does nothing that he is not empowered to do, and omits nothing that he is enjoined to do by the terms of his appointment. If the company conceives that it has any claim against the receiver and manager for breach of some duty owed by him to the company, the issue is not whether the receiver and manager has done or omitted to do anything which it would be wrongful in a manager of a company to do or omit, but whether he has exceeded or abused or wrongfully omitted to use the special powers and discretions vested in him pursuant to the contract of loan constituted by the debenture for the special purpose of enabling the assets comprised in the debenture holders' security to be preserved and realised.'

The duties owed by a receiver and manager do not compel him to adopt any particular course of action, by selling the whole or part of the mortgaged property or by carrying on the business of the company or by exercising any other powers and discretions vested in him. But since a mortgage is only security for a debt, a receiver and manager commits a breach of his duty if he abuses his powers by exercising them otherwise than 'for the special purpose of enabling the assets comprised in the debenture holders' security to be preserved and realised' for the benefit of the debenture holder. In the present case the evidence of the second defendant himself and the clear emphatic findings of Gault J [1989] 3 NZLR 710, 749, which have already been cited, show that the second defendant accepted appointment and acted as receiver and manager.

> 'not for the purpose of enforcing the security under the Westpac debenture but for the purpose of preventing the enforcement by the plaintiffs of the [FCC] debenture.'

This and other findings to similar effect establish that, ab initio and throughout his receivership, the second defendant did not exercise his powers for proper purposes. He was at all times in breach of the duty, which was pleaded against him, to exercise his powers in good faith for proper purposes.

Gault J rested his judgment not on breach of a duty to act in good faith for proper purposes but on negligence. He said, at pp 744, 747:

> 'on an application of negligence principles, a receiver owes a duty to the debenture holders to take reasonable care in dealing with the assets of the company. . . [The first defendant's] position is merely a specific example of the duty a mortgagee has to subsequent chargeholders to exercise its powers with reasonable care . . .'

Richardson J, delivering the judgment of the Court of Appeal [1990] 3 NZLR 265, 278–280, agreed that duties of care in negligence as defined by Gault J were owed by the second defendant as receiver and manager and by the first defendant as first debenture holder to the second defendant as second debenture holder. Richardson J agreed that the second defendant was in breach of his duty but, differing from Gault J, held that the first defendant had committed no breach.

The general duty of care said to be owed by a mortgagee to subsequent encumbrancers and the mortgagor in negligence is inconsistent with the right of the mortgagee and the duties which the courts applying equitable principles have imposed on the mortgagee. If a mortgagee enters into possession he is liable to account for rent on the basis of wilful default; he must keep mortgage premises in repair; he is liable for waste. Those duties were imposed to ensure that a mortgagee is diligent in discharging his mortgage and returning the property to the mortgagor. If a mortgagee exercises his power of sale in good faith for the purpose of protecting his security, he is not liable to the mortgagor even though he might have obtained a higher price and even though the terms might be regarded as disadvantageous to the mortgagor. *Cuckmere Brick Co Ltd v Mutual Finance Ltd* [1971] Ch 949 is Court of Appeal authority for the proposition that, if the mortgagee decides to sell, he must take reasonable care to obtain a proper price but is no authority for any wider proposition. A receiver exercising his power of sale also owes the same specific duties as the mortgagee. But that apart, the general duty of a receiver and manager appointed by a debenture holder, as defined by Jenkins LJ in *In re B. Johnson & Co (Builders) Ltd* [1955] Ch 634, 661, leaves no room for the imposition of a general duty to use reasonable care in dealing with the assets of the company. The duties imposed by equity on a mortgagee and on a receiver and manager would be quite unnecessary if there existed a general duty in negligence to take reasonable care in the exercise of powers and to take reasonable care in dealing with the assets of the mortgagor company.

Richardson J appreciated the contradictions and inconsistencies between the duties of a receiver and manager as set forth by Jenkins LJ in *In re B. Johnson & Co (Builders) Ltd* based on historical equitable principles and the suggested additional or alternative duty of care based on negligence. Richardson J said [1990] 3 NZLR 265, 276:

> 'The existence, nature and extent of the receiver's duty of care must be measured in relation to the primary objective of the receivership which is to enforce the security by recouping the moneys which it secures from the income or assets of the company subject to the security, and for that purpose by exercising incidental powers of management, and when recoupment is complete to hand the remaining property back to the control of the company.'

Their Lordships consider that it is not possible to measure a duty of care in relation to a primary objective which is quite inconsistent with that duty of care.

There is a great difference between managing a company for the benefit of a debenture holder and managing a company for the benefit of shareholders. If the debenture holder is dissatisfied with the policy or performance of his appointed receiver and manager, the appointment can be revoked. A dissatisfied second debenture holder may require the prior debenture to be assigned to him or may put the company into liquidation. A dissatisfied company may raise the money to pay off a debenture holder or put the company into liquidation. But if a receiver and manager decides at his discretion to manage and is allowed to manage and does manage in good faith with the object of preserving and realising the assets for the benefit of the debenture holder, he is subject to no further or greater liability.

...

The House of Lords has warned against the danger of extending the ambit of negligence so as to supplant or supplement other torts, contractual obligations, statutory duties or equitable rules in relation to every kind of damage including economic loss: see *CBS Songs Ltd v Amstrad Consumer Electronics Plc* [1988] AC 1013, 1059; *Caparo Industries Plc v Dickman* [1990] 2 AC 605 and *Murphy v Brentwood District Council* [1991] 1 AC 398. If the defined equitable duties attaching to mortgages and to receivers and managers appointed by debenture holders are replaced or supplemented by a liability in negligence the result will be confusion and injustice. A receiver and manager liable in negligence will be tempted to sell assets as speedily as possible for the purpose of repaying the mortgage debt, a decision which, whether negligent or not, does not expose him to a suit for damages but may be disadvantageous to the company. A receiver who is brave enough to manage will run the risk of being sued if the financial position of the company deteriorates, whether that deterioration be due to imperfect knowledge or bad advice or insufficient time or other circumstances. There will always be expert witnesses ready to testify with the benefit of hindsight that they would have acted differently and fared better.

A receiver and manager is appointed when the mortgagor company is in financial difficulties. He may know nothing of the trade carried on by the mortgagor company and nothing about the individual affairs of the company. He is dependent on information furnished by the directors and managers who must bear some responsibility for the financial difficulties of the company. Richardson J in the present case [1990] 3 NZLR 265, 284, in discussing the ambit of section 189 of the Companies Act 1955, said:

> 'There is a further justification for maintaining that clear distinction between the acts of the manager of the company and the acts of the receiver and manager of its property. The company has vicarious responsibility for the acts of the manager and in the exercise of those functions as manager the manager is not personally liable to other parties except for misfeasance. In contrast the receiver is personally liable on any contract entered into by him in the performance of his functions, except in so far as the contract otherwise provides (section 345(2)). In policy terms it may be considered entirely appropriate to confine the external sanction under section 189(1)(*c*) to officers of the company, leaving errant receivers and managers to their personal liability in respect of contracts, and recognising too that in the ordinary course poorly performing receivers are not likely to be given further assignments by debenture holders of other companies.'

Similar considerations apply to the first defendant. A mortgagee owes a general duty to subsequent encumbrancers and to the mortgagor to use his powers for the sole purpose of securing repayments of the moneys owing under his mortgage and a duty to act in good faith. He also owes the specific duties which equity has imposed on him in the exercise of his powers to go into possession and his powers of sale. It may well be that a mortgagee who appoints a receiver and manager, knowing that the receiver and manager intends to exercise his powers for the purpose of frustrating the activities of the second mortgagee or for some other improper purpose or who fails to revoke the appointment of a receiver and manager when the mortgagee knows that the receiver and manager is abusing his powers, may himself by guilty of bad faith but in the present case this possibility need not be explored.

The liability of the second defendant in the present case is firmly based not on negligence but on the breach of duty. There was overwhelming evidence that the receivership of the second defendant was inspired by him for improper purposes and carried on in bad faith, ultimately verging on fraud. The liability of the first defendant does not arise under negligence but as a result of the first defendant's breach of duty in failing to transfer the Westpac debenture to the first plaintiff at the end of March 1987. It is well settled that the mortgagor and all persons having any interest in the property subject to the mortgage or liable to pay the mortgage debt can redeem. It is now conceded that the first plaintiff was entitled to require the first defendant to assign the Westpac debenture to the first plaintiff on payment of all moneys due to the first defendant under the Westpac debenture. On 27 March 1987 the first plaintiff offered to purchase the Westpac debenture and to pay the first defendant all that was owing to it. It was faintly argued that the first defendant was entitled to refuse the offer because at a later stage it reasonably believed, so it was said, albeit wrongly, that the FCC debenture was void for non-registration. There is nothing in this point. The reason given by the second defendant on behalf of the first defendant for the refusal of the first defendant to assign the Westpac debenture to the first plaintiff as a subsequent charge holder was that 'we do not know of any right of assignment which subsequent charge holders have in respect of an earlier charge.' The second defendant is now older and the first defendant is now wiser.

. . .

In the result their Lordships are of the opinion that the appeal ought to be dismissed and the cross-appeal allowed and that the orders made by Gault J against the first and second defendants should be restored, . . .

Administration

Administration is a statutory rescue regime set out in Part II of the Insolvency Act 1986. It was enacted on the recommendation of the Cork Committee's proposals (Source 298) and after consideration by the Department of Trade and Industry (Source 299). The court has the power to make the order for administration for any of the purposes set out in s 8. The court first seemed wary of exercising this power (Source 300), but has since adopted a more sympathetic approach (Source 301). A debentureholder who has the power to appoint an administrative receiver may block a petition for administration (ss 9, 10) and may wish to have a floating charge for this purpose (Source 302). One problem with administration seems to be the expense, but the courts have attempted to reduce this (Source 303).

The administration order acts to prevent any enforcement proceedings against the company (ss 10, 11, Sources 304, 305). The administrator has wide powers (ss 14, 15, Sch 1) and must prepare proposals for the company's future. These proposals must be voted on by the creditors (ss 23, 24). Under s 27, any shareholder or creditor who believes he or she has been unfairly prejudiced by the administrator's actions, can apply to the court for relief.

SOURCE 298
Report of the Review Committee on Insolvency Law and Practice ('Cork Committee')

The Administrator
495. Elsewhere in this Report we have made a number of criticisms of the present law relating to floating charges, and we shall put forward various proposals for reform. There is, however, one aspect of the floating charge which we believe to

have been of outstanding benefit to the general public and to society as a whole; we refer to the power to appoint a receiver and manager of the whole property and undertaking of a company. This power is enjoyed by the holder of any well-drawn floating charge, but by no other creditor. Such receivers and managers are normally given extensive powers to manage and carry on the business of the company. In some cases, they have been able to restore an ailing enterprise to profitability, and return it to its former owners. In others, they have been able to dispose of the whole or part of the business as a going concern. In either case, the preservation of the profitable parts of the enterprise has been of advantage to the employees, the commercial community, and the general public.

496. None of these steps is possible in the absence of a floating charge. Where there is no such charge, the choice lies between an informal moratorium or a formal scheme of arrangement under the Act of 1948. Neither is wholly satisfactory. The latter is expensive and time consuming; the former is informal, is not binding on those creditors who do not assent, and can lead to problems in practice. Where neither course is practical, the directors of a company which is or appears to be insolvent have no option but to cease trading. We are satisfied that in a significant number of cases, companies have been forced into liquidation, and potentially viable businesses capable of being rescued have been closed down, for want of a floating charge under which a receiver and manager could have been appointed.

497. Accordingly, we propose that in all cases, and whether or not there is a floating charge in existence, provision should be made to enable a person (whom we shall call an Administrator) to be appointed whenever the circumstances justify such a course, with all the powers normally conferred upon a receiver and manager appointed under a floating charge, including power to carry on the business of the company and to borrow for that purpose.

498. Under our proposals, an Administrator may be appointed for all or any of the following reasons:

(a) to consider the reorganisation of the company and its management with a view to restoring profitability or maintaining employment;
(b) to ascertain whether a company of doubtful solvency can be restored to profitability;
(c) to make proposals for the most profitable realisation of assets for the benefit of creditors and shareholders;
(d) to carry on the business where this is in the public interest but it is unlikely that the business can be continued under the existing management.

499. The proposals which we put forward in the following paragraphs have been designed primarily with the corporate debtor in mind. We do not, however, intend that they should be so limited. We consider that the appointment of an Administrator may well be advantageous where a substantial business is carried on by a sole trader or in partnership. For simplicity, however, we shall refer to the debtor as 'the company'.

500. We propose that the power to appoint an Administrator should be vested in the Court, and should be exercisable only by an order of the Court made upon the application of an interested party. We consider that the application should be capable of being made by any creditor, by the company itself (pursuant to ordinary resolution of the members or by its Board, though not at the direct instance of individual directors), or by the Secretary of State for Trade. By a 'creditor' we mean a creditor, whether secured or unsecured, who is qualified to make an Insolvency Application . . . A creditor who is not so qualified or, in a suitable case, an individual director or shareholder, who can satisfy the Court that the assets are in jeopardy, should have the right to apply to the Court for leave to make an application for the appointment of an Administrator.

501. The right of the directors to apply for the appointment of an Administrator is of fundamental importance. Later in this Report we make proposals to augment the present provisions relating to fraudulent trading by a new concept of 'wrongful trading'. This will expose the directors to an increased risk of incurring personal liability if they allow their company to continue to trade while insolvent. One of the courses open to them, as we indicate below, will be to apply for the appointment of an Administrator; and it is important that their right to do so should be unfettered. Indeed, we have recommended elsewhere that the legislation should expressly provide that, if the directors at any time consider the company to be insolvent, they should have a duty to take immediate steps for the company to be placed in liquidation, receivership or administration.

. . .

503. It is expected that the new procedure will be used primarily in cases where the company has not granted a debenture secured by a floating charge, although it is not intended to be limited to such cases. Where a floating charge exists, however, notice of the application must also be served upon the debenture-holder.

504. Before making an appointment the Court must be satisfied that any holder of a floating charge on all or substantially all the assets of the company has had prior notice of the application and the opportunity to appoint a receiver and manager. It will be necessary to provide in the statute that any such floating charge shall be deemed to contain a power to appoint a receiver and manager in the event of application being made for the appointment of an Administrator. If the debenture-holder has already appointed a receiver and manager, or if he does so on receipt of notice of the application, no order for the appointment of an Administrator will normally be made; and further, the Court should not normally make an order for the appointment of an Administrator if a debenture-holder gives an undertaking forthwith to appoint a receiver and manager. Where a receiver has been appointed under a floating charge which does not extend to the whole of the assets necessary to enable the business to be carried on as a going concern, there may be a good case for the appointment of the receiver as Administrator. Once an Administrator is appointed, however, then until he is discharged by a further order of the Court, the power to appoint a receiver should cease to be exercisable by the debenture-holder.

SOURCE 299
A Revised Framework for Insolvency Law
The Administrator

29. One of the very significant benefits to which the floating charge has given rise has been the opportunity which the appointment of a receiver and manager under such a charge offers for the rescue and rehabilitation of the viable parts of

a company in difficulties. In several ways, however, receivership is not necessarily the complete remedy where a concern is confronted by serious financial problems but where there is a reasonable prospect of rehabilitation in whole or in part.

30. First, where there is no floating charge over the whole or substantially the whole of a company, no receiver and manager can be appointed and thus there may be no option but liquidation. Once a company is in liquidation, the prospect of maintaining any part of the business as a going concern is greatly reduced. Second, the position of a receiver and manager of a company is altered once that company is placed in liquidation, since he is no longer the agent of the company and his efforts to maintain the company, or parts of it, as a going concern are made correspondingly more difficult. Third, a receiver and manager's attempts to maintain a business in being may fail if fixed charge-holders, or others with title over assets which form part of the operating capacity of that business but which are not paid for, exercise their rights, and in so doing, make continued trading impossible. Finally, a receiver and manager appointed by a floating charge-holder acts principally in the interests of the charge-holder. Although decisions of the Courts have established that he also has obligations to others, there are circumstances when it would be desirable for the affairs of a company in difficulties to be conducted by an independently appointed insolvency practitioner.

31. In view of these considerations, the Government agrees with the Review Committee's recommendation that an alternative insolvency mechanism, to be known as the administrator procedure, should be established. The Government considers that this new procedure will facilitate the rehabilitation or re-organisation of a company in difficulties with a view to restoring it to profitability or will encourage the preservation of viable elements of a company as going concerns. The main elements of the administrator procedure are set out in the following paragraph.

32. The Court will be empowered to appoint an administrator to a company on the application of the company or a creditor of the company, where the company is insolvent or close to insolvency but where there is a reasonable prospect of rehabilitation or re-organisation of the company in whole or in part. No administrator will be appointed, however, where the holder of a floating charge wishes to exercise his right to appoint a receiver and manager. The task of the administrator will be in two stages. On appointment, he will assume the management of the company and undertake the preparation of a rescue or rehabilitation policy, or failing that, a policy for the most profitable realisation of assets in the interests of the company's creditors and shareholders. The administrator will then be required to submit his proposed policy to the company's unsecured creditors. If, in the light of his proposals, they vote in favour of his continued appointment, the administrator will so report to the Court, which will have the power to confirm his appointment subject to hearing views expressed by other interested parties. Once confirmed, the administrator's task will then be to carry out his policy. In the event of the administrator, or the unsecured creditors, deciding that his appointment is not the most appropriate insolvency procedure, he will so report to the Court which, depending on the circumstances, will make an order concerning the company's future status. During the currency of an administrator's appointment, no petition for winding up may be made without the leave of the Court. The appointment of the administrator will bring about a stay on all proceedings and actions and on creditors' rights to enforce security or

payment, or to levy execution, except where proceedings to levy distress commence prior to the appointment. In addition the rights of fixed charge-holders, owners of assets under a lease or hire purchase agreement or as a result of reservation of title clauses, will be suspended in order to give the administrator time to prepare and execute his plans. Provision will be made to protect the position of fixed charge-holders and others in the event that the administrator is not able to rehabilitate or reorganise a company and to restore it to profitability. The administrator will be under a duty to act at all times in the interests of the creditors and shareholders as a whole.

33. The Government considers that the introduction of the administrator procedure will provide a valuable addition to existing insolvency procedures. It will be of particular value in the case of a company in difficulties where no floating charge is in existence but where there is a good prospect of rehabilitating the business or of maintaining viable parts as going concerns. The administrator procedure may also provide a more effective method of achieving rehabilitation or re-organisation than receivership in appropriate cases in view of the protection the company will receive from legal actions and winding-up petitions, and from the temporary suspension of the rights of fixed charge-holders and others during the period of the administrator's appointment. Finally, the introduction of wrongful trading, explained in Chapter 2, will encourage directors to consider at an earlier stage the financial position and prospects of their companies. The availability of the administrator procedure will ensure that an alternative to receivership or liquidation will be available where there are reasonable grounds for supposing that rehabilitation or re-organisation of a company is achievable.

34. The Review Committee suggested that receivers, as well as administrators, should enjoy temporary protection from the exercise of the rights of fixed charge-holders and others and that continued trading by a receiver should be permitted after a company had been placed in liquidation, if sanctioned by the Court or the liquidator. These proposals are not acceptable. The Government believes that only a court-appointed official, the administrator, whose duty will be to act in the interests of all creditors and shareholders, should enjoy such temporary protection. In cases where post-liquidation trading might be appropriate in a receivership, a receiver of a company under threat of liquidation will be able to recommend to the holder of the floating charge that an application should be made to the Court for the appointment of an administrator.

SOURCE 300
Re Consumer & Industrial Press Ltd
[1988] BCLC 177

PETER GIBSON J: I have before me two petitions. The first in time was a winding-up petition presented on 16 June 1987 by a creditor who was an employee of the company. She was paid off, and on 22 July 1987 the Commissioners of Inland Revenue, for whom Mr Rayer James appears, were substituted as petitioners. They are creditors in the sum of £75,000 for PAYE tax and National Insurance contributions.

The second petition is one presented on 9 October 1987 by the company (for whom Mr Collings appears) which thereby seeks an administration order. The company is supported by two unsecured creditors with debts of £22,000 and £16,000 respectively. They appear by Mr Shuttleworth. There are two secured creditors of the company, one of whom is the company's bankers. Each has a debt of a little over £50,000. Neither secured creditor appears before me, nor has either of them appointed a receiver.

The debate before me has been confined to the question whether the court should make an administration order on the company's petition. If such an order is made, the winding-up petition must be dismissed (see s 11(1)(a) of the Insolvency Act 1986). If the court does not make that order it is not disputed that the winding-up order on the Revenue's petition must be made.

The power of the court to make an administration order is contained in s 8(1), ... Four purposes are specified in sub-s (3), three of which are claimed by the company in its petition to be relevant. They are '(a) the survival of the company, and the whole or any part of its undertaking, as a going concern', '(b) the approval of a voluntary arrangement under Part I', and, '(d) a more advantageous realisation of the company's assets than would be effected on a winding up'. Subsection (3) also provides that 'the order shall specify the purpose or purposes for which it is made'.

As I read s 8 the court must be satisfied on the evidence put before it that at least one of the purposes in s 8(3) is likely to be achieved if it is to make an administration order. That does not mean that it is merely possible that such purpose will be achieved; the evidence must go further than that to enable the court to hold that the purpose in question will more probably than not be achieved. Further, the court has to specify in the order the purpose which it is satisfied will be achieved. It is not a question of being satisfied that one purpose is likely to be achieved, and then adding in the order one or more of the other purposes which might perhaps be achieved, but in respect of which the evidence is less compelling.

If the conditions in s 8(1)(a) and (b) are satisfied the court then has a discretion whether to make an administration order. Counsel for the company argued that the court's discretion is limited by those conditions. In my judgment that is not correct. There are no words in s 8(1) limiting the considerations to which the court is to have regard. Once the conditions of (a) and (b) are satisfied the court has a complete discretion, and it must take account of all material circumstances. But of course, it will do so in order to further and not to frustrate the purposes of the 1986 Act.

I turn to the facts. The company publishes the magazine 'Pins and Needles', which, as its name implies, is concerned with knitting, needlework and dressmaking. The magazine has been published continuously since 1949. It has a considerable reputation in its field. In the calendar year 1986 the average monthly sales were nearly 33,000 copies. The title to the magazine is valuable and represents the company's largest asset. The company has, however, incurred substantial trading losses and it is heavily insolvent. The unaudited accounts of the company prepared by the directors show that at 30 April 1987 current liabilities amounted to £315,000, while current assets amounted to only £97,000. The balance sheet also shows that the company has other assets of £65,000, including a sum of £51,200 for what are called intangible assets, leaving a deficit as regards creditors of over £130,000. In a report prepared by independent accountants, Arthur Andersen & Co, which is put forward by the company, it is stated that the company's net liabilities are too large for it to trade out of its present difficulties. Accordingly, it is apparent that the condition in s 8(1)(a) is satisfied.

. . .

In the petition, and in the company's evidence in support of its petition, it is said that two of the purposes of the order would be to enable the company to survive and obtain the approval of the arrangement. I need not take up time with these matters, as counsel for the company accepts, as in my judgment he was bound to do, that the evidence falls a good deal short of that which would have been needed for the court to be able to find that those purposes or either of them are or is likely to be achieved. On the company's own evidence some £40,000 of external funding would have to be found, and there is nothing concrete in evidence, despite the lapse of time since the Revenue were substituted as petitioners, to suggest that that sum is likely to be found. Arthur Andersen & Co say no more than that they believe that there is a prospect that an appointment of joint administrators may lead to the approval of a voluntary arrangement. If the court is satisfied on para (*d*) of s 8(1) and makes an administration order, and if in the course of the administration it becomes apparent that further purposes within s 8(3) are likely to be achieved, an application under s 18(1) to amend the administration order can always be made.

The company now relies solely on para (*d*) of s 8(3). It says that the administrators would be likely to achieve a higher price than a liquidator because the administrators would be able to continue publishing the magazine, which it says can be published profitably. There is evidence to suggest that, by reason of a drastic cut-back in overheads that has been made, the publication of the magazine is now profitable. . . .

I think it likely that the administrators would want to publish the October edition and sell the business as a going concern, and that it is likely that there will be a more advantageous realisation of the company's assets thereby than in a winding up. Arthur Andersen & Co say that such a realisation would almost certainly be achieved. In my judgment therefore the statutory preconditions for the exercise of discretion are satisfied.

Ought I to exercise my discretion in favour of making an administration order? Counsel for the company supported by counsel for the unsecured creditors says that I should. Counsel for the Commissioners of Inland Revenue has argued to the contrary. He pointed out that the making of such an order would cause the winding-up petition to be dismissed, there being no power to stay that petition pending the administration; some debts at present likely to be preferential would cease to be preferential, whilst remaining unpaid. Further, he pointed to the fact that as the company accepts, the company has not only traded whilst insolvent, but also has continued to trade after the winding up petition was presented. It is said by a director that no one at the company became aware of the possible consequences of doing so. Counsel for the commissioners submitted that these were matters which a liquidator should investigate, but which an administrator could not. Counsel for the company submitted that none of this was relevant to the exercise of my discretion. I do not agree. It would seem to me to be absurd if the consequences of making the administration order instead of a winding up order were not taken into account when a court considers whether to exercise its discretion. Counsel for the Commissioners of Inland Revenue further submitted that the only true beneficiaries of the making of an administration order are likely to be the secured creditors, to which the proceeds of a more advantageous sale after a deduction of administration costs, are likely to go. He pointed out that the secured creditors had their own remedy and could put in a receiver to sell the assets, but had chosen not to do so. He submitted that the court should ignore them and allow the view of the majority creditor, in this case the Revenue, to prevail over the views of the opposing unsecured creditors.

I very much feel the force of submissions of counsel for the Commissioners of Inland Revenue, but I am not persuaded that I should accede to them. As matters now stand, on a sale by the liquidator there will almost certainly be nothing available to any creditor other than the secured creditor. If an administration order is made the administrators are likely to continue the business by publishing the October issue, and to achieve a much better price for the sale of the business or title, and probably achieve a useful profit on the October issue as well. I do not think I should ignore the benefit that would accrue to secured creditors when considering whether or make an administration order, although I accept that their interests weigh lighter in the scales than the interests of the other creditors. But the administration order, in addition to benefiting the secured creditors, will give at least the possibility of achieving some benefit for the preferential creditors and other unsecured creditors than would a liquidation. An administration order is intended to be of short duration, and if, as I would expect, the business or title is sold whilst the magazine continues to be published, and there remains a substantial deficiency as regards creditors, the company can then be put into liquidation, and any fraudulent or wrongful trading investigated by an independent liquidator. . . .

[Administration petition granted.]

SOURCE 301
Re Harris Simons Construction Ltd
[1989] BCLC 202

HOFFMANN J: On Monday afternoon I made an administration order under s 8 of the Insolvency Act 1986 in relation to Harris Simons Builders Ltd (the company). I gave no formal judgment at the time, but as the application appeared to raise a point of general interest on the construction of 1986 Act, I now give my reasons.

The company carries on business as builders. Over the past four years there has been a spectacular increase in turnover, from £830,000 in the year to April 1985, to £17m in the year to April 1987, and £27m in the year to April 1988. Almost all of this increased turnover has come from one client, a property developer called Berkley House plc, with which the directors had a close relationship. Recently the relationship has turned sour. There are disputes over a number of contracts and Berkley House has purported to dismiss the company and require its employees to leave their sites. It is also withholding sums running into several million pounds which the company says are due and in respect of which Berkley House says it has cross-claims. The effect on the company's cash flow has been that it is unable to pay its debts as they fall due and several writs and a statutory demand have been served. If no administration order is made, the company cannot carry on trading. There is no debenture holder who can be invited to appoint a receiver. The company will have to go into liquidation more or less immediately. The workforce will have to be dismissed and the contracts and work in progress will become a tangle of disputes and probably litigation. The report of the proposed administrator says that in those circumstances it would be extremely difficult to sell any part of the business.

If an administration order is made, the company will have what is usually called a breathing space but unless some source of funding can be found, will continue to have serious respiratory problems with its cash flow. It has however been able to negotiate at least an armistice with Berkley House by which the latter will, conditionally on an administration order being made, provide sufficient funding to enable the company to complete four current contracts on condition that it quietly removes itself from the other sites in dispute. It is hoped that the four remaining contracts will produce a profit and that it may thereby be possible to stabilise and preserve a business which can either survive or be sold to a third party. In the meanwhile, it may be possible to arrive at a negotiated settlement of the underlying dispute with Berkley House. The administration order is therefore proposed to achieve two of the purposes specified in s 8 of the 1986 Act, '(3)(*a*) the survival of the company, and the whole or any part of its undertaking, as a going concern', and '(3)(*d*) a more advantageous realisation of the company's assets than would be effected on a winding up.'

Section 8(1) gives the court jurisdiction to make an administration order if it is satisfied that a company 'is or is likely to become unable to pay its debts' and it considers that the making of an order 'would be likely to achieve' one or more of the purposes specified in s 8(3). I am satisfied on the evidence that the company is unable to pay its debts. Whether the order would be likely to achieve one of the specified objects is not so easy to answer. When the statute says that I must consider it likely, what degree of probability does this involve? In *Re Consumer & Industrial Press Ltd* Peter Gibson J said ([1988] BCLC 177 at 178):

> 'As I read s 8 the court must be satisfied on the evidence put before it that at least one of the purposes in s 8(3) is likely to be achieved if it is to make an administration order. That does not mean that it is merely possible that such purpose will be achieved; the evidence must go further than that to enable the court to hold that the purpose in question will more probably than not be achieved.'

The judge therefore required that on a scale of probability of 0 (impossibility) to I (absolute certainty) the likelihood of success should be more than 0.5. I naturally hesitate to disagree with Peter Gibson J particularly since he had the benefit of adversarial argument. But this is a new statute on which the judges of the Companies' Court are still feeling their way to a settled practice and I therefore think I should say that in my view he set the standard of probability too high. My reasons are as follows. First, 'likely' connotes probability but the particular degree of probability intended must be gathered from qualifying words (very likely, quite likely, more likely than not) or context. It cannot be a misuse of language to say that something is likely without intending to suggest that the probability of its happening exceeds 0.5, as in, 'I think that the favourite Golden Spurs at 5–1 is likely to win the Derby'. Second, the section requires the court to be 'satisfied' of the company's actual or likely insolvency but only to 'consider' that the order would be likely to achieve one of the stated purposes. There must have been a reason for this change of language and I think it was to indicate that a lower threshold of persuasion was needed in the latter case than the former. The first of the sentences I have quoted from the judgment of Peter Gibson J suggest that he did not take this variation into account. Third, some of the stated purposes are mutually exclusive and the probability of any one of them being achieved may be less than 0.5 but the probability of one or other of them being achieved may be more than 0.5. I doubt whether Parliament intended the courts to embark on such calculations of cumulative probabilities. Fourth, as Peter Gibson J said, s 8(1) only sets out the conditions to be satisfied before the court has jurisdiction. It still retains a discretion as to whether or not to make the order. It is therefore not unlikely that the legislature intended to set a modest threshold of probability to found jurisdiction and to rely on the court's discretion to make orders in cases in which, weighing all the circumstances, it seemed inappropriate to do so. Fifth, the report of the Insolvency Law Review Committee on *Insolvency Law and Practice* (Cmnd 8558) para 508, which recommended the introduction of administratorship, said that the new procedure was likely to be beneficial:

'. . . only in cases where there is a business of sufficient substance to justify the expense of an Administration, and where there is a real prospect of returning to profitability or selling as a going concern.'

Elsewhere the report speaks of an order being made if there is a 'reasonable possibility' of a scheme of reconstruction. I think that his kind of phraseology was intended to be reflected in the statutory phrase 'considers that [it] would be likely' in s 8(1).

For my part, therefore, I would hold that the requirements of s 8(1)(*b*) are satisfied if the court considers that there is a real prospect that one or more of the stated purposes may be achieved. It may be said that phrases like 'real prospect' lack precision compared with 0.5 on the scale of probability. But the courts are used to dealing in other contexts with such indications of the degree of persuasion they must feel. 'Prima facie case' and 'good arguable case' are well-known examples. Such phrases are like tempo markings in music; although there is inevitably a degree of subjectivity in the way they are interpreted, they are nevertheless meaningful and useful.

On the facts as they appear from the evidence before me, I think there is a real prospect that an administration order, coupled with the agreement with Berkley House, will enable the whole or part of the company's undertaking to survive or at least enable the administrator to effect a more advantageous realisation of the assets than would be effected in a winding up. Certainly the prospects for the company, its employees and creditors look bleak if no administration order is made and there has to be a winding up. Consequently, although I cannot say that it is more probable than not that one of the specified purposes will be achieved, I accept the opinion of the prospective administrator that, 'the making of an administration order offers the best prospect for preserving the company's future and maximising the realisation of the company's assets for the benefit of its creditors'. I therefore made the order.

SOURCE 302
Re Croftbell Ltd
[1990] BCLC 844

VINELOTT J: On 31 May 1989 Croftbell (the company) executed a debenture in favour of Benchmark Bank plc (Benchmark). By the debenture the company in consideration of Benchmark —

'affording or continuing to afford banking and/or other facilities [charged] by way of floating charge the whole of its undertaking and all its property and assets (collectively "the undertaking") as a continuing security for the payment and discharge [of all its indebtedness to Benchmark] both present and future howsoever arising.'

Benchmark was given power to appoint a receiver at any time if any obligations of the company had not been met when due or on the presentation of a petition for an administration order.

On 12 April 1990 the company presented a petition for an administration order. On 3 May Benchmark appointed joint receivers and immediately thereafter applied to dismiss the petition.

The question is whether the receivers appointed by Benchmark are receivers of —

'the whole or substantially the whole of [the] Company's property appointed by or on behalf of the holders of any debentures of the Company secured by a charge which, as created, was a floating charge'

within the meaning of s 29(2) of the Insolvency Act 1986. If they are, then Benchmark's application to dismiss the petition must succeed: see s 9(3) of the 1986 Act.

The context in which this question arises is shortly as follows. The company is a member of a group of which the parent is a company called Hastenberg's Group Ltd. In 1989 the company acquired the entire share capital of a company called Toller's Garage Ltd, which owns a valuable site. The cost to the company was £2.2m. Of this sum £1.7m was borrowed from Benchmark. A further £400,000 was borrowed from a company called Vertex Ltd. Further sums were borrowed from other lenders. It is said in an affidavit by Mr W D Gough, a director of the company and of its parent, that the company borrowed more than it needed to complete the purchase. Counsel (Mr Bannister) who appeared for the company told me that the company was left with a surplus of about £80,000. Mr Gough in his affidavit says that £14,150 of the surplus moneys was lent to another company in the group, Hastenberg's Development Ltd, and that the balance was applied in repaying a debt due to the parent company. The loan to Hastenberg's Development Ltd is said to have been extinguished by payments to and on behalf of the company by the parent company.

Mr Gough's evidence is that the company's only asset, apart from the shares of Toller's Garage Ltd, now consists of a sum of £4,764 owed to it by its parent company (which represents the balance of two credits, one of £12,344 representing value added tax payments on legal and other expenses incurred in the purchase of Toller's Garage Ltd, which were refunded to the parent company under group arrangements with the Customs and Excise, and £4,910, an insurance premium paid by the company on behalf of the parent company less a management fee of £12,000 owed to the parent company and £490 representing sundry small payments made by the parent company on its behalf). It is not easy to reconcile the balance said to be due from the parent company with a summary of the statement of affairs of the companies in the group annexed to the report of the proposed administrators, but nothing I think turns on these minor discrepancies.

The debenture was only one of three documents executed on 31 May 1989. The company also executed a document headed 'Pledge of Fluctuating Stocks, Shares and Securities' whereby it charged to Benchmark —

'all stocks and shares and all securities, marketable or otherwise, negotiable instruments, scrip, bills of lading, dock warrants, delivery orders, documents of title and policies which or the certificates of which are now or may at any time hereafter be lodged with or held by you or your agent or transferred to you or your nominees or registered in your or their names by or for us as security for all monies then or to become due to Benchmark.'

The charge extended to all dividends or interest or other payments or assets accruing in respect of the securities so charged. The company also executed a legal charge in favour of Vertex whereby it charged its shareholding in Toller's Garage Ltd to secure the loan of £400,000 from Vertex by way of a second fixed charge.

It is quite clear that the debenture, construed in isolation from the pledge, created a charge which, as created, was a floating charge on the whole of the company's property within s 29(2). It was suggested by counsel for the company at one stage in his argument that the debenture only created a charge on the assets of the company as at the date when it was executed. He relied on the absence of the words usually included in a debenture 'present and future' and 'all property and assets'. I do not think there is anything in that suggestion. It has been settled since the floating charge first emerged as a form of security that a charge on the undertaking of a company prima facie extends to all property which may become the property of the company as well as to the property of the company at the date of the charge: see *Re Panama New Zealand and Australian Royal Mail Co* (1870) LR 5 Ch App 318.

The first submission of counsel for the company was that the debenture, if construed together with the pledge and in the light of Mr Gough's evidence as to the purpose of the formation and as to the intended activities of the company, does not answer the description of a floating charge contained in the well-known and often-cited passage in the judgment of Romer LJ in *Re Yorkshire Woolcombers Association Ltd, Houldsworth v Yorkshire Woolcombers Association Ltd* [1903] 2 Ch 284 at 295:

> 'I certainly do not intend to attempt to give an exact definition of the term "floating charge," nor am I prepared to say that there will not be a floating charge within the meaning of [the Companies Act 1900] which does not contain all the three characteristics that I am about to mention, but I certainly think that if a charge has the three characteristics that I am about to mention it is a floating charge. (1.) If it is a charge on a class of assets of a company present and future; (2.) if that class is one which, in the ordinary course of the business of the company, would be changing from time to time; and (3.) if you find that by the charge it is contemplated that, until some future step is taken by or on behalf of those interested in the charge, the company may carry on its business in the ordinary way as far as concerns the particular class of assets I am dealing with.'

Counsel for the company (Mr Bannister) submitted that it is clear from the company's evidence and the surrounding circumstances that the company was acquired solely for the purpose of purchasing and holding the shares of Toller's Garage Ltd, that it has never carried on any trading activities, that the only transactions it has entered into, apart from the purchase of the shares, have been payments made on behalf of companies in the group or by companies in the group on its behalf, resulting in credit and the debit entries in inter-company accounts, and that in these circumstances it cannot be said that the debenture constituted a charge on a distinct class of assets which in the ordinary course of time would change, or that it was contemplated that the company would carry on business in the ordinary way with that class of assets until something was done to crystalise the charge, for the company in truth had no business.

It is important to bear in mind that in *Re Yorkshire Woolcombers Association Ltd* the question was whether the deed executed by the company created a charge on future book and other debts which was intended to attach to those debts as and when they came into existence or a charge which would float until some further step was taken and which as a floating charge would be void as against the company for want of registration. Romer LJ was therefore concerned not to define a floating charge for all purposes but to indicate the features which are material in distinguishing a specific charge extending to future assets from a floating charge. It is not suggested in the instant case that the debenture created a fixed or specific charge on assets then owned (other than the shares of Toller's Garage Ltd) or which might in future be owned by the company. It would have otherwise been impossible for the company to make the payments out of its surplus moneys which it made to the parent company or to enter into the other inter-company transactions within the group without the consent of Benchmark. Counsel's submission thus leads to the conclusion that the debenture had no operation at all. Counsel did not shrink from that conclusion. For my part I think it is sufficient to say that I can see no ground on which the court could conclude that a charge which according to the terms created a floating charge over the present and any future property of the company was wholly inoperative.

The alternative submission of counsel for the company was that even if the debenture did operate to create a floating charge on the assets of the company, other than shares of Toller's Garage Ltd, it should none the less be disregarded for the purposes of s 9 of the 1986 Act because it is mere artifice aimed at circumventing the purpose of Pt II of that Act. He submitted that the legislature intended that the court should have power to appoint an administrator if satisfied that the requirements of s 8 have been satisfied, save only where all or substantially all the assets of the company are comprised in a floating charge and the holder of the charge has power to appoint a receiver who by virtue of his powers under the debenture as enlarged by the 1986 Act will be in a position to continue the company's business. The power of the court should not be stultified, he said, by the device of tacking a floating charge onto a fixed charge over the company's sole or principal asset.

I do not find it necessary and it would not I think be appropriate to venture into the question what legislative purpose is to be inferred from precluding a court from appointing an administrator against the wishes of a debenture holder who has power to appoint an administrative receiver. As I understand counsel's argument it is not suggested that a debenture creating a floating charge (which I think this debenture did) falls outside s 29(2) merely because at the time when the receivers are appointed substantially the only asset of the company is subject to a fixed charge, securing a sum in excess of the likely value of that asset, for instance a factory in the possession of the company and used for the purposes of its business. The property of the company would then comprise the interest of the company as mortgagor and the question whether the holder of a floating charge has power to appoint a receiver over substantially the whole of the company's property cannot depend on the amount of the debt secured by the fixed charge relative to the value of the company's uncharged assets. Equally it cannot have been intended to exclude a floating charge which when created extended to future assets merely because at the creation of the charge the company had no assets or no assets which were not the subject of a fixed charge, for that would exclude the obvious and common case where the floating charge was created to finance the commencement of a company's intended business. Counsel for the company submitted that it is otherwise if it was contemplated when the charge was created that the company would not carry on any active business but would continue as a passive receptacle of an asset which was subject to a fixed charge in favour of the same debenture holder. In such circumstances, he said, the floating charge serves no purpose except to enable the debenture holder to frustrate the court's power to appoint an administrative receiver.

I do not think that the answer to the question whether the holder of a debenture, which on its face creates a floating charge, has power to appoint an administrative receiver can turn on the intentions of the company when the debenture was executed or the knowledge by the debenture holder of those intentions. The intentions of the company might change and the company might have substantial assets outside the scope of the fixed charge when the power to appoint a receiver is exercised.

. . .

[The application was granted.]

SOURCE 303
Practice Note
[1994] 1 All ER 324

SIR DONALD NICHOLLS V-C gave the following direction at the sitting of the court. Administration orders under Pt II of the Insolvency Act 1986 are intended primarily to facilitate the rescue and rehabilitation of insolvent but potentially viable businesses. It is of the greatest importance that this aim should not be frustrated by expense, and that the costs of obtaining an administration order should not operate as a disincentive or put the process out of the reach of smaller companies.

Rule 2.2 of the Insolvency Rules 1986, SI 1986/1925, provides that an application for an administration order may be supported by a report by an independent person to the effect that the appointment of an administrator for the company is expedient. It is the experience of the court that the contents of the r 2.2 report are sometimes unnecessarily elaborate and detailed. Because a report of this character is thought to be necessary, the preliminary investigation will often have been unduly protracted and extensive and, hence, expensive.

The extent of the necessary investigation and the amount of material to be provided to the court must be a matter for the judgment of the person who prepares the report and will vary from case to case. However, in the normal case, what the court needs is a concise assessment of the company's situation and of the prospects of an administration order achieving one or more of the statutory purposes. The latter will normally include an explanation of the availability of any finance required during the administration.

Every endeavour should be made to avoid disproportionate investigation and expense. In some cases a brief investigation and report will be all that is required. Where the court has insufficient material on which to base its decision, but the proposed administrator is in court, he may offer to supplement the material by giving oral evidence. In such a case he should subsequently provide a supplemental report covering the matters on which oral evidence was given so that this can be placed on the court file.

In suitable cases the court may appoint an administrator but require him to report back to the court within a short period so that the court can consider whether to allow the administration to continue or to discharge the order. In some cases the court may require the administrator to hold a meeting of creditors before reporting back to the court, both within a relatively short period.

It is the experience of the judges who sit in the Companies Court that, in general, a r 2.2 report is valuable as a safeguard in assisting the court to see whether the application has a sound basis. However, there may be straightforward cases in which such a report is not necessary because it would provide little assistance. Practitioners are reminded that the 1986 rules do not require that a r 2.2 report must be provided in every case.

This statement is made after consultation with the other judges of the Chancery Division.

SOURCE 304
Bristol Airport plc *v* Powdrill (Re Paramount Airways No 1)
[1990] 2 All ER 493

SIR NICOLAS BROWNE-WILKINSON V-C: This case raises a difficult question as to the interaction between the powers of an administrator of a company appointed by the court under Pt II of the Insolvency Act 1986 and the right of an airport to detain an aircraft for unpaid charges under s 88 of the Civil Aviation

Act 1982 (the statutory right of detention). The case has a wider importance since it is the first in which this court has had to consider the new administration procedure for dealing with insolvent companies introduced by the Insolvency Act 1985 and the rights of such administrator to possession of the assets of the company: but see *Air Ecosse Ltd v Civil Aviation Authority* (1987) 3 BCC 492, where the Court of Session had to consider a different point under the 1986 Act.

The Facts
I gratefully adopt the summary of the facts given in the skeleton argument lodged by the administrators.

Paramount Airways Ltd (Paramount) is a charter airline operating out of several United Kingdom airports including Bristol Airport (Bristol) and Birmingham International Airport (Birmingham).

On 7 August 1989 Paramount was insolvent. Its statement of affairs shows a deficiency as regards creditors on that date of over £11m. Among its unsecured creditors on that date were Bristol and Birmingham. Bristol was owed some £1,215,889. Of this sum just under £700,000 was owed in respect of landing fees etc and just over £500,000 was in respect of fuel. In respect of one of the detained aircraft (G-PATB) some £267,000 was owed in respect of landing charges etc and some £201,000 was owed in respect of fuel. On the same date Paramount was indebted to Birmingham for some £466,000 for airport charges. Of these about £160,000 was owed in respect of the aircraft detained by them (G-PATA). On 7 August 1989 none of the aircraft operated by Paramount were at Bristol or Birmingham. It follows that if Paramount had gone into liquidation on 7 August 1989 neither Bristol nor Birmingham would have had any aircraft capable of being detained under the 1982 Act; they would have been unsecured creditors in the liquidation.

On 7 August 1989 an administration order was made by Warner J under s 8 of the 1986 Act. The administration order was made for the following purposes (a) the survival of Paramount and the whole or any part of its undertaking as a going concern, (b) the approval of a voluntary arrangement under Pt I of the 1986 Act and (c) a more advantageous realisation of Paramount's assets than would be effected on a winding up. Two chartered accountants were appointed administrators under the order.

At the date of the administration order Paramount was the licensed operator of certain aircraft including an MD-83 (G-PATB), a Boeing 737 and another MD-83 (G-PATA). Paramount was operating these aircraft under a sublease from Irish Aerospace Leasing Ltd (Irish Aerospace) under leases expiring in about 1994. Irish Aerospace was itself the lessee of those aircraft. Air 2000 Ltd, the third respondent to this appeal, was the petitioning creditor.

On 7 August 1989 the administrators entered into an arrangement with Bristol whereby it was agreed that Paramount's aircraft would be permitted to land and depart from Bristol Airport in consideration of Paramount paying Bristol's standard charges. It is not alleged that this constituted a waiver by Bristol of its rights to detain the aircraft for charges incurred prior to the administration order. There was no similar arrangement made with Birmingham. After 7 August 1989 the administrators caused Paramount to continue its trading. Since that date Paramount has flown over 300,000 passengers to foreign destinations from 11 airports in the United Kingdom, including Bristol and Birmingham. In respect of all these flights £6.7m has been paid by Paramount in respect of airport charges and fuel to all the airports used, including substantial sums to both Bristol and Birmingham. All airport charges which have been incurred during the course of the administration, including all airport charges payable to Bristol and Birmingham, have been paid by the administrators. The debts now due to Bristol and Birmingham are the same debts that were due on 7 August 1989 in respect of charges incurred prior to the making of the administration order on 7 August 1989.

By the middle of October 1989 the administrators had formed the view that there was a real prospect of the sale of the business of Paramount being achieved on terms which would be beneficial to the general body of Paramount's creditors. Accordingly, notices were sent out to creditors calling the meeting required under s 23 of the Insolvency Act 1986 for Friday, 3 November 1989. On 30 October 1989 a meeting took place between representatives of four airports (including Bristol and Birmingham) at which an understanding was reached that none of them would exercise any power of detention until after the creditors' meeting on 3 November 1989.

On 2 November 1989 both Bristol and Birmingham became anxious that, as the holiday season was coming to an end, the aircraft might be about to leave the United Kingdom or otherwise be routed so as not to return to their respective airports. On that date there were two Paramount aircraft at Bristol, G-PATB and the Boeing 737. Bristol applied ex parte to Harman J for leave to detain the two aircraft and such leave was granted over the hearing of an inter partes application on Monday, 6 November 1989. Bristol permitted the Boeing 737 to leave Bristol and fly to Australia. G-PATB was detained and remained detained until 14 November 1989.

On the same day (2 November 1989) Paramount had aircraft G-PATA at Birmingham. This aircraft had charter commitments with a German firm for weekend return flights. In the course of the afternoon of 2 November Birmingham learned of the order made by Harman J. In conversations with a representative of the administrators Birmingham was informed that they could not detain G-PATA without leave of the court. Without obtaining the leave of the court, on the same afternoon Birmingham parked a lorry laden with concrete in front of G-PATA. At approximately 6 pm that evening the captain of G-PATA arrived at Birmingham and was served with a 'lien notice'. At about 8 pm on 2 November Birmingham obtained ex parte from Hodgson J an order giving Birmingham leave to detain G-PATA over the hearing of an inter partes application on Monday, 6 November, before the companies judge in London. G-PATA was detained by Birmingham down to 14 November 1989.

The meeting of Paramount's creditors summoned by the administrators took place on 3 November 1989. An offer for Paramount's business and assets was put before the meeting of creditors by the administrators. The meeting was attended by representatives from both Bristol and Birmingham. The offer was approved in principle by the creditors without dissent. The proposed sale was incapable of performance if the aircraft remained detained.

The applications for leave to detain by Bristol and Birmingham came before Harman J in the Companies Court on Monday, 6 November 1989, the respondents being the administrators, Irish Aerospace and Air 2000. The matter was argued for three days but, given the urgency of the matter, Harman J had to give an immediate judgment, which he delivered on Friday, 10 November 1989. The judge held that the airports required the leave of the court under s 11 of the 1986 Act before exercising their statutory right to detain the aircraft and, in the exercise of his discretion, refused to grant such leave. Birmingham and Bristol appeal against that decision.

Bristol and Birmingham immediately applied to this court to safeguard their position pending appeal. This court directed that the appeal should be heard on 21 November 1989 and that in the interim Bristol and Birmingham should have leave to detain the two aircraft until after the hearing of the appeal or until such earlier time as the sum of £350,000 should be paid into court or otherwise secured, the parties having agreed that in the event that £350,000 was so paid or secured all rights and claims of the airports in respect of the two aircraft should be transferred to that sum. The sum of £350,000 was so provided and the detention of the aircraft ceased on 14 November 1989.

Leave to appeal has been given by Harman J.

The Statutory Rights of Detention

Section 88(1) of the Civil Aviation Act 1982 provides as follows:

> 'Where default is made in the payment of airport charges incurred in respect of any aircraft at an aerodrome to which this section applies, the aerodrome authority may, subject to the provisions of this section — (*a*) detain, pending payment, either — (i) the aircraft in respect of which the charges were incurred (whether or not they were incurred by the person who is the operator of the aircraft at the time when the detention begins); or (ii) any other aircraft of which the person in default is the operator at the time when the detention begins; and (*b*) if the charges are not paid within 56 days of the date when the detention begins, sell the aircraft in order to satisfy the charges.'

Subsection (3) provides that the aircraft shall not be sold without the leave of the court, which must first be satisfied that a sum is due for airport charges, that default has been made in payment of such charges and that the aircraft is liable for sale under the section. Subsection (4) requires notice of any application for leave to sell to be given to persons whose interests may be affected by such sale so as to afford them an opportunity of becoming parties to such application. Subsection (6) provides that the proceeds of sale are to be applied in paying any customs or excise duty chargeable, the expenses of detaining, keeping and selling the aircraft, the airport charges which are unpaid and charges due by virtue of s 73 of the 1982 Act (which relate to charges for Eurocontrol). The surplus proceeds of sale are to be paid to or among the persons whose interests in the aircraft have been divested by reason of the sale. Subsections (7) and (8) provide that the power of detention and sale is exercisable in relation to the equipment on the aircraft and any stores and aircraft documents carried on the aircraft. Under sub-s (9) the power to detain is expressly made exercisable not only on the occasion on which the charges have been incurred but also on any subsequent occasion when the aircraft is on the aerodrome on which the charges were incurred or on any other aerodrome owned or managed by the same authority.

There are two points which should be noted at this stage. First, it is common ground that the sale of an aircraft under this section operates so as to divest all interests in the aircraft so as to vest full legal and equitable title to the aircraft in the purchaser.

. . .

Second, sub-s (1)(*a*)(ii) requires one to determine 'the time when the detention begins'. In *Havelet Leasing Ltd v Cardiff-Wales Airport Ltd* (28 June 1988, unreported) Phillips J held that, in order to exercise the statutory power of detention, the airport had to do some overt act evidencing the act of detention. He said:

> 'I hold that detention by an [airport] authority must be begun by some overt act. Such act need take no particular form. A simple declaration that the

aircraft was detained, had it been made to [the operator], would have sufficed; so would an administrative act that would de facto have prevented the aircraft being flown from the airport.'

In that case he held that the fixing to the aircraft of a 'lien notice' was the act of detention. That decision has not been challenged by either side in the present case and in my judgment is correct.

...

The administrators in this case contend that the exercise of the statutory right of detention under s 88 falls within either s 11(3)(c) (as being a step to enforce any security) or within s 11(3)(d) (as being the levying of a distress or 'other proceedings').

...

The Issues
A. *Under s 11(3)(c)*

...

(3) Is the exercise of the statutory right of detention 'a step taken to enforce any security' which requires the leave of the court under s 11?

B. *Under s 11(3)(d)*
(1) Does the detention of the aircraft constitute the levy of a distress?
(2) Does the detention of the aircraft constitute 'other proceedings' within the meaning of the subsection or does the word 'proceedings' mean only legal or quasi-legal actions?

C. *Discretion*
If the detention of the aircraft required the leave of the court under s 11(3), did the judge properly exercise his discretion by refusing such leave?

...

(3) *Is the exercise of the statutory right of detention a 'step taken to enforce' a security?*
Counsel for the airports submits that the overt act necessary to constitute the exercise of the statutory right of detention (ie the blocking of the aircraft or the service of a notice of lien) is not a step to enforce the security but a step to create or perfect the security. He submits that, in the present case, security was either created for the first time by the overt act of detention or, at least, such acts were only done to perfect what until then had been an inchoate security (ie a right to create a security by the overt act). The mere detention of an aircraft, says counsel, is not the taking of a step to enforce the security.

This is an important point since, to my mind, it raises the question of an administrator's right to possession of chattels which are subject to a possessory lien or similar right. Although there are special features of the statutory right of detention conferred by s 88, the starting point must be to discover what are the rights of the administrator to obtain possession of chattels from those claiming a right of retention the exercise of which involves no positive action by the creditor save a refusal to comply with a request to hand over the chattel. Is such a refusal a 'step . . . taken to enforce' the lien or other similar security? Although administrations involving aircraft are likely to be comparatively rare, nearly all administrations will raise the question whether, for example, company vehicles subject to a repairer's lien or goods consigned on the terms that the carrier has a lien on such goods can be withheld from the administrator unless he pays the debt in full.

If retention under such possessory lien does not require the leave of the court under s 11, this will be an exception to the normal rule. The administrator will be forced either to seek to run the business without the chattels so retained or to pay in full and at once the amount owed to the lien-holder. As in the present case, it may not be possible to run the business without the chattels. If the creditor claiming the lien is to be paid in full, he will be placed in a uniquely favourable position compared with all other creditors. During the administration an unsecured creditor cannot, without the leave of the court, enforce his debt by action so as to obtain immediate payment: see s 11(3)(*b*). Secured creditors cannot appoint a receiver or enforce their security in any other way: see s 11(3)(*b*) and (*c*). The policy of the 1986 Act is plainly to impose a moratorium on the payment of debts save to the extent that the administrator chooses to pay (in order, for example, to obtain further supplies from a creditor) or the court so directs.

Against that background, I turn to see what guidance is afforded by the words of the 1986 Act themselves. I suspect that, save in one regard, the draftsman may have overlooked the need for an administrator (as opposed to a liquidator) to obtain possession of chattels for the purpose of continuing to run the company's business. The only specific provision dealing with liens is s 246 which, so far as relevant, provides as follows:

'... (2) Subject as follows, a lien or other right to retain possession of any of the books, papers or other records of the company is unenforceable to the extent that its enforcement would deny possession of any books, papers or other records to the office-holder.

(3) This does not apply to a lien on documents which give a title to property and are held as such.'

The 'office-holder' is defined by sub-s (1) as meaning an administrator, liquidator or provisional liquidator, as the case may be.

Counsel for the airports relied on this section as indicating that, save in the case of documents, a possessory lien will be enforceable so as to deny the administrator possession of the chattel subject to the lien and that accordingly no leave would be required under s 11(3). In my judgment that is not necessarily the underlying assumption behind the section. Let me assume for the moment that the assertion of a right to retain a chattel under a lien is within s 11(3). The only consequence is that leave to enforce such right is required; apart from that restriction, the lien-holder's right to retain the chattel remains and may well be permitted by order of the court. However, in the case of documents falling within s 246(2) the right to retain as against the administrator is unenforceable: the holder of the lien over documents could not apply to the court under s 11(3) for leave to retain since under s 246(2) he has no right to retain which the court could give him leave to exercise. For that reason, in my judgment, there is no necessary conflict between s 246 and a construction of s 11(3)(*c*) which requires the leave of the court for the exercise of a right of retention under a possessory lien.

There is another feature of s 246(2) which in my judgment strongly supports the view that the exercise of a right to retain under a lien constitutes the enforcement of the security. Section 246(2) provides that 'a lien or other right to retain possession ... is *unenforceable* to the extent that its *enforcement*' would deny possession. The words I have emphasised show that in the 1986 Act the mere insistence by a lien-holder on his right to retain constitutes 'enforcement' of the lien. On ordinary principles, the same word used in different sections of the Act should normally be given the same meaning. Hence the word 'enforce', when used in s 11(3) in relation to a lien, prima facie includes the assertion by the lien-holder of his right to retain.

Therefore, both the limited guidance provided by the words of the 1986 Act and the desirability of giving effect to the statutory purpose of the administration procedure both point to leave being required under s 11(3)(c). There are, however, practical considerations which are said to point the other way. First, it is said that, by being forced to give up possession of the chattel, the person entitled to a possessory lien over it will lose his security: the loss of possession under a possessory lien involves the loss of the security: it cannot be right that the appointment of an administrator has the effect of turning a secured into an unsecured creditor. But this submission overlooks the fact that the only require-ment of s 11(3) is to require the leave of the court to the exercise of the right of retention. In the ordinary case where a lien-holder seeks to assert his lien from the ouset of the administration, on an application for leave under s 11(3), the court, if satisfied that the administrator needs possession of the chattel, would in the exercise of its discretion normally impose terms whereby the lien over the goods was retained, notwithstanding the loss of possession, or provided some other suitable security for the lien-holder.

Again, it is said that it would be ridiculous to require an application to the court in the case of every possessory lien, however small. In my judgment that would not be the consequence of upholding the administrator's claim in this case. An administrator in exercise of his powers (particularly those contained in paras 18 and 23 of Sch 1 to the 1986 Act) could agree with the lien-holder that possession of the chattel was to be given up on the terms that the lien-holder continued to enjoy a non-possessory lien over the chattel.

I therefore reach the conclusion that, in the case of an ordinary possessory lien, the assertion by the lien-holder of a right to retain constitutes the taking of a step to enforce his security within s 11(3) of the 1986 Act and therefore, in default of agreement with the administrator, requires the leave of the court.

Do the special features of the statutory right of detention under s 88 lead to a different conclusion in the present case? Although there are differences between the normal possessory lien and the statutory right of detention, in general the two rights are very similar, viz a passive right to retain a chattel against payment of a debt. Counsel for the airports urges that there are two matters (one technical, the other practical) which make this case different.

First, he submits that the overt act of detaining the aircraft is the act which creates the security, not one which enforces it. He submits that until there has been that overt act of detention, the airport has no security at all: it merely enjoys the statutory right to create the security by an act of detention. Therefore, he says, such detention cannot be a step taken to enforce the security. There was much discussion in the course of argument whether any security existed before the overt act of detention. It was suggested that the security existed at all times when relevant charges existed wherever the aircraft might be; alternatively, that the security came into existence when an aircraft touched down at the airport there being subsisting relevant charges which could give rise to a detention at that airport. I find such analyses artificial and unconvincing. In my judgment counsel for the airports is right in saying that the airports enjoyed no actual security until they detained the aircraft by an overt act of detention. But I am not persuaded that, just because the overt act of detention created or perfected the security, it was not also the taking of a step to enforce that security. There is no legal reason why the same act should not have a dual effect as being both the perfection of the security and a step taken to enforce it. Plainly, as a matter of commercial common sense, the detention of the aircraft in this case did enforce the right of detention in just the same way as does a refusal by a lien-holder to hand over the chattel. The artificiality of the argument can be demonstrated by considering what would be the position if, immediately after the notice of lien was served, the administrators had demanded the giving up of the aircraft. The refusal to meet such demand would have been indistinguishable from the refusal of a lien-holder to hand over the chattel subject to a possessory lien. It seems to me unnecessarily artificial to say that in this case there had to be a separate demand for the detained aircraft in order to constitute an enforcement of the security by the airport.

Counsel's second point concentrated on the mobility of aircraft. Once an aircraft has left the airport, the rights under s 88 come to an end unless and until it returns to that airport. The aircraft may have left the jurisdiction, never to return and be beyond the reach of any order of the court. Even if the aircraft returns to the United Kingdom, it may not return to the same airport. If, therefore, before exercising the statutory right of detention, the airport has to obtain the leave of the court, the aircraft may well have gone beyond recall even if the application is heard within hours and is successful. If, as Harman J held in the case of Birmingham, the detention of the aircraft before the leave of the court was obtained is a contempt of court as an interference with the possession of an officer of the court, the airport is placed in an impossible position.

These are powerful arguments. Plainly, an airport should not lose its rights under s 88 simply because there is no time to obtain prior leave of the court. But in my judgment, on a proper view of the matter the practical repercussions are not as serious as they are submitted to be. I think it unlikely that, after the judgment of this court has been digested, an administrator will seek to spirit away an aircraft without giving an airport time to apply ex parte for an interim order giving leave to detain, which will no doubt be granted on the usual cross-undertaking in damages. If, contrary to that prognosis, an administrator were to make such an attempt, in my judgment an airport would run no risk of being in contempt of court if at the same time as it detained the aircraft it made every effort to obtain the leave of the court which can normally be obtained in a matter of hours. I am unable to agree with the judge that Birmingham may have been in contempt of court in this case if, as I understand the position to have been, they were apprehensive that the aircraft was going to leave that airport almost immediately.

For these reasons, in my judgment the leave of the court to exercise the statutory power of detention contained in s 88 was required under s 11(3)(c). I should make it clear that this decision as to the right of detention under s 88 of the 1982 Act does not extend to other rights of detention under that Act, for example s 64(7) (operating without a licence) and s 78(5) (noise and vibration).

It is therefore strictly unnecessary to consider the position under section 11(3)(d), but since the judge primarily based his decision on para (d) it is desirable for me to do so.

B. The issues under s 11(3)(d)

(1) *Distress* The administrators claim that, by detaining the aircraft, the airports were levying a distress within the section and that therefore the leave of the court is required. This was the primary ground of the judge's decision. I am unable to agree with his view on this point. There is no doubt that the statutory right of detention has many similarities to the ancient remedy of distraint: it is a right for a creditor to exercise control over chattels, whereby the debtor is prevented from using them, as a pledge for the payment of a debt owed by the debtor to the creditor. But it lacks one essential feature of a distraint, namely that under the statutory right of detention the aircraft is not taken into the possession of the airport. Under s 88 the power is to detain, not to seize and detain. The airport can take all necessary steps to prevent the aircraft leaving and to prevent

any spares and documents being removed from it, but it has no right to exclude the owner from the aircraft completely. Therefore in my judgment the statutory right to detain is not strictly a right of distraint.

Moreover, although statutes have created statutory rights of distress, counsel could find no case in which a statutory provision had been held to be a right of distraint in the absence of clear words describing the right as a right to distrain. Distress is an ancient remedy and to a degree obsolescent. In my judgment in the absence of clear words in s 88 describing the right to detain as being a right of distress, it would be wrong to treat it as such.

(2) '*Other proceedings*' The administrators submit, and the judge held, that the detention of the aircraft required the leave of the court as being 'other proceedings . . . against the company or its property'.

I have no hesitation in rejecting that view. In my judgment the natural meaning of the words 'no other proceedings . . . may be commenced or continued' is that the proceedings in question are either legal proceedings or quasi-legal proceedings such as arbitration. It is true that the word 'proceedings' can, in certain contexts, refer to actions other than legal proceedings, eg proceedings of a meeting. In *Quazi v Quazi* [1979] 3 All ER 897, [1980] AC 744 the House of Lords held that a divorce by talaq in Pakistan constituted other proceedings within the statutory phrase 'judicial or other proceedings'. But in that phrase the word 'other' must have referred to non-judicial proceedings since judicial proceedings had already been expressly referred to. No such special feature is present in s 11(3)(d).

Further, the reference to the 'commencement' and 'continuation' of proceedings indicates that what Parliament had in mind was legal proceedings. The use of the word 'proceedings' in the plural together with the words 'commence' and 'continue' are far more appropriate to legal proceedings (which are normally so described) than to the doing of some act of a more general nature. Again, it is clear that the draftsman when he wished to refer to some activity other than 'proceedings' was well aware of the word 'steps' which he used in s 11(3)(c).

The judge took the view that the words 'other proceedings' covered —

> 'every sort of step against the company, its contracts or its property, which may be taken and the intention of Parliament by s 11 is to prevent all such, without the leave of the court or the consent of the administrators.'

In my judgment, however anxious one may be not to thwart the statutory purpose of an administration, the judge's formulation must be too wide. If the word 'proceedings' has this wide meaning, all the other detailed prohibitions in s 11(3) would be unnecessary. Moreover such a construction would introduce great uncertainty as to what constituted commencement or continuation of proceedings. Would the acceptance of a repudiation of a contract by the company constitute a 'proceeding'? Would a counter notice claiming a new tenancy under the Landlord and Tenant Act 1954 be a 'proceeding'? In my judgment, the judge's view would produce an undesirable uncertainty which, in view of my construction of s 11(3)(c), it is unnecessary to introduce into the Act.

C. Did the judge properly exercise his discretion by refusing leave to enforce?

The judge, in the exercise of his discretion, refused to grant the airports leave to enforce their security. He took the following matters into consideration. First, he referred to the fact that there was or might be a deficiency as against unsecured creditors of £11m or more. The judge had taken the view that the airports were not secured creditors and therefore should not be allowed to gain priority over the other unsecured creditors by detaining the aircraft. Next, he referred to the fact that the detention of the aircraft would prevent the realisation of the business as a going concern, which had been approved at the meeting of creditors, attended, without dissent, by representatives of both Birmingham and Bristol. Next, he took into account the fact that throughout the administration the airports had stood by and taken the benefit of the flying operations carried out by the administrator throughout the summer in return for which they had received very substantial sums in excess of what they would have received had the business gone into liquidation on 7 August. He treated the airports as 'blowing hot and cold', taking the benefits while they might and then seeking to assert inconsistent rights thereafter. Finally, as I have said, he took the view that Birmingham by obstructing the aircraft before obtaining the leave of the court was probably in contempt of court and took this into account.

In my judgment the judge took into account the relevant factors and did not take into account any irrelevant factors save the view, which I do not share, that Birmingham may have been in contempt of court. However, it is clear that that factor would have made no difference to the exercise of his discretion, since he pointed out expressly that the same matter could not be taken into account as against Bristol; yet he reached the same conclusion in relation to both airports. Therefore, in my judgment the exercise of his discretion is not reviewable in this court.

I would for myself go further and say that I completely agree with his decision. If, at the outset of an administration a secured creditor wishes to enforce his security in a way inconsistent with the achievement of the statutory purposes, he should make his position clear at the outset. To stand by and accept all the benefits of an administration and then, at the eleventh hour, seek to enforce a right which is inconsistent with the achievement of the statutory purpose is in my judgment unacceptable. The position in the present case is worse since on 7 August there were no aircraft at either Bristol or Birmingham; therefore at the commencement of the administration by the court the airports were unable to make themselves into secured creditors by exercising the statutory right of detention. Only as a result of the operations of the administrators, acting under the administration order, did the aircraft ever come to Bristol or Birmingham again. They are seeking to achieve an outcome where, as a result of the administration of the company under the order of the court, they achieve greater rights than they would have done had the company gone into liquidation on 7 August. Further, they have reaped substantial benefits by the continued opera- tion of the aircraft, giving rise to the payment by the administrators to both Bristol and Birmingham of substantial charges as they accrued due. In my judgment, whilst the administration procedure should not be used so far as possible to prejudice those who were secured creditors at the time when the administration order was made in lieu of a winding-up order, nor should it be used so as to give the unsecured creditors at that time security which they would not have enjoyed had it not been for the administration.

. . .

SOURCE 305
Re Atlantic Computer Systems plc (No 1)
[1991] BCLC 606

Leave applications: the general approach
There is one final matter to which we now turn. In the course of argument we were invited to give guidance on the principles to be applied on applications for

the grant of leave under s 11. It is an invitation to which we are reluctant to accede, for several reasons: first, Parliament has left at large the discretion given to the court, and it is not for us to cut down that discretion or, as it was put in argument, to confine it within a straitjacket. However much we emphasise that any observations are only guidelines, there is a danger that they may be treated as something more. Secondly, s 11(3)(c) and (d) applies to a very wide range of steps and proceedings, and the circumstances in which leave is sought will vary almost infinitely. Thirdly, it is the judges who sit in the Companies Court who have practical experience of the difficulties arising in the working out of this new jurisdiction, not the members of this court.

However, we have already drawn attention to the important role of the administrator in this field. He should respond speedily and responsibly to applications for consent under s 11. Parliament envisaged that in the first place s 11 matters should be dealt with by him. It is to be hoped, in the interests of all concerned, that applications to the court will become the exception rather than the rule. But we recognise that for this to be so, authorised insolvency practitioners and their legal advisers need more guidance than is available at present on what, in general, is the approach of the court on leave applications. We feel bound, therefore, to make some general observations regarding cases where leave is sought to exercise existing proprietary rights, including security rights, against a company in administration:

(1) It is in every case for the person who seeks leave to make out a case for him to be given leave.

(2) The prohibition in s 11(3)(c) and (d) is intended to assist the company, under the management of the administrator, to achieve the purpose for which the administration order was made. If granting leave to a lessor of land or the hirer of goods (a 'lessor') to exercise his proprietary rights and repossess his land or goods is unlikely to impede the achievement of that purpose, leave should normally be given.

(3) In other cases when a lessor seeks possession the court has to carry out a balancing exercise, balancing the legitimate interests of the lessor and the legitimate interests of the other creditors of the company (see Peter Gibson J in *Royal Trust Bank v Buchler* [1989] BCLC 130 at 135).

The metaphor employed here, for want of a better, is that of scales and weights. Lord Wilberforce adverted to the limitations of this metaphor in *Science Research Council v Nassé, BL Cars Ltd (formerly Leyland Cars) v Vyas* [1979] 3 All ER 673 at 681, [1980] AC 1028 at 1067. It must be kept in mind that the exercise under s 11 is not a mechanical one; each case calls for an exercise in judicial judgment, in which the court seeks to give effect to the purpose of the statutory provisions, having regard to the parties' interests and all the circumstances of the case. As already noted, the purpose of the prohibition is to enable or assist the company to achieve the object for which the administration order was made. The purpose of the power to give leave is to enable the court to relax the prohibition where it would be inequitable for the prohibition to apply.

(4) In carrying out the balancing exercise great importance, or weight, is normally to be given to the proprietary interests of the lessor. Sir Nicolas Browne-Wilkinson V-C observed in *Bristol Airport plc v Powdrill* [1990] BCLC 585 at 602, [1990] 2 All ER 493 at 507 that, so far as possible, the administration procedure should not be used to prejudice those who were secured creditors when the administration order was made in lieu of a winding-up order. The same is true regarding the proprietary interests of a lessor. The underlying principle here is that an administration for the benefit of unsecured creditors should not be conducted at the expense of those who have proprietary rights which they are

seeking to exercise, save to the extent that this may be unavoidable and even then this will usually be acceptable only to a strictly limited extent.

(5) Thus it will normally be a sufficient ground for the grant of leave if significant loss would be caused to the lessor by a refusal. For this purpose loss comprises any kind of financial loss, direct or indirect, including loss by reason of delay, and may extend to loss which is not financial. But if substantially greater loss would be caused to others by the grant of leave, or loss which is out of all proportion to the benefit which leave would confer on the lessor, that may outweigh the loss to the lessor caused by a refusal.

Our formulation was criticised in the course of the argument, and we certainly do not claim for it the status of a rule in those terms. At present we say only that it appears to us the nearest we can get to a formulation of what Parliament had in mind.

(6) In assessing these respective losses the court will have regard to matters such as: the financial position of the company, its ability to pay the rental arrears and the continuing rentals, the administrator's proposals, the period for which the administration order has already been in force and is expected to remain in force, the effect on the administration if leave were given, the effect on the applicant if leave were refused, the end result sought to be achieved by the administration, the prospects of that result being achieved, and the history of the administration so far.

(7) In considering these matters it will often be necessary to assess how probable the suggested consequences are. Thus if loss to the applicant is virtually certain if leave is refused, and loss to the others a remote possibility if leave is granted, that will be a powerful factor in favour of granting leave.

(8) This is not an exhaustive list. For example, the conduct of the parties may also be a material consideration in a particular case, as it was in *Bristol Airport v Powdrill.* There leave was refused on the ground that the applicants had accepted benefits under the administration, and had only sought to enforce their security at a later stage: indeed, they had only acquired their security as a result of the operations of the administrators. It behoves a lessor to make his position clear to the administrator at the outset of the administration and, if it should become necessary, to apply to the court promptly.

(9) The above considerations may be relevant not only to the decision whether leave should be granted or refused, but also to a decision to impose terms if leave is granted.

(10) The above considerations will also apply to a decision on whether to impose terms as a condition for refusing leave. Section 11(3)(*c*) and (*d*) makes no provision for terms being imposed if leave is refused, but the court has power to achieve that result. It may do so directly, by giving directions to the administrator: for instance, under s 17, or in response to an application by the administrator under s 14(3), or in exercise of its control over an administrator as an officer of the court. Or it may do so indirectly, by ordering that the applicant shall have leave unless the administrator is prepared to take this or that step in the conduct of the administration.

Cases where leave is refused but terms are imposed can be expected to arise frequently. For example, the permanent loss to a lessor flowing from his inability to recover his property will normally be small if the administrator is required to pay the current rent. In most cases this should be possible, since if the administration order has been rightly made the business should generally be sufficiently viable to hold down current outgoings. Such a term may therefore be a normal term to impose.

(11) The above observations are directed at a case such as the present where a lessor of land or the owner of goods is seeking to repossess his land or goods because of non-payment of rentals. A broadly similar approach will be applicable on many applications to enforce a security: for instance, an application by a mortgagee for possession of land. On such applications an important consideration will often be whether the applicant is fully secured. If he is, delay in enforcement is likely to be less prejudicial than in cases where his security is insufficient.

(12) In some cases there will be a dispute over the existence, validity or nature of the security which the applicant is seeking leave to enforce. It is not for the court on the leave application to seek to adjudicate upon that issue, unless (as in the present case, on the fixed or floating charge point) the issue raises a short point of law which it is convenient to determine without further ado. Otherwise the court needs to be satisfied only that the applicant has a seriously arguable case.

Scheme of Arrangement

This is set out in ss 425–427 of the Companies Act 1985. It is a long and complex procedure and until the passing of the Insolvency Act 1986 had largely fallen into abeyance as a rescue facility. The absence of any moratorium meant that any creditor could petition for the winding up of the company during the preparation of the Scheme. Now, if a company is in administration, it will be protected by a moratorium while steps are taken to put a Scheme in place.

Corporate Voluntary Arrangement ('CVA')

This was also created by the Insolvency Act 1986 (see Part I), and is a simplified version of the Scheme of Arrangement. It also suffers from not having a moratorium, and recent proposals by the Insolvency Service of the Department of Trade and Industry would, inter alia, legislate to add a moratorium to the CVA. The Insolvency Service issued a Consultative Document in October 1993 (Source 306). After extensive consultation, the proposals in that Document were revised in a further Consultative Document issued in April 1995 (Source 307).

SOURCE 306
Company Voluntary Arrangements and Administration Orders
(DTI Insolvency Service, October 1993)

Proposed Provisions for a New, Additional CVA Procedure
4.1 It is proposed that alternative provisions to the existing CVA procedure be introduced which would be additional to the existing procedure.

4.2 The legislation should provide the option of a moratorium with the minimum of formality by the filing of a notice in court. The notice would comprise the nominee's consent to act, his statement that there is a reasonable prospect of a successful CVA and the directors' statements that:

(a) no previous application has been made by the company for a moratorium in the period of 12 months ending with that day; and
(b) there are, to the directors' knowledge, no circumstances giving rise to the

possibility, in the event that the company should go into liquidation, of claims under:

    sections 238 and 242 (transactions at an undervalue)

    sections 239 and 243 (preferences)

    section 244 (extortionate credit transactions) and

    section 245 (floating charges invalid).

4.3 The moratorium would bind all creditors (including all secured creditors), would become effective on filing and would last for a period of 28 days. Creditors would be able to take action during the moratorium with the leave of the court. There would not be any court hearing but the filing in court, which should be advertised, would enable the court to adjudicate on any future disputes.

4.4 Directors would continue to manage the business, leaving it to the nominee to return to court if he considered a CVA was no longer a realistic prospect or that the directors had entered the process in bad faith. In this event the nominee would be required to inform all creditors of his decision and the reasons for the decision. The moratorium would end immediately, although views are sought in paragraph 2.10(a) on whether there should be three days' grace for floating chargeholders to appoint an administrative receiver before other creditors are allowed to take any action.

4.5 Statutory super priority could be introduced for funding provided during the moratorium — ie short term funding would have priority over other creditors (with the exception of the IP's costs which would be a first charge on the estate). Views are sought.

4.6 The nominee would call a meeting of the company's creditors within 28 days, either to approve proposals, or to approve an extension of the moratorium, or to put the company into liquidation or full administration (or a floating charge-holder could appoint an administrative receiver). A majority in excess of 75% in value of all creditors present in person or by proxy and voting would be required.

No meeting of shareholders would be held unless the company's balance sheet showed a net asset position, in which case more than 50% in value of the members present in person or by proxy and voting on the resolution, subject to any express provision in the articles, should be required to approve the scheme.

4.7 An extension of the moratorium would happen automatically (unless the court directed otherwise) if more than 75% in value of the creditors present in person or by proxy and voting agreed, but it would be limited to three months in all with a possible exceptional provision, subject to court satisfaction, for an extension to the moratorium to a maximum of six months.

4.8 If the proposal were accepted, the nominee would become supervisor and the CVA would proceed as currently.

4.9 A provision should be introduced to enable a creditors' committee to be formed at any time.

4.10 As now, application could be made to the court if the voluntary arrangement unfairly prejudiced the interests of a creditor, member or contributory of the company, or there was material irregularity at or in relation to a meeting.

4.11 Unknown or unnotified creditors would be bound, unless there would be a material effect on the agreed proposal or unless there had been deliberate concealment by the directors, at which time there would be an option to call a creditors' meeting to renegotiate the scheme.

4.12 Secured creditors should give the company seven days' notice of their intention to appoint an administrative receiver during which time the directors would be able to file for a CVA. The rights of secured creditors would be suspended during the moratorium, including the right of a floating charge-holder to appoint an administrative receiver (unless they obtained leave of the court). Secured creditors would be entitled to vote on the whole of their debt, and if no scheme is agreed floating chargeholders could then if they wished appoint an administrative receiver.

SOURCE 307
Revised Proposals for a New Company Voluntary Arrangement Procedure
(DTI Insolvency Service, April 1995)

The proposed new procedure would be available in addition to the existing CVA procedure set out in Part I of the Insolvency Act 1986 which would continue to be used where a moratorium is unnecessary and by administrators and liquidators.
The key elements of the new scheme are:

– An initial 28 day moratorium during which creditors will not be able to take action against the company (unless the court gives leave). This will provide a necessary breathing space for companies to assess rescue prospects and, if appropriate, come to a binding arrangement with creditors. The manage-ment will remain in control but will be subject to supervision and a restriction on the disposal of assets. There will be other safeguards to prevent abuse. The moratorium will be binding on all creditors, including secured creditors.
– Floating chargeholders will be required to give the company 5 working days notice of their intention to appoint an administrative receiver. This will give the company a short time to see whether a CVA is appropriate. The notice can be abridged where the company consents or where the court gives leave. There will be provisions to prevent disposal of assets during that period and penalties for abuse. An outline of the new procedure is given below. . . .

NEW CVA PROCEDURE — THE OUTLINE

(1) The directors of the company approach a potential nominee who assesses whether the company is suitable for a CVA.

(2) The nominee's assessment will be based on information supplied by the directors, any negotiations he considers appropriate with the company's bankers, major creditors and suppliers, and upon the availability of funding.

(3) If the nominee considers that a CVA should be proposed and that a stay is necessary or desirable, a 28 day moratorium can be obtained for the company by filing the following documents at court:

(a) notice of the prospective CVA;
(b) the prospective nominee's consent to act;
(c) a statement by the directors that the information they have supplied to the nominee is correct and the company has not had an earlier moratorium

which has expired or otherwise come to an end in the preceding 12 months;

(d) a statement by the nominee that in his opinion there is a reasonable prospect of a successful CVA and a creditors' meeting should be called;

(e) a statement that no administrative receiver, liquidator, administrator or supervisor is in office; and

(f) a statement that adequate funding is available for the period of the moratorium.

(4) The moratorium prevents any creditor from exercising any enforcement rights they might have against the company and its property without the leave of the court. In addition, no resolution may be passed, nor order made, for the winding up of the company.

(5) The suspension of the right to take action against the company and/or its property is not, however, to prevent set off by debtors/creditors whose debts/credits exist at the date the moratorium commences.

(6) Assets subject to a fixed or crystallised floating charge cannot be disposed of without either the consent of the chargeholder or the agreement of the court.

(7) Where such property is disposed of, the holder of the security will have rights over the sale proceeds and any other property of the company to protect against any shortfall over what would have been realised on a sale in the open market (as is presently the case with administrations).

(8) The moratorium must be advertised in the Gazette and a newspaper, and notice must be filed with the Registrar of Companies.

(9) A floating chargeholder must give the company 5 working days prior notice of its intention to appoint an administrative receiver unless there has been a moratorium within the previous 12 months.

(10) However, the 5 working days period can be abridged where the company consents to the appointment of an administrative receiver, or where the court gives leave.

(11) During the 5 working days period the company must not dispose of assets other than in the ordinary course of business unless the court grants leave. Specific penalties for unauthorised disposals will be created, including criminal sanctions, civil liability and disqualification.

(12) Meetings of creditors and shareholders must be held within 28 days of the start of the moratorium.

(13) The meetings will:

(a) accept or reject the proposal, as drafted or as modified in the meeting; or

(b) resolve to extend the moratorium beyond the initial 28 day period, with or without conditions but such an additional period is not to exceed 2 months; or

(c) resolve that the moratorium should come to an end.

The meeting may also, where a proposal is accepted or moratorium extended, elect a creditors' committee.

(14) An extension of the moratorium is automatic upon the nominee filing a notice at court indicating the creditors' consent.

(15) A majority in excess of 75% in value of all creditors present or represented and entitled to vote is required to pass any resolution.

(16) Secured creditors can vote for the full amount of their claim.

(17) The directors continue to manage the affairs of the company during the period of the moratorium, but their activities are to be supervised by the nominee. There will be a statutory base level of supervision. Further regulation of activities during the moratorium will be provided by:

(a) criminal sanctions and civil penalties to apply to directors who, for example, conceal, remove or destroy assets and/or records (analogous to compulsory liquidations);
(b) directors to be able to dispose of assets (other than in the ordinary course of business) only with the approval of the nominee, and either the court or the creditors' committee; and
(c) general provision for creditors and shareholders to apply to the courts for relief.

(18) Where a secured creditor has issued a 5 working days notice, the nominee will consider the view of that creditor on the level of supervision required before agreeing to act.

(19) A secured creditor, or any other creditor, can require an additional level of supervision over and above that considered appropriate by the nominee, but it will have to bear the additional cost.

(20) In addition, the level of supervision considered appropriate by the nominee should be endorsed or amended by more than 75% in value of the creditors at the first meeting and any resultant additional cost will be borne by the company.

(21) The nominee must withdraw his consent to act, thereby bringing the moratorium to an end, if he considers that, for whatever reason, a CVA is no longer a viable proposition. He will file notice of the termination at court.

(22) The arrangement is binding on all creditors, including unknown creditors, except creditors whose existence is deliberately concealed by the directors. It is also binding on all shareholders.

(23) The supervisor will be required to convene a further meeting of creditors where the effect of unknown claims would reduce the payment to creditors by 10% or more. At that meeting, creditors may decide either to continue the existing arrangement, bring it to an end, or accept a revised proposal (with or without modifications) which, when accepted, supersedes the existing arrangement.

(24) A meeting may not approve a proposal which would affect the right of a secured creditor to enforce its security without the concurrence of the creditor concerned.

(25) A meeting may not approve a proposal which results in a preferential debt (as defined by section 386 of the Insolvency Act 1986) being paid otherwise than in the usual order of priority afforded such debts or a preferential creditor being paid a lesser proportionate return than that of another preferential creditor unless the preferential creditor concerned agrees.

(26) Following either a nominee's withdrawal or rejection of the proposal, a floating chargeholder can appoint an administrative receiver in the following 12 months. This can be done without first having to give the company 5 working days notice. All other rights of other creditors, suppliers, landlords, shareholders etc are restored.

(27) Where the proposal is rejected by the meeting of creditors, or the moratorium expires, the moratorium is at an end and the nominee must immediately file notice of the termination at court.

(28) Termination of the moratorium whether following rejection of the proposal, by expiry, or by withdrawal of the nominee should be advertised in the

Gazette and a newspaper and a notice filed with the Registrar of Companies. Individual notice should also be given to all those who were notified of the moratorium.

PART III: LIQUIDATION

Getting into Liquidation

An insolvent company may recognise the inevitable and choose to go voluntarily (by special or extraordinary resolution) into liquidation ('creditors' voluntary winding up'). Alternatively, an unpaid creditor can petition the court for an order that the company be placed in liquidation ('compulsory winding up'). Solvent companies may also go into liquidation, either voluntarily ('members voluntary winding up') or compulsorily (for the grounds and the petitioners, see IA 1986, ss 122(1), 124). A case of a solvent company being forced into liquidation is highly likely to arise in a small company resembling a partnership where collaboration among the very few directors has broken down. One may seek the quasi-partnership remedy of having the company wound up on the grounds that this is just and equitable. This is, thus, a minority shareholder's remedy and is discussed above (pp 561ff).

Once established, with liquidators appointed, a creditors' voluntary winding up and a compulsory winding up will function in very similar ways, but obviously the latter will be under closer court control. A compulsory winding up permits a public inspection (under IA 1986, s 133), but a creditors' voluntary winding up does not. (A public inspection is a very rare occurrence). This may be one of the reasons why creditors occasionally petition for the compulsory winding up of a company already in creditors' voluntary winding up (Source 308).

An unpaid creditor whose claim exceeds £750 is, in theory, entitled to a compulsory winding-up order as of right ('ex debito iustitiae'), but occasionally a petition will be refused (Source 309). The courts also stress that the compulsory winding-up process is not appropriate where there is a genuine dispute as to whether the debt is actually owed (Source 310).

A voluntary winding up commences on the date on which the shareholders' resolution is passed. A compulsory winding up is backdated to the date on which the petition is presented. Since all transactions undertaken by the company after the commencement of the winding up are void, the presentation of a winding-up petition has the effect of freezing all the company's activities, unless a validation order is made by the court under IA 1986, s 127.

SOURCE 308
Re Falcon R J Developments Ltd
(Chancery Division 1987) [1987] BCLC 437

VINELOTT J: . . . A petition for the compulsory winding-up of the company was presented by Charrington & Co Ltd on 31 October 1986. It was founded on a judgment debt of just over £1700. The petition was served on 7 November. The date fixed for hearing on presentation of the petition was 8 December. Shortly before the petition was presented the directors of the company, that is Mr R. J. Johnson and his wife, had convened an extraordinary general meeting of the company for 27 November to consider a resolution for its winding-up, and a meeting of its creditors. Notices convening the meetings were sent out on 27 October.

At the extraordinary general meeting the resolution was duly passed. A Mr P. M. Hughes-Holland was appointed liquidator. The meeting of creditors followed immediately afterwards. Mr R. J. Johnson was the chairman of the board of directors and he took the chair at the meeting of the creditors, pursuant to section 588(3)(b) of the Companies Act 1985. A resolution was proposed by a creditor, Woodley Hill Construction Co Ltd, which I will call 'Woodley Hill', for the appointment of a Ms Bairstow of Arthur Young & Co as liquidator.

. . . at the meeting all the creditors who attended or who were represented by persons who attended the meeting except one (whose claim for some £6000 had been admitted by Mr Hughes-Holland) voted in favour of the resolution. But Mr R. J. Johnson held general proxies given to the chairman at the meeting and entitling him to exercise the creditors' votes at his discretion. On a proxy vote, the proxies held by Mr R. J. Johnson together with the votes exercised in respect of the in-house debt sufficed to defeat the resolution.

. . .

Some ten days after the creditors' meeting, on 8 December, the petition came before the court. An affidavit had been filed by Mr Hughes-Holland and an affidavit by Mr R. J. Johnson sworn on that day was produced at the hearing. The hearing was adjourned to 15 December to give Charringtons an opportunity of considering that evidence. In the interim, Charringtons, whose debt of course was comparatively small, decided that it did not wish to continue with the petition. Woodley Hill applied to be substituted. Charringtons was added to the list as a supporting creditor. The petition was stood over to 14 January and then to 20 January. On 15 December the names of 43 creditors appeared on the list (including those added to the list on the usual undertakings) as supporting creditors: there were 12 opposing creditors. Due to pressure of business, the petition was not heard on 20 January but was stood over to 2 February.

This case thus raises in an acute form the question whether if a voluntary liquidation has been commenced before the hearing of a petition a compulsory winding-up order should be made if supported by creditors with the largest stake in the outcome, and if so, what weight should be given to the views of the directors and others associated with the failed company.

I turn to the authorities. It is unnecessary to refer to any authorities prior to the decision of the Court of Appeal in *Re J. D. Swain Ltd*.[1]

In *Re Medisco Equipment Ltd*,[2] a company went into creditors' voluntary winding-up in February 1983. A petition was subsequently presented by a creditor with an undisputed debt of £105,000. The petition was heard in June 1983. At the hearing the petition was opposed by two creditors, both directors and shareholders, with debts amounting in the aggregate to just under £60,000. There were 13 small trade creditors who initially appeared to oppose the petition. At the adjourned hearing they played no part. Harman J refused to make a compulsory order.

. . . he posed the following question:

'If that is the principle which I have to consider and apply to this case, what

1 [1965] 1 WLR 909; [1965] 2 All ER 761
2 [1983] BCLC 305; (1983) 1 BCC, 98, 944

is there to show that the class remedy — and I do stress that in winding-up one is considering always a class remedy and not a private *lis* between the petitioner and the company — is inadequate?'

With the greatest respect to Harman J I am not satisfied that that is the correct approach. In *Re J. D. Swain Ltd* the Court of Appeal upheld the refusal of Pennycuick J to make a compulsory order not simply on the ground that the petitioning and supporting creditors would obtain a class remedy whether the voluntary winding-up was continued or was superseded by a compulsory winding-up, but upon the ground that the majority of the creditors preferred the continuance of the voluntary winding-up.

. . .

If a resolution for a voluntary winding-up has been passed, the assets of the company are held on the statutory trust for the creditors (in *Re J. D. Swain*, as in the present case, the unsecured creditors). The court should not lightly overrule the views of those with the largest stake in the assets of the company as to whether the assets should be administered in the course of a compulsory or in the course of voluntary winding-up. I think the explanation of the decision of Harman J[1] may be that he was satisfied that in the circumstances of that case the petitioning creditor (there were no supporting creditors) was acting unreasonably in persisting with the petition. By the time the petition was heard, the voluntary liquidator had been in office for some four or five months. Counsel for the petitioning creditor conceded that the switch to a compulsory order would delay distribution and add substantially to the costs. Harman J clearly took the view that it would be better for all the creditors, including the petitioning creditor, that the voluntary winding-up should be concluded as speedily as possible, and that the petitioning creditor was being perverse or even masochistic in persisting with the petition.

In two more recent cases, Hoffmann J has made a compulsory order even though a voluntary winding-up had been commenced when the petition was heard and even though no attack was made on the probity or the competence of the voluntary liquidator.

. . .

In *Re Lowestoft Traffic Services*[2] (as in *Medisco*) the voluntary winding-up commenced before the petition was presented. The creditors supporting and opposing were roughly equal in number, but the amount of the debt owed to the supporting creditors was over four times the amount owed to the opposing creditors. Morever, six out of ten of the opposing creditors were directors or employees of the company. There was evidence suggesting that the assets of the company had been transferred to a new company controlled by the same directors and shareholders as the old company, and prima facie evidence that the directors had been guilty of fraudulent trading. Hoffmann J rejected a submission that the onus was on the petitioning creditor. He said, . . .

'It was suggested that there is an onus on the petitioning creditor to justify the making of a winding-up order, but I am not sure that the concept of an onus can easily be applied to a case in which the discretion requires a number of matters to be taken into account. One of these must certainly be the number, value and quality of the creditors who favour a winding-up order as against those who do not. In this case the numbers are equal, but the quantity of the debts of those who favour a winding-up is very

---

1 In *Re Medisco*
2 [1986] BCLC 81; (1986) 2 BCC 98, 946

considerably greater than those who do not. In addition, it is, I think, proper to discount the opposition of those opposing creditors who are closely associated with the management of the company, particularly when, as in this case, it is said that the main reason why there should be an order for compulsory winding-up is the necessity for an independent investigation into their management.'

He made a compulsory order on the grounds that:

'It is important that where there are matters to be investigated the liquidator should do so with competence and integrity, but I think it is also in the public interest that the creditors should have confidence in his independence. It is well known, and a matter of frequent public sandal, that directors of insolvent companies occasionally succeed in transferring the assets and goodwill to a new company, often at the same premises, and start up in business again as if nothing had changed, leaving their creditors unpaid. Where it appears that something of that kind may have happened, and where, as in this case, there is prima facie evidence of a serious case of fraudulent trading by those directors, I think that the public interest requires that the liquidator should not only be independent. Certain criticisms have been made of the way in which Mr Edgar (the liquidator) has so far conducted this liquidation. But there does not seem to me to be anything to show that Mr Edgar has failed in his duties as liquidator. Nonetheless, through no fault whatever of Mr Edgar himself, the circumstances in which he was appointed understandably caused disquiet to the petitioning and supporting creditors, and I think it would be wrong for that state of disquiet to continue.'

In *Re Palmer Marine Surveys Ltd*[1] the petition preceded the notices convening the meetings to commence a voluntary winding-up. At the meeting of creditors, most of the creditors were excluded. One creditor who was admitted proposed the appointment of a member of a well-known firm of accountants as liquidator. That resolution was defeated by the use of proxy votes, although it was defeated by number and not value. The liquidator appointed by the members remained in office. At the hearing of the petition it was supported by three creditors with debts which far exceeded the debts due to the seven creditors who opposed. Two of the opposing creditors were companies controlled by the principal director. On the basis of the statement of affairs produced at the creditors' meeting the unsecured creditors had no prospect of receiving any dividend.

Hoffmann J summarised the decision of the Court of Appeal in *Re J. D. Swain Ltd* (which he described, incorrectly I think, as a case where the voluntary winding-up had commenced before the petition was presented) and referred to the decision of Harman J in *Re Medisco Equipment* in a passage which I should cite:

'Even if the creditors in favour of a continuation of the voluntary liquidation are a minority in value, the court may refuse a compulsory order if there appears to be no advantage to creditors in making one: see *Re Medisco Equipment Ltd*, in which the voluntary winding-up had been almost completed and a compulsory order would only have added to the expense. The court may also take into account not only the value of the debts but the possible or probable motives of the creditors in making their choice. Thus

---

1 [1986] 1 WLR 573; [1986] BCLC 106

creditors who are also shareholders or connected with the former management may have less weight given to their views than those who have no
interest except in their capacity as creditors.'

He summarised his reasons for making a compulsory order in the following
passage:

'Besides counting debts, I think I am also entitled to have regard to the
general principles of fairness and commercial morality which underlie the
details of the insolvency law as applied to companies. A judicial exercise of
discretion should not leave substantial independent creditors with a strong
and legitimate sense of grievance. In my judgment the continuation of the
voluntary winding-up would leave the petitioning creditor with a justifiable
feeling of unfair treatment in two respects. First, whatever may have been
the technical position under the winding-up Rules, the petitioning creditor
was entitled to be aggrieved at its exclusion from the creditors' meeting on
29 January. It is no answer that the result of the vote would have been the
same even if all the excluded creditors had been admitted. As a creditor
which stood to lose a very large sum of money, McKees (that is the
petitioning creditor) were in fairness entitled at least to be heard and to ask
questions. Secondly, in a case in which there is evidence to suggest that
assets have been transferred for inadequate value to an associated company,
the independent trade creditors should ordinarily be entitled to have the
company's affairs investigated by a liquidator who is not merely independent but who can be seen to be independent. The public is frequently
astonished by the ease with which unsuccessful businessmen appear to be
able to transfer the assets, goodwill, premises and employees of an insolvent
company to a pristine entity with which they continue trading as before,
leaving the creditors unpaid. This may be the price which has to be paid for
the entrepreneurial incentives of limited liability. But in cases in which it
appears to have happened, thorough investigation is required. Disap-
pointed creditors are bound to view with cynicism any investigation undertaken by a liquidator chosen by the very persons whose conduct is under
suspicion. There is no criticism in this case of the integrity or competence
of Mr Smith (the liquidator). But the fact that he was chosen by Mr Davis
(the majority shareholder) and that Mr Davis has gone to great lengths to
maintain him in office is itself enough to disqualify him in the eyes of the
petitioning and supporting creditors. Although this involves no reflection
on Mr Smith, I do not think that the creditors attitude can be simply
rejected as irrational. It is something which the court should take into
account.'

In *Re Lowestoft Traffic Services Co Ltd* and in *Re Palmer Marine Surveys Ltd* there
was a large preponderance in the aggregate amount to the debt owed to the
petitioning and supporting creditors over the amount owed to the opposing
creditors, and in both cases there were very strong reasons why the court should
not have interfered with the wishes of the majority. However, the observations of
Hoffmann J which I have cited afford valuable guidance as to the principles on
which the court's discretion should be exercised. In particular, the court is not
bound to give equal weight to all debts of equal amount. It must also have regard
to other interests which may influence the views of a particular creditor. And the
court is entitled to take into account 'general principles of fairness and morality
which underlie the details of insolvency law'.

The main ground relied on for making a compulsory order is that there are, it is said, matters which call for investigation in the winding-up which ought not to be left to a liquidator chosen by the directors, but should be conducted by somebody who is not only independent but seen to be independent.

. . .

Mr Goldblatt[1] submitted that the petitioning and supporting creditors had not shown that there was any sufficient reason to override the wishes of the majority of the creditors that the voluntary winding-up should continue. I accept that submission to this extent. If there had been a majority of outside creditors who wanted the voluntary winding-up to continue, their wishes would, I think, have prevailed against the petitioning and supporting creditors. No substantial reason has been advanced calling into question the ability and willingness of Mr Hughes-Holland to conduct the winding-up properly and fairly and if any investigation is called for it can conveniently and adequately be made in a voluntary winding-up (see *Re B. Karsberg Ltd*[2]).

But equally, if the wishes of Mr R. J. Johnson[3] and the associated companies are disregarded, I see no good reason why the wishes of the outside creditors should be overridden. The interposition of a compulsory winding-up may give rise to expense and delay and, of course, the outside creditors will lose the benefit of the postponement of the in-house debt. But it is for creditors to decide whether those advantages are outweighed by the advantage of having the official receiver take over the winding-up as provisional liquidator and of being able in due course to choose whether he or some other liquidator should continue in office at a meeting at which the voting will not be dominated by proxy votes exercised by Mr R. J. Johnson. I can see no reason why the views of the majority as to what is in their best interest should not prevail. There is no reason why the court should impose on them its own view as to what is in their best interests. That is a commercial decision. If that is right then the only question is whether the in-house debt should be taken into account and in effect given a determinative weight in favour of the continuance of voluntary winding-up.

I do not think it should. There are two reasons. First, Mr R. J. Johnson's preference for voluntary winding-up is not a preference founded on his interest or the interests of the associated companies as creditors. If there is a voluntary winding-up then the in-house debt would be postponed. Mr R. J. Johnson's preference for a winding-up is founded on reasons personal to himself and the associated companies; he is prepared to sacrifice the in-house debt in the expectation that, if there is a voluntary winding-up, and if the amount of the in-house debt is in effect added to the amount distributed to the outside creditors, his commercial reputation will suffer less than it otherwise would have done and he and his associated companies will be better placed in the future. A view founded on such considerations of personal advantage should not be allowed to outweigh the views of the majority of the other creditors as to what is in the interests of the creditors simply as creditors.

Secondly, the majority of the outside creditors would I think be left with a legitimate sense of grievance if, against their wishes, the winding-up of the company is left in the hands of a liquidator chosen and confirmed in office by the combined use of votes exercisable (whether by virtue of the in-house debt or by the use of general proxies) by the person who had control of the company during

---

1 Counsel for the opposing creditors
2 [1956] 1 WLR 57; [1955] 3 All ER 854
3 The controlling shareholder

its relatively brief life and whom they are entitled to treat as prima facie responsible for its insolvency.

In my judgment, the majority of outside creditors, without calling into question the probity or competence of Mr Hughes-Holland, are entitled to say that, faced with a choice between a compulsory winding-up and a voluntary winding-up conducted by a man chosen and put into office by Mr R. J. Johnson they prefer a compulsory winding-up.

Compulsory winding-up order granted.

SOURCE 309
Re Brendacot Ltd
(Chancery Division 1986) (1986) 2 BCC 99,164

HARMAN J: I have before me a petition for the compulsory winding-up of Brendacot Ltd. It raises a very unusual situation. The petitioning creditor was the landlord of the company and he petitions in respect of a debt of £5,028 which includes some sums in respect of rates and water rate. It appears quite likely that about £800 of the moneys included in the debt for rates and water rate is not in fact due because a void allowance was given by the relevant authority, and the undisputed amount of the debt appears to be about £4,200 or so.

The petition is opposed by the company (against whom the creditor is entitled *ex debito justitiae* to his order and whose opposition I therefore regard as of the slightest importance) and four opposing creditors whose debts total £22,000-odd. The opposition is thus in a majority in number and in value over the petitioning creditor. However, following the classic guidelines set out by Diplock LJ in *Re J D Swain Ltd*[1] the mere fact of a majority in number and value is not a sufficient reason to deprive the petitioning creditor of the class remedy of a winding-up which he seeks when there is not offered the class remedy in the form of a voluntary winding-up.

Here, the opposing creditors wish there to be neither a voluntary nor a compulsory winding-up. They give as their reason — they all being independent persons wholly unconnected with the company — that there is in progress an informal winding-up of the company. It has, I understand, ceased to trade due to differences between its directors, ceased to occupy the premises in respect of which the petition debt is founded and is undoubtedly insolvent — insolvent to a very substantial degree.

In those circumstances an informal creditors' meeting was held on 31 January of this year at which a substantial number of creditors attended, having been circularised with a notice of the meeting. At that meeting some ten creditors indicated that they would prefer an informal winding-up under the charge of a gentleman, Mr Shinegold, who trades as 'Mercantile Business Services' and is himself one of the opposing creditors, for the comparatively small sum of £930. Those ten were all, as far as one can see, independent trade creditors. Only three of them appear before me today. Two of the trade creditors attending indicated that they wished for a compulsory order to be made for the petition to succeed (it being already on foot). Thus, adding the petitioning creditor, who did not attend, there was a majority in number, ten-to-three, expressing their view at that informal meeting, and a majority in value of a very substantial amount — I think about £35,000 as against about £6,000 — against a compulsory order.

. . .

Mr Sheldon for the opposing creditors puts forward the point that there is a real commercial reason why it is in the interests of all the class of unsecured creditors that the order should not be made. He points out that there are debts to the Crown, in the form both of the Inland Revenue for PAYE and National Insurance contributions and of H.M. Customs & Excise for VAT, which debts are not at the moment preferential but which debts would probably (it is uncertain) become preferential to a substantial (it is undisclosed exactly how great an) extent upon an order being made or upon a resolution for a voluntary winding-up being passed. Those debts are of the order of £23,000 and if a substantial part of those debts were preferential it would very substantially erode the prospect that Mr Shinegold holds out of paying dividends to unsecured creditors regularly at a rate, he hopes, of around perhaps 40 per cent or a little more of their debts.

. . .

There is one further point which Mr Kay for the petitioner raises as being in favour of a compulsory order, and that is that there are at present garnishee proceedings with an order nisi in respect of some £5,000-odd claimed by a judgment creditor who has garnished the bank account of the company. If a compulsory order is made, there is no doubt whatever that that garnishee order nisi will never become absolute. It is suggested, on what appear to me to be sound grounds, that it may yet very well not be necessary to have a compulsory order in order to avoid the garnishee proceedings becoming absolute.

Mr Sheldon, supporting the affidavit of the opposing creditors' solicitor Mr Judge, says that Mr Judge's opinion put forward in his affidavit, that there are, not a guarantee, but good prospects that the garnishee order will not be made absolute and the order nisi will be set aside, is sound if there is an informal scheme for distribution amongst creditors going forward. Mr Sheldon has referred me to the White Book and the relevant passages in it. It does appear from those passages that there is, as Mr Judge says, certainly at the least a good chance — and probably, I think on the authorities, a fairly high chance — that the garnishee order will not be made absolute, if an informal scheme is in force. Mr Sheldon, of course, accepts that a guarantee is better than a high chance, but he says it is a very small difference and there is not a sufficient commercial reason in favour of a compulsory order in that small balance.

If it were the case that it were probable that the garnishee order would be made absolute if there were no compulsory order, that would be a powerful reason, as I see it, in favour of a compulsory order. I am satisfied by Mr Sheldon's submissions that Mr Judge's opinion is soundly based and that there are good prospects of avoiding the order becoming absolute: and therefore that reason for making a compulsory order does not press upon me.

Although this is a case where the class remedy is denied to a creditor who is entitled *ex debito justitiae* to his remedy as against the company, it is denied by a plain majority, both at the informal meeting of creditors and in the appearance before me, both in number and in value, who do put forward reasons which are properly described as good commercial reasons why the remedy should not be available. In my view the majority, in that circumstance, are entitled to have their voice prevail. And, following the guidelines set out by Diplock LJ, I shall refuse to make a compulsory order, and dismiss this petition.

[Petition dismissed.]

SOURCE 310
Re R A Foulds Ltd
(Chancery Division 1986) (1986) 2 BCC 99,269

HOFFMANN J: This is a motion to strike out a winding-up petition on the ground that it is based upon a disputed debt.

[The judge analysed the evidence and continued:]

Upon [the] evidence it seems to me clear that at the time when the petition was presented the petitioning creditor was unquestionably a creditor of the company, that is as to £1100 admitted in the evidence. Deducting, as I have said, at least £4500 from the claim for damage for the 'as fitted' drawings, it seems to me plain that the petitioning creditor was unquestionably owed a substantially larger amount.

At this point I think I should turn to the law. It has been the practice of the court, at any rate since the decision of Ungoed-Thomas J in *Mann v Goldstein*[1] to treat as an abuse of the process of the court a petition which is presented upon the basis of a debt which is bona fide disputed on substantial grounds. That is regarded as an improper use of the machinery of a winding-up petition. The reason is that the presentation of a winding-up petition puts very great pressure on the company and it is not right for that pressure to be used in order to induce the company to abandon a fairly arguable defence to the claim. However, that does not mean that the petitioning creditor must be able to show that it is owed any particular quantified amount. It was decided by Plowman J in *Re Tweeds Garages Ltd*[2] that it is sufficient if the petitioning creditor is definitely a creditor as to some part of its claim. In those circumstances it is a creditor and has the necessary *locus standi* to present a petition. Its presentation of the petition cannot therefore be said to be an abuse of the process of the court. The position may be different when at the hearing of the petition it is sought to rely upon failure to comply with a statutory notice under what is now section 518(1)(a) of the Companies Act 1985. Where on the hearing there is no other evidence of insolvency and the sole matter relied upon as justifying the making of a winding-up order is failure to comply with the statutory demand, it may be necessary for the petitioning creditor to demonstrate — and I think there is authority to support this — that some precise sum which ought to have been paid was in fact due. That is however not the case where the petitioning creditor simply relies upon showing in general that the company is insolvent. In this case, although statutory notices have been served, the petitioning creditor does not for the purposes of this motion seek to rely upon them. What it says is that the petition ought not at this stage to be struck out if it is shown that it may, on its eventual hearing, appear that the company is in fact insolvent without resort to the presumption created by section 518(1)(a).

The result therefore is that in accordance with the case of *Tweeds Garages* the petitioning creditor at the time when it presented its petition was a creditor and did have *locus standi* to present its petition. It could not therefore be struck out as an abuse of the process of the court, and in the ordinary way this motion would have to be dismissed. During the short adjournment, however, on the second day of the hearing of the motion the company, having regard to the way in which the figures have been analysed in the course of argument, made an open offer to the petitioning creditor to pay, by way of banker's draft, the sum of £10,129. The

1 [1968] 1 WLR 1091; [1968] 2 All ER 769
2 [1962] 1 Ch 406; [1962] 1 All ER 121

banker's draft was actually for £10,000 and the other £129 was offered on an undertaking by the solicitors. That, it was said, meant that there was now clearly a dispute as to the remaining part of the debt and therefore, on the basis of *Mann v Goldstein* the petitioning creditor no longer had *locus standi* to continue with the petition. While it may have been proper for the petition to have been presented originally, its further prosecution would be an abuse of the process of the court.

I think I should say quite openly that while I have loyally applied the principle in *Mann v Goldstein*, there have been occasions upon which I have felt uneasy about the consequences of doing so. A typical case (frequently within the construction industry) is that a petition is presented against a company which in fact is unable to pay its debts as they fall due and is under considerable pressure from its creditors. The creditors however, in the nature of things, do not know what each of them separately is doing or is owed and the company is able to deal with them separately. The company has overdraft facilities from its bank which are secured by a fixed and floating charge and the bank is not for the moment disposed to withdraw that facility. However, the company may be trading at a loss without the directors being in any way guilty of fraudulent trading, either because they do not have sufficient management information to know precisely how the company is faring or because they take an optimistic view of how future contracts will work out. At the same time the company is falling into arrears with payment of its PAYE and VAT. A petition is, as I say, presented and before advertisement a motion is launched to strike it out on the grounds that the debt is disputed. It comes before the courts with evidence indicating that there are conflicts of fact on affidavit and often raising questions which, for example, in a case in the construction industry, may be familiar to Official Referees but which require an experience which, at any rate speaking for myself, the Companies Court does not necessarily have. The result is that the court holds that there is a triable issue between the parties, the debt is disputed, and the petition is struck out. The company then goes on trading, the overdraft increases or there are further losses, there are further arrears in PAYE and VAT, which in the end rank as preferential debts, and when the company is finally wound up some months later there is a good deal less for unsecured creditors than there would have been if it had been wound up on the original petition. This flows from the fact that under the principle in *Mann v Goldstein* a petition based upon a disputed debt must be struck out without regard to the question of whether the company is solvent.

In this case there are two differences from the normal *Mann v Goldstein* situation. The first may be regarded as somewhat technical. That is that the debt as such is not disputed, at any rate as to the amount which has been certified. What is said is that there are cross-claims which, taking into account £10,000 odd which has now been tendered, would extinguish the remaining undisputed debt.

In *Re Euro Hotel (Belgravia) Limited*[1] Megarry J said that in such a case the principle did not require the petition to be struck out in the same way as if the basic debt had been disputed. They way he put it was:

> 'A disputed debt will not support a winding-up petition, and whether an undisputed debt that is overtopped by a disputed cross-debt will support a petition is for the exercise of a judicial discretion.'

I say that this is a somewhat technical distinction because on the face of it it is

---

1 [1975] 3 All ER 1075; [1975] STC 682

hard to see the difference between a disputed debt and a dispute which consists of alleging that by virtue of a set-off nothing is in fact owing. None the less that decision suggests that the court has a more general discretion than it would have in the ordinary *Mann v Goldstein* case. Secondly — and this I regard as a difference of substance rather than technicality — it cannot be said in this case that the presentation of the petition was an abuse of the process of the court. I have found that when the petition was presented the petitioning creditor undoubtedly had *locus standi* to do so. It is frequently said that in presenting a petition the creditor is not merely exercising a personal right but a class right on behalf of all creditors. That is why the petition is advertised, so that other creditors may have the opportunity to come in and oppose or support the making of the winding-up order, and on the hearing of the petition any winding-up order that is made is deemed to be made on behalf of all creditors and contributories. It therefore seems to me that if a petition has properly been presented the question of whether it should be allowed to go on to a hearing and be advertised, even though there has since been a payment in respect of the undisputed part of the debt, should be one for the discretion of the court and in exercising that discretion the court should take into account the evidence as to the solvency of the company. If it appears to the court likely that the company is insolvent and that upon the hearing of the petition even if the remaining debt to the petitioning creditor is held to be disputed and therefore not sufficient to found a petition, none the less there will be other creditors with undisputed debts who may be substituted and who will be entitled to an order, then the petition ought to be allowed to proceed. One is not in that case making a winding-up order upon the basis of the undisputed debt. One is merely refraining from striking out the petition until the evidence is complete and the views of other creditors can be ascertained.

I am of course conscious that if I allow the petition to proceed and be advertised and the company is not in fact able to pay its debts as they fall due, the chances are that it will be wound up, whereas if the petition were struck out now it may well be able to survive, and I suppose it is possible, because I do not know the exact state of the company's financial affairs, that it may be able to trade out of its difficulties. I am also conscious that this company, according to the evidence, employs about 18 people who would be affected by its ultimate winding-up. However, I must also bear in mind the injustices which would be caused to creditors along the lines that I indicated earlier if an insolvent company were allowed to continue to trade and increase its secured and preferential debt at the expense of the unsecured creditors. In this particular industry I think one must also bear in mind that companies which delay payment of their debts thereby cause hardship and sometimes insolvency to other persons in the industry who also have their employees.

[The judge then considered the evidence as to the company's solvency, and continued:]

> That being the state of the evidence as to the company's solvency and solvency being in my view a matter which in the circumstances of this case I can take into account in the exercise of my discretion, I think that this is a case in which the petition ought to go forward and the question of whether the company should be wound up or not decided, not today in a summary fashion upon these affidavits, but upon the date fixed for its hearing when the other creditors have been given the opportunity to make their views known. Therefore, in my judgment, the right order is that in spite of the offer which was made yesterday afternoon, I should

refuse to grant the injunction restraining advertisement or to strike out the petition.

The Conduct of the Liquidation

The liquidator has a vast array of statutory powers. There are the general powers set out in ss 165–169 of, and Sch 4 to the Insolvency Act 1986. In addition, the liquidator has powers to augment the estate by seeking to set aside the pre-liquidation transactions which have the effect of preferring one creditor to the others (ss 238–245, Source 311) and powers to seek contributions to the estate (a) from anyone responsible for causing the company to carry on business with intent to defraud creditors (s 213), and (b) from directors, including shadow directors, for failing to take all necessary steps to avoid further loss to creditors when they realised that insolvent liquidation was unavoidable ('wrongful trading', s 214). The liquidator's powers under ss 213 and 214 remove the protection of limited liability and are discussed in Chapter 2 (pp 62ff). The liquidator also has the power of disclaiming onerous contracts (ss 178–179).

SOURCE 311
Re M C Bacon
(Chancery Division) [1990] BCLC 324

MILLETT J: MC Bacon Ltd (the company) was formed in 1973 as part of a management buy-out by Mr Michael Creal (Mr Creal), Mr Sidney Glover (Mr Glover) and Mr Alex Knight (Mr Knight). It carried on business as a bacon importer and wholesaler. Mr Creal and Mr Glover were executive directors and ran the business. Mr Knight was a non-executive director who had helped to finance the buy-out, and his shareholding was eventually bought in by the company.

Traditional bacon was the cornerstone of the business for the first 10 years. In 1983, in response to the requirements of its principal customer, Dee Corporation, the company diversified into the supply of pre-packaged manufactured products such as gammon steaks, gammon joints and rashered bacon, and ran down the traditional side of the business. In December 1986 Dee Corporation, which by then was responsible for nearly 60% of the company's turnover, abruptly withdrew its custom. Mr Creal and Mr Glover considered putting the company into immediate liquidation but, after taking legal advice, they decided to continue trading. A substantial number of employees were made redundant and the company attempted to regain sales volume with reduced overheads, but it made substantial losses as well as incurring liability to make redundancy payments in the process. It struggled on for some months but was unsuccessful. It eventually went into creditors' voluntary liquidation on 24 August 1987 with an estimated deficiency as regards unsecured creditors of £329,435.

At the date of liquidation the company's overdraft at the second respondent, National Westminster Bank (the bank) stood at £235,530. The overdraft was secured by a debenture dated 20 May 1987 granted by the company. On 4 September 1987 the bank demanded payment and on the same day it appointed the first respondent as administrative receiver of the company. The applicant was appointed liquidator of the company at a meeting of creditors on 7 September 1987.

The applicant now claims to have the debenture set aside (i) under s 239 of the

Insolvency Act 1986 (the 1986 Act) as a voidable preference, or (ii) under s 238 of the 1986 Act as a transaction at an undervalue.

. . .

So far as I am aware, this is the first case under . . . section [239] and its meaning has been the subject of some debate before me. I shall therefore attempt to provide some guidance.

The section replaces s 44(1) of the Bankruptcy Act 1914, which in certain circumstances deemed fraudulent and avoided payments made and other transactions entered into in favour of a creditor 'with a view of giving such creditor . . . a preference over the other creditors'. Section 44(1) and its predecessors had been construed by the courts as requiring the person seeking to avoid the payment or other transaction to establish that it had been made 'with the dominant intention to prefer' the creditor.

Section 44(1) has been replaced and its language has been entirely recast. Every single word of significance, whether in the form of statutory definition or in its judicial exposition, has been jettisoned. 'View', 'dominant', 'intention' and even 'to prefer' have all been discarded. These are replaced by 'influenced', 'desire', and 'to produce in relation to that person the effect mentioned in sub-s (4)(*b*)'.

I therefore emphatically protest against the citation of cases decided under the old law. They cannot be of any assistance when the language of the statute has been so completely and deliberately changed. It may be that many of the cases which will come before the courts in future will be decided in the same way that they would have been decided under the old law. That may be so, but the grounds of decision will be different. What the court has to do is to interpret the language of the statute and apply it. It will no longer inquire whether there was 'a dominant intention to prefer' the creditor, but whether the company's decision was 'influenced by a desire to produce the effect mentioned in sub-s (4)(*b*)'.

This is a completely different test. It involves at least two radical departures from the old law. It is no longer necessary to establish a *dominant* intention to prefer. It is sufficient that the decision was *influenced* by the requisite desire. That is the first change. The second is that it is no longer sufficient to establish an *intention* to prefer. There must be a *desire* to produce the effect mentioned in the subsection.

This second change is made necessary by the first, for without it it would be virtually impossible to uphold the validity of a security taken in exchange for the injection of fresh funds into a company in financial difficulties. A man is taken to intend the necessary consequences of his actions, so that an intention to grant a security to a creditor necessarily involves an intention to prefer that creditor in the event of insolvency. The need to establish that such intention was dominant was essential under the old law to prevent perfectly proper transactions from being struck down. With the abolition of that requirement intention could not remain the relevant test. Desire has been substituted. That is a very different matter. Intention is objective, desire is subjective. A man can choose the lesser of two evils without desiring either.

It is not, however, sufficient to establish a desire to make the payment or grant the security which it is sought to avoid. There must have been a desire to produce the effect mentioned in the subsection, that is to say, to improve the creditor's position in the event of an insolvent liquidation. A man is not to be taken as *desiring* all the necessary consequences of his actions. Some consequences may be of advantage to him and be desired by him; others may not affect him and be matters of indifference to him; while still others may be positively disadvantageous to him and not be desired by him, but be regarded by him as the unavoidable price of obtaining the desired advantages. It will still be possible to provide assistance to a company in financial difficulties provided that the company is actuated only by proper commercial considerations. Under the new regime a transaction will not be set aside as a voidable preference unless the company positively wished to improve the creditor's position in the event of its own insolvent liquidation.

There is, of course, no need for there to be direct evidence of the requisite desire. Its existence may be inferred from the circumstances of the case just as the dominant intention could be inferred under the old law. But the mere presence of the requisite desire will not be sufficient by itself. It must have influenced the decision to enter into the transaction. It was submitted on behalf of the bank that it must have been the factor which 'tipped the scales'. I disagree. That is not what sub-s (5) says; it requires only that the desire should have influenced the decision. That requirement is satisfied if it was one of the factors which operated on the minds of those who made the decision. It need not have been the only factor or even the decisive one. In my judgment, it is not necessary to prove that, if the requisite desire had not been present, the company would not have entered into the transaction. That would be too high a test.

It was also submitted that the relevant time was the time when the debenture was created. That cannot be right. The relevant time was the time when the decision to grant it was made. In the present case that is not known with certainty. It was probably some time between 15 April and 20 May, although as early as 3 April Mr Glover and Mr Creal had resigned themselves to its inevitability. But it does not matter. If the requisite desire was operating at all, it was operating throughout.

The evidence

Mr Glover and Martin both gave evidence; Mr Creal did not. I accept Martin as a reliable witness. Mr Glover was far from reliable, but I accept him as an honest witness who tried his garrulous best to help the court. His recollection was poor and much of his evidence consisted of inaccurate reconstruction. It was chiefly valuable for the insights it gave of his own and others' motives. He was defensive in relation to his own responsibility for permitting the company to continue to trade and insisted that after 3 April he had ceased to be a director. I am satisfied that he remained a de facto director and that he was a party to and greatly influenced all decisions of importance in relation to financial matters. In relation to the bank's debenture, however, he did not take sides but gave his evidence fairly and impartially. He had either not worked out that it was in the interests of the pension fund, even if it were only an unsecured creditor, that the bank's debenture should be set aside, or, if he had, he did not allow it to affect his evidence.

I am satisfied that throughout the period from 15 April to 29 May Mr Glover, Mr Creal and Martin knew (i) that the company was probably insolvent and might not be able to avoid an insolvent liquidation; (ii) that its continuing to trade was entirely dependent on the continued support of the bank; (iii) that if the debenture which Mr Hill had asked for were not forthcoming the bank would withdraw its support; and (iv) that if the bank withdrew its support the company would be forced into immediate liquidation. I am also satisfied that they had decided to continue trading in a genuine belief that the company could be pulled round. It follows that they had no choice but to accede to the bank's request for a debenture. I accept Martin's evidence: 'It was viewed as a simple decision. Either we gave the bank a debenture or they called in the overdraft.'

That sufficiently explains the decision to grant the debenture and there is no justification for inferring any other reason. There is no evidence that either Martin or Mr Creal wanted to improve the bank's position in the event of an insolvent liquidation and there is no reason why they should. I find as a fact that in deciding to grant the debenture to the bank neither of them was motivated by any desire except the desire to avoid the calling in of the overdraft and to continue trading. That, however, is not the end of the matter. They were greatly influenced by Mr Glover's recommendation that the debenture should be granted, and I turn to examine his evidence to see whether he was influenced by a desire to improve the bank's position in the event of a liquidation for, if he was, then, in my judgment, the company's decision was similarly influenced, even though Mr Glover did not communicate any such desire to the others.

Mr Glover's evidence was to the same effect. He knew that if the company was to continue to trade it had no choice but to grant the debenture. He had a further reason for recommending it to the others. He believed that a debenture was not valid unless the company continued to trade for six months after it was given. Accordingly, he conceived the eccentric notion that if the bank took a debenture it would have to continue to support the company for a further six months.

. . .

I am satisfied that throughout the period Mr Glover's relationship with the bank was an arm's length one and that in dealing with the bank on the company's behalf he was not affected by personal financial considerations.

. . .

Conclusion

I dismiss the applicant's claim to set the debenture aside as a voidable preference.

3 Transaction at an undervalue

Section 238 of the 1986 Act is concerned with the depletion of a company's assets by transactions at an undervalue. Section 238(4) of the Act defines a transaction at an undervalue as follows:

> 'For the purposes of this section and section 241, a company enters into a transaction with a person at an undervalue if — (*a*) the company makes a gift to that person or otherwise enters into a transaction with that person on terms that provide for the company to receive no consideration, or (*b*) the company enters into a transaction with that person for a consideration the value of which, in money or money's worth, is significantly less than the value, in money or money's worth, of the consideration provided by the company.'

The granting of the debenture was not a gift, nor was it without consideration. The consideration consisted of the bank's forbearance from calling in the overdraft and its honouring of cheques and making of fresh advances to the company during the continuance of the facility. The applicant relies therefore on para (*b*).

To come within that paragraph the transaction must be (i) entered into by the company; (ii) for a consideration; (iii) the value of which measured in money or money's worth; (iv) is significantly less than the value; (v) also measured in money or money's worth; (vi) of the consideration provided by the company. It requires a comparison to be made between the value obtained by the company for the transaction and the value of consideration provided by the company. Both values must be measurable in money or money's worth and both must be considered from the company's point of view.

In my judgment, the applicant's claim to characterise the granting of the bank's debenture as a transaction at an undervalue is misconceived. The mere creation of a security over a company's assets does not deplete them and does not come within the paragraph. By charging its assets the company appropriates them to meet the liabilities due to the secured creditor and adversely affects the rights of other creditors in the event of insolvency. But it does not deplete its assets or diminish their value. It retains the right to redeem and the right to sell or remortgage the charged assets. All it loses is the ability to apply the proceeds otherwise than in satisfaction of the secured debt. That is not something capable of valuation in monetary terms and is not customarily disposed of for value.

In the present case the company did not suffer that loss by reason of the grant of the debenture. Once the bank had demanded a debenture the company could not have sold or charged its assets without applying the proceeds in reduction of the overdraft; had it attempted to do so, the bank would at once have called in the overdraft. By granting the debenture the company parted with nothing of value, and the value of the consideration which it received in return was incapable of being measured in money or money's worth.

Counsel for the applicant (Mr Vos) submitted that the consideration which the company received was, with hindsight, of no value. It merely gained time and with it the opportunity to lose more money. But he could not and did not claim that the company ought to have received a fee or other capital sum in return for the debenture. That gives the game away. The applicant's real complaint is not that the company entered into the transaction at an undervalue but that it entered into it at all.

In my judgment, the transaction does not fall within sub-s (4), and it is unnecessary to consider the application of sub-s (5) which provides a defence to the claim in certain circumstances.

4 Conclusion

In my judgment, the granting of the debenture to the bank was neither a voidable preference nor a transaction at an undervalue and I dismiss the application.

General Principles

It is a fundamental principle that all creditors should be treated equally and to this end the court will scrutinise any contract, scheme or arrangement which results in one creditor being more favourably treated than the others (Source 312). The liquidator's powers under ss 238–245, of the Insolvency Act 1986 are designed to further this fundamental principle.

Apart from IA 1986, s 214 (above), at common law it would seem that when the company is insolvent, the prime responsibility of the directors switches from the shareholders to the creditors (Source 313).

SOURCE 312
British Eagle International Airlines Ltd *v* Compagnie Nationale Air France
(House of Lords 1975) [1975] 1 WLR 758; [1975] 2 All ER 390

British Eagle International Airlines Ltd and the respondents, Compagnie Natio-
nale Air France, were airline operators and members of the International Air Transport Association, incorporated in Canada (hereinafter called IATA). IATA established a clearing house for the benefit of its members and both the appellants and the respondents became members of the clearing house on terms

that its regulations, rules of directions should be binding and should be deemed to constitute a contract between the appellants and the respondents respectively and IATA and every other member for the time. The obligation was repeated in similar language in regulation 18(b) of the Clearing House Manual of Procedure as follows:

> 'That it shall be deemed to be an express term of every contract agreement or arrangement for the time being subsisting between any two members in respect of which any debit or credit (being a debit or credit of a type for the time being handled by the clearing house) may arise that the amount of such debit or credit shall be payable or receivable by and through the medium of the clearing house in accordance with the regulations and current clearing procedure and not otherwise in any manner.'

At all material times the procedure of the clearing house provided for monthly clearances by balance clearing, ie the offsetting monthly of the total claimed by a member in respect of services supplied *for* all other members against the totals claimed against a member in respect of services supplied *by* all other members, so that in every case the result would be that a member would be concerned with a single figure, payable to or receivable by the clearing house.

LORD CROSS: . . . I turn now to the rival contentions on the point at issue. The liquidator of British Eagle relies on section 302 of the Companies Act 1948 [now s 107, Insolvency Act] which provides that, subject to the provisions of the Act as to preferential payments,

> 'the property of a company shall, on its winding up, be applied in satisfaction of its liabilities pari passu, and, subject to such application, shall, unless the articles otherwise provide, be distributed among the members according to their rights and interests in the company.'

He submits that the credits to which British Eagle was entitled and the debits to which it became liable in respect of its trading between October 1 and November 6 were, in substance, debts due to and from it, that to give effect to the clearing house arrangements with regard to them would result in what were in substance debts owing to the company being applied not for the general benefit of all creditors but exclusively for the benefit of what may be called the 'clearing house creditors' and that this would infringe the principle embodied in the section.

To this the clearing house — through Air France — replies that what passes into the control of the liquidator on a winding up is the property of the company subject to any rights over it created by the company in favour of others in good faith while it was a going concern; that the interline traffic agreement and the rules and regulations of the clearing house constituted a bona fide commercial contract between the members of the clearing house and IATA; that no one could suggest that the preference the 'clearing house creditors' admittedly obtain as a result of the contract was a 'fraudulent preference' within the meaning of section 302 of the Companies Act 1948 [now s 239, Insolvency Act]; and that the contract is as binding on the liquidator as it was on the company before it went into liquidation.

British Eagle then points out that even though there may be nothing in the Companies Act which deals expressly with a case of this sort the court can always refuse to give effect to provisions in contracts which achieve a distribution of the insolvent's property which runs counter to the principles of our insolvency legislation. In this connection they referred to the case of *Ex parte Mackay*, the headnote in which runs as follows:

'A. sold a patent to B. in consideration of B. paying royalties to A. B. at the same time lent A. £12,500; and it was agreed that B. should retain one-half of the royalties, as they became payable, towards satisfaction of the debt; provided that, if A. became bankrupt . . . B. might retain the whole of the royalties in satisfaction of the debt.'

A having become bankrupt, it was held that B had a lien on half of the royalties only and that the proviso that he might retain the whole of them in case of A's bankruptcy was void.

James LJ in his judgment, after holding that the charge on the first half of the royalties was good, continued as follows . . .

'But, on the other hand, it is equally clear to me that the charge cannot extend to the other moiety. If it were to be permitted that one creditor should obtain a preference in this way by some particular security, I confess I do not see why it might not be done in every case — why, in fact, every article sold to a bankrupt should not be sold under this stipulation that the price should be doubled in the event of his becoming bankrupt. It is contended that a creditor has a right to sell on these terms; but in my opinion a man is not allowed, by stipulation with a creditor, to provide for a different distribution of his effects in the event of bankruptcy from that which the law provides. It appears to me that this is a clear attempt to evade the operation of the bankruptcy laws.'

As Air France was not slow to point out, *Ex parte Mackay* was a very different case from this. There the provision which was impugned effected a change on bankruptcy. Property which up to the date of his bankruptcy was the unencumbered property of the insolvent became on his bankruptcy suddenly saddled with an incumbrance to the detriment of his general creditors and for the benefit of the particular creditor who received the new security. Here by contrast there was no change whatever on the winding-up; the same 'clearing house' provisions applied both before and after 8 November. The preference given to the 'clearing house creditors' in this case is, it was said, analogous to the charge on the first half of the royalties in *Ex parte Mackay* which was held not to have been affected in any way by the bankruptcy.

But an examination of the suggested analogy reveals a weakness in the respondents' case. It is true that if the respondents are right the 'clearing house' creditors will be treated as though they were creditors with valid charges on some of the book debts of British Eagle. But the parties to the 'clearing house' arrangements did not intend to give one another charges on some of each other's future book debts. The documents were not drawn so as to create charges but simply so as to set up by simple contract a method of settling each other's mutual indebtedness at monthly intervals. Moreover, if the documents had purported to create such charges, the charges — as the judge saw — would have been unenforceable against the liquidator for want of registration under section 95 of the Companies Act 1948. The 'clearing house' creditors are clearly not secured creditors. They are claiming nevertheless that they ought not to be treated in the liquidation as ordinary unsecured creditors but that they have achieved by the medium of the 'clearing house' agreement a position analogous to that of secured creditors without the need for the creation and registration of charges on the book debts in question. The respondents argue that the position which, according to them, the clearing house creditors have achieved, though it may be anomalous and unfair to the general body of unsecured creditors, is not forbidden by any provision in the Companies Act, and that the power of the court to go behind agreements, the results of which are repugnant to our insolvency legislation, is confined to cases in which the parties' dominant purpose was to evade its operation. I cannot accept this argument. In *Ex parte Mackay*, the charge on this second half of the royalties was — so to say — an animal known to the law which on its face put the charge in the position of a secured creditor. The court could only go behind it if it was satisfied — as was indeed obvious in that case — that it had been created deliberately in order to provide for a different distribution of the insolvent's property on his bankruptcy from that prescribed by the law. But what the respondents are saying here is that the parties to the 'clearing house' arrangements by agreeing that simple contract debts are to be satisfied in a particular way have succeeded in 'contracting out' of the provisions contained in section 302 for the payment of unsecured debts 'pari passu.' In such a context it is to my mind irrelevant that the parties to the 'clearing house' arrangements had good business reasons for entering into them and did not direct their minds to the question how the arrangements might be affected by the insolvency of one or more of the parties. Such a 'contracting out' must, to my mind, be contrary to public policy. The question is, in essence, whether what was called in argument the 'mini liquidation' flowing from the clearing house arrangements is to yield to or to prevail over the general liquidation. I cannot doubt that on principle the rules of the general liquidation should prevail. I would therefore hold that notwithstanding the clearing house arrangements. British Eagle on its liquidation became entitled to recover payment of the sums payable to it by other airlines for services rendered by it during that period and that airlines which had rendered services to it during that period became on the liquidation entitled to prove for the sums payable to them. So, while dismissing the appeal so far as concerns the September clearance, I would allow it so far as concerns the period from 1 October to 6 November.

SOURCE 313
West Mercia Safetywear Ltd (in liq) *v* Dodd
(Court of Appeal) [1988] BCLC 250

DILLON LJ: This is an appeal from a decision of his Honour Judge Roy Ward QC given in the Worcester County Court on 19 April 1987. The question he had to decide was a question concerning fraudulent preference and misfeasance arising in relation to the liquidation of a company called West Mercia Safetywear Ltd. The present appellant is the liquidator of that company. The respondent to the appeal is a Mr Albert James Dodd, who was at the material time a director of that company.

There is another company involved of which Mr Dodd was also a director, called A J Dodd & Co Ltd. The West Mercia company was, on the affidavits, a wholly-owned subsidiary of the Dodd company.

Both companies banked with Lloyds Bank. The account of the West Mercia company was in credit. The account of the Dodd company was very considerably overdrawn. The bank had a charge to secure the account of the Dodd company on the book debts of the Dodd company, and it also had a guarantee of the Dodd company's account from Mr Dodd himself. The book debts of the Dodd company included a debt which in early May 1984, the relevant time, amounted to about £30,000 due to the Dodd company from the West Mercia company.

In May 1984 both the West Mercia company and the Dodd company were in financial difficulties and, as Judge Ward found, insolvent. The directors, including Mr Dodd, called in an accountant, Mr Nigel Halls, to advise them and to take any necessary steps towards the liquidation of the companies. Mr Halls subsequently became liquidator of both companies when they were put into liquidation, and he is indeed the present appellant.

The evidence clearly establishes that Mr Halls explained very clearly to Mr Dodd and his co-director of the West Mercia company, a Mr Prescott, with whom this appeal is not concerned, that the company bank accounts of the West Mercia company were not thereafter to be operated. The judge says, and I entirely agree:

> 'I cannot believe that the directors thought that, whilst cheques were not to be drawn on either account, *transfers* of money between accounts would be permissible.'

The necessary steps were taken to put both companies into creditors' voluntary liquidation, and the requisite meetings to that end were held on 4 June 1984. In the meantime, however, on 21 May 1984 Mr Dodd instructed Lloyds Bank to transfer £4,000, which had just been paid in by a debtor to the West Mercia company's account, to the overdrawn account of the Dodd company. The plain and obvious intention of that was to reduce the overdraft of the Dodd company which Mr Dodd had personally guaranteed.

. . .

For my part I find helpful, and would approve, the statement of Street CJ in *Kinsela v Russell Kinsela Pty Ltd (in liq)* (1986) 4 NSWLR 722 at 730, where he said:

> 'In a solvent company the proprietary interests of the shareholders entitle them as a general body to be regarded as the company when questions of the duty of directors arise. If, as a general body, they authorise or ratify a particular action of the directors, there can be no challenge to the validity of what the directors have done. But where a company is insolvent the interests of the creditors intrude. They become prospectively entitled, through the mechanism of liquidation, to displace the power of the shareholders and directors to deal with the company's assets. It is in a practical sense their assets and not the shareholders' assets that, through the medium of the company, are under the management of the directors pending either liquidation, return to solvency, or the imposition of some alternative administration.'

In the present case, therefore, in my judgment Mr Dodd was guilty of breach of duty when, for his own purposes, he caused the £4,000 to be transferred in disregard of the interests of the general creditors of this insolvent company. Therefore the declaration sought in the notice of motion ought to be made as against Mr Dodd.

PART IV: THE INSOLVENCY PRACTITIONER PROFESSION

The Insolvency Act created the profession of insolvency practitioner. Anyone holding the office of liquidator, administrator, administrative receiver, supervisor or nominee of a Corporate Voluntary Arrangement must be a licensed insolvency practitioner (IA 1986, s 230, Pt XIII).

The Insolvency Act gives insolvency practitioners wide powers to insist on the maintenance of utilities supplies (s 233) and to extract information, books, papers etc which might assist the insolvency officer in carrying out his responsibilities (Sources 314, 315).

SOURCE 314
Re Cloverbay (No 2)
[1991] BCLC 135

SIR NICOLAS BROWNE-WILKINSON V-C: This is an appeal from a decision of Harman J sitting in the Companies Court (see sub nom *Re Cloverbay Ltd (No 3)* [1990] BCLC 471). The judge set aside an order made by the registrar under s 236(2)(*c*) of the Insolvency Act 1986 that Bank of Credit and Commerce International SA (BCCI) by two named persons attend to be examined on oath in connection with the affairs of Cloverbay Ltd. The application for that order was made by a Mr Withall and Mr Buller, who had been appointed administrators of Cloverbay by an order of Millett J dated 22 March 1989.

Cloverbay carried on business supplying air conditioning and refrigerating equipment to the Middle East. Its managing director was a Mr Zafar Zaid; his son, Jafar, also played a role in the business. Its bankers included BCCI. Accounts were held at the Brompton Road Branch of BCCI, where the manager at the relevant times was a Mr Rizvi and the assistant manager Mr Malik.

Charterhouse Export Finance Ltd and Charterhouse Export Credit Ltd (Charterhouse) confirmed contracts by suppliers to Cloverbay and provided credit to buyers from Cloverbay. Following the discovery of apparent irregularities, in July 1987 Charterhouse started proceedings in the Commercial Court against BCCI. In the course of that action, Charterhouse obtained orders under the Bankers' Books Evidence Act 1879 requiring the production of certain documents. Among the documents produced were cheques drawn by Cloverbay in favour of persons who, on investigation, claimed to have no knowledge of Cloverbay. Notwithstanding the fact that the crossings on some of the cheques do not appear to have been opened in accordance with Cloverbay's mandate to BCCI, some cheques appear to have been paid out in cash and others to have been indorsed over on behalf of the payees without the authority or knowledge of the payees.

. . .

. . . Charterhouse applied for and obtained the appointment of the joint administrators . . . [T]he administrators issued . . . a protective writ against BCCI claiming, inter alia, breach of the bank's mandate and knowing participation by BCCI in fraudulent breaches of trust.

The joint administrators then obtained from Hoffmann J an ex parte order under s 236 requiring BCCI to produce all books, records and memoranda relating to dealings with Cloverbay's accounts with BCCI. . . .

As a result of that order a large number of other documents were produced by BCCI. . . . The documents produced did not include any contemporaneous memoranda kept by BCCI recording the dealings with the accounts.

All the documents disclosed were put before counsel specialising in banking matters. He expressed the preliminary view that, on the face of it, BCCI's involvement appeared to be as bad a course of conduct on the part of any bank as he had seen but that the administrators would need to investigate further in order to establish whether BCCI had any explanation for what had occurred or, indeed, any other possible defences. Following that advice, the joint administrators applied for the oral examination under s 236 of Mr Rizvi and Mr Malik.

One of the joint administrators, Mr Withall, filed a confidential report in which he stated that he considered that such examination 'would be the only effective way of investigating the manner in which . . . [the] cheques were processed by BCCI', for the following reasons: (1) that the crucial questions are how, when and by whom the crossings on the cheques were opened and indorsed over on the payees' behalf. Those questions can only properly be answered by those who were present at the relevant time and who would understand the working practices of BCCI's branches. Mr Rizvi as the manager and Mr Malik as the assistant manager were the persons who could give such information; (2) it would appear that BCCI was involved in fraudulent activities by Mr Zaid in opening the cheques and indorsing them over. Accordingly, any claim against BCCI would depend on establishing the state of knowledge of BCCI, through its servants, in relation to those transactions.

Before explaining the reasons given by Harman J setting aside the order, I must refer in outline to the applicable law. Section 236(2) of the Insolvency Act 1986 provides

. . .

This provision has a long statutory history. Although the words of the section confer a general discretion on the court, over the years the courts have given certain guidance as to the proper basis for the exercise of the discretion. Most of the relevant authorities are reviewed by Slade J in *Re Castle New Homes Ltd* [1979] 2 All ER 775, [1979] 1 WLR 1075 and I will not repeat them. I am in agreement with much of the analysis of Slade J, in particular with the basic proposition that the exercise of the discretion involves the balancing of the requirements of the liquidator or administrator to obtain information on the one hand against the possible oppression to the person sought to be examined on the other. But Slade J went further and stated a more detailed rule for carrying out that balancing exercise in cases such as the present where there is a real possibility that the person seeking an order for examination will start an action against the person sought to be examined. He said ([1979] 2 All ER 775 at 788–789, [1979] 1 WLR 1075 at 1089–1090).

> 'Briefly, to summarise the principles relating to the "balance" question relevant for the present purposes, as I deduce them from the authorities, they are these. The court will always be concerned to avoid vexation, oppression or injustice in making an order under s 268. If the evidence shows that the purpose of a liquidator in seeking the examination is to achieve an advantage beyond that available to the ordinary litigant, in litigation which he has already commenced or which he has definitely decided to commence, the predisposition of the court may well be to refuse an immediate order for examination, unless the liquidator can show special grounds to the contrary. If, however, it appears from the evidence that the object of the liquidator is simply to elicit information which will enable or assist him to decide whether or not his company has a valid claim against a third party, the court will approach the liquidator's application with no such predisposition. While it will still be anxious in such a case to avoid oppression, it will also bear in mind that one of the very purposes of s 268 is to enable the liquidator "as effectively as possible and . . . with as little expense as possible and as much expedition as possible to complete his function as liquidator"; and that to assist him in this manner may inevitably involve giving him a degree of advantage which would not be available to an ordinary potential litigant.'

I will revert later to the merits of that test, but it appears that since that decision a practice has grown up of putting in evidence stating whether or not the applicant has reached a firm decision whether or not to sue. We were told that in practice the grant or refusal of an order under s 236 has come largely to depend on that point. So, in the present case, much evidence and argument was directed to the question whether or not the joint administrators had reached a firm decision to sue BCCI in any event. Before the judge, Mr Brisby for BCCI sought leave to cross-examine Mr Withall on his evidence that he had not yet reached a firm decision whether or not to pursue the case against BCCI beyond the issue of the protective writ. The judge refused to allow such cross-examination.

Although the judge accepted Mr Withall's evidence that he had made no firm decision on the matter, he said ([1990] BCLC 471 at 476):

> 'In my view I can properly conclude that the administrators have made a firm decision that they will not decide whether to sue BCCI until they have obtained all material that they can under the machinery of the 1986 Act. The question for me is whether in the face of a determination not to reach a decision but to go on exploring every opportunity to make good the potential claim against BCCI I should allow the order against BCCI to stand.'

Later he said (at 477–478)

> 'The cases show that the court has been much influenced by the oath of a liquidator that he has not decided whether or not to sue. None the less there must be a danger that gentlemen like Mr Withall, who is a very well-informed and capable professional, will resolve not to make any decision as to whether to litigate until they have obtained every piece of information that they can by use of the machinery of the 1986 Act. Such an observation in no way suggests bad faith on Mr Withall's part. He has a duty to the creditors and he should properly use all his professional knowledge and skill for their benefit. If it is for their benefit to know everything that can be disclosed before embarking upon litigation, so as to ensure that cases are brought only when success is nearly guaranteed, as it plainly is, then Mr Withall is doing his duty by using the machinery of the 1986 Act to discover all he can and by resolving that he will not decide on litigation until all avenues have been exhausted. In those circumstances any competent liquidator or administrator will always resolve not to decide whether or not to litigate until after he has obtained evidence by private examination. In those circumstances the court must in my judgment still consider the balance between oppression to the examinee or his company and assisting the liquidator. I find the clue to that balance in the word "need" emphasised earlier in Slade J's elucidation of Vaughan Williams J's decision [in *Re Franks, ex p Gittins* [1892] 1 QB 646] and in Vinelott J's quotation of Hoffmann J [in *Re J T Rhodes Ltd* [1987] BCLC 77 at 79–80]. If the court considers that the applicant does not need further information in order to take a rational decision whether or not to sue, but wants further information to improve his position, then in my judgment it is oppressive to order private examination. I am not convinced by the evidence in this case that Mr Withall and his partner "need" further information although they may reasonably "want" it.'

Mr Moss QC for the administrators, submits that there was no evidence to support the judge's finding that the joint administrators have decided not to decide until they have used the machinery of the Act to discover all they can. I accept this submission. The judge did not permit cross-examination of Mr

Withall's evidence and therefore it was never put to Mr Withall that he had decided not to decide. His evidence, which the judge accepted, was that he had not made up his mind on the question. The advice of counsel was that certain further evidence was required before taking the decision whether or not to sue. In my judgment the evidence does not justify any finding that the joint administrators had resolved not to reach a decision in order to facilitate the obtaining of an order under s 236.

In those circumstances, there is in my judgment a flaw in the judge's exercise of his discretion on the basis that he was exercising it. Having reached the erroneous conclusions as to the state of mind of the joint administrators, he posed himself the wrong question, viz ([1990] BCLC 471 at 476):

> 'whether in the face of a determination not to reach a decision but to go on exploring every opportunity to make good the potential claim against BCCI I should allow the order against BCCI to stand.'

Moreover in reaching his ultimate conclusion he wholly discounted the views of the joint administrators whereas the authorities show that, as officers of the court with detailed knowledge of all the circumstances of the company, their views should be afforded great weight by the court. Therefore in my judgment the exercise of the discretion by the judge cannot stand and we must exercise the discretion afresh.

Before doing so, I must first say something about the correct approach and in particular about the importance attached by Slade J to the question whether or not the applicant has reached a firm decision to sue. In my judgment experience has shown that test to be unsatisfactory, depending as it does on the subjective state of mind of the liquidator or administrator in each case. Although I am unable to accept the judge's finding that the joint administrators in this case had adopted the attitude which he attributed to them, in my judgment there must be a temptation to seek to get as much information as possible before taking a decision whether or not to sue. The more information there is as to the fact and possible defences to a claim the better informed will be any decision and the greater the likelihood of such decision being correct. It is the function of a liquidator or administrator to do his best for the creditors. True he is an officer of the court and must not act in any improper way but, like the judge, I can see nothing improper in a liquidator or administrator seeking to obtain as much information as possible before committing himself to proceedings. Moreover a test based on the subjective state of mind of the liquidator or administrator inevitably leads to undesirable disputes of fact, such as have arisen in this case, as to what is his state of mind. In my judgment therefore the test propounded in *Re Castle New Homes Ltd* [1979] 2 All ER 775, [1979] 1 WLR 1075 has not proved to be satisfactory and should not in future be applied.

Nor do I think that there is any other simple test that can be substituted. The words of the statute do not fetter the court's discretion in any way. Circumstances may vary infinitely. It is clear that in exercising the discretion the court has to balance the requirements of the liquidator against any possible oppression to the person to be examined. Such balancing depends on the relationship between the importance to the liquidator of obtaining the information on the one hand and the degree of oppression to the person sought to be examined on the other. If the information required is fundamental to any assessment of whether or not there is a cause of action and the degree of oppression is small (for example in the case of ordering premature discovery of documents) the balance will manifestly come down in favour of making the order. Conversely, if the liquidator is seeking merely to dot the i's and cross the t's of a fairly clear claim by examining the proposed defendant to discover his defence, the balance would come down against making the order. Of course, few cases will be so clear: it will be for the judge in each case to reach his own conclusion.

That said there are a number of points which in my judgment should be borne in mind in exercising the discretion. First, the reason for the inquisitorial jurisdiction contained in s 236 is that a liquidator or administrator comes into the company with no previous knowledge and frequently finds that the company's records are missing or defective. The purpose of s 236 is to enable him to get sufficient information to reconstitute the state of knowledge that the company should possess. In my judgment its purpose is not to put the company in a better position than it would have enjoyed if liquidation or administration had not supervened. In many cases an order under s 236 may have the *result* that the company is in such improved position, eg an order for discovery of documents made against a third party in order to reconstitute the company's own trading records may disclose the existence of claims which would otherwise remain hidden. But that is the *result* of the order not the *purpose* for which it is made.

Second, as a corollary to the first point, I do not think that the test of absolute 'need' as opposed to a reasonable requirement for the information is a workable or appropriate test. This was the determinative distinction relied upon by the judge. But if the applicant has to show an absolute 'need' this would lead to endless argument about whether the circumstances of each case disclose such need and would lead to the order being refused even in cases where the information would be of great utility to the applicant (short of absolute need) and could be obtained (eg by discovery of documents) without any great oppression to the person sought to be examined.

Third, in my judgment the case for making an order against an officer or former officer of the company will usually be stronger than it would be against a third party. Officers owe the company fiduciary duties and will often be in possession of information to which the company is entitled under the general law. Their special position as officers of the company is emphasised by s 235 of the Act, which imposes on them a statutory obligation to assist the liquidator or administrator. The enforcement of these duties owed by its officers to the company may require an order under s 236 even though it exposes such officers to the risk of personal liability. No such considerations apply when an order is sought against a third party. He owes no duty to the company. In an otherwise proper case he may be required to disclose documents or answer questions so as to provide the liquidator with the information necessary to carry out his functions even though this may have unfortunate repercussions for him. But he owes no general duty to give such information (apart from an order under s 236) and if by giving the information he risks exposing himself to liability this involves an element of oppression. That is not to say that an order cannot or should not be made against a third party. But it should be borne in mind that the degree of possible oppression is greater in his case.

Fourth, although the section treats the production of documents and the oral examination of witnesses together, an order for oral examination is much more likely to be oppressive than an order for the production of documents. An order for the production of documents involves only advancing the time of discovery if an action ensues: the liquidator is getting no more than any other litigant would get, save that he is getting it earlier. But oral examination provides the opportunity for pre-trial depositions which the liquidator would never otherwise be entitled to: the person examined has to answer on oath and his answers can both provide evidence in support of a subsequent claim brought by the liquidator and also form the basis of later cross-examination. In my judgment this greater risk of oppression when examination of witnesses is ordered calls for a more careful approach to such orders than to orders for the disclosure of documents.

In *Re J T Rhodes Ltd* [1987] BCLC 77 Hoffmann J suggested that the time may have come to reconsider whether oral examination is oppressive even if it does involve the risks which I have mentioned. He pointed to the change in attitudes since Victorian times and to the growth of investigatory powers such as those given to inspectors appointed by the Department of Trade and Industry. Those remarks were made in the context of a case where oral examination was sought of the 'moving light' and de facto director of the company; I have already said that in my view the fiduciary duties owed to the company by such a person may well justify a more stringent approach. But for myself I am unable to accept, in the absence of specific statutory authority, that it is not oppressive to require someone suspected of wrongdoing to prove the case against himself on oath before any proceedings are brought. In the exercise of its discretion, the court may consider that the legitimate requirements of the liquidator outweigh such oppression; but it remains oppressive.

How then should the discretion be exercised in this case? The administrators are seeking two forms of information, viz (a) an explanation of the unconventional markings on the cheques to verify how, as a matter of banking practice, they were dealt with, and (b) information as to the state of knowledge of the employees of BCCI with a view to establishing whether or not BCCI has knowingly participated in the fraud of Mr Zaid and is therefore liable as constructive trustee.

As to information in category (a) we were told that BCCI is now prepared to answer a reasonable questionnaire as to the markings on the cheques. That seems to me wholly adequate to give the administrators the information which they need and to which I would have thought they were in any event entitled from their bankers.

As to the information in category (b), it can only be obtained by oral examination of the witnesses. The exercise of the discretion whether or not to order such examination involves weighing the requirements of the administrators on the one hand against the degree of oppression involved in such examination on the other.

As to the administrators' requirements, we must of course pay great attention to the administrators' view that the information is required. But Mr Moss QC accepts that their views are not decisive. It would obviously be very helpful in any litigation against BCCI to know what its defence to the claim might be and to have sworn evidence available either to prove the case of knowing participation in fraudulent conduct or to provide material for cross-examination at a trial. It is true that the documents produced do not include contemporaneous memoranda recording the bank's dealings as would be the case with any normal bank. But the administrators already have the memorandum sent by BCCI to Charterhouse relating to certain of the cheques showing, in relation to those cheques, knowledge by employees of BCCI of the unconventional method whereby the crossings were opened and the cheques were indorsed over. Although this information does not extend to the cheques subsequently disclosed following the order of Hoffmann J, the administrators already have far more material than the ordinary litigant would have on which to reach a decision whether or not to sue BCCI as constructive trustee. The administrators already have as much information as the company would have had even if it had not become insolvent. The administrators are seeking to use the statutory procedure to get information which the company, if solvent, would not have been able to obtain before deciding whether or not to pursue the proceedings against BCCI.

When one turns to the other side of the balance, BCCI and its employees owe no fiduciary duties to the company: they are third parties against whom the company has already issued a writ, albeit a protective writ. The claim is to examine individuals whom, it is thought, may have knowingly participated in a fraud with a view to establishing such knowledge. In my judgment, to order pre-trial depositions from parties suspected of fraud or dishonest behaviour is very oppressive. The courts have always been astute to protect the interests of those accused of fraud in the civil courts and to require the plaintiff to prove his case against them. To use s 236 so as to run contrary to that attitude is, in my judgment, oppressive.

Accordingly in my judgment the scales clearly come down against making the order. The administrators can make at least as well informed a decision whether or not to pursue the action as an ordinary litigant: BCCI is suspected of dishonest conduct and would be required to answer questions relating to such conduct, thereby possibly building the case against itself. The requirements of the administrators are therefore not compelling whereas the degree of oppression to the proposed examinees is very considerable.

I therefore reach the same conclusion as the judge, but by a rather different route. I would dismiss the appeal.

McCOWAN LJ (dissenting): In my view, in an era of Department of Trade inquiries and legislation against insider dealing, the Court of Appeal should adopt the modern approach advocated by Hoffmann J.

For all the above reasons I conclude that Harman J's exercise of discretion is fatally flawed by being based on a misunderstanding of the law and a wrong finding of fact.

In exercising my discretion I would take into account the following factors: (1) the genuinely held view of an experienced and reputable office-holder that he requires this information; (2) the opinion that the joint administrators have received from a Queen's Counsel specialising in banking law that, on the face of it, BCCI's involvement in this matter appeared to be as bad a course of conduct on the part of any bank as he had seen, but that the administrators would need to investigate further in order to establish whether BCCI had any explanation for these occurrences or, indeed, any other possible defences; (3) the administrators in order to succeed in their action against BCCI would have to establish that BCCI through its officers knowingly assisted in the fraudulent design of Mr Zaid; (4) the memorandum sent by BCCI to the administrators is dated 24 February 1988 and deals with events which occurred five or six years earlier in the form of the writer of the memorandum reporting what he had been told by one officer of the bank about what that officer had been told by another officer; (5) the memorandum throws no light on whether those officers assisted Mr Zaid in his fraudulent design knowingly or innocently; (6) the memorandum does not deal with how the cheques were physically processed by BCCI or how, when or by whom the crossings on the cheques were opened or how, when or by whom those cheques were indorsed over on the payee's behalf; (7) the documents ordered to be disclosed by Vinelott J have not thrown light on any of these matters; (8) there are in this case no contemporary running memoranda as one would expect to find in the case of a United Kingdom bank.

In all those circumstances I see nothing unreasonable, oppressive or inequitable about the administrators' application for examination of the two named officers of BCCI. I would allow the appeal and order that the examination proceed.

SOURCE 315
British and Commonwealth Holdings (Nos 1 and 2)
(House of Lords) [1993] BCLC 168

LORD SLYNN OF HADLEY (with whose speech all the other Law Lords agreed):
...

The Court of Appeal (Ralph Gibson and Woolf LJJ (Nourse LJ dissenting)) allowed the appeal and restored the order of the registrar (see [1992] BCLC 641, [1992] Ch 342).

Nourse LJ did not accept that Browne-Wilkinson V-C had intended to lay down a rigid limitation on the exercise of the court's discretion. In his view, however, the decision in the *Cloverbay* case obliged the Court of Appeal to adopt the following approach as being correct for the court on application under s 236 ([1992] BCLC 641 at 655, [1992] Ch 342 at 360–361):

> 'The discretion must be exercised with a recognition that the primary purpose of s 236 is to enable office-holders to obtain the information which would have been obtainable by the company as a going concern. The convenient course is to inquire, first, whether on that approach, the registrar's order is oppressive to [the auditors], secondly, whether the documents required by the administrators are reasonably required for the discharge of their duties and, if so, whether their requirements outweigh any oppression to [the auditors].'

On that approach Nourse LJ considered that the claim was oppressive. The number of documents was vast. A claim was made against a firm of accountants who were never the auditors of B & C and the order was sought so that unspecified claims could be investigated. There was in his view no evidence to show that the documents were reasonably required by the administrators for the discharge of their duties.

Ralph Gibson LJ did not accept that the Vice-Chancellor in the *Cloverbay* case had intended to lay down a rule that no order could be made under s 236 if the purpose for which the office-holder claimed reasonably to require information sought included obtaining information the receipt of which would go beyond a reconstitution of knowledge which the company once had and was entitled in law to possess. That the information sought had been in the knowledge of the company, particularly if sought from an officer of the company, added weight to the applicant's case on the balancing exercise. Such a limitation could not, however, be derived from the section in its statutory context or from previous authority. The court had to weigh up all the circumstances in each case in order to decide whether an order for production should be made.

After a careful and detailed consideration of all the factors relied on by the administrators and by the auditors, Ralph Gibson LJ concluded that the order in the present case was not oppressive.
...

The first question on this appeal is whether the use of s 236 is limited in the way which Hoffmann J considered had been laid down by the Court of Appeal in the *Cloverbay* case.

It is, however, by no means certain that such a limitation was intended to be introduced by the Court of Appeal. It is true that on the one hand the Vice-

Chancellor defined the purpose of s 236 in terms which suggest such a limitation, as Hoffmann J thought, viz ([1991] BCLC 135 at 141, [1991] Ch 90 at 102):

> 'The purpose of s 236 is to enable [the administrators] to get sufficient information to reconstitute the state of knowledge that the company should possess. In my judgment its purpose is not to put the company in a better position than it would have enjoyed if liquidation or administration had not supervened',

and again, the Vice-Chancellor alluded to the same idea later ([1991] BCLC 135 at 143, [1991] Ch 90 at 104):

> 'The administrators are seeking to use the statutory procedure to get information which the company, if solvent, would not have been able to obtain before deciding whether or not to pursue the proceedings against BCCI.'

On the other hand both the Vice-Chancellor and Nourse LJ emphasised the importance of the balancing exercise. They both rejected the practice which had grown up since the decision of Slade J in *Re Castle New Homes Ltd* [1979] 2 All ER 775, [1979] 1 WLR 1075, whereby if the liquidator had sued or decided to sue he was refused an order, but if he had not done so but was seeking information to enable him to sue he was granted an order. Moreover, the Vice-Chancellor expressly agreed with much of the judgment of Slade J:

> '... in particular with the basic proposition that the exercise of the discretion involves the balancing of the requirements of the liquidator or administrator to obtain information on the one hand against the possible oppression to the person sought to be examined on the other.'

> . . .

Although the passages to which I first referred support the conclusion reached by Hoffmann J as to the effect of the judgment of the Court of Appeal, I do not think that reading the judgment overall such a limitation to 'reconstituting the company's knowledge' was intended to be laid down in the *Cloverbay* case.

In any event for my part I do not think that such a limitation exists.

The wording of the section contains no express limitation to documents which can be said to be part of a process of reconstituting the company's state of knowledge. The words are quite general. Thus s 236(2) refers to 'any person whom the court thinks capable of giving information concerning the promotion, formation, business, dealings, affairs or property of the company', and by sub-s (3) such a person may be ordered to produce 'any books, papers or other records in his possession or under his control relating to a company or the matters mentioned in paragraph (*c*) of the subsection'.

Nor do I see any support in earlier judgments which have been cited to us relating to the predecessors of s 236 or to comparable sections for such a limitation to 'reconstituting the company's knowledge'. On the contrary, for example, in *Re Gold Co* (1879) 12 Ch D 77 at 85 in a case under s 115 of the Companies Act 1862 (which enabled the court to summon any officer or any persons supposed to be capable of giving information concerning the transactions and trade dealings of the company) Jessel MR said:

> '... the whole object of the section is to assimilate the practice in winding-up to the practice in bankruptcy, which was established in order to enable assignees, who are now called trustees, in bankruptcy to find out facts before they brought an action, so as to avoid incurring the expense of some

hundreds of pounds in bringing an unsuccessful action, when they might, by examining a witness or two, have discovered at a trifling expense that an action could not succeed.'

Similarly, Chitty J said in *Re Imperial Continental Water Corp* (1886) 33 Ch D 314 at 316:

'Those extensive powers are conferred upon the Court for the beneficial winding-up of the company, for sometimes it happens that the liquidator is unable to obtain from unwilling persons the information which he requires.'

In *Re North Australian Territory Co* (1890) 45 Ch D 87 at 92, in relation to the same section, Bowen LJ said:

'The section which the Court is putting in force in the examination of a person under such circumstances is the section which places the decision as to an examination and as to its limits within the discretion of the Court. That being so, I do not think that we ought to attempt beforehand to classify all the occasions on which it may be proper to make such an order . . .'

. . .

In my opinion, although there may be some difference in the wording of these sections, the position under s 236 of the Insolvency Act 1986 is broadly the same as that under s 268 of the Companies Act 1948 as explained by Buckley J in *Re Rolls Razor Ltd* [1968] 3 All ER 698 at 700, in a passage subsequently approved by the Court of Appeal in *Re Esal (Commodities) Ltd* [1989] BCLC 59 at 64:

'The powers conferred by s 268 are powers directed to enabling the court to help a liquidator to discover the truth of the circumstances connected with the affairs of the company, information of trading, dealings, and so forth, in order that the liquidator may be able, as effectively as possible and, I think, with as little expense as possible . . . to complete his function as liquidator, to put the affairs of the company in order and to carry out the liquidation in all its various aspects, including, of course, the getting in of any assets of the company available in the liquidation. It is, therefore, appropriate for the liquidator, when he thinks that he may be under a duty to try to recover something from some officer or employee of a company, or some other person who is, in some way, concerned with the company's affairs, to be able to discover, with as little expense as possible and with as much ease as possible, the facts surrounding any such possible claim.'

These words, which reflect what was said by Jessel MR in 1879, seem to be wholly consistent not just with the wording of s 236 but also with the purposes of the administration as set out in s 8(3) of the 1986 Act and in particular:

'(*a*) the survival of the company, and the whole or any part of its undertaking, as a going concern . . . (*d*) a more advantageous realisation of the company's assets than would be effected in a winding-up . . .'

As Megarry J said in *Re Rolls Razor Ltd (No 2)* [1969] 3 All ER 1386 at 1396–1397, [1970] Ch 576 at 591–592:

'The process under s 268 is needed because of the difficulty in which the liquidator in an insolvent company is necessarily placed. He usually comes as a stranger to the affairs of a company which has sunk to its financial doom. In that process, it may well be that some of those concerned in the management of the company, and others as well, have been guilty of some misconduct or impropriety which is of relevance to the liquidation. Even those who are wholly innocent of any wrongdoing may have motives for concealing what was done. In any case, there are almost certain to be many transactions which are difficult to discover or to understand merely from the books and papers of the company. Accordingly, the legislature has provided this extraordinary process so as to enable the requisite information to be obtained. The examinees are not in any ordinary sense witnesses, and the ordinary standards of procedure do not apply. There is here an extraordinary and secret mode of obtaining information necessary for the proper conduct of the winding-up. The process, borrowed from the law of bankruptcy, can only be described as being sui generis.'

I am therefore of the opinion that the power of the court to make an order under s 236 is not limited to documents which can be said to be needed 'to reconstitute the state of the company's knowledge' even if that may be one of the purposes most clearly justifying the making of an order.

At the same time it is plain that there is an extraordinary power and that the discretion must be exercised after a careful balancing of the factors involved: on the one hand the reasonable requirements of the administrator to carry out his task, on the other the need to avoid making an order which is wholly unreasonable, unnecessary or 'oppressive' to the person concerned. The latter was stressed by Bowen LJ in *Re North Australian Territory Co* (1890) 45 Ch D 87 at 93:

'That is an inquisitorial power, which may work with great severity against third persons, and it seems to me to be obvious that such a section ought to be used with the greatest care, so as not unnecessarily to put in motion the machinery of justice when it is not wanted, or to put it in motion at a stage when it is not clear that it is wanted, and certainly not to put it in motion if unnecessary mischief is going to be done or hardship inflicted upon the third person who is called upon to appear and give information.'

. . .

The protection for the person called upon to produce documents lies, thus, not in a limitation by category of documents ('reconstituting the company's state of knowledge') but in the fact that the applicant must satisfy the court that, after balancing all the relevant factors, there is a proper case for such an order to be made. The proper case is one where the administrator reasonably requires to see the documents to carry out his functions and the production does not impose an unnecessary and unreasonable burden on the person required to produce them in the light of the administrator's requirements. An application is not necessarily unreasonable because it is inconvenient for the addressee of the application or causes him a lot of work or may make him vulnerable to future claims, or is addressed to a person who is not an officer or employee of or a contractor with the company in administration, but all these will be relevant factors, together no doubt with many others.

It is plain in the present case that Hoffmann J carried out the balancing exercise on the basis that he was entitled and bound to do so and, leaving aside the limitation on his powers which he subsequently felt that he had to observe, it seems to me that it is impossible to say that in carrying out that exercise he misdirected himself or came to a conclusion to which he could not reasonably have come in the exercise of his discretion. He followed the lines indicated by the Vice-Chancellor as to the exercise of the discretion and he balanced the various factors involved, reaching the conclusion on that basis that 'I would have no doubt that the registrar's order should stand'. The same result was reached after an independent exercise of discretion by Ralph Gibson LJ following a careful and detailed investigation of the factors relied on by the auditors and with that conclusion Woolf LJ, despite initial reservations as to the width of the order, agreed.

It seems to me that no grounds have been shown to justify your Lordships saying that Hoffmann J (in setting out his conclusion on the balancing exercise even though he felt inhibited from giving effect to it) and the majority in the Court of Appeal erred in law in a way which vitiates the exercise of the discretion involved. I would dismiss the appeal on that ground.

. . .

This may well be an exceptional order. The size of the financial crash, however, gives rise to an exceptional case. Creditors and investors stood to lose vast sums. It was the administrators' task to investigate 'what was the true financial position of Atlantic at the time of its acquisition and, if it was different from the way it was represented, how and why the truth was concealed' (see [1992] BCLC 314 at 317 per Hoffmann J). They need in this very complex situation to check the accuracy of the various financial documents and to know not only what representations were made but how accurate they were. Like Woolf LJ I find it difficult to see how the order can be cut down and remain effective. No way has been suggested to achieve this.

INDEX